HARRAP'S

MINI

Italian

DICTIONARY

HARRAP'S
MINI
Italian
DICTIONARY

HARRAP

Distributed in the United States by
Macmillan ▮ USA

Hanno collaborato alla redazione del presente dizionario
Annamaria Fallore Maiocchi e Ada Bichiacchi

First published as
Harrap's Compact Italian and English Dictionary
in 1968

First published in this edition in Great Britain 1988
by HARRAP BOOKS Ltd
43–45 Aonandale Street, Edinburgh EH7 4AZ
© Copyright 1967 U. Mursia & Co., Milano, Via Tadimo 29

Reprinted 1990, 1992, 1993, 1997

In the United States, ISBN 0-13-383332-1

Library of Congress Cataloging-in-Publication Data

Harrap's mini Italian dictionary.

p.   cm.
First published in 1968 as Harrap's compact Italian & English
dictionary; first published in this ed. in Great Britain 1988 by
Harrap Books Ltd., London.
ISBN 0-13-383332-1: $4.00
1. Italian language — Dictionaries — English.
2. English language — Dictionaries — Italian.
PF1840.H34 1990   89–70958
453'21 — dc20   CIP

MACMILLAN is a trademark of Macmillan, Inc. registered

NORME, REGOLE E INFORMAZIONI

NORME PER L'USO DEL DIZIONARIO

1. La parte iniziale del presente **Piccolo dizionario** comprende una serie di informazioni che valgono a completare l'opera, a facilitarne la consultazione o ad arricchire le conoscenze del lettore; tali si debbono considerare le **regole di pronuncia**, l'elenco dei **verbi irregolari inglesi**, la tabella di raffronto fra le **unità inglesi o americane** e il **sistema metrico**, le indicazioni relative al **sistema monetario inglese e americano**, l'elenco dei **numeri ordinali e cardinali** e, infine, l'**elenco delle abbreviazioni** usate nel dizionario stesso.

Inoltre comprende una serie di informazioni in inglese a facilitarne la consultazione per il lettore inglese.

2. La seconda parte comprende il **Compact English-Italian Dictionary** e reca in appendice un ampio elenco di **nomi propri, storici e geografici** (con la relativa traduzione in italiano), nonché l'elenco delle **sigle e abbreviazioni** usate nei **Paesi di lingua inglese** con l'indicazione dell'equivalente italiano.

3. La terza parte comprende il **Piccolo dizionario italiano-inglese** e reca in appendice un ampio elenco di **nomi propri, storici e geografici** (con la relativa traduzione in inglese), nonché l'elenco delle **sigle e abbreviazioni** usate in Italia con l'indicazione dell'equivalente italiano.

4. Nella parte **italiano-inglese**, i lemmi italiani non recano accento se si tratta di parole piane (es.: *violino, rosa, determinazione*); recano l'accento se si tratta di parole tronche (es.: *così, però, lassù*) o sdrucciole (es.: *richiùdere, rimpròvero, nàutico*) o bisdrucciole o terminanti in *ia, io* con l'accento sulla *i* (es.: *filosofìa, mormorìo*). Tali accenti sono tutti gravi, salvo nelle parole con accento su una *e*, nel qual caso ci si è attenuti a un criterio strettamente ortoepico (es.: *règola, desèrtico, maneggévole, pregévole*): si è, cioè, distinto fra accento grave (pronuncia aperta) e accento acuto (pronuncia chiusa).

5. Nel corpo delle singole voci sono stati ampiamente adottati, secondo la consuetudine generale dei grandi dizionari, i seguenti **segni grafici**:

a) la **doppia barra** (||) che sta a segnalare la peculiarità della fraseologia o una certa differenza di significato nell'ambito del lemma o il passaggio da un senso proprio a uno figurato o il passaggio dal significato corrente a uno più specialistico, infine, l'inizio dell'elencazione di parole composte e di analoghe associazioni semantiche;

b) i **numeri arabi in neretto** (1., 2., 3. ecc.) che valgono ad attirare l'attenzione sui diversi significati in cui è stato possibile articolare una determinata voce del dizionario;

c) la **losanga nera** (♦) che sta a indicare il cambiamento di natura grammaticale che sopravviene internamente a due omonimi appartenenti a un medesimo gruppo etimologico (es.: passaggio da sostantivo maschile a sostantivo femminile; da sostantivo ad aggettivo; da aggettivo ad avverbio; da verbo transitivo a verbo riflessivo ecc.);

d) gli **esponenti in numeri arabi** (¹, ², ³ ecc.) che servono a distinguere parole omonime appartenenti però a gruppi etimologici diversi.

6. In entrambe le parti, nel caso di sostantivi che abbiano **numero diverso** nelle due lingue, si è data l'indicazione del numero stesso sùbito dopo il lemma. Es.: **fare** *sm.* manners (*pl.*) - **postage** *s.* spese postali (*pl.*) - **embers** *s. pl.* brace (*sing.*).

7. Per i **plurali irregolari inglesi** si sono usati i seguenti criteri:

a) nella parte **inglese-italiano** si è fatta seguire al lemma, fra parentesi, la forma plurale irregolare, per esteso - es.: **child** *s.* (*pl.* children) - nei casi generali o abbreviata - es.: **diagnosis** *s.* (*pl.* -ses) - nei casi di parole derivanti da altre lingue antiche o moderne. Nel primo caso i plurali sono stati elencati anche come voce a sé e con rimando: es.: **children** V. *child*;

b) nella parte **italiano-inglese** si è fatta seguire alla traduzione, fra parentesi, la forma plurale irregolare, per esteso - es.: **bambino** *sm.* child (*pl.* children) - nei casi generali o abbreviata - es.: **diàgnosi** *sf.* diagnosis (*pl.* -ses) - nei casi di parole derivanti da altre lingue antiche o moderne.

8. Per i **verbi irregolari inglesi** si sono usati i seguenti criteri:

a) nella parte **inglese-italiano** si è fatta seguire al lemma, fra parentesi, il paradigma: es.: **to bring (brought, brought)**. Le due forme del passato remoto e del participio passato sono state elencate anche come voce a sé e con rimando: es.: **brought** V. *to bring*;

b) nella parte **italiano-inglese** si è fatta seguire alla traduzione, fra parentesi, l'indicazione dell'irregolarità - es.: **costare** *vi.* to cost (*v. irr.*) - a meno che lo stesso verbo inglese ricorra più volte nell'ambito della stessa voce ed escludendo inoltre i due verbi ausiliari *to be* e *to have* (per i quali ultimi si suppone una costante attenzione del lettore circa l'irregolarità).

9. Per i **comparativi** e i **superlativi irregolari inglesi** sono stati seguiti analoghi criteri.

REGOLE DI PRONUNCIA

Alfabeto

L'alfabeto inglese è composto di 26 lettere, 5 in più dell'alfabeto italiano e precisamente: *j, k, w, x, y*. L'elenco completo delle lettere è il seguente:

a	(pron. *ei*)	n	(pron. *en*)
b	(pron. *bi*, con la *i* allungata)	o	(pron. *ou*)
c	(pron. *si*, con la *i* allungata e la *s* aspra, come in *sordo*)	p	(pron. *pi*, con la *i* allungata)
d	(pron. *di*, con la *i* allungata)	q	(pron. *chiù*)
e	(pron. *i*, con la *i* allungata)	r	(pron. *ar*, con la *a* allungata)
f	(pron. *ef*)	s	(pron. *es*, con la *s* aspra)
g	(pron. *gi*, con la *i* allungata)	t	(pron. *ti*, con la *i* allungata)
h	(pron. *eic*, con la *c* dolce)	u	(pron. *iù*)
i	(pron. *ai*)	v	(pron. *vi*, con la *i* allungata)
j	(pron. *gei*)	w	(pron. *dabliu*)
k	(pron. *kei*)	x	(pron. *ecs*)
l	(pron. *el*)	y	(pron. *uai*)
m	(pron. *em*)	z	(pron. *sed*, con la *s* dolce, come in *rosa*).

La pronuncia inglese è particolarmente difficile da apprendere ed è altresì difficile dare norme precise per l'apprendimento della stessa. Diamo comunque, qui di seguito, un elenco delle vocali, dei gruppi vocalici, delle consonanti e di alcuni gruppi consonantici con indicazioni approssimative sulla pronuncia.

Vocali

La vocale A ha vari suoni:

1. **ei** in sillaba tonica aperta come nella parola *tale* (racconto); nei gruppi **ange** e **aste** come nelle parole *danger* (pericolo) e *baste* (fretta);

2. **e** aperta in sillaba tonica chiusa come nella parola *cat* (gatto);

3. ha un suono incerto tra e aperta e a in sillabe atone iniziali o mediane come nelle parole *about* (circa) e *final* (finale);

4. **a** allungata quando è seguita da r finale (r muta) come nelle parole *car* (automobile) e *far* (lontano);

5. **ea** se è seguita da re finale (e aperta e a appena accennate) come nelle parole *care* (cura) e *dare* (sfida);

6. **o** breve in molti vocaboli che cominciano con il gruppo **qua** come in *quality* (qualità) e in *quantity* (quantità);

7. **o** aperta e prolungata se seguita da l o ll come in *all* (tutto), *tall* (alto);

nel gruppo **alk** (l muta) come in *talk* (chiacchiera); preceduta da **w** (ma non seguita da **k** o **g**) come in *war* (guerra);

8. **a** allungata nei gruppi **ance**, **and**, **ant**, **ask**, **alf** (l muta), **ast**, **alm** (l muta), **aff**, **aft**, **asp** e **ath** quando la **a** è tonica;

9. **i** breve e velata nelle desinenze **age** e **ate** non accentate.

La vocale E ha vari suoni:

1. **i** allungata in sillaba tonica aperta come in *these* (questi) e nei mono-sillabi, come in *me* (me);

2. **e** aperta come nella parola italiana *bello*, in sillaba tonica chiusa, come in *let* (lasciare);

3. **i** come nella parola italiana *vita*, in sillaba atona, come in *repeat* (ri-petere);

4. **i** brevissima quando è preceduta da **s**, **z**, **c**, **ch**, **sh**, **g** e seguita da **s** come in *roses* (rose) e quando è tra due dentali come in *rested* (riposato);

5. **è** muta in fine di parola come in *love* (amore) e nelle desinenze **es**, **ed**, come in *loves* (amori) e *loved* (amato);

6. **eu** francese quando è seguita da **r** in sillaba tonica, come in *term* (termine);

7. **a** gutturale quando è nel gruppo **er** in fine di parola, come in *letter* (lettera);

8. **ia** con la **a** appena accennata quando è seguita da **re** in fine di parola come in *severe* (severo) e in *mere* (semplice).

La vocale I ha vari suoni:

1. **ai** in sillaba tonica aperta, come in *fine* (bello) e in sillaba chiusa quan-do è seguita dai gruppi **gh** (muto), come in *high* (alto); **ght** (gh muto) come in *night* (notte); **gn** (g muta), come in *sign* (segno); **ld**, come in *child* (bambino) e **nd**, come in *mind* (mente).

2. **i** breve in sillaba tonica chiusa, come in *tin* (stagno).

3. **eu** francese, se seguita da **r** come in *fir* (abete).

4. **aia**, se seguita da **re** come in *fire* (fuoco).

La vocale O ha vari suoni:

1. **ou** (con la **o** chiusa) in sillaba tonica aperta, come in *home* (casa) e se seguita da **ld** come in *cold* (freddo);

2. **o** aperta e breve in sillaba tonica chiusa come in *not* (non);

3. **ó** aperta e lunga se seguita da **r** come in *morning* (mattino);

4. **oa** se seguita da **re** in fine di parola come in *more* (più);

5. **eu** francese se preceduta da **w** e seguita da **r** come in *work* (lavoro);

6. **u** allungata nei seguenti vocaboli: *to do* (fare); *to move* (muovere); *to prove* (provare); *to lose* (perdere); *who* (chi); *two* (due); *tomb* (tomba); *womb* (grembo); *shoe* (scarpa); *wolf* (lupo); *woman* (donna);

7. a se preceduta da w e seguita da n come in *won* (vinto);

8. ua in *one* (uno).

La vocale U ha vari suoni:

1. iù in sillaba tonica aperta, come in *tune* (tono);

2. a in sillaba tonica chiusa, come in *but* (ma);

3. u allungata se preceduta da l o r, come in *Lucy* (Lucia) e *rule* (regola);

4. u breve, se preceduta da b, f, p e seguita da l, ll, sh, come in *bush* (cespuglio); *to push* (spingere); *bull* (toro); *full* (pieno); *to pull* (tirare);

5. eu francese se seguita da r in sillaba aperta, come in *fur* (pelliccia);

6. iua se seguita da re in fine di parola, come in *pure* (puro).

Gruppi vocalici

AI si pronuncia ea se seguito da r, come in *air* (aria).

AU, AW si pronunciano o allungata, come in *fraud* (frode) e *law* (legge).

EA si pronuncia e in circa 40 parole e loro composti; *bread* (pane); *dead* (morto); *death* (morte); *head* (testa); *heavy* (pesante) ecc.;
    i lunga in moltissime sillabe toniche: *beat* (calore); *meat* (carne);
    ei nelle seguenti parole: *great* (grande); *break* (rompere); *steak* (bistecca);
    eu francese se all'inizio di parola e seguito da r come in *earth* (terra); in molte parole suona però ia, come in *tear* (lacrima), o a allungata, come in *heart* (cuore).

EE si pronuncia i allungata, come in *feeling* (sentimento).

EI si pronuncia ei in genere, come in *rein* (briglia);
    i se preceduto da sibilante, come in *ceiling* (soffitto).

EY si pronuncia ei in sillaba tonica, come in *prey* (preda);
    i in sillaba atona, come in *money* (denaro). L'eccezione più comune è *key* (chiave) che si pronuncia ki.

EU, EW si pronunciano iù come in *Europe* (Europa) e in *new* (nuovo).

IE si pronuncia i allungata come in *piece* (pezzo).

OI, OY si pronunciano oi come in *soil* (suolo) e *royal* (reale).

OA si pronuncia ou come in *boat* (barca).

OO si pronuncia u allungata, come in *moon* (luna);
    u breve se seguita da k come in *book* (libro).
    Vi sono alcune eccezioni come *door* (porta) e *floor* (pavimento) dove il gruppo oo viene pronunciato oa e *blood* (sangue) e *flood* (alluvione) dove il gruppo oo viene pronunciato a.

OU, OW si pronunciano au come in *mouth* (bocca) e *now* (ora).

Consonanti

B è in generale pronunciata come in italiano; è però muta nei gruppi **bt** e **mb** in fine di parola, come in *debt* (debito) e *comb* (pettine).

C suona **s** aspra come nell'italiano *sordo* davanti a **e**, **i**, **y**, come in *cellar* (cantina), *city* (città) e *cyder* (sidro); suona **k** in fine di parola, come in *logic* (logico);
cce, **cci**, suonano **kse** e **ksi**;
ch suona **c** palatale come nell'italiano *città*, se seguito da vocale o in fine di parola; suona **k** in parole di origine greca o orientale. Suona **sc** come in italiano *sciare*, in parole di origine francese, come *machine* (macchina);
ck suona **k**;
tch suona **c** dolce.

G in fine di parola suona **g** gutturale come nell'italiano *gomma*;
ge, **gi** hanno suono palatale come nell'italiano *gesto*, *gita* in parole di origine latina; hanno suono gutturale in parole di origine germanica;
gh seguito da **t** o in fine di parola è muto;
gn ha la **g** muta quando le due lettere fanno parte della stessa sillaba, come in *sign* (segno); si pronunciano separate e la **g** ha suono gutturale quando le due lettere appartengono a due sillabe diverse, come in *signal* (segnale);
dge suona **g** palatale.

H è sempre aspirata tranne in *heir* (erede); *honest* (onesto); *honour* (onore) e *hour* (ora) e loro derivati.

J suona **g** palatale.

K è muta davanti a **n** come in *knee* (ginocchio).

L come in italiano.

M come in italiano.

N è nasale nei gruppi **ng** come in *ring* (anello) (la **g** è muta).

P suona **f** nei gruppi **ph**; è muta nel gruppo iniziale **psy**.

Q come in italiano.

R in genere, se mediana, non si pronuncia, ma allunga il suono della vocale che precede, come in *farm* (fattoria). Se è finale non si pronuncia.

S è in genere aspra all'inizio di parola o sillaba; è dolce se è posta tra due vocali;
sc suona **s** aspra se è seguita da **e**, **i**, **y**;
sh suona **sc** come nell'italiano *sciare*.
La **s** è muta in *aisle* (navata); *isle* e *island* (isola); *viscount* (visconte).

T ha due pronunce caratteristiche nel gruppo **th**:
a) un suono duro pronunciato con la lingua tra i denti, come in *thin* (sottile);
b) un suono dolce pronunciato con la lingua tra i denti, come in *this* (questo).

V come in italiano.

W in principio di parola suona **u** come in *west*; seguita da **r** è muta, come in *wrong* (sbagliato).

X finale ha il suono sordo **ks**; mediana può avere il suono sordo **ks** o il suono dolce **gs**; in principio di parola suona come la **s** dolce di *rosa*.

Y è semivocale; all'inizio di parola ha il suono consonantico **i**, come in *yes* (sì); ha tale suono anche in fine di polisillabi, come in *dignity* (dignità), e nel corpo della parola, come in *graveyard* (cimitero); in fine di monosillabi, invece, si pronuncia **ai**, come in *fly* (mosca) e in *cry* (grido).

Z **s** dolce di *rosa*.

Osservazioni

1. I gruppi finali **ble, cle, kle, gle** hanno la l appena accennata e le due consonanti vengono pronunciate staccate.
2. Nei gruppi **gua, gue, gui, build** e **cuit** finale la u è muta, come in *building* (fabbricato).
3. **ough** seguito da t si pronuncia o allungato, come in *thought* (pensiero); **ough** suona **of** in: *cough* (tosse) e *trough* (trogolo); suona **af** in: *enough* (abbastanza), *rough* (ruvido) e *tough* (duro); suona **au** in: *plough* (arare) e *bough* (ramo); suona **ou** in *though* (sebbene) e *dough* (pasta); suona u allungato in *through* (attraverso).
4. I gruppi **ci, sci, si, ti, xi** seguiti da vocale suonano **sc** come in *scelto*.
5. I gruppi finali **sten** e **stle** suonano **sn** e **sl**.
6. Il gruppo finale **sure** suona **ja** (j francese).
7. Il gruppo finale **ture** suona **cia** con la a allungata.

I SEGNI D'INTERPUNZIONE
(PUNCTUATION MARKS)

,	*comma*	virgola
;	*semicolon*	punto e virgola
:	*colon*	due punti
.	*full stop*	punto
?	*question mark*	punto di domanda
!	*exclamation mark*	punto esclamativo
'	*apostrophe*	apostrofo
—	*dash*	lineetta
-	*hyphen*	trattino d'unione
« »	*quotation marks*	virgolette basse o quadre
' '	*inverted commas*	virgolette alte o inglesi
( )	*brackets*	parentesi rotonde
[ ]	*square brackets*	parentesi quadre
*	*asterisk*	asterisco
...	*dots*	puntini
	new paragraph	a capo
	full stop and new paragraph	punto e a capo
	capital letter	lettera maiuscola
	small letter	lettera minuscola

VERBI IRREGOLARI INGLESI [1]

Infinito	Passato	Participio passato	
to **abide**	abode	abode	dimorare
to **arise**	arose	arisen	sorgere
to **awake***	awoke	awoke, awaked	svegliare, svegliarsi
to **be**	was	been	essere
to **bear**	bore	born, borne	sopportare, generare
to **beat**	beat	beaten, beat	battere
to **become**	became	become	diventare
to **befall**	befell	befallen	accadere
to **beget**	begot	begot, begotten	generare
to **begin**	began	begun	cominciare
to **behold**	beheld	beheld	mirare
to **bend**	bent	bent	piegare
to **bereave***	bereft	bereft	orbare
to **bet**	bet	bet	scommettere
to **bid**	bade, bid	bidden, bid	ordinare
to **bind**	bound	bound	(ri)legare
to **bite**	bit	bitten, bit	mordere
to **bleed**	bled	bled	sanguinare
to **blow**	blew	blown	soffiare
to **break**	broke	broken	rompere
to **breed**	bred	bred	allevare
to **bring**	brought	brought	portare
to **build**	built	built	costruire
to **burn***	burnt	burnt	bruciare
to **burst**	burst	burst	scoppiare
to **buy**	bought	bought	comperare
to **cast**	cast	cast	gettare, fondere
to **catch**	caught	caught	prendere, acchiappare
to **chide***	chid	chid	sgridare
to **choose**	chose	chosen	scegliere
to **cleave**	cleft	cleft	fendere
to **cling**	clung	clung	attaccarsi
to **come**	came	come	venire
to **cost**	cost	cost	costare
to **creep**	crept	crept	strisciare
to **cut**	cut	cut	tagliare
to **deal**	dealt	dealt	trattare, commerciare
to **dig***	dug	dug	scavare
to **do**	did	done	fare
to **draw**	drew	drawn	tirare, disegnare
to **dream***	dreamt	dreamt	sognare
to **drink**	drank	drunk	bere
to **drive**	drove	driven	guidare
to **dwell***	dwelt	dwelt	dimorare

[1] L'elenco, compilato per comodità del lettore, comprende i verbi di uso più comune. L'asterisco apposto accanto a un verbo indica l'esistenza, per il verbo stesso, di forme anche regolari.

to eat	ate, eat	eaten	mangiare
to fall	fell	fallen	cadere
to feed	fed	fed	nutrire
to feel	felt	felt	sentire, tastare
to fight	fought	fought	combattere
to find	found	found	trovare
to flee	fled	fled	fuggire
to fling	flung	flung	scagliare
to fly	flew	flown	volare
to forbid	forbade	forbidden	proibire
to forecast	forecast	forecast	predire
to forget	forgot	forgotten	dimenticare
to forgive	forgave	forgiven	perdonare
to forsake	forsook	forsaken	abbandonare
to freeze	froze	frozen	gelare
to get	got	got, gotten	ottenere, diventare
to gird	girt	girt	cingere
to give	gave	given	dare
to go	went	gone	andare
to grind	ground	ground	macinare
to grow	grew	grown	crescere, coltivare
to hang	hung	hung, hanged	appendere
to have	had	had	avere
to hear	heard	heard	udire
to hew*	hewed	hewn	recidere
to hide	hid	hidden, hid	nascondere
to hit	hit	hit	colpire
to hold	held	held	tenere, trattenere
to hurt	hurt	hurt	far male, ferire
to keep	kept	kept	tenere, conservare
to kneel*	knelt	knelt	inginocchiarsi
to knit*	knit	knit	lavorare a maglia
to know	knew	known	conoscere, sapere
to lay	laid	laid	deporre, posare
to lead	led	led	condurre, guidare
to lean	leant	leant	appoggiarsi, inclinarsi
to leap	leapt	leapt	saltare
to learn*	learnt	learnt	imparare
to leave	left	left	lasciare, partire
to lend	lent	lent	prestare
to let	let	let	lasciare
to lie	lay	lain	giacere, trovarsi
to light*	lit	lit	accendere
to lose	lost	lost	perdere
to make	made	made	fare
to mean	meant	meant	intendere, significare
to meet	met	met	incontrare
to mislay	mislaid	mislaid	smarrire
to mislead	misled	misled	sviare
to mistake	mistook	mistaken	sbagliare
to mow*	mowed	mown	falciare
to pay	paid	paid	pagare
to put	put	put	mettere

to read	read	read	leggere
to rend	rent	rent	strappare
to ride	rode	ridden	cavalcare
to ring	rang	rung	suonare
to rise	rose	risen	alzarsi, sorgere
to run	ran	run	correre
to saw	sawed	sawn	segare
to say	said	said	dire
to see	saw	seen	vedere
to seek	sought	sought	cercare
to sell	sold	sold	vendere
to send	sent	sent	mandare
to set	set	set	porre
to sew	sewed	sewn	cucire
to shake	shook	shaken	scuotere, tremare
to shear*	sheared	shorn	tosare
to shed	shed	shed	spargere
to shine	shone	shone	brillare, splendere
to shoe	shod	shod	calzare
to shoot	shot	shot	sparare
to show	showed	shown	mostrare
to shred	shred	shred	tagliuzzare
to shrink	shrank, shrunk	shrunk, shrunken	restringersi
to shut	shut	shut	chiudere
to sing	sang	sung	cantare
to sink	sank, sunk	sunk	affondare
to sit	sat	sat	sedere
to slay	slew	slain	trucidare
to sleep	slept	slept	dormire
to slink	slunk	slunk	svignarsela
to smell*	smelt	smelt	fiutare, odorare
to sow*	sowed	sown	seminare
to speak	spoke	spoken	parlare
to spell	spelt	spelt	compitare
to spend	spent	spent	spendere
to spill*	spilt	spilt	spandere, versare
to spin	spun, span	spun	filare
to spit	spat, spit	spat, spit	sputare
to split	split	split	spaccare
to spoil	spoilt	spoilt	guastare, viziare
to spread	spread	spread	diffondere, stendere
to spring	sprang	sprung	saltare
to stand	stood	stood	stare (in piedi)
to steal	stole	stolen	rubare
to stick	stuck	stuck	appiccicare
to sting	stung	stung	pungere
to stink	stank, stunk	stunk	puzzare
to strike	struck	struck	battere, colpire
to strive	strove	striven	sforzarsi
to swear	swore	sworn	giurare
to sweat*	sweat	sweat	sudare
to sweep	swept	swept	spazzare
to swell*	swelled	swollen	gonfiare
to swim	swam	swum	nuotare
to swing	swung	swung	dondolare
to take	took	taken	prendere

to teach	taught	taught	insegnare
to tear	tore	torn	lacerare
to tell	told	told	dire, raccontare
to think	thought	thought	pensare
to thrive	throve	thriven	prosperare
to throw	threw	thrown	gettare
to thrust	thrust	thrust	spingere, gettare
to tread	trode	trod, trodden	calpestare
to understand	understood	understood	capire
to upset	upset	upset	capovolgere
to wake	woke	woke, woken	svegliare, svegliarsi
to wear	wore	worn	indossare, logorare
to weave	wove	woven	intrecciare, tessere
to weep	wept	wept	piangere
to win	won	won	vincere
to wind	wound	wound	serpeggiare
to withdraw	withdrew	withdrawn	ritirare, ritirarsi
to wring	wrung	wrung	torcere
to write	wrote	written	scrivere

TABELLA DI RAFFRONTO
FRA LE UNITÀ INGLESI O AMERICANE
E IL SISTEMA METRICO

	denominazione delle unità inglesi o americane	valore	equivalenza col sistema metrico *	equivalenza del sistema metrico con le unità inglesi **
misure lineari	pollice (inch - in)	—	2,54 cm	0,3937 (cm)
	piede (foot - ft)	12 in	0,304 m	3,28 (m)
	yarda (yard - yd)	3 ft	0,914 m	1,09 (m)
	fathom	6 ft	1,828 m	0,546 (m)
	miglio terrestre (statute mile)	5280 ft	1,609 km	0,621 (km)
	miglio inglese	5000 ft	1,523 km	0,656 (km)
	nodo (nautical mile)	6080 ft	1,853 km	0,539 (km)
superfici	pollice quadr. (square inch - sq.in)	—	6,45 cm²	0,155 (cm²)
	piede quadr. (square foot - sq.ft)	144 sq.in	829 cm²	10,76 (m²)
	yarda quadr. (square yard - sq.yd)	1296 sq.in	0,836 m²	1,196 (m²)
	miglio quadr. (square mile)		2,59 km²	0,386 (km²)
volumi e capacità	pollice cubo (cubic inch - cu.in)	—	16,38 cm³	0,061 (cm³)
	piede cubo (cubic foot - cu.ft)	1728 cu.in	28,32 dm³	0,0353 (dm³)
	yarda cubica (cubic yard - cu.yd)	27 cu.ft	0,764 m³	1,308 (m³)
	register ton	100 cu.ft	2,852 m³	0,353 (m³)
	oncia fluida americana (U.S. fl.oz)	1,8 cu.in	29,57 cm³	0,0338 (cm³)
	oncia fluida inglese (imp. fl.oz)	1,73 cu.in	28,4 cm³	0,0353 (cm³)
	bushel	8 gals	28,3 l	0,035 (l)
	gallone americano (U.S. gal)	231 cu.in	3,78 l	0,26 (l)
	gallone inglese (imp. gal)	277 cu.in	4,54 l	0,22 (l)
	pinta (pint)	1/8 gal	0,47 l	2,11 (l)
pesi	oncia avoirdupois (ounce - oz)	—	28,35 g	0,0352 (g)
	oncia troy (ounce troy - oz)		31,1 g	0,0321 (g)
	libbra avoirdupois (pound - lb)	16 oz.a.d.p.	453 g	2,204 (kg)
	libbra troy (pound - lb)	12 oz.t.	373 g	2,679 (kg)
	tonnellata americana (short ton - ton)	2000 lbs	907 kg	0,102 (t)
	tonnellata ingl. (long ton - ton)	2240 lbs	1016 kg	0,984 (t)

Con la graduale introduzione del sistema metrico, le unità di misura inglesi e americane diventeranno progressivamente meno diffuse.

* Coefficiente per il quale si deve moltiplicare il valore della grandezza per ottenere la misura nel sistema metrico.

** Coefficiente per il quale si deve moltiplicare il valore espresso nell'unità metrica segnato tra parentesi per ottenere la misura nel sistema inglese.

SISTEMA MONETARIO INGLESE
(Denaro circolante)
Unità base = **pound**, sterlina.

Monete *(coins)*

½p piece (half-penny), duecentesima parte della sterlina;
1p piece (one penny), centesima parte sterlina;
2p piece (two pence), cinquantesima parte della sterlina;
5p piece (five pence), ventesima parte della sterlina;
10p piece (ten pence), decima parte della sterlina;
50p piece (fifty pence), metà della sterlina.

Banconote *(banknotes)*

pound note (£1), sterlina carta;
five-pound note (£5), cinque sterline;
ten-pound note (£10), dieci sterline;
twenty-pound note (£20), venti sterline.

Monete nominali *(nominal coins* – usate nelle parcelle dei professionisti, prezzi par articoli di lusso, per libri, ecc.)

guinea (£1.05, 105p), ghinea, centocinque pence;
half (a) guinea (52 ½p), mezza ghinea, cinquantadue pence e mezzo.

SISTEMA MONETARIO AMERICANO
(Denaro circolante)
Unità base = **dollar**, dollaro.

Rame *(copper)*:
cent o penny (1 c.), un centesimo di dollaro.

Lega di rame e nichel *(copper and nickel alloy)*:
nickel o five cents (5 c.), cinque centesimi di dollaro.

Argento *(silver)*:
dime (10 c.), dieci centesimi di dollaro;
quarter (25 c.), un quarto di dollaro;
half-dollar (50 c.), mezzo dollaro, cinquanta centesimi;
dollar ($ 1), dollaro (generalmente in banconota).

Banconote *(bills)*:
si hanno tagli da $ 1, 2, 5, 10, 20, 50, 100, 500.
Esistono inoltre, sebbene non in circolazione normale, banconote da $ 1,000, 5,000 e 10,000.

I NUMERI

CARDINALI

1	one
2	two
3	three
4	four
5	five
6	six
7	seven
8	eight
9	nine
10	ten
11	eleven
12	twelve
13	thirteen
14	fourteen
15	fifteen
16	sixteen
17	seventeen
18	eighteen
19	nineteen
20	twenty
21	twenty-one
22	twenty-two
30	thirty
40	forty
50	fifty
60	sixty
70	seventy
80	eighty
90	ninety
100	one hundred
101	one hundred and one
200	two hundred
1.000	one thousand
1.001	one thousand and one
1.010	one thousand and ten
10.000	ten thousand
100.000	one hundred thousand
200.000	two hundred thousand
1.000.000	one million

ORDINALI

1° -	1st -	the first
2° -	2nd -	the second
3° -	3rd -	the third
4° -	4th -	the fourth
5° -	5th -	the fifth
6° -	6th -	the sixth
7° -	7th -	the seventh
8° -	8th -	the eighth
9° -	9th -	the ninth
10° -	10th -	the tenth
11° -	11th -	the eleventh
12° -	12th -	the twelfth
13° -	13th -	the thirteenth
14° -	14th -	the fourteenth
15° -	15th -	the fifteenth
16° -	16th -	the sixteenth
17° -	17th -	the seventeenth
18° -	18th -	the eighteenth
19° -	19th -	the nineteenth
20° -	20th -	the twentieth
21° -	21st -	the twenty-first
22° -	22nd -	the twenty-second
30° -	30th -	the thirtieth
40° -	40th -	the fortieth
50° -	50th -	the fiftieth
60° -	60th -	the sixtieth
70° -	70th -	the seventieth
80° -	80th -	the eightieth
90° -	90th -	the ninetieth
100° -	100th -	the (one) hundredth
101° -	101st -	the one hundred and first
200° -	200th -	the two hundredth
1.000° -	1.000th -	the (one) thousandth
1.001° -	1.001st -	the one thousand and first
1.010° -	1.010th -	the one thousand and tenth
10.000° -	10,000th -	the ten thousandth
100.000° -	100,000th -	the one hundred thousandth
200.000° -	200,000th -	the two hundred thousandth
1.000.000° -	1,000,000th -	the one millionth

ELENCO DELLE ABBREVIAZIONI

abbr.	abbreviazione	*gen.*	genitivo
(aer.)	aeronautica	*general.*	generalmente
agg.	aggettivo	*(geogr.)*	geografia
(agr.)	agricoltura	*(geol.)*	geologia
(amer.)	americano, americanismo	*(geom.)*	geometria
		ger.	gerundio
amm.	amministrativo, amministrazione	*(gergo)*	gergo, gergale
		(giorn.)	giornalismo, giornalistico
(anat.)	anatomia		
(ant.)	anticamente, antiquato	*(giur.)*	giuridico
(arch.)	architettura	*(gramm.)*	grammatica
art.	articolo	*i.*	intransitivo
(arte)	arte, artistico	*id.*	idem
assol.	assoluto	*imp.*	impersonale
(astr.)	astronomia	*imperat.*	imperativo
attr.	attributo, attributivo	*ind.*	indicativo
aus.	ausiliare	*indef.*	indefinito
(auto)	automobilismo	*inf.*	infinito
avv.	avverbio	*int.*	interrogativo
(bot.)	botanica	*inter.*	interiezione, interiettivo
(biol.)	biologia	*(iron.)*	ironico
(chim.)	chimica	*irr.*	irregolare
(chir.)	chirurgia	*(itt.)*	ittiologia
(cine)	cinematografia	*(lat.)*	latino, latinismo
coll.	collettivo	*loc. avv.*	locuzione avverbiale
(comm.)	commercio, commerciale	*loc. cong.*	locuzione congiuntiva
comp.	comparativo	*loc. prep.*	locuzione prepositiva
compl.	complemento	*(lett.)*	letteratura, letterario
condiz.	condizionale	*m.*	maschile
cong.	congiunzione	*(mar.)*	marina, marittimo, marinaresco
(costr.)	costruzioni		
(cuc.)	cucina	*(mat.)*	matematica
(dial.)	dialettale	*(mecc.)*	meccanica
dif.	difettivo	*(med.)*	medicina
dim.	diminutivo	*(metal.)*	metallurgia
dimostr.	dimostrativo	*(mil.)*	militare
ecc., etc.	eccetera	*(min.)*	mineralogia, minerario
(eccl.)	ecclesiastico	*(mit.)*	mitologia
(econ.)	economia	*(mus.)*	musica
(edil.)	edilizia	*neg.*	negazione, negativo
(elettr.)	elettricità, elettrotecnica	*(neol.)*	neologismo
escl.	esclamativo, in esclamazione	*ogg.*	oggetto
		(ott.)	ottica
f.	femminile	*p.*	participio
(fam.)	familiare	*pass.*	passato
(farm.)	farmacia, farmaceutico	*pers.*	persona, **personale**
(ferr.)	ferrovia	*(pitt.)*	pittura
(fig.)	figurato	*pl.*	plurale
(fil.)	filosofia	*(poet.)*	poetico
(fis.)	fisica	*(pol.)*	politica
(foto)	fotografia	*(pop.)*	popolare
fut.	futuro	*poss.*	possessivo

pp.	participio passato	*sost.*	sostantivato
prep.	preposizione	*spec.*	specialmente
pred.	predicato, predicativo	*(sport)*	sport, sportivo
pres.	presente	*(spreg.)*	spregiativo
pron.	pronome, pronominale	*sthg.*	something
prov.	proverbio, proverbiale	*(stor.)*	storia
(psicol.)	psicologia	*superl.*	superlativo
qc.	qualcosa	*t.*	transitivo
qu.	qualcuno	*(teat.)*	teatro
r.	riflessivo	*(tec.)*	tecnica
(radio)	radiofonia	*(tel.)*	telefonia, telefono
rec.	reciproco	*(teol.)*	teologia
reg.	regolare	*(tip.)*	tipografia
rel.	relativo	*(tv.)*	televisione
(relig.)	religione	*(us.)*	uso, usato
s.	(dall'inglese) sostantivo	*v.*	verbo
s.	(dall'italiano) sostantivo	*V.*	vedi
	maschile e femminile	*(vezz.)*	vezzeggiativo
semidif.	semidifettivo	*v. dif.*	verbo difettivo
sf.	sostantivo femminile	*vi.*	verbo intransitivo
sm.	sostantivo maschile	*(v. irr.)*	verbo irregolare
(scherz.)	scherzoso	*(volg.)*	volgare
(scol.)	scolastico	*vr.*	verbo riflessivo
(scult.)	scultura	*v. semidif.*	verbo semidifettivo
sing.	singolare	*vt.*	verbo transitivo
so.	someone	*(zool.)*	zoologia
sogg.	soggetto		

INGLESE-ITALIANO

A

a *art.* 1. un, uno, una 2. un certo || *once a week*, una volta alla settimana.

A *s.* (*mus.*) la.

aback *avv.* alla sprovvista.

abacus *s.* 1. abaco 2. pallottoliere.

abandon *s.* abbandono.

to **abandon** *vt.* abbandonare.

to **abase** *vt.* abbassare, umiliare.

abasement *s.* umiliazione.

to **abash** *vt.* confondere.

abashment *s.* confusione.

to **abate** *vt.* diminuire. ♦ to **abate** *vi.* placarsi (*di tempo atmosferico*).

abatement *s.* diminuzione.

abbess *s.* badessa.

abbey *s.* abbazia.

abbot *s.* abate.

abbreviation *s.* abbreviazione.

to **abdicate** *vt.* e *vi.* 1. abdicare a 2. dimettersi.

abdication *s.* abdicazione.

abdomen *s.* addome.

abdominal *agg.* addominale.

to **abduct** *vt.* rapire.

abduction *s.* rapimento.

abductor *s.* 1. rapitore 2. (*anat.*) abduttore.

aberration *s.* aberrazione.

abetter *s.* fautore.

abeyance *s.* sospensione.

to **abhor** *vt.* aborrire.

abhorrence *s.* aborrimento.

to **abide** (**abode**, **abode**) *vi.* abitare || — by, conformarsi a.

ability *s.* abilità, capacità.

abject *agg.* abietto.

abjection *s.* abiezione.

abjuration *s.* abiura.

to **abjure** *vt.* abiurare.

ablation *s.* ablazione.

ablative *agg.* e *s.* ablativo.

able *agg.* capace || to be — to, essere in grado di, potere.

ablution *s.* abluzione.

abnegation *s.* 1. abnegazione 2. rinuncia.

abnormal *agg.* anormale.

aboard *avv.* e *prep.* a bordo.

abode V. to **abide**. ♦ **abode** *s.* dimora.

to **abolish** *vt.* abolire.

abolishment, **abolition** *s.* abolizione.

abolitionism *s.* abolizionismo.

abolitionist *agg.* e *s.* abolizionista.

abominable *agg.* abominevole.

to **abominate** *vt.* detestare.

abomination *s.* abominazione.

aboriginal *agg.* e *s.* aborigeno ||

to **abort** *vi.* abortire.

abortion *s.* aborto.

abortive *agg.* abortivo.

to **abound** *vi.* abbondare.

about *avv.* 1. circa 2. intorno || *to be* —, stare per. ♦ **about** *prep.* 1. intorno a 2. presso di 3. riguardo a.

above *prep.* 1. al di sopra di 2. più di || — *mentioned*, suddetto. ♦ **above** *avv.* in alto, sopra.

abrasion *s.* abrasione.

to **abridge** *vt.* 1. abbreviare 2. privare di.

abridg(e)ment *s.* 1. abbreviazione, sommario 2. privazione.

abroad *avv.* 1. all'estero 2. fuori.

to **abrogate** *vt.* abrogare.

abrogation *s.* abrogazione.

abrupt *agg.* 1. scosceso 2. brusco 3. inaspettato.

abruptness *s.* 1. ripidezza 2. rudezza 3. precipitazione.

abscess *s.* ascesso.

abscissa *s.* ascissa.

absence *s.* assenza.

absent *agg.* assente || — *minded*, distratto; — *mindedness*, distrazione.

to **absent** *vt.* to — *oneself*, assentarsi.

absenteeism *s.* assenteismo.

absinth(e) *s.* assenzio.

absolute *agg.* e *s.* assoluto.

absolution *s.* assoluzione.

absolutism *s.* assolutismo.

absolutist *agg.* e *s.* assolutista.

to **absolve** *vt.* assolvere.

to **absorb** *vt.* assorbire.

absorbent *agg.* e *s.* assorbente.

absorption *s.* assorbimento.

to **abstain** *vi.* astenersi.

abstemious *agg.* sobrio.

abstention *s.* astensione.

abstentionist *s.* astensionista.

abstinence *s.* astinenza.

abstract *agg.* astratto. ♦ **abstract** *s.* 1. astrazione 2. estratto.

to **abstract** *vt.* 1. astrarre 2. estrarre 3. sottrarre 4. riassumere.

abstraction *s.* 1. astrazione 2. distrazione 3. furto.

abstractly *avv.* astrattamente.

abstruse *agg.* astruso.

abstruseness *s.* astrusità.

absurd agg. assurdo.

absurdity s. assurdità.

absurdly avv. assurdamente.

abundance s. abbondanza.

abundant agg. abbondante.

abuse s. 1. abuso 2. ingiuria.

to abuse vt. 1. abusare 2. ingiuriare.

abusive agg. 1. abusivo 2. ingiurioso.

abysm, abyss s. abisso.

abysmal, abyssal agg. abissale.

academic agg. e s. accademico.

academician s. accademico.

academy s. accademia: — of music, conservatorio.

acanthus s. acanto.

acarus s. (pl. -ri) acaro.

to accelerate vt. accelerare.

acceleration s. accelerazione.

accelerative agg. accelerativo.

accelerator s. acceleratore.

accent s. accento.

to accent vt. 1. accentare 2. accentuare.

to accentuate V. to accent.

accentuation s. accentuazione.

to accept vt. accettare, approvare.

acceptable agg. accettabile.

acceptance s. 1. accettazione 2. consenso.

acceptation s. accezione, significato.

access s. accesso.

accessible agg. accessibile.

accession s. 1. assunzione (al trono) 2. adesione 3. aggiunta.

accessory agg. e s. 1. accessorio 2. complice.

accident s. 1. caso: by —, per caso 2. incidente 3. irregolarità.

accidental agg. accidentale.

to acclaim vt. acclamare.

acclamation s. acclamazione.

acclimation, acclimatization s. acclimazione, acclimatazione.

to acclimate, to acclimatize vt. acclimatare. ♦ **to acclimate, to acclimatize** vi. acclimatarsi.

to accommodate vt. 1. adattare 2. ospitare 3. fornire.

accommodating agg. accomodante.

accommodation s. 1. accomodamento 2. comodità 3. alloggio 4. (comm.) facilitazione.

accompaniment s. accompagnamento.

accompanist s. (mus.) accompagnatore.

to accompany vt. accompagnare

(anche mus.).

accomplice s. complice.

to accomplish vt. compiere, realizzare.

accomplishment s. 1. compimento 2. compitezza 3. dote.

accord s. accordo.

to accord vt. accordare. ♦ **to accord** vi. accordarsi.

accordance s. accordo.

accordant agg. concorde, conforme.

according agg. 1. concordante, conforme 2. armonioso. ♦ **according** avv. — as, secondo che; — to, secondo.

accordingly avv. 1. in conseguenza 2. conformemente.

accordion s. fisarmonica.

accordionist s. fisarmonicista.

account s. 1. (comm.) conto 2. (comm.) acconto 3. valore 4. resoconto || to take into —, prendere in considerazione; on — of, a causa di.

to account vt. considerare || to — for, essere responsabile di.

accountable agg. responsabile.

accountancy s. ragioneria.

accountant s. contabile || chartered —, ragioniere.

to accredit vt. accreditare.

to accrue vi. 1. derivare 2. accumularsi.

to accumulate vt. accumulare. ♦ **to accumulate** vi. accumularsi.

accumulation s. accumulazione.

accumulative agg. accumulativo.

accumulator s. accumulatore.

accuracy s. esattezza.

accurate agg. esatto.

accusation s. accusa.

accusative agg. e s. accusativo.

to accuse vt. accusare.

accused s. accusato.

accuser s. accusatore.

to accustom vt. abituare.

accustomed agg. 1. abituale 2. abituato.

ace s. asso.

acetone s. acetone.

acetylene s. acetilene.

ache s. dolore.

to ache vi. far male: my head aches, mi fa male la testa.

to achieve vt. 1. compiere 2. ottenere.

achievement s. 1. compimento 2. conseguimento 3. gesta.

aching agg. 1. doloroso 2. afflitto.

♦ **aching** *s.* dolore.
acid *agg.* e *s.* acido.
acidity *s.* acidità.
acidulous *agg.* acidulo.
to **acknowledge** *vt.* riconoscere ‖ *to — receipt of,* accusare ricevuta di.
acknowledg(e)ment *s.* riconoscimento.
acolyte *s.* accolito.
acorn *s.* ghianda.
acoustic(al) *agg.* acustico.
acoustics *s.* acustica.
to **acquaint** *vt.* informare ‖ *to become acquainted with,* fare la conoscenza di.
acquaintance *s.* conoscenza.
acquiescence *s.* acquiescenza.
to **acquire** *vt.* acquisire, acquistare.
acquisition *s.* acquisto.
to **acquit** *vt.* **1.** pagare **2.** liberare **3.** assolvere.
acquittal *s.* (*giur.*) assoluzione.
acquittance *s.* **1.** saldo **2.** quietanza.
acrid *agg.* acre.
acridity *s.* asprezza.
acrimony *s.* acrimonia.
acrobat *s.* acrobata.
acrobatic(al) *agg.* acrobatico.
acrobatics *s. pl.* acrobazia (*sing.*).
acropolis *s.* acropoli.
across *avv.* per traverso. ♦ **across** *prep.* attraverso ‖ *to come —.* incontrare.
act *s.* atto, legge.
to **act** *vt.* e *vi.* **1.** agire, fare **2.** (*teat.*) recitare.
acting *agg.* facente funzione di. ♦ **acting** *s.* **1.** azione **2.** (*teat.*) rappresentazione.
action *s.* **1.** azione **2.** (*giur.*) processo **3.** (*mecc.*) funzionamento.
active *agg.* attivo.
activism *s.* attivismo.
activist *s.* attivista.
activity *s.* attività.
actor *s.* attore.
actress *s.* attrice.
actual *agg.* reale.
actuality *s.* realtà.
actually *avv.* realmente.
to **actuate** *vt.* mettere in moto.
acuminate *agg.* acuminato.
acute *agg.* acuto.
ad *s.* V. *advertisement.*
adamantine *agg.* adamantino.
to **adapt** *vt.* adattare.
adaptable *agg.* adattabile.
adaptation *s.* adattamento.

to **add** *vt.* aggiungere ‖ *to — up.* fare una somma.
addendum *s.* (*pl.* -da) aggiunta.
adder *s.* vipera.
addict *s.* tossicomane.
addition *s.* **1.** (*mat.*) addizione **2.** aggiunta.
additional *agg.* supplementare.
address *s.* **1.** indirizzo **2.** abilità. ♦ **addresses** *s. pl.* omaggi.
to **address** *vt.* e *vi.* indirizzare, arringare. ♦ **to address** *vi.* rivolgersi.
addressee *s.* destinatario.
addresser *s.* mittente.
to **adduce** *vt.* addurre.
adenoids *s. pl.* adenoidi.
adept *agg.* e *s.* perito, esperto.
adequate *agg.* adeguato.
to **adhere** *vi.* aderire.
adherence *s.* aderenza, adesione.
adherent *agg.* e *s.* aderente.
adhesion *s.* V. *adherence.*
adhesive *agg.* e *s.* adesivo.
adipose *agg.* adiposo.
adjacent *agg.* adiacente.
adjective *agg.* **1.** aggettivale **2.** addizionale. ♦ **adjective** *s.* aggettivo.
to **adjoin** *vt.* **1.** aggiungere **2.** essere contiguo.
adjoining *agg.* adiacente.
to **adjourn** *vt.* aggiornare.
adjournment *s.* aggiornamento.
adjunct *s.* **1.** aggiunta **2.** aggiunto **3.** (*gramm.*) complemento.
adjuration *s.* implorazione.
to **adjust** *vt.* **1.** aggiustare **2.** adattare **3.** regolare.
adjustment *s.* **1.** adattamento, compromesso **2.** (*comm.*) liquidazione.
adjutant *s.* aiutante.
to **administer** *vt.* **1.** amministrare **2.** fornire. ♦ **to administer** *vi.* contribuire.
administration *s.* **1.** amministrazione **2.** somministrazione.
administrative *agg.* amministrativo.
administrator *s.* amministratore.
admirable *agg.* ammirabile.
admiral *s.* ammiraglio.
admiralty *s.* ammiragliato.
admiration *s.* ammirazione.
to **admire** *vt.* ammirare.
admirer *s.* ammiratore.
admiringly *avv.* con ammirazione.
admissible *agg.* ammissibile.
admission *s.* **1.** ammissione **2.** con-

fessione.

to **admit** *vt.* **1.** ammettere **2.** contenere.

admittance *s.* ammissione, ingresso.

to **admonish** *vt.* ammonire.

admonition *s.* ammonimento.

ado *s.* **1.** fatica **2.** confusione.

adolescence *s.* adolescenza.

adolescent *agg.* e *s.* adolescente.

to **adopt** *vt.* adottare.

adoption *s.* adozione.

adoptive *agg.* adottivo.

adorable *agg.* adorabile.

adoration *s.* adorazione.

to **adore** *vt.* adorare.

to **adorn** *vt.* adornare.

adornment *s.* ornamento.

adrenalin *s.* adrenalina.

adrift *avv.* alla deriva.

to **adulate** *vt.* adulare.

adulation *s.* adulazione.

adulator *s.* adulatore.

adult *agg.* e *s.* adulto.

to **adulterate** *vt.* adulterare.

adulteration *s.* adulterazione.

adulterer *s.* adultero.

adulteress *s.* adultera.

adulterine *agg.* adulterino.

adultery *s.* adulterio.

advance *s.* **1.** avanzamento **2.** anticipo **3.** approccio.

to **advance** *vt.* **1.** portar avanti **2.** anticipare (*denaro*) **3.** (*comm.*) aumentare. ♦ to **advance** *vi.* avanzare.

advancement *s.* **1.** avanzamento **2.** (*comm.*) rialzo.

advantage *s.* vantaggio || to take — of, approfittare di.

to **advantage** *vt.* avvantaggiare.

advantageous *agg.* vantaggioso.

advent *s.* avvento.

adventure *s.* avventura.

to **adventure** *vt.* rischiare. ♦ to **adventure** *vi.* avventurarsi.

adventurer *s.* avventuriero.

adventurous *agg.* avventuroso.

adverb *s.* avverbio.

adverbial *agg.* avverbiale.

adversary *s.* avversario.

adverse *agg.* avverso.

adversity *s.* avversità.

to **advert** *vi.* alludere, riferirsi.

to **advertise** *vt.* e *vi.* fare pubblicità a, divulgare.

advertisement *s.* **1.** avviso **2.** cartellone pubblicitario **3.** inserzione.

advertiser *s.* inserzionista.

advertising *agg.* pubblicitario. ♦ **advertising** *s.* pubblicità.

advice *s.* **1.** consiglio **2.** notizia.

advisability *s.* opportunità.

advisable *agg.* consigliabile.

to **advise** *vt.* **1.** consigliare **2.** avvisare || to — with so., consultarsi con qu.

advised *agg.* giudizioso.

adviser *s.* consigliere.

advocacy *s.* avvocatura.

advocate *s.* difensore.

aegis *s.* egida.

Aeolian *agg.* eolio.

to **aerate** *vt.* **1.** aerare **2.** gassare.

aeration *s.* **1.** aerazione **2.** (*chim.*) aggiunta di acido carbonico.

aerial *agg.* aereo. ♦ **aerial** *s.* (*radio*) antenna.

aerodrome *s.* aerodromo.

aerodynamics *s.* aerodinamica.

aeronaut *s.* aeronauta.

aeronautics *s.* aeronautica.

aeroplane *s.* aeroplano.

aerostat *s.* aerostato.

aerostatics *s.* aerostatica.

aesthete *s.* esteta.

aesthetic(al) *agg.* estetico.

aestheticism *s.* estetismo.

aesthetics *s.* estetica.

aestivation *s.* letargo estivo.

aether *s.* etere.

afar *avv.* lontano.

affability *s.* affabilità.

affable *agg.* affabile.

affair *s.* **1.** affare **2.** tresca.

to **affect**[1] *vt.* **1.** ostentare **2.** simulare.

to **affect**[2] *vt.* **1.** concernere **2.** commuovere **3.** (*med.*) intaccare.

affectation *s.* affettazione.

affected *agg.* **1.** affettato **2.** affetto **3.** commosso **4.** disposto.

affection *s.* **1.** affetto **2.** (*med.*) affezione.

affectionate *agg.* affezionato, affettuoso.

affective *agg.* affettivo.

to **affiliate** *vt.* affiliare. ♦ to **affiliate** *vi.* affiliarsi.

affiliation *s.* affiliazione.

affinity *s.* affinità, parentela.

to **affirm** *vt.* **1.** affermare **2.** ratificare.

affirmation *s.* **1.** affermazione **2.** ratificazione.

affirmative *agg.* affermativo || in the —, affermativamente.

to **affix** *vt.* aggiungere, apporre.

to **afflict** *vt.* affliggere.
affliction *s.* afflizione.
affluence *s.* **1.** affluenza **2.** abbondanza.
affluent *agg.* ricco. ◆ **affluent** *s.* (*geogr.*) affluente.
afflux *s.* afflusso.
to **afford** *vt.* offrire || can —, potersi permettere.
to **afforest** *vt.* imboschire.
afforestation *s.* imboschimento.
affront *s.* affronto || *to take* — *at*, offendersi per.
to **affront** *vt.* **1.** affrontare **2.** insultare.
afloat *avv.* a galla. ◆ **afloat** *agg.* **1.** galleggiante **2.** in circolazione.
afore *avv.* precedentemente. ◆ **afore** *prep.* prima di.
aforementioned, aforesaid *agg.* predetto.
afraid *agg.* spaventato || *to be* —, temere.
African *agg.* e *s.* africano.
after *agg.* seguente. ◆ **after** *prep.* **1.** dopo, dietro **2.** secondo **3.** alla maniera di. ◆ **after** *avv.* dopo. ◆ **after** *cong.* dopo che.
afternoon *s.* pomeriggio.
afterthought *s.* riflessione.
afterward(s) *avv.* poi.
again *avv.* ancora, di nuovo.
against *prep.* **1.** contro **2.** in previsione di.
agape *agg.* e *avv.* a bocca aperta.
age *s.* **1.** età **2.** secolo || *old* —, vecchiaia; *to be of* —, essere maggiorenne; *to be under* —, essere minorenne; *Middle Ages*, Medioevo.
to **age** *vt.* e *vi.* invecchiare.
aged *agg.* **1.** vecchio **2.** dell'età di.
agency *s.* **1.** causa, azione **2.** (*comm.*) agenzia, rappresentanza.
agent *s.* agente.
agglomerate *agg.* e *s.* agglomerato.
to **agglomerate** *vt.* agglomerare. ◆ to **agglomerate** *vi.* agglomerarsi.
agglomeration *s.* agglomerazione.
to **agglutinate** *vt.* agglutinare. ◆ to **agglutinate** *vi.* agglutinarsi.
to **aggravate** *vt.* **1.** aggravare **2.** irritare.
aggravation *s.* **1.** aggravamento **2.** esasperazione.
aggregate *agg.* e *s.* aggregato.
to **aggregate** *vt.* **1.** aggregare **2.** ammontare a. ◆ to **aggregate** *vi.* aggregarsi.

aggregation *s.* aggregazione.
aggression *s.* aggressione.
aggressive *agg.* aggressivo.
aggressiveness *s.* aggressività.
aggressor *s.* aggressore.
aghast *agg.* **1.** atterrito **2.** stupefatto.
agile *agg.* agile.
agility *s.* agilità.
to **agitate** *vt.* agitare.
agitation *s.* agitazione.
agitator *s.* agitatore.
agnostic *agg.* e *s.* agnostico.
ago *agg.* e *avv.* fa.
agonistic(al) *agg.* agonistico.
to **agonize** *vt.* tormentare. ◆ to **agonize** *vi.* **1.** tormentarsi **2.** agonizzare.
agony *s.* **1.** agonia **2.** dolore.
agrarian *agg.* e *s.* agrario.
to **agree** *vt.* e *vi.* **1.** accordarsi **2.** accettare **3.** essere adatto.
agreeable *agg.* **1.** gradevole **2.** conforme.
agreement *s.* **1.** accordo **2.** conformità **3.** consenso.
agricultural *agg.* agricolo.
agriculture *s.* agricoltura.
agronomist *s.* agronomo.
agronomy *s.* agronomia.
ague *s.* febbre malarica.
ahead *avv.* avanti.
aid *s.* aiuto.
to **aid** *vt.* aiutare, soccorrere.
to **ail** *vt.* affliggere. ◆ to **ail** *vi.* sentirsi male.
aileron *s.* alettone.
aim *s.* **1.** mira **2.** scopo.
to **aim** *vt.* e *vi.* **1.** mirare **2.** aspirare a.
aimless *agg.* senza scopo.
air *s.* aria || — *conditioning*, condizionamento d'aria; — *lift*, ponte aereo; —*line*, aviolinea; —*raid*, incursione aerea; — *mail*, posta aerea.
to **air** *vt.* aerare.
aircraft *s.* aereo, aerei || -*carrier*, portaerei.
airfield *s.* campo d'aviazione.
airiness *s.* leggerezza, disinvoltura.
airing *s.* **1.** ventilazione **2.** passeggiata.
to **air-mail** *vt.* trasportare per via aerea.
airman *s.* aviatore.
airport *s.* aeroporto.
airship *s.* aeronave.
airsickness *s.* mal d'aria.

airstrip *s.* pista (d'areoporto).

airtight *agg.* a tenuta d'aria.

airway *s.* via aerea.

airy *agg.* 1. arioso 2. aereo 3. gaio.

aisle *s.* navata (*laterale*).

ajar *avv.* socchiuso.

akin *agg.* 1. consanguineo 2. simile.

alacrity *s.* alacrità.

alarm *s.* allarme || —*clock*, sveglia; *to take* —, allarmarsi.

to alarm *vt.* allarmare.

alas *inter.* ahimè.

Albanian *agg.* e *s.* albanese.

albatross *s.* albatro.

albumen *s.* albume.

albumin *s.* albumina.

alchemist *s.* alchimista.

alchemy *s.* alchimia.

alcohol *s.* alcool: *wood* —, alcool metilico.

alcoholic *agg.* alcolico. ♦ **alcoholic** *sm.* alcolizzato.

alcoholism *s.* alcoolismo.

alcove *s.* alcova.

alder *s.* ontano.

alderman *s.* assessore.

ale *s.* birra || —*house*, birreria.

aleatory *agg.* aleatorio.

alembic *s.* alambicco.

alert *agg.* 1. all'erta 2. svelto. ♦ **alert** *s.* allarme.

algebraic(al) *agg.* algebrico.

alien *agg.* e *s.* 1. estraneo 2. straniero.

to alienate *vt.* alienare.

alienation *s.* alienazione.

alienist *s.* alienista.

alight *agg.* illuminato.

to alight *vi.* 1. scendere 2. posarsi, atterrare.

to align *vt.* allineare. ♦ **to align** *vi.* allinearsi.

alignment *s.* allineamento.

alike *agg.* simile. ♦ **alike** *avv.* similmente.

aliment *s.* alimento.

alimentary *agg.* alimentare.

alimentation *s.* alimentazione.

aliquot *agg.* e *s.* aliquota.

alive *agg.* 1. vivo 2. vivace 3. sensibile.

alkaline *agg.* alcalino.

all *agg.* tutto, tutti, ogni || — *the way*, lungo tutto il cammino. ♦ **all** *pron.* tutto, tutti || *not at* —, niente affatto; — *the better*, tanto meglio || — *of us*, noi tutti; *it is* — *up*, tutto è finito. ♦ **all** *avv.* completamente, interamente || —

right, va bene; — *but*, quasi. ♦ **all** *s.* tutto, totalità.

to allege *vt.* addurre.

allegiance *s.* fedeltà.

allegoric(al) *agg.* allegorico.

allegory *s.* allegoria.

allergic *agg.* allergico.

allergy *s.* allergia.

to alleviate *vt.* alleviare.

alleviation *s.* alleviamento.

alley *s.* vialetto, vicolo.

alliance *s.* 1. alleanza 2. unione.

allied *agg.* alleato.

alligator *s.* alligatore.

alliteration *s.* allitterazione.

alliterative *agg.* allitterativo.

to allocate *vt.* assegnare, distribuire.

allocution *s.* allocuzione.

to allot *vt.* assegnare.

allotment *s.* 1. distribuzione 2. lotto (*di terreno*).

to allow *vt.* 1. permettere 2. riconoscere 3. concedere.

allowance *s.* 1. permesso 2. assegno, indennità 3. razione 4. riconoscimento 5. sconto.

alloy *s.* (*metal.*) lega.

to allude *vi.* alludere.

to allure *vt.* attrarre.

allurement *s.* allettamento.

allusion *s.* allusione.

allusive *agg.* allusivo.

alluvion *s.* alluvione.

ally *s.* alleato.

to ally *vt.* 1. unire 2. alleare. ♦ **to ally** *vi.* allearsi.

almanac *s.* almanacco.

almighty *agg.* onnipotente: *the Almighty*, l'Onnipotente.

almond *s.* mandorla || — *tree*, mandorlo.

almost *avv.* quasi.

alms *s.* elemosina || — *house*, ospizio per i poveri; — *man*, accattone.

alone *agg.* e *avv.* solo.

along *avv.* e *prep.* 1. lungo 2. avanti.

alongside *avv.* (*mar.*) accanto, accosto. ♦ **alongside** *prep.* a fianco di, lungo.

aloof *avv.* a distanza. ♦ **aloof** *agg.* riservato, scontroso.

aloofness *s.* freddezza.

aloud *avv.* ad alta voce.

alp *s.* alpe.

alpha *s.* alfa.

alphabet *s.* alfabeto.

alphabetic(al) *agg.* alfabetico.

alpine *agg.* alpino.

already *avv.* già.

also *avv.* anche, inoltre.

altar *s.* altare || — -*boy*, chierichetto; — -*piece*, pala d'altare.

to **alter** *vt.* alterare. ♦ to **alter** *vi.* alterarsi, trasformarsi.

alteration *s.* alterazione.

altercation *s.* alterco.

alternacy *s.* alternanza.

alternate *agg.* alterno, alternato.

to **alternate** *vt.* alternare. ♦ to **alternate** *vi.* alternarsi.

alternation *s.* alternazione.

alternative *agg.* alternativo. ♦ **alternative** *s.* alternativa.

alternator *s.* (*elettr.*) alternatore.

although *cong.* benché.

altimeter *s.* altimetro.

altitude *s.* **1.** altitudine **2.** (*aer.*) quota.

altogether *avv.* interamente.

altruism *s.* altruismo.

altruist *s.* altruista.

altruistic *agg.* altruistico.

aluminium *s.* alluminio.

always *avv.* sempre.

amalgam *s.* amalgama.

to **amalgamate** *vt.* amalgamare. ♦ to **amalgamate** *vi.* amalgamarsi.

amalgamation *s.* amalgamazione.

amaranth *s.* amaranto.

to **amass** *vt.* ammucchiare.

amateur *agg. e s.* amatore, dilettante.

amateurism *s.* dilettantismo.

to **amaze** *vt.* stupire.

amazement *s.* sorpresa.

amazing *agg.* sorprendente.

Amazon *s.* amazzone.

ambages *s. pl.* ambagi.

ambassador *s.* ambasciatore.

amber *s.* ambra.

ambient *agg.* circostante. ♦ **ambient** *s.* ambiente.

ambiguity *s.* ambiguità.

ambiguous *agg.* ambiguo.

ambit *s.* ambito.

ambition *s.* ambizione.

ambitious *agg.* ambizioso.

ambivalence *s.* ambivalenza.

ambivalent *agg.* ambivalente.

amble *s.* ambio.

ambo *s.* ambone.

ambulance *s.* ambulanza.

ambush *s.* imboscata.

to **ambush** *vt. e vi.* tendere una imboscata (a).

to **ameliorate** *vt. e vi.* migliorare.

to **amend** *vt.* emendare. ♦ to **amend** *vi.* emendarsi.

amendment *s.* emendamento.

amends *s.* ammenda.

amenity *s.* amenità.

American *agg. e s.* americano.

Americanism *s.* americanismo.

amethyst *s.* ametista.

amiability *s.* amabilità.

amiable *agg.* amabile.

amiably *avv.* amabilmente.

amianthus *s.* amianto.

amicable *agg.* amichevole.

amid *prep.* in mezzo a, tra, fra.

amiss *avv.* a male; *to take sthg.* —, aversene a male. ♦ **amiss** *agg.* inopportuno, errato.

amity *s.* amicizia.

ammonia *s.* ammoniaca.

ammunition *s.* munizioni.

amnesty *s.* amnistia.

to **amnesty** *vt.* amnistiare.

amoeba *s.* ameba.

among(st) *prep.* tra, fra (*più di due*); in mezzo a.

amoral *agg.* amorale.

amorality *s.* amoralità.

amorous *agg.* amoroso.

amorphous *agg.* amorfo.

to **amortize** *vt.* (*comm.*) ammortizzare.

amount *s.* **1.** somma **2.** totale **3.** valore **4.** quantità.

to **amount** *vi.* **1.** ammontare **2.** equivalere.

amperometer *s.* amperometro.

amphibian *agg. e s.* anfibio.

amphibious *agg.* anfibio.

amphitheatre *s.* anfiteatro.

amphitryon *s.* anfitrione.

amphora *s.* anfora.

ample *agg.* ampio.

amplification *s.* amplificazione.

amplifier *s.* amplificatore.

to **amplify** *vt.* amplificare. ♦ to **amplify** *vi.* dilungarsi.

to **amputate** *vt.* amputare.

amputation *s.* amputazione.

amulet *s.* amuleto.

to **amuse** *vt.* divertire.

amusement *s.* divertimento.

an *art.* V. *a*.

anachronic *agg.* anacronistico.

anachronism *s.* anacronismo.

anachronistic(al) *agg.* anacronistico.

anaemia *s.* anemia.

anaemic *agg.* anemico.

anaesthesia *s.* anestesia.

anaesthetic *agg.* e *s.* anestetico.
anaesthetist *s.* anestesista.
to anaesthetize *vt.* anestetizzare.
anagram *s.* anagramma.
anal *agg.* anale.
analgesic *agg.* e *s.* analgesico.
analogic(al) *agg.* analogico.
analogous *agg.* analogo.
analogy *s.* analogia.
to analyse *vt.* analizzare.
analysis *s.* (*pl.* -ses) analisi.
analyst *s.* analista.
analytic(al) *agg.* analitico.
anarchic(al) *agg.* anarchico.
anarchism *s.* anarchia.
anarchist *s.* anarchico.
anarchy *s.* anarchia.
anathema *s.* anatema.
anatomic(al) *agg.* anatomico.
anatomist *s.* anatomista.
to anatomize *vt.* anatomizzare.
anatomy *s.* anatomia.
ancestor *s.* antenato.
ancestral *agg.* ancestrale.
ancestry *s.* stirpe.
anchor *s.* (*mar.*) ancora.
to anchor *vt.* ancorare. ♦ to anchor *vi.* ancorarsi.
anchorage *s.* ancoraggio.
anchoret *s.* anacoreta.
anchovy *s.* acciuga.
ancient *agg.* e *s.* antico.
and *cong.* e.
androgynous *agg.* androgino.
anecdote *s.* aneddoto.
anecdotic(al) *agg.* aneddotico.
anew *avv.* di nuovo.
anfractuosity *s.* anfrattuosità.
anfractuous *agg.* anfrattuoso.
angel *s.* angelo: guardian —, angelo custode.
angelic(al) *agg.* angelico.
anger *s.* collera.
to anger *vt.* irritare.
angle *s.* (*geom.*) angolo || at right angles, perpendicolarmente.
to angle *vi.* 1. pescare (con l'amo) 2. to — for, andare in cerca di.
angler *s.* pescatore (con l'amo).
Anglican *agg.* e *s.* anglicano.
Anglo-Saxon *agg.* e *s.* anglosassone.
angrily *avv.* irosamente.
angry *agg.* irato, arrabbiato || to get —, adirarsi.
anguish *s.* angoscia.
to anguish *vt.* angosciare. ♦ to anguish *vi.* angosciarsi.
angular *agg.* angolare.
anhydride *s.* anidride.

aniline *s.* anilina.
animadversion *s.* biasimo.
to animadvert *vi.* criticare: to — on so., sthg., criticare qu., qc.
animal *agg.* e *s.* animale.
to animate *vt.* animare.
animatedly *avv.* animatamente.
animation *s.* animazione.
animator *s.* animatore.
animism *s.* animismo.
animosity *s.* animosità.
anise *s.* anice.
ankle *s.* caviglia.
ankylosis *s.* anchilosi.
annals *s. pl.* annali.
Annelida *s. pl.* anellidi.
to annex *vt.* annettere.
annexation *s.* annessione.
to annihilate *vt.* annichilire.
annihilation *s.* annichilimento.
anniversary *s.* anniversario.
to annotate *vt.* e *vi.* annotare.
annotation *s.* annotazione.
to announce *vt.* annunciare.
announcement *s.* annuncio.
announcer *s.* annunciatore.
to annoy *vt.* infastidire.
annoyance *s.* fastidio.
annoying *agg.* fastidioso.
annual *agg.* annuale. ♦ annual *s.* annuario.
annuity *s.* rendita annuale.
to annul *vt.* annullare.
annulment *s.* annullamento.
to annunciate *vt.* annunciare.
annunciation *s.* annuncio, annunciazione.
anode *s.* anodo.
anodyne *agg.* e *s.* anodino.
to anoint *vt.* ungere, consacrare.
anomalous *agg.* anomalo.
anomaly *s.* anomalia.
anonym *s.* anonimo.
anonymous *agg.* anonimo.
another *agg.* e *pron.* un altro || one —, l'un l'altro.
answer *s.* risposta.
to answer *vt.* e *vi.* rispondere.
ant *s.* formica || --bear, formichiere.
antagonism *s.* antagonismo.
antagonist *s.* antagonista.
Antarctic *agg.* antartico.
antecedent *agg.* e *s.* antecedente. ♦ antecedents *s. pl.* antenati.
to antedate *vt.* 1. antidatare 2. anticipare.
antediluvian *agg.* e *s.* antidiluviano.

antelope s. antilope.
anteroom s. anticamera.
anthem s. inno.
anthological agg. antologico.
anthology s. antologia.
anthracite s. antracite.
anthropocentric agg. antropocentrico.
anthropologist s. antropologo.
anthropology s. antropologia.
anthropomorphic agg. antropomorfo.
anthropomorphism s. antropomorfismo.
anthropomorphous agg. antropomorfo.
anthropophagous agg. e s. (pl. -gi) antropofago.
anthropophagy s. antropofagia.
antiaesthetic agg. antiestetico.
anti-aircraft agg. antiaereo.
antibiotic agg. e s. antibiotico.
antibody s. anticorpo.
to **anticipate** vt. 1. anticipare 2. prevedere 3. pregustare.
anticipation s. 1. anticipo 2. previsione 3. pregustazione.
anticlerical agg. anticlericale.
anticlericalism s. anticlericalismo.
anticlerical s. anticlericale.
anticonceptive s. antifecondativo.
anticonstitutional agg. anticostituzionale.
anticyclone s. anticiclone.
anti-dazzle agg. antiabbagliante.
antidote s. antidoto.
anti-freeze s. anticongelante.
anti-gas agg. antigas.
antimilitarism s. antimilitarismo.
antimilitarist s. antimilitarista.
antimony s. antimonio.
antinomy s. antinomia.
antiparticle s. antiparticella.
antipathetic(al) agg. avverso.
antiphon(y) s. antifona.
antipodal agg. degli, agli antipodi.
antipode s. antipodo.
antiquarian agg. e s. antiquario.
antiquary s. antiquario.
antiquated agg. antiquato.
antique agg. antico. ♦ **antique** s. antichità ‖ — dealer, antiquario.
antiquity s. antichità.
antirheumatic agg. antireumatico.
anti-rust agg. e s. antiruggine.
anti-Semite s. antisemita.
anti-Semitism s. antisemitismo.
antiseptic agg. e s. antisettico.
antisocial agg. antisociale.

antispasmodic agg. e s. antispasmodico.
anti-tank agg. anticarro.
antitetanic agg. antitetanico.
anti-theft agg. e s. antifurto.
antithesis s. (pl. -ses) antitesi.
antithetic(al) agg. antitetico.
antitoxic agg. antitossico.
anus s. ano.
anvil s. incudine.
anxiety s. ansietà.
anxious agg. ansioso.
any agg. 1. qualunque 2. (in frasi neg.; int.; dubitative) qualche, nessuno, del ‖ at — rate, in ogni modo. ♦ **any** pron. 1. alcuno, nessuno 2. ne ‖ have you — bread?, hai del pane?; I haven't —, non ne ho.
anybody pron. 1. chiunque 2. (in frasi neg.; int.; dubitative) qualcuno, nessuno.
anyhow avv. e cong. comunque.
anyone pron. V. anybody.
anything pron. 1. qualunque cosa 2. (in frasi neg.; int.; dubitative) qualche cosa, niente.
anyway avv. in ogni modo, comunque.
anywhere avv. dovunque.
apace avv. presto.
apanage s. appannaggio.
apart avv. 1. a parte 2. lontano.
apartheid s. discriminazione razziale.
apartment s. alloggio (in affitto).
apathy s. apatia.
ape s. scimmia.
to **ape** vt. scimmiottare.
aperitif s. aperitivo.
apex s. apice.
aphaeresis s. aferesi.
aphonia s. afonia.
aphorism s. aforisma.
aphrodisiac agg. e s. afrodisiaco.
aphtha s. afta.
apiece avv. a testa.
apish agg. scimmiesco.
apocalypse s. apocalisse.
apocalyptic(al) agg. apocalittico.
apocrypha s. pl. libri apocrifi.
apocryphal agg. apocrifo.
apogee s. apogeo.
apologetic(al) agg. apologetico.
apologist s. apologista.
to **apologize** vi. scusarsi.
apologue s. apologo.
apology s. scusa.
apoplexy s. apoplessia.

apostasy s. apostasia.

apostate agg. e s. apostata.

apostle s. apostolo.

apostolate s. apostolato.

apostolic(al) agg. apostolico.

apostrophe s. apostrofo.

to **apostrophize** vt. apostrofare.

apothecary s. farmacista.

apotheosis s. (pl. -ses) apoteosi.

to **appal** vt. spaventare.

appalling agg. spaventoso.

apparatus s. apparato.

apparent agg. 1. visibile, evidente 2. (giur.) legittimo.

apparition s. apparizione.

appeal s. 1. appello 2. attrattiva.

to **appeal** vi. 1. appellarsi 2. attrarre.

appealing agg. 1. supplichevole 2. attraente.

to **appear** vi. 1. apparire 2. sembrare.

appearance s. 1. apparenza, aspetto 2. apparizione.

to **appease** vt. placare.

appeasement s. pacificazione, tregua.

appellative agg. e s. appellativo.

appendicitis s. appendicite.

appendix s. appendice.

appetite s. appetito.

appetizer s. aperitivo.

appetizing agg. appetitoso.

to **applaud** vt. e vi. applaudire.

applauding agg. plaudente.

applause s. applauso.

apple s. mela || *—tree*, melo.

appliance s. 1. applicazione 2. apparecchio.

applicant s. richiedente.

application s. 1. applicazione 2. domanda.

to **apply** vt. applicare. ♦ to **apply** vi. 1. applicarsi 2. rivolgersi.

to **appoint** vt. 1. fissare 2. nominare, assegnare.

appointee s. persona designata.

appointment s. 1. appuntamento 2. nomina 3. impiego.

apposition s. apposizione.

appraisal s. stima.

to **appraise** vt. stimare.

appreciable agg. apprezzabile.

to **appreciate** vt. 1. apprezzare 2. rendersi conto di. ♦ to **appreciate** vi. aumentare di valore.

appreciation s. 1. apprezzamento 2. aumento di valore.

to **apprehend** vt. assodare.

apprehension s. 1. apprensione 2. percezione 3. arresto.

apprehensive agg. 1. apprensivo 2. perspicace.

apprentice s. apprendista.

apprenticeship s. apprendistato.

approach s. 1. avvicinamento 2. approccio 3. impostazione (di una pratica ecc.).

to **approach** vt. avvicinare. ♦ to **approach** vi. avvicinarsi.

approachable agg. accessibile.

appropriate agg. appropriato.

to **appropriate** vt. 1. appropriarsi di 2. stanziare.

appropriation s. 1. appropriazione 2. stanziamento.

approval s. 1. approvazione 2. (comm.) prova: on —, in prova.

to **approve** vt. 1. approvare 2. mostrare.

approximate agg. approssimativo.

to **approximate** vt. approssimare. ♦ to **approximate** vi. approssimarsi.

approximation s. approssimazione.

approximative agg. approssimativo.

apricot s. albicocca || *—tree*, albicocco.

April s. aprile.

apron s. 1. grembiale 2. riparo 3. (teat.) proscenio.

apse s. abside.

apt agg. 1. atto 2. intelligente 3. proclive.

aptitude, aptness s. 1. idoneità 2. intelligenza 3. proprietà (di vocabolo).

aqualung s. autorespiratore.

aquamarine s. acquamarina.

aquarium s. acquario.

aquatic(al) agg. acquatico.

aqueduct s. acquedotto.

aqueous agg. acqueo, acquoso.

Arab agg. e s. arabo.

arabesque s. arabesco.

Arabian agg. e s. arabo.

Arabic agg. arabico.

arable agg. arabile.

arbiter s. arbitro.

arbitrage s. arbitraggio.

arbitrary agg. arbitrario.

to **arbitrate** vt. e vi. arbitrare.

arbitrator s. (giur.) arbitro.

arboreal, arboreous agg. arboreo.

arboriculture s. arboricoltura.

arbour s. pergolato.

arc s. arco.

arcade s. galleria.

Arcadian *agg. e s.* arcadico.
arch *s.* arco.
to arch *vt.* **1.** fabbricare ad arco **2.** inarcare. ♦ **to arch** *vi.* inarcarsi.
archaeologic(al) *agg.* archeologico.
archaeologist *s.* archeologo.
archaeology *s.* archeologia
archaic(al) *agg.* arcaico.
archaism *s.* arcaismo.
archangel *s.* arcangelo.
archbishop *s.* arcivescovo
archduke *s.* arciduca.
archer *s.* arciere.
archetype *s.* archetipo.
archipelago *s.* arcipelago.
architect *s.* architetto.
architectonic, architectural *agg* architettonico.
architecture *s.* architettura.
archive *s.* archivio.
archivist *s.* archivista.
Arctic *agg. e s.* artico.
ardent *agg.* ardente.
ardour *s.* ardore.
arduous *agg.* arduo.
area *s.* area.
arena *s.* (*arch.*) arena.
Areopagus *s.* areopago.
argent *s.* argenteo.
Argentine *agg. e s.* argentino.
argil *s.* argilla.
to argue *vi.* **1.** discutere **2.** ragionare. ♦ **to argue** *vt.* dimostrare.
argument *s.* **1.** discussione **2.** argomentazione.
arid *agg.* arido.
aridity *s.* aridità.
to arise (arose, arisen) *vi.* **1.** alzarsi **2.** (*fig.*) nascere.
aristocracy *s.* aristocrazia.
aristocrat *s.* aristocratico.
aristocratic(al) *agg.* aristocratico.
Aristotelian *agg. e s.* aristotelico.
arithmetic *s.* aritmetica.
arithmetic(al) *agg.* aritmetico.
arm¹ *s.* braccio || — -*in*- —, a braccetto.
arm² *s.* arma || *coat of arms*, stemma.
to arm *vt.* armare. ♦ **to arm** *vi.* armarsi.
armament *s.* armamento.
armchair *s.* poltrona.
armful *s.* bracciata.
armistice *s.* armistizio.
armless *agg.* inerme.
armlet *s.* braccialetto.
armour *s.* corazza.
to armour *vt.* corazzare || *armour-*

ed-car, autoblinda.
armoury *s.* **1.** arsenale **2.** armeria.
armpit *s.* ascella.
army *s.* esercito.
aromatic(al) *agg.* aromatico.
arose V. *to arise.*
around *avv.* intorno. ♦ **around** *prep.* **1.** intorno a **2.** circa.
to arouse *vt.* **1.** destare **2.** eccitare.
to arrange *vt.* **1.** accomodare **2.** predisporre **3.** (*mus.*) arrangiare.
arrangement *s.* **1.** accomodamento **2.** (*mus.*) arrangiamento **3.** dispositivo. ♦ **arrangements** *s. pl.* preparativi.
arras *s.* arazzo.
array *s.* **1.** apparato **2.** (*mil.*) spiegamento.
to array *vt.* **1.** ornare **2.** (*mil.*) schierare.
arrest *s.* arresto.
to arrest *vt.* arrestare.
arrival *s.* arrivo.
to arrive *vi.* arrivare.
arrogance *s.* arroganza.
arrogant *agg.* arrogante.
to arrogate *vt.* arrogarsi.
arrow *s.* freccia.
arsenal *s.* arsenale.
arsenic *s.* arsenico.
art *s.* arte.
arteriosclerosis *s.* arteriosclerosi.
artery *s.* arteria.
artesian *agg.* artesiano.
artful *agg.* **1.** abile **2.** artificioso **3.** astuto.
arthritic(al) *agg.* artritico.
arthritis *s.* artrite.
artichoke *s.* carciofo.
article *s.* articolo.
articulate *agg.* **1.** articolato **2.** chiaro.
to articulate *vt.* articolare. ♦ **to articulate** *vi.* articolarsi.
articulation *s.* articolazione.
artifice *s.* **1.** artificio **2.** abilità.
artificial *agg.* artificiale.
artificiality *s.* artificiosità.
artillery *s.* artiglieria.
artilleryman *s.* artigliere.
artist *s.* artista.
artistic(al) *agg.* artistico.
artistry *s.* abilità artistica.
artless *agg.* ingenuo.
Aryan *agg. e s.* ariano.
as *avv.* come || — ... —, tanto ... quanto; *so* — (*con infinito*), in modo da; — *for*, quanto a; — *far* —, sin dove, fino a; — *much*, al-

trettanto; — *well*, come pure. ♦
as *cong.* 1. poiché 2. mentre.
asbestos *s.* asbesto.
to **ascend** *vi.* ascendere. ♦ ᴧ
ascend *vt.* risalire, scalare.
ascendancy *s.* ascendente.
ascendant *agg. e s.* ascendente.
ascension *s.* ascensione.
ascent *s.* ascesa.
to **ascertain** *vt.* accertarsi di.
ascertainment *s.* accertamento.
ascetic *s.* asceta.
ascetic(al) *agg.* ascetico.
asceticism *s.* ascetismo.
to **ascribe** *vt.* ascrivere.
asepsis *s.* asepsi.
aseptic *agg. e s.* asettico.
asexual *agg.* asessuale.
ash *s.* cenere || — *-tray*, portacenere.
ash(-tree) *s.* frassino.
ashamed *agg.* vergognoso || *to be*
—, aver vergogna.
ashore *avv.* a terra.
ashy *agg.* cinereo.
Asiatic *agg. e s.* asiatico.
aside *avv.* a parte, da parte.
asininity *s.* asinità.
to **ask** *vt. e vi.* 1. chiedere 2. invitare || *to — so. for sthg.*, chiedere
a qu. qc.; *to — for trouble*, cercar fastidi.
askance *avv.* di traverso.
asker *s.* interrogante.
asleep *agg.* addormentato.
asocial *agg.* asociale.
asp *s.* aspide.
asparagus *s. coll.* asparago, asparagi.
aspect *s.* aspetto.
aspen *s.* pioppo tremulo.
aspergillum *s.* aspersorio.
asperity *s.* 1. asperità 2. (*fig.*)
asprezza.
aspersion *s.* 1. aspersione 2. calunnia.
asphalt *s.* asfalto.
asphyxia *s.* asfissia.
to **asphyxiate** *vt.* asfissiare.
aspirant *agg. e s.* aspirante.
to **aspirate** *vt.* aspirare.
aspiration *s.* aspirazione.
aspirator *s.* aspiratore.
to **aspire** *vi.* aspirare.
aspirin *s.* aspirina.
aspiring *agg.* ambizioso.
asquint *avv.* di traverso.
ass *s.* asino || *to make an — of oneself*, rendersi ridicolo.
to **assail** *vt.* assalire.

assailant, assailer *s.* assalitore.
assassin *s.* assassino.
to **assassinate** *vt.* assassinare.
assassination *s.* assassinio.
assault *s.* assalto, aggressione.
to **assault** *vt.* assalire.
assaulter *s.* assalitore.
to **assay** *vt.* saggiare.
assayer *s.* (as)saggiatore.
to **assemble** *vt.* riunire. ♦ to **assemble** *vi.* riunirsi.
assembly *s.* 1. assemblea 2. (*mil.*)
adunata 3. (*mecc.*) montaggio: —
line, catena di montaggio.
assent *s.* consenso.
to **assent** *vt.* approvare.
to **assert** *vt.* asserire || *to — oneself*, farsi valere.
assertion *s.* asserzione.
assertor *s.* assertore.
to **assess** *vt.* 1. tassare 2. (*comm.*)
ripartire.
assessment *s.* 1. valutazione 2. tassazione.
assessor *s.* agente delle tasse.
asset *s.* 1. bene, vantaggio. ♦ **assets** *s. pl.* patrimonio, attività
(*sing.*).
assiduity *s.* assiduità.
assiduous *agg.* assiduo.
to **assign** *vt.* 1. assegnare 2. trasferire 3. designare.
assignation *s.* 1. assegnazione 2.
(*giur.*) cessione 3. appuntamento.
assignment *s.* 1. assegnazione 2.
(*giur.*) cessione.
to **assist** *vt. e vi.* assistere.
assistance *s.* assistenza.
assistant *agg. e s.* assistente || *shop*
—, commesso.
assize *s.* 1. (*giur.*) seduta. ♦ **Assizes** *s. pl.* Assise.
associate *agg. e s.* associato.
to **associate** *vt.* associare. ♦ to
associate *vi.* associarsi.
association *s.* associazione.
assonance *s.* assonanza.
to **assort** *vt.* 1. assortire 2. classificare. ♦ to **assort** *vi.* 1. armonizzarsi 2. frequentare: *to — with
so.*, frequentare qu.
to **assume** *vt.* 1. assumere 2. fingere 3. presumere.

assuming *agg.* presuntuoso.
assumption *s.* 1. assunzione 2. finzione 3. supposizione 4. presunzione.
assurance *s.* 1. assicurazione 2. sicurezza 3. fiducia.
to **assure** *vt.* 1. assicurare 2. rassicurare.
assurer *s.* assicuratore.
asterisk *s.* asterisco.
astern *avv.* a poppa.
asteroid *s.* asteroide.
asthenia *s.* astenia.
asthma *s.* asma.
asthmatic *agg.* e *s.* asmatico.
astigmatic *agg.* astigmatico.
astigmatism *s.* astigmatismo.
astir *agg.* e *avv.* in moto.
to **astonish** *vt.* stupire.
astonishing *agg.* sorprendente.
astonishment *s.* sorpresa.
to **astound** *vt.* sbalordire.
astragal(us) *s.* astragalo.
astrakhan *s.* astracan.
astral *agg.* astrale.
astray *agg.* e *avv.* fuori strada.
astride *agg.* e *avv.* a cavalcioni. ♦
   astride *prep.* a cavalcioni di.
astringent *agg.* e *s.* astringente.
astrolabe *s.* astrolabio.
astrologer *s.* astrologo.
astrology *s.* astrologia.
astronaut *s.* astronauta.
astronautics *s.* astronautica.
astronomer *s.* astronomo.
astronomic(al) *agg.* astronomico.
astronomy *s.* astronomia.
astute *agg.* astuto.
asunder *avv.* 1. separatamente 2. in pezzi.
asylum *s.* 1. asilo, ricovero 2. manicomio.
asymmetric(al) *agg.* asimmetrico.
asymmetry *s.* asimmetria.
at *prep.* (*stato, tempo, modo*) a, da, in: *to arrive — a place,* arrivare in un luogo; *— that time,* in quel momento; *— will,* a volontà.
atavistic *agg.* atavico.
atavism *s.* atavismo.
ataxy *s.* atassia.
ate V. *to eat.*
atheism *s.* ateismo.
atheist *s.* ateo.
atheistic(al) *agg.* ateistico.
athlete *s.* atleta.
athletic *agg.* atletico.
athletics *s.* atletica.
atlas *s.* atlante.

atmosphere *s.* atmosfera.
atmospheric(al) *agg.* atmosferico.
atoll *s.* atollo.
atom *s.* atomo.
atomic(al) *agg.* atomico.
atomism *s.* atomismo.
to **atomize** *vt.* nebulizzare.
atomizer *s.* atomizzatore, nebulizzatore.
atomy *s.* atomo.
to **atone** *vt.* espiare.
atonement *s.* espiazione.
atonic *agg.* 1. atono 2. atonico.
atrocious *agg.* atroce.
atrocity *s.* atrocità.
atrophic *agg.* atrofico.
atrophy *s.* atrofia.
to **atrophy** *vt.* atrofizzare. ♦ to **atrophy** *vi.* atrofizzarsi.
atropin(e) *s.* atropina.
to **attach** *vt.* 1. attaccare, unire 2. attribuire 3. attrarre. ♦ to **attach** *vi.* attaccarsi.
attaché *s.* addetto.
attachment *s.* 1. attaccamento 2. (*mecc.*) accessorio.
attack *s.* attacco.
to **attack** *vt.* attaccare.
attacker *s.* assalitore.
to **attain** *vt.* raggiungere. ♦ to **attain** *vi.* giungere.
attainable *agg.* raggiungibile.
attainment *s.* 1. raggiungimento 2. cultura.
attempt *s.* 1. tentativo 2. attentato.
to **attempt** *vt.* 1. tentare 2. attentare a.
to **attend** *vi.* 1. badare a 2. obbedire ‖ *to — on,* essere al servizio di. ♦ to **attend** *vt.* 1. assistere 2. accompagnare 3. frequentare.
attendance *s.* 1. servizio 2. assistenza 3. frequenza.
attendant *s.* 1. servitore 2. assistente 3. assiduo frequentatore.
attention *s.* attenzione: *to pay —,* fare attenzione.
attentive *agg.* 1. attento 2. sollecito.
to **attenuate** *vt.* 1. assottigliare 2. attenuare. ♦ to **attenuate** *vi.* 1. assottigliarsi 2. attenuarsi.
attenuation *s.* 1. assottigliamento 2. attenuazione.
to **attest** *vt.* attestare.
attic *agg.* e *s.* attico.
to **attire** *vt.* vestire, agghindare. ♦ to **attire** *vi.* vestirsi.
attitude *s.* atteggiamento.

attorney s. 1. procura 2. procuratore || — (-at-law), procuratore legale.
to **attract** vt. attrarre.
attraction s. 1. attrazione 2. attrattiva.
attractive agg. attraente.
attribute s. attributo.
to **attribute** vt. attribuire.
attribution s. attribuzione.
attributive agg. attributivo. ♦ **attributive** s. attributo.
aubergine s. melanzana.
auction s. asta: — sale, vendita all'asta.
to **auction** vt. vendere all'asta.
auctioneer s. banditore.
audible agg. udibile.
audience s. 1. udienza 2. uditorio.
audiovisual agg. audiovisivo.
audit s. verifica, revisione.
audition s. audizione.
auditory agg. e s. uditorio.
auger s. trivella, succhiello.
to **augment** vt. aumentare. ♦ to **augment** vi. crescere.
augmentative agg. e s. accrescitivo.
to **augur** vt. e vi. predire.
august agg. augusto.
August s. agosto.
aunt s. zia || great- —, prozia.
auricle s. 1. padiglione auricolare 2. (med.) orecchietta.
auricular agg. auricolare.
auriferous agg. aurifero.
to **auscultate** vt. auscultare.
auscultation s. auscultazione.
auscultator s. stetoscopio.
auspice s. auspicio.
auspicious agg. propizio.
austere agg. austero.
austerity s. austerità.
austral agg. australe.
Australian agg. e s. australiano.
Austrian agg. e s. austriaco.
autarky s. autarchia.
authentic(al) agg. autentico.
to **authenticate** vt. autenticare.
authentication s. autenticazione.
authenticity s. autenticità.
author s. autore.
authoress s. autrice.
authoritative agg. 1. autoritario 2. autorevole.
authoritativeness s. autorevolezza.
authority s. autorità.
authorization s. autorizzazione.
to **authorize** vt. autorizzare.
authorless agg. anonimo.

authorship s. paternità (di un libro).
autobiographic(al) agg. autobiografico.
autobiography s. autobiografia.
autochthon s. autoctono.
autochthonous agg. autoctono.
autocracy s. autocrazia.
autocrat s. autocrate.
autocriticism s. autocritica.
autoeducation s. autoeducazione.
autofinancing s. autofinanziamento.
autograph s. autografo.
autography s. autografia.
autolesion s. autolesione.
automatic agg. automatico. ♦ **automatic** s. arma automatica.
automation s. automazione.
automatism s. automatismo.
automaton s. automa.
autonomist s. autonomista.
autonomous agg. autonomo.
autonomy s. autonomia.
autopsy s. autopsia.
auto-suggestion s. autosuggestione.
autumn s. autunno.
autumnal agg. autunnale.
auxiliary agg. e s. ausiliare.
avail s. utilità.
to **avail** vt. e vi. servire a || to — oneself of, approfittare di.
availability s. 1. disponibilità 2. validità.
available agg. 1. disponibile 2. valevole.
avalanche s. valanga.
avarice s. 1. avarizia 2. cupidigia.
avaricious agg. 1. avaro 2. cupido.
to **avenge** vt. vendicare.
avenger s. vendicatore.
avenue s. viale.
to **aver** vt. asserire, dichiarare.
average agg. medio. ♦ **average** s. 1. media 2. (comm.) avaria.
averse agg. avverso.
aversion s. avversione.
to **avert** vt. sviare.
aviary s. uccelliera.
aviation s. aviazione.
aviator s. aviatore.
avid agg. avido.
avidity s. avidità.
to **avoid** vt. 1. evitare 2. (giur.) annullare.
avoidable agg. 1. evitabile 2. (giur.) annullabile.
to **avow** vt. dichiarare, ammettere.
avowal s. dichiarazione, ammissione.

to **await** *vt.* attendere.

awake *agg.* 1. sveglio 2. conscio.

to **awake (awoke, awoke)** *vt.* svegliare. ♦ to **awake (awoke, awoke)** *vi.* svegliarsi.

to **awaken** *vt.* risvegliare, far aprire gli occhi. ♦ to **awaken** *vi.* risvegliarsi, aprire gli occhi.

awakening *s.* risveglio.

award *s.* 1. sentenza 2. ricompensa.

to **award** *vt.* aggiudicare.

aware *agg.* conscio.

away *avv.* via, lontano || *right —,* subito, seduta stante.

awe *s.* timore reverenziale.

awful *agg.* 1. terribile 2. imponente.

awkward *agg.* 1. goffo, imbarazzato 2. scomodo 3. inopportuno 4. delicato.

awkwardness *s.* 1. goffaggine 2. imbarazzo.

awl *s.* lesina.

awning *s.* tenda.

awoke V. *to awake.*

awry *agg.* 1. storto 2. bieco. ♦ **awry** *avv.* 1. per traverso 2. perversamente.

ax(e) *s.* scure.

axiom *s.* assioma.

axiomatic(al) *agg.* assiomatico.

axis *s.* (*pl.* axes) asse.

axle *s.* (*mecc.*) asse.

azimuth *s.* azimut.

azote *s.* azoto.

to **azotize** *vt.* azotare.

Aztec *agg.* e *s.* azteco.

azure *agg.* e *s.* azzurro.

B

b *s.* (*mus.*) si.

babble *s.* balbettio.

to **babble** *vi.* e *vt.* 1. balbettare 2. mormorare (*di acque*).

babe *s.* bambino.

babel *s.* babele.

baboon *s.* babbuino.

baby *s.* bimbo, neonato || *— sitter,* chi accudisce i bambini.

babyhood *s.* infanzia.

babyish *agg.* infantile.

baccarat *s.* baccarà.

Bacchanal *s.* 1. baccante 2. baccanale (*anche fig.*).

Bacchante *s.* baccante.

bacchic(al) *agg.* bacchico.

bachelor *s.* scapolo || *Bachelor of Arts,* titolo universitario in lettere.

bachelorhood *s.* celibato.

bacillus *s.* (*pl.* -li) bacillo.

back[1] *agg.* posteriore. ♦ **back** *avv.* dietro, indietro || *to be —,* essere di ritorno; *to go, to come —,* ritornare.

back[2] *s.* 1. dorso, schiena 2. spalle 3. rovescio 4. schienale 5. fondo.

to **back** *vt.* 1. sostenere 2. fare indietreggiare || *to — a bill,* avallare una cambiale. ♦ to **back** *vi.* indietreggiare || *— down,* abbandonare la contesa.

to **backbite** *vt.* denigrare.

backbiter *s.* calunniatore.

backbiting *agg.* maldicente. ♦ **backbiting** *s.* maldicenza.

backbone *s.* 1. spina dorsale 2. (*fig.*) fermezza.

backer *s.* 1. scommettitore 2. sostenitore.

backfire *s.* ritorno di fiamma.

background *s.* 1. sfondo 2. curriculum 3. ambiente.

backing *s.* 1. sostegno 2. marcia indietro.

backlash *s.* rimbalzo.

backslider *s.* apostata.

backward *agg.* 1. lento 2. tardo.

backward(s) *avv.* indietro.

backwash *s.* risacca.

bacon *s.* lardo affumicato, pancetta.

bacterial *agg.* batterico.

bacteriology *s.* batteriologia.

bacterium *s.* (*pl.* -ia) batterio.

bad (worse, worst) *agg.* 1. cattivo 2. brutto. ♦ **bad** *s.* 1. male 2. rovina.

bade V. *to bid.*

badge *s.* insegna.

badger *s.* tasso.

badly *avv.* male, malamente.

badness *s.* 1. cattiveria 2. cattiva qualità.

baffle *s.* (-plate) deflettore, diaframma.

to **baffle** *vt.* 1. eludere 2. confondere.

bag *s.* 1. sacco 2. borsa || *sleeping—,* sacco a pelo.

to **bag** *vt.* 1. gonfiare 2. rubare 3. insaccare.

baggage *s.* bagaglio.

bagpipe *s.* cornamusa.

bail[1] *s.* 1. cauzione 2. garante.

to **bail**[1] *vt.* 1. dar garanzia per 2.

affidare (*dietro cauzione*).

to **ball**[1] *vt.* e *vi.* (*mar.*) aggottare ‖ *to — out*, lanciarsi col paracadute.

bailiff *s.* 1. magistrato inquirente 2. ufficiale fiscale.

bain-marie *s.* bagnomaria.

bait *s.* 1. esca 2. sosta (*per ristoro*).

to **bait** *vt.* 1. adescare 2. tormentare. ♦ to **bait** *vi.* fermarsi (*per prendere ristoro*).

to **bake** *vt.* e *vi.* cuocere al forno.

baker *s.* fornaio.

bakery *s.* forno.

baking *s.* cottura al forno.

balance *s.* 1. bilancia 2. bilanciere 3. equilibrio 4. bilancio.

to **balance** *vt.* 1. pesare 2. pareggiare. ♦ to **balance** *vi.* 1. bilanciarsi 2. oscillare.

balanced *agg.* equilibrato.

balancer *s.* acrobata.

balcony *s.* 1. balcone 2. (*teat.*).balconata.

bald *agg.* 1. calvo, pelato 2. povero, nudo.

baldness *s.* 1. calvizie 2. (*fig.*) nudità.

baldric *s.* bandoliera.

bale *s.* (*comm.*) balla.

Balkan *agg.* balcanico.

ball *s.* 1. palla 2. ballo ‖ *— bearing*, cuscinetto a sfere.

to **ball** *vt.* appallottolare. ♦ to **ball** *vi.* appallottolarsi.

ballad *s.* ballata.

ballast *s.* zavorra.

to **ballast** *vt.* zavorrare.

ballet *s.* balletto ‖ *— dancer*, ballerino classico.

ballistics *s.* balistica.

balloon *s.* 1. pallone 2. lambicco 3. fumetto.

ballot *s.* 1. pallina, scheda (*per votazione*) 2. voto 3. scrutinio ‖ *— box*, urna.

to **ballot** *vt.* mettere in ballottaggio.

balm *s.* balsamo.

balm-cricket *s.* (*zool.*) cicala.

balmy *agg.* balsamico.

Baltic *agg.* baltico.

balustrade *s.* balaustrata.

bamboo *s.* bambù.

ban *s.* bando.

to **ban** *vt.* proibire.

banal *agg.* banale.

banality *s.* banalità.

banana *s.* 1. banana 2. banano.

band *s.* 1. legame 2. benda 3. nastro 4. banda.

to **band** *vt.* 1. legare 2. bendare.

bandage *s.* bendaggio.

to **bandage** *vt.* bendare.

banderole *s.* banderuola.

bandit *s.* bandito.

bandmaster *s.* capobanda.

bandog *s.* cane da guardia.

bandsman *s.* bandista.

bane *s.* 1. calamità 2. veleno.

baneful *agg.* velenoso.

bang *s.* 1. botta 2. detonazione.

to **bang** *vt.* e *vi.* sbattere violentemente.

banging *s.* 1. colpi violenti 2. detonazioni.

to **banish** *vt.* bandire, esiliare.

banishment *s.* bando, esilio.

banister *s.* ringhiera (*di scala*).

bank *s.* 1. banca 2. banco 3. argine 4. terrapieno.

to **bank** *vt.* 1. arginare 2. depositare in banca ‖ *to — upon*, contare su. ♦ to **bank** *vi.* gestire una banca.

bankbook *s.* libretto bancario.

banker *s.* banchiere.

banking *agg.* bancario. ♦ **banking** *s.* tecnica, professione bancaria.

bank note *s.* banconota.

bankrupt *agg.* e *s.* fallito ‖ *to go —*, fallire.

bankruptcy *s.* fallimento.

banner *s.* vessillo.

banns *s. pl.* pubblicazioni matrimoniali.

banquet *s.* banchetto.

to **banquet** *vi.* banchettare.

banter *s.* scherzo, beffa.

to **banter** *vt.* canzonare.

baptism *s.* battesimo.

baptist(e)ry *s.* battistero.

to **baptize** *vt.* battezzare.

bar *s.* 1. sbarra 2. diga 3. striscia 4. ostacolo 5. (*fig.*) tribunale 6. bar 7. (*mus.*) battuta.

to **bar** *vt.* 1. sbarrare 2. ostacolare 3. proibire.

barbarian *agg.* e *s.* barbaro.

barbaric *agg.* barbarico.

barbarism *s.* 1. barbarie 2. (*gramm.*) barbarismo.

barbarous *agg.* barbaro.

barbarousness *s.* barbarie.

barbecue *s.* 1. animale arrostito intero 2. festa campestre.

to **barbecue** *vt.* arrostire un animale intero.

barbed *agg.* dentato.

barber *s.* barbiere.

barbiturate s. barbiturico.

bard s. bardo, trovatore.

bare agg. **1.** nudo **2.** logoro.

to **bare** vt. **1.** denudare **2.** snudare **3.** smascherare.

barefoot agg. scalzo.

barehanded agg. e avv. **1.** a mano nuda **2.** senz'armi.

bareheaded agg. a capo scoperto.

barely avv. **1.** apertamente **2.** appena.

bargain s. affare.

to **bargain** vt. e vi. contrattare.

bargaining s. contrattazione.

barge s. chiatta.

baritone s. baritono.

bark[1] s. corteccia.

bark[2] s. latrato.

to **bark**[1] vt. scortecciare.

to **bark**[2] vi. latrare, abbaiare.

barking[1] s. scortecciamento.

barking[2] s. abbaiamento.

barley s. orzo.

barmaid s. barista (donna).

barman s. barista.

barn s. granaio.

barometer s. barometro.

barometric(al) agg. barometrico.

baron s. barone.

baroness s. baronessa.

baroque agg. e s. barocco.

barracks s. pl. caserma (sing.).

barrage s. sbarramento.

barrel s. **1.** barile **2.** cilindro **3.** canna (di arma da fuoco) || — -organ, organetto.

to **barrel** vt. mettere in barili.

barrelled agg. double- — gun, fucile a due canne.

barren agg. sterile.

barrenness s. sterilità.

barricade s. barricata.

to **barricade** vt. barricare.

barrier s. barriera || transonic —, muro del suono.

barrister s. avvocato (che può discutere cause nelle corti superiori).

barrow s. **1.** barella **2.** carriola.

barter s. baratto.

to **barter** vt. e vi. barattare.

basal agg. basilare.

basalt s. basalto.

base[1] agg. basso, vile.

base[2] s. base.

to **base** vt. basare.

baseless agg. senza base.

basement s. **1.** fondamento **2.** seminterrato.

baseness s. bassezza.

to **bash** vt. colpire.

bashful agg. timido.

bashfulness s. timidezza.

basic agg. **1.** fondamentale **2.** (chim.) basico.

basil s. basilico.

basilar agg. basilare.

basilisk s. basilisco.

basin s. **1.** bacino **2.** catino, lavabo || sugar —, zuccheriera.

basis s. (pl. -ses) base.

to **bask** vi. crogiolarsi (al sole, al fuoco).

basket s. cesto || —ball, pallacanestro; — -chair, poltroncina di vimini.

Basque agg. e s. basco.

bas-relief s. bassorilievo.

bass agg. e s. (mus.) basso.

bass s. pesce persico.

bassoon s. (mus.) fagotto.

bastard agg. e s. bastardo.

to **baste** vt. imbastire.

basting s. imbastitura.

bastion s. bastione.

bat[1] s. pipistrello.

bat[2] s. (sport) mazza.

batch s. **1.** infornata **2.** gruppo.

to **bate** vt. ridurre.

bath s. bagno || — -robe, accappatoio; — -tub, vasca da bagno.

to **bath** vt. bagnare. ♦ to **bath** vi. bagnarsi, fare il bagno.

to **bathe** s. bagno (in mare, lago ecc.).

to **bathe** vt. bagnare. ♦ to **bathe** vi. bagnarsi, fare il bagno (in mare, lago ecc.).

bather s. bagnante.

bathing s. il bagnarsi || — -suit, costume da bagno.

bathroom s. stanza da bagno.

bathysphere s. batisfera.

batiste s. batista.

batman s. attendente.

baton s. **1.** bastone **2.** bacchetta (di direttore d'orchestra).

batrachian s. batrace.

batsman s. (sport) battitore.

battalion s. battaglione.

to **batten** vt. (mar.) chiudere (i boccaporti).

batter s. (cuc.) pastella.

to **batter** vt. battere || to — down, abbattere; to — in, sfondare.

battering s. cannoneggiamento.

battery s. batteria || storage —, accumulatore.

battle s. battaglia.

to **battle** *vt.* e *vi.* combattere.

battledore *s.* racchetta di legno || — *and shuttlecock*, volano.

battlement *s.* (*arch.*) merlo.

battleship *s.* nave da guerra.

bauxite *s.* bauxite.

bawdiness *s.* oscenità.

bawdy *agg.* osceno || — *house*, bordello.

bawl *s.* grido.

to **bawl** *vt.* e *vi.* gridare, vociare.

bay[1] *s.* 1. baia 2. insenatura, recesso (*nelle montagne*).

bay[2] *s.* alloro || — *-tree*, lauro.

bay[3] *s.* 1. rientranza 2. campata || — *window*, bovindo.

bay[4] *s.* latrato || *at* —, senza scampo.

bay[5] *agg.* e *s.* baio.

to **bay**[1] *vt.* arginare.

to **bay**[2] *vi.* latrare.

bayonet *s.* baionetta.

baza(a)r *s.* 1. bazar 2. vendita di beneficenza.

to **be** (**was, been**) *vi.* 1. essere 2. stare 3. andare 4. costare: *how much is it?*, quanto costa? 5. dovere || *to* — *in*, essere in casa; *to* — *about*, stare per; *so be it*, così sia.

beach *s.* spiaggia.

beacon *s.* faro.

to **beacon** *vt.* guidare con segnalazioni luminose.

bead *s.* 1. goccia 2. perlina || — **beads** *s. pl.* rosario (*sing.*).

to **bead** *vt.* imperlare. ♦ to **bead** *vi.* imperlarsi.

beak *s.* 1. becco, rostro 2. beccuccio.

to **beak** *vt.* beccare.

beaker *s.* boccale.

beam *s.* 1. trave 2. raggio 3. asta (*di bilancia*) 4. fiancata (*di nave*).

to **beam** *vi.* brillare. ♦ to **beam** *vt.* irradiare.

beaming *agg.* raggiante.

bean *s.* fagiolo || *French* —, fagiolino; *coffee* —, grano di caffè.

bear *s.* orso.

to **bear**[1] *vt.* e *vi.* speculare al ribasso (*in Borsa*).

to **bear**[2] (**bore, born(e)**) *vt.* 1. portare 2. sopportare 3. generare. ♦ to **bear** (**bore, borne**) *vi.* 1. resistere 2. appoggiarsi 3. pazientare || *to* — *with*, aver pazienza con.

bearable *agg.* sopportabile.

beard *s.* 1. barba 2. chioma (*di cometa*).

to **beard** *vt.* affrontare, sfidare.

bearded *agg.* barbuto.

beardless *agg.* senza barba.

bearer *s.* portatore.

bearing *s.* 1. sopportazione 2. portamento 3. condotta 4. relazione 5. sostegno 6. raccolto || *to lose one's bearings*, perdere l'orientamento; *to take the bearings of a coast* (*mar.*), rilevare una costa.

beast *s.* bestia.

beastliness *s.* bestialità.

beastly *agg.* bestiale. ♦ **beastly** *avv.* bestialmente.

beat *s.* 1. battito 2. (*mus.*) battuta.

to **beat** (**beat, beat(en)**) *vt.* e *vi.* battere || *to* — *down*, abbattere; *to* — *back*, respingere.

beaten *agg.* abbattuto, vinto.

beater *s.* battitore.

beatification *s.* beatificazione.

beating *s.* 1. battito 2. bastonatura 3. sconfitta.

beatitude *s.* beatitudine.

beautiful *agg.* bello.

beautifully *avv.* magnificamente.

to **beautify** *vt.* abbellire. ♦ to **beautify** *vi.* abbellirsi.

beauty *s.* bellezza.

beaver *s.* castoro.

became V. *to become.*

because *cong.* perché || — *of*, a causa di.

beck[1] *s.* ruscello.

beck[2] *s.* cenno, gesto.

to **become** (**became, become**) *vi.* 1. divenire 2. avvenire. ♦ to **become** (**became, become**) *vt.* addirsi a.

becoming *agg.* adatto.

bed *s.* 1. letto 2. fondo 3. (*geol.*) strato || *double* —, letto matrimoniale || *flower*—, aiuola; — *-cover*, copriletto.

bedclothes *s. pl.* lenzuola.

bedlam *s.* manicomio.

bedouin *agg.* e *s.* beduino.

bedroom *s.* camera da letto.

bedside *s.* capezzale.

bedstead *s.* telaio del letto.

bedtime *s.* ora di andare a letto.

bee *s.* ape.

beech *s.* faggio || — *-marten*, faina.

beef *s.* manzo.

beefsteak *s.* bistecca.

beehive *s.* alveare.

beeline *s.* linea diretta, linea d'aria.

been V. *to be.*

beer *s.* birra.

beet *s.* barbabietola.

beetle *s.* coleottero, scarafaggio.

beetroot *s.* V. **beet**.

to **befall** (**befell**, **befallen**) *vt.* e *vi.* accadere.

before *avv.* prima, già || — -*mentioned*, già citato. ◆ **before** *prep.* 1. prima (di) 2. davanti a. ◆ **before** *cong.* 1. prima che 2. piuttosto che.

beforehand *avv.* anticipatamente.

to **beg** *vt.* e *vi.* 1. chiedere, pregare 2. elemosinare.

began V. *to* **begin**.

to **beget** (**begot**, **begot(ten)**) *vt.* generare.

beggar *s.* mendicante.

beggarly *agg.* misero. ◆ **beggarly** *avv.* miseramente.

beggary *s.* mendicità.

begging *agg.* mendicante. ◆ **begging** *s.* accattonaggio.

to **begin** (**began**, **begun**) *vt.* e *vi.* cominciare || *to* — *with*, in primo luogo, per cominciare.

beginner *s.* 1. iniziatore 2. principiante.

beginning *s.* inizio.

begot V. *to* **beget**.

begotten V. *to* **beget**.

to **begrime** *vt.* insudiciare.

begun V. *to* **begin**.

behalf *s.* profitto, favore: *on* — *of*, da parte di, a nome di.

to **behave** *vi.* comportarsi: *to* — *oneself*, comportarsi bene || *ill -behaved*, maleducato.

behaviour *s.* comportamento, condotta.

to **behead** *vt.* decapitare.

beheld V. *to* **behold**.

behind *avv.* dietro, indietro. ◆ **behind** *prep.* dietro (a). ◆ **behind** *s.* parte posteriore.

to **behold** (**beheld**, **beheld**) *vt.* guardare.

beholder *s.* spettatore.

to **behove** *vt. imp.* convenire, essere doveroso.

being *agg.* presente. ◆ **being** *s.* 1. esistenza 2. essere vivente.

belch *s.* 1. rutto 2. eruzione.

to **belch** *vi.* ruttare. ◆ to **belch** *vt.* eruttare.

belfry *s.* campanile.

Belgian *agg.* e *s.* belga.

to **belie** *vt.* 1. smentire 2. deludere.

belief *s.* credenza, fede.

to **believe** *vt.* e *vi.* credere, aver fede.

believer *s.* credente.

to **belittle** *vt.* sminuire.

bell *s.* 1. campana 2. campanello || — -*boy*, fattorino d'albergo; — -*ringer*, campanaro; — -*tower*, campanile.

belligerency *s.* belligeranza.

belligerent *agg.* e *s.* belligerante.

bellow *s.* muggito.

to **bellow** *vi.* muggire.

bellows *s. pl.* mantice, soffietto (*sing.*).

belly *s.* ventre.

to **belong** *vi.* 1. appartenere 2. concernere.

belongings *s. pl.* proprietà (*sing.*).

beloved *agg.* e *s.* amato.

below *avv.* giù, al di sotto. ◆ **below** *prep.* sotto: — *zero*, sotto zero.

belt *s.* 1. cintura 2. zona.

to **belt** *vt.* 1. cingere 2. staffilare.

to **bemire** *vt.* infangare. ◆ to **bemire** *vi.* impantanarsi.

bench *s.* 1. panca 2. banco 3. seggio 4. corte giudiziaria.

bend *s.* 1. curva 2. curvatura 3. (*mar.*) nodo.

to **bend** (**bent**, **bent**) *vt.* 1. piegare 2. tendere. ◆ to **bend** (**bent**, **bent**) *vi.* piegarsi.

bending *s.* V. **bend**.

beneath *avv.* e *prep.* V. **below**.

benediction *s.* benedizione.

benefactor *s.* benefattore.

benefactress *s.* benefattrice.

benefice *s.* beneficio.

beneficence *s.* beneficenza.

beneficent *agg.* benefico.

beneficiary *agg.* e *s.* beneficiario.

benefit *s.* 1. vantaggio 2. indennità 3. (*giur.*) beneficio.

to **benefit** *vt.* giovare, beneficare. ◆ to **benefit** *vi.* approfittare.

benevolence *s.* benevolenza.

benevolent *agg.* benevolo.

Bengal-light *s.* bengala.

benign *agg.* benigno.

benignity *s.* benignità.

bent V. *to* **bend**. ◆ **bent** *agg.* risoluto. ◆ **bent** *s.* inclinazione.

to **benumb** *vt.* intorpidire.

benumbing *s.* intorpidimento.

benzol *s.* benzolo.

to **bequeath** *vt.* lasciare per testamento.

bequest *s.* lascito.

Berber *agg.* e *s.* berbero.

to bereave (bereaved, bereft) *vt.* privare.

bergamot *s.* bergamotto.

berlin(e) *s.* berlina.

berry *s.* bacca.

berth *s.* 1. cuccetta 2. (*mar.*) ancoraggio 3. (*fig.*) posto.

to berth *vt.* ancorare.

beryllium *s.* berillio.

to beseech (besought, besought) *vt.* supplicare.

beseeching *s.* supplica.

to beseem *vt.* addirsi a.

beseeming *agg.* adàtto.

beside *prep.* 1. vicino a 2. fuori di.

besides *avv.* inoltre. ♦ **besides** *prep.* oltre a.

to besiege *vt.* assediare.

besieger *s.* assediante.

besought V. *to beseech*.

to besprinkle *vt.* spruzzare.

best *agg.* (*superl. di good*) il migliore ‖ — *seller*, libro molto venduto. ♦ **best** *s.* il meglio. ♦ **best** *avv.* 1. nel modo migliore 2. maggiormente.

bestial *agg.* bestiale.

bestiality *s.* bestialità.

to bestialize *vt.* abbrutire.

to bestir *vt.* agitare.

to bestow *vt.* concedere.

bestowal *s.* conferimento.

to bestrew (bestrewed, bestrewn) *vt.* cospargere, disseminare.

bet *s.* scommessa.

to bet (bet, bet) *vt. e vi.* scommettere.

to betake (betook, betaken) *vr.* — *oneself:* dirigersi, recarsi.

to betray *vt.* tradire.

betrayal *s.* tradimento.

betrayer *s.* traditore.

betrothal *s.* fidanzamento.

betrothed *agg. e s.* fidanzato.

better[1] *s.* scommettitore.

better[2] *agg.* (*comp. di good*) migliore. ♦ **better** *avv.* meglio ‖ *had* —, sarebbe meglio che; *all the* —, *so much the* —, tanto meglio. ♦ **better** *s.* 1. il meglio 2. superiore.

to better *vt. e vi.* migliorare.

between *avv.* in mezzo. ♦ **between** *prep.* tra, fra (*due cose, due persone*).

beverage *s.* bevanda.

bevy *s.* stormo, frotta.

to beware *vi.* guardarsi, diffidare.

to bewilder *vt.* sconcertare.

bewildering *agg.* sbalorditivo.

bewilderment *s.* confusione.

to bewitch *vt.* incantare.

bewitcher *s.* incantatore.

bewitching *agg.* affascinante.

beyond *avv.* più in là. ♦ **beyond** *prep.* al di là di. ♦ **beyond** *s.* l'al di là.

bias *s.* 1. pregiudizio 2. predisposizione.

to bias *vt.* influenzare.

bib *s.* bavaglino.

Bible *s.* Bibbia.

biblical *agg.* biblico.

bibliographic(al) *agg.* bibliografico.

bibliography *s.* bibliografia.

bicameral *agg.* bicamerale.

bicarbonate *s.* bicarbonato.

bicentennial *agg. e s.* bicentenario.

bicephalous *agg.* bicipite.

biceps *s.* bicipite.

to bicker *vi.* litigare.

bicoloured *agg.* bicolore.

biconcave *agg.* biconcavo.

bicycle *s.* bicicletta.

bid[1] *s.* 1. offerta (*a un'asta*) 2. appalto.

to bid[1] **(bid, bid)** *vt.* offrire (*a un'asta*). ♦ **to bid (bid, bid)** *vi.* fare offerta di appalto.

to bid[2] **(bade, bidden)** *vt. e vi.* 1. comandare 2. dire ‖ *to — good-bye*, accomiatarsi.

biennial *agg.* biennale.

biennium *s.* (*pl.* -biennia) biennio.

bier *s.* bara.

big *agg.* 1. grosso 2. gravido 3. importante.

bigamous *agg.* bigamo.

bigamy *s.* bigamia.

bigness *s.* grossezza.

bigot *s.* bigotto.

bigoted *agg.* bigotto, fanatico.

bilateral *agg.* bilaterale.

bilberry *s.* mirtillo.

bile *s.* bile.

bilingual *agg.* bilingue.

bilious *agg.* 1. biliare 2. collerico.

bill[1] *s.* becco.

bill[2] *s.* 1. progetto di legge 2. certi- 5. lista 6. affisso ‖ — *of lading*, polizza di carico; — *of rights*, dichiarazione dei diritti.

to bill *vt.* 1. fatturare 2. affiggere 3. (*teat.*) mettere in programma.

billhook *s.* falcetto.

billiard *agg.* di, da bigliardo: —

-cue, stecca da bigliardo.

billiards *s. pl.* bigliardo (*sing.*).

billion *s.* 1. bilione 2. (*amer.*) miliardo.

billow *s.* onda.

bimestrial *agg.* bimestrale.

bimonthly *agg.* e *s.* bimestrale. ♦ **bimonthly** *avv.* bimestralmente.

bin *s.* recipiente || *dust- —*, bidone della spazzatura.

bind *s.* 1. legame 2. fascia.

to bind (bound, bound) *vt.* 1. legare 2. fasciare 3. rilegare 4. obbligare.

binder *s.* 1. rilegatore 2. (*mecc.*) legatrice.

binding *agg.* impegnativo. ♦ **binding** *s.* 1. legame 2. fasciatura 3. rilegatura.

binocular *s.* binocolo.

binomial *s.* binomio.

biochemistry *s.* biochimica.

biographer *s.* biografo.

biographic(al) *agg.* biografico.

biography *s.* biografia.

biological *agg.* biologico.

biologist *s.* biologo.

biology *s.* biologia.

biophysics *s.* biofisica.

biosphere *s.* biosfera.

bipartite *agg.* bipartito.

bipartition *s.* bipartizione.

biped *agg.* e *s.* bipede.

biplane *s.* biplano.

bipolar *agg.* bipolare.

birch *s.* 1. betulla 2. verga.

bird *s.* uccello.

birdcage *s.* gabbia (*per uccelli*).

birdseed *s.* miglio.

birth *s.* 1. nascita 2. stirpe.

birthday *s.* compleanno.

birthmark *s.* voglia, segno caratteristico (*di persona*).

birthplace *s.* luogo di nascita.

biscuit *s.* biscotto.

bisection *s.* bisezione.

bisector *s.* bisettrice.

bisexual *agg.* ermafrodito.

bishop *s.* vescovo.

bishopric *s.* vescovato.

bismuth *s.* bismuto.

bison *s.* bisonte.

bistoury *s.* bisturi.

bistre *s.* bistro.

bit *s.* 1. pezzettino 2. un poco 3. (*mecc.*) parte tagliente di un utensile 4. morso (*del cavallo*).

bit V. *to bite*.

bitch *s.* cagna.

bite *s.* 1. morso 2. presa.

to bite (bit, bit(ten)) *vt.* mordere. ♦ **to bite (bit, bit(ten))** *vi.* abboccare || *to — in*, corrodere.

biting *agg.* 1. mordente 2. mordace.

bitten V. *to bite*.

bitter *agg.* 1. amaro 2. aspro 3. (*di clima*) rigido || *—sweet*, agrodolce. ♦ **bitter** *s.* amaro.

bitterish *agg.* amarognolo.

bitterness *s.* 1. amarezza 2. rancore 3. rigidità (*di clima*).

bitumen *s.* bitume.

bivalent *agg.* bivalente.

bivouac *s.* bivacco.

bi-weekly *agg.* e *s.* bisettimanale. ♦ **bi-weekly** *avv.* due volte alla settimana.

to blab *vt.* e *vi.* 1. chiacchierare 2. spifferare.

black *agg.* 1. nero 2. negro 3. (*fig.*) malvagio, minaccioso. ♦ **black** *s.* 1. colore nero 2. negro.

to black *vt.* annerire. ♦ **to black** *vi.* annerirsi.

to blackball *vt.* votare contro, bocciare.

blackberry *s.* mora selvatica.

blackbird *s.* merlo.

blackboard *s.* lavagna.

to blacken *vt.* 1. annerire 2. (*fig.*) diffamare. ♦ **to blacken** *vi.* diventare nero.

blackguard *s.* mascalzone.

blackish *agg.* nerastro.

blackleg *s.* 1. truffatore 2. crumiro.

blackmail *s.* ricatto.

to blackmail *vt.* ricattare.

blackmailer *s.* ricattatore.

blackness *s.* 1. nerezza 2. oscurità.

blackout *s.* oscuramento.

blacksmith *s.* fabbro ferraio.

bladder *s.* vescica.

blade *s.* 1. stelo 2. lama.

blamable *agg.* biasimevole.

blame *s.* 1. biasimo 2. colpa.

to blame *vt.* 1. biasimare 2. incolpare.

blameful *agg.* biasimevole.

blameless *agg.* irreprensibile.

bland *agg.* blando.

blandishment *s.* blandizie (*pl.*).

blandly *avv.* blandamente.

blank *agg.* 1. vuoto 2. in bianco || *— verse*, verso sciolto.. ♦ **blank** *s.* 1. vuoto 2. spazio in bianco 3. mira || *point- —*, di punto in bianco.

blanket *s.* coperta.

blankly *avv.* **1.** senza espressione **2.** decisamente.

blare *s.* squillo (*di tromba*).

to **blaspheme** *vt.* e *vi.* bestemmiare.

blasphemous *agg.* blasfemo.

blasphemously *avv.* empiamente.

blasphemy *s.* bestemmia, empietà.

blast *s.* **1.** raffica **2.** squillo **3.** scoppio **4.** flagello ‖ — *-furnace*, altoforno.

to **blast** *vt.* **1.** far esplodere **2.** rovinare.

blaze *s.* **1.** fiamma **2.** scoppio.

to **blaze** *vi.* ardere. ♦ to **blaze** *vt.* **1.** bruciare **2.** divulgare.

blazer *s.* giacca sportiva.

blazing *s.* **1.** fiamma **2.** splendore **3.** vanteria.

blazon *s.* **1.** blasone **2.** ostentazione.

bleach *s.* imbianchimento, candeggio.

to **bleach** *vt.* imbiancare, candeggiare. ♦ to **bleach** *vi.* imbiancarsi.

bleacher *s.* recipiente per candeggio.

bleaching *s.* V. *bleach*.

bleak *agg.* **1.** brullo **2.** desolato **3.** incolore.

bleakness *s.* **1.** freddezza **2.** squallore.

blear *agg.* **1.** cisposo **2.** ottuso.

bleat *s.* belato.

to **bleat** *vi.* belare.

to **bleed (bled, bled)** *vi.* sanguinare. ♦ to **bleed (bled, bled)** *vt.* salassare.

bleeding *s.* **1.** emorragia **2.** salasso **3.** fuga.

blemish *s.* difetto.

blend *s.* miscela.

to **blend** *vt.* mescolare. ♦ to **blend** *vi.* mescolarsi.

to **bless** *vt.* benedire.

blessed *agg.* beato, santo.

blessing *s.* benedizione.

blew V. to *blow*.

blind *agg.* cieco. ♦ **blind** *s.* **1.** tenda **2.** persiana **3.** paraocchi **4.** finzione.

to **blind** *vt.* **1.** accecare **2.** oscurare **3.** nascondere.

blindness *s.* cecità.

to **blink** *vi.* **1.** battere le palpebre **2.** lampeggiare **3.** (*fig.*) chiudere gli occhi.

blinker *s.* **1.** lampeggiatore **2.** paraocchi.

blinking *agg.* **1.** ammiccante **2.** scintillante. ♦ **blinking** *s.* ammicco.

bliss *s.* beatitudine.

blissful *agg.* **1.** beato **2.** delizioso.

blister *s.* bolla.

blithe *agg.* gaio.

blizzard *s.* tormenta (*di neve*).

block *s.* **1.** ceppo **2.** masso **3.** isolato (*di case*) **4.** ostacolo **5.** persona stupida ‖ — *letters*, stampatello.

to **block** *vt.* bloccare.

blockade *s.* blocco.

blockhead *s.* stupido.

blonde *s.* donna bionda.

blood *s.* sangue.

bloodhound *s.* segugio.

bloodless *agg.* **1.** esangue **2.** incruento **3.** (*fig.*) insensibile.

bloodshed *s.* spargimento di sangue.

bloodshot *agg.* iniettato di sangue.

bloody *agg.* **1.** sanguinante **2.** sanguinoso **3.** sanguinario **4.** maledetto.

bloom *s.* **1.** fiore **2.** rossore.

to **bloom** *vi.* **1.** fiorire **2.** arrossire.

blossom *s.* fiore.

to **blossom** *vi.* **1.** fiorire **2.** diventare.

blot *s.* macchia.

to **blot** *vt.* **1.** macchiare **2.** assorbire.

blotch *s.* **1.** macchia **2.** pustola.

blotting *s.* **1.** il macchiare **2.** l'asciugare ‖ — *-paper*, carta assorbente; — *-pad*, tampone di carta assorbente.

blouse *s.* camicetta.

blow *s.* **1.** soffio **2.** colpo **3.** fioritura ‖ *to come to blows*, venire alle mani.

to **blow (blew, blown)** *vt.* **1.** soffiare **2.** suonare (*strumenti a fiato*) ‖ *to — up*, (far) saltare in aria. ♦ to **blow (blew, blown)** *vi.* sbocciare.

blower *s.* **1.** soffiatore **2.** sfiatatoio.

blown V. to *blow*.

blowpipe *s.* **1.** cannello per soffiare **2.** cerbottana.

blue *agg.* **1.** azzurro, blu **2.** livido **3.** triste.

bluebell *s.* campanula.

bluebottle[1] *s.* fiordaliso.

bluebottle[2] *s.* tafano.

blueprint *s.* cianografia.

bluff *s.* ripida scogliera.

bluish *agg.* bluastro.

blunder *s.* errore.

blunt *agg.* **1.** smussato **2.** ottuso **3.** schietto.

blush *s.* rossore.

to **blush** vi. arrossire.

board s. 1. asse, tavola 2. vitto 3. pensione 4. consiglio, ministero 5. (mar.) bordo || on —, a bordo; full —, pensione completa. ♦ **boards** s. pl. palcoscenico (sing.).

to **board** vt. 1. fornire di assi 2. prendere a pensione 3. (mar.) abbordare. ♦ to **board** vi. 1. essere a pensione 2. imbarcarsi.

boarder s. pensionante.

boarding s. assito || —-house, pensione; —-school, collegio.

boast s. vanto.

to **boast** vt. vantare. ♦ to **boast** vi. vantarsi.

boaster s. spaccone.

boastful agg. vanaglorioso.

boastfulness s. millanteria.

boasting s. vanteria.

boat s. barca, battello || flying—, idrovolante; sauce—, salsiera; ferry—, traghetto.

boating s. canottaggio.

boatman s. barcaiolo.

boatswain s. nostromo.

to **bob** vi. dondolarsi, oscillare || to — up, venire a galla.

bobbin s. bobina.

bobsled s. guidoslitta.

bodice s. busto.

bodkin s. punteruolo, stiletto.

body s. 1. corpo 2. corporazione, ente 3. massa || —-belt, panciera.

bodymaker s. carrozziere.

Boeotian agg. e s. beota.

bog s.

boggy agg. paludoso.

bogy s. spauracchio.

boil s. bollitura.

to **boil** vt. e vi. bollire, ribollire || to — away, consumarsi; to — over, traboccare bollendo.

boiler s. bollitore, caldaia.

boiling agg. bollente. ♦ **boiling** s. ebollizione.

boisterous agg. 1. rumoroso 2. violento.

boisterousness s. fracasso.

bold agg. 1. audace 2. sfacciato 3. vigoroso || —-face, neretto.

boldness s. 1. audacia 2. sfacciataggine.

bolide s. bolide.

Bolshevism s. bolscevismo.

Bolshevist agg. e s. bolscevico.

bolster s. cuscino 2. supporto.

bolt s. 1. catenaccio 2. bullone 3. otturatore 4. freccia 5. fulmine.

to **bolt**[1] vt. 1. sprangare 2. imbullonare.

to **bolt**[2] vt. setacciare, vagliare.

bolter s. setaccio.

bomb s. bomba.

to **bomb** vt. bombardare.

to **bombard** vt. bombardare.

bombardier s. bombardiere.

bombardment s. bombardamento.

bombastic agg. ampolloso.

bomber s. bombardiere.

bond s. 1. vincolo 2. patto 3. (comm.) titolo 4. cauzione || —-holder, portatore di obbligazioni; goods in —, merci in attesa di sdoganamento.

bondage s. schiavitù.

bone s. 1. osso 2. lisca.

to **bone** vt. 1. disossare 2. spinare.

bonfire s. falò.

bonnet s. 1. cuffia 2. (auto) cofano.

bonus s. gratifica || cost of living —, carovita.

bony agg. 1. osseo 2. ossuto.

bonze s. bonzo.

booby s. sciocco.

book s. 1. libro 2. registro || note-—, taccuino; copy- —, quaderno.

to **book** vt. 1. registrare 2. prenotare.

bookbinding s. rilegatura.

bookcase s. libreria.

booking s. 1. registrazione 2. prenotazione || — -office, biglietteria.

bookish agg. 1. studioso 2. libresco.

bookkeeper s. contabile.

bookkeeping s. contabilità.

booklet s. libretto.

bookmaker s. allibratore.

bookseller s. libraio.

bookshelf s. (pl. -lves) scaffale.

bookshop s. libreria.

bookstall s. edicola, bancarella (di libri).

boom s. 1. rombo 2. periodo di prosperità.

to **boom** vi. 1. rimbombare 2. essere in periodo di prosperità.

boor s. persona zotica.

boorish agg. rustico.

boorishness s. rozzezza.

boot s. 1. stivale, scarpa 2. (auto) portabagagli.

bootblack s. lustrascarpe.

booth s. baracca || telephone —, cabina telefonica.

booty s. bottino.

border s. 1. orlo 2. frontiera.

to **border** vt. orlare || to — on, confinare con.

borderer s. abitante di confine.

bordering s. 1. il bordare 2. il confinare.

bore V. to bear.

bore[1] s. 1. buco 2. calibro (di arma).

bore[2] s. 1. seccatura 2. seccatore.

to **bore**[1] vt. forare.

to **bore**[2] vt. annoiare.

boreal agg. boreale.

boredom s. noia.

boric agg. borico.

boring[1] agg. noioso.

boring[2] s. perforazione || — test, son.aggio.

born V. to bear. ◆ **born** agg. nato, generato || to be —, nascere.

borne V. to bear.

borough s. 1. municipio 2. circoscrizione elettorale.

to **borrow** vt. prendere a prestito.

borrower s. chi prende a prestito.

bosom s. seno || — friend, amico intimo.

boss[1] s. 1. protuberanza 2. (arch.) bugna.

boss[2] s. capo, padrone.

bossy[1] agg. a bugnato.

bossy[2] agg. (gergo) prepotente.

botanist s. botanico.

botany s. botanica.

botch s. pasticcio.

to **botch** vt. 1. rattoppare 2. arruffare.

botcher s. pasticcione.

both agg. e pron. entrambi, tutti e due. ◆ **both** avv. nel medesimo tempo || — ... and, sia... sia, tanto... quanto.

bother s. seccatura.

to **bother** vt. infastidire. ◆ to **bother** vi. preoccuparsi.

bothersome agg. fastidioso.

bottle s. bottiglia || feeding- —, poppatoio; — -feeding, allattamento artificiale.

to **bottle** vt. imbottigliare.

bottling s. imbottigliamento.

bottom s. 1. inferiore 2. basilare. ◆ **bottom** s. 1. fondo 2. fondamento 3. deretano 4. (mar.) chiglia.

to **bottom** vt. 1. mettere il fondo (a) 2. impagliare 3. capire. ◆ to **bottom** vi. posare, essere posato.

bottomless agg. 1. senza fondo 2. senza fine.

bough s. ramo (d'albero).

bought V. to buy.

boulder s. macigno.

boulevard s. viale.

bounce s. 1. balzo 2. vanteria.

to **bounce** vt. far rimbalzare. ◆ to **bounce** vi. 1. rimbalzare 2. gloriarsi.

bouncer s. fanfarone.

bound[1] s. limite, confine.

bound[2] s. salto.

bound[3] V. to bind.

bound[4] agg. 1. destinato 2. diretto a 3. certo.

to **bound**[1] vt. confinare, limitare.

to **bound**[2] vi. balzare.

boundary s. limite, frontiera.

boundless agg. illimitato.

bounteous agg. generoso.

bounty s. generosità.

bourgeois agg. e s. borghese.

bourgeoisie s. borghesia.

bow[1] s. 1. arco 2. archetto 3. fiocco || -window, bovindo.

bow[2] s. inchino.

bow[3] s. prua.

to **bow** vt. piegare. ◆ to **bow** vi. 1. piegarsi 2. inclinarsi.

bowels s. pl. viscere.

bower s. 1. pergolato 2. dimora.

bowl[1] s. ciotola.

bowl[2] s. boccia.

to **bowl** vt. far rotolare. ◆ to **bowl** vi. 1. rotolare 2. giocare a bocce.

bowler s. giocatore di bocce || — hat, bombetta.

bowling s. gioco delle bocce.

bowman s. arciere.

bowshot s. tiro d'arco.

box[1] s. 1. scatola 2. stanzetta 3. stalla 4. (teat.) palco 5. (giur.) banco || letter- —, buca per le lettere; money- —, salvadanaio; strong- —, cassaforte.

box[2] s. pugno, ceffone.

to **box**[1] vt. mettere in scatola.

to **box**[2] vt. schiaffeggiare. ◆ to **box** vi. fare del pugilato.

boxer s. pugile.

boxing s. pugilato.

boy s. ragazzo.

to **boycott** vt. boicottare.

boyhood s. fanciullezza.

boyish agg. fanciullesco.

bra s. reggipetto.

brace s. 1. sostegno 2. coppia, paio 3. (mar.) braccio. ◆ **braces** s. pl. bretelle.

to **brace** *vt.* 1. legare 2. fortificare.

bracelet *s.* braccialetto.

brachycardia *s.* brachicardia.

bracket *s.* 1. mensola, sostegno 2. parentesi.

brackish *agg.* salato, salso.

brag *s.* 1. millanteria 2. millantatore.

to **brag** *vt.* vantare. ♦ to **brag** *vi.* vantarsi.

braggart *agg.* e *s.* spaccone.

bragging *s.* millanteria.

braid *s.* 1. treccia 2. gallone.

to **braid** *vt.* 1. intrecciare 2. guarnire.

brain *s.* cervello.

brainless *agg.* scervellato.

brake[1] *s.* 1. felce 2. boschetto.

brake[2] *s.* freno.

to **brake** *vt.* frenare.

brakesman *s.* frenatore.

bramble *s.* rovo.

bran *s.* crusca.

branch *s.* 1. ramo 2. filiale.

to **branch** *vt.* ramificare. ♦ to **branch** *vi.* ramificarsi || to — out, estendersi (*di attività commerciale, affari*).

branching *s.* ramificazione.

brand *s.* 1. tizzone 2. marchio (*a fuoco*) 3. marca || — -new, nuovo fiammante.

to **brand** *vt.* 1. marchiare 2. stigmatizzare.

to **brandish** *vt.* brandire.

brass *agg.* 1. di ottone 2. (*fig.*) sfacciato. ♦ **brass** *s.* 1. ottone 2. (*mecc.*) bronzina 3. (*fig.*) sfacciataggine || — band, fanfara

brassy *agg.* V. *brass*.

bravado *s.* bravata.

brave *agg.* e *s.* prode, coraggioso.

bravely *avv.* coraggiosamente.

bravery *s.* 1. coraggio 2. splendore.

brawl *s.* rissa.

to **brawl** *vi.* rissare.

brawn *s.* muscolo, forza muscolare.

brawny *agg.* muscoloso.

bray *s.* raglio.

to **bray**[1] *vi.* 1. ragliare 2. (*fig.*) stonare.

to **bray**[2] *vt.* frantumare, sminuzzare.

brazen *agg.* V. *brass*.

brazier[1] *s.* calderaio.

brazier[2] *s.* braciere.

Brazilian *agg.* e *s.* brasiliar. *s.*

breach *s.* 1. rottura 2. breccia 3. infrazione || — of promise, rottura di fidanzamento.

bread *s.* pane.

to **bread** *vt.* rimpanare.

breadth *s.* 1. larghezza 2. altezza (*di stoffe*).

breadthwise *avv.* in larghezza (*di stoffe*).

break *s.* 1. rottura 2. interruzione, intervallo 3. infrazione || — -up, collasso, smembramento, fine.

to **break** (broke, broken) *vt.* 1. rompere 2. interrompere 3. domare 4. rovinare. ♦ to **break** (broke, broken) *vi.* 1. rompersi 2. irrompere || to — down, demolire, (*auto*) restare in panne, esaurirsi; to — off, mandare a monte; to — up, fare a pezzi.

breakdown *s.* 1. collasso 2. rottura 3. dissesto || *nervous* —, esaurimento nervoso.

breaker *s.* 1. rompitore 2. violatore 3. domatore 4. (*mecc.*) macchina rompitrice 5. (*mar.*) frangente 6. (*elett.*) interruttore.

breakfast *s.* prima colazione.

to **breakfast** *vi.* fare la prima colazione.

breaking *s.* 1. rottura 2. (*comm.*) fallimento.

breakneck *agg.* a rotta di collo.

breakwater *s.* frangiflutti.

breast *s.* petto || — -bone, sterno.

breasted *agg.* dal petto || *double-*—, a doppio petto.

breath *s.* 1. soffio 2. respiro.

breathable *agg.* respirabile.

to **breathe** *vi.* 1. respirare 2. spirare. ♦ to **breathe** *vt.* 1. infondere 2. sussurrare.

breathing *s.* V. *breath*.

breathless *agg.* 1. ansante 2. esanime.

breathlessness *s.* affanno.

bred V. to *breed*. ♦ **bred** *agg.* ill-—, maleducato.

breech *s.* 1. parte posteriore 2. culatta (*di arma*).

breeches *s. pl.* calzoni.

breed *s.* razza.

to **breed** (bred, bred) *vt.* 1. generare 2. allevare. ♦ to **breed** (bred, bred) *vi.* nascere.

breeder *s.* chi genera 2. allevatore.

breeding *s.* 1. generazione 2. allevamento 3. educazione.

breeze *s.* brezza.

breezy *agg.* 1. ventilato 2. cordiale.

brethren *s. pl.* confratelli.

breviary s. breviario.
brevity s. brevità.
brew s. **1.** mistura **2.** fermentazione (di birra).
to **brew** vt. **1.** mescolare **2.** (fig.) macchinare. ♦ to **brew** vi. fare la birra.
brewer s. birraio.
brewery s. fabbrica di birra.
bribe s. dono (a scopo di corruzione), allettamento.
to **bribe** vt. corrompere.
briber s. corruttore.
bribery s. corruzione.
brick s. mattone.
bricklayer s. muratore.
brickwork s. muratura in mattoni.
brickyard s. mattonaia
bride s. sposa.
bridegroom s. sposo.
bridge s. ponte || swing—, ponte girevole; toll—, ponte a pedaggio; — -head, testa di ponte
bridle s. briglia, freno.
to **bridle** vt. imbrigliare.
bridling s. imbrigliatura.
brief agg. breve. ♦ **brief** s. riassunto.
to **brief** vt. **1.** riassumere **2.** (giur.) nominare (il proprio avvocato) **3.** dare istruzioni.
briefness s. brevità, concisione.
brier s. **1.** rovo **2.** rosa selvatica.
brig s. brigantino.
brigade s. brigata.
bright agg. **1.** chiaro, splendente **2.** vivace.
to **brighten** vt. **1.** far brillare **2.** animare. ♦ to **brighten** vi. **1.** brillare **2.** animarsi.
brightness s. **1.** splendore **2.** gaiezza.
brill s. (itt.) rombo.
brilliance, brilliancy s. brillantezza.
brilliant agg. e s. brillante.
brilliantine s. brillantina.
brim s. **1.** orlo **2.** ala (di cappello).
brimful agg. colmo.
brindled agg. pezzato.
brine s. acqua salata.
to **bring (brought, brought)** vt. **1.** portare **2.** indurre || to — about, causare; to — back, richiamare alla memoria; to — forth, dare alla luce; to — up, educare, allevare.
brink s. orlo.
brisk agg. **1.** vivace **2.** frizzante.
briskness s. vivacità.

bristle s. setola.
to **bristle** vi. essere irto di.
bristly agg. **1.** setoloso **2.** ruvido.
British agg. britannico.
Briton agg. e s. britanno.
broad agg. **1.** ampio **2.** chiaro **3.** marcato **4.** volgare || — daylight, pieno giorno. ♦ **broad** s. larghezza. ♦ **broad** avv. ampiamente.
broadcast s. **1.** radiodiffusione **2.** radiocomunicazione.
to **broadcast (broadcast, broadcast)** (anche reg.) vt. e vi. radiotrasmettere.
broadcaster s. trasmettitore.
broadcasting s. radiodiffusione.
to **broaden** vt. allargare. ♦ to **broaden** vi. allargarsi, estendersi.
broadness s. **1.** larghezza **2.** grossolanità.
broadside s. (mar.) **1.** bordo, fiancata **2.** bordata.
brocade s. broccato.
bro(c)coli s. broccolo.
broil s. rissa.
to **broil** vt. cuocere alla griglia. ♦ to **broil** vi. abbrustolirsi (al sole).
broke V. to **break.**
broken V. to **break.** ♦ **broken** agg. **1.** variabile (di tempo) **2.** accidentato (di terreno) **3.** indebolito **4.** avvilito **5.** scorretto.
broker s. **1.** (comm.) agente **2.** mediatore.
bromide s. bromuro.
bromine s. bromo.
bronchial agg. bronchiale.
bronchia s. pl. bronchi.
bronchitis s. bronchite.
broncho-pneumonia s. broncopolmonia.
bronze s. bronzo.
to **bronze** vt. abbronzare. ♦ to **bronze** vi. abbronzarsi.
brooch s. spilla.
brood s. covata.
to **brood** vt. **1.** covare **2.** (fig.) rimuginare, meditare.
brooding s. **1.** cova **2.** meditazione.
brook s. ruscello.
to **brook** vt. sopportare, tollerare.
brooklet s. ruscelletto.
broom s. **1.** ginestra **2.** scopa.
broth s. brodo.
brothel s. bordello.
brother s. **1.** fratello **2.** collega || — -in-law, cognato; half- —, fratellastro.

brotherhood s. 1. fratellanza 2. confraternita.

brotherlike agg. fraterno.

brotherly agg. fraterno. ♦ **brotherly** avv. fraternamente.

brought V. to bring.

brow s. fronte. ♦ **brows** s. pl. sopracciglia.

brown agg. 1. bruno 2. marrone. ♦ **brown** s. marrone.

to brown vt. 1. rendere bruno 2. rosolare. ♦ **to brown** vi. 1. diventare bruno 2. abbronzarsi

to browse vt. e vi. brucare.

bruise s. contusione.

to bruise vt. ammaccare. ♦ **to bruise** vi. ammaccarsi.

bruiser s. 1. pugilatore 2. (fig.) gradasso.

brush s. 1. spazzola, spazzolino 2. spazzolata 3. pennello 4. rissa || — -up, ripasso.

to brush vt. 1. spazzolare 2. sfiorare || to — aside (fig.), ignorare; to — up, ripassare.

brushwood s. sottobosco.

brushy agg. 1. ispido 2. folto (di bosco).

brusque agg. brusco.

brutal agg. brutale.

brutality s. brutalità.

to brutalize vt. 1. abbrutire 2. maltrattare. ♦ **to brutalize** vi. abbrutirsi.

brute agg. brutale. ♦ **brute** s. bruto.

brutish agg. brutale, rozzo.

bubble s. 1. bolla 2. gorgoglio.

to bubble vi. gorgogliare || to — over, traboccare.

bubo s. bubbone.

bubonic agg. bubbonico.

buccaneer s. bucaniere.

buck s. 1. daino 2. maschio (di molti animali).

to buck vi. sgroppare.

bucket s. secchio.

buckle s. fibbia.

to buckle vt. 1. affibbiare 2. piegare. ♦ **to buckle** vi. piegarsi.

bucolic agg. bucolico.

bud s. 1. gemma 2. germe.

to bud vi. germogliare.

Buddhism s. buddismo.

Buddhist agg. e s. buddista.

budget s. 1. raccolta (di documenti) 2. bilancio.

buffalo s. bufalo.

buffer s. respingente.

buffet[1] s. schiaffo.

buffet[2] s. credenza.

to buffet vt. schiaffeggiare.

buffoon s. buffone.

bug s. 1. coleottero 2. cimice || big —, (gergo) pezzo grosso.

bugbear s. spauracchio.

bugger s. sodomita.

build s. costruzione, struttura.

to build (built, built) vt. costruire || to — up, murare.

builder s. costruttore.

building agg. edilizio. ♦ **building** s. edificio.

built V. to build.

bulb s. 1. bulbo 2. lampadina || — socket, portalampada.

Bulgarian agg. e s. bulgaro.

bulge s. gonfiore.

to bulge vi. gonfiarsi. ♦ **to bulge** vt. 1. sporgere 2. gonfiare.

bulgy agg. rigonfio.

bulk s. 1. massa 2. carico.

bulkhead s. paratia.

bulky agg. massiccio.

bull s. 1. toro 2. maschio (di alcuni mammiferi) || —'s eye, oblò.

bulldog s. mastino.

bullet s. pallottola.

bulletin s. bollettino || news —, giornale radio.

bullfight s. corrida.

bullfighter s. torero.

bullock s. torello.

bully agg. borioso.

to bully vt. e vi. fare il prepotente (verso).

bulwark s. 1. bastione 2. (mar.) parapetto.

bumble-bee s. calabrone.

bump s. 1. urto 2. bernoccolo.

to bump vt. e vi. urtare, andare a sbattere contro.

bumper s. 1. paraurti 2. respingente.

bun s. 1. focaccia 2. crocchia.

bunch s. 1. mazzo 2. grappolo.

bundle s. 1. fagotto 2. fascio.

to bundle vt. riunire in fascio, fare un involto.

bung s. tappo.

bungler agg. e s. confusionario.

bunny s. coniglietto.

buoy s. boa.

buoyancy s. 1. galleggiabilità 2. ottimismo.

buoyant agg. 1. galleggiante 2. ottimista.

burden s. 1. peso 2. tonnellaggio.

to **burden** vt. caricare.
burdensome agg. gravoso.
bureau s. (pl. bureaux) ufficio.
bureaucracy s. burocrazia.
bureaucrat s. burocrate.
bureaucratic agg. burocratico.
burglar s. scassinatore (notturno).
burglary s. furto (notturno) con scasso.
to **burgle** vt. e vi. svaligiare con scasso.
burgomaster s. borgomastro.
burial s. sepoltura || — -ground, cimitero; — -service, ufficio funebre.
burin s. bulino.
burly agg. corpulento.
burn s. ustione.
to **burn** (**burnt, burnt**) (anche reg.) vt. e vi. bruciare, ardere.
burner s. bruciatore.
burning s. 1. incendio 2. (metal.) fusione.
to **burnish** vt. lustrare.
burnt V. to burn.
burrow s. tana, buca.
bursar s. economo.
bursary s. 1. ufficio dell'economato 2. borsa di studio.
burst s. 1. scoppio 2. squarcio.
to **burst** (**burst, burst**) vt. 1. far esplodere 2. sfondare. ♦ to **burst** (**burst, burst**) vi. 1. scoppiare 2. irrompere.
bursting s. scoppio.
to **bury** vt. seppellire.
bus s. autobus.
busby s. colbac.
bush s. cespuglio.
bushel s. staio.
bushy agg. folto.
busily avv. attivamente.
business s. 1. affare 2. mestiere 3. ditta 4. scopo || —-man, uomo d'affari; — -like, metodico, sistematico.
bust s. busto.
bustle s. trambusto.
to **bustle** vi. agitarsi.
busy agg. occupato.
to **busy** vt. occupare.
busybody s. ficcanaso.
but cong. ma. ♦ but avv. solo. ♦ but prep. tranne || — for, se non fosse per; — that, se non; cannot —, non poter far a meno di; all —, pressoché.
butane s. butano.
butcher s. macellaio.
butchery s. macello.

butler s. maggiordomo.
butt[1] s. 1. calcio (di arma) 2. impugnatura (di utensile) 3. mozzicone.
butt[2] s. urto.
to **butt** vt. e vi. cozzare.
butter s. burro.
to **butter** vt. imburrare.
buttercup s. ranuncolo.
butterfly s. farfalla.
buttery agg. burroso.
buttock s. natica.
button s. bottone.
to **button** vt. abbottonare.
button-hole s. occhiello.
to **button-hole** vt. 1. fare asole a 2. (fig.) attaccar bottone.
button-holer s. attaccabottoni.
buttress s. contrafforte.
buxom agg. formoso, avvenente (di donna).
to **buy** (**bought, bought**) vt. comprare || to — off, riscattare; to — up, accaparrare.
buyable agg. acquistabile.
buyer s. acquirente.
buzz s. ronzio.
buzzard s. poiana.
to **buzz** vi. e vt. ronzare, bisbigliare.
buzzer s. 1. insetto che ronza 2. cicala, segnale acustico.
by avv. 1. vicino 2. da parte, in disparte || — and —, fra poco; — and large, complessivamente. ♦ by prep. 1. (agente, causa, mezzo) per, da, con, di || a book (written) — Shakespeare, un libro di Shakespeare; to travel — train, viaggiare col treno 2. (tempo) entro, per, durante || — day — day, di giorno in giorno; — night, di notte 3. (luogo) vicino a, a fianco di, attraverso || a house — the sea, una casa sul mare. ♦ by agg. secondario.
bye-bye inter. arrivederci.
bygone agg. e s. passato.
by-line s. (giorn.) firma.
byname s. soprannome.
by-pass s. 1. circonvallazione 2. deviazione.
by-product s. sottoprodotto.
byroad s. strada secondaria.
byssus s. bisso.
bystander s. spettatore.
bystreet s. viuzza.
byway s. via traversa.
byword s. proverbio, epiteto.
bywork s. lavoro supplementare (e tempo perso).
Byzantine agg. e s. bizantino.

C

C (*mus.*) do.
cab *s.* vettura di piazza.
cabal *s.* intrigo, cospirazione.
cabbage *s.* cavolo.
cab(b)ala *s.* cabala.
cab(b)alistic *agg.* cabalistico.
cabin *s.* 1. capanna 2. (*aer.; fer.; mar.*) cabina.
cabinet *s.* 1. stanzino 2. stipo, armadietto 3. (*pol.*) gabinetto, consiglio dei ministri || — -maker, ebanista; — -minister, membro del gabinetto.
cable *s.* 1. cavo 2. cablogramma || — -way, teleferica.
to cable *vt.* e *vi.* 1. fornire di cavo 2. trasmettere un cablogramma.
cablegram *s.* cablogramma.
cabman *s.* tassista.
caboose (*mar.*) cambusa.
cabotage *s.* cabotaggio.
cacao *s.* cacao.
cacophony *s.* cacofonia.
cactus *s.* cactus.
cadaverous *agg.* 1. cadaverico 2. esangue.
cadence *s.* cadenza, ritmo.
cadet *s.* cadetto.
caducity *s.* caducità.
Caesarean *agg.* cesareo, imperiale || — operation, parto cesareo.
caesura *s.* cesura.
café *s.* caffè (*locale pubblico*).
caffeine *s.* caffeina.
cage *s.* 1. gabbia 2. impalcatura.
to cage *vt.* mettere in gabbia.
cake *s.* torta, focaccia.
calamary *s.* calamaro.
calamitous *agg.* calamitoso.
calamity *s.* calamità.
calcareous *agg.* calcareo.
calcification *s.* calcificazione.
to calcify *vt.* calcificare. ♦ to calcify *vi.* calcificarsi.
calcination *s.* calcinazione.
to calcine *V.* to *calcify.*
calcite *s.* calcite.
calcium *s.* calcio.
to calculate *vt.* 1. calcolare 2. contare. ♦ to calculate *vi.* fare affidamento.
calculated *agg.* 1. calcolato 2. premeditato 3. (*fig.*) idoneo.
calculating *agg.* calcolatore || — machine, macchina calcolatrice.
calculation *s.* calcolo.

calculator *s.* calcolatore, calcolatrice.
calendar *s.* calendario, almanacco.
calf[1] *s.* (*pl.* calves) vitello.
calf[2] *s.* polpaccio.
to calibrate *vt.* 1. calibrare 2. (*mecc.*) tarare.
calibration *s.* calibratura, taratura.
calibre *s.* calibro.
calico *s.* calicò.
call *s.* 1. richiamo, chiamata 2. breve visita: to pay (*v. irr.*) so. a —, fare una breve visita a qu. 3. (*giur.*) appello 4. (*mil.*) adunata 5. (*mar.*) scalo || — -bird, uccello da richiamo; — box, cabina telefonica; — up, chiamata alle armi; trunk —, chiamata intercontinentale.
to call *vt.* e *vi.* 1. chiamare, richiamare: to — aside, chiamare in disparte; to — to arms, chiamare alle armi; to — to mind, richiamare alla mente 2. esortare, ordinare || to — into being, creare; to — out, chiamare ad alta voce, esclamare; to — up, telefonare; to — at, fare scalo a; to — for, passare a prendere; to — on, fare una breve visita a; to — upon, implorare, invocare.
caller *s.* visitatore, visitatrice.
calligrapher *s.* calligrafo.
calligraphic *agg.* calligrafico.
calling *s.* 1. appello 2. mestiere, professione 3. vocazione.
callosity *s.* 1. callosità 2. (*fig.*) insensibilità.
callous *agg.* 1. calloso 2. (*fig.*) insensibile.
calm *agg.* calmo. ♦ calm *s.* calma.
to calm *vt.* calmare. ♦ to calm *vi.* to — down, calmarsi (*di tempesta ecc.*).
calming *agg.* calmante.
calmly *avv.* con calma.
calmness *s.* calma, tranquillità.
calorific *agg.* calorifico.
calorimeter *s.* calorimetro.
calory *s.* caloria.
to calumniate *vt.* calunniare.
Calvary *s.* Calvario.
calves *V.* calf.
Calvinism *s.* calvinismo.
Calvinist *agg.* e *s.* calvinista.
came *V.* to come.
camel *s.* cammello.
camellia *s.* camelia.
cameo *s.* cammeo.
camera *s.* 1. (*foto*) macchina foto-

grafica **2.** (*giur.*) Camera di Consiglio.

camisole *s.* corpetto, farsetto.

camouflage *s.* **1.** mascheramento **2.** (*mil.*) mimetizzazione.

to camouflage *vt.* **1.** mascherare **2.** (*mil.*) mimetizzare.

camp *s.* (*mil.*) campo **2.** campeggio || — *-bed*, brandina.

to camp *vt.* (*mil.*) accampare. ♦ **to camp** *vi.* **1.** accamparsi **2.** attendarsi.

campaign *s.* (*mil.*) campagna.

camper *s.* campeggiatore.

camphor *s.* canfora.

camping *s.* **1.** (*mil.*) accampamento **2.** campeggio.

can[1] *s.* recipiente di latta, bidone.

can[2] *v. dif.* (*ind. cong. pres.*) **could** (*ind. cong. pass. e condiz.*) potere, essere in grado di.

Canadian *agg. e s.* canadese.

canal *s.* canale.

canalization *s.* canalizzazione.

to canalize *vt.* canalizzare.

canary *agg.* giallo canarino. ♦ **canary** *s.* canarino.

to cancel *vt.* annullare, cancellare.

cancellation *s.* annullamento, cancellatura.

cancer *s.* cancro.

candid *agg.* sincero, candido.

candidate *s.* candidato.

candidature *s.* candidatura.

candidly *avv.* sinceramente, candidamente.

candied *agg.* candito.

candle *s.* candela || — *-end*, moccolo; — *-holder*, candelabro; *by* — *-light*, a lume di candela.

candlestick *s.* candeliere.

candour *s.* candore, ingenuità.

candy *s.* candito.

to candy *vt.* candire. ♦ **to candy** *vi.* cristallizzarsi (*di zucchero*).

cane *s.* **1.** giunco, canna **2.** bastone da passeggio.

to cane *vt.* bastonare (*con una canna*).

canine *s.* dente canino.

caning *s.* bastonatura.

canned *agg.* conservato in scatola.

cannibal *s.* cannibale.

cannibalism *s.* cannibalismo.

cannon *s.* **1.** cannone **2.** carambola (*al biliardo*).

to cannon *vi.* **1.** cannoneggiare **2.** far carambola.

canoe *s.* canoa.

canon *s.* **1.** canone **2.** (*eccl.*) canonico: — *law*, diritto canonico.

canonical *agg.* canonico.

to canonize *vt.* canonizzare.

canopy *s.* **1.** baldacchino **2.** volta (*del cielo*).

cant *s.* **1.** (*arch.*) angolo esterno **2.** inclinazione **3.** gergo.

canteen *s.* **1.** (*mil.*) dispensa **2.** mensa aziendale.

canvas *s.* **1.** canovaccio **2.** (*mar.*) velatura **3.** tela **4.** tendone.

canyon *s.* burrone.

cap *s.* **1.** berretto **2.** (*arch.*) capitello **3.** (*mecc.; elettr.*) cappuccio, capsula.

capability *s.* capacità, abilità.

capable *agg.* abile, capace.

capacitor *s.* condensatore.

capacity *s.* **1.** capacità **2.** (*elettr.*) potenza (*di motore*).

cape[1] *s.* capo, promontorio.

cape[2] *s.* cappa.

caper[1] *s.* cappero.

caper[2] *s.* piroetta, capriola.

to caper *vi.* far capriole.

capercaillie *s.* gallo cedrone.

capillarity *s.* capillarità.

capillary *agg.* capillare. ♦ **capillary** *s.* (*anat.*) vaso capillare.

capital[1] *agg. e s.* capitale.

capital[2] *s.* (*arch.*) capitello.

capitalism *s.* capitalismo.

capitalist *s.* capitalista.

capitalistic *agg.* capitalistico.

to capitalize *vt.* capitalizzare.

capitular *s.* capitolare.

capitulary *s.* capitolare.

to capitulate *vi.* capitolare.

capitulation *s.* capitolazione.

capon *s.* cappone.

caprice *s.* capriccio.

to capsize *vt.* capovolgere. ♦ **to capsize** *vi.* capovolgersi.

capstan *s.* argano.

capsule *s.* capsula.

to capsule *vt.* incapsulare.

captain *s.* **1.** capitano **2.** (*comm.*) magnate.

captious *agg.* capzioso.

to captivate *vt.* cattivare, ammaliare.

captivating *agg.* cattivante, ammaliante.

captive *s.* prigioniero: *to take* —, far prigioniero.

captivity *s.* prigionia, cattività.

capture *s.* cattura.

to capture *vt.* far prigioniero, pren-

dere (*di città* ecc.).
Capuchin s. 1. (*eccl.*) Cappuccino 2. scimmia cappuccina.
car s. 1. carro 2. automobile 3. (*ferr.*) vagone || —*licence*, permesso di circolazione; *dining*—, vagone ristorante; *sleeping*—, vagone letto.
carabin s. carabina.
carabineer s. carabiniere.
to caracole vi. caracollare.
carafe s. caraffa.
caramel s. caramello.
carat s. carato.
caravan s. 1. carovana 2. carro (*di zingari* ecc.).
caravel s. caravella.
carbon s. carbonio || —*paper*, carta carbone.
carbonate s. carbonato.
carboniferous agg. carbonifero
to carbonize vt. carbonizzare.
carbuncle s. carbonchio.
carburation s. carburazione.
carburetter, carburettor s. carburatore.
carcase s. carcassa.
carcinogen s. sostanza cancerogena.
card s. 1. cartoncino, biglietto 2. carta da giuoco.
to card vt. schedare.
cardan s. cardano || —*joint*, giunto cardanico.
cardboard s. cartone.
cardiac agg. cardiaco.
cardigan s. giacca di lana.
cardinal agg. e s. cardinale.
cardiogram s. cardiogramma
cardiologist s. cardiologo.
cardiopathy s. cardiopatia.
care s. 1. cura, attenzione, protezione: *take* —!, attenzione!; *to take* — *of*, aver cura 2. preoccupazione || — *-free*, senza pensieri; — *-worn*, pieno di pensieri.
to care vi. curarsi, interessarsi.
career s. 1. carriera 2. andatura veloce.
careful agg. 1. accurato 2. prudente.
carefully avv. 1. accuratamente 2. attentamente.
careless agg. noncurante.
carelessly avv. negligentemente.
carelessness s. trascuratezza.
caress s. carezza.
to caress vt. accarezzare.
caressing agg. carezzevole.
caretaker s. guardiano, custode.
caricature s. caricatura.

Carmelite s. carmelitano.
carmine agg. e s. carminio.
carnage s. carneficina, strage.
carnal agg. carnale, sensuale.
carnation agg. carnicino. ♦ **carnation** s. garofano.
carnival s. carnevale.
carnivore s. carnivoro.
carnivorous agg. carnivoro.
carol s. canto, inno.
carotid s. carotide.
carousel s. carosello.
carp s. carpa.
carpenter s. carpentiere, falegname.
carpet s. tappeto || *bedside* —, scendiletto.
carriage s. 1. carrozza, vettura 2. (*comm.*) trasporto.
carrier s. 1. portatore, spedizioniere 2. (*mecc.*) trasportatore 3. supporto.
carrion s. carogna.
carrot s. carota.
carry s. portata (*di arma da fuoco* ecc.).
to carry vt. e vi. 1. portare (*un peso*), trasportare 2. trasmettere (*suoni*) || *to* — *about*, portare addosso; *to* — *on*, continuare; *to* — *out*, eseguire, realizzare, compiere; *to* — *through*, portare a buon fine.
carrying s. trasporto.
cart s. carro.
cartel s. (*econ.; pol.*) cartello.
cartilage s. cartilagine.
cartography s. cartografia.
cartomancy s. cartomanzia.
carton s. scatola di cartone.
cartoon s. 1. vignetta 2. (*cine*) disegno animato.
cartridge s. 1. cartuccia 2. (*foto*) rotolo.
to carve vt. e vi. scolpire, incidere, cesellare.
carver s. intagliatore, scultore (*in legno e avorio*).
carving s. scultura, intaglio (*in legno e avorio*).
caryatid s. cariatide.
cascade s. piccola cascata (*d'acqua*).
case[1] s. 1. caso, avvenimento 2. (*giur.*) causa.
case[2] s. 1. astuccio 2. cassa, cassetta.
to case vt. imballare.
casement s. telaio di finestra (*a due battenti*), finestra.

cash s. cassa, contanti || — *on delivery*, pagamento alla consegna; *by ready* —, in contanti.

to cash vt. incassare, riscuotere.

cashier s. cassiere.

to cashier vt. destituire.

casing s. involucro, copertura.

cask s. barile, botte.

casket s. scrigno.

cassation s. cassazione.

cassock s. tunica (*del clero anglicano*).

cast s. 1. getto, lancio 2. (*metal.*) gettata, stampo 3. complesso (*di attori*) || — *-iron*, ghisa.

to cast (**cast, cast**) vt. e vi. 1. gettare, lanciare 2. (*metal.*) fondere (*in stampo*) || *to* — *aside*, gettare da parte; *to* — *down*, abbassare (*gli occhi*).

castanets s. pl. nacchere.

castaway agg. arenato, respinto. ♦

castaway s. naufrago, reprobo.

caste s. casta.

caster s. V. castor.

to castigate vt. castigare, punire.

casting s. 1. il gettare 2. (*metal.*) getto, colata 3. distribuzione (*delle parti agli attori*).

castle s. castello.

castor s. 1. pepaiuola, saliera 2. rotella da mobili.

castor-oil s. olio di ricino.

to castrate vt. castrare.

casual agg. casuale, fortuito.

casually avv. per caso.

casualness s. irregolarità, noncuranza.

casualty s. 1. infortunio 2. infortunato.

casuistry s. casistica.

cat s. gatto.

cataclysm s. cataclisma.

catacomb s. catacomba.

catalepsy s. catalessi.

cataleptic agg. e s. catalettico.

catalogue s. catalogo.

to catalogue vt. e vi. catalogare.

catalyst s. catalizzatore.

cataplasm s. cataplasma.

catapult s. catapulta.

cataract s. cateratta.

catarrh s. catarro.

catastrophe s. catastrofe, calamità.

catastrophic(al) agg. catastrofico.

catch s. 1. presa, cattura 2. trappola || — *-as* — *-can*, lotta libera.

to catch (**caught, caught**) vt. 1. afferrare, acchiappare, prendere: *to*

— *the train*, prendere il treno 2. pescare, sorprendere.

catching agg. 1. attraente 2. orecchiabile (*di melodia*) 3. (*med.*) contagioso.

catchy agg. 1. attraente 2. orecchiabile (*di melodia*) 3. insidioso.

catechism s. catechismo.

to catechize vt. catechizzare.

catechumen s. catecumeno.

categoric(al) agg. categorico.

category s. categoria.

to cater vi. 1. provvedere cibo 2. procurare svaghi.

caterpillar s. 1. bruco 2. (*mecc.*) cingolo 3. trattore a cingoli.

catharsis s. catarsi.

cathartic agg. catartico.

cathedral s. cattedrale.

Catherine-wheel s. girandola.

cathode s. catodo.

cathodic agg. catodico.

catholic agg. e s. cattolico.

Catholicism s. cattolicesimo.

cation s. catione.

cattish agg. felino.

cattle s. bestiame, armenti || — *-dealer*, negoziante di bestiame; — *-lifter*, ladro di bestiame.

caught V. *to catch*.

cauldron s. caldaia.

cauliflower s. cavolfiore.

causal agg. causale.

causality s. causalità.

causative agg. causativo.

cause s. 1. causa, ragione, motivo 2. (*giur.*) processo, causa.

to cause vt. causare, cagionare.

causeway s. strada rialzata.

caustic agg. caustico (*anche fig.*).

caustically avv. causticamente (*anche fig.*).

causticity s. causticità (*anche fig.*).

cauterization s. cauterizzazione.

to cauterize vt. cauterizzare.

caution s. 1. prudenza, cautela 2. cauzione, garanzia || — *-money*, cauzione, pegno.

to caution vt. mettere in guardia.

cautious agg. cauto, prudente.

cautiously avv. cautamente.

cavalier s. cavaliere.

cavalry s. cavalleria.

cave s. caverna, spelonca.

to cave vt. e vi. scavare || *to* — *in*, sprofondare.

cavernous agg. cavernoso (*anche fig.*).

caviar(e) s. caviale.

cavil s. cavillo.

to **cavil** vi. cavillare.

cavity s. cavità.

cavy s. cavia.

cayman s. caimano.

to **cease** vt. e vi. cessare, finire.

cedar s. cedro.

cedilla s. cediglia.

ceiling s. soffitto.

to **celebrate** vt. e vi. celebrare, solennizzare.

celebrated agg. famoso.

celebration s. celebrazione.

celebrity s. celebrità, persona famosa.

celerity s. celerità.

celery s. sedano.

celestial agg. celestiale, paradisiaco.

celibacy s. celibato.

cell s. 1. cella 2. cellula.

cellar s. cantina.

cellarman s. cantiniere.

cellular agg. cellulare, alveolare.

cellulitis s. cellulite.

celluloid agg. e s. celluloide.

cellulose s. cellulosa.

Celt s. celta.

Celtic agg. celtico.

cement s. 1. cemento 2. stucco, mastice.

to **cement** vt. cementare (anche fig.).

cemetery s. cimitero.

to **cense** vt. incensare.

censer s. turibolo.

censor s. censore.

to **censor** vt. censurare.

censorial agg. censorio.

censorship s. censura, censorato.

censure s. censura.

to **censure** vt. censurare.

census s. censo.

cent s. centesimo (di dollaro).

centaur s. centauro.

centenarian agg. e s. centenario.

centenary agg. e s. centenario.

centennial agg. centennale.

centesimal agg. centesimale.

centigrade agg. centigrado.

centigramme s. centigrammo.

centilitre s. centilitro.

centimetre s. centimetro.

central agg. 1. centrale 2. fondamentale.

centralism s. accentramento.

centralization s. concentrazione (di poteri).

to **centralize** vt. e vi. accentrare.

centre s. centro, parte centrale, interno.

centrifugal agg. centrifugo.

centripetal agg. centripeto.

centrism s. centrismo.

to **centuplicate** vt. centuplicare.

centurion s. centurione.

century s. 1. secolo 2. (stor.) centuria.

cephalalgia s. cefalea.

ceramics s. (arte della) ceramica.

cereal agg. e s. cereale.

cerebral agg. cerebrale.

cerebro-spinal agg. cerebro-spinale.

cerebrum s. cervello.

ceremonial agg. da cerimonia. ♦ **ceremonial** s. cerimoniale.

ceremonious agg. cerimonioso.

ceremony s. cerimonia   to stand on —, far complimenti.

certain agg. 1. certo, sicuro 2. indeterminato, certo.

certainly avv. certamente.

certainty s. certezza.

certificate s. certificato.

to **certify** vt. certificare, attestare.

certitude s. certezza.

cervical agg. cervicale. ♦ **cervical** s. vertebra cervicale. ♦ **cervicals** s. pl. nervi cervicali.

cessation s. cessazione.

cession s. cessione.

cess-pit, cess-pool s. pozzo nero.

cetacean agg. di cetaceo. ♦ **cetacean** s. cetaceo.

to **chafe** vt. 1. riscaldare 2. irritare.

to **chafe** vi. 1. strofinarsi 2. irritarsi.

chaff s. 1. pula, paglia trinciata 2. (fig.) oggetto di nessun valore.

chaffer s. contrattazione, baratto.

chain s. 1. catena 2. serie, concatenamento.

to **chain** vt. 1. incatenare 2. (fig.) mettere in ceppi.

chain-stores s. pl. catene (di negozi o grandi magazzini).

chair s. sedia: deck— —, sedia a sdraio; easy— —, poltrona 2. cattedra (universitaria).

chairman s. presidente (di consiglio, assemblea ecc.).

chalice s. calice.

chalk s. 1. gesso 2. (min.) calcare || —-drawing, disegno a pastello; — -stone (pat.), calcolo.

chalky agg. gessoso.

challenge s. 1. sfida 2. (mil.) intimazione.

to **challenge** vt. 1. sfidare 2. (mil.) intimare.

challenger *s.* sfidatore, sfidante.

chamber *s.* 1. sala, aula 2. (*pol.; comm.*) camera || —*-music*, musica da camera; —*maid*, cameriera (*specialmente d'albergo*).

chamberlain *s.* 1. ciambellano 2. tesoriere.

chameleon *s.* camaleonte.

chamois *s.* camoscio.

champion *s.* 1. campione 2. difensore.

championship *s.* campionato.

chance *s.* 1. avvenimento fortuito, caso 2. occasione.

to **chance** *vi.* accadere.

chancellery *s.* cancelleria.

chancellor *s.* cancelliere.

chancery *s.* cancelleria.

chandelier *s.* candeliere, lampadario.

change *s.* 1. cambio, mutamento || — *for a* —, tanto per cambiare 2. moneta spicciola.

to **change** *vt. e vi.* cambiare.

changeability *s.* mutabilità.

changeable *agg.* 1. mutabile 2. incostante (*di tempo*).

changing *agg.* cangiante, mutevole.
♦ **changing** *s.* cambio.

channel *s.* 1. canale, stretto. ♦ **channels** *s. pl.* vie di comunicazione.

chant *s.* canto, cantilena.

to **channel** *vt.* 1. fare canali 2. incanalare.

chaos *s.* caos.

chap[1] *s.* (*fam.*) individuo, ragazzo.

chap[2] *s.* screpolatura.

chapel *s.* cappella.

chaplain *s.* cappellano.

chaplet *s.* ghirlanda, corona (*di fiori*).

chapter *s.* capitolo.

to **char** *vt.* carbonizzare. ♦ to **char** *vi.* carbonizzarsi.

character *s.* 1. carattere, indole 2. scrittura 3. (*lett.*) personaggio.

characteristic *agg.* caratteristico.
♦ **characteristic** *s.* caratteristica.

characterization *s.* caratterizzazione.

to **characterize** *vt.* caratterizzare.

charade *s.* sciarada.

charcoal *s.* carbone di legna.

charge *s.* 1. prezzo richiesto, spesa 2. incarico, sorveglianza 3. (*giur.*) accusa.

to **charge** *vt.* 1. far pagare, addebitare 2. incaricare 3. accusare: *to*

— *so. with a crime*, accusare qu. di un delitto.

chargeable *agg.* 1. a carico di, da addebitarsi a 2. accusabile.

chariot *s.* cocchio.

charitable *agg.* caritatevole.

charitably *avv.* caritatevolmente.

charity *s.* 1. carità, benevolenza 2. istituzione benefica.

charlatan *s.* ciarlatano.

charm *s.* 1. fascino 2. incantesimo, malia.

to **charm** *vt.* 1. affascinare 2. sottoporre a magia.

charming *agg.* affascinante.

charmingly *avv.* in modo affascinante.

charnel(-house) *s.* ossario.

chart *s.* 1. grafico 2. carta marina.

charter *s.* 1. licenza, brevetto 2. carta costituzionale.

chartography *s.* cartografia.

charwoman *s.* domestica ad ore.

charwork *s.* lavoro di domestica ad ore.

chase *s.* 1. inseguimento, caccia 2. riserva di caccia, cacciagione.

to **chase**[1] *vt.* inseguire, cacciare.

to **chase**[2] *vt.* cesellare.

chaser[1] *s.* cacciatore, inseguitore.

chaser[2] *s.* cesellatore.

chasing *s.* 1. cesellatura 2. filettatura (*di una vite*).

chasm *s.* baratro, abisso.

chaste *agg.* casto, puro.

chastely *avv.* castamente, virtuosamente.

chastity *s.* castità.

chat *s.* chiacchiera.

to **chat** *vi.* chiacchierare.

chatter *s.* 1. chiacchiera, chiacchierio 2. il battere dei denti.

to **chatter** *vi.* 1. chiacchierare 2. battere i denti.

chatterbox *s.* chiacchierone, chiacchierona.

chattering *s.* 1. chiacchierio 2. il battere dei denti.

chauvinism *s.* sciovinismo.

chauvinist *s.* sciovinista.

cheap *agg. e avv.* a buon mercato.

cheaply *avv.* economicamente, in modo poco costoso.

cheat *s.* 1. frode 2. imbroglione.

to **cheat** *vt. e vi.* imbrogliare.

cheater *s.* truffatore, baro.

cheating *s.* inganno.

check[1] *s.* 1. scacco 2. controllo, verifica 3. scontrino, contromarca.

check² s. disegno a scacchi.
to **check** vi. dare scacco. ♦ to **check** vt. controllare, verificare.
checked agg. quadrettato.
checkmate s. scacco matto.
to **checkmate** vt. dare scacco matto.
cheek s. guancia.
cheekily avv. sfacciatamente.
cheeky agg. sfacciato.
to **cheer** vt. rallegrare, incoraggiare. ♦ to **cheer** vi. essere di buon umore, rallegrarsi.
cheerful agg. di buon umore.
cheerfully avv. allegramente.
cheerfulness s. buon umore.
cheering agg. incoraggiante. ♦ **cheering** s. acclamazioni (pl.).
cheese s. formaggio.
cheetah s. ghepardo.
chemical agg. chimico.
chemically avv. chimicamente.
chemicals s. pl. prodotti chimici.
chemisette s. camicetta.
chemist s. 1. chimico 2. farmacista.
chemistry s. chimica.
cheque s. assegno: to cash a —, cambiare un assegno; — -book, libretto d'assegni; blank —, assegno in bianco; crossed —, assegno sbarrato.
to **cherish** vt. 1. (fig.) nutrire 2. curare teneramente, coccolare.
cherry s. ciliegia.
cherub s. cherubino.
chess s. giuoco degli scacchi || — -board, scacchiera; — -men, pezzi degli scacchi.
chest s. 1. cassetta, cassone 2. torace.
chestnut agg. castano. ♦ **chestnut** s. 1. castagno 2. castagna.
to **chew** vt. e vi. masticare.
chicanery s. cavillo (legale).
chick s. 1. pulcino 2. (fig.) bambino.
chicken s. gallinella, pollo.
chicory s. cicoria.
to **chide** (chid, chid) (anche reg.) vt. e vi. redarguire, sgridare.
chief agg. principale. ♦ **chief** s. capo, comandante.
chiefly avv. principalmente.
chieftain s. capo (di tribù, clan ecc.).
chilblain s. gelone.
child s. (pl. children) 1. bambino, bambina 2. figlio, figlia.
childhood s. infanzia.
childish agg. infantile.

childishness s. fanciullaggine, puerilità.
childless agg. senza figli.
childlike agg. infantile.
children V. child.
Chilean agg. e s. cileno.
chill s. 1. colpo di freddo 2. (metal.) conchiglia.
to **chill** vt. 1. raffreddare, agghiacciare (anche fig.) 2. (metal.) fondere in conchiglia. ♦ to **chill** vi. raffreddarsi.
chilled agg. 1. congelato 2. (metal.) fuso in conchiglia.
chilliness s. 1. freddo 2. (fig.) freddezza.
chilly agg. 1. freddoloso (di persona) 2. fresco (di tempo).
chime s. scampanio.
to **chime** vt. e vi. scampanare, suonare a festa.
chiming s. lo scampanare.
chimney s. camino, comignolo || — -sweeper, spazzacamino.
chimpanzee s. scimpanzè.
chin s. mento || — -strap, sottogola.
china s. 1. porcellana fine 2. (fam.) stoviglie di porcellana.
chinchilla s. cincillà.
chine s. spina dorsale.
Chinese agg. e s. cinese.
chink s. fessura, crepa.
chip s. 1. scheggia 2. (cuc.) patatina fritta.
to **chip** vt. 1. scheggiare 2. rompere. ♦ to **chip** vi. scheggiarsi, frantumarsi.
chiromancer s. chiromante.
chiromancy s. chiromanzia.
chiropodist s. pedicure.
chirp s. 1. cinguettio, pigolio 2. stridio, il frinire (di cicale ecc.).
to **chirp** vi. 1. cinguettare, pigolare 2. frinire, stridere (di cicale ecc.).
chisel s. cesello.
to **chisel** vt. cesellare.
chiseller s. cesellatore.
chitterlings s. pl. trippa.
chivalrous agg. cavalleresco.
chivalry s. 1. cavalleria 2. condotta cavalleresca.
chloride s. cloruro.
chlorine s. cloro.
chlorite s. clorito.
chloroform s. cloroformio.
chlorophyl(l) s. clorofilla.
chock s. 1. cuneo, bietta 2. (mar.) passacavi.
chocolate agg. 1. di cioccolato 2.

color cioccolata. ♦ **chocolate** s. cioccolato: *cake of —*, tavoletta di cioccolato.

choice agg. di prima qualità, scelto. ♦ **choice** s. 1. scelta 2. la cosa scelta 3. assortimento.

choir s. coro.

choke s. 1. soffocamento 2. strozzatura (*di tubo*).

to choke vt. 1. soffocare (*anche fig.*) 2. ingorgare. ♦ **to choke** v' ostruirsi.

choker s. soffocatore.

cholera s. colera.

cholesterol s. colesterolo.

to choose (chose, chosen) vt. scegliere.

chooser s. chi sceglie.

chop s. 1. (*cuc.*) braciola 2. colpo (*di scure ecc.*).

to chop vt. e vi. 1. fendere, tagliare 2. (*cuc.*) tritare || *to — down*, abbattere (*alberi*); *to — off*, tagliar via.

chopper s. 1. ascia 2. chi taglia con l'ascia 3. tagliatrice.

choppy agg. 1. screpolato 2. increspato (*del mare*).

choral agg. corale.

chord s. 1. (*mus.; anat.; geom.*) corda 2. (*mus.*) accordo.

choreographer s. coreografo.

choreographic agg. coreografico.

choreography s. coreografia.

chorus s. coro || *-singer*, corista.

chose V. *to choose*.

chosen V. *to choose*.

chrism s. crisma.

to christen vt. battezzare.

Christendom s. cristianità.

christening s. battesimo.

Christian agg. e s. cristiano || *— name*, nome di battesimo.

Christianity s. cristianesimo.

to christianize vt. convertire al cristianesimo.

Christmas s. Natale.

chromatic agg. cromatico.

chromatically avv. cromaticamente.

chromatism s. cromatismo.

chromatography s. cromatografia.

chrome s. cromo.

to chrome vt. cromare.

chromium s. cromo || *— -plated*, cromato; *-plating*, cromatura.

chromolithograph s. cromolitografia.

chromosome s. cromosoma.

chromosphere s. cromosfera.

chronic agg. cronico (*anche fig.*).

chronicle s. cronaca.

chronicler s. cronista.

chronologic(al) agg. cronologico.

chronologically avv. cronologicamente.

chronology s. cronologia.

chronometer s. cronometro.

chrysalid s. crisalide.

chrysanthemum s. crisantemo.

chubby agg. paffuto.

church s. 1. chiesa 2. comunità religiosa || *— -going*, assiduità ai servizi religiosi; *— -living*, beneficio ecclesiastico; *— -service*, funzione religiosa.

churchman s. 1. ecclesiastico 2. membro della chiesa anglicana.

churchy agg. bigotto.

churchyard s. cimitero.

chyle s. (*fisiol.*) chilo.

ciborium s. ciborio.

cicada s. cicala.

to cicatrize vt. cicatrizzare. ♦ **to cicatrize** vi. cicatrizzarsi.

cider s. sidro.

cigar s. sigaro || *— -case*, portasigari, *— -end*, mozzicone; *— -holder*, bocchino per sigari.

cigarette s. sigaretta || *— -case*, portasigarette, *— -end*, mozzicone, *— -holder*, bocchino; *— -paper*, cartina per sigaretta.

cilice s. cilicio.

cinder s. 1. brace 2. scoria.

cine-camera s. macchina da presa.

cinema s. cinematografo.

cinematograph s. 1. proiettore cinematografico 2. macchina da presa.

cinematographer s. 1. operatore cinematografico 2. cineasta.

cinematographic agg. cinematografico.

cinematography s. cinematografia.

cine-projector s. proiettore cinematografico.

cinerary agg. cinerario.

cinnabar s. cinabro.

cinnamon s. cannella.

cipher s. 1. cifrario 2. monogramma 3. (*mat.; anche fig.*) zero, nullità.

to cipher vt. e vi. cifrare.

circle s. 1. cerchio, circolo (*anche fig.*) 2. orbita (*dei pianeti*) 3. galleria (*di teatro*).

circlet s. cerchietto.

circuit s. 1. cinta, circonvallazione 2. rivoluzione, rotazione (di astri) 3. (elettr.; sport) circuito.

circular agg. circolare. ♦ **circular** s. lettera circolare.

to **circulate** vt. mettere in circolazione, diffondere. ♦ to **circulate** vi. circolare.

circulating agg. circolante.

circulation s. 1. circolazione 2. diffusione 3. (giorn.) tiratura.

circulatory agg. circolatorio.

to **circumcise** vt. circoncidere.

circumcision s. circoncisione.

circumference s. circonferenza.

circumflex agg. circonflesso.

circumlocution s. circonlocuzione.

to **circumnavigate** vt. circumnavigare.

circumnavigation s. circumnavigazione.

circumnavigator s. circumnavigatore.

to **circumscribe** vt. circoscrivere.

circumscription s. circoscrizione.

circumspect agg. circospetto.

circumspection s. circospezione.

circumstance s. circostanza.

circumstantial agg. 1. circostanziale 2. circostanziato.

circumstantiality s. abbondanza di particolari.

circumstantially avv. circostanziatamente.

to **circumvent** vt. circuire.

circumvention s. raggiro.

circumvolution s. circonvoluzione.

circus s. 1. circo, arena 2. piazza rotonda.

cirrhosis s. cirrosi.

cisalpine agg. cisalpino.

cistern s. cisterna.

citadel s. cittadella.

to **cite** vt. citare.

citizen s. cittadino.

citizenhood s. cittadinanza.

citizenship s. diritto di cittadinanza.

citrate s. citrato.

citric agg. citrico.

citron s. cedro.

city s. 1. città (grande) 2. centro di grande traffico di una città.

civic agg. civico.

civil agg. civile, cortese.

civilian agg. e s. civile, borghese.

civility s. civiltà, cortesia.

civilization s. civilizzazione, civiltà.

to **civilize** vt. civilizzare.

civilly avv. civilmente.

civism s. civismo.

claim s. 1. richiesta 2. (giur.) rivendicazione 3. (comm.) reclamo.

to **claim** vt. 1. esigere, chiedere 2. (giur.) rivendicare 3. (comm.) reclamare.

claimant s. 1. rivendicatore 2. richiedente.

clairvoyance s. chiaroveggenza.

clairvoyant agg. e s. chiaroveggente.

to **clamber** vi. arrampicarsi.

clammy agg. vischioso.

clamour s. clamore, vocio.

to **clamour** vt. e vi. vociferare.

clan s. gruppo familiare, tribù.

clandestine agg. clandestino.

to **clang** vi. emettere un suono, un grido. ♦ to **clang** vt. far risonare.

clangour s. fragore.

to **clank** vi. tintinnare. ♦ to **clank** vt. far tintinnare.

clap s. 1. applauso 2. rumore improvviso 3. piccolo colpo (con la mano).

to **clap** vt. e vi. 1. applaudire 2. dare un colpo (con la mano) 3. battere (le ali).

clapper s. 1. battente (di porta) 2. (teat.) membro della « claque ».

claret s. 1. color rosso-violetto 2. vino chiaretto.

clarification s. chiarificazione.

to **clarify** vt. chiarificare. ♦ to **clarify** vi. chiarificarsi.

clarinet s. clarinetto.

clarity s. chiarità.

clash s. 1. cozzo, urto 2. scontro (d'opinioni).

to **clash** vt. e vi. 1. cozzare, far strepito 2. scontrarsi (d'opinioni).

clasp s. fermaglio, fibbia.

to **clasp** vt. afferrare.

class s. 1. classe, categoria 2. (scol.) classe 3. (fig.) distinzione.

classic agg. e s. classico.

classical agg. classico.

classically avv. classicamente.

classicism s. classicismo.

classification s. classificazione.

to **classify** vt. classificare.

classmate s. compagno di classe.

classroom s. aula.

classy agg. (fam.) di classe.

clatter s. fracasso.

to **clatter** vi. far fracasso.

clause s. clausola.

claustrophobia s. claustrofobia.

claw *s.* 1. artiglio, zampa con artigli 2. uncino 3. chela.
to claw *vt.* artigliare.
clawed *agg.* munito di artigli.
clay *s.* argilla: *fire* —, argilla refrattaria || — *pigeon*, piattello.
clayey *agg.* argilloso.
clean *agg.* 1. pulito 2. netto, nitido 3. *(fig.)* puro, schietto.
to clean *vt.* pulire.
cleaner *s.* pulitore, pulitrice || *dry*—, smacchiatore a secco.
cleaning *s.* pulitura.
cleanliness *s.* pulizia.
cleanly *agg.* pulito. ♦ **cleanly** *avv.* in modo pulito.
cleanness *s.* 1. pulizia *(anche fig.)* 2. nitidezza.
to cleanse *vt.* 1. pulire 2. purificare.
cleanser *s.* 1. pulitore 2. detersivo.
cleansing *agg.* purificante. ♦ **cleansing** *s.* 1. purificazione 2. depurazione.
clear *agg.* 1. chiaro, limpido 2. distinto, evidente || — *-cut*, nettamente stagliato; — *-sighted*, dalla vista buona.
to clear *vt.* 1. chiarire, schiarire 2. discolpare 3. *(comm.)* svincolare || *to* — *away*, sparecchiare, dissiparsi *(di nebbia); to* — *up*, rassettare *(una stanza)*, chiarire *(un malinteso).* ♦ **to clear** *vi.* schiarirsi.
clearance *s.* 1. chiarificazione 2. sgombero 3. *(comm.)* sdoganamento.
clearing *s.* 1. chiarimento 2. rimozione.
clearly *avv.* chiaramente.
clearness *s.* 1. chiarezza 2. *(fig.)* limpidezza.
cleavage *s.* 1. spaccatura 2. *(min.)* clivaggio.
to cleave *(cleft, cleft) vt.* e *vi.* fendere, spaccare.
cleft *s.* fenditura.
clemency *s.* clemenza.
clement *agg.* 1. clemente 2. dolce, gentile *(di carattere)* 3. mite *(di tempo).*
to clench *vt.* 1. stringere *(mani, denti ecc.)* 2. ribadire.
clergy *s.* clero.
clergyman *s.* ecclesiastico.
clerical *agg.* 1. clericale 2. impiegatizio.
clericalism *s.* clericalismo.
clerk *s.* impiegato || *chief* —, ca-

poufficio.
to clerk *vi.* lavorare come impiegato.
clever *agg.* intelligente, abile, ingegnoso.
cleverly *avv.* intelligentemente.
cleverness *s.* intelligenza, abilità, ingegnosità.
clew *s.* gomitolo *(di filo).*
click *s.* scatto, rumore secco.
client *s.* cliente.
cliff *s.* scogliera.
climate *s.* clima.
climatic *agg.* climatico.
climax *s.* apice, culmine.
climb *s.* 1. rampa 2. ascesa.
to climb *vt.* e *vi.* 1. arrampicarsi 2. scalare *(anche fig.).*
climber *s.* 1. scalatore 2. *(fig.)* arrivista 3. pianta rampicante.
climbing *s.* 1. scalata 2. *(fig.)* arrivismo. ♦ **climbing** *agg.* rampicante.
to cling *(clung, clung) vi.* attaccarsi, aggrapparsi *(anche fig.): to* — *to a hope*, aggrapparsi ad una speranza.
clinical *agg.* clinico.
clinician *s.* clinico.
clinking *s.* tintinnio.
clip *s.* 1. fermaglio, molletta || *hair* —, forcina per capelli 2. graffa *(per ferite)* 3. tosatura *(di pecore).*
to clip *vt.* 1. tenere insieme *(con un fermaglio)* 2. tosare *(pecore ecc.).*
clipper *s.* 1. tosatore 2. *(mar.)* "clipper". ♦ **clippers** *s. pl.* 1. forbici 2. macchinetta per tosare *(sing.).*
cloak *s.* 1. mantello 2. *(fig.)* manto, velo.
clock *s.* orologio *(da muro, da tavolo)* || *alarm-* —, sveglia.
clockwise *agg.* in senso orario || *counter-* —, in senso antiorario.
clockwork *s.* meccanismo a orologeria.
clod *s.* zolla.
clog *s.* 1. impedimento, intoppo 2. zoccolo.
to clog *vt.* ostruire, impedire *(anche fig.).* ♦ **to clog** *vi.* inceparsi.
cloister *s.* chiostro.
close *agg.* 1. chiuso 2. serrato: — *combat*, combattimento corpo a corpo 3. afoso, viziato *(di aria)* 4. intimo: — *friend*, amico intimo 5. accurato, attento — *fitting*, aderente *(di vestiti);* —

-mouthed, riservato; — -shaven, rasato con cura.

close s. 1. spazio cintato 2. fine, termine 3. corpo a corpo.

close avv. vicino, presso.

to close vt. chiudere || to — up, turare, sbarrare (di strada). ♦ to close vi. chiudersi || to — in, avvicinarsi, accorciarsi (di giorni); to — with, venire a un accordo.

closed agg. chiuso.

closely avv. 1. da vicino 2. attentamente.

closeness s. 1. afa, mancanza d'aria 2. compattezza 3. intimità 4. vicinanza 5. accuratezza.

closet s. 1. studio, salotto privato 2. armadio a muro 3. gabinetto.

close-up s. (cine) primo piano.

closing s. chiusura (di negozi, teatri ecc.).

clot s. grumo.

to clot vt. raggrumare, coagulare. ♦ to clot vi. raggrumarsi, coagularsi.

cloth s. tessuto, stoffa, tela || (table-) —, tovaglia.

to clothe vt. vestire.

clothes s. pl. abiti, indumenti || -book, attaccapanni; —-line, corda (per stendere il bucato); —-peg, molletta (fermabucato).

clothing s. 1. vestiario 2. copertura.

cloud s. 1. nuvola, nube 2. nugolo (di insetti).

to cloud vt. e vi. annuvolare, oscurare || to — (up, over), annuvolarsi.

clouded agg. 1. coperto (di nubi) 2. torbido (di liquidi).

cloudily avv. nebulosamente.

cloudy agg. 1. nuvoloso 2. torbido.

clover s. trifoglio.

clown s. pagliaccio.

clownish agg. pagliaccesco.

club s. 1. mazza, randello 2. circolo, associazione 3. (carte) fiori.

clue s. 1. indizio, traccia 2. filo di un racconto.

clumsily avv. goffamente.

clumsiness s. goffaggine.

clumsy agg. goffo, senza grazia.

clung V. to cling.

cluster s. 1. grappolo (d'uva), mazzo (di fiori), gruppo 2. folla, capannello (di gente) 3. sciame.

clutch s. 1. stretta, grinfia 2. (auto) frizione.

to clutch vt. e vi. afferrare, asserrarsi, agguantare.

coach s. 1. carrozza, cocchio 2. pullman 3. carrozza ferroviaria 4. (sport) allenatore, istruttore || -house, rimessa; mourning- —, carro funebre; stage- —, diligenza.

coachman s. cocchiere.

coachwork s. carrozzeria.

coadjutor s. coadiutore.

coagulant s. sostanza coagulante.

to coagulate vt. coagulare. ♦ to coagulate vi. coagularsi.

coagulation s. coagulazione.

coagulator s. coagulante.

coal s. carbone: — -bed, bacino carbonifero; — -black, nero come il carbone; — -fed, alimentato a carbone; — -mine, miniera di carbone.

to coalesce vi. 1. coalizzarsi, unirsi 2. fondersi.

coalition s. coalizione.

coarse agg. 1. grossolano, rozzo 2. ruvido, grosso (di materiale).

coarsely avv. grossolanamente.

coarseness s. 1. grossolanità 2. ruvidezza (di stoffe ecc.).

coast s. costa || —-guard, polizia costiera.

coastal agg. costiero.

coaster s. 1. nave cabotiera 2. sottobicchiere.

coat s. 1. giacca, soprabito 2. manto (anche fig.), pelliccia (di animale) 3. rivestimento, intonaco || — of arms, stemma.

to coat vt. rivestire, coprire.

coating s. rivestimento, mano di vernice.

to coax vt. blandire, circuire. ♦ to coax vi. far moine.

coaxial agg. coassiale.

cobalt s. cobalto.

cobble s. ciottolo.

to cobble vt. 1. pavimentare (con ciottoli) 2. rappezzare (scarpe).

cobbler s. ciabattino.

cobra s. cobra.

cobweb s. ragnatela.

cocaine s. cocaina.

coccyx s. (pl. -cyges) coccige.

cock s. 1. gallo 2. cane di fucile.

cockade s. coccarda.

cockatoo s. cacatoa.

cockboat s. (mar.) lancia.

cockerel s. galletto.

cock-eyed agg. strabico.

cockish agg. sfrontato.

cockney *agg.* e *s.* dialetto londinese.

cockpit *s.* 1. arena (*per combattimento di galli*) 2. (*mar.*) castello di poppa.

cockroach *s.* scarafaggio.

cockscomb *s.* 1. cresta (*di gallo*) 2. (*fig.*) zerbinotto.

cocktail *s.* 1. cavallo con coda mozzata 2. cocktail.

cocoa *s.* cacao.

coconut *s.* noce di cocco.

cocoon *s.* bozzolo.

cod *s.* merluzzo.

code *s.* codice.

to code *vt.* 1. codificare 2. cifrare (*un dispaccio*).

codeine *s.* codeina.

codex *s.* codice, manoscritto antico.

codfish *s.* merluzzo.

codicil *s.* codicillo.

codification *s.* codificazione.

to codify *vt.* codificare.

co-director *s.* condirettore.

co-education *s.* istruzione nella scuola mista.

co-educational *agg.* (*scol.*) misto.

coefficient *agg.* e *s.* coefficiente.

coenobium *s.* cenobio.

coercible *agg.* coercibile.

coercion *s.* coercizione.

coercive *agg.* coercitivo.

coeval *agg.* e *s.* coevo.

to coexist *vi.* coesistere.

coexistence *s.* coesistenza.

coffee *s.* caffè: — *-bean*, chicco di caffè; — *-grounds*, fondi di caffè || — *-house*, caffè, bar; — *-mill*, macinino; — *-pot*, caffettiera.

coffer *s.* cassa, cofano.

coffin *s.* bara.

cog *s.* dente (*di ruota*).

cognate *agg.* e *s.* consanguineo, congiunto.

cognition *s.* cognizione.

cognitive *agg.* avente conoscenza.

cognizable *agg.* 1. conoscibile 2. (*giur.*) entro la giurisdizione di una corte.

to cohabit *vi.* coabitare.

cohabitation *s.* coabitazione.

coheir *s.* coerede.

coheiress *s.* (*donna*) coerede.

coherence *s.* 1. coerenza 2. aderenza.

coherent *agg.* 1. coerente 2. aderente.

coherently *avv.* coerentemente.

cohesion *s.* coesione.

cohesive *agg.* coesivo.

cohort *s.* coorte.

coil *s.* 1. rotolo, spira 2. (*elettr.; mecc.*) bobina.

coin *s.* moneta (*di metallo*).

to coin *vt.* coniare (*anche fig.*).

coinage *s.* conio.

to coincide *vi.* coincidere.

coincidence *s.* coincidenza.

coiner *s.* falsario.

colander *s.* colino.

cold *agg.* 1. freddo: *to be* —, aver freddo 2. freddo (*di carattere*), apatico: *in* — *blood*, a sangue freddo. ◆ **cold** *s.* 1. freddo 2. raffreddore: *to catch a* —, prendere il raffreddore.

coldness *s.* freddezza (*anche fig.*).

Coleoptera *s. pl.* coleotteri.

colic *s.* colica.

colitis *s.* colite.

to collaborate *vi.* collaborare.

collaboration *s.* collaborazione.

collaborationist *s.* collaborazionista.

collaborator *s.* collaboratore.

collapse *s.* 1. crollo (*anche fig.*) 2. collasso.

to collapse *vi.* crollare (*anche fig.*).

collar *s.* 1. colletto 2. collare.

to collate *vt.* 1. collezionare, confrontare 2. riordinare (*pagine di un'opera*).

collateral *agg.* collaterale.

colleague *s.* collega.

to collect *vt.* 1. riunire 2. incassare, riscuotere 3. fare una raccolta. ◆ **to collect** *vi.* 1. riunirsi 2. riscuotere.

collecting *s.* il raccogliere: *stamp* —, il raccogliere francobolli.

collection *s.* 1. raccolta, collezione 2. riunione di persone 3. questua, colletta.

collective *agg.* collettivo || — *title* (*tip.*), titolo generale.

collectivism *s.* collettivismo.

collectivity *s.* collettività.

collectivization *s.* collettivizzazione.

to collectivize *vt.* collettivizzare.

collector *s.* 1. collezionista 2. esattore.

college *s.* 1. collegio 2. scuola secondaria (*con internato*).

collegial *agg.* collegiale.

collier *s.* minatore.

colliery *s.* miniera di carbone.

collimator *s.* collimatore.

collision *s.* **1.** collisione **2.** urto, conflitto (*d'interessi*).

collocation *s.* collocazione.

colloidal *agg.* colloidale.

colloquial *agg.* d'uso corrente, familiare.

colloquialism *s.* espressione familiare.

colloquially *avv.* nella lingua parlata.

colloquy *s.* colloquio.

collusion *s.* collusione.

colon *s.* (*gramm.*) due punti.

colonel *s.* colonnello.

colonial *agg.* coloniale.

colonialism *s.* sistema coloniale.

colonialist *s.* colonialista.

colonist *s.* **1.** colono **2.** colonizzatore.

colonization *s.* colonizzazione.

to **colonize** *vt.* colonizzare. ♦ to **colonize** *vi.* stabilirsi in colonia.

colonizer *s.* colonizzatore.

colonnade *s.* colonnato.

colony *s.* colonia.

colossal *agg.* colossale.

colossus *s.* colosso.

colour *s.* **1.** colore **2.** colorito || *-bearer*, portabandiera; — *-blind*, daltonico; — *-print*, stampa a colori. ♦ **colours** *s. pl.* bandiera (*sing.*) || *with the* —, sotto le armi.

to **colour** *vt.* colorare, tingere. ♦ to **colour** *vi.* colorirsi, prender colore.

colourable *agg.* verosimile.

colouration *s.* colorazione.

coloured *agg.* colorato, colorito (*anche fig.*).

colourful *agg.* colorito, pittoresco.

colouring *s.* **1.** colorante **2.** coloramento.

colourless *agg.* incolore.

colt *s.* **1.** puledro **2.** (*fig.*) novellino.

columbarium *s.* (*pl. -ria*) colombario.

column *s.* colonna (*anche fig.*).

columnist *s.* giornalista (*che cura una rubrica*).

coma *s.* coma.

comatose *agg.* comatoso.

comb *s.* **1.** pettine **2.** cresta (*gallo, onde ecc.*).

to **comb** *vt.* pettinare. ♦ to **comb** *vi.* frangersi (*di onde*) || *to — one's hair*, pettinarsi.

combat *s.* combattimento, lotta.

combination *s.* **1.** combinazione **2.** associazione.

to **combine** *vt.* **1.** unire **2.** (*chim.*) combinare **3.** contribuire. ♦ to **combine** *vi.* **1.** unirsi **2.** combinarsi.

combing *s.* pettinata.

comb-out *s.* rastrellamento.

combustible *agg.* e *s.* combustibile.

combustion *s.* combustione.

to **come (came, come)** *vi.* venire, arrivare, giungere, provenire || *to — about*, accadere; *to — across*, incontrare per caso; *to — along* (*fam.*), capitare; *to — back*, ritornare; *to — down*, scendere; *to — in*, entrare, salire (*di prezzi*); *to — on*, avanzare, sopraggiungere (*di malattie, stagioni ecc.*), entrare in scena (*di attori*); *to — through*, superare; *to — under*, essere soggetti, essere catalogati; *to — upon*, trovare per caso.

comedian *s.* autore, attore di commedie.

comedy *s.* commedia.

comeliness *s.* avvenenza.

comely *agg.* avvenente.

comer *s.* chi viene.

comet *s.* cometa.

comfit *s.* confetto.

comfort *s.* **1.** conforto **2.** comodità.

to **comfort** *vt.* **1.** confortare **2.** ristorare.

comfortable *agg.* comodo, confortevole || *to be —*, sentirsi a proprio agio.

comfortably *avv.* comodamente.

comforting *agg.* confortante.

comic *agg.* comico, buffo. ♦ **comic** *s.* **1.** attore comico **2.** il ridicolo, il comico. ♦ **comics** *s. pl.* (*fam.*) fumetti.

comical *agg.* comico, buffo.

comicality *s.* comicità.

coming *agg.* prossimo, futuro. ♦ **coming** *s.* **1.** venuta, arrivo || *— away*, partenza; *— back*, ritorno; *— down*, discesa, calo (*dei prezzi*).

comity *s.* cortesia, gentilezza.

comma *s.* virgola || *inverted commas*, virgolette.

command *s.* **1.** comando, ordine **2.** padronanza.

to **command** *vt.* e *vi.* **1.** comandare **2.** dominare (*anche fig.*).

commandant *s.* comandante.

commander *s.* comandante.

commandership *s.* funzioni di comandante.

commandment s. comandamento.

to **commemorate** vt. commemorare.

commemoration s. commemorazione.

commemorative agg. commemorativo.

to **commend** vt. lodare, encomiare.

commendable agg. lodevole.

commendably avv. lodevolmente.

commendation s. elogio, lode.

commendatory agg. laudativo.

commensal s. commensale.

commensurability s. commensurabilità.

commensurable agg. commensurabile.

commensurate agg. proporzionato.

comment s. 1. commento 2. critica.

to **comment** vt. e vi. commentare: to — up (on) a test, commentare un testo.

commentary s. commentario.

commentation s. annotazione, commento.

commentator s. 1. commentatore 2. radiocronista.

commerce s. commercio.

commercial agg. commerciale.

commercialism s. mercantilismo.

commercialist s. commercialista.

to **commercialize** vt. rendere commerciabile.

commercially avv. commercialmente.

commination s. comminazione.

to **commiserate** vt. e vi. commiserare.

commissary s. commissario, delegato.

commissaryship s. commissariato.

commission s. 1. commissione, comitato 2. commissione, incarico || — agent (o merchant), commissionario.

to **commission** vt. 1. commissionare 2. delegare.

commissioned agg. munito di autorità || non- — officer, sottufficiale.

commissioner s. (pol.) delegato.

to **commit** vt. 1. affidare, rimettere: to — one's soul to God, rimettere la propria anima a Dio 2. commettere.

commitment, committal s. 1. consegna 2. incarico.

committed agg. (neol.) impegnato.

committee s. comitato.

commodity s. merce, oggetto di prima necessità || free commodities, merci esenti da dogana.

common agg. 1. comune 2. solito, abituale || — law, legge consacrata dalla consuetudine.

commoner s. 1. cittadino (non nobile) 2. membro della Camera dei Comuni.

commonness s. 1. banalità 2. frequenza (di un avvenimento).

commonplace s. luogo comune.

commons s. pl. il popolo (sing.) || the House of —, la Camera dei Comuni.

commonwealth s. 1. confederazione 2. repubblica (anche fig.).

commotion s. 1. agitazione, confusione 2. insurrezione, tumulto.

communal agg. della comunità.

commune s. comune.

communicability s. comunicabilità.

communicable agg. comunicabile.

to **communicate** vt. comunicare, trasmettere (malattie, calore ecc.).
♦ to **communicate** vi. mettersi in comunicazione.

communication s. 1. comunicazione, informazione 2. relazione, rapporto.

communicative agg. comunicativo.

communicativeness s. comunicativa.

communion s. comunione, comunanza || Holy Communion, Eucaristia.

communism s. comunismo.

communist s. comunista.

communistic agg. comunistico.

community s. 1. comunanza (di beni ecc.) 2. collettività, società 3. (eccl.) comunità.

commutability s. permutabilità, commutabilità.

commutable agg. permutabile, commutabile.

commutative agg. commutativo.

commutator s. commutatore.

to **commute** vt. commutare.

compact[1] s. patto, contratto.

compact[2] agg. 1. compatto 2. ridotto.

compactness s. 1. compattezza 2. concisione (di stile).

companion[1] s. compagno.

companion[2] s. (mar.) boccaporto: — -way, scaletta (di boccaporto), scalandrone.

companionable agg. socievole.

companionship s. amicizia, cameratismo.

company s. 1. compagnia 2. comitiva 3. (comm.) società.

comparable agg. paragonabile.

comparative agg. 1. comparativo 2. comparato. ♦ **comparative** s. (gramm.) comparativo.

comparatively avv. 1. comparativamente 2. relativamente.

to **compare** vt. paragonare, verificare. ♦ to **compare** vi. competere, rivaleggiare, reggere al confronto.

comparison s. 1. paragone, confronto 2. (gramm.) comparazione.

compartment s. compartimento, scompartimento.

compass s. 1. circonferenza, spazio, estensione 2. bussola. ♦ **compasses** s. pl. (a pair of —) compasso (sing.).

to **compass** vt. circondare.

compassion s. compassione: out of —, per compassione.

compassionate agg. compassionevole.

to **compassionate** vt. compassionare.

compassionately avv. con compassione.

compatibility s. compatibilità.

compatible agg. compatibile.

compatibly avv. compatibilmente.

to **compel** vt. costringere, obbligare.

compelling agg. irresistibile.

compendious agg. compendioso.

to **compensate** vt. ricompensare, risarcire. ♦ to **compensate** vi. supplire.

compensation s. 1. compenso 2. (mecc.) compensazione 3. indennità, risarcimento.

compensator s. compensatore.

compensatory agg. compensativo.

to **compete** vi. competere, gareggiare.

competence s. 1. competenza 2. mezzi sufficienti per vivere (pl.).

competent agg. competente, abile.

competently avv. con competenza.

competition s. 1. competizione, gara 2. rivalità.

competitive agg. 1. di competizione 2. (comm.) di concorrenza.

competitively avv. per mezzo di concorso.

competitor s. concorrente, rivale.

compilation s. compilazione.

to **compile** vt. compilare.

compiler s. compilatore.

complacency s. 1. soddisfazione 2. compiacenza di sé.

complacent agg. 1. compiacente 2. soddisfatto di sé.

to **complain** vi. lagnarsi, dolersi.

complaint s. 1. lamento 2. reclamo.

complaisant agg. compiacente.

complement s. complemento.

complemental agg. complementare.

complementary agg. complementare.

complete agg. completo.

to **complete** vt. 1. completare 2. riempire (moduli ecc.).

completely avv. completamente.

completeness s. completezza.

completion s. compimento.

complex agg. 1. complicato 2. (gramm.) composto. ♦ **complex** s. complesso.

complexion s. carnagione, colorito.

complexity s. complessità.

compliance s. 1. condiscendenza 2. servilismo.

compliant agg. 1. compiacente 2. servile.

to **complicate** vt. complicare.

complicated agg. complicato.

complication s. complicazione.

complicity s. complicità.

compliment s. complimento: to pay so. a —, far un complimento a qu.

to **compliment** vt. complimentare, congratularsi con.

complimentary agg. 1. complimentoso 2. di favore: — tickets, biglietti di favore.

to **comply** vi. accondiscendere, conformarsi.

component agg. e s. componente.

to **comport** vi. comportarsi.

to **compose** vt. 1. comporre, costituire 2. (mus.) comporre || to — a quarrel, comporre una vertenza.

composed agg. 1. composto 2. calmo.

composer s. compositore.

composing agg. calmante. ♦ **composing** s. 1. il comporre 2. (tip.) composizione.

composite agg. composto.

composition s. 1. composizione 2. compromesso 3. concordato, intesa.

compositor s. (tip.) compositore.

composure s. posatezza, sangue freddo.

compote *s.* conserva di frutta.

compound 1. miscela **2.** (*chim.*) composto **3.** (*gramm.*) parola composta.

to **compound** *vt.* e *vi.* **1.** comporre, mescolare **2.** combinare (*ingredienti, elementi ecc.*).

to **comprehend** *vt.* **1.** contenere **2.** capire.

comprehensibility *s.* comprensibilità.

comprehensible *agg.* **1.** comprensibile **2.** delimitato.

comprehension *s.* **1.** comprensione **2.** portata.

comprehensive *agg.* **1.** di vasta portata **2.** comprensivo.

comprehensively *avv.* comprensivamente.

compress *s.* compressa (*di garza*).

to **compress** *vt.* **1.** comprimere **2.** (*fig.*) condensare (*idee ecc.*).

compressibility *s.* compressibilità.

compression *s.* **1.** compressione **2.** (*fig.*) concentrazione.

to **comprise** *vt.* contenere, includere.

compromise *s.* compromesso.

to **compromise** *vt.* compromettere. ♦ to **compromise** *vi.* venire a un compromesso.

compromising *agg.* compromettente.

compulsion *s.* costrizione: *under —*, per costrizione.

compulsive *agg.* coercitivo.

compulsory *agg.* obbligatorio.

compunction *s.* compunzione.

computable *agg.* calcolabile.

computation *s.* calcolo.

to **compute** *vt.* computare, calcolare.

computer *s.* calcolatore.

comrade *s.* camerata, compagno.

comradeship *s.* cameratismo.

to **concatenate** *vt.* concatenare.

concatenation *s.* concatenazione.

concave *agg.* concavo.

to **conceal** *vt.* nascondere.

concealment *s.* **1.** occultamento **2.** nascondiglio.

conceit *s.* vanità, presunzione.

conceited *agg.* presuntuoso, vanitoso.

conceivability *s.* concepibilità.

conceivable *agg.* concepibile.

to **conceive** *vt.* **1.** concepire, generare **2.** immaginare, ide re.

to **concentrate** *vt.* **1.** concentrare **2.** convergere. ♦ to **concentrate** *vi.* concentrarsi.

concentration *s.* **1.** concentrazione **2.** concentramento.

concentric *agg.* concentrico.

concept *s.* concetto.

conception *s.* **1.** concezione, concepimento **2.** concetto.

conceptional *agg.* concezionale.

conceptual *agg.* concettuale.

conceptualism *s.* concettualismo.

concern *s.* **1.** interesse, rapporto **2.** affare **3.** sollecitudine **4.** (*comm.*) ditta, azienda.

to **concern** *vt.* concernere, riguardare.

concerned *agg.* **1.** interessato **2.** ansioso, preoccupato || *as far as I am —*, per quanto mi riguarda.

concerning *prep.* riguardo a, circa.

concert *s.* **1.** concerto **2.** accordo.

concerted *agg.* **1.** (*mus.*) concertato **2.** convenuto.

concession *s.* concessione.

concessionary *agg.* e *s.* concessionario.

concettism *s.* concettismo.

conch *s.* conchiglia, mollusco.

conchoid *s.* concoide.

conchoidal *agg.* concoidale.

conciliar *agg.* conciliare.

to **conciliate** *vt.* conciliare.

conciliation *s.* conciliazione.

conciliator *s.* conciliatore, conciliatrice.

conciliatory *agg.* conciliante.

concise *agg.* conciso, succinto.

concision *s.* concisione.

conclave *s.* conclave.

to **conclude** *vt.* terminare, concludere. ♦ to **conclude** *vi.* terminare, concludersi.

conclusion *s.* conclusione.

conclusive *agg.* conclusivo.

to **concoct** *vt.* **1.** mescolare (*di ingredienti*) **2.** preparare, tramare.

concomitance *s.* concomitanza.

concomitant *agg.* concomitante.

concomitantly *avv.* simultaneamente.

concord *s.* **1.** concordia **2.** (*mus.*) accordo **3.** (*gramm.*) concordanza.

concordant *agg.* **1.** concorde **2.** (*mus.*) armonioso.

concordat *s.* concordato.

concourse *s.* concorso, affluenza (*di persone ecc.*).

concrete *agg.* concreto. ♦ **concrete** *s.* calcestruzzo.

concreteness s. concretezza.

concretion s. concrezione.

concubinage s. concubinato.

concubine s. concubina.

concupiscence s. concupiscenza.

to concur vi. concorrere, contribuire (di cause, avvenimenti).

concurrence s. **1.** concorso (di circostanze) **2.** cooperazione (di persone) **3.** (geom.) convergenza.

concurrent agg. concorrente, simultaneo.

to concuss vt. **1.** urtare **2.** (med.) provocare un trauma **3.** intimidire.

concussion s. **1.** urto **2.** (med.) commozione cerebrale, trauma.

to condemn vt. **1.** condannare **2.** biasimare, censurare.

condemnable agg. **1.** condannabile **2.** censurabile.

condemnation s. **1.** condanna **2.** biasimo, censura.

condensability s. condensabilità.

condensable agg. condensabile.

condensate s. (fis.; chim.) condensamento.

condensation s. condensazione.

to condense vt. condensare, abbreviare. ♦ **to condense** vi. condensarsi, concentrarsi.

condenser s. condensatore.

to condescend vi. accondiscendere.

condescending agg. condiscendente.

condescendingly avv. con condiscendenza.

condescension s. **1.** condiscendenza **2.** affabilità.

condition s. condizione, clausola: on — that, a condizione che.

to condition vt. condizionare.

conditional agg. e s. condizionale.

conditionally avv. condizionatamente.

conditioned agg. condizionato: — air, aria condizionata.

conditioning s. **1.** condizionatura (di tessili) **2.** condizionamento.

condolence s. condoglianza.

conduct s. **1.** condotta, comportamento **2.** metodo.

to conduct vi. **1.** condurre, guidare, dirigere **2.** (fis.) condurre, trasmettere. ♦ **to conduct** vt. **1.** comportarsi **2.** indicare la via.

conductibility s. conducibilità.

conductivity s. conducibilità.

conductor s. **1.** guida (di persone) **2.** (mus.) direttore **3.** bigliettario.

conduit s. **1.** conduttura **2.** passaggio segreto.

cone s. **1.** cono **2.** pigna.

to confabulate vi. confabulare.

confectionary agg. di pasticceria.

confectioner s. pasticciere.

confectionery s. pasticceria.

confederate agg. confederato. ♦ **confederate** s. **1.** confederato **2.** complice.

to confederate vt. confederare. ♦ **to confederate** vi. confederarsi.

confederation s. confederazione.

to confer vt. conferire, dare. ♦ **to confer** vi. conferire, consultarsi.

conference s. **1.** conferenza **2.** congresso.

to confess vt. e vi. confessare, professare.

confessedly avv. apertamente, dichiaratamente.

confession s. confessione, professione: — of faith, professione di fede.

confessional agg. e s. confessionale.

confessionary agg. confessionale.

confessor s. **1.** confessore **2.** chi si confessa.

confetti s. pl. coriandoli.

confidant s. confidente.

to confide vt. confidare. ♦ **to confide** vi. confidarsi: to — in so., confidarsi con qu.

confidence s. **1.** fiducia **2.** confidenza **3.** sicurezza in se stessi.

confident agg. fiducioso.

confidential agg. confidenziale, riservato.

confidently avv. con sicurezza, con fiducia.

confiding agg. senza sospetti.

configuration s. configurazione.

to configure vt. configurare.

to confine vt. relegare, limitare. ♦ **to confine** vi. confinare, essere contiguo.

confinement s. **1.** reclusione **2.** limitazione **3.** puerperio.

to confirm vt. **1.** confermare **2.** cresimare.

confirmation s. **1.** conferma **2.** cresima **3.** (pol.; giur.) ratifica.

confirmatory agg. confermativo.

confiscable agg. confiscabile.

to confiscate vt. confiscare.

confiscation s. confisca.

conflagration s. conflagrazione.

conflict s. conflitto, contrasto.

confluence s. 1. confluenza 2. incrocio (di strade ecc.).

confluent agg. confluente.

to **conform** vt. conformare. ♦ to **conform** vi. conformarsi, ottemperare.

conformation s. 1. conformazione 2. adattamento.

conformist s. conformista.

conformity s. 1. conformità 2. conformismo.

to **confound** vt. 1. confondere, disorientare 2. sconvolgere.

confounded agg. attonito, confuso.

confraternity s. confraternita.

to **confront** vt. 1. affrontare 2. trovarsi di fronte a.

confrontation s. confronto.

Confucianism s. confucianesimo.

to **confuse** vt. 1. disorientare, sconcertare 2. confondere.

confusedly avv. confusamente.

confusion s. 1. disordine, confusione 2. turbamento.

confutation s. confutazione.

to **confute** vt. confutare.

to **congeal** vt. ghiacciare. ♦ to **congeal** vi. gelarsi.

congenial agg. 1. congeniale, affine 2. amabile, simpatico.

congeniality s. 1. affinità 2. carattere simpatico.

congenially avv. amabilmente.

congenital agg. congenito.

conger s. anguilla marina.

congeries s. congerie.

to **congest** vt. congestionare. ♦ to **congest** vi. congestionarsi.

congested agg. congestionato.

congestion s. congestione.

to **conglobate** vt. conglobare. ♦ to **conglobate** vi. conglobarsi.

conglobation s. conglobazione.

to **conglomerate** vt. conglomerare. ♦ to **conglomerate** vi. conglomerarsi.

conglomeration s. conglomerazione.

to **congratulate** vt. congratulare, congratularsi con.

congratulation s. congratulazione.

congratulatory agg. congratulatorio.

to **congregate** vt. adunare. ♦ to **congregate** vi. adunarsi.

congregation s. 1. unione, adunata, assemblea 2. (relig.) congregazione.

congregational agg. della congregazione.

congress s. congresso, riunione.

congressional agg. di congresso.

congruence s. congruenza.

congruent agg. congruente, conforme.

congruity s. conformità.

congruous agg. congruente, conforme.

conic(al) agg. conico.

conifer s. conifera.

coniferous agg. conifero.

conjecture s. congettura.

to **conjecture** vt. o vi. congetturare, ipotizzare.

conjointly avv. congiuntamente.

conjugal agg. coniugale.

conjugate agg. congiunto. ♦ **conjugate** s. 1. (mat.) coniugato 2. (biol.) fusione.

to **conjugate** vt. coniugare. ♦ to **conjugate** vi. coniugarsi.

conjugation s. coniugazione.

conjunction s. congiunzione.

conjunctiva s. (anat.) congiuntiva.

conjunctive agg. 1. (biol.) connettivo 2. (gramm.) congiuntivo. ♦ **conjunctive** s. congiuntivo.

conjunctivitis s. congiuntivite.

conjuncture s. congiuntura, circostanza.

conjuration s. 1. incantesimo 2. evocazione solenne.

to **conjure** vt. 1. scongiurare 2. evocare. ♦ to **conjure** vi. fare giochi di prestigio.

conjurer s. prestigiatore.

conjuring s. prestidigitazione.

connatural agg. connaturale.

to **connect** vt. 1. connettere, collegare, unire 2. associare (mentalmente) 3. (tel.) avere relazioni, collegarsi 2. (ferr.) far coincidenza.

connecting agg. che connette. ♦ **connecting** s. (elettr.) collegamento.

connection s. 1. collegamento, connessione 2. relazione, parentela 3. coincidenza 4. (comm.) clientela.

connective agg. connettivo.

conning-tower s. (mar.) torretta di comando.

connivance s. connivenza.

to **connive** vi. essere connivente.

connotation s. significato implicito.

to **connote** vt. implicare, significare.

to **conquer** *vt.* conquistare.

conqueror *s.* conquistatore.

conquest *s.* conquista.

consanguine *agg.* consanguineo.

consanguinity *s.* consanguineità.

conscience *s.* coscienza: *for —' sake*, per scrupolo di coscienza; *to be — -stricken*, sentirsi rimordere la coscienza.

conscienceless *agg.* senza scrupoli.

conscientious *agg.* scrupoloso || *— objector*, obiettore di coscienza.

conscientiously *avv.* coscienziosamente.

conscious *agg.* consapevole, conscio.

consciousness *s.* coscienza, consapevolezza.

conscript *agg.* e *s.* coscritto.

conscription *s.* coscrizione.

to **consecrate** *vt.* consacrare, dedicare.

consecration *s.* consacrazione, dedizione.

consecutive *agg.* consecutivo.

consecutively *avv.* consecutivamente.

consensual *agg.* consensuale.

consensus *s.* consenso, accordo || *— of opinion*, unanimità.

consent *s.* consenso, accordo || *by mutual —*, amichevolmente.

to **consent** *vi.* acconsentire.

consequence *s.* 1. conseguenza, effetto 2. importanza.

consequent *agg.* conseguente, risultante.

consequential *agg.* consequenziale.

consequently *avv.* di conseguenza.

conservatism *s.* conservatorismo.

conservative *agg.* conservativo. ♦ Conservative *s.* conservatore.

conservator *s.* 1. conservatore 2. sovrintendente (*di museo ecc.*).

conserve *s.* conserva di frutta.

to **consider** *vt.* considerare, riflettere, stimare.

considerable *agg.* considerevole, importante.

considerate *agg.* rispettoso, pieno di riguardi.

consideration *s.* 1. considerazione 2. rimunerazione 3. (*comm.*) provvigione.

considering *prep.* tenuto conto di, considerando.

to **consign** *vt.* 1. (*comm.*) inviare, consegnare 2. depositare (*soldi in banca*).

consignation *s.* 1. (*comm.*) pagamento 2. consegna (*di merce*).

consignee *s.* consegnatario.

consigner *s.* mittente.

consignment *s.* 1. invio, spedizione 2. consegna, deposito.

to **consist** *vi.* consistere, essere composto.

consistence, consistency *s.* 1. consistenza, compattezza 2. costanza.

consistent *agg.* coerente, logico.

consistently *avv.* coerentemente.

consistory *s.* concistoro.

consolation *s.* consolazione.

consolatory *agg.* consolante.

to **console** *vt.* consolare.

to **consolidate** *vt.* consolidare. ♦ to **consolidate** *vi.* consolidarsi.

consolidation *s.* consolidazione.

consoling *agg.* consolante.

consonance *s.* consonanza, accordo.

consonant *agg.* consono. ♦ **consonant** *s.* consonante.

consort *s.* 1. consorte 2. compagno, collega.

to **consort** *vi.* associarsi, unirsi. ♦ to **consort** *vt.* associare, unire.

conspicuous *agg.* cospicuo, notevole.

conspicuousness *s.* cospicuità.

conspiracy *s.* congiura.

conspirator *s.* cospiratore.

to **conspire** *vt.* e *vi.* cospirare.

constable *s.* 1. agente di polizia 2. conestabile.

constabulary *s.* corpo della polizia.

constancy *s.* costanza.

constant *agg.* costante, fedele. ♦ **constant** *s.* (*mat.*) costante.

constantly *agg.* costantemente.

constellation *s.* costellazione.

consternation *s.* costernazione.

constipation *s.* stitichezza.

constituency *s.* 1. gli elettori (*pl.*) 2. circoscrizione elettorale.

constituent *agg.* costituente. ♦ **constituent** *s.* 1. elemento costitutivo 2. (*pol.*) elettore.

to **constitute** *vt.* 1. costituire 2. eleggere.

constitution *s.* 1. costituzione, statuto 2. costituzione, composizione (*del corpo, dell'aria ecc.*).

constitutional *agg.* costituzionale.

constitutionalism *s.* costituzionalismo.

constitutionality *s.* costituzionalità.

constitutive agg. costitutivo.
to constrain vt. costringere.
constrained agg. costretto, forzato.
constraint s. 1. costrizione 2. imbarazzo.
to constrict vt. costringere.
constriction s. costrizione.
to construct vt. costruire (anche fig.).
construction s. 1. costruzione 2. (giur.) interpretazione.
constructive agg. costruttivo.
to construe vt. 1. costruire grammaticalmente 2. interpretare. ♦ **to construe** vi. fare l'analisi grammaticale.
consuetudinary agg. consuetudinario: — **law**, diritto consuetudinario.
consul s. console.
consular agg. consolare.
consulate s. consolato.
to consult vt. consultare. ♦ **to consult** vi. consultarsi.
consultation s. 1. consultazione 2. consulto.
consultative agg. consultativo.
consulting agg. consulente || — **-room**, ambulatorio.
to consume vt. consumare. ♦ **to consume** vi. consumarsi.
consumer s. consumatore, utente.
consummate agg. consumato, perfetto.
consumption s. 1. consumo 2. sciupio 3. distruzione 4. tubercolosi.
consumptive s. tisico, tubercolotico.
contact s. contatto, relazione.
to contact vt. e vi. mettere, mettersi in contatto con, prender contatto.
contagion s. contagio.
contagious agg. contagioso.
to contain vt. 1. contenere, comprendere 2. reprimere, frenare (i sentimenti).
contained agg. frenato, contenuto (di comportamento).
container s. recipiente.
contamination s. contaminazione.
to contemplate vt. e vi. contemplare, meditare.
contemplation s. contemplazione.
contemplative agg. contemplativo.
contemplator s. contemplatore.
contemporaneousness s. contemporaneità.
contemporary agg. e s. contemporaneo.

contempt s. disprezzo || — **of Court** (giur.), vilipendio della Corte.
contemptibility s. spregevolezza.
contemptible agg. spregevole.
contemptuous agg. sprezzante.
contemptuously avv. sprezzantemente.
to contend vi. 1. contendere. ♦ **to contend** vt. sostenere, affermare.
contending agg. contendente, rivale.
content s. 1. volume, capacità 2. contenuto. ♦ **contents** s. pl. indice (di libro) (sing.). ♦ **content** agg. contento, soddisfatto.
to content vt. contentare, soddisfare.
contented agg. contento, pago.
contention s. 1. contesa 2. emulazione 3. controversia.
contentious agg. litigioso.
contest s. contestazione, contesa.
to contest vt. contestare, contendere. ♦ **to contest** vi. competere, rivaleggiare.
context s. contesto.
contiguity s. contiguità.
continence s. continenza.
continent agg. continente. ♦ **continent** s. (geogr.) continente.
continental agg. e s. continentale.
contingency s. contingenza, caso.
contingent agg. eventuale, imprevisto.
continual agg. continuo.
continuation s. continuazione, seguito.
to continue vt. e vi. continuare, far continuare.
continuity s. 1. continuità 2. (cine) sceneggiatura.
continuous agg. continuo.
to contort vt. contorcere.
contortion s. contorsione.
contortionist s. contorsionista.
contour s. contorno, profilo.
contraband s. contrabbando.
contraceptive s. anticoncezionale.
contract s. contratto, patto.
to contract vt. 1. contrarre (matrimonio, amicizia ecc.) 2. (comm.) contrattare 3. contrarre, restringere. ♦ **to contract** vi. contrarsi, restringersi.
contractile agg. contrattile.
contraction s. accorciamento.
contractor s. 1. contraente 2. appaltatore 3. imprenditore.

contractual *agg.* contrattuale.
to **contradict** *vt.* contraddire.
contradiction *s.* contraddizione.
contradictory *agg.* contraddittorio.
to **contraindicate** *vt.* controindicare.
contraindication *s.* controindicazione.
contraposition *s.* opposizione, antitesi.
contrarily *avv.* contrariamente.
contrary *agg.* contrario, opposto.
♦ **contrary** *s.* il contrario: *on the* —, al contrario. ♦ **contrary** *avv.* contrariamente, all'opposto.
contrast *s.* contrasto, opposizione.
to **contrast** *vt. e vi.* far contrasto, mettere in contrasto.
to **contravene** *vt.* contravvenire.
to **contribute** *vt.* contribuire. ♦ to **contribute** *vi.* collaborare (*a un giornale*).
contribution *s.* **1.** contributo **2.** (*comm.*) apporto di capitale **3.** collaborazione (*a un giornale*).
contributor *s.* **1.** contributore **2.** collaboratore (*di giornale ecc.*).
contrite *agg.* contrito.
contrition *s.* contrizione.
contrivance *s.* **1.** espediente **2.** apparato, congegno **3.** invenzione.
to **contrive** *vt.* escogitare. ♦ to **contrive** *vi.* adoperarsi, riuscire.
control *s.* autorità, influenza, dominio, controllo || — *device* (*mecc.*), dispositivo di controllo; — *room*, camera di manovra; *birth-* —, limitazione delle nascite; *self-* —, autocontrollo. ♦ **controls** *s. pl.* (*mecc.*) comandi.
to **control** *vt.* controllare, dirigere.
controller *s.* controllore, sovrintendente.
controversial *agg.* controverso.
controversy *s.* controversia, polemica.
controvertible *agg.* controvertibile.
contumacious *agg.* **1.** insubordinato **2.** contumace.
contumacy *s.* **1.** ribellione **2.** contumacia.
contumely *s.* onta, contumelia.
contusion *s.* contusione.
contusive *agg.* contundente.
convalescence *s.* convalescenza.
convalescent *agg. e s.* convalescente.
to **convene** *vt.* **1.** convocare, riunire **2.** (*giur.*) citare. ♦ to **convene**
vi. riunirsi, incontrarsi.
convenience *s.* **1.** comodo, vantaggio. ♦ **conveniences** *s. pl.* comodità.
convenient *agg.* conveniente, comodo, adatto.
convent *s.* convento.
conventicle *s.* conventicola.
convention *s.* **1.** patto, convenzione **2.** assemblea **3.** regola (*di gioco*). ♦ **conventions** *s. pl.* convenzioni (*sociali*).
conventional *agg.* convenzionale, comune.
conventionality *s.* convenzionalità.
conventual *agg. e s.* conventuale.
to **converge** *vi.* convergere. ♦ to **converge** *vt.* far convergere.
convergence *s.* convergenza.
convergent *agg.* convergente.
conversation *s.* conversazione.
converse *agg. e s.* inverso, contrario.
conversely *avv.* viceversa.
conversion *s.* conversione, trasformazione.
convert *s.* convertito.
to **convert** *vt.* **1.** convertire **2.** trasformare.
converter *s.* **1.** convertitore **2.** (*elettr.; mecc.*) convertitore, trasformatore.
convertible *agg.* convertibile || — *car*, automobile decappottabile.
convex *agg.* convesso.
convexity *s.* convessità.
to **convey** *vt.* **1.** trasportare, convogliare **2.** trasmettere (*suoni, odori ecc.*) **3.** dare l'idea, suggerire.
conveyable *agg.* trasportabile, trasmissibile.
conveyance *s.* **1.** trasporto **2.** trasmissione **3.** convogliamento.
conveyancer *s.* notaio.
conveyer *s.* **1.** trasportatore **2.** trasmettitore **3.** convogliatore.
convict *s.* condannato, forzato.
to **convict** *vt.* condannare, dichiarare colpevole.
conviction *s.* **1.** (*giur.*) verdetto di colpevolezza, condanna **2.** convinzione.
to **convince** *vt.* convincere.
convincing *agg.* convincente.
convincingly *avv.* in modo convincente.
convivial *agg.* allegro, conviviale, gioviale.
conviviality *s.* giovialità.

convivially *avv.* convivialmente.

to **convocate** *vt.* convocare.

convocation *s.* convocazione.

convolution *s.* circonvoluzione.

convoy *s.* 1. (*mar.; mil.*) convoglio 2. scorta.

to **convoy** *vt.* 1. (*mar.; mil.*) convogliare 2. scortare.

convulsion *s.* 1. convulsione 2. rivolgimento.

convulsive *agg.* convulso.

to **coo** *vi.* tubare.

cook *s.* cuoco, cuoca: *head —,* capocuoco.

to **cook** *vt.* e *vi.* cucinare, cuocere.

cookery *s.* arte culinaria, cucina.

cooking *s.* 1. cottura 2. arte culinaria, cucina.

cool *agg.* 1. fresco 2. leggero (*di abito*) 3. calmo 4. freddo, senza entusiasmo 5. sfacciato.

to **cool** *vt.* 1. rinfrescare 2. calmare. ♦ to **cool** *vi.* 1. rinfrescarsi 2. calmarsi.

cooling *agg.* rinfrescante. ♦ **cooling** *s.* abbassamento di temperatura.

coolness *s.* 1. frescura 2. freddezza, calma, sangue freddo.

coop *s.* stia.

to **coop** *vt.* mettere nella stia.

cooper *s.* bottaio.

to **co-operate** *vi.* cooperare.

co-operation *s.* cooperazione.

co-operative *agg.* cooperativo.

co-operator *s.* cooperatore.

to **co-opt** *vt.* eleggere membro (*di comitato*).

co-ordinate *agg.* 1. dello stesso rango 2. coordinato. ♦ **co-ordinate** *s.* (*mat.*) coordinata.

to **co-ordinate** *vt.* coordinare.

co-ordination *s.* coordinazione.

co-ordinative *agg.* coordinativo.

co-owner *s.* comproprietario.

co-ownership *s.* comproprietà.

cop¹ *s.* cima (*di collina ecc.*).

cop² *s.* (*gergo*) poliziotto.

copartnership *s.* società, associazione.

to **cope** *vi.* fronteggiare, tener testa.

co-pilot *s.* (*aer.*) secondo pilota.

copper *s.* 1. rame 2. moneta di rame.

to **copper** *vt.* rivestire di rame.

copperplate *s.* 1. lastra di rame (*per incisione*) 2. incisione in rame.

Coptic *agg.* copto.

copulation *s.* copulazione.

copulative *agg.* copulativo.

copy *s.* 1. copia, trascrizione 2. riproduzione 3. esemplare || *—-book,* quaderno; *—-reader,* revisore di stampa; *fair —,* bella copia; *rough —,* brutta copia.

to **copy** *vt.* 1. copiare 2. imitare.

copyist *s.* copista.

copyright *s.* diritto d'autore, proprietà letteraria.

coquetry *s.* civetteria.

coral *s.* corallo.

cord *s.* corda, spago || *spinal —,* midollo spinale.

cordage *s.* cordame.

cordial *agg.* cordiale. ♦ **cordial** *s.* (*bevanda*) cordiale.

cordiality *s.* cordialità.

cordially *avv.* cordialmente.

cordon *s.* cordone.

core *s.* 1. torsolo 2. centro, cuore.

co-respondent *s.* (*giur.*) correo (*in adulterio*).

coriaceous *agg.* coriaceo.

cork *s.* 1. sughero 2. tappo, turacciolo || *— jacket,* cintura di salvataggio.

corkscrew *s.* cavatappi, cavaturaccioli.

cormorant *s.* cormorano.

corn¹ *s.* 1. grano 2. cereale || *ear of —,* spiga di grano; *—-cob,* pannocchia.

corn² *s.* callo, durone.

cornea *s.* cornea.

corner *s.* 1. angolo 2. (*comm.*) accaparramento (*di merci*).

to **corner** *vt.* 1. mettere, spingere in un angolo 2. (*fig.*) mettere con le spalle al muro. ♦ to **corner** *vi.* formare un angolo.

cornet *s.* cornetta.

cornice *s.* cornicione.

corolla *s.* corolla.

corollary *s.* corollario.

coronary *agg.* coronario.

coronation *s.* incoronazione.

coroner *s.* magistrato inquirente.

corporal¹ *agg.* corporale.

corporal² *s.* caporale.

corporation *s.* 1. corporazione 2. azienda municipale.

corporative *agg.* corporativo: *— system,* sistema corporativo.

corporeal *agg.* corporeo.

corpse *s.* cadavere.

corpulent *agg.* corpulento.

corpuscle *s.* corpuscolo.

corral *s.* recinto (*per bestiame*).

correct *agg.* corretto.

to correct *vt.* correggere.

correction *s.* correzione, rettifica.

corrective *agg.* e *s.* correttivo.

correctness *s.* correttezza.

corrector *s.* correttore: — *of the press* (*tip.*), correttore di bozze.

to correlate *vt.* essere, mettere in correlazione. ♦ **to correlate** *vi.* essere in correlazione.

correlation *s.* correlazione.

correlative *agg.* correlativo.

to correspond *vi.* **1.** corrispondere, essere in rapporti epistolari **2.** rispondere a (*esigenze ecc.*) **3.** equivalere.

correspondence *s.* **1.** corrispondenza **2.** accordo, rispondanza.

correspondent *s.* corrispondente.

corridor *s.* corridoio.

corroborant *agg.* corroborante.

corroboration *s.* conferma, convalida.

to corrode *vt.* corrodere. ♦ **to corrode** *vi.* corrodersi.

corrosion *s.* corrosione.

corrosive *agg.* e *s.* corrosivo.

to corrugate *vt.* corrugare.

corrugation *s.* corrugamento.

corrupt *agg.* corrotto, guasto, depravato.

to corrupt *vt.* corrompere, alterare. ♦ **to corrupt** *vi.* corrompersi, alterarsi.

corruption *s.* corruzione.

corsair *s.* corsaro.

corset *s.* corsetto.

cortisone *s.* cortisone.

corvette *s.* corvetta.

corvine *agg.* corvino.

coryphaeus *s.* (*pl.* -aei) corifeo.

cosecant *s.* cosecante.

cosily *avv.* comodamente.

cosine *s.* coseno.

cosmetic *agg.* e *s.* cosmetico.

cosmic(al) *agg.* cosmico.

cosmogony *s.* cosmogonia.

cosmographer *s.* cosmografo.

cosmography *s.* cosmografia.

cosmology *s.* cosmologia.

cosmopolitan *agg.* e *s.* cosmopolita.

cosmopolitanism *s.* cosmopolitismo.

cosmopolite *agg.* e *s.* cosmopolita.

cosmopolitism *s.* cosmopolitismo.

cosmos *s.* cosmo.

Cossack *s.* cosacco.

cost *s.* costo, prezzo || — *of living*, carovita; *at all costs*, ad ogni costo;

extra —, spesa supplementare.

to cost (**cost, cost**) *vt.* e *vi.* costare.

costal *agg.* costale.

coster, costermonger *s.* venditore ambulante (*di frutta, verdura ecc.*).

costly *agg.* costoso.

costume *s.* **1.** costume **2.** abito.

cosy *agg.* comodo, intimo.

cot¹ *s.* capanna.

cot² **1.** (*mar.*) cuccetta **2.** culla.

cotangent *s.* cotangente.

cotenant *s.* coaffittuario.

cothurnus *s.* (*pl.*-ni) coturno.

cottage *s.* villino.

cotton *s.* cotone || — *-mill*, cotonificio; — *-spinner*, operaio di filatura; — *-wool*, ovatta; — *-waste*, cascame.

couch *s.* divano.

cough *s.* tosse.

to cough *vt.* e *vi.* tossire.

could *v. can.*

council *s.* **1.** consiglio (*adunanza di persone*) **2.** (*eccl.*) concilio.

councillor *s.* consigliere.

counsel *s.* **1.** consultazione **2.** consiglio **3.** legale.

to counsel *vt.* e *vi.* consigliare.

counsellor *s.* **1.** consigliere **2.** legale.

count¹ *s.* **1.** conto, calcolo **2.** (*pol.*) scrutinio **3.** (*giur.*) capo d'accusa.

count² *s.* conte.

to count *vt.* e *vi.* **1.** contare, calcolare **2.** considerare, avere importanza.

countable *agg.* numerabile.

countenance *s.* espressione del volto, aria.

counter¹ *s.* **1.** calcolatore, contatore || *revolution* —, contagiri.

counter² *s.* volta di poppa.

counter³ *s.* **1.** banco, cassa (*di negozio*) **2.** sportello **3.** gettone (*da gioco*).

counter⁴ *agg.* contrario, opposto || — *clockwise*, in senso antiorario; — *poison*, antidoto. ♦ **counter** *avv.* in senso ontario.

to counteract *vt.* agir contro, contrapporsi a.

counter-attack *s.* contrattacco.

to counter-attack *vt.* e *vi.* contrattaccare.

counterbalance *s.* contrappeso.

to counterbalance *vt.* controbilanciare.

counterblow *s.* contraccolpo.

countercharge s. controaccusa.

counterfeit agg. contraffatto, simulato. ♦ **counterfeit** s. contraffazione, simulazione.

counterfeiter s. 1. falsario 2. simulatore.

counterfoil s. matrice.

countermand s. revoca, contrordine.

counterpane s. copriletto.

counterpart s. 1. sostituto 2. duplicato, sosia 3. complemento.

counterpoint s. contrappunto.

countershaft s. contralbero.

countersign s. contrassegno.

counterweight s. contrappeso.

countess s. contessa.

countless agg. innumerevole.

countrified agg. campagnolo, rurale.

country s. 1. paese, regione 2. campagna 3. patria 4. nazione.

countryman s. 1. compaesano, compatriota 2. contadino.

countryside s. campagna.

countrywoman s. 1. compaesana, compatriota 2. contadina.

county s. contea, provincia.

coup s. 1. colpo 2. (fig.) impressione.

couple s. coppia, paio.

to couple vt. accoppiare. ♦ **to couple** vi. accoppiarsi.

coupling s. accoppiamento.

coupon s. cedola, tagliando.

courage s. coraggio, ardire.

courageous agg. coraggioso.

course s. 1. corso (del tempo), corso (di lezioni, conferenze) 2. serie 3. portata (dei pasti) 4. (sport) circuito || of —, naturalmente; in due — a tempo debito.

court s. 1. corte, cortile 2. (giur.) corte || — of justice, tribunale.

to court vt. corteggiare.

courtier s. cortigiano.

courting s. corteggiamento.

courtyard s. cortile.

courtship s. corteggiamento.

cousin s. cugino, cugina.

cove s. 1. insenatura 2. grotta.

covenant s. convenzione, patto.

cover s. 1. coperta, copertura 2. calotta 3. copertina (di libro) 4. riparo, ricovero 5. coperto (a tavola).

to cover vt. 1. coprire, ricoprire 2. proteggere 3. percorrere 4. nascondere 5. comprendere, includere.

covering s. copertura, rivestimento.

coverlet s. copriletto.

covert s. ricovero, rifugio.

covertly avv. nascostamente.

to covet vt. agognare.

covetousness s. cupidigia.

cow s. mucca, vacca || — bell, campanaccio; — -grass, trifoglio di campo; — -shed, stalla.

coward s. codardo, vile.

cowardice s. codardia, viltà.

cowardly agg. codardo. ♦ **cowardly** avv. vilmente.

cowboy s. bovaro.

cowherd s. vaccaro.

cowl s. 1. cappuccio, tonaca (di frate) 2. (auto; aer.) cofano del motore.

coxswain s. timoniere.

coy agg. timido, riservato.

crab s. granchio.

crabbed agg. sgarbato, bisbetico.

crack s. 1. schianto, detonazione, schiocco 2. incrinatura, rottura.

to crack vt. schiantare, rompere, incrinare 2. schioccare. ♦ **to crack** vi. 1. screpolarsi, spezzarsi 2. scricchiolare.

cracked agg. 1. incrinato 2. fesso (di voce).

cracker s. petardo || nut-crackers, schiaccianoci; — of jokes, burlone.

crackle s. 1. crepitio 2. screpolatura, incrinatura.

to crackle vi. scoppiettare, scricchiolare. ♦ **to crackle** vt. screpolare.

crackling s. scoppiettio.

cradle s. culla (anche fig.).

craft s. 1. abilità, mestiere, professione 2. astuzia, inganno.

craftsman s. artigiano.

craftsmanship s. artigianato.

crafty agg. astuto, abile.

crag s. rupe, cresta.

to cram vt. riempire, stipare, rimpinzare. ♦ **to cram** vi. rimpinzarsi.

cramp s. crampo.

to cramp vt. (fig.) bloccare, paralizzare.

crane s. gru (anche mecc.).

to crane vt. e vi. 1. sollevare o abbassare (mediante una gru) 2. allungare (il collo).

cranium s. cranio.

crank¹ s. manovella, manubrio.

crank² agg. 1. piegato 2. disinnestato.

to **crank** vt. e vi. **1.** piegare a gomito **2.** mettere in moto (con manovella).

cranking s. avviamento (di motore).

crash s. **1.** strepito, fracasso **2.** caduta **3.** scontro, collisione **4.** rovina (anche morale).

to **crash** vt. e vi. **1.** abbattere, precipitare, crollare con grande rumore **2.** scontrare, scontrarsi.

crate s. cassa da imballaggio.

crater s. cratere.

to **crawl** vi. **1.** strisciare, andar carponi **2.** brulicare **3.** avere la pelle d'oca.

crawl s. **1.** strisciamento **2.** (nuoto) « crawl ».

crayfish s. gambero (d'acqua dolce).

craze s. mania, smania.

craziness s. pazzia, follia.

crazy agg. **1.** folle **2.** maniaco, entusiasta.

to **creak** vi. cigolare, stridere.

cream s. **1.** panna, crema **2.** ogni sostanza densa e untuosa.

creamery s. caseificio.

creamy agg. cremoso.

crease s. piega, grinza.

to **crease** vt. fare pieghe, sgualcire. ✦ to **crease** vi. sgualcirsi.

to **create** vt. **1.** creare, produrre, suscitare **2.** nominare.

creation s. **1.** creazione **2.** universo, natura, il creato.

creative agg. creativo.

creator s. creatore.

creature s. **1.** essere vivente **2.** creatura (anche fig.), favorito.

credence s. credenza, fede.

credentials s. pl. credenziali.

credibility s. credibilità.

credible agg. credibile.

credit s. **1.** fiducia **2.** credito, reputazione, autorità **3.** (comm.) fido, credito.

to **credit** vt. **1.** prestar fede **2.** attribuire **3.** (comm.) accreditare

creditor s. creditore.

credulity s. credulità.

credulous agg. credulo.

creed s. credo, credenza religiosa.

creek s. **1.** insenatura **2.** (amer.) torrente.

to **creep** (**crept**, **crept**) vi. **1.** strisciare, avanzare lentamente **2.** arrampicarsi (di piante) || to — along, avanzare strisciando; to — away, allontanarsi strisciando.

creeper s. **1.** rettile, verme **2.** persona strisciante **3.** pianta rampicante.

creepy agg. **1.** strisciante **2.** che dà i brividi.

to **cremate** vt. cremare.

cremation s. cremazione.

crematory s. crematoio.

creole agg. e s. creolo.

crept V. to creep.

crepuscular agg. crepuscolare.

crescent agg. **1.** crescente **2.** a mezzaluna. ✦ **crescent** s. **1.** luna crescente **2.** mezzaluna (emblema turco) **3.** strada a semicerchio.

cress s. crescione.

crest s. **1.** cresta **2.** ciuffo, pennacchio **3.** criniera.

to **crest** vt. ornare di pennacchio. ✦ to **crest** vi. incresparsi (di onde).

crevasse s. crepaccio.

crevice s. fessura.

crew¹ s. equipaggio, ciurma.

crew² V. to crow.

crib s. **1.** greppia **2.** presepio **3.** stalla, capanna.

crick s. crampo || a — in the neck, torcicollo.

cricket s. grillo.

crime s. delitto, crimine.

criminal agg. e s. criminale.

criminalist s. penalista.

criminality s. criminalità.

criminology s. criminologia.

crimson s. cremisi.

to **cringe** vi. (fig.) farsi piccolo, umiliarsi.

cripple agg. e s. storpio, zoppo.

to **cripple** vt. storpiare. ✦ to **cripple** vi. essere zoppo.

crisis s. crisi.

crisp agg. **1.** croccante **2.** crespo **3.** tonificante. ✦ **crisp** s. patatina fritta, croccante.

criss-cross agg. incrociato.

critic s. critico.

critical agg. critico.

criticism s. critica.

to **criticize** vt. criticare.

critique s. critica, recensione.

croak s. gracidamento.

to **croak** vt. e vi. **1.** gracidare **2.** (fig.) brontolare.

Croatian agg. e s. croato.

crochet s. lavoro all'uncinetto || —-hook (o — -pin), uncinetto.

crock¹ s. coccio, vaso di terracotta.

crock² s. **1.** ronzino **2.** persona vecchia e malandata.

crock[3] *s.* fuliggine, sudiciume.
crockery *s.* terraglia.
crocodile *s.* coccodrillo.
croft *s.* piccolo podere, campicello.
crook *s.* 1. gancio, uncino 2. curva, flessione 3. (*gergo*) truffatore.
crookback *s.* gobba.
crooked *agg.* 1. curvo, storto, deforme 2. (*fig.*) perverso.
crookedly *avv.* 1. tortuosamente 2. indirettamente 3. perversamente.
crop *s.* 1. raccolto, messe 2. gozzo (*di uccello*) 3. (*fig.*) gruppo 4. rapata (*di capelli*).
to crop *vt.* 1. mietere 2. tosare.
cropper[1] *s.* mietitore.
cropper[2] *s.* (*fam.*) capitombolo.
cross *agg.* 1. obliquo, trasversale 2. adirato || — -bar, traversa; — -road, incrocio. ♦ cross *s.* 1. croce 2. tribolazione, pena.
to cross *vt.* e *vi.* 1. fare il segno della croce 2. attraversare 3. incrociare 4. cancellare || to — one's legs, accavallare le gambe.
crossbeam *s.* trave maestra.
crossbelt *s.* cartucciera a tracolla.
crossbow *s.* balestra.
crossbreed *s.* ibrido, incrocio.
cross-country *agg.* campestre.
cross-examination *s.* controinterrogatorio.
to cross-examine *vt.* controinterrogare.
cross-hatch *s.* tratteggio.
crossing *s.* 1. passaggio, traversata 2. incrocio || level —, passaggio a livello.
crossly *avv.* di malumore.
crosswise *avv.* 1. di traverso 2. a forma di croce.
crossword *s.* parole incrociate (*pl.*) || — puzzle, cruciverba.
crouch *s.* l'accovacciarsi.
to crouch *vi.* accovacciarsi, rannicchiarsi.
crow[1] *s.* corvo, cornacchia || a white —, una mosca bianca; to eat (v. irr.) a —, inghiottire un rospo.
crow[2] *s.* canto del gallo.
to crow (crew, crowed) *vi.* cantare (*del gallo*).
crowd *s.* folla, massa, moltitudine.
to crowd *vt.* affollare. ♦ to crowd *vi.* affollarsi, accalcarsi || to — together, stringere insieme.
crown *s.* 1. corona 2. cocuzzolo 3. coronamento, successo 4. (*moneta*) corona: half a —, mezza corona.

to crown *vt.* 1. incoronare 2. coronare, ricompensare.
crowning *s.* 1. incoronazione 2. coronamento.
crucial *agg.* cruciale.
crucible *s.* 1. crogiuolo 2. (*fig.*) dura prova.
crucifix *s.* crocifisso.
crucifixion *s.* crocifissione.
to crucify *vt.* crocifiggere.
crude *agg.* grezzo, rozzo, primitivo.
crudity *s.* asprezza.
cruel *agg.* crudele.
cruelty *s.* crudeltà.
cruet *s.* ampolla.
cruise *s.* crociera: to go on a —, fare una crociera.
cruiser *s.* incrociatore.
cruising *s.* crociera.
crumb *s.* 1. briciola 2. mollica.
to crumb *vt.* 1. sbriciolare 2. impanare.
to crumble *vt.* sbriciolare. ♦ to crumble *vi.* sbriciolarsi.
crumbly *agg.* friabile.
to crumple *vt.* spiegazzare. ♦ to crumple *vi.* spiegazzarsi.
to crunch *vt.* e *vi.* sgranocchiare rumorosamente.
crusade *s.* crociata.
crusader *s.* crociato.
crush *s.* 1. folla, calca 2. frantumazione 3. (*gergo*) cotta.
to crush *vt.* 1. frantumare, torchiare 2. (*fig.*) annientare, sconfiggere. ♦ to crush *vi.* accalcarsi, affollarsi.
crushing *agg.* schiacciante (*anche fig.*).
crust *s.* 1. crosta 2. incrostazione.
Crustacea *s. pl.* crostacei.
crutch *s.* 1. gruccia, stampella 2. forcella (*di ramo*).
cry *s.* grido, lamento, pianto || within —, a portata di voce.
to cry *vt.* e *vi.* 1. gridare 2. piangere || to — out, alzare la voce, protestare.
crypt *s.* cripta.
cryptogam *s.* crittogama.
cryptogram *s.* crittogramma.
cryptography *s.* crittografia.
crystal *agg.* cristallino. ♦ crystal *s.* cristallo || — work, cristalleria.
crystalline *agg.* cristallino (*anche fig.*).
crystallization *s.* cristallizzazione.
to crystallize *vt.* cristallizzare. ♦ to crystallize *vi.* cristallizzarsi.

crystallography *s.* cristallografia.
cub *s.* 1. volpacchiotto 2. (*fam.*) ragazzaccio.
cubage *s.* cubatura.
Cuban *agg.* e *s.* cubano.
cubature *s.* cubatura.
cube *s.* cubo || — *root*, radice cubica.
cubic *agg.* cubico.
cubism *s.* cubismo.
cubit *s.* cubito.
cuckold *s.* becco, cornuto.
to cuckold *vt.* tradire (*il marito*).
cuckoo *s.* cuculo.
cucumber *s.* cetriolo.
cudgel *s.* randello.
to cudgel *vt.* randellare.
cuff *s.* polsino (*di camicia*).
cuirass *s.* corazza.
cuirassier *s.* corazziere.
culinary *agg.* culinario.
to cull *vt.* scegliere.
culminant *agg.* culminante.
to culminate *vi.* culminare, giungere al culmine.
culottes *s. pl.* gonna pantaloni.
culprit *s.* 1. colpevole 2. imputato.
cult *s.* culto.
cultivable *agg.* coltivabile.
to cultivate *vt.* coltivare (*anche fig.*).
cultivation *s.* coltivazione.
cultural *agg.* culturale.
culture *s.* 1. coltura, coltivazione 2. cultura.
cultured *agg.* colto, educato.
cumbersome *agg.* ingombrante.
cumulative *agg.* cumulativo.
cumulus *s.* (*pl.* -li) cumulo.
cuneiform *agg.* cuneiforme.
cunette *s.* cunetta (*di trincea*).
cunning *agg.* astuto, furbo. ♦ **cunning** *s.* astuzia.
cup *s.* 1. tazza 2. (*sport*) coppa, trofeo || — *bearer*, coppiere; *tea* —, tazza da tè.
cupboard *s.* credenza, armadio.
cupel *s.* coppella.
cupidity *s.* cupidigia.
cupreous *agg.* cupreo.
cupric *agg.* ramico.
cur *s.* 1. cane bastardo 2. mascalzone.
curable *agg.* curabile.
curacy *s.* vicariato, cura.
curare *s.* curaro.
curate *s.* curato, vicario.
curative *agg.* curativo.
curator *s.* direttore (*di museo, istituto ecc.*).

curb *s.* 1. cordone del marciapiede 2. freno (*fig.*) || — *-bit*, morso della briglia.
curd *s.* giuncata.
to curdle *vt.* cagliare, coagulare. ♦ **to curdle** *vi.* cagliarsi, coagularsi.
curdy *agg.* cagliato, coagulato.
cure *s.* 1. cura, rimedio: *to take a* —, fare una cura 2. (*eccl.*) cura 3. vulcanizzazione (*di gomma*).
to cure *vt.* 1. curare, rimediare 2. salare, affumicare (*di cibi*) 3. vulcanizzare (*una gomma*). ♦ **to cure** *vi.* curarsi.
cureless *agg.* incurabile.
curette *s.* (*chir.*) raschiatoio.
curfew *s.* coprifuoco.
curio *s.* oggetto raro.
curiosity *s.* curiosità: *out of* —, per curiosità.
curious *agg.* 1. curioso 2. strano, singolare.
curl *s.* 1. ricciolo 2. curva, spirale.
to curl *vt.* 1. arricciare 2. torcere. ♦ **to curl** *vi.* 1. arricciarsi 2. torcersi 3. sollevarsi in spire.
curler *s.* ferro per arricciare i capelli, bigodino.
curly *agg.* 1. ricciuto 2. a spirale.
currency *s.* 1. (*comm.*) circolazione monetaria 2. corso, credito, voga.
current *agg.* corrente. ♦ **current** *s.* corrente (*anche fig.*) || *alternating* —, corrente alternata; *direct* —, corrente continua.
currently *avv.* comunemente.
curriculum *s.* curriculum.
to curry *vt.* 1. strigliare 2. conciare (*di cuoio*).
curry-comb *s.* striglia.
curse *s.* maledizione, anatema: *a* — *upon him!*, sia maledetto!
to curse *vt.* 1. maledire 2. scomunicare. ♦ **to curse** *vi.* imprecare, pronunciare bestemmie.
cursed *agg.* maledetto.
cursive *agg.* e *s.* corsivo.
to curtail *vt.* accorciare, abbreviare.
curtain *s.* 1. tenda, tendina 2. cortina 3. siparío || — *-call*, chiamata alla ribalta.
curtain-raiser *s.* avanspettacolo.
curtly *avv.* brevemente, bruscamente.
curtsey *s.* riverenza, inchino (*di donna*).
curve *s.* curva, svolta.
to curve *vt.* curvare. ♦ **to curve** *vi.*

curvarsi.
curvet *s.* falcata.
curvilinear *agg.* curvilineo.
cushion *s.* cuscino.
cusp *s.* 1. cuspide 2. (*geom.*) vertice.
custard *s.* crema (*di uova e latte*).
custody *s.* 1. custodia, vigilanza 2. arresto, detenzione.
custom *s.* costume, consuetudine. ♦ **customs** *s. pl.* dogana (*sing.*) || — -**house officer**, doganiere.
customary *agg.* 1. abituale, d'uso comune 2. (*giur.*) consuetudinario.
customer *s.* cliente, avventore.
cut *s.* 1. taglio 2. decurtazione 3. (*sport*) colpo secco.
to cut (**cut, cut**) *vt. e vi.* 1. tagliare, tagliarsi || **to — a poor figure**, fare una brutta figura 2. (*comm.*) ridurre 3. praticare un'apertura || **to — down**, abbattere; **to — out**, ritagliare; **to — up**, trinciare (*il pollo*), sradicare (*alberi*).
cutlet *s.* costoletta.
cut-off *s.* 1. scorciatoia 2. ritaglio di giornale.
cutter¹ *s.* 1. tagliatore 2. (*mecc.*) fresa.
cutter² *s.* (*mar.*) "cutter".
cut-throat *agg.* spietato. ♦ **cut-throat** *s.* tagliagole.
cutting *agg.* tagliente, sferzante. ♦ **cutting** *s.* 1. taglio, incisione 2. ritaglio, truciolo 3. (*comm.*) riduzione.
cuttlefish *s.* seppia.
cyanide *s.* cianuro.
cybernetics *s.* cibernetica.
cycle *s.* ciclo.
cycling *s.* ciclismo.
cyclostyle *s.* ciclostile.
cyclotron *s.* ciclotrone.
cyclist *s.* ciclista.
cyclometer *s.* contachilometri.
cylinder *s.* 1. cilindro 2. rullo.
cylindrical *agg.* cilindrico.
cynic *agg. e s.* cinico.
cynicism *s.* cinismo.
cypress *s.* cipresso.
Cyprian *agg. e s.* cipriota.
Cyrillic *agg.* cirillico.
cyst *s.* cisti.
cystitis *s.* cistite.
cytology *s.* citologia.
Czar *s.* zar.
Czech *agg. e s.* ceco.
Czecho-Slovak *agg. e s.* cecoslovacco.

D

D *s.* (*mus.*) re.
dab *s.* 1. colpo 2. macchia.
to dab *vt.* 1. sfiorare 2. applicare.
to dabble *vt.* inumidire. ♦ **to dabble** *vi.* 1. inumidirsi 2. sguazzare || **to — in** (**at**), dilettarsi di.
dachshund *s.* cane bassotto.
dad(dy) *s.* (*fam.*) papà, babbo.
daffodil *s.* narciso selvatico.
daft *agg.* sciocco, pazzoide.
dagger *s.* 1. pugnale 2. (*tip.*) croce || **at daggers drawn**, ai ferri corti.
daguerreotype *s.* dagherrotipo.
daguerreotypy *s.* dagherrotipia.
dahlia *s.* dalia.
daily *agg.* quotidiano, giornaliero. ♦ **daily** *s.* (*giornale*) quotidiano. ♦ **daily** *avv.* ogni giorno.
daintily *avv.* delicatamente.
daintiness *s.* squisitezza.
dainty *agg.* 1. squisito 2. esigente 3. raffinato (*di gusti*). ♦ **dainty** *s.* leccornia.
dairy *s.* latteria.
dairymaid *s.* lattaia.
dairyman *s.* lattaio.
dais *s.* piattaforma.
daisy *s.* margherita.
dalliance *s.* amoreggiamento.
to dally *vi.* gingillarsi, oziare.
Dalmatian *agg. e s.* dalmata.
daltonism *s.* daltonismo.
dam¹ *s.* diga, sbarramento.
dam² *s.* madre (*di animali*).
to dam *vt.* arginare.
damage *s.* danno. ♦ **damages** *pl.* (*giur.*) indennizzo, risarcimento (*sing.*).
to damage *vt.* danneggiare.
damaging *agg.* dannoso.
damask *s.* damasco.
to damask *vt.* damascare.
dame *s.* dama, gentildonna.
damn *s.* maledizione.
to damn *vt.* 1. dannare 2. (*spesso scritto d-*) maledire, mandare all'inferno.
damnation *s.* dannazione.
damnatory *agg.* compromettente (*di prove*).
damp *agg.* umido. ♦ **damp** *s.* 1. umidità 2. (*fig.*) depressione || **fire—**, grisù.
to damp *vt.* 1. inumidire 2. (*fig.*) deprimere, smorzare.

damper s. 1. regolatore (*di stufa, fornace ecc.*) 2. (*mus.*) sordina.

dampness s. umidità.

dance s. danza.

to dance *vt.* e *vi.* danzare || **to — attendance on**, essere a disposizione di.

dancer s. ballerino.

dancing s. danza.

dandelion s. (*bot.*) soffione.

dandruff s. forfora.

dandy *agg.* elegante, raffinato. ◆ **dandy** s. zerbinotto.

Dane s. danese.

danger s. pericolo.

dangerous *agg.* pericoloso.

to dangle *vi.* ciondolare, penzolare ◆ **to dangle** *vt.* far penzolare.

dangling *agg.* penzolante.

Danish *agg.* danese.

dank *agg.* umido.

Dantean, Dantesque *agg.* dantesco.

dapple s. macchia || **-grey**, leardo pomellato.

to dapple *vt.* chiazzare.

dare (**dared, durst**) *v. dif.* osare.

to dare *vt.* 1. affrontare 2. sfidare.

daredevil s. scavezzacollo.

daring *agg.* audace. ◆ **daring** s. audacia.

dark *agg.* 1. scuro 2. triste 3. segreto. ◆ **dark** s. 1. oscurità 2. (*fig.*) ignoranza.

to darken *vt.* oscurare. ◆ **to darken** *vi.* oscurarsi.

darkling *agg.* oscuro. ◆ **darkling** *avv.* nell'oscurità.

darkness s. oscurità.

darling *agg.* e s. caro.

darn s. rammendo.

to darn *vt.* rammendare.

darnel s. loglio.

darner s. rammendatrice.

darning s. rammendo.

dart s. 1. dardo 2. slancio.

to dart *vt.* lanciare. ◆ **to dart** *vi.* lanciarsi (*in avanti*).

darting *agg.* dardeggiante.

Darwinism s. darwinismo.

dash s. 1. slancio 2. attacco 3. tonfo 4. spruzzo 5. lineetta || **-board**, cruscotto (*di automobili*).

to dash *vt.* 1. frantumare 2. macchiare. ◆ **to dash** *vi.* 1. precipitarsi 2. infrangersi.

dashing *agg.* impetuoso.

dastard s. vigliacco, furfante.

date[1] s. 1. data 2. appuntamento || **up to —**, aggiornato; **out of —**, antiquato.

date[1] s. dattero.

to date *vt.* e *vi.* datare || **to — a girl**, dare un appuntamento a una ragazza.

dating s. datazione.

dative *agg.* e s. dativo.

datum s. (*pl.* **data**) dato, elemento.

to daub *vt.* 1. intonacare 2. impiastrare.

dauber s. imbrattatore.

daughter s. figlia || **-in-law**, nuora; **grand-** (*di nonni*), nipotina.

to daunt *vt.* spaventare, intimidire.

dauntless *agg.* intrepido.

to dawdle *vi.* oziare, bighellonare.

dawn s. alba.

to dawn *vi.* 1. albeggiare 2. apparire, balenare (*nella mente*).

day s. giorno || **— labourer**, lavoratore a giornata; **the — after tomorrow**, dopodomani; **the — before yesterday**, l'altro ieri; **this week**, oggi a otto; **— off**, giorno di riposo; **— out**, giorno di libera uscita.

daybook s. (*comm.*) brogliaccio.

daybreak s. alba.

daydream s. fantasticheria.

to daydream *vi.* fantasticare.

daydreamer s. sognatore.

daylight s. luce del giorno.

daylong *agg.* che dura tutto il giorno. ◆ **daylong** *avv.* per tutto il giorno.

daytime s. giornata.

daze s. sbalordimento.

to daze *vt.* sbalordire.

dazzle s. 1. abbagliamento || **— lamps** (*auto*), fari abbaglianti.

to dazzle *vt.* abbagliare.

deacon s. diacono.

dead *agg.* 1. morto 2. assoluto || **— drunk**, ubriaco fradicio. ◆ **dead** *avv.* assolutamente || **— sure**, arcisicuro.

to deaden *vt.* 1. attutire 2. isolare (*acusticamente*). ◆ **to deaden** *vi.* attutirsi.

deadening s. isolamento acustico.

deadline s. 1. linea non superabile 2. scadenza, termine massimo.

deadly *agg.* mortale. ◆ **deadly** *avv.* mortalmente.

deadness s. torpore.

deaf *agg.* sordo.

to deafen *vt.* assordare.

deaf-mute s. sordomuto.

deafness s. sordità.

deal s. 1. quantità 2. accordo 3. affare 4. mano (*del gioco delle carte*) || *a great* —, moltissimo.

to **deal** (dealt, dealt) *vt.* distribuire, dare. ♦ to **deal** (dealt, dealt) *vi.* trattare, comportarsi || *to* — *in*, commerciare in.

dealer s. 1. commerciante 2. mazziere (*delle carte*).

dealing s. 1. commercio 2. distribuzione 3. relazione || *double-* —, slealtà.

dealt V. to deal.

deambulatory *agg.* deambulatorio.

dean s. 1. decano 2. preside (*di facoltà universitaria*).

dear *agg.* caro || — *me!*, povero me!

dearly *avv.* 1. caramente 2. a caro prezzo.

dearness s. amorevolezza.

dearth s. penuria.

death s. morte || — *-rattles*, rantoli dell'agonia; — *-warrant*, ordine di esecuzione capitale.

deathly *agg.* e *avv.* V. deadly.

to **debase** *vt.* 1. avvilire 2. svalutare.

to **debar** *vt.* escludere, privare.

to **debark** *vt.* e *vi.* sbarcare.

to **debate** s. dibattito.

to **debate** *vt.* e *vi.* 1. discutere 2. ponderare.

debauch s. intemperanza, corruzione.

debauched *agg.* corrotto.

debauchery s. 1. corruzione 2. dissolutezza.

debenture s. (*comm.*) obbligazione.

debit s. debito.

to **debit** *vt.* addebitare.

to **debouch** *vi.* sfociare.

debris s. detriti (*pl.*).

debt s. debito.

debtor s. debitore.

début s. debutto.

decadence s. decadenza.

decadent *agg.* e s. decadente.

decagram(m)e s. decagrammo.

decahedron s. decaedro.

to **decalcify** *vt.* decalcificare.

decalitre s. decalitro.

decalogue s. decalogo.

decametre s. decametro.

to **decamp** *vi.* levare le tende.

to **decant** *vt.* travasare.

decantation s. decantazione.

decanter s. caraffa.

to **decapitate** *vt.* decapitare.

decasyllabic *agg.* decasillabico.

decay s. 1. decadimento 2. rovina 3. carie (*dei denti*).

to **decay** *vt.* 1. far decadere 2. mandare in rovina. ♦ to **decay** *vi.* 1. decadere 2. andare in rovina 3. cariarsi.

decayable *agg.* deperibile.

decease s. decesso.

to **decease** *vi.* morire.

deceit s. 1. inganno 2. falsità.

deceitful *agg.* 1. ingannevole 2. falso.

to **deceive** *vt.* ingannare.

deceiving *agg.* ingannatore.

to **decelerate** *vt.* e *vi.* rallentare.

deceleration s. rallentamento.

decelerator s. rallentatore.

December s. dicembre.

decency s. decenza. ♦ **decencies** s. *pl.* convenienze.

decennary *agg.* decennale. ♦ **decennary** s. decennio.

decennial *agg.* e s. decennale.

decent *agg.* decente || *a* — *fellow*, un buon diavolo.

decentralization s. decentramento.

to **decentralize** *vt.* decentrare.

deception s. inganno.

deceptive *agg.* ingannevole.

to **decide** *vt.* decidere. ♦ to **decide** *vi.* decidersi, pronunciarsi.

decigram(me) s. decigrammo.

decimal *agg.* e s. decimale.

to **decimate** *vt.* decimare.

decimation s. decimazione.

decimetre s. decimetro.

to **decipher** *vt.* decifrare.

deciphering s. decifrazione.

decision s. decisione.

decisive *agg.* 1. decisivo 2. deciso.

deck s. (*mar.*) ponte, coperta || — *-chair*, sedia a sdraio; *quarter-* —, cassero.

to **deck** *vt.* ornare.

decker s. *double-* —, autobus a due piani.

to **declaim** *vt.* e *vi.* declamare.

declaimer s. declamatore.

declamation s. declamazione.

declamatory *agg.* declamatorio.

declaration s. dichiarazione.

to **declare** *vt.* e *vi.* dichiarare.

declension s. 1. declino 2. (*gramm.*) declinazione.

declinable *agg.* declinabile.

declination s. 1. inclinazione 2. declino.

decline s. declino, deperimento.

to **decline** vt. e vi. declinare.
declining s. 1. declinazione 2. deperimento 3. rifiuto.
declivity s. declivio.
to **decode** vt. decifrare, tradurre (testi in codice).
decolorization s. decolorazione.
decoloration s. decolorazione.
to **decolour(ize)** vt. decolorare.
decomposable agg. scomponibile.
to **decompose** vt. 1. decomporre 2. scomporre. ♦ to **decompose** vi. 1. decomporsi 2. scomporsi.
decomposition s. decomposizione.
to **deconsecrate** vt. sconsacrare.
to **decorate** vt. decorare.
decoration s. decorazione.
decorative agg. decorativo.
decorator s. decoratore.
decorous agg. decoroso.
decoy s. esca, richiamo.
decrease s. diminuzione.
to **decrease** vt. e vi. diminuire.
decree s. decreto.
to **decree** vt. decretare.
decrepit agg. decrepito.
decrepitude s. decrepitezza.
to **decry** vt. stigmatizzare, denigrare.
to **decuple** vt. decuplicare.
to **dedicate** vt. dedicare.
dedicatee s. persona a cui è dedicato qc.
dedication s. 1. dedica 2. consacrazione.
dedicative, dedicatory agg. dedicatorio.
to **deduce** vt. 1. dedurre 2. derivare.
to **deduct** vt. detrarre.
deduction s. 1. deduzione 2. detrazione.
deductive agg. deduttivo.
deed s. atto, azione.
to **deem** vt. giudicare.
deep agg. 1. profondo 2. cupo ‖ —freeze, surgelamento; — mourning, lutto stretto. ♦ **deep** s. abisso, profondità. ♦ **deep** avv. profondamente ‖ — into the night, fino a notte tarda.
to **deepen** vt. 1. approfondire 2. incupire. ♦ to **deepen** vi. 1. approfondirsi 2. incupirsi.
deeply avv. profondamente.
deepness s. profondità.
deep-rooted agg. radicato.
deer s. cervo ‖ (fallow) —, daino.
to **deface** vt. sfregiare.

defacement s. sfregio.
defamation s. diffamazione.
defamatory agg. diffamatorio.
to **defame** vt. diffamare.
defamer s. diffamatore.
default s. 1. mancanza 2. inadempienza 3. (giur.) contumacia: judgement by —, giudizio in contumacia.
defaulting agg. (comm.) insolvente.
defeat s. 1. sconfitta 2. fallimento.
to **defeat** vt. 1. sconfiggere 2. frustrare.
defeatism s. disfattismo.
defeatist agg. e s. disfattista.
to **defecate** vt. purificare. ♦ to **defecate** vi. defecare.
defect s. difetto.
defection s. defezione.
defective agg. 1. difettoso 2. (gramm.) difettivo. ♦ **defective** s. anormale.
defence s. difesa.
defenceless agg. indifeso.
to **defend** vt. difendere.
defendant s. imputato.
defender s. difensore.
defenestration s. defenestrazione.
defensible agg. difensibile.
defensive agg. difensivo. ♦ **defensive** s. difensiva.
to **defer**[1] vt. e vi. differire ‖ deferred payment, pagamento a rate.
to **defer**[2] vt. rimettere. ♦ to **defer** vi. rimettersi.
deference s. deferenza.
deferential agg. deferente.
deferment s. differimento.
defiance s. sfida.
defiant agg. ardito.
deficiency s. 1. deficienza 2. disavanzo.
deficient agg. e s. deficiente.
deficit s. (comm.) disavanzo.
to **defile** vi. marciare in fila. ♦ to **defile** vt. 1. insozzare 2. profanare.
defilement s. 1. contaminazione 2. profanazione.
definable agg. definibile.
to **define** vt. definire.
definite agg. definito.
definitely avv. in modo preciso.
definiteness s. precisione.
definition s. 1. definizione 2. nitidezza.
definitive agg. definitivo.
to **deflagrate** vt. far deflagrare. ♦ to **deflagrate** vi. deflagrare.

deflagration s. deflagrazione.
to deflate vt. sgonfiare. ♦ **to deflate** vi. sgonfiarsi.
deflation s. 1. sgonfiamento 2. deflazione.
to deflect vt. e vi. deviare.
deflection s. deviazione.
defloration s. deflorazione.
to deflower vt. 1. deflorare 2. devastare 3. spogliare (dei fiori).
to deforest vt. disboscare.
deforestation s. diboscamento.
to deform vt. deformare. ♦ **to deform** vi. deformarsi.
deformation s. deformazione.
deformed agg. deforme.
deformity s. deformità.
to defraud vt. defraudare.
defrauder s. frodatore.
to defray vt. pagare, risarcire.
defrayal s. pagamento, risarcimento.
to defrost vt. sgelare.
defroster s. riscaldatore.
deft agg. abile, destro.
to defy vt. sfidare.
degenerate agg. e s. degenerato.
to degenerate vt. e vi. degenerare.
degeneration s. degenerazione.
degradation s. degradazione.
to degrade vt. degradare.
degree s. 1. grado 2. rango 3. laurea, diploma || by degrees, gradatamente.
to dehydrate vt. disidratare.
dehydration s. disidratazione.
to deify vt. deificare.
deism s. deismo.
deity s. divinità.
to deject vt. abbattere, scoraggiare.
dejected agg. triste, abbattuto.
dejectedly avv. con aria abbattuta.
dejection s. abbattimento.
delation s. delazione.
delator s. delatore.
delay s. 1. ritardo 2. proroga.
to delay vt. e vi. ritardare.
delegacy s. delegazione.
delegate s. delegato.
to delegate vt. delegare.
delegation s. delegazione.
to delete vt. cancellare (anche fig.).
deliberate agg. 1. deliberato 2. cauto.
to deliberate vt. e vi. deliberare.
deliberately avv. deliberatamente.
deliberation s. 1. deliberazione 2. ponderatezza.
delicacy s. 1. delicatezza 2. ghiottoneria.

delicate agg. 1. delicato 2. esigente.
delicatessen s. pl. 1. ghiottonerie 2. salumeria (sing.).
delicious agg. delizioso.
delict s. (giur.) delitto.
delight s. delizia, gioia.
to delight vt. deliziare. ♦ **to delight** vi. dilettarsi.
delighted agg. lietissimo, entusiasta.
delightful agg. delizioso.
to delimit(ate) vt. delimitare.
delimitation s. delimitazione.
to delineate vt. delineare.
delineation s. delineazione.
delinquency s. 1. delinquenza 2. colpevolezza.
delinquent agg. colpevole. ♦ **delinquent** s. delinquente.
delirious agg. delirante.
deliriously avv. in modo delirante.
delirium s. delirio, frenesia.
to deliver vt. 1. liberare 2. consegnare 3. partorire 4. pronunciare (un discorso).
deliverance s. liberazione.
delivery s. 1. liberazione 2. consegna 3. parto 4. resa 5. dizione, pronuncia || — -man, fattorino.
deltoid agg. triangolare.
to delude vt. ingannare.
deluge s. diluvio.
delusion s. illusione.
delusive agg. illusorio.
to delve vt. scavare, esumare. ♦ **to delve** vi. compiere ricerche, frugare.
demagnetization s. demagnetizzazione.
to demagnetize vt. demagnetizzare.
demagogic(al) agg. demagogico.
demagogue s. demagogo.
demagogy s. demagogia.
demand s. 1. domanda 2. esigenza || on —, a richiesta.
to demand vt. 1. domandare 2. esigere.
demarcation s. demarcazione.
demeanour s. contegno.
demented s. demerito.
demesne s. dominio, proprietà terriera.
demigod s. semidio.
demijohn s. damigiana.
demilitarization s. smilitarizzazione.
to demilitarize vt. smilitarizzare.
demise s. 1. trapasso (di proprietà)

2. decesso.

demiurge *s.* demiurgo.

demobilization *s.* smobilitazione.

to demobilize *vt.* smobilitare.

democracy *s.* democrazia.

democrat *s.* democratico.

democratic(al) *agg.* democratico.

democratization *s.* democratizzazione.

to democratize *vt.* democratizzare.

demographic(al) *agg.* demografico.

demography *s.* demografia.

to demolish *vt.* demolire.

demolisher *s.* demolitore.

demolition *s.* demolizione.

demon *s.* demonio.

demoniac(al) *agg.* demoniaco.

demonology *s.* demonologia.

demonstrability *s.* dimostrabilità.

demonstrable *agg.* dimostrabile.

demonstrant *s.* dimostrante.

to demonstrate *vt. e vi.* dimostrare.

demonstration *s.* dimostrazione.

demonstrative *agg.* 1. dimostrativo 2. espansivo.

demonstrativeness *s.* 1. dimostrazione 2. espansività.

demonstrator *s.* 1. dimostratore 2. dimostrante.

demoralization *s.* 1. depravazione 2. demoralizzazione.

to demoralize *vt.* 1. depravare 2. demoralizzare.

to demur *vi.* titubare, esitare.

demure *agg.* riservato, pudico.

demureness *s.* riservatezza, pudore.

den *s.* tana.

to denationalize *vt.* snazionalizzare.

to denature *vt.* denaturare.

deniable *agg.* negabile.

denial *s.* rifiuto || *self-* —, abnegazione.

to denigrate *vt.* denigrare.

denigration *s.* denigrazione.

denigrator *s.* denigratore.

to denominate *vt.* denominare.

denomination *s.* 1. denominazione 2. setta 3. valore (*di monete*).

denominational *agg.* confessionale.

denominative *agg.* denominativo.

denominator *s.* denominatore.

denotation *s.* 1. indicazione 2. significato.

to denote *vt.* denotare, indicare.

to denounce *vt.* denunciare.

dense *agg.* 1. denso 2. opaco 3. stupido.

density *s.* 1. densità 2. opacità 3.

stupidità.

dent *s.* incavo, tacca.

dental *agg. e s.* dentale.

dentary *agg.* dentario.

dentine *s.* dentina.

dentist *s.* dentista.

dentistry *s.* odontoiatria.

dentition *s.* dentizione.

denture *s.* dentiera.

denudation *s.* denudazione.

to denude *vt.* denudare.

denunciation *s.* denunzia.

to deny *vt.* negare, rifiutare.

deodorant *agg. e s.* deodorante.

to deodorize *vt.* deodorare.

deontology *s.* deontologia.

deoxidization *s.* disossidazione.

to deoxidize *vt.* disossidare.

to depart *vi.* partire, allontanarsi.

department *s.* 1. reparto 2. (*amer.*) ministero || *— store*, grande magazzino.

departure *s.* 1. partenza 2. allontanamento.

to depend *vi.* 1. dipendere: *it all depends on circumstances*, tutto dipende dalle circostanze 2. contare: *— on so.*, contare su qu.

dependable *agg.* fidato.

dependant *agg. e s.* dipendente.

dependence *s.* 1. dipendenza 2. fiducia.

dependency *s.* territorio dipendente.

dependent *agg.* dipendente.

to depict *vt.* dipingere.

to depilate *vt.* depilare.

depilatory *agg. e s.* depilatorio.

to deplete *vt.* 1. vuotare 2. esaurire.

depletion *s.* esaurimento.

deplorable *agg.* deplorevole.

to deplore *vt.* deplorare.

to deploy *vt.* schierare, spiegare. ♦ to deploy *vi.* schierarsi (*di truppe ecc.*).

to depone *vt.* deporre (*in un processo*).

deponent *s.* testimone.

to depopulate *vt.* spopolare.

to deport *vt.* deportare || *to — oneself*, comportarsi.

deportation *s.* deportazione.

deportment *s.* atteggiamento.

deposal *s.* deposizione.

to depose *vt. e vi.* deporre.

deposit *s.* deposito.

to deposit *vt.* depositare.

deposition *s.* 1. deposizione 2. deposito.

depositor *s.* depositante.

depot *s.* deposito.

to deprave *vt.* depravare.

depravity *s.* depravazione.

deprecable *agg.* deprecabile.

to deprecate *vt.* disapprovare.

deprecation *s.* disapprovazione.

deprecative, deprecatory *agg.* disapprovante.

to depreciate *vt.* svalutare. ♦ **to depreciate** *vi.* svalutarsi.

depreciation *s.* 1. svalutazione 2. ammortamento: — *charge*, quota d'ammortamento.

depreciative, depreciatory *agg.* spregiativo.

depredation *s.* saccheggio.

depredatory *agg.* predatorio.

to depress *vt.* 1. deprimere 2. abbassare.

depression *s.* 1. depressione 2. (*econ.*) crisi.

depressor *s.* depressore.

deprivation *s.* privazione.

to deprive *vt.* privare.

depth *s.* 1. profondità 2. (*mar.*) fondale.

to depurate *vt.* depurare. ♦ **to depurate** *vi.* depurarsi.

depuration *s.* depurazione.

depurative *agg. e s.* depurativo.

depurator *s.* depuratore.

deputation *s.* delega.

to depute *vt.* deputare.

deputy *s.* 1. deputato 2. sostituto.

derailment *s.* deragliamento.

to derange *vt.* sconvolgere.

derangement *s.* sconvolgimento.

deratization *s.* derattizzazione.

to deride *vt.* deridere.

derision *s.* 1. derisione 2. zimbello.

derisive, derisory *agg.* derisorio.

derivable *agg.* derivabile.

derivation *s.* derivazione.

derivative *agg. e s.* derivato.

derivatively *avv.* per derivazione.

to derive *vt. e vi.* derivare.

derm *s.* derma.

dermatologist *s.* dermatologo.

dermatology *s.* dermatologia.

to derogate *vi.* derogare.

derogation *s.* deroga.

derogatory *agg.* derogatorio.

derrick *s.* 1. argano 2. torre di trivellazione.

descant *s.* 1. melodia 2. dissertazione.

to descend *vt. e vi.* (di)scendere ‖

to — upon so., aggredire qu.

descendance *s.* discendenza.

descendant *s.* discendente.

descent *s.* 1. discesa 2. incursione 3. lignaggio 4. caduta.

describable *agg.* descrivibile.

to describe *vt.* descrivere.

description *s.* descrizione.

descriptive *agg.* descrittivo.

to descry *vt.* scoprire.

to desecrate *vt.* profanare.

desert[1] *agg.* deserto. ♦ **desert** *s.* deserto.

desert[2] *s.* 1. merito 2. compenso.

to desert *vt.* abbandonare. ♦ **to desert** *vi.* disertare.

deserted *agg.* deserto.

deserter *s.* disertore.

desertion *s.* 1. abbandono 2. diserzione.

to deserve *vt.* meritare.

deservedly *avv.* meritatamente.

deserving *agg.* meritevole.

design *s.* disegno.

to design *vt.* 1. destinare 2. progettare 3. disegnare.

designate *agg.* designato.

to designate *vt.* 1. designare 2. indicare.

designation *s.* designazione.

designer *s.* disegnatore.

designing *agg.* astuto. ♦ **designing** *s.* 1. disegno 2. complotto.

desirable *agg.* desiderabile.

desire *s.* desiderio.

to desire *vt.* 1. desiderare 2. domandare.

desirous *agg.* desideroso.

to desist *vi.* desistere.

desk *s.* 1. scrivania 2. cassa ‖ *school- master's —*, cattedra (*di insegnante*).

desolate *agg.* desolato.

to desolate *vt.* 1. affliggere 2. devastare.

desolation *s.* desolazione.

despair *s.* disperazione.

to despair *vi.* disperare.

despairing *agg.* disperato.

desperate *agg.* disperato.

despicable *agg.* spregevole.

despicableness *s.* spregevolezza.

despisable *agg.* spregevole.

to despise *vt.* disprezzare.

despite *prep.* malgrado.

despiteful *agg.* maligno, dispettoso.

despondency *s.* scoraggiamento.

despondent *agg.* scoraggiato.

despot *s.* despota.

despotic(al) *agg.* dispotico.
despotism *s.* dispotismo.
destination *s.* destinazione.
to **destine** *vt.* destinare.
destiny *s.* destino.
destitute *agg.* 1. povero 2. privo.
destitution *s.* 1. povertà 2. privazione.
to **destroy** *vt.* distruggere.
destroyable *agg.* distruggibile.
destroyer *s.* 1. distruttore 2. cacciatorpediniere.
destroying *agg.* distruttore.
destruction *s.* distruzione, rovina.
destructive *agg.* distruttivo.
destructor *s.* distruttore.
desuetude *s.* disuso.
desultory *agg.* saltuario.
to **detach** *vt.* distaccare.
detachable *agg.* staccabile.
detached *agg.* 1. distaccato 2. isolato.
detachment *s.* 1. distacco 2. (*mil.*) distaccamento.
detail *s.* 1. dettaglio, particolare 2. pattuglia.
to **detail** *vt.* 1. dettagliare 2. (*mil.*) distaccare (*una pattuglia*).
to **detain** *vt.* 1. detenere 2. trattenere.
to **detect** *vt.* scoprire.
detectable *agg.* scopribile.
detection *s.* scoperta.
detective *s.* investigatore || — *novel*, romanzo poliziesco.
detector *s.* (*radio*) rivelatore.
detent *s.* (*mecc.*) arpione.
detention *s.* 1. detenzione 2. ritardo forzato.
to **deter** *vt.* trattenere.
to **deterge** *vt.* detergere.
detergent *agg.* e *s.* detergente, detersivo.
to **deteriorate** *vt.* deteriorare. ◆ to **deteriorate** *vi.* deteriorarsi.
deterioration *s.* deterioramento.
determinable *agg.* determinabile.
determinant *s.* causa determinante.
determinate *agg.* determinato.
determination *s.* determinazione.
determinative *agg.* determinativo.
to **determine** *vt.* determinare, decidere. ◆ to **determine** *vi.* risolversi || *to — on*, fissarsi su.
determined *agg.* deciso.
determinism *s.* determinismo.
determinist *agg.* e *s.* determinista.
deterrent *agg.* e *s.* (*neol.*) deterrente.

detersive *agg.* e *s.* detersivo.
to **detest** *vt.* detestare.
detestable *agg.* detestabile.
detestation *s.* 1. odio 2. esecrazione.
dethronement *s.* deposizione (*dal trono*).
to **detonate** *vt.* e *vi.* esplodere.
detonator *s.* detonatore.
detour *s.* deviazione, giravolta.
to **detract** *vt.* e *vi.* diminuire.
detraction *s.* detrazione.
detractor *s.* detrattore.
detriment *s.* detrimento.
detrimental *agg.* dannoso.
to **devaluate** *vt.* svalutare.
devaluation *s.* svalutazione.
to **devastate** *vt.* devastare.
devastation *s.* devastazione.
to **develop** *vt.* sviluppare. ◆ to **develop** *vi.* svilupparsi.
developer *s.* sviluppatore.
development *s.* sviluppo.
to **deviate** *vt.* e *vi.* deviare.
deviation *s.* deviazione.
deviationism *s.* deviazionismo.
device *s.* 1. trovata 2. dispositivo. ◆ **devices** *s. pl.* capriccio, inclinazione (*sing.*).
devil *s.* diavolo.
devilish *agg.* diabolico.
devious *agg.* 1. remoto 2. errante.
to **devise** *vt.* 1. escogitare 2. lasciare in eredità.
deviser *s.* inventore.
devising *s.* invenzione.
devoid *agg.* privo.
devolution *s.* 1. trasmissione (*di beni*) 2. degenerazione.
to **devolve** *vt.* trasmettere. ◆ to **devolve** *vi.* trasferirsi.
to **devote** *vt.* dedicare.
devoted *agg.* 1. devoto 2. votato.
devotion *s.* devozione.
devotional *agg.* devoto.
to **devour** *vt.* divorare.
devourer *s.* divoratore.
devout *agg.* devoto, pio, religioso.
dew *s.* rugiada.
dewy *agg.* rugiadoso.
dexterity *s.* destrezza.
dexterous *agg.* destro.
dextrin(e) *s.* destrina.
diabetes *s.* diabete.
diabetic *agg.* e *s.* diabetico.
diabolic(al) *agg.* diabolico.
diadem *s.* diadema.
to **diagnose** *vt.* diagnosticare.
diagnosis *s.* (*pl.* -es) diagnosi.

diagnostic *agg.* diagnostico.
diagonal *agg.* e *s.* diagonale.
diagram *s.* diagramma.
dial *s.* quadrante.
to dial *vt.* comporre (*un numero telefonico*) || *to — so.,* telefonare a qu.
dialect *s.* dialetto.
dialectal *agg.* dialettale.
dialectic(al) *agg.* dialettico.
dialectics *s.* dialettica.
dialogue *s.* dialogo.
to dialogue *vt.* e *vi.* dialogare.
diameter *s.* diametro.
diametrically *avv.* diametralmente.
diamond *s.* 1. diamante 2. losanga.
diaper *s.* 1. arabesco 2. pannolino.
diaphanous *agg.* diafano.
diaphragm *s.* diaframma.
diapositive *s.* diapositiva.
diarchy *s.* diarchia.
diarist *s.* diarista.
diarrhoea *s.* diarrea.
diary *s.* diario.
diatribe *s.* diatriba.
dice V. *die.*
to dice *vt.* 1. giocare ai dadi 2. tagliare a dadi 3. quadrettare.
dictaphone *s.* dittafono.
dictate *s.* dettame.
to dictate *vt.* e *vi.* dettare.
dictation *s.* 1. dettato 2. dettame.
dictator *s.* dittatore.
dictatorial *agg.* dittatoriale.
dictatorship *s.* dittatura.
diction *s.* 1. stile 2. dizione.
dictionary *s.* dizionario.
dictograph *s.* dittografo.
did V. *to do.*
didactic *agg.* didattico.
didactics *s.* didattica.
die *s.* (*pl.* dice) dado.
to die *vi.* morire || *to — away,* svanire; *to — out,* estinguersi.
dielectric *agg.* e *s.* dielettrico.
diet *s.* dieta.
to diet *vt.* mettere a dieta. ♦ **to diet** *vi.* essere a dieta.
dietarian *s.* chi sta a dieta.
dietary *agg.* dietetico. ♦ **dietary** *s.* dieta.
dietetic(al) *agg.* dietetico.
differ *vi.* differire.
difference *s.* 1. differenza 2. divergenza.
different *agg.* differente.
differential *agg.* e *s.* differenziale.
to differentiate *vt.* differenziare. ♦ **to differentiate** *vi.* differen-

ziarsi.
differentiation *s.* differenziazione.
differently *avv.* differentemente.
differing *agg.* 1. differente, discordante.
difficult *agg.* difficile.
difficulty *s.* difficoltà.
diffidence *s.* timidezza.
diffident *agg.* esitante.
diffraction *s.* difrazione.
diffuse *agg.* diffuso.
to diffuse *vt.* diffondere. ♦ **to diffuse** *vi.* diffondersi.
diffusedly, diffusely *avv.* 1. diffusamente 2. ovunque.
diffuser *s.* (*foto*) diffusore.
diffusion *s.* 1. diffusione 2. prolissità.
diffusive *agg.* 1. diffusivo 2. prolisso.
diffusor *s.* diffusore.
to dig (dug, dug) *vt.* vangare, scavare || *to — in,* affondare; *to — out,* estrarre.
digest *s.* 1. sommario 2. condensato.
to digest *vt.* classificare, condensare, redigere. ♦ **to digest** *vt.* e *vi.* digerire.
digestibility *s.* digeribilità.
digestible *agg.* digeribile.
digestion *s.* digestione.
digestive *agg.* e *s.* digestivo.
digger *s.* 1. zappatore 2. scavatrice.
digging *s.* 1. scavo 2. miniera. ♦ **diggings** *s. pl.* (*gergo*) alloggio (*sing.*).
digital *agg.* digitale.
dignified *agg.* dignitoso.
to dignify *vt.* elevare, nobilitare.
dignitary *s.* dignitario.
dignity *s.* 1. dignità 2. dignitario.
digression *s.* digressione.
digressive *agg.* digressivo.
dike *s.* diga.
to dike *vt.* arginare.
to dilapidate *vt.* dilapidare. ♦ **to dilapidate** *vi.* andare in rovina.
dilatability *s.* dilatabilità.
dilatable *agg.* dilatabile.
dilatation *s.* dilatazione.
to dilate *vt.* dilatare. ♦ **to dilate** *vi.* dilatarsi.
dilatory *agg.* 1. dilatorio 2. lento.
diligence *s.* diligenza.
diligent *agg.* diligente.
diluent *agg.* e *s.* diluente.
to dilute *vt.* diluire.
dilution *s.* 1. diluzione 2. sostanza

diluita.

diluvial *agg.* diluviale.

dim *agg.* **1.** debole **2.** appannato **3.** oscuro.

to **dim** *vt.* **1.** indebolire **2.** oscurare. ♦ to **dim** *vi.* **1.** indebolirsi **2.** oscurarsi.

dime *s.* quarto di dollaro.

dimension *s.* dimensione.

dimeter *s.* dimetro.

to **diminish** *vt.* e *vi.* diminuire.

diminishable *agg.* diminuibile.

diminution *s.* diminuzione.

diminutive *agg.* minuscolo. ♦ **diminutive** *s.* diminutivo.

dimissory *agg.* dimissorio.

dimly *avv.* **1.** debolmente **2.** oscuramente.

dimness *s.* **1.** debolezza **2.** offuscamento (*di vista*).

dimple *s.* fossetta.

din *s.* baccano.

to **din** *vt.* e *vi.* rintronare.

to **dine** *vi.* pranzare.

diner *s.* commensale.

to **ding** *vt.* e *vi.* suonare, scampanellare.

dingy *agg.* scuro, sporco.

dining *s.* il pranzare || - -room, sala da pranzo.

dinner *s.* pranzo || - -wagon, carrello (*per i pasti*) || - -car, vagone ristorante.

dinosaur *s.* dinosauro.

dint *s.* tacca || by - of, a forza di.

diocesan *agg.* e *s.* diocesano.

diocese *s.* diocesi.

diode *s.* diodo.

Dionysiac, Dionysian *agg.* dionisiaco.

diopter *s.* diottria.

dioptric *agg.* diottrico.

dioxid(e) *s.* biossido.

dip *s.* **1.** bagno **2.** inclinazione **3.** (*aer.*) picchiata **4.** tuffo.

to **dip** *vt.* **1.** immergere **2.** abbassare. ♦ to **dip** *vi.* **1.** immergersi **2.** abbassarsi **3.** tuffarsi.

diphtheria *s.* difterite.

diphtheric *agg.* difterico.

diphthong *s.* dittongo.

diplomacy *s.* diplomazia.

diplomat *s.* diplomatico.

diplomatic *agg.* diplomatico.

diplomatically *avv.* diplomaticamente.

diplomatics *s.* diplomazia.

diplomatist *s.* diplomatico.

dipody *s.* dipodia.

dipper *s.* **1.** tuffatore **2.** mestolo || the Big -, l'Orsa Maggiore.

dipsomaniac *s.* dipsomane.

dipteral *agg.* dittero.

diptych *s.* dittico.

dire *agg.* terribile, orrendo.

direct *agg.* diretto.

to **direct** *vt.* **1.** dirigere **2.** ordinare.

direction *s.* **1.** direzione **2.** indicazione.

directional *agg.* direzionale.

directive *agg.* direttivo. ♦ **directive** *s.* direttiva.

directly *avv.* **1.** direttamente **2.** subito.

director *s.* **1.** direttore **2.** regista.

directorial *agg.* direttivo.

directory *agg.* direttivo. ♦ **directory** *s.* **1.** (*tel.*) guida **2.** (*amer.*) consiglio di amministrazione.

direful *agg.* orrendo.

dirge *s.* canto funebre.

diriment *agg.* dirimento.

dirt *s.* sporcizia.

dirtiness *s.* sozzura.

dirty *agg.* **1.** sporco **2.** brutto **3.** sboccato.

to **dirty** *vt.* sporcare. ♦ to **dirty** *vi.* sporcarsi.

disability *s.* **1.** incapacità **2.** invalidità.

to **disable** *vt.* rendere incapace, inabile.

to **disabuse** *vt.* disingannare.

to **disaccustom** *vt.* disabituare.

disadvantage *s.* svantaggio.

disadvantageous *agg.* svantaggioso.

to **disagree** *vi.* dissentire.

disagreeable *agg.* sgradevole.

disagreeableness *s.* sgradevolezza.

disagreement *s.* dissenso.

to **disappear** *vi.* scomparire.

disappearance *s.* sparizione.

to **disappoint** *vt.* deludere.

disappointingly *avv.* in modo deludente.

disappointment *s.* delusione.

disapprobation, disapproval *s.* disapprovazione.

to **disapprove** *vt.* e *vi.* disapprovare.

disapprovingly *avv.* con disapprovazione.

to **disarm** *vt.* e *vi.* disarmare.

disarmament *s.* disarmo.

to **disarrange** *vt.* scompigliare.

disarrangement *s.* scompiglio.

disarray *s.* scompiglio, confusione.

to **disassemble** *vt.* smontare.
disassembling *s.* smontaggio.
disaster *s.* disastro.
disastrous *agg.* disastroso.
to **disavow** *vt.* ripudiare.
to **disband** *vt.* sciogliere. ♦ to **disband** *vi.* sbandarsi.
disbelief *s.* incredulità.
to **disbelieve** *vt. e vi.* non credere.
disbeliever *s.* incredulo.
disbursement *s.* pagamento.
to **discard** *vt.* scartare.
to **discern** *vt.* discernere.
discernible *agg.* visibile.
discernment *s.* discernimento.
discharge *s.* 1. scarico 2. scarica 3. congedo 4. assoluzione 5. liberazione 6. pagamento.
to **discharge** *vt.* 1. scaricare 2. congedare 3. assolvere 4. liberare. ♦ to **discharge** *vi.* scaricarsi.
disciple *s.* discepolo.
disciplinable *agg.* disciplinabile.
disciplinary *agg.* disciplinare.
discipline *s.* disciplina.
to **disclaim** *vt.* rifiutare, declinare *(responsabilità)*.
disclaimer *s.* rinuncia, rifiuto.
to **disclose** *vt.* svelare.
disclosure *s.* rivelazione.
discold *agg. e s.* discolo.
to **discolour** *vt.* scolorire. ♦ to **discolour** *vi.* scolorirsi.
discolouration *s.* scoloramento.
to **discomfit** *vt.* 1. sconfiggere 2. disorientare.
to **discomfort** *vt.* mettere a disagio.
to **discompose** *vt.* agitare.
to **disconcert** *vt.* turbare.
to **disconnect** *vt.* separare, disunire.
disconnected *agg.* 1. sconnesso 2. disinnestato.
disconnectedness *s.* sconnessione.
disconsolate *agg.* sconsolato.
discontent *s.* scontento.
to **discontinue** *vt. e vi.* cessare.
discontinuity *s.* discontinuità.
discontinuous *agg.* discontinuo.
discord *s.* 1. discordia, dissenso 2. *(mus.)* dissonanza.
discordance *s.* 1. disaccordo 2. discordanza *(di suoni)*.
discordant *agg.* discorde.
discordantly *avv.* in disaccordo.
discount *s.* sconto || at a —, sottocosto.
to **discount** *vt.* 1. scontare 2. tenere in poco conto.

discountable *agg.* 1. scontabile 2. poco attendibile.
to **discourage** *vt.* scoraggiare.
discouragement *s.* scoraggiamento.
to **discover** *vt.* scoprire.
discoverer *s.* scopritore.
discovery *s.* scoperta.
discredit *s.* 1. discredito 2. dubbio.
to **discredit** *vt.* 1. screditare 2. mettere in dubbio.
discreditable *agg.* vergognoso, infamante.
discreet *agg.* prudente, discreto.
discrepancy *s.* disaccordo.
discrete *agg.* separato, distinto.
discretion *s.* 1. discrezione 2. saggezza.
discretionary *agg.* discrezionale.
discriminate *agg.* discriminato.
to **discriminate** *vt. e vi.* discriminare.
discriminating *agg.* 1. sagace 2. discriminante.
discrimination *s.* 1. discriminazione 2. discernimento.
discursive *agg.* divagante.
discus *s.* disco || — *-thrower*, discobolo.
to **discuss** *vt.* discutere.
discussion *s.* discussione.
disdain *s.* sdegno.
to **disdain** *vt.* disdegnare.
disdainful *agg.* sdegnoso.
disease *s.* malattia.
to **disembark** *vt. e vi.* sbarcare.
to **disembarrass** *vt.* sbarazzare.
to **disembody** *vt.* 1. disincarnare 2. congedare.
to **disembowel** *vt.* sventrare.
disembowelment *s.* sventramento.
to **disenchant** *vt.* disincantare.
disenchantment *s.* disincanto.
to **disengage** *vt.* 1. disimpegnare 2. disinnestare. ♦ to **disengage** *vi.* liberarsi.
disengagement *s.* 1. liberazione 2. disinnesto.
to **disentangle** *vt.* 1. districare. ♦ to **disentangle** *vi.* districarsi.
disentanglement *s.* districamento.
to **disesteem** *vt.* disistima.
to **disesteem** *vt.* disprezzare.
disfavour *s.* 1. disgrazia 2. disapprovazione.
to **disfigure** *vt.* sfigurare.
disfigurement *s.* deturpamento.
to **disfranchise** *vt.* privare dei diritti *(civili o di voto)*.
to **disgorge** *vt.* 1. emettere 2. vomi-

tare (*anche fig.*).

disgrace *s.* 1. vergogna 2. disgrazia.

to disgrace *vt.* disonorare.

disgraceful *agg.* vergognoso.

disgregation *s.* disgregazione.

disguise *s.* travestimento || *in* —, travestito, camuffato.

to disguise *vt.* mascherare.

disgust *s.* disgusto.

to disgust *vt.* disgustare.

disgustedly *avv.* con disgusto.

disgustful, disgusting *agg.* disgustoso.

dish *s.* 1. piatto 2. vivanda || —-*washer*, lavapiatti.

to dish *vt.* servire || *to — up*, servire in tavola.

to disharmonize *vt.* disarmonizzare.

to dishearten *vt.* scoraggiare.

disheartenment *s.* scoraggiamento.

to dishevel *vt.* arruffare.

dishonest *agg.* disonesto.

dishonesty *s.* disonestà.

dishonour *s.* 1. disonore 2. mancato pagamento.

to dishonour · *vt.* 1. disonorare 2. rifiutare di pagare.

dishonourable *agg.* disonorevole.

dishonourableness *s.* disonorabilità.

disillusion(ment) *s.* disillusione

to disinfect *vt.* disinfettare.

disinfectant *s.* disinfettante.

disinfection *s.* disinfezione.

to disinfest *vt.* disinfestare.

disinfestation *s.* disinfestazione.

to disinherit *vt.* diseredare.

to disintegrate *vt.* disintegrare. ◆ **to disintegrate** *vi.* disintegrarsi.

disintegration *s.* disintegrazione.

disintegrator *s.* disintegratore.

to disinter *vt.* dissotterrare.

disinterested *agg.* disinteressato.

disinterment *s.* dissotterramento.

to disjoin *vt.* disgiungere. ◆ **to disjoin** *vi.* disgiungersi.

to disjoint *vt.* 1. disgregare 2. disarticolare. ◆ **to disjoint** *vi.* disgregarsi.

disjunction *s.* separazione.

disjunctive *agg.* disgiuntivo.

disjunctively *avv.* disgiuntamente.

disk *s.* disco.

dislike *s.* avversione.

to dislike *vt.* detestare, provar avversione per.

to dislocate *vt.* 1. spostare 2. slogare 3. disorganizzare.

dislocation *s.* 1. dislocazione 2. slogatura 3. disorganizzazione.

to dislodge *vt.* sloggiare.

disloyal *agg.* sleale.

disloyalty *s.* slealtà.

dismal *agg.* tetro.

to dismantle *vt.* smantellare.

dismantlement *s.* smantellamento.

to dismast *vt.* (*mar.*) disalberare.

dismay *s.* costernazione.

to dismay *vt.* costernare.

to dismember *vt.* smembrare.

dismemberment *s.* smembramento.

to dismiss *vt.* 1. congedare 2. licenziare 3. bandire.

dismissal *s.* 1. congedo 2. licenziamento 3. destituzione 4. rigetto.

to dismount *vt.* e *vi.* smontare.

disobedience *s.* disubbidienza.

disobedient *agg.* disubbidiente.

to disobey *vt.* disubbidire.

to disoblige *vt.* essere scortese con.

disobliging *agg.* scortese.

disorder *s.* 1. disordine 2. disturbo.

to disorder *vt.* 1. scompigliare 2. disturbare.

disorderly *agg.* 1. disordinato 2. turbolento.

disorganization *s.* disorganizzazione.

to disorganize *vt.* disorganizzare.

to disorient(ate) *vt.* disorientare.

disorientation *s.* disorientamento.

to disown *vt.* rinnegare.

disowning *s.* rinnegamento.

to disparage *vt.* 1. deprezzare 2. screditare.

disparagement *s.* 1. deprezzamento 2. denigrazione.

disparaging *agg.* 1. sprezzante 2. denigratorio.

disparate *agg.* disparato.

disparity *s.* disparità.

dispassionate *agg.* spassionato.

to dispatch *vt.* 1. spedizione 2. dispaccio 3. disbrigo 4. celerità.

to dispatch *vt.* 1. spedire 2. sbrigare.

to dispel *vt.* dissipare.

dispensary *s.* dispensario.

dispensation *s.* 1. (*eccl.*) dispensa 2. distribuzione 3. beneficio.

to dispense *vt.* dispensare. ◆ **to dispense** *vi.* fare a meno di: *to — with so.*, fare a meno di qu.

dispersal *s.* dispersione.

to disperse *vt.* disperdere. ◆ **to disperse** *vi.* disperdersi.

dispersion *s.* dispersione.

dispersive *agg.* dispersivo.

dispirited *agg.* depresso.

to **displace** *vt.* 1. spostare 2. destituire.

displacement *s.* 1. spostamento 2. sostituzione 3. (*mar.*) dislocamento.

display *s.* mostra, esibizione.

to **display** *vt.* mostrare, esporre.

to **displease** *vt.* dispiacere.

displeasing *agg.* spiacevole.

displeasure *s.* dispiacere.

disposal *s.* 1. disposizione 2. cessione.

to **dispose** *vt.* e *vi.* disporre || *to — of*, disfarsi di, smerciare.

disposition *s.* 1. disposizione 2. indole.

to **dispossess** *vt.* spogliare.

dispossession *s.* 1. spoliazione 2. (*giur.*) esproprio.

disproportion *s.* sproporzione.

disproportionate, disproportioned *agg.* sproporzionato.

to **disprove** *vt.* 1. confutare 2. dimostrare la falsità di.

disputable *agg.* discutibile.

dispute *s.* controversia, disputa.

to **dispute** *vt.* 1. disputare 2. contestare.

disqualification *s.* 1. incapacità 2. (*giur.*) interdizione 3. squalifica.

to **disqualify** *vt.* 1. rendere incapace 2. (*giur.*) interdire 3. squalificare.

disquieting *agg.* inquietante.

disquisition *s.* 1. disquisizione 2. inchiesta.

to **disregard** *s.* noncuranza.

to **disregard** *vt.* ignorare.

disreputable *agg.* 1. sconveniente 2. screditato.

disreputably *avv.* disonorevolmente.

disrepute *s.* discredito.

disrespectful *agg.* irrispettoso.

to **disrobe** *vt.* svestire. ♦ to **disrobe** *vi.* svestirsi.

disruption *s.* rottura.

disruptive *agg.* 1. che sembra 2. dirompente.

dissatisfaction *s.* insoddisfazione.

dissatisfactory *agg.* insoddisfacente.

dissatisfied *agg.* scontento.

to **dissatisfy** *vt.* scontentare.

to **dissect** *vt.* sezionare.

dissection *s.* 1. sezionamento 2. parte sezionata.

to **dissemble** *vt.* e *vi.* dissimulare,
ignorare.

dissembling *s.* dissimulazione. ♦ **dissembling** *agg.* ipocrita.

dissemblingly *avv.* ingannevolmente.

to **disseminate** *vt.* (dis)seminare.

dissemination *s.* disseminazione.

disseminator *s.* propagatore.

dissension *s.* divergenza.

dissent *s.* 1. dissenso 2. (*relig.*) separazione, scisma.

to **dissent** *vi.* dissentire.

dissenter *s.* dissidente.

dissenting *agg.* dissenziente.

to **dissertate** *vi.* dissertare.

dissertation *s.* dissertazione.

dissertator *s.* dissertatore.

disservice *s.* cattivo servizio.

to **dissever** *vt.* scindere. ♦ to **dissever** *vi.* scindersi.

dissidence *s.* dissidio.

dissident *agg.* e *s.* dissidente.

dissimilar *agg.* dissimile.

dissimilarity *s.* dissomiglianza.

dissimilation *s.* dissimilazione.

to **dissimulate** *vt.* e *vi.* dissimulare.

dissimulation *s.* dissimulazione.

dissimulator *s.* dissimulatore.

to **dissipate** *vt.* dissipare. ♦ to **dissipate** *vi.* dissiparsi.

dissipation *s.* dissipazione.

dissociable *agg.* 1. dissociabile 2. riservato.

to **dissociate** *vt.* dissociare. ♦ to **dissociate** *vi.* dissociarsi.

dissociation *s.* 1. dissociazione 2. sdoppiamento (*della personalità*).

dissolubility *s.* dissolubilità.

dissoluble *agg.* dissolubile.

dissolute *agg.* dissoluto.

dissoluteness *s.* dissolutezza.

dissolution *s.* dissoluzione.

to **dissolve** *vt.* dissolvere. ♦ to **dissolve** *vi.* dissolversi.

dissolvent *agg.* e *s.* dissolvente.

dissonance *s.* dissonanza.

dissonant *agg.* dissonante.

to **dissuade** *vt.* dissuadere.

dissuasion *s.* dissuasione.

dissyllabic *agg.* bisillabico.

dissyllable *s.* bisillabo.

dissymmetry *s.* asimmetria.

distaff *s.* conocchia.

distance *s.* distanza || *long- — call*, telefonata interurbana; *at a —*, da lontano.

distant *agg.* 1. lontano 2. riservato.

distantly *avv.* (da) lontano.

distaste *s.* ripugnanza.

distasteful *agg.* repellente.
distemper[1] *s.* **1.** turbamento fisico **2.** cimurro **3.** tumulto.
distemper[2] *s.* tempera.
to distend *vt.* distendere. ♦ **to distend** *vi.* distendersi.
to distil(l) *vt.* e *vi.* (di)stillare.
distillate *s.* distillato.
distillation *s.* distillazione.
distiller *s.* distillatore.
distillery *s.* distilleria.
distinct *agg.* distinto.
distinction *s.* distinzione.
distinctive *agg.* distintivo.
to distinguish *vt.* e *vi.* distinguere.
distinguished *agg.* **1.** distinto **2.** illustre.
to distort *vt.* distorcere.
distortion *s.* distorsione.
to distract *vt.* **1.** distrarre **2.** turbare, far impazzire.
distraction *s.* **1.** distrazione **2.** follia: *to love to —,* amare alla follia.
to distrain *vi.* sequestrare.
distrait *agg.* distratto, smarrito.
distraught *agg.* **1.** folle **2.** sconvolto.
distress *s.* **1.** angoscia **2.** pericolo **3.** sequestro.
to distress *vt.* **1.** affliggere **2.** sequestrare.
distressful *agg.* penoso.
distributable *agg.* distribuibile.
to distribute *vt.* distribuire.
distribution *s.* distribuzione.
distributive *agg.* distributivo.
distributor *s.* distributore.
district *s.* distretto.
distrust *s.* diffidenza.
to distrust *vt.* diffidare di.
distrustful *agg.* diffidente.
to disturb *vt.* **1.** disturbare **2.** turbare.
disturbance *s.* agitazione.
disturber *s.* disturbatore.
disunion *s.* separazione.
to disunite *vt.* disunire. ♦ **to disunite** *vi.* separarsi.
disunited *agg.* disunito.
disuse *s.* disuso.
disused *agg.* disusato.
ditch *s.* fosso ‖ *to die in the last —.* resistere ad oltranza.
to ditch *vi.* scavare fossi.
dithyramb *s.* ditirambo.
dithyrambic *agg.* ditirambico.
ditty *s.* **1.** canzone **2.** poemetto.
diuretic *agg.* e *s.* diuretico.
diurnal *agg.* **1.** diurno **2.** quotidiano.

diuturnal *agg.* diuturno.
diuturnity *s.* diuturnità.
divan *s.* divano.
dive *s.* **1.** tuffo **2.** (*aer.*) picchiata.
to dive *vi.* **1.** tuffarsi **2.** (*aer.*) lanciarsi in picchiata.
diver *s.* **1.** tuffatore **2.** palombaro.
to diverge *vi.* divergere.
divergence *s.* divergenza.
divergent *agg.* divergente.
diverse *agg.* **1.** diverso **2.** mutevole.
to diversify *vt.* rendere diverso.
diversion *s.* **1.** diversione **2.** passatempo.
diversity *s.* diversità.
to divert *vt.* **1.** deviare **2.** divertire.
to divest *vt.* spogliare.
to divide *vt.* dividere. ♦ **to divide** *vi.* dividersi.
dividend *s.* dividendo.
dividing *s.* divisione.
divination *s.* divinazione.
divinatory *agg.* divinatorio.
divine *agg.* divino. ♦ **divine** *s.* (*eccl.*) teologo.
to divine *vt.* e *vi.* predire.
diviner *s.* indovino ‖ *water —,* rabdomante.
diving *s.* tuffo ‖ *— -bell,* campana subacquea; *— -board,* trampolino.
divining *s.* divinazione.
divinity *s.* **1.** divinità **2.** teologia.
divisibility *s.* divisibilità.
divisible *agg.* divisibile.
division *s.* divisione.
divisional *agg.* di divisione.
divisor *s.* divisore.
divorce *s.* divorzio.
to divorce *vt.* divorziare.
divulgation *s.* divulgazione.
to divulge *vt.* divulgare.
divulger *s.* divulgatore.
dizzily *avv.* vertiginosamente.
dizziness *s.* vertigine.
dizzy *agg.* **1.** vertiginoso **2.** preso da vertigine **3.** stordito.
to do (**did, done**) *vt.* e *vi.* **1.** (*v. aus. in frasi int., neg., int.-neg.*) *— you understand English?,* capisci l'inglese?; *I do not* (*I don't*), non capisco; *he does not* (*he doesn't*) *speak English,* non parla l'inglese **2.** (*uso enfatico*) *I do study!,* studio veramente! **3.** (*sostitutivo*) *he said he would come and he did,* disse che sarebbe venuto e venne **4.** fare (*in senso generale, astratto*) *what are you doing?,* che cosa stai facendo?; *to*

— one's duty, fare il proprio dovere 5. bastare: *that will do*, ciò
basta 6. addirsi, convenire: *this
house will do me*, questa casa mi
va bene || *to — without*, fare a
meno.

docile *agg.* docile.

docility *s.* docilità.

dock[1] *s.* bacino: *dry* —, bacino di
carenaggio || *— -master*, capitano
di porto; *wet* —, darsena.

dock[2] *s.* banco degli imputati (*in
tribunale*).

docker *s.* scaricatore.

docket *s.* 1. (*giur.*) estratto verbale
2. etichetta.

dockyard *s.* cantiere.

doctor *s.* dottore.

doctoral *agg.* dottorale.

doctorate *s.* dottorato.

doctrinaire *agg.* e *s.* dottrinario.

doctrinal *agg.* dottrinale.

doctrine *s.* dottrina.

document *s.* documento.

to document *vt.* documentare.

documentary *agg.* e *s.* documentario.

documentation *s.* documentazione.

to dodder *vi.* tremare, vacillare.

dodecagon *s.* dodecagono.

dodecahedron *s.* dodecaedro.

dodge *s.* 1. schivata 2. balzo.

to dodge *vt.* schivare. ◆ **to dodge**
vi. scansarsi.

doe *s.* femmina (*di daino, cervo ecc.*).

doer *s.* chi agisce, chi fa.

dog *s.* 1. cane 2. (*mecc.*) gancio ||
— -cart, calesse; *— -catcher*, accalappiacani; *— -days*, giorni di ca-
nicola; *— -ear*, orecchia (*a una
pagina*); *— -tired*, stanco morto.

to dog *vt.* inseguire.

dogged *agg.* ostinato.

doggerel *s.* filastrocca.

dogmatic(al) *agg.* dogmatico.

dogmatism *s.* dogmatismo.

doily *s.* tovagliolino.

doings *s. pl.* azioni, imprese.

dole *s.* 1. ripartizione 2. sussidio.

doleful *agg.* triste.

dolichocephalic *agg.* dolicocefalo.

doll *s.* bambola.

dollar *s.* dollaro.

dolly *s.* 1. bambola 2. (*cine*) carrello.

dolomitic *agg.* dolomitico.

dolphin *s.* 1. delfino 2. boa.

dolt *s.* stupido.

domain *s.* dominio.

dome *s.* cupola.

domestic *agg.* 1. domestico 2. nazionale. ◆ **domestic** *s.* domestico.

domicile *s.* domicilio.

domiciliary *agg.* domiciliare.

dominant *agg.* dominante.

to dominate *vt.* e *vi.* dominare.

domination *s.* dominazione.

domineering *agg.* dispotico.

Dominican *agg.* e *s.* domenicano.

dominion *s.* dominio, possedimento
(*di territorio*).

donation *s.* donazione.

donative *s.* dono.

done V. **to do** || *over* —, troppo
cotto; *under* —, poco cotto.

donjon *s.* torrione.

donkey *s.* asino.

donor *s.* donatore.

doodle *s.* ghirigoro.

doom *s.* 1. destino 2. giudizio.

to doom *vt.* condannare.

doomsday *s.* giudizio universale.

door *s.* porta, portiera || *— -keeper*,
portinaio; *— -post*, stipite; *—
-way*, soglia.

dope *s.* 1. vernice 2. stupefacente.

to dope *vt.* 1. verniciare 2. drogare.

doping *s.* drogaggio.

Doric *agg.* dorico.

dormer (window) *s.* abbaino.

dormitory *s.* dormitorio.

dormouse *s.* (*pl. dormice*) ghiro.

dorsal *agg.* dorsale.

dosage *s.* dosaggio.

to dose *vt.* 1. dosare 2. adulterare.

dosimeter *s.* dosatore.

dossal *s.* dossale.

dossier *s.* incartamento.

dot *s.* punto, puntino.

to dot *vt.* punteggiare.

dotage *s.* 1. rimbambimento 2. infatuazione.

dotal *agg.* dotale.

doting *agg.* 1. senile 2. infatuato.
◆ **doting** *s.* senilità.

double *agg.* doppio. ◆ **double** *s.*
1. doppio 2. (*cine*) controfigura.
◆ **double** *avv.* 1. doppiamente
2. in due.

to double *vt.* 1. raddoppiare 2. doppiare 3. piegare. ◆ **to double** *vi.*
1. raddoppiarsi 2. piegarsi.

double-dealing *s.* imbroglio.

doubleness *s.* doppiezza.

doubling *s.* raddoppiamento.

doubly *avv.* doppiamente.

doubt *s.* dubbio || *no* —, indubbia-
mente.

to doubt *vt.* e *vi.* dubitare.

doubtful *agg.* incerto, dubbio.

doubtfulness *s.* dubbiosità.

doubtless *agg.* indubbio. ◆ **doubtless** *avv.* indubbiamente.

dough *s.* pasta.

dove *s.* colomba || — *-cot(e)*, colombaia.

dowdy *agg.* sciatto.

dower *s.* dote.

down¹ *s.* 1. duna 2. collina.

down² *s.* 1. piumino 2. lanugine.

down³ *agg.* 1. diretto verso il basso 2. depresso.

down⁴ *avv.* (in) giù || — *with!*, abbasso: — *with the tyrant!*, abbasso il tiranno! ◆ **down** *prep.* giù per.

to down *vt.* abbattere, rovesciare.

downcast *agg.* abbattuto.

downfall *s.* rovescio.

downhearted *agg.* scoraggiato.

downhill *agg.* discendente, inclinato. ◆ **downhill** *avv.* in discesa.

downpour *s.* acquazzone.

downright *agg.* vero, sincero. ◆ **downright** *avv.* completamente.

downstairs *avv.* giù. ◆ **downstairs** *agg.* dabbasso. ◆ **downstairs** *s.* pianterreno.

downtrodden *agg.* calpestato, oppresso.

downward *agg.* in giù, discendente.

downward(s) *avv.* in giù.

downy¹ *agg.* ondulato.

downy² *agg.* 1. lanuginoso 2. morbido.

dowry *s.* dote.

dowser *s.* rabdomante.

doze *s.* sonnellino.

to doze *vi.* sonnecchiare.

dozen *s.* dozzina.

drab *s.* 1. sciattona 2. sgualdrina.

draff *s.* feccia.

draft *s.* 1. tiro 2. sorso 3. abbozzo 4. corrente d'aria 5. (*comm.*) tratta 6. (*mar.*) pescaggio.

to draft *vt.* 1. tirare 2. abbozzare.

drag *s.* 1. erpice 2. (*mar.*) draga 3. ostacolo.

to drag *vt.* 1. trascinare 2. dragare. ◆ **to drag** *vi.* trascinarsi || *to — on*, tirare in lungo.

to draggle *vt.* inzaccherare. ◆ **to draggle** *vi.* inzaccherarsi.

dragon *s.* drago || — *-fly*, libellula.

drain *s.* 1. canale, fogna, fuga.

to drain *vt.* prosciugare. ◆ **to drain** *vi.* 1. prosciugarsi 2. defluire.

drainage *s.* 1. fognatura 2. drenaggio.

draining *s.* 1. scolatura 2. drenaggio.

dram *s.* dramma (*unità di peso*).

drama *s.* dramma.

dramatic(al) *agg.* drammatico.

dramatics *s. pl.* produzioni drammatiche (*di dilettanti*).

dramatist *s.* drammaturgo.

to dramatize *vt. e vi.* drammatizzare.

dramaturgy *s.* drammaturgia.

drank V. *to drink.*

to drape *vt.* drappeggiare.

draper *s.* negoziante di tessuti.

drapery *s.* 1. tessuti 2. drappeggi.

drastic *agg.* drastico.

draught *s.* V. *draft.* ◆ **draughts** *s. pl.* gioco della dama (*sing.*).

draught-board *s.* scacchiera.

draw *s.* 1. tiro 2. estrazione 3. attrazione.

to draw (drew, drawn) *vt.* 1. tirare 2. attirare 3. disegnare 4. estrarre 5. (*comm.*) emettere || *to — up*, compilare. ◆ **to draw (drew, drawn)** *vi.* tirarsi || *to — on*, avvicinarsi; *to — in*, ritirarsi; *to — up*, fermarsi.

drawback *s.* ostacolo.

drawbridge *s.* ponte levatoio.

drawer *s.* 1. estrattore 2. disegnatore 3. cassetto.

drawers *s. pl.* mutande.

drawing *s.* 1. disegno 2. estrazione 3. attrazione || — *-pen*, tiralinee; — *-pin*, puntina da disegno.

drawing-room *s.* salotto.

to drawl *vt.* strascicare la voce.

drawn V. *to draw.*

dread *s.* spavento.

dreadful *agg.* terribile.

dreadnought *s.* 1. impavido 2. (*mar.*) corazzata.

dream *s.* sogno.

to dream (dreamt, dreamt) (*anche reg.*) *vt. e vi.* sognare.

dreamer *s.* sognatore.

dreamt V. *to dream.*

dreamless *agg.* senza sogni.

dreamy *agg.* 1. sognante 2. vago.

dreariness *s.* tristezza.

dreary *agg.* tetro, squallido.

dredge *s.* draga.

to dredge¹ *vt. e vi.* dragare.

to dredge² *vt.* cospargere, spolverizzare.

dredger¹ *s.* draga.

dredger² *s.* spolverizzatore.

dredging *s.* dragaggio.

dregs *s. pl.* **1.** feccia (*sing.*) **2.** sedimento (*sing.*).

to drench *vt.* inzuppare || **to get drenched**, inzupparsi.

dress *s.* abito, abbigliamento.

to dress *vt.* **1.** vestire **2.** bendare **3.** condire, rifinire. ♦ **to dress** *vi.* vestirsi.

dressing *s.* **1.** abbigliamento **2.** medicazione **3.** condimento || *—-gown*, vestaglia; *—table*, toletta.

dressmaker *s.* sarta.

dressmaking *s.* sartoria.

drew V. *to draw.*

dribble *s.* **1.** gocciolamento **2.** (*sport*) palleggio.

to dribble *vt.* e *vi.* **1.** stillare **2.** (*sport*) palleggiare.

dribbling *s.* V. *dribble.*

drier *s.* essiccatore.

drift *s.* **1.** spinta **2.** deriva **3.** raffica **4.** (*fig.*) significato.

to drift *vt.* sospingere. ♦ **to drift** *vi.* andare alla deriva, essere trascinato.

drill *s.* **1.** trapano, trivella **2.** esercitazione.

to drill *vt.* **1.** trapanare, trivellare **2.** esercitare.

drilling *s.* **1.** trapanazione, trivellazione **2.** esercitazione || *— machine*, trapano.

drink *s.* **1.** il bere **2.** bevanda.

to drink (drank, drunk) *vt.* e *vi.* bere.

drinkable *agg.* bevibile.

drinker *s.* bevitore.

drinking *s.* il bere.

drip *s.* gocciolamento.

to drip *vt.* e *vi.* gocciolare.

dripping *s.* gocciolio.

drive *s.* **1.** gita (*in auto*) **2.** viale (*carrozzabile*) **3.** spinta.

to drive (drove, driven) *vt.* **1.** condurre **2.** guidare **3.** azionare || *to — away*, scacciare; *to — in*, conficcare. ♦ **to drive (drove, driven)** *vi.* andare (*in veicolo*) || *to — off*, partire (*in veicolo*); *to — up*, arrivare (*in veicolo*).

drive-in *s.* cinema, banca ecc. in cui si entra in auto.

driver *s.* conducente.

driving *s.* **1.** guida **2.** comando.

drizzle *s.* pioggerella.

to drizzle *vi.* piovigginare.

drizzly *agg.* piovigginoso.

droll *agg.* buffo.

drollery *s.* **1.** buffoneria **2.** scherzo.

dromedary *s.* dromedario.

drone *s.* **1.** fuco **2.** ronzio.

to drone *vt.* e *vi.* ronzare.

to droop *vt.* abbassare. ♦ **to droop** *vi.* afflosciarsi, languire.

drooping *agg.* **1.** pendente, abbassato **2.** abbattuto.

drop *s.* **1.** goccia **2.** caduta **3.** ribasso.

to drop *vt.* lasciar cadere. ♦ **to drop** *vi.* cadere || *to — in*, fare una visitina; *to — away*, scomparire.

dropper *s.* contagocce.

dropsical *agg.* idropico.

dropsy *s.* idropisia.

dross *s.* scoria.

drought *s.* siccità.

drove V. *to drive.*

to drown *vt.* **1.** annegare **2.** smorzare. ♦ **to drown** *vi.* annegare.

drowning *s.* annegamento.

to drowse *vi.* sonnecchiare, assopirsi.

drowsily *avv.* in modo sonnolento.

drowsiness *s.* sonnolenza.

drowsy *agg.* sonnolento.

to drub *vt.* percuotere, bastonare.

drudge *s.* sgobbone.

to drudge *vi.* sfacchinare.

drudgery *s.* lavoro faticoso.

drug *s.* **1.** medicina **2.** droga || *—-store*, farmacia (*in cui si vendono articoli vari*).

to drug *vt.* drogare.

druggist *s.* farmacista.

Druid *s.* druido.

drum *s.* **1.** tamburo **2.** timpano.

to drum *vi.* suonare il tamburo. ♦ **to drum** *vt.* (*fig.*) inculcare.

drummer *s.* tamburino.

drumming *s.* tamburreggiamento.

drunk V. *to drink.* ♦ **drunk** *agg.* ubriaco.

drunkard *s.* ubriacone.

drunken *agg.* ubriaco.

drunkenness *s.* ubriachezza.

dry *agg.* asciutto, arido, secco || *— cleaning*, lavaggio a secco.

to dry *vt.* **1.** seccare **2.** asciugare. ♦ **to dry** *vi.* **1.** seccarsi **2.** asciugarsi || *to — up*, ammutolire.

dryad *s.* driade.

drying *agg.* essiccante. ♦ **drying** *s.* essiccamento.

dual *agg.* duplice.

dualism *s.* dualismo.

dualist *s.* dualista.

dualistic *agg.* dualistico.

duality s. dualità.

to dub[1] vt. creare cavaliere.

to dub[2] vt. (cine) doppiare.

dubbing s. doppiaggio.

dubious agg. 1. dubbio 2. dubbioso.

dubiousness s. dubbiosità.

dubitative agg. dubitativo.

ducal agg. ducale.

duchess s. duchessa.

duchy s. ducato.

duck[1] s. anitra.

duck[2] s. tela.

duck[3] s. tuffo.

to duck vt. 1. tuffare 2. piegare. ♦
   to duck vi. 1. tuffarsi 2. piegarsi.

duckling s. anatroccolo.

duct s. condotto.

ductile agg. duttile.

ductility s. duttilità.

due agg. e s. dovuto || to be —, do-
   ver arrivare; to fall —, scadere.

duel s. duello.

to duel vi. duella.e.

duet s. duetto.

dug V. to dig.

duke s. duca.

dukedom s. ducato.

dull agg. 1. tardo, sciocco 2. sordo
   3. triste 4. noioso 5. opaco.

to dull vt. 1. istupidire 2. intorpidire 3. smorzare. ♦ **to dull** vi.
   1. istupidirsi 2. intorpidirsi 3.
   smorzarsi.

dullard s. imbecille.

dul(l)ness s. 1. lentezza 2. noia
   3. opacità 4. ottusità.

dully avv. 1. ottusamente 2. lentamente 3. in modo noioso 4. debolmente.

duly avv. debitamente.

dumb agg. muto || — -show, pan-
   tomima.

to dumbfound vt. confondere.

dumbness s. mutismo.

dumb-waiter s. montavivande.

dummy agg. 1. muto 2. falso. ♦
   dummy s. fantoccio.

dump s. 1. colpo sordo 2. ammasso.

dumping s. « dumping » (tipo di
   vendita concorrenziale sui mercati
   esteri).

dunce s. ignorante.

dune s. duna.

dung s. 1. sterco 2. letame.

dungarees s. pl. tuta (da lavoro)
   (sing.).

dungeon s. 1. torrione 2. prigione
   sotterranea.

dunghill s. letamaio.

to dunk vt. e vi. inzuppare.

duodenal agg. duodenale.

duodenum s. (pl. -na) duodeno.

dupe s. gonzo.

duplex agg. duplice.

duplicate agg. doppio. ♦ **duplicate** s. duplicato.

to duplicate vt. duplicare.

duplication s. 1. raddoppiamento
   2. riproduzione.

duplicator s. copialettere.

duplicity s. doppiezza.

durability s. durata.

durable agg. durevole.

duralumin s. duralluminio.

duration s. durata.

duress s. 1. prigionia 2. coercizione.

during prep. durante.

durst V. dare.

dusk s. 1. oscurità 2. crepuscolo.

dusky agg. oscuro.

dust s. polvere || — -bin, pattu-
   miera.

to dust vt. 1. impolverare 2. spolverare. ♦ **to dust** vi. impolverarsi.

duster s. 1. strofinaccio (per la polvere) 2. polverizzatore.

dustman s. spazzino.

dusty agg. polveroso.

Dutch agg. olandese.

Dutchman s. olandese.

dutiful agg. rispettoso.

duty s. 1. ubbidienza 2. dovere 3.
   tassa.

duumvirate s. duumvirato.

dwarf s. nano.

dwarfish agg. nano.

to dwell (dwelt, dwelt) vi. 1.
   abitare 2. fermarsi.

dweller s. abitatore.

dwelling s. abitazione.

dwelt V. to dwell.

dye s. tintura.

to dye vt. tingere. ♦ **to dye** vi. tin-
   gersi.

dyer s. tintore.

dyerworks s. pl. tintoria (sing.).

dying agg. morente.

dynamic(al) agg. dinamico.

dynamics s. dinamica.

dynamism s. dinamismo.

dynamite s. dinamite.

dynamiter s. dinamitardo.

dynamo s. dinamo.

dynamometer s. dinamometro.

dynast s. dinasta.

dynastic(al) agg. dinastico.

dynasty s. dinastia.

dyne s. dina.

dysenteric agg. dissenterico.
dysentery s. dissenteria.
dyspepsia s. dispepsia.
dyspeptic(al) agg. dispeptico.

E

E (mus.) mi.
each agg. ogni, ciascuno. ♦ **each** pron. ognuno, ciascuno || — other, l'un l'altro.
eager agg. 1. ardente, appassionato 2. avido, desideroso.
eagerly avv. 1. ardentemente 2. avidamente.
eagerness s. 1. ardore 2. impazienza, premura.
eagle s. aquila.
ear[1] orecchio || — -ache mal d'orecchi — -drum; timpano; — -ring, orecchino; — -vax, cerume; within — -shot, a portata di voce.
ear[2] s. spiga (di grano).
earl s. conte.
earldom s. 1. titolo di conte 2. contea.
early agg. 1. primo, il principio, la prima parte (di qualsiasi tempo) 2. mattiniero 3. prematuro 4. remoto || — train, treno del primo mattino.
early avv. 1. presto, di buon'ora, per tempo 2. al principio.
earmark s. 1. marchio, caratteristica 2. (comm.) contrassegno.
to **earn** vt. guadagnare, meritare.
earnest agg. 1. serio, zelante 2. ardente. ♦ **earnest** s. caparra, pegno.
earnestly avv. 1. seriamente 2. con ardore.
earnestness s. 1. serietà 2. ardore.
earnings s. pl. 1. guadagni 2. (comm.) utili.
earth s. 1. terra, mondo 2. terreno.
earth-bound agg. radicato, attaccato ai beni terreni.
earthen agg. di terra, di terracotta.
earthenware s. terraglia.
earthly agg. terrestre.
earthquake s. terremoto.
earthworm s. lombrico.
earthy agg. terroso, di terra.
ease s. 1. tranquillità (di spirito),

benessere 2. facilità, agevolezza 3. sollievo.
to **ease** vt. e vi. 1. alleviare, calmare 2. liberare, alleggerire.
easeful agg. tranquillo.
easel s. cavalletto, telaio.
easily avv. 1. facilmente, comodamente.
easiness s. 1. comodità, benessere 2. facilità.
east s. est, oriente: the Far East, l'Estremo Oriente. ♦ **east** avv. ad est, verso est.
Easter s. Pasqua.
easterly agg. dell'est, dall'est, orientale.
eastern agg. dell'est, orientale.
eastward agg. verso est.
easy agg. 1. facile 2. agiato, modo 3. piacevole.
easy avv. facilmente, comodamente.
easygoing agg. facilone, indolente.
to **eat** (ate, eaten) vt. e vi. 1. mangiare 2. rodere, corrodere.
eatable agg. mangiabile, commestibile.
eatables s. pl. vivande, viveri.
eaten V. to eat.
eater s. mangiatore.
eating s. il mangiare.
eaves s. pl. gronda, cornicione (sing.).
to **eavesdrop** vi. origliare.
ebb s. 1. riflusso, l'abbassarsi della marea 2. (fig.) decadenza || — -tide, bassa marea.
ebbing agg. 1. defluente 2. in declino.
ebonist s. ebanista.
ebonite s. ebanite.
ebony s. ebano.
ebullition s. ebollizione.
eccentric agg. e s. eccentrico (anche fig.).
eccentricity s. eccentricità.
ecclesiastic agg. e s. ecclesiastico.
ecclesiastical agg. ecclesiastico.
echelon s. scaglione.
echinoderm s. echinoderma.
echo s. eco.
to **echo** vt. e vi. 1. far eco (a) 2. echeggiare.
eclectic agg. e s. eclettico.
eclecticism s. eclettismo.
eclipse s. eclissi.
to **eclipse** vt. eclissare.
ecliptic agg. eclittico.
eclogue s. egloga.
ecology s. ecologia.

economic *agg.* economico.
economical *agg.* economico.
economics *s.* scienze economiche.
economist *s.* economista.
to economize *vt. e vi.* economizzare.
economy *s.* economia.
ecstasy *s.* estasi.
ecstatic *agg.* estatico.
ecstatically *avv.* estaticamente.
ecumenic(al) *agg.* ecumenico.
eczema *s.* eczema.
eddy *s.* **1.** turbine d'aria, vortice **2.** gorgo, risucchio.
edge *s.* **1.** orlo, margine **2.** ciglio, sponda **3.** taglio (*di lama*) **4.** spigolo.
to edge *vt. e vi.* **1.** bordare, fare un bordo **2.** affilare, arrotare, aguzzare (*anche fig.*).
edged *agg.* affilato, tagliente || *double— —*, a doppio taglio (*anche fig.*).
edgeless *agg.* **1.** senza bordo **2.** smussato, che non taglia.
edging *s.* orlatura, fettuccia.
edible *agg.* mangereccio.
edibles *s. pl.* commestibili.
edict *s.* editto.
edifice *s.* edificio (*anche fig.*).
edifying *agg.* edificante.
to edit *vt.* **1.** pubblicare, curare (*un libro*) **2.** redigere **3.** (*cine*) montare.
editing *s.* **1.** redazione, commento (*di un testo*) **2.** direzione (*di un giornale, ecc.*).
edition *s.* edizione.
editor *s.* **1.** commentatore, curatore (*di un testo*) **2.** direttore, redattore (*di un giornale*).
editorial *s.* editoriale, articolo di fondo. ♦ **editorial** *agg.* editoriale.
editorship *s.* direzione, redazione (*di giornali*).
to educate *vt.* **1.** istruire, educare **2.** affinare, esercitare.
educated *agg.* **1.** istruito, colto **2.** addestrato (*di animali*).
education *s.* **1.** cultura, educazione **2.** istruzione, insegnamento.
educational *agg.* educativo.
educative *agg.* istruttivo.
educator *s.* educatore.
to educe *vt.* estrarre, sviluppare.
educible *agg.* che si può estrarre.
to edulcorate *vt.* dolcificare.
eel *s.* anguilla.
eerie, eery *agg.* irreale, sovrannaturale.

to efface *vt.* cancellare, distruggere.
effect *s.* **1.** effetto, risultato **2.** impressione. ♦ **effects** *s. pl.* effetti personali.
to effect *vt.* effettuare, eseguire.
effective *agg.* **1.** efficace **2.** effettivo.
effectiveness *s.* efficacia.
effectual *agg.* efficace.
effectuality *s.* efficacia, validità.
effectuation *s.* effettuazione.
effeminacy *s.* effeminatezza.
effeminate *agg.* effeminato.
effervescence *s.* **1.** effervescenza **2.** (*fig.*) eccitamento.
effete *agg.* logoro, esaurito.
efficacious *agg.* efficace.
efficaciousness *s.* **1.** efficacia **2.** rendimento (*di una macchina*).
efficiency *s.* efficienza, rendimento.
efficient *agg.* **1.** efficiente, di alto rendimento **2.** abile, capace.
effigy *s.* effigie.
to effloresce *vi.* fiorire, germogliare.
effluent *s.* defluente.
effort *s.* sforzo, fatica.
effortless *agg.* senza sforzo, facile.
effrontery *s.* sfrontatezza.
effulgence *s.* splendore.
effusion *s.* effusione, esuberanza.
effusive *agg.* espansivo, esultante.
egg *s.* uovo || *boiled —*, uovo alla coque; *hard-boiled —*, uovo sodo.
to egg *vt.* — *on so.*, istigare, incitare qu.
egocentric *agg.* egocentrico.
egocentrism *s.* egocentrismo.
egoism *s.* egoismo.
egoist *s.* egoista.
egoistic(al) *agg.* egoistico.
egotism *s.* egotismo.
egotist *s.* egotista.
egregious *agg.* insigne, eminente.
egress *s.* uscita.
Egyptian *agg. e s.* egiziano.
eider-down *s.* piumino (*da letto*).
eight *agg.* otto.
eighteen *agg.* diciotto.
eighteenth *agg.* diciottesimo.
eighth *agg.* ottavo.
eightieth *agg.* ottantesimo.
eighty *agg.* ottanta.
either *agg.* **1.** l'uno o l'altro **2.** ciascuno dei due, tutti e due. ♦ **either** *avv.* anche, pure. ♦ **either** *avv.* (*in frasi neg.*) neanche, neppure. ♦ **either** *cong.* (*seguito da or*) o, oppure.
to ejaculate *vt.* **1.** eiaculare **2.** e-

sclamare.

ejaculation *s.* **1.** eiaculazione **2.** esclamazione.

to eject *vt.* gettar fuori.

ejection *s.* **1.** espulsione **2.** (*fig.*) destituzione.

ejector *s.* espulsore.

elaborate *agg.* elaborato, accurato.

to elaborate *vt.* e *vi.* elaborare.

elaboration *s.* elaborazione.

to elapse *vi.* trascorrere, passare (*del tempo*).

elastic *agg.* elastico (*anche fig.*).

elasticity *s.* elasticità.

to elate *vt.* inebriare, esaltare.

elbow *s.* gomito.

to elbow *vt.* e *vi.* spingere con il gomito, andare avanti a gomitate.

elder *agg.* (*comp. di old*) maggiore, più vecchio (*tra due persone*). ♦ **elder** *s.* maggiore, più vecchio (*fra due*).

elderly *agg.* attempato.

eldest *agg.* (*superl. di old*) maggiore (*tra fratelli*), primogenito.

elect *agg.* eletto, scelto.

to elect *vt.* eleggere.

election *s.* **1.** elezione **2.** scelta.

elective *agg.* **1.** elettivo **2.** elettorale.

elector *s.* elettore.

electoral *agg.* elettorale.

electorate *s.* elettorato.

electric(al) *agg.* elettrico.

electrician *s.* elettricista.

electricity *s.* elettricità.

to electrify *vt.* **1.** elettrificare **2.** elettrizzare.

electrization *s.* elettrizzazione.

electrocardiogram *s.* elettrocardiogramma.

to electrocute *vt.* fulminare mediante elettricità.

electrocution *s.* elettroesecuzione.

electrode *s.* elettrodo.

electrodynamics *s.* elettrodinamica.

electrolysis *s.* elettrolisi.

electro-magnet *s.* elettromagnete.

electromagnetic *agg.* elettromagnetico.

electron *s.* elettrone.

electronic *agg.* elettronico.

electronics *s.* elettronica.

electrostatics *s.* elettrostatica.

elegance *s.* eleganza.

elegant *agg.* elegante, raffinato.

elegiac *agg.* elegiaco.

elegy *s.* elegia.

element *s.* **1.** elemento **2.** principio costitutivo.

elemental *agg.* **1.** dei quattro elementi **2.** elementare **3.** fondamentale.

elementary *agg.* elementare.

elephant *s.* elefante.

elephantiasis *s.* elefantiasi.

elephantine *agg.* elefantesco.

to elevate *vt.* innalzare, elevare (*anche fig.*).

elevated *agg.* **1.** elevato **2.** sopraelevato.

elevation *s.* **1.** elevazione **2.** collina, luogo alto.

elevator *s.* ascensore, montacarichi.

eleven *agg.* undici.

elevenses *s.* (*fam.*) spuntino a metà mattina.

eleventh *agg.* undicesimo.

elf *s.* (*pl.* elves) elfo, folletto.

elfish *agg.* **1.** incantato **2.** vivace.

to elicit *vt.* estrarre, strappare.

eligibility *s.* eleggibilità.

eligible *agg.* eleggibile.

to eliminate *vt.* eliminare.

elimination *s.* eliminazione.

elision *s.* elisione.

elixir *s.* elisir.

elk *s.* alce.

ellipse *s.* ellisse.

ellipsis *s.* ellissi.

elliptic(al) *agg.* ellittico.

elm *s.* olmo.

elocution *s.* **1.** elocuzione **2.** dizione.

to elope *vi.* fuggire (*con un amante*).

elopement *s.* fuga (*con un amante*).

eloquence *s.* eloquenza.

eloquent *agg.* eloquente (*anche fig.*).

else *avv.* (*dopo avv. e pron. int., indef.*) altro.

elsewhere *avv.* altrove.

to elude *vt.* eludere, schivare.

elusive *agg.* **1.** elusivo, ambiguo **2.** sfuggevole.

elytron *s.* (*pl.* elytra) elitra.

Elzevir *agg.* e *s.* elzeviro.

to emaciate *vt.* far deperire, far dimagrire.

emaciated *agg.* emaciato.

to emanate *vi.* emanare.

emanation *s.* emanazione.

to emancipate *vt.* emancipare.

emancipation *s.* emancipazione.

to embalm *vt.* **1.** imbalsamare **2.** profumare.

embalmer *s.* imbalsamatore.

embankment *s.* **1.** argine, diga **2.** alzaia.

embarcation *s.* imbarco.

embargo *s.* embargo, fermo.

to **embark** *vt.* imbarcare (*truppe, merci*). ♦ to **embark** *vi.* imbarcarsi.

embarkation *s.* imbarco.

to **embarrass** *vt.* mettere in imbarazzo.

embarrassing *agg.* imbarazzante.

embarrassment *s.* **1.** imbarazzo **2.** difficoltà.

embassy *s.* ambasciata.

to **embattle** *vt.* disporre in ordine di battaglia, fortificare.

to **embed** *vt.* incassare, conficcare.

to **embellish** *vt.* abbellire, ornare.

embellishment *s.* abbellimento, ornamento.

ember *s.* tizzone. ♦ **embers** *s. pl.* brace (*sing.*).

embezzler *s.* malversatore.

to **embitter** *vt.* **1.** rendere amaro **2.** (*fig.*) amareggiare.

embitterment *s.* amarezza, inasprimento.

to **emblazon** *vt.* **1.** decorare **2.** celebrare.

emblem *s.* emblema, simbolo (*fig.*).

emblematic(al) *agg.* emblematico.

embodiment *s.* **1.** incarnazione **2.** incorporamento.

to **embody** *vt.* **1.** incarnare **2.** personificare **3.** incorporare.

to **embolden** *vt.* incoraggiare.

embolism *s.* embolia.

embolus *s.* (*pl.* -li) embolo.

to **emboss** *vt.* **1.** scolpire **2.** stampare in rilievo.

embossed *agg.* **1.** sbalzato **2.** fatto in rilievo.

embrace *s.* abbraccio, amplesso.

to **embrace** *vt.* abbracciare (*anche fig.*). ♦ to **embrace** *vi.* abbracciarsi.

embrasure *s.* **1.** vano (*di porta, finestra*) **2.** feritoia.

to **embroider** *vt.* ricamare.

embroiderer *s.* ricamatore.

embroidery *s.* ricamo.

to **embroil** *vt.* coinvolgere in una disputa.

embryo *s.* embrione.

embryonic *agg.* embrionale (*anche fig.*).

to **emend** *vt.* emendare.

emendation *s.* emendamento.

emerald *s.* smeraldo.

to **emerge** *vi.* **1.** emergere, affiorare **2.** (*fig.*) risultare.

emergency *s.* emergenza, caso imprevisto || — *-door,* uscita di sicurezza; — *means,* mezzi di fortuna.

emersion *s.* emersione.

emery *s.* smeriglio || — *-paper,* carta smerigliata.

emetic *agg.* e *s.* emetico.

emigrant *agg.* e *s.* emigrante.

to **emigrate** *vi.* emigrare.

emigration *s.* emigrazione.

eminence *s.* **1.** luogo, parte eminente **2.** (*anat.*) protuberanza **3.** (*fig.*) eminenza, eccellenza.

eminent *agg.* eminente (*anche fig.*).

eminently *avv.* eminentemente.

emir *s.* emiro.

emissary *s.* emissario, agente segreto.

emission *s.* emissione.

to **emit** *vt.* **1.** emettere **2.** esalare.

emollient *agg.* e *s.* emolliente.

emolument *s.* remunerazione, salario.

emotion *s.* emozione, turbamento.

emotional *agg.* **1.** emotivo, impressionabile **2.** commovente.

emotionalism *s.* emotività.

emotionally *avv.* con emozione.

emotive *agg.* **1.** commovente **2.** emotivo.

emperor *s.* imperatore.

emphasis *s.* **1.** accentuazione, rilievo **2.** enfasi.

to **emphasize** *vt.* accentuare.

emphatic *agg.* **1.** accentuato **2.** enfatico.

emphysema *s.* enfisema.

emphyteusis *s.* enfiteusi.

empire *s.* impero.

empiric *s.* empirico.

empirical *agg.* empirico.

empiricism *s.* empirismo.

emplacement *s.* **1.** collocazione **2.** (*mil.*) piazzuola.

employ *s.* impiego: *out of* —, senza impiego.

to **employ** *vt.* **1.** impiegare, adoperare **2.** assumere.

employee *s.* impiegato.

employer *s.* datore di lavoro.

employment *s.* impiego, occupazione.

to **empoison** *vt.* avvelenare.

emporium *s.* **1.** centro commerciale **2.** emporio.

to **empower** *vt.* dare pieni poteri a.

emptiness *s.* 1. vuoto 2. vanità.

empty *agg.* 1. vuoto 2. vano 3. vacante || − −*handed*, a mani vuote.

to empty *vt.* vuotare. ♦ **to empty** *vi.* vuotarsi.

to emulate *vt.* emulare.

emulation *s.* emulazione.

emulator *s.* emulatore.

emulous *agg.* emulo.

to emulsify *vt.* emulsionare.

emulsion *s.* emulsione.

emulsive *agg.* emulsivo.

to enable *vt.* mettere in grado.

to enact *vt.* decretare, emanare (*una legge*).

enactment *s.* 1. promulgazione 2. legge.

enamel *s.* smalto.

to enamel *vt.* smaltare.

to encamp *vi.* accamparsi.

encaustic *agg.* encaustico.

encephalic *agg.* encefalico.

encephalitis *s.* encefalite.

to enchant *vt.* incantare, affascinare.

enchanter *s.* incantatore, mago.

enchanting *agg.* incantevole.

enchantment *s.* incanto, incantesimo.

enchantress *s.* incantatrice.

to encircle *vt.* circondare, cingere.

enclitic *agg.* enclitico.

to enclose *vt.* 1. racchiudere, cingere 2. accludere.

enclosed *agg.* 1. racchiuso, circondato 2. accluso.

enclosure *s.* 1. recinto, staccionata 2. allegato.

encomiast *s.* encomiasta.

to encompass *vt.* circondare (*anche fig.*).

encore *avv.* (*teat.*) bis.

to encore *vt.* chiedere il bis.

encounter *s.* scontro.

to encourage *vt.* incoraggiare, animare.

encouragement *s.* incoraggiamento.

encouraging *agg.* incoraggiante.

to encroach *vt.* 1. usurpare, invadere 2. (*giur.*) ledere.

to encrust *vt.* incrostare.

to encumber *vt.* 1. ingombrare, imbarazzare 2. ostruire.

encumbrance *s.* ingombro, impedimento.

encyclic(al) *agg.* enciclico. ♦ **encyclic(al)** *s.* enciclica.

encyclop(a)edia *s.* enciclopedia.

encyclop(a)edic(al) *agg.* enciclo-

pedico.

end *s.* 1. estremità, fine, termine 2. scopo, mira 3. morte.

to end *vt.* e *vi.* finire, concludere.

to endanger *vt.* mettere in pericolo, compromettere.

to endear *vt.* affezionare, rendere caro.

endearing *agg.* affettuoso, tenero.

endearment *s.* tenerezza. ♦ **endearments** *s. pl.* blandizie.

to endeavo(u)r *vi.* sforzarsi. ♦ **to endeavo(u)r** *vt.* tentare.

endemic *agg.* endemico.

ending *agg.* finale, ultimo. ♦ **ending** *s.* fine, conclusione.

endless *agg.* senza fine, eterno, continuo.

endocarditis *s.* endocardite.

endocardium *s.* endocardio.

endocarp *s.* endocarpo.

endocrine *agg.* endocrino.

endocrinology *s.* endocrinologia.

endogeny *s.* endogenesi.

to endorse *vt.* (*comm.*) girare, vistare.

endorsee *s.* (*comm.*) giratario.

endorsement *s.* (*comm.*) girata.

endorser *s.* (*comm.*) girante.

to endow *vt.* 1. dotare 2. fare una donazione.

endowment *s.* 1. costituzione di dote, donazione 2. (*fig.*) talento.

endurance *s.* 1. resistenza, sopportazione 2. durata.

to endure *vt.* tollerare, sopportare. ♦ **to endure** *vi.* resistere, durare.

enduring *agg.* 1. tollerante, paziente 2. durevole.

enema *s.* clistere.

enemy *agg.* e *s.* nemico.

energetic(al) *agg.* 1. energico 2. energetico.

to energize *vt.* infondere energia.

energumen *s.* energumeno.

energy *s.* energia, forza.

to enervate *vt.* snervare, indebolire.

enervation *s.* indebolimento.

to enfeeble *vt.* indebolire.

to enfold *vt.* 1. avvolgere 2. cingere.

to enforce *vt.* 1. imporre, far rispettare 2. mettere in vigore (*una legge*).

to enframe *vt.* incorniciare.

to enfranchise *vt.* affrancare, liberare.

enfranchisement *s.* affrancamento,

liberazione.

to engage *vt.* 1. impegnare 2. ingaggiare 3. attrarre (*l'attenzione*). ♦ **to engage** *vi.* impegnarsi ‖ **to — in conversation**, prendere parte alla conversazione.

engaged *agg.* 1. impegnato 2. fidanzato 3. occupato, riservato.

engagement *s.* 1. impegno 2. fidanzamento 3. assunzione, impiego.

engaging *agg.* attraente, avvincente.

engagingly *avv.* in modo attraente.

to engender *vt.* produrre, causare.

engine *s.* 1. macchina, motore 2. (*ferr.*) locomotrice ‖ **fire —**, autopompa.

engineer *s.* 1. ingegnere 2. tecnico.

engineering *s.* 1. ingegneria 2. costruzione meccanica.

English *agg.* inglese. ♦ **English** *s.* lingua inglese.

Englishman *s.* (*uomo*) inglese.

Englishwoman *s.* (*donna*) inglese.

to engrave *vt.* 1. intagliare, incidere 2. (*fig.*) imprimere.

engraver *s.* incisore.

engraving *s.* arte dell'incisione ‖ **wood— —**, xilografia.

to engross *vt.* 1. copiare (*un atto legale*), redigere (*un documento*) 2. assorbire (*l'attenzione*).

engrossment *s.* copiatura (*di documento*).

to enhance *vt.* accrescere.

enigma *s.* enigma.

enigmatic(al) *agg.* enigmatico.

to enjoy *vt.* 1. godere, gioire 2. gustare, provar piacere di ‖ **to — oneself**, divertirsi.

enjoyable *agg.* piacevole, gradevole.

enjoyably *avv.* piacevolmente.

enjoyment *s.* godimento, piacere.

to enkindle *vt.* infiammare, eccitare. ♦ **to enkindle** *vi.* infiammarsi, eccitarsi.

to enlarge *vt.* 1. allargare, ampliare 2. (*foto*) ingrandire. ♦ **to enlarge** *vi.* allargarsi, ampliarsi.

enlargement *s.* 1. allargamento 2. (*foto*) ingrandimento.

enlarger *s.* (*foto*) ingranditore.

to enlighten *vt.* rischiarare, illuminare (*anche fig.*).

enlightenment *s.* 1. spiegazione, schiarimento 2. (*lett.*) l'illuminismo.

to enlist *vt.* arruolare. ♦ **to enlist** *vi.* arruolarsi.

enlistment *s.* arruolamento, ingaggio.

to enliven *vt.* rianimare, ravvivare.

to enmesh *vt.* impegolare, irretire.

enmity *s.* ostilità, inimicizia.

to ennoble *vt.* nobilitare.

enormity *s.* mostruosità.

enormous *agg.* enorme, immenso.

enough *avv.* abbastanza, sufficientemente. ♦ **enough** *agg.* sufficiente. ♦ **enough** *s.* il necessario, quanto basta.

to enrage *vt.* far arrabbiare, esasperare.

to enrapture *vt.* rapire, estasiare.

to enrich *vt.* 1. arricchire (*anche fig.*) 2. abbellire.

enrichment *s.* 1. arricchimento 2. abbellimento.

to enrol *vt.* 1. arruolare, ingaggiare 2. iscrivere.

enrolment *s.* 1. arruolamento, iscrizione 2. (*giur.*) registrazione.

ensign *s.* 1. bandiera, stendardo 2. portabandiera.

to enslave *vt.* assoggettare, far schiavo (*anche fig.*).

enslavement *s.* asservimento, schiavitù (*anche fig.*).

to ensnare *vt.* adescare, intrappolare (*anche fig.*).

to ensue *vt. e vi.* seguire.

to ensure *vt.* assicurare, garantire.

entail *s.* eredità, ordine di successione (*vincolato*).

to entangle *vt.* impigliare, intralciare (*anche fig.*).

entanglement *s.* groviglio, impiccio.

to enter *vt. e vi.* 1. entrare, penetrare 2. iscrivere 3. (*comm.*) registrare ‖ **to — upon**, intraprendere (*una carriera*).

enteric *agg.* enterico.

enteritis *s.* enterite.

enterocolitis *s.* enterocolite.

enterogastritis *s.* gastroenterite.

enterprise *s.* 1. impresa 2. iniziativa, intraprendenza.

enterprising *agg.* intraprendente.

to entertain *vt.* 1. ricevere, ospitare 2. intrattenere, divertire 3. carezzare (*un'idea*), nutrire (*dubbi, speranze*).

entertainer *s.* 1. anfitrione, ospite 2. comico.

entertaining *agg.* divertente.

entertainment *s.* 1. trattenimento, spettacolo 2. ricevimento, festa 3. divertimento.

to **enthral** *vt.* (*fig.*) affascinare, incantare.

enthralment *s.* incanto, malìa.

to **enthrone** *vt.* mettere sul trono.

enthronement *s.* investitura, intronizzazione.

enthusiasm *s.* entusiasmo.

enthusiast *s.* entusiasta.

enthusiastic(al) *agg.* entusiastico.

enthusiastically *avv.* entusiasticamente.

to **entice** *vt.* sedurre, allettare.

enticement *s.* 1. attrattiva 2. adescamento, istigazione.

enticing *agg.* seducente, attraente.

entire *agg.* intero, completo.

entirely *avv.* interamente, completamente.

to **entitle** *vt.* 1. intitolare (*un libro*) 2. dare un titolo.

entity *s.* entità, esistenza.

entomological *agg.* entomologico.

entomologist *s.* entomologo.

entomology *s.* entomologia.

entrails *s. pl.* intestino (*sing.*), visceri.

entrance *s.* 1. ingresso, entrata 2. ammissione ‖ — *hall*, vestibolo.

to **entrap** *vt.* prendere in trappola, truffare.

to **entreat** *vt.* pregare, supplicare.

entreaty *s.* supplica, istanza.

to **entrench** *vt.* e *vi.* trincerare, fortificare (*anche fig.*) ‖ *to* — *upon*, usurpare.

entrepreneur *s.* 1. (*teat.*) impresario 2. imprenditore.

to **entrust** *vt.* affidare, commettere.

entry *s.* 1. entrata 2. ingresso, passaggio 3. (*comm.*) registrazione.

to **entwine** *vt.* attorcigliare, intrecciare. ♦ to **entwine** *vi.* arrotolarsi.

to **enucleate** *vt.* spiegare, chiarire.

enucleation *s.* spiegazione, chiarimento.

to **enumerate** *vt.* enumerare.

enumeration *s.* enumerazione.

enumerator *s.* numeratore.

to **enunciate** *vt.* enunciare, proclamare.

enunciation *s.* enunciazione.

to **envelop** *vt.* avvolgere, avviluppare.

envelope *s.* busta, involucro.

envelopment *s.* avvolgimento.

enviable *agg.* invidiabile.

envious *agg.* invidioso.

to **environ** *vt.* circondare, accerchiare.

environment *s.* ambiente.

environs *s. pl.* dintorni.

envy *s.* invidia.

to **envy** *vt.* invidiare.

enzyme *s.* enzima.

epaulet(te) *s.* (*mil.*) spallina.

ephebe *s.* efebo.

ephemeral *agg.* effimero.

ephemeris *s.* (*pl.* -ides) effemeride.

epic *agg.* epico. ♦ **epic** *s.* poema epico.

epically *avv.* epicamente.

epicentre *s.* epicentro.

epicurean *agg.* e *s.* epicureo.

epidemic(al) *agg.* epidemico.

epidemically *avv.* epidemicamente.

epidermal *agg.* epidermico.

epidermis *s.* epidermide.

epigastric *agg.* epigastrico.

epigram *s.* epigramma.

epigrammatic *agg.* epigrammatico.

epigrammatist *s.* epigrammista.

epigraph *s.* epigrafe.

epigraphy *s.* epigrafia.

epilepsy *s.* epilessia.

epileptic *agg.* epilettico.

epilogue *s.* epilogo.

Epiphany *s.* Epifania.

episcopacy *s.* episcopato.

episcopal *agg.* episcopale.

episcopate *s.* episcopato.

episode *s.* episodio.

episodic(al) *agg.* episodico.

epistle *s.* epistola.

epistolary *agg.* epistolare.

epitaph *s.* epitaffio.

epithalamium *s.* epitalamio.

epithet *s.* epiteto.

epitome *s.* epitome, riassunto.

epoch *s.* epoca, età.

epopee *s.* epopea.

equability *s.* uguaglianza, uniformità.

equal *agg.* uguale, simile, stesso. ♦ **equal** *s.* pari (*di rango*).

equality *s.* uguaglianza, parità.

equalization *s.* eguagliamento.

to **equalize** *vt.* e *vi.* uguagliare.

equally *avv.* ugualmente, imparzialmente.

equanimity *s.* equanimità.

equanimous *agg.* equanime.

equation *s.* 1. equazione 2. pareggio.

equator *s.* equatore.

equatorial *agg.* equatoriale.

equestrian *agg.* equestre.

equidistant *agg.* equidistante.

equilateral *agg.* equilatero.

equine *agg.* equino.

equinoctial *agg.* equinoziale.

equinox *s.* equinozio.

to equip *vt.* 1. equipaggiare 2. fornire, arredare.

equipment *s.* 1. equipaggiamento 2. attrezzatura.

equipoise *s.* equilibrio.

equipollent *agg.* equipollente.

equitation *s.* equitazione.

equity *s.* giustizia, equità.

equivalence *s.* equivalenza.

equivalent *agg. e s.* equivalente.

equivocal *agg.* 1. ambiguo, equivoco 2. sospetto, losco.

equivocally *avv.* 1. ambiguamente 2. in modo losco.

to equivocate *vi.* equivocare, giocare sull'equivoco.

equivocation *s.* 1. l'equivocare 2. equivoco.

equivoke *s.* 1. gioco di parole 2. ambiguità (*d'espressione*).

era *s.* era, epoca.

eradicable *agg.* estirpabile.

to eradicate *vt.* sradicare, estirpare.

to erase *vt.* raschiare, cancellare.

eraser *s.* 1. raschietto 2. gomma per cancellare.

erasure *s.* raschiatura, cancellatura.

erect *agg.* diritto, ritto.

to erect *vt.* 1. raddrizzare 2. costruire.

erection *s.* 1. raddrizzamento 2. erezione.

eremite *s.* eremita.

ermine *s.* ermellino.

to erode *vt.* corrodere, logorare.

erosion *s.* erosione.

erosive *agg.* corrosivo.

erotic *agg.* erotico.

eroticism *s.* erotismo.

to err *vi.* 1. sbagliare 2. errare, vagabondare.

errand *s.* commissione || — -boy, fattorino.

errant *agg.* 1. errante 2. che sbaglia.

erratic *agg.* 1. erratico 2. irregolare.

erratically *avv.* 1. irregolarmente 2. eccentricamente.

erring *agg.* 1. errante 2. che sbaglia.

erroneous *agg.* erroneo.

error *s.* 1. errore 2. torto.

erudite *agg.* erudito.

erudition *s.* erudizione.

to erupt *vi.* eruttare.

eruption *s.* eruzione.

eruptive *agg.* eruttivo.

escalade *s.* scalata.

escalator *s.* scala mobile.

escape *s.* 1. fuga, evasione 2. scampo, salvezza.

to escape *vt. e vi.* 1. fuggire, evadere 2. scampare.

escapism *s.* evasione dalla realtà.

escapist *s.* chi cerca di evadere dalla realtà.

eschatology *s.* escatologia.

to eschew *vt.* evitare, astenersi da.

escort *s.* scorta.

to escort *vt.* scortare, accompagnare.

Eskimo *s.* esquimese.

esoteric *agg.* esoterico.

especial *agg.* speciale.

especially *avv.* specialmente.

espionage *s.* spionaggio.

esplanade *s.* spianata.

to espy *vt.* scorgere, avvistare.

esquire *s.* (*titolo di cortesia*) John Smith *Esq.*, egregio sig. John Smith.

essay *s.* 1. esperimento, prova 2. (*lett.*) saggio.

to essay *vt.* provare, mettere alla prova.

essayist *s.* saggista.

essence *s.* essenza.

essential *agg.* essenziale.

to establish *vt.* 1. affermare (*un diritto ecc.*) 2. instaurare 3. (*comm.*) fondare, costituire.

established *agg.* 1. stabilito, affermato 2. fondato.

establishment *s.* 1. affermazione, conferma 2. instaurazione 3. stabilimento, azienda.

estate *s.* 1. terra, proprietà (*terriera*) 2. stato, gruppo politico 3. condizione, classe sociale || — *agent*, mediatore.

esteem *s.* stima, considerazione.

to esteem *vt.* 1. stimare, tenere in gran conto 2. considerare.

estimable *agg.* degno di stima.

estimate *s.* 1. stima, giudizio 2. (*comm.*) preventivo.

to estimate *vt.* 1. stimare, valutare 2. preventivare.

estimator *s.* perito, stimatore.

to estrange *vt.* alienare, alienarsi, allontanare.

estrangement *s.* alienazione, allontanamento.

estuary *s.* estuario.

etching *s.* acquaforte.

eternal *agg.* eterno.

eternity *s.* eternità.

ether s. etere.
ethereal agg. etereo.
ethic(al) agg. etico.
ethics s. etica.
Ethiopian agg. etiopico. ♦ **Ethiopian** s. etiope.
Ethiopic agg. etiopico.
ethnic(al) agg. etnico.
ethnography s. etnografia.
ethnologist s. etnologo.
ethnology s. etnologia.
ethylene s. etilene.
ethylic agg. etilico.
etiquette s. 1. etichetta 2. cerimoniale.
Etrurian, Etruscan agg. e s. etrusco.
etymologic(al) agg. etimologico.
etymology s. etimologia.
eucalyptus s. eucalipto.
Eucharist s. Eucaristia.
eucharistic(al) agg. eucaristico.
eugenics s. eugenetica.
eulogist s. elogiatore.
to eulogize vt. elogiare.
eulogy s. elogio, panegirico.
eunuch s. eunuco.
euphemism s. eufemismo.
euphonic agg. eufonico.
euphony s. eufonia.
euphoria s. euforia.
euphuism s. eufuismo.
euphuist s. affettato.
euphuistic agg. affettato, ricercato (di stile).
European agg. e s. europeo.
Eurovision s. eurovisione.
euthanasia s. eutanasia.
to evacuate vt. e vi. evacuare, sfollare.
evacuation s. evacuazione, sfollamento.
to evade vt. evitare, schivare, eludere.
to evaluate vt. valutare.
evaluation s. valutazione.
evanescent agg. evanescente.
evangelic(al) agg. evangelico.
evangelist s. evangelista.
evangelistic agg. di un evangelista, missionario.
evangelization s. evangelizzazione.
to evangelize vt. evangelizzare.
to evaporate vi. evaporare. ♦ **to evaporate** vt. far evaporare.
evaporation s. evaporazione.
evasion s. 1. evasione, scappatoia 2. scusa, pretesto.
evasive agg. evasivo.

evasively avv. evasivamente.
evasiveness s. ambiguità.
eve s. vigilia.
even agg. 1. uguale, uniforme, costante, regolare 2. pari, equo. ♦ **even** avv. 1. ancora (con comp.) 2. persino, anche || — as, nel momento in cui.
evening s. 1. sera, serata 2. (fig.) declino, fine.
evenly avv. in modo uguale, uniformemente.
evensong s. vespro.
event s. 1. caso, eventualità 2. avvenimento 3. (sport) prova.
eventful agg. ricco di avvenimenti, movimentato.
eventual agg. finale, definitivo.
eventuality s. eventualità.
eventually avv. alla fine.
ever avv. 1. mai 2. sempre.
evergreen s. sempreverde.
everlasting agg. eterno.
everliving agg. immortale.
evermore avv. perpetuamente.
every agg. ogni, ciascuno, tutti.
everybody pron. indef. ognuno, tutti.
everyday agg. di tutti i giorni, quotidiano.
everyone pron. indef. V. everybody.
everything pron. indef. ogni cosa, tutto.
everywhere avv. ovunque.
to evict vt. sfrattare, espellere.
eviction s. sfratto.
evidence s. 1. evidenza 2. prova.
to evidence vt. provare, dimostrare.
evident agg. evidente, chiaro.
evil agg. cattivo, malvagio || — eye, malocchio. ♦ **evil** s. male, peccato.
to evince vt. evirare.
to evoke vt. evocare.
evocation s. evocazione.
evocative agg. evocatore.
to evoke vt. evocare.
evolution s. evoluzione.
evolutional agg. evolutivo.
evolutionism s. evoluzionismo.
to evolve vt. evolvere. ♦ **to evolve** vi. evolversi.
evolvement s. evoluzione, sviluppo.
ewe s. pecora (femmina).
to exacerbate vt. esacerbare, inasprire.
exacerbation s. esacerbazione, inasprimento.
exact agg. 1. esatto, giusto 2. puntuale, rigoroso.

to **exact** vt. 1. esigere 2. rendere necessario.

exacting agg. 1. esigente 2. impegnativo.

exaction s. esazione, estorsione.

exactitude s. esattezza, precisione.

exactly avv. esattamente.

exactness s. esattezza, precisione.

to **exaggerate** vt. esagerare, ingrandire.

exaggeration s. esagerazione.

to **exalt** vt. 1. innalzare, elevare 2. esaltare, lodare.

exaltation s. 1. innalzamento 2. esaltazione.

exalted agg. 1. elevato (di grado ecc.) 2. esaltato, eccitato.

examination s. 1. esame, ispezione 2. esame scolastico 3. (giur.) interrogatorio.

to **examine** vt. 1. verificare, ispezionare 2. esaminare 3. (giur.) istruire un processo.

examiner s. esaminatore.

example s. esempio.

to **exasperate** vt. 1. peggiorare, aggravare 2. esasperare.

exasperatingly avv. in modo esasperante.

exasperation s. esasperazione.

to **excavate** vt. scavare, fare scavi (archeologici).

excavation s. 1. scavo 2. fossa, buca.

excavator s. 1. operaio scavatore 2. (mecc.) escavatore.

to **exceed** vt. e vi. 1. eccedere, superare (i limiti) 2. essere superiore.

exceeding agg. esagerato.

exceedingly avv. eccessivamente, troppo.

to **excel** vt. superare. ♦ to **excel** vi. primeggiare.

excellence s. 1. eccellenza 2. pregio, superiorità.

Excellency s. (titolo) Eccellenza.

excellent agg. eccellente.

except prep. eccetto, tranne.

to **except** vt. ecc.ttuare, escludere. ♦ to **except** vi. obiettare, sollevare eccezioni.

excepting prep. eccetto, tranne.

exception s. eccezione.

exceptional agg. eccezionale, straordinario.

excerpt s. brano scelto.

excess s. 1. eccesso, intemperanza 2. supplemento.

exchange s. 1. scambio 2. (finanza)

excessive agg. eccessivo, smoderato. cambio 3. borsa, mercato || bill of —, cambiale; — -broker, agente di cambio.

to **exchange** vt. cambiare, scambiare. ♦ to **exchange** vi. fare un cambio.

exchangeable agg. scambiabile.

exchanger s. cambiavalute.

exchequer s. Tesoro, Scacchiere, fisco.

excise s. imposta indiretta || — duty, dazio.

to **excise**[1] vt. tassare.

to **excise**[2] vt. estirpare, mutilare (un testo).

exciseman s. daziere, funzionario degli uffici delle imposte.

excision s. taglio, recisione.

excitability s. eccitabilità.

excitable agg. eccitabile.

excitant agg. e s. eccitante.

excitation s. eccitazione.

to **excite** vt. 1. provocare, far nascere (una rivolta, un sentimento ecc.) 2. eccitare, animare.

excited agg. eccitato.

excitement s. eccitazione.

to **exclaim** vt. e vi. esclamare.

exclamation s. esclamazione.

exclamatory agg. esclamativo.

to **exclude** vt. escludere.

exclusion s. esclusione.

exclusive agg. 1. altezzoso 2. chiuso, scelto (di ambiente) 3. esclusivo.

exclusiveness s. esclusività.

to **excogitate** vt. escogitare.

excommunicable agg. scomunicabile.

excommunicate agg. e s. scomunicato.

to **excommunicate** vt. scomunicare.

excommunication s. scomunica.

excrement s. escremento.

excrescence s. escrescenza, protuberanza.

excruciating agg. tormentoso, straziante.

to **exculpate** vt. giustificare, scolpare.

excursion s. 1. escursione, gita 2. (mil.) sortita.

excursionist s. escursionista, gitante.

excusable agg. scusabile.

excuse s. 1. scusa, giustificazione 2.

pretesto.

to **excuse** *vt.* scusare, giustificare.

execrable *agg.* esecrabile.

to **execrate** *vt.* e *vi.* 1. esecrare, detestare 2. maledire.

execration *s.* 1. esecrazione 2. maledizione.

executant *s.* esecutore.

to **execute** *vt.* 1. eseguire; mettere in esecuzione 2. (*giur.*) convalidare 3. giustiziare.

execution *s.* 1. compimento, attuazione 2. esecuzione.

executioner *s.* esecutore, boia.

executive *agg.* esecutivo.

executor *s.* esecutore.

exedra *s.* esedra.

exegesis *s.* (*pl.* -ses) esegesi.

exegete *s.* esegeta.

exemplary *agg.* esemplare.

exemplification *s.* esemplificazione.

to **exemplify** *vt.* esemplificare.

exempt *agg.* esente, esonerato.

to **exempt** *vt.* esentare, esonerare.

exemption *s.* esenzione, esonero.

exequies *s. pl.* esequie.

exercise *s.* esercizio, esercitazione ‖ — -book, quaderno.

to **exercise** *vt.* esercitare, usare. ♦ to **exercise** *vi.* esercitarsi, allenarsi.

exercitation *s.* esercizio, uso (*di una facoltà*).

to **exert** *vt.* esercitare.

exertion *s.* 1. esercizio (*di autorità*) 2. sforzo.

exhalation *s.* esalazione.

to **exhale** *vt.* e *vi.* esalare, emettere.

exhaust *s.* 1. (*mecc.*) scarico, scappamento 2. apparato aspiratore.

to **exhaust** *vt.* e *vi.* 1. aspirare (*aria, gas ecc.*) 2. esaurire (*anche fig.*).

exhausted *agg.* 1. aspirato 2. esausto, spossato.

exhausting *agg.* che esaurisce.

exhaustion *s.* 1. aspirazione 2. esaurimento.

exhaustive *agg.* 1. esauriente 2. spossante.

exhibit *s.* 1. insieme di oggetti in mostra 2. (*giur.*) documento.

to **exhibit** *vt.* 1. esibire, mostrare 2. (*giur.*) produrre (*documenti ecc.*).

exhibition *s.* 1. presentazione (*di documenti*) 2. esposizione, mostra.

exhibitionism *s.* esibizionismo.

exhibitionist *s.* esibizionista.

exhibitor *s.* espositore.

to **exhilarate** *vt.* rallegrare, esilarare.

exhilarating *agg.* esilarante.

to **exhort** *vt.* esortare, ammonire.

exhortation *s.* esortazione.

exhortative *agg.* esortativo.

exhumation *s.* esumazione.

to **exhume** *vt.* esumare.

exigence *s.* 1. esigenza, necessità 2. situazione critica.

exigent *agg.* 1. pressante, urgente 2. esigente.

exigible *agg.* esigibile.

exiguity *s.* esiguità.

exiguous *agg.* esiguo.

exile *s.* 1. esilio, bando 2. esule.

to **exile** *vt.* esiliare.

to **exist** *vi.* esistere.

existence *s.* esistenza.

existent *agg.* esistente.

existential *agg.* esistenziale.

existentialism *s.* esistenzialismo.

existentialist *agg.* e *s.* esistenzialista.

existing *agg.* esistente, attuale.

exit *s.* uscita.

exode, exodus *s.* esodo.

exogenous *agg.* esogeno.

to **exonerate** *vt.* 1. esonerare, dispensare 2. giustificare.

exoneration *s.* 1. dispensa, esonero 2. giustificazione.

exorbitant *agg.* esorbitante.

to **exorcise** *vt.* esorcizzare.

exorciser *s.* esorcista.

exorcism *s.* esorcismo.

exorcist *s.* esorcista.

exothermic *agg.* esotermico.

exotic *agg.* esotico.

exoticism *s.* esotismo.

to **expand** *vt.* espandere, dilatare, allargare. ♦ to **expand** *vi.* espandersi, dilagare, dilatarsi, allargarsi, svilupparsi.

expanse *s.* distesa, estensione, spazio.

expansion *s.* espansione, dilatazione, allargamento.

expansionism *s.* espansionismo.

expansive *agg.* 1. espansivo 2. dilatabile.

to **expatiate** *vi.* 1. errare, vagabondare 2. parlare e scrivere diffusamente.

expatiation *s.* 1. dissertazione 2. prolissità.

expatriate *agg.* e *s.* espatriato.

to **expatriate** *vt.* esiliare. ♦ to

expatriate *vi.* espatriare.

expatriation *s.* espatrio.

to expect *vt.* 1. aspettare, aspettarsi 2. esigere, insistere 3. pensare, credere || *to — somebody to come*, prevedere la venuta di qu.

expectance *s.* aspettativa, attesa.

expectant *s.* 1. chi attende 2. candidato.

expectation *s.* attesa, aspettativa. ◆ **expectations** *s. pl.* speranze.

expectorant *agg. e s.* espettorante.

expectoration *s.* espettorazione.

expediency *s.* 1. convenienza 2. opportunismo.

expedient *s.* espediente, ripiego.

to expedite *vt.* affrettare.

expedition *s.* 1. spedizione 2. prontezza, celerità.

expeditious *s.* svelto, sbrigativo.

to expel *vt.* espellere, cacciare.

expense *s.* 1. spesa, sborso 2. (*fig.*) sacrificio, prezzo.

expensive *agg.* costoso, caro.

experience *s.* esperienza.

to experience *vt.* sperimentare, provare.

experienced *agg.* pratico, esperto.

experiment *s.* esperimento, prova.

experimental *agg.* sperimentale.

experimentation *s.* sperimentismo.

experimentalist *s.* sperimentalista.

experimentation *s.* sperimentazione.

expert *agg.* esperto. ◆ **expert** *s.* esperto, perito, competente.

expertly *avv.* abilmente.

to explate *vt.* espiare.

explation *s.* espiazione.

explatory *agg.* espiatorio.

expiration *s.* 1. fine, scadenza 2. espirazione.

expiratory *agg.* espiratorio.

to expire *vt. e vi.* 1. finire, scadere 2. spirare, morire.

expiring *agg.* 1. che scade 2. spirante, morente.

expiry *s.* fine, cessazione.

to explain *vt. e vi.* spiegare, chiarire.

explanation *s.* spiegazione, delucidazione.

expletive *agg.* espletivo, pleonastico. ◆ **expletive** *s.* 1. imprecazione 2. pleonasmo.

explicable *agg.* spiegabile.

to explicate *vt.* sviluppare (*un prin-*

cipio, un'idea ecc.).

explication *s.* spiegazione, sviluppo.

explicit *agg.* esplicito, chiaro.

to explode *vt.* esplodere, far esplodere. ◆ **to explode** *vi.* scoppiare, esplodere.

to exploit *vt.* 1. utilizzare, sfruttare 2. approfittare di.

exploitation *s.* sfruttamento, utilizzazione.

exploiter *s.* 1. chi valorizza (*idea, invenzione ecc.*) 2. sfruttatore.

exploration *s.* esplorazione.

to explore *vt.* esplorare.

explorer *s.* esploratore, esploratrice.

explosion *s.* esplosione, scoppio.

explosive *agg. e s.* esplosivo.

exponent *s.* 1. divulgatore 2. esponente.

exponential *agg.* esponenziale.

export *s.* esportazione.

to export *vt.* esportare.

exportation *s.* esportazione.

exporter *s.* esportatore.

to expose *vt.* 1. esporre 2. (*foto*) impressionare.

exposé *s.* esposto, resoconto.

exposition *s.* 1. spiegazione, commento 2. mostra, esposizione.

expositive *agg.* espositivo.

expositor *s.* commentatore.

expository *agg.* esplicativo.

exposure *s.* 1. esposizione (*al freddo, al caldo ecc.*) 2. mostra 3. (*foto*) (*tempo di*) esposizione.

to expound *vt.* spiegare (*una teoria*).

express *agg.* 1. chiaro, preciso 2. espresso, diretto. ◆ **express** *s.* espresso, corriere || — *train*, direttissimo.

to express *vt.* esprimere, manifestare.

expression *s.* espressione.

expressionism *s.* espressionismo.

expressionist *s.* espressionista.

expressive *agg.* espressivo, significativo.

expressly *avv.* espressamente.

to expropriate *vt.* espropriare.

expropriation *s.* espropriazione.

expulsion *s.* espulsione.

expulsive *agg.* espulsivo.

expunction *s.* cancellatura.

to expurgate *vt.* espurgare (*uno scritto*).

expurgation *s.* espurgazione (*di uno scritto*).

exquisite *agg.* 1. squisito 2. fine, sensibile. ◆ **exquisite** *s.* raffinato.

exquisiteness *s.* squisitezza, finezza.

extant *agg.* ancora esistente.

extemporaneous, extemporary *agg.* estemporaneo.

extempore *agg.* improvvisato.

extemporization *s.* improvvisazione.

to extemporize *vt.* e *vi.* improvvisare.

to extend *vt.* 1. estendere, allungare, prolungare. ◆ to extend *vi.* estendersi, allungarsi, prolungarsi.

extendible *agg.* estendibile.

extensible *agg.* estensibile.

extension *s.* 1. estensione, allungamento 2. (*comm.*) proroga.

extensive *agg.* 1. esteso, ampio 2. estensivo.

extent *s.* 1. estensione 2. volume 3. limite, grado.

to extenuate *vt.* attenuare.

extenuation *s.* attenuazione.

exterior *agg.* esterno, esteriore. ◆ exterior *s.* 1. l'esterno 2. esteriorità.

exteriority *s.* esteriorità.

exteriorization *s.* esteriorizzazione.

to exteriorize *vt.* esternare.

to exterminate *vt.* sterminare.

extermination *s.* sterminio.

external *agg.* esteriore, esterno.

externality *s.* superficialità.

to externalize *vt.* esternare.

externally *avv.* esternamente, esteriormente.

exterritorial *agg.* estraterritoriale.

extinct *agg.* 1. estinto 2. spento.

extinction *s.* estinzione.

to extinguish *vt.* 1. estinguere, spegnere 2. pagare, ammortizzare.

extinguisher *s.* spegnitore, estintore.

to extirpate *vt.* estirpare, sradicare.

extirpation *s.* estirpazione, sradicamento.

to extol *vt.* lodare, magnificare.

to extort *vt.* estorcere, strappare.

extorter *s.* chi estorce.

extortion *s.* estorsione.

extortioner *s.* ricattatore.

extra *agg.* 1. straordinario 2. in più, extra. ◆ extra *s.* 1. supplemento 2. (*giorn.*) edizione straordinaria 3. (*cine*) comparsa. ◆ extra *avv.* extra, di più, in più, insolitamente.

extract *s.* 1. estratto 2. citazione.

to extract *vt.* estrarre, togliere.

extractable *agg.* estraibile.

extraction *s.* 1. estrazione 2. origine, stirpe.

extractive *agg.* estrattivo.

extractor *s.* estrattore.

to extradite *vt.* estradare.

extradition *s.* estradizione.

extraneous *agg.* estraneo.

extraordinary *agg.* straordinario, eccezionale.

extraterritorial *agg.* estraterritoriale.

extraterritoriality *s.* estraterritorialità.

extravagance *s.* 1. prodigalità, sperpero 2. stravaganza.

extravagant *agg.* 1. prodigo 2. stravagante.

extreme *agg.* 1. estremo, ultimo 2. grave. ◆ extreme *s.* estremo, estremità.

extremely *avv.* estremamente.

extremism *s.* estremismo.

extremist *s.* estremista.

extremity *s.* estremità.

extrinsic(al) *agg.* estrinseco.

extrovert *s.* estroverso.

to extrude *vt.* estromettere.

exuberance *s.* esuberanza.

exuberant *agg.* 1. copioso, abbondante 2. esuberante, pieno di vita.

exudation *s.* essudazione.

to exude *vt.* e *vi.* trasudare.

to exult *vi.* gioire, esultare.

exultant *agg.* esultante.

exultation *s.* esultanza.

eye *s.* occhio.

eyeball *s.* bulbo oculare.

eyebrow *s.* sopracciglio.

eyeglass *s.* lente, monocolo.

eyehole *s.* orbita, occhiaia.

eyelash *s.* ciglio.

eyelet *s.* occhiello, asola.

eyelid *s.* palpebra.

eyesight *s.* vista.

eyesore *s.* cosa brutta e spiacevole.

eyewitness *s.* testimone oculare.

F

F *s.* (*mus.*) fa.

fable *s.* favola.

fabled *agg.* 1. mitico 2. inventato.

fabric *s.* 1. tessuto 2. manufatto 3.

struttura **4.** fabbricazione.

to **fabricate** *vt.* **1.** fabbricare **2.** inventare.

fabrication *s.* **1.** fabbricazione **2.** invenzione.

fabulist *s.* **1.** favolista **2.** bugiardo.

fabulosity *s.* favolosità.

fabulous *agg.* favoloso.

façade *s.* facciata.

face *s.* **1.** faccia **2.** aspetto **3.** sfrontatezza **4.** facciata **5.** quadrante (*di orologio*) ‖ *to pull faces*, fare boccacce ‖ *— -powder*, cipria; — *value*, (*comm.*) valore nominale.

to **face** *vt.* **1.** fronteggiare **2.** affrontare **3.** ricoprire ‖ *to — about*, fare dietro-front.

facet *s.* sfaccettatura.

facetious *agg.* faceto.

facetiousness *s.* lepidezza.

facial *agg.* facciale.

facile *agg.* **1.** facile **2.** pronto **3.** accomodante.

to **facilitate** *vt.* facilitare.

facilitation *s.* facilitazione.

facility *s.* facilità. ♦ **facilities** *s. pl.* facilitazioni.

facing *agg.* che sta di fronte. ♦ **facing** *s.* rivestimento. ♦ **facings** *s. pl.* mostrine.

fact *s.* **1.** fatto **2.** realtà ‖ *in —*, infatti, di fatto; *as a matter of —*, effettivamente.

faction *s.* **1.** fazione **2.** faziosità.

factious *agg.* fazioso.

factiousness *s.* faziosità.

factitious *agg.* fittizio.

factitiousness *s.* artificiosità.

factor *s.* **1.** fattore **2.** agente.

factory *s.* fabbrica.

factual *agg.* effettivo.

facultative *agg.* **1.** facoltativo **2.** casuale.

faculty *s.* facoltà.

fad *s.* **1.** mania **2.** capriccio.

faddist *s.* maniaco.

faddy *agg.* capriccioso.

fade *s.* (*radio*) variazione graduale.

to **fade** *vi.* **1.** appassire **2.** sbiadire **3.** svanire ‖ *to — in* (*cine*) aprire in dissolvenza; *to — out*, (*cine*) chiudere in dissolvenza. ♦ to **fade** *vt.* **1.** far sbiadire **2.** far svanire.

fading *s.* **1.** appassimento **2.** scolorimento **3.** affievolimento **4.** dissolvenza.

to **fag** *vt.* affaticare. ♦ to **fag** *vi.* **1.** affaticarsi **2.** sfacchinare.

fag(g)ot *s.* fascina.

faience *s.* terracotta.

fail *s.* fallo.

to **fail** *vi.* **1.** fallire **2.** mancare, venir meno **3.** indebolirsi **4.** esser bocciato. ♦ to **fail** *vt.* **1.** mancare di **2.** bocciare **3.** abbandonare.

failing[1] *agg.* debole. ♦ **failing** *s.* **1.** debolezza **2.** mancanza **3.** fallimento.

failing[2] *prep.* in mancanza di.

failure *s.* **1.** fallimento **2.** incapacità **3.** mancanza **4.** indebolimento **5.** guasto ‖ *to be a —*, essere un fallito.

fain *agg.* contento, disposto. ♦ **fain** *avv.* volentieri ‖ *I would — stay*, preferirei restare.

faint *agg.* **1.** debole **2.** timido **3.** vago.

faint *s.* svenimento ‖ *— -hearted*, codardo.

to **faint** *vi.* svenire.

faintness *s.* **1.** debolezza **2.** timidezza.

fair[1] *agg.* **1.** onesto **2.** biondo **3.** gentile **4.** bello **5.** sereno (*di tempo*) **6.** (*comm.*) libero ‖ *— -play*, comportamento leale. ♦ **fair** *avv.* **1.** con onestà **2.** con precisione.

fair[2] *s.* fiera ‖ *fun —*, Luna Park.

fairly *avv.* **1.** onestamente **2.** abbastanza.

fairness *s.* **1.** bellezza **2.** onestà **3.** color biondo **4.** bianchezza (*di carnagione*).

fairway *s.* canale navigabile.

fairy *agg.* **1.** fatato **2.** immaginario. ♦ **fairy** *s.* fata ‖ *— -tale*, fiaba.

fairyland *s.* paese delle fate.

fairylike *agg.* simile a fata.

faith *s.* **1.** fede **2.** promessa ‖ *— -healer*, guaritore.

faithful *agg.* **1.** fedele **2.** degno di fiducia.

faithfulness *s.* fedeltà.

faithless *agg.* **1.** senza fede **2.** sleale.

to **fake** *vt.* (*gergo*) falsificare.

fakir *s.* fachiro.

falcon *s.* falcone.

falconry *s.* falconeria.

fall *s.* **1.** caduta, cascata **2.** (*amer.*) autunno.

to **fall** (**fell, fallen**) *vi.* **1.** cadere **2.** abbassarsi **3.** capitare in sorte **4.** dividersi ‖ *to — back*, ritirarsi; *to — behind*, restare indietro; *to — in with*, imbattersi; *to — short*, essere insufficiente; to — away, deperire; to — down, far fiasco; to — due, scadere.

fallacious agg. fallace.

fallaciousness s. fallacia.

fallacy s. 1. fallacia 2. errore 3. sofisma.

fallen V. to fall.

fallibility s. fallibilità.

fallible agg. fallibile.

falling agg. cadente. ♦ **falling** s. caduta || — back, ripiegamento; — off, diminuzione; — short, insufficienza.

fall-out s. pioggia radioattiva.

fallow agg. incolto.

false agg. 1. falso 2. stonato 3. ingannevole || — bottom, doppio fondo.

falsehood s. falsità.

falsely avv. falsamente.

falseness s. falsità.

falsifiable agg. falsificabile.

falsification s. falsificazione.

falsifier s. falsificatore.

to **falsify** vt. 1. falsificare 2. smentire.

falsity s. falsità.

to **falter** vi. vacillare. ♦ to **falter** vt. balbettare.

fame s. fama.

famed agg. celebre.

familiar agg. familiare. ♦ **familiar** s. amico intimo || to be — with, esser pratico di.

familiarity s. familiarità.

familiarization s. familiarità.

to **familiarize** vt. familiarizzare.

family s. famiglia.

famine s. carestia.

to **famish** vt. far morire di fame. ♦ to **famish** vi. morire di fame.

famous agg. famoso.

fan¹ s. 1. ventaglio 2. ventilatore 3. pala (d'olica).

fan² s. (gergo) tifoso, ammiratore.

to **fan** vt. 1. sventolare 2. (agr.) vagliare.

fanatic agg. e s. fanatico.

fanatical agg. fanatico.

fanaticism s. fanatismo.

to **fanaticize** vt. rendere fanatico. ♦ to **fanaticize** vi. agire da fanatico.

fanciful agg. 1. fantasioso 2. fantastico.

fancifulness s. 1. fantasia 2. capriccio.

fancy agg. 1. immaginario 2. stra-

vagante 3. decorato. ♦ **fancy** s. 1. fantasia 2. capriccio 3. inclinazione || — ball, ballo in costume; — -dress, costume.

to **fancy** vt. 1. immaginare 2. ritenere.

fang s. 1. zanna 2. dente (velenoso).

fanning s. ventilazione.

fantastic(al) agg. 1. immaginario 2. bizzarro.

to **fantasticate** vt. e vi. fantasticare.

fantasy s. 1. fantasia 2. capriccio.

far agg. (farther, farthest) (further, furthest) lontano. ♦ **far** avv. 1. lontano 2. di gran lunga || — away, — off, lontano; as — as, fino a, per quanto; so —, finora; — -gone, a uno stadio avanzato (di malattie).

farce s. farsa.

farcical agg. farsesco.

farcicality s. qualità farsesca.

fare s. 1. tariffa 2. vitto 3. passeggero || bill of —, lista delle vivande.

to **fare** vi. 1. andare 2. riuscire 3. nutrirsi || to — badly, andar male.

farewell s. congedo. ♦ **farewell** inter. addio.

farfetched agg. remoto.

farinaceous agg. farinaceo.

farinose agg. farinoso.

farm s. fattoria || — -yard, aia. to **farm** vt. coltivare. ♦ to **farm** vi. fare l'agricoltore.

farmer s. agricoltore.

farmhouse s. casa colonica.

farming s. agricoltura.

farmstead s. cascina.

farraginous agg. farraginoso.

farrier s. maniscalco.

farsighted agg. e s. presbite.

farther agg. (comp. di far) più lontano, ulteriore. ♦ **farther** avv. 1. (di) più 2. più lontano 3. inoltre.

farthermost agg. il più lontano.

farthest agg. (superl. di far) il più lontano, estremo. ♦ **farthest** avv. (il) più lontano.

farthing s. "farthing" (moneta inglese: un quarto di penny).

fascicle s. fascicolo.

to **fascinate** vt. affascinare.

fascinating agg. affascinante.

fascination s. fascino.

fascinator s. affascinatore.

fascism s. fascismo.

fascist agg. e s. fascista.

fashion *s.* **1.** modo **2.** abitudine **3.** moda || − *-plate*, figurino; *a man of* −, un uomo di mondo.

to fashion *vt.* foggiare.

fashionable *agg.* **1.** alla moda **2.** elegante.

fast *agg.* **1.** fermo **2.** fedele **3.** inalterabile **4.** rapido **5.** (*fig.*) dissoluto **6.** in anticipo (*di orologio*). ♦ **fast** *avv.* **1.** fermamente **2.** fortemente **3.** velocemente **4.** in modo dissoluto.

fast *s.* digiuno.

to fast *vi.* digiunare.

to fasten *vt.* **1.** attaccare **2.** allacciare **3.** chiudere **4.** fissare. ♦ **to fasten** *vi.* **1.** allacciarsi **2.** chiudersi **3.** fissarsi.

fastener *s.* **1.** fermaglio **2.** legaccio, chiusura || *snap* −, automatico.

fastening *s.* **1.** legatura **2.** gancio, chiavistello.

faster *s.* digiunatore.

fastidious *agg.* schizzinoso.

fastidiousness *s.* schizzinosità.

fastness *s.* **1.** velocità **2.** fermezza **3.** solidità **4.** dissolutezza.

fat *agg.* **1.** grasso **2.** (*fig.*) proficuo. ♦ **fat** *s.* grasso || − *-head*, zuccone.

to fat V. **to fatten**.

fatal *agg.* fatale.

fatalism *s.* fatalismo.

fatalist *s.* fatalista.

fatalistic *agg.* fatalistico.

fatality *s.* **1.** fatalità **2.** fatalismo.

fatally *avv.* **1.** in modo fatale **2.** fatalmente.

fate *s.* fato.

father *s.* padre || − *-in-law*, suocero.

fatherhood *s.* paternità.

fatherland *s.* madrepatria.

fatherless *agg.* senza padre.

fatherlike *agg.* paterno. ♦ **fatherlike** *avv.* paternamente.

fatherly *agg.* e *avv.* V. *fatherlike*.

fathom *s.* (*mar.*) braccio (*misura di profondità*).

to fathom *vt.* scandagliare.

fathomless *agg.* **1.** incommensurabile **2.** incomprensibile.

fatidic(al) *agg.* fatidico.

fatigue *s.* fatica.

to fatigue *vt.* affaticare. ♦ **to fatigue** *vi.* affaticarsi.

fatness *s.* grassezza.

to fatten *vt.* ingrassare. ♦ **to fatten** *vi.* ingrassarsi.

fattener *s.* ingrassatore.

fattening *s.* ingrassamento.

fattiness *s.* grassezza.

fatty *agg.* grasso.

fatuity *s.* fatuità.

fatuous *agg.* fatuo.

fault *s.* **1.** fallo **2.** colpa **3.** difetto || − *-finder*, criticone.

faultiness *s.* imperfezione.

faultless *agg.* **1.** perfetto **2.** irreprensibile.

faulty *agg.* difettoso.

faun *s.* fauno.

favour *s.* favore.

to favour *vt.* **1.** favorire **2.** sostenere **3.** (*fam.*) assomigliare a.

favourable *agg.* favorevole.

favourite *agg.* e *s.* favorito.

favouritism *s.* favoritismo.

fawn *s.* cerbiatto.

to fawn *vt.* fare le feste || *to* − *on*, adulare.

fawner *s.* adulatore.

fawning *s.* servilismo.

fear *s.* paura, timore.

to fear *vt.* e *vi.* temere, aver paura.

fearful *agg.* **1.** terribile **2.** timoroso.

fearfulness *s.* **1.** aspetto terribile **2.** timore.

fearless *agg.* intrepido.

feasibility *s.* fattibilità.

feasible *agg.* fattibile.

feast *s.* **1.** festa **2.** banchetto.

to feast *vt.* **1.** rallegrare **2.** festeggiare. ♦ **to feast** *vi.* banchettare.

feaster *s.* convitato.

feat *s.* impresa, prodezza.

feather *s.* penna, piuma.

to feather *vt.* **1.** coprire di penne, piume **2.** (*mar.*) spalare.

feathered *agg.* **1.** pennuto **2.** (*fig.*) alato.

feathering *s.* piumaggio.

featherless *agg.* implume.

feature *s.* **1.** lineamento **2.** (*cine*) attrazione **3.** caratteristica || − *film*, parte principale di un film.

to feature *vt.* **1.** caratterizzare **2.** (*teat.*) dare una parte importante a.

featureless *agg.* senza caratteristiche.

febrifuge *s.* febbrifugo.

febrile *agg.* febbrile.

February *s.* febbraio.

fecal *agg.* fecale.

fecund *agg.* fecondo.

to fecundate *vt.* fecondare.

fecundation *s.* fecondazione.

fecundity s. fecondità.
fed V. to feed.
federacy s. federazione.
federal agg. federale.
federalism s. federalismo.
federate agg. confederato.
to federate vt. confederare. ◆ to
federate vi. confederarsi.
federation s. (con)federazione.
federative agg. federativo.
fee s. 1. onorario 2. tassa 3. (giur.)
proprietà ereditaria.
feeble agg. debole.
feebleness s. debolezza.
feed s. 1. alimentazione 2. pascolo.
to feed (fed, fed) vt. 1. nutrire
2. pascere 3. rifornire || to be fed
up, essere stufo. ◆ to feed (fed,
fed) vi. nutrirsi || to — up, in-
grassare.
feeder s. 1. ciò che, chi nutre 2.
cavo di alimentazione 3. affluente
4. serbatoio.
feeding s. alimentazione.
feel s. tatto.
to feel (felt, felt) vt. 1. sentire
(coi tatto o col sentimento) 2. tastare, sondare. ◆ to feel (felt,
felt) vi. 1. sentirsi 2. andare a tastoni.
feeling agg. sensibile. ◆ feeling s.
1. sentimento 2. sensibilità 3. sensazione.
feet V. foot.
to feign vt. 1. inventare 2. falsificare. ◆ to feign vi. fingersi.
feignedly avv. simulatamente.
feigner s. simulatore.
feint s. 1. finta 2. simulazione.
to feint vi. fare una finta.
feldspar s. feldspato.
to felicitate vt. felicitare con || to
— so. on sthg., felicitarsi con qu.
di qc.
felicitation s. felicitazione.
felicitous agg. appropriato.
feline agg. e s. felino.
fell[1] V. to fall.
fell[2] agg. 1. crudele 2. funesto.
to fell vt. abbattere.
felling s. taglio (di un bosco).
fellow s. 1. individuo 2. compagno,
collega || -citizen, concittadi-
no; — -creature, simile; a good
—, un buon diavolo.
fellowship s. 1. amicizia 2. associazione.
felon agg. e s. criminale.
felony s. crimine, delitto.

felt[1] V. to feel.
felt[2] s. feltro.
to felt vt. feltrare.
felucca s. feluca.
female agg. 1. femminile 2. (mecc.)
femmina. ◆ female s. femmina.
feminine agg. e s. femminile.
femininity s. femminilità.
feminism s. femminismo.
femur s. femore.
fen s. palude || -berry, mirtillo;
— -fire, fuoco fatuo.
fence s. 1. recinto 2. scherma 3.
(fam.) ricettatore.
to fence vt. cintare. ◆ to fence vi.
tirar di scherma.
fencer s. schermidore.
fencing s. 1. cinta 2. scherma.
fender s. 1. riparo 2. paraurti 3.
(mar.) parabordo.
fennel s. finocchio.
feracity s. feracità.
feral[1] agg. ferale, funesto.
feral[2] agg. ferino.
ferial agg. feriale.
ferine agg. ferino.
ferment s. fermento.
to ferment vi. 1. fermentare 2. agitarsi. ◆ to ferment vt. 1. far fermentare 2. eccitare.
fermentation s. 1. fermentazione 2.
fermento.
fermentative agg. fermentativo.
fern s. felce.
ferocious agg. feroce.
ferocity s. ferocia.
ferreous agg. 1. ferroso 2. ferreo.
ferret[1] s. furetto.
ferret[2] s. nastro, fettuccia.
ferro-concrete s. cemento armato.
ferrous agg. ferroso.
ferruginous agg. ferruginoso.
ferry s. traghetto.
to ferry vt. e vi. traghettare.
ferryman s. traghettatore.
fertile agg. fertile.
fertility s. fertilità.
fertilization s. fertilizzazione.
to fertilize vt. 1. fertilizzare 2. fecondare.
fertilizer s. fertilizzante.
fervency s. fervore.
fervent, fervid agg. ardente.
fervour s. ardore.
festal agg. festivo.
fester s. suppurazione, piaga.
to fester vi. suppurare (di ferita).
festival s. 1. festa 2. festival.
festive agg. 1. festivo 2. festoso.

festivity *s.* festività. ◆ **festivities** *s. pl.* festeggiamenti.

festoon *s.* festone.

to fetch *vt.* 1. andare a prendere 2. tirare 3. fruttare, rendere || *to — back*, riportare.

fetid *agg.* fetido.

fetish *s.* feticcio.

fetishism *s.* feticismo.

fetishist *s.* feticista.

fetter *s.* ceppo, catena.

to fetter *vt.* incatenare.

fettle *s.* condizione || *in fine —*, in forma.

feud[1] *s.* ostilità.

feud[2] *s.* feudo.

feudal *agg.* feudale.

feudalism *s.* feudalesimo.

feudality *s.* 1. feudalesimo 2. feudo.

feudatory *agg.* e *s.* feudatario.

fever *s.* febbre || *to be in a —*, avere la febbre.

feverish *agg.* 1. febbricitante 2. febbrile.

few *agg.* e *pron.* pochi || *a —*, alcuni; *quite a —*, un numero considerevole; *a good —*, parecchi.

fewness *s.* scarsità, esiguità.

fiancé *s.* fidanzato.

fib *s.* fandonia.

to fib *vi.* dire fandonie.

fibre *s.* fibra.

fibroid, fibrous *agg.* fibroso.

fickle *agg.* incostante.

fickleness *s.* incostanza.

fictile *agg.* fittile.

fiction *s.* 1. narrativa 2. finzione.

fictional *agg.* immaginario.

fictitious *agg.* fittizio.

fiddle *s.* violino || *fit as a —*, in ottima salute.

to fiddle *vi.* 1. suonare il violino 2. gingillarsi.

fiddler *s.* violinista.

fiddlestick *s.* archetto. ◆ **fiddlesticks** *s. pl.* sciocchezze.

fidelity *s.* fedeltà.

to fidget *vt.* agitare. ◆ **to fidget** *vi.* agitarsi.

fidgety *agg.* irrequieto.

fiduciary *agg.* e *s.* fiduciario.

field *s.* campo || *— -glass*, binocolo; *— -day*, giorno di esercitazioni; *— -officer*, ufficiale superiore.

fiend *s.* demonio.

fiendish *agg.* diabolico.

fierce *agg.* 1. fiero 2. selvaggio 3. ardente.

fierceness *s.* 1. ferocia 2. ardore.

fiery *agg.* 1. di fuoco 2. focoso 3. infiammabile.

fife *s.* piffero.

fifteen *agg.* e *s.* quindici.

fifteenth *agg.* e *s.* quindicesimo.

fifth *agg.* e *s.* quinto.

fiftieth *agg.* e *s.* cinquantesimo.

fifty *agg.* e *s.* cinquanta || *— - —*, a metà.

fig[1] *s.* fico.

fig[2] *s.* tenuta, vestiario.

fight *s.* 1. lotta 2. spirito combattivo.

to fight (fought, fought) *vt.* e *vi.* combattere || *to — down*, vincere; *to — off*, respingere; *to — shy of*, tenersi alla larga da.

fighter *s.* 1. combattente 2. (*aer.*) caccia.

fighting *s.* combattimento, rissa.

figuration *s.* figurazione.

figurative *agg.* 1. figurativo 2. figurato.

figure *s.* 1. figura, forma 2. cifra 3. diagramma.

to figure *vt.* raffigurare. ◆ **to figure** *vi.* 1. immaginarsi 2. passare per.

figurehead *s.* 1. prestanome 2. (*mar.*) polena.

filament *s.* filamento.

filamentary, filamentous *agg.* filamentoso.

filcher *s.* ladruncolo.

file[1] *s.* lima.

file[2] *s.* 1. schedario, archivio 2. fila 3. raccolta.

to file[1] *vt.* limare.

to file[2] *vt.* 1. archiviare 2. ordinare. ◆ **to file** *vi.* marciare in fila.

filial *agg.* filiale.

filiation *s.* filiazione.

filibuster *s.* filibustiere.

filigree *s.* filigrana.

filing[1] *s.* limatura.

filing[2] *s.* 1. archiviazione 2. sfilata.

fill *s.* sazietà.

to fill *vt.* 1. riempire 2. occupare 3. otturare (*di denti*) || *to — in*, *to — up*, riempire, compilare. ◆ **to fill** *vi.* riempirsi.

fillet *s.* 1. nastro 2. (*cuc.*) filetto.

filling *s.* 1. riempitura 2. otturazione 3. (*cuc.*) ripieno || *— station*, stazione di rifornimento.

fillip *s.* 1. schiocco (*delle dita*) 2. stimolo.

film *s.* 1. pellicola 2. velo 3. membrana.

to film *vt.* 1. coprire con una pellicola 2. filmare. ◆ to film vi. 1. coprirsi con una pellicola 2. girare un film.

filmy agg. velato.

filter s. filtro.

to **filter** vt. e vi. filtrare.

filth s. sozzura.

filthily avv. in modo sudicio.

filthiness s. 1. sozzura 2. corruzione morale.

filthy agg. 1. sozzo 2. corrotto.

filtration s. filtrazione.

fin s. 1. pinna 2. (mecc.) aletta.

final agg. e s. finale.

finalist s. finalista.

finality s. 1. finalità 2. carattere definitivo.

finally avv. alla fine.

finance s. finanza.

to **finance** vt. finanziare.

financial agg. finanziario.

financier s. 1. finanziere 2. finanziatore.

financing s. finanziamento.

finch s. fringuello.

find s. scoperta, ritrovamento.

to **find (found, found)** vt. 1. trovare 2. provvedere 3. ritenere || to — out, scoprire.

finding s. 1. scoperta 2. sentenza.

fine¹ agg. 1. bello 2. fine. ◆ **fine** avv. bene.

fine² s. multa.

to **fine¹** vt. raffinare. ◆ **fine** vi. raffinarsi.

to **fine²** vt. multare.

finely avv. 1. bene 2. finemente.

finger s. dito || — -print, impronta digitale; — -tip, punta delle dita; — -post, cartello segnavia.

to **finger** vt. 1. toccare con le dita 2. rubare || to be light-fingered (fig.), avere le mani lunghe.

finish s. 1. fine 2. finezza 3. finitura.

to **finish** vt. e vi. finire.

finished agg. (fig.) perfetto.

finishing agg. ultimo, conclusivo. ◆ **finishing** s. (ri)finitura.

finite agg. limitato.

Finn s. finlandese.

Finnic, Finnish agg. finlandese.

fir (-tree) s. abete || — -wood, abetaia.

fire s. 1. fuoco 2. incendio || on —, in fiamme; — -guard, parafuoco; — -plug, bocca da incendio; — -station, caserma dei pompieri; — -works, fuochi d'artificio.

to **fire** vt. 1. dar fuoco 2. far fuoco

3. (fig.) infiammare. ◆ to **fire** vi. 1. prender fuoco 2. (fig.) infiammarsi.

firedamp s. grisù.

fire escape s. 1. scala di sicurezza 2. scala dei pompieri.

firefly s. lucciola.

fireman s. pompiere.

fireplace s. caminetto.

fireproof agg. incombustibile.

fireside s. angolo del focolare.

firewood s. legna da ardere.

firing s. 1. accensione 2. sparo 3. alimentazione (di un fuoco) || — squad, plotone d'esecuzione.

firm¹ agg. 1. fisso 2. solido 3. deciso.

firm² s. azienda, ditta.

firmament s. firmamento.

firmly avv. 1. fermamente 2. solidamente.

firmness s. 1. fermezza 2. stabilità.

first agg. primo || — -aid, pronto soccorso; — -born, primogenito; — -class, di prima qualità; — -name, nome di battesimo. ◆ **first** avv. 1. prima di tutto 2. per la prima volta || at —, sulle prime. ◆ **first** s. 1. primo 2. principio.

firth s. fiordo.

fiscal agg. fiscale.

fish s. pesce || — -hook, amo.

to **fish** vi. 1. pescare 2. cercare. ◆ to **fish** vt. pescare.

fisher s. pescatore.

fisherman s. pescatore.

fishery s. pesca.

fishing s. pesca || — -boat, peschereccio; — -line, lenza.

fishmonger s. pescivendolo.

fishy agg. 1. di pesce 2. pescoso 3. (fig.) equivoco.

fission s. fissione.

fist s. pugno.

fit¹ agg. 1. adatto 2. pronto.

fit² s. 1. giusta misura 2. attacco, accesso (di febbre, ira ecc.).

to **fit** vt. 1. adattare 2. andar bene a 3. provare || to — out, equipaggiare.

fitful agg. 1. irregolare 2. spasmodico.

fitfulness s. irregolarità.

fitness s. convenienza.

fitter s. 1. aggiustatore 2. montatore.

fitting agg. adatto, conveniente. ◆ **fitting** s. 1. adattamento, prova 2. equipaggiamento. ◆ **fittings**

s. pl. **1.** accessori **2.** arredamento (*sing.*).

five *agg.* e *s.* cinque.

fix *s.* **1.** difficoltà **2.** (*mar.*) punto.

to fix *vt.* fissare || — *up*, sistemare, riparare. ♦ **to fix** *vi.* stabilirsi.

fixation *s.* fissazione.

fixed *agg.* **1.** fisso **2.** stabilito.

fixer *s.* **1.** montatore **2.** fissatore.

fixing *s.* **1.** collocamento **2.** messa in opera **3.** fissaggio.

fixity *s.* **1.** stabilità **2.** fissità.

fizz *s.* **1.** effervescenza **2.** bevanda effervescente.

to fizz *vi.* frizzare.

fjord *s.* fiordo.

flabbiness *s.* **1.** mollezza **2.** fiacchezza (*di carattere ecc.*).

flabby *agg.* **1.** floscio **2.** fiacco.

flaccid *agg.* flaccido.

flaccidness *s.* flaccidezza.

flag¹ *s.* bandiera || — *ship*, nave ammiraglia.

flag² *s.* lastra di pietra (*per pavimentazione*).

to flag¹ *vt.* **1.** imbandierare **2.** pavesare. ♦ **to flag** *vi.* **1.** pendere **2.** avvizzire.

to flag² *vt.* lastricare.

to flagellate *vt.* flagellare.

flagellation *s.* flagellazione.

flagellator *s.* flagellatore.

flagrancy *s.* flagranza.

flagrant *agg.* flagrante.

flagstaff *s.* asta di bandiera.

flair *s.* fiuto, intuizione.

flake *s.* **1.** fiocco (*di neve, lana ecc.*) **2.** favilla **3.** lamina **4.** scaglia.

to flake *vt.* **1.** sfaldare **2.** squamare **3.** coprire di fiocchi. ♦ **to flake** *vi.* **1.** sfaldarsi **2.** squamarsi **3.** cadere in fiocchi.

flaky *agg.* **1.** a falde **2.** a lamine, a scaglie.

flame *s.* fiamma || — *thrower*, lanciafiamme.

to flame *vi.* fiammeggiare.

flaming *agg.* ardente.

flange *s.* orlo, frangia.

flank *s.* fianco.

to flank *vt.* **1.** fiancheggiare **2.** (*mil.*) attaccare il fianco di.

flannel *s.* flanella. ♦ **flannels** *s. pl.* calzoni di flanella.

flap *s.* **1.** lembo, falda **2.** colpo, agitazione **3.** linguetta **4.** (*aer.*) alettone.

flare *s.* **1.** fiammata improvvisa **2.**

chiarore.

to flare *vi.* **1.** brillare (*di luce incerta*) **2.** agitarsi **3.** divampare.

flash *s.* **1.** lampo **2.** chiusa || — *back*, scena retrospettiva; — *light*, lampo al magnesio.

to flash *vt.* **1.** proiettare **2.** diffondere. ♦ **to flash** *vi.* **1.** lampeggiare **2.** muoversi rapidamente.

flashing *agg.* risplendente. ♦ **flashing** *s.* splendore, scintillio.

flask *s.* fiasca.

flat¹ *agg.* **1.** piatto, piano **2.** disteso **3.** deciso **4.** sgonfio (*di pneumatico*).

flat² *s.* **1.** superficie piana **2.** pianura **3.** bassofondo **4.** chiatta **5.** appartamento **6.** (*mus.*) bemolle || — *iron*, ferro da stiro.

flatly *avv.* **1.** pianamente **2.** scialbamente **3.** recisamente.

flatness *s.* **1.** piattezza **2.** decisione.

to flatten *vt.* **1.** appiattire **2.** smorzare. ♦ **to flatten** *vi.* **1.** appiattirsi **2.** indebolirsi.

to flatter *vt.* **1.** adulare **2.** illudere.

flatterer *s.* adulatore.

flattery *s.* adulazione.

flatulence, flatulency *s.* **1.** flatulenza **2.** vanità.

flatus *s.* flatulenza.

to flaunt *vt.* **1.** sventolare **2.** ostentare.

flavour *s.* gusto, aroma.

to flavour *vt.* aromatizzare, dare gusto a.

flavoured *agg.* **1.** profumato **2.** saporito.

flavouring *s.* **1.** aroma **2.** condimento.

flavourless *agg.* insipido.

flaw *s.* **1.** screpolatura **2.** falla, pecca.

flawless *agg.* perfetto.

flax *s.* lino.

flaxen *agg.* **1.** di lino **2.** biondo.

to flay *vt.* **1.** scorticare **2.** criticare aspramente.

flea *s.* pulce || — *bite* (*fig.*), inezia.

fleck *s.* **1.** macchia **2.** scaglia.

to flee (fled, fled) *vt.* **1.** abbandonare **2.** evitare, schivare. ♦ **to flee (fled, fled)** *vi.* **1.** fuggire **2.** svanire.

fleece *s.* vello.

fleecy *agg.* lanoso.

to fleer *vt.* e *vi.* far beffe (a).

fleet *s.* flotta.

fleeting *agg.* fugace.

Flemish *agg.* fiammingo.

flesh *s.* carne ‖ *to lose* —, dimagrire; *to put on* —, ingrassare.

fleshiness *s.* 1. carnosità 2. corpulenza.

fleshless *agg.* scarno.

fleshly *agg.* carnale, sensuale.

flew V. *to fly.*

to flex *vt.* flettere, piegare. ♦ to flex *vi.* flettersi.

flexibility *s.* 1. flessibilità 2. docilità.

flexible *agg.* 1. flessibile 2. docile.

flexion *s.* 1. flessione 2. curva.

flexuosity *s.* flessuosità.

flexuous *agg.* flessuoso.

flicker *s.* tremolio, bagliore.

to flicker *vi.* 1. tremolare 2. guizzare. ♦ to flicker *vt.* far tremolare.

flight[1] *s.* 1. volo 2. stormo 3. rampa (*di scale*).

flight[2] *s.* fuga.

flimsiness *s.* leggerezza, frivolezza.

flimsy *agg.* leggero, sottile.

to flinch *vi.* indietreggiare, ritirarsi.

fling *s.* 1. getto 2. beffa 3. tentativo.

to fling (flung, flung) *vt.* gettare. ‖ *to* — *open*, spalancare. ♦ to fling (flung, flung) *vi.* gettarsi.

flint *s.* selce, pietra focaia.

to flip *vt.* 1. far schioccare 2. sbattere.

flippancy *s.* leggerezza.

flippant *agg.* leggero.

flipper *s.* pinna.

flirt *s.* 1. movimento rapido 2. amoreggiamento.

to flirt *vt.* muovere rapidamente. ♦ to flirt *vi.* amoreggiare.

flirtation *s.* amoreggiamento.

to flit *vi.* 1. volare 2. scorrere.

float *s.* galleggiante.

to float *vt.* 1. trasportare 2. inondare 3. (*comm.*) varare (*un progetto ecc.*). ♦ to float *vi.* 1. galleggiare 2. spandersi.

floatage *s.* 1. galleggiamento 2. relitto.

floatation *s.* (*comm.*) varo.

floater *s.* galleggiante.

floating *agg.* 1. galleggiante 2. oscillante, fluttuante.

flock *s.* 1. bioccolo 2. gregge 3. cascame.

to flock *vi.* affollarsi.

floe *s.* banchisa.

to flog *vt.* fustigare ‖ *to* — *a dead horse*, fare una fatica inutile.

flogger *s.* fustigatore.

flood *s.* inondazione, diluvio.

to flood *vt.* inondare. ♦ to flood *vi.* straripare.

flooding *s.* 1. inondazione 2. emorragia.

floodlight *s.* illuminazione con riflettore.

flood tide *s.* flusso della marea.

floor *s.* 1. pavimento 2. piano ‖ —*lamp*, lampada a stelo.

to floor *vt.* pavimentare.

flooring *s.* impiantito.

flop *s.* 1. tonfo 2. insuccesso.

floral *agg.* floreale.

floriculture *s.* floricultura.

floriculturist *s.* floricultore.

florid *agg.* 1. florido 2. fiorito (*di stile*).

floridity *s.* floridezza.

florin *s.* fiorino.

florist *s.* fiorista.

flotilla *s.* flottiglia.

to flounce *vi.* agitarsi ‖ *to* — *out*, andarsene furibondo.

flour *s.* farina ‖ *potato*— *,* fecola.

to flour *vt.* 1. infarinare 2. macinare.

flourish *s.* 1. ornamento 2. squillo di tromba.

to flourish *vi.* 1. prosperare 2. essere attivo.

flourishing *agg.* 1. fiorente 2. pomposo.

floury *agg.* 1. farinoso 2. infarinato.

flow *s.* corrente, flusso.

to flow *vi.* 1. scorrere 2. derivare da. ♦ to flow *vt.* inondare.

flower *s.* fiore ‖ —*-bed*, aiuola; —*-bud*, bocciuolo.

to flower *vi.* fiorire. ♦ to flower *vt.* infiorare.

flowering *agg.* in fiore. ♦ flowering *s.* fioritura.

flowerless *agg.* senza fiori.

flowery *agg.* fiorito.

flowing *agg.* 1. fluente 2. fluido.

flown V. *to fly.*

flu *s.* influenza.

to fluctuate *vi.* 1. fluttuare 2. ondeggiare.

fluctuation *s.* oscillazione.

flue *s.* condotto per l'aria.

fluency *s.* 1. fluidità 2. scioltezza.

fluent *agg.* 1. fluente 2. dalla parola facile.

fluently *avv.* 1. fluentemente 2. speditamente.

fluff *s.* peluria.

fluffy *agg.* **1.** soffice, vaporoso **2.** coperto di peluria.

fluid *agg.* e *s.* fluido.

fluidity *s.* fluidità.

flung V. *to* fling.

fluorescence *s.* fluorescenza.

fluorescent *agg.* fluorescente.

fluoride *s.* fluoruro.

fluorine *s.* fluoro.

flurry *s.* **1.** ventata **2.** agitazione.

to flurry *vt.* agitare.

flush *agg.* **1.** abbondante **2.** pieno di vita **3.** a pari livello **4.** ben fornito. ♦ **flush** *s.* **1.** flusso **2.** vampata **3.** vigore.

to flush *vt.* **1.** lavare **2.** far scorrere **3.** rianimare. ♦ **to flush** *vi.* **1.** scorrere **2.** arrossire.

flute *s.* **1.** flauto **2.** increspatura.

fluted *agg.* **1.** flautato **2.** increspato.

flutter *s.* **1.** battito, movimento rapido **2.** eccitazione.

to flutter *vt.* agitare. ♦ **to flutter** *vi.* **1.** agitarsi **2.** battere le ali.

fluttering *agg.* **1.** svolazzante **2.** palpitante. ♦ **fluttering** *s.* **1.** svolazzamento **2.** palpitazione.

fluxion *s.* flusso.

fly¹ *s.* **1.** volo **2.** calesse **3.** *(mecc.)* volano.

fly² *s.* mosca.

to fly (flew, flown) *vi.* volare. ♦ **to fly (flew, flown)** *vt.* **1.** far volare **2.** sventolare || *to — about*, svolazzare; *to — away*, fuggire; *to off* *(aer.)*, decollare.

flying *agg.* **1.** rapido **2.** sventolante || *—boat*, idrovolante.

flypaper *s.* carta moschicida.

foam *s.* schiuma || *— rubber* gommapiuma.

to foam *vi.* spumeggiare.

foamy *agg.* spumeggiante.

focal *agg.* focale.

focus *s.* **1.** fuoco **2.** focolaio.

to focus *vt.* mettere a fuoco.

fodder *s.* foraggio.

to fodder *vt.* foraggiare.

foe *s.* nemico.

foetus *s.* feto.

fog *s.* nebbia.

foggy *agg.* nebbioso *(anche fig.)*.

foible *s.* debolezza.

foil¹ *s.* **1.** fioretto **2.** traccia.

foil² *s.* lamina.

fold¹ *s.* ovile.

fold² *s.* **1.** piega **2.** spira.

to fold¹ *vt.* **1.** piegare **2.** avvolgere **3.** abbracciare. ♦ **to fold** *vi.* piegarsi.

to fold² *vt.* chiudere nell'ovile.

folder *s.* **1.** volantino **2.** cartelletta.

folding *agg.* pieghevole. ♦ **folding** *s.* **1.** piega, piegatura **2.** avvolgimento **3.** abbraccio.

foliage *s.* fogliame.

folio *s.* *(tip.)* fo(g)lio.

folk *s.* gente, popolo.

folklore *s.* folclore.

folkloristic *agg.* folcloristico.

to follow *vt.* e *vi.* seguire.

follower *s.* seguace.

following *agg.* seguente. ♦ **following** *s.* seguito.

folly *s.* follia.

to foment *vt.* fomentare.

fomentation *s.* fomentazione.

fomenter *s.* fomentatore.

fond *agg.* **1.** amante **2.** affettuoso.

to fondle *vt.* vezzeggiare.

fondly *avv.* **1.** amorevolmente **2.** ingenuamente.

fondness *s.* tenerezza, amore.

font *s.* **1.** fonte battesimale **2.** acquasantiera.

food *s.* cibo.

foodstuff *s.* alimenti *(pl.)*.

fool *s.* **1.** sciocco **2.** buffone || *to make a — of*, beffarsi di.

to fool *vt.* ingannare. ♦ **to fool** *vi.* fare lo sciocco || *to — away*, sperperare.

foolery *s.* follia.

foolhardiness *s.* folle temerarietà.

foolhardy *agg.* temerario.

foolish *agg.* sciocco.

foolishness *s.* sciocchezza.

foot *s.* *(pl.* feet) **1.** piede **2.** zampa || *on —*, a piedi.

football *s.* pallone.

footballer *s.* calciatore.

foot-bath *s.* pediluvio.

footboard *s.* predellino.

footbridge *s.* cavalcavia.

footfall *s.* passo.

footing *s.* punto d'appoggio.

footlights *s. pl.* luci della ribalta.

footman *s.* domestico.

footmark *s.* orma.

footnote *s.* poscritto.

footpath *s.* sentiero.

footprint, footstep *s.* orma.

footstool *s.* sgabello.

footway *s.* passaggio pedonale.

fop *s.* damerino.

foppery *s.* fatuità.

foppish *agg.* fatuo.

for¹ *prep.* per || *— all that*, ciò nonostante; *as* —, in quanto a.

for[1] *cong.* poiché.

forage *s.* foraggio.

foray *s.* incursione, saccheggio.

forbade V. *to forbid.*

to **forbear** (**forbore, forborne**) *vi.* 1. astenersi 2. essere paziente.

forbearance *s.* 1. astensione 2. pazienza.

forbearing *agg.* paziente.

to **forbid** (**forbade, forbidden**) *vt.* proibire, impedire.

forbidding *agg.* 1. severo 2. ripugnante.

forbore V. *to forbear.*

forborne V. *to forbear.*

force *s.* forza. ♦ **forces** *s. pl.* truppe ‖ *the Armed Forces,* le Forze Armate.

to **force** *vt.* 1. forzare 2. costringere ‖ *to* — *back,* respingere; *to* — *in,* sfondare; *to* — *on,* far avanzare.

forceful *agg.* forte.

forceps *s.* 1. forcipe 2. pinza.

forcible *agg.* 1. violento 2. potente.

ford *s.* guado.

to **ford** *vt.* guadare.

fordable *agg.* guadabile.

fore *agg.* anteriore. ♦ **fore** *s.* prua.

forearm *s.* avambraccio.

to **forearm** *vt.* premunire.

to **forebode** *vt.* presagire (*un male*).

foreboding *s.* presagio.

forecast *s.* previsione.

to **forecast** (**forecast, forecast**) *vt.* prevedere.

forecastle *s.* castello di prua.

forefather *s.* antenato.

forefinger *s.* indice.

foreground *s.* primo piano.

forehead *s.* fronte.

foreign *agg.* 1. straniero 2. estraneo ‖ — *Office,* Ministero degli Esteri.

foreigner *s.* straniero.

forelock *s.* ciuffo.

foreman *s.* caposquadra, caporeparto.

foremast *s.* albero di trinchetto.

forename *s.* nome di battesimo.

forensic(al) *agg.* forense.

to **forerun** (**foreran, forerun**) *vt.* precorrere.

forerunner *s.* 1. precursore 2. messaggero.

foresail *s.* vela di trinchetto.

to **foresee** (**foresaw, foreseen**) *vt.* prevedere.

foreseeable *agg.* prevedibile.

foreseeing *s.* previsione.

foreseen V. *to foresee.*

to **foreshadow** *vt.* adombrare.

foreshortening *s.* scorcio.

foresight *s.* 1. previsione 2. previdenza.

forest *s.* foresta.

forestal *agg.* forestale.

to **forestall** *vt.* 1. prevenire 2. accaparrare.

forestalling *s.* 1. anticipazione 2. accaparramento.

forester *s.* 1. guardia forestale 2. abitante di foreste.

forestry *s.* 1. foresta 2. silvicultura.

foretaste *s.* pregustazione.

to **foretaste** *vt.* pregustare.

to **foretell** (**foretold, foretold**) *vt.* predire.

forethought *agg.* premeditato. ♦ **forethought** *s.* 1. premeditazione 2. previdenza.

foretold V. *to foretell.*

forever *avv.* per sempre.

to **forewarn** *vt.* avvertire.

foreword *s.* prefazione.

forfeit *s.* 1. perdita 2. ammenda 3. penitenza.

forfeiture *s.* 1. multa 2. confisca.

to **forgather** *vi.* riunirsi, associarsi.

forgave V. *to forgive.*

forge *s.* fucina.

to **forge** *vt.* 1. foggiare, fabbricare 2. contraffare.

forger *s.* 1. fabbro 2. falsario.

forgery *s.* contraffazione.

to **forget** (**forgot, forgotten**) *vt.* e *vi.* dimenticare, dimenticarsi.

forgetful *agg.* 1. immemore 2. negligente.

forgetfulness *s.* 1. oblio 2. negligenza.

forget-me-not *s.* non-ti-scordar-di-me.

to **forgive** (**forgave, forgiven**) *vt.* perdonare.

forgiveness *s.* perdono.

forgot V. *to forget.*

forgotten V. *to forget.*

fork *s.* 1. forchetta 2. forca 3. forcella 4. biforcazione.

to **fork** *vi.* biforcarsi ‖ *to* — *out,* (*gergo*) pagare. ♦ to **fork** *vt.* biforcare.

forked *agg.* biforcuto.

forlorn *agg.* abbandonato.

form *s.* 1. forma 2. modulo 3. banco.

to **form** *vt.* formare. ♦ to **form** *vi.* formarsi.
formal *agg.* formale || — *dress*, abito da cerimonia.
formalism *s.* formalismo.
formalist *s.* formalista.
formality *s.* formalità.
to **formalize** *vt.* 1. formare 2. formalizzare.
format *s.* formato.
formation *s.* formazione.
formative *agg.* formativo.
forme *s.* (*tip.*) forma di stampa.
former[1] *agg. e pron.* precedente, il primo (*fra due*).
former[2] *s.* 1. artefice 2. stampo.
formerly *avv.* precedentemente.
formic *agg.* formico.
formidable *agg.* 1. formidabile 2. spaventoso.
formless *agg.* informe.
formulary *s.* formulario.
to **formulate** *vt.* formulare.
formulation *s.* formulazione.
to **forsake** (**forsook**, **forsaken**) *vt.* abbandonare.
forsaking *s.* abbandono.
forsook V. *to forsake.*
to **forswear** (**forswore**, **forsworn**) *vt.* 1. abiurare 2. spergiurare.
fort *s.* (*mil.*) fortezza.
forth *avv.* 1. avanti 2. fuori || *and so* —, e così via.
forthcoming *agg.* prossimo.
fortieth *agg. e s.* quarantesimo.
fortification *s.* fortificazione.
to **fortify** *vt.* fortificare.
fortitude *s.* forza d'animo.
fortnight *s.* due settimane.
fortnightly *agg.* quindicinale. ♦ **fortnightly** *avv.* ogni due settimane.
fortress *s.* (*mil.*) fortezza.
fortuitous *agg.* fortuito.
fortunate *agg.* 1. fortunato 2. propizio.
fortune *s.* 1. sorte: *to tell fortunes*, predire la sorte 2. fortuna.
fortune-teller *s.* indovino.
forty *agg. e s.* quaranta.
forward *agg.* 1. avanzato 2. precoce 3. pronto.
to **forward** *vt.* 1. promuovere 2. spedire.
forwarder *s.* spedizioniere.
forwarding *s.* spedizione.
forward(s) *avv.* avanti, in avanti.
fossil *agg. e s.* fossile.

fossilization *s.* fossilizzazione.
to **fossilize** *vt.* fossilizzare. ♦ to **fossilize** *vi.* fossilizzarsi.
to **foster** *vt.* 1. favorire 2. allevare, nutrire.
fought V. *to fight.*
foul *agg.* 1. sporco 2. tempestoso.
foulmouthed *agg.* sboccato.
to **foul** *vt.* 1. sporcare 2. urtare. ♦ to **foul** *vi.* 1. sporcarsi 2. urtarsi.
found V. *to find.*
to **found**[1] *vt.* fondare.
to **found**[2] *vt.* fondere.
foundation *s.* 1. fondazione 2. fondamenta 3. fondamento.
founder[1] *s.* fondatore.
founder[2] *s.* fonditore.
to **founder** *vi.* crollare. ♦ to **founder** *vt.* affondare.
foundling *s.* trovatello || —*hospital*, brefotrofio.
foundry *s.* fonderia.
fountain *s.* 1. fontana 2. sorgente || —*pen*, penna stilografica.
four *agg. e s.* quattro || —*banded*, quadrumane; — *footed*, quadrupede.
fourscore *agg.* ottanta.
fourteen *agg. e s.* quattordici.
fourteenth *agg. e s.* quattordicesimo.
fourth *agg. e s.* quarto.
fowl *s.* pollo, pollame.
fox *s.* volpe: —*hunt*, caccia alla volpe.
foxglove *s.* digitale.
foxy *agg.* 1. volpino 2. rossiccio 3. scolorito 4. aspro.
foyer *s.* ridotto.
fraction *s.* frazione.
fractional *agg.* frazionario.
to **fractionize** *vt.* frazionare.
fracture *s.* frattura.
to **fracture** *vt.* fratturare. ♦ to **fracture** *vi.* fratturarsi.
fragile *agg.* fragile.
fragility *s.* fragilità.
fragment *s.* frammento.
fragmentary *agg.* frammentario.
fragrance *s.* fragranza.
fragrant *agg.* fragrante.
frail *agg.* 1. debole 2. caduco.
frailness, frailty *s.* debolezza.
frame *s.* 1. cornice 2. struttura, intelaiatura.
to **frame** *vt.* 1. incorniciare 2. formare.
framework *s.* struttura.
framing *s.* incorniciatura.

franc *s.* franco.

franchise *s.* franchigia.

Franciscan *agg.* e *s.* francescano.

frank *agg.* franco.

frankness *s.* franchezza.

frantic *agg.* frenetico.

fraternal *agg.* fraterno.

fraternity *s.* 1. fraternità 2. confraternita.

fraternization *s.* affratellamento.

to fraternize *vi.* fraternizzare.

fratricidal *agg.* fratricida.

fratricide *s.* 1. fratricida 2. fratricidio.

fraud *s.* 1. frode 2. impostura 3. (*fam.*) impostore.

fraudulence *s.* frode.

fraudulent *agg.* fraudolento.

fray *s.* zuffa.

to fray *vt.* consumare. ♦ **to fray** *vi.* consumarsi.

freak *s.* 1. capriccio 2. macchiolina.

freakish, freaky *agg.* capriccioso.

freckle *s.* lentiggine.

freckled, freckly *agg.* lentigginoso.

free *agg.* 1. libero 2. (*comm.*) franco 3. abbondante 4. gratuito || — *on board*, franco porto. ♦ **free** *avv.* gratuitamente.

to free *vt.* liberare.

freedom *s.* libertà.

freely *avv.* 1. liberamente 2. gratuitamente.

freemason *s.* massone.

freemasonry *s.* massoneria.

freethinker *s.* libero pensatore.

freethinking *s.* libertà di pensiero.

freetrade *s.* libero scambio.

freetrader *s.* libero scambista.

freeze *s.* gelo, congelamento.

to freeze (froze, frozen) *vt.* e *vi.* 1. gelare 2. (*imp.*) far freddo.

freezer *s.* cella frigorifera.

freezing *agg.* glaciale, congelante. ♦ **freezing** *s.* congelamento.

freight *s.* 1. trasporto 2. nolo.

to freight *vt.* 1. trasportare 2. noleggiare 3. caricare.

French *agg.* francese. ♦ **French** *s.* lingua francese.

to frenchify *vt.* francesizzare. ♦ **to frenchify** *vi.* francesizzarsi.

Frenchman *s.* francese (*uomo*).

Frenchwoman *s.* francese (*donna*).

frenzied *agg.* frenetico.

frenzy *s.* frenesia, delirio.

frequency *s.* frequenza.

frequent *agg.* frequente.

to frequent *vt.* frequentare.

fresco *s.* affresco.

fresh *agg.* fresco, nuovo, puro || — *water*, acqua dolce. ♦ **fresh** *s.* sorgente.

fresh-water *agg.* d'acqua dolce.

to freshen *vt.* 1. rinfrescare 2. desalinizzare. ♦ **to freshen** *vi.* rinfrescarsi.

freshly *avv.* 1. in modo fresco 2. recentemente.

freshman *s.* matricola.

freshness *s.* 1. freschezza 2. inesperienza.

fret¹ *s.* agitazione.

fret² *s.* 1. fregio 2. traforo.

to fret¹ *vt.* rodere. ♦ **to fret** *vi.* 1. affliggersi 2. agitarsi.

to fret² *vt.* 1. ornare 2. traforare.

fretful *agg.* irritabile.

fretfully *avv.* con irritazione.

fretfulness *s.* irritabilità.

fretwork *s.* intaglio ornamentale.

friability *s.* friabilità.

friable *agg.* friabile.

friar *s.* frate || *Black* —, domenicano; *Grey* —, francescano; *White* —, carmelitano.

friction *s.* frizione, attrito.

Friday *s.* venerdì; *Good* —, Venerdì Santo.

fried *agg.* fritto.

friend *s.* amico || *to make friends*, fare amicizia; *the Society of Friends*, i quaccheri.

friendless *agg.* senza amici.

friendliness *s.* cordialità.

friendly *agg.* amichevole. ♦ **friendly** *avv.* amichevolmente.

friendship *s.* amicizia.

frigate *s.* fregata.

fright *s.* spavento.

to frighten *vt.* spaventare.

frightful *agg.* spaventevole.

frightfulness *s.* spavento.

frigid *agg.* 1. glaciale 2. frigido.

frigidity *s.* 1. freddezza 2. frigidità.

frill *s.* 1. fronzolo 2. gala increspata.

to frill *vt.* ornare di gale.

fringe *s.* 1. frangia 2. bordo.

to fringe *vt.* ornare.

frippery *s.* cianfrusaglie (*pl.*).

to frisk *vi.* fare capriole.

frisky *agg.* gaio.

frivolity *s.* frivolezza.

frivolous *agg.* frivolo.

frizzly, frizzy *agg.* crespo.

frock *s.* 1. abito 2. tonaca.

frog¹ *s.* rana.

frog² s. alamaro.

frogman s. sommozzatore.

frolic s. scherzo.

frolicsome agg. scherzoso.

from prep. da, di.

front agg. anteriore. ♦ front s. 1. fronte 2. sfrontatezza.

to front vt. fronteggiare.

frontal agg. frontale.

frontier s. frontiera.

frontispiece s. frontespizio.

frost s. 1. gelo 2. brina || —bite, congelamento; hoar- —, brinata.

to frost vt. 1. gelare 2. (cuc.) glassare 3. smerigliare.

frosty agg. 1. gelato 2. gelido 3. canuto.

froth s. 1. schiuma 2. frivolezza.

to froth vi. far schiuma.

frothy agg. 1. schiumoso 2. leggero.

frown s. 1. l'aggrottare le ciglia 2. cipiglio.

to frown vi. 1. aggrottare le ciglia 2. acciglarsi.

frowning agg. acciglato.

froze V. to freeze.

frozen V. to freeze.

fructiferous agg. fruttifero.

to fructify vi. fruttificare. ♦ to fructify vt. fertilizzare.

frugal agg. frugale.

frugalist s. persona frugale.

frugality s. frugalità.

fruit s. 1. frutta 2. frutto.

fruiterer s. fruttivendolo.

fruitful agg. 1. fruttifero 2. fertile 3. redditizio.

fruitfulness s. 1. fertilità 2. vantaggio.

fruition s. 1. godimento 2. realizzazione.

fruitless agg. infruttuoso.

to frustrate vt. frustrare.

frustration s. frustrazione.

frustum s. (pl. -ta) (geom.) tronco.

fry s. fritto, frittura.

to fry vt. e vi. friggere.

fudge s. fandonia, sciocchezza.

to fudge vt. rattoppare.

fuel s. combustibile || —oil, nafta.

to fuel vt. alimentare di combustibile.

fugacity s. fugacità.

fugitive agg. 1. fuggitivo 2. effimero. ♦ fugitive s. 1. fuggitivo 2. rifugiato.

fugitiveness s. fuggevolezza.

fugue s. (mus.) fuga.

fulcrum s. (pl. fulcra) fulcro.

to fulfil vt. 1. compiere 2. adempiere, esaurire.

fulfilment s. 1. compimento 2. adempimento, esaudimento.

fulgency s. fulgidezza.

fulgent agg. fulgente.

fulgid agg. fulgido.

fulguration s. folgorazione.

full agg. pieno || — up, completo; — -stop, punto. ♦ full avv. interamente. ♦ full s. 1. intero 2. massimo.

fullness s. pienezza.

fully avv. completamente.

fulminant agg. fulminante.

fulmination s. 1. fulminazione 2. imprecazione.

fumarole s. fumarola.

to fumble vi. annaspare. ♦ to fumble vt. maneggiare goffamente.

fume s. 1. fumo 2. eccitazione.

to fume vi. 1. fumare 2. irritarsi.

fun s. 1. divertimento 2. facezia || to make — of so., canzonare qu.; to have good —, divertirsi molto.

funambulism s. funambolismo.

funambulist s. funambolo.

function s. funzione.

to function vi. 1. funzionare 2. fungere da.

functional agg. funzionale.

functionary s. funzionario.

fund s. fondo, riserva.

to fund vt. 1. accumulare 2. investire in obbligazioni.

fundament s. base.

fundamental agg. fondamentale. ♦ fundamental s. fondamento.

funeral agg. funebre. ♦ funeral s. funerale.

funerary, funereal agg. funereo.

funicular agg. e s. funicolare.

funnel s. 1. imbuto 2. camino, ciminiera.

funny agg. 1. comico 2. strano.

fur s. 1. pelliccia 2. patina, rivestimento.

to fur vt. coprire con pelliccia.

furbelow s. falpalà.

furious agg. furioso.

to furl vt. 1. piegare, chiudere 2. ammainare (vele ecc.). ♦ to furl vi. piegarsi, chiudersi.

furnace s. fornace.

to furnish vt. 1. fornire 2. ammobiliare.

furnisher s. fornitore.

furnishings s. pl. arredamento (sing.).

furniture *s.* 1. mobilio 2. contenuto.

furrier *s.* pellicciaio.

furriery *s.* pellicceria.

furrow *s.* 1. solco 2. scia.

to **furrow** *vt.* 1. solcare 2. arare.

further *agg.* (*comp. di far*) 1. più lontano 2. ulteriore. ♦ **further** *avv.* 1. più in là 2. ancora.

to **further** *vt.* favorire.

furthermore *avv.* inoltre.

furthermost *agg.* il più lontano.

furthest *agg.* (*superl. di far*) estremo. ♦ **furthest** *avv.* all'estremo limite.

furtive *agg.* furtivo.

furunculosis *s.* furuncolosi.

fury *s.* furia.

fuse *s.* 1. valvola, fusibile 2. spoletta 3. miccia.

to **fuse** *vt.* 1. fondere 2. liquefare. ♦ to **fuse** *vi.* 1. fondersi 2. saltare (*di valvola*).

fuselage *s.* fusoliera.

fusible *agg.* fusibile.

fusion *s.* fusione.

fuss *s.* 1. trambusto 2. smancerie.

to **fuss** *vi.* far confusione. ♦ to **fuss** *vt.* irritare.

fussily *avv.* 1. con inutile scalpore 2. con esagerata importanza.

fussy *agg.* 1. che fa confusione 2. meticoloso.

fusty *agg.* stantio.

futility *s.* futilità.

future *agg.* e *s.* futuro.

futurism *s.* futurismo.

fuzz *s.* lanuggine.

fuzzily *avv.* confusamente.

fuzziness *s.* 1. increspatura (*di capelli*) 2. (*foto*) sfocatura.

fuzzy *a* *g.* 1. lanuginoso 2. confuso 3. (*foto*) sfocato.

G

G *s.* (*mus.*) sol.

to **gabble** *vt.* e *vi.* parlare in modo confuso.

gabbler *s.* chiacchierone.

gable *s.* frontone.

gadfly *s.* 1. tafano 2. (*fig.*) persona irritante.

gadget *s.* aggeggio.

Gael *s.* gaelico.

Gaelic *agg.* e *s.* gaelico.

gaff *s.* uncino, rampone.

gag *s.* 1. bavaglio 2. improvvisazione 3. trovata geniale.

to **gag** *vt.* imbavagliare. ♦ to **gag** *vi.* improvvisare (*motti di spirito*).

gage *s.* garanzia.

to **gage** *vt.* dare in pegno.

gaiety *s.* gaiezza. ♦ **gaieties** *s. pl.* divertimenti.

gaily *avv.* gaiamente.

gain *s.* 1. guadagno 2. aumento, miglioramento.

to **gain** *vt.* e *vi.* 1. guadagnare 2. aumentare || **to — on**, guadagnar terreno su.

gainer *s.* chi guadagna.

gainful *agg.* lucroso.

gainings *s. pl.* guadagni.

to **gainsay** *vt.* contraddire.

gainsaying *s.* contraddizione.

gait *s.* andatura.

gaiter *s.* ghetta.

galalith *s.* galalite.

galantine *s.* galantina.

galaxy *s.* galassia.

gale *s.* tempesta.

galenic *agg.* galenico.

Galilean *agg.* e *s.* galileo.

gall[1] *s.* bile, fiele || **— -bladder**, cistifellea.

gall[2] *s.* scorticatura 2. irritazione.

to **gall** *vt.* irritare. ♦ to **gall** *vi.* irritarsi.

gallant *agg.* 1. prode 2. galante. ♦ **gallant** *s.* uomo di mondo.

gallantry *s.* 1. galanteria 2. coraggio 3. atto, discorso amoroso.

galleon *s.* galeone.

gallery *s.* galleria || **picture-**, pinacoteca.

galley *s.* 1. (*mar.*) galea 2. (*mar.*) cambusa 3. (*tip.*) vantaggio || **— proof** (*tip.*), bozza in colonna; **— slave**, galeotto.

Gallic *agg.* e *s.* gallico.

gallicism *s.* francesismo.

gallinacean *agg.* e *s.* gallinaceo.

gallium *s.* gallio.

gallon *s.* gallone (*misura*).

galloon *s.* gallone (*ornamento*).

gallooned *agg.* gallonato.

gallop *s.* 1. galoppo: **at a —**, al galoppo 2. galoppata.

to **gallop** *vt.* far galoppare. ♦ to **gallop** *vi.* galoppare.

gallows *s. pl.* patibolo (*sing.*).

galore *s.* abbondanza. ♦ **galore** *avv.* in abbondanza.

galosh(e) *s.* galoscia.

galvanic(al) *agg.* **1.** galvanico **2.** *(fig.)* galvanizzante.

galvanization *s.* galvanizzazione.

to galvanize *vt.* galvanizzare.

galvanometer *s.* galvanometro.

galvanoplastic *agg.* galvanoplastico.

gamble *s.* gioco d'azzardo.

to gamble *vt. e vi.* giocare (*d'azzardo*).

gambler *s.* giocatore d'azzardo.

gambling *s.* V. **gamble** || — *-house,* casa da gioco.

gambol *s.* piroetta.

game *agg.* risoluto. ♦ **game** *s.* **1.** gioco *(con regole),* mano *(in una partita)* **2.** *(fig.)* progetto **3.** selvaggina *(coll.).*

to game *v.* to gamble.

gamekeeper *s.* guardacaccia.

gamely *avv.* coraggiosamente.

gamesome *agg.* scherzoso.

gamester *s.* giocatore.

gammon *s.* *(mar.)* trinca di bompresso.

gang *s.* **1.** squadra **2.** banda.

to gang *vt. e vi.* formare una banda.

ganglion *s.* *(pl.* ganglia) ganglio.

gangrene *s.* cancrena.

to gangrene *vi.* andare in cancrena.

gangster *s.* bandito.

gangsterism *s.* banditismo.

gangway *s.* **1.** passaggio *(tra file di sedie ecc.)* **2.** *(mar.)* passerella.

gaol *s.* prigione.

to gaol *vt.* imprigionare.

gaoler *s.* carceriere.

gap *s.* **1.** apertura, breccia **2.** intervallo **3.** divergenza **4.** lacuna.

gape *s.* **1.** sbadiglio **2.** apertura **3.** stupore.

to gape *vi.* **1.** spalancare la bocca **2.** sbadigliare **3.** restare a bocca aperta.

gaping *agg.* **1.** aperto **2.** stupito.

garage *s.* autorimessa || — *keeper,* garagista.

garb *s.* costume.

garbage *s.* rifiuto.

garden *s.* giardino.

to garden *vi.* fare del giardinaggio.

gardener *s.* giardiniere.

gardening *s.* giardinaggio.

gargarism *s.* gargarismo.

gargle *s.* liquido per gargarismi.

to gargle *vt. e vi.* gargarizzare.

gargoyle *s.* doccione.

garish *agg.* **1.** abbagliante **2.** appariscente.

garland *s.* ghirlanda.

garlic *s.* aglio.

garment *s.* abito, indumento.

garnet[1] *s.* granato.

garnet[2] *s.* *(mar.)* paranco.

to garnish *vt.* guarnire.

garnish(ment) *s.* ornamento.

garret *s.* soffitta.

garrison *s.* guarnigione.

to garrison *vt.* presidiare.

garrulity *s.* garrulità.

garrulous *agg.* garrulo.

garter *s.* giarrettiera || *knight o, the Garter,* Cavaliere dell'Ordine della Giarrettiera.

gas *s.* gas || — *-fitter,* gassista; — *-mask,* maschera antigas; — *-meter,* contatore del gas.

to gas *vt.* **1.** fornire di gas **2.** asfissiare col gas.

Gascon *agg. e s.* guascone.

gasconade *s.* guasconata.

gaseous *agg.* gassoso.

gash *s.* sfregio.

to gash *vt.* sfregiare.

gas oil *s.* gasolio.

gasoline *s.* *(amer.)* benzina.

gasp *s.* respiro affannoso.

to gasp *vi.* **1.** ansare **2.** restare senza fiato **3.** parlare affannosamente.

gassy *agg.* gassoso.

gastric *agg.* gastrico.

gastritis *s.* gastrite.

gastroenteritis *s.* gastroenterite.

gastronome *s.* gastronomo.

gastronomic(al) *agg.* gastronomico.

gastronomy *s.* gastronomia.

gate *s.* **1.** cancello **2.** porta.

gatekeeper *s.* portiere, custode.

gateway *s.* portone, ingresso.

to gather *vt.* **1.** raccogliere **2.** acquistare **3.** dedurre. ♦ **to gather** *vi.* raccogliersi.

gathering *s.* **1.** raccolta **2.** *(med.)* ascesso.

gaud *s.* fronzolo.

gaudiness *s.* sfarzo.

gaudy *agg.* sfarzoso. ♦ **gaudy** *s.* festa *(universitaria).*

gauge *s.* **1.** misura **2.** calibro **3.** *(ferr.)* scartamento **4.** pescaggio || *narrow —,* scartamento ridotto.

to gauge *vt.* misurare.

gaunt *agg.* scarno.

gauze *s.* garza, velo, mussolina.

gauzy *agg.* trasparente.

gave V. to give.

gay *agg.* **1.** gaio **2.** licenzioso.

gayety *s.* gaiezza.

gaze s. sguardo fisso.

to gaze vi. fissare.

gazelle s. gazzella.

gazette s. gazzetta.

gazetteer s. 1. giornalista 2. dizionario geografico.

gear s. 1. meccanismo 2. (auto) marcia, cambio 3. (mecc.) ingranaggio.

to gear vt. ingranare || to — up, down, aumentare, diminuire la velocità.

gearing s. ingranaggio, innesto.

geese V. goose.

gelatin(e) s. gelatina.

gelatinous agg. gelatinoso.

to geld vt. castrare.

gelid agg. gelido.

gem s. gemma.

gemmy agg. pieno di gemme.

gender s. genere.

genderless agg. di genere comune.

genealogical agg. genealogico.

genealogy s. genealogia.

generable agg. generabile.

general agg. e s. generale.

generality s. 1. generalità 2. maggioranza.

generalization s. generalizzazione.

to generalize vt. e vi. generalizzare.

generally avv. generalmente.

to generate vt. generare.

generation s. generazione.

generative agg. generativo.

generator s. generatore.

generic(al) agg. generico.

generosity s. generosità.

generous agg. 1. generoso 2. abbondante.

genesis s. (pl. -ses) genesi.

genetic(al) agg. genetico.

genetics s. genetica.

genial agg. 1. gioviale 2. geniale 3. mite (di clima).

geniality s. 1. giovialità 2. mitezza (di clima).

genital agg. e s. genitale.

genitive agg. e s. genitivo.

genius s. genio.

genocide s. genocidio.

genre s. genere.

genteel agg. raffinato.

gentian s. genziana.

gentile agg. e s. pagano.

gentility s. signorilità.

gentle agg. 1. nobile 2. garbato 3. moderato 4. facile.

gentleman s. 1. signore 2. gentiluomo.

gentlemanlike, gentlemanly agg.

da gentiluomo.

gentleness s. gentilezza.

gentlewoman s. gentildonna.

gently avv. 1. gentilmente, con delicatezza 2. gradualmente.

gentry s. classe gentilizia.

to genuflect vi. genuflettersi.

genuflection s. genuflessione.

genuine agg. 1. autentico 2. sincero 3. puro.

genuineness s. 1. autenticità 2. sincerità.

genus s. (pl. -nera) genere.

geodesy s. geodesia.

geographer s. geografo.

geographic(al) agg. geografico.

geography s. geografia.

geologic(al) agg. geologico.

geologist s. geologo.

geology s. geologia.

geometer s. geometra.

geometric(al) agg. geometrico.

geometrician s. geometra.

geometry s. geometria.

geophysics s. geofisica.

geopolitics s. geopolitica.

georgic agg. georgico.

geranium s. geranio.

gerent s. gerente.

germ s. germe.

german agg. germano.

German agg. e s. tedesco.

Germanic agg. germanico.

Germanism s. germanesimo.

Germanist s. germanista.

germanium s. germanio.

germinal agg. germinale.

to germinate vt. far germinare. ◆ to germinate vi. germinare.

germination s. germinazione.

gerontology s. gerontologia.

gerund s. gerundio.

gerundial agg. gerundivo.

gerundive agg. e s. gerundivo.

gestation s. gestazione.

to gesticulate vi. gesticolare.

gesticulation s. gesticolazione.

gesture s. 1. gesto 2. il gestire.

to gesture vi. far gesti.

to get (got, got) vt. 1. ottenere, procurare 2. prendere 3. portare 4. fare. ◆ to get (got, got) vi. 1. andare 2. divenire || to — off, scendere; to — over, scavalcare; to — out, (far) uscire; to — up, alzarsi; to — married, sposarsi; to — hold of, impossessarsi di.

getaway s. 1. fuga 2. (sport) partenza.

gettable *agg.* ottenibile.

get-up *s.* 1. equipaggiamento 2. presentazione (*di libro, giornale ecc.*).

geyser *s.* 1. geyser 2. scaldabagno.

ghastliness *s.* 1. aspetto spaventoso 2. pallore spettrale.

ghastly *agg.* 1. spaventoso 2. spettrale.

gherkin *s.* cetriolo.

Ghibelline *agg. e s.* ghibellino.

ghost *s.* 1. spirito 2. spettro || *to give up the —*, spirare.

ghostliness *s.* 1. l'essere spettrale 2. spiritualità.

ghostly *agg.* 1. spettrale 2. spirituale.

giant *s.* gigante.

giantism *s.* gigantismo.

gibbet *s.* patibolo.

to gibbet *vt.* 1. impiccare 2. (*fig.*) mettere alla berlina.

gibbosity *s.* gibbosità.

gibbous *agg.* gibboso.

gibe *s.* scherno.

to gibe *vt. e vi.* schernire.

giblets *s. pl.* regaglie.

giddily *avv.* vertiginosamente.

giddiness *s.* 1. capogiro 2. (*fig.*) frivolezza.

giddy *agg.* 1. stordito 2. vertiginoso 3. frivolo.

to giddy *vt.* stordire. ◆ **to giddy** *vi.* aver le vertigini.

gift *s.* 1. dono 2. dote.

to gift *vt.* dotare.

gig[1] *s.* 1. calessino 2. (*mar.*) iole.

gig[2] *s.* rampone, fiocina.

gigantean, gigantic *agg.* gigantesco.

giggle *s.* risatina.

to giggle *vi.* fare risatine.

to gild (gilt, gilt) (*anche reg.*) *vt.* (in)dorare.

gilder *s.* doratore.

gilding *s.* doratura.

gill *s.* 1. branchia 2. pappagorgia.

gilt V. *to gild.*

gilt *s.* doratura.

gimlet *s.* succhiello.

gin[1] *s.* "gin" (*liquore*).

gin[2] *s.* 1. elevatore 2. trappola (*per animali*).

ginger *s.* zenzero.

gingerly *agg.* cauto. ◆ **gingerly** *avv.* cautamente.

gipsy *s.* zingaro.

gipsydom *s.* gli zingari (*pl.*).

gipsyish *agg.* zingaresco.

giraffe *s.* giraffa.

to gird (girt, girt) (*anche reg.*) *vt.* cingere.

girder *s.* 1. trave maestra 2. sbarra.

girdle *s.* 1. cintura 2. reggicalze.

to girdle *vt.* cingere.

girl *s.* ragazza || *flower —*, fioraia.

girlhood *s.* adolescenza (*di ragazza*).

Girondist *agg. e s.* girondino.

girt V. *to gird.*

girth *s.* 1. circonferenza 2. cinghia.

to give (gave, given) *vt.* dare || *to — in*, cedere; *to — out*, annunciare, venir meno; *to — up*, smettere, abbandonare; *to — birth to*, generare; *to — oneself up*, costituirsi (*alla polizia*); *to — oneself up to*, dedicarsi (a); *to — off*, emettere (*luce ecc.*).

giver *s.* datore.

glacial *agg.* glaciale.

glaciation *s.* glaciazione.

glacier *s.* ghiacciaio.

glacis *s.* spalto.

glad *agg.* lieto.

to gladden *vt.* rallegrare. ◆ **to gladden** *vi.* rallegrarsi.

glade *s.* radura.

gladiator *s.* gladiatore.

gladiolus *s.* (*pl.* -li) gladiolo.

gladly *avv.* con piacere.

gladness *s.* contentezza.

glair *s.* albume.

gladsome *agg.* gioioso.

glair *s.* albume.

glamorous *agg.* affascinante.

glamour *s.* 1. fascino 2. incantesimo

glance *s.* 1. occhiata 2. colpo obliquo.

to glance *vt. e vi.* 1. gettare uno sguardo 2. sfiorare 3. balenare || *to — off*, sorvolare su.

gland *s.* 1. ghiandola 2. ghianda.

glandiferous *agg.* ghiandifero.

glandular *agg.* glandolare.

glare *s.* 1. luce abbagliante 2. sguardo truce 3. abbagliamento.

to glare *vi.* 1. splendere 2. guardare torvamente.

glaring *agg.* 1. abbagliante 2. evidente.

glass *s.* 1. vetro 2. bicchiere 3. specchio || *—-ware*, articoli in vetro; *— -work*, fabbrica di vetro; *— -paper*, carta vetrata. ◆ **glasses** *s. pl.* occhiali, cannocchiale (*sing.*).

to glass *vt.* 1. specchiare 2. imbottigliare.

glassy *agg.* 1. vitreo 2. cristallino.

glaucous *agg.* glauco.
glaze *s.* superficie vetrosa.
to glaze *vt.* **1.** smaltare **2.** mettere vetri a. ♦ **to glaze** *vi.* diventare vitreo.
glazier *s.* vetraio.
glazy *agg.* vitreo.
gleam *s.* barlume.
to gleam *vi.* scintillare.
gleamy *agg.* scintillante.
to glean *vt.* e *vi.* spigolare.
gleaner *s.* spigolatore.
gleaning *s.* spigolatura.
glee *s.* allegria.
gleeful *agg.* allegro.
glib *agg.* **1.** liscio **2.** facondo **3.** sciolto.
glibness *s.* **1.** disinvoltura **2.** facondia.
glide *s.* scivolata.
to glide *vt.* **1.** far scorrere **2.** trascorrere. ♦ **to glide** *vi.* **1.** scivolare **2.** passare.
glider *s.* aliante.
gliding *agg.* scorrevole. ♦ **gliding** *s.* volo a vela.
glimmer *s.* barlume.
to glimmer *vi.* brillare.
glimpse *s.* **1.** visione **2.** occhiata **3.** vaga idea.
to glimpse *vt.* e *vi.* intravedere.
glitter *s.* scintillio.
to glitter *vi.* scintillare.
gloaming *s.* crepuscolo.
to gloat *vi.* fissare avidamente.
global *agg.* globale.
globe *s.* **1.** globo **2.** pianeta.
globous, globular *agg.* sferico.
globule *s.* globulo.
gloom *s.* **1.** oscurità **2.** tristezza.
to gloom *vt.* **1.** oscurare **2.** rattristare. ♦ **to gloom** *vi.* **1.** oscurarsi **2.** rattristarsi.
gloomy *agg.* cupo.
glorification *s.* glorificazione.
to glorify *vt.* glorificare.
glorious *agg.* **1.** glorioso **2.** splendido.
gloriousness *s.* V. glory.
glory *s.* **1.** gloria **2.** splendore.
to glory *vi.* vantarsi.
gloss *s.* **1.** glossa **2.** lucentezza **3.** apparenza.
glossarist *s.* glossatore.
glossary *s.* glossario.
glossy *agg.* lucido.
glottis *s.* glottide.
glottologist *s.* glottologo.
glottology *s.* glottologia.

glove *s.* guanto ‖ *to be hand in — with*, essere molto intimo con.
gloved *agg.* inguantato.
glover *s.* guantaio.
glow *s.* **1.** calore **2.** splendore **3.** colorito ‖ *—worm*, lucciola.
to glow *vi.* ardere.
glucose *s.* glucosio.
glue *s.* colla.
to glue *vt.* incollare.
glut *s.* **1.** scorpacciata **2.** saturazione.
to glut *vt.* **1.** saziare **2.** saturare. ♦ **to glut** *vi.* fare una scorpacciata.
gluten *s.* glutine.
gluteus *s.* (*pl.* glutei) gluteo.
glutton *s.* ghiottone.
gluttonous *agg.* ghiottone.
gluttony *s.* ghiottoneria.
glycerin(e) *s.* glicerina.
glycogen *s.* glicogeno.
gnarled *agg.* nodoso.
to gnash *vt.* e *vi.* digrignare.
gnat *s.* zanzara.
to gnaw *vt.* rodere.
gnawing *agg.* **1.** rosicante **2.** corrodente.
gnome[1] *s.* gnomo.
gnome[2] *s.* massima.
gnomic *agg.* gnomico.
gnosis *s.* gnosi.
gnostic *agg.* e *s.* gnostico.
gnosticism *s.* gnosticismo.
go *s.* **1.** movimento **2.** energia **3.** colpo ‖ *—between*, intermediario; *— -by*, evasione; *— -cart*, girello.
to go (**went, gone**) *vi.* **1.** andare **2.** divenire ‖ *to — by*, passare; *to — for*, andare a cercare; *to — on*, continuare.
goad *s.* pungolo.
to goad *vt.* stimolare.
goal *s.* **1.** traguardo **2.** (*sport*) rete ‖ *- -keeper*, portiere.
goat *s.* capra.
goatish *agg.* **1.** caprino **2.** lascivo.
to gobble *vt.* trangugiare, inghiottire.
goblin *s.* folletto.
god *s.* **1.** dio, divinità **2.** Dio.
godchild *s.* (*pl.* -children) figlioccio.
goddaughter *s.* figlioccia.
goddess *s.* dea.
godfather *s.* padrino.
godless *agg.* **1.** ateo **2.** empio.
godlike *agg.* divino.
godliness *s.* devozione.
godly *agg.* religioso.
godmother *s.* madrina.

godown s. deposito.

godsend s. dono del cielo.

godship s. divinità.

godson s. figlioccio.

goggle agg. **1.** stralunato **2.** sporgente (di occhi).

to goggle vt. stralunare. ♦ **to goggle** vi. essere sporgenti (di occhi).

goggles s. pl. occhiali di protezione.

going s. **1.** l'andare **2.** partenza.

goitre s. gozzo.

goitrous agg. gozzuto.

gold s. d'oro. ♦ **gold** s. oro || — -field, zona aurifera; — -dig-r, cercatore d'oro.

golden agg. dorato, d'oro.

goldfinch s. cardellino.

goldsmith s. orefice.

gone V. to go.

gonfalon s. gonfalone.

goniometer s. goniometro.

goniometry s. goniometria.

good (better, best) agg. **1.** buono **2.** bravo **3.** bello. ♦ **good** inter. bene!

good s. **1.** bene **2.** utilità || for —, per sempre.

good-bye inter. e s. addio, arrivederci.

good-for-nothing s. buono a nulla.

goodly agg. bello.

goodness s. **1.** bontà **2.** il meglio || my —!, Dio mio!

goods s. pl. merce (sing.).

goodwill s. **1.** buona volontà **2.** benevolenza.

goody agg. troppo buono. ♦ **goody** inter. bene!

goose s. (pl. geese) oca.

gooseberry s. uva spina.

goose-step s. passo dell'oca.

gore s. sangue rappreso.

gorge s. gola.

to gorge V. to glut.

gorgeous agg. magnifico.

gorgeousness s. magnificenza.

gospel s. vangelo.

gossamer s. ragnatela.

gossip s. **1.** pettegolezzo **2.** pettegolo.

to gossip vi. far pettegolezzi.

gossiper s. pettegolo.

gossipy agg. pettegolo.

got V. to get.

Gothic agg. e s. gotico.

gothicism s. **1.** stile gotico **2.** rozzezza.

gouache s. guazzo.

gouge s. sgorbia.

gourd s. zucca.

gourmand s. goloso.

gourmet s. buongustaio.

gout s. **1.** gotta **2.** goccia.

gouty agg. gottoso.

to govern vt. **1.** governare **2.** controllare **3.** (gramm.) reggere.

governable agg. docile.

governess s. istitutrice.

government s. governo.

governmental agg. governativo.

governor s. **1.** governatore **2.** regolatore.

gown s. **1.** veste **2.** toga || dressing-—, veste da camera; night- —, camicia da notte.

grab s. presa.

to grab vt. **1.** afferrare **2.** (mecc.) bloccare.

grace s. grazia.

to grace vt. adornare.

graceful agg. grazioso.

gracefulness s. grazia.

graceless agg. **1.** sgraziato **2.** depravato.

gracile agg. gracile.

gracility s. gracilità.

gracious agg. benigno || good —!, mio Dio!

gradation s. gradazione.

grade s. **1.** grado **2.** pendio.

to grade vt. **1.** graduare **2.** livellare.

gradient agg. che sale, scende gradatamente. ♦ **gradient** s. pendenza.

gradual agg. graduale.

graduality s. gradualità.

graduate s. laureato.

to graduate vt. **1.** graduare **2.** laureare. ♦ **to graduate** vi. laurearsi.

graduation s. **1.** graduazione **2.** laurea.

graft s. innesto.

to graft vt. innestare.

grain s. **1.** granaglie (pl.) **2.** chicco **3.** grano.

grainy agg. **1.** granuloso **2.** granoso.

gram s. grammo.

Gramineae s. pl. graminacee.

grammar s. grammatica.

grammarian s. grammatico.

grammatic(al) agg. grammaticale.

gramophone s. grammofono.

granary s. granaio.

grand agg. **1.** grande **2.** nobile || -aunt, prozia; — -uncle, prozio; — -nephew, pronipote (maschio); — -niece, pronipote (femmina).

grandchild s. (pl. -children) nipote (di nonni).

granddaughter s. nipote (femmina) (di nonni).

grandeur s. grandiosità.

grandfather s. nonno.

grandiloquence s. magniloquenza.

grandiloquent agg. magniloquente.

grandiose agg. grandioso.

grandiosity s. grandiosità.

grandmother s. nonna.

grandmotherly agg. protettivo.

grandparents s. pl. nonni.

grandson s. nipote (maschio) (di nonni).

grange s. fattoria, casa colonica.

granite s. granito.

granitic agg. granitico.

granivorous agg. granivoro.

grant s. concessione.

to **grant** vt. concedere || to take for granted, dare per scontato.

granular agg. granulare.

granularity s. granulosità.

to **granulate** vt. granulare. ♦ to **granulate** vi. granularsi.

granulation s. granulazione.

granulous agg. granuloso.

grape s. 1. acino || -shot, mitraglia. ♦ **grapes** s. pl. uva.

grapefruit s. pompelmo.

grapevine s. 1. vigna 2. (fam.) notizia ufficiosa.

graph s. grafico.

graphic(al) agg. 1. grafico 2. pittoresco.

graphite s. grafite.

graphologist s. grafologo.

graphology s. grafologia.

graphomania s. grafomania.

graphomaniac s. grafomane.

grapnel s. (mar.) grappino.

to **grapple** vt. afferrare. ♦ to **grapple** vi. lottare.

grappling s. (mar.) aggancio || -irons, grappini d'abbordaggio.

grasp s. 1. stretta 2. manico 3. potere.

to **grasp** vt. e vi. afferrare.

grasping agg. avido.

grass s. erba.

grasshopper s. cavalletta.

grass-widow s. donna separata dal marito.

grassy agg. erboso.

grate s. 1. grata 2. graticola.

to **grate** vt. 1. fornire di grata 2. grattugiare. ♦ to **grate** vi. stridere.

grateful agg. grato.

gratefulness s. gratitudine.

grater s. grattugia.

to **gratify** vt. 1. ricompensare 2. appagare.

gratifying agg. soddisfacente.

grating[1] agg. 1. irritante 2. stridente. ♦ **grating** s. stridore.

grating[2] s. 1. grata 2. (ott.) reticolo.

gratitude s. gratitudine.

gratuitous agg. gratuito.

gratuity s. mancia.

grave[1] agg. grave.

grave[2] s. tomba.

gravel s. ghiaia.

to **gravel** vt. inghiaiare.

gravelly agg. ghiaioso.

graven agg. intagliato.

graver s. 1. incisore 2. bulino.

gravestone s. pietra tombale.

graveyard s. cimitero.

gravid agg. gravido.

to **gravitate** vi. gravitare.

gravitation s. gravitazione.

gravitational agg. gravitazionale.

gravity s. gravità.

gravy s. sugo.

gray agg. e s. grigio.

to **graze**[1] vt. 1. colpo di striscio 2. escoriazione.

to **graze**[1] vt. e vi. 1. graffiare 2. sfiorare.

to **graze**[2] vt. e vi. pascolare, condurre al pascolo.

grazier s. allevatore (di bestiame).

grazing[1] s. abrasione.

grazing[2] s. pascolo.

grease s. grasso.

to **grease** vt. ungere, lubrificare.

greaser s. ingrassatore.

greasiness s. untuosità.

greasy agg. 1. grasso 2. unto, untuoso 3. scivoloso.

great agg. grande || -grandchild, pronipote (di nonni); -grandfather, bisnonno; -grandmother, bisnonna.

greatness s. grandezza.

Grecian agg. e s. greco.

greed(iness) s. avidità.

greedy agg. avido.

Greek agg. e s. greco.

green agg. 1. verde 2. inesperto 3. vigoroso 4. recente. ♦ **green** s. prato. ♦ **greens** s. pl. frasche, verdura (sing.).

greenery s. 1. vegetazione 2. serra.

greengrocer s. erbivendolo.

greenhouse s. serra.

greenish *agg.* verdastro.
greenness *s.* 1. color verde 2. acerbezza 3. ingenuità 4. vigore.
greenroom *s.* (*teat.*) camerino.
to greet *vt.* e *vi.* salutare.
greeting *s.* saluto.
Gregorian *agg.* gregoriano.
grenadier *s.* granatiere.
grenadine *s.* granatina.
grew V. *to grow.*
grey *agg.* e *s.* grigio.
greyhound *s.* levriere.
greyness *s.* grigiore.
grid *s.* griglia.
gridiron *s.* graticola.
grief *s.* 1. dolore 2. fallimento || *to come to —*, fare fiasco.
grievance *s.* 1. lagnanza 2. torto.
to grieve *vt.* affliggere. ♦ **to grieve** *vi.* affliggersi.
grievous *agg.* 1. doloroso 2. grave.
griffon *s.* grifone.
grill *s.* 1. graticola 2. cibo ai ferri || *— -room*, rosticceria.
to grill *vt.* e *vi.* arrostire (*alla graticola*).
grille *s.* inferriata.
grim *agg.* cupo.
grimace *s.* smorfia.
grime *s.* sudiciume.
to grime *vt.* insudiciare.
grimly *avv.* cupamente.
grimy *agg.* sudicio.
grin *s.* 1. largo sorriso 2. sogghigno.
to grin *vi.* 1. fare un largo sorriso 2. sogghignare.
to grind (ground, ground) *vt.* 1. macinare 2. molare 3. digrignare 4. (*fig.*) opprimere.
grinder *s.* 1. mola 2. molare 3. arrotino || *organ- —*, suonatore di organetto.
grinding *agg.* irritante. ♦ **grinding** *s.* 1. macinatura 2. stridore 3. affilatura 4. (*fig.*) oppressione.
grindstone *s.* mola.
grip *s.* 1. stretta 2. manico 3. (*fig.*) padronanza || *to lose one's grips*, perdere le staffe.
to grip *vt.* e *vi.* afferrare.
gripe *s.* 1. presa 2. freno. ♦ **gripes** *s. pl.* colica (*sing.*).
gripper *s.* pinza.
grist *s.* grano da macinare || *to bring — to one's mill*, tirar l'acqua al proprio mulino.
grit *s.* sabbia, arenaria.
grizzly *agg.* grigio. ♦ **grizzly** *s.* orso grigio.

groan *s.* gemito.
to groan *vi.* gemere.
groaning *s.* gemito.
grocer *s.* droghiere.
grocery *s.* drogheria. ♦ **groceries** *s. pl.* droghe e coloniali.
groggy *agg.* vacillante.
groin *s.* inguine.
groom *s.* stalliere.
to groom *vt.* strigliare.
groove *s.* solco.
to grope *vi.* brancolare.
gropingly *avv.* a tastoni.
gross *agg.* 1. grossolano 2. pesante 3. lussureggiante 4. (*comm.*) lordo.
grotesque *agg.* grottesco.
grotto *s.* grotta.
ground[1] V. *to grind.*
ground[2] *s.* 1. suolo, terreno 2. distanza, territorio 3. motivi, ragioni (*general. pl.*) || *— -floor*, pianterreno.
to ground *vt.* fondare. ♦ **to ground** *vi.* 1. fondarsi 2. arenarsi.
grounded *agg.* interrato.
groundless *agg.* infondato.
groundlessness *s.* infondatezza.
grounds *s. pl.* 1. fondi, sedimenti 2. parco (*sing.*).
group *s.* gruppo.
to group *vt.* raggruppare. ♦ **to group** *vi.* raggrupparsi.
grouping *s.* raggruppamento.
grove *s.* boschetto || *olive —*, oliveto.
to grovel *vi.* 1. strisciare a terra 2. (*fig.*) umiliarsi.
grovelling *s.* strisciamento. ♦ **grovelling** *agg.* 1. strisciante 2. (*fig.*) abbietto.
to grow (grew, grown) *vi.* 1. crescere 2. diventare || *to — better*, migliorare; *to — old*, invecchiare; *to — up*, crescere, diventare maturo (*di persone*). ♦ **to grow (grew, grown)** *vt.* coltivare.
grower *s.* coltivatore.
growing *s.* coltivazione.
growl *s.* brontolio.
to growl *vt.* e *vi.* brontolare.
growler *s.* brontolone.
grown V. *to grow.*
grown-up *agg.* e *s.* adulto.
growth *s.* 1. crescita 2. produzione.
grub *s.* 1. verme 2. larva.
to grub *vt.* e *vi.* scavare.
grubby *agg.* 1. bacato 2. sporco.
grudge *s.* malanimo || *to bear a — against so.*, nutrire rancore verso

qu.

to **grudge** *vt.* 1. dare a malincuore 2. invidiare.

grudging *agg.* 1. riluttante 2. invidioso.

gruesome *agg.* raccapricciante.

gruff *agg.* burbero.

grumble *s.* brontolio.

to **grumble** *vt. e vi.* brontolare.

grumbler *s.* brontolone.

grumbling *s.* brontolio.

grumpy *agg.* burbero, tetro.

grunt *s.* grugnito.

to **grunt** *vt. e vi.* grugnire.

gruyère *s.* gruviera.

guarantee *s.* 1. garanzia 2. garante.

to **guarantee** *vt.* garantire.

guard *s.* 1. guardia 2. capotreno 3. parapetto.

to **guard** *vt.* custodire.

guardian *s.* 1. guardiano 2. tutore.

guardianship *s.* 1. protezione 2. tutela.

guardless *agg.* indifeso.

guardrail *s.* 1. spartitraffico 2. corrimano (*di scala*).

Guelph *s.* guelfo.

guerrilla *s.* 1. guerriglia 2. guerrigliere.

guess *s.* supposizione.

to **guess** *vt. e vi.* 1. supporre 2. indovinare.

guess-work *s.* congettura.

guest *s.* ospite || — *-house*, pensione.

guffaw *s.* riso sguaiato.

guide *s.* guida.

to **guide** *vt.* guidare.

guild *s.* corporazione.

guile *s.* insidia.

guileful *agg.* insidioso.

guileless *agg.* sincero.

guillotine *s.* ghigliottina.

guilt *s.* colpa.

guiltiness *s.* colpevolezza.

guiltless *agg.* innocente.

guilty *agg.* colpevole.

guinea *s.* ghinea.

Guinea-pig *s.* cavia.

guise *s.* 1. aspetto, apparenza 2. falso aspetto.

guitar *s.* chitarra.

guitarist *s.* chitarrista.

gulf *s.* golfo.

gull¹ *s.* gabbiano.

gull² *s.* sciocco.

to **gull** *vt.* truffare.

gully *s.* condotto (*di scolo*) || —

-hole, tombino.

gulp *s.* 1. boccone 2. sorso.

to **gulp** *vt.* inghiottire.

gum¹ *s.* gengiva.

gum² *s.* gomma.

to **gum** *vt.* ingommare.

gummy *agg.* gommoso.

gun *s.* 1. cannone 2. fucile 3. rivoltella, pistola || — *-barrel*, canna da fucile; — *-carriage*, affusto di cannone.

gunfire *s.* sparatoria.

gunner *s.* artigliere.

gunpowder *s.* polvere da sparo.

gun-room *s.* armeria.

gunshot *s.* colpo di arma da fuoco.

gunsmith *s.* armaiolo.

gurgle *s.* gorgoglio.

to **gurgle** *vi.* gorgogliare.

gush *s.* 1. getto 2. effusione.

to **gush** *vi.* 1. sgorgare 2. essere espansivo.

gusher *s.* pozzo petrolifero.

gushing *agg.* 1. sgorgante 2. esuberante.

gust *s.* 1. raffica 2. (*fig.*) impeto.

gustative, gustatory *agg.* gustativo.

gusty *agg.* ventoso.

gut *s.* budello.

to **gut** *vt.* sventrare.

gutter *s.* 1. grondaia 2. rigagnolo.

to **gutter** *vt.* scanalare. ♦ to **gutter** *vi.* colare.

guttural *agg. e s.* gutturale.

to **guzzle** *vt.* tracannare.

gymkhana *s.* gincana.

gymnasium *s.* palestra.

gymnast *s.* ginnasta.

gymnastic(al) *agg.* ginnastico.

gymnastics *s.* ginnastica.

gynaeceum *s.* (*pl.* -cea) gineceo.

gynaecologic *agg.* ginecologico.

gynaecologist *s.* ginecologo.

gynaecology *s.* ginecologia.

gypsy *s.*, V. *gipsy*.

to **gyrate** *vi.* girare.

gyroscope *s.* giroscopio.

gyves *s. pl.* ceppi, catene.

H

haberdasher *s.* merciaio.

haberdashery *s.* merceria.

habit *s.* 1. abitudine 2. temperamen-

to **3.** costume.
habitable *agg.* abitabile.
habitation *s.* abitazione.
habitual *agg.* abituale, consueto.
habitude *s.* abitudine.
hack[1] *s.* **1.** tacca, incisione **2.** piccone, mazza **3.** tosse secca.
hack[2] *s.* **1.** ronzino **2.** (*fig.*) scribacchino.
to **hack**[1] *vt.* sminuzzare. ♦ to **hack** *vi.* tossire a colpi secchi.
to **hack**[2] *vt.* e *vi.* **1.** adoperare cavalli da nolo **2.** adibire a un lavoro da scribacchino.
hackney *s.* **1.** cavallo da nolo **2.** vettura da nolo.
hacksaw *s.* seghetto.
had V. *to have.*
haematoma *s.* ematoma.
haemoglobin *s.* emoglobina.
haemophilia *s.* emofilia.
haemoptysis *s.* emottisi.
haemorrhage *s.* emorragia.
haemorrhoids *s. pl.* emorroidi.
haemostasia *s.* emostasi.
haemostatic *agg.* e *s.* emostatico.
haft *s.* manico, impugnatura.
hag *s.* **1.** strega, megera **2.** (*zool.*) lampreda.
haggard *agg.* sparuto, emaciato.
to **haggle** *vi.* mercanteggiare.
hagiographer *s.* agiografo.
hagiography *s.* agiografia.
hail[1] *s.* grandine || — *-stone*, chicco di grandine; — *-storm*, grandinata.
hail[2] *inter.* salve!, salute!
to **hail**[1] *vi.* grandinare.
to **hail**[2] *vt.* e *vi.* salutare, chiamare.
hair *s.* **1.** capelli, capigliatura **2.** pelo, crine, setola || — *-breadth*, spessore di un capello; — *-cut*, taglio dei capelli; — *-do*, acconciatura.
hairdresser *s.* parrucchiere.
hairiness *s.* pelosità.
hairless *agg.* senza capelli.
hairpin *s.* forcella (*per capelli*).
hairy *agg.* **1.** capelluto **2.** peloso.
halation *s.* alone.
halberd *s.* alabarda.
hale *agg.* robusto, gagliardo.
half *agg.* mezzo.
half *s.* (*pl.* **halves**) metà, mezzo. ♦
half *avv.* a mezzo, a metà || — *-brother*, fratellastro; — *-length*, di media lunghezza; — *-mast*, a mezz'asta; — *-pay*, stipendio ridotto; — *-processed*, semilavorato; — *-sister*, sorellastra; — *-year*, se-

mestre.
halfpenny *s.* mezzo penny.
halfway *agg.* e *avv.* a mezza strada.
hall *s.* **1.** sala, salone **2.** refettorio, sala di ritrovo.
hallo! *int.* pronto (*al telefono*).
to **hallow** *vt.* santificare.
to **hallucinate** *vt.* allucinare.
hallucination *s.* allucinazione.
halo *s.* alone, aureola.
to **halt**[1] *vt.* fermare. ♦ to **halt** *vi.* fermarsi.
to **halt**[2] *vi.* zoppicare.
halter *s.* **1.** capestro **2.** cavezza.
to **halve** *vt.* dividere a metà.
halyard *s.* (*mar.*) drizza.
ham *s.* **1.** prosciutto. ♦ **hams** *s. pl.* natiche.
hamlet *s.* piccolo villaggio.
hammer *s.* martello, martelletto: — *-blow*, colpo di martello, di maglio || *to bring under the* —, mettere all'asta.
to **hammer** *vt.* e *vi.* martellare.
hammering *s.* martellamento.
hammock *s.* amaca.
hamper[1] *s.* cesta.
hamper[2] *s.* impedimento.
to **hamper** *vt.* imbarazzare, ostacolare.
to **hamstring** *vt.* azzoppare.
hand *s.* **1.** mano: *hands off!*, via le mani!; *hands up!*, mani in alto! **2.** operaio, lavoratore **3.** calligrafia || *at* —, a portata di mano; *first* —, di prima mano.
to **hand** *vt.* porgere, dare || *to — in*, consegnare; *to — out*, distribuire; *to — over*, rimettere.
handbag *s.* borsetta.
handbill *s.* volantino.
handbook *s.* manuale.
handcuffs *s. pl.* manette.
to **handcuff** *vt.* mettere le manette.
handful *s.* **1.** manciata **2.** piccolo numero (*di persone*).
handgrip *s.* stretta di mano, morsa della mano.
handicap *s.* svantaggio.
to **handicap** *vt.* svantaggiare, ostacolare.
handicraft *s.* **1.** lavoro manuale **2.** abilità manuale.
handicraftsman *s.* artigiano.
handily *avv.* **1.** abilmente **2.** a portata di mano.
handiwork *s.* lavoro fatto a mano.
handkerchief *s.* fazzoletto.
handle *s.* **1.** manico, impugnatura

2. (*fig.*) pretesto || — -*bar*, manubrio (*di bicicletta*).

to handle *vt.* **1.** maneggiare **2.** comportarsi verso.

handler *s.* manipolatore.

handling *s.* **1.** maneggiamento **2.** maniera di trattare.

handmade *agg.* fatto a mano.

handrail *s.* corrimano.

handshake *s.* stretta di mano.

handsome *agg.* bello, di bell'aspetto.

handwriting *s.* calligrafia.

handy *agg.* **1.** abile, destro **2.** a portata di mano || — -*man*, factotum.

hang *s.* inclinazione, pendio.

to hang (**hung, hung**) *vt.* appendere, attaccare.

to hang (**hung, hung**) *vi.* **1.** pendere **2.** appoggiarsi. ◆ **to hang** (*reg.*) *vt.* impiccare.

hanger *s.* gancio, uncino || — *on*, seguace, parassita; *dress*—, attaccacapanni; *paper*—, tappezziere.

hanging *agg.* pendente, sospeso. ◆ **hanging** *s.* impiccagione.

hangman *s.* boia, carnefice.

hank *s.* matassa.

hapless *agg.* sfortunato.

to happen *vi.* avvenire, accadere.

happening *s.* avvenimento.

happily *avv.* felicemente.

happiness *s.* felicità.

happy *agg.* felice, contento.

harangue *s.* arringa.

to harangue *vt.* e *vi.* arringare, pronunciare un discorso solenne.

to harass *vt.* tormentare, molestare.

harbinger *s.* precursore.

harbour *s.* **1.** porto **2.** (*fig.*) rifugio.

to harbour *vt.* **1.** accogliere, dare asilo a **2.** nutrire (*pensieri ecc.*). ◆ **to harbour** *vi.* entrare in porto.

hard *agg.* **1.** duro **2.** severo, spietato **3.** difficile **4.** rigido (*di tempo*). ◆ **hard** *avv.* **1.** energicamente **2.** con difficoltà, duramente **3.** vicino, accanto || — -*boiled*, bollito fino a diventar duro; — -*headed*, ostinato; — -*set*, in bisogno.

to harden *vt.* indurire. ◆ **to harden** *vi.* indurirsi.

hardening *agg.* temprante. ◆ **hardening** *s.* tempra.

hardihood *s.* ardire, coraggio.

hardily *avv.* arditamente.

hardiness *s.* **1.** ardire **2.** robustezza.

hardly *avv.* **1.** a stento, a malapena **2.** quasi **3.** duramente, severamente.

hardness *s.* durezza (*anche fig.*).

hardship *s.* **1.** avversità **2.** stento.

hardware *s.* ferramenta.

hardy *agg.* ardito.

hare *s.* lepre || — -*brained*, scervellato; — -*lip*, labbro leporino.

to hark *vt.* e *vi.* ascoltare || *to* — *back*, risalire a (*col pensiero*).

harlequin *s.* arlecchino.

harlequinade *s.* arlecchinata.

harlot *s.* prostituta.

harm *s.* danno (*morale e fisico*) || *out of* — 's *way*, in salvo.

to harm *vt.* far male, far torto.

harmful *agg.* nocivo, dannoso.

harmfulness *s.* l'essere nocivo.

harmless *agg.* innocuo.

harmonic *agg.* **1.** armonico, armonioso **2.** (*mat.*) in progressione.

harmonious *agg.* armonioso.

harmonium *s.* armonium.

to harmonize *vt.* armonizzare. ◆ **to harmonize** *vi.* armonizzarsi.

harmony *s.* armonia, accordo.

harness *s.* finimenti (*pl.*).

to harness *vt.* bardare, mettere i finimenti a.

harp *s.* arpa.

harpist *s.* arpista.

harpoon *s.* rampone, fiocina.

harpsichord *s.* clavicembalo.

harrow *s.* erpice.

harsh *agg.* **1.** duro, ruvido **2.** aspro **3.** discordante (*di suono*).

harshness *s.* asprezza, durezza.

harvest *s.* raccolto, messe.

harvester *s.* **1.** mietitore **2.** mietitrice meccanica.

haste *s.* fretta, rapidità || *to make* —, far presto.

to haste, to hasten *vt.* affrettare. ◆ **to haste, to hasten** *vi.* affrettarsi.

hastily *avv.* **1.** frettolosamente **2.** precipitosamente.

hasty *agg.* **1.** frettoloso, affrettato **2.** avventato, impetuoso.

hat *s.* cappello.

hatch *s.* **1.** portello, mezza porta **2.** (*mar.*) boccaporto.

hatchet *s.* accetta.

hate *s.* odio.

to hate *vt.* odiare, avere in odio.

hateful *agg.* **1.** odioso **2.** pieno di odio.

hatred *s.* odio.

hatstand *s.* attaccapanni.

hatter *s.* cappellaio.

haughtily *avv.* altezzosamente.

haughtiness s. alterigia, boria.
haughty agg. altezzoso, arrogante.
haul s. 1. trazione, tiro 2. raccolta, retata.
to **haul** vt. tirare, trainare. ♦ to **haul** vi. cambiare (di vento).
haulage s. 1. trasporto 2. costo del trasporto.
haunt s. 1. ricovero, ritiro 2. covo, tana.
to **haunt** vt. 1. frequentare assiduamente 2. perseguitare (di ricordi, pensieri ecc.).
haunted agg. 1. frequentato 2. perseguitato.
haunting agg. che perseguita.
to **have** (had, had) vt. 1. (ausiliare) avere: I — gone, sono andato; I — not (I haven't) read the book, non ho letto il libro 2. avere, possedere || to — breakfast, far colazione 3. dovere: I — to go there, devo andarci 4. ricevere, ottenere || had better, sarebbe meglio che; I had rather, preferirei.
haven s. (fig.) porto, rifugio.
havoc s. strage, rovina.
hawk s. 1. falco, sparviero 2. (fig.) avvoltoio.
hawker[1] s. falconiere.
hawker[2] venditore ambulante.
hawser s. gomena.
hawthorn s. biancospino.
hay s. fieno, paglia || — -loft, fienile; — -making, falciatura.
haycock s. mucchio di fieno.
hayseed s. seme di erba.
haystack s. mucchio di fieno.
hazard s. 1. azzardo, rischio 2. giuoco di dadi.
to **hazard** vt. azzardare, arrischiare.
haze s. foschia, nebbia.
hazel s. nocciuolo || — -nut, nocciuola.
hazily avv. indistintamente.
haziness s. 1. foschia 2. (fig.) confusione.
hazy agg. 1. nebbioso 2. indistinto (anche fig.).
he pron. sogg. m. egli, lui, colui.
head s. 1. testa 2. capo, direttore 3. individuo 4. parte alta di una cosa 5. capo, unità di bestiame || — -first, a capofitto; — -master, direttore di una scuola; — -money, taglia; — -work, lavoro mentale.
to **head** vt. 1. colpire con la testa 2. dirigere, comandare 3. intestare. ♦ to **head** vi. dirigersi.

headache s. mal di testa.
headed agg. munito di testa || hot- —, esaltato; pig- —, ostinato; swollen- —, tronfio; wrong- —, caparbio.
heading s. 1. intestazione, titolo (di un capitolo) 2. (aer.) rotta.
headland s. promontorio.
headless agg. senza testa (anche fig.).
headlight s. faro anteriore.
headline s. intestazione di capitolo, articolo.
headlong avv. a capofitto, precipitosamente.
headquarters s. pl. quartier generale (sing.).
headstone s. pietra tombale.
to **heal** vt. 1. guarire, curare 2. (fig.) sanare. ♦ to **heal** vi. 1. guarire 2. sanarsi.
healer s. guaritore.
healing agg. salutare.
health s. 1. salute 2. salvezza divina.
healthful agg. salubre.
healthily avv. salubremente.
healthiness s. 1. salute 2. salubrità.
healthy agg. 1. sano, robusto 2. salutare.
heap s. mucchio, cumulo.
to **heap** vt. ammucchiare, accumulare.
to **hear** (heard, heard) vt. e vi. 1. sentire, udire 2. sentir dire, venire a sapere.
hearing s. 1. udito 2. udienza.
hearsay s. diceria, voce.
hearse s. carro funebre.
heart s. 1. cuore (anche fig.) 2. affetto, coraggio 3. centro, parte principale || — -beat, pulsazione; — -break, crepacuore; — -breaking, straziante; — -failure, collasso cardiaco; — -felt, sincero, di cuore.
heartache s. angoscia, angustia.
heartburn s. bruciore di stomaco.
hearted agg. dal cuore, di cuore || broken- —, desolato; chicken- —, pauroso; down- —, depresso; lion- —, dal cuore di leone; whole- —, generoso.
to **hearten** vt. incoraggiare. ♦ to **hearten** vi. prendere coraggio.
hearth s. 1. focolare (anche fig.) 2. (metal.) crogiuolo, letto di fusione.
heartily avv. cordialmente.
heartiness s. 1. cordialità.

heartless *agg.* senza cuore.

hearty *agg.* 1. sincero, cordiale 2. sano, robusto.

heat *s.* 1. calore, caldo 2. animosità || — -*stroke*, colpo di calore; — -*wave*, ondata di calore.

to heat *vt.* 1. scaldare 2. animare. ♦ **to heat** *vi.* 1. scaldarsi 2. animarsi.

heater *s.* bollitore, riscaldatore.

heath *s.* brughiera.

heathen *agg.* e *s.* pagano.

heather *s.* erica.

heating *s.* riscaldamento.

heave *s.* 1. sforzo 2. rigonfiamento (*di onde*) 3. sollevamento.

heaven *s.* 1. cielo, paradiso (*anche fig.*) 2. stato di grazia.

heavenly *agg.* divino, celeste.

heavenward *agg.* rivolto al cielo.

heavily *avv.* pesantemente, gravemente.

heaviness *s.* pesantezza.

heavy *agg.* 1. pesante 2. violento, forte 3. fangoso, pesante (*di terreno*).

Hebrew *agg.* e *s.* ebreo.

hecatomb *s.* ecatombe.

hectare *s.* ettaro.

hectic *agg.* 1. tisico, etico 2. febbricitante.

hectogram(me) *s.* ettogrammo.

hectolitre *s.* ettolitro.

hectometre *s.* ettometro.

hedge *s.* 1. siepe 2. barriera.

to hedge *vt.* circondare con una siepe. ♦ **to hedge** *vi.* essere evasivo.

hedgehog *s.* riccio, porcospino.

hedonism *s.* edonismo.

hedonist *s.* edonista.

heed *s.* attenzione, cura.

heedful *agg.* attento, vigile.

heedless *agg.* sventato.

heedlessness *s.* sventatezza, trascuratezza.

heel *s.* 1. calcagno, tallone 2. sperone (*di uccelli*).

Hegelian *agg.* hegeliano.

hegemony *s.* egemonia.

heifer *s.* giovenca.

heigh *inter.* ehi!

height *s.* 1. altezza 2. altitudine 3. altura, collina 4. sommità, il più alto grado.

to heighten *vt.* 1. innalzare 2. accrescere, intensificare. ♦ **to heighten** *vi.* innalzarsi.

heinous *agg.* atroce.

heir *s.* erede.

heiress *s.* ereditiera.

held V. *to hold*.

helicoid *agg.* elicoidale.

helicopter *s.* elicottero.

heliocentric(al) *agg.* eliocentrico.

heliotherapy *s.* elioterapia.

heliport *s.* eliporto.

helium *s.* elio.

hell *s.* inferno (*anche fig.*).

Hellenic *agg.* ellenico.

Hellenism *s.* ellenismo.

Hellenist *s.* ellenista.

hellish *agg.* infernale.

hello *inter.* salve!

helm[1] *s.* elmo, casco.

helm[2] *s.* timone (*anche fig.*).

helmet *s.* elmetto, casco.

helmsman *s.* timoniere.

help *s.* aiuto, soccorso.

to help *vt.* 1. aiutare, soccorrere 2. servire (*cibo*) || *cannot* —, non poter fare a meno di; *to* — *oneself to*, servirsi di (*cibo*).

helper *s.* aiutante.

helpful *agg.* utile, servizievole.

helpless *agg.* senza aiuto, indifeso.

helpmate *s.* collaboratore.

Helvetic *agg.* elvetico.

hem[1] *s.* orlo, bordo.

hem[2] *inter.* ehm!.

to hem[1] *vt.* orlare || *to* — *in*, circondare, accerchiare.

to hem[2] *vi.* schiarirsi la gola.

hemicycle *s.* emiciclo.

hemiplegia *s.* emiplegia.

hemisphere *s.* emisfero.

hemispheric(al) *agg.* emisferico.

hemlock *s.* cicuta.

hemp *s.* canapa.

hen *s.* 1. gallina 2. femmina (*di uccelli*) || — -*house*, pollaio.

hence *avv.* 1. di qui, da questo momento 2. donde.

henceforth *avv.* d'ora innanzi.

hendecasyllabic *agg.* endecasillabico.

hendecasyllable *s.* endecasillabo.

henna *s.* alcanna.

hepatic *agg.* epatico.

hepatitis *s.* epatite.

heptagon *s.* ettagono.

heptagonal *agg.* ettagonale.

her *agg. poss. f.* suo, sua, suoi, sue. ♦ **her** *pron. compl. f.* la, lei, le, colei.

herald *s.* 1. araldo 2. nunzio 3. (*fig.*) precursore.

heraldic *agg.* araldico.

herb *s.* 1. erba 2. pianta medicinale.

herbaceous *agg.* erbaceo.

herbal *agg.* di erba.

herbarium *s.* erbario.

herbivorous *agg.* erbivoro.

herborist *s.* erborista.

Herculean *agg.* erculeo.

herd *s.* gregge, mandria.

herdsman *s.* mandriano.

here *avv.* qui, qua || — *I am*, eccomi.

hereabouts *avv.* qui intorno.

hereafter *avv.* d'ora innanzi.

hereby *avv.* 1. con questo mezzo 2. qui vicino.

hereditary *agg.* ereditario.

heredity *s.* (*biol.*) ereditarietà.

herein *avv.* 1. in questo 2. (*comm.*) nella presente.

heresiarch *s.* eresiarca.

heresy *s.* eresia.

heretic(al) *agg.* e *s.* eretico.

herewith *avv.* qui accluso.

heritable *agg.* ereditabile.

heritage *s.* eredità.

hermaphrodite *agg.* e *s.* ermafrodito.

hermeneutics *s.* ermeneutica.

hermetic(al) *agg.* ermetico.

hermetically *avv.* ermeticamente.

hermit *s.* eremita.

hermitage *s.* eremo, eremitaggio.

hernia *s.* ernia.

hernial *agg.* erniario.

hero *s.* eroe.

heroic(al) *agg.* eroico.

heroin *s.* (*chim.*) eroina.

heroine *s.* eroina.

heroism *s.* eroismo.

heron *s.* airone.

herpes *s.* erpete.

herring *s.* aringa || — *-bone*, spina di pesce (*nei tessuti ecc.*).

hers *pron. poss. f.* il suo, la sua, i suoi, le sue.

herself *pron. r. f.* 1. se stessa, sé, si 2. ella stessa.

hesitant *agg.* esitante.

to hesitate *vi.* esitare.

hesitatingly *avv.* con esitazione.

hesitation *s.* esitazione.

heteroclite *agg.* eteroclito.

heterodox *agg.* eterodosso.

heterodoxy *s.* eterodossia.

heterogeneity *s.* eterogeneità.

heterogen°ous *agg.* eterogeneo.

to hew (hewed, hewn) *vt.* fendere, recidere || — *down*, abbat-

tere.

hexagon *s.* esagono.

hexagonal *agg.* esagonale.

hexahedron *s.* esaedro.

hexameter *s.*,esametro.

hiatus *s.* iato.

to hibernate *vi.* (*zool.*) cadere in letargo invernale.

hibernation *s.* 1. svernamento 2. ibernazione.

hiccough, hiccup *s.* singhiozzo, singulto.

hid V. *to hide*.

hidden V. *to hide*.

hide[1] *s.* pelle, cuoio.

hide[2] *s.* nascondiglio || — *-and-seek*, rimpiattino.

to hide[1] **(hid, hidden)** *vt.* nascondere, celare. ♦ **to hide (hid, hidden)** *vi.* nascondersi, celarsi.

to hide[2] *vt.* 1. spellare, scorticare 2. frustare.

hideous *agg.* orrendo, odioso.

hideousness *s.* odiosità, aspetto orribile.

hiding *s.* il nascondere.

hierarchy *s.* gerarchia.

hieratic *agg.* ieratico.

hieroglyph *s.* geroglifico.

hieroglyphic(al) *agg.* geroglifico.

high *agg.* 1. alto, elevato (*anche fig.*) 2. altezzoso 3. forte, intenso (*di luce, colori*) || — *-born*, di alto lignaggio; — *-class*, di prim'ordine; — *-coloured*, dal colore acceso; — *-hearted*, pieno di coraggio; — *-life*, vita di alta società; — *school*, scuola media; — *sea*, mare aperto; — *-speed*, ad alta velocità. ♦ **high** *avv.* 1. alto, in alto 2. fortemente.

highbrow *agg.* e *s.* intellettuale.

highland *s.* regione montuosa.

highlander *s.* montanaro.

highly *avv.* 1. molto, assai 2. altamente, nobilmente.

highness *s.* 1. altezza, elevatezza 2. eccellenza, valore.

highway *s.* strada maestra.

highwayman *s.* bandito, rapinatore.

hilarious *agg.* ilare.

hill *s.* collina, altura.

hillock *s.* collinetta.

hillside *s.* pendio.

hilltop *s.* sommità della collina.

hilly *agg.* collinoso.

hilt *s.* elsa.

him *pron. pers. m.* lo, lui, gli, colui, sé.

himself *pron. r. m.* 1. si, sé, se

stesso **2.** egli stesso.

hind[1] *s.* cerva, daina.

hind[2] *s.* colono, fattore.

hind(er) *agg.* posteriore.

to **hinder** *vt. e vi.* **1.** impedire, ostruire **2.** imbarazzare.

hindrance *s.* ostacolo, impaccio.

Hindu *agg. e s.* indù.

hinge *s.* **1.** cardine **2.** (*fig.*) perno.

to **hinge** *vt.* munire di cardini. ♦ to **hinge** *vi.* **1.** girare sui cardini **2.** essere imperniato.

hint *s.* **1.** cenno, allusione **2.** consiglio.

to **hint** *vt. e vi.* alludere, accennare, suggerire.

hinterland *s.* retroterra.

hip *s.* anca, fianco.

hippocampus *s.* (*pl.* -pi.) ippocampo.

hippopotamus *s.* ippopotamo.

hire *s.* affitto, nolo.

to **hire** *vt.* prendere a servizio, noleggiare.

hireling *s.* mercenario.

his *agg. poss. m.* suo, sua, suoi, sue. ♦ **his** *pron. poss. m.* il suo, la sua, i suoi, le sue.

Hispanic *agg.* ispanico.

Hispanicism *s.* ispanismo.

Hispanist *s.* ispanista.

hispid *agg.* ispido.

hiss *s.* sibilo, fischio.

to **hiss** *vt. e vi.* **1.** sibilare **2.** fischiare.

histology *s.* istologia.

historian *s.* storico.

historic(al) *agg.* storico.

historicity *s.* storicità.

historiographer *s.* storiografo.

historiography *s.* storiografia.

history *s.* storia.

histrion *s.* istrione.

histrionic(al) *agg.* istrionico.

histrionism *s.* istrionismo.

hit *s.* **1.** colpo, botta **2.** osservazione sarcastica **3.** caso fortunato **4.** (*teat.*) successo.

to **hit** (**hit**, **hit**) *vt. e vi.* **1.** battere, picchiare **2.** urtare, venire a contatto **3.** (*fig.*) toccare, colpire || to — the mark, colpire nel segno.

hitch *s.* **1.** colpo, strattone, balzo repentino **2.** nodo.

to **hitch** *vt.* **1.** muovere a sbalzi **2.** legare, attaccare. ♦ to **hitch** *vi.* muoversi a sbalzi.

to **hitchhike** *vi.* fare l'autostop.

hitchhiker *s.* autostoppista.

hitchhiking *s.* autostop.

hive *s.* **1.** alveare, arnia **2.** sciame (*anche fig.*).

hives *s. pi.* orticaria, eruzione cutanea.

hoar *s.* candore, vecchiaia || --frost, brina.

hoard *s.* gruzzolo.

to **hoard** *vt.* ammassare, ammucchiare. ♦ to **hoard** *vi.* ammucchiarsi.

hoarder *s.* incettatore.

hoarding *s.* recinto provvisorio.

hoarse *agg.* rauco, fioco.

hoarseness *s.* raucedine.

hoary *agg.* **1.** bianco, canuto **2.** venerando.

hobble *s.* **1.** zoppicamento **2.** imbarazzo.

to **hobble** *vi.* zoppicare. ♦ to **hobble** *vt.* azzoppare.

hobby *s.* svago preferito, passatempo.

hobnail *s.* chiodo (*per scarponi*).

hobnailed *agg.* chiodato.

hodman *s.* manovale.

hoe *s.* zappa.

to **hoe** *vt.* zappare, estirpare le erbacce.

hog *s.* maiale.

hogshead *s.* barilotto (*per tabacco, zucchero*).

hoist *s.* montacarichi.

to **hoist** *vt.* alzare, sollevare.

hold[1] *s.* **1.** presa **2.** (*fig.*) ascendente.

hold[2] *s.* (*mar.*) stiva.

to **hold** (**held**, **held**) *vt. e vi.* **1.** tenere, sostenere **2.** contenere **3.** ritenere, credere, pensare **4.** occupare una carica, possedere **5.** resistere, aggrapparsi || to — up, sollevare; to — back, esitare.

holder *s.* **1.** possessore, detentore, proprietario **2.** sostegno, supporto **3.** dente canino.

holdings *s. pl.* beni, titoli.

hold-up *s.* intoppo nel traffico, panna di automobile.

hole *s.* **1.** foro, apertura, buco **2.** antro, tana.

holiday *s.* **1.** festa, giorno festivo **2.** vacanza.

holiness *s.* santità.

hollow *agg.* **1.** concavo, infossato **2.** cupo, cavernoso **3.** (*fig.*) falso, irreale, vuoto.

to **hollow** *vt.* scavare, incavare.

hollow *avv.* (*fam.*) completamente.

hollowness *s.* **1.** cavità **2.** timbro

cavernoso (*di voce*).

holly *s.* agrifoglio.

holocaust *s.* olocausto.

holograph *agg.* e *s.* documento olografo.

holy *agg.* santo, sacro.

homage *s.* omaggio.

home[1] *s.* **1.** casa, focolare domestico **2.** patria **3.** rifugio, asilo, ospizio.

home[2] *agg.* domestico, casalingo.

home[3] *avv.* **1.** a casa, in patria **2.** direttamente, al segno ‖ — -*born*, indigeno, locale; — -*bred*, allevato in casa; — -*made*, fatto in casa; — -*market*, mercato nazionale; — -*town*, città natia; — -*trade*, commercio interno

homeland *s.* patria.

homeless *agg.* senza casa.

homelike *agg.* domestico, familiare.

homely *agg.* **1.** semplice, modesto **2.** domestico.

homeopathic *agg.* omeopatico

homeopathy *s.* omeopatia.

Homeric *agg.* omerico.

homesick *agg.* nostalgico.

homesickness *s.* nostalgia.

homeward *agg.* e *avv.* verso casa, verso la patria.

homework *s. coll.* compiti per casa.

homicidal *agg.* omicida.

homicide *s.* omicidio.

homily *s.* omelia.

homogeneity *s.* omogeneità.

homogeneous *agg.* omogeneo.

to homogenize *vt.* omogeneizzare.

to homologate *vt.* omologare.

homologation *s.* omologazione.

homologous *agg.* omologo.

homology *s.* omologia.

homonymous *agg.* omonimo.

homonymy *s.* omonimia.

homosexual *agg.* e *s.* omosessuale.

homosexuality *s.* omosessualità.

homy *agg.* casalingo.

honest *agg.* **1.** onesto, integro **2.** leale.

honesty *s.* **1.** onestà, probità **2.** lealtà.

honey *s.* miele.

honeycomb *s.* favo.

honeyed *agg.* **1.** coperto di miele **2.** (*fig.*) sdolcinato, adulatorio.

honeymoon *s.* luna di miele.

honeysuckle *s.* caprifoglio.

honorary *agg.* onorario, onorifico.

honorific *agg.* onorifico.

honour *s.* **1.** onore, reputazione **2.** stima, reverenza **3.** Eccellenza.

to honour *vt.* onorare, fare onore a.

honourable *agg.* stimato, onorevole.

honourableness *s.* onorabilità.

hood *s.* cappuccio.

to hood *vt.* incappucciare, fornire di cappuccio.

hoof *s.* zoccolo (*di animale*).

hook *s.* **1.** uncino, gancio **2.** amo **3.** tagliola **4.** falce per grano ‖ *by — or by crook*, di riffa o di raffa.

to hook *vt.* agganciare. ♦ **to hook** *vi.* agganciarsi.

hooked *agg.* **1.** fornito di uncini **2.** adunco, uncinato.

hoop *s.* collare, cerchio (*di botte, ruota ecc.*).

to hoop *vt.* cerchiare (*una botte*).

to hoot *vt.* e *vi.* **1.** urlare, gridare **2.** suonare il clacson.

hop[1] *s.* salto (*su una gamba sola*).

hop[2] *s.* luppolo.

to hop *vt.* e *vi.* saltare su una gamba sola.

hope *s.* speranza.

to hope *vt.* e *vi.* sperare, essere fiducioso.

hopeful *agg.* pieno di speranza, fiducioso.

hopefulness *s.* fiducia, buona speranza.

hopeless *agg.* senza speranza, irrimediabile.

hopelessness *s.* disperazione.

hopper *s.* persona od insetto che saltella.

horde *s.* orda.

horizon *s.* orizzonte.

horizontal *agg.* orizzontale.

horizontally *avv.* orizzontalmente.

hormone *s.* ormone.

horn *s.* **1.** corno, tentacolo, antenna **2.** (*mus.*) corno, tromba.

to horn *vt.* **1.** fornire di corna **2.** ferire con le corna.

hornet *s.* vespa, calabrone.

hornpipe *s.* cornamusa.

horology *s.* orologeria.

horoscope *s.* oroscopo: *to cast a —*, fare un oroscopo.

horrible *agg.* **1.** orribile, orrendo **2.** (*fam.*) eccessivo.

horribly *avv.* orribilmente.

horrid *agg.* orrido, orrendo.

horrific *agg.* orribile, orripilante.

to horrify *vt.* **1.** atterrire, incutere timore **2.** scandalizzare.

horror *s.* **1.** orrore, spavento **2.** cosa orribile ‖ — -*stricken*, atterrito.

hors-d'oeuvre s. antipasto.

horse s. cavallo || — -bean, fava; — -boy, mozzo di stalla; — -chestnut, ippocastano; — -doctor, veterinario; — -race, corsa ippica; — -shoe, ferro di cavallo.

horseback s. dorso di cavallo || on —, a cavallo.

horseman s. cavaliere.

horticultural agg. attinente all'orticultura.

horticulture s. orticultura.

hosanna inter. osanna.

hose s. 1. idrante 2. calze (pl.).

hosier s. commerciante in calze.

hosiery s. maglieria.

hospice s. alloggio, ospizio.

hospitable agg. ospitale.

hospital s. ospedale.

hospitality s. ospitalità.

host[1] s. folla, moltitudine.

host[2] s. ospite, anfitrione.

hostage s. ostaggio.

hostel s. pensionato (per giovani, studenti, militari ecc.).

hostess s. 1. ospite, padrona di casa 2. assistente di volo.

hostile agg. ostile, nemico.

hostility s. inimicizia, ostilità.

hot agg. 1. caldo, ardente 2. forte, piccante 3. violento, impetuoso || — -headed, scalmanato.

hotel s. albergo || — -keeper, albergatore.

hothead s. testa calda.

hothouse s. serra.

hotly avv. caldamente.

hotspur s. persona impulsiva.

hound s. bracco, segugio.

to hound vt. cacciare (con bracchi).

hour s. 1. ora 2. periodo. ◆ **hours** s. pl. orario (sing.).

hourly agg. 1. continuo 2. all'ora 3. ad ogni ora. ◆ **hourly** avv. 1. continuamente 2. ad ogni ora 3. d'ora in ora.

house s. 1. casa, abitazione 2. albergo, pensione 3. clinica 4. convento 5. casato, dinastia 6. teatro 7. (comm.) ditta 8. (mar.) tuga.

to house vt. 1. alloggiare, ricevere in casa 2. (fig.) offrire un rifugio. ◆ **to house** vi. 1. prendere alloggio 2. rifugiarsi.

housebreaker s. scassinatore.

housebreaking s. demolizione edilizia.

household s. famiglia: Royal Household, la famiglia reale.

householder s. capofamiglia.

housekeeper s. governante, domestica.

housekeeping s. il governo della casa.

houseless agg. senza casa.

housemaid s. domestica, cameriera.

housewife s. (pl. -wives) massaia, casalinga.

housework s. lavoro domestico.

housing s. 1. il ricevere, l'accogliere 2. alloggio, rifugio, riparo.

hovel s. 1. tana 2. baracca.

to hover vi. 1. librarsi, svolazzare 2. gironzolare.

how avv. come, in che modo.

however avv. 1. comunque 2. però, tuttavia.

howitzer s. obice.

howl s. urlo, grido.

to howl vt. e vi. urlare, ululare.

howling agg. urlante, ululante.

hub s. mozzo di ruota.

hubbub s. tumulto, fracasso.

huddle s. calca, folla.

to huddle vt. ammucchiare. ◆ **to huddle** vi. affollarsi, accalcarsi.

hue s. tinta, colore.

hug s. abbraccio.

to hug vt. abbracciare (anche fig.) || — to — oneself, compiacersi.

huge agg. enorme, vasto.

hugeness s. grandezza, enormità.

hull s. scafo.

hullabaloo s. tumulto, fracasso.

hullo inter. 1. (fam.) salve 2. (tel.) pronto.

hum s. ronzio, mormorio.

to hum vt. e vi. 1. ronzare, mormorare 2. cantare a bocca chiusa.

human agg. 1. umano 2. sensibile.

humane agg. umano, compassionevole.

humaneness s. benevolenza, umanità.

humanism s. umanesimo.

humanist s. umanista.

humanistic agg. umanistico.

humanitarian agg. filantropico, umanitario.

humanity s. 1. umanità, il genere umano 2. bontà, benevolenza.

to humanize vt. 1. rendere umano 2. adattare alla natura umana. ◆ **to humanize** vi. acquisire sentimenti migliori.

humankind s. il genere umano.

humble agg. umile, modesto.

to humble vt. umiliare.

humbleness s. umiltà.

humbly avv. umilmente.

humbug s. frode, impostura.

humdrum s. monotonia, tedio. ◆
humdrum agg. monotono.

humeral agg. omerale.

humerus s. (pl. -ri) omero.

humid agg. umido.

humidity s. umidità.

to **humiliate** vt. umiliare, mortificare.

humiliation s. umiliazione.

humility s. umiltà.

humming agg. ronzante. ◆ **humming** s. ronzio.

humorist s. umorista.

humorous agg. arguto, dotato di senso dell'umorismo.

humour s. 1. umorismo 2. umore.

hump s. 1. gobba, gibbosità 2. collinetta, cresta.

humpback s. 1. gobba 2. gobbo.

hunch s. gobba, gibbosità.

hunchback s. persona gobba.

hundred agg. cento. ◆ **hundred** s. centinaio.

hundredth agg. centesimo.

hung V. to hang.

Hungarian agg. e s. ungherese.

hunger s. 1. fame, appetito 2. (fig.) ingordigia.

hungrily avv. 1. con grande appetito 2. avidamente.

hungry agg. 1. affamato || to be —, aver fame 2. (fig.) avido, bramoso.

hunt s. 1. caccia 2. ricerca, inseguimento.

to **hunt** vt. e vi. 1. cacciare, andare a caccia 2. cercare affannosamente.

hunter s. cacciatore (anche fig.).

hunting s. 1. caccia 2. ricerca.

huntsman s. cacciatore.

hurdle s. ostacolo (anche fig.).

hurl s. lancio violento.

to **hurl** vt. lanciare, scagliare (anche fig.).

hurrah inter. urrah!

hurricane s. uragano, ciclone (anche fig.).

hurried agg. affrettato, precipitoso.

hurry s. fretta, precipitazione: to be in a —, aver fretta.

to **hurry** vt. affrettare. ◆ to **hurry** vi. affrettarsi || — up!, fa presto!

hurt s. lesione, ferita (anche fig.).

to **hurt** (hurt, hurt) vt. e vi. 1. dolere 2. recar dolore, offendere.

hurtful agg. 1. dannoso 2. offensivo.

husband s. marito.

husbandry s. 1. agricoltura 2. amministrazione domestica.

hush inter. silenzio.

to **hush** vt. 1. zittire, tacere 2. (fig.) calmare.

husk s. 1. guscio, baccello 2. involucro 3. (pl.) rifiuti.

to **husk** vt. sgusciare, sbucciare.

husky agg. rugoso, secco.

hussar s. ussaro.

hut s. 1. capanna, casupola 2. rifugio alpino.

hyacinth s. giacinto.

hybrid agg. e s. ibrido.

hybridism s. ibridismo.

hybridization s. ibridazione.

hydra s. idra.

hydrangea s. ortensia.

hydrant s. idrante.

hydrate s. idrato.

to **hydrate** vt. idratare.

hydraulic agg. idraulico.

hydraulics s. idraulica.

hydric agg. contenente idrogeno.

hydrocarbon s. idrocarburo.

hydrocephalus s. idrocefalo.

hydroelectric agg. idroelettrico.

hydrofluoric agg. fluoridrico.

hydrofoil boat s. aliscafo.

hydrogen s. idrogeno.

hydrology s. idrologia.

hydrolysis s. (pl. -ses) idrolisi.

hydrostatic(al) agg. idrostatico.

hyena s. iena.

hygiene s. igiene.

hygienics s. la scienza dell'igiene.

hygienist s. igienista.

hygrometry s. igrometria.

hymn s. inno.

hyperbole s. iperbole.

hyperbolic(al) agg. iperbolico.

hyperborean agg. e s. iperboreo.

hypercritical agg. ipercritico.

hypermetropy s. ipermetropia.

hypernutrition s. supernutrizione.

hypersensitive agg. ipersensibile.

hypersensitivity s. ipersensibilità.

hypertension s. ipertensione.

hypertrophy s. ipertrofia.

hyphen s. lineetta d'unione.

hypnosis s. (pl. -ses) ipnosi.

hypnotic agg. e s. ipnotico.

hypnotism s. ipnotismo.

to **hypnotize** vt. ipnotizzare.

hypochondria s. ipocondria.

hypochondriac agg. e s. ipocondriaco.

hypocrisy s. ipocrisia.

hypocrite s. ipocrita.
hypocritic(al) agg. ipocrita.
hypodermic agg. ipodermico.
hypodermoclysis s. ipodermoclisi.
hyposulphite s. iposolfito.
hypotenuse s. ipotenusa.
hypothecary agg. ipotecario.
to hypothecate vt. ipotecare.
hypothesis s. (pl. -ses) ipotesi.
to hypothesize vi. fare ipotesi.
hypothetic(al) agg. ipotetico.
hypothetically avv. ipoteticamente.
hysteria s. isterismo.
hysteric(al) agg. isterico.
hysterics s. attacco isterico.

I

I pron. pers. io.
iamb s. giambo.
iambic agg. giambico.
Iberian agg. e s. iberico.
ice s. ghiaccio || — box, ghiacciaia; —
  -breaker, rompighiaccio; —
  -cream, gelato.
to ice vt. 1. ghiacciare 2. (cuc.) glassare.
iceboat s. nave rompighiaccio.
Icelander s. islandese.
Icelandic agg. islandese.
ichtyologist s. ittiologo.
ichthyology s. ittiologia.
icicle s. ghiacciuolo.
iciness s. gelo.
icing s. glassatura.
icon s. icona.
iconoclast s. iconoclasta.
iconoclastic agg. iconoclastico.
iconography s. iconografia.
icy agg. gelido, gelato.
idea s. idea.
ideal agg. e s. ideale.
idealism s. idealismo.
idealist s. idealista.
idealistic(al) agg. idealistico.
idealization s. idealizzazione.
to idealize vt. idealizzare.
ideally avv. idealmente.
to ideate vt. ideare.
ideation s. ideazione.
identic(al) agg. identico.
identifiable agg. identificabile.
identification s. identificazione.
to identify vt. identificare || to —
  oneself with, immedesimarsi con.

identity s. identità.
ideogram s. ideogramma.
ideography s. ideografia.
ideologic(al) agg. ideologico.
ideologist s. ideologo.
ideology s. ideologia.
idiocy s. idiozia.
idiom s. 1. idioma 2. idiotismo.
idiomatic(al) agg. idiomatico.
idiosyncrasy s. idiosincrasia.
idiot s. idiota.
idiotic(al) agg. idiota.
idle agg. 1. ozioso 2. vano.
to idle vi. oziare.
idleness s. 1. ozio 2. futilità.
idler s. ozioso.
idly avv. oziosamente.
idol s. idolo.
idolater s. idolatra.
to idolatrize vt. idolatrare.
idolatrous agg. idolatrico.
idolatry, idolism s. idolatria.
idyl(l) s. idillio.
idyllic agg. idillico.
if cong. se || as —, come se.
igneous agg. igneo.
to ignite vt. accendere. ♦ to ignite
  vi. accendersi.
ignition s. accensione || battery
  coil —, spinterogeno.
ignobility s. ignobilità.
ignoble agg. ignobile.
ignominious agg. ignominioso.
ignominy, ignomy s. ignominia.
ignorance s. ignoranza.
ignorant agg. ignorante.
to ignore vt. ignorare.
ilex s. leccio.
iliac agg. iliaco.
ill (worse, worst) agg. 1. ammala-
  to 2. cattivo. ♦ ill avv. male ||
  — -advised, sconsiderato; — disposed, malevolo; — -fated, sfortunato; — -mannered, maleducato.
  ♦ ill s. male.
illation s. illazione.
illegal agg. 1. illegale 2. illecito.
illegality s. illegalità.
illegible agg. illeggibile.
illegitimacy s. illegittimità.
illegitimate agg. illegittimo.
illiberal agg. 1. illiberale 2. meschino.
illiberality s. 1. illiberalità 2. meschinità.
illicit agg. illecito.
illimitable agg. illimitato.
illiteracy s. 1. analfabetismo 2. i-
  gnoranza.

illiterate agg. e s. 1. analfabeta 2. ignorante.
illness s. malattia.
illogical agg. illogico.
illogicality s. illogicità.
to **ill-treat** vt. maltrattare.
to **illuminate** vt. illuminare.
illumination s. illuminazione.
to **illumine** vt. illuminare.
illuminism s. illuminismo.
ill-usage s. maltrattamento.
to **ill-use** vt. maltrattare.
illusion s. illusione.
illusionism s. illusionismo.
illusionist s. illusionista.
illusive agg. illusorio.
illusiveness s. illusorietà.
illusory agg. illusorio.
to **illustrate** vt. illustrare.
illustration s. illustrazione.
illustrative agg. illustrativo.
illustrator s. illustratore.
illustrious agg. illustre.
ill-will s. malevolenza.
ill-wisher s. malevolo.
image s. immagine.
to **image** vt. 1. immaginare 2. descrivere 3. riflettere.
imagery s. raffigurazione.
imaginable agg. immaginabile.
imaginary agg. immaginario.
imagination s. immaginazione.
imaginative agg. immaginativo.
to **imagine** vt. e vi. immaginare.
imagining s. immaginazione.
imbecile agg. e s. 1. debole 2. imbecille.
imbecility s. debolezza 2. imbecillità.
to **imbibe** vt. assorbire. ♦ to **imbibe** vi. imbeversi.
to **imbue** vt. impregnare.
imitable agg. imitabile.
to **imitate** vt. imitare.
imitation s. imitazione.
imitative agg. imitativo.
imitator s. imitatore.
immaculate agg. immacolato.
immanence s. immanenza.
immanent agg. immanente.
immanentism s. immanentismo.
immaterial agg. 1. immateriale 2. irrilevante.
immaterialism s. immaterialismo.
immaterialist s. immaterialista.
immateriality s. immaterialità.
immature agg. immaturo.
immaturity s. immaturità.
immeasurability s. incommensura-

bilità.
immeasurable agg. incommensurabile.
immediacy s. 1. immediatezza 2. rapporto diretto.
immediate agg. 1. immediato 2. diretto.
immediateness s. V. immediacy.
immemorial agg. immemorabile.
immense agg. immenso.
immenseness, immensity s. immensità.
immensurability s. immensurabilità.
immensurable agg. immensurabile.
to **immerge**, to **immerse** vt. immergere. ♦ to **immerge** vi. immergersi.
immersion s. 1. immersione 2. eclisse.
immigrant agg. e s. immigrante.
to **immigrate** vi. immigrare.
immigration s. immigrazione.
imminence s. 1. imminenza 2. pericolo.
imminent agg. 1. imminente 2. sovrastante.
immobile agg. immobile.
immobility s. immobilità.
immobilization s. immobilizzazione.
to **immobilize** vt. immobilizzare.
immoderate agg. smodato.
immoderateness s. smoderatezza.
immodest agg. 1. immodesto 2. indecente.
immodesty s. 1. immodestia 2. indecenza.
to **immolate** vt. immolare.
immolation s. immolazione.
immolator s. immolatore.
immoral agg. immorale.
immorality s. immoralità.
immortal agg. e s. immortale.
immortality s. immortalità.
immortalization s. l'immortalare.
to **immortalize** vt. immortalare.
immovability s. 1. immobilità 2. inamovibilità.
immovable agg. 1. immobile 2. inamovibile.
immovables s. pl. beni immobili.
immune agg. 1. immune 2. esente.
immunity s. 1. immunità 2. esenzione.
immunization s. immunizzazione.
to **immunize** vt. immunizzare.
to **immure** vt. 1. murare 2. impri-

gionare 3. chiudere fra mura.

immutability *s.* immutabilità.

immutable *agg.* immutabile.

imp *s.* diavoletto.

impact *s.* urto, collisione.

to **impact** *vt.* conficcare.

to **impair** *vt.* menomare.

impairment *s.* menomazione.

to **impale** *vt.* impalare.

impalpability *s.* impalpabilità.

impalpable *agg.* impalpabile.

imparity *s.* imparità.

to **impart** *vt.* 1. impartire 2. rivelare.

impartial *agg.* imparziale.

impartiality *s.* imparzialità.

impassable *agg.* invalicabile, impraticabile.

impassibility *s.* impassibilità.

impassible *agg.* impassibile.

to **impassion** *vt.* appassionare.

impassionate, impassioned *agg.* eccitato, ardente.

impassive *agg.* impassibile.

impatience *s.* 1. impazienza 2. avversione.

impatient *agg.* 1. impaziente 2. intollerante.

impavid *agg.* impavido.

to **impeach** *vt.* 1. imputare 2. biasimare ‖ *to — so. for high treason,* accusare qu. di alto tradimento.

impeachable *agg.* accusabile.

impeacher *s.* accusatore.

impeachment *s.* accusa.

impeccability *s.* impeccabilità.

impeccable *agg.* impeccabile.

impecunious *agg.* povero.

to **impede** *vt.* 1. impedire 2. ostacolare.

impediment *s.* impedimento.

to **impel** *vt.* spingere, incitare.

impellent *agg.* impellente. ♦ **impellent** *s.* incentivo.

to **impend** *vi.* incombere.

impendence *s.* imminenza.

impendent *agg.* incombente.

impenetrability *s.* impenetrabilità.

impenetrable *agg.* impenetrabile.

impenitence *s.* impenitenza.

impenitent *agg.* impenitente.

imperative *agg.* e *s.* imperativo.

imperator *s.* imperatore.

imperceptibility *s.* impercettibilità.

imperceptible *agg.* impercettibile.

imperfect *agg.* 1. imperfetto 2. incompiuto.

imperfection *s.* 1. imperfezione 2.

incompiutezza.

imperial *agg.* imperiale.

imperialism *s.* imperialismo.

imperialist *s.* imperialista.

imperialistic *agg.* imperialistico.

to **imperil** *vt.* mettere in pericolo.

imperious *agg.* 1. imperioso 2. impellente.

imperiousness *s.* 1. imperiosità 2. urgenza.

imperishability *s.* indistruttibilità.

imperishable *agg.* indistruttibile, imperituro.

impermeability *s.* impermeabilità.

impermeable *agg.* impermeabile.

impersonal *agg.* impersonale.

impersonality *s.* l'essere impersonale.

to **impersonate** *vt.* impersonare.

impersonation *s.* personificazione.

impertinence *s.* 1. impertinenza 2. non pertinenza.

impertinent *agg.* 1. impertinente 2. non pertinente.

imperturbability *s.* imperturbabilità.

imperturbable *agg.* imperturbabile.

impervious *agg.* 1. impervio 2. impermeabile.

to **impetrate** *vt.* impetrare.

impetration *s.* impetrazione.

impetuosity *s.* impetuosità.

impetuous *agg.* impetuoso.

impetus *s.* impeto.

impiety *s.* empietà.

impious *agg.* empio.

impish *agg.* birichino.

implacability *s.* implacabilità.

implacable *agg.* implacabile.

to **implant** *vt.* 1. impiantare 2. inculcare.

implement *s.* utensile.

to **implement** *vt.* 1. compiere 2. attrezzare.

to **implicate** *vt.* implicare.

implication *s.* implicazione.

implicit, implied *agg.* implicito.

to **implore** *vt.* implorare.

imploring *agg.* supplichevole.

to **imply** *vt.* implicare.

impolite *agg.* scortese.

impoliteness *s.* scortesia.

impolitic *agg.* impolitico.

imponderability *s.* imponderabilità.

imponderable *agg.* imponderabile.

import *s.* 1. importanza 2. significato 3. (*comm.*) importazione.

to **import** *vt.* 1. importare 2. si-

gnificare **3.** (*comm.*) importare.
importance *s.* importanza.
important *agg.* importante.
importer *s.* importatore.
importunate, importune *agg.* urgente.
to **importune** *vt.* importunare.
importunity *s.* **1.** insistenza **2.** urgenza.
to **impose** *vt.* **1.** imporre **2.** (*tip.*) impaginare. ♦ to **impose** *vi.* imporsi || *to — on,* ingannare.
imposing *agg.* imponente.
imposition *s.* **1.** imposizione **2.** imposta **3.** inganno **4.** (*tip.*) messa in macchina.
impossibility *s.* impossibilità.
impossible *agg.* impossibile.
impostor *s.* impostore.
imposture *s.* impostura.
impotence *s.* impotenza.
impotent *agg.* impotente.
to **impoverish** *vt.* impoverire.
impoverishment *s.* impoverimento.
impracticability *s.* **1.** inattuabilità **2.** impraticabilità **3.** intrattabilità.
impracticable *agg.* **1.** inattuabile **2.** impraticabile **3.** intrattabile.
imprecation *s.* imprecazione.
imprecatory *agg.* imprecatorio.
impregnable *agg.* inespugnabile.
to **impregnate** *vt.* **1.** impregnare **2.** fecondare.
impregnation *s.* fecondazione.
to **impress** *vt.* **1.** imprimere, stampare **2.** impressionare.
impression *s.* **1.** impressione **2.** ristampa.
impressionability *s.* impressionabilità.
impressionable *agg.* impressionabile.
impressionism *s.* impressionismo.
impressionist *agg.* e *s.* impressionista.
impressive *agg.* impressionante.
imprint *s.* **1.** impronta **2.** stampa.
to **imprint** *vt.* **1.** imprimere **2.** stampare.
to **imprison** *vt.* imprigionare.
imprisonment *s.* prigionia.
improbability *s.* improbabilità.
improbable *agg.* improbabile.
improbably *avv.* improbabilmente.
impromptu *agg.* improvvisato. ♦ **impromptu** *s.* improvvisazione.
improper *agg.* **1.** erroneo **2.** inadatto **3.** sconveniente, irregolare.

impropriety *s.* **1.** scorrettezza **2.** sconvenienza.
to **improve** *vt.* **1.** migliorare **2.** valorizzare. ♦ to **improve** *vi.* migliorare, perfezionarsi.
improvement *s.* miglioramento.
improvidence *s.* imprevidenza.
improvident *agg.* imprevidente.
improvisation *s.* improvvisazione.
improvisator *s.* improvvisatore.
to **improvise** *vt.* e *vi.* improvvisare.
imprudence *s.* imprudenza.
imprudent *agg.* imprudente.
impudence *s.* impudenza.
impudent *agg.* impudente.
to **impugn** *vt.* (*giur.*) impugnare.
impugnable *agg.* (*giur.*) impugnabile.
impugner *s.* oppositore.
impulse, impulsion *s.* impulso.
impulsive *agg.* impulsivo.
impulsiveness, impulsivity *s.* impulsività.
impunity *s.* impunità.
impure *agg.* impuro.
impurity *s.* impurità.
imputable *agg.* imputabile.
imputation *s.* imputazione.
to **impute** *vt.* imputare.
in *avv.* e *prep.* a, in, dentro, entro, durante || *to be — Paris,* essere a Parigi; *the best — the world,* il migliore del mondo; *— my opinion,* secondo me; *— all,* in tutto; *— that,* in quanto che.
inability *s.* incapacità.
inaccessibility *s.* inaccessibilità.
inaccessible *agg.* inaccessibile.
inaccuracy *s.* inesattezza.
inaccurate *agg.* inesatto.
inaction *s.* inattività.
inactive *agg.* inattivo.
inactivity *s.* inattività.
inadaptability *s.* inadattabilità.
inadequacy *s.* inadeguatezza.
inadequate *agg.* inadeguato.
inadmissibility *s.* inammissibilità.
inadmissible *agg.* inammissibile.
inadvertence *s.* inavvertenza.
inadvertent *agg.* **1.** disattento **2.** involontario.
inalienability *s.* inalienabilità.
inalienable *agg.* inalienabile.
inalterability *s.* inalterabilità.
inalterable *agg.* inalterabile.
inane *agg.* e *s.* vuoto.
inanimate *agg.* **1.** inanimato **2.** fiacco.
inanity *s.* inanità.

inappeasable *agg.* implacabile.
inappellable *agg.* inappellabile.
inappetence *s.* inappetenza.
inapplicable *agg.* inapplicabile.
inappropriate *agg.* inadeguato.
inapt *agg.* **1.** inadatto **2.** inetto.
inarticulate *agg.* inarticolato.
inattention *s.* **1.** disattenzione **2.** negligenza.
inattentive *agg.* **1.** disattento **2.** negligente.
inaudible *agg.* impercettibile.
inaugural *agg.* inaugurale.
to inaugurate *vt.* inaugurare.
inauguration *s.* inaugurazione.
inboard *agg.* interno. ◆ **inboard** *avv.* internamente.
inborn, inbred *agg.* innato.
incalculable *agg.* **1.** incalcolabile **2.** incerto.
incandescence *s.* incandescenza.
incandescent *agg.* incandescente.
incantation *s.* incantesimo.
incapability *s.* incapacità.
incapable *agg.* incapace.
incapacity *s.* incapacità.
to incarnate *vt.* **1.** incarnare **2.** realizzare.
incarnation *s.* incarnazione.
incatenation *s.* incatenamento.
incautious *agg.* incauto.
incendiary *agg. e s.* **1.** incendiario **2.** sovversivo.
incensation *s.* incensamento.
incense *s.* incenso.
to incense[1] *vt.* incensare.
to incense[2] *vt.* provocare.
incensurable *agg.* incensurabile.
incentive *agg.* stimolante. ◆ **incentive** *s.* incentivo.
incertitude *s.* incertezza.
incessant *agg.* incessante.
incest *s.* incesto.
incestuous *agg.* incestuoso.
inch *s.* pollice (*misura*).
incidence *s.* incidenza.
incident *agg.* probabile. ◆ **incident** *s.* avvenimento.
incidental *agg.* fortuito. ◆ **incidental** *s.* caso.
incipient *agg.* incipiente.
to incise *vt.* incidere.
incisive *agg.* incisivo.
incisiveness *s.* incisività.
incisor *s.* incisivo.
incitation *s.* incitamento.
to incite *vt.* incitare.
incivility *s.* villania.
inclemency *s.* inclemenza.

inclement *agg.* inclemente.
inclinable *agg.* incline.
inclination *s.* inclinazione.
to incline *vt.* inclinare. ◆ **to incline** *vi.* propendere.
inclined *agg.* **1.** inclinato **2.** incline.
to include *vt.* includere.
included *agg.* incluso, compreso.
inclusion *s.* inclusione.
inclusive *agg.* compreso.
incoherence *s.* incoerenza.
incoherent *agg.* incoerente.
incombustible *agg.* incombustibile.
income *s.* rendita, reddito || — -*tax*, imposta sul reddito.
incoming *s.* entrata. ◆ **incoming** *agg.* entrante.
incommensurability *s.* incommensurabilità.
incommensurable *agg.* incommensurabile.
incommensurate *agg.* **1.** inadeguato **2.** smisurato.
incommunicability *s.* incomunicabilità.
incommunicable *agg.* incomunicabile.
incommutable *agg.* incommutabile.
incomparable *agg.* incomparabile.
incompatibility *s.* incompatibilità.
incompatible *agg.* incompatibile.
incompetence *s.* incompetenza.
incompetent *agg. e s.* incompetente.
incomplete *agg.* incompleto.
incompleteness, incompletion *s.* incompletezza.
incomprehensibility *s.* incomprensibilità.
incomprehensible *agg.* incomprensibile.
incomprehension *s.* incomprensione.
inconceivability *s.* inconcepibilità.
inconceivable *agg.* inconcepibile.
inconclusive *agg.* inconcludente.
inconclusiveness *s.* inconcludenza.
incongruity *s.* incongruenza.
incongruous *agg.* incongruo.
inconsequence *s.* incongruenza.
inconsequent *agg.* incongruente.
inconsequential *agg.* **1.** incoerente **2.** irrilevante.
inconsiderate *agg.* sconsiderato.
inconsistence *s.* incoerenza.
inconsistent *agg.* incoerente.
inconsolable *agg.* inconsolabile.
inconstancy *s.* incostanza.
inconstant *agg.* incostante.

incontestability *s.* incontestabilità.

incontestable *agg.* incontestabile.

incontinence *s.* incontinenza.

incontinent *agg.* incontinente.

incontinently *avv.* smoderatamente.

incontrollable *agg.* incontrollabile.

incontrovertible *agg.* incontrovertibile.

inconvenience *s.* 1. disturbo 2. scomodità.

to **inconvenience** *vt.* scomodare.

inconvenient *agg.* incomodo.

inconvertible *agg.* inconvertibile.

to **incorporate** *vt.* 1. incorporare 2. (*comm.*) costituire. ◆ to **incorporate** *vi.* incorporarsi.

incorporated *agg.* 1. (*comm.*) anonimo 2. incorporato.

incorporation *s.* 1. incorporazione 2. (*comm.*) costituzione.

incorporeal *agg.* incorporeo.

incorrect *agg.* scorretto.

incorrectness *s.* scorrettezza.

incorrigible *agg.* incorreggibile.

incorrupt *agg.* incorrotto.

incorruptibility *s.* incorruttibilità.

incorruptible *agg.* incorruttibile.

increase *s.* aumento.

to **increase** *vt.* e *vi.* aumentare.

increasing *agg.* crescente.

increasingly *avv.* sempre più.

incredibility *s.* incredibilità.

incredible *agg.* incredibile.

incredulity *s.* incredulità.

incredulous *agg.* incredulo.

increment *s.* incremento.

to **incriminate** *vt.* incriminare.

incrimination *s.* incriminazione.

incriminatory *agg.* incriminante.

incrustation *s.* incrostazione.

incubation *s.* incubazione.

incubator *s.* incubatrice.

to **inculcate** *vt.* inculcare.

inculcation *s.* inculcazione.

inculpable *agg.* innocente.

inculpation *s.* accusa.

incumbent *agg.* incombente.

to **incur** *vt.* incorrere in.

incurability *s.* incurabilità.

incurable *agg.* incurabile.

incursion *s.* incursione.

indebted *agg.* 1. indebitato 2. obligato.

indecency *s.* indecenza.

indecent *agg.* indecente.

indecipherable *agg.* indecifrabile.

indecision *s.* indecisione.

indecisive *agg.* 1. indeciso 2. non decisivo.

indeclinable *agg.* indeclinabile.

indecomposable *agg.* indecomponibile.

indecorous *agg.* indecoroso.

indeed *avv.* in verità, davvero.

indefatigable *agg.* infaticabile.

indefeasible *agg.* irrevocabile.

indefinable *agg.* indefinibile.

indefinite *agg.* indefinito.

indefiniteness *s.* indeterminatezza.

indelible *agg.* indelebile.

indelicacy *s.* 1. rozzezza 2. sconvenienza.

indelicate *agg.* 1. sgarbato 2. sconveniente.

to **indemnify** *vt.* 1. indennizzare 2. assicurare.

indemnity *s.* 1. indennità 2. assicurazione.

indemonstrable *agg.* indimostrabile.

indent *s.* 1. dentellatura 2. incavo 3. (*comm.*) ordinazione 4. (*tip.*) capoverso.

to **indent** *vt.* 1. dentellare, frastagliare 2. intagliare 3. (*comm.*) ordinare (*merci*).

indentation, indention *s.* 1. dentellatura 2. incisione.

indenture *s.* 1. dentellatura 2. contratto.

independence *s.* indipendenza.

independent *agg.* e *s.* indipendente.

indescribable *agg.* indescrivibile.

indestructibility *s.* indistruttibilità.

indestructible *agg.* indistruttibile.

indeterminable *agg.* indeterminabile.

indeterminate *agg.* indeterminato.

indetermination *s.* indeterminazione.

index *s.* indice.

Indian *agg.* e *s.* indiano.

to **indicate** *vt.* indicare.

indicating *agg.* indicatore.

indication *s.* 1. indicazione 2. segno.

indicative *agg.* e *s.* indicativo.

indicator *s.* indicatore.

to **indict** *vt.* accusare.

indictment *s.* (*giur.*) accusa.

indifference *s.* 1. indifferenza 2. imparzialità 3. mancanza di valore.

indifferent *agg.* 1. indifferente 2.

imparziale 3. mediocre.

indifferentism s. indifferentismo.

indifferentist s. indifferentista.

indigence s. indigenza.

indigenous agg. indigeno.

indigent agg. indigente.

indigestible agg. indigesto.

indigestion s. dispepsia.

indignant agg. indignato.

indignation s. indignazione.

indignity s. 1. indegnità 2. offesa.

indigo s. indaco.

indirect agg. 1. indiretto 2. tortuoso.

indiscernible agg. indistinguibile.

indiscipline s. indisciplina.

indiscreet agg. 1. sconsiderato 2. indiscreto.

indiscrete agg. compatto.

indiscretion s. 1. sconsideratezza 2. indiscrezione.

indiscriminate agg. indiscriminato.

indispensable agg. indispensabile.

indisposed agg. indisposto.

indisposition s. 1. avversione 2. indisposizione.

indisputability s. ipdiscutibilità.

indisputable agg. indiscutibile.

indisputed agg. indiscusso.

indissolubility s. indissolubilità.

indissoluble agg. indissolubile.

indistinct agg. indistinto.

indistinguishable agg. indistinguibile.

individual agg. individuale. ◆ **individual** s. individuo.

individualism s. individualismo.

individualist agg. e s. individualista.

individualistic agg. individualistico.

individuality s. individualità.

individualization s. individualizzazione.

to **individualize** vt. individualizzare.

indivisibility s. indivisibilità.

indivisible agg. indivisibile.

indocility s. indocilità.

Indo-European agg. e s. indo-europeo.

indolence s. indolenza.

indolent agg. indolente.

indomitable agg. indomabile.

indoor agg. in casa.

indoors avv. in casa.

indraft, indraught s. risucchio, vortice.

indubitable agg. indubitabile.

to **induce** vt. indurre.

inducement s. 1. allettamento 2. movente.

induction s. 1. induzione 2. insediamento.

inductive agg. induttivo.

inductor s. induttore.

to **indulge** vt. essere indulgente verso. ◆ to **indulge** vi. indulgere.

indulgence s. 1. indulgenza 2. proroga.

indulgent agg. indulgente.

indult s. indulto.

industrial agg. industriale. ◆ **industrial** s. lavoratore dell'industria.

industrialism s. industrialismo.

industr'alist s. industriale.

industr alization s. industrializzazione.

to **industrialize** vt. industrializzare.

industrious agg. industrioso.

industry s. 1. industria 2. operosità, diligenza.

inebriate agg. e s. ubriaco.

to **inebriate** vt. inebriare.

inedited agg. inedito.

ineffable agg. ineffabile.

ineffective agg. 1. inefficace 2. inefficiente.

ineffectiveness s. 1. inefficacia 2. inefficienza.

ineffectual agg. inutile.

inefficacy s. inefficacia.

inefficient agg. V. *ineffective.*

inelegance s. ineleganza.

inelegant agg. inelegante.

ineligibility s. ineleggibilità.

ineligible agg. ineleggibile.

ineluctable agg. ineluttabile.

inept agg. inadatto.

ineptitude, ineptness s. inettitudine.

inequality s. disuguaglianza.

inequity s. ingiustizia.

ineradicable agg. inestirpabile.

inerrability s. infallibilità.

inerrable agg. infallibile.

inert agg. inerte.

inertness s. inerzia.

inescapable agg. inevitabile.

inestimable agg. inestimabile.

inevitability s. inevitabilità.

inevitable agg. inevitabile.

inevitableness s. inevitabilità.

inexact agg. inesatto.

inexactitude s. inesattezza.

inexcusability s. inescusabilità.

inexcusable agg. imperdonabile.

inexecutable *agg.* ineseguibile.
inexhaustibility *s.* inesauribilità.
inexhaustible *agg.* inesauribile.
inexistence *s.* inesistenza.
inexistent *agg.* inesistente.
inexorability *s.* inesorabilità.
inexorable *agg.* inesorabile.
inexpedient *agg.* inopportuno.
inexpensive *agg.* poco costoso.
inexperience *s.* inesperienza.
inexperienced, inexpert *agg.* inesperto.
inexpiable *agg.* inespiabile.
inexplicable *agg.* inesplicabile.
inexplorable *agg.* inesplorabile.
inexpressible *agg.* inesprimibile.
inexpressive *agg.* inespressivo.
inexpressiveness *s.* inespressività.
inexpugnability *s.* inespugnabilità.
inexpugnable *agg.* inespugnabile.
inextinguishable *agg.* inestinguibile.
inextricable *agg.* inestricabile.
infallibility *s.* infallibilità.
infallible *agg.* infallibile.
infamous *agg.* infame.
infamy *s.* infamia.
infancy *s.* infanzia.
infant *agg.* infantile. ♦ **infant** *s.* 1. neonato 2. (*giur.*) minore.
infanticide *s.* 1. infanticida 2. infanticidio.
infantile *agg.* infantile.
infantilism *s.* infantilismo.
infantry *s.* fanteria || — *man*, fante.
infarct *s.* infarto.
to **infatuate** *vt.* infatuare.
infatuation *s.* infatuazione.
to **infect** *vt.* contagiare.
infection *s.* contagio.
infectious *agg.* contagioso.
infective *agg.* infettivo.
infecund *agg.* infecondo.
infelicitous *agg.* infelice.
infelicity *s.* infelicità.
to **infer** *vt.* dedurre.
inferable *agg.* deducibile.
inference *s.* deduzione.
inferior *agg.* e *s.* inferiore.
inferiority *s.* inferiorità.
infernal *agg.* infernale.
to **infest** *vt.* infestare.
infestation *s.* infestamento.
infidel *s.* e *s.* infedele.
infidelity *s.* 1. miscredenza 2. infedeltà.
to **infiltrate** *vt.* infiltrare. ♦ to **infiltrate** *vi.* infiltrarsi.
infiltration *s.* infiltrazione.

infinite *agg.* e *s.* infinito.
infinitesimal *agg.* infinitesimale.
infinitive *agg.* e *s.* infinito.
infinitude *s.* infinità.
infinity *s.* infinità, infinito.
infirm *agg.* 1. infermo 2. irresoluto.
infirmary *s.* infermeria.
infirmity *s.* 1. infermità 2. irresolutezza.
to **inflame** *vt.* infiammare. ♦ to **inflame** *vi.* infiammarsi.
inflammability *s.* infiammabilità.
inflammable *agg.* infiammabile.
inflammation *s.* 1. l'infiammare, l'infiammarsi 2. infiammazione.
inflammatory *agg.* infiammatorio.
to **inflate** *vt.* gonfiare.
inflation *s.* 1. gonfiore, gonfiatura 2. (*comm.*) inflazione.
inflationary *agg.* inflazionistico.
to **inflect** *vt.* 1. flettere 2. modulare.
inflection *s.* 1. flessione 2. inflessione.
inflexibility *s.* inflessibilità.
inflexible *agg.* inflessibile.
to **inflict** *vt.* infliggere.
infliction *s.* 1. inflizione 2. pena.
inflorescence *s.* infiorescenza.
influence *s.* 1. influenza 2. (*elettr.*) induzione.
to **influence** *vt.* influenzare.
influential *agg.* influente.
influenza *s.* (*med.*) influenza.
influx *s.* 1. affluenza 2. sbocco (*di fiume*).
inform *agg.* informe.
to **inform** *vt.* 1. informare 2. dar forma a.
informal *agg.* non ufficiale.
informality *s.* assenza di formalità.
information *s.* (*solo sing.*) 1. informazione 2. sapere 3. accusa.
informative, informatory *agg.* informativo.
informed *agg.* istruito.
informer *s.* 1. informatore 2. accusatore.
infraction *s.* 1. infrazione 2. violazione.
infrangibility *s.* infrangibilità.
infrangible *agg.* 1. infrangibile 2. inviolabile.
infrared *agg.* infrarosso.
infrequent *agg.* raro.
to **infringe** *vt.* violare.
infringement *s.* violazione.
infringer *s.* trasgressore.
infructuous *agg.* infruttuoso.

to **infuse** *vt.* 1. versare 2. infondere 3. mettere in infusione.
infusible *agg.* infusibile.
infusion *s.* 1. infusione 2. infuso.
ingenious *agg.* ingegnoso.
ingenuity *s.* ingegnosità.
ingenuous *agg.* 1. ingenuo 2. franco.
ingenuousness *s.* ingenuità.
to **ingest** *vt.* ingerire.
ingestion *s.* ingestione.
inglorious *agg.* inglorioso.
ingot *s.* lingotto.
ingratitude *s.* ingratitudine.
ingredient *s.* ingrediente.
inguen *s.* inguine.
inguinal *agg.* inguinale.
to **inhabit** *vt.* abitare.
inhabitable *agg.* abitabile.
inhabitancy *s.* domicilio.
inhabitant *s.* abitante.
inhalant *s.* 1. inalatore 2. sostanza da inalare.
inhalation *s.* inalazione.
to **inhale** *vt.* e *vi.* 1. aspirare 2. inalare.
inhaler *s.* inalatore.
inherent *agg.* inerente.
to **inherit** *vt.* e *vi.* ereditare.
inheritance *s.* eredità.
to **inhibit** *vt.* 1. inibire 2. interdire.
inhibition *s.* 1. inibizione 2. interdizione.
inhibitory *agg.* inibitorio.
inhospitable *agg.* inospitale.
inhospitality *s.* inospitalità.
inhuman *agg.* inumano.
inhumanity *s.* inumanità.
inhumation *s.* inumazione.
inimical *agg.* nemico.
inimitable *agg.* inimitabile.
iniquitous *agg.* iniquo.
iniquity *s.* iniquità.
initial *agg.* e *s.* iniziale.
to **initial** *vt.* siglare.
initiate *agg.* e *s.* iniziato.
to **initiate** *vt.* iniziare.
initiation *s.* 1. inizio 2. iniziazione.
initiative *agg.* introduttivo. ♦ **initiative** *s.* iniziativa.
initiator *s.* iniziatore.
to **inject** *vt.* iniettare.
injection *s.* iniezione.
injector *s.* iniettore.
injunction *s.* ingiunzione.
to **injure** *vt.* ledere, ferire.
injurer *s.* 1. danneggiatore 2. feritore.
injury *s.* 1. torto, danno 2. ferita.

injustice *s.* ingiustizia.
ink *s.* inchiostro || — -*pot*, calamaio.
inkholder *s.* calamaio.
inkling *s.* indizio.
inky *agg.* 1. di, simile a inchiostro 2. macchiato d'inchiostro.
inlaid *agg.* e *s.* interno. ♦ **inland** *avv.* all'interno.
inlay *s.* intarsio.
to **inlay (inlaid, inlaid)** *vt.* intarsiare.
inlet *s.* 1. piccola insenatura 2. apertura.
inmate *s.* 1. inquilino 2. ricoverato.
inmost *agg.* più interno.
inn *s.* locanda || — -*keeper*, locandiere; — *of court*, scuola di legge.
innate *agg.* innato.
innavigable *agg.* non navigabile.
inner *agg.* interno, intimo.
innermost *agg.* V. *inmost*.
innervation *s.* innervazione.
innocence *s.* innocenza.
innocent *agg.* e *s.* innocente.
innocuity *s.* innocuità.
innocuous *agg.* innocuo.
innominate *agg.* innominato.
to **innovate** *vt.* e *vi.* innovare.
innovation *s.* innovazione.
innovator *s.* innovatore.
innumerability *s.* innumerabilità.
innumerable *agg.* innumerevole.
inobservance *s.* 1. inosservanza 2. disattenzione.
inobservant *agg.* 1. inosservante 2. disattento.
to **inoculate** *vt.* 1. inoculare 2. inculcare.
inoculation *s.* inoculazione.
inodorous *agg.* inodoro.
inoffensive *agg.* inoffensivo.
inopportune *agg.* inopportuno.
inopportuneness *s.* inopportunità.
inordinate *agg.* smoderato.
inorganic *agg.* inorganico.
inoxidizable *agg.* inossidabile.
inpouring *agg.* affluente. ♦ **inpouring** *s.* afflusso.
input *s.* (*mecc.; elettr.*) alimentazione, entrata.
inquest *s.* 1. inchiesta 2. giuria.
inquietude *s.* inquietudine.
to **inquire** *vt.* e *vi.* chiedere || *to* — *after*, chiedere informazioni su; *to* — *into*, indagare su.
inquirer *s.* investigatore.
inquiring *agg.* 1. indagatore 2. cu-

rioso.

inquiry s. 1. ricerca 2. domanda 3. inchiesta.

inquisition s. 1. ricerca 2. inchiesta.

inquisitive agg. V. *inquiring*.

inquisitiveness s. curiosità.

inrush s. irruzione.

insalubrity s. insalubrità.

insane agg. insano.

insanitary agg. malsano.

insanity s. insania.

insatiability s. insaziabilità.

insatiable, insatiate agg. insaziabile.

to **inscribe** vt. 1. iscrivere 2. scolpire 3. dedicare.

inscription s. 1. iscrizione 2. dedica.

inscrutability s. inscrutabilità.

inscrutable agg. inscrutabile.

inscrutableness s. inscrutabilità.

insect s. insetto.

insecticide s. insetticida.

insectivorous agg. insettivoro.

insecure agg. insicuro.

insecurity s. insicurezza.

insensate agg. 1. insensibile 2. insensato.

insensibility s. insensibilità.

insensible agg. 1. insensibile 2. inconscio.

insensitive agg. insensibile.

inseparable agg. inseparabile.

insert s. inserzione.

to **insert** vt. inserire.

insertion s. inserzione.

to **inset** (**inset, inset**) vt. inserire.

inside agg. e s. interno. ♦ **inside** avv. e prep. dentro.

insidious agg. insidioso.

insight s. 1. intuito 2. penetrazione.

insignificant agg. insignificante.

insincere agg. insincero.

insincerity s. falsità.

to **insinuate** vt. insinuare.

insinuation s. insinuazione.

insinuative agg. insinuante.

insipid agg. insipido.

insipidity, insipidness s. insipidezza.

insipience s. insipienza.

insipient agg. insipiente.

to **insist** vi. insistere.

insistence s. insistenza.

insistent agg. insistente.

insolation s. insolazione.

insolence s. insolenza.

insolent agg. e s. insolente.

insolubility s. insolubilità.

insoluble agg. insolubile.

insolvable agg. insolubile.

insolvency s. insolvenza.

insolvent agg. insolvente. ♦ **insolvent** s. debitore insolvente.

insomnia s. insonnia.

to **inspect** vt. ispezionare.

inspection s. ispezione.

inspector s. ispettore.

inspectoral agg. di ispettore, di ispezione.

inspectorate s. ispettorato.

inspiration s. 1. inspirazione 2. ispirazione.

to **inspire** vt. 1. inspirare 2. ispirare.

inspirer s. ispiratore.

inspiring agg. ispiratore.

instability s. instabilità.

to **install** vt. installare.

installation s. installazione.

instalment s. 1. rata 2. puntata.

instance s. 1. esempio 2. caso 3. istanza.

instancy s. 1. urgenza 2. insistenza.

instant agg. 1. urgente 2. corrente. ♦ **instant** s. istante.

instantaneous agg. istantaneo.

instantly avv. all'istante. ♦ **instantly** cong. non appena che.

instead avv. invece.

instep s. 1. collo del piede 2. collo di scarpa.

to **instigate** vt. istigare.

instigation s. istigazione.

instigator s. istigatore.

to **instil(l)** vt. instillare.

instinct agg. imbevuto. ♦ **instinct** s. istinto.

instinctive agg. istintivo.

institute s. istituto. ♦ **institutes** s. pl. istituzioni.

to **institute** vt. istituire.

institution s. istituto.

institutional agg. istituzionale.

institutor s. istitutore.

to **instruct** vt. 1. istruire 2. informare 3. ordinare.

instruction s. istruzione.

instructive agg. istruttivo.

instructor s. istruttore.

instrument s. 1. strumento 2. atto giuridico.

to **instrument** vt. 1. strumentare 2. redigere.

instrumental agg. 1. strumentale 2. utile.

instrumentation s. 1. orchestrazione 2. uso di strumenti.

insubordinate *agg.* insubordinato.

insubordination *s.* insubordinazione.

insubstantial *agg.* incorporeo.

insufferable *agg.* insopportabile.

insufficiency *s.* insufficienza.

insufficient *agg.* insufficiente.

insular *agg.* 1. insulare 2. (*fig.*) di mentalità ristretta.

to **insulate** *vt.* isolare.

insulation *s.* isolamento.

insulator *s.* isolatore.

insulin *s.* insulina.

insult *s.* insulto.

to **insult** *vt.* insultare.

insuperable *agg.* insuperabile.

insuppressible *agg.* insopprimibile.

insurance *s.* assicurazione.

insurant *s.* assicurato.

to **insure** *vt.* assicurare.

insurer *s.* assicuratore.

insurgency *s.* insurrezione.

insurgent *agg.* e *s.* insorto.

insurmountable *agg.* insormontabile.

insurrection *s.* insurrezione.

insurrectional, insurrectionary *agg.* insurrezionale.

insurrectionist *s.* insorto.

intact *agg.* intatto.

intake *s.* 1. presa 2. energia assorbita.

intangible *agg.* intangibile.

integrable *agg.* integrabile.

integral *agg.* integrale.

integrant *agg.* integrante.

to **integrate** *vt.* integrare.

integration *s.* integrazione.

integrity *s.* integrità.

intellect *s.* intelletto.

intellective *agg.* intellettivo.

intellectual *agg.* e *s.* intellettuale.

intellectualism *s.* intellettualismo.

intelligence *s.* 1. intelligenza 2. informazioni (*pl.*).

intelligent *agg.* intelligente.

intelligibility *agg.* intelligibilità.

intelligible *agg.* intelligibile.

intemperance *s.* intemperanza.

intemperate *agg.* 1. smoderato 2. rigido (*di clima*).

to **intend** *vt.* 1. intendere 2. destinare.

intendant *s.* intendente.

intended *agg.* progettato.

intense *agg.* intenso.

intensification *s.* intensificazione.

to **intensify** *vt.* intensificare. ◆ to

intensify *vi.* intensificarsi.

intensity *s.* 1. intensità 2. vigore.

intensive *agg.* intensivo, intenso.

intent *agg.* intento, dedito. ◆ **intent** *s.* intenzione, scopo.

intention *s.* intenzione.

intentional *agg.* intenzionale.

intently *avv.* intensamente.

to **inter** *vt.* seppellire.

to **intercalate** *vt.* intercalare.

to **intercede** *vi.* intercedere.

to **intercept** *vt.* intercettare.

interception *s.* intercettamento.

interceptor *s.* intercettatore.

intercession *s.* intercessione.

intercessor *s.* intercessore.

interchange *s.* scambio.

to **interchange** *vt.* scambiare. ◆ to **interchange** *vi.* scambiarsi.

interchangeable *agg.* scambievole.

intercom *s.* citofono.

intercommunication *s.* intercomunicazione.

intercontinental *agg.* intercontinentale.

intercostal *agg.* intercostale.

intercourse *s.* rapporto, relazione || *trade* —, scambi commerciali.

interdependence *s.* interdipendenza.

interdependent *agg.* interdipendente.

interdict *s.* 1. interdizione 2. interdetto 3. proibizione.

to **interdict** *vt.* 1. interdire 2. proibire.

interdiction *s.* V. *interdict*.

interest *s.* interesse.

to **interest** *vt.* interessare.

interested *agg.* interessato || *those* —, gli interessati.

interesting *agg.* interessante.

to **interfere** *vi.* 1. interferire 2. scontrarsi.

interference *s.* 1. interferenza 2. collisione.

interior *agg.* e *s.* interno.

to **interject** *vt.* intromettere.

interjection *s.* intromissione.

to **interlace** *vt.* intrecciare. ◆ to **interlace** *vi.* intrecciarsi.

interlacing *s.* intreccio.

to **interline** *vt.* interlineare.

interlinear *agg.* interlineare.

interlineation *s.* interlineazione.

to **interlink** *vt.* concatenare.

to **interlock** *vt.* sincronizzare.

interlocution *s.* interlocuzione.

interlocutor *s.* interlocutore.

to **interlope** *vi.* immischiarsi.
interlude *s.* 1. intervallo 2. intermezzo.
intermarriage *s.* matrimonio tra membri di famiglie, razze diverse.
to **intermarry** *vt.* e *vi.* imparentarsi per mezzo di matrimonio.
to **intermeddle** *vi.* intromettersi.
intermeddler *s.* intrigante.
intermediary *agg.* intermedio, frapposto. ♦ **intermediary** *s.* 1. intermediario, mediatore 2. cosa intermedia.
intermediate *agg.* V. *intermediary.*
intermediation *s.* mediazione.
interment *s.* sepoltura.
interminable *agg.* interminabile.
to **intermingle** *vt.* mescolare. ♦ to **intermingle** *vi.* mescolarsi.
intermission *s.* sosta, pausa.
to **intermit** *vt.* interrompere. ♦ to **intermit** *vi.* interrompersi, essere intermittente.
intermittence *s.* intermittenza.
intermittent *agg.* intermittente.
to **intern** *vt.* internare.
internal *agg.* interno.
international *agg.* internazionale.
internationalism *s.* internazionalismo.
internationalist *s.* internazionalista.
to **internationalize** *vt.* internazionalizzare.
internment *s.* internamento.
to **interpellate** *vt.* interpellare.
interpellation *s.* interpellanza.
interphone *s.* citofono.
interplanetary *agg.* interplanetario.
interplay *s.* azione reciproca.
to **interpolate** *vt.* interpolare.
interpolation *s.* interpolazione.
to **interpose** *vt.* interporre. ♦ to **interpose** *vi.* interporsi.
interposition *s.* interposizione.
to **interpret** *vt.* interpretare. ♦ to **interpret** *vi.* fare l'interprete.
interpretation *s.* interpretazione.
interpretative *agg.* interpretativo.
interpreter *s.* interprete.
interpunction *s.* interpunzione.
interregnum *s.* 1. interregno 2. intervallo.
interrelation *s.* relazione.
interrelationship *s.* interdipendenza.
to **interrogate** *vt.* interrogare.
interrogation *s.* interrogazione || — -mark, punto interrogativo.

interrogative *agg.* e *s.* interrogativo.
interrogatory *agg.* interrogativo. ♦ **interrogatory** *s.* 1. interrogazione 2. interrogatorio.
to **interrupt** *vt.* e *vi.* interrompere.
interrupter *s.* interruttore.
interruption *s.* interruzione.
to **intersect** *vt.* intersecare. ♦ to **intersect** *vi.* intersecarsi.
intersection *s.* intersezione.
interspace *s.* intervallo, spazio.
to **intersperse** *vt.* cospargere.
interstice *s.* interstizio.
to **intertwine** *vt.* attorcigliare. ♦ to **intertwine** *vi.* attorcigliarsi.
interurban *agg.* interurbano.
interval *s.* intervallo.
to **intervene** *vi.* intervenire.
intervener *s.* chi interviene.
intervention *s.* intervento.
interventionist *s.* interventista.
interview *s.* intervista.
to **interview** *vt.* intervistare.
interviewer *s.* intervistatore.
to **interweave (interwove, interwoven)** *vt.* intessere, intrecciare.
intestinal *agg.* intestinale.
intestine *agg.* e *s.* intestino.
intimacy *s.* intimità.
intimate *agg.* intimo. ♦ **intimate** *s.* amico intimo.
to **intimate** *vt.* 1. intimare 2. accennare.
intimation *s.* 1. intimazione 2. preannunzio.
intimidation *s.* intimidazione.
intimidatory *agg.* intimidatorio.
into *prep.* in, dentro || *to go — the, park,* entrare nel parco; *far — the night,* fino a tarda notte.
intolerable *agg.* intollerabile.
intolerance *s.* intolleranza.
intolerant *agg.* e *s.* intollerante.
to **intonate** *vt.* intonare.
intonation *s.* intonazione.
to **intone** *vt.* intonare.
to **intoxicate** *vt.* inebriare.
intoxication *s.* ebbrezza.
intractable *agg.* intrattabile.
intramuscular *agg.* intramuscolare.
intransgressible *agg.* che non può essere trasgredito.
intransigence *s.* intransigenza.
intransigent *agg.* e *s.* intransigente.
intransitive *agg.* intransitivo.
intravenous *agg.* endovenoso.
intrepid *agg.* intrepido.

intrepidity s. intrepidezza.
intricacy s. complicazione.
intricate agg. intricato.
intrigant s. intrigante.
intrigue s. intrigo.
to intrigue vt. 1. ingannare 2. rendere perplesso 3. affascinare. ♦ to intrigue vi. avere una tresca.
intriguer s. intrigante.
intrinsic agg. intrinseco.
to introduce vt. 1. introdurre 2. presentare.
introduction s. 1. introduzione 2. presentazione.
introductive, introductory agg. introduttivo.
intromission s. interferenza.
to intromit vt. introdurre.
to introspect vi. autoesaminarsi.
introspection s. introspezione.
introspective agg. introspettivo.
introversion s. introversione.
introvert agg. e s. introverso.
to intrude vt. imporre. ♦ to intrude vi. intromettersi.
intruder s. 1. intruso 2. importuno.
intrusion s. intrusione.
intrusive agg. 1. intruso 2. importuno.
intrusiveness s. indiscrezione.
intuition s. intuizione.
intuitional agg. intuitivo.
intuitionism s. intuizionismo.
intuitive agg. intuitivo.
to inundate vt. inondare.
inundation s. inondazione.
inurbane agg. inurbano.
inurbanity s. inurbanità.
to inure vt. abituare. ♦ to inure vi. venire in uso.
inurement s. abitudine.
inutility s. inutilità.
to invade vt. 1. invadere 2. violare.
invader s. invasore.
invalid agg. 1. invalido 2. nullo. ♦ invalid s. invalido.
to invalid vt. 1. rendere invalido 2. riformare.
to invalidate vt. invalidare.
invalidation s. invalidazione.
invalidity s. invalidità.
invaluable agg. inestimabile.
invariability s. invariabilità.
invariable agg. invariabile.
invasion s. invasione.
invective s. invettiva.
to inveigh vi. inveire.

to invent vt. inventare.
invention s. 1. invenzione 2. inventiva.
inventive agg. inventivo.
inventor s. inventore.
inventory s. inventario.
to inventory vt. fare l'inventario di.
inverse agg. e s. inverso.
inversion s. inversione.
invert agg. e s. invertito.
to invert vt. invertire.
invertebrate agg. e s. invertebrato.
invertible agg. invertibile.
to invest vt. 1. investire 2. rivestire.
to investigate vt. e vi. investigare.
investigation s. investigazione.
investigative agg. investigativo.
investigator s. investigatore.
investiture s. investitura.
investment s. investimento.
investor s. investitore.
inveterate agg. inveterato.
invidious agg. odioso.
invidiousness s. odiosità.
to invigorate vt. rinvigorire.
invigorator agg. rinforzante.
invincibility s. invincibilità.
invincible agg. invincibile.
inviolability s. inviolabilità.
inviolable agg. inviolabile.
inviolate agg. inviolato.
invisibility s. invisibilità.
invisible agg. invisibile.
invitation s. invito.
to invite vt. 1. invitare 2. provocare.
invocation s. invocazione.
invoice s. fattura.
to invoice vt. fatturare.
to invoke vt. 1. invocare 2. evocare.
involuntary s. involontario.
involute agg. 1. involuto 2. a spirale.
involution s. 1. involuzione 2. intrico 3. (mat.) elevazione a potenza.
to involve vt. 1. avvolgere 2. implicare 3. complicare.
invulnerability s. invulnerabilità.
invulnerable agg. invulnerabile.
inward agg. interiore.
inwardness s. interiorità.
inwards avv. internamente.
iodine s. iodio.
to iodize vt. iodare.
ion s. ione.
Ionic agg. ionico.

ionization s. ionizzazione.

ionosphere s. ionosfera.

Iranian agg. e s. iraniano.

Iraqi agg. e s. iracheno.

irascibility s. irascibilità.

irascible agg. irascibile.

irate agg. adirato.

ireful agg. irato.

iridescence s. iridescenza.

iridescent agg. iridescente.

iris s. iride.

Irish agg. irlandese.

Irishman s. irlandese.

irksome agg. noioso.

iron agg. di ferro. ♦ **iron** s. ferro || — -foundry, ferriera. ♦ **irons** s. pl. catene.

to **iron** vt. 1. rivestire di ferro 2. stirare.

ironclad agg. corazzato. ♦ **ironclad** s. corazzata.

ironic(al) agg. ironico.

ironing s. stiratura.

ironmonger s. negoziante in ferramenta.

ironsmith s. fabbro ferraio.

ironware s. ferramenta.

ironwork s. lavoro in ferro. ♦ **ironworks** s. pl. ferriera (sing.).

irony s. ironia.

to **irradiate** vt. irradiare. ♦ to **irradiate** vi. risplendere.

irradiation s. 1. illuminazione 2. irradiazione.

irrational agg. irrazionale.

irrationalism, irrationality s. irrazionalità.

irrealizable agg. irrealizzabile.

irreconcilability s. inconciliabilità.

irreconcilable agg. inconciliabile.

irrecoverable agg. 1. irrecuperabile 2. irrimediabile.

irredentism s. irredentismo.

irredentist s. irredentista.

irreducible agg. irriducibile.

irreflection s. irriflessione.

irreflective agg. irriflessivo.

irrefutable agg. irrefutabile.

irregular agg. e s. irregolare.

irregularity s. irregolarità.

irrelevant agg. 1. non pertinente 2. insignificante.

irreligious agg. irreligioso.

irremediable agg. irrimediabile.

irremissible agg. irremissibile.

irremovability s. irremovibilità.

irremovable agg. irremovibile.

irreparable agg. irreparabile.

irreplaceable agg. insostituibile.

irreprehensible agg. irreprensibile.

irrepressible agg. irrefrenabile.

irrepressibleness s. irrefrenabilità.

irreproachable agg. irreprensibile.

irreprovable agg. irreprensibile.

irresistible agg. irresistibile.

irresolute agg. irresoluto.

irresoluteness, irresolution s. irresolutezza.

irresolvable agg. insolubile.

irrespective agg. noncurante.

irresponsibility s. irresponsabilità.

irresponsible agg. 1. irresponsabile 2. insolubile.

irresponsive agg. che non risponde.

irretrievable agg. irrecuperabile.

irreverence s. irriverenza.

irreverent agg. irriverente.

irreversibility s. irreversibilità.

irreversible agg. irreversibile.

irrevocable agg. irrevocabile.

irrigable agg. irrigabile.

to **irrigate** vt. irrigare.

irrigation s. irrigazione.

irritability s. irritabilità.

irritable agg. irritabile.

irritant agg. e s. irritante.

to **irritate** vt. irritare.

irritation s. irritazione.

irritative agg. irritante.

irruption s. irruzione.

Islamic agg. islamico.

Islamism s. islamismo.

island s. 1. isola 2. salvagente stradale.

islander s. isolano.

isle s. piccola isola || the British Isles, le isole britanniche.

islet s. isolotto.

isochronism s. isocronismo.

to **isolate** vt. isolare.

isolation s. isolamento.

isolationism s. isolazionismo.

isolationist s. isolazionista.

isolator s. isolatore.

isomorphism s. isomorfismo.

isomorphous agg. isomorfo.

isosceles agg. isoscele.

isotherm s. isoterma.

isothermal agg. isotermico.

isotope s. isotopo.

isotrope s. isotropo.

Israeli agg. e s. israeliano.

Israelite s. israelita.

issue s. 1. uscita, sbocco, foce 2. conclusione 3. prole, stirpe 4. problema 5. emissione, pubblicazione.

to **issue** vt. 1. emettere, pubblicare 2. rilasciare. ♦ to **issue** vi. 1.

uscire 2. risultare 3. discendere.

issueless *agg.* 1. senza sbocco 2. senza prole.

isthmus *s.* istmo.

it *pron. neutro* esso, essa, ciò, lo, gli, le, ne, sé || *I don't believe* —, non ci credo; — *is raining*, piove; — *is Sunday*, è domenica.

Italian *agg. e s.* italiano.

to **italicize** *vt. e vi.* 1. stampare in corsivo 2. sottolineare.

itch *s.* 1. prurito 2. scabbia.

to **itch** *vi.* 1. prudere 2. aver voglia di.

itching *s.* prurito.

item *s. (comm.)* voce.

to **itemize** *vt.* specificare, elencare.

to **iterate** *vt.* ripetere.

itinerant *agg.* ambulante.

itinerary *s.* itinerario.

its *agg. e pron. poss. neutro* suo, sua, suoi, sue.

itself *pron. r. neutro* esso stesso, essa stessa, sé, si || *by* —, da solo.

ivory *s.* avorio.

ivy *s.* edera.

J

jab *s.* 1. stoccata 2. colpo improvviso.

jack *s.* 1. *(fam.)* marinaio 2. fante *(gioco delle carte)* 3. bandiera *(di nave)* 4. maschio *(di certi animali)* 5. uomo di fatica 6. *(mecc.)* cricco.

jackal *s.* sciacallo.

jackass *s.* somaro.

jackdaw *s.* cornacchia.

jacket *s.* 1. giacchetta 2. rivestimento protettivo, isolante.

Jacobin *s.* giacobino.

jade¹ *s.* giada.

jade² *s.* 1. cavallo, ronzino 2. megera.

to **jag** *vt.* frastagliare, dentellare.

jaguar *s.* giaguaro.

jail *s.* carcere.

to **jail** *vt.* incarcerare.

jailer *s.* carceriere.

to **jam** *vt.* premere, serrare, pigiare. ♦ to **jam** *vi.* bloccarsi, incepparsi.

jam¹ *s.* marmellata.

jam² *s.* 1. ammasso 2. compressione 3. ingorgo.

jamb *s.* stipite.

Jansenism *s.* giansenismo.

Jansenist *s.* giansenista.

January *s.* gennaio.

Japanese *agg. e s.* giapponese.

jar *s.* rumore aspro, stridio.

to **jar** *vi.* 1. discordare 2. stridere. ♦ to **jar** *vt.* 1. far discordare 2. far stridere.

jargon *s.* 1. gergo 2. linguaggio professionale.

jarring *agg.* discorde, stridente.

jasmin(e) *s.* gelsomino.

jasper *s.* diaspro.

jaundice *s.* itterizia.

javelin *s.* giavellotto.

jaw *s.* 1. mascella, mandibola 2. morsa, ganascia. ♦ **jaws** *s. pl.* stretta, gola.

jealous *agg.* geloso.

jealously *avv.* gelosamente.

jealousness, jealousy *s.* gelosia.

jeer *s.* beffa, scherno.

jelly *s.* gelatina *(anche di frutta)*.

to **jeopardize** *vt.* mettere a repentaglio.

jeopardy *s.* rischio, pericolo.

jerk *s.* 1. scatto, strattone 2. spinta 3. sussulto, tic nervoso.

to **jerk** *vt.* dare uno strattone. ♦ to **jerk** *vi.* sobbalzare || *to* — *along*, avanzare a scatti.

jerky *agg.* 1. sussultante 2. convulso.

jersey *s.* camicetta a maglia con maniche.

jest *s.* facezia, scherzo.

to **jest** *vi.* scherzare, dire delle facezie.

jester *s.* burlone.

jestful *agg.* incline allo scherzo.

Jesuit *s.* gesuita.

Jesuitical *agg.* gesuitico.

jet¹ *agg.* nero lucido.

jet² *s.* 1. getto, spruzzo 2. spruzzatore || — *engine*, motore a reazione; — *plane*, aeroplano a reazione.

to **jet** *vt.* schizzare, sprizzare. ♦ to **jet** *vi.* slanciarsi.

jetty *s.* molo || *landing* —, imbarcadero.

Jew *s.* ebreo.

jewel *s.* gioiello.

jewelcase *s.* scrigno.

jeweller *s.* gioielliere.

jewellery *s.* 1. gioielli 2. commercio delle gemme.

Jewish *agg.* ebraico, ebreo.

to **jib** *vi.* recalcitrare, impuntarsi.

jig *s.* 1. giga 2. *(mecc.)* maschera.

jigsaw s. sega da traforo.

to jingle vt. far tintinnare. ♦ to jingle vi. tintinnare.

job s. 1. lavoro, impiego 2. (fam.) faccenda, situazione.

jobber s. 1. noleggiatore 2. lavoratore a cottimo 3. trafficante disonesto.

jockey s. fantino.

jocose agg. giocoso, allegro.

jocosity s. giocondità.

jocund agg. giocondo, gaio.

jocundity s. allegria, giocondità.

join s. giuntura.

to join vt. 1. unire 2. raggiungere. ♦ to join vi. 1. unirsi 2. essere contiguo.

joiner s. falegname.

joinery s. falegnameria.

joining s. congiunzione.

joint agg. unito, associato || — account, conto di partecipazione; — -heir, coerede; — -stock, capitale sociale; — -tenant, comproprietario.

joint s. 1. giuntura, congiunzione 2. trancio di carne 3. articolazione.

jointer s. pialla.

jointly avv. unitamente.

joke s. scherzo, burla, facezia.

to joke vt. burlarsi di, canzonare. ♦ to joke vi. celiare.

joker s. tipo ameno, burlone.

jolly agg. gaio, vivace.

to jolt vt. far sobbalzare, scuotere. ♦ to jolt vi. traballare.

to jostle vt. spingere. ♦ to jostle vi. spingersi.

journal s. 1. giornale 2. diario.

journalism s. giornalismo.

journalist s. giornalista.

journalistic agg. giornalistico.

journey s. viaggio (general. per terra).

to journey vi. fare un viaggio.

journey-(man) s. operaio specializzato.

jovial agg. gioviale, allegro.

joviality s. giovialità.

jowl¹ s. 1. mascella 2. guancia.

jowl² s. gozzo.

joy s. gioia, contentezza.

joyful agg. giulivo, allegro.

joyfully avv. gaiamente, allegramente.

joyless agg. mesto, senza gioia.

joyous agg. gioioso, gaio.

joyously avv. gioiosamente.

jubilant agg. giubilante, trionfante.

to jubilate vi. esultare.

jubilation s. giubilo.

jubilee s. giubileo.

Judaic agg. giudaico.

Judaism s. giudaismo.

judge s. 1. giudice 2. intenditore.

to judge vt. e vi. 1. fare da giudice, giudicare 2. supporre, stimare.

judgement s. 1. giudizio 2. verdetto, sentenza 3. parere.

judicial agg. giudiziale, giudiziario.

judiciary agg. giudiziario. ♦ judiciary s. magistratura.

judicious agg. giudizioso.

jug s. 1. boccale 2. caraffa, bricco.

juggler s. 1. giocoliere 2. impostore.

jugular agg. e s. giugulare.

juice s. succo (di frutta ecc.).

juiciness s. succosità.

juicy agg. succoso.

jujube s. giuggiola.

Julian agg. giuliano.

July s. luglio.

jumble s. guazzabuglio.

jump s. salto, balzo: high — (sport), salto in alto.

to jump vt. 1. saltare, superare con un salto 2. mangiare (giuoco della dama). ♦ to jump vi. 1. saltare 2. trasalire.

jumper¹ s. saltatore.

jumper² s. maglione.

jumping agg. saltatore.

junction s. 1. congiunzione 2. nodo ferroviario.

juncture s. 1. articolazione 2. (fig.) congiuntura, momento critico.

June s. giugno.

jungle s. giungla.

junior agg. 1. minore, di secondaria importanza 2. il più giovane. ♦ junior s. 1. cadetto 2. minore.

juniper s. ginepro.

junk¹ s. 1. avanzo, rifiuto 2. gomena vecchia 3. carne salata.

junk² s. (mar.) giunca.

juridic(al) agg. giuridico.

jurisdiction s. giurisdizione.

jurisdictional agg. giurisdizionale.

jurisprudence s. giurisprudenza.

jurisprudent s. giurisprudente.

jurisprudential agg. legale.

jurist s. giurista.

jury s. giuria, giurì.

juryman s. giurato.

just agg. giusto, retto. ♦ just avv. appena, appunto, esattamente || — now, proprio ora; — so., proprio così; — then, proprio allora.

justice s. giustizia, imparzialità.
justiciable agg. processabile.
justiciary agg. giudiziario.
justifiability s. legittimità di difesa.
justifiable agg. giustificabile, legittimo || — homicide, omicidio per legittima difesa.
justification s. giustificazione.
justificative agg. giustificativo.
to **justify** vt. 1. giustificare 2. difendere 3. perdonare.
justly avv. giustamente, esattamente.
jut s. sporgenza.
to **jut** vt. e vi. sporgere.
jute s. iuta.
juvenile agg. giovanile.
juxtaposition s. accostamento.

K

kaleidoscope s. caleidoscopio.
kalends s. pl. calende.
kangaroo s. canguro.
kaolin(e) s. caolino.
karting s. andare in « go-kart ».
kathode s. catodo.
keel s. 1. chiglia 2. chiatta (da carbone).
to **keel** vt. 1. rovesciare 2. (mar.) carenare.
keen agg. 1. aguzzo, affilato 2. pungente 3. forte 4. appassionato 5. acuto.
keenly avv. 1. in modo penetrante 2. dolorosamente 3. avidamente 4. (comm.) al minimo.
keenness s. 1. sottigliezza 2. intensità 3. ardore 4. acume.
keep s. 1. sostentamento 2. torrione.
to **keep (kept, kept)** vi. 1. restare 2. conservarsi || to — on, continuare; to — off, tenersi in disparte. ♦ to **keep (kept, kept)** vt. 1. tenere 2. mantenere 3. custodire 4. rispettare || to — back, dissimulare; to — up, tener alto, sostenere.
keeper s. guardiano.
keeping s. 1. sorveglianza 2. mantenimento 3. armonia.
keepsake s. oggetto ricordo.
keg s. barilotto.
kennel s. 1. canile 2. muta di cani 3. rigagnolo.

to **kennel** vt. tenere in un canile.
♦ to **kennel** vi. rintanarsi.
kepi s. chepì.
kept V. to **keep**.
kerbstone s. cordonatura (del marciapiede).
kerchief s. fazzoletto.
kernel s. 1. gheriglio 2. seme 3. (fig.) essenza.
kettle s. bollitore, bricco.
key s. 1. chiave 2. tasto || — money, buonuscita.
to **key** vt. 1. (mecc.) inchiavettare 2. (mus.) accordare 3. chiudere a chiave || to — up (fig.), eccitare.
keyboard s. tastiera.
keyed agg. 1. munito di chiavi 2. (mus.) a tasti.
keyhole s. buco della serratura.
keyless agg. senza chiave.
keystone s. chiave di volta.
kick s. 1. calcio 2. rinculo || — off (sport), calcio d'inizio.
to **kick** vt. prendere a calci. ♦ to **kick** vi. 1. tirar calci 2. rinculare (di armi) 3. recalcitrare.
kicker s. chi scalcia.
kid[1] s. 1. capretto 2. bimbo.
kid[2] s. tinozza.
to **kidnap** vt. rapire.
kidnapper s. rapitore.
kidnapping s. ratto.
kidney s. 1. rene 2. temperamento || stones in the kidneys, calcoli renali.
kier s. caldaia.
to **kill** vt. 1. uccidere 2. respingere 3. smorzare 4. fermare.
killer s. uccisore || lady-—, dongiovanni.
killing agg. mortale. ♦ **killing** s. uccisione.
killjoy s. guastafeste.
kiln s. fornace.
kilo, kilogram(me) s. chilo(grammo).
kilometer s. chilometro.
kilt s. gonnellino degli scozzesi.
kin agg. consanguineo, affine. ♦ **kin** s. parentela.
kind[1] agg. gentile || very — of you, molto gentile da parte tua.
kind[2] s. specie, tipo.
to **kindle** vt. accendere. ♦ to **kindle** vi. accendersi.
kindliness s. gentilezza.
kindling s. 1. accensione 2. legna facilmente infiammabile.
kindly agg. gentile. ♦ **kindly** avv.

gentilmente.

kindness *s.* gentilezza.

kindred *agg.* **1.** imparentato **2.** affine. ♦ **kindred** *s.* parentela.

kinematics *s.* cinematica.

kinetic *agg.* cinetico.

kinetics *s.* cinetica.

king *s.* re ‖ *king's English*, la lingua inglese ufficiale.

kingdom *s.* regno.

kinghood *s.* regalità.

kingly *agg.* regale, regio.

kingship *s.* regalità.

kinless *agg.* senza parenti.

kinsfolk *s. pl.* parenti.

kinship *s.* parentela.

kinsman *s.* parente.

kinswoman *s.* parente (*donna*).

kiosk *s.* chiosco ‖ *newspaper —*, edicola.

kipper *s.* aringa, salmone affumicato.

to kipper *vt.* affumicare (*pesce*).

kiss *s.* bacio.

to kiss *vt.* baciare ‖ *to — the dust*, mordere la polvere.

kit *s.* **1.** cassetta **2.** equipaggiamento.

kitchen *s.* cucina ‖ *— garden*, orto.

kitchener *s.* cuciniere.

kitchenette *s.* cucinino.

kitchenware *s.* batteria da cucina.

kite *s.* **1.** nibbio **2.** aquilone **3.** aliante.

kitten *s.* gattino.

kleptomania *s.* cleptomania.

kleptomaniac *agg. e s.* cleptomane.

knack *s.* **1.** abilità **2.** dispositivo ingegnoso.

knapsack *s.* zaino (*per soldati*).

knave *s.* furfante.

knavery *s.* disonestà.

knavish *agg.* disonesto.

to knead *vt.* impastare.

kneader *s.* **1.** chi impasta **2.** impastatrice.

kneading *s.* impasto ‖ *— trough*, madia.

knee *s.* **1.** ginocchio **2.** tubo a gomito ‖ *— cap*, rotula, ginocchiera.

to kneel (knelt, knelt) *vi.* inginocchiarsi.

kneeler *s.* **1.** chi s'inginocchia **2.** inginocchiatoio.

knell *s.* rintocco funebre.

to knell *vt.* chiamare a raccolta. ♦ **to knell** *vi.* sonare a morto.

knelt *V. to kneel.*

knew *V. to know.*

knickerbockers *s. pl.* calzoni alla zuava.

knick-knack *s.* ninnolo.

knick-knackery *s.* cianfrusaglie.

knife *s.* (*pl.* knives) **1.** coltello **2.** bisturi ‖ *pen— ,* temperino; *pruning— ,* falcetto ‖ *— -grinder*, arrotino.

to knife *vt.* **1.** tagliare **2.** accoltellare.

knight *s.* cavaliere.

knighthood *s.* **1.** rango di cavaliere **2.** cavalleria.

knightliness *s.* cavalleria.

knightly *agg.* cavalleresco. ♦ **knightly** *avv.* cavallerescamente.

to knit (knit, knit) (*anche reg.*) *vt.* **1.** lavorare a maglia **2.** corrugare **3.** unire. ♦ **to knit (knit, knit)** (*anche reg.*) *vi.* unirsi, saldarsi.

knitter *s.* **1.** magliaia **2.** telaio per maglieria.

knitting *s.* lavoro a maglia.

knitwear *s.* maglieria.

knob *s.* **1.** protuberanza **2.** pomo, manopola.

knobby *agg.* nodoso.

knock *s.* **1.** colpo **2.** (*mecc.*) battito in testa.

to knock *vt.* urtare. ♦ **to knock** *vi.* **1.** bussare **2.** detonare ‖ *to — down*, abbattere; *to — out*, sopraffare.

knocker *s.* battente.

knot *s.* **1.** nodo **2.** coccarda **3.** gruppo **4.** difficoltà.

to knot *vt.* annodare. ♦ **to knot** *vi.* annodarsi.

knottiness *s.* **1.** nodosità **2.** (*fig.*) difficoltà.

knotty *agg.* **1.** nodoso **2.** (*fig.*) difficile.

to know (knew, known) *vt.* **1.** conoscere **2.** sapere **3.** riconoscere ‖ *to — of*, aver sentito parlare di; *to — about*, essere al corrente di.

knowable *agg.* **1.** comprensibile **2.** riconoscibile.

knowing *agg.* **1.** intelligente **2.** istruito.

knowledge *s.* conoscenza.

known *V. to know.*

knuckle *s.* articolazione, nocca ‖ *— duster*, pugno di ferro.

to knuckle *vi.* **1.** (*fig.*) cedere **2.** applicarsi ‖ *to — under*, sottomettersi.

knurl *s.* zigrinatura.
to knurl *vt.* zigrinare.
Korean *agg.* e *s.* coreano.

L

la *s.* (*mus.*) la.
label *s.* etichetta.
to label *vt.* 1. mettere l'etichetta a 2. classificare.
labial *agg.* e *s.* labiale.
laboratory *s.* laboratorio.
laborious *agg.* laborioso.
laboriousness *s.* laboriosità.
labour *s.* 1. lavoro, fatica 2. mano d'opera 3. doglie (*pl.*) || *hard —,* lavori forzati; *— party,* partito laborista.
to labour *vi.* 1. lavorare, faticare 2. avere le doglie. ♦ **to labour** *vt.* elaborare, sviluppare.
laboured *agg.* 1. elaborato 2. penoso.
labourer *s.* lavoratore.
labouring *agg.* laborioso.
labourism *s.* laburismo.
labourist *s.* laburista.
labyrinth *s.* labirinto.
lace *s.* 1. laccio 2. pizzo 3. passamaneria.
to lace *vt.* 1. allacciare 2. guarnire con merletti, galloni.
to lacerate *vt.* lacerare.
lachrymal *agg.* lacrimale.
lachrymator *s.* gas lacrimogeno.
lack *s.* mancanza.
to lack *vt.* mancare di. ♦ **to lack** *vi.* mancare, scarseggiare.
lacker *s.* 1. lacca 2. oggetto laccato.
to lacker *vt.* laccare.
laconic(al) *agg.* laconico.
to lacquer V. *to lacker.*
lactation *s.* 1. lattazione 2. allattamento.
lacteal, lacteous *agg.* latteo.
lactose *s.* lattosio.
lacunar *agg.* lacunoso. ♦ **lacunar** *s.* soffitto a cassettoni.
lacustrine *agg.* lacustre.
lacy *agg.* simile a pizzo.
lad *s.* ragazzo.
ladder *s.* 1. scala a pioli 2. smagliatura.
to ladder *vt.* munire di scala. ♦ **to**

ladder *vi.* smagliarsi.
to lade (laded, laden) *vt.* caricare.
laden *agg.* (*fig.*) oppresso.
lading *s.* carico: *bill of —,* polizza di carico.
ladle *s.* mestolo.
to ladle *vt.* versare con un mestolo.
lady *s.* signora || *Our Lady,* la Madonna; *— doctor,* dottoressa.
ladybird *s.* coccinella.
ladykiller *s.* (*fam.*) dongiovanni.
ladylike *agg.* signorile, raffinato.
ladyship *s.* 1. rango di nobildonna 2. Signoria.
lag *s.* ritardo, rallentamento.
to lag *vi.* ritardare, restare indietro.
laggard *agg.* e *s.* pigro.
lagoon *s.* laguna.
to laicize *vt.* laicizzare.
laid V. *to lay.*
lain V. *to lie.*
lair *s.* tana.
laity *s.* 1. i laici 2. i profani.
lake *s.* lago.
laky *agg.* lacustre.
lamb *s.* agnello.
lambent *agg.* 1. lambente 2. scintillante.
lame *agg.* 1. zoppo 2. (*fig.*) debole (*di argomenti*).
to lame *vt.* storpiare.
lamellar *agg.* lamellare.
lameness *s.* 1. zoppaggine 2. imperfezione.
lament *s.* lamento.
to lament *vt.* lamentare. ♦ **to lament** *vi.* lamentarsi.
lamentable *agg.* lamentevole.
lamentation *s.* lamento.
lamented *agg.* 1. deplorato 2. compianto.
to laminate *vt.* laminare.
lamination *s.* 1. laminazione 2. lamina.
lamp *s.* lampada || *—-black,* nerofumo; *— -shade,* paralume.
lamplight *s.* luce artificiale.
lampoon *s.* libello.
lamprey *s.* lampreda.
lance *s.* 1. lancia 2. fiocina.
to lance *vt.* (*med.*) incidere.
lancer *s.* lanciere.
lancet *s.* bisturi.
land *s.* 1. terra 2. paese, contrada 3. campagna, terreno || *—-surveying,* agrimensura; *— surveyor,* agrimensore.
to land *vi.* 1. sbarcare 2. atterrare. ♦ **to land** *vt.* 1. sbarcare 2. de-

porre 3. prendere possesso di.

landed *agg.* fondiario.

landing *s.* 1. sbarco 2. atterraggio 3. pianerottolo || — *-stage*, pontile di sbarco; — *-strip*, pista d'atterraggio.

landlady *s.* 1. padrona di casa 2. albergatrice.

landless *agg.* senza terreni.

landlord *s.* 1. padrone di casa, di terra 2. albergatore.

landmark *s.* 1. punto di riferimento 2. pietra miliare.

landowner *s.* proprietario terriero.

landscape *s.* paesaggio || — *-painter*, paesaggista.

landslide, landslip *s.* frana.

lane *s.* 1. viottolo, vicolo 2. (*mar.*) rotta 3. corsia (*di strada*).

language *s.* linguaggio.

languid *agg.* languido.

languish *s.* languore.

to **languish** *vi.* languire.

languor *s.* languore.

languorous *agg.* languido.

lank *agg.* 1. allampanato 2. liscio (*di capelli*).

lanolin(e) *s.* lanolina.

lantern *s.* lanterna.

lap[1] *s.* 1. grembo 2. valletta 3. lembo.

lap[2] *s.* 1. sovrapposizione 2. (*sport*) giro di pista.

to **lap** *vt.* 1. piegare 2. avvolgere 3. lambire 4. bere avidamente. ♦ to **lap** *vi.* ripiegarsi.

laparotomy *s.* laparatomia.

lapel *s.* risvolto (*di giacca, soprabito*).

lapidary *agg.* lapidario. ♦ **lapidary** *s.* tagliatore di pietre.

lapidation *s.* lapidazione.

Lapp *agg.* e *s.* lappone.

lappet *s.* 1. falda 2. lobo dell'orecchio.

lapse *s.* 1. errore 2. intervallo.

to **lapse** *vi.* 1. errare 2. scivolare.

larboard *s.* fiancata sinistra (*di nave*).

larceny *s.* furto.

larch *s.* larice.

lard *s.* lardo.

to **lard** *vt.* 1. ungere con lardo 2. lardellare.

larder *s.* dispensa.

large *agg.* 1. largo 2. grande, ampio 3. generoso || *at* —, in genere; *to be at* —, essere in libertà.

largeness *s.* 1. ampiezza, grandezza 2. generosità.

lark *s.* allodola.

laryngitis *s.* laringite.

larynx *s.* laringe.

lascivious *agg.* lascivo.

lasciviousness *s.* lascivia.

lash *s.* 1. frusta 2. frustata 3. (*eye*)—, ciglio.

to **lash** *vt.* frustare || *to* — *at*, sferzare.

lashing *s.* 1. frustata 2. legatura.

lass, lassie *s.* ragazzina.

last *agg.* (*superl. di* late) 1. ultimo 2. scorso 3. massimo || *the* — *but one*, il penultimo. ♦ **last** *s.* 1. fine 2. ultimo. ♦ **last** *avv.* 1. ultimo 2. l'ultima volta || *at* —, alla fine.

to **last** *vi.* durare.

lasting *agg.* durevole. ♦ **lasting** *s.* durata.

latch *s.* chiavistello.

late (later, latter; latest, last) *agg.* 1. tardi 2. in ritardo 3. tardo 4. precedente 5. defunto. ♦ **late** *avv.* 1. tardi 2. in ritardo.

lately *avv.* recentemente.

latent *agg.* latente.

later *agg.* (*comp. di* late) posteriore. ♦ **later** *avv.* più tardi.

lateral *agg.* laterale.

latest *agg.* (*superl. di* late) ultimo, recentissimo || *at the* —, al più tardi.

latex *s.* lattice.

lathe *s.* tornio.

lather *s.* schiuma.

to **lather** *vt.* insaponare. ♦ to **lather** *vi.* schiumare.

Latin *agg.* e *s.* latino.

Latinism *s.* latinismo.

Latinist *s.* latinista.

Latinity *s.* latinità.

latitude *s.* 1. latitudine 2. ampiezza.

latter *agg.* (*comp. di* late) 1. posteriore 2. ultimo 3. secondo.

latterly *avv.* recentemente.

lattice *s.* grata, traliccio.

latticed *agg.* munito di grata.

laudable *agg.* lodevole.

laudanum *s.* laudano.

laudatory *agg.* laudatorio.

laugh *s.* risata.

to **laugh** *vi.* ridere || *to* — *at*, deridere.

laughable *agg.* comico.

laughing *s.* risata || — *-stock*, zimbello.

laughter *s.* riso || *to burst into* —, scoppiare a ridere.

launch[1] s. varo.

launch[2] s. (mar.) lancia.

to launch vt. 1. lanciare 2. varare.

to launder vt. e vi. 1. fare il bucato 2. lavare e stirare.

launderette s. lavanderia con macchine automatiche.

laundress s. lavandaia.

laundry s. 1. lavanderia 2. bucato.

laureate agg. coronato d'alloro.

laurel s. lauro, alloro.

to laurel vt. coronare d'alloro.

lavatory s. gabinetto.

lavender s. lavanda.

lavish agg. prodigo.

to lavish vt. prodigare.

lavishness s. prodigalità.

law s. 1. legge 2. professione legale 3. processo, causa || — -court, tribunale; to go to —, ricorrere in giudizio.

lawful agg. 1. legale 2. legittimo.

lawfulness s. 1. legalità 2. legittimità.

lawgiver s. legislatore.

lawless agg. 1. illegale 2. sregolato.

lawn s. 1. prato (rasato).

lawsuit s. (giur.) processo.

lawyer s. avvocato.

lax agg. allentato.

laxative agg. e s. lassativo.

laxity s. 1. negligenza 2. rilassatezza.

lay V. to lie.

lay agg. 1. laico 2. profano || — -brother, converso; — -sister, conversa. ♦ **lay** s. configurazione.

to lay (laid, laid) vt. 1. porre 2. deporre 3. preparare 4. calmare || to — aside, mettere da parte; to — out, stendere, spendere.

lay-by s. piazzola di sosta.

layer s. 1. strato 2. gallina che fa uova 3. (mil.) puntatore.

laying s. 1. posa 2. covata.

layoff s. stagione morta (di lavoro).

layout s. 1. esposizione 2. schema.

lazaret s. lazzaretto.

laziness s. pigrizia.

lazy agg. pigro.

lead[1] s. 1. piombo 2. grafite || red-, minio; white- —, biacca.

lead[2] s. 1. comando 2. guinzaglio 3. mano (di carte).

to lead[1] vt. impiombare.

to lead[2] (led, led) vt. 1. condurre, capeggiare 2. indurre.

leaden agg. di piombo, plumbeo.

leader s. 1. capo 2. articolo di fondo.

leadership s. direzione.

leading[1] agg. 1. dominante 2. primo. ♦ **leading** s. guida.

leading[2] s. impiombatura.

leaf s. (pl. leaves) 1. foglia 2. foglio.

to leaf vt. sfogliare. ♦ **to leaf** vi. mettere le foglie.

leafless agg. senza foglie.

leaflet s. 1. fogliolina 2. volantino.

league s. lega.

to league vi. allearsi.

leak s. 1. fessura 2. (mar.) falla 3. perdita.

to leak vi. perdere || to — out, trapelare.

leakage s. 1. colatura 2. dispersione.

leaky agg. che cola, perde.

lean[1] agg. magro, esile.

lean[2] s. inclinazione.

to lean (leant, leant) (anche reg.) vt. e vi. 1. pendere 2. appoggiarsi 3. sporgersi 4. inclinare.

leaning s. 1. inclinazione 2. l'appoggiarsi.

leanness s. magrezza.

leant V. to lean.

leap s. 1. salto || — -year, anno bisestile.

to leap (leapt, leapt) (anche reg.) vt. e vi. saltare.

to learn (learnt, learnt) (anche reg.) vt. e vi. imparare, apprendere.

learned agg. colto.

learner s. allievo.

learning s. cultura.

learnt V. to learn.

lease s. 1. contratto d'affitto 2. durata (di contratto) || on —, in affitto.

to lease vt. affittare.

leash s. guinzaglio.

to leash vt. tenere al guinzaglio.

least agg. (superl. di little) il minimo. ♦ **least** s. (il) meno. ♦ **least** avv. (il) meno.

leather s. 1. cuoio 2. oggetto in cuoio || patent —, vernice.

leathern agg. di cuoio.

leave s. 1. permesso 2. congedo. ♦ **to leave** (left, left) vt. lasciare. ♦ **to leave** (left, left) vi. partire || to — off, smettere.

leaven s. 1. lievito 2. (fig.) fermento.

to leaven vt. far lievitare.

leaves V. *leaf.*
leaving s. partenza.
lecherous *agg.* lascivo.
lechery s. lascivia.
lecture s. 1. conferenza 2. lezione 3. improvero.
to lecture *vt.* rimproverare. ♦ **to lecture** *vi.* fare una conferenza.
lecturer s. 1. conferenziere 2. lettore universitario.
led V. *to lead.*
ledger s. (*comm.*) libro mastro.
lee s. feccia.
leech s. sanguisuga (*anche fig.*).
to leer *vt.* e *vi.* guardare di sbieco.
leeward *agg.* e *avv.* sottovento.
leeway s. deriva.
left *agg.* sinistro. ♦ **left** s. sinistra || *—handed,* mancino.
left V. *to leave.*
leftist s. (*pol.*) uomo di sinistra.
leg s. 1. gamba 2. (*cuc.*) cosciotto || *to pull so.'s —,* canzonare qu.
legacy s. legato.
legal *agg.* legale.
legality s. legalità.
legalization s. legalizzazione.
to legalize *vt.* legalizzare.
legatee s. legatario.
legation s. legazione.
legend s. leggenda.
legendary *agg.* leggendario.
leggins s. pl. gambali.
legible *agg.* leggibile.
legion s. legione.
legionary *agg.* e s. legionario.
to legislate *vi.* fare leggi. ♦ **to legislate** *vt.* trasformare per mezzo di leggi.
legislation s. legislazione.
legislative *agg.* legislativo.
legislator s. legislatore.
legislature s. 1. legislatura 2. corpo legislativo.
legitimacy s. legittimità.
legitimate *agg.* legittimo.
to legitimate *vt.* legittimare.
legitimation s. legittimazione.
legume s. legume.
leguminous *agg.* leguminoso.
leisure s. 1. agio 2. tempo libero.
leisurely *agg.* e *avv.* con comodo.
lemon s. limone.
lemonade s. limonata.
to lend (**lent, lent**) *vt.* prestare.
lender s. prestatore.
length s. 1. lunghezza 2. durata, spazio di tempo || *at —,* alla fine.
to lengthen *vt.* allungare. ♦ **to**

lengthen *vi.* allungarsi.
lengthy *agg.* lungo, prolisso.
lenient *agg.* 1. emolliente 2. mite.
lenitive *agg.* e s. calmante.
lens s. 1. (*ott.*) lente 2. (*foto*) obiettivo.
lent V. *to lend.*
Lent s. quaresima.
lentil s. lenticchia.
leonine *agg.* leonino.
leopard s. 1. leopardo 2. gattopardo.
leper s. lebbroso || *— hospital,* lebbrosario.
leporine *agg.* leporino.
leprosy s. lebbra.
leprous *agg.* lebbroso.
lesbian *agg.* e s. lesbica.
lesion s. lesione.
less *agg.* (*comp. di little*) minore, meno. ♦ **less** s. meno. ♦ **less** *avv.* meno. ♦ **less** *prep.* meno.
lessee s. affittuario.
to lessen *vt.* e *vi.* diminuire.
lesser *agg.* minore.
lesson s. lezione.
lest *cong.* per paura che.
to let (**let, let**) *vt.* 1. lasciare, permettere 2. affittare || *to — in,* far entrare; *to — off,* lasciar andare; *to — out,* lasciar uscire.
lethal *agg.* letale.
lethargy s. letargo.
letter s. lettera.
lettered *agg.* 1. letterato 2. intestato.
lettuce s. lattuga.
leucocyte s. leucocito.
leucocythaemia, leukemia s. leucemia.
levant s. levante.
level *agg.* 1. livellato 2. a livello 3. regolato. ♦ **level** s. 1. livello 2. superficie piana 3. livella || *on a — with,* sullo stesso piano di.
to level *vt.* 1. livellare 2. puntare (*un'arma*).
levelling s. 1. livellamento 2. puntamento (*di arma*).
lever s. 1. manubrio 2. leva.
to lever *vi.* far leva.
to levigate *vt.* 1. levigare 2. polverizzare.
levigation s. 1. levigazione 2. polverizzazione.
levity s. leggerezza.
levy s. 1. leva 2. imposta.
to levy *vt.* 1. arruolare 2. imporre (*di tasse*).

lewd *agg.* impudico.

lewdness *s.* impudicizia.

lexical *agg.* lessicale.

lexicographer *s.* lessicografo.

lexicography *s.* lessicografia.

lexicology *s.* lessicologia.

lexicon *s.* lessico.

liability *s.* **1.** obbligo **2.** tendenza **3.** (*giur.*) responsabilità. ♦ **liabilities** *s. pl.* passività (*sing.*).

liable *agg.* **1.** soggetto a **2.** (*giur.*) responsabile.

liar *s.* bugiardo.

libation *s.* libagione.

libel *s.* **1.** libello **2.** (*giur.*) diffamazione.

to libel *vt.* **1.** scrivere un libello contro **2.** (*giur.*) sporgere querela.

liberal *agg.* **1.** liberale **2.** umanistico. ♦ **liberal** *s.* liberale.

liberalism *s.* liberalismo.

liberalist *s.* liberalista.

liberality *s.* liberalità.

to liberalize *vt.* rendere liberale.

to liberate *vt.* liberare.

liberation *s.* liberazione.

liberator *s.* liberatore.

liberticide *s.* **1.** liberticida **2.** liberticidio.

libertinage *s.* libertinaggio.

libertine *agg. e s.* libertino.

libertinism *s.* libertinaggio.

liberty *s.* libertà.

libidinous *agg.* libidinoso.

libido *s.* libidine.

librarian *s.* bibliotecario.

library *s.* biblioteca || *film —,* cineteca; *record —,* discoteca.

lice V. *louse.*

licence *s.* licenza || *driving —,* patente automobilistica.

to license *vt.* dare una licenza a.

licensed *agg.* autorizzato.

licentious *agg.* licenzioso.

licentiousness *s.* dissolutezza.

lichen *s.* lichene.

lick *s.* leccata.

to lick *vt.* **1.** leccare **2.** lambire.

lid *s.* coperchio.

lie[1] *s.* menzogna || *the —,* smentita.

lie[2] *s.* posizione.

to lie[1] *vi.* mentire.

to lie[2] (lay, lain) *vi.* giacere, trovarsi || *to — down,* coricarsi; *to — in,* partorire.

lieutenant *s.* tenente.

life *s.* (*pl.* lives) vita || *— belt,* cintura di salvataggio; *— preserver,* salvagente.

lifeboat *s.* lancia di salvataggio.

lifeless *agg.* senza vita.

lifelike *agg.* vivido.

lift *s.* **1.** ascensore **2.** passaggio (*su un veicolo*) **3.** sollevamento.

to lift *vt.* **1.** alzare **2.** rubare. ♦ **to lift** *vi.* alzarsi.

light[1] *agg.* **1.** chiaro **2.** biondo **3.** leggero **4.** agile **5.** insignificante.

light[2] *s.* **1.** luce **2.** fuoco **3.** lampada || *traffic lights,* semaforo.

to light (lit, lit) (*anche reg.*) *vt.* **1.** accendere **2.** illuminare. ♦ **to light (lit, lit)** (*anche reg.*) *vi.* **1.** accendersi **2.** illuminarsi **3.** posarsi.

to lighten *vt.* **1.** alleggerire, alleviare **2.** illuminare. ♦ **to lighten** *vi.* **1.** alleggerirsi **2.** illuminarsi **3.** (*imp.*) lampeggiare.

lighter *s.* **1.** accenditore **2.** (*mar.*) chiatta.

lighthouse *s.* faro.

lighting *s.* **1.** accensione **2.** luce (*di quadro*).

lightless *agg.* oscuro.

lightness *s.* **1.** leggerezza **2.** gaiezza **3.** illuminazione.

lightning *s.* fulmine || *— rod,* parafulmine.

Ligurian *agg. e s.* ligure.

like *agg.* **1.** simile **2.** caratteristico di. ♦ **like** *prep.* come || *— this, — that,* così; *to feel —,* aver voglia di; *to look —,* avere l'aria di.

like *s.* simile. ♦ **likes** *s. pl.* gusti.

to like *vt.* piacere. ♦ **to like** *vi.* volere.

likelihood *s.* probabilità.

likely *agg.* **1.** probabile **2.** adatto. ♦ **likely** *avv.* probabilmente.

likeness *s.* **1.** somiglianza **2.** immagine.

likewise *avv.* **1.** allo stesso modo **2.** anche.

liking *s.* **1.** gusto **2.** preferenza.

lilac *agg. e s.* lilla.

lily *agg.* bianco. ♦ **lily** *s.* giglio || *water —,* ninfea.

limb *s.* **1.** membro **2.** ramo.

lime[1] *s.* **1.** calce **2.** pania.

lime[2] *s.* cedro.

lime[3] *s.* tiglio.

to lime *vt.* **1.** cementare **2.** invischiare.

limelight *s.* luce della ribalta.

limestone *s.* calcare.

limit *s.* limite.

to limit *vt.* limitare.

limitary agg. **1.** limitato **2.** limitativo **3.** situato alla frontiera.

limitation s. limitazione.

limitative agg. limitativo.

limited agg. limitato || — company, società a responsabilità limitata; — monarchy, monarchia costituzionale.

limp agg. molle.

to **limp** vi. zoppicare.

limpid agg. limpido.

limpidity s. limpidezza.

limping s. zoppicamento.

line s. **1.** linea, riga **2.** ruga **3.** discendenza **4.** attività **5.** verso **6.** (comm.) articolo.

to **line** vt. **1.** rigare **2.** fiancheggiare **3.** foderare || to — up, allineare, allinearsi.

lineage s. lignaggio.

lineal agg. in linea diretta.

lineament s. lineamento.

linear agg. lineare.

linen agg. di lino. ♦ **linen** s. **1.** tela di lino **2.** biancheria.

liner s. **1.** transatlantico **2.** aereo di linea.

to **linger** vt. e vi. indugiare.

linguist s. linguista.

linguistic(al) agg. linguistico.

linguistics s. linguistica.

liniment s. linimento.

lining s. **1.** rigatura **2.** allineamento **3.** fodera **4.** rivestimento.

link s. **1.** anello **2.** (fig.) legame || cuff-links, gemelli da polso.

to **link** vt. collegare. ♦ to **link** vi. collegarsi.

linotyping s. linotipia.

linotypist s. linotipista.

lint s. garza.

lintel s. architrave.

lion s. leone.

lioness s. leonessa.

lip s. **1.** labbro **2.** margine || --stick, rossetto per labbra.

to **lip** vt. **1.** toccare (con le labbra) **2.** sussurrare.

liquefaction s. liquefazione.

to **liquefy** vt. liquefare. ♦ to **liquefy** vi. liquefarsi.

liqueur s. rosolio.

liquid agg. **1.** liquido **2.** chiaro **3.** armonioso **4.** instabile. ♦ **liquid** s. liquido.

to **liquidate** vt. liquidare.

liquidation s. liquidazione.

liquidator s. liquidatore.

liquor s. **1.** liquido **2.** bevanda alcolica.

liquorice s. liquirizia.

to **lisp** vi. parlare bleso.

lisping agg. bleso. ♦ **lisping** s. pronuncia blesa.

list¹ s. **1.** lista **2.** striscia **3.** cimosa. ♦ **lists** s. pl. lizza (sing.).

list² s. (mar.) sbandamento.

to **list¹** vt. elencare, catalogare.

to **list²** vi. (mar.) sbandare.

to **listen** vi. ascoltare: to — to so., ascoltare qu.; to — in, ascoltare la radio.

listener s. ascoltatore.

listening s. ascolto.

listless agg. disattento.

lit V. to light.

litany s. litania.

literal agg. **1.** letterale **2.** prosaico **3.** di lettera alfabetica.

literalism s. interpretazione letterale.

literary agg. letterario.

literate agg. e s. letterato.

literature s. letteratura.

lithe agg. agile.

lithograph s. litografia.

to **lithograph** vt. litografare.

lithographic(al) agg. litografico.

lithography s. (arte della) litografia.

litigant s. (giur.) contendente.

litmus s. tornasole.

litre s. litro.

litter s. **1.** lettiga, barella **2.** strame **3.** rifiuti **4.** figliata.

little (less, least) agg. **1.** piccolo **2.** breve **3.** poco || a —, un po' di. ♦ **little** s. poco. ♦ **little** avv. poco || a —, piuttosto.

liturgic(al) agg. liturgico.

liturgy s. liturgia.

live agg. **1.** vivo **2.** ardente **3.** carico (di armi).

to **live** vi. e vt. vivere, abitare.

livelihood s. mezzi di sussistenza.

liveliness s. vivacità.

lively agg. vivace.

liver s. fegato.

livery¹ agg. bilioso.

livery² s. **1.** livrea **2.** (giur.) passaggio di proprietà.

lives V. life.

livestock s. bestiame.

livid agg. livido.

living agg. **1.** vivo **2.** perfetto (di somiglianza). ♦ **living** s. **1.** mezzo di mantenimento **2.** vita || --room, soggiorno.

lizard s. lucertola.
llama s. (zool.) lama.
load s. 1. carico, peso 2. (elettr.) carica, tensione.
to load vt. 1. caricare 2. adulterare.
loader s. caricatore.
loading s. caricamento.
loadstar s. stella polare.
loaf s. (pl. loaves) pagnotta || sugar- —, pan di zucchero.
to loaf vi. oziare.
loafer s. fannullone.
loan s. prestito: on —, a prestito.
to loan vt. prestare.
loath agg. riluttante.
to loathe vt. detestare.
loathing s. disgusto.
loathsome agg. 1. odioso 2. disgustoso.
loaves V. loaf.
lobby s. anticamera.
lobe s. lobo.
lobster s. aragosta.
local agg. e s. locale.
locality s. località.
to localize vt. localizzare.
to locate vt. 1. situare 2. individuare 3. indicare.
location s. 1. posizione 2. locazione.
lock[1] s. 1. ricciolo 2. fiocco.
lock[2] s. 1. serratura 2. diga 3. otturatore (di arma).
to lock vt. serrare. ◆ **to lock** vi. (mecc.) inceparsi.
locker s. armadio, bauletto a chiave.
locket s. medaglione.
lockout s. (econ.) serrata.
locomotion s. locomozione.
locomotive agg. locomotorio. ◆ **locomotive** s. locomotiva.
locust s. locusta || — -tree, carrubo, robinia.
locution s. locuzione.
lodge s. 1. loggia 2. padiglione.
to lodge vt. 1. alloggiare 2. collocare. ◆ **to lodge** vi. 1. alloggiare 2. entrare.
lodging s. alloggio, dimora.
loftiness s. 1. altezza 2. nobiltà.
lofty agg. 1. alto, elevato 2. orgoglioso, altero.
log s. ceppo || — -book, giornale di bordo.
logarithm s. logaritmo.
logic s. logica.
logical agg. logico.
logistic(al) agg. logistico.

logistics s. pl. (mil.) logistica (sing.).
logomachy s. logomachia.
loin s. lombo. ◆ **loins** s. pl. reni.
to loiter vt. sprecare (tempo ecc.). ◆ **to loiter** vi. bighellonare, oziare.
loitering s. il bighellonare, l'andare a zonzo.
Lombard agg. e s. lombardo.
Londoner s. londinese.
Londonese agg. londinese.
loneliness s. solitudine.
lonely, lonesome agg. solo, solitario.
long agg. lungo || — -distance call, telefonata interurbana. ◆ **long** s. molto tempo. ◆ **long** avv. a lungo || how —?, quanto tempo?; all day —, tutto il giorno; as — as, fino a, purché; so —!, arrivederci!; before —, tra poco.
to long vi. desiderare ardentemente: to — for sthg., desiderare ardentemente qc.
longanimity s. longanimità.
longboat s. lancia.
longevity s. longevità.
longevous agg. longevo.
longing agg. bramoso. ◆ **longing** s. brama.
longitude s. longitudine.
longitudinal agg. longitudinale.
long-sighted agg. 1. presbite 2. preveggente.
look s. sguardo. ◆ **looks** s. pl. aspetto (sing.).
to look vi. 1. sembrare 2. guardare || to — after, badare a; to — at, guardare; to — for, cercare; to — forward to, non veder l'ora di; to — like, somigliare; to — up, consultare (orario, dizionario ecc.); to — through, esaminare attentamente; to — up to, rispettare; to — down on, disprezzare.
looker-on s. spettatore.
looking-glass s. specchio.
lookout s. 1. guardia 2. vista panoramica 3. prospettiva.
loom s. telaio.
to loom vt. tessere. ◆ **to loom** vi. apparire indistintamente.
loop s. 1. cappio 2. gancio.
loophole s. feritoia.
loose agg. 1. sciolto 2. ampio 3. vago 4. licenzioso 5. allentato.
to loose vt. 1. sciogliere 2. liberare 3. lanciare.

to **loosen** *vt.* **1.** sciogliere **2.** allentare.

looseness *s.* **1.** scioltezza **2.** ampiezza **3.** libertinaggio **4.** imprecisione.

to **lop** *vt.* potare, mozzare.

loquacious *agg.* loquace.

loquacity *s.* loquacità.

lord *s.* **1.** signore **2.** Pari || — *Mayor*, sindaco.

to **lord** *vt.* dominare.

lordly *agg.* **1.** fastoso, imponente **2.** altero.

lordship *s.* signoria, autorità.

lorry *s.* autocarro.

to **lose** (**lost, lost**) *vt.* e *vi.* perdere.

loser *s.* perdente.

losing, loss *s.* perdita.

lost V. *to lose.*

lot *s.* **1.** sorte **2.** parte **3.** lotto (*di terreno ecc.*) || *a — of*, una quantità di.

to **lot** *vt.* lottizzare.

lotion *s.* lozione.

lottery *s.* lotteria.

loud *agg.* forte, fragoroso, rumoroso || —*speaker*, altoparlante. ♦ **loud(ly)** *avv.* ad alta voce.

lounge *s.* **1.** atrio (*di albergo, teat. ecc.*) **2.** lo stare in ozio.

to **lounge** *vi.* bighellonare.

lounger *s.* fannullone.

louse *s.* (*pl.* **lice**) pidocchio.

lousy *agg.* pidocchioso.

lovable *agg.* amabile.

love *s.* amore.

to **love** *vt.* amare.

loveless *agg.* senza amore.

loveliness *s.* bellezza.

lovely *agg.* bello.

lover *s.* amante, innamorato.

loving *agg.* amoroso.

lovingness *s.* affettuosità.

low[1] *agg.* **1.** basso **2.** debole || —*spirited*, depresso. ♦ **low** *avv.* **1.** in basso **2.** a voce bassa **3.** a basso prezzo.

low[2] *s.* muggito.

to **low** *vi.* muggire.

to **lower** *vt.* **1.** abbassare **2.** abbattere. ♦ **to lower** *vi.* abbattersi.

lowering *s.* abbassamento.

lowland *s.* pianura.

lowly *agg.* **1.** basso **2.** umile. ♦ **lowly** *avv.* umilmente.

loyal *agg.* leale.

loyalty *s.* lealtà.

lozenge *s.* **1.** (*geom.*) rombo **2.** pastiglia.

lubber *s.* zoticone.

lubricant *agg.* e *s.* lubrificante.

to **lubricate** *vt.* lubrificare.

lubricating, lubrication *s.* lubrificazione.

lubricator *s.* lubrificatore.

lubricity *s.* **1.** viscosità **2.** (*fig.*) lascivia.

lubricous *agg.* lubrico.

lucent *agg.* lucente.

lucid *agg.* lucido, chiaro.

lucidity *s.* lucidità, chiarezza.

luck *s.* **1.** sorte **2.** fortuna || *to be in* —, *out of* —, essere fortunato, sfortunato.

luckily *avv.* fortunatamente.

luckless *agg.* sfortunato.

lucky *agg.* fortunato.

lucrative *agg.* lucrativo.

to **lucubrate** *vi.* fare delle elucubrazioni.

lucubration *s.* elucubrazione.

ludicrous *agg.* ridicolo.

ludicrousness *s.* comicità.

luggage *s.* bagaglio.

lugubrious *agg.* lugubre.

lukewarm *agg.* tiepido, apatico.

to **lull** *vt.* **1.** cullare **2.** calmare.

lullaby *s.* ninna-nanna.

lumbago *s.* lombaggine.

lumbar *agg.* lombare.

lumber *s.* **1.** cianfrusaglie (*pl.*) **2.** legname || —*room*, ripostiglio.

to **lumber** *vt.* **1.** ammucchiare **2.** ingombrare. ♦ **to lumber** *vi.* **1.** tagliare legname **2.** muoversi pesantemente e rumorosamente.

lumbering *s.* commercio di legname.

luminary *s.* **1.** corpo luminoso **2.** luminare.

luminous *agg.* luminoso.

luminousness *s.* luminosità.

lump *s.* **1.** mucchio **2.** gonfiore **3.** zolletta **4.** (*comm.*) blocco **5.** persona goffa.

to **lump** *vt.* ammassare. ♦ **to lump** *vi.* raggrumarsi.

lumpy *agg.* **1.** granuloso **2.** increspato (*di mare*) **3.** pesante.

lunacy *s.* pazzia.

lunar *agg.* lunare.

lunatic *agg.* e *s.* pazzo.

lunation *s.* lunazione.

lunch *s.* seconda colazione, pasto del mezzogiorno.

to **lunch** *vi.* fare la seconda colazione. ♦ **to lunch** *vt.* offrire la colazione a.

luncheon s. spuntino.

lunette s. (arch.) lunetta.

lung s. polmone: iron —, polmone d'acciaio.

lupine s. lupino.

lure s. esca.

to lure vt. adescare.

lurid agg. 1. spettrale 2. orribile.

lurk s. nascondiglio.

to lurk vi. nascondersi.

luscious agg. 1. dolce 2. sensuale.

lust s. 1. lussuria 2. brama.

to lust vi. bramare: to — for so., sthg., bramare qu., qc.

lustful agg. 1. sensuale 2. bramoso.

lustfulness s. 1. sensualità 2. brama.

lustral agg. lustrale.

lustre[1] s. lustro, splendore.

lustre[2] s. lustro, quinquennio.

lusty agg. vigoroso, gagliardo.

lute s. liuto.

Lutheran agg. e s. luterano.

Lutheranism s. luteranesimo.

to luxate vt. (med.) lussare.

luxation s. lussazione.

luxuriant agg. lussureggiante.

to luxuriate vi. lussureggiare || to — in, deliziarsi di.

luxurious agg. lussuoso, sontuoso.

luxury s. 1. lusso 2. oggetto di lusso.

lye s. lisciva.

lying[1] agg. bugiardo.

lying[2] agg. giacente, situato.

lymph s. linfa.

lymphatic agg. linfatico. ◆ **lymphatic** s. vaso linfatico.

to lynch vt. linciare.

lynch law s. linciaggio.

lynx s. lince.

lyre s. lira.

lyric(al) agg. lirico. ◆ **lyric** s. lirica.

lyricism, lyrism s. lirismo.

lyrist s. poeta lirico.

M

macabre agg. macabro.

macaroni s. maccheroni.

macaroon s. amaretto.

mace s. mazza || - -bearer, mazziere.

to macerate vt. macerare. ◆ **to**

macerate vi. macerarsi.

maceration s. macerazione.

Machiavellian agg. machiavellico.

Machiavellism s. machiavellismo.

to machinate vt. macchinare.

machination s. macchinazione.

machine s. macchina || sewing- —, macchina da cucire.

to machine vt. e vi. lavorare a macchina.

machine-gun s. mitragliatrice.

to machine-gun vt. mitragliare.

machine-gunner s. mitragliere.

machinery s. 1. macchinario 2. meccanismo.

machining s. lavorazione (a macchina).

machinist s. macchinista.

mackerel s. sgombro || - -sky, cielo a pecorelle.

mackintosh s. impermeabile.

macrocephalic agg. macrocefalo.

macrocosm s. macrocosmo.

macrocosmic agg. macrocosmico.

macromolecule s. macromolecola.

macroscopic agg. macroscopico.

to maculate vt. maculare.

maculation s. maculamento.

mad agg. 1. pazzo 2. idrofobo || to go —, impazzire.

madam s. signora.

madcap s. scervellato.

to madden vt. far impazzire. ◆ **to madden** vi. diventare matto.

madding agg. folle.

made V. to make.

madhouse s. manicomio.

madly avv. pazzamente.

madman s. pazzo.

madness s. 1. pazzia 2. idrofobia.

madrepore s. madrepora.

madrigal s. madrigale.

Maecenas s. mecenate.

magazine s. 1. magazzino 2. rivista 3. arsenale.

maggot s. 1. bruco 2. (fig.) capriccio.

maggoty agg. 1. bacato 2. (fig.) capriccioso.

magic s. magia.

magic(al) agg. magico.

magician s. mago.

magisterial agg. 1. di magistrato 2. autoritario.

magistracy s. magistratura.

magistrate s. magistrato.

magistrature s. magistratura.

magnanimity s. magnanimità.

magnanimous agg. magnanimo.

magnesium s. magnesio.

magnet s. magnete, calamita.

magnetic(al) agg. magnetico.

magnetism s. magnetismo.

magnetization s. 1. magnetizzazione 2. forza d'attrazione.

to **magnetize** vt. magnetizzare.

magnetizer s. magnetizzatore.

magneto s. magnete.

magnetometer s. magnetometro.

magnification s. 1. esaltazione 2. ingrandimento.

magnificence s. magnificenza.

magnificent agg. magnifico.

magnifier s. 1. esaltatore 2. lente d'ingrandimento.

to **magnify** vt. 1. esaltare 2. ingrandire.

magniloquence s. magniloquenza.

magniloquent agg. magniloquente.

magnitude s. grandezza.

magpie s. gazza.

Magyar agg. e s. magiaro.

mahogany s. mogano.

maid s. 1. fanciulla 2. cameriera || old —, zitella.

maiden[1] agg. 1. vergine, puro 2. esordiente.

maiden[2] s. fanciulla || — name, nome da ragazza.

maidenhead, maidenhood s. verginità.

maidenliness s. modestia, verecondia.

maidenly agg. verginale.

maidservant s. cameriera.

maieutics s. maieutica.

maigre agg. magro.

mail s. posta || — -train, treno postale.

to **mail** vt. mandare per posta.

to **maim** vt. storpiare.

main[1] agg. 1. principale 2. vigoroso || — road, strada maestra.

main[2] s. 1. alto mare 2. l'essenziale 3. condotto principale.

mainland s. terraferma.

mainly avv. principalmente.

mainmast s. (mar.) albero maestro.

mainsail s. vela maestra.

mainspring s. molla principale.

to **maintain** vt. 1. mantenere 2. asserire.

maintenance s. 1. mantenimento 2. manutenzione 3. difesa.

maize s. granoturco.

majestic(al) agg. maestoso.

majesty s. maestà.

major agg. maggiore, principale. ◆

major s. 1. maggiorenne 2. (mil.) maggiore.

majority s. 1. maggioranza 2. maggiore età.

make s. 1. fattura 2. costituzione 3. marca.

to **make (made, made)** vt. e vi. 1. fare 2. rendere 3. fabbricare || to — for, dirigersi; to — up, preparare, truccare; to — up for, compensare per || to — oneself understood, farsi capire; to — to confess, obbligare qu. a confessare; to — so. do what one likes, far fare a qu. ciò che si vuole.

make-believe s. finzione.

maker s. 1. creatore 2. costruttore || — -up, truccatore.

makeshift s. espediente.

make-up s. 1. composizione 2. trucco 3. (tip.) impaginazione.

making s. 1. fattura 2. formazione. ◆ **makings** s. pl. il necessario (sing.).

maladjusted agg. 1. disadatto 2. disadattato.

maladjustment s. inadattabilità.

maladministration s. cattiva amministrazione.

maladroit agg. maldestro.

malady s. malattia.

malaise s. malessere.

Malayan agg. e s. malese.

malcontent agg. e s. malcontento.

male agg. maschio, maschile. ◆ **male** s. maschio.

malediction s. maledizione.

malefactor s. malfattore.

malefic agg. malefico.

maleficence s. malvagità.

maleficent agg. malefico.

malevolence s. malevolenza.

malevolent agg. malevolo.

malformation s. malformazione.

malformed agg. malformato.

malice s. 1. malignità 2. astio: to bear — to so., nutrire rancore verso qu.

malicious agg. 1. maligno 2. premeditato.

malign agg. maligno.

malignancy s. malignità.

malignant agg. maligno.

malignity s. V. malignancy.

malleability s. malleabilità.

malleable agg. malleabile.

mallet s. mazzuolo.

mallow s. malva.

malnutrition s. malnutrizione.

malpractice s. pratica illecita.

malt s. malto.

Malthusian agg. e s. maltusiano.

Malthusianism s. maltusianesimo.

maltose s. maltosio.

to **maltreat** vt. maltrattare.

maltreatment s. maltrattamento.

malversation s. malversazione.

mama s. mamma.

mamma[1] s. mamma.

mamma[2] s. mammella.

mammal s. mammifero.

mammalian agg. e s. màmmifero.

mammiferous agg. mammifero.

mammoth agg. enorme. ♦ **mammoth** s. mammut.

mammy s. mammina.

man s. (pl. men) 1. uomo 2. marito || — -bour, ora lavorativa; — of-war, nave da guerra.

to **man** vt. munire, equipaggiare (di uomini).

manacle s. manetta.

to **manacle** vt. ammanettare.

to **manage** vt. 1. dirigere 2. maneggiare 3. riuscire. ♦ to **manage** vi. destreggiarsi, cavarsela.

manageable agg. 1. maneggevole 2. fattibile.

management s. 1. direzione, amministrazione 2. abilità.

manager s. 1. direttore 2. amministratore 3. impresario 4. organizzatore.

manageress s. 1. direttrice 2. amministratrice.

managerial agg. direttivo.

managership s. 1. direzione 2. amministrazione.

managing agg. dirigente || — director, consigliere delegato.

mandarin s. mandarino.

mandatary s. mandatario.

mandate s. mandato.

mandator s. mandante.

mandatory agg. e s. mandatario.

mandible s. mandibola.

mandolin s. mandolino.

mandrake s. mandragora.

mandrel s. anima metallica.

mandrill s. mandrillo.

mane s. criniera.

manful agg. valoroso.

manganate s. manganato.

mange s. rogna.

manger s. mangiatoia.

to **mangle** vt. 1. lacerare 2. storpiare.

mangy agg. 1. lacero 2. rognoso 3. spregevole.

to **manhandle** vt. manovrare (a mano).

manhole s. botola.

manhood s. 1. virilità 2. vigore 3. genere umano.

maniac agg. e s. maniaco, pazzo.

Manich(a)eism s. manicheismo.

manicurist s. manicure.

manifest agg. manifesto.

to **manifest** vt. manifestare.

manifestant s. manifestante.

manifestation s. manifestazione.

manifold agg. molteplice.

manifoldness s. molteplicità.

manikin s. 1. omiciattolo 2. manichino.

maniple s. manipolo.

to **manipulate** vt. manipolare.

manipulation s. manipolazione.

manipulator s. manipolatore.

mankind s. umanità.

manlike agg. 1. civile 2. antropomorfo.

manliness s. virilità.

manly agg. maschio, virile.

manner s. 1. maniera 2. contegno. ♦ **manners** s. pl. 1. modi 2. usanze.

mannered agg. manierato || ill- —, maleducato.

mannerism s. manierismo.

mannerly agg. cortese.

manoeuvrable agg. manovrabile.

manoeuvre s. manovra.

to **manoeuvre** vt. manovrare. ♦ to **manoeuvre** vi. fare le manovre.

manoeuvrer s. stratega.

manometer s. manometro.

manor s. feudo || — -house, castello.

manorial agg. feudale.

mansard s. mansarda.

manservant s. domestico.

mansion s. palazzo.

manslaughter s. omicidio preter-intenzionale.

mantelpiece, mantelshelf s. mensola di caminetto.

mantle s. manto, mantello.

to **mantle** vt. ammantare. ♦ to **mantle** vi. coprirsi.

manual agg. e s. manuale.

manufactory s. fabbrica.

manufacturable agg. fabbricabile.

manufacture s. 1. manifattura 2. manufatto.

to **manufacture** vt. fabbricare.

manufacturer s. fabbricante.

manufacturing *agg.* manifatturiero. ◆ **manufacturing** *s.* fabbricazione.

manure *s.* concime.

manuscript *agg. e s.* manoscritto.

many (more, most) *agg. e pron.* molti || — *a*, più di uno; — *-sided*, molteplice; *so* —, tanti; *too* —, troppi; *as* — *as*, tanti... quanti; *how* —?, quanti?

map *s.* carta geografica.

maple *s.* acero.

to mar *vt.* guastare.

marathon *s.* maratona.

to maraud *vt. e vi.* saccheggiare.

marauder *s.* predatore.

marble *s.* 1. marmo 2. biglia.

to marble *vt.* marmorizzare.

marble-cutter *s.* marmista.

March *s.* marzo.

march[1] *s.* confine.

march[2] *s.* marcia.

to march *vi.* 1. camminare 2. marciare || *to* — *in*, entrare marciando.

marching *agg.* in, di marcia.

marchioness *s.* marchesa.

mare *s.* cavalla.

margarine *s.* margarina.

margin *s.* margine.

marginal *agg.* marginale.

marine *agg.* marino, marittimo. ◆ **marine** *s.* 1. marina 2. fante di marina.

marital *agg.* maritale.

maritime *agg.* marittimo.

mark *s.* 1. segno 2. bersaglio 3. voto 4. marchio 5. importanza 6. marco || *question* —, punto interrogativo.

to mark *vt.* 1. segnare 2. dare i voti a 3. scegliere 4. osservare.

marked *agg.* notevole.

marker *s.* 1. chi segna 2. segnalibro.

market *s.* mercato.

to market *vt.* 1. vendere al mercato 2. introdurre sul mercato. ◆ **to market** *vi.* comprare, vendere sul mercato.

marketing *s.* 1. compra-vendita 2. « marketing » (*ricerche di mercato*).

marking *s.* segno.

marksman *s.* tiratore scelto.

marl *s.* marna.

marmalade *s.* marmellata (*d'arance*).

marmoreal *agg.* marmoreo.

marmot *s.* marmotta.

to maroon *vt.* abbandonare un luogo deserto.

marquee *s.* tendone.

marquess, marquis *s.* marchese.

marquise *s.* marchesa.

marriage *s.* matrimonio, unione.

married *agg.* 1. sposato 2. coniugale.

marrow *s.* midollo || (*vegetable*) —, zucca.

to marry *vt.* sposare. ◆ **to marry** *vi.* sposarsi.

marsh *s.* palude || — *-fever*, malaria; — *gas*, metano.

marshal *s.* maresciallo.

to marshal *vt.* 1. schierare 2. introdurre.

marshy *agg.* paludoso.

marsupial *agg. e s.* marsupiale.

marten *s.* martora.

martial *agg.* 1. marziale 2. di Marte.

Martian *agg. e s.* marziano.

martyr *s.* martire.

martyrdom *s.* martirio.

to martyrize *vt.* martirizzare.

martyrology *s.* martirologio.

marvel *s.* meraviglia.

to marvel *vi.* meravigliarsi.

marvellous *agg.* meraviglioso.

Marxism *s.* marxismo.

Marxist *agg. e s.* marxista.

marzipan *s.* marzapane.

mascot(te) *s.* mascotte.

masculine *agg. e s.* maschile.

masculinity *s.* mascolinità.

mash *s.* 1. mistura 2. puré.

to mash *vt.* 1. mescolare 2. schiacciare.

mask *s.* maschera.

to mask *vt.* mascherare.

masking *s.* il mascherarsi.

masochism *s.* masochismo.

mason *s.* muratore || *Free Mason*, massone.

masonry *s.* 1. arte del muratore 2. costruzione in muratura 3. massoneria.

masquerade *s.* mascherata.

to masquerade *vi.* 1. mascherarsi 2. fingersi.

mass[1] *s.* messa.

mass[2] *s.* massa, ammasso.

to mass *vt.* ammassare. ◆ **to mass** *vi.* ammassarsi.

massacre *s.* massacro.

to massacre *vt.* massacrare.

massage *s.* massaggio.

to massage *vt.* massaggiare.

masseur s. massaggiatore.

masseuse s. massaggiatrice.

massif s. massiccio.

massive agg. 1. massiccio 2. potente.

massiveness s. compattezza.

to **mass-produce** vt. produrre in serie.

mass-producer s. produttore in serie.

mass-production s. produzione in serie.

massy agg. massiccio.

mast s. (mar.) albero.

to **mast** vt. (mar.) alberare.

master s. 1. padrone 2. maestro ‖ — builder, capomastro; Master of Arts, laureato in lettere.

to **master** vt. 1. conoscere a fondo 2. dominare.

masterful agg. 1. autoritario 2. abile.

masterhood s. padronanza.

masterly agg. magistrale.

masterpiece s. capolavoro.

mastership s. 1. autorità 2. abilità.

masterstroke s. colpo magistrale.

mastery s. 1. maestria 2. signoria.

mastication s. masticazione.

mastiff s. mastino.

mastitis s. mastite.

mastodon s. mastodonte.

mastoid s. mastoide.

mastoiditis s. mastoidite.

masturbation s. masturbazione.

mat s. stuoia ‖ door- —, zerbino.

to **mat** vt. 1. intrecciare 2. coprire con stuoie 3. smerigliare.

match[1] s. 1. gara, incontro 2. avversario 3. l'uguale 4. matrimonio.

match[2] s. fiammifero.

to **match** vt. 1. accoppiare, maritare 2. uguagliare. ♦ to **match** vi. 1. accoppiarsi 2. accordarsi 3. rivaleggiare.

matchless agg. impareggiabile.

mate s. 1. compagno 2. aiuto 3. (mar.) ufficiale in seconda.

to **mate** vt. accoppiare. ♦ to **mate** vi. accoppiarsi.

material agg. 1. materiale 2. essenziale. ♦ **material** s. 1. materia, materiale 2. stoffa. ♦ **materials** s. pl. articoli ‖ raw —, materie prime.

materialism s. materialismo.

materialist agg. e s. materialista.

materialistic agg. materialistico.

materialization s. materializzazione.

to **materialize** vt. materializzare. ♦ to **materialize** vi. 1. materializzarsi 2. avverarsi.

maternal agg. materno.

maternity s. maternità.

mathematic(al) agg. matematico.

mathematician s. matematico.

mathematics s. matematica.

matriarchy s. matriarcato.

matricidal agg. matricida.

matricide s. 1. matricida 2. matricidio.

to **matriculate** vt. immatricolare. ♦ to **matriculate** vi. immatricolarsi.

matriculation s. immatricolazione.

matrimonial agg. matrimoniale.

matrimony s. matrimonio.

matrix s. 1. matrice 2. (anat.) utero.

matron s. 1. matrona 2. direttrice 3. governante.

matronal, matronly agg. matronale.

matter s. 1. materia 2. faccenda ‖ what is the — with you?, che cosa vi succede?; what is the —?, che succede?

to **matter** vi. 1. importare: it matters little, poco importa 2. (med.) suppurare.

matter-of-fact agg. pratico.

matting s. stuoia.

mattock s. piccone.

mattress s. materasso.

to **maturate** vi. 1. maturare 2. suppurare.

maturation s. 1. maturazione 2. suppurazione.

mature agg. maturo.

to **mature** vt. e vi. maturare.

maturity s. 1. maturità 2. (comm.) scadenza.

matutine agg. mattutino.

maudlin agg. 1. sdolcinato 2. querulo.

to **maunder** vi. 1. parlare a vanvera 2. girovagare.

mausoleum s. mausoleo.

mawkish agg. 1. nauseante 2. sdolcinato.

mawkishness s. 1. sapore nauseante 2. sdolcinatezza.

maxim s. massima.

maximalist s. massimalista.

maximum agg. e s. massimo.

May s. maggio ‖ — Day, primo maggio.

may (might) v. dif. potere (pres. ind. e congiuntivo) || — I go out?, posso uscire?; he — arrive to day, può darsi che arrivi oggi; — he live to repent it, possa egli vivere tanto da pentirsene

maybe avv. forse.

maybug s. maggiolino.

mayflower s. biancospino.

mayonnaise s. maionese.

mayor s. sindaco.

maze s. labirinto.

to **maze** vt. disorientare, confondere.

mazily avv. confusamente.

mazy agg. intricato.

me pron. pers. me, mi.

meadow s. prato.

meagre agg. 1. magro 2. scarso.

meal¹ s. farina.

meal² s. pasto.

mealy agg. 1. farinoso 2. infarinato 3. pallido 4. chiazzato.

mean¹ agg. 1. meschino 2. mediocre.

mean² s. punto medio, mezzo. ◆ **means** s. pl. mezzi || by no means, ben lungi da.

to **mean (meant, meant)** vt. e vi. 1. intendere, significare 2. destinare.

meander s. meandro.

to **meander** vi. serpeggiare.

meaning agg. 1. disposto 2. significativo. ◆ **meaning** s. 1. significato 2. idea.

meaningful agg. significativo.

meaningless agg. senza senso.

meanly avv. 1. meschinamente 2. umilmente.

meanness s. meschinità.

meant V. to mean.

meantime s. frattempo. ◆ **meantime** avv. frattanto.

meanwhile avv. frattanto.

measles s. morbillo || German —, rosolia.

measurable agg. misurabile.

measure s. 1. misura 2. ritmo.

to **measure** vt. e vi. misurare.

measureless agg. smisurato.

measurement s. misurazione.

measurer s. misuratore.

meat s. carne.

meaty agg. 1. polposo 2. sostanzioso.

mechanic s. meccanico.

mechanical agg. meccanico.

mechanics s. meccanica.

mechanism s. 1. meccanismo 2.

mechanization s. meccanizzazione.

to **mechanize** vt. meccanizzare.

medal s. medaglia.

to **meddle** vi. immischiarsi.

meddler s. intrigante.

meddlesome agg. importuno.

medi(a)eval agg. medievale.

medi(a)evalism s. medievalismo.

medi(a)evalist s. medievalista.

medial agg. medio.

median agg. mediano.

mediate agg. mediato.

to **mediate** vt. conseguire con mediazione. ◆ to **mediate** vi. fare da intermediario.

mediation s. mediazione.

mediator s. mediatore.

medical agg. medico.

medicament s. medicamento.

medication s. medicazione.

medicative agg. curativo.

medicinal agg. medicinale.

medicine s. medicina || —-man, stregone.

mediocrity s. mediocrità.

to **meditate** vt. e vi. meditare.

meditation s. meditazione.

meditative agg. meditativo.

Mediterranean agg. mediterraneo.

medium agg. medio. ◆ **medium** s. mezzo.

mediumistic agg. medianico.

medlar s. nespola || —-tree, nespolo.

medley agg. misto. ◆ **medley** s. miscuglio.

medulla s. midollo.

medullar(y) agg. midollare.

meek agg. mite.

meekness s. mansuetudine.

to **meet (met, met)** vt. 1. incontrare 2. far fronte a. ◆ to **meet (met, met)** vi. incontrarsi || to — with, imbattersi in.

meeting s. 1. incontro 2. riunione || political —, comizio.

megalomaniac s. megalomane.

megaphone s. megafono.

melancholic agg. malinconico.

melancholy agg. malinconico. ◆ **melancholy** s. malinconia.

mellifluous agg. mellifluo.

mellow agg. 1. maturo 2. pastoso 3. ubertoso.

to **mellow** vt. e vi. maturare.

mellowness s. 1. maturità 2. pastosità 3. ubertosità.

melodic agg. melodico.

melodious *agg.* melodioso.

melodiousness *s.* melodiosità.

melodrama *s.* melodramma.

melodramatic *agg.* melodrammatico.

melody *s.* melodia.

melomaniac *s.* melomane.

melon *s.* melone || *water- —*, anguria.

melt *s.* fusione.

to melt *vt.* 1. sciogliere 2. intenerire. ♦ **to melt** *vi.* 1. sciogliersi 2. intenerirsi || *to — away*, svanire.

melter *s.* fonditore.

melting *s.* fusione || *- -pot*, crogiuolo.

meltingly *avv.* teneramente.

member *s.* membro.

membership *s.* 1. qualifica di membro 2. i membri.

membrane *s.* membrana.

memoirs *s. pl.* memorie.

memorable *agg.* memorabile.

memorandum *s.* (*pl.* -da) promemoria.

memorial *agg.* commemorativo. ♦ **memorial** *s.* 1. monumento 2. memoriale.

memorialist *s.* memorialista.

to memorize *vt.* imparare a memoria.

memory *s.* memoria.

men V. *man.*

menace *s.* minaccia.

to menace *vt.* e *vi.* minacciare.

menacing *agg.* minaccioso.

menagerie *s.* serraglio.

mend *s.* rattoppo.

to mend *vt.* 1. riparare 2. correggere. ♦ **to mend** *vi.* 1. correggersi 2. migliorare.

mendacious *agg.* mendace.

mendacity *s.* 1. abitudine di mentire 2. bugia.

mender *s.* 1. riparatore 2. rammendatrice.

mendicant *agg.* e *s.* mendicante.

mendicity *s.* mendicità.

mending *s.* 1. riparazione 2. rammendo.

menial *agg.* servile. ♦ **menial** *s.* servo.

meninx *s.* (*pl.* meninges) meninge.

meniscus *s.* menisco.

menopause *s.* menopausa.

menses *s. pl.* mestruazioni.

menstruation *s.* mestruazione.

mental *agg.* mentale || *— -hospi-*

tal, manicomio.

mentality *s.* 1. mentalità 2. intelligenza.

menthol *s.* mentolo.

mention *s.* menzione || *don't — it*, non c'è di che (*risposta a « grazie »*).

to mention *vt.* nominare.

mentionable *agg.* menzionabile.

mentor *s.* mentore.

mephitic *agg.* mefitico.

mercantile *agg.* mercantile.

mercantilism *s.* mercantilismo.

mercenary *agg.* e *s.* mercenario.

merchandise *s.* merce.

to merchandise *vt.* e *vi.* commerciare.

merchant *s.* mercante || *— ship*, nave mercantile.

merciful *agg.* pietoso.

merciless *agg.* spietato.

mercury *s.* mercurio.

mercy *s.* pietà, misericordia.

mere¹ *agg.* 1. mero 2. solo.

mere² *s.* confine.

mere³ *s.* laghetto, stagno.

to merge *vt.* assorbire. ♦ **to merge** *vi.* 1. essere assortito 2. immergersi.

merger *s.* (*comm.*) fusione (*di società*).

meridian *agg.* 1. meridiano 2. culminante. ♦ **meridian** *s.* 1. meridiano 2. culmine.

meridional *agg.* e *s.* meridionale.

merit *s.* merito.

to merit *vt.* meritare.

meritorious *agg.* meritorio.

mermaid *s.* sirena.

merman *s.* tritone.

merrily *avv.* allegramente.

merry *agg.* gaio.

merry-go-round *s.* giostra.

merrymaking *s.* festa.

mesh *s.* maglia. ♦ **meshes** *s. pl.* reti.

mesocarp *s.* mesocarpo.

mesozoic *agg.* e *s.* mesozoico.

mess *s.* 1. mensa 2. confusione 3. pasticcio.

to mess *vt.* mettere in disordine || *to — up*, mettere a soqquadro.

message *s.* 1. messaggio 2. commissione.

messenger *s.* messaggero || *— -boy*, fattorino.

Messiah *s.* Messia.

Messianic *agg.* messianico.

mestizo *s.* meticcio.

met V. *to meet.*
metabolism s. metabolismo.
metal s. **1.** metallo **2.** pietrisco.
metallic *agg.* metallico.
metallization s. metallizzazione.
to **metallize** *vt.* metallizzare.
metalloid s. metalloide.
metallurgic(al) *agg.* metallurgico.
metallurgist s. metallurgico.
metallurgy s. metallurgia.
metamorphic *agg.* metamorfico.
metamorphism s. metamorfismo.
metamorphosis s. (*pl.* -ses) metamorfosi.
metaphor s. metafora.
metaphoric(al) *agg.* metaforico.
metaphysic(al) *agg.* metafisico.
metaphysics s. metafisica.
metapsychic(al) *agg.* metapsichico.
metapsychics s. metapsichica.
metastasis s. (*pl.* -ses) metastasi.
metayage s. mezzadria.
metayer s. mezzadro.
mete s. segno di confine ‖ *metes and bounds* (*giur.*), limiti e confini.
metempsychosis s. metempsicosi.
meteor s. meteora.
meteoric *agg.* **1.** meteorico **2.** transitorio.
meteorold s. meteorite.
meteorologic(al) *agg.* meteorologico.
meteorologist s. meteorologo.
meteorology s. meteorologia.
meter s. **1.** contatore **2.** tassametro.
methane s. metano.
method s. metodo.
methodic(al) *agg.* metodico.
methodist s. metodista.
methodological *agg.* metodologico.
methodology s. metodologia.
meticulosity s. meticolosità.
meticulous *agg.* meticoloso.
metre s. **1.** metro **2.** (*mus.*) tempo.
metrical *agg.* metrico.
metrics s. metrica.
metronome s. metronomo.
metropolis s. metropoli.
metropolitan *agg.* metropolitano.
♦ **metropolitan** s. abitante di una metropoli.
mettle s. tempra.
mettled, mettlesome *agg.* focoso.
mew¹ s. gabbiano.
mew² s. miagolio.
to **mew¹** *vt.* rinchiudere in gabbia.
to **mew²** *vi.* miagolare.
to **mewl** *vi.* vagire.

Mexican *agg.* e s. messicano.
mezzanine s. mezzanino.
miaul s. miagolio.
mice V. *mouse.*
microbe s. microbo.
microbial *agg.* microbico.
microbiology s. microbiologia.
microcosm s. microcosmo.
micrometer s. micrometro.
micrometry s. micrometria.
micro-organism s. microorganismo.
microphone s. microfono.
microphotography s. microfotografia.
microscope s. microscopio.
microscopic(al) *agg.* microscopico.
microscopy s. microscopia.
mid *agg.* medio, mezzo.
midday s. mezzogiorno.
middle *agg.* medio ‖ *Middle Ages,* medioevo; — *aged,* di mezza età.
♦ **middle** s. **1.** mezzo **2.** cintola.
middle class s. borghesia.
middleman s. intermediario.
middling *agg.* medio.
midge s. moscerino.
midget s. nano.
midland *agg.* centrale. ♦ **midlands** s. *pl.* regione centrale (*sing.*).
midnight s. mezzanotte.
midriff s. **1.** diaframma **2.** costume da bagno a due pezzi.
midshipman s. guardiamarina.
midst s. mezzo.
midsummer s. solstizio d'estate.
midway *agg.* e *avv.* a mezza strada.
mid-week *agg.* di metà settimana.
midwife s. (*pl.* -wives) levatrice.
midwinter s. solstizio d'inverno.
mien s. portamento.
might s. potenza.
might V. *may.*
mighty *agg.* potente.
migrant *agg.* e s. migratore.
to **migrate** *vi.* (e)migrare.
migration s. (e)migrazione.
migratory *agg.* migratore.
milady s. nobildonna.
mild *agg.* dolce.
mildew s. muffa.
mildness s. dolcezza.
mile s. miglio.
milestone s. pietra miliare.
milfoil s. millefoglio.
miliary *agg.* migliare.
militant *agg.* militante. ♦ **militant** s. attivista.

militarily *avv.* militarmente.

militarism *s.* militarismo.

militarist *s.* militarista.

militarization *s.* militarizzazione.

to **militarize** *vt.* militarizzare.

military *agg.* e *s.* militare.

militiaman *s.* milite.

milk *s.* latte || *— -jug*, lattiera.

to **milk** *vt.* mungere. ♦ to **milk** *vi.* 1. produrre latte 2. mungere.

milker *s.* 1. mungitore 2. mucca da latte.

milking *s.* mungitura.

milkmaid *s.* mungitrice.

milkman *s.* lattaio.

milky *agg.* 1. latteo 2. (*fig.*) gentile || *the Milky Way*, la Via Lattea.

mill *s.* 1. mulino 2. macinino 3. fabbrica || *saw— —*, segheria.

to **mill** *vt.* 1. macinare 2. segare 3. frullare.

millenary *agg.* millenario. ♦ **millenary** *s.* 1. millennio 2. millenario.

millennium *s.* millennio.

millepede *s.* millepiedi.

miller *s.* mugnaio 2. fresatore 3. fresa.

millet *s.* (*bot.*) miglio.

milliard *s.* 1. miliardo 2. (*amer.*) bilione.

milligram(me) *s.* milligrammo.

millimetre *s.* millimetro.

milliner *s.* modista.

millinery *s.* modisteria.

milling *s.* 1. macinatura 2. fresatura.

million *s.* milione.

millionaire *s.* milionario.

millstone *s.* macina.

mime *s.* mimo.

to **mime** *vi.* e *vt.* mimare.

to **mimeograph** *vt.* ciclostilare.

mimetic *agg.* mimetico.

mimic *agg.* imitativo || *— art*, mimica. ♦ **mimic** *s.* imitatore.

to **mimic (mimicked, mimicked)** *vt.* imitare.

mimicry *s.* 1. imitazione 2. mimetismo.

minaret *s.* minareto.

minatory *agg.* minatorio.

mince *s.* carne tritata.

to **mince** *vt.* 1. tritare 2. tagliuzzare 3. mitigare. ♦ to **mince** *vi.* camminare, parlare in modo affettato.

mincer *s.* tritacarne.

mincing *agg.* affettato.

mind *s.* 1. mente 2. opinione.

to **mind** *vt.* 1. badare a 2. spiacere || *never —!*, non importa!; *I do not —*, non mi preoccupo di.

minded *agg.* incline || *broad— —*, di larghe vedute; *narrow— —*, di idee ristrette || *if you are so —*, se la pensate cosl.

mindful *agg.* memore.

mindless *agg.* 1. disattento 2. stupido.

mine[1] *pron. poss.* il mio, la mia, i miei, le mie || *a friend of —*, un mio amico.

mine[2] *s.* 1. miniera 2. mina || *— -sweeper*, dragamine.

to **mine** *vt.* 1. scavare 2. estrarre 3. minare.

miner *s.* minatore.

mineral *agg.* e *s.* minerale.

to **mineralize** *vt.* mineralizzare.

mineralogy *s.* mineralogia.

to **mingle** *vt.* mescolare. ♦ to **mingle** *vi.* mescolarsi.

miniature *agg.* in miniatura. ♦ **miniature** *s.* miniatura.

to **miniature** *vt.* e *vi.* fare miniature.

miniaturist *s.* miniaturista.

minim *s.* 1. (*mus.*) minima 2. quantità minima 3. inezia.

minimal *agg.* minimo.

to **minimize** *vt.* minimizzare.

minimum *s.* (*pl.* -ma) minimo.

mining *agg.* minerario. ♦ **mining** *s.* 1. scavo 2. estrazione 3. posa di mine.

minion *s.* favorito.

miniskirt *s.* minigonna.

minister *s.* ministro.

to **minister** *vi.* assistere.

ministerial *agg.* ministeriale.

ministry *s.* ministero.

mink *s.* visone.

minor *agg.* minore. ♦ **minor** *s.* minorenne.

minority *s.* 1. minoranza 2. età minore.

minstrel *s.* menestrello.

mint[1] *s.* zecca.

mint[2] *s.* menta.

to **mint** *vt.* coniare.

mintage *s.* conio.

minuend *s.* minuendo.

minuet *s.* minuetto.

minus *s.* e *prep.* meno.

minute *agg.* minuto, minuscolo.

minute *s.* 1. minuto 2. nota || *— -band*, lancetta dei minuti.

minutely[1] *avv.* minutamente.

minutely[2] *avv.* di minuto in minuto.

minuteness *s.* 1. minutezza 2. minuziosità.

miracle *s.* miracolo.

miraculous *agg.* miracoloso.

mirage *s.* miraggio.

mire *s.* fango.

to mire *vt.* infangare. ♦ **to mire** *vi.* infangarsi.

mirror *s.* specchio || *driving-* —, specchietto retrovisore.

to mirror *vt.* rispecchiare.

mirth *s.* allegria.

mirthful *agg.* allegro.

mirthless *agg.* triste.

miry *agg.* fangoso.

misadventure *s.* disavventura.

misanthrope *s.* misantropo.

misanthropy *s.* misantropia.

misapplication *s.* applicazione erronea.

to misapply *vt.* applicare erroneamente.

misapprehension *s.* malinteso.

misbehaviour *s.* cattivo contegno.

misbelief *s.* falsa credenza.

to misbelieve *vi.* avere una falsa credenza.

misbeliever *s.* miscredente.

misbelieving *agg.* eretico.

to miscalculate *vt.* e *vi.* calcolare male.

miscarriage *s.* 1. disguido 2. fallimento 3. aborto.

to miscarry *vi.* 1. smarrirsi 2. fallire 3. abortire.

miscellaneous *agg.* miscellaneo.

miscellany *s.* miscellanea.

mischance *s.* sfortuna.

mischief *s.* 1. danno, male 2. malizia 3. birichinata.

mischievous *agg.* 1. nocivo 2. malizioso.

misconduct *s.* cattiva condotta.

miscount *s.* conteggio errato.

misdeed *s.* misfatto.

to misdirect *vt.* mandare in direzione sbagliata.

misdirection *s.* indicazione sbagliata.

misdoing *s.* misfatto.

miser *s.* avaro.

miserable *agg.* 1. triste 2. miserabile.

miserliness *s.* avarizia.

miserly *agg.* avaro.

misery *s.* 1. miseria 2. sofferenza.

misfire *s.* cilecca.

misfit *s.* 1. cosa che si adatta male 2. (*fig.*) pesce fuor d'acqua.

misfortune *s.* sventura.

to misgive (misgave, misgiven) *vt.* preoccupare. ♦ **to misgive (misgave, misgiven)** *vi.* preoccuparsi.

misgiving *s.* 1. presentimento 2. timore.

to misgovern *vt.* governare male.

misgovernment *s.* malgoverno.

to misguide *vt.* 1. guidare male 2. traviare.

to mishandle *vt.* maltrattare.

mishap *s.* infortunio.

to misinform *vt.* informare male.

misinformation *s.* informazione sbagliata.

to misinterpret *vt.* interpretare male.

misinterpretation *s.* interpretazione errata.

to misjudge *vt.* giudicare male.

misjudgement *s.* giudizio erroneo.

to mislay (mislaid, mislaid) *vt.* smarrire.

to mislead (misled, misled) *vt.* 1. traviare 2. ingannare.

misogamy *s.* misogamia.

misogynist *s.* misogino.

misogyny *s.* misoginia.

misoneism *s.* misoneismo.

to misplace *vt.* collocare male, fuori posto.

misplacement *s.* spostamento.

misprint *s.* errore di stampa, refuso.

to misprint *vt.* stampare con errori.

to mispronounce *vt.* pronunciare male.

mispronunciation *s.* pronuncia scorretta.

misquotation *s.* citazione erronea.

to misquote *vt.* citare erroneamente.

to misread (misread, misread) *vt.* leggere erroneamente.

mesreading *s.* falsa interpretazione.

to misrepresent *vt.* travisare.

misrepresentation *s.* travisamento.

miss[1] *s.* 1. colpo mancato 2. difetto.

miss[2] *s.* signorina: *Miss Jane Smith*, la signorina Jane Smith.

to miss *vt.* 1. mancare (*il colpo*) 2. perdere 3. notare, sentire la mancanza di **4.** evitare.

missal s. messale.

missile s. missile.

missing agg. mancante || the —, i dispersi.

mission s. missione.

missionary agg. e s. missionario.

missioner s. missionario.

to **misspell** vt. sbagliare l'ortografia.

mist s. **1.** bruma **2.** pioggerella **3.** appannamento.

to **mist** vt. appannare. ♦ to **mist** vi. appannarsi.

mistakable agg. suscettibile d'errore.

mistake s. errore.

to **mistake (mistook, mistaken)** vt. **1.** sbagliare **2.** scambiare **3.** non capire.

mistaken agg. **1.** in errore **2.** erroneo.

mister s. signore: Mr. Brown, il signor Brown.

mistletoe s. vischio.

mistook V. to mistake.

mistral s. maestrale.

mistranslation s. traduzione errata.

mistress s. **1.** signora: Mrs. Brown, la signora Brown **2.** insegnante **3.** amante.

mistrust s. diffidenza.

to **mistrust** vt. e vi. diffidare di, sospettare.

mistrustful agg. diffidente.

misty agg. **1.** nebbioso **2.** confuso.

to **misunderstand (misunderstood, misunderstood)** vt. e vi. fraintendere.

misunderstanding s. **1.** malinteso **2.** disaccordo.

misunderstood V. to misunderstand.

misusage, misuse s. **1.** cattivo uso **2.** maltrattamento.

to **misuse** vt. **1.** usar male **2.** maltrattare.

to **miswrite (miswrote, miswritten)** vt. scrivere scorrettamente.

mithridatic agg. immunizzante (contro veleni).

mithridatism s. immunizzazione (contro un veleno).

to **mitigate** vt. mitigare.

mitigation s. mitigazione.

mitral agg. mitrale.

mitre s. **1.** (eccl.) mitra **2.** giunto ad angolo.

mitt(en) s. manopola, guantone.

to **mix** vt. mescolare || to — up, confondere. ♦ to **mix** vi. mescolarsi.

mixed agg. misto, eterogeneo.

mixer s. (mecc.) mescolatore.

mixing s. mescolanza.

mixture s. **1.** mescolanza **2.** miscela.

mizzen s. (mar.) mezzana.

mnemonic agg. mnemonico.

mnemonics s. mnemonica.

moan s. gemito.

to **moan** vt. e vi. gemere.

moanful agg. lamentoso.

moaning s. lamento.

moat s. fossato.

mob s. **1.** folla **2.** plebaglia.

to **mob** vt. **1.** assalire **2.** affollare.

mobile agg. **1.** mobile **2.** mutevole.

mobility s. **1.** mobilità **2.** mutevolezza.

mobilization s. mobilitazione.

to **mobilize** vt. mobilitare.

moccasin s. mocassino.

mock agg. **1.** ironico **2.** finto || — -heroic, eroicomico. ♦ **mock** s. **1.** derisione **2.** imitazione.

to **mock** vt. e vi. beffare, prendersi gioco di.

mocker s. burlone.

mockery s. **1.** derisione **2.** contraffazione.

mocking agg. beffardo.

modal agg. modale.

modality s. modalità.

model s. modello. ♦ **model** s. **1.** modello **2.** copia.

to **model** vt. modellare.

modeller s. **1.** modellatore **2.** modellista.

modelling s. **1.** modellatura **2.** creazione di modelli.

moderate agg. e s. moderato.

to **moderate** vt. moderare. ♦ to **moderate** vi. moderarsi.

moderateness s. moderatezza.

moderation s. moderazione.

moderator s. moderatore.

modern agg. e s. moderno.

modernism s. modernismo.

modernist s. modernista.

modernity s. modernità.

modernization s. **1.** rimodernamento **2.** aggiornamento.

to **modernize** vt. modernizzare. ♦ to **modernize** vi. modernizzarsi.

modest agg. **1.** modesto **2.** pudico.

modesty s. 1. modestia 2. pudore.
modifiable agg. modificabile.
modification s. modificazione.
modifier s. modificatore.
to **modify** vt. modificare.
to **modulate** vt. e vi. modulare.
modulation s. modulazione.
modulator s. modulatore.
mofette s. mofeta.
Mohammedan agg. e s. maomettano.
moist agg. umido.
to **moisten** vt. inumidire. ♦ to **moisten** vi. inumidirsi.
moistness s. umidità.
moisture s. vapore umido.
molar agg. e s. molare.
molasses s. melassa.
mole[1] s. neo.
mole[2] s. talpa.
mole[3] s. molo.
molecular agg. molecolare.
molecule s. molecola.
moleskin s. 1. pelle di talpa 2. fustagno. ♦ **moleskins** s. pl. calzoni di fustagno.
to **molest** vt. molestare.
molestation s. molestia.
molester s. molestatore.
to **mollify** vt. addolcire.
mollusc s. mollusco.
molybdenum s. molibdeno.
moment s. 1. momento 2. importanza.
momentary agg. momentaneo.
momentous agg. importante.
monachal agg. monacale.
monad s. monade.
monarch s. monarca.
monarchic(al) agg. monarchico.
monarchist s. monarchico.
monarchy s. monarchia.
monastery s. monastero.
monastic(al) agg. monastico.
Monday s. lunedì.
monetary agg. monetario.
monetization s. monetazione.
to **monetize** vt. monetizzare.
money s. denaro || —-bag, portamonete; — -order, vaglia; earnest —, caparra; paper —, valuta cartacea; ready —, contanti.
moneyed agg. 1. di, in denaro 2. ricco.
moneyless agg. squattrinato.
monger s. mercante || fish —, pescivendolo.
Mongolian agg. e s. mongolo.
mongolism s. mongolismo.

mongoloid agg. e s. mongoloide.
mongrel agg. misto. ♦ **mongrel** s. 1. bastardo 2. incrocio.
monism s. monismo.
monition s. 1. ammonizione 2. (giur.) citazione.
monitor s. 1. consigliere 2. capoclasse 3. dispositivo di controllo.
monitory agg. ammonitore.
monk s. monaco.
monkey s. scimmia.
monkeyish agg. scimmiesco.
monkhood s. mónacato.
monkish agg. monastico, manacale.
monochromatic agg. monocromatico.
monochrome s. monocromia.
monocle s. monocolo.
monody s. monodia.
monogamist s. monogamo.
monogamy s. monogamia.
monogram s. monogramma.
monograph s. monografia.
monographic(al) agg. monografico.
monolith s. monolito.
monolithic agg. monolitico.
monologue s. monologo.
monometallic agg. monometallico.
monomial s. monomio.
monomolecular agg. monomolecolare.
monoplane s. monoplano.
monopolist s. monopolista.
to **monopolize** vt. monopolizzare.
monopoly s. monopolio.
monorail s. monorotaia.
monosyllabic agg. monosillabico.
monosyllable s. monosillabo.
monotheism s. monoteismo.
monotheist s. monoteista.
monotheistic(al) agg. monoteistico.
monotone s. tono uniforme.
monotonous agg. monotono.
monotony s. 1. tono uniforme 2. monotonia.
monotype s. monotipo.
monsoon s. monsone.
monster agg. colossale. ♦ **monster** s. mostro.
monstrance s. ostensorio.
monstrosity s. mostruosità.
monstrous agg. mostruoso.
montage s. montaggio.
month s. mese.
monthly agg. e s. mensile. ♦ **monthly** avv. mensilmente.
monument s. monumento.
monumental agg. monumentale.

mood s. 1. umore 2. (gramm.) modo.
◆ **moods** s. pl. capricci.

moodily avv. di malumore.

moodiness s. malumore.

moody agg. di malumore.

moon s. luna.

to **moon** vi. 1. gingillarsi 2. allunare || to — about, bighellonare.

mooncalf s. (pl. -lves) idiota.

mooning s. vagabondaggio.

moonlight s. chiaro di luna.

moonlit agg. illuminato dalla luna.

moonshine s. V. moonlight.

moonshiny agg. V. moonlit.

moony agg. 1. lunare 2. distratto.

Moor s. moro.

moor s. brughiera.

to **moor** vt. e vi. ormeggiare.

moorage s. ormeggio. ◆ **moorings** s. pl. 1. gomena (sing.) 2. ormeggi.

mop¹ s. 1. scopa 2. zazzera.

mop² s. smorfia.

to **mop**¹ vt. 1. pulire 2. asciugare || to — up (mil.), rastrellare.

to **mop**² vi. fare smorfie.

mope s. 1. persona avvilita 2. tristezza.

to **mope** vt. avvilire. ◆ to **mope** vi. avvilirsi.

mopish agg. avvilito.

moraine s. morena.

moral agg. e s. morale. ◆ **moral** s. 1. morale 2. principio morale. ◆ **morals** s. pl. costumi.

morale s. il morale.

moralism s. moralismo.

moralist s. moralista.

moralistic agg. moralistico.

morality s. moralità.

moralization s. moralizzazione.

to **moralize** vt. moralizzare. ◆ to **moralize** vi. trarre la morale.

morass s. palude.

moratory agg. moratorio.

moratorium s. (pl. -ria) moratoria.

moray s. murena.

morbid agg. 1. morboso 2. patologico.

morbidity s. 1. morbosità 2. stato patologico.

mordacity, mordancy s. mordacità.

mordant agg. e s. mordente.

more (comp. di much, many) agg., pron. e avv. più, di più, maggiormente || — and —, sempre più; once —, ancora una volta.

moreover avv. inoltre.

morganatic agg. morganatico.

morgue s. obitorio.

Mormon agg. e s. mormone.

morning s. mattino.

Moroccan agg. e s. marocchino.

moron s. deficiente.

morose agg. tetro.

morphia, morphine s. morfina.

morphinomaniac agg. e s. morfinomane.

morphologic(al) agg. morfologico.

morphology s. morfologia.

morsel s. boccone.

mortal agg. e s. mortale.

mortality s. mortalità.

mortally avv. mortalmente.

mortar¹ s. mortaio.

mortar² s. calcina.

mortgage s. ipoteca.

to **mortgage** vt. ipotecare.

mortagagee s. creditore ipotecario.

mortgager s. debitore ipotecario.

mortification s. mortificazione.

to **mortify** vt. 1. mortificare 2. incancrenire. ◆ to **mortify** vi. 1. mortificarsi 2. incancrenirsi.

mortuary agg. mortuario. ◆ **mortuary** s. camera mortuaria.

mosaic agg. musivo. ◆ **mosaic** s. mosaico.

Moslem agg. e s. mussulmano.

mosque s. moschea.

mosquito s. zanzara || — -net, zanzariera.

moss s. 1. acquitrino 2. muschio.

mossy agg. muscoso.

most agg. e pron. (superl. di much, many) il più, la maggior parte di, il massimo. ◆ **most** avv. 1. il più 2. molto 3. maggiormente.

mostly avv. per lo più.

mote s. particella.

moth s. 1. falena 2. tignola.

mother s. madre || — -country, madrepatria; — -in-law, suocera.

motherhood s. maternità.

motherless agg. senza madre.

motherly agg. materno.

mothproof agg. inattaccabile dalle tarme.

motif s. motivo.

motion s. 1. moto, movimento 2. mozione || — -picture, film.

motionless agg. immobile.

to **motivate** vt. 1. motivare 2. stimolare.

motivation s. 1. motivazione 2. stimolo.

motive agg. motore. ◆ **motive** s.

motivo, movente.

motley *agg.* 1. screziato 2. eterogeneo. ♦ **motley** *s.* miscuglio.

motor *agg.* e *s.* motore ‖ — *-cycle*, motocicletta; — *-car*, automobile, — *-boat*, motobarca; — *ship*, motonave.

to **motor** *vi.* andare in automobile.

motoring *s.* automobilismo.

motorist *s.* automobilista.

motorization *s.* motorizzazione.

to **motorize** *vt.* motorizzare.

mottle *s.* chiazza.

to **mottle** *vt.* chiazzare.

moufflon *s.* muflone.

mould[1] *s.* stampo.

mould[2] *s.* muffa.

mould[3] *s.* terriccio.

to **mould**[1] *vt.* modellare.

to **mould**[2] *vi.* ammuffire.

moulding *s.* 1. il modellare 2. cornice 3. fusione.

mouldy *agg.* ammuffito.

mound *s.* monticello.

mount[1] *s.* monte, montagna.

mount[2] 1. cavalcatura 2. intelaiatura 3. affusto di cannone 4. montatura.

to **mount** *vt.* salire. ♦ to **mount** *vi.* 1. montare 2. ammontare.

mountain *s.* montagna.

mountaineer *s.* 1. montanaro 2. alpinista.

mountaineering *s.* alpinismo.

mountainous *agg.* montuoso.

mountebank *s.* ciarlatano.

mounter *s.* montatore.

to **mourn** *vt.* e *vi.* piangere.

mourner *s.* chi è in lutto.

mournful *agg.* lugubre.

mourning *s.* 1. dolore 2. lutto: *to go into* —, mettere il lutto.

mouse *s.* (*pl.* mice) topo.

moustache *s.* baffi (*pl.*).

mouth *s.* bocca.

to **mouth** *vt.* declamare. ♦ to **mouth** *vi.* fare smorfie.

mouthful *s.* boccone.

mouthpiece *s.* 1. bocchino 2. portavoce.

movable *agg.* mobile.

movables *s. pl.* beni mobili.

move *s.* 1. movimento 2. mossa 3. trasloco.

to **move** *vt.* 1. muovere 2. commuovere. ♦ to **move** *vi.* 1. muoversi

movement *s.* 1. movimento, moto. 2. traslocare 3. commuoversi.

mover *s.* promotore.

movie *s.* film. ♦ **movies** *s. pl.* cinema (*sing.*).

moving *s.* 1. spostamento 2. trasloco.

mow *s.* covone.

to **mow** (**mowed, mown**) *vt.* falciare.

mower *s.* falciatore.

mowing *s.* falciatura.

mown V. to **mow**.

much (more, most) *agg.*, *s.* e *avv.* molto ‖ *so* —, tanto; *too* —, troppo; *as* — *as*, tanto quanto; *how* —?, quanto?

muck *s.* letame.

mucous *agg.* mucoso.

mucus *s.* muco.

mud *s.* fango ‖ — *-guard*, parafango.

to **mud** *vt.* infangare.

muddle *s.* confusione, pasticcio.

to **muddle** *vt.* confondere.

muddleheaded *agg.* confusionario.

muddler *s.* confusionario.

muddy *agg.* 1. fangoso 2. torbido 3. infangato.

to **muddy** *vt.* infangare.

muff[1] *s.* manicotto.

muff[2] *s.* 1. colpo mancato 2. babbeo.

to **muffle** *vt.* 1. avvolgere 2. smorzare.

muffler *s.* 1. sciarpa 2. guantone 3. silenziatore.

mug *s.* (*fam.*) faccia ‖ — *shot* (*tv*), primo piano.

mulberry *s.* mora ‖ — (*-tree*) gelso.

mule *s.* mulo.

mulish *agg.* (*fig.*) testardo.

muller *s.* pestello.

multiform *agg.* multiforme.

multimillionaire *s.* multimilionario.

multiple *agg.* e *s.* multiplo.

multiplicable *agg.* moltiplicabile.

multiplicand *s.* moltiplicando.

multiplication *s.* moltiplicazione.

multiplicity *s.* molteplicità.

multiplier *s.* moltiplicatore.

to **multiply** *vt.* moltiplicare. ♦ to **multiply** *vi.* moltiplicarsi.

multitude *s.* moltitudine.

multitudinous *agg.* 1. innumerevole 2. vasto.

mumble *s.* borbottio.

to **mumble** *vt.* e *vi.* borbottare.

mumbling *s.* V. *mumble*.

mummer *s.* guitto.

mummification s. mummificazione.
to **mummify** vt. mummificare.
mummy[1] s. mummia.
mummy[2] s. mammina.
mumps s. pl. orecchioni.
to **munch** vt. e vi. biascicare.
municipal agg. municipale.
municipality s. municipalità.
municipalization s. municipalizzazione.
to **municipalize** vt. municipalizzare.
munificence s. munificenza.
munificent agg. munifico.
munitions s. pl. munizioni.
mural agg. murale. ♦ **mural** s. affresco.
murder s. assassinio.
to **murder** vt. assassinare.
murderer s. assassino.
murderous agg. omicida.
muriatic agg. muriatico.
murky agg. tenebroso.
murmur s. 1. mormorio 2. brontolio.
to **murmur** vt. mormorare. ♦ to **murmur** vi. brontolare.
murmuring s. V. murmur.
muscat(el) s. moscato.
muscle s. muscolo.
muscled agg. muscoloso.
muscular agg. 1. muscolare 2. muscoloso.
musculature s. muscolatura.
Muse s. musa.
to **muse** vi. meditare.
museum s. museo.
mushroom s. fungo.
mushy agg. infrollito.
music s. musica.
musical agg. 1. musicale 2. appassionato di musica.
musicality s. musicalità.
musician s. musicista || street —, suonatore ambulante.
musicologist s. musicologo.
musicology s. musicologia.
musing agg. meditabondo. ♦ **musing** s. meditazione.
musk s. muschio.
musket s. moschetto.
musketeer s. moschettiere.
musky agg. muschiato.
Muslim agg. e s. mussulmano.
muslin s. mussola.
muss s. stato di confusione.
mussel s. mitilo.
must[1] s. mosto.
must[2] s. muffa.

must v. dif. (pres. ind.) dovere || be — return here, deve ritornare qui, it — be true, deve essere vero; you — know him!, non puoi non conoscerlo!
mustard s. senape.
muster s. adunata.
to **muster** vt. adunare. ♦ to **muster** vi. adunarsi.
mutability s. mutabilità.
mutable agg. mutevole.
mutation s. cambiamento.
mute agg. muto. ♦ **mute** s. 1. muto 2. sordina.
to **mutilate** vt. mutilare.
mutilation s. mutilazione.
mutineer s. ammutinato.
mutinous agg. ammutinato, ribelle.
mutiny s. ammutinamento.
to **mutiny** vi. ammutinarsi.
mutism s. mutismo.
to **mutter** V. to murmur.
mutton s. montone.
mutual agg. 1. reciproco 2. comune.
muzzle s. 1. muso 2. museruola 3. bocca (di arma).
to **muzzle** vt. mettere la museruola a.
my agg. poss. mio, mia, miei, mie.
mycosis s. (pl. -ses) micosi.
myocardial agg. miocardico.
myocarditis s. miocardite.
myocardium s. miocardio.
myopia s. miopia.
myopic agg. miope.
myosote s. miosotide.
myriad s. miriade.
myriagram s. miriagrammo.
myriametre s. miriametro.
Myriapoda s. pl. miriapodi.
myrrh s. mirra.
myrtle s. mirto.
myself pron. r. io stesso, me stesso, mi.
mysterious agg. misterioso.
mystery s. mistero.
mystic agg. e s. mistico.
mystical agg. mistico.
mysticism s. misticismo.
mystification s. mistificazione.
mystifier s. mistificatore.
to **mystify** vt. 1. disorientare 2. avvolgere nel mistero.
myth s. mito.
mythic(al) agg. mitico.
to **mythicize** vt. volgere in mito.
mythologic(al) agg. mitologico.
to **mythologize** vi. studiare i miti.
mythology s. mitologia.

mythomania s. mitomania.
mythomaniac agg. e s. mitomane.

N

nabob s. nababbo.
nacre s. madreperla.
to nag vt. e vi. brontolare.
naiad s. naiade.
nail s. 1. unghia, artiglio 2. chiodo.
to nail vt. 1. inchiodare 2. munire di chiodi.
nailer s. fabbricante di chiodi.
naïve agg. ingenuo, semplice.
naiveté s. ingenuità.
naked agg. 1. nudo, spogliato 2. spoglio, indifeso.
nakedness s. nudità.
name s. 1. nome 2. fama, reputazione || — -day, onomastico; full —, generalità.
to name vt. 1. nominare, dare un nome 2. designare.
nameless agg. 1. senza nome 2. innominabile.
namely avv. cioè.
nanny s. bambinaia, balia.
nap[1] s. siesta, sonnellino.
nap[2] s. pelo (di stoffe).
to nap vi. schiacciare un sonnellino, sonnecchiare.
nape s. nuca.
naphtha s. nafta.
napkin s. 1. tovagliolo: — -ring, anello per tovagliolo 2. pannolino.
narcissism s. narcisismo.
narcosis, narcotism s. narcosi.
narcotic agg. s. narcotico.
narcotization s. narcotizzazione.
to narcotize vt. narcotizzare.
to narrate vt. narrare.
narration s. narrazione, racconto.
narrative agg. narrativo. ♦ **narrative** s. resoconto, narrazione.
narrator s. narratore.
narrow agg. 1. stretto, angusto, stretto (anche fig.) 2. esatto, minuzioso || — -minded, di idee ristrette. ♦ **narrow** s. stretto, strettoia.
to narrow vt. stringere, ridurre. ♦ **to narrow** vi. stringersi, contrarsi.
narrowness s. strettezza, limitatezza.
narwhal s. narvalo.
nasal agg. nasale. ♦ **nasal** s. 1.

suono nasale 2. osso nasale.
nascent agg. nascente.
nastily avv. 1. sgradevolmente 2. con cattiveria.
nastiness s. 1. cattivo gusto 2. cattiveria.
nasty agg. 1. sporco, sgradevole 2. cattivo, tempestoso (di tempo).
natal agg. natale.
natality s. natalità.
natant agg. natante.
natation s. nuoto.
natatorial agg. natatorio.
nation s. nazione.
national agg. nazionale.
nationalism s. nazionalismo.
nationalist s. nazionalista.
nationality s. 1. nazionalità 2. patriottismo.
nationalization s. 1. nazionalizzazione 2. naturalizzazione.
to nationalize vt. 1. nazionalizzare 2. naturalizzare.
native agg. 1. innato 2. natio, indigeno. ♦ **native** s. indigeno, nativo.
nativity s. nascita, natività.
natural agg. 1. naturale, fisico 2. spontaneo 3. istintivo, innato.
naturalism s. naturalismo.
naturalist s. naturalista.
naturalistic agg. naturalistico.
naturalization s. 1. naturalizzazione 2. acclimatamento.
to naturalize vi. 1. naturalizzare 2. acclimatare.
nature s. 1. natura 2. carattere, temperamento || good —, bontà.
natured agg. di natura, per natura || good —, buono, di buon carattere.
naturism s. naturismo, nudismo.
naturist s. naturista.
naughtily avv. con cattiveria.
naughtiness s. cattiveria.
naughty agg. cattivo, impertinente.
to nauseate vt. nauseare, disgustare. ♦ **to nauseate** vi. avere la nausea, disgustarsi.
nauseating agg. nauseabondo.
nautical agg. nautico.
naval agg. navale.
nave[1] s. mozzo di ruota.
nave[2] s. navata centrale (di chiesa).
navel s. 1. ombelico 2. (fig.) centro.
navigability s. navigabilità.
navigable agg. navigabile.
to navigate vt. e vi. 1. navigare 2. regolare la rotta.

navigation s. 1. navigazione 2. rotta.

navigator s. navigatore, ufficiale di rotta.

navvy s. sterratore.

navy s. marina da guerra, flotta.

nay avv. anzi, non solo.

Nazi agg. e s. nazista.

Neapolitan agg. e s. napoletano.

near agg. 1. vicino, prossimo 2. affine, intimo 3. fedele, esatto. ♦ **near** prep. vicino a, presso a. ♦ **near** avv. vicino, presso, accanto.

to **near** vt. e vi. avvicinarsi (a).

nearby agg. avv. prep. assai vicino.

nearly avv. quasi.

neat agg. 1. pulito, lindo 2. grazioso, di buon gusto 3. chiaro, conciso.

neatly avv. 1. lindamente, ordinatamente 2. con semplicità, con buon gusto 3. concisamente.

neatness s. 1. pulizia, ordine 2. grazia, armonia 3. semplicità 4. concisione.

nebula s. nebulosa.

nebular agg. nebulare.

nebulosity s. nebulosità.

nebulous agg. nebuloso, vago.

necessary agg. necessario.

to **necessitate** vt. 1. rendere necessario 2. obbligare.

necessity s. necessità.

neck s. collo ǁ stiff —, torcicollo.

neckerchief s. fazzoletto da collo.

necklace s. collana, vezzo.

neckline s. scollatura.

necktie s. cravatta.

necrology s. necrologia.

necromancer s. negromante.

necromancy s. negromanzia.

necropolis s. necropoli.

necrosis s. (pl. -ses) necrosi.

nectar s. nettare.

need s. necessità, bisogno.

to **need** vt. e vi. essere necessario, occorrere, abbisognare, mancare di.

needful agg. necessario, indispensabile.

neediness s. bisogno, povertà.

needle s. 1. ago 2. puntina di grammofono.

to **needle** vt. 1. cucire, pungere (con un ago) 2. irritare.

needleful s. gugliata.

needless agg. inutile, superfluo.

needlewoman s. cucitrice.

needlework s. lavoro ad ago.

needs avv. necessariamente.

needy agg. povero, indigente.

ne'er avv. (contrazione di never) mai.

negation s. diniego.

negative agg. negativo. ♦ **negative** s. 1. negazione 2. qualità negativa.

neglect s. negligenza, trascuratezza.

to **neglect** vt. trascurare.

neglectful agg. negligente, noncurante.

negligence s. negligenza, trascuratezza.

negligent agg. negligente, trascurato.

negligible agg. trascurabile.

negotiable agg. negoziabile.

to **negotiate** vt. e vi. negoziare, trattare.

negotiation s. trattativa.

negress s. negra.

negro agg. e s. negro.

negroid agg. negroide.

neigh s. nitrito.

to **neigh** vi. nitrire.

neighbour s. vicino.

to **neighbour** vi. essere vicini di casa.

neighbourhood s. 1. i vicini, vicinato 2. paraggi, dintorni (pl.).

neighbouring agg. vicino, contiguo.

neither[1] agg. né l'uno né l'altro.

neither[2] avv. né, neppure, nemmeno: — ... nor, né ... né.

nemesis s. (pl. -ses) nemesi.

neo-classic(al) agg. neoclassico.

neo-classicism s. neoclassicismo.

neo-criticism s. neocriticismo.

neolithic agg. neolitico.

neologism s. neologismo.

neology s. neologia.

neon s. neon.

neophyte s. neofito.

neoplatonic agg. neoplatonico.

Neoplatonism s. neoplatonismo.

neopositivism s. neopositivismo.

neorealism s. neorealismo.

neorealist s. neorealista.

nephew s. nipote (di zio).

nephritic agg. nefritico.

nephritis s. nefrite.

nepotism s. nepotismo.

nerve s. 1. nervo 2. nervatura 3. forza, energia, sangue freddo.

to **nerve** vt. tonificare, rinvigorire.

nerveless agg. snervato, inerte.

nervous agg. 1. nervoso 2. forte, vigoroso 3. timido, apprensivo.

nervously avv. 1. nervosamente 2.

timidamente.

nervousness s. 1. nervosismo, irritazione 2. timidezza.

nervy agg. 1. muscoloso, forte 2. nervoso.

nescient agg. ignorante.

nest s. 1. nido 2. (fig.) covo, tana 3. colonia (di uccelli, insetti ecc.).

to nest vi. fare il nido, nidificare.

to nestle vt. ospitare. ♦ **to nestle** vi. annidarsi, rifugiarsi.

nestling s. uccellino di nido.

net[1] agg. e s. netto.

net[2] s. 1. rete 2. (fig.) trappola.

to net vt. 1. coprire con reti 2. pescare con reti.

netful s. retata.

netting s. rete, reticolato.

nettle s. ortica || — rash, orticaria.

to nettle vt. pungere (di ortica).

network s. rete, reticolato.

neuralgia s. nevralgia.

neuralgic agg. nevralgico.

neurasthenia s. nevrastenia.

neurasthenic agg. nevrastenico.

neuritis s. nevrite.

neurologist s. neurologo.

neurology s. neurologia.

neuropathic agg. neuropatico.

neuropathology s. neuropatologia.

neurosis s. (pl. -ses) nevrosi.

neurotic agg. neuropatico.

neuter s. parola neutra, neutro.

neutral agg. neutrale.

neutralism s. neutralismo.

neutralist s. neutralista.

neutrality s. neutralità.

neutralization s. neutralizzazione.

to neutralize vt. neutralizzare.

neutron s. neutrone.

never avv. mai, giammai || — again, mai più; — mind, non importa; now or —, ora o mai più; — -ending, eterno.

nevermore avv. mai più.

nevertheless avv. nonostante, ciò nondimeno.

new agg. nuovo, recente || — -born, neonato; — -comer, nuovo venuto; — -made, appena fatto.

newish agg. piuttosto nuovo.

newly avv. recentemente.

news s. notizia, notizie || — -man, strillone (di giornali); — -reel, cinegiornale.

newsmonger s. persona pettegola e curiosa.

newspaper s. giornale, quotidiano.

New Zealander s. neozelandese.

next agg. 1. prossimo, vicino, il più vicino 2. futuro, venturo 3. primo, contiguo. ♦ **next** avv. dopo, in seguito, poi. ♦ **next** prep. presso, accanto.

nib s. pennino.

nibble s. morso.

to nibble vt. 1. mordicchiare, sgranocchiare 2. abboccare.

nibbler s. roditore.

nice agg. 1. piacevole, bello, simpatico 2. buono, gustoso 3. accurato, minuzioso.

nicely avv. 1. amabilmente, piacevolmente 2. esattamente.

nicety s. 1. finezza, precisione. ♦ **niceties** s. pl. minuzie.

niche s. nicchia.

nick s. tacca, intaccatura || in the — of time, al momento giusto.

to nick vt. 1. intaccare 2. colpire, afferrare al momento opportuno.

nickel s. nichel.

to nickel vt. nichelare.

nickname s. soprannome, nomignolo.

to nickname vt. soprannominare.

nicotine s. nicotina.

niece s. nipote (femmina) (di zio).

niggard agg. spilorcio.

niggardliness s. spilorceria.

niggardly agg. avaro, spilorcio.

nigger s. (spreg.) negro.

night s. 1. notte, sera 2. buio, oscurità || by —, di notte, good —, buona notte; — -bird, uccello notturno, nottambulo; — -dress, camicia da notte; — -shift, turno di notte.

nightcap s. berretto da notte.

nightfall s. tramonto.

nightingale s. usignolo.

nightly agg. notturno. ♦ **nightly** avv. di notte.

nightmare s. incubo.

nightpiece s. « notturno » (dipinto che rappresenta una scena notturna).

nihilism s. nichilismo.

nihilist s. nichilista.

nimble agg. 1. agile, leggero 2. acuto, sveglio.

nimbleness s. 1. agilità 2. prontezza, acutezza.

nimbly avv. 1. agilmente, leggermente 2. prontamente.

nine agg. nove.

ninepins s. pl. birilli.

nineteen agg. diciannove.

nineteenth *agg.* e *s.* diciannovesimo.

ninetieth *agg.* novantesimo.

ninety *agg.* novanta.

ninth *agg.* nono.

nip *s.* 1. pizzicotto, morso 2. stretta, presa 3. morso (*di freddo, gelo ecc.*).

to nip *vt.* 1. pizzicare, mordere (*anche di freddo ecc.*) 2. stroncare.

nipple *s.* capezzolo.

nitrate *s.* nitrato.

nitric *agg.* nitrico.

nitrite *s.* (*chim.*) nitrito.

nitroglycerin(e) *s.* nitroglicerina.

no *agg.* nessuno. ♦ **no** *avv.* 1. no 2. in nessun modo.

nobiliary *agg.* nobiliare.

nobility *s.* nobiltà (*anche fig.*).

noble *agg.* 1. nobile (*anche fig.*) 2. superbo, grandioso. ♦ **noble** *s.* nobile.

nobleman *s.* nobiluomo.

nobleness *s.* nobiltà (*anche fig.*).

noblewoman *s.* nobildonna.

nobly *avv.* nobilmente.

nobody *pron. indef.* nessuno.

nocturnal *agg.* notturno.

nocturne *s.* (*pitt.; mus.*) notturno.

nod *s.* 1. cenno del capo 2. ordine, comando.

to nod *vt.* e *vi.* 1. annuire col capo 2. assopirsi, chinare il capo dal sonno 3. inclinarsi (*di edifici ecc.*).

nodding *agg.* chinato, inclinato. ♦ **nodding** *s.* cenno del capo.

nodose *agg.* nodoso.

nodosity *s.* nodosità.

nodular *agg.* a forma di nodo.

nodule *s.* nodulo.

noise *s.* rumore, fragore, chiasso.

noiseless *agg.* senza rumore, silenzioso.

noisily *avv.* rumorosamente.

noisy *agg.* 1. rumoroso, turbolento 2. (*fig.*) vistoso, chiassoso.

nomad *agg.* e *s.* nomade.

nomadism *s.* nomadismo.

nomenclature *s.* nomenclatura.

nominal *agg.* nominale.

nominalism *s.* nominalismo.

nominalist *s.* nominalista.

nominalistic *agg.* nominalistico.

nominative *agg.* e *s.* nominativo.

nominator *s.* nominatore.

nonagenarian *agg.* e *s.* nonagenario.

non-aligned *agg.* non allineato.

non-alignment *s.* non allineamento.

non-appearance *s.* contumacia.

non-attendance *s.* assenza.

non-committal *agg.* evasivo.

non-conducting *agg.* isolante, non conduttore.

non-conductor *s.* isolante.

nonconformist *agg.* e *s.* anticonformista.

nonconformity *s.* anticonformismo.

non-delivery *s.* mancata consegna.

none *pron. sing.* e *pl.* nessuno, non uno. ♦ **none** *avv.* niente affatto.

nonentity *s.* 1. cosa o persona insignificante 2. inesistenza.

non-existence *s.* inesistenza.

non-resistance *s.* resistenza passiva.

nonsense *s.* assurdità, sciocchezza.

nonsensical *agg.* assurdo, sciocco.

non-stop *agg.* continuo, senza fermate. ♦ **non-stop** *avv.* di continuo, senza fermate.

non-transferable *agg.* non trasferibile.

noodle *s.* sciocco, gonzo.

nook *s.* 1. cantuccio, angolo 2. ripostiglio.

noon *s.* mezzogiorno.

noose *s.* 1. nodo scorsoio 2. tranello.

nor *cong.* né, neppure || *neither I — he*, né io né lui.

normal *agg.* 1. normale, regolare 2. perpendicolare.

normality *s.* normalità.

normalization *s.* normalizzazione.

to normalize *vt.* normalizzare.

Norman *agg.* e *s.* normanno.

normative *agg.* normativo.

north *s.* nord, settentrione || *— wind*, vento di tramontana.

north-east *s.* nord-est.

northerly *agg.* del nord, settentrionale. ♦ **northerly** *avv.* verso il nord.

northern *agg.* nordico, settentrionale.

northerner *s.* abitante del nord.

northward(s) *agg.* e *avv.* verso nord.

Norwegian *agg.* e *s.* norvegese.

nose *s.* 1. naso 2. muso (*di animali*) 3. prua (*mar.*).

to nose *vt.* e *vi.* 1. fiutare 2. indagare 3. ficcare il naso.

nostril *s.* narice.

not *avv.* non || *— at all*, niente affatto.

notability s. notabilità.

notable agg. degno di nota, notevole.

notarial agg. notarile.

notary s. notaio.

notation s. 1. (mus.) notazione 2. (mat.) numerazione.

notch s. tacca, dentellatura.

to **notch** vt. 1. intaccare 2. intagliare.

note s. 1. (mus.) nota, tono 2. marchio, segno 3. nota, appunto, commento 4. (comm.) cedola, acconto 5. banconota.

to **note** vt. notare.

notebook s. taccuino.

notehead s. intestazione.

noteless agg. privo di interesse.

noteworthiness s. importanza.

noteworthy agg. notevole.

nothing pron. indef. nulla, niente, nessuna cosa.

nothingness s. 1. il nulla 2. nullità.

notice s. 1. avviso, avvertimento 2. (giur.) intimazione 3. licenziamento 4. attenzione, cura 5. recensione || — -board, cartello pubblicitario, tabella.

to **notice** vt. 1. osservare, fare attenzione a 2. recensire.

noticeable agg. notevole.

notifiable agg. da denunciarsi.

notification s. notifica.

to **notify** vt. notificare; far sapere.

notion s. 1. nozione 2. idea, teoria.

notional agg. 1. immaginario 2. speculativo.

notoriety s. notorietà.

notorious agg. 1. noto, conosciuto 2. famigerato.

notoriously avv. notoriamente.

notwithstanding prep. nonostante, malgrado.

nougat s. torrone.

nought s. 1. nulla 2. (mat.) zero.

noumenon s. (pl. -ena) noumeno.

noun s. (gramm.) nome, sostantivo.

to **nourish** vt. nutrire (anche fig.).

nourishing agg. nutriente.

nourishment s. nutrimento.

novel s. romanzo.

novelist s. romanziere.

to **novelize** vt. romanzare.

novelty s. novità.

November s. novembre.

novice s. 1. (eccl.) novizio 2. apprendista.

novitiate s. noviziato.

now avv. 1. ora, adesso, subito, al presente 2. allora 3. a dire il vero. ♦ **now** cong. ora che. ♦ **now** s. ora, il presente.

nowadays avv. al giorno d'oggi.

nowhere avv. in nessun luogo.

noxious agg. nocivo, dannoso.

nozzle s. becco, beccuccio (di teiera, pompa ecc.).

nuclear agg. nucleare.

nuclein s. nucleina.

nucleonics s. pl. fisica nucleare.

nucleus s. (pl. -ei) 1. nucleo 2. nocciolo, centro.

nude agg. 1. nudo 2. (fig.) semplice. ♦ **nude** s. (pitt.; scult.) nudo.

nudism s. nudismo.

nudist agg. e s. nudista.

nugget s. pepita.

nuisance s. 1. noia, seccatura 2. danno.

null agg. nullo.

nullification s. annullamento.

to **nullify** vt. annullare.

nullity s. 1. nullità 2. il non essere valido.

numb agg. 1. intorpidito, intirizzito 2. tramortito, intontito.

to **numb** vt. 1. intorpidire, intirizzire 2. (fig.) istupidire.

number s. 1. numero, cifra 2. numero, quantità 3. numero di giornale.

to **number** vt. 1. contare, numerare 2. annoverare 3. ammontare.

numberless agg. innumerevole.

numbness s. torpore (anche fig.).

numerable agg. numerabile, calcolabile.

numeral agg. e s. numerale.

numerator s. numeratore.

numerical agg. numerico.

numerically avv. numericamente.

numerous agg. numeroso.

numismatic agg. numismatico.

numismatics s. numismatica.

numismatist s. numismatico.

numismatology s. numismatica.

nun s. 1. monaca, suora 2. piccione dal cappuccio.

nuncio s. (eccl.) nunzio.

nunnery s. convento (di suore).

nuptial agg. nuziale.

nuptials s. pl. nozze, sponsali.

nurse s. 1. nutrice, balia 2. infermiera.

to **nurse** vt. 1. allattare, nutrire 2. allevare 3. curare (ammalati).

nursling s. lattante.

nursery *s.* **1.** camera dei bambini **2.** scuola materna **3.** vivaio || — *rhyme,* filastrocca per bambini.

nursing *agg.* **1.** che allatta, nutre **2.** che cura || — *home,* casa di cura. ♦ **nursing** *s.* **1.** allattamento **2.** il curare **3.** professione di infermiera.

nurture *s.* vitto, nutrimento.

to nurture *vt.* nutrire, allevare.

nut *s.* **1.** noce **2.** (*mecc.*) dado.

nutcracker *s.* schiaccianoci.

nutmeg *s.* noce moscata.

nutrition *s.* nutrizione.

nutritive *agg.* nutritivo.

nutshell *s.* guscio di noce.

nylon *s.* nailon.

nymph *s.* ninfa.

O

oak *s.* quercia.

oakum *s.* stoppa.

oar *s.* remo || — *blade,* pala di remo.

to oar *vi.* remare.

oarsman *s.* rematore.

oasis *s.* (*pl.* -ses) oasi.

oats *s. pl.* avena (*sing.*).

oath *s.* **1.** giuramento **2.** bestemmia.

obduracy *s.* **1.** inesorabilità **2.** ostinazione.

obdurate *agg.* **1.** inesorabile **2.** ostinato.

obedience *s.* ubbidienza.

obedient *agg.* ubbidiente.

obeisance *s.* riverenza.

obelisk *s.* obelisco.

obese *agg.* obeso.

obesity *s.* obesità.

to obey *vt. e vi.* ubbidire.

to obfuscate *vt.* **1.** offuscare **2.** confondere.

obituary *s.* necrologio.

object *s.* oggetto.

to object *vt. e vi.* obiettare.

objectification *s.* oggettivazione.

to objectify *vt.* oggettivare.

objection *s.* **1.** obiezione **2.** avversione.

objectionable *agg.* **1.** biasimevole **2.** sgradevole.

objective *agg.* oggettivo. ♦ **objective** *s.* obiettivo.

objectiveness *s.* oggettività.

objectivism *s.* oggettivismo.

objectivity *s.* oggettività.

objector *s.* oppositore || *conscientious* —, obiettore di coscienza.

obligation *s.* obbligo.

obligatoriness *s.* obbligatorietà.

obligatory *agg.* obbligatorio.

to oblige *vt.* **1.** obbligare **2.** fare un favore a.

obliging *agg.* cortese.

oblique *agg.* obliquo.

obliqueness, obliquity *s.* obliquità.

to obliterate *vt.* cancellare.

obliteration *s.* cancellatura.

oblivion *s.* oblio || *Act of* —, amnistia.

oblivious *agg.* dimentico.

oblong *agg.* **1.** oblungo **2.** rettangolare. ♦ **oblong** *s.* (*geom.*) rettangolo.

obnoxious *agg.* odioso.

obscene *agg.* osceno.

obscenity *s.* oscenità.

obscurantism *s.* oscurantismo.

obscurantist *agg. e s.* oscurantista.

obscuration *s.* oscuramento.

obscure *agg.* oscuro. ♦ **obscure** *s.* oscurità.

to obscure *vt.* oscurare.

obscurity *s.* oscurità.

obsecration *s.* supplica.

obsequies *s. pl.* esequie.

obsequious *agg.* ossequioso.

observable *agg.* **1.** visibile **2.** notevole.

observance *s.* **1.** osservanza **2.** (*relig.*) regola.

observant *agg.* osservante.

observation *s.* osservazione.

observatory *s.* osservatorio.

to observe *vt. e vi.* osservare.

observer *s.* osservatore.

observing *agg.* attento.

to obsess *vt.* ossessionare.

obsession *s.* ossessione.

obsessive *agg.* ossessivo.

obsolescence *s.* disuso.

obsolescent *agg.* che sta cadendo in disuso.

obsolete *agg.* **1.** antiquato **2.** scaduto (*di prezzi*).

obstacle *s.* ostacolo.

obstetric(al) *agg.* ostetrico.

obstetrician *s.* ostetrico.

obstetrics *s.* ostetricia.

obstinacy *s.* ostinazione.

obstinate *agg.* ostinato.

to obstruct *vt.* **1.** ostruire **2.** ritardare 3. intasare.

obstruction s. ostruzione, ostacolo.

obstructionism s. ostruzionismo.

obstructionist s. ostruzionista.

to obtain vt. ottenere. ♦ **to obtain** vi. prevalere.

obtainable agg. ottenibile.

to obtrude vt. imporre. ♦ **to obtrude** vi. 1. imporsi 2. intromettersi.

obtruder s. 1. intruso 2. importuno.

obtrusion s. intrusione.

obtrusive agg. 1. intruso 2. importuno.

obtrusiveness s. 1. intrusione 2. invadenza.

to obtund vt. ottundere.

obtundent agg. ottundente.

to obturate vt. otturare.

obturation s. otturazione.

obturator s. otturatore.

obtuse agg. 1. ottuso 2. sordo.

obtuseness s. ottusità.

to obviate vt. ovviare.

obvious agg. ovvio.

obviousness s. chiarezza.

occasion s. 1. occasione 2. motivo.

occasional agg. occasionale.

occident s. occidente.

occidental agg. occidentale.

occidentalism s. occidentalismo.

to occidentalize vt. occidentalizzare.

occidentally avv. all'occidentale.

occipital agg. occipitale.

occiput s. (pl. -pita) occipite.

to occlude vt. occludere.

occlusion s. occlusione.

occlusive agg. occlusivo.

occult agg. occulto.

to occult vt. occultare. ♦ **to occult** vi. occultarsi.

occultation s. occultamento.

occultism s. occultismo.

occultist s. occultista.

occupant s. occupante.

occupation s. occupazione.

occupational agg. professionale.

occupier s. occupante.

to occupy vt. occupare: to — oneself with, occuparsi di.

to occur vi. 1. accadere 2. venire in mente 3. ricorrere.

occurrence s. avvenimento.

ocean s. oceano.

oceanic agg. oceanico.

oceanography s. oceanografia.

ocellus s. (pl. -li) ocello.

ochre s. ocra.

octagon s. ottagono.

octagonal agg. ottagonale.

octahedron s. ottaedro.

octane s. ottano.

octave s. ottava.

October s. ottobre.

octogenarian agg. e s. ottuagenario.

octonarian agg. e s. ottonario.

octonary agg. di otto in otto. ♦ **octonary** s. strofa di otto versi.

octopus s. (pl. -pi) polipo, piovra.

octosyllabic agg. ottosillabico.

octosyllable s. verso, parola di otto sillabe.

ocular agg. e s. oculare.

oculate(d) agg. maculato.

oculist s. oculista.

oculistic agg. oculistico.

odalisque s. odalisca.

odd agg. 1. dispari 2. scompagnato 3. in più 4. occasionale 5. bizzarro. ♦ **odd** s. cosa extra.

oddity, oddness s. stranezza.

odds s. pl. 1. differenza 2. disaccordo 3. pronostico || — and ends, rimanenze.

ode s. ode.

odious agg. odioso.

odontological agg. odontoiatrico.

odontologist s. odontoiatra.

odontology s. odontoiatria.

odoriferous agg. odorifero.

odorous agg. odoroso.

odour s. odore.

odourless agg. inodoro.

oedema s. edema.

oenologist s. enologo.

oenology s. enologia.

oesophagus s. (pl. -gi) esofago.

of prep. 1. di 2. (tempo) a, in 3. da parte di: very kind — you, molto gentile da parte vostra || — late, ultimamente.

off avv. 1. lontano, via 2. completamente || to be —, essere finito, fermo, in libertà. ♦ **off** prep. 1. lontano, via da 2. giù da. ♦ **off** agg. 1. destro 2. esterno 3. lontano 4. secondario 5. libero || — day, giorno di libertà.

offence s. 1. offesa 2. colpa, delitto 3. scandalo.

offenceless agg. 1. inoffensivo 2. innocente.

to offend vt. offendere. ♦ **to offend** vi. 1. peccare 2. violare la legge.

offender s. 1. peccatore 2. colpevole.

offensive *agg.* 1. offensivo 2. sgradevole. ♦ **offensive** *s.* offensiva.

offensiveness *s.* aggressività.

offer *s.* offerta.

to offer *vt.* offrire. ♦ **to offer** *vi.* offrirsi.

offerer *s.* offerente.

offering *s.* offerta.

offertory *s.* offertorio.

offhand *agg.* 1. improvvisato 2. spontaneo. ♦ **offhand** *avv.* lì per lì.

office *s.* ufficio, carica || **box-** —, botteghino.

officer *s.* ufficiale, funzionario || *non-commissioned* —, sottufficiale.

official *agg.* ufficiale. ♦ **official** *s.* funzionario.

officiant *s.* ufficiante.

to officiate *vi.* 1. esercitare le funzioni di 2. (*relig.*) ufficiare.

officious *agg.* 1. ufficioso 2. intrigante.

offing *s.* (*mar.*) largo.

offscourings *s. pl.* rifiuti, scarti.

offset *s.* 1. compenso 2. sperone (*di monte*) 3. germoglio, progenie 4. (*tip.*) fotolito.

offshoot *s.* 1. germoglio 2. ramo.

offshore *agg.* 1. di terra 2. lontano dalla costa. ♦ **offshore** *avv.* al largo.

offside *s.* (*sport*) fuori gioco.

offspring *s.* 1. prole 2. frutto.

often *avv.* spesso || *how* —?, quante volte?

ogive *s.* ogiva.

oil *s.* 1. olio 2. petrolio || — *cloth,* tela cerata; — *field,* giacimento petrolifero; — *mill,* frantoio; — *paper,* carta oleata; — *pipeline,* oleodotto.

to oil *vt.* ungere, oliare.

oiler *s.* oliatore.

oily *agg.* oleoso, untuoso.

ointment *s.* unguento.

O.K. *avv.* bene: *to be* —, andar bene.

old (**elder**, **older**; **eldest**, **oldest**) *agg.* vecchio || *how* — *are you?,* quanti anni hai?; — *-fashioned,* antiquato. ♦ **old** *s.* passato.

oldish *agg.* attempato.

oleander *s.* oleandro.

oleograph *s.* oleografia.

oleographic *agg.* oleografico.

olfactory *agg.* olfattivo.

oligarch *s.* oligarca.

oligarchic(al) *agg.* oligarchico.

oligarchy *s.* oligarchia.

olive *agg.* 1. d'oliva 2. olivastro. ♦ **olive** *s.* 1. oliva 2. (*-tree*) olivo.

Olympiad *s.* olimpiade.

Olympian *agg.* olimpico, olimpionico. ♦ **Olympian** *s.* olimpionico.

Olympic *agg.* V. *Olympian*.

omelet(te) *s.* frittata.

omen *s.* auspicio.

ominous *agg.* di cattivo augurio.

omission *s.* omissione.

to omit *vt.* omettere.

omnipotence *s.* onnipotenza.

omnipotent *agg.* e *s.* onnipotente.

omnipresent *agg.* onnipresente.

omniscience *s.* onniscienza.

omniscient *agg.* e *s.* onnisciente.

omnivorous *agg.* onnivoro.

on *prep.* 1. su 2. a, in, di, per || *on purpose,* apposta. ♦ **on** *avv.* 1. su, indosso 2. (in) avanti || *to be* —, essere in funzione, essere rappresentato; *and so* —, eccetera.

once *avv.* una volta || *at* —, subito; *all at* —, improvvisamente. ♦ **once** *cong.* una volta che.

on-coming *agg.* prossimo.

one *agg.* 1. uno 2. uno solo. ♦ **one** *pron.* 1. (*dimostr.*) questo, quello 2. (*indef.*) (l') uno || — *by* —, uno a uno. ♦ **one** *s.* uno || — *John Brown,* un certo John Brown.

one-eyed *agg.* guercio.

oneness *s.* unità, unicità.

onerous *agg.* oneroso.

oneself *pron. r.* se stesso.

one-sided *agg.* unilaterale.

one-sidely *avv.* unilateralmente.

oneway *agg.* a senso unico.

ongoings *s. pl.* avvenimenti.

onion *s.* cipolla || *spring-* —, cipollina.

onlooker *s.* spettatore.

only *agg.* e *avv.* solo.

onomastic *agg.* onomastico.

onomatopoeia *s.* onomatopea.

onomatopoeic *agg.* onomatopeico.

onset *s.* 1. attacco 2. inizio.

onto *prep.* su, in cima a.

ontological *agg.* ontologico.

ontology *s.* ontologia.

onus *s.* onere.

onward *agg.* avanzato.

onward(s) *avv.* avanti.

onyx *s.* onice.

to ooze *vt.* e *vi.* stillare || *to* — *out,* trapelare.

oozy *agg.* melmoso.

opacity *s.* opacità.

opal s. opale.

opalescent agg. opalescente.

opaque agg. opaco.

open agg. aperto || — wide —, spalancato; in the — air, all'aperto.

to open vt. aprire. ♦ **to open** vi. aprirsi.

open-handed agg. generoso.

opening s. 1. apertura 2. radura.

openly avv. apertamente.

open-minded agg. di larghe vedute.

open-mindedness s. larghezza di vedute.

openness s. 1. apertura 2. franchezza.

opera s. opera lirica || — -house, teatro dell'opera; — glass, binocolo.

to operate vt. 1. operare 2. far funzionare 3. gestire. ♦ **to operate** vi. 1. operare 2. funzionare.

operatic agg. di opera.

operation s. 1. operazione 2. funzionamento 3. azione.

operative agg. 1. attivo 2. operatono, operaio (meccanico). — sentenza. ♦ **operative** s. artigianista, telegrafista.

operator s. 1. operatore 2. telefonio || — part, dispositivo di una

ophthalmia s. oftalmia.

ophthalmic agg. oftalmico.

ophthalmology s. oftalmologia, oculistica.

ophthalmoscopy s. oftalmoscopia.

opiate agg. 1. oppiato 2. soporifero. ♦ **opiate** s. narcotico.

opinion s. opinione.

opinionated, opinionative agg. ostinato.

opium s. oppio.

opponent s. avversario.

opportune agg. opportuno.

opportunism s. opportunismo.

opportunist s. opportunista.

opportunist(ic) agg. opportunistico.

opportunity s. occasione.

opposable agg. opponibile.

to oppose vt. opporre. ♦ **to oppose** vi. opporsi.

opposed agg. 1. opposto 2. ostile.

opposer s. oppositore.

opposite agg. e s. opposto. ♦ **opposite** avv. di fronte. ♦ **opposite** prep. di fronte a, dirimpetto a.

opposition s. opposizione.

to oppress vt. opprimere.

oppression s. oppressione.

oppressive agg. opprimente.

oppressor s. oppressore.

opprobrious agg. obbrobrioso.

to opt vi. optare.

optic(al) agg. ottico.

optician s. ottico.

optics s. ottica.

optimism s. ottimismo.

optimist agg. e s. ottimista.

optimistic(al) agg. ottimistico.

option s. opzione.

optional agg. facoltativo.

opulence s. opulenza.

opulent agg. opulento.

or cong. o, oppure || either... —, sia... sia.

oracle s. oracolo.

oracular agg. profetico.

oral agg. e s. orale.

orange s. 1. arancia 2. arancio.

orangeade s. aranciata.

orangery s. aranceto.

oration s. discorso.

orator s. oratore.

oratorical agg. oratorio.

oratory[1] s. oratorio.

oratory[2] s. oratoria.

orb s. 1. cerchio 2. sfera.

orbit s. orbita.

orbital agg. orbitale.

orchard s. frutteto.

orchestra s. orchestra.

orchestral agg. orchestrale.

to orchestrate vt. orchestrare.

orchestration s. orchestrazione.

orchid, orchis s. orchidea.

to ordain vt. ordinare (anche eccl.).

ordeal s. 1. ordalia 2. dura prova.

order s. 1. ordine 2. classe || in — that, affinché; in — to, allo scopo di; postal —, vaglia postale; made to —, eseguito su ordinazione. ♦ **orders** s. pl. (relig.) ordini: to take —, farsi prete.

to order vt. 1. ordinare 2. riordinare.

ordering s. ordinamento.

orderly agg. ordinato. ♦ **orderly** s. 1. (mil.) ordinanza 2. (mil.) attendente.

ordinal agg. e s. ordinale.

ordinance s. 1. ordinanza 2. (relig.) rito.

ordinary agg. ordinario. ♦ **ordinary** s. 1. condizione ordinaria 2. pranzo a prezzo fisso.

ordinate s. ordinata.

ordination *s.* **1.** ordine **2.** (*relig.*) ordinazione.

ore *s.* minerale.

organ *s.* organo || barrel— —, organetto; mouth— —, armonica.

organic *agg.* organico.

organism *s.* organismo.

organist *s.* organista.

organizable *agg.* organizzabile.

organization *s.* organizzazione.

to organize *vt.* organizzare. ♦ **to organize** *vi.* organizzarsi.

organizer *s.* organizzatore.

organzine *s.* organzino.

orgasm *s.* orgasmo.

orgeat *s.* orzata.

orgiastic *agg.* orgiastico.

orgy *s.* orgia.

orient *s.* oriente.

to orient *vt.* **1.** orientare **2.** volgere verso oriente.

oriental *agg. e s.* orientale.

orientalist *s.* orientalista.

orientation *s.* orientamento.

orifice *s.* orifizio.

origan *s.* origano.

origin *s.* origine.

original *agg. e s.* originale.

originality *s.* originalità.

originally *avv.* **1.** originalmente **2.** originariamente.

to originate *vt.* dare origine. ♦ **to originate** *vi.* aver origine.

originator *s.* iniziatore.

ornament *s.* ornamento.

ornamental *agg.* ornamentale.

ornamentation *s.* decorazione.

ornate *agg.* ornato.

ornithological *agg.* ornitologico.

ornithologist *s.* ornitologo.

ornithology *s.* ornitologia.

orographic(al) *agg.* orografico.

orography *s.* orografia.

orphan *agg. e s.* orfano.

orphanage *s.* **1.** la condizione di orfano **2.** orfanotrofio.

orthodox *agg.* ortodosso.

orthodoxy *s.* ortodossia.

orthogonal *agg.* ortogonale.

orthographic(al) *agg.* **1.** ortografico **2.** ortogonale.

orthography *s.* **1.** ortografia **2.** (*geom.*) proiezione ortogonale.

ortho(p)(a)edic(al) *agg.* ortopedico.

ortho(p)(a)edics *s.* ortopedia.

ortho(p)(a)edist *s.* ortopedico.

to oscillate *vi.* oscillare.

oscillation *s.* oscillazione.

oscillator *s.* oscillatore.

oscillatory *agg.* oscillatorio.

oscillograph *s.* oscillografo.

osier *s.* vimine.

osmose, osmosis *s.* osmosi.

osseous *agg.* osseo.

ossification *s.* ossificazione.

to ossify *vt.* ossificare. ♦ **to ossify** *vi.* ossificarsi.

ostensible *agg.* apparente.

ostensory *s.* ostensorio.

ostentation *s.* ostentazione.

ostentatious *agg.* ostentato.

osteological *agg.* osteologico.

osteology *s.* osteologia.

ostracism *s.* ostracismo.

to ostracize *vt.* dare l'ostracismo a.

ostrich *s.* struzzo.

other *agg. e pron.* altro || each —, l'un l'altro; every — day, un giorno no sì e un giorno no. ♦ **others** *pron. pl.* altri || some... —..., gli uni... gli altri.

otherwise *agg.* diverso. ♦ **otherwise** *avv.* altrimenti.

otherworld *s.* mondo ultraterreno.

otitis *s.* otite.

otorhinolaryngologist *s.* otorinolaringoiatra.

otter *s.* lontra.

Ottoman *agg. e s.* ottomano.

ought *s.* zero.

ought *v. dif.* (*condiz.*) dovere: you — to wait, dovresti aspettare.

ounce *s.* oncia.

our *agg. poss.* nostro, nostra, nostri, nostre.

ours *pron. poss.* il nostro, la nostra, i nostri, le nostre.

ourselves *pron. r. pl.* noi stessi.

out *agg.* esterno. ♦ **out** *avv.* fuori. ♦ **out** (*of*) *prep.* **1.** fuori (*di*) **2.** senza **3.** per || — -of-date, fuori moda; — -of-work, disoccupato; — -of-the-way, remoto.

to outbid (**outbade, outbidden**) *vt.* offrire di più.

outboard *agg. e avv.* fuoribordo.

outbreak *s.* **1.** scoppio **2.** sommossa.

outburst *s.* scoppio.

outcast *s.* proscritto.

to outclass *vt.* surclassare.

outcome *s.* risultato.

outcry *s.* grido, scalpore.

outdid V. to outdo.

to outdistance *vt.* distanziare.

to outdo (**outdid, outdone**) *vt.* superare.

outdoor *agg.* all'aperto.

outdoors *avv.* all'aperto.

outer *agg.* esteriore.

outfit(ting) *s.* equipaggiamento.

to outfit *vt.* rifornire di equipaggiamento. ♦ **to outfit** *vi.* rifornirsi di equipaggiamento.

outfitter *s.* fornitore.

to outfly (outflew, outflown) *vt.* sorpassare nel volo.

outgone V. *to outgo.*

outgo *s.* uscita.

to outgo (outwent, outgone) *vt.* sorpassare.

outgoing *agg.* uscente, in partenza.

to outgrow (outgrew, outgrown) *vt.* **1.** diventare troppo grande per **2.** sorpassare *(in statura).*

outgrowth *s.* **1.** escrescenza **2.** risultato.

outhouse *s.* **1.** tettoia **2.** dipendenza.

outing *s.* escursione ‖ — *clothes*, abiti sportivi.

outlandish *agg.* **1.** strano **2.** remoto.

outlaw *s.* fuorilegge.

outlawry *s.* (*giur.*) proscrizione.

outlay *s.* spesa.

outlet *s.* **1.** sbocco **2.** cortile.

outline *s.* **1.** contorno **2.** schema **3.** lineamento.

to outline *vt.* **1.** delineare **2.** abbozzare.

outliner *s.* bozzettista.

to outlive *vt.* sopravvivere a.

outlook *s.* **1.** veduta **2.** prospettiva **3.** vigilanza.

to outnumber *vt.* superare numericamente.

outpost *s.* avamposto.

outpour *s.* **1.** scroscio di pioggia **2.** (*fig.*) sfogo.

output *s.* produzione, rendimento.

outrage *s.* oltraggio.

to outrage *vt.* oltraggiare.

outrageous *agg.* **1.** oltraggioso **2.** violento.

outrageousness *s.* **1.** oltraggio **2.** violenza.

outran V. *to outrun.*

to outrange *vt.* avere una portata maggiore di.

to outreach *vt.* sorpassare.

outrider *s.* battistrada.

outright *agg.* **1.** franco **2.** completo. ♦ **outright** *avv.* **1.** francamente **2.** completamente.

outrightness *s.* **1.** immediatezza **2.** franchezza.

outroar *s.* fracasso.

to outrun (outran, outrun) *vt.* oltrepassare.

outrush *s.* fuga.

to outsell (outsold, outsold) *vt.* **1.** vendere in quantità superiore **2.** vendere a prezzo superiore.

outset *s.* esordio.

to outshine (outshone, outshone) *vt.* eclissare (*anche fig.*).

outside *agg.* e *s.* **1.** esterno **2.** massimo. ♦ **outside** *avv.* **1.** all'esterno **2.** all'aperto. ♦ **outside** *prep.* fuori di.

outsider *s.* **1.** profano **2.** es[...]neo **3.** (*sport*) non favorito.

outsize *agg.* fuori misura. ♦ **outsize** *s.* taglia fuori misura.

outskirt *s.* orlo. ♦ **outskirts** *s. pl.* periferia (*sing.*).

outsold V. *to outsell.*

outspoken *agg.* franco.

to outspread (outspread, outspread) *vt.* spiegare. ♦ **to outspread (outspread, outspread)** *vi.* spiegarsi.

outstanding *agg.* **1.** prominente **2.** resistente **3.** in sospeso.

to outstretch *vt.* distendere.

to outstrip *vt.* superare (*in velocità*).

outward *agg.* e *s.* esterno. ♦ **outward(s)** *avv.* esternamente.

outwent V. *to outgo.*

oval *agg.* e *s.* ovale.

ovary *s.* ovaia.

ovation *s.* ovazione.

oven *s.* forno.

over *avv.* **1.** di sopra **2.** eccessivamente ‖ *to be* —, essere finito; — *and* — *again*, più e più volte. ♦ **over** *prep.* **1.** su **2.** più di **3.** durante ‖ — *there*, dall'altra parte; — *and above*, oltre a.

overalls *s. pl.* tuta da lavoro (*sing.*).

overate V. *to overeat.*

to overbear (overbore, overborne) *vt.* dominare, sopraffare.

overbearing *agg.* imperioso.

overbearingness *s.* imperiosità.

overboard *avv.* in mare.

overbore V. *to overbear.*

overborne V. *to overbear.*

to overburden *vt.* sovraccaricare.

overcame V. *to overcome.*

overcast *agg.* scuro, nuvoloso.

to overcast (overcast, overcast) *vt.* oscurare. ♦ **to overcast (overcast, overcast)** *vi.* oscurarsi.

overcharge s. 1. sovraccarico 2. sovrapprezzo.

to overcharge vt. 1. sovraccaricare 2. far pagare troppo caro.

to overcloud vi. rannuvolarsi.

overcoat s. soprabito.

to overcome (overcame, overcome) vt. superare, vincere.

overcoming s. superamento, vittoria.

overconfident agg. troppo sicuro di sé.

overcredulity s. credulità eccessiva.

overcrowded agg. sovraffollato.

overcrowding s. sovraffollamento.

to overdo (overdid, overdone) vt. 1. esagerare 2. stancare.

overdone agg. troppo cotto.

overdose s. dose eccessiva.

overdrank V. to overdrink.

to overdraw (overdrew, overdrawn) vt. 1. esagerare 2. scoprire il conto in banca.

to overdrink (overdrank, overdrunk) vi. bere troppo.

overdue agg. scaduto.

to overeat (overate, overeaten) vi. mangiare troppo.

to overestimate vt. sopravvalutare.

overexcitability s. sovreccitabilità.

overexcitable agg. sovreccitabile.

to overexcite vt. sovreccitare.

overexcitement s. sovreccitazione.

to overexert vt. stancare.

to overexpose vt. sovresporre.

overfeeding s. superalimentazione.

overflow V. to overfly.

to overflow vt. inondare. ♦ to overflow vi. traboccare.

overflowing s. inondazione.

to overfly (overflew, overflown) vt. 1. sorvolare 2. superare in volo.

overfond agg. troppo appassionato.

to overgrow (overgrew, overgrown) vt. 1. coprire 2. superare. ♦ to overgrow (overgrew, overgrown) vi. 1. coprirsi 2. crescere troppo.

overgrowth s. 1. crescita eccessiva 2. vegetazione sovrabbondante.

overhang s. sporgenza, aggetto.

to overhang (overhung, overhung) vt. 1. sovrastare 2. ornare con tendaggi ecc.

to overhaul vt. 1. revisionare 2. sorpassare.

overhaul(ing) s. revisione.

overheard agg. 1. alto 2. (comm.) generale. ♦ overhead avv. in alto.

to overhear (overheard, overheard) vt. 1. udire per caso 2. origliare.

to overheat vt. surriscaldare. ♦ to overheat vi. surriscaldarsi.

overheating s. surriscaldamento.

overhung V. to overhang.

overindulgence s. eccessiva indulgenza.

overladen agg. sovraccarico.

overland avv. via terra.

overlap s. sovrapposizione.

overlay s. copertura.

to overleap vt. saltare di là da.

overload s. sovraccarico.

to overload vt. sovraccaricare.

to overlook vt. 1. guardare dall'alto 2. trascurare 3. ispezionare.

overlooker s. ispettore.

overnight agg. 1. compiuto durante la notte 2. per una notte. ♦ overnight avv. durante la notte.

overpaid V. to overpay.

to overpass vt. 1. attraversare 2. sorpassare 3. trasgredire.

overpast agg. passato.

to overpay (overpaid, overpaid) vt. pagare più del dovuto.

overpayment s. pagamento eccessivo.

overpeopled agg. sovrappopolato.

overplus s. soprappiù.

overpopulated agg. sovrappopolato.

overpopulation s. sovrappopolazione.

to overpower V. to overbear.

overpowering agg. 1. schiacciante 2. prepotente.

overpressure s. sovrapressione.

to overprint vt. sovrastampare.

to overprize vt. sopravvalutare.

to overproduce vt. produrre in eccesso.

overproduction s. sovraproduzione.

overproud agg. troppo orgoglioso.

overran V. to overrun.

to overrate vt. sopravvalutare.

to overreach vt. 1. oltrepassare 2. imbrogliare.

to overrule vt. 1. dirigere 2. annullare 3. dominare.

to overrun (overran, overrun) vt. 1. invadere 2. devastare 3. oltrepassare.

oversaw V. *to oversee.*
oversea(s) *agg. e avv.* d'oltremare.
to oversee (oversaw, overseen) *vt.* ispezionare.
overseer *s.* 1. ispettore 2. capo squadra.
to overset (overset, overset) *vt.* rovesciare. ♦ **to overset (overset, overset)** *vi.* rovesciarsi.
to overshadow *vt.* 1. ombreggiare 2. adombrare 3. proteggere.
overshoe *s.* soprascarpa.
to overshoot (overshot, overshot) *vt.* lanciare di là da || **to — the mark,** passare i limiti.
overside *avv.* lungo il fianco.
oversight *s.* 1. svista 2. sorveglianza.
to oversleep (overslept, overslept) *vi.* dormire oltre l'ora fissata.
to overspread (overspread, over-re. ♦ **to overspread (overspread, overspread)** *vi.* spargersi.
to overstate *vt.* esagerare.
to overtake (overtook, overtaken) *vt.* 1. cogliere 2. superare.
overtaking *s.* sorpasso: **no —,** divieto di sorpasso.
overthrew V. *to overthrow.*
overthrow *s.* 1. rovesciamento 2. disfatta.
to overthrow (overthrew, overthrown) *vt.* 1. rovesciare 2. sconfiggere.
overtime *s.* straordinario (*orario di lavoro*).
overtook V. *to overtake.*
to overturn V. *to overthrow.*
overturnable *agg.* rovesciabile.
overturn(ing) *s.* rovesciamento.
overweary *agg.* stremato.
overweight *agg.* che supera il peso. ♦ **overweight** *s.* sovraccarico.
to overwhelm *vt.* 1. sommergere 2. sopraffare.
overwhelming *agg.* schiacciante.
overwork *s.* 1. lavoro eccessivo 2. straordinario.
to overwork *vt.* 1. far lavorare troppo 2. far eccessivo uso di. ♦ **to overwork** *vi.* lavorare troppo.
to overwrite (overwrote, overwritten) *vi.* scrivere troppo.
overwrought *agg.* 1. esausto 2. ricercato (*di stile*).
ovine *agg.* ovino.
oviparous *agg.* oviparo.

ovulation *s.* ovulazione.
ovule *s.* ovulo.
to owe *vt.* dovere, essere debitore di || **you must pay what is owing,** dovete pagare il vostro debito.
owing *agg.* dovuto.
owing to *prep.* a causa di.
owl *s.* gufo.
own *agg. e pron.* proprio.
to own *vt.* 1. possedere 2. ammettere || **to — to,** confessare.
owner *s.* proprietario || **shipowner,** armatore.
ownership *s.* proprietà.
ox (*pl.* oxen) *s.* bue.
oxidation *s.* ossidazione.
oxide *s.* ossido.
oxidizable *agg.* ossidabile.
to oxidize *vt.* ossidare. ♦ **to oxidize** *vi.* ossidarsi.
oxygen *s.* ossigeno || **— tent,** tenda ad ossigeno.
to oxygenate *vt.* ossigenare.
oxygenation *s.* ossigenazione.
to oxygenize *vt.* ossigenare.
oxyhydrogen *agg.* ossidrico: **— blowpipe,** cannello ossidrico.
oyster *s.* 1. ostrica 2. persona silenziosa, riservata.
ozone *s.* ozono.
to ozonize *vt.* ozonizzare.

P

pace *s.* passo.
to pace *vi.* andare al passo. ♦ **to pace** *vt.* percorrere. ♦ **to pace** *vi.* andare al passo, marciare.
paced *agg.* misurato (*a passi*) || **slow—,** a passi lenti.
pachyderm *s.* pachiderma.
pacific *agg.* pacifico.
to pacificate *vt.* pacificare.
pacification *s.* pacificazione.
pacificator, pacifier *s.* pacificatore.
pacificatory *agg.* conciliante.
pacifism *s.* pacifismo.
pacifist *agg. e s.* pacifista.
to pacify *vt.* pacificare.
pack *s.* 1. pacco, balla, fagotto 2. carico 3. imballaggio 4. muta (*di cani*) 5. (*med.*) impacco || **— -ice,** banchisa; **— -saddle,** basto.
to pack *vt.* 1. impacchettare 2. im-

ballare 3. raggruppare. ◆ to **pack**
vi. raggrupparsi ‖ *to — up*, fare
i bagagli.
package *s.* 1. imballaggio 2. pacco.
to **package** *vt.* 1. imballare 2. impacchettare.
packer *s.* 1. imballatore 2. impacchettatrice (*macchina*).
packet *s.* 1. pacchetto 2. (*mar.*) —
(*-boat*), postale.
packing *s.* 1. imballaggio 2. (*mecc.*)
guarnizione 3. (*mar.*) baderna ‖
— *-free*, franco d'imballaggio. ‖
pact *s.* patto.
pad[1] *s.* 1. imbottitura 2. zampa (*di*
cane, lupo, volpe) 3. (*med.*) tampone.
pad[2] *s.* rumore sordo.
to **pad** *vt.* imbottire.
paddle *s.* 1. pala 2. pagaia.
to **paddle** *vi.* remare con pagaie.
paddy *s.* risaia.
padlock *s.* lucchetto.
to **padlock** *vt.* chiudere con lucchetto.
paediatric *agg.* pediatrico.
paediatrician *s.* pediatra.
paediatrics *s.* pediatria.
paediatrist *s.* pediatra.
pagan *agg.* e *s.* pagano.
paganism *s.* paganesimo.
page[1] *s.* paggio.
page[2] *s.* pagina.
to **page** *vt.* 1. (*tip.*) impaginare 2.
numerare le pagine.
pageant *s.* 1. (*teat.*) scena (*di sa-*
cra rappresentazione) 2. parata,
corteo.
pageantry *s.* 1. pompa, fasto 2.
ostentazione.
to **paginate** *vt.* V. *to page*.
pagination *s.* 1. paginatura 2. impaginazione.
paid V. *to pay*.
pail *s.* secchio.
paillasse *s.* pagliericcio.
pain *s.* 1. pena 2. dolore, sofferenza.
◆ **pains** *s. pl.* doglie.
to **pain** *vt.* far male, far soffrire.
painful *agg.* penoso.
painless *agg.* indolore.
painstaking *agg.* diligente. ◆
painstaking *s.* cura.
paint *s.* 1. pittura 2. belletto.
to **paint** *vt.* dipingere. ◆ to **paint**
vi. imbellettarsi.
painter *s.* 1. pittore 2. imbianchino.
painting *s.* 1. pittura 2. dipinto,
quadro.

paintress *s.* pittrice.
pair *s.* paio, coppia.
to **pair** *vt.* accoppiare. ◆ to **pair**
vi. accoppiarsi.
palace *s.* palazzo.
paladin *s.* paladino.
palatable *agg.* 1. gustoso 2. (*fig.*)
gradevole.
palatal *agg.* e *s.* palatale.
palatalization *s.* palatalizzazione.
palate *s.* palato.
pale[1] *agg.* pallido.
pale[2] *s.* 1. palo 2. palizzata.
to **pale** *vt.* far impallidire. ◆ to
pale *vi.* impallidire.
paleness *s.* pallore.
paleochristian *agg.* paleocristiano.
paleographer *s.* paleografo.
paleography *s.* paleografia.
paleolithic *agg.* paleolitico.
paleologist *s.* paleologo.
paleology *s.* paleologia.
paleontologic(al) *agg.* paleontologico.
paleontologist *s.* paleontologo.
paleontology *s.* paleontologia.
paleozoic *agg.* paleozoico.
palette *s.* tavolozza.
palfrey *s.* palafreno.
palinode *s.* palinodia.
palisade *s.* palizzata.
pall *s.* 1. drappo funebre 2. (*eccl.*)
pallio.
to **pall**[1] *vt.* coprire con un drappo.
to **pall**[2] *vt.* saziare. ◆ to **pall** *vi.*
saziarsi.
pallet[1] *s.* pagliericcio.
pallet[2] *s.* 1. paletta 2. tavolozza.
to **palliate** *vt.* 1. attenuare 2. scusare.
palliation *s.* 1. attenuazione 2. scusante.
palliative *agg.* e *s.* palliativo.
pallid *agg.* pallido.
pallor *s.* pallore.
palm[1] *s.* palma (*anche fig.*).
palm[2] *s.* (*anat.*) palmo.
to **palm** *vt.* toccare con la mano.
palmaceous *agg.* (*bot.*) di palma.
palmar *agg.* palmare.
palmate, palmated, *agg.* palmato.
palmiped *agg.* e *s.* palmipede.
palmistry *s.* chiromanzia.
palmy *agg.* 1. coperto di palme 2.
prosperoso, vittorioso.
palpability *s.* palpabilità.
palpable *agg.* palpabile.
to **palpate** *vt.* palpare.
to **palpitate** *vi.* palpitare.

palpitation *s.* palpitazione.
palsy *s.* paralisi.
to palsy *vt.* paralizzare.
to palter *vi.* tergiversare.
paltriness *s.* meschinità.
paltry *agg.* meschino.
to pamper *vt.* viziare.
pamphlet *s.* opuscolo.
pamphleteer *s.* autore di opuscoli.
pan *s.* 1. padella 2. vaschetta 3. bacino 4. piatto di bilancia || *baking* —, teglia.
pancake *s.* frittella.
panchromatic *agg.* pancromatico.
pancreatic *agg.* pancreatico.
pandemonium *s.* pandemonio.
pander *s.* mezzano, ruffiano.
to pander *vi.* fare il mezzano.
pane *s.* 1. lastra di vetro 2. (*edil.*) pannello 3. faccia (*di brillante*).
panegyric *s.* panegirico.
panegyric(al) *agg.* laudativo.
panel *s.* 1. pannello 2. (*neol.*) commissione, comitato 3. (*giur.*) lista di giurati.
pang *s.* 1. fitta 2. (*fig.*) stretta al cuore.
panic *agg.* e *s.* panico.
panicky *agg.* allarmato.
panicle *s.* pannocchia.
panification *s.* panificazione.
pannier *s.* paniere.
panoramic *agg.* panoramico.
pansy *s.* viola del pensiero.
pant *s.* 1. palpito 2. ansito.
to pant *vi.* 1. palpitare 2. ansimare.
pantagruelian *agg.* pantagruelico.
pantheism *s.* panteismo.
pantheist *s.* panteista.
pantheistic(al) *agg.* panteistico.
panther *s.* pantera.
panties *s. pl.* (*fam.*) mutandine.
panting *s.* 1. palpitazione 2. ansito 3. ansia.
pantograph *s.* pantografo.
pantomime *s.* pantomima.
pantry *s.* dispensa.
pants *s. pl.* (*fam.*) mutande.
pap *s.* pappa.
papacy *s.* papato.
papal *agg.* papale.
paper *s.* 1. carta 2. prova d'esame
paper *s.* 1. carta 2. certificato, documento 3. prova d'esame 4. giornale || — *back*, libro in brossura; — *board*, cartone; — *hanger*, tappezziere; — *hanging*, tappezzeria.
to paper *vt.* 1. incartare 2. tappezzare.

papery *agg.* cartaceo.
papillary *agg.* papillare.
papism *s.* papismo.
papist *s.* papista.
papyrology *s.* papirologia.
papyrus *s.* (*pl.* -ri) papiro.
parable *s.* parabola.
parabolic(al) *agg.* 1. parabolico 2. di parabola.
paraboloid *s.* paraboloide.
parachute *s.* paracadute.
to parachute *vt.* paracadutare. ◆
to parachute *vi.* paracadutarsi.
parachutism *s.* paracadutismo.
parachutist *s.* paracadutista.
parade *s.* 1. (*mil.*) parata 2. mostra, sfoggio 3. viale, passeggiata.
to parade *vt.* disporre in parata. ◆
to parade *vi.* marciare in parata.
paradigm *s.* paradigma.
paradisaic(al) *agg.* paradisiaco.
paradise *s.* paradiso.
paradisiac(al) *agg.* paradisiaco.
paradox *s.* paradosso.
paradoxical *agg.* paradossale.
paraffin *s.* paraffina.
paragon *s.* modello (*di perfezione ecc.*).
paragraph *s.* paragrafo.
to paragraph *vt.* dividere in paragrafi.
parallel *agg.* parallelo. ◆ **parallel** *s.* 1. parallelo 2. paragone.
to parallel *vt.* 1. mettere in posizione parallela 2. paragonare.
parallelepiped *s.* parallelepipedo.
parallelism *s.* parallelismo.
parallelogram *s.* parallelogramma.
paralogism *s.* paralogismo.
to paralyse *vt.* paralizzare.
paralysis *s.* (*pl.* -ses) paralisi.
paralytic *agg.* e *s.* paralitico.
parameter *s.* parametro.
paramount *agg.* supremo. ◆ **paramount** *s.* capo supremo.
paramour *s.* amante.
paranoia *s.* paranoia.
paranoiac *agg.* e *s.* paranoico.
paranymph *s.* paraninfo.
parapet *s.* parapetto.
paraphrase *s.* parafrasi.
to paraphrase *vt.* e *vi.* parafrasare.
parasite *s.* parassita.
parasitic(al) *agg.* parassitico.
parasitism *s.* parassitismo.
parasol *s.* parasole.
paratrooper *s.* paracadutista.
paratyphoid *s.* paratifo.

parcel s. 1. pacco 2. lotto, appezzamento di terreno 3. gruppo.

to parcel vt. spartire.

parcelling s. spartizione.

parcener s. coerede.

to parch vt. 1. arrostire 2. disseccare. ♦ **to parch** vi. 1. bruciarsi 2. disseccarsi.

parchment s. pergamena.

pardon s. perdono.

to pardon vt. perdonare.

pardonable agg. perdonabile.

to pare vt. 1. tagliare 2. sbucciare.

parenchyma s. parenchima.

parent s. 1. genitore 2. causa, origine.

parentage s. 1. discendenza 2. nascita.

parental agg. paterno, materno.

parenthesis s. (pl. -ses) parentesi.

parenthetic(al) agg. parentetico.

parenthood s. paternità, maternità.

parentless agg. orfano.

paresis s. paresi.

pariah s. paria.

parietal agg. parietale.

parish s. parrocchia || — priest, parroco.

parishioner s. parrocchiano.

Parisian agg. e s. parigino.

parisyllabic agg. e s. parisillabo.

parity s. parità.

park s. 1. parco 2. posteggio.

to park vt. 1. adibire a parco 2. parcheggiare.

parking s. parcheggio || no —, divieto di sosta.

parkway s. (amer.) viale.

parley s. colloquio.

to parley vi. parlamentare.

parliament s. parlamento.

parliamentarian s. parlamentare.

parliamentarianism s. parlamentarismo.

parliamentary agg. parlamentare.

parlour s. 1. salotto 2. parlatorio || beauty —, istituto di bellezza.

Parmesan agg. parmigiano.

parochial agg. 1. parrocchiale 2. (fig.) ristretto.

parochialism s. ristrettezza di vedute.

parodist s. parodista.

parody s. parodia.

to parody vt. parodiare.

parole s. 1. parola d'onore 2. parola d'ordine.

paroxysm s. parossismo.

parricidal agg. parricida.

parricide s. 1. parricidio 2. parricida.

parrot s. pappagallo.

to parrot vt. ripetere pappagallescamente.

to parry vt. parare, schivare.

parsley s. prezzemolo.

parson s. parroco (anglicano).

parsonage s. (eccl.) canonica, parrocchia.

part s. parte. ♦ **to part** vt. dividere. ♦ **to part** vi. dividersi.

to partake (**partook, partaken**) vi. partecipare, prendere parte.

parthenogenesis s. partenogenesi.

partial agg. parziale.

partiality s. parzialità.

partially avv. parzialmente.

participant agg. e s. partecipante.

to participate vi. 1. partecipare 2. condividere.

participation s. partecipazione.

participial agg. participiale.

participle s. participio.

particle s. particella (anche gramm.).

particular agg. 1. particolare 2. particolareggiato 3. esigente. ♦ **particular** s. particolare.

particularism s. particolarismo.

particularist s. particolarista.

particularity s. 1. particolarità 2. meticolosità.

to particularize vt. e vi. dettagliare.

parting s. separazione.

partisan agg. e s. partigiano.

partition s. 1. divisione 2. tramezzo.

to partition vt. dividere.

partitive agg. e s. partitivo.

partly avv. in parte.

partner s. 1. socio 2. coniuge.

partnership s. 1. associazione 2. (comm.) società.

partook V. to partake.

partridge s. pernice.

parturient agg. partoriente.

parturition s. parto.

party s. 1. parte 2. partito 3. brigata 4. trattenimento 5. pattuglia.

pasha s. pascià.

pass¹ s. passo, gola.

pass² s. 1. passaggio 2. trapasso 3. promozione 4. lasciapassare.

to pass vt. e vi. passare || to — away, sparire; to — by, passar oltre.

passable *agg.* passabile.
passage *s.* 1. passaggio 2. corridoio 3. brano.
passementerie *s.* passamaneria.
passenger *s.* passeggero.
passer *s.* — *-by*, passante.
passible *agg.* passibile.
passing *agg.* 1. passeggero 2. casuale. ♦ **passing** *s.* passaggio.
passion *s.* passione || — *-flower*, passiflora.
passional *agg.* passionale.
passionate *agg.* appassionato, passionale.
passionless *agg.* impassibile.
passive *agg.* e *s.* passivo.
passivism, passivity *s.* passività.
passport *s.* passaporto.
password *s.* parola d'ordine.
past *agg.* passato. ♦ **past** *s.* passato. ♦ **past** *avv.* vicino. ♦ **past** *prep.* al di là di.
paste *s.* pasta || — *tooth* —, dentifricio.
to paste *vt.* 1. incollare, appiccicare 2. (*gergo*) attaccare.
pasteboard *agg.* di cartone. ♦ **pasteboard** *s.* cartone.
pastel *s.* pastello.
pasteurization *s.* pastorizzazione.
to pasteurize *vt.* pastorizzare.
pastime *s.* passatempo.
pastoral *agg.* e *s.* pastorale.
pastry *s.* dolci (*pl.*).
pasture *s.* pascolo.
to pasture *vt.* e *vi.* pascolare.
pasty *agg.* pastoso. ♦ **pasty** *s.* (*cuc.*) pasticcio.
pat *agg.* adatto. ♦ **pat** *avv.* esattamente. ♦ **pat** *s.* 1. colpetto 2. panetto di burro.
to pat *vt.* battere leggermente.
patch *s.* 1. pezza, toppa 2. macchia.
to patch *vt.* aggiustare, rattoppare, raffazzonare.
patching *s.* rattoppo.
patchy *agg.* 1. rappezzato 2. a macchie.
patent *agg.* 1. chiaro, manifesto, evidente 2. brevettato. ♦ **patent** *s.* brevetto.
to patent *vt.* brevettare.
patentee *s.* detentore di brevetto.
paternal *agg.* paterno.
paternalism *s.* paternalismo.
paternalistic *agg.* paternalistico.
paternity *s.* paternità.
path *s.* 1. sentiero 2. pista 3. percorso, traiettoria.
pathetic *agg.* patetico.
pathfinder *s.* esploratore.
pathless *agg.* 1. senza sentieri 2. inesplorato.
pathogenic *agg.* patogeno.
pathologic(al) *agg.* patologico.
pathologist *s.* patologo.
pathology *s.* patologia.
pathway *s.* sentiero.
patience *s.* pazienza.
patient *agg.* 1. paziente 2. suscettibile. ♦ **patient** *s.* paziente.
patriarch *s.* patriarca.
patriarchal *agg.* patriarcale.
patriarchate *s.* patriarcato.
patrician *agg.* e *s.* patrizio.
patricide *s.* V. *parricide*.
patrimonial *agg.* patrimoniale.
patrimony *s.* patrimonio.
patriot *s.* patriota.
patriotic *agg.* patriottico.
patriotism *s.* patriottismo.
patrol *s.* pattuglia, ronda.
to patrol *vt.* e *vi.* pattugliare, fare la ronda.
patron *s.* patrono.
patronage *s.* patronato.
patronal *agg.* patronale.
patroness *s.* patronessa.
to patronize *vt.* 1. patrocinare 2. trattare con condiscendenza.
patronizing *agg.* 1. protettivo 2. condiscendente.
patter[1] *s.* gergo.
patter[2] *s.* picchiettio.
to patter *vi.* picchiettare.
pattern *s.* 1. modello, campione 2. disegno (*di stoffa ecc.*).
to pattern *vt.* modellare (su).
paunch *s.* pancia.
pauper *s.* povero.
pauperism *s.* povertà.
pause *s.* pausa.
to pause *vi.* 1. fare una pausa 2. esitare, indugiare.
pauseless *agg.* incessante.
to pave *vt.* 1. pavimentare 2. (*fig.*) appianare.
pavement *s.* 1. pavimentazione 2. marciapiede.
paver *s.* lastricatore.
pavilion *s.* padiglione.
paving *s.* pavimentazione.
paw *s.* zampa.
to paw *vt.* dare zampate. ♦ **to paw** *vi.* scalpitare (*di cavalli*).
pawn *s.* 1. pegno 2. pedina (*di scacchi*).

to **pawn** vt. impegnare (*dare in pegno*).

pawnbroker s. prestatore su pegno.

pawnbroking s. il prestare su pegno.

pawner s. chi dà qualcosa in pegno.

pawnshop s. agenzia di prestiti su pegno.

pay s. paga.

to **pay (paid, paid)** vt. e vi. 1. pagare 2. rendere, fruttare || to — off, liquidare.

payable agg. 1. pagabile 2. redditizio.

payee s. creditore.

payer s. pagatore.

paying out s. esborso.

payment s. pagamento.

payoff s. 1. giorno di paga 2. liquidazione.

payroll s. libro paga.

pea s. pisello || *chick* —, cece.

peace s. pace.

peaceable agg. pacifico.

peaceful s. pacifico, tranquillo.

peacefulness s. pace, calma.

peaceless agg. agitato.

peacemaker s. pacificatore.

peach s. (*bot.*) pesca.

peach-tree s. pesco.

peachy agg. simile a pesca.

peacock s. pavone.

to **peacock** vi. pavoneggiarsi.

peak s. 1. picco 2. punta 3. visiera.

peaky agg. appuntito.

peal s. 1. scampanio 2. scoppio, fragore, scroscio (*di risa, applausi*).

to **peal** vi. scampanare. ♦ to **peal** vt. far rimbombare.

peanut s. arachide.

pear s. pera.

pear-tree s. pero.

pearl s. perla.

to **pearl** vt. imperlare, ornare di perle. ♦ to **pearl** vi. imperlarsi.

pearly agg. 1. perlaceo 2. ricco di perle.

peasant s. contadino.

peasantry s. 1. condizione di contadino 2. i contadini (*pl.*).

peat s. torba || — -*bog*, torbiera.

pebble s. 1. ciottolo 2. cristallo di rocca.

to **pebble** vt. coprire con ciottoli.

peccary s. pecari.

peck s. beccata.

to **peck** vt. e vi. beccare.

pectoral agg. e s. pettorale.

peculation s. peculato.

peculiar agg. 1. particolare 2. strano.

peculiarity s. 1. particolarità 2. bizzarria, eccentricità.

pecuniary agg. pecuniario.

pedagogic(al) agg. pedagogico.

pedagogics s. pedagogia.

pedagogist s. pedagogista.

pedagogue s. pedagogo.

pedagogy s. pedagogia.

pedal s. pedale.

to **pedal** vt. e vi. pedalare.

pedant s. pedante.

pedantic agg. pedante.

pedantry s. pedanteria.

pedestal s. piedistallo.

pedestrian agg. pedestre. ♦ **pedestrian** s. pedone.

pediatrics ecc. V. *paediatrics* ecc.

pediment s. (*arch.*) frontone.

pedlar s. venditore ambulante.

peel s. buccia.

to **peel** vt. sbucciare. ♦ to **peel** vi. sbucciarsi.

peeling s. buccia.

peep[1] s. 1. sguardo furtivo 2. fessura.

peep[2] s. pigolio.

to **peep**[1] vi. 1. guardare furtivamente 2. far capolino.

to **peep**[2] vi. pigolare.

peeper[1] s. ficcanaso, persona curiosa.

peeper[2] s. picciondino.

peer s. 1. pari 2. Pari, membro della Camera dei Lord.

to **peer** vt. uguagliare. ♦ to **peer** vi. 1. scrutare 2. far capolino.

peerage s. 1. i Pari 2. nobiltà.

peerless agg. senza pari.

peevish agg. irritabile.

peg s. piuolo.

to **peg** vt. fissare.

pejorative agg. e s. peggiorativo.

pelagic agg. oceanico.

pelican s. pellicano.

pellet s. 1. pallottolina (*di carta ecc.*) 2. pallottola 3. pillola.

pellucid agg. trasparente.

pelt[1] s. colpo (*di proiettile ecc.*).

pelt[2] s. pelle (*di animale*).

to **pelt** vt. colpire.

pelvic agg. pelvico.

pelvis s. bacino.

pen[1] s. penna || -*nib*, pennino; *fountain*- —, penna stilografica.

pen[2] s. recinto (*per animali*).

to **pen**[1] vt. scrivere.

to **pen**[1] vt. rinchiudere animali in un recinto.

penal *agg.* penale.
to **penalize** *vt.* (*sport.*) penalizzare.
penalty *s.* penalità, punizione.
penance *s.* penitenza.
pence *s.* V. *penny.*
pencil *s.* matita.
pendant, pendent *agg. e s.* pendente.
pending *prep.* **1.** durante **2.** fino a.
pendular *agg.* pendolare.
pendulous *agg.* pendulo.
pendulum *s.* pendolo || — *-clock,* pendola.
penetrable *agg.* penetrabile.
to **penetrate** *vt. e vi.* penetrare.
penetration *s.* penetrazione.
penetrative *agg.* penetrante.
penguin *s.* pinguino.
penicillin *s.* penicillina.
peninsula *s.* penisola.
peninsular *agg.* peninsulare.
penis *s.* pene.
penitence *s.* penitenza.
penitent *agg. e s.* penitente.
penitential *agg.* penitenziale.
penitentiary *agg.* penitenziale. ♦ **penitentiary** *s.* (*eccl.*) penitenziere **2.** riformatorio **3.** (*amer.*) penitenziario.
penknife *s.* (*pl.* -knives) temperino.
pennant *s.* (*mar.*) pennone.
penniless *agg.* senza un soldo.
pennon *s.* pennone.
penny *s.* (*numero delle monete*), **pence** (*loro valore*) *s.* "penny".
pension *s.* pensione.
to **pension** *vt.* pensionare.
pensionable *agg.* pensionabile.
pensioner *s.* pensionato.
pensive *agg.* pensoso.
pent *agg.* chiuso.
pentagon *s.* pentagono.
pentagonal *agg.* pentagonale.
pentagram *s.* pentagono.
pentahedron *s.* pentaedro.
pentameter *s.* pentametro.
pentane *s.* pentano.
pentathlon *s.* pentatlon.
Pentecost *s.* Pentecoste.
Pentecostal *agg.* pentecostale.
penthouse *s.* tettoia.
pentode *s.* (*elettr.*) pentodo.
pentose *s.* pentosio.
penult(imate) *agg. e s.* penultimo.
penury *s.* povertà.
peony *s.* peonia.
people *s.* (*costruzione al pl.*) **1.** popolo **2.** gente **3.** folla.
to **people** *vt.* popolare.

pepper *s.* pepe || — *-mill,* macina-pepe.
to **pepper** *vt.* condire con pepe.
peppercorn *s.* grano di pepe.
peppermint *s.* menta peperita.
peppery *agg.* **1.** pepato **2.** collerico.
pepsin(e) *s.* pepsina.
per *prep.* per: — *cent,* per cento.
peracid *s.* peracido.
to **perambulate** *vt.* **1.** attraversare **2.** ispezionare. ♦ to **perambulate** *vi.* passeggiare.
perambulation *s.* **1.** ispezione **2.** passeggiata.
perambulator *s.* carrozzella per bambini.
percale *s.* percalle.
perceivable *agg.* percettibile.
to **perceive** *vt.* percepire, scorgere. ♦ to **perceive** *vi.* accorgersi.
percentage *s.* percentuale.
perceptible *agg.* percettibile.
perception *s.* percezione.
perceptive *agg.* percettivo.
perch[1] *s.* gruccia.
to **perch** *vi.* appollaiarsi.
perchlorate *s.* perclorato.
percipience *s.* percezione.
to **percolate** *vt. e vi.* filtrare, colare.
percolator *s.* filtro.
percussion *s.* percussione || — *-pin,* percussore.
perdition *s.* perdizione.
perdurable *agg.* durevole.
to **peregrinate** *vi.* peregrinare.
peregrination *s.* peregrinazione.
peremptory *agg.* perentorio.
perennial *agg.* perenne.
perfect *agg.* perfetto.
to **perfect** *vt.* perfezionare.
perfectibility *s.* perfettibilità.
perfectible *agg.* perfettibile.
perfecting *s.* **1.** perfezionamento **2.** completamento.
perfection *s.* **1.** perfezione **2.** perfezionamento.
perfectionism *s.* perfezionismo.
perfectionist *s.* perfezionista.
perfectly *avv.* perfettamente.
perfidious *agg.* perfido, sleale.
perfidy *s.* perfidia, slealtà.
to **perforate** *vt.* perforare.
perforation *s.* perforazione.
to **perform** *vt.* **1.** eseguire **2.** (*teat.*) rappresentare.
performable *agg.* **1.** eseguibile **2.** rappresentabile.

performance s. 1. esecuzione 2. atto 3. (*teat.*) rappresentazione.
performer s. 1 esecutore 2. attore.
performing *agg.* ammaestrato.
perfume s. profumo.
to perfume *vt.* profumare.
perfumer s. profumiere.
perfumery s. 1. profumeria 2. profumi.
perfunctory *agg.* superficiale.
to perfuse *vt.* aspergere.
perfusion s. aspersione.
perhaps *avv.* forse.
pericardium s. pericardio.
perigee s. perigeo.
peril s. pericolo.
perilous *agg.* pericoloso.
perimeter s. perimetro.
period s. 1. periodo 2. ora di lezione 3. stadio, fase (*di una malattia*) 4. (*gramm.*) punto.
periodic *agg.* periodico.
periodical *agg.* e s. periodico.
periodicity s. periodicità.
peripheral *agg.* periferico.
periphery s. 1. perimetro 2. superficie.
periphrase, periphrasis s. (*pl.* -ses) perifrasi.
periphrastic *agg.* perifrastico.
periscope s. periscopio.
to perish *vi.* perire.
perishable *agg.* 1. deperibile 2. mortale.
perishables s. *pl.* merci deteriorabili.
peristyle s. peristilio.
peritonitis s. peritonite.
periwig s. parrucca.
periwigged *agg.* imparruccato.
periwinkle s. pervinca.
to perjure *vt.* giurare falsamente.
perjurer, perjury s. spergiuro.
permanence s. permanenza.
permanent *agg.* permanente.
permanganate s. permanganato.
permeability s. permeabilità.
permeable *agg.* permeabile.
to permeate *vt.* permeare. ♦ **to permeate** *vi.* permearsi.
permission, permit s. permesso.
to permit *vt.* e *vi.* permettere.
to permute *vt.* permutare.
pernicious *agg.* pernicioso.
to perorate *vi.* perorare.
peroration s. perorazione.
peroxid(e) s. perossido ‖ *hydrogen* —, acqua ossigenata.
to peroxide *vt.* ossigenare.

perpendicular *agg.* perpendicolare. ♦ **perpendicular** s. 1. perpendicolare 2. filo a piombo.
perpendicularity s. perpendicolarità.
to perpetrate *vt.* perpetrare.
perpetration s. perpetrazione.
perpetual *agg.* perpetuo.
to perpetuate *vt.* perpetuare.
perpetuity s. 1. perpetuità 2. rendita vitalizia.
to perplex *vt.* 1. rendere perplesso 2. complicare.
perplexed *agg.* perplesso.
perplexity s. 1. perplessità 2. complicazione.
to persecute *vt.* perseguitare.
persecution s. persecuzione.
persecutor s. persecutore.
perseverance s. perseveranza.
to persevere *vi.* perseverare.
Persian *agg.* e s. persiano.
persimmon s. (*bot.*) cachi.
to persist *vi.* persistere.
persistence s. persistenza.
persistent *agg.* persistente.
person s. persona.
personable *agg.* ben fatto.
personage s. personaggio.
personal *agg.* personale.
personality s. personalità.
personalization s. personificazione.
to personalize *vt.* personificare.
personally *avv.* personalmente.
personification s. personificazione.
to personify *vt.* personificare.
personnel s. personale.
perspective *agg.* prospettico. ♦ **perspective** s. prospettiva.
perspicacious *agg.* perspicace.
perspicacity s. perspicacia.
perspicuity s. perspicuità.
perspicuous *agg.* perspicuo.
perspiration s. traspirazione.
to perspire *vt.* e *vi.* sudare, trasudare.
to persuade *vt.* persuadere.
persuasion s. 1. persuasione 2. credenza.
persuasive *agg.* persuasivo.
pert *agg.* impertinente.
to pertain *vi.* appartenere.
pertinacious *agg.* pertinace.
pertinacy, pertinacity s. pertinacia.
pertinence s. pertinenza.
pertinent *agg.* pertinente.
pertly *avv.* insolentemente.
pertness s. insolenza.

to **perturb** *vt.* perturbare.
perturbation *s.* perturbazione.
perusal *s.* lettura attenta.
to **peruse** *vt.* leggere attentamente.
to **pervade** *vt.* pervadere.
pervasion *s.* penetrazione.
pervasive *agg.* penetrante.
perverse *agg.* **1.** perverso **2.** errato **3.** ostinato.
perversion *s.* perversione.
perversity *s.* perversità.
pervert *s.* **1.** pervertito **2.** apostata.
to **pervert** *vt.* pervertire.
pessimism *s.* pessimismo.
pessimist *s.* pessimista.
pessimistic *agg.* pessimistico.
pessimistically *avv.* in modo pessimistico.
pest *s.* peste (*anche fig.*).
to **pester** *vt.* importunare.
pestiferous *agg.* pestifero.
pestilence *s.* pestilenza.
pestilent *agg.* **1.** nocivo **2.** molesto.
pestilential *agg.* pestilenziale.
pestle *s.* pestello.
pet *agg.* e *s.* favorito || — *name*, vezzeggiativo.
to **pet** *vt.* vezzeggiare.
petal *s.* petalo.
petard *s.* petardo.
petition *s.* petizione, istanza.
to **petition** *vt.* e *vi.* fare una petizione (a).
petitioner *s.* postulante.
to **petrify** *vt.* pietrificare. ♦ to **petrify** *vi.* pietrificarsi.
petrography *s.* petrografia.
petrol *s.* benzina.
petticoat *s.* sottoveste.
pettifogger *s.* azzeccagarbugli.
petty *agg.* **1.** meschino **2.** subalterno.
petulant *agg.* petulante.
pew *s.* banco (*di chiesa*).
pewter *s.* peltro.
phagocyte *s.* fagocita.
phalanstery *s.* falansterio.
phalanx *s.* (*pl.* -ges) falange.
phallic *agg.* fallico.
phantasm *s.* fantasma.
phantasmagoria *s.* fantasmagoria.
phantasmagorial, phantasmagoric(al) *agg.* fantasmagorico.
phantom *s.* **1.** fantasma **2.** apparizione.
Pharaoh *s.* faraone.
Pharisee *s.* fariseo.
pharmaceutic(al) *agg.* farmaceutico.

pharmaceutics *s.* farmaceutica.
pharmacology *s.* farmacologia.
pharmacopoeia *s.* farmacopea.
pharmacy *s.* farmacia.
pharyngitis *s.* faringite.
pharynx *s.* (*pl.* -ges) faringe.
phase *s.* fase.
pheasant *s.* fagiano.
phenic *agg.* fenico.
phenol *s.* fenolo.
phenomenal *agg.* **1.** fenomenico **2.** fenomenale.
phenomenalism *s.* fenomenismo.
phenomenology *s.* fenomenologia.
phenomenon *s.* (*pl.* -na) fenomeno.
phial *s.* fiala.
to **philander** *vi.* fare il cascamorto.
philanderer *s.* cascamorto.
philanthrope *s.* filantropo.
philanthropic(al) *agg.* filantropico.
philanthropism *s.* filantropia.
philanthropist *s.* filantropo.
philanthropy *s.* filantropia.
philatelic(al) *agg.* filatelico.
philatelist *s.* filatelico.
philately *s.* filatelia.
philharmonic *agg.* filarmonico.
philippic *s.* filippica.
Philippine *agg.* filippino.
philologian, philologist *s.* filologo.
philology *s.* filologia.
philosopher *s.* filosofo.
philosophic(al) *agg.* filosofico.
philosophist *s.* pseudofilosofo.
to **philosophize** *vi.* filosofare.
philosophy *s.* filosofia.
phlebitis *s.* flebite.
phleboclysis *s.* fleboclisi.
phlegm *s.* flemma.
phlegmatic(al) *agg.* flemmatico.
phlegmon *s.* flemmone.
phlogistic *agg.* flogistico.
phobia *s.* fobia.
phoenix *s.* fenice.
phone *s.* V. *telephone*.
phones *s. pl.* cuffie.
phoneme *s.* fonema.
phonetics *s.* fonetica.
phonogram *s.* fonogramma.
phonograph *s.* fonografo.
phonology *s.* fonologia.
phosphate *s.* fosfato.
phosphor *s.* fosforo.
phosphorescence *s.* fosforescenza.
phosphorescent *agg.* fosforescente.
phosphoric *agg.* fosforico.
phosphorous *agg.* fosforoso.

PHOTO 204 **PILING**

photo s. foto.
photocell s. cellula fotoelettrica.
photocopy s. fotocopia.
photoelectric(al) agg. fotoelettrico.
photogenic agg. fotogenico.
photograph s. fotografia.
to photograph vt. fotografare.
photographer s. fotografo.
photography s. fotografia (come arte).
photometry s. fotometria.
photomontage s. fotomontaggio.
phrase s. 1. locuzione, frase 2. stile.
to phrase vt. esprimere.
phraseology s. fraseologia.
phrenetic(al) agg. frenetico.
phrenologist s. frenologo.
phrenology s. frenologia.
phthisiology s. tisiologia.
phthisis s. tisi.
phylloxera s. fillossera.
physic s. medicina.
physical agg. fisico.
physician s. medico.
physicist s. fisico.
physics s. fisica.
physiognomist s. fisionomista.
physiognomy s. fisionomia.
physiologic(al) agg. fisiologico.
physiologist s. fisiologo.
physiology s. fisiologia.
physiotherapy s. fisioterapia.
physique s. fisico.
pianist s. pianista.
picaresque agg. picaresco.
pick[1] s. 1. piccone 2. colpo di piccone || tooth —, stuzzicadenti.
pick[2] s. scelta, il meglio (di qc.).
to pick vt. 1. scavare 2. pulire 3. raccogliere 4. rubare.
pickax(e) s. piccone.
picker s. 1. piccone 2. zappatore 3. raccoglitore.
picket s. 1. piolo, palo 2. (mil.) picchetto.
pickle s. 1. salamoia 2. sottaceti (pl.).
to pickle vt. mettere in salamoia, sotto aceto.
picklock s. 1. scassinatore 2. grimaldello.
pickpocket s. borsaiolo.
pickup s. 1. raccolta 2. (mecc.) accelerazione 3. fonorivelatore.
pictorial agg. 1. illustrato 2. pittorico. ♦ **pictorial** s. giornale illustrato.
picture s. 1. quadro, dipinto, ritrat-

to 2. illustrazione. ♦ **pictures** s. pl. cinema (sing.) || —, fook, libro illustrato.
to picture vt. dipingere || to — to oneself, immaginarsi, figurarsi.
picturesque agg. pittoresco.
pidgin agg. — English, inglese scorretto (usato tra cinesi ed europei).
pie[1] s. pica, gazza.
pie[2] s. torta, pasticcio.
pie[3] s. (tip.) refuso.
piece s. 1. pezzo 2. pezza (di tessuto) || by the —, a cottimo.
to piece vt. rappezzare, raggiustare.
piecemeal avv. pezzo per pezzo. ♦ **piecemeal** agg. frammentario.
piecework s. (lavoro a) cottimo.
pieceworker s. cottimista.
pied agg. screziato.
pier s. 1. molo 2. pilone || —-glass, specchiera.
to pierce vt. 1. forare 2. trafiggere.
piercer s. 1. punzone 2. punzonatore.
piercing agg. penetrante. ♦ **piercing** s. perforamento.
pietism s. pietismo.
piety s. pietà, reverenza.
pig s. 1. maiale 2. (metal.) lingotto.
pigeon s. piccione || — -house, piccionaia; carrier —, piccione viaggiatore.
pigeonhole s. 1. colombaia 2. casella 3. (giur.) casellario.
to pigeonhole vt. incasellare.
piggish agg. porcino.
pigheaded agg. testardo.
pigment s. pigmento.
pigmentation s. pigmentazione.
pigmy agg. e s. pigmeo.
pigsty s. porcile.
pike[1] s. picca.
pike[2] s. (amer.) pedaggio.
pilaster s. pilastro.
pile s. 1. mucchio 2. fabbricato 3. rogo 4. (elettr.) pila 5. (fig.) gruzzolo.
to pile[1] vt. ammucchiare. ♦ **to pile** vi. ammucchiarsi.
to pile[2] vt. conficcare pali in, fare palizzate.
piles s. pl. emorroidi.
to pilfer vt. e vi. rubacchiare.
pilferer s. ladruncolo.
pilgrim s. pellegrino.
pilgrimage s. pellegrinaggio.
piling[1] s. ammucchiamento.
piling[2] s. palificazione di sostegno.

pill s. pillola: contraceptive (pill), pillola anticoncezionale.

pillage s. 1. saccheggio 2. bottino.

to **pillage** vt. saccheggiare.

pillar s. colonna, pilastro || — -box, cassetta delle lettere.

pillory s. berlina.

to **pillory** vt. mettere alla berlina.

pillow s. cuscino, guanciale || — -case, federa.

pilot s. pilota.

to **pilot** vt. pilotare.

pilotage s. pilotaggio.

pimple s. foruncolo.

pin s. 1. spillo 2. perno || pins and needles, formicolio.

to **pin** vt. 1. puntare 2. (fig.) inchiodare.

pinafore s. grembiulino.

pinaster s. pinastro.

to **pincer** vt. attanagliare.

pincers s. pl. tenaglie.

pinch s. 1. pizzico, pizzicotto 2. (fig.) angustia.

to **pinch** vt. 1. pizzicare 2. stringere 3. causare dolore. ♦ to **pinch** vi. essere avaro.

pinchbeck s. principesbecco.

pincushion s. puntaspilli.

Pindaric agg. pindarico.

pine s. pino || — -apple, ananasso; — -cone, pigna; — -wood, pineta.

to **pine** vi. struggersi.

pinion[1] s. penna remigante.

pinion[2] s. (mecc.) pignone.

to **pinion** vt. tarpare le ali a.

pink agg. rosa. ♦ **pink** s. 1. colore rosa 2. garofano 3. (fig.) quintessenza.

to **pink** vt. 1. traforare 2. trafiggere.

pinky agg. roseo.

pinnacle s. 1. pinnacolo 2. sommità.

pinpoint s. capocchia di spillo.

pint s. pinta.

pioneer s. pioniere.

pious agg. 1. pio 2. pietoso.

piousness s. pietà.

pip s. seme di frutto.

to **pip** vi. pigolare.

pipage s. 1. tubatura 2. trasporto per tubatura.

pipe s. 1. tubo 2. pipa 3. strumento a fiato 4. condotta.

to **pipe** vi. suonare (piffero ecc.) 2. stridere. ♦ to **pipe** vt. 1. suonare 2. trasportare con tubature 3. fornire di tubature.

pipeline s. oleodotto.

piper s. pifferaio.

pipet(te) s. (chim.) pipetta.

piping agg. 1. flautato 2. acuto. ♦ **piping** s. 1. suono (di piffero ecc.) 2. suono acuto 3. tubatura.

piquancy s. gusto piccante.

piquant agg. piccante.

pique s. ripicco, risentimento.

piracy s. 1. pirateria 2. plagio.

pirate s. 1. pirata 2. plagiario.

pirogue s. piroga.

pirouette s. piroetta.

to **pirouette** vi. piroettare.

pistil s. pistillo.

pistol s. pistola.

piston s. pistone.

pit s. 1. fossa 2. cavità 3. platea.

to **pit** vt. 1. bucare 2. mettere in una fossa.

pitch[1] s. 1. lancio 2. beccheggio 3. (mecc.) passo 4. (mus.) intonazione 5. inclinazione.

pitch[2] s. pece, bitume || — -dark, nero come la pece.

to **pitch**[1] vt. 1. sistemare 2. gettare 3. intonare. ♦ to **pitch** vi. 1. beccheggiare 2. (aer.) picchiare.

to **pitch**[2] vt. impeciare.

pitcher s. brocca.

pitchfork s. forcone.

to **pitchfork** vt. 1. rimuovere 2. spingere (col forcone).

pitching s. beccheggio.

pitchy agg. 1. impeciato 2. simile a pece.

piteous agg. pietoso.

pitfall s. trappola.

pith s. 1. midollo 2. (fig.) essenza.

pithy agg. (fig.) vigoroso.

pitiable, pitiful agg. pietoso.

pitiless agg. spietato.

pittance s. poco denaro.

pitted agg. butterato.

pity s. pietà || what a —!, che peccato!

to **pity** vt. aver pietà di, compatire.

pitying agg. pietoso.

pivot s. cardine.

to **pivot** vt. montare su cardini. ♦ to **pivot** vi. girare su cardini.

placable agg. placabile.

placard s. manifesto.

to **placate** vt. placare.

placatory agg. conciliante.

place s. 1. posto 2. brano || to take —, aver luogo, accadere.

to **place** *vt.* mettere, porre, situare.

placement *s.* collocamento.

placid *agg.* placido.

placidity *s.* placidità.

placing *s.* sistemazione.

plagiarism *s.* plagio.

plagiarist *s.* plagiario.

to **plagiarize** *vt.* plagiare.

plagiary *s.* 1. plagio 2. plagiario.

plague *s.* peste.

to **plague** *vt.* affliggere.

plaguer *s.* tormentatore.

plaid *s.* 1. mantello scozzese 2. tessuto a quadri.

plain *agg.* 1. piano, chiaro, evidente 2. semplice 3. comune, scialbo. ♦ **plain** *s.* pianura. ♦ **plain** *avv.* 1. chiaramente 2. semplicemente.

plain-clothes *s. pl.* abiti borghesi.

plainness *s.* 1. chiarezza 2. semplicità 3. aspetto scialbo.

plaint *s.* 1. lamento, lagnanza 2. (*giur.*) querela.

plaintiff *s.* (*giur.*) attore (*nei processi civili*).

plaintive *agg.* lamentoso.

plait *s.* 1. piega (*di abiti*) 2. treccia.

to **plait** *vt.* 1. pieghettare 2. intrecciare.

plan *s.* 1. piano, progetto 2. pianta (*di una città*).

to **plan** *vt.* progettare.

plane[1] *agg.* piano. ♦ **plane** *s.* 1. piano 2. aereo.

plane[2] *s.* pialla.

plane[3] *s.* — -*tree*, platano.

to **plane**[1] *vi.* volare.

to **plane**[2] *vt.* piallare.

planer *s.* (*mecc.*) piallatrice.

planet *s.* (*astr.*) pianeta.

planetary *agg.* planetario.

planimetric(al) *agg.* planimetrico.

planimetry *s.* planimetria.

planisphere *s.* planisfero.

plank *s.* tavola, asse.

to **plank** *vt.* coprire di tavole.

planking *s.* tavolato.

plankton *s.* (*biol.*) plancton.

planner *s.* progettista.

planning *s.* progettazione.

plant *s.* 1. pianta 2. impianto, apparato 3. fabbrica, stabilimento.

to **plant** *vt.* (im)piantare.

plantation *s.* piantagione.

planter *s.* 1. piantatore 2. colonizzatore.

plantigrade *agg. e s.* plantigrado.

plaque *s.* placca.

plash *s.* pozzanghera.

plaster *s.* 1. cerotto 2. gesso 3. intonaco.

to **plaster** *vt.* 1. incerottare 2. ingessare 3. intonacare 4. ricoprire.

plastering *s.* 1. intonacatura 2. ingessatura.

plastic *agg.* plastico, malleabile.

plasticine *s.* plastilina.

plasticity *s.* plasticità.

to **plasticize** *vt.* rendere plastico.

plastics *s. pl.* materie plastiche.

plate *s.* 1. lastra, lamina 2. piatto 3. tavola fuori testo 4. targa 5. squama 6. vasellame.

to **plate** *vt.* 1. placcare 2. rivestire di piastre.

plateau *s.* altipiano.

platen *s.* 1. piastra metallica 2. rullo di macchina da scrivere.

platform *s.* 1. piattaforma 2. (*ferr.*) marciapiede 3. impalcatura 4. (*amer.*) programma politico.

plating *s.* 1. placcatura 2. rivestimento metallico.

to **platinize** *vt.* platinare.

platinum *s.* platino.

platitude *s.* banalità.

Platonic *agg.* platonico.

Platonism *s.* platonismo.

platoon *s.* plotone.

plausibility *s.* plausibilità.

plausible *agg.* plausibile.

play *s.* 1. gioco 2. dramma 3. (*mus.*) esecuzione 4. azione || — *bill*, cartellone teatrale; — *time*, ricreazione.

to **play** *vt. e vi.* 1. giocare 2. recitare 3. agire 4. suonare || *to* —*down*, dare poca importanza a.

playboy *s.* (*fam.*) gaudente.

player *s.* 1. giocatore 2. attore 3. suonatore.

playful *agg.* giocoso.

playfulness *s.* allegria.

playground *s.* terreno di giochi.

playhouse *s.* teatro.

playing *s.* 1. gioco 2. rappresentazione 3. (*mus.*) esecuzione.

plaything *s.* giocattolo.

playwright, playwriter *s.* commediografo.

plea *s.* 1. giustificazione 2. (*giur.*) eccezione difensiva.

to **plead** *vt.* 1. patrocinare 2. addurre a pretesto 3. (*giur.*) perorare (*una causa*). ♦ to **plead** *vi.* 1. difendersi 2. supplicare.

pleader *s.* patrocinatore.

pleading *agg.* supplichevole. ♦

pleading s. difesa. ♦ **pleadings** s. pl. comparse.

pleasant agg. piacevole.

pleasantry s. piacevolezza.

to please vt. e vi. piacere (a) || — God, a Dio piacendo.

pleased agg. lieto.

pleasing agg. piacevole.

pleasure s. piacere.

pleat s. piega (di abiti ecc.).

to pleat vt. pieghettare.

plebeian agg. e s. plebeo.

plebiscitary agg. plebiscitario.

plebiscite s. plebiscito.

plectrum s. plettro.

pledge s. **1.** pegno **2.** promessa **3.** brindisi.

to pledge vt. **1.** impegnare **2.** brindare a.

pledgee s. (giur.) creditore pignoratizio.

plenary agg. plenario || — session, seduta plenaria.

plenilune s. plenilunio.

plenipotentiary agg. e s. plenipotenziario.

plentiful agg. abbondante.

plenty s. abbondanza, quantità.

pleonasm s. pleonasma.

pleonastic agg. pleonastico.

plethora s. pletora.

plethoric agg. pletorico.

pleurisy s. pleurite.

plexus s. plesso.

pliability s. pieghevolezza.

pliable agg. pieghevole.

pliancy s. V. pliability.

pliant s. V. pliable.

pliers s. pl. pinze.

plight[1] s. situazione critica.

plight[2] s. impegno, promessa.

to plight vt. impegnare, promettere.

plod s. **1.** passo pesante **2.** lavoro faticoso.

to plod vt. e vi. **1.** camminare faticosamente **2.** sgobbare.

plodder s. **1.** chi cammina faticosamente **2.** sgobbone.

plot s. **1.** appezzamento **2.** trama **3.** congiura.

to plot vt. e vi. **1.** fare la pianta di **2.** tramare.

plotter s. cospiratore.

plough s. aratro.

to plough vt. e vi. **1.** arare **2.** solcare.

ploughing s. aratura.

ploughman s. aratore.

ploughshare s. vomere.

plover s. piviere.

pluck s. **1.** strappo **2.** coraggio.

to pluck vt. **1.** strappare **2.** spennare **3.** tirare || to — up, sradicare.

plucky agg. coraggioso.

plug s. **1.** tappo (di lavandino ecc.) **2.** (elettr.; tel.) spina || spark(ing)— (mecc.), candela.

to plug vt. **1.** tappare **2.** tamponare || to — in, inserire la corrente; to — away, sgobbare:

plugging s. chiusura.

plum s. **1.** prugna, susina **2.** uva passa **3.** (fig.) il meglio.

plumage s. piumaggio.

plumb agg. **1.** a piombo **2.** completo. ♦ **plumb** s. **1.** filo a piombo **2.** scandaglio. ♦ **plumb** avv. **1.** a piombo **2.** esattamente.

to plumb vt. **1.** rendere verticale **2.** scandagliare **3.** impiombare.

plumber s. idraulico.

plumbery s. negozio di idraulico.

plumbing s. **1.** piombatura **2.** lavori idraulici.

plumbum s. piombo.

plume s. piuma, penna.

plummet s. piombino.

plump[1] agg. grassottello.

plump[2] agg. brusco, netto.

♦ **plump** avv. **1.** improvvisamente **2.** direttamente.

to plump vt. **1.** ingrassare **2.** far cadere. ♦ **to plump** vi. **1.** ingrassare **2.** cadere.

to plunder v. depredare.

plunderer s. saccheggiatore.

plunge s. tuffo.

to plunge vt. tuffare. ♦ **to plunge** vi. tuffarsi.

plunger s. **1.** tuffatore **2.** stantuffo.

plunk s. colpo metallico.

to plunk vt. far cadere pesantemente. ♦ **to plunk** vi. cadere pesantemente.

plural agg. e s. plurale.

pluralism s. pluralismo.

plurality s. pluralità.

plus agg. **1.** in più **2.** (elettr.) positivo || — value, plusvalore. ♦ **plus** s. **1.** più **2.** quantità positiva. ♦ **plus** prep. più.

plush s. « peluche », felpa.

plutocracy s. plutocrazia.

plutocrat s. plutocrate.

ply s. piega || — -wood, compensato.

to ply vt. **1.** maneggiare **2.** importunare. ♦ **to ply** vi. **1.** lavorare assiduamente 2. fare la spola.

pneumatic *agg.* e *s.* pneumatico.

pneumonia *s.* polmonite.

pneumothorax *s.* pneumotorace.

to poach *vt.* 1. calpestare 2. cacciare di frodo 3. interferire.

poacher *s.* bracconiere.

poaching *s.* bracconaggio.

pocket *s.* 1. tasca 2. buca (*di biliardo*) || — -book, lib:o tascabile.

to pocket *vt.* 1. intascare 2. nascondere, soffocare (*sentimenti ecc.*).

pocketful *s.* tascata.

pod *s.* 1. baccello 2. gruppetto.

poem *s.* 1. poesia 2. poema.

poet *s.* poeta.

poetic(al) *agg.* poetico.

poetic(s) *s.* poetica.

poetry *s.* poesia.

poignant *agg.* 1. pungente 2. commovente.

point *s.* 1. punto 2. punta, estremità 3. caratteristica.

to point *vt.* 1. indicare, segnare a dito 2. appuntire 3. dirigere || *to — out*, indicare, porre in rilievo.

point-blank *agg.* diretto. ◆ **point-blank** *avv.* direttamente.

pointed *agg.* 1. appuntito 2. mordace 3. evidente.

pointer *s.* 1. indicatore 2. lancetta (*di orologio*).

pointless *agg.* 1. spuntato 2. inutile, senza scopo.

pointsman *s.* (*ferr.*) deviatore.

poise *s.* equilibrio.

to poise *vt.* bilanciare. ◆ **to poise** *vi.* bilanciarsi.

poison *s.* veleno.

to poison *vt.* avvelenare.

poisoning *agg.* velenoso. ◆ **poisoning** *s.* avvelenamento.

poisonous *agg.* velenoso (*anche fig.*).

poke *s.* spinta, urto.

to poke *vt.* e *vi.* 1. spingere 2. andare a tastoni.

poker *s.* attizzatoio.

poky *agg.* meschino.

polar *agg.* polare.

polarity *s.* polarità.

polarization *s.* polarizzazione.

to polarize *vt.* polarizzare.

pole¹ *s.* palo

pole² *s.* polo.

Pole³ *s.* polacco.

polecat *s.* puzzola.

polemic *s.* 1. polemica 2. polemista.

polemic(al) *agg.* polemico.

polemi(ci)st *s.* polemista.

to polemize *vi.* polemizzare.

police *s.* polizia || — -*force*, corpo di polizia.

police court *s.* pretura.

policeman *s.* poliziotto.

policy¹ *s.* 1. linea di condotta 2. sagacia.

policy² *s.* polizza.

polio(myelitis) *s.* poliomielite.

Polish¹ *agg.* polacco.

polish² *s.* 1. lucidatura 2. lucido 3. raffinatezza || *shoe* —, lucido per le scarpe.

to polish *vt.* 1. lucidare 2. raffinare. ◆ **to polish** *vi.* 1. divenire lucido 2. raffinarsi.

polisher *s.* 1. lucidatore 2. lucido.

polishing *s.* lucidatura.

polite *agg.* cortese.

politeness *s.* cortesia.

politic *agg.* abile.

political *agg.* politico.

politician *s.* uomo politico.

politics *s.* politica.

poll *s.* 1. votazione, scrutinio 2. referendum.

to poll *vt.* radere. ◆ **to poll** *vi.* votare, raccogliere voti.

pollen *s.* polline.

to pollinate *vt.* impollinare.

pollination *s.* impollinazione.

to pollute *vt.* contaminare.

pollution *s.* contaminazione.

polyandry *s.* poliandria.

polychrome *agg.* policromo.

polychromy *s.* policromia.

polyclinic *s.* policlinico.

polygamist *s.* poligamo.

polygamous *agg.* poligamo.

polygamy *s.* poligamia.

polyglot *agg.* e *s.* poliglotta.

polygon *s.* poligono.

polyhedral *agg.* poliedrico.

polyhedron *s.* poliedro.

polymerization *s.* polimerizzazione.

polymorphic *agg.* polimorfo.

polymorphism *s.* polimorfismo.

polyp *s.* polipo.

polyphonic *agg.* polifonico.

polyphony *s.* polifonia.

polysyllabic(al) *agg.* polisillabico.

polysyllable *s.* polisillabo.

polytechnic *agg.* e *s.* politecnico.

polytheism *s.* politeismo.

polytheist *s.* politeista.

polytheistic(al) *agg.* politeistico.

polyvalent *agg.* polivalente.

pomade *s.* pomata.

to **pomade** *vt.* impomatare.

pomegranate *s.* **1.** melagrana **2.** melograno.

pomp *s.* pompa, fasto.

pomposity *s.* pomposità.

pompous *agg.* pomposo.

pond *s.* stagno.

to **pond** *vt.* e *vi.* stagnare.

to **ponder** *vt.* e *vi.* ponderare.

ponderable *agg.* ponderabile.

ponderous *agg.* ponderoso.

pontiff *s.* pontefice.

pontifical *agg.* pontificio. ♦ **pontifical** *s.* pontificato.

pontificate *s.* pontificato.

to **pontificate** *vi.* pontificare.

pontoon *s.* pontone.

pony *s.* « pony », piccolo cavallo.

poodle *s.* barboncino.

pool[1] *s.* **1.** stagno **2.** pozza || *swimming* —, piscina.

pool[2] *s.* (*comm.*) **1.** fondo comune **2.** (*comm.*) consorzio, sindacato.

poor *agg.* povero.

poorly *avv.* male.

poorness *s.* povertà.

pop *s.* scoppio.

to **pop** *vi.* scoppiare. ♦ to **pop** *vt.* **1.** far scoppiare **2.** ficcare.

popcorn *s.* fiocco di granoturco.

pope *s.* papa.

popery *s.* papismo.

poplar *s.* pioppo.

poppied *agg.* coperto di papaveri.

poppy *s.* papavero.

populace *s.* plebaglia.

popular *agg.* popolare.

popularity *s.* popolarità.

popularization *s.* popolarizzazione.

to **popularize** *vt.* popolarizzare.

to **populate** *vt.* popolare.

population *s.* popolazione.

Populism *s.* populismo.

Populist *s.* populista.

populous *agg.* popoloso.

porch *s.* portico.

porcupine *s.* porcospino.

pore *s.* poro.

to **pore** *vi.* esaminare.

pork *s.* carne di maiale.

pornographic *agg.* pornografico.

pornography *s.* pornografia.

porosity *s.* porosità.

porous *agg.* poroso.

porphyry *s.* porfido.

port[1] *s.* porto.

port[2] *s.* **1.** (*mecc.*) apertura, foro **2.** (*mar.*) portello.

port[3] *s.* fianco sinistro di nave.

portable *agg.* portatile.

portal *s.* portale.

portcullis *s.* saracinesca (*di fortezza*).

to **portend** *vt.* preannunciare.

portent *s.* **1.** presagio **2.** portento.

portentous *agg.* **1.** sinistro **2.** portentoso.

porter[1] *s.* facchino.

porter[2] *s.* custode, portiere.

porter[3] *s.* birra scura.

portfolio *s.* **1.** cartella, busta **2.** (*pol.*) portafoglio.

porthole *s.* **1.** (*mar.*) portello **2.** feritoia.

portion *s.* porzione, parte.

to **portion** *vt.* dividere, distribuire.

portrait *s.* ritratto.

portraitist *s.* ritrattista.

to **portray** *vt.* ritrarre.

portrayal *s.* ritratto.

portrayer *s.* ritrattista.

Portuguese *agg.* e *s.* portoghese.

pose *s.* posa.

to **pose**[1] *vt.* proporre.

to **pose**[2] *vi.* posare.

poser *s.* posatore.

position *s.* posizione.

positive *agg.* **1.** positivo **2.** sicuro. ♦ **positive** *s.* **1.** realtà **2.** (*foto*) positiva.

positivism *s.* positivismo.

positivist *s.* positivista.

positivistic *agg.* positivistico.

posology *s.* posologia.

to **possess** *vt.* possedere.

possessed *agg.* indemoniato.

possession *s.* possesso.

possessive *agg.* possessivo.

possessor *s.* possessore.

possibility *s.* possibilità.

possible *agg.* possibile.

possibly *avv.* possibilmente.

post[1] *s.* **1.** posta, corrispondenza || — *card*, cartolina; *by return of* —, a giro di posta.

post[2] *s.* **1.** palo, sostegno, puntello **2.** stipite || *sign*- —, indicatore stradale.

to **post**[1] *vt.* imbucare, inviare per posta.

to **post**[2] *vt.* affiggere.

postage *s.* spese postali (*pl.*).

postage stamp *s.* francobollo.

postal *agg.* postale.

to **postdate** *vt.* posdatare.

poster *s.* **1.** affisso **2.** attacchino.

poste-restante *s.* fermo posta.

posterior *agg.* posteriore.
posterity *s.* posterità.
postern *s.* postierla.
post-free *agg.* franco di porto.
posthumous *agg.* postumo.
postil(l)ion *s.* postiglione.
postman *s.* postino.
postmark *s.* timbro postale.
postmaster *s.* direttore di ufficio postale.
to **postpone** *vt.* rimandare.
postponement *s.* rinvio.
to **post-score** *vt.* (*cine*) sonorizzare.
postscript *s.* poscritto.
postulate *s.* postulato.
to **postulate** *vt.* 1. porre come postulato 2. chiedere.
postulator *s.* postulante.
posture *s.* posizione.
to **posture** *vi.* assumere una posizione.
post-war *agg.* postbellico.
posy *s.* mazzolino di fiori.
pot *s.* 1. recipiente 2. pentola || —-bellied, panciuto.
to **pot** *vt.* conservare (*in vaso*).
potable *agg.* potabile.
potash *s.* potassa.
potassic *agg.* potassico.
potassium *s.* potassio.
potato *s.* patata.
potent *agg.* potente.
potential *agg.* e *s.* potenziale.
potentiality *s.* potenzialità.
potion *s.* pozione.
potter *s.* vasaio.
pottery *s.* 1. terraglie 2. fabbrica di terraglie.
pouch *s.* borsa.
to **pouch** *vt.* intascare.
poulterer *s.* pollivendolo.
poultry *s.* pollame.
pounce *s.* balzo.
to **pounce** *vi.* avventarsi su, contro.
pound[1] *s.* 1. libbra 2. sterlina.
pound[2] *s.* recinto.
to **pound**[1] *vt.* e *vi.* pestare.
to **pound**[2] *vt.* rinchiudere.
pour *s.* acquazzone.
to **pour** *vt.* versare. ♦ to **pour** *vi.* 1. versarsi 2. diluviare.
pout *s.* broncio.
to **pout** *vi.* fare il broncio.
poverty *s.* povertà.
powder *s.* 1. polvere 2. cipria, talco.
to **powder** *vt.* 1. polverizzare 2. incipriare. ♦ to **powder** *vi.* 1. pol-

verizzarsi 2. incipriarsi.
powdery *agg.* 1. friabile 2. polveroso.
power *s.* potenza, potere || *horse* —, cavallo vapore; — *-station*, centrale elettrica.
to **power** *vt.* motorizzare.
powerful *agg.* potente.
powerless *agg.* debole.
pox *s.* sifilide || *chicken*- —, varicella, *small*- —, vaiolo.
practicability *s.* praticabilità.
practicable *agg.* 1. praticabile 2. fattibile.
practical *agg.* pratico.
practicality *s.* praticità.
practice *s.* 1. pratica 2. abitudine, regola 3. esercizio 4. professione 5. (*coll.*) clienti (*di medico ecc.*).
to **practise** *vt.* 1. praticare 2. esercitare. ♦ to **practise** *vi.* esercitarsi.
practitioner *s.* professionista.
praetorian *s.* pretoriano.
pragmatic(al) *agg.* prammatico.
pragmatism *s.* pragmatismo.
pragmatist *agg.* e *s.* pragmatista.
prairie *s.* prateria.
praise *s.* lode.
to **praise** *vt.* lodare.
praiser *s.* lodatore.
praiseworthy *agg.* lodevole.
prance *s.* impennata.
prank *s.* monelleria.
to **prank** *vt.* ornare, agghindare vistosamente. ♦ to **prank** *vi.* mettersi in mostra.
prate *s.* chiacchiera, sproloquio.
to **prate** *vi.* chiacchierare, proferire parole senza senso.
prattle *s.* balbettio.
to **prattle** *vt.* e *vi.* balbettare.
praxis *s.* prassi.
to **pray** *vt.* e *vi.* pregare.
prayer *s.* preghiera.
to **preach** *vt.* e *vi.* predicare.
preacher *s.* predicatore.
to **preachify** *vi.* predicare in modo noioso.
preaching *s.* predicazione.
preachy *agg.* (*fam.*) incline a far prediche.
to **pre-announce** *vt.* preannunziare.
to **prearrange** *vt.* predisporre.
prearrangement *s.* predisposizione.
prebend *s.* prebenda.
prebendary *s.* prebendario.
precarious *agg.* precario.

precariousness s. precarietà.
precatory agg. supplichevole.
precaution s. precauzione.
precautional agg. precauzionale.
to **precede** vt. e vi. precedere.
precedence s. precedenza.
precedent agg. e s. precedente.
preceding agg. precedente.
precept s. precetto.
preceptive agg. istruttivo
preceptor s. precettore.
precession s. precessione.
precinct s. 1. recinto 2. limiti 3. vicinanze (pl.).
preciosity s. preziosità.
precious agg. prezioso.
preciousness s. preziosità.
precipice s. precipizio.
precipitate agg. e s. precipitato.
to **precipitate** vt. e vi. precipitare.
precipitation s. precipitazione.
precipitous agg. ripido.
précis s. riassunto.
precise agg. preciso.
precision s. precisione.
to **preclude** vt. precludere.
precocious agg. precoce.
precociousness, precocity s. precocità.
preconceived agg. preconcetto.
precursor s. precursore, predecessore.
precursory agg. 1. preliminare 2. premonitore.
predaceous agg. rapace.
to **predate** vt. predatare.
predatory agg. rapace.
to **predecease** vt. premorire a.
predecessor s. predecessore.
to **predesignate** vt. predesignare.
predestination s. predestinazione.
to **predestine** vt. predestinare.
predetermination s. predeterminazione.
to **predetermine** vt. predeterminare.
predicable agg. asseribile.
predicament s. situazione scabrosa.
predicate agg. e s. predicato.
to **predicate** vt. 1. asserire 2. implicare.
predication s. affermazione.
predicative agg. 1. predicativo 2. affermativo.
predicatory agg. predicatorio.
to **predict** vt. e vi. predire.
prediction s. predizione.
predilection s. predilezione.

to **predispose** vt. predisporre.
predisposition s. predisposizione.
predominance s. predominanza.
to **predominate** vi. predominare.
pre-eminence s. preminenza.
pre-eminent agg. preminente.
pre-emption s. prelazione, priorità.
to **pre-engage** vt. impegnare in anticipo.
to **pre-establish** vt. prestabilire.
to **pre-exist** vi. preesistere.
pre-existence s. preesistenza.
to **prefabricate** vt. prefabbricare.
prefabricated agg. — house, casa prefabbricata.
preface s. prefazione.
to **preface** vt. 1. fare una prefazione a 2. iniziare.
prefatory agg. introduttivo.
prefect s. prefetto.
prefecture s. prefettura.
to **prefer** vt. 1. preferire 2. promuovere, elevare.
preferable agg. preferibile.
preference s. preferenza.
preferential agg. preferenziale.
preferment s. avanzamento, promozione.
prefiguration s. prefigurazione.
to **prefigure** vt. prefigurare.
prefix s. prefisso.
pregnancy s. 1. gravidanza 2. (fig.) significato, importanza.
pregnant agg. 1. incinta 2. significativo, importante 3. fecondo.
prehension s. 1. prensione 2. apprendimento.
prehistoric(al) agg. preistorico.
prehistory s. preistoria.
prejudice s. pregiudizio.
to **prejudice** vt. 1. pregiudicare 2. influenzare.
prejudicial agg. pregiudizievole.
prelate s. prelato.
prelatic(al) agg. prelatizio.
preliminary agg. preliminare. ♦
preliminaries s. pl. preliminari.
prelude s. preludio.
to **prelude** vt. preludere. ♦ to **prelude** vi. eseguire un preludio.
premature agg. prematuro.
to **premeditate** vt. premeditare.
premeditation s. premeditazione.
premier s. primo ministro.
premise s. 1. premessa 2. stabile con terreni annessi.
to **premise** vt. premettere.
premolar agg. e s. premolare.
premonitory agg. premonitore.

preoccupation s. preoccupazione.

to preoccupy vt. 1. preoccupare 2. occupare in precedenza.

preparation s. preparazione, preparativo.

preparative, preparatory agg. preparatorio.

to prepare vt. preparare. ♦ **to prepare** vi. prepararsi.

preponderance s. preponderanza.

preponderant agg. preponderante.

preposition s. preposizione.

prepositional agg. di preposizione.

to prepossess vt. 1. occupare in precedenza 2. influenzare.

prepossessing agg. attraente.

prepossession s. prevenzione.

preposterous agg. assurdo.

prepotence s. predominio.

prepotent agg. predominante.

Pre-Raphaeli(ti)sm s. preraffaellismo.

prerogative agg. privilegiato. ♦ **prerogative** s. prerogativa.

presage s. presagio.

presbyope s. presbite.

presbyopic agg. presbite.

Presbyterian agg. e s. presbiteriano.

Presbyterianism s. presbiterianismo.

presbytery s. presbiterio.

prescience s. prescienza.

to prescribe vt. prescrivere.

prescript s. ordinanza.

prescription s. prescrizione.

presence s. presenza.

present[1] agg. presente || — -day, contemporaneo. ♦ **present** s. presente, tempo presente || at —, attualmente. ♦ **presents** s. pl. (giur.) documento (sing.).

present[2] s. dono, regalo.

to present vt. 1. presentare 2. regalare.

presentable agg. presentabile.

presentation s. 1. presentazione 2. dono.

presenter s. 1. presentatore 2. donatore.

presentiment s. presentimento.

presently avv. presto, quanto prima.

presentment s. presentazione.

preservable agg. conservabile.

preservation s. conservazione.

preservative agg. e s. preservativo.

preserve s. 1. riserva 2. conserva (di pomodoro, frutta ecc.).

to preserve vt. 1. preservare 2. conservare 3. mettere in conserva.

to preside vi. presiedere.

presidency s. presidenza.

president s. presidente.

presidential agg. presidenziale.

press s. 1. stretta, pressione 2. pressa 3. (fig.) stampa 4. calca, ressa || — conference, conferenza stampa.

to press vt. 1. premere, comprimere 2. costringere. ♦ **to press** vi. affollarsi.

pressing agg. 1. urgente 2. insistente.

pressman s. 1. cronista (di giornale) 2. (tip.) stampatore.

pressure s. pressione || — -cooker, pentola a pressione.

to pressurize vt. pressurizzare.

prestige s. prestigio.

presumable agg. presumibile.

to presume vt. e vi. 1. presumere 2. avere la presunzione di.

presuming agg. presuntuoso.

presumption s. 1. presunzione 2. supposizione.

presumptive agg. presunto.

presumptuous agg. presuntuoso.

presumptuousness s. presunzione.

to presuppose vt. presupporre.

presupposition s. presupposizione.

pretence s. 1. pretesa 2. pretesto 3. simulazione.

to pretend vi. 1. pretendere 2. fingere.

pretender s. 1. pretendente 2. simulatore.

pretension s. 1. pretesa 2. presunzione.

pretentious agg. pretenzioso.

preternatural agg. soprannaturale.

pretext s. pretesto.

prettiness s. grazia.

pretty agg. grazioso. ♦ **pretty** avv. abbastanza.

to prevail vi. prevalere.

prevailing agg. 1. prevalente 2. efficace.

prevalence s. prevalenza.

to prevaricate vi. 1. tergiversare 2. mentire.

prevarication s. 1. tergiversazione 2. menzogna.

prevaricator s. 1. chi tergiversa 2. mentitore.

to prevent vt. impedire.

prevention s. 1. impedimento 2. prevenzione.

preventive agg. preventivo.

preview s. anteprima.
previous agg. precedente.
prevision s. previsione.
pre-war agg. prebellico.
prey s. preda.
to **prey** vi. **1.** (de)predare **2.** (fig.) consumare.
price s. prezzo, costo.
to **price** vt. fissare il prezzo di.
priceless agg. inestimabile.
prick s. **1.** punta **2.** puntura **3.** (fig.) pungolo, rimorso.
to **prick** vt. **1.** pungere **2.** segnare **3.** rizzare le orecchie. ♦ to **prick** vi. **1.** formicolare **2.** pungersi.
prickle s. **1.** spina **2.** pungiglione.
prickly agg. pungente.
pride s. orgoglio.
to **pride** vt. to — oneself upon, essere orgoglioso di.
priest s. prete.
priesthood s. **1.** clero **2.** sacerdozio.
prig s. presuntuoso.
prim agg. affettato.
primary agg. primo, primario.
primate s. (eccl.) primate.
prime agg. **1.** primo **2.** di prima qualità. ♦ **prime** s. **1.** principio **2.** (fig.) fiore.
to **prime** vt. caricare, innescare.
primer[1] s. sillabario.
primer[2] s. innesco.
primeval agg. primordiale.
primigenial agg. primigenio.
priming s. **1.** innesco **2.** prima mano (di vernice ecc.).
primitive agg. e s. primitivo.
primitiveness s. primitività.
primogeniture s. primogenitura.
primordial agg. primordiale.
primrose s. primula.
prince s. principe.
princely agg. principesco.
princess s. principessa.
principal agg. principale. ♦ **principal** s. **1.** principale, direttore **2.** (edil.) trave maestra **3.** (comm.) mandante.
principality s. principato.
principle s. principio.
print s. **1.** impronta **2.** stampa **3.** stampatello **4.** (foto) copia.
to **print** vt. **1.** stampare **2.** scrivere a stampatello **3.** imprimere.
printer s. **1.** tipografo **2.** (mecc.) stampatrice.
printing s. **1.** stampa **2.** tiratura || — -press, pressa tipografica.
prior agg. precedente. ♦ **prior** s.

priore. ♦ **prior** avv. prima.
priorate s. priorato.
prioress s. priora.
priority s. priorità.
prism s. prisma.
prismatic(al) agg. prismatico.
prison s. prigione.
prisoner s. prigioniero.
privacy s. **1.** intimità **2.** riserbo.
private agg. **1.** privato **2.** appartato **3.** segreto, riservato, personale. ♦ **private** s. soldato semplice.
privation s. privazione.
privative agg. privativo.
privilege s. privilegio.
to **privilege** vt. privilegiare.
privy agg. **1.** nascosto **2.** al corrente di.*
prize s. premio.
to **prize** vt. stimare.
probabilism s. probabilismo.
probability s. probabilità.
probable agg. probabile.
probate s. omologazione.
probation s. prova.
probative agg. probativo.
probatory agg. probatorio.
probe s. sonda.
to **probe** vt. sondare.
probity s. probità.
problem s. problema.
problematic(al) agg. problematico.
procedural agg. procedurale.
procedure s. **1.** procedimento **2.** procedura.
to **proceed** vi. **1.** procedere **2.** provenire.
proceeding s. V. procedure.
proceeds s. pl. profitto (sing.).
process s. **1.** procedimento **2.** processo.
to **process** vt. **1.** processare **2.** (chim.) trattare.
procession s. processione.
processionary s. (zool.) processionaria.
proclaim s. proclama.
to **proclaim** vt. proclamare.
proclamation s. proclama(zione).
proconsul s. proconsole.
to **procrastinate** vt. e vi. procrastinare.
procrastination s. procrastinazione.
to **procreate** vt. procreare.
procreation s. procreazione.
procreator s. procreatore.
proctor s. **1.** censore **2.** (giur.) procuratore.

procurator s. procuratore.

to procure vt. 1. procurare, procurarsi 2. adescare.

procurer s. mezzano.

prod s. pungolo.

to prod vt. pungolare.

prodigal agg. e s. prodigo.

prodigality s. prodigalità.

prodigious agg. 1. prodigioso 2. enorme.

prodigiousness s. prodigiosità.

prodigy s. prodigio.

produce s. prodotto || *farm* —, prodotto agricolo; *raw* —, materia prima.

to produce vt. 1. produrre 2. presentare.

producer s. 1. produttore 2. (*teat.*) regista.

product s. prodotto.

production s. 1. esibizione 2. produzione.

productive agg. produttivo.

productivity s. produttività.

proem s. proemio.

profanation s. profanazione.

profane agg. 1. profano 2. empio.

to profane vt. profanare.

profaner s. profanatore.

profanity s. 1. profanità 2. empietà.

to profess vt. 1. professare 2. pretendere.

profession s. professione.

professional agg. professionale || — *man*, professionista. ♦ **professional** s. professionista.

professionalism s. professionismo.

professor s. professore (*d'università*).

professorial agg. professorale.

proficiency s. competenza || — *in English*, buona conoscenza dell'inglese.

proficient agg. e s. esperto, competente.

profile s. profilo.

to profile vt. 1. profilare 2. tracciare il profilo di.

profit s. profitto, guadagno.

to profit vt. giovare. ♦ **to profit** vi. approfittare.

profitable agg. vantaggioso.

profiteer s. profittatore.

profligacy s. 1. sregolatezza 2. spergero.

profligate agg. e s. 1. dissoluto 2. scialacquatore.

profound agg. profondo.

profuse agg. 1. abbondante 2. prodigo.

profusion s. 1. profusione 2. prodigalità.

progenitor s. progenitore.

progeny s. progenie.

prognathism s. prognatismo.

prognathous agg. prognato.

prognosis s. (*pl.* -ses) prognosi.

prognostic agg. rivelatore. ♦ **prognostic** s. 1. pronostico 2. sintomo.

prognostication s. 1. pronostico 2. prognosi.

program(me) s. programma.

to program(me) vt. programmare.

programming s. programmazione.

programmist s. programmista.

progress s. 1. progresso 2. avanzata 3. sviluppo 4. andamento, corso.

to progress vi. 1. progredire 2. avanzare 3. svilupparsi.

progression s. 1. progressione 2. avanzamento.

progressive agg. progressivo, progressista. ♦ **progressive** s. progressista.

to prohibit vt. proibire.

prohibition s. 1. proibizione 2. proibizionismo.

prohibitionist s. proibizionista.

prohibitive agg. proibitivo.

project s. progetto.

to project vt. 1. progettare 2. proiettare. ♦ **to project** vi. sporgere.

projectile s. proiettile.

projection s. 1. progetto 2. proiezione.

projector s. 1. progettista 2. proiettore.

proletarian agg. e s. proletario.

proletariat s. proletariato.

to proliferate vt. proliferare. ♦ **to proliferate** vi. moltiplicarsi.

proliferation s. proliferazione.

prolific agg. prolifico.

prolix agg. prolisso.

prolixity s. prolissità.

prologue s. prologo.

to prolong vt. 1. prolungare 2. (*comm.*) prorogare.

promenade s. passeggiata, passeggio pubblico, lungomare.

prominence s. prominenza.

prominent agg. prominente.

promiscuity s. promiscuità.

promiscuous agg. promiscuo.

promise s. promessa.

to promise vt. e vi. promettere.

promissory *agg.* contenente una promessa || — *note* (*comm.*), pagherò cambiario.

promontory *s.* promontorio.

to **promote** *vt.* **1.** promuovere **2.** dare impulso, favorire.

promoter *s.* promotore.

promotion *s.* **1.** promozione **2.** incoraggiamento.

prompt *agg.* **1.** sollecito **2.** (*comm.*) in contanti. ♦ **prompt** *s.* **1.** (*comm.*) termine di pagamento **2.** suggerimento.

to **prompt** *vt.* **1.** spingere **2.** suggerire.

prompter *s.* suggeritore.

promptness *s.* prontezza.

to **promulgate** *vt.* promulgare.

promulgation *s.* promulgazione.

promulgator *s.* promulgatore.

prone *agg.* prono.

prong *s.* **1.** dente (*di forca*) **2.** forca.

pronominal *agg.* pronominale.

pronoun *s.* pronome.

to **pronounce** *vt.* **1.** pronunciare **2.** dichiarare. ♦ to **pronounce** *vi.* pronunciarsi.

pronouncement *s.* dichiarazione.

pronouncing, pronunciation *s.* pronuncia.

proof *agg.* a prova di. ♦ **proof** *s.* **1.** prova **2.** bozza **3.** gradazione alcoolica || —*reader*, correttore di bozze; *burden of* — (*giur.*), onere della prova.

prop *s.* puntello.

to **prop** *vt.* **1.** sostenere **2.** appoggiare.

propaedeutic(al) *agg.* propedeutico.

propaedeutics *s.* propedeutica.

propagandist *s.* propagandista.

to **propagandize** *vt.* propagandare.

to **propagate** *vt.* propagare. ♦ to **propagate** *vi.* propagarsi.

propagation *s.* **1.** propagazione **2.** (*bot.; zool.*) riproduzione.

propagator *s.* propagatore.

propane *s.* propano.

to **propel** *vt.* spingere avanti.

propellent *agg.* e *s.* propulsore, propellente.

propeller *s.* propulsore || (*screw-*) —, elica.

propensity *s.* propensione.

proper *agg.* **1.** proprio **2.** adatto **3.** corretto **4.** propriamente detto.

property *s.* **1.** proprietà **2.** (*teat.*) costumi, arredi per la scena (*pl.*) ||

real —, beni immobili (*pl.*).

prophecy *s.* profezia.

to **prophesy** *vt.* e *vi.* profetizzare.

prophet *s.* profeta.

prophetic(al) *agg.* profetico.

prophylactic *agg.* e *s.* profilattico.

prophylaxis *s.* profilassi.

to **propitiate** *vt.* propiziare.

propitiation *s.* propiziazione.

propitiator *s.* propiziatore.

propitiatory *agg.* propiziatorio.

propitious *agg.* propizio.

proportion *s.* **1.** proporzione **2.** parte. ♦ **proportions** *s. pl.* dimensioni.

to **proportion** *vt.* **1.** proporzionare **2.** dividere in parti proporzionate.

proportional *agg.* proporzionale.

proportionality *s.* proporzionalità.

proportionate *agg.* proporzionato.

to **proportionate** *V.* to *proportion.*

proportioning *s.* proporzionamento.

proposal *s.* proposta.

to **propose** *vt.* proporre. ♦ to **propose** *vi.* **1.** prefiggersi, intendere **2.** fare richiesta di matrimonio || *to* — *the health of so.*, bere alla salute di qu.

proposition *s.* **1.** proposta **2.** proposizione **3.** asserzione **4.** problema.

proprietary *agg.* di proprietà. ♦ **proprietary** *s.* proprietario || — *rights*, diritti di proprietà.

proprietor *s.* proprietario.

propriety *s.* **1.** proprietà **2.** opportunità **3.** decoro, decenza. ♦ **proprieties** *s. pl.* convenienze.

propulsion *s.* propulsione.

propulsive *agg.* propulsivo.

propylaeum *s.* (*pl. -laea*) propileo.

propylene *s.* propilene.

prosaic *agg.* prosaico.

prosaism *s.* prosaicità.

proscenium *s.* (*pl. -nia*) proscenio.

to **proscribe** *vt.* **1.** bandire **2.** vietare.

proscription *s.* **1.** proscrizione **2.** proibizione.

prose *s.* **1.** prosa **2.** prosaicità || — *writer*, prosatore.

prosecutable *agg.* perseguibile.

to **prosecute** *vt.* **1.** proseguire **2.** perseguire.

prosecution *s.* **1.** proseguimento **2.** processo **3.** (*giur.*) accusa.

prosecutor *s.* **1.** prosecutore **2.** accusatore || *Public* — (*giur.*), l'accusa pubblica.

proselyte s. proselito.
proselytism s. proselitismo.
prosiness s. 1. prosaicità 2. banalità.
prosody s. prosodia.
prospect s. 1. panorama 2. prospettiva 3. speranza, aspettativa.
to prospect vt. 1. esplorare 2. ricercare.
prospecting s. ricerca.
prospective agg. 1. futuro 2. eventuale.
to prosper vt. far prosperare. ♦ **to prosper** vi. prosperare.
prosperity s. prosperità.
prosperous agg. prospero.
prostate s. prostata.
prostatic agg. prostatico.
prosthesis s. (med.) protesi.
prostitute s. prostituta.
to prostitute vt. prostituire.
prostitution s. prostituzione.
prostrate agg. prostrato.
to prostrate vt. prostrare.
prostration s. 1. prostrazione 2. prosternazione.
prostyle agg. e s. prostilo.
prosy agg. 1. prosaico 2. noioso.
protagonist s. protagonista.
to protect vt. proteggere.
protection s. 1. protezione 2. salvacondotto.
protectionism s. protezionismo.
protectionist s. protezionista.
protective agg. protettivo.
protector s. protettore.
protectorate s. protettorato.
protectory s. patronato.
protein s. proteina.
protest s. 1. protesta 2. (comm.) protesto.
to protest vt. e vi. protestare.
protestant agg. e s. protestante.
Protestantism s. protestantesimo.
protestation s. dichiarazione.
protocol s. protocollo.
proton s. protone.
protoplasm s. protoplasma.
prototype s. prototipo.
Protozoa s. pl. protozoi.
to protract vt. 1. protrarre 2. rilevare.
protraction s. 1. protrazione 2. rilievo.
protractor s. 1. protrattore 2. goniometro.
to protrude vt. 1. sporgere 2. imporre. ♦ **to protrude** vi. 1. sporgersi 2. imporsi.

protrusion, protuberance s. protuberanza.
proud agg. orgoglioso, superbo.
to prove vt. 1. provare, verificare 2. omologare. ♦ **to prove** vi. risultare.
provender s. foraggio, biada.
proverb s. proverbio.
proverbial agg. proverbiale.
to provide vi. 1. provvedere 2. premunirsi 3. stabilire (di leggi). ♦ **to provide** vt. 1. procurare 2. rifornire.
provided cong. purché, a patto che.
providence s. 1. provvidenza 2. previdenza.
provident agg. 1. provvido 2. previdente.
providential agg. provvidenziale.
province s. 1. provincia 2. (fig.) sfera, campo d'attività.
provincial agg. e s. provinciale.
provincialism s. provincialismo.
provision s. 1. preparativo 2. provvedimento 3. clausola 4. (giur.) disposizione. ♦ **provisions** s. pl. provviste.
to provision vt. approvvigionare.
provisional agg. provvisorio.
provisioning s. approvvigionamento.
provocation s. provocazione.
provocative agg. 1. provocante 2. stimolante.
provocativeness s. provocazione.
to provoke vt. 1. provocare 2. irritare.
provoker s. provocatore.
provost s. prevosto.
prow s. prora.
prowess s. prodezza, valore.
proximity s. prossimità.
proxy s. 1. procura 2. procuratore.
prude s. persona eccessivamente pudica.
prudence s. prudenza.
prudent agg. prudente.
prudential agg. prudenziale.
prudentials s. pl. provvedimenti precauzionali.
prudery s. ritrosia eccessiva.
prudish agg. pudibondo.
prune s. prugna secca.
to prune vt. potare.
pruner s. potatore.
pruning s. potatura ‖ — -book, falcetto.
prussic agg. prussico.
pry[1] s. ficcanaso.

pry² s. leva.

to **pry**¹ vi. indagare.

to **pry**² vt. muovere con una leva.

psalm s. salmo.

psalmody s. salmodia.

pseudonym s. pseudonimo.

psyche s. psiche.

psychiatric(al) agg. psichiatrico.

psychiatrist s. psichiatra.

psychiatry s. psichiatria.

psychic s. 1. medium 2. psicologia.

psychic(al) agg. psichico.

psychoanalysis s. psicanalisi.

psychoanalyst s. psicanalista.

psychoanalytic(al) agg. psicanalitico.

to **psychoanalyze** vt. psicanalizzare.

psychologic(al) agg. psicologico.

psychologist s. psicologo.

psychology s. psicologia.

psychometry s. psicometria.

psychopathic agg. e s. psicopatico.

psychopathology s. psicopatologia.

psychopathy s. psicopatia.

psychosis s. psicosi.

psychotherapy s. psicoterapia.

ptisan s. tisana.

pub s. bar (*in Gran Bretagna*).

puberty s. pubertà.

pubis s. (pl. -bes) pube.

public agg. e s. pubblico ‖ *the reading* —, i lettori (pl.).

publican s. 1. oste 2. (*stor.*) pubblicano.

publication s. pubblicazione.

publicity s. pubblicità.

to **publish** vt. 1. pubblicare 2. divulgare.

publishable agg. pubblicabile.

publisher s. editore.

pucker s. ruga, grinza.

to **pucker** vt. raggrinzare, corrugare. ♦ to **pucker** vi. raggrinzarsi, corrugarsi.

pudding s. 1. budino 2. pasticcio ‖ *black* —, sanguinaccio.

puddle s. 1. pozzanghera 2. malta.

to **puddle** vt. 1. infangare 2. coprire di malta.

puerility s. puerilità.

Puerto Rican agg. e s. portoricano.

puff s. 1. soffio, sbuffo 2. piumino.

to **puff** vi. 1. sbuffare 2. gonfiarsi. ♦ to **puff** vt. 1. soffiare 2. gonfiare.

puffy agg. 1. gonfio 2. ansimante 3. paffuto, grasso.

pugilist s. pugile.

pugnacious agg. pugnace.

pugnacity s. combattività.

puke s. vomito.

to **puke** vt. e vi. vomitare.

pull s. 1. strappo 2. sforzo, tensione 3. maniglia (*di cassetto*).

to **pull** vt. 1. tirare 2. strappare ‖ *to* — *down*, demolire. ♦ to **pull** vi. 1. trascinarsi 2. remare ‖ *to* — *back*, ritirarsi; *to* — *up*, fermarsi.

puller s. (*mecc.*) estrattore.

pulley s. puleggia.

pulmonary agg. polmonare.

pulp s. polpa.

to **pulp** vt. ridurre in polpa. ♦ to **pulp** vi. diventare polposo.

pulpit s. pulpito.

pulpy agg. polposo.

pulsation s. pulsazione.

pulsatory agg. pulsante.

pulse s. 1. pulsazione, polso, battito 2. (*radio*) impulso.

to **pulse** vi. pulsare.

to **pulverize** vt. polverizzare. ♦ to **pulverize** vi. polverizzarsi.

pumice s. pomice.

pump s. pompa ‖ *petrol* —, distributore di benzina.

to **pump** vt. e vi. pompare ‖ *to* — *up*, gonfiare.

pumpkin s. zucca.

pun s. gioco di parole.

punch¹ s. punteruolo.

punch² s. pugno.

punch³ s. « punch » (*bevanda alcoolica*).

to **punch**¹ vt. (per)forare.

to **punch**² vt. prendere a pugni.

punching s. perforazione.

punctilio s. meticolosità.

punctilious agg. meticoloso.

punctual agg. puntuale.

punctuality s. puntualità.

punctually avv. puntualmente.

to **punctuate** vt. 1. punteggiare 2. (*fig.*) sottolineare.

punctuation s. punteggiatura.

puncture s. 1. puntura 2. foratura.

to **puncture** vt. 1. pungere 2. forare.

pungency s. 1. asprezza 2. acutezza (*di dolore*).

pungent agg. 1. pungente 2. acuto, cocente 3. piccante.

to **punish** vt. punire.

punishable agg. punibile.

punishment s. punizione.

punitive, punitory agg. punitivo.

punt s. chiatta.

punter s. puntatore (*di corse ecc.*).
puny *agg.* sparuto.
pup s. cucciolo.
pupil¹ s. 1. allievo 2. (*giur.*) pupillo.
pupil² s. pupilla.
pupil(l)age s. (*giur.*) minorità:
child in —, bambino sotto tutela.
pupil(l)ary *agg.* (*giur.*) pupillare.
puppet s. burattino || *— show*, spettacolo di burattini; *— player*, burattinaio.
puppy s. cucciolo.
purchase s. acquisto.
to purchase *vt.* acquistare.
purchaser s. acquirente.
purchasing s. acquisto || *— power*, potere di acquisto.
pure *agg.* puro, schietto, casto.
purely *avv.* puramente, semplicemente.
purgative *agg.* purgativo. ♦ **purgative** s. purgante.
purgatory s. purgatorio.
purge s. 1. purga 2. epurazione.
to purge *vt.* 1. purgare 2. epurare.
♦ **to purge** *vi.* purgarsi.
purification s. purificazione.
purificatory *agg.* purificatore.
to purify *vt.* purificare.
purism s. purismo.
purist s. purista.
Puritan *agg.* e s. puritano.
Puritanism s. puritanismo.
purity s. purezza.
to purloin *vt.* rubare.
purloiner s. frodatore.
purple *agg.* 1. purpureo, paonazzo 2. ornato. ♦ **purple** s. porpora.
to purple *vt.* imporporare. ♦ **to purple** *vi.* imporpòrarsi.
purport s. significato.
to purport *vt.* 1. significare 2. pretendere.
purpose s. 1. intenzione, scopo 2. fermezza || *on —*, di proposito.
to purpose *vi.* proporsi (*di*).
purposeful *agg.* 1. premeditato 2. avveduto.
purposefully *avv.* intenzionalmente, espressamente.
purposeless *agg.* 1. inutile 2. senza intenzione.
purpurin s. porporina.
to purr *vi.* fare le fusa.
purse s. borsellino.
to purse *vt.* contrarre. ♦ **to purse** *vi.* incresparsi, contrarsi.
purser s. commissario di bordo.
pursuant *agg.* conforme.

to pursue *vt.* 1. (in)seguire 2. continuare.
pursuer s. 1. inseguitore 2. continuatore.
pursuit s. 1. inseguimento 2. occupazione, impiego.
purulence s. suppurazione.
purulent *agg.* purulento.
push s. 1. spinta, influenza, pressione 2. bisogno 3. (*elettr.*) pulsante.
to push *vt.* 1. spingere, incalzare, fare pressione 2. lanciare (*una moda, un articolo ecc.*) ♦ **to push** *vi.* spingersi.
pusher s. chi, ciò che spinge.
pusillanimity s. pusillanimità.
pusillanimous *agg.* pusillanime.
puss(y) s. micino.
pustule s. pustola.
to put (**put, put**) *vt.* 1. mettere, porre 2. esporre, sottoporre || *to — off*, rimandare, togliere (*vestiti ecc.*); *to — on*, indossare, accendere; *to — through*, mettere in comunicazione telefonica; *to — up*, alzare. ♦ **to put** (**put, put**) *vi.* dirigersi.
putative *agg.* putativo.
putrefaction s. putrefazione.
to putrefy *vt.* putrefare. ♦ **to putrefy** *vi.* putrefarsi.
putrescence s. putrescenza.
putrescible *agg.* putrescibile.
putrid *agg.* putrido.
putridness s. putridità.
puttees s. *pl.* mollettiere.
putty s. mastice, stucco.
puzzle s. 1. enigma 2. imbarazzo 3. intrigo.
to puzzle *vt.* imbarazzare. ♦ **to puzzle** *vi.* essere imbarazzato.
pygmy *agg.* e s. pigmeo.
pyjamas s. *pl.* pigiama (*sing.*).
pylon s. pilone || *steel —*, traliccio.
pylorus s. piloro.
pyorrh(o)ea s. piorrea.
pyramid s. piramide.
pyramidal *agg.* piramidale.
pyre s. pira.
pyrites s. pirite.
pyrography s. pirografia.
pyromancy s. piromanzia.
pyromaniac s. piromane.
pyrope s. piropo.
pyrotechnic(al) *agg.* pirotecnico.
pyrotechnics s. pirotecnica.
Pythagorean *agg.* e s. pitagorico.
python s. pitone.
pyx s. pisside.

Q

quack[1] s. ciarlatano.
quack[2] s. schiamazzare (di anitra).
to quack[1] vi. fare il ciarlatano.
to quack[2] vi. schiamazzare (di anitra).
quadrangle s. quadrangolo.
quadrangular agg. quadrangolare.
quadrant s. quadrante.
quadrennial agg. quadriennale.
quadrilateral agg. e s. quadrilatero.
quadrille s. quadriglia.
quadrumane s. quadrumane.
quadrumanous agg. quadrumane.
quadruped agg. e s. quadrupede.
quadruple agg. e s. quadruplo.
to quadruple vt. quadruplicare. ◆
to quadruple vi. quadruplicarsi.
quagmire s. pantano.
quail s. quaglia.
to quail vi. avvilirsi, sgomentarsi.
quaint agg. strano, bizzarro.
quake s. scossa, tremito.
to quake vi. 1. avere i brividi 2. tremare (anche di terra).
Quaker s. Quacchero.
quaky agg. tremante.
qualifiable agg. qualificabile.
qualification s. 1. qualificazione, capacità, requisito 2. condizione, riserva 3. qualifica.
qualified agg. 1. qualificato, competente 2. limitato || — acceptance (comm.) accettazione con riserva.
qualifier s. (gramm.) parola che modifica.
to qualify vt. 1. qualificare, definire 2. abilitare 3. (giur.) autorizzare. ◆ to qualify vi. 1. qualificarsi 2. abilitarsi.
qualitative agg. qualitativo.
quality s. qualità, caratteristica.
qualm s. 1. nausea 2. scrupolo.
qualmish agg. 1. soggetto a nausee 2. nauseante 3. scrupoloso.
quantitative agg. quantitativo.
quantity s. quantità.
quarantine s. quarantena.
quarrel s. lite, contesa.
to quarrel vi. litigare, venire a contesa.
quarreller s. attaccabrighe, contendente.
quarrelsome agg. attaccabrighe, rissoso.
quarry[1] s. 1. cava 2. (fig.) fonte d'informazione.

quarry[2] s. selvaggina, preda.
to quarry vt. 1. cavare (pietre, marmo ecc.) 2. ricavare informazioni da.
quarter s. 1. quarto: a — of an hour, un quarto d'ora 2. quartiere, rione. ◆ quarters s. pl. 1. alloggio 2. (mil.) acquartieramento.
to quarter vt. e vi. 1. dividere in quattro parti 2. alloggiare 3. (mil.) acquartierarsi.
quarterly agg. trimestrale. ◆ quarterly s. pubblicazione trimestrale. ◆ quarterly avv. trimestralmente.
quartermaster s. 1. commissario 2. quartiermastro.
quartet s. quartetto.
quartz s. quarzo.
to quash vt. (giur.) annullare.
quaternary agg. quaternario.
quatrain s. quartina.
quaver s. trillo, vibrazione.
to quaver vt. e vi. 1. vibrare, tremare (di voce) 2. gorgheggiare.
quay s. banchina, molo.
queasy agg. 1. nauseabondo 2. schizzinoso.
queen s. regina.
queenlike agg. regale.
queenly agg. regale, da regina.
queer agg. strano, eccentrico.
to queer vt. mettere in ridicolo.
queerly avv. stranamente.
to quench vt. 1. spegnere, estinguere 2. calmare.
quencher s. estintore.
quenchless agg. inestinguibile.
querulous agg. querulo, gemebondo.
query s. domanda, quesito.
to query vt. e vi. 1. chiedere, indagare 2. mettere in dubbio.
quest s. ricerca.
to quest vt. e vi. cercare, far ricerche.
question s. 1. domanda, interrogazione 2. dubbio, obiezione 3. questione, problema || — mark, punto interrogativo.
to question vt. 1. interrogare 2. mettere in dubbio.
questionable agg. incerto, discutibile.
questionably avv. discutibilmente.
questionary s. questionario.
queue s. 1. coda 2. fila di persone: to stand in a —, fare la coda.
to queue vt. e vi. fare la coda, mettere in coda.

quibble s. giuoco di parole, doppio senso.

to quibble vi. 1. fare giuochi di parole 2. cavillare.

quibbling agg. a doppio senso.

quick agg. 1. rapido, veloce 2. pronto, intelligente, acuto || — -eyed, dagli occhi penetranti; — -eared, dall'orecchio fino; — -lime, calce viva; — -sighted, dalla vista acuta; — -tempered, irascibile.

to quicken vt. 1. affrettare 2. animare. ♦ **to quicken** vi. 1. affrettarsi 2. animarsi.

quickly avv. rapidamente, prontamente.

quickness s. 1. rapidità 2. vivacità, acutezza.

quicksand s. sabbia mobile.

quickset s. siepe di sempreverdi.

quicksilver s. mercurio, argento vivo (anche fig.).

quickstep s. passo cadenzato.

quickthorn s. biancospino.

quiescence s. quiescenza.

quiescent agg. quiescente.

quiescently avv. tranquillamente.

quiet agg. 1. quieto, tranquillo 2. sobrio, tenue (di colore) 3. docile, dolce.

to quiet vt. acquietare. ♦ **to quiet** vi. acquietarsi.

quietism s. quietismo.

quietist s. quietista.

quietly avv. tranquillamente, con calma.

quietness s. quiete, tranquillità.

quill s. 1. penna, penna d'oca 2. piccolo galleggiante (per canna da pesca).

to quill vt. pieghettare, increspare.

quilt s. trapunta.

to quilt vt. trapuntare.

quince s. cotogna || — jam, marmellata di cotogne.

quinine s. chinino.

quinquennial agg. quinquennale.

quintal s. quintale.

quintessence s. quintessenza.

quintet s. quintetto.

quintuple agg. e s. quintuplo.

to quintuple vt. quintuplicare. ♦ **to quintuple** vi. quintuplicarsi.

quisling s. collaborazionista.

to quit vt. 1. abbandonare, lasciare 2. quietanzare, saldare.

quite avv. 1. completamente, interamente 2. piuttosto, abbastanza || — young, giovanissimo; to be

— well, stare proprio bene.

quiver s. fremito, brivido.

to quiver vt. e vi. 1. tremare, fremere 2. palpitare.

quivering agg. fremente, tremolante. ♦ **quivering** s. tremolio.

quixotic agg. donchisciottesco.

quiz s. (pl. quizzes) burlone.

to quiz vt. burlare.

quotation s. 1. citazione 2. (comm.) quotazione.

quote s. (fam.) citazione. ♦ **quotes** s. pl. virgolette.

to quote vt. 1. citare 2. (comm.) quotare (in borsa).

quotidian agg. quotidiano.

quotient s. quoziente.

R

rabbi s. rabbino.

rabbit s. coniglio.

rabble s. plebaglia.

to rabble vt. assaltare, linciare.

rabid agg. 1. rabbioso 2. irragionevole 3. idrofobo.

rabidity s. 1. rabbia 2. fanatismo.

rabies s. idrofobia.

race¹ s. 1. corso 2. corsa || — -meeting, concorso ippico.

race² s. razza.

to race vi. 1. correre 2. imballarsi (di motori) 3. prendere parte a una corsa 4. allevare cavalli da corsa.

racecourse s. ippodromo.

racehorse s. cavallo da corsa.

racer s. 1. corridore 2. cavallo da corsa 3. mezzo da corsa.

racial agg. razziale.

racialism s. razzismo.

racialist s. razzista.

racially avv. dal punto di vista razziale.

racily avv. vivacemente.

raciness s. vivacità.

racing s. corsa || — car, automobile da corsa.

racism s. razzismo.

racist s. razzista.

rack¹ s. 1. rastrelliera 2. reticella portabagagli 3. (mecc.) cremagliera || clothes —, attaccapanni.

rack² s. ruota, strumento di tortura.

rack³ s. nembo, nuvolaglia.

rack⁴ s. rovina, distruzione.

to **rack**[1] *vt.* **1.** torturare **2.** pretendere troppo.

to **rack**[2] *vi.* fuggire (*di nubi*).

racket[1] *s.* racchetta.

racket[2] *s.* **1.** fracasso **2.** baldoria **3.** (*gergo*) associazione a delinquere.

racy *agg.* **1.** genuino **2.** vivace, pungente.

radial *agg.* radiale.

radiance *s.* radiosità.

radiant *agg.* **1.** radiante **2.** raggiante.

to **radiate** *vt.* e *vi.* irradiare.

radiation *s.* (ir)radiazione.

radiator *s.* radiatore.

radical *agg.* e *s.* radicale.

radicalism *s.* radicalismo.

radio *s.* radio || — *beacon*, radiofaro; — *control*, radiocomando; — *operator*, radiotelegrafista.

radioactive *agg.* radioattivo.

radioactivity *s.* radioattività.

radioengineering *s.* radiotecnica.

radiogoniometer *s.* radiogoniometro.

radiogram *s.* **1.** marconigramma **2.** radiogrammofono.

radiograph *s.* radiografia.

radiography *s.* radiografia.

radiologist *s.* radiologo.

radiology *s.* radiologia.

radioscopy *s.* radioscopia.

radiostatics *s. pl.* disturbi atmosferici.

radiotelegraphy *s.* radiotelegrafia.

radiotelephony *s.* radiotelefonia.

radiotherapeutics *s.* radioterapia.

radish *s.* ravanello.

radium *s.* radio.

radius *s.* raggio.

raffia *s.* rafia.

raft *s.* zattera || — *bridge*, ponte di barche.

rag *s.* straccio.

ragamuffin *s.* pezzente.

rage *s.* **1.** furore **2.** passione.

to **rage** *vi.* infuriare || *the plague raged*, la peste infieriva.

ragged *agg.* **1.** lacero **2.** frastagliato **3.** spettinato **4.** rozzo.

raggedly *avv.* **1.** a brandelli **2.** in modo non uniforme.

raggedness *s.* **1.** cenciosità **2.** ineguaglianza.

raging *agg.* furioso.

raid *s.* incursione, scorreria.

to **raid** *vt.* e *vi.* fare un'incursione.

rail, railing *s.* **1.** sbarra **2.** ringhiera **3.** rotaia || *to go by* —, viaggiare per ferrovia.

raillery *s.* canzonatura.

railroad, railway *s.* ferrovia || — *companies*, società ferroviarie.

railwayman *s.* ferroviere.

rain *s.* pioggia || *it looks like* —, vuol piovere; *to be drenched with* —, essere inzuppato || — *-glass*, barometro.

to **rain** *v. imp.* piovere. ♦ to **rain** *vt.* far piovere.

rainbow *s.* arcobaleno.

raincoat *s.* impermeabile.

rainfall *s.* **1.** piovosità **2.** scroscio di pioggia.

rainproof *agg.* impermeabile.

rainy *agg.* piovoso.

raise *s.* aumento.

to **raise** *vt.* **1.** alzare **2.** innalzare **3.** allevare **4.** coltivare **5.** (*mil.*) arruolare.

raisin *s.* uva passa.

raising *s.* **1.** innalzamento **2.** aumento **3.** allevamento **4.** coltivazione **5.** educazione.

rake[1] *s.* rastrello.

rake[2] *s.* inclinazione.

rake[3] *s.* libertino.

to **rake**[1] *vt.* **1.** rastrellare **2.** raschiare || *to* — *up*, ammucchiare.

to **rake**[2] *vi.* essere inclinato.

rally[1] *s.* riunione, raduno.

rally[2] *s.* canzonatura.

to **rally**[1] *vt.* raccogliere. ♦ to **rally** *vi.* rianimarsi.

to **rally**[2] *vt.* canzonare.

ram *s.* ariete **2.** (*mar.*) sperone.

to **ram** *vt.* **1.** (*mar.*) speronare **2.** conficcare **3.** comprimere.

ramble *s.* vagabondaggio.

to **ramble** *vi.* **1.** vagare **2.** divagare.

rambler *s.* **1.** vagabondo **2.** rampicante.

rambling *agg.* **1.** errante **2.** sconnesso || — *thoughts*, divagazioni.

ramification *s.* ramificazione.

to **ramify** *vt.* ramificare. ♦ to **ramify** *vi.* ramificarsi.

rammer *s.* (*mil.*) pestello.

ramp[1] *s.* rampa.

ramp[2] *s.* (*gergo*) truffa.

rampage *s.* contegno iroso.

rampant *agg.* **1.** rampante **2.** violento **3.** predominante **4.** lussureggiante.

rampart *s.* bastione.

to **rampart** *vt.* fortificare.

ramshackle *agg.* sgangherato, che cade in rovina.

ran V. *to run*.

rancid *agg.* rancido.

rancour *s.* rancore.

rand *s.* soletta (*di scarpa*).

random *agg.* fatto a caso || *at* —, a casaccio.

rang V. *to ring*.

range *s.* 1. fila 2. catena (*di monti*) 3. spazio 4. sfera, raggio 5. gamma 6. fornello 7. (*aer.*) autonomia.

to range *vt.* 1. allineare 2. classificare 3. puntare. ♦ **to range** *vi.* 1. vagare 2. avere una portata di 3. oscillare (*di prezzi*).

ranger *s.* 1. guardia forestale 2. vagabondo.

rank *agg.* 1. rigoglioso 2. volgare 3. puzzolente. ♦ **rank** *s.* 1. fila 2. rango, grado 3. truppa.

to rank *vi.* 1. schierarsi 2. essere classificato.

to ransack *vt.* 1. frugare 2. saccheggiare.

ransom *s.* riscatto.

to ransom *vt.* riscattare.

to rant *vt.* e *vi.* declamare.

rap *s.* colpo.

to rap *vt.* e *vi.* 1. battere 2. bussare.

rapacious *agg.* rapace.

rapacity *s.* rapacità.

rape[1] *s.* violenza carnale.

rape[2] *s.* rapa.

to rape *vt.* violentare.

rapid *agg.* rapido. ♦ **rapid** *s.* rapida.

rapidity *s.* rapidità.

rapt *agg.* rapito.

raptorial *agg.* rapace.

rapture *s.* rapimento.

rare *agg.* 1. raro 2. rarefatto.

rarefaction *s.* rarefazione.

to rarefy *vt.* 1. rarefare 2. raffinare. ♦ **to rarefy** *vi.* rarefarsi.

rarely *avv.* 1. raramente 2. in modo eccellente.

rareness, rarity *s.* 1. rarità 2. rarefazione.

rascal *s.* furfante.

rascalism, rascality *s.* furfanteria.

rash *agg.* avventato. ♦ **rash** *s.* eruzione cutanea.

rashness *s.* avventatezza.

rasp *s.* 1. raspa 2. stridore.

to rasp *vt.* 1. raspare 2. irritare.

raspberry *s.* lampone.

rasping *agg.* stridente.

rat *s.* 1. topo 2. (*fig.*) traditore.

rate *s.* 1. tasso, quota 2. tassa 3. prezzo, tariffa 4. ritmo, andamento

|| *first* —, di prim'ordine; — *of discount*, tasso di sconto.

to rate[1] *vt.* 1. stimare 2. tassare 3. classificare.

to rate[2] *vt.* redarguire.

rateable *agg.* soggetto ad imposta.

ratepayer *s.* contribuente.

rather *avv.* piuttosto || *I had* —, preferirei; *I would* — *not*, non ci tengo.

ratification *s.* ratifica.

to ratify *vt.* ratificare.

rating[1] *s.* 1. stima 2. tassa 3. classificazione.

rating[2] *s.* sgridata.

ratio *s.* rapporto.

ration *s.* razione.

to ration *vt.* razionare.

rational *agg.* razionale.

rationalism *s.* razionalismo.

rationalist *s.* razionalista.

rationality *s.* razionalità.

to rationalize *vt.* 1. razionalizzare 2. spiegare razionalmente.

rationally *avv.* razionalmente.

rattle *s.* 1. sonaglio 2. rantolo 3. tintinnio.

to rattle *vt.* far risuonare. ♦ **to rattle** *vi.* 1. risuonare 2. cianciare.

rattling *agg.* 1. vivace 2. tintinnante.

ravage *s.* rovina.

to ravage *vt.* devastare.

rave *s.* delirio.

to rave *vt.* declamare. ♦ **to rave** *vi.* delirare || — *about sthg.*, andar pazzo per qc.

ravel *s.* 1. groviglio 2. lembo sfilacciato.

to ravel *vt.* ingarbugliare. ♦ **to ravel** *vi.* sfilacciarsi.

raven *s.* corvo.

to raven *vt.* e *vi.* saccheggiare.

ravenous *agg.* vorace.

ravine *s.* burrone.

raving *agg.* delirante. ♦ **raving** *s.* delirio.

to ravish *vt.* 1. rapire 2. violentare.

ravisher *s.* rapitore.

ravishing *agg.* (*fig.*) affascinante.

ravishment *s.* 1. rapimento 2. stupro.

raw *agg.* 1. crudo 2. greggio 3. inesperto 4. a nudo. ♦ **raw** *s.* punto vivo.

rawness *s.* 1. crudezza 2. rozzezza 3. inesperienza 4. escoriazione.

ray[1] *s.* 1. raggio 2. lampo.

ray[2] *s.* (*zool.*) razza.

to **ray** *vt.* irradiare. ♦ to **ray** *vi.* irradiarsi.

to **raze** *vt.* radere al suolo.

razor *s.* rasoio || — *-blade*, lametta.

to **reabsorb** *vt.* riassorbire.

reach *s.* 1. portata 2. penetrazione || *beyond my* —, irraggiungibile.

to **reach** *vt.* 1. raggiungere 2. porgere. ♦ to **reach** *vi.* estendersi.

to **react** *vi.* reagire.

reaction *s.* reazione.

reactionary *agg.* e *s.* reazionario.

reactive *agg.* reattivo.

read *agg.* colto. ♦ **read** *s.* lettura.

to **read** (**read, read**) *vt.* 1. leggere 2. interpretare 3. segnare || *to* — *over*, rileggere; *to* — *through*, esaminare.

readable *agg.* 1. leggibile 2. interessante.

reader *s.* 1. lettore 2. libro di lettura.

readily *avv.* prontamente.

readiness *s.* prontezza.

reading *s.* 1. lettura 2. interpretazione || — *-desk*, leggio.

to **readjust** *vt.* riaggiustare.

readjustment *s.* riordinamento.

to **readmit** *vt.* riammettere.

readmittance *s.* riammissione.

ready *agg.* pronto || — *-made*, confezionato; — *money*, contanti; — *-made clothes*, abito preconfezionato; — *-built*, prefabbricato.

to **ready** *vt.* preparare.

to **reaffirm** *vt.* riaffermare.

reafforestation *s.* rimboschimento.

reagent *s.* reagente.

real *agg.* e *s.* reale || — *estate*, beni immobili (*pl.*).

realism *s.* realismo.

realist *s.* realista.

realistic *agg.* realistico.

reality *s.* 1. realtà 2. realismo.

realizable *agg.* realizzabile.

realization *s.* 1. realizzazione 2. percezione.

to **realize** *vt.* 1. accorgersi di 2. realizzare 3. capire.

really *avv.* realmente.

realm *s.* reame.

realty *s.* beni immobili (*pl.*).

ream *s.* (*tip.*) risma.

to **reap** *vt.* 1. mietere 2. fare il raccolto (*anche fig.*).

reaper *s.* mietitore.

reaping *s.* mietitura.

to **reappear** *vi.* riapparire.

to **reappoint** *vt.* rinominare.

rear *agg.* posteriore. ♦ **rear** *s.* 1. retroguardia 2. retro.

to **rear** *vt.* 1. alzare, innalzare 2. allevare 3. coltivare.

to **rearm** *vt.* riarmare.

rearmament *s.* riarmo.

to **rearrange** *vt.* riordinare.

rearrangement *s.* riordinamento.

reason *s.* 1. ragione 2. causa, motivo 3. raziocinio.

to **reason** *vt.* e *vi.* 1. ragionare 2. persuadere || *to* — *about a subject*, discutere di un argomento.

reasonable *agg.* ragionevole.

reasonableness *s.* ragionevolezza.

reasonably *avv.* ragionevolmente.

reasoning *s.* ragionamento.

to **reassert** *vt.* riasserire.

reassurance *s.* rassicurazione.

to **reassure** *vt.* rassicurare.

to **reawaken** *vt.* risvegliare. ♦ to **reawaken** *vi.* risvegliarsi.

rebate *s.* riduzione, sconto.

rebel *agg.* e *s.* ribelle.

to **rebel** *vi.* ribellarsi.

rebellion *s.* ribellione.

rebellious *agg.* ribelle.

to **rebind** (**rebound, rebound**) *vt.* rilegare (*un libro*).

rebirth *s.* rinascita.

reborn *agg.* rinato.

rebound[1] V. to **rebind**.

rebound[2] *s.* rimbalzo.

to **rebound** *vi.* rimbalzare.

rebuff *s.* diniego, mortificazione.

to **rebuild** (**rebuilt, rebuilt**) *vt.* ricostruire.

rebuke *s.* rimprovero.

to **rebuke** *vt.* rimproverare.

to **rebut** *vt.* respingere, rifiutare.

recalcitrant *agg.* recalcitrante.

to **recalcitrate** *vi.* recalcitrare.

recall *s.* 1. richiamo 2. revoca.

to **recall** *vt.* 1. richiamare 2. rievocare, far tornare alla memoria.

to **recant** *vt.* e *vi.* ritrattare.

recantation *s.* ritrattazione.

to **recapitulate** *vt.* e *vi.* ricapitolare.

recapitulation *s.* ricapitolazione.

recapture *s.* riconquista.

to **recapture** *vt.* riconquistare.

recast *s.* nuova forma.

to **recast** (**recast, recast**) *vt.* 1. rifondere 2. rimaneggiare.

to **recede** *vi.* 1. indietreggiare 2. diminuire.

receding *agg.* **1.** rientrante **2.** sfuggente.

receipt *s.* **1.** ricevimento **2.** ricevuta **3.** ricetta.

to receipt *vt.* quietanzare.

to receive *vt.* **1.** ricevere **2.** accettare.

receiver *s.* **1.** ricevitore **2.** *(giur.)* ricettatore.

receiving *s.* ricezione.

recension *s.* revisione.

recent *agg.* recente.

receptacle *s.* ricettacolo.

reception *s.* **1.** ricevimento **2.** ricezione **3.** accoglienza.

receptive *agg.* ricettivo.

receptivity *s.* ricettività.

recess *s.* **1.** intervallo **2.** rientranza **3.** recesso.

recession *s.* **1.** ritiro **2.** recessione.

recessive *agg.* retrocedente.

recharge *s.* ricarica.

to recharge *vt.* ricaricare.

to rechristen *vt.* ribattezzare.

recipe *s.* ricetta.

recipient *agg. e s.* ricevente.

reciprocal *agg.* reciproco. ◆ **reciprocal** *s.* *(mat.)* numero reciproco.

to reciprocate *vt.* **1.** contraccambiare **2.** muovere alternativamente. ◆ **to reciprocate** *vi.* muoversi alternativamente.

reciprocating *agg.* *(mecc.)* alternativo.

reciprocation *s.* **1.** moto alterno **2.** scambio.

reciprocity *s.* reciprocità.

recital *s.* **1.** relazione **2.** recitazione.

recitation *s.* **1.** recitazione **2.** recita **3.** narrazione.

recitative *agg. e s.* recitativo.

to recite *vt.* **1.** recitare **2.** riferire.

reckless *agg.* incurante.

recklessness *s.* noncuranza.

to reckon *vt.* **1.** contare, computare **2.** considerare.

reckoner *s.* calcolatore.

reckoning *s.* conto.

reclaim *s.* rivendicazione.

to reclaim *vt.* **1.** redimere **2.** bonificare **3.** rivendicare.

reclamation *s.* **1.** redenzione **2.** bonifica **3.** rivendicazione.

to recline *vt.* chinare. ◆ **to recline** *vi.* chinarsi.

reclining *agg.* chinato.

recluse *agg.* recluso. ◆ **recluse** *s.* eremita.

reclusion *s.* **1.** reclusione **2.** eremo.

recognition *s.* riconoscimento.

recognizable *agg.* riconoscibile.

to recognize *vt.* riconoscere.

recoil *s.* **1.** il ritrarsi **2.** rinculo.

to recoil *vi.* **1.** ritrarsi **2.** ricadere **3.** rinculare.

to recollect *vt.* **1.** raccogliere **2.** ricordare || *to — oneself*, riaversi.

recollection *s.* ricordo.

to recommence *vt. e vi.* ricominciare.

to recommend *vt.* raccomandare.

recommendation *s.* raccomandazione.

recommendatory *agg.* raccomandatorio.

recompense *s.* **1.** ricompensa **2.** risarcimento.

to recompense *vt.* **1.** ricompensare **2.** risarcire.

to recompose *vt.* ricomporre.

recomposition *s.* ricomposizione.

to reconcile *vt.* (ri)conciliare || *to — oneself*, rassegnarsi.

reconcilement *s.* **1.** riconciliazione **2.** rassegnazione.

reconnaissance *s.* ricognizione.

to reconnoitre *vt. e vi.* perlustrare.

to reconquer *vt.* riconquistare.

reconquest *s.* riconquista.

to reconsider *vt.* riconsiderare.

reconsideration *s.* revisione.

reconstitute *vt.* ricostituire.

to reconstruct *vt.* ricostruire.

reconstruction *s.* ricostruzione.

reconversion *s.* riconversione.

to reconvert *vt.* riconvertire.

record *s.* **1.** registrazione **2.** documento **3.** passato **4.** disco || *— player*, giradischi.

to record *vt.* registrare.

recorder *s.* **1.** cancelliere **2.** registratore **3.** archivista || *tape —*, magnetofono.

recording *s.* registrazione.

recordist *s.* *(cine)* tecnico del suono.

recourse *s.* ricorso.

to recover *vt.* ricuperare, riacquistare, riscoprire. ◆ **to recover** *vi.* ristabilirsi.

recoverable *agg.* **1.** ricuperabile **2.** guaribile.

recovery *s.* **1.** recupero **2.** guarigione **3.** *(giur.)* rivendicazione.

to recreate *vt.* divertire. ◆ **to recreate** *vi.* divertirsi.

to re-create *vt.* ricreare.

recreation *s.* ricreazione.

recreative *agg.* ricreativo.
to recriminate *vi.* recriminare.
recrimination *s.* recriminazione.
recrudescence *s.* recrudescenza.
recrudescent *agg.* che rincrudisce.
recruit *s.* recluta.
to recruit *vt.* 1. reclutare 2. rinforzare. ♦ **to recruit** *vi.* ristabilirsi.
recruitment *s.* reclutamento.
rectangle *s.* rettangolo.
rectangular *agg.* rettangolare.
rectification *s.* rettificazione.
rectifier *s.* (*mecc.*) rettificatrice.
to rectify *vt.* rettificare.
rectilineal *agg.* rettilineo.
rectitude *s.* rettitudine.
rector *s.* 1. rettore 2. parroco.
rectorate *s.* rettorato.
rectorship *s.* rettorato.
rectory *s.* 1. presbiterio 2. (*eccl.*) beneficio.
to recur *vi.* ritornare.
recurrence *s.* ricorso.
recurrent *agg.* ricorrente.
recusant *agg.* e *s.* dissidente.
red *agg.* e *s.* rosso || *-bot,* rovente; *—-lead,* minio; *—-letter day,* giorno festivo. ♦ **Reds** *s. pl.* comunisti.
to redact *vt.* 1. redigere 2. revisionare.
redactor *s.* redattore.
to redden *vt.* arrossare. ♦ **to redden** *vi.* arrossire.
reddish *agg.* rossiccio.
to redeem *vt.* 1. riscattare 2. ricuperare 3. estinguere: *to — a mortgage,* estinguere un'ipoteca.
redeemable *agg.* 1. riscattabile 2. ricuperabile.
redeemer *s.* redentore.
redemption *s.* 1. redenzione 2. (*comm.*) rimborso 3. (*giur.*) riscatto.
redness *s.* rossore.
to redouble *vt.* e *vi.* raddoppiare.
redress *s.* riparazione.
to redress *vt.* riparare, rimediare.
redskin *agg.* e *s.* pellerossa.
to reduce *vt.* 1. ridurre 2. degradare.
reduced *agg.* ridotto.
reducer *s.* riduttore.
reduction *s.* 1. riduzione 2. degradazione.
redundance *s.* sovrabbondanza.
redundant *agg.* ridondante.
redwood *s.* sequoia.
to re-echo *vt.* e *vi.* riecheggiare.
reed *s.* canna || *broken —,* perso-

na infida; *— -pipe,* zampogna.
re-edification *s.* riedificazione.
to re-edify *vt.* riedificare.
to re-educate *vt.* rieducare.
reef *s.* secca || *coral —,* banco di coralli.
to reek *vi.* puzzare. ♦ **to reek** *vt.* trasudare.
reel *s.* 1. bobina 2. giro vorticoso || *news —,* cinegiornale.
to reel *vt.* avvolgere || *to — off,* snocciolare. ♦ **to reel** *vi.* girare.
to re-elect *vt.* rieleggere.
to re-emerge *vi.* riemergere.
to re-enact *vt.* richiamare in vigore (*una legge*).
to re-enter *vt.* rientrare.
re-entrance *s.* rientro.
re-entry *s.* 1. rientro 2. nuova registrazione.
to re-establish *vt.* ristabilire.
re-establishment *s.* ristabilimento.
re-examination *s.* riesame.
to re-examine *vt.* riesaminare.
refectory *s.* refettorio.
to refer *vt.* 1. attribuire 2. rimandare. ♦ **to refer** *vi.* 1. riferirsi 2. rivolgersi.
referable *agg.* riferibile.
referee *s.* arbitro.
to referee *vt.* e *vi.* arbitrare.
reference *s.* 1. riferimento 2. consultazione 3. referenza 4. (*giur.*) rinvio.
referential *agg.* riferentesi a.
refill *s.* ricambio.
to refill *vt.* riempire di nuovo.
to refine *vt.* raffinare. ♦ **to refine** *vi.* raffinarsi.
refined *agg.* 1. raffinato 2. colto.
refinement *s.* 1. raffinamento 2. raffinatezza.
refiner *s.* raffinatore.
refinery *s.* raffineria.
refit *s.* riparazione.
to refit *vt.* riparare.
to reflect *vt.* e *vi* 1. riflettere 2. meditare.
reflection *s.* 1. riflessione, riflesso 2. biasimo || *to cast reflections on so.,* criticare qu.
reflective *agg.* riflessivo.
reflector *s.* riflettore.
reflex *agg.* e *s.* riflesso.
reflorescence *s.* rifioritura.
reflux *s.* riflusso.
reform *s.* riforma.
to reform *vt.* riformare.
reformation *s.* riforma.

reformational *agg.* di riforma.

reformatory *agg.* riformativo. ♦ **reformatory** *s.* riformatorio.

reformer *s.* riformatore.

to **refract** *vt.* rifrangere.

refraction *s.* rifrazione.

refractivity *s.* rifrangibilità.

refractor *s.* rifrattore.

refractory *agg.* 1. refrattario 2. ostinato.

refrain *s.* ritornello.

to **refrain** *vi.* trattenersi, astenersi.

to **refresh** *vt.* 1. rinfrescare 2. rinvigorire. ♦ to **refresh** *vi.* 1. rinvigorirsi 2. rifornirsi.

refreshment *s.* ristoro. ♦ **refreshments** *s. pl.* cibo, bevanda (*sing.*).

refrigerant *agg.* e *s.* refrigerante.

to **refrigerate** *vt.* refrigerare.

refrigeration *s.* refrigerazione.

refrigerator *s.* frigorifero.

refrigeratory *agg.* refrigerante.

to **refuel** *vt.* rifornire di carburante. ♦ to **refuel** *vi.* rifornirsi di carburante.

refuge *s.* rifugio.

refugee *s.* rifugiato, profugo.

refulgence *s.* fulgore.

refulgent *agg.* rifulgente.

refund *s.* rimborso.

to **refund** *vt.* rimborsare.

refusable *agg.* rifiutabile.

refusal *s.* 1. rifiuto 2. diritto di opzione.

refuse *s.* rifiuto.

to **refuse** *vt.* rifiutare. ♦ to **refuse** *vi.* rifiutarsi.

refuser *s.* ricusante.

refutal *s.* confutazione.

to **refute** *vt.* confutare.

to **regain** *vt.* riguadagnare.

regal *agg.* regale.

regality *s.* regalità.

regally *avv.* regalmente.

regard *s.* 1. considerazione 2. sguardo ‖ *with — to,* riguardo a. ♦ **regards** *s. pl.* saluti.

to **regard** *vt.* 1. considerare 2. riguardare 3. osservare.

regardful *agg.* 1. attento 2. rispettoso.

regardless *agg.* senza riguardo. ♦ **regardless** *avv.* senza riguardo a, senza badare a.

regatta *s.* regata.

regelation *s.* ricongelamento.

regency *s.* reggenza.

to **regenerate** *vt.* rigenerare. ♦ to **regenerate** *vi.* rigenerarsi.

regeneration *s.* rigenerazione.

regenerative *agg.* rigeneratore.

regenerator *s.* rigeneratore.

regent *agg.* e *s.* reggente.

regicide *s.* 1. regicida 2. regicidio.

regimen *s.* regime.

regiment *s.* reggimento.

to **regiment** *vt.* 1. irreggimentare 2. disciplinare.

regimental *agg.* reggimentale.

regimentals *s. pl.* (*mil.*) uniforme (*sing.*).

region *s.* regione.

regional *agg.* regionale.

register *s.* registro.

to **register** *vt.* registrare, iscrivere. ♦ to **register** *vi.* iscriversi.

registrar *s.* 1. segretario 2. ufficiale di stato civile.

registration *s.* registrazione, iscrizione.

registry *s.* 1. registrazione 2. ufficio del Registro.

regnant *agg.* regnante.

regress *s.* retrocessione.

to **regress** *vi.* retrocedere.

regression *s.* regresso.

regressive *agg.* regressivo.

regret *s.* rammarico.

to **regret** *vt.* 1. rimpiangere 2. rammaricarsi di.

regretful *agg.* pieno di rammarico.

regular *agg.* e *s.* regolare.

regularity *s.* regolarità.

regularization *s.* regolarizzazione.

to **regularize** *vt.* regolarizzare.

regularly *avv.* regolarmente.

to **regulate** *vt.* regolare.

regulation *s.* 1. regolamento 2. regolazione.

regulative *agg.* e *s.* regolatore.

regulator *s.* regolatore.

to **rehabilitate** *vt.* 1. riabilitare 2. ripristinare.

rehabilitation *s.* 1. riabilitazione 2. ripristino.

rehearsal *s.* 1. ripetizione 2. (*teat.*) prova.

to **rehearse** *vt.* 1. ripetere 2. provare.

reign *s.* regno.

to **reign** *vi.* regnare.

to **reimburse** *vt.* rimborsare.

reimbursement *s.* rimborso.

rein *s.* redine.

to **rein** *vt.* tenere a freno.

to **reincarnate** *vt.* reincarnare.

reincarnation *s.* reincarnazione.

reindeer *s.* renna.

to **reinforce** vt. rinforzare.
reinforce(ment) s. rinforzo.
to **reinstate** vt. ristabilire.
to **reintegrate** vt. reintegrare.
reinvestment s. nuovo investimento.
to **reinvigorate** vt. rinvigorire.
reinvigoration s. rinvigorimento.
to **reiterate** vt. reiterare.
reiteration s. reiterazione.
reject s. persona, cosa rifiutata.
to **reject** vt. rifiutare.
rejection s. rifiuto.
to **rejoice** vt. rallegrare. ♦ to
rejoice vi. rallegrarsi.
rejoicing s. allegria 2. festa.
rejuvenation s. ringiovanimento.
relapse s. ricaduta.
to **relapse** vi. 1. ricadere 2. avere
una ricaduta.
to **relate** vt. 1. narrare 2. mettere
in relazione. ♦ to **relate** vi. aver
rapporto con.
relater s. narratore.
relation s. 1. relazione 2. parente.
relationship s. 1. relazione 2. parentela.
relative agg. relativo. ♦ **relative**
s. parente.
relativism s. relativismo.
relativity s. relatività.
to **relax** vt. 1. rilassare 2. allentare.
♦ to **relax** vi. rilassarsi.
relaxation s. 1. rilassamento 2. svago 3. mitigazione.
relay s. 1. turno 2. rjcambio 3. (radio) collegamento.
to **relay** vt. (radio) collegare.
release s. 1. liberazione 2. quietanza 3. cessione 4. scarico.
to **release** vt. 1. liberare 2. cedere.
releasee s. cessionario.
to **relegate** vt. 1. relegare 2. rimettere.
relegation s. relegazione.
relentless agg. inflessibile.
to **relent** vi. impietosirsi.
relevance s. 1. relazione 2. pertinenza.
relevant agg. 1. relativo 2. pertinente.
reliability s. attendibilità.
reliable agg. attendibile, fidato.
reliance s. 1. fede 2. persona, cosa
di fiducia.
relic s. reliquia.
relief[1] s. 1. sollievo 2. aiuto 3. esenzione 4. cambio.
relief[2] s. 1. rilievo 2. (pitt.) pro-

spettiva.
to **relieve** vt. 1. alleviare, sollevare
2. aiutare 3. dare il cambio a 4.
dare rilievo a.
reliever s. soccorritore.
relieving agg. 1. che allevia, soccorre 2. (mil.) che dà il cambio.
religion s. religione.
religiosity s. religiosità.
religious agg. e s. religioso.
to **relinquish** vt. abbandonare.
relinquishment s. abbandono.
reliquary s. reliquario.
reliques s. pl. resti.
relish s. 1. gusto 2. sapore, profumo, aroma 3. condimento.
to **relish** vt. 1. gustare 2. insaporire.
to **relive** vt. e vi. rivivere.
to **reload** vt. ricaricare.
to **reluct** vi. essere riluttante.
reluctance s. riluttanza.
reluctant agg. riluttante.
reluctantly avv. con riluttanza.
to **rely** vi. fidarsi.
remade V. to remake.
to **remain** vi. rimanere, restare.
remainder s. resto, avanzo, rimanenza.
remains s. pl. resti.
to **remake** (remade, remade) vt.
rifare.
remark s. nota, osservazione, commento.
to **remark** vt. e vi. osservare.
remarkable agg. notevole.
remarkableness s. ragguardevolezza.
remarkably avv. notevolmente.
to **remarry** vt. risposare. ♦ to
remarry vi. risposarsi.
remediable agg. rimediabile.
remedy s. rimedio, cura.
to **remedy** vt. rimediare.
to **remember** vt. ricordare. ♦ to
remember vi. ricordarsi.
remembrance s. ricordo.
to **remind** vt. ricordare (qc. a qu.),
far ricordare, rammentare.
reminder s. ricordo, promemoria.
remindful agg. 1. memore 2. che
fa ricordare.
reminiscence s. ricordo.
reminiscent agg. che ricorda.
remise s. (giur.) cessione.
to **remise** vt. (giur.) rinunciare a,
cedere (diritti ecc.).
remiss agg. negligente.
remissible agg. remissibile.

remission s. 1. remissione 2. esonero, annullamento 3. (med.) remissione.

remissive agg. indulgente.

to **remit** vt. rimettere. ♦ to **remit** vi. diminuire, mitigarsi.

remittal s. (giur.) remissione (condono).

remittance s. rimessa (di denaro).

remittent agg. (med.) intermittente.

remnant agg. rimanente. ♦ **remnant** s. resto, rimanenza, avanzo.

to **remodel** vt. rimodellare.

remonstrance s. rimostranza.

to **remonstrate** vi. protestare.

remonstration s. rimostranza.

remorse s. rimorso.

remorseful agg. pieno di rimorso.

remorseless agg. senza rimorsi.

remote agg. remoto.

remoteness s. distanza, lontananza.

remotion s. rimozione, allontanamento.

remount s. rimonta (di cavalli).

to **remount** vt. e vi. 1. rimontare (a cavallo, in bicicletta) 2. risalire.

removable agg. rimovibile.

removal s. 1. rimozione 2. trasferimento, trasloco.

remove s. 1. trasferimento 2. grado (di parentela).

to **remove** vt. rimuovere. ♦ to **remove** vi. trasferirsi.

removed agg. lontano.

remover s. chi, ciò che toglie.

to **remunerate** vt. rimunerare.

remuneration s. rimunerazione.

remunerative agg. rimunerativo.

renaissance s. rinascimento.

renal agg. renale.

to **rename** vt. rinominare.

to **rend (rent, rent)** vt. lacerare. ♦ to **rend (rent, rent)** vi. lacerarsi.

to **render** vt. 1. rendere 2. consegnare.

rendering s. 1. restituzione 2. resa.

renegade s. rinnegato.

to **renew** vt. rinnovare. ♦ to **renew** vi. rinnovarsi.

renewable agg. rinnovabile.

renewal s. 1. rinnovo 2. ripresa.

renewer s. rinnovatore.

renitency s. riluttanza.

renitent agg. renitente, riluttante.

rennet s. ranetta.

to **renounce** vt. 1. rinunciare a 2. ripudiare.

renouncement s. rinuncia.

to **renovate** vt. rinnovare.

renown s. rinomanza, fama.

renowned agg. rinomato, famoso.

rent[1] s. affitto.

rent[2] s. 1. strappo, squarcio 2. spaccatura.

rent[3] V. to rend.

to **rent** vt. affittare. ♦ to **rent** vi. essere affittato.

rental s. affitto.

renunciation s. rinuncia.

to **reoccupy** vt. rioccupare.

to **reopen** vt. riaprire. ♦ to **reopen** vi. riaprirsi.

reopening s. riapertura.

reorganization s. riassetto, riorganizzazione.

repaid V. to repay.

repair s. 1. riparazione, restaurazione 2. stato, condizione.

to **repair** vt. riparare, restaurare.

repairer s. riparatore.

reparation s. riparazione.

repartee s. replica arguta.

repartition s. ripartizione.

to **repatriate** vt. e vi. rimpatriare.

repatriation s. rimpatrio.

to **repay (repaid, repaid)** vt. ripagare.

repayable agg. ripagabile.

repeal s. revoca.

to **repeal** vt. revocare.

repealer s. revocatore.

repeat s. ripetizione.

to **repeat** vt. ripetere. ♦ to **repeat** vi. ripetersi.

repeater s. 1. ripetitore 2. ripetente 3. arma a ripetizione.

repeating agg. 1. a ripetizione 2. periodico (di numero).

to **repel** vt. respingere.

repellent agg. repellente.

to **repent** vt. e vi. pentirsi.

repentance s. pentimento.

repentant agg. pentito.

repenter s. penitente.

repercussion s. ripercussione.

repercussive agg. ripercussivo.

repertoire s. repertorio.

repertory s. 1. repertorio 2. raccolta.

repetition s. ripetizione.

to **repine** vi. lamentarsi.

to **replace** vt. 1. ricollocare 2. rimpiazzare, sostituire.

replaceable agg. sostituibile.

replacement s. 1. ricollocamento 2. sostituzione.

replete *agg.* pieno.

repletion *s.* pienezza.

replication *s.* replica.

reply *s.* risposta.

to **reply** *vi.* rispondere.

report *s.* 1. diceria 2. reputazione 3. rapporto 4. scoppio.

to **report** *vt.* riportare. ♦ to **report** *vi.* 1. stendere rapporto 2. fare il cronista 3. presentarsi.

reporter *s.* cronista (*di giornale*).

to **repose** *vt.* porre. ♦ to **repose** *vi.* riposare.

to **reprehend** *vt.* rimproverare.

reprehensible *agg.* biasimevole.

reprehension *s.* biasimo.

to **represent** *vt.* rappresentare, raffigurare.

representation *s.* 1. rappresentazione 2. rappresentanza.

representative *agg.* rappresentativo. ♦ **representative** *s.* rappresentante.

to **repress** *vt.* reprimere.

repressed *agg.* represso.

repressible *agg.* reprimibile.

repression *s.* repressione.

repressive *agg.* repressivo.

reprimand *s.* rimprovero.

reprint *s.* ristampa.

to **reprint** *vt.* ristampare.

reprisal *s.* rappresaglia.

reproach *s.* 1. rimprovero 2. discredito.

to **reproach** *vt.* 1. rimproverare 2. discreditare.

reproachable *agg.* riprovevole.

reproachful *agg.* di rimprovero.

reprobate *agg.* corrotto. ♦ **reprobate** *s.* reprobo.

to **reprobate** *vt.* 1. riprovare 2. dannare.

reprobation *s.* 1. riprovazione 2. dannazione.

to **reproduce** *vt.* riprodurre. ♦ to **reproduce** *vi.* riprodursi.

reproducer *s.* riproduttore.

reproducible *agg.* riproducibile.

reproduction *s.* riproduzione.

reproductive *agg.* riproduttivo.

reproof *s.* rimprovero.

to **reprove** *vt.* rimproverare.

reptile *agg.* strisciante. ♦ **reptile** *s.* rettile.

republic *s.* repubblica.

republican *agg. e s.* repubblicano.

republication *s.* ripubblicazione.

to **republish** *vt.* ripubblicare.

to **repudiate** *vt.* ripudiare.

repudiation *s.* ripudio.

repugnance *s.* 1. ripugnanza 2. incompatibilità.

repugnant *agg.* 1. ripugnante 2. incompatibile.

repulse *s.* ripulsa, rifiuto.

to **repulse** *vt.* respingere.

repulsion *s.* repulsione.

repulsive *agg.* ripulsivo.

reputable *agg.* onorato.

reputation *s.* reputazione.

repute *s.* fama.

to **repute** *vt.* reputare.

reputed *agg.* 1. supposto 2. putativo.

request *s.* richiesta.

to **request** *vt.* (ri)chiedere.

to **require** *vt.* 1. richiedere 2. ordinare, obbligare.

requirement *s.* 1. richiesta 2. requisito.

requisite *agg.* richiesto. ♦ **requisite** *s.* requisito.

requisition *s.* 1. richiesta 2. requisito 3. requisizione.

to **requisition** *vt.* requisire.

requital *s.* 1. contraccambio 2. ricompensa.

to **requite** *vt.* 1. ricompensare 2. contraccambiare.

to **reread** (**reread, reread**) *vt.* rileggere.

to **rescind** *vt.* rescindere.

rescission *s.* rescissione.

rescue *s.* 1. liberazione 2. soccorso.

to **rescue** *vt.* 1. liberare 2. riacquistare 3. soccorrere.

research *s.* ricerca || — *work*, lavoro di ricerca.

to **research** *vi.* fare ricerche.

researcher *s.* ricercatore.

to **resell** (**resold, resold**) *vt.* rivendere.

resemblance *s.* rassomiglianza.

to **resemble** *vt.* assomigliare a.

to **resent** *vt.* risentirsi di.

resentful *agg.* 1. risentito 2. permaloso.

resentment *s.* risentimento.

reservation *s.* 1. riserva 2. prenotazione.

reserve *s.* 1. riserva 2. riserbo.

to **reserve** *vt.* riservare.

reservoir *s.* serbatoio.

to **reset** (**reset, reset**) *vt.* 1. rimettere a posto 2. (*tip.*) ricomporre.

to **resettle** *vt.* risistemare. ♦ to **resettle** *vi.* risistemarsi.

resettlement *s.* risistemazione.

to **reshape** *vt.* dare nuova forma a.
to **reside** *vi.* risiedere.
residence *s.* residenza.
resident *agg.* e *s.* residente.
residential *agg.* residenziale.
residual *agg.* residuo. ♦ **residual** *s.* 1. residuo 2. resto.
residue *s.* residuo, avanzo.
to **resign** *vt.* 1. consegnare 2. rinunciare || *to — oneself*, rassegnarsi. ♦ to **resign** *vi.* dimettersi.
resignation *s.* 1. dimissioni (*pl.*) 2. rinuncia 3. rassegnazione.
resigned *agg.* rassegnato.
resilience, resiliency *s.* elasticità.
resilient *agg.* elastico.
resin *s.* resina.
resinous *agg.* resinoso.
resipiscence *s.* resipiscenza.
resipiscent *agg.* resipiscente.
resist *s.* sostanza protettiva.
to **resist** *vt.* e *vi.* resistere.
resistance *s.* resistenza.
resistant, resistent *agg.* resistente.
resistive *agg.* resistente.
resold V. to *resell*.
to **resole** *vt.* risolare.
resolubile *agg.* (ri)solubile.
resolute *agg.* risoluto.
resoluteness *s.* risolutezza.
resolution *s.* 1. risolutezza 2. risoluzione 3. scissione.
resolutive *agg.* risolutivo.
resolvable *agg.* risolvibile.
resolve *s.* risoluzione.
to **resolve** *vt.* 1. risolvere 2. scindere. ♦ to **resolve** *vi.* risolversi.
resolvent *agg.* e *s.* solvente.
resonance *s.* risonanza.
resonant *agg.* risonante.
to **resorb** *vt.* riassorbire.
resorbent *agg.* riassorbente.
resort *s.* 1. ricorso 2. risorsa 3. ritrovo 4. luogo di soggiorno.
to **resort** *vi.* 1. ricorrere 2. recarsi.
to **resound** *vi.* risuonare. ♦ to **resound** *vt.* proclamare.
resource *s.* risorsa.
resourceful *agg.* pieno di risorse.
resourceless *agg.* senza risorse.
respect *s.* 1. rispetto, stima 2. aspetto 3. punto di vista.
to **respect** *vt.* rispettare.
respectability *s.* 1. rispettabilità 2. convenzioni sociali (*pl.*).
respectable *agg.* rispettabile.
respectful *agg.* rispettoso.
respecting *prep.* rispetto a.
respective *agg.* rispettivo.

respiration *s.* respirazione.
respirator *s.* respiratore.
respiratory *agg.* respiratorio.
respite *s.* 1. dilazione 2. tregua.
to **respite** *vt.* concedere una dilazione, una tregua a.
resplendent *agg.* risplendente.
respond *s.* responsorio.
to **respond** *vi.* rispondere.
respondence *s.* rispondenza.
respondent *agg.* 1. rispondente 2. sensibile. ♦ **respondent** *s.* (*giur.*) convenuto.
response *s.* risposta.
responsibility *s.* responsabilità.
responsible *agg.* 1. responsabile 2. di responsabilità.
responsive *agg.* rispondente.
responsory *s.* responsorio.
rest[1] *s.* 1. riposo 2. appoggio.
rest[2] *s.* resto, residuo.
to **rest** *vt.* 1. riposare 2. appoggiare. ♦ to **rest** *vi.* 1. riposarsi 2. appoggiarsi.
to **restate** *vt.* riesporre.
restaurant *s.* ristorante || *— -car*, vagone ristorante.
restful *agg.* tranquillo.
restfulness *s.* tranquillità.
resting-place *s.* luogo di riposo.
restitution *s.* restituzione.
restive *agg.* 1. restio 2. irrequieto.
restless *agg.* 1. irrequieto 2. incessante.
restlessness *s.* irrequietezza.
restorable *agg.* 1. restituibile 2. restaurabile.
restoration *s.* 1. restituzione 2. restauro 3. restaurazione 4. ricostruzione.
to **restore** *vt.* 1. restituire 2. restaurare 3. ricostruire 4. ristabilire.
to **restrain** *vt.* 1. trattenere 2. confinare.
restrainable *agg.* reprimibile.
restraint *s.* 1. freno 2. detenzione.
to **restrict** *vt.* limitare.
restrictedly *avv.* limitatamente.
restriction *s.* restrizione.
restrictive *agg.* restrittivo.
result *s.* risultato.
to **result** *vi.* 1. risultare 2. risolversi.
resultant *agg.* e *s.* risultante.
resultful *agg.* utile, efficace.
resultless *agg.* inutile, inefficace.
to **resume** *vt.* riprendere.
resummons *s.* nuova convocazione.
resumption *s.* ripresa.

resurgent *agg.* risorgente.

to **resurrect** *vt.* (*fam.*) risuscitare.

resurrection *s.* risurrezione.

resurrectional *agg.* di risurrezione.

to **resuscitate** *vt.* e *vi.* risuscitare.

resuscitation *s.* risuscitamento.

to **ret** *vt.* macerare.

retail *s.* vendita al minuto || *by* —, al minuto.

to **retail** *vt.* e *vi.* vendere al minuto.

retailer *s.* dettagliante.

to **retain** *vt.* trattenere, conservare.

retainable *agg.* trattenibile, conservabile.

retainer *s.* caparra, anticipo.

retaining *agg.* — *wall*, muro di sostegno.

retake *s.* (*cine*) replica di una ripresa.

to **retake** (**retook, retaken**) *vt.* 1. riprendere 2. (*cine*) ripetere una ripresa.

to **retaliate** *vi.* far rappresaglia.

retaliation *s.* rappresaglia.

retaliative, retaliatory *agg.* vendicativo.

retard *s.* ritardo.

to **retard** *vt.* e *vi.* ritardare.

to **retaste** *vt.* riassaggiare.

to **retch** *vi.* avere conati di vomito.

to **retell** (**retold, retold**) *vt.* ripetere.

retention *s.* 1. ritenzione 2. memoria.

retentive *agg.* 1. che trattiene 2. tenace (*di memoria*).

reticence, reticency *s.* reticenza.

reticent *agg.* reticente.

reticle *s.* (*ott.*) reticolo.

reticular *agg.* reticolare.

reticulate *agg.* reticolato.

reticulum *s.* (*pl.* -la) reticolo.

retinue *s.* seguito.

to **retire** *vt.* ritirare. ♦ to **retire** *vi.* ritirarsi.

retired *agg.* 1. ritirato 2. a riposo, in ritiro.

retirement *s.* 1. ritiro 2. collocamento a riposo 3. (*mil.*) ritirata.

retiring *agg.* 1. riservato 2. che si ritira, uscente.

retold V. to *retell*.

retook V. to *retake*.

retorsion *s.* ritorsione.

retort *s.* storta.

to **retort** *vt.* ritorcere. ♦ to **retort** *vi.* ribattere.

retort(ion) *s.* ritorsione.

retouch *s.* ritocco.

to **retouch** *vt.* ritoccare.

to **retrace** *vt.* ripercorrere, risalire.

to **retract** *vt.* 1. ritrarre 2. ritrattare. ♦ to **retract** *vi.* ritrarsi.

retractable *agg.* ritraibile 2. ritrattabile.

retractation *s.* ritrattazione.

retractile *agg.* retrattile.

retractor *s.* (*med.*) divaricatore.

to **retread** (**retrod, retrodden**) *vt.* ripercorrere.

retreat *s.* eremo, luogo appartato.

to **retreat** *vi.* ritirarsi, retrocedere.

retreating *agg.* sfuggente. ♦ **retreating** *s.* (*mil.*) ritirata.

retribution *s.* punizione.

retrievable *agg.* 1. ricuperabile 2. riparabile.

retrieval *s.* 1. ricupero (*di beni*) 2. riparazione.

to **retrieve** *vt.* 1. ricuperare 2. riparare.

retroaction *s.* 1. reazione 2. azione retroattiva.

retroactive *agg.* retroattivo.

to **retrocede** *vi.* retrocedere.

to **retrocede²** *vt.* restituire.

retrocession¹ *s.* retrocessione.

retrocession² *s.* restituzione.

retrod V. to *retread*.

retrodden V. to *retread*.

retrospect(ion) *s.* sguardo retrospettivo.

retrospective *agg.* retrospettivo.

retroversion *s.* retroversione.

return *s.* 1. ritorno 2. restituzione 3. guadagno, profitto 4. relazione || — *journey*, viaggio di ritorno; *election returns*, risultati elettorali.

to **return** *vi.* 1. ritornare 2. rispondere, ricambiare, replicare. ♦ to **return** *vt.* 1. restituire, rimandare 2. produrre, fruttare 3. (*pol.*) eleggere.

reunion *s.* riunione.

to **reunite** *vt.* riunire. ♦ to **reunite** *vi.* riunirsi.

revaluation *s.* rivalutazione.

to **revalue** *vt.* rivalutare.

to **reveal** *vt.* rivelare.

revel *s.* baldoria.

to **revel** *vi.* far baldoria.

revelation *s.* rivelazione.

reveller *s.* chi fa baldoria.

revelry *s.* baldoria.

revenge *s.* vendetta.

to **revenge** *vt.* vendicare. ♦ to **revenge** *vi.* vendicarsi.

revengeful *agg.* vendicativo.

revenger s. vendicatore.

revenue s. 1. entrata 2. fisco.

to **reverberate** vt. e vi. riverberare.

reverberation s. riverberazione, riverbero.

to **revere** vt. riverire.

reverence s. riverenza.

to **reverence** vt. riverire.

reverend agg. reverendo.

reverent(ial) agg. riverente.

reverie s. fantasticheria.

reversal s. 1. rovesciamento 2. (giur.) annullamento.

reverse agg. e s. rovescio || — gear, retromarcia.

to **reverse** vt. rovesciare. ♦ to **reverse** vi. innestare la retromarcia.

reversibility s. reversibilità.

reversible agg. reversibile, rovesciabile.

reversion s. reversione.

to **revert** vi. ritornare.

review s. 1. revisione 2. recensione 3. rivista, periodico 4. (mil.) rivista.

to **review** vt. 1. rivedere 2. recensire 3. (mil.) passare in rivista.

reviewal s. revisione, recensione.

reviewer s. recensore, revisore.

to **revile** vt. e vi. ingiuriare.

to **revise** vt. rivedere, modificare.

reviser s. revisore.

revision s. revisione, correzione.

revival s. 1. ripristino 2. ripresa 3. rinascita.

to **revive** vt. e vi. resuscitare.

reviver s. chi, ciò che rinvigorisce.

revivification s. rinascita.

to **revivify** vt. ravvivare.

revocable agg. revocabile.

revocation s. revoca.

revocatory agg. revocatorio.

to **revoke** vt. revocare.

revolt s. rivolta.

to **revolt** vt. disgustare. ♦ to **revolt** vi. rivoltarsi.

revolution s. rivoluzione.

revolutionary agg. e s. rivoluzionario.

to **revolutionize** vt. rivoluzionare.

to **revolve** vt. meditare. ♦ to **revolve** vi. girare, rotare.

revolver s. rivoltella.

revolving agg. 1. rotante 2. rotativo.

revulsion s. 1. revulsione 2. mutamento.

revulsive agg. revulsivo.

reward s. ricompensa.

to **reward** vt. ricompensare.

rewarding agg. rimunerativo. ♦ **rewarding** s. rimunerazione.

to **rewrite (rewrote, rewritten)** vt. riscrivere.

rhagades s. pl. ragadi.

rhapsody s. rapsodia.

rheostat s. reostato.

rhetoric s. retorica.

rhetorical agg. retorico.

rhetorician s. retore.

rheumatic agg. e s. reumatico.

rheumatism s. reumatismo.

rhinitis s. rinite.

rhinoceros s. rinoceronte.

rhizome s. rizoma.

rhododendron s. rododendro.

rhomb s. rombo.

rhombic(al) agg. rombico.

rhombohedron s. (pl. -dra) romboedro.

rhombold agg. e s. romboide.

rhubarb s. rabarbaro.

rhyme s. rima.

to **rhyme** vt. far rimare. ♦ to **rhyme** vi. rimare.

rhymer s. rimatore.

Rhynchota s. pl. rincoti.

rhythm s. ritmo.

rhythmic(al) agg. ritmico.

rib s. 1. costola 2. costa, nervatura 3. stecca.

to **rib** vt. 1. munire (di coste ecc.) 2. scanalare.

ribbing s. 1. nervatura 2. rigatura.

ribbon s. nastro.

rice s. riso || — -field (o — -swamp), risaia.

rich agg. ricco.

richly avv. riccamente.

richness s. ricchezza.

rick s. bica.

ricket(s) s. rachitismo.

rickety agg. 1. rachitico 2. malsicuro.

to **rid (rid, rid)** vt. liberare || to get — of, sbarazzarsi di.

ridden V. to ride.

riddle[1] s. indovinello.

riddle[2] s. vaglio, crivello.

to **riddle**[1] vt. risolvere.

to **riddle**[2] vt. 1. vagliare 2. setacciare.

ride s. passeggiata, percorso (a cavallo, su un veicolo).

to **ride (rode, ridden)** vt. 1. montare (cavallo, bicicletta) 2. percorrere (a cavallo, su un veicolo) 3.

(*fig.*) opprimere. ♦ **to ride (rode, ridden)** *vi.* andare (*a cavallo, su un veicolo*).

rider *s.* cavaliere, fantino.

ridge *s.* cresta, catena di monti.

ridicule *s.* ridicolo.

to ridicule *vt.* schernire.

ridiculous *agg.* ridicolo.

riding *s.* corsa (*a cavallo, in veicolo*).

rifle *s.* fucile.

rifleman *s.* fuciliere.

rift *s.* crepa.

rigging *s.* attrezzatura.

right[1] *agg.* **1.** giusto **2.** (*geom.*) retto **3.** destro.

right[2] *s.* **1.** il giusto, il bene **2.** diritto **3.** destra, mano destra, lato destro.

right[3] *avv.* **1.** giustamente, bene **2.** direttamente **3.** proprio **4.** a destra.

righteous *agg.* giusto.

righteousness *s.* rettitudine.

rightful *agg.* **1.** legittimo **2.** giusto.

rightly *avv.* **1.** rettamente **2.** esattamente.

rigid *agg.* rigido.

rigidity, rigor *s.* rigidità.

rigorism *s.* rigorismo.

rigorist *s.* rigorista.

rigorous *agg.* rigido.

rigour *s.* rigore.

rim *s.* bordo, orlo.

to rim *vt.* bordare, cerchiare.

rind *s.* **1.** buccia **2.** corteccia **3.** crosta **4.** cotenna.

to rind *vt.* **1.** sbucciare **2.** scortecciare.

ring[1] *s.* **1.** anello, cerchio **2.** pista.

ring[2] *s.* **1.** scampanellata **2.** (*fig.*) accento, tono.

to ring[1] *vt.* circondare.

to ring[2] **(rang, rung)** *vt.* suonare || *to — up*, telefonare. ♦ **to ring (rang, rung)** *vi.* risuonare.

ringleader *s.* capobanda.

rink *s.* pista di pattinaggio.

to rinse *vt.* sciacquare.

rinsing *s.* risciacquatura.

riot *s.* **1.** rivolta **2.** gazzarra.

to riot *vi.* **1.** tumultuare **2.** gozzovigliare.

rioter *s.* rivoltoso.

riotous *agg.* **1.** tumultuante **2.** sregolato.

rip *s.* lacerazione, scucitura, strappo.

to rip *vt.* lacerare. ♦ **to rip** *vi.* lacerarsi.

ripe *agg.* maturo.

to ripen *vt. e vi.* maturare.

ripeness *s.* maturità.

ripple *s.* **1.** increspatura, ondulatura **2.** gorgoglio.

to ripple *vt.* increspare, ondulare. ♦ **to ripple** *vi.* incresparsi, ondularsi.

rise *s.* **1.** il sorgere **2.** salita, ascesa **3.** aumento **4.** sorgente.

to rise (rose, risen) *vi.* **1.** sorgere **2.** aumentare.

riser *s.* chi si alza.

risible *agg.* risibile.

rising *s.* **1.** sorgere **2.** salita, ascesa **3.** aumento **4.** rivolta.

risk *s.* rischio.

to risk *vt.* rischiare.

risky *agg.* rischioso.

rissole *s.* polpetta.

rite *s.* rito.

ritual *agg. e s.* rituale.

rival *agg. e s.* rivale.

to rival *vt.* rivaleggiare.

rivalry, rivalry *s.* rivalità.

river *s.* fiume.

riverside *s.* lungofiume.

to rivet *vt.* **1.** ribadire **2.** fissare.

rivulet *s.* fiumicello.

road *s.* strada || *— -bed*, fondo stradale; *— sign*, cartello stradale.

roadstead *s.* (*mar.*) rada.

roadway *s.* carreggiata.

to roam *vt. e vi.* vagare (*per*).

roar *s.* **1.** ruggito **2.** rombo.

to roar *vt. e vi.* **1.** ruggire **2.** tuonare || *to — with laughter*, ridere fragorosamente.

roaring *agg.* **1.** rumoroso **2.** ruggente, mugghiante. ♦ **roaring** *s.* V. *roar.*

roast *agg. e s.* arrosto.

to roast *vt.* **1.** arrostire **2.** tostare. ♦ **to roast** *vi.* arrostirsi.

roasting *agg.* rovente. ♦ **roasting** *s.* **1.** arrostimento **2.** torrefazione.

to rob *vt.* derubare. ♦ **to rob** *vi.* rubare.

robber *s.* ladro.

robbery *s.* furto.

robe *s.* **1.** toga **2.** vestiti (*pl.*).

to robe *vt.* vestire. ♦ **to robe** *vi.* vestirsi.

robin *s.* pettirosso.

robust *agg.* **1.** robusto **2.** faticoso.

robustness *s.* robustezza.

rock[1] *s.* **1.** roccia **2.** rocca.

rock[2] *s.* dondolìo.

to rock *vt.* cullare, dondolare. ♦

to **rock** vi. dondolarsi, oscillare, barcollare.

rocker s. 1. chi culla, dondola 2. dondolo (di sedia ecc.) 3. (mecc.) bilanciere.

rocket s. razzo.

rocking agg. 1. a dondolo 2. vacillante. ♦ **rocking** s. oscillazione, dondolio.

rocky agg. roccioso.

rod s. verga || fishing- —, canna da pesca.

rode V. to ride.

rodent agg. e s. roditore.

roe[1] s. capriolo maschio.

roe[2] s. uova di pesce.

rogue s. briccone.

roguery s. bricconeria.

roguish agg. bricconesco.

role s. 1. (teat.) ruolo, parte 2. funzione.

roll[1] s. 1. rotolo 2. elenco, lista 3. rullo, cilindro.

roll[2] s. 1. (mar.; aer.) rollio 2. rullo (di tamburo).

to **roll** vt. 1. far rotolare 2. arrotolare 3. spianare. ♦ to **roll** vi. 1. rotolare 2. arrotolarsi 3. ruotare 4. rollare 5. rullare.

roller s. 1. rullo, cilindro 2. cavallone || — skates, schettini.

rolling s. 1. (ar)rotolamento 2. — -mill, laminatoio; — pin, matterello.

Roman agg. e s. romano.

Romance agg. romanzo, neolatino.

romance s. 1. poema cavalleresco, racconto fantastico 2. avventura romanzesca 3. idillio 4. poesia 5. (mus.) romanza.

Romanesque agg. e s. romanico.

Romanian agg. e s. romeno.

Romanic agg. romanico.

Romanist s. romanista.

Romansh agg. e s. ladino.

romantic agg. e s. romantico.

romanticism s. romanticismo.

to **romanticize** vt. romanzare.

to **romp** vi. giocare rumorosamente.

rompish agg. chiassoso.

rood s. croce.

roof s. tetto || — -garden, giardino pensile.

to **roof** vt. 1. coprire con un tetto 2. ospitare.

rook s. cornacchia.

room s. 1. stanza 2. spazio 3. possibilità.

to **room** vt. e vi. (amer.) alloggiare.

roomy agg. spazioso.

root s. radice.

to **root**[1] vt. piantare || to — away, out, up, sradicare. ♦ to **root** vi. mettere radice.

to **root**[2] vt. e vi. grufolare.

rope s. fune, corda || — -dancer, funambolo.

to **rope** vt. legare.

rosary s. 1. roseto 2. (eccl.) rosario.

rose agg. e s. rosa || — -bush, rosaio; — -diamond, rosetta; — -window, rosone.

rose V. to rise.

rosemary s. rosmarino.

roseola s. rosolia.

rosery s. roseto.

rosette s. 1. rosetta 2. (arch.) rosone 3. coccarda.

rosewood s. palissandro.

rosin s. pece greca.

rostrum s. (pl. rostra o rostrums) rostro.

rosy agg. roseo.

rot s. putrefazione.

to **rot** vt. e vi. imputridire.

rotary agg. rotante. ♦ **rotary** s. — (press), rotativa.

to **rotate** vt. e vi. rotare.

rotation s. rotazione.

rotative, rotatory agg. rotatorio.

rote s. abitudine, memoria meccanica.

rotogravure s. rotocalco.

rotor s. rotore.

rotten agg. marcio.

rottenness s. marciume.

rotund agg. 1. rotondo 2. enfatico.

rouble s. rublo.

rouge s. rossetto.

rough agg. 1. irregolare, ruvido, scabro 2. tempestoso 3. rozzo.

to **rough** vt. irruvidire || to — it (fam.), vivere primitivamente.

to **roughen** vt. irruvidire. ♦ to **roughen** vi. irruvidirsi.

to **rough-hew** vt. abbozzare.

roughly avv. ruvidamente.

roughness s. 1. ruvidezza 2. rudezza 3. inclemenza (di tempo).

round agg. 1. rotondo 2. intero 3. franco 4. vigoroso 5. considerevole. ♦ **round** s. 1. cerchio 2. sfera 3. ciclo 4. giro, ronda.

round avv. intorno. ♦ **round** prep. intorno a.

to **round** vt. arrotondare. ♦ to **round** vi. 1. arrotondarsi 2. girare

3. svilupparsi.

roundabout *agg.* indiretto. ◆
roundabout *s.* giostra.

roundly *avv.* 1. vigorosamente 2. francamente.

roundness *s.* 1. rotondità 2. scorrevolezza 3. franchezza.

to **rouse** *vt.* (ri)svegliare (*anche fig.*).
◆ to **rouse** *vi.* (ri)svegliarsi.

rouser *s.* ridestatore.

rousing *agg.* stimolante.

rout *s.* 1. plebaglia 2. tumulto 3. rotta.

to **rout** *vt.* sconfiggere.

route *s.* via, rotta.

routinist *s.* abitudinario.

rove *s.* vagabondaggio.

to **rove** *vt.* e *vi.* vagare.

rover *s.* 1. vagabondo 2. pirata.

roving *s.* vagabondaggio.

row[1] *s.* fila.

row[2] *s.* remata, gita in barca.

to **row** *vt.* trasportare (*remando*). ◆
to **row** *vi.* remare.

rowdy *agg.* e *s.* turbolento.

rower *s.* rematore.

rowlock *s.* scalmo.

royal *agg.* regale, reale.

royalist *s.* realista.

royalty *s.* 1. regalità 2. i reali 3. diritto d'autore.

rub *s.* 1. fregata, grattata 2. ineguaglianza 3. ostacolo, difficoltà.

to **rub** *vt.* fregare. ◆ to **rub** *vi.* fregarsi.

rubber *s.* 1. massaggiatore 2. strofinaccio 3. gomma ‖ — -solution, mastice.

rubbish *s.* rifiuti (*pl.*).

rubble *s.* pietrisco.

ruby *s.* rubino.

rucksack *s.* zaino.

rudder *s.* timone.

ruddy *agg.* rosso, rubicondo.

rude *agg.* 1. rude, violento 2. rudimentale 3. grezzo.

rudeness *s.* 1. rozzezza 2. violenza.

rudiment *s.* rudimento.

rudimentary *agg.* rudimentale.

ruffian *agg.* brutale. ◆ **ruffian** *s.* ribaldo.

ruffle *s.* 1. increspatura 2. sconvolgimento 3. tumulto.

to **ruffle** *vt.* 1. increspare 2. arruffare 3. agitare.

rug *s.* 1. coperta 2. tappetino.

rugged *agg.* 1. ruvido 2. scompigliato 3. austero 4. rozzo.

ruggedness *s.* 1. ruvidezza 2. auste-

rità 3. rudezza.

ruin *s.* rovina.

to **ruin** *vt.* e *vi.* rovinare.

ruinous *agg.* 1. rovinoso 2. in rovina.

rule *s.* 1. regola 2. dominio 3. riga da disegno.

to **rule** *vt.* 1. governare, dominare 2. rigare.

ruler *s.* 1. dominatore 2. regolo.

ruling *s.* 1. governo 2. decisione.

Rumanian *agg.* e *s.* romeno.

rumble *s.* 1. rombo 2. brontolio.

to **rumble** *vt.* e *vi.* 1. rombare 2. brontolare.

rumbling *s.* V. *rumble.*

rumen *s.* rumine.

ruminant *agg.* e *s.* ruminante.

to **ruminate** *vt* e *vi.* ruminare.

rummage *s.* ricerca, perquisizione.

to **rummage** *vt.* e *vi.* 1. rovistare 2. perquisire.

rumour *s.* diceria.

to **rumour** *vt.* far correre la voce.

rump *s.* 1. posteriore 2. resto.

to **rumple** *vt.* 1. spiegazzare 2. arruffare.

run *s.* 1. corsa 2. percorso, giro 3. andamento 4. periodo 5. richiesta.

to **run** (ran, run) *vi.* 1. correre 2. colare 3. diventare 4. estendersi 5. essere in vigore, durare. ◆ to **run** (ran, run) *vt.* 1. far funzionare 2. dirigere 3. seguire 4. passare ‖ *to* — *in*, rodare; *to* — *over*, investire.

runaway *agg.* 1. fuggitivo 2. decisivo. ◆ **runaway** *s.* 1. fuggitivo 2. fuga.

rung[1] *s.* 1. piolo 2. raggio (*di ruota*).

rung[2] V. *to ring.*

runnel *s.* ruscello.

runner *s.* 1. corridore 2. messo 3. passatoia 4. pattino 5. carrello.

running *s.* 1. corsa 2. esercizio 3. flusso ‖ — *-in*, rodaggio.

runway *s.* pista.

rupture *s.* rottura.

rural *agg.* rurale.

rush[1] *s.* giunco.

rush[2] *s.* 1. attacco 2. impeto 3. afflusso ‖ — *-hours*, ore di punta.

to **rush** *vt.* spingere. ◆ to **rush** *vi.* precipitarsi.

rushy *agg.* 1. di giunchi 2. folto di giunchi.

Russian *agg.* e *s.* russo.

rust *s.* ruggine.

to **rust** *vt.* arrugginire. ♦ to **rust** *vi.* arrugginirsi.

rustic(al) *agg.* rustico. ♦ **rustic(al)** *s.* campagnolo.

rustle *s.* fruscio, stormire (*di foglie*).

to **rustle** *vt.* far frusciare. ♦ to **rustle** *vi.* frusciare.

rusty *agg.* **1.** rugginoso **2.** (*fig.*) ombroso.

ruthless *agg.* spietato.

ruthlessness *s.* crudeltà.

rye *s.* segale.

S

Sabbath *s.* il giorno della settimana dedicato al riposo.

sable *s.* zibellino.

sabot *s.* zoccolo.

sabotage *s.* sabotaggio.

to **sabotage** *vt. e vi.* sabotare.

saboteur *s.* sabotatore.

sabre *s.* sciabola || *-cut*, sciabolata.

to **sabre** *vt.* sciabolare.

saccharin(e) *s.* saccarina.

saccharose *s.* saccarosio.

sacerdotal *agg.* sacerdotale.

sack[1] *s.* **1.** sacco **2.** (*gergo*) licenziamento.

sack[2] *s.* (*mil.*) sacco, saccheggio.

sack[3] *s.* vino bianco delle Canarie.

to **sack**[1] *vt.* **1.** insaccare **2.** (*gergo*) licenziare.

to **sack**[2] *vt.* (*mil.*) saccheggiare.

sacking[1] *s.* tela da sacco.

sacking[2] *s.* saccheggio.

sacral[1] *agg.* (*anat.*) sacro.

sacral[2] *agg.* rituale.

sacrament *s.* sacramento.

sacramental *agg.* sacramentale.

sacred *agg.* **1.** sacro, religioso **2.** consacrato, dedicato.

sacrifice *s.* **1.** sacrificio **2.** abnegazione.

to **sacrifice** *vt. e vi.* **1.** sacrificare, immolare **2.** rinunziare.

sacrilege *s.* sacrilegio.

sacrist *s.* sagrestano.

sacristy *s.* sagrestia.

sacrosanct *agg.* sacrosanto.

sad *agg.* triste, mesto || *to make so. —*, rattristare qu.

to **sadden** *vt.* rattristare. ♦ to **sadden** *vi.* rattristarsi.

saddle *s.* **1.** sella, sellino **2.** giogaia.

to **saddle** *vt.* sellare, mettere in sella.

saddler *s.* sellaio.

sadism *s.* sadismo.

sadist *s.* sadico.

sadistic *agg.* sadico.

sadly *avv.* tristemente, mestamente.

sadness *s.* tristezza, mestizia.

safe *s.* **1.** sicuro, al riparo **2.** salvo, intatto **3.** innocuo || *— and sound,* sano e salvo; *— -conduct,* salvacondotto; *— -deposit,* cassetta di sicurezza. ♦ **safe** *s.* **1.** cassaforte **2.** sicura (*di armi*).

safeguard *s.* salvaguardia.

to **safeguard** *vt.* salvaguardare, difendere.

safekeeping *s.* custodia.

safety *s.* sicurezza, salvezza, scampo || *— belt,* cintura di sicurezza; *— device,* dispositivo di sicurezza; *— -pin,* spilla di sicurezza.

saffron *s.* zafferano.

sag *s.* **1.** abbassamento, cedimento **2.** (*mar.*) scarroccio.

sagacious *agg.* acuto, sagace.

sagaciousness, sagacity *s.* sagacia, perspicacia.

sage[1] *s.* salvia.

sage[2] *s.* saggio, dotto.

said V. *to say.*

sail[1] *s.* vela, velatura || *to set* (*v. irr.*) *—,* spiegare le vele, salpare; *to strike* (*v. irr.*) *—,* ammainare le vele.

sail[2] *s.* gita su imbarcazione a vela.

to **sail** *vt. e vi.* **1.** veleggiare, navigare, costeggiare **2.** salpare **3.** volare, veleggiare (*di uccelli, nuvole ecc.*).

sailer *s.* veliero.

sailing *s.* **1.** navigazione, traversata **2.** partenza (*di navi*).

sailor *s.* marinaio.

sailplane *s.* veleggiatore.

saint *agg. e s.* santo.

to **saint** *vt.* canonizzare, santificare.

sainthood, saintliness *s.* santità.

saintly *agg.* santo, di santo.

sake *s.* **1.** amore, interesse **2.** riguardo, rispetto || *for God's —,* per l'amor di Dio.

salaam *s.* riverenza, salamelecco.

salacious *agg.* salace, lascivo.

salad *s.* insalata || *fruit —,* macedonia di frutta.

salamander *s.* salamandra.

salariat s. categorie salariate.

salary s. stipendio.

sale s. 1. vendita || *bill of* —, fattura; *on* —, in vendita 2. asta: — *by auction*, vendita all'asta 3. liquidazione, svendita.

sal(e)able agg. vendibile, commerciabile.

salesman s. venditore, commesso.

saleswoman s. venditrice, commessa.

salicylate s. salicilato.

salient agg. 1. sporgente, prominente 2. saliente, notevole.

saline agg. salino, salso.

salinity s. salsedine, salinità.

saliva s. saliva.

salivary agg. salivare.

salivation s. salivazione.

sallow agg. giallastro.

sally s. 1. (mil.) sortita 2. escursione.

to **sally** vi. fare una sortita || *to* — *forth*, uscire (per una passeggiata).

salmon s. salmone.

saloon s. salone || *dancing* —, sala da ballo.

salt s. sale. ♦ **salt** agg. 1. salato 2. sotto sale 3. (fig.) amaro, piccante || —*cellar*, saliera; —-*mine*, salina.

to **salt** vt. 1. salare, cospargere di sale 2. rendere piccante (anche fig.).

salting s. palude costiera.

saltish agg. salmastro, salaticcio.

saltness s. salsedine.

saltpetre s. salnitro.

salty agg. sala:o, salmastro 2. piccante (anche fig.).

salubrious agg. salubre.

salutary agg. salutare.

salutation s. saluto.

salute s. saluto, gesto di saluto || *to fire a* —, salutare a salve.

to **salute** vt. salutare, dare il benvenuto.

salvage s. salvataggio (di navi, carico ecc.).

salvation s. salvezza (anche relig.).

salve s. unguento, balsamo.

same agg. medesimo, stesso, uguale || *at the* — *time*, allo stesso tempo. ♦ **same** pron. lo stesso, il medesimo.

samely agg. monotono, uniforme.

sameness s. 1. somiglianza 2. monotonia.

sample s. campione, modello, esemplare || — *book*, campionario.

sanatorium s. sanatorio.

sanatory agg. curativo.

sanctification s. santificazione.

to **sanctify** vt. santificare.

sanction s. 1. autorizzazione, approvazione 2. (giur.) ratifica 3. sanzione.

to **sanction** vt. 1. autorizzare 2. (giur.) ratificare 3. aggiungere sanzioni penali (ad una legge).

sanctity s. santità.

sanctuary s. 1. santuario 2. asilo, rifugio.

sand s. sabbia, rena || — *bath*, bagno di sabbia. ♦ **sands** s. pl. spiaggia (sing.).

to **sand** vt. 1. coprire di sabbia 2. arenare 3. smerigliare.

sandal s. sandalo.

sandpaper s. carta vetrata.

sandstone s. arenaria.

sandy agg. sabbioso.

sane agg. sano di mente, sensato.

saneness, sanity s. sanità (di mente), equilibrio.

sang V. to sing.

sanguinary agg. sanguinario, crudele.

sanguine agg. sanguigno.

sanguineous agg. del sangue, sanguigno.

sanitarian s. igienista. ♦ **sanitarian** agg. igienico.

sanitarist s. igienista.

sanitary agg. igienico, sanitario.

sanity s. V. saneness.

sank V. to sink.

Sanscrit, Sanskrit agg. e s. Sanscrito.

santon s. santone.

sap s. 1. linfa, succo 2. (fig.) vigore.

sapful agg. 1. succoso 2. vigoroso.

sapid agg. sapido, gustoso (anche fig.).

sapient agg. pedante.

sapless agg. 1. secco, avvizzito 2. fiacco.

saponification s. saponificazione.

to **saponify** vt. saponificare.

Sapphic agg. saffico.

sapphire s. zaffiro.

saraband s. sarabanda.

Saracen agg. e s. saraceno.

sarcasm s. sarcasmo.

sarcastic agg. sarcastico.

sarcophagus s. (pl. -gi) sarcofago.

sardine s. sardina.
sardonic agg. sardonico.
sash[1] s. fascia, cintura.
sash[2] s. telaio scorrevole (di finestra).
sat V. to sit.
satanic(al) agg. satanico.
satchel s. cartella (di scolaro).
to **sate** vt. saziare.
satellite s. satellite.
satiable agg. saziabile.
to **satiate** vt. saziare, satollare.
satiety s. sazietà.
satin s. raso.
satire s. satira.
satiric(al) agg. satirico.
satirist s. autore di satire.
to **satirize** vt. satireggiare.
satisfaction s. 1. soddisfazione 2.
riparazione 3. (giur.) estinzione.
satisfactory agg. soddisfacente.
satisfiable agg. che può essere soddisfatto.
to **satisfy** vt. soddisfare, appagare
|| to — a claim, accogliere un re-
clamo. ♦ to **satisfy** vi. fare ammenda.
satrap s. satrapo.
saturate agg. saturo.
to **saturate** vt. saturare, impregnare.
saturation s. saturazione.
Saturday s. sabato.
satyr s. satiro.
satyric agg. satiresco.
sauce s. salsa, intingolo.
saucepan s. casseruola.
saucer s. piattino, sottocoppa.
saucily avv. sfacciatamente.
saucy agg. sfacciato, insolente.
sauerkraut s. crauti.
to **saunter** vi. bighellonare.
saunterer s. bighellone.
sausage s. salsiccia, salame.
savage agg. 1. selvaggio, barbaro 2.
feroce, crudele. ♦ **savage** s. selvaggio.
savagely avv. selvaggiamente, barba-
ramente.
savannah s. savana.
save prep. salvo, tranne, eccetto.
to **save** vt. e vi. 1. salvare, difendere
2. conservare, risparmiare.
saving s. liberazione, salvezza. ♦
savings s. pl. risparmi.
saviour s. salvatore, redentore.
to **savour** vi. aver sapore.
savoury agg. saporito, piccante.
saw s. sega || —-mill, segheria.
to **saw** (sawed, sawn) vt. e vi.

segare.
sawdust s. segatura.
sawn V. to saw.
sawyer s. segatore.
Saxon agg. e s. sassone.
saxophone s. sassofono.
say s. il dire, detto, parola.
to **say** (said, said) vt. e vi. 1. dire, affermare 2. esprimere un'o-
pinione || to — out, dire aperta-
mente.
saying s. proverbio, massima: as the
— goes, come dice il proverbio.
scabbard s. fodero.
scabby agg. coperto di croste.
scabies s. scabbia.
scaffold s. 1. impalcatura 2. patibolo, forca.
to **scaffold** vt. erigere impalcature.
scaffolding s. impalcatura.
scald s. scottatura.
to **scald** vt. 1. scottare 2. sterilizzare con acqua bollente. ♦ to
scald vi. scottarsi.
scale[1] s. piatto (di bilancia). ♦
scales s. pl. bilancia (sing.).
scale[2] s. scaglia.
scale[3] s. scala, misura, gradazione.
to **scale**[1] vt. e vi. pesare.
to **scale**[2] vt. squamare, scrostare. ♦
to **scale** vi. squamarsi, scrostarsi.
to **scale**[3] vt. 1. scalare 2. graduare
|| to — down, diminuire; to —
up, aumentare.
scalene agg. e s. scaleno.
scallop s. 1. conchiglia 2. dentellatura, festone, smerlo (di stoffa).
to **scallop** vt. 1. tagliare a festone
2. cuocere pesce in conchiglia.
scalp s. 1. cranio, cuoio capelluto
2. scalpo.
to **scalp** vt. 1. scalpare 2. criticare
aspramente.
scalpel s. bisturi.
to **scan** vt. 1. scandire (versi)
2. esaminare, scrutare.
scandal s. 1. scandalo 2. maldicenza
3. (giur.) diffamazione.
to **scandalize** vt. scandalizzare.
scandalous agg. scandaloso.
Scandinavian agg. e s. scandinavo.
scanning s. 1. scansione (di versi)
2. osservazione || —-line, (tv), li-
nea di scansione.
scansion s. scansione.
scantily avv. debolmente, scarsamente.
scantiness s. insufficienza, scarsezza.

scanty *agg.* **1.** scarso, insufficiente **2.** esiguo, angusto.

scapegoat *s.* capro espiatorio.

scapegrace *s.* **1.** scapestrato **2.** monello.

scapular *agg.* scapolare.

scar *s.* cicatrice, sfregio.

to scar *vt.* cicatrizzare **2.** sfregiare. ♦ **to scar** *vi.* cicatrizzarsi.

scarab *s.* scarabeo.

scarce *agg.* insufficiente, scarso.

scarcely *avv.* appena, a fatica, a malapena.

scare *s.* terrore, sgomento.

to scare *vt.* spaventare, sgomentare.

scarecrow *s.* **1.** spaventapasseri **2.** spauracchio.

scarf *s.* sciarpa, fascia.

to scarify *vt.* scarificare.

scarlet *agg.* scarlatto, porporino ‖ — *-fever,* scarlattina.

scarp(e) *s.* scarpata.

to scatter *vt.* **1.** spargere **2.** mettere in fuga, disperdere. ♦ **to scatter** *vi.* spargersi, diffondersi.

scattered *agg.* sparso, disseminato.

scattering *s.* sparpagliamento, dispersione.

scenario *s.* sceneggiatura ‖ — *writer,* sceneggiatore.

scene *s.* **1.** scena **2.** episodio **3.** scenario, quinta **4.** vista, panorama ‖ — *-painter,* scenografo.

scenery *s.* **1.** scenario **2.** prospettiva, veduta.

scenographer *s.* scenografo.

scenographic *agg.* scenografico.

scenography *s.* scenografia.

scent *s.* **1.** odore, profumo **2.** traccia, pista (*anche fig.*).

to scent *vt.* **1.** fiutare, seguire la traccia **2.** profumare.

scented *agg.* profumato.

scentless *agg.* inodoro.

sceptical *agg.* scettico.

scepticism *s.* scetticismo.

sceptre *s.* scettro.

schedule *s.* **1.** catalogo, distinta, elenco **2.** (*amer.*) orario **3.** inventario.

to schedule *vt.* comporre una lista, un catalogo.

schematic(al) *agg.* schematico.

schematism *s.* schematismo.

scheme *s.* **1.** schema **2.** piano, progetto.

to scheme *vt.* e *vi.* **1.** progettare, fare un piano **2.** tramare.

schism *s.* scisma.

schismatic(al) *s.* scismatico.

schizophrenic *agg.* e *s.* schizofrenico.

scholar *s.* studioso, letterato.

scholarly *agg.* dotto, istruito.

scholarship *s.* **1.** dottrina, sapere **2.** borsa di studio.

scholastic *agg.* **1.** scolastico, pedante **2.** (*fil.*) scolastico.

scholastically *avv.* scolasticamente, secondo la scolastica.

scholasticism *s.* (*fil.*) scolastica.

school *s.* **1.** scuola, classe **2.** lezione, ora di lezione ‖ — *-book,* libro di testo; — *-mate,* compagno di scuola; — *-report,* pagella; — *-term,* trimestre; — *-time,* periodo scolastico; *boarding-* —, collegio; *grammar-* —, ginnasio; *night-* —, serale.

to school *vt.* **1.** istruire **2.** controllare, disciplinare.

schoolboy *s.* scolaro.

schoolfellow *s.* compagno di scuola.

schoolmaster *s.* maestro, insegnante.

schoolmistress *s.* maestra, insegnante.

schoolroom *s.* aula scolastica.

schooner *s.* (*mar.*) goletta.

science *s.* scienza ‖ — *fiction,* fantascienza; *man of* —, scienziato.

scientific *agg.* scientifico.

scientifically *avv.* scientificamente.

scientism *s.* scientismo.

scientist *s.* scienziato.

scimitar *s.* scimitarra.

scion *s.* **1.** germoglio **2.** rampollo, discendente.

scission *s.* scissione, divisione.

scissors *s. pl.* forbici, cesoie.

sclerosis *s.* (*pl.* -ses) sclerosi.

sclerotic *agg.* sclerotico.

scoff *s.* derisione, scherno.

to scoff *vt.* e *vi.* deridere, schernire ‖ — *at so.,* farsi beffe di qu.

scold *s.* donna bisbetica.

to scold *vt.* sgridare, rimproverare. ♦ **to scold** *vi.* essere adirato.

scolding *s.* sgridata, rimprovero.

scoliosis *s.* scoliosi.

scooter *s.* **1.** monopattino **2.** motoretta.

scope *s.* **1.** portata, possibilità **2.** prospettiva, sfera, campo.

scorbutic *agg.* scorbutico.

scorch *s.* bruciatura, scottatura.

to scorch *vt.* e *vi.* **1.** bruciacchiare **2.** inaridire (*di sole, gelo ecc.*).

scorching *agg.* 1. bruciante, ardente 2. *(fig.)* caustico, mordace.

score *s.* 1. tacca, scanalatura 2. linea, segno, linea di partenza, limite *(in corse, giuochi ecc.)* 3. *(sport)* punteggio 4. *(mus.)* spartito.

to score *vt. e vi.* 1. intaccare, intagliare 2. marcare, segnare 3. *(sport)* segnare il punteggio 4. *(mus.)* orchestrare ‖ *to — up,* mettere in conto.

scorer *s.* *(sport)* marcatore.

scorn *s.* 1. disprezzo, disdegno 2. scherno.

to scorn *vt.* disprezzare, disdegnare.

scornful *agg.* sprezzante, sdegnoso.

scorpion *s.* scorpione ‖ *— -fish,* scorfano.

Scot *s.* scozzese.

Scotch *agg.* scozzese.

Scotsman *s.* *(uomo)* scozzese.

Scottish *agg.* scozzese.

scoundrel *s.* furfante, farabutto.

scourge *s.* *(fig.)* flagello.

to scourge *vt.* sferzare, flagellare.

scout *s.* esploratore, ricognitore.

to scout *vi.* andare in esplorazione, in ricognizione. ♦ *to scout vt.* perlustrare.

scowl *s.* cipiglio, sguardo torvo.

to scowl *vt. e vi.* aggrottare le ciglia, guardare torvamente.

scramble *s.* 1. arrampicata 2. contesa, gara.

to scramble *vt.* 1. arraffare 2. mescolare alla rinfusa. ♦ *to scramble vi.* 1. inerpicarsi 2. gareggiare 3. *(cuc.)* strapazzare *(le uova).*

scrap *s.* pezzetto, frammento ‖ *—-heap,* mucchio di rifiuti.

scraps *s. pl.* rimasugli, scarti.

scrape *s.* 1. graffio, scalfittura 2. raschio.

to scrape *vt. e vi.* 1. raschiare, grattare 2. levigare 3. sfregare, strisciare ‖ *to — a living,* sbarcare il lunario.

scraper *s.* 1. raschietto 2. strimpellatore.

scraping *s.* raschiatura.

scratch *s.* 1. graffiatura, graffio 2. grattata 3. colpo fortunato *(al giuoco).*

to scratch *vt. e vi.* 1. graffiare 2. *(fig.)* scalfire 3. grattare.

scrawl *s.* scarabocchio, sgorbio.

to scrawl *vt. e vi.* 1. scarabocchiare 2. scribacchiare.

scrawler *s.* chi scarabocchia.

scrawly *agg.* scarabocchiato ‖ *— writing (fam.),* scritto a zampe di gallina.

scream *s.* grido acuto, strillo.

to scream *vt. e vi.* 1. gridare, strillare 2. fischiare *(di locomotiva).*

screamer *s.* strillone.

screaming *agg.* 1. strillante, urlante 2. sguaiato.

screech *s.* 1. grido, strillo acuto 2. stridore.

screen *s.* 1. paravento 2. *(cine; tv)* schermo 3. *(mil.)* scorta.

to screen *vt. e vi.* 1. riparare, schermare 2. vagliare.

screenings *s. pl.* materiale vagliato *(sing.).*

screenplay *s.* *(cine)* sceneggiatura.

screenwriter *s.* sceneggiatore.

screw *s.* 1. vite 2. cavatappi, succhiello 3. elica.

to screw *vt.* 1. avvitare, stringere 2. torcere. ♦ *to screw vi.* torcersi ‖ *to — out,* svitare.

screwdriver *s.* cacciavite.

screwy *agg.* 1. brillo 2. tirchio, spilorcio.

scribble *s.* sgorbio, scarabocchio *(anche fig.).*

to scribble *vt. e vi.* scarabocchiare.

scribe *s.* copista.

scriber *s.* punta a tracciare.

scrip[1] *s.* 1. pezzo di carta 2. frammento di uno scritto.

scrip[2] *s.* certificato provvisorio, cedola.

scripture *s.* la sacra Scrittura.

to scrounge *vt. e vi.* rubacchiare.

scrounger *s.* ladruncolo, scroccone.

scrub *s.* 1. boscaglia 2. povero diavolo *(fam.).*

to scrub *vt. e vi.* sfregare.

scrubby *agg.* esile, debole.

scruff *s.* nuca, collottola.

scruple *s.* scrupolo.

scrupolosity *s.* scrupolosità.

scrupulous *agg.* scrupoloso.

to scrutinize *vt.* scrutinare, esaminare.

scrutiny *s.* 1. esame minuzioso 2. scrutinio 3. esame *(di una legge).*

scuffle *s.* zuffa, tafferuglio.

to scuffle *vi.* azzuffarsi.

scullery *s.* retrocucina ‖ *— -boy, -maid,* sguattero, sguattera.

sculptor *s.* scultore.

sculptress *s.* scultrice.

sculptural *agg.* scultorio, statuario.

sculpture s. scultura.

to **sculpture** vt. e vi. scolpire.

scum s. 1. schiuma, spuma 2. feccia (anche fig.).

to **scum** vt. e vi. 1. schiumare, far schiuma 2. produrre feccia.

scummer s. schiumarola.

scurf s. 1. squama, forfora 2. incrostazioni (pl.).

scurrility s. scurrilità, volgarità.

scurrilous agg. scurrile, triviale.

to **scurry** vi. precipitarsi.

scurvy agg. spregevole, meschino.

scuttle[1] s. recipiente per carbone.

scuttle[2] s. 1. (mar.) portellino 2. botola.

scuttle[3] s. fuga precipitosa.

to **scuttle**[1] vt. produrre falle (in una nave).

to **scuttle**[2] vi. correre via precipitosamente.

sea s. mare || — -bear, orso polare; — -biscuit, galletta; — calf, foca; — fight, battaglia navale; — food, frutti di mare; — front, lungomare; — quake, maremoto; — storm, mareggiata.

seacoast s. costa, spiaggia.

seafarer s. navigante, navigatore.

seafaring s. viaggi per mare.

seahorse s. ippocampo.

seal[1] s. foca.

seal[2] s. 1. sigillo, timbro 2. (fig.) suggello, vincolo.

to **seal**[1] vi. andare a caccia di foche.

to **seal**[2] vt. 1. sigillare 2. suggellare || to — one's fate, decidere la propria sorte.

sealing s. suggellamento || -wax, ceralacca.

seam s. 1. cucitura 2. sutura.

to **seam** vt. 1. unire con cucitura 2. rigare, segnare.

seamen s. pl. equipaggio (di una nave).

seamanship s. arte della navigazione.

seamless agg. senza cucitura.

seamstress s. cucitrice.

seaplane s. idrovolante.

seaport s. porto marittimo.

search s. 1. ricerca, indagine 2. perquisizione, visita doganale || — warrant, mandato di perquisizione.

to **search** vt. e vi. cercare, perlustrare, perquisire || to — out, rinvenire, scovare.

searcher s. ricercatore.

searching agg. indagatore, inquisitorio. ♦ **searching** s. 1. ricerca, esame 2. sondaggio.

searchlight s. riflettore.

seashore s. spiaggia, lido.

seasickness s. mal di mare.

seaside s. spiaggia, riva.

season s. stagione, epoca || — bill (teat.), cartellone; — ticket, abbonamento stagionale.

to **season** vt. 1. stagionare 2. acclimatare 3. condire. ♦ to **season** vi. 1. stagionarsi 2. invecchiarsi (di vino).

seasonable agg. 1. di stagione 2. opportuno.

seasonal agg. stagionale.

seasoned agg. 1. stagionato 2. condito.

seasoning s. 1. stagionatura 2. condimento.

seat s. 1. sedile, posto 2. seggio 3. sede.

to **seat** vt. 1. mettere a sedere 2. insediare, collocare.

seaward agg. che va verso il mare.

seaweed s. alga marina.

sebaceous agg. sebaceo.

secant agg. e s. secante.

to **secede** vi. separarsi, ritirarsi.

seceder s. secessionista, separatista.

secession s. secessione, scissione.

secessionism s. secessionismo.

to **seclude** vt. 1. appartare, isolare 2. rinchiudere.

secluded agg. appartato, isolato, solitario.

seclusion s. 1. isolamento 2. solitudine.

seclusive agg. che serve ad isolare.

second[1] s. minuto secondo.

second[2] agg. secondo.

secondary agg. secondario.

secrecy s. 1. segretezza 2. riserbo.

secret agg. 1. segreto 2. nascosto, intimo. ♦ **secret** s. segreto.

secretariat(e) s. 1. segretariato 2. segreteria.

secretary s. 1. segretario 2. ministro (preposto ad un dicastero).

to **secrete**[1] vt. secernere.

to **secrete**[2] vt. occultare, nascondere.

secretion s. secrezione.

secretly avv. 1. segretamente 2. in modo reticente.

sect s. setta.

sectarian s. settario.

sectarianism s. spirito di setta.

sectary s. settario.

section *s.* 1. sezione, parte 2. paragrafo 3. regione, quartiere.

to section *vt.* sezionare.

sectional *agg.* 1. parziale, di classe 2. a sezioni.

sector *s.* settore.

secular *agg.* 1. secolare 2. laico 3. mondano, profano. ♦ **secular** *s.* laico.

secularism *s.* secolarismo.

secularist *agg.* e *s.* laico.

to secularize *vt.* laicizzare.

secure *agg.* 1. sicuro, certo 2. salvo.

to secure *vt.* 1. assicurare, salvaguardare 2. (*giur.; cómm.*) garantire 3. mettere al sicuro.

security *s.* 1. sicurezza, protezione 2. certezza 3. garanzia, cauzione. ♦ **securities** *s. pl.* titoli, valori.

sedan *s.* — (-*chair*), portantina.

sedate *agg.* 1. posato, composto 2. grave, serio.

sedative *agg.* e *s.* sedativo.

sedentary *agg.* e *s.* sedentario.

sediment *s.* sedimento.

sedimentary *agg.* sedimentario.

sedimentation *s.* sedimentazione.

sedition *s.* sedizione.

seditious *agg.* sedizioso.

to seduce *vt.* sedurre, corrompere.

seduction *s.* seduzione.

sedulous *agg.* assiduo.

to see (saw, seen) *vt.* e *vi.* 1. vedere, scorgere 2. capire, rendersi conto di 3. esaminare, giudicare 4. fare in modo che || to — *about*, assumersi l'incarico di; to — *off*, accompagnare (*alla partenza*); to — *over*, ispezionare; to — *through* (*fig.*), indovinare, penetrare.

see *s.* (*eccl.*) sede, diocesi.

seed *s.* 1. seme, semenza 2. (*fig.*) principio, germe 3. stirpe.

seedy *agg.* pieno di semi.

to seek (sought, sought) *vt.* e *vi.* 1. cercare, andare alla ricerca di 2. ottenere 3. chiedere, ricorrere a || to — *for sthg.*, ricercare qc.

seeker *s.* cercatore.

to seem *vi.* sembrare, apparire.

seeming *agg.* apparente, esteriore.

seemliness *s.* decenza, decoro.

seemly *agg.* decoroso, decente.

seen V. *to see.*

segment *s.* segmento, sezione.

segmentation *s.* segmentazione.

to segregate *vt.* segregare, separare. ♦ **to segregate** *vi.* separarsi, scindersi.

segregation *s.* segregazione.

seismograph *s.* sismografo.

seismologist *s.* sismologo.

seismology *s.* sismologia.

seizable *agg.* afferrabile.

to seize *vt.* e *vi.* afferrare, prendere 2. capire, comprendere 3. (*giur.*) avere in possesso, sequestrare.

seizing *s.* 1. atto dell'afferrare 2. conquista, cattura.

seizure *s.* 1. (*giur.*) confisca, sequestro 2. conquista, cattura.

seldom *avv.* raramente.

select *agg.* 1. scelto, selezionato 2. schizzinoso.

to select *vt.* selezionare.

selection *s.* selezione, scelta.

selective *agg.* selettivo.

selectivity *s.* selettività.

selector *s.* selettore.

self *s.* (*pl.* selves) l'io, l'individuo. ♦ **self** *agg.* 1. della stessa materia 2. uniforme.

self-conceit *s.* presunzione.

self-control *s.* autocontrollo.

self-defence *s.* legittima difesa.

self-denial *s.* abnegazione.

self-determination *s.* autodeterminazione.

self-educated *agg.* autodidatta.

self-examination *s.* esame di coscienza.

self-government *s.* (*pol.*) autogoverno.

self-help *s.* (*giur.*) legittima difesa.

selfish *agg.* egoistico.

selfishness *s.* egoismo.

self-portrait *s.* autoritratto.

sell *s.* (*fam.*) delusione.

to sell (sold, sold) *vt.* e *vi.* 1. vendere 2. (*fig.*) vendere, tradire || to — *off* (*comm.*), liquidare.

seller *s.* 1. venditore 2. articolo che si vende.

selling *s.* vendita, smercio || — *up*, vendita fallimentare.

selves V. *self.*

semantic *agg.* semantico.

semantics *agg.* semantica.

semester *s.* semestre.

semi *prefisso* semi, mezzo, metà.

semicircle *s.* semicerchio.

semicircular *agg.* semicircolare.

semicolon *s.* punto e virgola.

semifinal *agg.* e *s.* semifinale.

seminar *s.* seminario (*d'università*).

seminarist *s.* seminarista.

seminary *s.* seminario.

semination *s.* semina.

Semite *agg. e s.* semita.

Semitic *agg.* semitico.

Semitism *s.* semitismo.

semitone *s.* semitono.

semivowel *s.* semivocale.

senate *s.* senato.

senator *s.* senatore.

senatorial *agg.* senatoriale.

to send (sent, sent) *vt. e vi.* mandare, inviare, spedire || *to — away*, congedare; *to — back*, rinviare; *to — for*, mandare a chiamare; *to — off*, inviare (*per lettera*); *to — out*, emettere.

sender *s.* **1.** mandante, mittente **2.** (*comm.*) spedizioniere **3.** (*radio, tv.*) emittente.

sending *s.* **1.** invio **2.** (*comm.*) spedizione **3.** (*radio, tv.*) trasmissione.

senescence *s.* senescenza.

senile *agg.* senile.

senility *s.* senilità.

senior *agg.* **1.** più vecchio, più anziano **2.** più ragguardevole, che ha più anzianità. ♦ **senior** *s.* **1.** decano, anziano **2.** il superiore.

seniority *s.* anzianità (*d'anni, di grado*).

sensation *s.* **1.** senso, sensazione **2.** colpo, impressione.

sensational *agg.* **1.** che dipende dai sensi **2.** sensazionale.

sense *s.* **1.** senso, sensazione, impressione **2.** conoscenza **3.** significato || *common —*, buon senso. ♦ **senses** *s. pl.* facoltà mentale (*sing.*).

senseful *agg.* significativo.

senseless *agg.* **1.** inanimato **2.** insensato.

sensibility *s.* **1.** sensibilità, sensitività **2.** emotività.

sensible *agg.* **1.** sensato, giudizioso **2.** percettibile **3.** notevole, considerevole **4.** consapevole.

sensibly *avv.* **1.** assennatamente **2.** percettibilmente.

sensism *s.* sensismo.

sensist *s.* sensista.

sensitive *agg.* **1.** sensitivo, sensibile **2.** suscettibile, impressionabile.

sensitively *avv.* sensibilmente.

sensitiveness *s.* **1.** sensibilità **2.** suscettibilità.

to sensitize *vt.* sensibilizzare.

sensitizer *s.* (*foto*) sensibilizzatore.

sensorial *agg.* sensorio.

sensory *agg.* sensoriale.

sensual *agg.* sensuale.

sensualism *s.* sensualismo.

sensuality *s.* sensualità.

sensually *avv.* sensualmente, voluttuosamente.

sensuous *agg.* sensoriale, voluttuoso.

sent V. *to send*.

sentence *s.* **1.** giudizio, sentenza **2.** (*gramm.*) frase || *to pass a —*, pronunciare una sentenza.

to sentence *vt.* giudicare, pronunciare una sentenza contro.

sententious *agg.* sentenzioso.

sententiously *avv.* sentenziosamente.

sentient *agg.* senziente, sensibile.

sentiment *s.* **1.** sentimento **2.** opinione, parere.

sentimental *agg.* sentimentale, romantico.

sentimentalism *s.* sentimentalismo.

sentimentalist *s.* persona sentimentale.

sentimentality *s.* sentimentalità.

sentinel *s.* sentinella, guardia.

sentry *s.* sentinella, guardia, scolta || *— box*, garitta.

separate *agg.* separato, staccato.

to separate *vt.* separare. ♦ **to separate** *vi.* separarsi.

separately *avv.* separatamente.

separation *s.* separazione, divisione.

separatism *s.* separatismo.

September *s.* settembre.

septicaemia *s.* setticemia.

septuagenarian *agg. e s.* settuagenario.

septuagenary *agg.* settuagenario.

septum *s.* (*pl.* -ta) diaframma.

sepulchral *agg.* sepolcrale.

sepulchre *s.* sepolcro.

sequacious *agg.* pedissequo, servile.

sequel *s.* **1.** conseguenza **2.** seguito.

sequence *s.* **1.** successione, sequela **2.** sequenza.

to sequestrate *vt.* sequestrare, confiscare.

sequestration *s.* sequestro, confisca.

sequin *s.* lustrino.

seraphic(al) *agg.* serafico.

serenade *s.* serenata.

serene *agg.* **1.** sereno, senza nubi **2.** calmo, tranquillo.

serenely *avv.* serenamente.

serenity *s.* **1.** serenità, limpidezza **2.** tranquillità.

sergeant *s.* **1.** sergente **2.** brigadiere.

serial *s.* romanzo a puntate, pubblicazione periodica.

serially *avv.* 1. in serie 2. periodicamente.

sericulture *s.* sericoltura.

sericulturist *s.* sericoltore.

series *s.* serie, successione.

serigraphy *s.* serigrafia.

serious *agg.* 1. serio, pensieroso 2. grave, importante.

seriousness *s.* 1. serietà 2. gravità.

sermon *s.* sermone, predica.

serotherapy *s.* sieroterapia.

serous *agg.* sieroso.

serpent *s.* serpente.

serum *s.* siero.

servant *s.* servo, servitore.

to **serve** *vt.* e *vi.* 1. servire, essere al servizio di 2. servire, essere utile 3. essere sotto le armi 4. (*giur.*) notificare (*di atti*) || to — out, distribuire.

server *s.* 1. chi serve 2. chierico 3. vassoio.

service *s.* 1. servizio (*anche militare*) 2. servigio, favore 3. funzione religiosa 4. (*giur.*) notifica. ♦ **Services** *s. pl.* forze armate.

serviceable *agg.* utile, pratico.

serviette *s.* tovagliolo.

servile *agg.* servile.

servilism *s.* servilismo.

servility *s.* servilità.

serving *s.* 1. il servire 2. servizio (*di tavola*).

servitude *s.* servitù, schiavitù.

session *s.* sessione, seduta. ♦ **sessions** *s. pl.* (*giur.*) udienze.

set *s.* 1. fermo, fisso 2. stabilito, prestabilito 3. studiato, preparato. ♦ **set** *s.* 1. il solidificarsi 2. forma, serie 3. gruppo 4. direzione, corso 5. (*poet.*) tramonto 6. serie completa, insieme: *a — of teeth*, una dentiera; *the complete — of Shakespeare's works*, la raccolta completa delle opere di Shakespeare.

to **set** (**set**, **set**) *vt.* e *vi.* 1. mettere, porre, collocare 2. sistemare, mettere a punto 3. tramontare (*anche fig.*) || to — about, accingersi; to — back, impedire; to — in, incominciare; to — out, esporre; to — up, fissare, installare; to — aside (*giur.*), annullare; to — off, compensare.

set-back *s.* contrattempo.

set-down *s.* rimprovero.

set-off *s.* 1. contrasto 2. compensazione.

setting *s.* 1. messa in opera, montaggio 2. ambiente 3. scenario, messa in scena 4. incastonatura.

to **settle** *vt.* e *vi.* 1. fissare, decidere, determinare 2. saldare, liquidare (*conti, questioni ecc.*) 3. sistemare, sistemarsi 4. stabilire 5. calmare, calmarsi 6. depositare, depositarsi (*di sedimenti ecc.*) || to — down, stabilirsi (*in un luogo*).

settled *agg.* fissato, stabilito.

settlement *s.* 1. determinazione 2. saldo, liquidazione 3. sistemazione 4. lo stabilirsi (*in un luogo*) 5. colonia, distretto 6. (*giur.*) transazione || *financial* —, regolamento di conti.

settler *s.* 1. chi decide 2. colonizzatore.

settling *s.* 1. stabilizzazione 2. saldo, pagamento.

set-to *s.* zuffa.

setup *s.* disposizione, organizzazione.

seven *agg.* sette.

sevenfold *agg.* settuplo. ♦ **sevenfold** *avv.* sette volte tanto.

seventeen *agg.* diciassette.

seventeenth *agg.* diciassettesimo.

seventh *agg.* settimo.

seventieth *agg.* settantesimo.

seventy *agg.* settanta.

to **sever** *vt.* staccare, dividere. ♦ to **sever** *vi.* staccarsi, dividersi.

several *agg.* 1. parecchi, diversi (*pl.*) 2. separato, distinto. ♦ **several** *pron.* alcuni, diversi (*pl.*) || — of them, alcuni di loro.

severally *avv.* separatamente, individualmente.

severe *agg.* 1. severo, austero 2. violento, forte 3. rigido (*di clima*).

severely *avv.* 1. severamente 2. violentemente.

severity *s.* 1. severità, durezza 2. violenza.

to **sew** (**sewed**, **sewn**) *vt.* e *vi.* cucire.

sewage *s.* acque di scolatura.

sewer[1] *s.* chi cuce, cucitrice.

sewer[2] *s.* 1. canale artificiale di drenaggio 2. fogna.

sewing *s.* 1. il cucire 2. lavoro di cucito.

sewn V. to *sew.*

sex *s.* sesso.

sexagenarian *agg.* e *s.* sessagenario.

sextet(te) *s.* sestetto.

sexton *s.* sagrestano.

sextuple *agg.* e *s.* sestuplo.

sexual *agg.* sessuale.

shabbiness *s.* **1.** l'essere male in arnese **2.** meschinità.

shabby *agg.* **1.** male in arnese, cencioso **2.** meschino, gretto.

shackles *s. pl.* **1.** manette, ceppi **2.** (*fig.*) impedimenti.

shade *s.* **1.** ombra (*anche fig.*) **2.** sfumatura (*di colore, significato ecc.*) **3.** spirito, ombra **4.** schermo, riparo || *eye-- --*, visiera.

to shade *vt.* e *vi.* **1.** ombreggiare, riparare (*da luce, calore*) **2.** velare, oscurare (*anche fig.*).

shadiness *s.* ombrosità.

shading *s.* **1.** l'ombreggiare **2.** ombreggiatura, sfumatura.

shadow *s.* ombra (*anche fig.*). ◆ **shadows** *s. pl.* oscurità.

to shadow *vt.* pedinare, seguire come un'ombra.

shadowy *agg.* **1.** ombroso, ombreggiato **2.** indistinto, vago.

shady *agg.* ombreggiato, all'ombra.

shaft[1] *s.* **1.** lancia, giavellotto **2.** fulmine **3.** gambo, stelo **4.** asta, bastone **5.** (*mecc.*) albero.

shaft[2] *s.* sfiatatoio, condotto.

shaggy *agg.* **1.** ispido, irsuto **2.** peloso (*di tessuto*) **3.** incolto.

Shah *s.* scià.

shake *s.* **1.** scossa, scuotimento **2.** tremore, tremito **3.** frullato.

to shake (shook, shaken) *vt.* e *vi.* **1.** scuotere, agitare (*liquidi*) **2.** tremare, far tremare **3.** turbare **4.** indebolire.

shakily *avv.* instabilmente.

shaking *agg.* tremante, vacillante. ◆ **shaking** *s.* scossa, scuotimento.

shaky *agg.* **1.** instabile, tremolante **2.** malsicuro.

shall *v. dif.* **1.** (*aus. per le prime pers. del fut. predicente*) *I -- go to England next summer*, andrò in Inghilterra l'estate prossima; *we -- work next week*, lavoreremo la prossima settimana **2.** (*aus. per le seconde e terze pers. del fut. volitivo*) *you -- go to bed!*, andrai a letto! **3.** dovere: *you -- wait for me*, devi aspettarmi.

shallow *agg.* **1.** poco profondo, basso **2.** (*fig.*) superficiale.

sham *s.* **1.** finta, inganno **2.** ipocrita.

shaman *s.* sciamano.

shambles *s. pl.* **1.** mattatoio (*sing.*) **2.** carneficina (*sing.*).

shame *s.* **1.** vergogna, pudore **2.** disonore.

to shame *vt.* **1.** svergognare, far arrossire **2.** disonorare.

shamefaced *agg.* **1.** vergognoso **2.** timido.

shameful *agg.* vergognoso, disonorevole.

shameless *agg.* svergognato, sfacciato.

shamelessly *avv.* sfacciatamente.

shank *s.* **1.** gamba, stinco **2.** gambo, stelo **3.** fusto (*di colonna*) || *-- -bone*, tibia.

shape *s.* forma, figura.

to shape *vt.* e *vi.* creare, dar forma a.

shapeless *agg.* informe.

shapely *agg.* ben fatto.

share *s.* **1.** parte, porzione **2.** (*comm.*) azione, titolo.

to share *vt.* dividere, spartire. ◆ **to share** *vi.* partecipare, condividere.

shareholder *s.* azionista.

share-out *s.* distribuzione.

shark *s.* **1.** squalo, pescecane **2.** (*fig.*) profittatore.

sharp *agg.* **1.** tagliente, affilato **2.** aguzzo **3.** scosceso, ripido **4.** netto, chiaro **5.** intelligente, acuto.

sharp *avv.* puntualmente, in punto.

to sharpen *vt.* **1.** affilare, aguzzare **2.** (*fig.*) rendere più acuto.

sharper *s.* imbroglione.

sharply *avv.* acutamente.

sharpness *s.* **1.** filo, affilatura **2.** acutezza **3.** vivacità, intelligenza.

sharp-sighted *agg.* dalla vista acuta.

to shatter *vt.* frantumare. ◆ **to shatter** *vi.* frantumarsi.

shattering *s.* disintegrazione.

shave[1] *s.* **1.** il radersi, rasatura.

shave[2] *s.* pialla.

to shave[1] *vt.* radere. ◆ **to shave** *vi.* radersi.

to shave[2] *vt.* piallare.

shaven *agg.* **1.** rasato **2.** (*eccl.*) tonsurato.

shaving *s.* **1.** il radersi **2.** truciolo.

shawl *s.* scialle.

she *pron. pers. f.* ella, lei, colei. ◆ **she** *attr. indicante il sesso degli animali*: *a -- -bear*, un'orsa.

sheaf *s.* (*pl.* **sheaves**) **1.** fascio, covone **2.** (*geom.*) fascio (*di rette ecc.*).

to shear (sheared, shorn) *vt.* **1.** cesoiare, tranciare **2.** tosare.

shearing s. recisione, taglio.

shears s. pl. cesoie, forbici.

sheath s. guaina, fodero.

to **sheathe** vt. **1.** mettere nel fodero **2.** rivestire di.

sheaves V. sheaf.

to **shed (shed, shed)** vt. **1.** versare, spandere **2.** lasciar cadere.

shed s. tettoia, capannone.

shedding s. **1.** spargimento **2.** perdita, caduta (di foglie ecc.).

sheen s. splendore, lucentezza.

sheep s. (anche pl.) **1.** pecora, ovino **2.** (fig.) persona debole, timorosa.

sheepish agg. timido, impacciato.

sheepskin s. **1.** pelle di pecora **2.** cartapecora.

sheer[1] agg. **1.** puro, semplice, mero **2.** liscio, non diluito (di bevande).

sheer[2] s. virata, cambiamento di rotta.

sheet s. **1.** lenzuolo **2.** foglio **3.** lamina, lamiera.

sheik(h) s. sceicco.

shelf s. (pl. shelves) mensola, scaffale.

shell s. **1.** conchiglia, guscio **2.** involucro, carcassa **3.** bossolo (di cartuccia) **4.** (fig.) apparenza.

to **shell** vt. e vi. sgusciare, sgranare.

shelter s. **1.** riparo, rifugio **2.** pensilina.

to **shelter** vt. riparare. ♦ to **shelter** vi. ripararsi.

to **shelve** vt. **1.** provvedere di scaffali **2.** mettere negli scaffali.

shelves V. shelf.

shelving s. scaffalatura.

shepherd s. pastore, pecoraio.

sherbet s. sorbetto.

shield s. **1.** scudo **2.** (fig.) protezione.

to **shield** vt. proteggere, difendere.

shift s. **1.** cambiamento, sostituzione **2.** risorsa, espediente **3.** turno (di lavoro).

to **shift** vt. **1.** spostare **2.** cambiare. ♦ to **shift** vi. **1.** spostarsi **2.** arrangiarsi.

shilling s. scellino.

shilly-shally vi. tentennare.

to **shimmer** vi. luccicare, mandare bagliori.

to **shine (shone, shone)** vt. e vi. **1.** splendere, brillare (anche fig.) **2.** essere brillante.

shine s. **1.** splendore, luminosità **2.** luce del sole.

Shintoist s. scintoista.

shiny agg. splendente, rilucente.

ship s. nave, bastimento || convoy——, nave scorta; flag——, nave ammiraglia; landing——, nave da sbarco.

to **ship** vt. **1.** imbarcare **2.** (comm.) spedire. ♦ to **ship** vi. imbarcarsi.

shipboard s. bordo.

shipboy s. mozzo.

shipbuilder s. costruttore navale.

shipmate s. compagno di bordo.

shipment s. imbarco, spedizione di merci.

shipping s. **1.** forze navali (pl.) **2.** imbarco, spedizione.

shipwreck s. naufragio.

to **shipwreck** vi. naufragare.

shipyard s. cantiere navale.

shirker s. scansafatiche.

shirt s. camicia (da uomo).

shiver[1] s. scheggia.

shiver[2] s. brivido, fremito.

to **shiver**[1] vt. frantumare. ♦ to **shiver** vi. frantumarsi.

to **shiver**[2] vt. e vi. rabbrividire, tremare.

shivering s. V. shiver.

shivery agg. **1.** fragile **2.** tremante.

shoal[1] s. secca, bassofondo.

shoal[2] s. banco (di pesci).

shock s. **1.** urto, collisione **2.** forte impressione, violenta emozione.

to **shock** vt. **1.** colpire, disgustare **2.** provocare un collasso. ♦ to **shock** vi. scandalizzarsi **2.** scontrarsi.

shocking agg. **1.** che colpisce **2.** disgustoso.

shoe s. scarpa, calzatura || horse——, ferro di cavallo.

shoeblack s. lustrascarpe.

shoemaker s. calzolaio.

shoe-string s. laccio (da scarpe).

shone V. to shine.

shook V. to shake.

shoot s. **1.** spedizione di caccia **2.** virgulto **3.** puntura, fitta.

to **shoot (shot, shot)** vt. e vi. **1.** lanciare **2.** sparare, uccidere sparando **3.** cacciare **4.** fare un'istantanea.

shooter s. cacciatore.

shooting s. **1.** tiro, sparo **2.** caccia **3.** il fotografare, il girare un film.

shop s. **1.** bottega, negozio **2.** officina, laboratorio || ——-assistant, commesso; ——-book, libro dei conti; ——-lifter, taccheggiatore; ——-window, vetrina.

shopkeeper s. negoziante.

shopman s. commesso di negozio.

shopping s. compere, acquisti (pl.).

shore s. spiaggia, lido.

shorn V. to shear.

short agg. **1.** corto, breve **2.** basso, piccolo (di statura) **3.** conciso **4.** brusco, rude. ♦ **short** s. **1.** compendio **2.** (cine) cortometraggio.

short avv. **1.** bruscamente, improvvisamente **2.** (comm.) allo scoperto.

shortage s. mancanza, carenza.

short-circuit s. corto circuito.

short-cut s. scorciatoia.

short-dated agg. (comm.) a breve scadenza.

to **shorten** vt. accorciare, abbreviare.

shortening s. accorciamento, abbreviazione.

shorthand s. stenografia.

shortly avv. **1.** fra breve **2.** brevemente.

shortness s. brevità.

short-sighted agg. miope.

shot[1] V. to shoot.

shot[2] s. **1.** sparo, colpo **2.** proiettile **3.** ripresa cinematografica.

shotgun s. fucile da caccia.

should s. dif. **1.** (aus. per le prime pers. del condiz.) I — be very happy, sarei felicissimo **2.** dovere: it — be so, dovrebbe essere così.

shoulder s. spalla.

to **shoulder** vt. e vi. **1.** spingere con le spalle **2.** portare sulle sp.lle.

shout s. grido, chiasso.

to **shout** vt. e vi. gridare, urlare.

shove s. spinta, urto.

to **shove** vt. spingere. ♦ to **shove** vi. spingersi.

shovel s. pala.

to **shovel** vt. spalare.

shoveller s. spalatore.

show s. **1.** mostra, esibizione **2.** apparenza **3.** pompa, ostentazione || — case, bacheca; — down, chiarificazione; — off, esibizionismo.

to **show** (showed, shown) vt. e vi. **1.** mostrare, far vedere **2.** rappresentare, indicare **3.** dimostrare, provare **4.** apparire, farsi vedere || to — down, mettere le carte in tavola; to — off, darsi delle arie.

shower s. acquazzone, rovescio.

showman s. presentatore.

shown V. to show.

showy agg. fastoso, appariscente.

shrank V. to shrink.

shred s. brandello, frammento.

shrew s. bisbetica.

shrewd agg. sagace, accorto.

shrewdly avv. sagacemente.

shrewdness s. sagacia, accortezza.

shrewish agg. brontolone.

shriek s. grido, strillo, suono lacerante.

to **shriek** vt. e vi. gridare, stridere.

shrill agg. stridulo, acuto.

to **shrill** vt. e vi. strillare, stridere.

shrimp s. gamberetto.

shrine s. reliquiario.

shrink s. restringimento.

to **shrink** (shrank, shrunk) vt. e vi. **1.** restringere, restringersi, contrarre **2.** indietreggiare.

shrinkable agg. restringibile.

shrinkage s. **1.** diminuzione, restringimento **2.** (comm.) deprezzamento.

shrinking s. contrazione, ritiro.

shroud s. sudario.

shrub s. arbusto, cespuglio.

shrubbery s. boscaglia d'arbusti.

shrug s. spallucciata.

to **shrug** vi. alzare le spalle.

shrunk V. to shrink.

shudder s. brivido.

to **shudder** vi. rabbrividire.

shuffle s. **1.** passo strascicato **2.** scompiglio **3.** il mescolare (le carte).

to **shuffle** vt. e vi. **1.** muoversi a fatica **2.** mescolare, scompigliare.

to **shun** vt. sfuggire, scansare.

shunt s. **1.** (elett.) derivazione **2.** (ferr.) scambio.

to **shunt** vt. e vi. **1.** (elett.) inserire in derivazione **2.** (ferr.) smistare, smistarsi.

shut agg. ben chiuso.

to **shut** (shut, shut) vt. e vi. chiudere, serrare || shut up!, tacil

shutter s. imposta, persiana.

shuttle s. spola, navetta.

shy agg. riservato, timido.

to **shy** vt. spaventare. ♦ to **shy** vi. scartare (di cavallo).

shyly avv. timidamente.

shyness s. timidezza, scontrosità.

Siberian agg. e s. siberiano.

sibilant agg. e s. sibilante.

Sibylline agg. sibillino.

Sicilian agg. e s. siciliano.

sick agg. **1.** ammalato **2.** nauseato || to fall —, ammalarsi.

to **sicken** *vt.* e *vi.* **1.** far ammalare, ammalarsi **2.** sfiorire **3.** sentir nausea.

sickening *agg.* nauseabondo, rivoltante.

sickle *s.* falce.

sickly *agg.* **1.** malaticcio **2.** pallido, debole **3.** nauseante.

sickness *s.* malattia.

side *s.* **1.** lato, fianco **2.** parte, partito, fazione **3.** discendenza || *-door*, porta laterale; — *-face*, profilo; — *-look*, occhiata in tralice; — *-note*, nota marginale; — *-post*, stipite.

sideboard *s.* credenza.

sidecar *s.* motocarrozzetta.

sidelong *agg.* laterale, obliquo.

sidereal *agg.* sidereo.

sideways *avv.* lateralmente, obliquamente.

to **sidle** *vi.* camminare di fianco, andare a sghembo || *to — up to so.*, avvicinarsi furtivamente a qu.

siege *s.* assedio.

sieve *s.* setaccio, crivello.

to **sieve** *vt.* setacciare, crivellare.

to **sift** *vt.* e *vi.* setacciare **2.** filtrare (*di luce, polvere ecc.*).

sigh *s.* sospiro.

to **sigh** *vt.* e *vi.* **1.** sospirare **2.** sibilare.

sight *s.* **1.** vista, visione **2.** veduta, panorama **3.** colpo d'occhio **4.** mirino.

to **sight** *vt.* e *vi.* **1.** avvistare **2.** prendere la mira.

sighted *agg.* **1.** fornito di vista || *long* —, presbite; *short* —, miope.

sightless *agg.* senza vista.

sign *s.* **1.** segno, cenno **2.** indicazione, traccia || *traffic* —, segnale stradale.

to **sign** *vt.* e *vi.* firmare, segnare, sottoscrivere.

signal *s.* segnale, segno.

to **signal** *vt.* segnalare. ♦ to **signal** *vi.* far segnali.

signalman *s.* segnalatore.

signatory *s.* firmatario.

signature *s.* **1.** firma, sigla **2.** (*tip.*) segnatura.

signboard *s.* insegna (*di albergo, negozio ecc.*).

significant *agg.* espressivo, significativo.

to **signify** *vt.* e *vi.* **1.** significare, voler dire **2.** denotare, indicare, presagire **3.** importare.

silence *s.* silenzio.

to **silence** *vt.* far tacere, imporre il silenzio.

silencer *s.* silenziatore.

silent *agg.* **1.** silenzioso, taciturno **2.** muto.

silently *avv.* silenziosamente.

silhouette *s.* profilo, contorno.

silica *s.* silice.

silicate *s.* silicato.

silicon *s.* silicio.

silicosis *s.* silicosi.

silk *s.* seta.

silken *agg.* serico, di seta.

silkworm *s.* baco da seta || *-breeding*, sericoltura.

silky *agg.* di seta, serico.

sill *s.* basamento, soglia.

silliness *s.* stupidità, sciocchezza.

silly *agg.* sciocco, stupido.

to **silo** *vt.* conservare, mettere in silo.

silt *s.* melma.

silver *s.* argento, argenteria || *-plate*, argenteria; — *-plating*, argentatura || *quick* —, mercurio.

to **silver** *vt.* inargentare. ♦ to **silver** *vi.* inargentarsi.

silverware *s.* oggetti d'argento.

silvery *agg.* argenteo.

similar *agg.* simile, analogo.

similarity *s.* somiglianza, similitudine.

similitude *s.* **1.** similitudine **2.** somiglianza.

simoniac *agg.* e *s.* simoniaco.

simony *s.* simonia.

to **simper** *vi.* parlare in modo affettato.

simple *agg.* **1.** semplice, elementare **2.** sincero **3.** autentico.

simpleton *s.* sempliciotto.

simplicity *s.* semplicità, candore.

simplification *s.* semplificazione.

to **simplify** *vt.* semplificare.

simply *avv.* semplicemente.

simulation *s.* simulazione.

simulator *s.* simulatore.

simultaneity *s.* simultaneità.

simultaneous *agg.* simultaneo.

sin *s.* **1.** peccato, colpa **2.** offesa.

to **sin** *vi.* peccare.

since *avv.* da allora, da allora in poi || *long* —, molto tempo fa. ♦ **since** *cong.* **1.** da quando **2.** poiché. ♦ **since** *prep.* da, fin da.

sincere *agg.* sincero, schietto.

sincerely *avv.* sinceramente || *yours* —, cordialmente vostro (*nelle lettere*).

sincerity *s.* sincerità.
sinew *s.* **1.** tendine, nervo **2.** (*fig.*) vigore, nerbo.
sinful *agg.* peccaminoso, colpevole.
sinfully *avv.* peccaminosamente.
to **sing** (**sang, sung**) *vt. e vi.* cantare.
to **singe** *vt.* bruciacchiare, strinare (*anche fig.*). ♦ to **singe** *vi.* bruciarsi.
singer *s.* cantante.
singing *s.* **1.** canto **2.** fischio (*del vento ecc.*).
single *agg.* **1.** solo, unico **2.** individuale, particolare **3.** celibe ‖ *every — day*, tutti i giorni.
to **single** *vt.* distinguere, scegliere: *to — out sthg.*, scegliere qc.
singleness *s.* **1.** unicità **2.** sincerità.
singly *avv.* **1.** separatamente, ad uno ad uno **2.** da solo, senza aiuto.
singsong *s.* cantilena, canto monotono.
singular *agg.* **1.** singolare, solo **2.** eccezionale **3.** bizzarro, strano.
singularity *s.* **1.** singolarità, rarità **2.** particolarità **3.** stranezza.
singularly *avv.* singolarmente.
sinister *agg.* sinistro, funesto, di cattivo augurio.
sink *s.* **1.** lavandino, acquaio **2.** scolo.
to **sink** (**sank, sunk**) *vi.* **1.** affondare, andare a fondo **2.** sprofondare **3.** abbassare, abbassarsi, calare **4.** cadere, cedere (*di terreno, muro ecc.*).
sinner *s.* peccatore.
sinuous *agg.* sinuoso.
sinus *s.* **1.** cavità **2.** seno.
sip *s.* sorso.
to **sip** *vt. e vi.* sorseggiare.
siphon *s.* sifone.
sir *s.* **1.** (*vocativo*) signore **2.** « sir » (*titolo*).
siren *s.* sirena.
siroc *s.* scirocco.
sirup *s.* sciroppo.
sister *s.* **1.** sorella **2.** suora ‖ *— -in- law*, cognata.
sisterhood *s.* congregazione religiosa di suore.
sisterly *avv.* da sorella, amorevolmente.
to **sit** (**sat, sat**) *vt. e vi.* **1.** sedere, stare seduto, far sedere **2.** essere in seduta **3.** appollaiarsi, posare **4.** covare ‖ *to — out*, rimanere fino alla fine; *to — up*, rimanere al-

zato.
site *s.* area fabbricabile.
sitting *s.* **1.** posa, seduta **2.** adunanza ‖ *— -room*, stanza di soggiorno. ♦ **sittings** *s. pl.* sessioni (*di una Corte*).
situated *agg.* **1.** situato, collocato **2.** in una certa situazione (*di persona*).
situation *s.* **1.** situazione, posizione **2.** stato, circostanza **3.** posto, impiego: *to apply for a —*, fare una domanda di impiego.
six *agg.* sei.
sixfold *agg.* sestuplo. ♦ **sixfold** *avv.* sei volte tanto.
sixpence *s.* moneta da sei « pence », mezzo scellino.
sixpenny *agg.* del valore di sei « pence ».
sixteen *agg.* sedici.
sixteenth *agg.* sedicesimo.
sixth *agg.* sesto.
sixtieth *agg.* sessantesimo.
sixty *agg.* sessanta.
size *s.* **1.** grandezza, misura, dimensione **2.** formato, taglia **3.** colla.
to **size** *vt.* allineare ‖ *to — up*, valutare.
sizzle *s.* sfrigolio.
skate *s.* pattino ‖ *roller —*, pattino a rotelle.
to **skate** *vi.* pattinare.
skating *s.* pattinaggio.
skein *s.* matassa.
skeleton *s.* scheletro (*anche fig.*).
to **skeletonize** *vt.* scheletrire. ‖
to **skeletonize** *vi.* scheletrirsi (*anche fig.*).
skeptic *agg. e s.* scettico.
skeptical *agg.* scettico.
skepticism *s.* scetticismo.
sketch *s.* **1.** schizzo, abbozzo **2.** scenetta.
to **sketch** *vt.* abbozzare, schizzare.
skewness *s.* asimmetria.
ski *s.* sci ‖ *— -lift*, sciovia.
to **ski** *vi.* sciare.
skier *s.* sciatore.
skiff *s.* (*mar.*) schifo.
skilful *agg.* abile, esperto.
skilfully *avv.* abilmente.
skilfulness *s.* abilità.
skill *s.* abilità, destrezza.
skilled *agg.* esperto, abile, versato ‖ *— worker*, operaio specializzato.
to **skim** *vt. e vi.* **1.** schiumare, scremare **2.** rasentare, sfiorare.
skimmer *s.* schiumarola.

skimming s. scrematura.

skin s. pelle, cute.

to **skin** vt. e vi. scuoiare || to — over, rimarginarsi (di ferite).

skinny agg. magro, scarno.

to **skip** vt. e vi. fare un balzo, saltare alla corda || to — a few pages, saltare qualche pagina.

skirmish s. scaramuccia.

skirt s. 1. sottana, gonna 2. orlo, lembo.

to **skirt** vt. e vi. orlare, costeggiare.

skittish agg. capriccioso, frivolo.

skittles s. pl. birilli.

skull s. cranio, teschio || — -cap, papalina.

sky s. cielo, firmamento.

skylark s. allodola.

skylight s. lucernario.

skyline s. linea, profilo (di montagne ecc.).

skyman s. paracadutista.

skyscraper s. grattacielo.

skyward agg. e avv. verso il cielo.

slab s. 1. lastra, piastra 2. pezzo, fetta.

slack agg. 1. molle, allentato 2. debole, fiacco 3. (comm.) calmo, stagnante, debole. ♦ **slack** s. (comm.) stagione morta.

to **slacken** vt. 1. allentare, mollare 2. diminuire. ♦ to **slacken** vi. 1. allentarsi 2. smorzarsi.

slacker s. fannullone.

slain V. to **slay.**

slam s. sbatacchiamento.

to **slam** vt. sbattere, chiudere violentemente. ♦ to **slam** vi. chiudersi violentemente.

slander s. 1. calunnia 2. (giur.) diffamazione.

to **slander** vt. 1. calunniare 2. (giur.) diffamare.

slanderer s. 1. calunniatore 2. (giur.) diffamatore.

slanderous agg. calunnioso, maldicente.

slang s. gergo.

slant s. pendenza, inclinazione.

to **slant** vt. e vi. essere in pendenza, inclinare.

slanting agg. inclinato, obliquo, sghembo.

slap s. schiaffo, ceffone.

to **slap** vt. 1. schiaffeggiare 2. sbattere.

slash s. 1. taglio, sfregio 2. frustata.

to **slash** vt. tagliare, fendere.

slate s. ardesia, tegola d'ardesia.

slaughter s. 1. macello 2. carneficina, massacro.

to **slaughter** vt. 1. macellare 2. massacrare.

slaughterer s. 1. macellatore 2. massacratore.

slaughterhouse s. mattatoio.

Slav agg. e s. slavo.

slave s. schiavo.

slaver[1] s. schiavista.

slaver[2] s. saliva, bava.

slavery s. schiavitù.

to **slay (slew, slain)** vt. ammazzare.

sleek agg. lucido, levigato.

sleep s. sonno, dormita || — -walker, sonnambulo.

to **sleep (slept, slept)** vt. e vi. 1. dormire, riposare 2. passare la notte.

sleeper s. 1. dormiente, dormiglione 2. (ferr.) traversina 3. (ferr.) vettura letto.

sleepily avv. con aria assonnata.

sleeping agg. dormiente, addormentato || — bag, sacco a pelo; — -berth, cuccetta; — -car, vagone letto; — -draught, sonnifero.

sleepless agg. insonne.

sleeplessness s. insonnia.

sleepy agg. assonnato, sonnolento.

sleet s. nevischio.

sleeve s. manica.

sleeved agg. con maniche.

sleigh s. slitta.

slender agg. 1. magro, snello 2. debole, fiacco.

slenderness s. 1. snellezza, magrezza 2. debolezza.

slept V. to **sleep.**

slew V. to **slay.**

slice s. pezzo, fetta, porzione.

to **slice** vt. affettare.

slicer s. affettatrice.

slid V. to **slide.**

slide s. 1. scivolata 2. pendenza 3. scivolo 4. (mecc.) carrello, pattino.

to **slide (slid, slid)** vt. e vi. 1. scivolare, far scivolare, scorrere, far scorrere 2. sfuggire.

sliding agg. scorrevole.

slight agg. 1. esile, minuto, magro 2. leggero, scarso.

slim agg. 1. magro, sottile 2. debole.

slime s. melma, limo.

slimy agg. fangoso, viscoso.

sling[1] s. fionda.

sling[2] *s.* cinghia.

to **sling**[1] (**slung, slung**) *vt.* scagliare con la fionda.

to **sling**[2] *vt.* sospendere, appendere.

to **slink** (**slunk, slunk**) *vi.* sgattaiolare.

slip[1] *s.* 1. innesto 2. (*tip.*) bozza in colonna.

slip[2] *s.* 1. scalo, molo 2. guinzaglio 3. sottoveste 4. scivolone 5. papera, lapsus.

to **slip** *vt.* e *vi.* 1. scivolare, inciampare 2. entrare, uscire furtivamente 3. sguisciare, liberarsi || *to — away*, scorrere (*di tempo*).

slipper *s.* pantofola.

slippery *agg.* sdrucciolevole, viscido (*anche fig.*).

slipshod *agg.* 1. scalcagnato 2. trasandato.

slit *s.* fessura, fenditura.

to **slit** (**slit, slit**) *vt.* fendere.

slope *s.* pendenza, pendio.

to **slope** *vi.* essere in pendenza, inclinarsi.

sloping *agg.* inclinato, obliquo.

slot *s.* fessura, scanalatura || — *-machine*, distributore automatico a gettoni.

sloth *s.* pigrizia, indolenza.

slothful *agg.* pigro, indolente.

slouch *s.* andatura dinoccolata.

slouching *agg.* dinoccolato, goffo.

slovenliness *s.* sciatteria, sporcizia.

slovenly *agg.* sciatto, sudicio.

slow *agg.* 1. lento 2. tardo, ottuso || — *-down*, rallentamento; — *-match*, miccia.

to **slow** *vt.* e *vi.* to — *up* o *down*, rallentare.

slowly *avv.* lentamente.

slowness *s.* lentezza, pigrizia.

sluggish *agg.* pigro, tardo, indolente.

sluggishness *s.* pigrizia, indolenza.

slum *s.* vicolo, tugurio. ♦ **slums** *s. pl.* quartieri poveri (*di una città*).

slumber *s.* dormiveglia, assopimento.

to **slumber** *vt.* e *vi.* dormire, dormicchiare.

slung V. *to* sling.

slunk V. *to* slink.

slush *s.* poltiglia, fango.

sly *agg.* 1. astuto, malizioso 2. infido.

smack *s.* 1. sapore, aroma 2. schiocco 3. schiaffo.

to **smack** *vt.* e *vi.* 1. schioccare 2. schioccare baci 3. schiaffeggiare.

small *agg.* 1. piccolo, minuto 2. leggero, debole 3. poco, scarso 4. di poca importanza.

small-arms *s. pl.* armi portatili.

smallness *s.* piccolezza.

smallpox *s.* vaiolo.

smart *agg.* 1. acuto, pungente 2. vivace, sveglio 3. elegante.

to **smarten** *vt.* e *vi.* abbellire || *to — up*, rianimarsi, farsi bello.

smartness *s.* 1. acutezza, vivacità, brio 2. eleganza.

smash *s.* 1. urto, scontro 2. rovina.

to **smash** *vt.* 1. frantumare, fracassare 2. sconfiggere, annientare. ♦ to **smash** *vi.* 1. frantumarsi 2. sfasciarsi 3. crollare.

smasher *s.* 1. chi frantuma 2. (*fam.*) caso eccezionale.

smear *s.* macchia, imbrattatura.

to **smear** *vt.* macchiare, imbrattare.

smell *s.* 1. odorato, olfatto 2. odore.

to **smell** (**smelt, smelt**) *vt.* e *vi.* 1. fiutare, sentire l'odore 2. avere odore || *to — of*, sapere di; *to — out*, scovare.

smile *s.* sorriso.

to **smile** *vt.* e *vi.* sorridere || *fortune smil'ed on you*, la fortuna ti fu favorevole.

smiling *agg.* sorridente, sereno.

smirch *s.* onta, macchia.

to **smite** (**smote, smitten**) *vt.* e *vi.* 1. colpire, percuotere 2. sconfiggere, sgominare || *to — down*, abbattere.

smith *s.* fabbro.

smitten V. *to* smite.

smoke *s.* 1. fumo 2. fumata || — *-stack*, fumaiolo.

to **smoke** *vt.* e *vi.* 1. fumare 2. affumicare.

smoker *s.* fumatore, fumatrice.

smoking *s.* il fumare. ♦ **smoking** *agg.* fumante.

smoky *agg.* 1. fumoso 2. affumicato, annerito dal fumo 3. che sa di fumo.

smooth *agg.* 1. liscio, levigato 2. omogeneo 3. armonioso (*di suono*) 4. mellifluo 5. calmo, tranquillo (*di mare*).

to **smooth** *vt.* 1. lisciare, spianare 2. appianare.

smoothing *s.* lisciatura, spianatura.

smoothly *avv.* 1. pianamente 2. armonicamente 3. in modo mellifluo.

smoothness *s.* 1. levigatezza 2. armonia (*di verso, suono*) 3. affabilità.

smote V. *to smite*.

to smother *vt.* e *vi.* **1.** soffocare, opprimere **2.** ricoprire.

to smoulder *vi.* ardere sotto la cenere.

to smuggle *vt.* e *vi.* contrabbandare.

smuggler *s.* contrabbandiere.

smuggling *s.* contrabbando.

smut *s.* fuliggine.

snack *s.* **1.** boccone, porzione **2.** spuntino || — *-bar*, tavola calda.

snail *s.* chiocciola, lumaca.

snake *s.* serpente.

snakily *avv.* **1.** tortuosamente **2.** (*fig.*) slealmente.

snaky *agg.* serpentino.

snap *s.* **1.** colpo secco, morso, schiocco **2.** scatto **3.** fermaglio, fibbia.

to snap *vt.* e *vi.* **1.** schioccare, far schioccare **2.** aprirsi di colpo, spezzare con un colpo secco **3.** (*foto*) scattare un'istantanea.

snapshot *s.* (*foto*) istantanea.

snare *s.* **1.** trappola, rete **2.** insidia, tentazione.

to snare *vt.* prendere in trappola, al laccio (*anche fig.*).

snarl *s.* ringhio.

to snarl *vi.* ringhiare.

snatch *s.* **1.** strappo, strattone **2.** brano, frammento.

to snatch *vt.* e *vi.* afferrare, ghermire || *to — off*, strappare.

sneak *s.* persona malfida.

sneer *s.* sogghigno beffardo.

to sneer *vt.* e *vi.* sorridere beffardamente, schernire.

sneeze *s.* starnuto.

to sneeze *vi.* starnutire.

to sniff *vt.* e *vi.* fiutare || *to — at sthg.* annusare qc.

snip *s.* **1.** ritaglio, scampolo **2.** forbiciata.

to snip *vt.* tagliuzzare.

snobbery *s.* snobismo.

to snore *vi.* russare.

snort *s.* sbuffo, rumore sbuffante.

to snort *vt.* e *vi.* sbuffare.

snout *s.* muso, grugno.

snow *s.* neve, nevicata || — *plough*, spazzaneve; — *-slide*, valanga.

to snow *v. imp.* nevicare || *it is snowing*, nevica.

snowfall *s.* nevicata.

snowflake *s.* fiocco di neve.

snowy *agg.* **1.** nevoso, coperto di neve **2.** niveo.

snuff *s.* **1.** l'aspirare col naso **2.** tabacco da fiuto || — *-box*, tabacchiera.

to snuff¹ *vt.* e *vi.* **1.** annusare aspirando **2.** fiutare tabacco.

to snuff² *vt.* e *vi.* smoccolare (*una candela*).

to snuffle *vi.* e *vi.* pronunciare con tono nasale.

snug *agg.* **1.** comodo **2.** confortevole **3.** nascosto.

to snuggle *vi.* **1.** rannicchiarsi **2.** accoccolarsi.

so *avv.* così, tanto, talmente || — *far*, fino ad ora; — *long as*, a patto che; || —, in tal caso; *that being* —, stando così le cose.

to soak *vt.* **1.** immergere **2.** bagnare. ♦ **to soak** *vi.* **1.** inzupparsi, imbeversi **2.** bagnarsi.

soaking *agg.* **1.** che bagna, che inzuppa **2.** bagnato. ♦ **soaking** *s.* immersione, bagnatura.

soap *s.* sapone || — *dish*, portasapone.

to soap *vt.* insaponare. ♦ **to soap** *vi.* insaponarsi.

soapbox *s.* **1.** cassa per sapone **2.** (*fam.*) palco improvvisato per oratori (*da strada*).

soapsuds *s. pl.* saponata (*sing.*).

soapwort *s.* saponaria.

sob *s.* singhiozzo.

to sob *s.* e *vi.* singhiozzare.

sober *agg.* **1.** sobrio (*nel bere*) **2.** calmo, composto.

sobriety *s.* **1.** sobrietà (*nel bere*) **2.** moderazione, calma.

so-called *agg.* cosiddetto.

sociability *s.* socievolezza.

sociable *agg.* socievole.

social *agg.* **1.** sociale **2.** socievole.

socialism *s.* socialismo.

socialist *s.* socialista.

sociality *s.* socievolezza.

to socialize *vt.* socializzare.

society *s.* **1.** società, compagnia **2.** strato sociale **3.** associazione.

sociological *agg.* sociologico.

sociologist *s.* sociologo.

sociology *s.* sociologia.

sock *s.* **1.** calzino, calza corta **2.** soletta.

socket *s.* **1.** cavità **2.** (*elett.*) presa di corrente, portalampada **3.** (*anat.*) orbita.

Socratic *agg.* e *s.* socratico.

sod *s.* zolla erbosa.

soda *s.* carbonato di sodio.

sodium s. sodio.

soft agg. 1. molle, tenero 2. liscio, morbido, soffice 3. dolce, mite ‖ — -boiled (egg), uovo alla coque.

to **soften** vt. 1. ammollire, ammorbidire 2. calmare, raddolcire. ♦ to **soften** vi. 1. ammorbidirsi 2. intenerirsi.

softening agg. che rende molle. ♦ **softening** s. 1. ammorbidimento 2. intenerimento.

softly avv. 1. teneramente 2. sommessamente 3. pian piano.

softness s. 1. morbidezza 2. dolcezza, mitezza.

soil[1] s. 1. suolo, terreno 2. macchia (anche fig.).

to **soil** vt. macchiare. ♦ to **soil** vi. macchiarsi.

sojourn s. soggiorno.

to **sojourn** vi. soggiornare.

solace s. sollievo, conforto.

to **solace** vt. consolare.

solar agg. solare.

sold V. to **sell**.

solder s. lega per saldatura.

to **solder** vt. saldare.

soldering s. saldatura.

soldier s. 1. soldato 2. stratega ‖ foot- —, soldato di fanteria; horse- —, soldato di cavalleria.

soldierlike agg. militaresco.

soldiery s. coll. soldatesca, truppe.

sole[1] s. solo, unico.

sole[2] s. suola, pianta del piede.

sole[3] s. sogliola.

solecism s. solecismo.

solely avv. solamente.

solemn agg. solenne, serio, grave.

solemnity s. solennità.

to **solemnize** vt. solennizzare.

solemnly avv. solennemente.

sol-fa s. solfeggio.

to **sol-fa** vt. e vi. solfeggiare.

to **solicit** vt. 1. sollecitare 2. adescare. ♦ to **solicit** vi. fare sollecitazioni.

solicitation s. 1. sollecitazione 2. invito, adescamento.

solicitor s. 1. sollecitatore 2. procuratore legale.

solicitous agg. 1. sollecito 2. ansioso, desideroso.

solid agg. 1. solido, compatto 2. reale, fondato. ♦ **solid** s. solido.

solidarity s. solidarietà.

solidary agg. solidale.

solidification s. solidificazione.

to **solidify** vt. solidificare. ♦ to **so-**

lidify vi. solidificarsi.

solidity s. 1. solidità 2. (comm.) solvenza.

solidly avv. 1. solidamente 2. all'unanimità.

soliloquy s. soliloquio.

solitaire s. solitario (pietra preziosa e giuoco delle carte).

solitary agg. 1. solo, unico 2. solitario 3. isolato, romito.

solitude s. solitudine, isolamento.

soloist s. solista.

solstice s. solstizio.

solubility s. solubilità.

soluble agg. 1. solubile 2. scomponibile 3. risolvibile.

solution s. 1. (chim.) soluzione 2. risolvimento.

solvability s. 1. (comm.) solvibilità 2. solubilità 3. risolvibilità.

solvable agg. 1. (comm.) solvibile 2. solubile 3. risolvibile.

to **solve** vt. risolvere, chiarire.

solvency s. (comm.) solvibilità.

solvent agg. 1. (comm.) solvibile 2. solvente. ♦ **solvent** s. solvente.

somatic(al) agg. somatico.

somatology s. somatologia.

sombre agg. 1. fosco, scuro 2. (fig.) tetro, triste.

some agg. 1. qualche, alcuni, certi 2. un certo, qualsiasi 3. (partitivo) un po' di, del, della, dei, degli, delle. ♦ **some** pron. 1. alcuni, alcune 2. un po'. ♦ **some** avv. circa.

somebody pron. indef. qualcuno.

somehow avv. in qualche modo, in un modo o nell'altro.

someone pron. indef. qualcuno: — else, qualcun altro.

somersault s. 1. salto mortale, capriola 2. (aer.) capottamento 3. (auto) ribaltamento.

to **somersault**, to **somerset** vi. 1. fare salti mortali 2. (aer.) capottare 3. (auto.) ribaltare.

something pron. indef. qualche cosa.

sometime avv. 1. un tempo 2. presto o tardi, un giorno o l'altro.

sometimes avv. qualche volta, alcune volte.

someway avv. in un modo o nell'altro.

somewhat pron. ind. un poco.

somewhere avv. in qualche luogo.

somnambulism s. sonnambulismo.

somnambulist s. sonnambulo.

somnolent *agg.* 1. sonnolento 2. assopito.

son *s.* figlio, figliolo || — *-in-law*, genero.

song *s.* canto, canzone.

songbook *s.* canzoniere.

songful *agg.* 1. melodioso 2. che ama cantare.

songster *s.* cantante (*uomo*).

sonnet *s.* sonetto.

sonority *s.* sonorità.

sonorous *agg.* sonoro, risonante.

sonorously *avv.* sonoramente.

soon (*comp. di* soon) *avv.* presto, tra poco || *the sooner the better*, prima è meglio è; *sooner or later*, presto o tardi; *I had sooner*, preferirei; *as — as*, non appena.

soot *s.* fuliggine.

to **soot** *vt.* macchiare, sporcare di fuliggine.

to **soothe** *vt.* calmare, placare.

soothsayer *s.* indovino.

sooty *agg.* fuligginoso.

sophism *s.* sofisma.

sophist *s.* sofista (*anche fig.*).

sophistic(al) *agg.* sofistico, pedante.

sophisticated *agg.* 1. sofisticato, raffinato 2. adulterato.

sophistry *s.* sofisma.

sorcerer *s.* stregone, mago.

sorceress *s.* strega, maga.

sorcery *s.* stregoneria, sortilegio.

sordid *agg.* 1. sordido, avaro 2. vile, meschino.

sore *agg.* 1. doloroso, dolorante, infiammato 2. triste, addolorato 3. estremo, intenso.

sorrel *s.* sauro.

sorrow *s.* 1. dispiacere, dolore 2. rincrescimento 3. sventura.

to **sorrow** *vi.* affliggersi, addolorarsi.

sorrowful *agg.* 1. triste, infelice 2. penoso, doloroso.

sorry *agg.* spiacente, dolente || *sorry!*, scusate!; *to be* —, dispiacersi.

sort *s.* sorta, specie.

to **sort** *vt.* raggruppare, selezionare.

♦ to **sort** *vi.* accordarsi, adattarsi.

sought V. *to seek.*

soul *s.* 1. anima, animo, spirito 2. essenza, personificazione.

sound[1] *avv.* profondamente.

sound[2] *agg.* 1. sano, intero, in buono stato 2. buono, solido 3. profondo, completo || — *-beaded* equilibra-

to, — *-minded*, di buon senso.

sound[3] *s.* suono, rumore || — *wave*, onda sonora.

sound[4] *s.* sondaggio.

sound[5] *s.* braccio di mare, stretto.

to **sound**[1] *vt. e vi.* 1. suonare, risuonare 2. sembrare, aver l'aria di.

to **sound**[2] *vt. e vi.* sondare, scandagliare.

sounding *agg.* sonoro, sonante, risonante.

soundless *agg.* muto, senza suono.

soundly *avv.* 1. sanamente 2. profondamente.

soundness *s.* 1. buona condizione (*di salute*) 2. solidità (*di argomento*).

soup *s.* zuppa, minestra.

sour *agg.* 1. acido, aspro, acerbo 2. bisbetico.

to **sour** *vt. e vi.* 1. inacidire 2. inasprire, esacerbare.

source *s.* 1. fonte, sorgente 2. origine.

sourdine *s.* (*mus.*) sordina.

sourish *agg.* acidulo.

sourness *s.* acidità.

south *s.* sud, mezzogiorno.

southern *agg.* del sud, meridionale.

southerner *s.* abitante del sud, meridionale.

southward *avv.* verso sud.

sovereign *s.* sovrano.

sovereignty *s.* sovranità.

sow *s.* scrofa.

to **sow** (**sowed, sown**) *vt. e vi.* seminare, piantare.

sowing *s.* seminagione.

sown V. *to sow.*

spa *s.* sorgente minerale.

space *s.* spazio || — *-ship*, astronave.

to **space** *vt.* spaziare, disporre ad intervalli.

spaceman *s.* astronauta.

spacesuit *s.* tuta spaziale.

spacial *agg.* spaziale.

spacing *s.* spaziatura, interlineatura.

spacious *agg.* spazioso, ampio.

spade *s.* vanga, badile.

span V. *to spin.*

span *s.* 1. spanna, palmo 2. breve spazio di tempo.

to **span** *vt.* 1. misurare a spanne 2. attraversare.

spangle *s.* lustrino.

Spaniard *s.* spagnolo.

Spanish *agg.* spagnolo.

to **spank** *vt.* (*fam.*) sculacciare.

spar[1] s. (mar.) antenna.

spar[2] s. incontro di pugilato.

spare agg. 1. parco, frugale 2. d'avanzo, disponibile, in più || — room, camera in più (per gli ospiti); — time, tempo disponibile; — wheel, ruota di scorta.

to **spare** vt. 1. economizzare, risparmiare 2. privarsi, fare a meno di. ♦ to **spare** vi. essere frugale.

sparing agg. 1. parco, frugale 2. limitato, moderato.

spark s. 1. scintilla, favilla 2. (fig.) lampo, barlume.

to **spark** vi. scintillare, emettere scintille.

sparkle s. scintilla, favilla.

to **sparkle** vi. 1. emettere scintille (di fuoco) 2. sfavillare, brillare, risplendere (anche fig.).

sparkler s. stella filante.

sparkling agg. scintillante, vivace (anche fig.).

sparrow s. passero || — -hawk, sparviero.

Spartan agg. e s. spartano.

spasm s. 1. spasmo 2. attacco, spasimo (anche fig.).

spasmodic(al) agg. spasmodico.

spastic agg. spastico.

spat V. to spit.

spatial agg. spaziale.

spatiality s. spazialità.

spatter s. 1. schizzo 2. sgocciolio.

to **spatter** vt. e vi. 1. schizzare, inzaccherare 2. gocciolare.

to **speak (spoke, spoken)** vt. e vi. 1. parlare 2. esprimere, rivelare || to — at, alludere a; to — out, parlare francamente; to — to, garantire; to — up, alzare la voce.

speaker s. parlatore, oratore, annunciatore || the — of the House of Commons, il Presidente della Camera dei Comuni.

speaking agg. parlante, espressivo, eloquente. ♦ **speaking** s. 1. il parlare, discorso 2. eloquenza, declamazione.

spear s. 1. lancia, alabarda, asta 2. fiocina.

to **spear** vt. 1. trafiggere (con lancia) 2. fiocinare.

special agg. 1. speciale, particolare 2. eccezionale, straordinario.

specialist s. specialista.

speciality s. specialità, particolarità.

to **specialize** vt. specializzare. ♦ to

specialize vi. specializzarsi.

specially avv. specialmente, soprattutto.

specialty s. 1. (comm.) specialità 2. (giur.) contratto sigillato.

species s. 1. specie, classe 2. sorta, genere, tipo.

specific agg. specifico, particolare.

specification s. 1. specificazione 2. descrizione dettagliata.

to **specify** vt. specificare, precisare.

specimen s. modello, esemplare.

speck s. 1. macchiolina, punto 2. granello (di polvere ecc.).

speckled agg. macchiato, screziato.

speckless agg. senza macchia (anche fig.).

spectacle s. spettacolo, vista. ♦ **spectacles** s. pl. occhiali: to put on one's —, mettersi gli occhiali.

spectacled agg. che porta gli occhiali.

spectacular agg. spettacolare.

spectator s. spettatore.

spectral agg. spettrale.

spectre s. spettro, fantasma.

specular agg. speculare.

to **speculate** vt. e vi. 1. meditare, considerare 2. (comm.) speculare.

speculation s. 1. speculazione, meditazione 2. (comm.) speculazione.

speculative agg. contemplativo, speculativo (anche comm.).

speculator s. 1. spirito speculatore 2. (comm.) speculatore.

sped V. to speed.

speech s. 1. parola, favella 2. discorso, arringa 3. linguaggio.

speechless agg. senza parola, muto (anche fig.).

speed s. velocità, rapidità.

to **speed** vi. affrettarsi. ♦ to **speed (sped, sped)** vt. 1. aiutare 2. affrettare 3. regolare la velocità || to — up the work, affrettare i lavori.

speedometer s. tachimetro.

speedway s. pista, circuito (di autodromo).

speedy agg. rapido, pronto.

spell[1] s. incantesimo.

spell[2] s. 1. turno di lavoro 2. intervallo.

to **spell (spelt, spelt)** (anche reg.) vt. e vi. compitare, sillabare.

to **spellbind (spellbound, spellbound)** vt. incantare, affascinare.

spelling s. 1. compitazione 2. ortografia.

spelt V. *to spell*.

to spend (spent, spent) *vt.* e *vi.* 1. spendere, sborsare 2. dedicare, impiegare 3. passare, trascorrere.

sperm *s.* sperma.

sphenoid *agg.* e *s.* sfenoide.

sphere *s.* sfera, globo.

spheric(al) *agg.* sferico.

sphericity *s.* sfericità.

sphincter *s.* sfintere.

Sphinx *s.* sfinge (*anche fig.*).

spice *s.* 1. aroma 2. (*fig.*) sapore, gusto 3. spezie (*pl.*).

to spice *vt.* 1. condire con spezie 2. (*fig.*) dar gusto a, rendere interessante.

spicery *s.* spezie, aromi (*pl.*).

spicily *avv.* 1. aromaticamente 2. (*fig.*) gustosamente.

spiciness *s.* 1. aroma, profumo 2. (*fam.*) arguzia.

spick-and-span *agg.* (*fam.*) lindo, lucente.

spicy *agg.* 1. aromatico, piccante 2. (*fig.*) arguto, mordace.

spider *s.* ragno.

spidery *agg.* 1. simile a ragno 2. infestato da ragni.

spike[1] *s.* punta, aculeo.

spike[2] *s.* spiga.

to spike *vt.* inchiodare || *to — so.'s guns*, guastare i piani di qu.

to spill (spilt, spilt) *vt.* 1. versare 2. disarcionare. ♦ **to spill (spilt, spilt)** *vi.* versarsi, traboccare.

spin *s.* (*aer.*) avvitamento.

to spin (span, spun) *vt.* e *vi.* 1. filare (*cotone ecc.*) 2. (*mecc.*) lavorare al tornio 3. girare, far girare.

spinach *s.* spinacio.

spinal *agg.* spinale.

spindle *s.* 1. fuso, fusello 2. (*mecc.*) asse, mandrino.

spine *s.* 1. spina, lisca 2. spina dorsale.

spineless *agg.* 1. senza spine 2. senza spina dorsale 3. (*fam.*) debole, molle.

spinner *s.* 1. ragno filatore 2. (*aer.*) ogiva filatore.

spinning *s.* 1. filatura, filato 2. movimento rotatorio || *— -mill*, filanda.

spinster *s.* 1. filatrice 2. donna nubile, zitella.

spiral *agg.* spirale, a spirale. ♦ **spiral** *s.* spirale.

spire[1] *s.* guglia, cuspide.

spire[2] *s.* spira, spirale.

spirit *s.* 1. spirito, anima 2. folletto, fantasma 3. genio, intelletto 4. coraggio, vigore.

spirits[1] *s. pl.* umore, stato d'animo (*sing.*).

spirits[2] *s. pl.* bevande fortemente alcooliche.

spirited *agg.* brioso, vivace || *high- —*, fiero; *poor- —*, depresso.

spiritism *s.* spiritismo.

spiritual *agg.* spirituale.

spiritualism *s.* 1. spiritualismo 2. spiritismo.

spiritualist *s.* 1. spiritualista 2. spiritista.

spirituality *s.* spiritualità.

spit *s.* sputo, saliva.

to spit (spat, spat) *vi.* sputare.

spite *s.* dispetto, ripicco: *out of —*, per dispetto; *in — of*, a dispetto di.

spiteful *agg.* dispettoso.

spittle V. *spit*.

spittoon *s.* sputacchiera.

splash *s.* 1. schizzo, spruzzo 2. tonfo.

to splash *vt.* e *vi.* **A.** schizzare, spruzzare 2. inzaccherare, infangare. ♦ **to splash** *vi.* 1. spruzzare 2. cadere con un tonfo.

splashy *agg.* bagnato, fangoso.

splay *agg.* largo e piatto. ♦ **splay** *s.* (*arch.*) strombatura.

to splay *vt.* (*arch.*) strombare. ♦ **to splay** *vi.* essere in posizione obliqua.

spleen *s.* 1. milza 2. (*fig.*) malumore, umore nero.

splendid *agg.* splendido, magnifico.

splendour *s.* splendore, lustro.

splenetic *agg.* e *s.* splenetico, bilioso.

splinter *s.* scheggia, frantume.

split *agg.* spaccato, diviso. ♦ **split** *s.* 1. fessura, crepaccio 2. scissione.

to split (split, split) *vt.* 1. fendere 2. spaccare, frazionare || *to — hairs*, spaccare un capello in quattro; *to — one's sides (with laughing)*, ridere a crepapelle. ♦ **to split (split, split)** *vi.* fendersi.

splitting *agg.* che si fende, che fende. ♦ **splitting** *s.* fessura, spaccatura.

spoil(s) *s.* spoglia, preda.

to spoil (spoilt, spoilt) (anche reg.) vt. e vi. **1.** rovinare, alterare, sciupare, viziare **2.** saccheggiare, predare.

spoilt agg. **1.** guasto, avariato **2.** viziato.

spoke s. **1.** raggio (di ruota) **2.** piolo (di scala).

spoke V. to speak.

spoken V. to speak.

spokesman s. portavoce.

spoliation s. ruberia, saccheggio.

sponge s. spugna, colpo di spugna.

to sponge vt. **1.** pulire, lavare con la spugna **2.** fare spugnature **3.** (fig.; fam.) scroccare.

sponger s. **1.** pescatore di spugne **2.** scroccone.

spongy agg. spugnoso, poroso.

sponsor s. **1.** padrino, madrina **2.** (giur.) garante, mallevadore.

to sponsor vt. **1.** essere garante di **2.** offrire (programmi radio, tv).

sponsorial agg. **1.** di garanzia **2.** di padrino, di madrina.

sponsorship s. **1.** garanzia **2.** qualità di padrino, di madrina.

spontaneity s. spontaneità.

spontaneous agg. spontaneo.

spontaneously avv. spontaneamente.

spool s. rocchetto, bobina.

spoon s. cucchiaio.

to spoon vt. prendere con un cucchiaio.

spoon-fed agg. coccolato, viziato.

spoonful s. cucchiaiata.

sporadic agg. sporadico, raro.

sport s. **1.** giuoco, divertimento **2.** scherzo **3.** sport. ♦ **sports** s. pl gare, incontri.

to sport vi. **1.** scherzare **2.** giocare **3.** fare dello sport.

sporting agg. sportivo.

sportive agg. **1.** gioviale **2.** sportivo.

sportsman s. **1.** sportivo **2.** uomo animato da spirito sportivo.

sportsmanlike agg. caratteristico di uno sportivo.

sportswoman s. donna sportiva.

spot s. **1.** luogo, località **2.** macchia (anche fig.) ‖ on the —, sul colpo.

to spot vt. macchiare, punteggiare. ♦ **to spot** vi. macchiarsi.

spotless agg. senza macchia, immacolato (anche fig.).

spotlight s. riflettore, luce della ribalta.

spotty agg. macchiato, chiazzato.

spout s. **1.** tubo di scarico, grondaia **2.** getto, colonna (d'acqua).

to spout vt. scaricare, emettere. ♦ **to spout** vi. scaturire, zampillare.

sprain s. distorsione, strappo muscolare.

to sprain vt. storcere, slogare.

sprang V. to spring.

sprawl vi. sdraiarsi in modo scomposto.

spray s. **1.** spruzzo, schiuma **2.** getto vaporizzato (di acqua ecc.) **3.** spruzzatore.

to spray vt. **1.** polverizzare, vaporizzare **2.** aspergere, spruzzare.

sprayer s. spruzzatore.

spread agg. steso, aperto, spiegato.

to spread (spread, spread) vt. **1.** stendere, spiegare, spalmare **2.** (fig.) spargere, diffondere. ♦ **to spread (spread, spread)** vi. stendersi, spiegarsi.

spreader s. spruzzatore.

spreading agg. che si propaga. ♦ **spreading** s. (fig.) propagazione.

spree s. baldoria.

sprig s. **1.** ramoscello **2.** (fig.) rampollo.

spring s. **1.** sorgente, fonte **2.** primavera **3.** salto, balzo **4.** molla, elasticità ‖ — -board, trampolino; — -head, fontana; — -mattress, materasso a molle.

to spring (sprang, sprung) vi. **1.** nascere, discendere, scaturire (di acqua) **2.** saltare **3.** scattare ‖ to — up, crescere (di piante). ♦ **to spring (sprang, sprung)** vt. **1.** far scattare (con una molla) **2.** far brillare (una mina) **3.** saltare.

springiness s. elasticità.

springy agg. **1.** pieno di sorgenti **2.** elastico.

sprinkle s. aspersione, spruzzatina.

to sprinkle vt. e vi. spruzzare, aspergere.

sprinkler s. **1.** spruzzatore, innaffiatoio **2.** aspersorio.

sprint s. (sport) scatto finale.

to sprout vi. germogliare. ♦ **to sprout** vt. far germogliare.

to spruce vt. adornare, agghindare.

sprung V. to spring. ♦ **sprung** agg. **1.** a molla **2.** spaccato.

spun V. to spin.

spur s. **1.** sperone **2.** (fig.) sprone.

to spur vt. **1.** spronare **2.** (fig.) incitare.

to **spurn** *vt. e vi.* disdegnare, trattare con disprezzo.

spurt *s.* getto, vampata.

spy *s.* spia.

to **spy** *vt. e vi.* spiare, fare la spia.

squabble *s.* battibecco, lite.

to **squabble** *vi.* accapigliarsi, venire a parole.

squad *s.* squadra, plotone.

squalid *agg.* squallido, miserabile.

squall *s.* urlo, strepito.

squalor *s.* squallore.

to **squander** *vt.* sprecare, scialacquare.

squanderer *s.* sciupone, sperperatore.

square *agg.* 1. quadrato 2. robusto, massiccio 3. perpendicolare. ◆

square *s.* 1. quadrato 2. piazza 3. squadra || -built, tarchiato; --root, radice quadrata; --shouldered, dalle spalle larghe e diritte. ◆ **square** *avv.* ad angolo retto, in squadra.

to **square** *vt. e vi.* 1. quadrare, squadrare 2. pareggiare un conto 3. elevare al quadrato.

squared *agg.* 1. squadrato, quadrato 2. elevato al quadrato.

squash *s.* 1. cosa schiacciata 2. spremuta (*di frutta*): *orange* —, spremuta d'arancio.

to **squash** *vt.* 1. schiacciare, spiaccicare 2. spremere.

squat *agg.* rannicchiato, accoccolato.

to **squat** *vi.* accovacciarsi, accoccolarsi.

squatter *s.* pioniere.

squeak *s.* 1. grido acuto 2. pigolio, squittio, guaito 3. cigolio.

to **squeak** *vt. e vi.* 1. strillare in tono acuto 2. squittire, guaire 3. cigolare.

squeaky *agg.* 1. che strilla 2. che guaisce, squittisce 3. cigolante.

squeamish *agg.* 1. soggetto a nausee 2. schizzinoso.

squeeze *s.* 1. compressione 2. spremitura 3. stretta, abbraccio.

to **squeeze** *vt.* 1. spremere 2. stringere, abbracciare. ◆ **squeeze** *vi.* accalcarsi.

squeezer *s.* 1. ciò che preme 2. (*mecc.*) torchio.

squid *s.* seppia.

squint *agg.* strabico. ◆ **squint** *s.* strabismo.

to **squint** *vi.* essere strabico. ◆ to **squint** *vt.* guardare di traverso.

squire *s.* gentiluomo, nobiluomo (*di campagna*).

squirrel *s.* scoiattolo.

stab *s.* coltellata, pugnalata.

to **stab** *vt.* pugnalare, accoltellare.

to **stabilize** *vt.* stabilizzare.

stabilizer *s.* stabilizzatore.

stable¹ *agg.* stabile, permanente.

stable² *s.* scuderia, stalla.

stack *s.* mucchio, cumulo || *chimney* —, ciminiera.

to **stack** *vt.* ammucchiare, accumulare.

staff *s.* 1. bastone, sostegno (*anche fig.*) 2. stato maggiore 3. personale (*di ufficio ecc.*) || *editorial* —, corpo redazionale; *flag* —, asta della bandiera.

stag *s.* cervo.

stage *s.* 1. piattaforma 2. palcoscenico 3. (*fig.*) campo d'azione, scena 4. stadio, grado 5. tappa || -direction, didascalia; — -director, regista (*teat.*); — -effect, effetto scenico; — -name, nome d'arte; landing— (*mar.*), pontile.

to **stage** *vt.* 1. mettere in scena 2. inscenare (*una dimostrazione ecc.*).

stagger *s.* barcollamento, andatura a zig-zag.

to **stagger** *vi.* 1. vacillare 2. dubitare, esitare. ◆ to **stagger** *vt.* far vacillare.

staginess *s.* teatralità.

staging *s.* 1. (*teat.*) messa in scena 2. (*edil.*) impalcatura.

stagnancy *s.* ristagno.

stagnant *agg.* stagnante.

to **stagnate** *vi.* ristagnare.

stagnation *s.* ristagno, stasi.

staid *agg.* posato, serio.

stain *s.* 1. scolorimento, macchia 2. (*fig.*) taccia, onta.

to **stain** *vt.* 1. macchiare 2. tingere. ◆ to **stain** *vi.* macchiarsi, sporcarsi.

stained *agg.* macchiato, sporco.

stainless *agg.* senza macchia.

stair *s.* scalino, gradino. ◆ **stairs** *s. pl.* scale || *winding*—, scala a chiocciola; *flight of* —, rampa di scale.

staircase *s.* 1. scala, scalone 2. tromba delle scale.

stairway *s.* scalinata.

stake¹ *s.* 1. palo, paletto 2. piccola incudine.

stake² *s.* posta, scommessa || *at* —, in giuoco. ◆ **stakes** *s. pl.* (*ippica*) premio, corsa.

to **stake**[1] vt. cintare, chiudere (con una palizzata).

to **stake**[2] vt. mettere in giuoco, scommettere.

stale agg. 1. vecchio, stantio 2. (fig.) trito, caduto in disuso.

stalk[1] s. stelo, gambo.

stalk[2] s. andatura rigida e maestosa.

stall s. 1. stalla 2. bancarella, chiosco.

stammer s. balbuzie, balbettamento.

to **stammer** vt. e vi. 1. balbettare 2. farfugliare.

stammering agg. balbuziente. ♦ **stammering** s. balbuzie.

stamp s. 1. impronta, segno 2. francobollo, bollo 3. stampo || --collector, filatelico; — -paper, carta bollata.

to **stamp** vt. 1. imprimere, incidere 2. (fig.) dare l'impronta 3. timbrare || to — down, calpestare. ♦ to **stamp** vi. battere i piedi.

stamping s. 1. scalpitio 2. timbratura.

stand s. 1. pausa, fermata 2. punto di vista 3. posizione, luogo (d'appostamento) 4. palco, tribuna 5. bancarella, chiosco || test- —, banco di prova.

to **stand** (stood, stood) vi. 1. essere, stare in piedi 2. stare, trovarsi 3. fermarsi, indugiare 4. conservarsi, rimaner valido || to — by, stare accanto, restare fedele a; to — for, significare, implicare; to — out, resistere, tener duro, spiccare. ♦ to **stand** (stood, stood) vt. sopportare, resistere.

standard s. 1. stendardo, bandiera 2. modello, campione 3. livello, qualità 4. supporto, base 5. tipo.

standardization s. standardizzazione.

stand-by s. scorta, riserva.

standing agg. 1. eretto, che sta in piedi 2. fermo, inattivo 3. fisso, immutabile. ♦ **standing** s. 1. posizione eretta 2. posizione, rango 3. periodo di tempo.

standoffish agg. riservato, altezzoso.

standpoint s. 1. luogo di osservazione 2. punto di vista.

standstill agg. in riposo, fermo. ♦ **standstill** s. arresto, fermata.

stank V. to **stink**.

staple s. 1. prodotto principale (di un paese ecc.) 2. (fig.) argomento principale (di una conversazione).

star s. 1. stella, astro 2. (fig.) fortuna, destino 3. (tip.) asterisco.

to **star** vt. 1. costellare 2. segnare con un asterisco. ♦ to **star** vi. (cine, teat.) avere il ruolo di protagonista.

starboard agg. di dritta. ♦ **starboard** s. (mar.) dritta.

starch s. 1. amido 2. (fig.) rigidezza, formalismo.

to **starch** vt. 1. inamidare 2. (fig.) rendere formale.

starchiness s. 1. inamidatura 2. (fig.) formalismo, rigidità.

stardom s. divismo.

stare s. sguardo fisso.

to **stare** vt. guardare intensamente, fissare. ♦ to **stare** vi. sgranare gli occhi.

starfish s. stella di mare.

staring agg. 1. fisso, stupefatto 2. sgargiante, vistoso.

staringly avv. fissamente, con occhi sbarrati.

stark agg. 1. rigido, duro 2. completo, vero e proprio.

starless agg. senza stelle.

starlet s. 1. piccola stella 2. (cine) stellina.

starlight agg. stellato, stellare. ♦ **starlight** s. luce stellare.

starlike agg. simile a stella.

starlit agg. illuminato dalle stelle.

starred agg. 1. stellato, adorno di stelle 2. a stella.

starry agg. stellato, trapunto di stelle, brillante come una stella.

start s. 1. inizio, partenza 2. soprassalto || by fits and starts, irregolarmente 3. vantaggio dato all'inizio di una corsa 4. (mecc.) avviamento.

to **start** vi. 1. partire, mettersi in viaggio 2. cominciare 3. trasalire || to — up, spuntare all'improvviso. ♦ to **start** vt. 1. cominciare 2. far trasalire.

starter s. 1. iniziatore, fondatore 2. (sport) "starter", mossiere.

starting s. 1. inizio, partenza 2. debutto 3. (mecc.) messa in moto, avviamento.

startle s. trasalimento.

to **startle** vt. spaventare, far trasalire. ♦ to **startle** vi. spaventarsi, trasalire.

startling *agg.* impressionante, sorprendente.

starvation *s.* inedia, fame.

to starve *vi.* 1. morire di fame 2. (*fig.*) bramare. ◆ **to starve** *vt.* far morire di fame.

state *s.* 1. stato, condizione 2. governo, nazione 3. rango, dignità || *-control*, statalizzazione; — *documents*, documenti ufficiali; — *-prisoner*, prigioniero politico; — *-trial*, processo politico.

to state *vt.* 1. affermare, dichiarare 2. stabilire.

stateless *agg.* 1. senza patria 2. senza pompa 3. apolide.

stately *agg.* nobile, signorile.

statement *s.* 1. esposto, relazione 2. asserzione, affermazione 3. (*giur.*) deposizione, esposizione dei fatti.

statesman *s.* statista.

static(al) *agg.* statico.

statics *s.* statica.

station *s.* 1. posto, luogo, base 2. stazione 3. condizione sociale || *petrol* —, stazione di rifornimento; *through* —, stazione di transito.

stationary *agg.* stazionario.

stationer *s.* cartolaio || —'*s* (*shop*), cartoleria.

stationery *s.* articoli di cancelleria.

station house *s.* guardina.

stationmaster *s.* capostazione.

statist *s.* statista.

statistic(al) *agg.* statistico.

statistically *avv.* statisticamente.

statistics *s.* 1. scienza della statistica 2. statistiche (*pl.*).

statuary *agg.* statuario, scultorio.

statue *s.* statua.

statuesque *agg.* statuario.

stature *s.* statura.

status *s.* 1. stato, condizione sociale 2. situazione.

statute *s.* statuto, regolamento.

statutory *agg.* statutario.

to staunch *vt.* 1. arrestare 2. stagnare. ◆ **to staunch** *vi.* stagnarsi.

stave *s.* 1. doga (*di botte*) 2. piolo (*di scala*) 3. strofa.

stay¹ *s.* 1. soggiorno 2. pausa.

stay² *s.* 1. sostegno, supporto 2. (*mecc.*) puntello.

to stay¹ *vi.* 1. fermarsi, sostare, soggiornare 2. resistere || *to — away*, essere assente; *to — in*, stare in casa, (*mil.*) essere consegnato; *to*

— *up*, vegliare. ◆ **to stay** *vt.* 1. arrestare, fermare 2. resistere.

to stay² *vt.* (*mecc.*) puntellare.

steadfast *agg.* fermo, risoluto.

steadfastly *avv.* stabilmente, fermamente.

steadfastness *s.* fermezza, tenacia.

steadily *avv.* 1. saldamente, fermamente 2. costantemente.

steadiness *s.* 1. fermezza, sicurezza 2. assiduità, perseveranza.

steading *s.* tenuta agricola.

steady *agg.* 1. fermo, saldo 2. equilibrato 3. continuo, regolare 4. fedele, assiduo.

to steady *vt.* rafforzare, rendere fermo, equilibrato. ◆ **to steady** *vi.* rafforzarsi.

steak *s.* bistecca.

to steal (**stole, stolen**) *vt.* e *vi.* rubare || *to — along*, camminare furtivamente; *to — away*, svignarsela; *to — upon*, avvicinarsi pian piano.

stealing *s.* furto || *cattle* (*o borse*)- *-*—, abigeato.

stealthily *avv.* furtivamente.

stealthy *agg.* furtivo.

steam *s.* vapore: — *-engine*, macchina a vapore.

to steam *vt.* 1. esporre al vapore 2. cucinare al vapore. ◆ **to steam** *vi.* emettere vapore.

steamboat *s.* imbarcazione a vapore.

steamer *s.* nave a vapore.

steamship *s.* piroscafo.

steamtight *agg.* a tenuta di vapore.

steamy *agg.* 1. che esala vapore 2. appannato, umido.

stearic *agg.* stearico.

steel *s.* 1. acciaio 2. arma, spada 3. acciarino || — *cap*, elmetto; — *company*, acciaieria || *stainless* —, acciaio inossidabile.

steelwork *s.* lavoro, struttura in acciaio.

steelwork *s. pl.* acciaieria (*sing.*).

steely *agg.* 1. di acciaio, simile ad acciaio 2. (*fig.*) severissimo.

steelyard *s.* stadera.

steep¹ *agg.* 1. ripido, scosceso 2. (*fig.*) ambizioso, arduo 3. esorbitante (*di prezzi*).

steep² *s.* macerazione, l'inzuppare.

to steep *vt.* immergere (*anche fig.*), inzuppare.

steeple *s.* guglia, campanile.

steeplechase *s.* (*ippica*) corsa ad

ostacoli.

steer s. bue giovane, manzo.

to steer vt. **1.** governare, manovrare **2.** dirigere. ♦ **to steer** vi. **1.** dirigersi **2.** (auto) sterzare.

steering s. guida, governo (dello sterzo, del timone).

stem s. **1.** tronco, gambo, stelo **2.** cannello (di pipa) **3.** (mar.) prua.

to stem vt. arrestare, arginare.

stench s. puzzo, tanfo.

step s. **1.** passo (anche fig.), andatura **2.** orma, impronta **3.** provvedimento **4.** gradino || to be in — with so., tenere il passo con qu.; — by —, gradualmente; in — (elett.), in fase.

to step vi. camminare || to — aside, farsi da parte; to — forward, avanzare; to — in, montare (su un veicolo). ♦ **to step** vt. misurare a passi.

stepbrother s. fratellastro.

stepchild s. (pl. -children) figliastro.

stepdaughter s. figliastra.

stepfather s. patrigno.

stepmother s. matrigna.

stepsister s. sorellastra.

stepson s. figliastro.

stereophonic agg. stereofonico.

stereophony s. stereofonia.

stereoscope s. stereoscopio.

stereotype s. stereotipo.

sterile agg. sterile.

sterility s. sterilità.

to sterilize vt. rendere sterile, sterilizzare.

stern[1] agg. severo, austero.

stern[2] s. (mar.) poppa.

sternly avv. severamente.

sternness s. severità, austerità.

stethoscope s. stetoscopio.

stevedore s. scaricatore (di porto).

stew s. (cuc.) umido, stufato.

to stew vt. e vi. cuocere in umido.

steward s. **1.** amministratore, intendente **2.** (aer., mar.) cameriere di bordo.

stewardess s. **1.** dispensiera **2.** (aer., mar.) cameriera di bordo.

stick s. **1.** bastone **2.** bastoncino **3.** barra, stecca.

to stick (stuck, stuck) vt. **1.** ficcare, conficcare **2.** infilare **3.** incollare, appiccicare. ♦ **to stick** (stuck, stuck) vi. **1.** fissarsi, conficcarsi **2.** incollarsi.

stickiness s. viscosità, adesività.

sticky agg. **1.** appiccicaticcio, visco-

so **2.** poco accomodante.

stiff agg. **1.** rigido, duro **2.** (fig.) inflessibile **3.** indolenzito, intorpidito **4.** freddo, riservato || — collar, colletto duro; — neck, torcicollo.

to stiffen vt. **1.** indurire **2.** indolenzire, intorpidire **3.** rassodare. ♦ **to stiffen** vi. **1.** indurirsi, irrigidirsi (anche fig.) **2.** rassodarsi.

stiffness s. **1.** durezza, rigidezza **2.** intorpidimento.

to stifle vt. **1.** soffocare **2.** (fig.) reprimere. ♦ **to stifle** vi. sentirsi soffocare.

stifling agg. soffocante.

to stigmatize vt. **1.** marchiare **2.** stigmatizzare.

stile s. scaletta.

still[1] agg. tranquillo, calmo, silenzioso || -life (pitt.), natura morta.

still[2] avv. **1.** ancora, tuttora **2.** tuttavia, nondimeno.

still[3] s. alambicco.

to still vt. acquietare, calmare. ♦ **to still** vi. acquietarsi, calmarsi.

stillness s. calma, quiete.

stilt s. trampolo.

stimulant s. **1.** stimolante **2.** bevanda alcolica.

to stimulate vt. stimolare, incitare.

stimulus s. (pl.- li) stimolo, incentivo.

sting s. **1.** pungiglione, aculeo **2.** puntura d'insetto **3.** dolore acuto **4.** pungolo, stimolo.

to sting (stung, stung) vt. e vi. **1.** pungere **2.** colpire, ferire (anche fig.).

stinginess s. avarizia, spilorceria.

stinging agg. pungente, mordace.

stingy agg. avaro, taccagno.

stink s. puzzo, fetore.

to stink (stank, stunk) vt. e vi. puzzare, riempire di puzzo.

stinking agg. puzzolente, fetido.

to stipulate vt. e vi. stipulare.

stipulation s. stipulazione, patto.

stir s. **1.** il rimescolare, l'attizzare || to give a —, dare una rimescolata **2.** animazione, tumulto.

to stir vt. **1.** rimescolare **2.** muovere, agitare. ♦ **to stir** vi. muoversi, agitarsi.

stirabout agg. indaffarato.

stirrer s. incitatore, istigatore.

stirring agg. eccitante.

stirrup s. staffa.

stitch s. **1.** punto **2.** maglia.

stock s. 1. rifornimento, provvista ‖ to be out of —, essere sprovvisto 2. titoli, azioni (pl.) 3. tronco, ceppo 4. (fig.) stirpe.

to stock vt. 1. approvvigionare 2. tenere in magazzino.

stockbroker s. agente di cambio.

stockbroking s. professione dell'agente di cambio.

stock company s. società per azioni.

Stock Exchange s. Borsa valori.

stockfish s. stoccafisso.

stockholder s. azionista.

stocking s. calza lunga.

stoic agg. e s. stoico.

stoicism s. stoicismo.

stoker s. fuochista.

stole V. to steal.

stolen V. to steal.

stolid agg. 1. imperturbabile 2. sciocco.

stolidity s. flemma.

stomach s. stomaco: — -ache, mal di stomaco.

stomatitis s. stomatite.

stomatology s. stomatologia.

stone s. 1. pietra, ciottolo, sasso 2. nocciolo 3. (med.) calcolo ‖ — -blind, completamente cieco; — -breaker, spaccapietre; — cutter, tagliapietre.

to stone vt. 1. lapidare 2. rivestire di pietra 3. snocciolare.

stoneless agg. senza nocciolo.

stoneware s. ceramica.

stony agg. 1. pietroso, sassoso 2. (fig.) duro, insensibile.

stood V. to stand.

stool s. sgabello, seggiolino.

stoop s. curvatura, inchino.

to stoop vi. 1. curvare, inchinarsi 2. (fig.) accondiscendere, abbassarsi.

stop s. 1. sosta, arresto 2. segno di punteggiatura ‖ — watch, cronometro.

to stop vt. 1. fermare 2. turare o otturare 3. impedire. ♦ to stop vi. fermarsi.

stopper s. 1. tappo, turacciolo 2. otturatore.

stopping s. 1. otturazione 2. (comm.) cessazione, sospensione (di pagamenti ecc.).

storage s. 1. immagazzinamento 2. deposito, magazzino.

store s. 1. provvista, riserva 2. magazzino ‖ — -keeper, magazziniere; — -ship, nave da carico.

to store vt. 1. fornire, rifornire 2. immagazzinare, mettere da parte (anche fig.).

storehouse s. magazzino, deposito.

storey s. piano (di edificio).

stork s. cicogna.

storm s. 1. tempesta, temporale 2. tumulto, agitazione.

to storm vi. 1. infuriare, scatenarsi 2. (fam.) adirarsi. ♦ to storm vt. attaccare.

stormy agg. tempestoso, burrascoso.

story s. storia, racconto, novella, favola ‖ to tell stories, contar frottole.

stoup s. acquasantiera.

stout agg. 1. forte, robusto, resistente 2. fermo, risoluto 3. grosso, tozzo.

stove s. 1. stufa 2. cucina economica: gas-—, cucina a gas.

to stove vt. mettere in forno, stufa.

to stow vt. stivare, riempire.

stowage s. (mar.) stivaggio.

straddle s. posizione a gambe divaricate, il mettersi a cavalcioni.

to straddle vt. stare a cavalcioni di. ♦ to straddle vi. mettersi a gambe divaricate.

straight[1] agg. 1. diritto, rettilineo 2. onesto, retto 3. ordinato ‖ a — whisky, un whisky liscio.

straight[2] s. 1. posizione diritta 2. (fig.) condotta onesta.

straight[3] avv. 1. diritto, in linea retta 2. direttamente.

to straighten vt. raddrizzare. ♦ to straighten vi. raddrizzarsi.

straightforward agg. 1. diritto, diretto 2. schietto, leale.

straightforwardly avv. 1. in linea retta 2. francamente, schiettamente.

strain s. 1. tensione (anche fig.) 2. sforzo, fatica 3. distorsione, strappo muscolare.

to strain vt. 1. sottoporre a tensione 2. sforzare. ♦ to strain vi. sforzarsi.

strained agg. 1. teso 2. indebolito 3. non spontaneo, forzato.

strainer s. colino, filtro.

strait s. (geogr.) stretto. ♦ to strand vi. incagliarsi.

stranding s. incagliamento (di una nave).

strange agg. 1. strano, bizzarro 2. estraneo, sconosciuto.

stranger s. estraneo, sconosciuto, forestiero.

to **strangle** vt. strangolare.

strangling s. strangolamento.

strap s. 1. cinghia, correggia 2. maniglia a pendaglio (su tram ecc.).

to **strap** vt. legare con cinghia.

stratagem s. stratagemma.

strategic(al) agg. strategico.

strategist s. stratega.

strategy s. strategia.

stratification s. stratificazione.

to **stratify** vt. stratificare.

stratosphere s. stratosfera.

stratospheric agg. stratosferico.

stratum s. (pl. -ta) 1. strato 2. strato sociale.

straw s. 1. paglia 2. fuscello, cannuccia || — (-hat), paglietta; — -colour, giallo paglierino.

strawberry s. fragola.

stray agg. 1. smarrito, randagio 2. casuale. ♦ **stray** s. animale domestico smarrito.

to **stray** vi. vagare, vagabondare (anche fig.).

streak s. 1. striscia, striatura 2. vena (anche fig.).

to **streak** vt. 1. striare 2. venare.

stream s. 1. corso d'acqua, ruscello 2. flusso, fiotto 3. corrente (anche fig.).

to **stream** vi. 1. scorrere, fluire 2. ondeggiare || to — out, effondersi. ♦ to **stream** vt. far scorrere.

street s. via, strada || one-way —, strada a senso unico.

streetwalker s. passeggiatrice.

strength s. 1. forza, vigore 2. solidità, tenacia.

to **strengthen** vt. rafforzare, irrobustire. ♦ to **strengthen** vi. rafforzarsi, irrobustirsi.

strengthening agg. fortificante.

strenuous agg. strenuo, energico.

strenuously avv. strenuamente.

strenuousness s. vigore.

streptococcus s. (pl. -cci) streptococco.

streptomycin s. streptomicina.

stress s. 1. sforzo, pressione 2. enfasi 3. accento tonico.

to **stress** vt. 1. forzare 2. accentuare 3. porre in rilievo.

stretch s. 1. stiramento, tensione 2. spazio di tempo 3. distesa, estensione.

to **stretch** vt. tirare, tendere, stendere. ♦ to **stretch** vi. estendersi.

stretcher s. 1. tenditore 2. lettiga.

to **strew** (**strewed, strewn**) vt. spargere, sparpagliare.

strict agg. 1. preciso, esatto 2. (fig.) severo, rigido.

strictly avv. 1. esattamente 2. severamente.

stridden V. to **stride**.

stride s. 1. passo lungo, andatura || to make great strides, avanzare a grandi passi.

to **stride** (**strode, stridden**) vi. camminare a grandi passi.

strident agg. stridente.

strife s. contesa, lotta.

strike s. 1. sciopero 2. scoperta (di giacimento) 3. attacco aereo.

to **strike** (**struck, struck**) vt. e vi. 1. battere, colpire 2. (fig.) impressionare, colpire 3. suonare le ore 4. accendere (un fiammifero) 5. scioperare || to — down, abbattere; to — in, frapporsi.

striker s. 1. scioperante 2. (mecc.) percussore.

striking agg. sorprendente.

string s. 1. spago, cordicella 2. laccio 3. (mus.) corda.

to **string** (**strung, strung**) vt. e vi. 1. legare con corde 2. accordare (uno strumento) || to — up, impiccare.

strip s. striscia, nastro.

to **strip** vt. svestire. ♦ to **strip** vi. svestirsi.

stripe s. 1. striscia, lista.

to **stripe** vt. rigare, listare.

striped agg. a righe, a strisce.

to **strive** (**strove, striven**) vi. sforzarsi.

strode V. to **stride**.

stroke s. 1. colpo, percossa 2. movimento 3. bracciata (al nuoto), remata, battuta (al tennis) 4. tratto (di penna ecc.) 5. rintocco (d'orologio) 6. (med.) colpo 7. carezza.

to **stroke**[1] vt. vogare in cadenza.

to **stroke**[2] vt. accarezzare, lisciare.

stroll s. passeggiatina, quattro passi.

to **stroll** vi. gironzolare.

strolling agg. errante, girovago.

strong agg. forte, robusto, energico.

stronghold s. roccaforte.

strontium s. stronzio.

strove V. to **strive**.

struck V. to **strike**.

structural agg. strutturale.

structure s. 1. struttura 2. costruzione.

struggle s. 1. lotta, combattimento 2. sforzo || *hand-to-hand* —, lotta corpo a corpo.

to struggle vi. 1. lottare, divincolarsi 2. (fig.) sforzarsi.

struggler s. contendente, chi lotta.

to strum vt. e vi. strimpellare.

strumpet s. prostituta.

strung V. *to string*.

strut s. andatura solenne.

to strut vi. incedere con sussiego.

stub s. 1. ceppo 2. mozzicone.

stubble s. stoppia.

stubborn agg. ostinato, cocciuto, tenace, ribelle.

stubbornness s. caparbietà, tenacia.

to stucco vt. stuccare.

stuck V. *to stick*.

stud s. 1. chiodo a capocchia larga 2. bottoncino (*da camicia*).

to stud vt. guarnire di borchie.

student s. studente.

studentship s. borsa di studio.

studied agg. 1. studiato, ricercato 2. colto.

studio s. 1. studio (*d'artista*) 2. teatro di posa.

studious agg. studioso, diligente.

study s. 1. studio 2. esame attento, investigazione.

to study vt. e vi. 1. studiare 2. esaminare attentamente.

stuff s. 1. sostanza, materia prima 2. cosa, roba 3. stoffa, tessuto.

to stuff vt. 1. imbottire 2. (cuc.) farcire 3. rimpinzare.

stuffing s. 1. imbottitura 2. (cuc.) ripieno.

stuffy agg. afoso || — *air*, aria viziata.

to stumble vi. 1. inciampare 2. (fig.) fare passi falsi.

stump s. 1. ceppo, tronco 2. radice (*di dente*) 3. piattaforma, podio.

to stun vt. stordire, tramortire.

stung V. *to sting*.

stunk V. *to stink*.

stunt s. (gergo) 1. bravata, esibizione 2. trovata pubblicitaria, notizia sensazionale.

stupefaction s. 1. stupore 2. torpore provocato da stupefacenti.

to stupefy vt. 1. istupidire 2. abbrutire. ♦ **to stupefy** vi. 1. istupidirsi 2. abbrutirsi.

stupendous agg. splendido, stupendo.

stupid agg. stupido, ottuso.

stupidity s. stupidità.

stupidly avv. stupidamente.

sturdy agg. 1. vigoroso, forte 2. risoluto.

to stutter vt. e vi. balbettare.

stuttering s. balbuzie.

sty s. porcile.

style s. 1. stile (*anche fig.*) 2. modello, genere 3. moda.

to style vt. chiamare, denominare.

stylist s. stilista.

stylistic agg. stilistico.

stylization s. stilizzazione.

to stylize vt. stilizzare.

stylographic agg. stilografico.

stylus s. stilo.

subalpine agg. subalpino.

subaltern s. subalterno.

subaquatic agg. subacqueo.

subclass s. sottoclasse.

subcommission s. sottocommissione.

subcommissioner s. vice-commissario.

subcommittee s. sottocomitato.

subconscious agg. e s. subcosciente.

subcutaneous agg. sottocutaneo.

subdeacon s. suddiacono.

to subdivide vt. suddividere. ♦ **to subdivide** vi. suddividersi.

subdivisible agg. suddivisibile.

subdivision s. suddivisione.

subdual s. 1. soggiogamento 2. attenuazione.

to subdue vt. 1. conquistare, soggiogare 2. ridurre, attenuare.

subgovernor s. vicegovernatore.

subject[1] agg. 1. soggetto, assoggettato 2. sottoposto, esposto a.

subject[2] 1. argomento, materia di studio 2. (gramm.) soggetto 3. suddito.

to subject vt. 1. assoggettare 2. esporre.

subjection s. 1. assoggettamento 2. dipendenza.

subjective agg. soggettivo.

subjectivism s. soggettivismo.

subjunctive s. congiuntivo.

sublease s. subaffitto.

to sublease vt. subaffittare.

to sublet (sublet, sublet) vt. subaffittare.

sublieutenancy s. grado di sottotenente.

sublieutenant s. sottotenente.

sublimate agg. e s. sublimato.

to sublimate vt. sublimare.

sublime agg. e s. sublime.

sublimity s. sublimità.

submarine agg. subacqueo. ♦ **submarine** s. sommergibile.

submariner s. sommergibilista.

to **submerge** vt. immergere, sommergere. ♦ to **submerge** vi. immergersi.

submergence s. sommersione.

submersible agg. affondabile.

submersion s. immersione.

submission s. sottomissione, docilità.

submissive agg. remissivo, docile.

submissively avv. in modo remissivo.

submissiveness s. sottomissione.

to **submit** vt. sottomettere, sottoporre. ♦ to **submit** vi. sottomettersi, assoggettarsi.

submultiple agg. e s. sottomultiplo.

subnormal agg. al di sotto della norma.

subordinacy s. subordinazione.

subordinate agg. subordinato. ♦ **subordinate** s. subalterno, inferiore.

to **subordinate** vt. subordinare.

subordination s. subordinazione.

to **suborn** vt. subornare, corrompere.

subornation s. subornazione.

subplot s. trama secondaria.

to **subscribe** vt. e vi. 1. sottoscrivere, firmare 2. aderire, trovarsi d'accordo 3. abbonarsi.

subscriber s. 1. the —, il sottoscritto 2. abbonato.

subscription s. 1. sottoscrizione 2. abbonamento 3. consenso.

subsequence s. susseguenza.

subsequent agg. successivo, ulteriore.

subsequently avv. successivamente.

to **subside** vi. 1. calare, decrescere 2. quietarsi 3. cadere (sul fondo), depositare (di liquidi).

subsidiary agg. sussidiario, supplementare, ausiliario.

to **subsidize** vt. sussidiare.

subsidy s. sussidio.

to **subsist** vt. e vi. sussistere.

subsistence s. esistenza, sussistenza.

subsistent agg. sussistente.

subsoil s. sottosuolo.

subspecies s. sottospecie.

substance s. 1. sostanza, essenza 2. contenuto, l'essenziale 3. solidità, fondamento.

substantial agg. 1. sostanzioso, solido 2. importante, notevole.

substantialism s. sostanzialismo.

substantiality s. 1. sostanzialità 2. concretezza.

substantially avv. sostanzialmente.

substantive agg. considerevole, reale. ♦ **substantive** s. (gramm.) sostantivo.

substitute s. 1. sostituto 2. surrogato, imitazione.

to **substitute** vt. e vi. sostituire.

substitution s. sostituzione.

substratum s. (pl. -ta) 1. strato (anche fig.).

subtenancy s. subaffitto.

subtenant s. subaffittuario.

subterfuge s. sotterfugio.

subterranean agg. sotterraneo.

sub-title s. sottotitolo, didascalia.

subtile agg. 1. penetrante, acuto, sottile 2. elusivo, indefinibile.

subtleness s. 1. sottigliezza, acutezza 2. carattere elusivo.

subtlety s. sottigliezza.

subtly avv. 1. acutamente, sottilmente 2. elusivamente.

to **subtract** vt. sottrarre, detrarre.

subtraction s. sottrazione.

subtractive agg. sottrattivo.

subtrahend s. sottraendo.

suburb s. sobborgo. ♦ **suburbs** s. pl. periferia (sing.).

suburban agg. suburbano, periferico.

subversion s. sovversione.

subversive agg. sovversivo.

to **subvert** vt. sovvertire.

subway s. 1. sottopassaggio 2. (amer.) metropolitana.

to **succeed** vt. succedere a, seguire, subentrare a. ♦ to **succeed** vi. 1. succedere, seguire 2. riuscire, aver successo.

success s. successo, riuscita.

successful agg. che ha successo.

successfully avv. con successo.

succession s. successione, serie.

successive agg. successivo, seguente.

successively avv. successivamente.

successor s. successore.

succint agg. succinto, conciso.

succulent agg. succulento.

to **succumb** vi. soccombere, soggiacere.

succursal s. succursale.

such agg. tale, simile: — that, — as, tale che, tale da. ♦ **such** pron. tale, tali, questo, quello, questa, quella, questi, quelli, queste, quelle.

suchlike *agg.* simile, dello stesso genere.

suck *s.* succhiata, poppata.

to **suck** *vt.* e *vi.* 1. succhiare, poppare 2. assorbire.

sucker *s.* 1. (*mecc.*) pistone 2. ventosa.

to **suckle** *vt.* allattare.

suckling *s.* lattante.

sudden *agg.* improvviso, inaspettato.

♦ **sudden** *s.* evento improvviso.

suddenly *avv.* inaspettatamente.

suddenness *s.* subitaneità.

to **sue** *vt.* e *vi.* 1. ricorrere in giudizio 2. sollecitare.

to **suffer** *vt.* e *vi.* 1. subire, patire 2. tollerare 3. soffrire.

suffering *s.* 1. sofferenza, pena 2. tolleranza.

sufficiency *s.* sufficienza.

sufficient *agg.* sufficiente.

suffix *s.* (*gramm.*) suffisso.

to **suffocate** *vt.* e *vi.* soffocare.

suffocation *s.* soffocamento.

suffrage *s.* 1. suffragio, diritto di voto 2. preghiera.

to **suffuse** *vt.* coprire, cospargere.

sugar *s.* 1. zucchero 2. (*fig.*) atteggiamento mellifluo || — *-beet*, barbabietola da zucchero; — *-cane*, canna da zucchero; — *-tongs*, mollette per lo zucchero; *lump* —, zucchero in zollette.

to **sugar** *vt.* 1. inzuccherare 2. (*fig.*) addolcire, adulare.

sugariness *s.* 1. dolcezza 2. mellifluità.

sugary *agg.* 1. zuccheroso, zuccherino 2. (*fig.*) mellifluo.

to **suggest** *vt.* 1. suggerire 2. far nascere un'idea 3. insinuare.

suggestible *agg.* suggeribile, suggestionabile.

suggestion *s.* 1. suggerimento 2. suggestione 3. associazione di idee.

suggestive *agg.* stimolante, che ispira.

suggestiveness *s.* carattere allusivo.

suicidal *agg.* suicida, che ha tendenze al suicidio.

suicide *s.* 1. suicidio 2. suicida.

suit *s.* 1. domanda, preghiera 2. (*giur.*) causa 3. abito completo (*da uomo*) || — *-case*, valigia.

to **suit** *vt.* adattare, convenire a, far comodo a. ♦ to **suit** *vi.* essere conveniente, accordarsi, adattarsi.

suitability *s.* convenienza.

suitable *agg.* adatto, idoneo.

suitably *avv.* appropriatamente.

suite *s.* 1. seguito, corteo 2. serie.

suitor *s.* 1. postulante 2. corteggiatore.

sulkiness *s.* malumore.

sulks *s. pl.* malumore, broncio (*sing.*).

sulky[1] *agg.* 1. imbronciato, scontroso 2. tetro.

sulky[2] *s.* "sulky", sediolo.

sullen *agg.* 1. accigliato 2. tetro.

sullenly *avv.* accigliato, di malumore.

sulphate *s.* solfato.

sulphide *s.* solfuro.

sulphite *s.* solfito.

sulphonamide *s.* sulfamidico.

sulphur *s.* zolfo || — *-mine* (*o* — *-pit*), solfatara.

to **sulphur**, to **sulphurate** *vt.* solforare.

sulphuric *agg.* solforico.

sulphurous *agg.* solforoso.

sultan *s.* sultano.

sultanate *s.* sultanato.

sultriness *s.* afa, caldo soffocante.

sultry *agg.* afoso, soffocante.

sum *s.* 1. somma, quantità (*di denaro*) 2. addizione.

to **sum** *vt.* e *vi.* sommare, addizionare || to — *up*, riassumere.

summarily *avv.* sommariamente.

to **summarize** *vt.* e *vi.* riassumere.

summary *s.* sommario, ricapitolazione.

summer *s.* estate.

to **summer** *vi.* trascorrere l'estate.

summertime *s.* stagione estiva.

summit *s.* 1. cima, vetta 2. (*fig.*) culmine || *at the* — (*pol.*), al vertice.

to **summon** *vt.* 1. chiamare, mandare a chiamare 2. convocare 3. (*giur.*) citare.

summons *s.* 1. (*giur.*) citazione, ingiunzione 2. convocazione.

sumptuous *agg.* sontuoso.

sumptuously *avv.* sontuosamente.

sumptuousness *s.* sontuosità.

sun *s.* sole || — *-bath*, bagno di sole; — *-glasses*, occhiali da sole.

to **sun** *vt.* esporre al sole. ♦ to **sun** *vi.* esporsi al sole.

to **sun-bathe** *vi.* fare i bagni di sole.

sunbeam *s.* raggio di sole.

sunbow *s.* arcobaleno.

sunburn *s.* 1. abbronzatura 2. scottatura (solare).

sunburnt *agg.* **1.** abbronzato **2.** scottato dal sole.

sunburst *s.* sprazzo di sole.

Sunday *s.* domenica.

to sunder *vt.* separare, recidere. ♦
to sunder *vi.* separarsi, scindersi.

sundry *agg.* parecchi, vari.

sunflower *s.* girasole.

sung V. *to* sing.

sunk V. *to* sink.

sunlight *s.* luce del sole.

sunlit *agg.* soleggiato.

sunny *agg.* luminoso, soleggiato.

sunproof *agg.* inalterabile al sole.

sunrise *s.* il sorgere del sole.

sunset *s.* tramonto (*anche fig.*).

sunshade *s.* parasole.

sunshine *s.* luce del sole.

sunspot *s.* macchia solare.

sunstroke *s.* insolazione.

sun-worship *s.* culto del Sole.

sup *s.* sorso, goccia.

to sup¹ *vt.* e *vi.* sorseggiare.

to sup² *vi.* cenare.

superable *agg.* superabile.

to superabound *vi.* sovrabbondare.

superabundance *s.* sovrabbondanza.

superabundant *agg.* sovrabbondante.

superb *agg.* superbo, magnifico.

superciliary *agg.* sopracciliare.

supercilious *agg.* altero.

superelevation *s.* sopraelevazione.

superficial *agg.* superficiale, poco profondo.

superficiality *s.* superficialità.

superfluous *agg.* superfluo.

superhuman *agg.* sovrumano.

to superimpose *vt.* sovrapporre.

superintendence *s.* sovrintendenza.

superintendent *s.* sovrintendente.

superior *agg.* superiore.

superiority *s.* superiorità.

superlative *agg.* superlativo.

superman *s.* superuomo.

supermarket *s.* supermercato.

supermundane *agg.* ultraterreno.

supernatural *agg.* soprannaturale.

supernutrition *s.* supernutrizione.

to supersede *vt.* rimpiazzare.

supersensitive *agg.* ipersensibile.

supersensitiveness *s.* ipersensibilità.

supersession *s.* sostituzione.

supersonic *agg.* ultrasonoro, supersonico.

superstition *s.* superstizione.

superstitious *agg.* superstizioso.

superstructure *s.* sovrastruttura.

supertax *s.* soprattassa.

superterrestrial *agg.* ultraterreno.

to supervise *vt.* e *vi.* sovrintendere.

supervision *s.* sorveglianza, sovrintendenza.

supervisor *s.* sovrintendente.

supervisory *agg.* di controllo.

supine *agg.* supino (*anche fig.*).

supinely *avv.* supinamente.

supper *s.* cena || to have —, cenare;
— -time, ora di cena.

to supplant *vt.* soppiantare.

supple *agg.* **1.** pieghevole, flessibile **2.** elastico (*anche fig.*).

supplement *s.* supplemento.

supplementary *agg.* supplementare.

suppliant *agg.* supplichevole. ♦
suppliant *s.* supplicante.

supply *s.* **1.** rifornimento, approvvigionamento **2.** (*comm.*) fornitura **3.** sostituto, supplente.

to supply *vt.* fornire, rifornire. ♦
to supply *vi.* fare da sostituto.

support *s.* sostegno, appoggio || *in — of*, in favore di.

to support *vt.* **1.** sostenere, reggere **2.** dare appoggio a **3.** mantenere.

supportable *agg.* sostenibile, sopportabile.

supporter *s.* **1.** sostegno **2.** fautore, sostenitore.

to suppose *vt.* supporre, presupporre, presumere.

supposed *agg.* presunto, supposto.

supposition *s.* supposizione, ipotesi.

suppository *s.* (*med.*) supposta.

to suppress *vt.* **1.** sopprimere, reprimere **2.** (*fig.*) soffocare, trattenere.

suppression *s.* **1.** soppressione **2.** il mettere a tacere.

to suppurate *vi.* suppurare.

suppuration *s.* suppurazione.

suprarenal *agg.* surrenale.

supremacy *s.* supremazia.

supreme *agg.* sommo, supremo.

surcharge *s.* **1.** sovraccarico **2.** soprattassa **3.** sovrapprezzo.

sure *agg.* sicuro, certo, fidato.

surely *avv.* sicuramente, certamente.

surety *s.* garanzia, pegno.

suretyship *s.* garanzia.

surf *s.* **1.** risacca **2.** spuma dei marosi.

surface *s.* superficie (*anche fig.*).

surfeit *s.* **1.** eccesso **2.** sazietà. ♦
to surfeit *vt.* saziare. ♦ to sur-

felt *vi.* saziarsi.

surge *s.* **1.** maroso, cavallone **2.** (*fig.*) impeto.

to surge *vi.* gonfiarsi, sollevarsi, tumultuare.

surgeon *s.* chirurgo.

surgery *s.* chirurgia.

surgical *agg.* chirurgico.

surlily *avv.* sgarbatamente.

surly *agg.* sgarbato.

to surmount *vt.* sormontare, superare.

surname *s.* **1.** cognome **2.** soprannome.

to surname *vt.* soprannominare.

to surpass *vt.* sorpassare, superare.

surpassing *agg.* superiore, eccellente.

surpassingly *avv.* straordinariamente.

surplus *s.* **1.** sovrappiù, eccedenza **2.** residuati di guerra.

surprise *s.* **1.** sorpresa **2.** stupore, meraviglia.

to surprise *vt.* **1.** sorprendere, cogliere all'improvviso **2.** stupire.

surprisedly *avv.* con sorpresa.

surprising *agg.* sorprendente.

surrealism *s.* surrealismo.

surrealist *agg.* e *s.* surrealista.

surrender *s.* **1.** resa, capitolazione **2.** abbandono, cessione.

to surrender *vt.* cedere, consegnare. ♦ **to surrender** *vi.* arrendersi.

surreptitious *agg.* clandestino, furtivo.

surrogate *s.* sostituto, supplente.

surround *s.* bordura, bordo.

to surround *vt.* **1.** circondare **2.** accerchiare.

surrounding *agg.* circostante. ♦ **surroundings** *s. pl.* dintorni.

survey *s.* esame, sguardo generale.

to survey *vt.* e *vi.* esaminare, fare rivelazioni.

surveyor *s.* ispettore.

survival *s.* **1.** sopravvivenza **2.** avanzo, reliquia.

to survive *vi.* sopravvivere. ♦ **to survive** *vt.* vivere più a lungo di.

survivor *s.* superstite.

susceptibility *s.* suscettibilità.

susceptible *agg.* **1.** suscettibile **2.** impressionabile.

suspect *agg.* sospetto. ♦ **suspect** *s.* persona sospetta.

to suspect *vt.* sospettare. ♦ **to suspect** *vi.* essere sospettoso.

to suspend *vt.* **1.** appendere, tenere

sospeso **2.** sospendere.

suspender *s.* giarrettiera, bretella.

suspense *s.* incertezza, attesa ansiosa.

suspension *s.* sospensione.

suspensive *agg.* sospensivo.

suspicion *s.* sospetto, dubbio.

suspicious *agg.* sospettoso, diffidente.

suspiciously *avv.* sospettosamente.

to sustain *vt.* **1.** mantenere, sostenere **2.** prolungare **3.** reggere.

sustainable *agg.* sostenibile.

sustenance *s.* mezzi di sussistenza (*pl.*).

suture *s.* sutura.

to suture *vt.* suturare.

swab *s.* **1.** strofinaccio **2.** (*mar.*) radazza **3.** (*med.*) tampone.

to swab *vt.* pulire, strofinare.

swag *s.* movimento ondeggiante.

swagger *agg.* sgargiante.

to swagger *vi.* **1.** pavoneggiarsi **2.** gloriarsi.

swallow[1] *s.* rondine.

swallow[2] *s.* **1.** baratro **2.** deglutizione.

to swallow *vt.* e *vi.* **1.** deglutire, inghiottire **2.** (*fig.*) ingoiare.

swam V. to *swim*.

swamp *s.* palude || — *-fever*, febbre malarica.

to swamp *vt.* inondare, inzuppare. ♦ **to swamp** *vi.* affondare (*anche fig.*).

swan *s.* cigno || — *song*, canto del cigno.

swarm *s.* sciame, folla.

to swarm *vi.* **1.** sciamare **2.** pullulare, brulicare, essere affollato.

swash *s.* **1.** sciacquio **2.** gradassata.

to swash *vt.* **1.** spruzzare, sguazzare **2.** turbinare, infrangersi. ♦ **to swash** *vt.* far sguazzare.

to swat *vt.* colpire, schiacciare (*mosche ecc.*).

swathe *s.* benda, fascia.

to swathe *vt.* bendare, fasciare.

sway *s.* **1.** oscillazione **2.** potere, potenza, preponderanza.

to sway *vt.* **1.** sballottolare **2.** dominare, influenzare **3.** maneggiare, impugnare **4.** (*mar.*) issare. ♦ **to sway** *vi.* **1.** ondeggiare **2.** propendere **3.** predominare.

swear *s.* bestemmia, imprecazione.

to swear (swore, sworn) *vt.* e *vi.* **1.** giurare, far giurare **2.** imprecare, bestemmiare.

sweat *s.* sudore, traspirazione.

to **sweat** *vt.* e *vi.* traspirare, sudare, sfacchinare.

sweater *s.* 1. chi suda 2. maglione di lana.

sweating *s.* sudore || - *bath*, bagno turco.

sweaty *agg.* 1. sudato 2. che fa sudare.

Swede *s.* svedese.

Swedish *agg.* svedese.

sweep *s.* 1. scopata 2. movimento circolare 3. curva, distesa.

to **sweep** (swept, swept) *vi.* 1. spazzare, scopare 2. muoversi rapidamente 3. estendersi. ♦ to **sweep** (swept, swept) *vt.* 1. spazzare 2. sfiorare.

sweeping *agg.* 1. vasto 2. completo 3. rapido, impetuoso (*di corrente*). ♦ **sweepings** *s. pl.* rifiuti.

sweet *agg.* 1. dolce, amabile 2. piacevole, gentile. ♦ **sweet** *s.* 1. dolce, torta 2. caramella.

to **sweeten** *vt.* 1. zuccherare 2. addolcire. ♦ to **sweeten** *vi.* addolcirsi.

sweetening *s.* 1. addolcimento 2. sostanza che addolcisce.

sweetheart *s.* innamorato.

sweetly *avv.* dolcemente.

sweetmeat *s.* dolciumi, frutta candita.

sweetness *s.* 1. sapore dolce 2. dolcezza, amabilità.

swell *s.* 1. rigonfiamento 2. il gonfiarsi (*dell'acqua ecc.*).

to **swell** (swelled, swollen) *vi.* 1. gonfiarsi 2. crescere, aumentare. ♦ to **swell** (swelled, swollen) *vt.* gonfiare.

swelling *s.* rigonfiamento, ingrossamento.

swept V. to *sweep*.

to **swerve** *vt.* deviare. ♦ to **swerve** *vi.* fare uno scarto.

swift *agg.* rapido, veloce.

swim *s.* nuotata.

to **swim** (swam, swum) *vi.* nuotare. ♦ to **swim** (swam, swum) *vt.* attraversare a nuoto.

swimmer *s.* nuotatore.

swimming *s.* nuoto || - *belt*, salvagente; - *pool*, piscina.

swindle *s.* truffa, frode.

to **swindle** *vt.* e *vi.* truffare.

swindler *s.* truffatore.

swine *s.* maiale, porco || - *herd*, porcaro.

swing *s.* 1. oscillazione 2. libertà d'azione 3. altalena.

to **swing** (swung, swung) *vi.* 1. dondolare, oscillare 2. ruotare 3. camminare dondolandosi. ♦ to **swing** (swung, swung) *vt.* 1. far dondolare 2. far ruotare.

swinging *s.* dondolio.

swish *s.* 1. sibilo 2. sferzata.

Swiss *agg.* svizzero.

switch *s.* 1. verga, frustino 2. (*elett.*) interruttore.

to **switch** *vt.* e *vi.* 1. colpire con un frustino 2. muovere bruscamente 3. (*ferr.*) smistare || to - *off*, spegnere (*la luce*); to - *on*, accendere (*la luce*).

swollen V. to *swell*.

swoon *s.* svenimento.

to **swoon** *vi.* svenire.

to **swoop** *vi.* calare improvvisamente, abbattersi.

sword *s.* spada.

swore V. to *swear*.

sworn V. to *swear*.

swum V. to *swim*.

swung V. to *swing*.

sycamore *s.* sicomoro.

syllable *s.* sillaba.

syllogism *s.* sillogismo.

syllogistic *agg.* sillogistico.

to **syllogize** *vt.* e *vi.* sillogizzare.

sylph *s.* silfo, silfide.

sylvan *agg.* silvano, silvestre.

symbiosis *s.* simbiosi.

symbol *s.* simbolo.

symbolic(al) *agg.* simbolico.

symbolism *s.* simbolismo.

to **symbolize** *vt.* simboleggiare.

symmetric(al) *agg.* simmetrico.

symmetry *s.* simmetria.

sympathetic *agg.* 1. sensibile, comprensivo 2. congeniale, adatto.

to **sympathize** *vi.* condividere i sentimenti altrui.

sympathizer *s.* 1. chi è comprensivo 2. simpatizzante (*di un partito ecc.*).

sympathy *s.* 1. comprensione, partecipazione 2. condoglianze (*pl.*).

symphonic *agg.* sinfonico.

symphony *s.* sinfonia.

symposium *s.* simposio, banchetto.

symptom *s.* sintomo.

symptomatic(al) *agg.* sintomatico.

synagogue *s.* sinagoga.

synchronism *s.* sincronismo.

synchronization *s.* sincronizzazione.

to **synchronize** *vt.* e *vi.* sincronizzare.

to **syncopate** *vt.* sincopare.

syncope *s.* sincope.

syndicalism *s.* sindacalismo.

syndicate *s.* sindacato.

synod *s.* sinodo.

synonym *s.* sinonimo.

synonymous *agg.* sinonimo.

synonymy *s.* sinonimia.

synovitis *s.* sinovite.

syntactic(al) *agg.* sintattico.

syntax *s.* sintassi.

synthesis *s.* (*pl.* -ses) sintesi.

to **synthesize** *vt.* sintetizzare.

synthetic(al) *agg.* sintetico.

syntony *s.* sintonia.

syphilis *s.* sifilide.

syphilitic *agg.* sifilitico.

Syrian *agg.* e *s.* siriano.

syringe *s.* siringa.

syrup *s.* sciroppo.

syrupy *agg.* sciropposo.

system *s.* 1. sistema 2. metodo || *railway* —, rete ferroviaria.

systematic(al) *agg.* sistematico, metodico.

systematically *avv.* sistematicamente, metodicamente.

systematization *s.* sistemazione.

to **systematize** *vt.* ridurre a sistema.

T

tab *s.* 1. linguetta (*di scarpa*) 2. (*mil.*) mostrina 3. talloncino.

tabernacle *s.* 1. tabernacolo 2. tempio.

table *s.* 1. tavola 2. tavolata 3. tabella 4. || —*cloth*, tovaglia; *time—*, orario.

tablet *s.* 1. tavoletta 2. pastiglia, compressa.

tabloid *s.* pasticca.

taboo *s.* e *agg.* tabù.

tabular *agg.* 1. a forma di tabella 2. catalogato 3. piano, piatto.

tabulate *agg.* piano.

to **tabulate** *vt.* disporre in tabelle.

tabulation *s.* classificazione.

tabulator *s.* tabulatore.

tachometer *s.* tachimetro.

tachycardia *s.* tachicardia.

tacit *agg.* tacito.

taciturn *agg.* taciturno.

tack *s.* 1. chiodo 2. imbastitura 3. bordata 4. (*fig.*) linea di condotta.

to **tack** *vt.* 1. inchiodare 2. imbastire. ◆ to **tack** *vi.* 1. bordeggiare 2. virare.

tacking *s.* 1. l'inchiodare 2. imbastitura 3. bordeggio.

tackle *s.* 1. arnesi (*pl.*) 2. (*mar.*) paranco.

to **tackle** *vt.* 1. afferrare 2. affrontare (*difficoltà ecc.*).

tacky *agg.* viscoso.

tact *s.* tatto.

tactful *agg.* pieno di tatto.

tactical *agg.* tattico.

tactician *s.* tattico.

tactics *s.* tattica.

tactile *agg.* 1. tattile 2. tangibile.

tactility *s.* 1. tattilità 2. tangibilità.

tactless *agg.* senza tatto.

tactlessness *s.* mancanza di tatto.

tactual *agg.* tattile.

tadpole *s.* (*zool.*) girino.

tag *s.* 1. lembo pendente 2. cartellino 3. aggiunta 4. luogo comune || *licence* —, bollo di circolazione.

to **tag** *vt.* mettere cartellini a.

tail *s.* coda || —*coat*, marsina.

to **tail** *vt.* munire di coda. ◆ to **tail** *vi.* 1. essere in coda 2. seguire da presso || *to* — *away*, affievolirsi.

tailor *s.* sarto || —*made costume*, tailleur.

to **tailor** *vi.* fare il sarto. ◆ to **tailor** *vt.* fare un abito.

taint *s.* 1. infezione 2. tara 3. marchio.

to **taint** *vt.* guastare. ◆ to **taint** *vi.* guastarsi.

taintless *agg.* incontaminato.

take *s.* 1. presa 2. incasso 3. (*cine*) ripresa.

to **take** (**took**, **taken**) *vt.* 1. prendere 2. portare 3. accompagnare 4. necessitare || *to* — *after*, assomigliare; *to* — *in*, ricevere, ridurre, capire; *to* — *off*, togliere, decollare; *to* — *on*, assumere; *to* — *to*, darsi a.

take-off *s.* (*aer.*) decollo.

taking *agg.* 1. attraente 2. contagioso. ◆ **taking** *s.* 1. presa 2. incasso.

talc(um) *s.* talco || *talcum powder*, talco in polvere.

tale s. racconto, storia, novella.

talent s. talento.

talented agg. che ha talento.

talentless agg. senza talento.

tales s. pl. (giur.) giudici supplenti.

talisman s. talismano.

talk s. 1. conversazione 2. chiacchiera.

to talk vt. e vi. parlare, conversare, discutere || to — out, discutere a fondo.

talkative agg. loquace.

talkativeness s. loquacità.

talker s. 1. parlatore 2. chiacchierone.

talkies s. pl. (gergo) film sonoro (sing.).

talking s. conversazione.

talky agg. loquace.

tall agg. 1. alto 2. incredibile.

tallness s. altezza, statura.

tallow s. sego.

tally s. 1. tacca 2. cartellino, talloncino, etichetta.

to tally vt. registrare. ♦ to tally vi. combaciare.

tallyshop s. negozio che vende a rate.

talon s. 1. artiglio 2. (mecc.) dente 3. (comm.) matrice.

tamarind s. tamarindo.

tambourine s. tamburello.

tame agg. 1. domesticato 2. mansueto 3. insipido, banale.

to tame vt. domare, addomesticare. ♦ to tame vi. ammansirsi.

tameable agg. addomesticabile.

tameless agg. indomito.

tamely avv. docilmente.

tameness s. 1. docilità 2. banalità.

tamer s. domatore.

taming s. addomesticamento.

to tamp vt. pigiare.

tamper s. pestello.

to tamper vi. 1. manomettere 2. immischiarsi: to — with, immischiarsi in 3. corrompere.

tamperer s. 1. falsificatore 2. corruttore 3. ficcanaso.

tampering s. 1. manomissione 2. corruzione.

tampon s. tampone.

tan agg. marrone rossiccio. ♦ tan s. 1. tannino 2. concia 3. abbronzatura.

to tan vt. 1. conciare 2. abbronzare. ♦ to tan vi. abbronzarsi.

tanning s. abbronzatura.

tang[1] s. 1. punta 2. odore, sapore penetrante.

tang[2] s. suono acuto.

to tang vt. far risuonare. ♦ to tang vi. risuonare.

tangency s. tangenza.

tangent agg. e s. tangente.

tangential agg. tangenziale.

tangerine s. mandarino.

tangibility s. tangibilità.

tangible agg. tangibile.

tangle s. groviglio.

to tangle vt. 1. aggrovigliare 2. intrappolare. ♦ to tangle vi. aggrovigliarsi.

tanglesome, tangly agg. ingarbugliato.

tank s. 1. serbatoio, cisterna 2. carro armato || —-truck, autobotte.

tankard s. boccale.

tanker s. nave cisterna || air —, aerocisterna; oil —, petroliera.

tanner s. conciatore.

tannery s. conceria.

tannin s. tannino.

tanning s. concia.

to tantalize vt. tormentare.

tantalizing agg. allettante.

tantamount agg. equivalente.

tap[1] s. rubinetto, spina.

tap[2] s. colpetto.

to tap[1] vt. 1. spillare 2. forare.

to tap[2] vt. battere leggermente.

tape s. nastro || —-recorder, magnetofono; recording —, nastro magnetico.

to tape vt. 1. legare con un nastro 2. misurare con un nastro 3. incidere su nastro magnetico.

taper agg. conico, rastremato ♦ taper s. 1. candela 2. conicità, rastremazione.

to taper vt. assottigliare. ♦ to taper vi. assottigliarsi, restringersi.

tapestry s. arazzo.

tapeworm s. tenia.

tapir s. tapiro.

tar s. catrame.

to tar vt. incatramare.

tardiness s. 1. lentezza 2. indolenza.

tardy agg. 1. lento 2. svogliato.

tare s. tara.

target s. bersaglio.

tariff s. tariffa.

tarnish s. 1. appannamento 2. macchia.

to tarnish vi. 1. appannarsi 2. macchiarsi. ♦ to tarnish vt. 1. macchiare **2.** inquinare.

tarpaulin s. telone impermeabile.

tarry agg. **1.** catramato **2.** simile a cᵔtrame.

to **tarry** vi. indugiare.

tart agg. aspro.

tart s. torta di frutta, crostata.

tartan¹ s. tessuto scozzese.

tartan² s. (mar.) tartana.

tartar agg. e s. tartaro.

tartaric agg. tartarico.

tartlet s. pasticcino.

tartly avv. in modo acido.

task s. compito, dovere, impresa.

to **task** vt. **1.** assegnare un compito a **2.** affaticare.

task-work s. lavoro a cottimo.

tassel s. **1.** nappa **2.** segnalibro.

to **tassel** vt. adornare di nappe.

taste s. **1.** gusto **2.** assaggio.

to **taste** vt. **1.** gustare **2.** assaggiare. ♦ to **taste** vi. sapere di.

tasteful agg. raffinato.

tastefulness s. buon gusto.

tasteless agg. **1.** insipido **2.** di cattivo gusto.

tastelessness s. **1.** scipitezza **2.** mancanza di gusto.

taster s. assaggiatore.

tasty agg. **1.** saporito **2.** (gergo) di buon gusto.

tatter s. cencio.

to **tatter** vt. stracciare. ♦ to **tatter** vi. cadere a pezzi.

tattery agg. stracciato.

tattle s. chiacchiera.

to **tattle** vi. chiacchierare.

tattler s. chiacchierone.

tattoo¹ s. tatuaggio.

tattoo² s. (mil.) **1.** ritirata **2.** carosello militare.

to **tattoo**¹ vt. tatuare.

to **tattoo**² vi. tamburellare.

taught V. to **teach**.

taunt s. sarcasmo.

to **taunt** vt. **1.** rimproverare **2.** schernire.

taunting agg. beffardo. ♦ **taunting** s. rimprovero sarcastico.

taut agg. **1.** teso **2.** in ordine.

to **tauten** vt. tendere. ♦ to **tauten** vi. tendersi.

tautness s. tensione.

tautologic(al) agg. tautologico.

tautology s. tautologia.

tavern s. taverna || — -keeper, oste.

taw s. biglia.

tawdry agg. sgargiante.

tawny agg. bruno fulvo.

tax s. **1.** tassa **2.** peso || — -payer, contribuente.

to **tax** vt. **1.** tassare **2.** accusare.

taxability s. tassabilità.

taxable agg. tassabile.

taxation s. tassazione.

taxi s. tassì || — -driver, tassista; (aer.) — track, pista di rullaggio.

to **taxi** vi. (aer.) rullare.

taxicab s. autopubblica.

taximeter s. tassametro.

tea s. tè || — -pot, teiera; high —, cena fredda; — -set, servizio da tè.

to **teach (taught, taught)** vt. insegnare.

teachable agg. **1.** che apprende facilmente **2.** che si insegna facilmente.

teacher s. insegnante.

teachership s. insegnamento.

teaching agg. che insegna. ♦ **teaching** s. insegnamento.

teacup s. tazza da tè.

team s. **1.** squadra **2.** tiro (di cavalli).

to **team** vt. aggiogare, accoppiarsi, raggrupparsi. ♦ to **team** vi. accoppiarsi, associarsi.

tear¹ s. **1.** lacrima **2.** goccia || — -gas, gas lacrimogeno.

tear² s. strappo, lacerazione.

to **tear (tore, torn)** vt. strappare, lacerare. ♦ to **tear (tore, torn)** vi. strapparsi.

tearful agg. lacrimoso.

tearing agg. violento. ♦ **tearing** s. strappo, lacerazione.

tear-off s. parte da staccare.

tease s. chi stuzzica.

to **tease** vt. **1.** stuzzicare **2.** cardare (lana ecc.).

teaser s. **1.** seccatore **2.** cardatore **3.** questione difficile.

teaspoon s. cucchiaino da tè.

technical agg. tecnico.

technicality s. tecnicismo.

technician s. tecnico.

technique s. tecnica.

technological agg. tecnologico.

technology s. tecnologia.

tectonics s. **1.** edilizia **2.** tettonica.

tedious agg. tedioso.

tediousness s. tedio.

to **teem** vi. brulicare.

teen-ager s. adolescente.

teens s. pl. età da tredici a diciannove anni.

teeth V. **tooth**.

teething s. dentizione.

teetotal(l)er *s.* astemio.

telecast *s.* teletrasmissione || — *news*, telegiornale.

to **telecast (telecast, telecast)** *vt.* teletrasmettere.

telecommunication *s.* telecomunicazione.

telecontrol *s.* telecomando.

telegram *s.* telegramma.

telegraph *s.* telegrafo.

to **telegraph** *vt.* e *vi.* telegrafare.

telegraphic *agg.* telegrafico.

telegraphist *s.* telegrafista.

telegraphy *s.* telegrafia.

telemeter *s.* telemetro.

telepathy *s.* telepatia.

telephone *s.* telefono || — *booth*, cabina telefonica; — *book*, elenco telefonico.

to **telephone** *vt.* e *vi.* telefonare.

telephonist *s.* telefonista.

telephony *s.* telefonia.

telephoto *s.* telefoto.

telephotograph *s.* telefotografia.

telescope *s.* telescopio.

to **telescope** *vi.* incastrarsi.

teletype *s.* telescrivente.

teletyper *s.* telescriventista.

teletypewriter *s.* telescrivente.

to **teleview** *vt.* e *vi.* guardare la televisione.

televiewer *s.* telespettatore.

to **televise** *vt.* riprendere con la televisione.

television *s.* televisione || — *set*, televisore.

televisional *agg.* televisivo.

to **tell (told, told)** *vt.* e *vi.* **1.** dire **2.** raccontare **3.** distinguere.

teller *s.* **1.** narratore **2.** *(comm.)* cassiere.

telling *agg.* efficace. ♦ **telling** *s.* **1.** il raccontare **2.** rivelazione.

telltale *s.* **1.** chiacchierone **2.** *(tec.)* controllore.

telluric *agg.* tellurico.

telpher *s.* cabina di funivia.

telpherage *s.* trasporto per teleferica.

temper *s.* **1.** indole **2.** umore **3.** collera **4.** moderazione.

to **temper** *vt.* temperare.

temperament *s.* temperamento.

temperamental *agg.* capriccioso.

temperance *s.* temperanza.

temperate *agg.* temperato *(di clima)* **2.** moderato.

temperature *s.* temperatura || *to have a* —, avere la febbre.

tempered *agg.* **1.** temprato **2.** moderato **3.** di indole, umore || *quick* —, irritabile.

tempest *s.* tempesta.

temple[1] *s.* tempio.

temple[2] *s. (anat.)* tempia.

temporal *agg.* temporale.

temporariness *s.* temporaneità.

temporary *agg.* temporaneo.

temporization *s.* temporeggiamento.

to **temporize** *vi.* temporeggiare.

to **tempt** *vt.* tentare.

temptation *s.* tentazione.

tempter *s.* tentatore.

tempting *agg.* seducente.

ten *agg.* e *s.* dieci.

tenacious *agg.* **1.** tenace **2.** viscoso.

tenacity *s.* tenacia.

tenancy *s.* locazione.

tenant *s.* **1.** proprietario **2.** locatario.

to **tend**[1] *vt.* curare, badare a, custodire.

to **tend**[2] *vi.* tendere.

tendency *s.* tendenza.

tendential, tendentious *agg.* tendenzioso.

tender[1] *agg.* tenero || — *of*, sollecito verso.

tender[2] *s.* **1.** guardiano, custode **2.** nave di appoggio.

tender[3] *s.* offerta, proposta.

to **tender** *vt.* offrire, presentare.

tenderness *s.* **1.** tenerezza **2.** delicatezza.

tendon *s. (anat.)* tendine.

tendril *s.* viticcio.

tenebrous *agg.* tenebroso.

tenement *s.* **1.** podere **2.** abitazione.

tenor *s.* **1.** tenore *(di vita ecc.)* **2.** *(giur.)* copia esatta **3.** *(mus.)* tenore.

tense[1] *agg.* teso.

tense[2] *s. (gramm.)* tempo.

to **tense** *vt.* tendere. ♦ to **tense** *vi.* tendersi.

tension *s.* tensione.

tent *s.* tenda.

tentacle *s.* tentacolo.

tentative *agg.* sperimentale. ♦ **tentative** *s.* tentativo, prova.

tenth *agg.* e *s.* decimo.

tenuity *s.* **1.** tenuità **2.** rarefazione **3.** fluidità.

tenuous *agg.* **1.** tenue **2.** rarefatto **3.** fluido.

tenure *s.* **1.** possesso **2.** gestione.

tepid *agg.* tiepido.
tepidity *s.* tepidezza.
tercet *s.* terzina.
tergal *agg.* dorsale.
to **tergiversate** *vi.* tergiversare.
tergiversation *s.* tergiversazione.
term *s.* 1. termine 2. (*scol.*) trimestre 3. (*giur.*) sessione 4. condizione. ♦ **terms** *s. pl.* rapporti.
to **term** *vt.* definire.
terminable *agg.* terminabile.
terminal *agg.* estremo. ♦ **terminal** *s.* 1. estremità 2. stazione di testa, capolinea 3. (*elettr.*) morsetto.
to **terminate** *vt.* 1. limitare 2. terminare. ♦ to **terminate** *vi.* 1. essere limitato 2. terminare.
termination *s.* 1. termine 2. (*gramm.*) desinenza.
terminator *s.* 1. chi termina 2. limite.
terminology *s.* terminologia.
terminus *s.* (*pl.* -ni) 1. capolinea 2. meta.
termite *s.* (*zool.*) termite.
tern *s.* terno.
ternary *agg.* ternario.
terrace *s.* 1. terrapieno 2. terrazzo (*sul tetto*) 3. fila di case.
terraqueous *agg.* terracqueo.
terrestrial *agg.* e *s.* terrestre.
terrible *agg.* terribile.
terrific *agg.* 1. spaventoso 2. (*fam.*) straordinario.
to **terrify** *vt.* atterrire.
territorial *agg.* territoriale.
territory *s.* territorio.
terror *s.* terrore.
terrorism *s.* terrorismo.
terrorist *s.* terrorista.
terroristic *agg.* terroristico.
to **terrorize** *vt.* terrorizzare.
terse *agg.* conciso.
terseness *s.* concisione.
tertiary *agg.* e *s.* terziario.
test *s.* 1. prova, esperimento, saggio 2. "test", reattivo psicologico || — *driver*, collaudatore; — *film*, provino; — *-tube*, provetta.
to **test** *vt.* 1. controllare 2. mettere alla prova 3. analizzare.
testament *s.* testamento.
testamentary *agg.* testamentario.
tester *s.* 1. collaudatore 2. apparecchio di misura 3. baldacchino.
testicle *s.* testicolo.
to **testify** *vt.* e *vi.* testimoniare.
testimonial *s.* 1. benservito 2. dono.
testimony *s.* testimonianza.

testing *s.* collaudo, prova.
tetanic(al) *agg.* tetanico.
tetanus *s.* tetano.
tetchy *agg.* stizzoso.
tetrahedron *s.* tetraedro.
tetralogy *s.* tetralogia.
Teutonic *agg.* teutonico.
text *s.* 1. testo 2. argomento.
textile *agg.* e *s.* tessile.
textual *agg.* testuale.
texture *s.* trama, tessuto.
thallium *s.* tallio.
than *cong.* che, di, di quello che (non), di quanto (non): *he is older — you*, è più vecchio di te.
to **thank** *vt.* ringraziare || — *you!*, grazie!
thankful *agg.* riconoscente.
thankfulness *s.* riconoscenza.
thankless *agg.* ingrato.
thanks *s. pl.* grazie, ringraziamenti.
thanksgiving *s.* ringraziamento.
that *agg.* (*pl.* those) quello, quella. ♦ **that** *pron. dimostr.* quello, questo, ciò. ♦ **that** *pron. rel.* che, il quale, la quale, i quali, le quali.
that *cong.* 1. che 2. affinché 3. purché.
thatch *s.* copertura di paglia (*per tetti*).
to **thatch** *vt.* coprire con paglia.
thaumaturge *s.* taumaturgo.
thaumaturgic(al) *agg.* taumaturgico.
thaw *s.* sgelo, disgelo.
to **thaw** *vt.* sgelare. ♦ to **thaw** *vi.* sgelarsi.
the *art.* il, lo, la, i, gli, le.
theatre *s.* teatro.
theatrical *agg.* teatrale.
theft *s.* furto.
their *agg. poss.* loro.
theirs *pron. poss.* il, la loro; i, le loro.
theism *s.* teismo.
them *pron.* loro, li, le, sé.
thematic *agg.* tematico.
theme *s.* tema.
themselves *pron. r.* 1. se stessi, se stesse, sé, si 2. essi stessi, esse stesse.
then *avv.* 1. allora 2. poi.
theocracy *s.* teocrazia.
theocratic(al) *agg.* teocratico.
theologian *s.* teologo.
theologic(al) *agg.* teologico.
theology *s.* teologia.
theorem *s.* teorema.

theoretic(al) *agg.* teorico.

theoretics *s.* teoretica.

theorist *s.* teorico.

to **theorize** *vi.* teorizzare.

theory *s.* teoria.

therapeutic(al) *agg.* terapeutico.

therapeutics *s.* terapeutica.

therapy *s.* terapia.

there *avv.* 1. là, lì 2. ci, vi 3. in ciò. ♦ **there** *inter.* ecco! su!

thereabout(s) *avv.* 1. là vicino 2. all'incirca.

thereby *avv.* per mezzo di, perciò.

therefore *avv.* quindi, dunque.

thereupon *avv.* al che, tosto.

thermal *agg.* termico, termale.

thermic *agg.* termico.

thermionic *agg.* termoionico.

thermodynamics *s.* termodinamica.

thermoelectric *agg.* termoelettrico.

thermometer *s.* termometro.

thermonuclear *agg.* termonucleare.

thermostat *s.* termostato.

these (*pl. di* this), questi, queste.

thesis *s.* (*pl. -ses*) tesi, dissertazione.

thews *s. pl.* muscoli.

they *pron. pers.* 1. essi, esse, loro 2. (*in costruzioni impersonali*) si: — *say,* si dice.

thick *agg.* spesso, grosso: *a — book,* un grosso libro 2. fitto, folto 3. denso, torbido.

to **thicken** *vt.* ispessire, addensare. ♦ to **thicken** *vi.* ispessirsi, addensarsi.

thickening *s.* ispessimento.

thicket *s.* boschetto.

thickly *avv.* fittamente, densamente.

thickness *s.* 1. spessore, grossezza 2. densità 3. strato.

thickset *agg.* 1. fitto, spesso 2. tarchiato.

thief *s.* (*pl. thieves*) ladro.

to **thieve** *vt. e vi.* rubare, essere ladro.

thievish *agg.* ladresco.

thigh *s.* coscia || — *bone,* femore.

thimble *s.* ditale.

thin *agg.* 1. sottile 2. magro, snello 3. rado, raro 4. fluido, rarefatto 5. debole, fiacco.

to **thin** *vt. e vi.* 1. assottigliare, assottigliarsi, dimagrire 2. diradare, sfoltire. ♦ to **thin** *vt.* 1. assottigliare 2. diradare, sfoltire. ♦ to **thin** *vi.* 1. assottigliarsi 2. diradarsi.

thing *s.* 1. cosa, oggetto 2. argomen-

to, soggetto.

to **think** (**thought, thought**) *vt. e vi.* 1. pensare, riflettere 2. ritenere, considerare 3. credere, aspettarsi || *to — of,* pensare, avere in animo di; *to — ill of so.,* avere una cattiva opinione di qu.; *to — out,* escogitare; *to — over,* riflettere.

thinkable *agg.* concepibile, immaginabile.

thinker *s.* pensatore.

thinking *agg.* pensante, ragionevole ♦ **thinking** *s.* pensiero, riflessione, opinione.

thinness *s.* sottigliezza, tenuità, magrezza, radezza.

third *agg. e s.* terzo.

thirdly *avv.* in terzo luogo.

third-rate *agg.* di terz'ordine.

thirst *s.* 1. sete, arsura 2. (*fig.*) avidità.

thirsty *agg.* assetato || to be —, aver sete; *to be — for* (*fig.*), bramare.

thirteen *agg.* tredici.

thirteenth *agg.* tredicesimo.

thirtieth *agg.* trentesimo.

thirty *agg.* trenta.

this *agg. e pron. dimostr.* (*pl. these*) questo, questa.

Thomism *s.* tomismo.

Thomist *s.* tomista.

thorax *s.* torace.

thorn *s.* spina (*anche fig.*).

thorny *agg.* spinoso (*anche fig.*).

thorough *agg.* 1. completo, totale 2. perfetto, esperto 3. meticoloso.

thoroughbred *agg.* 1. purosangue (*di cavallo*) 2. di antico lignaggio. ♦ **thoroughbred** *s.* purosangue.

thoroughfare *s.* arteria di grande traffico || *no —,* passaggio vietato.

those (*pl. di that*) quelli, quelle.

though *avv.* comunque, tuttavia. ♦ **though** *cong.* benché, sebbene.

thought V. *to think.*

thought *s.* 1. pensiero, riflessione 2. idea, parere 3. concezione.

thoughtful *agg.* 1. pensoso, pensieroso 2. sollecito.

thoughtless *agg.* sconsiderato, sventato, negligente.

thoughtlessness *s.* sconsideratezza, negligenza.

thousand *agg.* mille. ♦ **thousand** *s.* migliaio.

thrall *s.* schiavo.

to **thrash** *vt. e vi.* 1. battere, sferzare **2.** (*mar.*) navigare contro vento **3.** trebbiare **4.** bastonare || *to — out*, dibattere.

thrasher *s.* trebbiatore.

thrashing machine *s.* trebbiatrice.

thread *s.* **1.** filo (*anche fig.*) **2.** vena, filone.

to thread *vt.* **1.** infilare **2.** far passare attraverso.

threadbare *agg.* **1.** consumato, consunto **2.** (*fig.*) vieto, trito.

threading *s.* filettatura.

threadlike *agg.* filiforme.

threat *s.* minaccia.

to threaten *vt. e vi.* minacciare.

threatening *agg.* minaccioso.

three *agg. e s.* tre.

threescore *agg.* sessanta.

to thresh *vt. e vi.* trebbiare.

threshold *s.* **1.** soglia, limitare **2.** (*fig.*) esordio, inizio.

threw V. *to throw*.

thrice *avv.* tre volte.

thriftiness *s.* economia, parsimonia.

thrifty *agg.* frugale, economo.

thrill *s.* brivido, palpito.

to thrill *vt.* far fremere, elettrizzare. ♦ **to thrill** *vi.* fremere, vibrare, emozionarsi.

thriller *s.* (*gergo*) storia, film sensazionale, poliziesco.

thrilling *agg.* **1.** sensazionale, emozionante **2.** penetrante.

to thrive (**throve, thriven**) *vi.* **1.** prosperare, fiorire **2.** crescere vigorosamente.

thriving *agg.* **1.** prospero, fiorente **2.** rigoglioso.

throat *s.* gola || *— wash*, gargarismo; *sore —*, mal di gola.

throaty *agg.* gutturale.

throb *s.* battito, pulsazione, fremito.

to throb *vi.* battere, pulsare, fremere.

throbbing *agg.* palpitante, vibrante (*anche fig.*).

thrombosis *s.* trombosi.

throne *s.* trono.

throng *s.* folla, moltitudine.

to throng *vt.* affollare, stipare. ♦ **to throng** *vi.* affollarsi, affluire.

to throttle *vt.* strozzare, strangolare.

through *avv.* **1.** attraverso, da una parte all'altra **2.** (*ferr.*) direttamente || *— train*, treno diretto. ♦ **through** *prep.* **1.** attraverso, per **2.** durante, per tutta la durata di

3. per mezzo.

throughout *avv.* da un capo all'altro, dal principio alla fine. ♦ **throughout** *prep.* in ogni parte di, durante tutto il, dal principio alla fine di.

throve V. *to thrive*.

throw *s.* lancio, gittata (*di missile ecc.*), tiro.

to throw (**threw, thrown**) *vt. e vi.* **1.** gettare, scagliare, proiettare **2.** atterrare, rovesciare || *to — away*, buttar via; *to — off*, buttar fuori; *to — out* espellere.

throwback *s.* **1.** movimento brusco all'indietro **2.** ostacolo.

thrown V. *to throw*.

thrush *s.* tordo.

thrust *s.* **1.** colpo, botta **2.** colpo con arma appuntita.

to thrust (**thrust, thrust**) *vt. e vi.* **1.** spingere, ficcare **2.** frapporre **3.** forzare.

thud *s.* tonfo, rumore sordo.

to thud *vi.* fare un rumore sordo.

thumb *s.* pollice.

to thumb *vt.* **1.** lasciare ditate su (*un foglio ecc.*) **2.** strimpellare.

thump *s.* rumore sordo.

to thump *vt.* battere, percuotere, dar pugni.

thumping *agg.* pesante.

thunder *s.* **1.** tuono: *a peal of —*, un colpo di tuono **2.** scoppio, rombo **3.** fulmine (*anche fig.*).

to thunder *vt. e vi.* **1.** tuonare, rimbombare **2.** minacciare.

thunderbolt *s.* fulmine, saetta (*anche fig.*).

thundering *agg.* **1.** tonante, fulminante **2.** (*fam.*) straordinario.

thundery *agg.* minaccioso.

Thursday *s.* giovedì.

thus *avv.* così, in questo modo.

to thwart *vt.* opporsi a, ostacolare.

thyme *s.* timo.

thyroid *s.* tiroide.

tibia *s.* tibia.

tick *s.* tic-tac, ticchettio (*di orologio*).

to tick *vt. e vi.* ticchettare.

ticket *s.* **1.** biglietto, tessera, scontrino **2.** (*mil.*) congedo || *—-collector*, bigliettario; *— -inspector*, controllore; *single —*, biglietto di andata.

to ticket *vt.* **1.** mettere il cartellino del prezzo a **2.** fornire di biglietto.

ticking s. traliccio.

tickle s. solletico.

to tickle vt. fare il solletico, solleticare (anche fig.). ♦ **to tickle** vi. prudere.

tickler s. 1. chi solletica 2. questione delicata.

ticklish agg. 1. sensibile al solletico 2. scabroso.

tide s. 1. marea 2. (fig.) corrente, corso || — -gauge, mareografo.

to tide vi. salire, crescere come la marea.

tidily avv. lindamente.

tidings s. pl. novità.

tidy agg. ordinato, preciso, pulito.

to tidy vt. riordinare, mettere in ordine.

tie s. 1. laccio, legaccio 2. cravatta 3. (fig.) legame 4. (ferr.) traversina.

to tie vt. 1. legare, allacciare, congiungere (anche fig.) 2. annodare.

tied agg. vincolato, invita.

tier s. ordine, fila (di posti).

to tier vt. allineare.

tiff s. stizza, bisticcio || to be in a —, essere in collera.

to tiff vi. essere stizzito.

tiger s. tigre.

tight agg. 1. impermeabile, a perfetta tenuta 2. teso, tirato 3. stretto, aderente, attillato 4. scarso, a corto di denaro 5. (gergo) ubriaco. ♦ **tight** avv. 1. ermeticamente 2. in maniera tesa.

to tighten vt. 1. serrare 2. tirare, tendere. ♦ **to tighten** vi. 1. serrarsi 2. tendersi.

tightly avv. ermeticamente, strettamente.

tightness s. 1. impermeabilità, tenuta 2. tensione 3. (gergo) ubriachezza.

tights s. pl. calzamaglia.

tigress s. tigre (femmina).

tile s. 1. tegola, mattonella, piastrella 2. (fam.) cappello a cilindro.

to tile vt. coprire di tegole, piastrelle.

tilemaking s. fabbricazione di tegole.

tilery s. fabbrica di tegole.

tiling s. tegolato, piastrellatura.

till¹ prep. fino a: — now, fino ad ora. ♦ **till** cong. finché, fino al momento in cui.

till² s. cassetto in cui si custodisce il denaro.

to till vt. dissodare, arare.

tillage s. 1. dissodamento, aratura 2. terreno coltivato.

tiller s. 1. aratore 2. (mar.) barra del timone.

tilt¹ s. tenda, tendone.

tilt² s. 1. torneo, giostra 2. contesa, disputa 3. inclinazione, pendenza.

to tilt vt. 1. inclinare 2. rovesciare. ♦ **to tilt** vi. 1. oscillare 2. (mar.) beccheggiare.

timber s. 1. legname da costruzione 2. bosco con alberi d'alto fusto 3. trave 4. (fig.) tempra, carattere 5. (mar.) costola || — -work, costruzione in legno.

to timber vt. rivestire di legno.

timbre s. timbro (di suoni).

time s. 1. tempo, periodo di tempo, circostanza, epoca, età 2. volta, volte 3. orario, ora || with —, col passar del tempo; from — to —, di tanto in tanto; as times go, coi tempi che corrono; at times, a volte; in good —, per tempo; what — is it?, che ore sono?

to time vt. fissare l'orario di. ♦ **to time** vi. tenere il tempo.

timekeeper s. 1. cronometro 2. cronometrista.

timeliness s. tempestività.

timely agg. opportuno, tempestivo.

timepiece s. orologio (da tavolo).

timer s. cronometrista.

time-study agg. — engineer, analista tempi.

timid agg. timido.

timidity s. timidezza.

timing s. 1. calcolo del tempo (di pose fotografiche ecc.) 2. (mecc.) messa in fase.

timorous agg. timoroso.

tin s. 1. stagno, latta 2. recipiente, scatola.

to tin vt. 1. stagnare 2. conservare in scatola.

tincture s. 1. (chim.) tintura, soluzione alcolica 2. tinta 3. sfumatura, traccia 4. gusto, aroma.

to tincture vt. 1. tingere, colorare 2. aromatizzare.

tinder s. esca (per fuoco).

tinge s. 1. sfumatura, tocco 2. (fig.) pizzico.

to tinge vt. dare una sfumatura a (anche fig.).

to tingle vt. 1. pizzicare 2. far tintinnare. ♦ **to tingle** vi. arrossire (di guance).

tink s. tintinnio.

tinker s. calderaio (*ambulante*), stagnino.

to tinker vt. rabberciare, riparare.

tinkle s. tintinnio.

to tinkle vt. far tintinnare. ◆ **to tinkle** vi. tintinnare.

tinkling s. tintinnio.

tinsel agg. vistoso, sgargiante. ◆ **tinsel** s. orpello (*anche fig.*).

tint s. tinta, colore delicato, sfumatura.

to tint vt. colorire, tinteggiare.

tiny agg. minuscolo.

tip¹ s. 1. punta, cima 2. puntale.

tip² s. 1. immondezzaio 2. inclinazione.

tip³ s. mancia.

to tip¹ vt. toccare, battere leggermente.

to tip² vt. 1. rovesciare 2. inclinare. ◆ **to tip** vi. 1. rovesciarsi 2. inclinarsi.

to tip³ vt. e vi. 1. dare la mancia 2. (*gergo*) dare, passare.

tippet s. mantellina.

tipsy agg. ubriaco.

tiptoe s. punta dei piedi: *on* —, in punta di piedi.

to tiptoe vi. camminare in punta di piedi.

tire¹ s. 1. cerchione di ruota 2. pneumatico || *flat* —, gomma a terra.

to tire¹ vt. stancare, annoiare. ◆ **to tire** vi. stancarsi, annoiarsi.

to tire² vt. fornire di cerchione, di pneumatico.

tired agg. stanco, affaticato, esausto || *to be* — *out*, essere stanco morto.

tireless agg. instancabile.

tiresome agg. faticoso, stancante, noioso.

tissue s. tessuto || — *paper*, carta velina.

Titan s. titano, gigante.

titanic agg. titanico (*anche fig.*).

title s. 1. titolo 2. titolo, grado, qualifica.

to title vt. 1. intitolare, intestare 2. conferire un titolo.

titular agg. titolare.

to prep. 1. (con verbo di moto) a, in, da 2. verso, per 3. (di tempo) fino a 4. (paragone, rapporto) contro a 5. riguardo a || — *all appearances*, stando alle apparenze; — *my despair*, con mia disperazione; — *this end*, a questo scopo.

toad s. rospo.

toady s. adulatore.

to toady vt. adulare, comportarsi servilmente.

toast¹ s. pane abbrustolito, crostino.

toast² s. brindisi.

to toast¹ vt. abbrustolire, tostare.

to toast² vt. e vi. fare un brindisi.

toaster s. tostapane.

tobacco s. tabacco || — *box*, tabacchiera.

tobacconist s. tabaccaio || —'s *shop*, tabaccheria.

tocsin s. segnale d'allarme.

today s. oggi. ◆ **today** avv. oggigiorno.

toddle s. andatura incerta, vacillante.

to toddle vi. camminare a passi incerti, passeggiare.

toe s. dito del piede.

together avv. assieme, insieme, unitamente.

toil¹ s. fatica, duro lavoro || — *worn*, sfinito dalla fatica.

toil² s. laccio, trappola (*anche fig.*).

to toil¹ vi. faticare, lavorare duramente.

to toil² vt. prendere in trappola (*anche fig.*).

toilet s. 1. toletta, pulizia 2. abbigliamento 3. bagno, gabinetto || — *paper*, carta igienica.

toilsome agg. faticoso, laborioso.

token s. 1. segno, simbolo 2. prova, pegno, ricordo.

tolerable agg. 1. tollerabile 2. discreto.

tolerance s. tolleranza.

tolerant agg. tollerante.

to tolerate vt. tollerare, sopportare.

toleration s. tolleranza.

toll¹ s. pedaggio, dazio, gabella.

toll² s. rintocco (*di campane*).

to toll vt. suonare. ◆ **to toll** vi. rintoccare.

tomato s. pomodoro.

tomb s. tomba.

tomboy s. ragazza indiavolata.

tome s. tomo, volume.

tomfool agg. e s. sciocco, banale.

tommy s. 1. pane, pagnotta 2. provviste (*che l'operaio porta da casa*) (pl.).

tommy-gun s. fucile mitragliatore, mitra.

tomorrow s. e avv. domani.

ton s. tonnellata.

tonality s. tonalità.

tone s. tono, timbro, accento.

to **tone** vt. e vi. 1. (mus.) dare il tono, intonare, accordare 2. (pitt.) sfumare.

toneless agg. inespressivo, privo di colore, senza vigore.

tongs s. pl. pinze, molle, tenaglie.

tongue s. 1. lingua 2. lingua, linguaggio 3. lingua (di terra, fuoco) || — -tied, muto, taciturno; — -twister, scioglilingua.

to **tongue** vt. leccare, lambire.

tonic agg. tonico, corroborante. ♦ **tonic** s. (med.) tonico, energetico.

tonight avv. e s. stanotte, stasera.

tonnage s. tonnellaggio, stazza.

tonsil s. tonsilla.

tonsillitis s. tonsillite.

tonsure s. tonsura.

to **tonsure** vt. tonsurare.

too avv. 1. troppo 2. anche, pure 3. inoltre.

took V. to take.

tool s. 1. arnese, attrezzo, utensile 2. (fig.) strumento.

tooth s. (pl. teeth) 1. dente, zanna 2. dente (di pettine, forchetta ecc.) || — -paste, dentifricio; — -pick, stuzzicadenti.

toothache s. mal di denti.

toothbrush s. spazzolino da denti.

toothing s. dentatura, dentellatura.

toothless agg. sdentato.

toothy agg. dai denti sporgenti.

top[1] s. 1. cima, sommità 2. (fig.) apice 3. parte superiore, "capote" di automobile.

top[2] s. trottola.

topaz s. topazio.

topic s. argomento, soggetto.

topical agg. d'attualità.

topographer s. topografo.

topographic(al) agg. topografico.

topography s. topografia.

topology s. topologia.

toponymy s. toponomastica.

topsail s. vela di gabbia.

topsyturvy agg. sottosopra, capovolto. ♦ **topsyturvy** s. capovolgimento, disordine, scompiglio. ♦ **topsyturvy** avv. sottosopra.

to **topsyturvy** vt. mettere sossopra.

toque s. berretto, tocco.

torch s. torcia, fiaccola || electric —, lampadina tascabile.

torchlight s. luce di fiaccole, torce || — procession, fiaccolata.

tore V. to tear.

torment s. tormento, tortura.

to **torment** vt. tormentare.

torn V. to tear.

tornado s. ciclone.

torpedo s. 1. (zool.) torpedine 2. (mar.) siluro || — -boat, torpediniera; — boat destroyer, cacciatorpediniere.

to **torpedo** vt. silurare.

torpid agg. torpido, apatico.

torpor s. torpore.

torrefaction s. torrefazione.

to **torrefy** vt. torrefare.

torrent s. torrente (anche fig.).

torrential agg. torrenziale.

torrid agg. torrido.

torsion s. torsione.

tortoise s. tartaruga.

torture s. tortura, tormento (anche fig.).

to **torture** vt. torturare, tormentare.

torturous agg. tormentoso.

toss s. 1. lancio 2. movimento del capo.

to **toss** vt. 1. gettare, lanciare 2. agitare, scuotere 3. disarcionare. ♦ to **toss** vi. 1. agitarsi, smaniare 2. tirare a sorte 3. (mar.) beccheggiare.

total agg. totale, completo. ♦ **total** s. totale.

totalitarian agg. totalitario.

totalitarianism s. totalitarismo.

totality s. totalità.

totalizator s. totalizzatore.

to **totalize** vt. e vi. totalizzare.

totalizer s. totalizzatore.

to **totter** vi. camminare barcollando.

tottering agg. vacillante, malsicuro.

touch s. 1. tocco, colpetto 2. tatto 3. contatto, rapporto.

to **touch** vt. 1. toccare 2. sfiorare 3. (fig.) colpire, commuovere. ♦ to **touch** vi. essere in contatto, confinare.

touchiness s. suscettibilità.

touching agg. toccante, commovente. ♦ **touching** prep. riguardo a.

touchstone s. pietra di paragone.

touchwood s. esca (per accendere il fuoco).

touchy agg. permaloso.

tough agg. 1. duro 2. forte, robusto 3. (fig.) inflessibile 4. difficile 5. violento.

to **toughen** vt. indurire. ♦ to **toughen** vi. indurirsi.

toughness s. 1. durezza 2. inflessibilità.

tour s. giro, viaggio, escursione.

to **tour** vt. e vi. fare un viaggio.

tourism s. turismo.

tourist s. turista.

tourmalin(e) s. tormalina.

tournament s. torneo.

to **tousle** vt. scompigliare, arruffare.

tow s. rimorchio.

toward(s) prep. 1. verso, in direzione di 2. riguardo a 3. verso, circa (di tempo).

towel s. asciugamano || — -borse, porta-asciugamano.

tower s. torre.

to **tower** vi. torreggiare.

towing s. rimorchio.

town s. 1. città 2. cittadinanza || — -council, consiglio comunale; — -planning, piano regolatore; chief —, capoluogo.

townhall s. municipio.

townhouse s. residenza di città.

townscape s. veduta (di città).

townsfolk s. abitanti di una città.

township s. territorio, giurisdizione di una città.

townsman s. cittadino.

townspeople s. cittadinanza.

townward(s) avv. verso la città.

toxic(al) agg. tossico.

toxicity s. tossicità.

toxicologist s. tossicologo.

toxicology s. tossicologia.

toxin s. tossina.

toy s. 1. giocattolo 2. bazzecola, storiella.

to **toy** vi. giocherellare, trastullarsi.

toyish agg. 1. simile a giocattolo 2. insignificante.

toyshop s. negozio di giocattoli.

trabeation s. trabeazione.

trace s. traccia, orma.

to **trace** vt. 1. tracciare 2. seguire le tracce 3. rintracciare || to — back, risalire.

traceable agg. 1. rintracciabile 2. che si può tracciare.

trachea s. trachea.

tracheal agg. tracheale.

tracheitis s. tracheite.

trachyte s. trachite.

tracing s. 1. tracciato 2. calco, ricalco.

track s. 1. traccia, orma 2. sentiero, corso (anche fig.) 3. (sport) pista 4. (ferr.) binario || sound — (cine), colonna sonora.

to **track** vt. 1. inseguire, pedinare 2. tracciare un sentiero. ♦ to **track** vi. posare i binari.

tract¹ s. periodo, tratto, spazio.

tract² s. opuscolo.

tractability s. arrendevolezza.

tractable agg. arrendevole.

traction s. 1. trazione 2. contrazione.

tractor s. trattore.

trade s. 1. mestiere 2. commercio, traffico 3. commercianti (pl.) || — bank, banca commerciale; — dispute, vertenza sindacale; — -mark, marchio di fabbrica; — -show (cine), anteprima per la critica; free- —, libero scambio.

to **trade** vt. e vi. commerciare, negoziare.

trader s. 1. commerciante 2. nave mercantile.

trading s. commercio.

tradition s. tradizione.

traditional agg. tradizionale.

traditionalism s. tradizionalismo.

traditionalist s. tradizionalista.

to **traduce** vt. calunniare.

traffic s. 1. traffico, commercio 2. traffico, circolazione || — lights, semaforo; — jam, ingorgo stradale.

tragedian s. 1. tragediografo 2. attore tragico.

tragedy s. tragedia.

tragic(al) agg. tragico.

tragicomedy s. tragicommedia.

tragicomic(al) agg. tragicomico.

trail s. 1. traccia, striscia 2. pista, orma 3. cammino, sentiero.

to **trail** vt. 1. trascinare 2. seguire le tracce di. ♦ to **trail** vi. trascinarsi.

trailer s. 1. inseguitore, cacciatore 2. rimorchio 3. (cine) film di prossima programmazione.

train s. 1. treno: express — (o fast —), rapido; slow —, accelerato 2. seguito, corteo 3. serie, successione, fila.

to **train** vt. 1. allevare, educare 2. esercitare, allenare, addestrare. ♦ to **train** vi. 1. esercitarsi, allenarsi 2. viaggiare in ferrovia.

trainer s. istruttore, allenatore.

training s. educazione, ammaestramento, allenamento.

trait s. tratto, fattezza, caratteristica.

traitor s. traditore.

trajectory s. traiettoria.

tram s. 1. tram 2. carrello da miniera || — -conductor, tranviere.

trammel s. 1. tramaglio 2. intoppo.

tramp s. 1. calpestio 2. viaggio a piedi.

to **tramp** vt. 1. camminare pesantemente 2. viaggiare a piedi 3. vagabondare.

trample s. calpestio.

to **trample** vt. 1. calpestare 2. (fig.) offendere. ♦ to **trample** vi. camminare pesantemente.

tramway s. tranvia.

to **tranquillize** vt. tranquillizzare.

tranquillizer s. (med.) tranquillante.

to **transact** vt. e vi. negoziare, trattare affari.

transaction s. 1. affare, operazione 2. (giur.) transazione 3. atti (di congresso ecc.) (pl.).

transactor s. negoziatore.

transalpine agg. e s. transalpino.

transatlantic agg. transatlantico.

to **transcend** vt. trascendere, superare.

transcendence s. trascendenza.

transcendent agg. trascendente.

transcendental agg. trascendentale.

transcendentalism s. trascendentalismo.

transcontinental agg. transcontinentale.

to **transcribe** vt. trascrivere.

transcript s. riproduzione, copia.

transcription s. trascrizione.

transept s. transetto.

transfer s. 1. trasferimento, cessione 2. (giur.) trapasso 3. decalcomania.

to **transfer** vt. trasferire, cedere.

transferable agg. trasferibile.

transfiguration s. trasfigurazione.

to **transfigure** vt. trasfigurare.

to **transfix** vt. trafiggere.

transfocator s. (cine) teleobiettivo.

to **transform** vt. trasformare.

transformable agg. trasformabile.

transformation s. trasformazione.

transformer s. trasformatore.

transformism s. trasformismo.

to **transfuse** vt. 1. travasare 2. fare una trasfusione (di sangue).

transfusion s. trasfusione.

to **transgress** vt. trasgredire. ♦ to **transgress** vi. commettere una violenza, peccare.

transgression s. trasgressione.

transgressor s. trasgressore.

transient agg. passeggero, transitorio.

transistor s. (radio) transistor.

transit s. 1. transito, passaggio 2. trasporto.

transition s. transizione.

transitive agg. transitivo.

transitory agg. transitorio.

translatable agg. traducibile.

to **translate** vt. tradurre.

translation s. 1. traduzione 2. trasferimento, assunzione (al cielo).

translator s. traduttore.

translucent agg. traslucido, diafano, trasparente.

to **transmigrate** vi. trasmigrare.

transmigration s. trasmigrazione.

transmissible agg. trasmissibile.

transmission s. trasmissione.

to **transmit** vt. trasmettere.

transmitter s. trasmettitore.

transoceanic agg. transoceanico.

transparence s. trasparenza.

transparent agg. 1. trasparente, limpido 2. chiaro, evidente.

to **transpire** vt. e vi. traspirare.

to **transplant** vt. trapiantare.

transplantation s. trapianto.

transport s. 1. trasporto (anche fig.) 2. mezzo di trasporto.

transportable agg. trasportabile.

transposal s. trasposizione.

transposition s. trasposizione (di parole, cifre ecc.).

transubstantiation s. transustanziazione.

transversal agg. e s. trasversale.

trap s. trappola || — -door, botola.

to **trap** vt. prendere in trappola.

trapezium s. trapezio.

trapper s. chi tende trappole.

trash[1] s. rifiuto.

trash[2] s. guinzaglio.

to **trash** vt. sfrondare.

trashy agg. senza valore.

traumatic agg. traumatico.

travel s. 1. viaggi (pl.): — agency, agenzia di viaggi 2. (mecc.) corsa.

to **travel** vi. viaggiare.

traveller s. viaggiatore.

travelling agg. 1. viaggiante 2. di, da viaggio 3. mobile. ♦ **travelling** s. il viaggiare.

traverse agg. trasversale. ♦ **traverse** s. 1. trasversale 2. traversata.

to **traverse** vt. 1. traversare 2. muovere lateralmente. ♦ to **traverse** vi. 1. fare una traversata 2. muoversi lateralmente 3. girare su un perno.

travertin(e) s. travertino.

travesty s. parodia.

trawl s. (mar.) strascico.

trawler s. peschereccio a strascico.

tray s. vassoio ‖ *ash-* —, portacenere.

treacherous agg. traditore, sleale.

treacherousness, treachery s. tradimento, slealtà.

tread s. 1. passo 2. suola 3. battistrada.

to tread (trod, trodden) vt. e vi. camminare. ♦ **to tread (trod, trodden)** vt. 1. percorrere 2. calpestare.

treadle s. pedale.

treason s. tradimento.

treasure s. tesoro.

to treasure vt. 1. ammassare 2. custodire gelosamente.

treasurer s. tesoriere.

treasury s. 1. tesoreria 2. Ministero del Tesoro.

treat s. festa.

to treat vt. 1. trattare 2. offrire.

treatise s. trattato.

treatment s. 1. trattamento 2. (med.) cura.

treaty s. trattato.

treble agg. 1. triplo, triplice 2. (mus.) di soprano, parte di soprano.

to treble vt. triplicare. ♦ **to treble** vi. triplicarsi.

tree s. 1. albero 2. trave ‖ *— frog*, raganella.

trefoil s. trifoglio.

trellis s. graticcio.

tremble s. tremito.

to tremble vi. tremare.

trembling agg. tremante, tremolante. ♦ **trembling** s. tremito.

tremendous agg. tremendo.

tremor s. tremore.

tremulous agg. tremulo.

trench s. 1. fosso 2. trincea.

to trench vt. e vi. scavare, solcare, scavare trincee.

trenchant agg. tagliente, incisivo, efficace.

trencher s. tagliere.

trend s. direzione, orientamento, tendenza.

to trend vi. tendere.

trepan s. trapano.

to trepan vt. trapanare.

trepidation s. 1. tremito 2. trepidazione.

trespass s. 1. trasgressione 2. violazione.

to trespass vi. 1. commettere una violazione 2. peccare.

trespasser s. 1. trasgressore 2. peccatore.

trestle s. 1. cavalletto 2. intelaiatura.

trial s. 1. processo 2. prova, esperimento.

triangle s. triangolo.

triangular agg. triangolare.

triangulation s. triangolazione.

tribal agg. tribale.

tribe s. tribù.

tribune[1] s. tribuno.

tribune[2] s. tribuna.

tributary agg. e s. tributario.

tribute s. tributo.

trichromatic agg. tricromico.

trick s. 1. trucco 2. imbroglio 3. mania.

to trick vt. ingannare.

trickery s. inganno.

trickish agg. scaltro.

trickle s. gocciolio.

to trickle vi. gocciolare.

tricky agg. 1. scaltro 2. intricato.

tricolour agg. e s. tricolore.

tricycle s. triciclo.

trident s. tridente.

tridimensional agg. tridimensionale.

triennial agg. triennale.

trifle s. sciocchezza.

to trifle vi. scherzare.

trifler s. persona leggera.

trifling agg. 1. insignificante 2. frivolo.

trigeminal agg. e s. trigemino.

trigeminus s. trigemino.

trigger s. grilletto.

trigonometry s. trigonometria.

trihedron s. triedro.

trill s. trillo.

to trill vt. e vi. trillare.

trillion s. 1. trilione 2. (amer.) bilione.

trilogy s. trilogia.

trim agg. ordinato. ♦ **trim** s. 1. ordine 2. assetto 3. (cine) taglio.

to trim vt. 1. ordinare 2. tagliare.

trimester s. trimestre.

trimmer s. decoratore.

trimming s. 1. guarnizione 2. bastonatura.

trinity s. trinità.

trinket s. ninnolo.

trinomial s. trinomio.

trip s. 1. gita, viaggio 2. passo agile 3. passo falso.

to trip vi. 1. saltellare 2. inciampare. ♦ **to trip** vt. 1. far inciam-

pare 2. (*mecc.*) liberare.
tripartite *agg.* tripartito.
tripartition *s.* tripartizione.
tripe *s.* 1. trippa 2. (*gergo*) ciarpame, sciocchezze (*pl.*).
triple *agg.* triplo.
to triple *vt.* triplicare. ♦ **to triple** *vi.* triplicarsi.
triplicate *agg.* triplicato. ♦ **triplicate** *s.* triplice copia.
to triplicate *vt.* triplicare.
tripod *s.* 1. treppiede 2. tripode.
tripper *s.* gitante.
triptych *s.* trittico.
trisyllabic(al) *agg.* trisillabico.
trite *agg.* trito.
to triturate *vt.* triturare.
triumph *s.* trionfo.
to triumph *vi.* trionfare.
triumphant *agg.* trionfante.
triumvir *s.* triumviro.
triumvirate *s.* triumvirato.
trivalent *agg.* trivalente.
trivial *agg.* banale.
triviality *s.* banalità.
trod V. *to* **tread**.
trodden V. *to* **tread**.
troglodyte *s.* troglodita.
troglodytic(al) *agg.* trogloditico.
trolley *s.* carrello || — *bus*, filobus; — *line*, linea tranviaria.
troop *s.* 1. gruppo 2. truppe (*pl.*).
to troop *vi.* 1. radunarsi 2. sfilare.
trophy *s.* trofeo.
tropic *agg.* tropico.
tropical *agg.* tropicale.
tropism *s.* tropismo.
troposphere *s.* troposfera.
trot *s.* trotto.
to trot *vt.* far trottare. ♦ **to trot** *vi.* trottare.
trotter *s.* trottatore.
trouble *s.* guaio, disturbo.
to trouble *vt.* disturbare. ♦ **to trouble** *vi.* preoccuparsi.
troublesome *agg.* fastidioso.
trough *s.* 1. truogolo 2. condotto, solco 3. depressione (*atmosferica*).
trousers *s. pl.* calzoni
trout *s.* trota.
trowel *s.* cazzuola.
truce *s.* tregua.
truck¹ *s.* baratto, scambio.
truck¹ *s.* 1. carrello 2. (*amer.*) autocarro.
to truck¹ *vt.* barattare.
to truck² *vt.* trasportare (*su carrello*)
trucker *s.* camionista.
truculent *agg.* truculento.

to trudge *vi.* camminare faticosamente.
true *agg.* vero, esatto || *out of* —, sfasato.
truffle *s.* tartufo.
truly *avv.* 1. veramente 2. esattamente.
to trump *vt.* ingannare || *to* — *up a charge*, inventare un'accusa.
trumpery *agg.* illusorio. ♦ **trumpery** *s.* orpello.
trumpet *s.* tromba.
to trumpet *vi.* 1. suonare la tromba 2. barrire. ♦ **to trumpet** *vt.* strombazzare.
trumpeter *s.* trombettiere.
truncate *agg.* tronco, troncato.
truncheon *s.* manganello.
trunk *s.* 1. tronco 2. baule 3. proboscide || — *-call*, comunicazione interurbana. ♦ **trunks** *s. pl.* calzoni corti.
truss *s.* 1. fascio 2. (*arch.*) capriata.
trust *s.* 1. fede, fiducia 2. incarico di fiducia 3. (*econ.*) "trust", consorzio monopolistico.
to trust *vt. e vi.* confidare, fidarsi di, dar credito || *to* — *so. with sthg.*, affidare qc. a qu.
trustee *s.* 1. (*comm.*) fiduciario 2. (*giur.*) curatore.
truster *s.* chi si fida.
trustful *agg.* fiducioso.
trustworthy *agg.* degno di fiducia.
truth *s.* verità.
truthful *agg.* 1. vero 2. fedele.
try *s.* tentativo || — *-on*, prova (*di abiti*); — *-out* (*mecc.*), prova.
to try *vt.* provare, tentare || *to* — *for sthg.*, cercare di ottenere qc.; *to* — *on*, provare (*di abiti*); *to* — *out*, sottoporre a dura prova.
trying *agg.* 1. difficile 2. difficilmente sopportabile.
tub *s.* tinozza, vasca.
tube *s.* 1. tubo 2. camera d'aria 3. (*fam.*) ferrovia sotterranea.
tuber *s.* 1. tubero 2. tubercolo.
tubercular *agg.* 1. tubercolare 2. tubercoloso.
tuberculosis *s.* tubercolosi.
tuberculous *agg.* tubercoloso.
tubing *s.* tubatura.
tubular, tubulous *agg.* tubolare.
tuck *s.* piega (*di abito*).
to tuck *vt.* 1. (ri)piegare 2. pigiare || *to* — *up*, rimboccare.
Tuesday *s.* martedì.
tuff *s.* tufo vulcanico.

tuft s. 1. ciuffo 2. fiocco 3. cespuglio.

tug s. strappo || — -of-war, tiro alla fune.

to tug vt. e vi. 1. tirare 2. dare strattoni.

tugboat s. (mar.) rimorchiatore.

tuition s. istruzione.

tulip s. tulipano.

tumble s. 1. caduta 2. confusione.

to tumble vi. 1. cadere 2. agitarsi 3. precipitarsi 4. fare acrobazie. ♦ **to tumble** vt. 1. far cadere 2. scompigliare.

tumble-down agg. in rovina.

tumbler s. 1. acrobata 2. bicchiere (senza piede).

tumefaction s. tumefazione.

to tumefy vt. tumefare. ♦ **to tumefy** vi. tumefarsi.

tumescence s. tumescenza.

tumescent agg. gonfio.

tumid agg. tumido.

tumidity s. gonfiore.

tumour s. tumore.

tumult s. tumulto.

tumultuous agg. tumultuoso.

tumulus s. (pl. -li) tumulo.

tun s. botte.

tuna s. tonno.

tune s. 1. tono 2. accordo 3. motivo || in —, intonato; out of —, stonato.

to tune vt. (mus.) accordare || to — up, mettere a punto. ♦ **to tune** vi. essere in armonia.

tuneful agg. armonioso.

tuner s. 1. (mus.) accordatore 2. (radio) sintonizzatore.

tungsten s. tungsteno.

tunic s. tunica.

Tunisian agg. e s. tunisino.

to tunnel vi. costruire un tunnel. ♦ **to tunnel** vt. perforare.

tunny s. tonno.

turban s. turbante.

turbid agg. torbido.

turbidity s. torbidezza.

turbine s. turbina.

turbojet s. turbogetto || — engine, turboreattore.

turbulence s. turbolenza.

turbulent agg. turbolento.

tureen s. zuppiera.

turf s. 1. zolla erbosa 2. torba 3. campo da corse || — -accountant, allibratore.

turgid agg. turgido.

turgidity s. turgidezza.

Turk agg. e s. turco.

turkey s. tacchino.

Turkish agg. turco.

turmoil s. agitazione.

turn s. 1. giro 2. curva 3. turno 4. servizio 5. attitudine || — -out, assemblea, sciopero, produzione; — -table, piattaforma girevole, giradischi.

to turn vi. 1. girarsi, volgersi 2. diventare. ♦ **to turn** vt. 1. girare, volgere 2. mutare 3. tornire || to — off, chiudere, spegnere; to — on, aprire, accendere; to — down, abbassare; to — out, scacciare, produrre, spegnere, risultare; to — over, rovesciare.

turnabout s. 1. giostra 2. inversione (di rotta).

turncoat s. voltagabbana.

turner s. tornitore.

turning s. 1. giro, svolta 2. tornitura.

turning-point s. svolta decisiva, momento critico.

turnip s. rapa.

turnkey s. secondino.

turnout s. 1. folla 2. equipaggio.

turnover s. 1. rovesciamento 2. (comm.) giro 3. torta.

turnpike s. strada a pedaggio.

turnspit s. girarrosto.

turpentine s. trementina.

turpitude s. turpitudine.

turquoise s. turchese.

turret s. torretta.

turtle s. 1. tartaruga 2. — (-dove), tortora.

Tuscan agg. e s. toscano.

tusk s. zanna.

tussle s. zuffa.

to tussle vi. azzuffarsi.

tutelar(y) agg. tutelare.

tutor s. istitutore.

to tutor vt. 1. istruire 2. controllare.

tutorial agg. di istitutore.

tutorship s. mansione di istitutore.

twang s. 1. suono acuto 2. suono nasale.

to twang vi. 1. avere un suono acuto 2. parlare con voce nasale.

tweet s. cinguettio.

to tweet vi. cinguettare.

tweezers s. pl. pinzette.

twelfth agg. e s. dodicesimo.

twelve agg. e s. dodici.

twentieth agg. e s. ventesimo.

twenty agg. e s. venti.

twice *avv.* due volte.

twig *s.* ramoscello.

twilight *s.* **1.** crepuscolo **2.** luce fioca.

twin *agg.* e *s.* gemello.

to twin *vt.* accoppiare. ♦ **to twin** *vi.* accoppiarsi.

twine *s.* **1.** spago, corda **2.** groviglio.

twinge *s.* fitta, dolore.

twinkle *s.* **1.** scintillio **2.** ammicco || *in a* —, in un batter d'occhio.

to twinkle *vi.* **1.** scintillare **2.** ammiccare.

twinkling *s.* balenio.

twirl *s.* piroetta, rotazione.

to twirl *vt.* e *vi.* girare, roteare.

twist *s.* **1.** filo ritorto **2.** torsione **3.** curva.

to twist *vt.* **1.** torcere **2.** travisare. ♦ **to twist** *vi.* **1.** torcersi **2.** serpeggiare.

twister *s.* **1.** torcitore **2.** truffatore.

twisty *agg.* **1.** tortuoso **2.** disonesto.

to twit *vt.* biasimare.

twitch *s.* **1.** strattone **2.** tic nervoso.

twitter *s.* **1.** pigolio **2.** agitazione.

to twitter *vi.* **1.** pigolare **2.** essere ansioso.

two *agg.* e *s.* due.

twofold *agg.* doppio. ♦ **twofold** *avv.* doppiamente.

twopence *s.* due penny (*valore*).

tycoon *s.* (*amer.*) magnate.

type *s.* **1.** tipo **2.** simbolo **3.** (*tip.*) carattere tipografico || — *setting* (*tip.*), composizione.

to type *vt.* **1.** rappresentare **2.** dattilografare.

written) *vt.* e *vi.* dattilografare.

to typewrite (**typewrote**, **typewritten**) *vt.* e *vi.* dattilografare.

typewriter *s.* dattilografo.

typewriting *s.* dattilografia.

typewritten V. **to typewrite**.

typewrote V. **to typewrite**.

typhoon *s.* tifone.

typhus *s.* tifo.

typic(al) *agg.* tipico.

to typify *vt.* **1.** incarnare **2.** esemplificare.

typist *s.* dattilografo.

typographer *s.* tipografo.

typographic(al) *agg.* tipografico.

typography *s.* tipografia.

tyrannic(al) *agg.* tirannico.

tyrannicide *s.* **1.** tirannicida **2.** tirannicidio.

to tyrannize *vt.* e *vi.* tiranneggiare.

tyrannous *agg.* tirannico.

tyranny *s.* tirannia.

tyrant *s.* tiranno.

tyre *s.* V. *tire*.

Tyrrhene, Tyrrhenian *agg.* e *s.* tirreno.

Tzigane *agg.* e *s.* tzigano.

U

ubication *s.* ubicazione.

ugliness *s.* bruttezza.

ugly *agg.* **1.** brutto **2.** vile, turpe.

ulcer *s.* ulcera, piaga (*anche fig.*).

to ulcerate *vt.* ulcerare. ♦ **to ulcerate** *vi.* ulcerarsi.

ulceration *s.* ulcerazione.

ulcerous *agg.* ulceroso.

ulna *s.* (*pl.* -ae) (*anat.*) ulna.

ultimate *agg.* ultimo, finale, definitivo.

ultra *agg.* ultra, estremo, eccessivo. ♦ **ultra** *s.* estremista.

ultramarine *agg.* oltremarino.

ultramontane *agg.* e *s.* oltremontano.

ultramundane *agg.* oltremondano.

ultra-red *agg.* infrarosso.

ultrasonic *agg.* ultrasonico.

ultraviolet *agg.* ultravioletto.

umbilical *agg.* ombelicale.

umbrella *s.* ombrello || — *-stand*, portaombrelli.

umpire *s.* (*giur.; sport*) arbitro.

unabashed *agg.* imperturbato.

unabated *agg.* non diminuito, non scemato.

unable *agg.* incapace, inabile.

unabridged *agg.* non abbreviato, completo || — *edition*, edizione integrale.

unacceptable *agg.* inaccettabile.

unaccomplished *agg.* incompleto, incompiuto.

unaccountability *s.* inesplicabilità.

unaccountable *agg.* inesplicabile.

unaccustomed *agg.* non abituale, insolito.

unachievable *agg.* ineseguibile.

unacquainted *agg.* **1.** ignaro di, non al corrente di **2.** sconosciuto, poco familiare.

unacquired *agg.* non acquisito, innato.

unactive *agg.* inattivo.

unadapted *agg.* inadatto.

unadorned *agg.* disadorno.

unadvisable *agg.* non consigliabile, inopportuno.

unaffected *agg.* 1. senza affettazione, semplice 2. insensibile.

unafraid *agg.* impavido.

unalienable *agg.* inalienabile.

unallied *agg.* senza relazione, senza connessione.

unalterable *agg.* inalterabile.

unamendable *agg.* incorreggibile.

to unanchor *vi.* togliere l'ancora. ◆ **to unanchor** *vt.* disancorare.

unanimated *agg.* inanimato.

unanimity *s.* unanimità.

unanimous *agg.* unanime.

unannounced *agg.* non annunciato, imprevisto.

unanswerable *agg.* 1. a cui non si può rispondere 2. irrefutabile.

unanswered *agg.* senza risposta.

unappealable *agg.* inappellabile.

unappeasable *agg.* implacabile.

unappeased *agg.* insoddisfatto.

unapplied *agg.* non impiegato, inapplicato.

unappreciated *agg.* non apprezzato, incompreso.

unapprehensive *agg.* 1. lento nell'apprendere 2. non apprensivo.

unapproachable *agg.* inaccessibile.

unapt *agg.* 1. inadatto 2. inetto.

unargued *agg.* indiscusso.

to unarm *vt.* disarmare.

unarmed *agg.* disarmato, inerme.

unartful *agg.* privo di artifici, ingenuo.

unascertainable *agg.* non verificabile.

unascertained *agg.* sconosciuto, non accertato.

unasked *agg.* non richiesto.

unaspiring *agg.* senza ambizione.

unassailable *agg.* inattaccabile.

unassailed *agg.* inattaccato.

unasserted *agg.* non asserito.

unassuming *agg.* modesto, senza pretese.

unattackable *agg.* inattaccabile.

unattainable *agg.* inaccessibile.

unattempted *agg.* intentato.

unauthorized *agg.* 1. non autorizzato 2. illecito.

unavailable *agg.* 1. inutile, vano 2. non disponibile.

unavenged *agg.* impunito.

unavoidable *agg.* inevitabile.

unaware *agg.* inconsapevole, inconscio.

unawareness *s.* inconsapevolezza.

unawares *avv.* inconsapevolmente, inconsciamente.

unbalance *s.* squilibrio.

to unbalance *vt.* sbilanciare.

to unbandage *vt.* sbendare.

unbearable *agg.* insopportabile.

unbeaten *agg.* 1. insuperato, non battuto 2. non frequentato.

unbecoming *agg.* disdicevole.

unbelief *s.* incredulità, scetticismo.

unbelievable *agg.* incredibile.

unbelieving *agg.* incredulo, scettico.

to unbend (unbent, unbent) *vt.* 1. raddrizzare 2. allentare, slegare. ◆ **to unbend (unbent, unbent)** *vi.* raddrizzarsi.

unbias(s)ed *agg.* imparziale, senza preconcetti.

to unbind (unbound, unbound) *vt.* sciogliere, slegare.

to unbolt *vt.* disserrare, aprire.

unborn *agg.* non nato, nascituro, che deve venire.

to unbosom *vt.* rivelare, confidare. ◆ **to unbosom** *vi.* sfogarsi: *to — oneself to so.*, aprirsi con qu.

unbound V. *to unbind.*

unbreakable *agg.* infrangibile.

unbreathable *agg.* irrespirabile.

to unbreech *vt.* togliere i calzoni.

to unbridle *vt.* sbrigliare, dare libero corso a (*anche fig.*).

unbridled *agg.* incontrollato, senza briglia.

unbroken *agg.* 1. intatto, intero, inviolato 2. incessante.

unbruised *agg.* non ammaccato, illeso.

to unbuckle *vt.* sfibbiare, slacciare.

to unburden *vt.* 1. scaricare, alleggerire 2. (*fig.*) alleviare.

unburied *agg.* insepolto.

to unbury *vt.* disseppellire.

to unbutton *vt.* sbottonare. ◆ **to unbutton** *vi.* sbottonarsi.

uncalled *agg.* non chiamato, non invitato: *— for*, superfluo, gratuito.

uncanny *agg.* misterioso, irreale.

uncared-for *agg.* negletto, abbandonato.

unceasing *agg.* incessante.

uncensurable *agg.* incensurabile.

uncertain *agg.* 1. incerto, malsicuro 2. instabile.

uncertainty *s.* 1. incertezza 2. irresolutezza.

to unchain *vt.* sciogliere da catene.

unchanged *agg.* immutato.

uncharged *agg.* **1.** non carico **2.** non incriminato.

uncharitable *agg.* poco caritatevole.

to **uncharm** *vt.* liberare da un incantesimo.

unchaste *agg.* impuro.

unchecked *agg.* sfrenato.

uncivil *agg.* **1.** scortese, maleducato **2.** indecoroso.

uncivilized *agg.* non civilizzato.

to **unclasp** *vt.* slacciare. ♦ to **unclasp** *vi.* allentare la stretta.

uncle *s.* zio.

uncombed *agg.* spettinato.

uncomely *agg.* **1.** sgraziato **2.** sconveniente.

uncomfortable *agg.* **1.** scomodo, a disagio **2.** spiacevole.

uncommon *agg.* insolito, raro.

uncompared *agg.* incomparato.

uncompelled *agg.* non costretto, spontaneo.

unconcerned *agg.* indifferente, noncurante.

unconcerning *agg.* irrilevante, che non interessa.

unconditional *agg.* incondizionato.

uncongenial *agg.* **1.** antipatico, spiacevole **2.** non congeniale.

unconquerable *agg.* invincibile, indomabile.

unconquered *agg.* invitto, indomito.

unconscionable *agg.* **1.** irragionevole **2.** senza scrupoli.

unconscious *agg.* **1.** inconscio, ignaro **2.** privo di sensi. ♦ **unconscious** *s.* inconscio.

unconsciousness *s.* **1.** inconsapevolezza **2.** stato di incoscienza.

unconsolable *agg.* inconsolabile.

unconstitutional *agg.* incostituzionale.

unconstrained *agg.* **1.** non costretto, libero **2.** disinvolto.

unconstraint *s.* **1.** assenza di costrizione, libertà **2.** spontaneità.

uncontrollable *agg.* incontrollabile.

uncontrolled *agg.* senza controllo, sfrenato.

unconventional *agg.* non convenzionale, disinvolto.

unconvertible *agg.* inconvertibile.

unconvincing *agg.* non convincente.

to **uncork** *vt.* sturare, stappare.

uncountable *agg.* innumerevole.

to **uncouple** *vt.* **1.** sguinzagliare **2.** staccare.

uncouth *agg.* **1.** ordinario, rozzo **2.** desolato.

to **uncover** *vt.* **1.** scoprire **2.** spogliare. ♦ to **uncover** *vi.* togliersi il cappello.

uncovered *agg.* **1.** scoperto, senza tetto **2.** spogliato **3.** senza cappello.

unction *s.* **1.** unzione **2.** unguento.

unctuous *agg.* grasso, untuoso (*anche fig.*).

uncultivable *agg.* non coltivabile.

uncultivated *agg.* incolto, non coltivato.

uncut *agg.* intonso, non tagliato.

undaunted *agg.* intrepido, impavido.

to **undeceive** *vt.* disingannare.

undecided *agg.* **1.** indeciso, non risolto **2.** indefinito **3.** irresoluto.

undeclinable *agg.* indeclinabile.

undecomposable *agg.* indecomponibile.

undefended *agg.* **1.** indifeso **2.** (*giur.*) non assistito da difesa legale.

undeniable *agg.* innegabile.

under *prep.* **1.** sotto, al di sotto di **2.** in corso di **3.** meno di. ♦ **under** *avv.* sotto, al di sotto ‖ —-age, minorenne.

underbrush *s.* sottobosco.

to **undercharge** *vt.* far pagare troppo poco.

underclothes *s. pl.* biancheria intima (*sing.*).

undercover *agg.* segreto.

undercurrent *s.* **1.** corrente sottomarina **2.** (*fig.*) attività, tendenza nascosta.

to **underdo** (**underdid, underdone**) *vt.* e *vi.* **1.** agire in modo insufficiente **2.** cuocere poco.

underdone V. to **underdo**. ♦ **underdone** *agg.* poco cotto.

to **underestimate** *vt.* sottovalutare.

underfed *agg.* denutrito.

to **underfeed** (**underfed, underfed**) *vt.* nutrire insufficientemente.

to **undergo** (**underwent, undergone**) *vt.* **1.** subire, essere sottoposto a **2.** sopportare.

undergraduate *s.* studente universitario.

underground *agg.* sotterraneo. ♦ **underground** *s.* **1.** sottosuolo **2.** metropolitana.

underground *avv.* 1. sottoterra 2. (*pol.*) clandestinamente.

underhand *agg.* 1. clandestino, segreto 2. furbo, astuto. ♦ **underhand** *avv.* segretamente, clandestinamente.

to underline *vt.* sottolineare.

underlining *s.* sottolineatura.

undermentioned *agg.* sottoindicato.

to undermine *vt.* 1. minare, scalzare 2. (*fig.*) indebolire, insidiare.

underneath *avv.* di sotto, al di sotto.

to underpay (underpaid, underpaid) *vt.* pagare inadeguatamente.

to underrate *vt.* sottovalutare.

underscriber *s.* sottoscrittore.

undersea *agg.* sottomarino.

to undersell (undersold, undersold) *vt.* svendere.

undershrub *s.* sottobosco.

undersignature *s.* firma in calce.

undersold V. *to undersell.*

to understand (understood, understood) *vt.* e *vi.* 1. capire, comprendere 2. dedurre, supporre 3. sentir dire.

understandable *agg.* comprensibile.

understanding *s.* 1. comprensione 2. patto, intesa || *on this* —, a queste condizioni.

to understate *vt.* minimizzare.

understatement *s.* attenuazione del vero.

understood V. *to understand.*

to undertake (undertook, undertaken) *vt.* e *vi.* 1. intraprendere 2. incaricarsi di 3. prendere in appalto.

undertaker *s.* 1. impresario 2. imprenditore di pompe funebri.

undertaking *s.* 1. l'intraprendere 2. (*comm.*) impresa 3. (*giur.*) promessa, obbligazione.

undertook V. *to undertake.*

undervaluation *s.* 1. scarsa stima 2. svalutazione.

to undervalue *vt.* sottovalutare.

underwater *agg.* subacqueo || *fishing* —, pesca subacquea.

underwent V. *to undergo.*

underworld *s.* 1. bassifondi (*pl.*) 2. oltretomba.

to underwrite (underwrote, underwritten) *vt.* e *vi.* 1. sottoscrivere, firmare 2. (*comm.*) assicurare.

undeserved *agg.* immeritato.

undeserving *agg.* immeritevole.

undesirable *agg.* indesiderabile.

undestroyable *agg.* indistruttibile.

undetected *agg.* non scoperto.

undetermined *agg.* 1. indeterminato 2. indeciso.

undid V. *to undo.*

undies *s. pl.* biancheria intima (*sing.*)

undine *s.* ondina.

undisciplined *agg.* indisciplinato.

undiscriminating *agg.* che non distingue, che non fa distinzioni.

undiscussed *agg.* indiscusso.

indisputed *agg.* incontestato.

undissembled *agg.* non dissimulato.

undistinguished *agg.* indistinto.

undisturbed *agg.* indisturbato.

undividable *agg.* indivisibile.

to undo (undid, undone) *vt.* 1. disfare, sciogliere 2. annullare, rovinare.

undoing *s.* 1. disfacimento 2. rovina.

undone[1] V. *to undo.* ♦ **undone** *agg.* disfatto, rovinato.

undone[2] *agg.* incompiuto.

undoubtable *agg.* indubitabile.

undoubted *agg.* indubbio.

undreamed *agg.* non sognato, impensato.

to undress *vt.* svestire. ♦ **to undress** *vi.* svestirsi.

undue *agg.* 1. non dovuto, indebito 2. inadatto.

to undulate *vi.* 1. ondeggiare 2. essere ondulato.

undulation *s.* ondulazione.

undulatory *agg.* ondulatorio.

unduly *avv.* indebitamente.

to unearth *vt.* 1. dissotterrare, portare alla luce 2. far uscire dalla tana (*un animale*).

unearthly *agg.* ultraterreno || *hour*, ora impossibile.

uneasily *avv.* 1. a disagio, con difficoltà 2. con ansia.

uneasiness *s.* 1. disagio, pena 2. ansia.

uneasy *agg.* 1. a disagio 2. ansioso, inquieto.

uneatable *agg.* immangiabile.

uneducated *agg.* rozzo, ignorante.

uneffected *agg.* non effettuato.

unembarrassed *agg.* a proprio agio, disinvolto.

unemployed *agg.* 1. disoccupato 2. non usato.

unemployment *s.* disoccupazione

|| — *benefit*, sussidio di disoccupazione.

unending agg. eterno, senza fine.

unequal agg. 1. ineguale 2. inadeguato, incapace.

unequalled agg. ineguagliato.

unerring agg. infallibile, sicuro.

uneven agg. 1. ineguale, irregolare 2. ruvido, non livellato.

unevenness s. 1. disuguaglianza, irregolarità 2. dislivello.

uneventful agg. pacifico, senza avvenimenti importanti.

unexceptionable agg. ineccepibile.

unexhausted agg. inesausto.

unexpected agg. inatteso.

unexpensive agg. poco costoso.

unexplored agg. inesplorato.

unextinguishable agg. inestinguibile.

unfadable agg. 1. che non può appassire 2. solido (di colore).

unfading agg. 1. che non appassisce 2. che non sbiadisce.

unfailing agg. 1. infallibile, sicuro 2. immancabile.

unfair agg. sleale: — *competition*, concorrenza sleale.

unfairness s. slealtà, ingiustizia.

unfaithful agg. 1. infedele, sleale 2. inesatto.

unfaithfulness s. 1. infedeltà 2. inesattezza.

unfaltering agg. fermo, non esitante.

unfamiliar agg. poco familiare.

unfashionable agg. fuori moda.

to **unfasten** vt. slacciare, slegare. ♦ to **unfasten** vi. slacciarsi, slegarsi.

unfathomable agg. insondabile.

unfavourable agg. sfavorevole.

unfeeling agg. insensibile, spietato.

unfinished agg. 1. incompleto 2. non rifinito.

unfit agg. 1. inadatto, disadatto 2. inabile.

unfitness s. 1. inidoneità 2. debole costituzione.

to **unfold** vt. 1. aprire, schiudere 2. svelare. ♦ to **unfold** vi. 1. aprirsi, schiudersi 2. svelarsi.

unforbearing agg. insofferente, impaziente.

unforeseeing agg. imprevidente.

unforeseen agg. imprevisto.

unforgettable agg. indimenticabile.

unforgiving agg. senza misericordia.

unforgotten agg. inobliato.

unfortunate agg. sfortunato.

unfortunately avv. sfortunatamente.

unfounded agg. infondato.

to **unfreeze (unfroze, unfrozen)** vt. disgelare, scongelare. ♦ to **unfreeze (unfroze, unfrozen)** vi. disgelarsi.

unfrequent agg. infrequente.

unfriendly agg. poco amichevole.

to **unfrock** vt. spretare.

unfroze V. to *unfreeze*.

unfrozen V. to *unfreeze*.

unfruitful agg. infruttuoso.

unfruitfulness s. infruttuosità.

to **unfurl** vt. e vi. spiegare, spiegarsi (di bandiere ecc.).

unfurnished agg. 1. non ammobiliato 2. sfornito.

ungainly agg. goffo, maldestro.

ungentlemanlike agg. indegno di un gentiluomo.

ungirt agg. senza cintura.

to **unglue** vt. scollare. ♦ to **unglue** vi. scollarsi.

ungodly agg. 1. empio 2. malvagio.

ungraceful agg. sgraziato.

ungrammatical agg. sgrammaticato.

ungrateful agg. ingrato.

ungrounded agg. 1. infondato 2. senza preparazione.

unguarded agg. sguarnito, senza difesa.

unguent s. unguento.

unhandy agg. 1. maldestro 2. poco maneggevole.

unhappiness s. infelicità.

unhappy agg. infelice, triste.

unharmed agg. intatto, illeso.

unharmful agg. innocuo.

unhealthily avv. in modo malsano, poco igienicamente.

unhealthy agg. 1. malsano, insalubre 2. (fig.) dannoso 3. malaticcio.

unheard agg. 1. non udito 2. non ascoltato 3. sconosciuto, strano || — *of*, inaudito.

to **unhinge** vt. scardinare.

unholy agg. profano, empio.

to **unhook** vt. sganciare. ♦ to **unhook** vi. sganciarsi.

unhoped agg. insperato, inatteso.

to **unhorse** vt. 1. disarcionare 2. staccare i cavalli da (*carrozza*).

unhuman agg. sovrumano.

unhurt agg. illeso, incolume.

unhurtful agg. innocuo.

unicellular *agg.* unicellulare.

unification *s.* unificazione.

uniform *agg.* uniforme, costante. ♦ **uniform** *s.* uniforme, divisa.

to uniform *vt.* uniformare.

uniformity *s.* uniformità.

to unify *vt.* unificare.

unilateral *agg.* unilaterale.

unilaterally *avv.* unilateralmente.

unimaginable *agg.* inimmaginabile.

unimpaired *agg.* inalterato, intatto.

unimpassioned *agg.* spassionato, calmo.

unimpeachable *agg.* incensurabile.

unimportance *s.* scarsa importanza.

unimportant *agg.* privo d'importanza.

unimposing *agg.* poco imponente, che non fa soggezione.

uninhabitable *agg.* inabitabile.

uninhabited *agg.* disabitato.

uninominal *agg.* uninominale.

unintelligent *agg.* stupido.

unintelligible *agg.* inintelligibile.

unintended *agg.* 1. involontario 2. *(giur.)* non intenzionale.

uninteresting *agg.* non interessante.

uninviting *agg.* poco attraente.

union *s.* unione, associazione, lega || *(trade)* —, sindacato; *the Union Jack*, la bandiera del Regno Unito.

unionism *s.* tendenza ad unirsi.

unionist *s.* unionista.

uniparous *agg.* uniparo.

unique *agg.* 1. unico, solo 2. eccezionale.

uniqueness *s.* unicità.

unisexual *agg.* unisessuale.

unison *s.* 1. *(mus.)* unisono 2. *(fig.)* concordia.

unit *s.* 1. unità, unità di misura 2. complesso, insieme.

unitary *agg.* unitario.

to unite *vt.* unire. ♦ **to unite** *vi.* 1. unirsi 2. mettersi d'accordo.

united *agg.* unito, collegato.

unity *s.* 1. unità 2. armonia.

universal *agg.* universale.

universality *s.* universalità.

to universalize *vt.* universalizzare.

universe *s.* universo.

university *s.* università.

univocal *agg.* univoco, non ambiguo.

to unjoint *vt.* disgiungere.

unjust *agg.* ingiusto.

unjustifiable *agg.* ingiustificabile.

unjustified *agg.* ingiustificato.

unkempt *agg.* trascurato, sciatto.

unkind *agg.* 1. sgarbato, scortese 2. crudele.

unkindness *s.* scortesia.

unknown *agg.* sconosciuto, ignoto.

unlawful *agg.* illegale.

to unlearn (unlearnt, unlearnt) *(anche reg.)* *vt.* disimparare.

unleavened *agg.* non lievitato || — *bread*, pane azzimo.

unless *cong.* a meno che, salvo che.

unlike *agg.* dissimile, diverso. ♦ **unlike** *avv.* diversamente. ♦ **unlike** *prep.* diversamente da.

unlikelihood *s.* inverosimilianza, improbabilità.

unlikely *agg.* inverosimile, improbabile.

unlimited *agg.* illimitato, sconfinato.

to unline *vt.* sfoderare.

unlined¹ *agg.* senza fodera.

unlined² *agg.* senza rughe.

unliterary *agg.* non letterario.

to unload *vt.* 1. scaricare 2. *(fig.)* alleggerire.

to unlock *vt.* aprire *(con chiave)*.

unlooked-for *agg.* imprevisto.

to unloose *vt.* slegare.

unlosable *agg.* che non può essere perso.

unlovable *agg.* poco amabile, antipatico.

unlucky *agg.* 1. sfortunato 2. di cattivo augurio.

to unman *vt.* 1. evirare 2. abbrutire 3. togliere forza.

unmarred *agg.* non sciupato.

unmarried *agg.* non coniugato.

to unmask *vt.* togliere la maschera *(anche fig.)*. ♦ **to unmask** *vi.* togliersi la maschera.

unmatched *agg.* senza rivali.

unmentionable *agg.* innominabile, irripetibile.

unmerciful *agg.* spietato.

unmethodical *agg.* non metodico.

unminded *agg.* negletto.

unmindful *agg.* 1. immemore 2. incurante.

unmistakable *agg.* indubbio, inequivocabile.

to unmoor *vt.* e *vi.* togliere gli ormeggi a.

to unnail *vt.* schiodare.

unnatural *agg.* innaturale, contro natura.

unnavigable *agg.* non navigabile.

unnecessary *agg.* non necessario.

unneeded *agg.* inutile, non necessario.

to **unnerve** *vt.* snervare.

unnoticed *agg.* inosservato.

unobjectionable *agg.* ineccepibile.

unobliging *agg.* poco compiacente.

unobservant *agg.* **1.** inosservante **2.** distratto.

unobserved *agg.* inosservato.

unobtrusive *agg.* discreto, modesto.

unoffending *agg.* inoffensivo.

unofficial *agg.* ufficioso.

to **unpack** *vt. e vi.* **1.** disfare (*le valigie*) **2.** disimballare.

umpalatable *agg.* di gusto sgradevole.

unpardonable *agg.* imperdonabile.

unpaved *agg.* non lastricato.

unperceivable *agg.* impercettibile.

unperceived *agg.* inavvertito.

unperishable *agg.* duraturo, imperituro.

unpleasant *agg.* spiacevole, sgradevole.

unpliable *agg.* poco pieghevole.

unpoetic(al) *agg.* poco poetico.

to **unpoison** *vt.* svelenire.

unpolluted *agg.* incontaminato.

unpopular *agg.* impopolare.

unpopularity *s.* impopolarità.

unprecise *agg.* impreciso.

unpredictable *agg.* imprevedibile.

unpredicted *agg.* imprevisto.

unpremeditated *agg.* non premeditato.

unprepared *agg.* impreparato.

unpreparedness *s.* impreparazione.

unprepossessed *agg.* senza prevenzioni.

unprepossessing *agg.* senza attrattive, antipatico.

unpresentable *agg.* impresentabile.

unpriestly *agg.* che non si addice a un prete.

unprincely *agg.* che non si addice a un principe.

unprintable *agg.* non adatto ad essere pubblicato.

unproductive *agg.* improduttivo.

unprofitable *agg.* poco vantaggioso.

unprofitableness *s.* infruttuosità.

unpronounceable *agg.* impronunciabile.

unprovable *agg.* indimostrabile.

unpublished *agg.* inedito.

unqualified *agg.* **1.** incompetente **2.** non abilitato **3.** (*giur.*) senza restrizioni.

to **unqualify** *vt.* **1.** inabilitare **2.** squalificare.

unquenchable *agg.* inestinguibile, insaziabile (*anche fig.*).

unquestionable *agg.* incontestabile, indiscutibile.

unquestioned *agg.* indiscusso.

unquiet *agg.* inquieto.

unquoted *agg.* **1.** non citato **2.** (*comm.*) non quotato (*di titoli*).

to **unravel** *vt.* districare. ♦ to **unravel** *vi.* districarsi.

unreachable *agg.* irraggiungibile.

unready *agg.* **1.** impreparato **2.** tardo, lento.

unreal *agg.* irreale.

unreality *s.* irrealtà.

unrealizable *agg.* irrealizzabile.

unreasonable *agg.* irragionevole.

unrecognizable *agg.* irriconoscibile.

unredeemed *agg.* **1.** irredento **2.** non controbilanciato **3.** (*comm.*) non estinto.

unrelated *agg.* senza rapporti, senza legami.

unreliable *agg.* **1.** non fidato **2.** inattendibile.

unrepealed *agg.* (*giur.*) non abrogato.

unrequired *agg.* non richiesto.

unrest *s.* inquietudine.

unrestrained *agg.* non represso.

unrestricted *agg.* senza limitazioni.

unrevenged *agg.* invendicato.

unripe *agg.* immaturo, acerbo (*anche fig.*).

unrivalled *agg.* impareggiabile.

to **unroll** *vt.* svolgere. ♦ to **unroll** *vi.* svolgersi.

unruly *agg.* sregolato, indisciplinato.

to **unsaddle** *vt.* dissellare, disarcionare.

unsafe *agg.* malsicuro.

unsatisfied *agg.* **1.** insoddisfatto **2.** non convinto.

unsavoury *agg.* insipido, scipito.

unscholarly *agg.* **1.** indegno di un letterato **2.** non erudito.

to **unscrew** *vt.* svitare.

unscriptural *agg.* non conforme alle Sacre Scritture.

to **unseal** *vt.* dissigillare.

unseasonable *agg.* **1.** fuori stagione **2.** (*fig.*) intempestivo.

unseemliness *s.* indecenza.

unseemly *agg.* sconveniente, indecente.

unseizable *agg.* inafferrabile.

unselfish *agg.* disinteressato.

unselfishness *s.* disinteresse.

unsettled *agg.* **1.** disordinato **2.** sconvolto, turbato **3.** mutevole, indeciso.

to unsew (unsewed, unsewn) *vt.* scucire.

unshaken *agg.* non scosso, fermo.

to unsheathe *vt.* sguainare.

to unshoe (unshod, unshod) *vt.* **1.** togliere le scarpe **2.** togliere i ferri a (*un cavallo*).

unshrinkable *agg.* irrestringibile.

unskilfulness *s.* incapacità, imperizia.

unskilled *agg.* inesperto, inabile.

unsocial *agg.* asociale.

unsold *agg.* invenduto.

to unsolder *vt.* dissaldare.

unsolved *agg.* insoluto.

unsound *agg.* **1.** malsano, malato **2.** guasto, avariato.

unspeakable *agg.* **1.** inesprimibile **2.** inqualificabile.

unstable *agg.* **1.** instabile **2.** (*fig.*) mutevole.

unsteadiness *agg.* incostanza, volubilità.

unsteady *agg.* instabile, incostante.

unsubstantial *agg.* **1.** inconsistente **2.** illusorio.

unsuccessful *agg.* mal riuscito, sfortunato.

unsuitable *agg.* inadatto, non appropriato.

unsure *agg.* **1.** malsicuro, precario **2.** incerto.

unsurpassed *agg.* insorpassato.

unsuspected *agg.* insospettato, non sospetto.

unsustainable *agg.* insostenibile.

untamable *agg.* indomabile.

untame *agg.* selvaggio, non addomesticato.

untaught *agg.* poco istruito, ignorante.

unteachable *agg.* **1.** difficile da insegnare **2.** non educabile.

unthinkable *agg.* inimmaginabile.

to unthread *vt.* sfilare, togliere il filo a.

untidily *avv.* disordinatamente.

untidy *agg.* disordinato, trasandato.

to untie *vt.* slegare. ♦ **to untie** *vi.* slegarsi.

until *prep.* fino a. ♦ **until** *cong.* finché.

untimeliness *s.* intempestività, inopportunità.

untimely *agg.* **1.** prematuro **2.** inopportuno. ♦ **untimely** *avv.* **1.** pre-

maturamente **2.** inopportunamente.

untiring *agg.* instancabile.

untitled *agg.* senza titolo.

to untomb *vt.* dissotterrare.

untouchable *agg.* **1.** intoccabile **2.** (*fig.*) irraggiungibile.

untouched *agg.* **1.** non toccato, intatto **2.** illeso, indenne.

untoward *agg.* **1.** restio, caparbio **2.** infausto.

untranslatable *agg.* intraducibile.

untravelled *agg.* che non ha viaggiato.

untrodden *agg.* non calpestato, non battuto.

untrue *agg.* **1.** falso, menzognero **2.** infedele.

untrustworthy *agg.* indegno di fiducia.

to untune *vt.* scordare (*uno strumento musicale*).

unusable *agg.* inutilizzabile.

unusual *agg.* insolito, inusitato.

unutterable *agg.* indescrivibile, impronunciabile.

unvarying *agg.* invariabile.

to unveil *vt.* **1.** togliere il velo a **2.** (*fig.*) rivelare.

unwary *agg.* incauto, sconsiderato.

unwatchful *agg.* non vigilante, disattento.

unweaned *agg.* non svezzato.

unweary *agg.* non stanco, indefesso.

unwell *agg.* indisposto, ammalato.

unwieldy *agg.* **1.** ingombrante **2.** impacciato.

unwilling *agg.* **1.** riluttante **2.** involontario.

unwillingly *avv.* malvolentieri.

unwillingness *s.* **1.** riluttanza **2.** malavoglia.

to unwind (unwound, unwound) *vt.* srotolare. ♦ **to unwind (unwound, unwound)** *vi.* srotolarsi.

unwise *agg.* malaccorto.

unwitting *agg.* inconsapevole.

unworldly *agg.* spirituale, non mondano.

unworthy *agg.* indegno, spregevole.

unwound *V. to unwind.*

to unwrap *vt.* disfare, svolgere.

unwritten *agg.* non scritto || — *law*, legge tramandata oralmente.

unwrought *agg.* **1.** non lavorato **2.** grezzo.

up[1] *avv.* **1.** su, in su, in alto **2.** in piedi || — *to*, fino a; *hurry* —, spicciati; *the game is* —, tutto è perduto. ♦ **up** *prep.* su, su per, in cima a || — *now,* fino ad ora.

up² *agg.* ascendente, che va verso l'alto || — *-train,* treno per Londra.

up-and-down *agg.* **1.** che va in su e in giù **2.** oscillante.

to upbraid *vt.* rimproverare.

upheaval *s.* **1.** sollevamento **2.** agitazione.

uphill *agg.* **1.** in salita **2.** (*fig.*) difficile. ♦ **uphill** *avv.* in salita. ♦ **uphill** *s.* salita.

to uphold (upheld, upheld) *vt.* **1.** sostenere, sorreggere **2.** (*fig.*) appoggiare, patrocinare.

to upholster *vt.* tappezzare, imbottire.

upholsterer *s.* tappezziere.

upholstery *s.* tappezzeria, imbottitura.

upkeep *agg.* mantenimento, manutenzione.

upland *agg.* montuoso. ♦ **upland** *s.* zona montuosa.

upon *prep.* V. *on*.

upper *agg.* **1.** superiore, più alto **2.** più lontano (*dall'ingresso ecc.*) || *the Upper House,* la Camera dei Lords.

uppercut *s.* (*sport*) "uppercut", colpo dal basso in alto.

upright *agg.* **1.** ritto, diritto, eretto **2.** retto, integro. ♦ **upright** *avv.* in piedi, perpendicolarmente.

uprightness *s.* **1.** perpendicolarità **2.** rettitudine.

uproar *s.* tumulto, chiasso.

uproarious *agg.* tumultuoso, chiassoso.

to uproot *vt.* sradicare, svellere.

ups and downs *s. pl.* **1.** ondulazioni (*del terreno*) **2.** (*fig.*) vicissitudini, alti e bassi.

to upset (upset, upset) *vt.* **1.** rovesciare **2.** disturbare, sconvolgere. ♦ **to upset (upset, upset)** *vi.* rovesciarsi, capovolgersi.

upset *agg.* **1.** rovesciato, capovolto **2.** (*fig.*) sconvolto, turbato. ♦ **upset** *s.* **1.** rovesciamento **2.** disordine.

upshot *s.* esito, risultato.

upside-down *avv.* capovolto, sottosopra.

upstairs *agg. e avv.* al piano superiore, di sopra.

upstanding *agg.* **1.** eretto, diritto **2.** (*fig.*) franco, leale.

up-to-date *agg.* aggiornato, all'ultima moda.

upward(s) *agg.* ascendente, rivolto verso l'alto. ♦ **upward** *avv.* **1.** in su, in alto **2.** al di sopra.

uranium *s.* uranio.

urban *agg.* urbano, di città.

urbane *agg.* urbano, cortese.

urbanity *s.* urbanità, cortesia.

urbanization *s.* urbanizzazione.

to urbanize *vt.* urbanizzare.

urchin *s.* monello.

uretic *agg. e s.* diuretico.

urge *s.* **1.** impulso, stimolo **2.** spinta, sprone.

to urge *vt. e vi.* **1.** spingere, stimolare **2.** consigliare, raccomandare.

urgency *s.* **1.** urgenza, premura **2.** bisogno urgente, necessità.

urgent *agg.* urgente, pressante.

uric *agg.* urico.

to urinate *vi.* orinare.

urine *s.* orina.

urn *s.* **1.** urna **2.** bricco.

us *pron. pers. compl. pl.* ci, noi: *three of* —, tre di noi.

usable *agg.* usabile, servibile.

usage *s.* **1.** uso, trattamento, impiego **2.** usanza.

use *s.* **1.** uso, impiego **2.** utilità, vantaggio **3.** (*giur.*) usufrutto.

to use *vt.* **1.** usare, adoperare **2.** trattare || *to* — *up,* consumare.

used *agg.* **1.** usato, adoperato **2.** abituato || —*up,* esaurito.

useful *agg.* utile, pratico.

usefulness *s.* utilità, vantaggio.

useless *agg.* inutile, vano.

uselessness *s.* inutilità.

user *s.* **1.** utente **2.** (*giur.*) usufruttuario.

usher *s.* usciere.

to usher *vt.* precedere (*in qualità di usciere*).

usual *agg.* usuale, abituale || *as* —, come al solito.

usually *avv.* di solito, abitualmente.

usufruct *s.* (*giur.*) usufrutto.

usufructuary *agg. e s.* usufruttuario.

usurer *s.* usuraio.

to usurp *vt.* usurpare.

usurpation *s.* usurpazione.

usurper *s.* usurpatore.

usury *s.* usura (*anche fig.*).

utensil *s.* utensile, arnese.

uterine *agg.* uterino.

uterus *s.* (*pl.* -ri) utero.

utilitarian *s.* utilitarista.

utilitarianism *s.* utilitarismo.

utility *s.* utilità, vantaggio.

utilizable *agg.* utilizzabile.

utilization *s.* utilizzazione.

to **utilize** *vt.* utilizzare.

utmost *agg. e s.* 1. estremo, ultimo 2. massimo, sommo || *to do one's* —, fare del proprio meglio.

Utopian *s.* utopista.

utter *agg.* completo, totale.

to **utter** *vt.* 1. emettere 2. esprimere, pronunciare.

utterable *agg.* esprimibile.

utterance *s.* espressione, sfogo.

uttering *s.* 1. messa in circolazione 2. spaccio (*di assegni ecc.*).

utterly *avv.* completamente, totalmente.

uttermost *agg. e s.* V. *utmost.*

uxoricide *s.* 1. uxoricida 2. uxoricidio.

V

vacancy *s.* 1. vuoto, lacuna 2. posto vacante || *no* —, completo (*di alberghi ecc.*).

vacant *agg.* 1. vuoto, vacante 2. non occupato.

to **vacate** *vt.* lasciar vacante, sgomberare || *to* — *a seat*, dare le dimissioni.

vacation *s.* 1. il ritirarsi, il lasciar libero 2. (*amer.*) vacanze: *long* —, vacanze estive (*pl.*).

to **vaccinate** *vt. e vi.* vaccinare.

vaccination *s.* vaccinazione.

vaccine *s.* vaccino.

to **vacillate** *vi.* 1. vacillare 2. (*fig.*) esitare.

vacillating *agg.* 1. vacillante 2. incostante, irresoluto.

vacillation *s.* 1. vacillamento 2. esitazione.

vacillatory *agg.* V. *vacillating.*

vacuity *s.* vacuità (*anche fig.*).

vacuous *agg.* 1. vacuo, vuoto 2. sciocco, ozioso.

vacuum *s.* vuoto pneumatico || — *cleaner*, aspirapolvere.

vagabond *s.* viandante, vagabondo.

vagary *s.* fantasticheria, capriccio.

vagrancy *s.* vagabondaggio, accattonaggio.

vagrant *agg. e s.* vagabondo.

vague *agg.* vago, impreciso.

vaguely *avv.* vagamente.

vagueness *s.* indeterminatezza.

vain *agg.* 1. vano, inutile 2. vanitoso.

vainglorious *agg.* vanaglorioso.

vainglory *s.* vanagloria.

vainly *avv.* 1. inutilmente 2. vanitosamente.

valance *s.* 1. drappeggio 2. cortina (*di un letto*).

valediction *s.* addio, commiato.

valedictory *agg.* d'addio, di saluto. ♦ **valedictory** *s.* discorso d'addio.

valence *s.* (*chim.*) valenza.

valerian *s.* valeriana.

valet *s.* valletto.

valiant *agg.* valoroso, prode.

valid *agg.* valido, legittimo.

to **validate** *vt.* render valido, convalidare.

validity *s.* validità.

validly *avv.* validamente.

valley *s.* valle, vallata.

valorization *s.* valorizzazione.

to **valorize** *vt.* valorizzare.

valour *s.* valore.

valuable *agg.* 1. di valore, prezioso 2. valutabile.

valuation *s.* 1. valutazione, stima 2. considerazione.

value *s.* 1. valore, prezzo 2. (*fig.*) pregio, importanza || — *in exchange*, valore effettivo.

to **value** *vt.* 1. valutare, stimare 2. considerare, dar valore.

valueless *agg.* di nessun valore.

valuer *s.* estimatore.

valve *s.* 1. valvola 2. valva.

vamp¹ *s.* 1. rappezzamento 2. (*mus.*) accompagnamento.

vamp² *s.* (*gergo*) donna fatale.

vampire *s.* vampiro.

van *s.* 1. furgone 2. vagone ferroviario || *luggage* —, bagagliaio; *prison* —, cellulare.

Vandal *agg. e s.* vandalo.

Vandalic *agg.* vandalico.

vandalism *s.* vandalismo.

vane *s.* 1. banderuola 2. pala (*di mulino a vento ecc.*).

vanguard *s.* avanguardia (*anche fig.*).

vanilla *s.* vaniglia.

to **vanish** *vi.* svanire, sparire.

vanishing *s.* il dileguarsi, lo sparire.

vanity *s.* vanità || — *case*, borsetta col necessario per il trucco.

to **vanquish** *vt.* vincere, conquistare.

vanquisher *s.* conquistatore

vantage *s.* vantaggio.

vapid *agg.* insulso.

vaporization *s.* evaporazione. ♦ to **vaporize** *vt.* far evaporare. ♦ to **vaporize** *vi.* 1. evaporare 2. (*fig.*) volatilizzarsi.

vaporizer *s.* vaporizzatore.

vaporous *agg.* vaporoso.

vapour *s.* vapore, esalazione.

to **vapour** *vi.* 1. evaporare 2. (*fig.*) vantarsi.

vapouring *agg.* che evapora. ♦ **vapouring** *s.* vanteria.

vapourish *agg.* 1. pieno di vapori 2. depresso.

vapours *s. pl.* depressione (*sing.*), allucinazioni.

variability *s.* variabilità, mutevolezza.

variable *agg.* variabile, incostante.

variance *s.* 1. variazione 2. disaccordo.

variant *agg.* differente, contrastante. ♦ **variant** *s.* variante.

variation *s.* variazione, modificazione. ♦ **variations** *s. pl.* (*mat.*) variazioni.

varicoloured *agg.* variopinto.

varicose *agg.* varicoso.

varied *agg.* 1. vario, variato 2. variopinto.

to **variegate** *vt.* variegare, screziare.

variegated *agg.* variegato, screziato.

variegation *s.* screziatura.

variety *s.* varietà, diversità || — **show** (*teat.*), spettacolo di varietà.

various *agg.* alcuni, molti (*pl.*).

variously *avv.* variamente.

varnish *s.* 1. vernice, lacca 2. (*fig.*) apparenza, aspetto esteriore || **nail** —, smalto per unghie.

to **varnish** *vt.* 1. verniciare, laccare 2. (*fig.*) mascherare.

varnishing *s.* verniciatura, laccatura.

to **vary** *vt.* variare, cambiare. ♦ to **vary** *vi.* essere differente.

vase *s.* vaso.

vaseline *s.* vaselina.

vassal *s.* vassallo.

vassallage *s.* vassallaggio.

vast *agg.* ampio, immenso, vasto.

vastness *s.* vastità.

vat *s.* tino, tinozza.

vault¹ *s.* 1. volta, soffitto a volta 2. cantina 3. sepolcro 4. (*fig.*) volta celeste.

vault² *s.* volteggio.

to **vault** *vi.* volteggiare. ♦ to **vault** *vt.* saltare.

vaulting *s.* 1. il costruire volte 2. costruzione a volta.

to **vaunt** *vt.* vantare. ♦ to **vaunt** *vi.* vantarsi.

veal *s.* (*cuc.*) vitello.

vector *s.* vettore.

vectorial *agg.* vettoriale.

veer *s.* 1. cambiamento di direzione 2. (*mar.*) virata.

to **veer** *vi.* 1. cambiare direzione 2. (*mar.*) virare.

vegetable *agg.* vegetale. ♦ **vegetable** *s.* 1. vegetale 2. ortaggio. ♦ **vegetables** *s. pl.* verdura (*sing.*).

vegetal *agg.* vegetale.

vegetarian *agg.* e *s.* vegetariano.

to **vegetate** *vi.* vegetare (*anche fig.*).

vegetation *s.* 1. vegetazione 2. il vegetare.

vegetative *agg.* vegetativo.

vehemence *s.* veemenza.

vehement *agg.* veemente, impetuoso.

vehicle *s.* veicolo.

veil *s.* 1. velo, cortina 2. (*fig.*) apparenza, pretesto.

to **veil** *vt.* 1. velare, coprire 2. (*fig.*) dissimulare, nascondere.

veiling *s.* 1. il velare 2. velo, schermo.

vein *s.* (*anat.; geol.; fig.*) vena 2. venatura, nervatura.

to **vein** *vt.* venare, coprire di venature.

veined *agg.* 1. venato 2. con venature, nervature.

velleity *s.* velleità.

velocipede *s.* velocipede.

velocity *s.* velocità.

velvet *agg.* di velluto, vellutato. ♦ **velvet** *s.* velluto.

velvety *agg.* vellutato, morbido.

venal *agg.* venale.

venality *s.* venalità.

to **vend** *vt.* vendere.

vendor *s.* venditore.

to **veneer** *vt.* 1. impiallacciare 2. (*fig.*) mascherare.

veneer, veneering *s.* 1. impiallacciatura 2. (*fig.*) maschera, vernice.

venerable *agg.* venerabile.

to **venerate** *vt.* venerare.

veneration *s.* venerazione.

venereal *agg.* venereo.

Venetian *agg.* e *s.* veneziano || —

blinds, shades, persiana alla veneziana.

vengeance *s.* vendetta || *to take — on so.,* vendicarsi di qu.

vengeful *agg.* vendicativo, vendicatore.

venial *agg.* veniale.

venom *s.* veleno (*di animali*).

venomous *agg.* velenoso.

venous *agg.* **1.** venoso **2.** con nervature.

vent[1] *s.* spacco, apertura (*di abito*).

vent[2] *s.* **1.** sbocco, apertura, foro **2.** (*fig.*) sfogo || *to give — to,* dar libero corso a.

to vent *vt.* **1.** svuotare, esalare **2.** (*fig.*) sfogare.

to ventilate *vt.* **1.** ventilare **2.** (*fig.*) discutere, rendere manifesto.

ventilation *s.* **1.** ventilazione **2.** discussione.

ventral *agg.* ventrale, addominale.

ventricle *s.* ventricolo.

ventriloquism *s.* ventriloquio.

ventriloquist *s.* ventriloquo.

venture *s.* **1.** avventura, azzardo **2.** (*comm.*) speculazione.

to venture *vt.* avventurare, arrischiare. ♦ **to venture** *vi.* avventurarsi, arrischiarsi.

venturer *s.* avventuriero.

venue *s.* sede giurisdizionale.

veracious *agg.* verace.

veracity *s.* veracità.

veranda(h) *s.* veranda.

verb *s.* verbo.

verbal *agg.* **1.** verbale **2.** orale, a parole.

verbally *avv.* verbalmente, oralmente.

verbiage *s.* verbosità.

verbose *agg.* verboso, prolisso

verdant *agg.* verdeggiante.

verdict *s.* verdetto.

verdigris *s.* verderame.

verge *s.* **1.** orlo, limite || *on the — of,* sul punto di **2.** bacchetta, verga.

to verge *vi.* **1.** confinare, essere contiguo, adiacente **2.** (*fig.*) rasentare: *to — on madness,* rasentare la pazzia.

verifiable *agg.* verificabile.

verification *s.* verifica.

verifier *s.* verificatore.

to verify *vt.* **1.** verificare, controllare **2.** (*giur.*) autenticare.

verily *avv.* in verità.

verisimilar *agg.* verosimile.

verisimilitude *s.* verosimiglianza.

verism *s.* verismo.

veritable *agg.* vero, genuino.

verity *s.* verità, realtà.

vermiform *agg.* vermiforme.

vermin *s. coll.* insetti parassiti.

verminous *agg.* infestato da parassiti.

vernacular *s.* vernacolo, dialetto nativo. ♦ **vernacular** *agg.* vernacolo, nativo.

versatile *agg.* versatile, multiforme.

versatility *s.* versatilità.

verse *s.* **1.** verso **2.** strofa **3.** componimento in versi.

versification *s.* versificazione.

to versify *vt.* e *vi.* **1.** comporre in versi **2.** narrare in versi.

version *s.* versione, traduzione.

vertebra *s.* (*pl. -ae*) vertebra.

vertebral *agg.* vertebrale.

vertebrate *agg.* e *s.* vertebrato.

vertex *s.* (*pl. -tices*) vertice, apice, sommità.

vertical *agg.* verticale. ♦ **vertical** *s.* piano verticale, verticale.

verticality *s.* posizione verticale, perpendicolarità.

very *agg.* **1.** vero e proprio, autentico **2.** (*uso enfatico*) esatto, stesso: *at that — moment,* in quello stesso istante. ♦ **very** *avv.* molto, assai.

vessel *s.* **1.** vaso, recipiente **2.** nave, vascello.

vest *s.* **1.** panciotto **2.** camiciola, davantino.

to vest *vt.* **1.** conferire, investire **2.** (*giur.*) assegnare **3.** parare (*di altari ecc.*). ♦ **to vest** *vi.* passare per eredità.

vestal *s.* vestale.

vestibule *s.* vestibolo, entrata, portico di chiesa.

vestige *s.* vestigio, traccia.

vestment *s.* veste (*spec. liturgica*).

vestry *s.* **1.** sagrestia **2.** assemblea parrocchiale.

vesture *s.* rivestimento, veste.

veteran *agg.* e *s.* veterano.

veterinary *agg.* e *s.* veterinario.

to vex *vt.* **1.** vessare, opprimere **2.** irritare.

vexation *s.* **1.** vessazione, oppressione **2.** irritazione.

vexatious *agg.* **1.** irritante, fastidioso **2.** (*giur.*) vessatorio.

vexed *agg.* **1.** vessato, oppresso **2.** irritato.

via *prep.* per, via, attraverso: — *air mail*, per via aerea.

viability *s.* vitalità.

viable *agg.* vitale.

viaduct *s.* viadotto.

vial *s.* fiala.

viand *s.* vivanda, cibo.

vibrant *agg.* vibrante, tremante.

to **vibrate** *vi.* vibrare, risuonare. ♦ to **vibrate** *vt.* far vibrare.

vibration *s.* vibrazione, tremolio.

vibrator *s.* vibratore.

vibratory *agg.* **1.** vibratorio **2.** vibrante.

vicar *s.* **1.** curato (*nella Chiesa d'Inghilterra*) **2.** vicario (*Chiesa Cattolica*).

vicariate *s.* vicariato.

vice[1] *s.* **1.** immoralità, depravazione **2.** vizio.

vice[2] *s.* (*mecc.*) morsa.

vice[3] *s.* sostituto, vice.

vice[4] *prep.* in luogo di.

viceroy *s.* viceré.

vicinity *s.* **1.** vicinanza, prossimità **2.** affinità.

vicious *agg.* **1.** vizioso, immorale **2.** maligno **3.** bizzarro (*di animali*) **4.** difettoso, scorretto.

vicissitude *s.* vicissitudine.

victim *s.* vittima.

victor *s.* vincitore.

victorious *agg.* vittorioso.

victory *s.* vittoria.

to **victual** *vt.* vettovagliare, approvvigionare. ♦ to **victual** *vi.* approvvigionarsi.

victualling *s.* vettovagliamento, approvvigionamento.

victuals *s. pl.* vettovaglie, viveri.

to **vie** *vi.* gareggiare.

view *s.* **1.** vista, sguardo **2.** veduta, panorama **3.** opinione **4.** scopo, mira **5.** (*giur.*) sopralluogo || *point of* —, punto di vista; — *-finder* (*foto*), mirino.

to **view** *vt.* **1.** guardare attentamente **2.** esaminare.

viewer *s.* **1.** chi guarda **2.** telespettatore **3.** ispettore.

viewless *agg.* **1.** senza vista (*di casa ecc.*) **2.** invisibile.

viewpoint *s.* punto di vista.

vigil *s.* veglia.

vigilance *s.* vigilanza.

vigilant *agg.* vigilante, vigile.

vigorous *agg.* vigoroso, forte.

Viking *s.* vichingo.

vigour *s.* vigore, energia.

vigorously *avv.* vigorosamente.

vile *agg.* vile, spregevole.

vileness *s.* viltà, bassezza.

to **vilify** *vt.* diffamare.

villa *s.* villa.

village *s.* villaggio, paese.

villager *s.* abitante di villaggio.

villain *s.* furfante, scellerato.

villainous *agg.* scellerato, infame.

villainy *s.* scelleratezza.

to **vindicate** *vt.* **1.** rivendicare **2.** giustificare, difendere.

vindication *s.* **1.** rivendicazione **2.** giustificazione, difesa.

vindictive *agg.* vendicativo.

vine *s.* vite || — *-leaf*, pampino; — *-dresser*, vignaiuolo.

vinegar *s.* aceto.

vinery *s.* serra per viti.

vineyard *s.* vigneto, vigna.

vintage *s.* **1.** vendemmia **2.** annata.

vintager *s.* vendemmiatore.

vintner *s.* vinaio.

to **violate** *vt.* **1.** violare, trasgredire **2.** profanare.

violation *s.* **1.** violazione, trasgressione **2.** profanazione.

violator *s.* **1.** violatore, trasgressore **2.** profanatore.

violence *s.* violenza, veemenza.

violent *agg.* violento, impetuoso.

violet *agg.* violetto, viola. ♦ **violet** *s.* viola mammola.

violin *s.* violino.

violoncellist *s.* violoncellista.

viper *s.* vipera (*anche fig.*).

virgin *agg.* e *s.* vergine.

virginal *agg.* verginale.

virginity *s.* verginità.

virile *agg.* virile.

virility *s.* virilità.

virtual *agg.* virtuale, effettivo.

virtuality *s.* potenzialità, virtualità.

virtue *s.* **1.** virtù, moralità, forza d'animo **2.** qualità, merito.

virtuosity *s.* virtuosismo.

virtuous *agg.* virtuoso, morale.

virulence *s.* virulenza.

virulent *agg.* virulento.

virus *s.* virus.

visa *s.* visto consolare.

to **visa** *vt.* vistare (*un passaporto*).

visceral *agg.* viscerale.

viscid *agg.* viscido.

viscidity *s.* viscidità.

viscose *s.* viscosa.

viscosity *s.* viscosità.

viscount *s.* visconte.

viscous *agg.* viscoso.

visibility s. visibilità.

visible agg. visibile, evidente, manifesto.

vision s. 1. visione, immaginazione 2. vista, capacità visiva.

visional agg. irreale.

visionary s. visionario.

visit s. visita: *to pay a* —, fare una visita.

to visit vt. e vi. visitare, fare una visita.

visitation s. 1. visita ufficiale 2. castigo divino.

visitor s. visitatore, ospite.

visor s. visiera.

visual agg. visuale, visivo.

to visualize vt. 1. rendere visibile 2. prospettare. ♦ **to visualize** vi. diventare visibile.

vital agg. vitale, essenziale.

vitality s. vitalità.

to vitalize vt. vivificare.

vitals s. pl. organi vitali.

vitamin s. vitamina.

to vitiate vt. 1. viziare 2. (giur.) invalidare.

vitiation s. 1. corruzione 2. (giur.) l'invalidare.

viticulture s. viticoltura.

vitreous agg. vitreo.

vitrifiable agg. vetrificabile.

vitrification s. vetrificazione.

to vitrify vt. vetrificare. ♦ **to vitrify** vi. vetrificarsi.

vitriol s. vetriolo.

to vituperate vt. vituperare.

vituperation s. invettiva, biasimo.

vivacious agg. vivace, vispo.

vivacity s. vivacità, brio.

vivid agg. 1. vivace, vigoroso 2. vivido, colorito.

to vivify vt. vivificare, animare.

viviparous agg. viviparo.

vivisection s. vivisezione.

vixen s. 1. volpe femmina 2. megera.

vocabulary s. vocabolario.

vocal agg. vocale.

vocalization s. vocalizzazione.

to vocalize vt. e vi. vocalizzare.

vocation s. 1. vocazione 2. attitudine, inclinazione 3. professione.

vocational agg. professionale.

vocative agg. e s. vocativo.

vociferous agg. clamoroso, vociferante.

vogue s. voga, moda.

voice s. voce || *with one* —, all'unanimità.

to voice vt. esprimere, dire.

voiced agg. 1. dalla voce: *deep* —, dalla voce profonda 2. sonoro.

voiceless agg. senza voce, muto.

void agg. 1. vuoto 2. privo 3. (giur.) nullo. ♦ **void** s. il vuoto.

to void vt. 1. vuotare, liberare 2. abrogare.

volatile agg. 1. volatile, alato 2. (fig.) incostante. ♦ **volatile** s. 1. volatile 2. (chim.) sostanza volatile.

to volatilize vt. volatilizzare. ♦ **to volatilize** vi. volatilizzarsi.

volcano s. vulcano.

volley s. 1. scarica, raffica, salva || — -*ball*, palla a volo.

voltage s. (elettr.) voltaggio, tensione.

voltameter s. voltametro.

volubility s. speditezza (di eloquio), loquacità.

voluble agg. spedito (di eloquio), loquace.

volume s. 1. volume 2. tomo, libro 3. massa.

volumetric(al) agg. volumetrico.

voluminous agg. 1. in molti volumi 2. (fig.) fecondo (di scrittore) 3. voluminoso.

voluntarily avv. volontariamente.

voluntary agg. 1. volontario, spontaneo 2. voluto, fatto di proposito 3. mantenuto da contributi non statali. ♦ **voluntary** s. azione volontaria.

volunteer s. volontario.

to volunteer vi. 1. offrirsi volontariamente 2. arruolarsi volontario.

voluptuary agg. 1. voluttuario 2. voluttuoso.

voluptuous agg. voluttuoso, sensuale.

voluptuousness s. voluttà, sensualità.

volute s. voluta, spirale.

vomit s. vomito.

to vomit vt. e vi. vomitare (anche fig.).

voracious agg. ingordo, vorace.

vortex s. vortice, gorgo.

vortical agg. vorticoso.

votary s. seguace, devoto.

vote s. voto, votazione.

to vote vt. e vi. votare.

voter s. elettore.

votive agg. votivo.

to vouch vt. e vi. 1. attestare, garantire 2. (giur.) citare come garante.

voucher s. **1.** testimone **2.** documento giustificativo.

to vouchsafe vt. concedere.

vow s. voto.

to vow vi. fare un voto.

vowel s. vocale.

voyage s. viaggio (spec. per via d'acqua) || outward —, viaggio di andata; home —, viaggio di ritorno.

to voyage vi. fare una traversata, navigare.

vulcanization s. vulcanizzazione.

vulgar agg. volgare, triviale.

vulgarism, vulgarity s. volgarità.

to vulgarize vt. **1.** rendere volgare **2.** divulgare.

vulnerability s. vulnerabilità.

vulnerable agg. vulnerabile.

vulture s. avvoltoio.

W

to wabble vi. vacillare, traballare.

wad s. **1.** tampone **2.** imbottitura **3.** rotolo (di banconote).

to wad vt. **1.** tamponare **2.** imbottire.

wadable agg. guadabile.

wadding s. ovatta.

waddle s. andatura ondeggiante.

to waddle vi. camminare ondeggiando.

wade s. guado.

to wade vt. guadare. ◆ **to wade** vi. procedere faticosamente.

wader s. **1.** chi passa a guado **2.** (zool.) trampoliere. ◆ **waders** s. pl. stivaloni impermeabili.

wading s. il guadare.

wafer s. **1.** cialda **2.** disco adesivo.

waft s. soffio.

to waft vt. sospingere. ◆ **to waft** vi. fluttuare.

wag s. **1.** cenno **2.** scodinzolio.

to wag vt. scuotere. ◆ **to wag** vi. scuotersi || to have a wagging tongue, avere la lingua troppo lunga.

to wage vt. intraprendere (guerra).

to wager vt. e vi. scommettere.

wages s. pl. salario (sing.) || —-earner, salariato.

to waggle V. to wag.

wag(g)on s. carro || tea- —, car-

rello da tè.

waif s. relitto (anche fig.).

wail s. gemito.

to wail vt. e vi. gemere.

wainscot s. rivestimento in legno.

to wainscot vt. rivestire in legno.

waist s. cintola.

waistband s. cintura.

waistbelt s. cinturone.

waistcoat s. panciotto.

wait s. **1.** attesa **2.** agguato.

to wait vt. e vi. (for so., sthg.) aspettare (qu., qc.) || to — on, servire.

waiter s. **1.** cameriere **2.** vassoio.

waiting s. attesa || — -room, sala d'aspetto; to keep —, fare aspettare.

waitress s. cameriera.

o waive vt. rinunciare a, mettere da parte.

wake¹ s. **1.** scia **2.** pista.

wake² s. **1.** risveglio **2.** veglia (funebre).

to wake (waked e woke, waked, woke(n)) vt. svegliare. ◆ **to wake (waked e woke, waked, woke(n))** vi. svegliarsi.

wakeful agg. sveglio.

wakefulness s. veglia.

to waken V. to wake.

wakening s. risveglio.

waking agg. sveglio. ◆ **waking** s. **1.** risveglio **2.** veglia.

walk s. **1.** passeggiata **2.** andatura **3.** (fig.) rango || to take a —, fare una passeggiata.

to walk vi. passeggiare, andare a piedi || to — off, andarsene.

walker s. camminatore.

walkie-talkie s. (radio) trasmettitore-ricevitore portatile.

walking s. il camminare || — tour, escursione a piedi.

walkover s. facile vittoria.

wall s. muro || — paper, carta da parato; main —, muro maestro.

to wall vt. circondare di mura || to — up, murare.

wallet s. portafoglio.

wall-eye s. glaucoma.

Walloon agg. e s. vallone.

to wallop vt. **1.** bastonare **2.** percuotere, sculacciare.

wallow s. pantano.

to wallow vi. sguazzare.

walnut s. noce.

walrus s. tricheco.

waltz s. valzer.

to **waltz** *vi.* ballare il valzer.

wan *agg.* pallido.

to **wan** *vi.* impallidire.

wand *s.* bacchetta magica.

wander *s.* vagabondaggio.

to **wander** *vi.* 1. vagare 2. vaneggiare.

wanderer *s.* vagabondo.

wandering *agg.* 1. errante 2. delirante. ♦ **wandering** *s.* 1. vagabondaggio 2. delirio.

wane *s.* declino.

to **wane** *vi.* 1. declinare 2. decrescere 3. essere in fase calante.

to **wangle** *vt.* ottenere con intrighi.

want *s.* 1. mancanza 2. bisogno: *to be in — of*, aver bisogno di.

to **want** *vt.* 1. volere 2. aver bisogno di 3. mancare.

wanted *agg.* ricercato: *to be — by the police*, essere ricercato dalla polizia.

wanting *prep.* senza, in mancanza di.

wanton *agg.* 1. licenzioso 2. capriccioso 3. arbitrario 4. lascivo.

to **wanton** *vi.* 1. scherzare 2. comportarsi dissolutamente.

wantonness *s.* 1. dissolutezza 2. capriccio.

war *s.* guerra: *— Office*, Ministero della Guerra.

to **war** *vi.* guerreggiare.

warble *s.* trillo.

to **warble** *vt.* e *vi.* trillare.

warbling *agg.* melodioso. ♦ **warbling** *s.* gorgheggio.

ward *s.* 1. guardia 2. reparto 3. rione 4. tutela 5. pupillo.

to **ward** *vt.* parare: *to — off a blow*, parare un colpo.

warden *s.* 1. guardiano 2. direttore 3. governatore.

wardenship *s.* carica di direttore, governatore.

warder *s.* 1. guardiano 2. carceriere.

wardrobe *s.* guardaroba.

wardroom *s.* (*mar.*) quadrato ufficiali.

wardship *s.* tutela.

ware *agg.* conscio, circospetto.

to **ware** *vt.* fare attenzione a.

wares *s. pl.* 1. articoli 2. vasellame (*sing.*).

warehouse *s.* magazzino.

to **warehouse** *vt.* depositare in magazzino.

warehouseman *s.* 1. magazziniere 2. commerciante all'ingrosso.

warfare *s.* operazione bellica.

warfaring *agg.* bellicoso.

warily *avv.* cautamente.

wariness *s.* cautela.

warlike *agg.* guerriero.

warlikeness *s.* bellicosità.

warlock *s.* stregone.

warm *agg.* 1. caldo 2. animato.

to **warm** *vt.* 1. scaldare 2. animare. ♦ to **warm** *vi.* 1. scaldarsi 2. animarsi.

warmer *s.* riscaldatore.

warm-hearted *agg.* bonario, cordiale.

warming *s.* riscaldamento.

warmonger *s.* guerrafondaio.

warmth *s.* calore.

to **warn** *vt.* avvertire: *to — off*, invitare ad allontanarsi.

warning *s.* (pre)avviso ‖ *— light*, spia luminosa.

warp *s.* 1. ordito 2. deformazione.

to **warp** *vt.* 1. curvare 2. (*fig.*) alterare. ♦ to **warp** *vi.* 1. curvarsi 2. (*fig.*) alterarsi.

warpath *s.* sentiero di guerra.

warping *s.* deformazione, pervertimento.

warrant *s.* 1. garanzia, garante 2. (*giur.; comm.*) ordine, autorizzazione.

to **warrant** *vt.* 1. garantire 2. giustificare.

warrantable *agg.* 1. giustificabile 2. legittimo.

warrantee *s.* chi riceve una garanzia.

warranter, -tor *s.* garante.

warranty *s.* 1. garanzia 2. autorizzazione.

warrior *s.* guerriero.

warship *s.* nave da guerra.

wart *s.* verruca.

wartime *s.* tempo di guerra.

wary *agg.* cauto.

was V. *to be.*

wash *s.* 1. lavata 2. bucato 3. sciacquio 4. brodaglia 5. mano (*di colore*).

to **wash** *vt.* 1. lavare 2. bagnare 3. gettare. ♦ to **wash** *vi.* 1. lavarsi 2. essere lavabile ‖ *to — up*, rigovernare (*le stoviglie*); *to — over*, sommergere.

washable *agg.* lavabile.

washbasin *s.* catino.

washboard *s.* asse per lavare.

washer *s.* 1. lavandaio 2. (*mecc.*) lavatrice 3. (*mecc.*) rondella.

washerwoman s. lavandaia.

washhouse s. lavanderia.

washing s. **1.** lavaggio **2.** bucato **3.** risciacquatura || — -machine, lavatrice.

whashout s. erosione, dilatamento.

washroom s. **1.** lavanderia **2.** gabinetto.

washstand s. lavabo.

washy agg. **1.** annacquato **2.** scialbo.

wasp s. vespa.

waspish agg. pungente.

waspishness s. irascibilità.

wastage s. logorio.

waste agg. **1.** deserto **2.** di scarto. ♦ **waste** s. **1.** spreco **2.** scarto **3.** deserto || — -basket, cestino per rifiuti; — -paper, carta straccia.

to waste vt. **1.** consumare **2.** sprecare **3.** rovinare. ♦ **to waste** vi. **1.** consumarsi **2.** rovinarsi.

wasteful agg. **1.** rovinoso **2.** prodigo.

waster s. dissipatore.

wasting agg. **1.** logorante **2.** devastante. ♦ **wasting** s. **1.** sciupio **2.** deperimento **3.** devastazione.

watch s. **1.** orologio (da polso) **2.** guardia || — -fire, fuoco di bivacco; to be on the —, stare in guardia.

to watch vt. **1.** osservare **2.** stare a guardia di. ♦ **to watch** vi. **1.** vegliare **2.** aspettare.

watcher s. **1.** spettatore **2.** sorvegliante.

watchful agg. attento.

watchfulness s. **1.** vigilanza **2.** cautela.

watchmaker s. orologiaio.

watchman s. guardia (notturna).

watchword s. parola d'ordine.

water s. acqua || to hold —, non fare acqua, (fig.) essere logico; — -bottle, borraccia; — -colour, acquarello; — -colourist, acquarellista; — -closet, gabinetto; — -gate, chiusa; — -line, linea di galleggiamento; — -meadow, marcita; — -polo, pallanuoto; drinking —, acqua potabile.

to water vt. **1.** bagnare **2.** diluire **3.** abbeverare **4.** secernere || to make one's mouth —, far venire l'acquolina in bocca. ♦ **to water** vi. **1.** abbeverarsi **2.** riempirsi d'acqua.

waterfall s. cascata.

watering s. **1.** annaffiamento **2.** diluizione **3.** abbeverarsi **4.** rifornimento d'acqua **5.** secrezione || — -can, — -pot, annaffiatoio.

waterman s. (pl. -men) barcaiolo.

watermark s. **1.** filigrana **2.** indicatore di livello **3.** livello d'acqua.

watermelon s. anguria.

waterproof agg. e s. impermeabile.

to waterproof vt. impermeabilizzare.

watershed s. **1.** spartiacque **2.** bacino idrico.

watertight agg. stagno.

waterway s. canale navigabile.

waterworks s. pl. impianto idrico (sing.).

watery agg. **1.** acquoso **2.** lacrimoso.

wattle s. **1.** fascina **2.** vimine.

wave s. **1.** onda, ondata **2.** cenno (della mano).

to wave vi. **1.** ondeggiare **2.** far cenno (con la mano). ♦ **to wave** vt. **1.** far ondeggiare **2.** ondulare **3.** chiamare (con un cenno di mano).

waved agg. ondulato.

wave-length s. lunghezza d'onda.

waveless agg. liscio.

wavelet s. piccola onda.

wavelike agg. ondeggiante.

to waver vi. vacillare.

wavering s. **1.** oscillazione **2.** esitazione.

wavily avv. a onde.

waviness s. ondulazione.

waving s. **1.** ondeggiamento, ondulazione **2.** sventolio **3.** cenno.

wavy agg. **1.** ondulato **2.** ondeggiante.

wax s. **1.** cera **2.** paraffina.

to wax[1] vt. incerare.

to wax[2] vi. **1.** crescere **2.** aumentare.

waxen agg. di, come cera.

way s. **1.** via **2.** maniera **3.** punto di vista **4.** stato || to make —, far posto; this —, per di qua; in a —, in un certo senso; by the —, tra parentesi; one —, senso unico; out of the —, fuori mano.

waybill s. lista dei passeggeri.

wayfarer s. viandante.

to waylay vt. tendere un agguato a.

wayside s. margine della strada.

wayward agg. **1.** indocile **2.** capriccioso.

waywardness s. ostinazione.

we pron. sogg. noi.

weak *agg.* 1. debole 2. diluito.

to weaken *vi.* indebolirsi. ◆ to weaken *vt.* indebolire.

weakling *s.* persona debole.

weakly *agg.* debole.

weakness *s.* debolezza.

weal¹ *s.* benessere, prosperità.

weal² *s.* livido.

wealth *s.* ricchezza.

wealthy *agg.* ricco.

to wean *vt.* 1. svezzare 2. togliere il vizio a.

weaning *s.* svezzamento.

weapon *s.* arma.

wear *s.* 1. uso, usura 2. durata 3. abbigliamento.

to wear (wore, worn) *vt.* 1. indossare 2. logorare 3. stancare || *to — out,* logorare, stancare. ◆ to wear (wore, worn) *vi.* 1. logorarsi 2. stancarsi 3. durare || *to — out,* logorarsi, stancarsi.

wearily *avv.* stancamente.

weariness *s.* 1. stanchezza 2. tedio.

wearing *agg.* 1. logorante 2. da indossare. ◆ wearing *s.* 1. logorio 2. l'indossare.

wearisome *agg.* 1. faticoso 2. tedioso.

weary *agg.* 1. stanco 2. annoiato.

to weary *vt.* 1. affaticare 2. annoiare. ◆ to weary *vi.* 1. affaticarsi 2. annoiarsi.

weasel *s.* donnola.

weather *s.* tempo (*atmosferico*) || *— -glass,* barometro; *— report,* bollettino meteorologico.

to weather *vt.* 1. esporre all'aria 2. superare || *to — a storm,* resistere a una burrasca. ◆ to weather *vi.* alterarsi.

weathercock *s.* banderuola.

weathering *s.* alterazione (*di tempo*).

weave *s.* tessuto.

to weave (wove, woven) *vt.* 1. tessere, intrecciare 2. (*fig.*) ideare.

weaver *s.* tessitore.

weaving *s.* 1. tessitura 2. orditura.

web *s.* 1. tela 2. (*fig.*) trama 3. membrana || *cob —,* ragnatela.

to wed *vt.* sposare. ◆ to wed *vi.* sposarsi.

wedding *s.* nozze (*pl.*) || *—-breakfast,* rinfresco di nozze; *— -ring,* fede nuziale.

wedge *s.* cuneo.

to wedge *vt.* 1. incuneare 2. fendere con cunei.

wedlock *s.* vincolo matrimoniale.

Wednesday *s.* mercoledì.

wee *agg.* minuscolo || *a — bit,* un tantino.

weed *s.* erbaccia. ◆ weeds *s. pl.* gramaglie.

to weed *vt.* 1. sarchiare 2. estirpare.

weeding *s.* sarchiatura.

week *s.* settimana || *today —,* oggi a otto; *— in — out,* una settimana dopo l'altra.

weekday *s.* giorno feriale.

week-end *s.* fine settimana.

weekly *agg.* e *s.* settimanale. ◆ weekly *avv.* settimanalmente.

weep *s.* pianto.

to weep (wept, wept) *vt.* e *vi.* 1. piangere 2. trasudare || *to — out,* piangere disperatamente.

weeper *s.* 1. chi piange 2. velo, nastro di lutto.

weeping *s.* 1. pianto 2. trasudamento.

weft *s.* trama (*di tessuto*).

to weigh *vt.* e *vi.* 1. pesare 2. (*fig.*) ponderare || *to — down,* piegare; *to — anchor* (*mar.*), levar l'ancora.

weigh-house *s.* pesa pubblica.

weighing *s.* pesatura || *-machine,* pesa.

weight *s.* 1. peso 2. importanza || *to put on —,* ingrassare.

to weight *vt.* appesantire, caricare.

weightiness *s.* 1. pesantezza 2. (*fig.*) importanza.

weightless *agg.* senza peso.

weighty *agg.* 1. pesante 2. (*fig.*) importante.

weir *s.* chiusa, diga.

weird *agg.* 1. fatale 2. misterioso.

welcome *agg.* gradito. ◆ welcome *s.* benvenuto.

to welcome *vt.* dare il benvenuto a, gradire.

to weld *vt.* saldare. ◆ to weld *vi.* saldarsi.

welding *s.* saldatura.

welfare *s.* benessere || *— contributions,* oneri previdenziali; *— state,* stato assistenziale; *— work,* assistenza sociale.

well¹ *s.* 1. fonte, pozzo 2. tromba delle scale.

well² *avv.* e *s.* bene || *as —,* pure; *as — as,* oltre a, oltre che; *to be —,* star bene; *to get —,* guarire.

to well *vi.* sgorgare.

well-advised *agg.* saggio.

well-being *s.* benessere.

well-bred *agg.* educato.
well-doing *s.* buona condotta.
well-done *agg.* (*cuc.*) ben cotto.
well-meaning *agg.* ben intenzionato.
well-off *agg.* agiato.
well-read *agg.* colto, ben educato.
well-timed *agg.* opportuno.
well-to-do *agg.* agiato.
Welsh *agg.* gallese.
Welshman *s.* gallese.
went V. *to go.*
wept V. *to weep.*
were V. *to be* || *as it —,* per così dire.
west *agg.* occidentale. ♦ **west** *avv.* a, verso ovest. ♦ **west** *s.* ovest.
westerly *agg.* 1. dall'ovest 2. verso ovest. ♦ **westerly** *avv.* verso ovest.
western *agg.* occidentale.
westerner *s.* occidentale.
to westernize *vt.* occidentalizzare. ♦ **to westernize** *vi.* occidentalizzarsi.
westward *agg. e avv.* verso ovest.
westwards *avv.* verso ovest.
wet *agg.* 1. umido 2. piovoso || *— blanket,* guastafeste. ♦ **wet** *s.* 1. umidità 2. tempo piovoso.
to wet *vt.* bagnare. ♦ **to wet** *vi.* bagnarsi.
wet-nurse *s.* nutrice.
wetting *s.* bagnatura.
whale *s.* balena || *— -boat,* baleniera.
to whale *vi.* andare a caccia di balene.
whalebone *s.* stecca di balena.
whaler *s.* 1. baleniere 2. baleniera.
wharf *s.* banchina.
to wharf *vt.* attraccare.
what *agg.* 1. (*int.*) quale? quali? che? 2. (*rel.*) (quello) ... che 3. (*escl.*) che! ♦ **what** *pron.* 1. (*int.*) che?, che cosa? 2. (*rel.*) ciò che 3. (*escl.*) quanto! || *— for?,* perché mai?; *— is he?,* che cosa fa? ♦ **what** *inter.* come!
whatever *agg.* qualunque. ♦ **whatever** *pron.* qualunque cosa. ♦ **whatever** *avv.* affatto.
whatsoever V. *whatever.*
wheat *s.* grano.
to wheedle *vt.* lusingare.
wheel *s.* 1. ruota 2. volante || *wheels within wheels,* retroscena.
to wheel *vt.* 1. far ruotare 2. spingere (*su un veicolo a ruote*). ♦

to wheel *vi.* ruotare.
wheelbarrow *s.* carriola.
wheeze *s.* respiro affannoso.
to wheeze *vi.* ansimare.
whelp *s.* cucciolo.
when *avv. e cong.* quando.
whence *avv.* da dove.
whenever *avv.* tutte le volte che.
where *avv.* dove.
whereabout(s) *avv. e cong.* dove. ♦ **whereabout(s)** *s.* luogo.
whereas *cong.* mentre.
whereby *avv.* 1. (*int.*) come? 2. (*rel.*) per cui.
wherefore *avv.* 1. (*int.*) perché 2. (*rel.*) perciò.
wherein *avv.* 1. (*int.*) come? dove? 2. (*rel.*) in cui.
whereof *avv.* 1. (*int.*) di che? 2. (*rel.*) di cui.
whereon *avv.* 1. (*int.*) su che? 2. (*rel.*) su cui.
whereto *avv.* 1. (*int.*) verso dove? a che scopo? 2. (*rel.*) a cui.
whereupon *avv.* 1. (*int.*) su che? 2. (*rel.*) dopo di che.
wherever *avv.* dovunque.
whet *s.* 1. affilatura 2. (*fig.*) stimolante.
to whet *vt.* 1. affilare 2. stimolare.
whether *cong.* se || *— ... or, o...o.*
whey *s.* siero (*del latte*).
which *agg.* 1. (*int.*) quale?, quali? 2. (*rel.*) il, la quale, i, le quali. ♦ **which** *pron.* 1. (*int.*) quale?, quali?, chi? 2. (*rel.*) il, la quale, i, le quali; il che || *I cannot tell — is —,* non so distinguerli l'uno dall'altro.
whichever *agg.* qualunque. ♦ **whichever** *pron.* qualunque cosa.
whiff *s.* 1. soffio 2. sbuffo.
to whiff *vt. e vi.* 1. soffiare 2. emettere sbuffi.
whig *agg. e s.* (*pol. inglese*) liberale.
while *cong.* 1. mentre 2. sebbene. ♦ **while** *s.* momento || *once in a —,* una volta tanto; *the —,* frattanto.
to while *vt.* — *away the time,* ammazzare il tempo.
whilst V. *while.*
whim *s.* capriccio.
whimper *s.* 1. piagnucolio 2. uggiolio.
to whimper *vi.* 1. piagnucolare 2. uggiolare.
whimsical *agg.* stravagante.

whimsicality *s.* stravaganza.
whimsy *agg.* capriccioso. ◆ **whimsy** *s.* capriccio.
whine *s.* piagnisteo.
to whine V. *to whimper.*
whinny *s.* nitrito.
to whinny *vi.* nitrire.
whip *s.* frusta.
to whip *vt.* 1. frustare 2. frullare. ◆ **to whip** *vi.* precipitarsi || *to — away*, partire improvvisamente; *to — out*, pronunciare con violenza, tirar fuori.
whipper-snapper *s.* gradasso.
whirl *s.* 1. vortice 2. *(fig.)* confusione.
to whirl *vt.* 1. far roteare 2. trascinare. ◆ **to whirl** *vi.* 1. roteare 2. correr via 3. *(fig.)* esser confuso.
whirligig *s.* giostra.
whirlpool *s.* gorgo.
whirlwind *s.* turbine.
whir(r) *s.* 1. ronzio 2. frullio *(d'ali)* 3. rombo *(di motore)*.
to whir(r) *vi.* 1. ronzare 2. frullare *(d'ali)* 3. rombare *(di motore)*.
whisk *s.* 1. scopino 2. frullino 3. movimento rapido.
to whisk *vt.* 1. spazzare 2. *(cuc.)* frullare 3. agitare. ◆ **to whisk** *vi.* guizzare via.
whisker *s.* 1. basetta 2. baffo.
whisper *s.* 1. mormorio 2. diceria.
to whisper *vt.* e *vi.* mormorare, bisbigliare.
whistle *s.* fischio.
to whistle *vt.* e *vi.* 1. fischiare 2. chiamare con un fischio.
whistler *s.* 1. chi fischia 2. marmotta canadese.
whit *s.* 1. inezia 2. atomo.
Whit *agg.* di Pentecoste.
white *agg.* e *s.* bianco || *— feather*, viltà; *— -livered*, codardo.
to whiten *vt.* e *vi.* imbiancare.
whitener *s.* 1. imbianchino 2. candeggiante.
whiteness *s.* bianchezza.
whitening *s.* 1. imbiancamento 2. candeggiamento.
whitesmith *s.* lattoniere.
whitethorn *s.* biancospino.
whitewash *s.* 1. calce 2. *(fig.)* riabilitazione.
to whitewash *vt.* 1. imbiancare 2. *(fig.)* riabilitare.
whitewasher *s.* imbianchino.
whitewashing *s.* 1. imbiancatura 2. riabilitazione.

whiting *s.* calce.
whitish *agg.* biancastro.
whitlow *s.* patereccio.
Whitsunday *s.* Pentecoste.
whiz *s.* sibilo.
who *pron.* 1. *(int.)* chi? 2. *(rel.)* il, la quale, i, le quali.
whoever *pron.* chiunque.
whole *agg.* tutto, intero. ◆ **whole** *s.* 1. il tutto, l'intero 2. il complesso || *as a —*, nell'insieme; *on the —*, nel complesso.
wholeness *s.* totalità.
wholesale *agg.* e *avv.* all'ingrosso. ◆ **wholesale** *s.* vendita all'ingrosso.
to wholesale *vt.* e *vi.* vendere all'ingrosso.
wholesaler *s.* venditore all'ingrosso.
wholesome *agg.* salutare.
wholly *avv.* totalmente.
whom *pron. compl.* di who.
whomever *pron. compl.* chiunque.
whomsoever V. *whomever.*
whoop *s.* ululato.
whooping-cough *s.* pertosse.
whorl *s.* spirale.
whose *pron.* 1. *(int.)* di chi? 2. *(rel.)* del, della quale, dei, delle quali.
whosoever *pron.* di chiunque.
whosoever V. *whoever.*
why *avv.* 1. *(int.)* perché? 2. *(rel.)* per cui. ◆ **why** *cong.* perché. ◆ **why** *inter.* perbacco.
wick *s.* lucignolo.
wicked *agg.* malvagio.
wickedness *s.* malvagità.
wicker *s.* vimine.
wicket *s.* 1. sportello 2. cancelletto.
wide *agg.* 1. largo 2. alto *(di tessuto)* 3. spalancato: *— open*, spalancato. ◆ **wide** *avv.* largamente.
wide-awake *agg.* 1. completamente sveglio 2. *(fig.)* vigilante.
widely *avv.* largamente.
to widen *vt.* allargare. ◆ **to widen** *vi.* allargarsi.
widespread *agg.* esteso.
widow *s.* vedova.
widower *s.* vedovo.
widowhood *s.* vedovanza.
width *s.* 1. larghezza 2. altezza *(di stoffa)*.
to wield *vt.* 1. brandire 2. esercitare *(autorità ecc.)*.
wife *s.* *(pl.* wives) moglie.
wig *s.* *(fam.)* sgridata.

wild *agg.* **1.** selvaggio, selvatico **2.** agitato **3.** pazzo **4.** avventato **5.** disordinato. ♦ **wild** *s.* deserto. ♦ **wild** *avv.* **1.** selvaggiamente **2.** impulsivamente **3.** sfrenatamente.

wilderness *s.* deserto.

wild-goose chase *s.* impresa vana, impossibile.

wildness *s.* **1.** selvatichezza **2.** furore.

wile *s.* astuzia.

wilful *agg.* **1.** ostinato **2.** premeditato.

wilfulness *s.* **1.** ostinazione **2.** premeditazione.

will *s.* **1.** volontà **2.** testamento || *free* —, libero arbitrio.

will *v.* ausiliare (*usato per il futuro*) *he* — *be*, egli sarà **2.** *v.* dif. volere: *I* — *go*, io voglio andare, io andrò (*futuro volitivo*).

to will *vt.* e *vi.* **1.** disporre **2.** lasciare per testamento.

willed *agg.* *strong* —, di forte volontà.

willing *agg.* **1.** volonteroso **2.** disposto || — *or not*, volente o nolente.

willingly *avv.* volentieri.

willow *s.* — -(*tree*), salice: *weeping* —, salice piangente.

willy-nilly *agg.* e *avv.* volente o nolente.

wily *agg.* astuto.

wimple *s.* **1.** soggolo **2.** arricciatura.

to win (won, won) *vt.* e *vi.* vincere || *to* — *back*, riconquistare.

wince *s.* sussulto.

to wince *vi.* trasalire.

winch *s.* **1.** argano **2.** manovella.

wind¹ *s.* **1.** vento **2.** respiro || *to get* — *of*, aver sentore di; — -*breaker*, giacca a vento; — -*cone*, manica a vento.

wind² *s.* **1.** svolta, curva **2.** giro di carica.

to wind¹ *vt.* **1.** fiutare **2.** sfiatare.

to wind² (wound, wound) *vt.* **1.** avvolgere **2.** (*una molla*) caricare **3.** girare || *to* — *off*, svolgere. ♦ **to wind (wound, wound)** *vi.* **1.** serpeggiare **2.** avvolgersi || *to* — *off*, svolgersi.

windbag *s.* **1.** otre (*di cornamusa*) **2.** (*fig.*) parolaio.

winder *s.* **1.** manovella **2.** avvolgitore.

winding *agg.* tortuoso. ♦ **winding** *s.* **1.** tortuosità **2.** tornante **3.** spira **4.** caricamento **5.** ritorcitura.

windlass *s.* argano.

windmill *s.* mulino a vento.

window *s.* finestra, finestrino || — -*dresser*, vetrinista; *French-* —, porta finestra.

windpipe *s.* trachea.

windscreen *s.* parabrezza || — *wiper*, tergicristallo.

windshield *s.* (*amer.*) parabrezza.

windward *agg.* contro vento. ♦ **windward** *s.* sopravvento.

windy *agg.* **1.** ventoso **2.** verboso.

wine *s.* vino.

wing *s.* **1.** ala **2.** battente (*di porta*) **3.** (*teat.*) quinta || *on the* —, in volo; *to take* —, spiccare il volo.

winged *agg.* alato.

wink *s.* **1.** battito di palpebre **2.** ammicco **3.** (*fig.*) istante.

to wink *vi.* **1.** battere le palpebre **2.** ammiccare **3.** scintillare.

winner *s.* vincitore.

winning *agg.* **1.** vincitore **2.** suadente. ♦ **winning** *s.* vittoria.

to winnow *vt.* e *vi.* vagliare.

winsome *agg.* incantevole.

winter *s.* inverno. ♦ **winter** *agg.* invernale.

to winter *vi.* svernare.

wintered *agg.* gelato.

winterly V. *wintry.*

wintriness *s.* rigore invernale.

wintry *agg.* invernale, fred.lo.

wipe *s.* **1.** asciugatura **2.** spolverata.

to wipe *vt.* **1.** asciugare **2.** strofinare || *to* — *off*, cancellare.

wiper *s.* **1.** chi pulisce **2.** strofinaccio.

wire *s.* **1.** filo metallico **2.** telegramma || — *netting*, rete metallica; *barbed* —, filo spinato.

to wire *vt.* e *vi.* **1.** legare con filo metallico **2.** prendere in trappola **3.** telegrafare.

wired *agg.* munito di filo metallico, di rete metallica.

wireless *agg.* senza fili. ♦ **wireless** *s.* radiotelegrafia.

to wireless *vt.* e *vi.* radiotelegrafare.

wire-puller *s.* intrigante, eminenza grigia.

wiry *agg.* **1.** di, simile a filo metallico **2.** (*fig.*) resistente.

wisdom *s.* saggezza.

wise *agg.* **1.** saggio **2.** edotto, informato.

wise *s.* modo, maniera.

wiseacre *s.* saccente.

wisely *avv.* saggiamente.

wish *s.* 1. desiderio 2. augurio: *best wishes*, i migliori auguri.

to **wish** *vt.* e *vi.* 1. desiderare 2. augurare || *I wish I were*, vorrei essere; *I wish I had*, vorrei avere; *I wish I could*, vorrei potere.

wisher *s.* 1. chi desidera 2. chi augura.

wishful *agg.* desideroso.

wishing *agg.* desideroso. ◆ **wishing** *s.* desiderio.

wistaria *s.* glicine.

wistful *agg.* 1. desideroso 2. pensoso.

wistfully *avv.* 1. con desiderio 2. pensosamente.

wistfulness *s.* 1. bramosia 2. raccoglimento.

wit *s.* 1. ingegno 2. spirito 3. persona di spirito || *to live by one's wits*, vivere di espedienti; *to be at one's wits' end*, non saper più cosa fare.

witch *s.* strega.

to **witch** *vt.* stregare.

witchcraft *s.* 1. stregoneria 2. fascino.

witch-doctor *s.* stregone.

witchery *s.* V. *witchcraft*.

witching *agg.* magico.

with *prep.* 1. con 2. presso 3. a causa di, per, da.

to **withdraw** (**withdrew, withdrawn**) *vt.* ritirare. ◆ to **withdraw** (**withdrew, withdrawn**) *vi.* ritirarsi.

withdrawal *s.* 1. ritirata, ritiro 2. ritrattazione.

withdrawn V. to *withdraw*.

withdrew V. to *withdraw*.

withe *s.* vimine.

to **wither** *vt.* e *vi.* avvizzire.

withering *s.* avvizzimento.

to **withhold** (**withheld, withheld**) *vt.* 1. trattenere 2. rifiutare 3. nascondere.

within *prep.* entro. ◆ **within** *avv.* dentro.

without *prep.* senza, senza di. ◆ **without** *cong.* senza (che). ◆ **without** *avv.* fuori.

to **withstand** (**withstood, withstood**) *vt.* resistere a, fronteggiare.

withstander *s.* oppositore.

withstood V. to *withstand*.

witness *s.* 1. testimone: *eye— —*, testimone oculare 2. testimonianza.

to **witness** *vt.* 1. essere testimone a 2. mostrare. ◆ to **witness** *vi.* testimoniare.

witticism *s.* arguzia.

wittily *avv.* spiritosamente.

wittiness *s.* spirito.

wittingly *avv.* consapevolmente.

witty *agg.* spiritoso.

wives V. *wife*.

wizard *s.* mago.

to **wobble** V. to *wabble*.

woe *s.* dolore.

woeful *agg.* doloroso.

woke V. to *wake*.

woken V. to *wake*.

wolf *s.* (*pl.* wolves) lupo || *she— —*, lupa.

to **wolf** *vt.* divorare.

wolfish *agg.* da lupo.

woman *s.* (*pl.* women) donna.

womanhood *s.* 1. femminilità 2. maturità (*della donna*) 3. condizione di donna.

womanish *agg.* 1. effeminato 2. femminile.

womankind *s.* le donne (*in genere*).

womanlike *agg.* femminile. ◆ **womanlike** *avv.* femminilmente.

womanliness *s.* femminilità.

womanly *agg.* femminile.

womb *s.* 1. ventre 2. grembo 3. utero.

women V. *woman*.

won V. to *win*.

wonder *s.* 1. prodigio 2. meraviglia.

to **wonder** *vi.* 1. domandarsi 2. stupirsi.

wonderful *agg.* meraviglioso.

wonderingly *avv.* con meraviglia.

wonderland *s.* paese delle meraviglie.

wondrous *agg.* mirabile.

wont *agg.* abituato. ◆ **wont** *s.* abitudine.

wonted *agg.* abituato, abituale.

to **woo** *vt.* corteggiare.

wood *s.* 1. bosco 2. legno || *— -cutter*, boscaiolo.

woodcock *s.* beccaccia.

woodcut *s.* 1. incisione su legno 2. xilografia.

wooden *agg.* di legno.

woodiness *s.* 1. boscosità 2. legnosità.

woodland *s.* terreno boscoso.

woodman *s.* 1. guardaboschi 2. tagialegna.

woodpecker *s.* picchio.

woodwork *s.* lavoro in legno.
woody *agg.* 1. boscoso 2. legnoso.
wooer *s.* corteggiatore.
wool *s.* 1. lana 2. peluria di animale || *cotton* —, ovatta.
wool(l)en *agg.* di lana. ◆ **wool(l)en** *s.* stoffa di lana.
woolly *agg.* 1. di lana, lanoso 2. (*fig.*) confuso.
word *s.* parola || *by* — *of mouth*, oralmente.
to word *vt.* esprimere.
wordiness *s.* verbosità.
wording *s.* espressione.
wordy *agg.* verboso.
wore V. *to wear.*
work *s.* lavoro || *out of* —, disoccupato. ◆ **works** *s. pl.* 1. meccanismo (*sing.*) 2. fabbrica, officina (*sing.*).
to work *vt.* 1. lavorare 2. far funzionare 3. dirigere || *to* — *in,* introdurre; *to* — *off,* liberarsi di; *to* — *out,* calcolare; *to* — *up,* elaborare. ◆ **to work** *vi.* 1. lavorare 2. funzionare 3. agitarsi.
workable *agg.* 1. eseguibile 2. lavorabile.
workaday *agg.* lavorativo.
workday *s.* giorno feriale.
worker *s.* lavoratore || *skilled* —, operaio qualificato.
workhouse *s.* ospizio di mendicità.
working *agg.* 1. laborioso 2. funzionante. ◆ **working** *s.* 1. lavorio 2. funzionamento 3. lavorazione || — *clothes,* abiti da lavoro; — *expenses,* spese d'esercizio.
workless *agg.* senza lavoro.
workman *s.* operaio.
workmanship *s.* 1. abilità 2. fattura.
workroom *s.* laboratorio.
workshop *s.* officina.
workwoman *s.* operaia.
world *s.* mondo: *all over the* —, in tutto il mondo.
worldliness *s.* 1. condizione terrena 2. mondanità.
worldly *agg.* 1. terreno 2. mondano.
world-wide *agg.* diffuso, noto in tutto il mondo.
worm *s.* verme || — *screw,* vite senza fine.
to worm *vt.* carpire || *to* — *one's way,* insinuarsi.
wormwood *s.* assenzio.
worn V. *to wear.* ◆ **worn** *agg.* 1.

consumato 2. indebolito || — *out,* logoro, (*fig.*) esausto.
worried *agg.* 1. preoccupato 2. tormentato.
worrier *s.* seccatore.
worrisome *agg.* 1. irritante 2. preoccupato.
worry *s.* 1. ansia 2. guaio.
to worry *vt.* tormentare. ◆ **to worry** *vi.* preoccuparsi.
worrying *agg.* 1. preoccupante 2. tormentoso.
worse *agg.* (*comp.* di bad e ill) peggiore, peggio. ◆ **worse** *avv.* e *s.* peggio || *all the* —, tanto peggio; *so much the* — *for,* tanto peggio per; *none the* —, ugualmente; — *and* —, di male in peggio.
worship *s.* adorazione.
to worship *vt.* e *vi.* adorare, venerare.
worshipper *s.* 1. adoratore 2. fedele.
worst *agg.* (*superl.* di bad e ill) peggiore, pessimo. ◆ **worst** *avv.* e *s.* peggio || *at (the)* —, nella peggiore delle ipotesi.
worsted *agg.* di lana pettinata.
worth *agg.* degno. ◆ **worth** *s.* valore.
worthily *avv.* degnamente.
worthiness *s.* 1. valore 2. dignità.
worthless *agg.* 1. senza valore 2. indegno.
worthlessness *s.* 1. mancanza di valore 2. indegnità.
worthy *agg.* degno, meritevole. ◆ **worthy** *s.* persona illustre.
would *v. dif.* 1. (ausiliare del *condiz.*) *he* — *go,* egli andrebbe 2. (*passato ind. imperfetto, congiuntivo, condiz.*) volere 3. (*imperfetto ind.*) solere: *he* — *come every day,* soleva venire ogni giorno.
would-be *agg.* sedicente.
wound *s.* ferita.
to wound *vt.* ferire.
wound V. *to wind.*
wove V. *to weave.*
woven V. *to weave.*
wrack *s.* distruzione, rovina.
to wrangle *vi.* discutere.
wrangler *s.* attaccabrighe.
wrap *s.* sciarpa, coperta, mantello.
to wrap *vt.* avvolgere || *to* — *up,* impacchettare. ◆ **to wrap** *vi.* avvolgersi.
wrapper *s.* 1. imballatore 2. carta da imballo 3. copertina.

wrapping *s.* involucro || — *paper*, carta da imballaggio.

wrath *s.* ira.

wrathful *agg.* irato.

wrathfulness *s.* ira

wreath *s.* ghirlanda.

to wreathe *vt.* 1. intrecciare 2. inghirlandare 3. attorcigliare. ♦ **to wreathe** *vi.* innalzarsi in spire.

wreathy *agg.* 1. inghirlandato 2. a forma di ghirlanda.

wreck *s.* 1. naufragio (*anche fig.*) 2. relitto.

to wreck *vt.* rovinare. ♦ **to wreck** *vi.* naufragare.

wreckage V. *wreck.*

wren *s.* scricciolo.

wrench *s.* 1. strappo 2. (*mecc.*) chiave inglese.

to wrench, to wrest *vt.* 1. strappare 2. torcere.

wrestle *s.* lotta.

to wrestle *vi.* lottare.

wrestler *s.* lottatore.

wrestling *s.* (*sport.*) lotta.

wretch *s.* disgraziato.

wretched *agg.* 1. disgraziato 2. scadente.

wretchedness *s.* 1. disgrazia 2. squallore.

wriggle *s.* contorsione.

to wriggle *vt.* contorcere. ♦ **to wriggle** *vi.* 1. contorcersi 2. (*fig.*) dar risposte evasive.

wring *s.* 1. torsione 2. dolore acuto.

to wring (wrung, wrung) *vt.* 1. torcere 2. estorcere 3. stringere || *to — out*, spremere, (*fig.*) strappare.

wringer *s.* 1. torcitore 2. torchio.

wringing *agg.* lancinante (*di dolore*). ♦ **wringing** *s.* torcitura.

wrinkle[1] *s.* 1. ruga 2. grinza

wrinkle[2] *s.* stratagemma.

to wrinkle *vt.* 1. corrugare 2. splegazzare. ♦ **to wrinkle** *vi.* corrugarsi.

wrinkled, wrinkly *agg.* 1. corrugato 2. rugoso.

wrinkledness *s.* rugosità.

wrist *s.* polso.

wristband *s.* polsino.

to write (wrote, written) *vt.* scrivere || *to — back*, rispondere; *to — down*, annotare, descrivere; *to — off*, cancellare; *to — out*, copiare, emettere un assegno.

writer *s.* scrittore.

writhe *s.* contorcimento.

to writhe *vt.* contorcere. ♦ **to writhe** *vi.* 1. contorcersi 2. (*fig.*) fremere.

writing *s.* 1. lo scrivere 2. scrittura 3. scritto || — *desk*, scrivania; — *paper*, carta da lettere.

written V. *to write.*

wrong *agg.* 1. sbagliato 2. ingiusto 3. illegale. ♦ **wrong** *avv.* 1. erroneamente 2. ingiustamente

wrong *s.* 1. torto 2. male || — *doer*, peccatore, offensore; — *doing*, peccato, offesa.

to wrong *vt.* 1. far torto a 2. imbrogliare.

wrongful *agg.* V. *wrong.*

wrongfulness *s.* ingiustizia.

wrongly *avv.* V. *wrong.*

wrote V. *to write.*

wrought *agg.* lavorato || — *iron*, ferro battuto.

wrung V. *to wring.*

wry *agg.* storto.

to wry *vt.* contorcere. ♦ **to wry** *vi.* contorcersi.

wryly *avv.* per traverso.

X

xenophobe *s.* xenofobo.

xenophobia *s.* xenofobia.

xerophilous *agg.* xerofilo.

X-ray *agg. attr.* a, di raggi X.

to X-ray *vt.* sottoporre a raggi X.

X-rays *s. pl.* raggi X.

xylograph *s.* xilografia.

xylographer *s.* xilografo.

xylographic(al) *agg.* xilografico.

xylography *s.* xilografia.

xylophone *s.* xilofono.

xylophonist *s.* xilofonista.

Y

yacht *s.* panfilo.

to yacht *vi.* fare crociere su panfilo.

yachtsman *s.* (*pl.* -men) proprietario di panfilo.

to yank *vt.* e *vi.* strappare, dare uno

strattone.

yap s. guaito.

to **yap** vi. guaire.

yard s. 1. iarda 2. cortile 3. cantiere: ship- —, cantiere navale.

yarn s. 1. filo 2. (fig.) storia.

yawl s. (naut.) iole, piccola imbarcazione.

yawn s. 1. sbadiglio 2. apertura.

to **yawn** vi. 1. sbadigliare 2. aprirsi.

yawning agg. 1. sonnolento 2. spalancato.

yea avv. sì.

year s. anno: — by —, di anno in anno; all the — round, per tutto l'anno; New Year's Day, Capodanno.

yearbook s. annuario.

yearling agg. di un anno d'età.

yearling s. animale di un anno.

yearlong agg. che dura un anno.

yearly agg. annuale. ♦ **yearly** avv. annualmente.

to **yearn** vi. languire || to — for, after sthg., bramare qc.

yearning s. brama. ♦ **yearning** agg. bramoso.

yeast s. 1. lievito 2. fermento.

to **yeast** vi. 1. lievitare 2. fermentare.

yell s. urlo.

to **yell** vt. e vi. urlare.

yeller s. urlatore.

yellow agg. e s. giallo.

to **yellow** vt. e vi. ingiallire.

yellowish agg. giallastro.

yelp s. guaito.

to **yelp** vi. guaire.

yeoman s. piccolo proprietario terriero.

yes avv. sì.

yesterday avv. e s. ieri: the day before —, l'altro ieri; — week, ieri a otto.

yet avv. 1. ancora 2. già || as —, finora. ♦ **yet** cong. tuttavia.

yew s. — (-tree) tasso.

yield s. 1. produzione 2. (comm.) rendita.

to **yield** vt. e vi. 1. produrre, rendere 2. cedere || to — oneself up, arrendersi.

yielding agg. 1. pieghevole 2. docile.

yoke s. 1. giogo 2. barra (del timone) 3. coppia (di animali).

to **yoke** vt. aggiogare.

yolk s. tuorlo.

yonder agg. quello là, di laggiù. ♦ **yonder** avv. là.

you pron. pers. 1. tu, te, ti 2. voi, ve, vi 3. (forma di cortesia) Lei, Loro.

young agg. giovane || — people, i giovani (in genere).

youngster s. giovanetto.

your agg. poss. 1. tuo 2. vostro 3. (forma di cortesia) Suo.

yours pron. poss. 1. tuo 2. vostro 3. (forma di cortesia) Suo, Loro || — truly, — faithfully, distinti saluti.

yourself pron. r. 1. tu stesso, ti, te, te stesso 2. (forma di cortesia) Lei stesso.

yourselves pron. r. 1. voi stessi, vi 2. (forma di cortesia) Loro stessi.

youth s. 1. gioventù 2. ragazzo.

youthful agg. 1. giovane 2. giovanile.

youthfulness s. aspetto giovanile.

Yugoslav agg. e s. iugoslavo.

Z

zeal s. zelo.

zealot s. fanatico.

zealous agg. zelante.

zed s. zeta.

zenith s. zenit.

zephyr s. zeffiro.

zero s. 1. zero 2. (fig.) nullità.

zest s. 1. gusto 2. aroma.

zigzag agg. e avv. a zigzag.

to **zigzag** vi. andare a zigzag.

zinc s. zinco.

to **zinc** vt. zincare.

zincking s. zincatura.

zincograph s. zincografia.

to **zincograph** vt. imprimere su lastre di zinco.

zincographer s. zincografo.

zincography s. zincografia.

Zionism s. sionismo.

Zionist s. e agg. sionista.

zip s. fischio || — (-fastener), cerniera lampo.

to **zip** vi. sibilare.

zipper s. cerniera lampo.

zircon s. zircone.

zirconium s. zirconio.

zodiac s. zodiaco.

zodiacal agg. zodiacale.

zonal, zonary *agg.* zonale.
zonate(d) *agg.* a zone.
zonation *s.* zonatura.
zone *s.* zona.
zoo *s.* zoo.
zoological *agg.* zoologico.
zoologist *s.* zoologo.
zoology *s.* zoologia.
zoom *s.* **1.** rombo **2.** (*aer.*) salita a candela.
to zoom *vi.* **1.** rombare **2.** (*aer.*) salire a candela.

zoomorphic *agg.* zoomorfo.
zoomorphism *s.* zoomorfismo.
zoophilist *s.* zoofilo.
zoophilous *agg.* zoofilo.
zoophily *s.* zoofilia.
zoophobia *s.* zoofobia.
zootechnic *agg.* zootecnico.
zootechnics, zootechny *s.* zootecnica.
zootomic(al) *agg.* zootomico.
zouave *s.* zuavo.
zygoma *s.* (*pl.* zygomata) zigomò.

NOMI PROPRI, STORICI E GEOGRAFICI

Abel Abele.
Abraham Abramo.
Abyssinia .Abissinia.
Achilles Achille.
Adam Adamo.
Adolph Adolfo.
Adonis Adone.
Adriatic Sea Mar Adriatico.
Aegean Sea Mar Egeo
Aeneas Enea.
Aeschylus Eschilo.
Aesop Esopo.
Afghanistan Afganistan.
Agamemnon Agamennone.
Agatha Agata.
Agnes Agnese.
Ajax Aiace.
Albert Alberto
Aldous Aldo.
Alec, Alex *dim. di* Alexander.
Alexander Alessandro.
Alexandra Alessandra.
Alexis Alessio.
Alfred Alfredo.
Algiers Algeri.
Alps *pl.* Alpi.
Alsace Alsazia.
Amazon Rio delle Amazzoni.
Ambrose Ambrogio.
Andes *pl.* Ande.
Andrew Andrea.
Andy *dim. di* Andrew.
Angel Angelo.
Ann(e) Anna.
Annie *dim. di* Ann(e).
Antarctica Antartide.
Anthony Antonio.
Antoninus Antonino.
Antony Antonio.
Apennines *pl.* Appennini.
Aphrodite Afrodite.
Apulia Puglia.
Aragon Aragona.
Archimedes Archimede.
Ariadne Arianna.
Aristophanes Aristofane.
Aristotle Aristotele.
Armand Armando.
Arnold Arnaldo.
Arthur Arturo.
Athens Atene.
Atlantic Atlantico.

Augustin Agostino.
Augustus Augusto.
Azores *pl.* Azzorre.

Babel Babele.
Babylon Babilonia.
Bacchus Bacco.
Balearic Islands Baleari.
Balkans *pl.* Balcani.
Balthazar Baldassarre.
Baltic Sea Mar Baltico.
Baltimore Baltimora.
Baptist Battista.
Barcelona Barcellona.
Barnabas, Barnaby Barnaba.
Bartholomew Bartolomeo.
Basel Basilea.
Basil Basilio.
Beatrix Beatrice.
Belgium Belgio.
Belgrade Belgrado.
Benedict Benedetto.
Bengal Bengala.
Ben *dim. di* Benjamin.
Benjamin Beniamino.
Benny *dim. di* Benjamin.
Berlin Berlino.
Bermudas *pl.* Bermude.
Bern Berna.
Bernard Bernardo.
Bertha Berta.
Bess *dim. di* Elizabeth.
Bethlehem Betlemme.
Betty *dim. di* Elizabeth.
Bill(y) *dim. di* William.
Blanche Bianca.
Bob(by) *dim. di* Robert.
Bohemia Boemia.
Boniface Bonifacio.
Bosporus Bosforo.
Brandenburg Brandeburgo.
Brazil Brasile.
Brittany Bretagna.
Brutus Bruto.
Burma Birmania.

Cadiz Cadice.
Caesar Cesare.
Cain Caino.
Caius Caio.

Calvin Calvino.
Cambodia Cambogia.
Canada Canadà.
Capitol Campidoglio.
Caribbean Sea Mar dei Caraibi.
Caroline Carolina.
Carpathian Mountains *pl.* Carpazi.
Carthage Cartagine.
Cashmere Cascemir.
Caspian Sea Mar Caspio.
Cassiopea Cassiopea.
Cassius Cassio.
Catherine Caterina.
Cato Catone.
Caucasus Caucaso.
Cecil Cecilio.
Channel (The) La Manica.
Charlemagne Carlomagno.
Charles Carlo.
Charlie *dim. di* Charles.
Charlotte Carlotta.
Chile Cile.
China Cina.
Christ Cristo.
Christine Cristina.
Christopher Cristoforo.
Cicero Cicerone.
Cinderella Cenerentola.
Clara Clara, Chiara.
Claude, Claudius Claudio.
Clement Clemente.
Clementine Clementina.
Clytemnestra Clitennestra.
Cologne Colonia.
Connie *dim. di* Constance.
Conrad Corrado.
Constance Costanza.
Constantine Costantino.
Constantinople Costantinopoli.
Corinth Corinto.
Cornelius Cornelio.
Cornwall Cornovaglia.
Crete Creta.
Cynthia Cinzia.
Cyprus Cipro.
Cyril Cirillo.
Cyrus Ciro.
Czechoslovakia Cecoslovacchia.

Daisy *dim. di* Margaret.
Damascus Damasco.
Damocles Damocle.
Dan *dim. di* Daniel.
Daniel Daniele.
Danny *dim. di* Daniel.
Danube Danubio.
Danzig Danzica.

Daphne Dafne.
Dardanelles *pl.* Dardanelli.
Darius Dario.
Dave *dim. di* David.
Deb(by) *dim. di* Deborah.
Deborah Debora.
Delphi Delfo.
Democritus Democrito.
Demosthenes Demostene.
Denmark Danimarca.
Dick *dim. di* Richard.
Dido Didone.
Diocletian Diocleziano.
Diogenes Diogene.
Dionysius Dionigi, Dionisio.
Dominic Domenico.
Domitian Domiziano.
Dorothy Dorotea.
Dublin Dublino.

Ed(dy) *dim. di* Edmund, Edward.
Edgar Edgardo.
Edinburgh Edimburgo.
Edmund Edmondo.
Edward Edoardo.
Egypt Egitto.
Eire (Stato Libero di) Irlanda.
Eleanor Eleonora.
Electra Elettra.
Elias, Elijah Elia.
Eliza Elisa.
Elizabeth Elisabetta.
Emanuel Emanuele.
Emily Emilia.
England Inghilterra.
Epaminondas Epaminonda.
Epicurus Epicuro.
Erasmus Erasmo.
Ernest Ernesto.
Esther Ester.
Ethiopia Etiopia.
Euclid Euclide.
Eugene Eugenio.
Euphrates Eufrate.
Euripides Euripide.
Europe Europa.
Eve Eva.
Evelyn Evelina.
Ezekiel Ezechiele.

Faust(us) Fausto.
Felix Felice.
Ferdinand Ferdinando.
Finland Finlandia.
Florence Firenze.
France Francia.
Frances Francesca.

Francis Francesco.
Frank Franco.
Frankfurt Francoforte.
Fred(dy) *dim. di* Frederic.
Frederic Federico.

Gabriel Gabriele.
Galilee Galilea.
Gascony Guascogna.
Gaule Gallia.
Geneva Ginevra.
Genoa Genova.
Geoffrey Goffredo.
George Giorgio.
Gerard Gerardo.
Germany Germania.
Gibraltar Gibilterra.
Gilbert Gilberto.
Golgotha Golgota.
Goliath Golia.
Grace Grazia.
Great Britain Gran Bretagna.
Greece Grecia.
Greenland Groenlandia.
Gregory Gregorio.
Guiana Guaiana.
Gustavus Gustavo.
Guy Guido.

Hadrian Adriano.
Hague (The) L'Aia.
Hamburg Amburgo.
Hamlet Amleto.
Hannibal Annibale.
Harcld Aroldo.
Harriet Enrichetta.
Harry *dim. di* Harold, Henry.
Hebrides *pl.* Ebridi.
Hector Ettore.
Helen Elena.
Hellas Ellade.
Henrietta Enrichetta.
Henry Arrigo, Enrico.
Heraclitus Eraclito.
Herbert Erberto.
Hercules Ercole.
Hermes Ermete.
Herod Erode.
Herodotus Erodoto.
Hesiod Esiodo.
Hilary Ilario.
Himalaya Imalaia.
Hindustan Indostan.
Hippolytus Ippolito.
Holland Olanda.
Homer Omero.
Horace, Horatio Orazio.

Hubert Uberto.
Hugh Ugo.
Humbert Umberto.
Hungary Ungheria.

Icarus Icaro.
Iceland Islanda.
Ignatius Ignazio.
Innocent Innocente.
Ionian Sea Mar Ionio.
Ireland Irlanda.
Iris Iride.
Isaac Isacco.
Isabel Isabella.
Isaiah Isaia.
Ishmael Ismaele.
Isis Iside.
Israel Israele.
Italy Italia.

Jack(ie) *dim. di* John.
Jacob Giacobbe.
Jamaica Giamaica.
James Giacomo.
Jane Giovanna.
Janet *dim. di* Jane.
Japan Giappone.
Jason Giasone.
Java Giava.
Jean Giovanna.
Jeffrey Goffredo.
Jehovah Geova.
Jenny *dim. di* Jean.
Jeremiah Geremia.
Jericho Gerico.
Jerome Gerolamo.
Jerry *dim. di* Gerard, Jerome.
Jerusalem Gerusalemme.
Jesus Gesù.
Jim(my) *dim. di* James.
Jo *dim. di* Josephine.
Joan Giovanna.
Job Giobbe.
Joe *dim. di* Joseph.
John Giovanni.
Johnny *dim. di* John.
Jonah, Jonas Giona.
Jonathan Gionata.
Jordan Giordano.
Joseph Giuseppe.
Josephine Giuseppina.
Joshua Giosuè.
Jove Giove.
Judas, Jude Giuda.
Judea Giudea.
Judith Giuditta.
Judy *dim. di* Judith.

Julia Giulia.
Julian Giuliano.
Juliana Giuliana.
Julie Giulia.
Juliet Giulietta.
Julius Giulio.
Juno Giunone.
Jupiter Giove.
Juvenal Giovenale.

Kashmir Cascemir.
Kate, Kitty *dim. di* Catherine.
Korea Corea.

Lambert Lamberto.
Laocoon Laocoonte.
Lapland Lapponia.
Larry *dim. di* Lawrence.
Latium Lazio.
Launcelot Lancillotto.
Lausanne Losanna.
Lawrence Lorenzo.
Lazarus Lazzaro.
Leander Leandro.
Lebanon Libano.
Leghorn Livorno.
Leo(n) Leone.
Leonard Leonardo.
Leonidas Leonida.
Leopold Leopoldo.
Lethe Lete.
Letitia Letizia.
Lewis Luigi.
Libya Libia.
Liège Liegi.
Lisbon Lisbona.
Livy Livio.
Liza, Lizzie, Liz(zy), *dim. di* Elizabeth.
Lombardy Lombardia.
London Londra.
Lou *dim. di* Louise.
Louis Luigi.
Louise Luigia, Luisa.
Louvain Lovanio.
Lucerne Lucerna.
Lucian Luciano.
Lucifer Lucifero.
Lucius Lucio.
Lucretius Lucrezio.
Lucy Lucia.
Luke Luca.
Luther Lutero.
Luxemburg Lussemburgo.
Lycurgus Licurgo.
Lydia Lidia.
Lyons Lione.

Magdalene Maddalena.
Mag(gie) *dim. di* Margaret.
Majorca Maiorca.
Malaya Malesia.
Manchuria Manciuria.
Manfred Manfredi.
Mantua Mantova.
Marathon Maratona.
Marcellus Marcello.
Margaret Margherita.
Margie *dim. di* Margaret.
Marianne Marianna.
Marius Mario.
Mark Marco.
Mars Marte.
Martha Marta.
Martial Marziale.
Martin Martino.
Mary Maria.
Matilda Matilde.
Matt *dim. di* Matthew.
Matthew Matteo.
Matty *dim. di* Martha, Matilda.
Maurice Maurizio.
Max *dim. di* Maximilian.
Maximilian Massimiliano.
May *dim. di* Mary.
Mediterranean Mediterraneo.
Meg *dim. di* Margaret.
Menelaus Menelao.
Mephistopheles Mefistofele.
Mercury Mercurio.
Merlin Merlino.
Methuselah Matusalemme.
Meuse Mosa.
Mexico Messico.
Michael Michele.
Mick(ey) *dim. di* Michael.
Midas Mida.
Mike *dim. di* Michael.
Milan Milano.
Minos Minosse.
Minotaur Minotauro.
Mithridates Mitridate.
Mohammed Maometto.
Moll(y) *dim. di* Mary.
Moluccas *pl.* Molucche.
Monaco (Principato di) Monaco.
Morocco Marocco.
Moscow Mosca.
Moses Mosè.
Mozambique Mozambico.
Munich Monaco di Baviera.
Mycenae Micene.

Naples Napoli.
Napoleon Napoleone.
Narcissus Narciso.

Nell(y) *dim. di* Helen.
Neptune Nettuno.
Nero Nerone.
Netherlands *pl.* Paesi Bassi.
Newfoundland Terranova.
New Zealand Nuova Zelanda.
Nice Nizza.
Nicholas Nicola.
Nick *dim. di* Nicholas.
Nile Nilo.
Noah Noè.
Normandy Normandia.
Norway Norvegia.

Oedipus Edipo.
Oliver Oliviero.
Olympus Olimpo.
Ophelia Ofelia.
Orestes Oreste.
Orion Orione.
Orkneys *pl.* Orcadi.
Orpheus Orfeo.
Osiris Osiride.
Oswald Osvaldo.
Othello Otello.
Ovid Ovidio.

Pacific Pacifico.
Paddy *dim. di* Patrick.
Padua Padova.
Palestine Palestina.
Pancras Pancrazio.
Papua Papuasia.
Paris[1] Paride.
Paris[2] Parigi.
Parnassus Parnaso.
Parthenon Partenone.
Pat *dim. di* Patricia, Patrick.
Patricia Patrizia.
Patrick Patrizio.
Paul Paolo.
Paula Paola.
Pauline Paolina.
Peg(gy) *dim. di* Margaret.
Peking Pechino.
Peloponnesus Peloponneso.
Pennsylvania Pensilvania.
Pericles Pericle.
Perseus Perseo.
Peru Perù.
Pete *dim. di* Peter.
Peter Pietro.
Phaedra Fedra.
Pharsalus Farsalo.
Philadelphia Filadelfia.
Philip Filippo.
Philippi Filippi.

Philippines *pl.* Filippine.
Piedmont Piemonte.
Pigmalion Pigmalione.
Pindar Pindaro.
Piraeus Pireo.
Pius Pio.
Plato Platone.
Pliny Plinio.
Plutarch Plutarco.
Poland Polonia.
Poll(y) *dim. di* Mary.
Polynesia Polinesia.
Pompey Pompeo.
Portugal Portogallo.
Prague Praga.
Prometheus Prometeo.
Ptolemy Tolomeo.
Pyrenees *pl.* Pirenei.
Pythagoras Pitagora.

Quentin Quintino.

Rachel Rachele.
Ramses Ramsete.
Raphael Raffaele, Raffaello.
Raymond Raimondo.
Remus Remo.
Rhine Reno.
Rhodes Rodi.
Rhone Rodano.
Richard Riccardo.
Rob *dim. di* Robert.
Robert Roberto.
Roderick Rodrigo.
Roger Ruggero.
Roland Orlando, Rolando.
Rome Roma.
Romulus Romolo.
Rosalie Rosalia.
Rosalind Rosalinda.
Rose Rosa.
Roumania Romania.
Roxana Rossana.
Rudolph Rodolfo.
Rudy *dim. di* Rudolph.

Sadie, Sally *dim. di* Sarah.
Sam *dim. di* Samuel.
Samson Sansone.
Samuel Samuele.
Sappho Saffo.
Sarah Sara.
Sardinia Sardegna.
Satan Satana.
Saturn Saturno.
Savoy Savoia.

Saxony Sassonia.
Scipion Scipione.
Scotland Scozia.
Sean Giovanni.
Sebastian Sebastiano.
Sibyl Sibilla.
Sicily Sicilia.
Silvester Silvestro.
Simeon Simeone.
Simon Simone.
Simplon Sempione.
Smyrna Smirne.
Socrates Socrate.
Sodom Sodoma.
Solomon Salomone.
Somaliland Somalia.
Sophia Sofia.
Sophocles Sofocle.
Soudan Sudan.
Spain Spagna.
Stephen Stefano.
Steve *dim. di* Stephen.
Stockholm Stoccolma.
Strasbourg Strasburgo.
Sue *dim. di* Susan(nah).
Sulla Silla.
Susy *dim. di* Susan(nah).
Susan(nah) Susanna.
Sweden Svezia.
Switzerland Svizzera.
Sylvia Silvia.
Syracuse Siracusa.
Syria Siria.

Tacitus Tacito.
Tangier(s) Tangeri.
Ted(dy) *dim. di* Edward.
Telemachus Telemaco.
Terence Terenzio.
Tess *dim. di* Theresa.
Thailand Tailandia.
Thames Tamigi.
Thebes Tebe.
Themistocles Temistocle.
Theodoric Teodorico.
Theresa Teresa.
Thermopylae *pl.* Termopili.
Theseus Teseo.
Thomas Tommaso.
Tiber Tevere.
Tiberius Tiberio.
Tirol Tirolo.
Titian Tiziano.
Titus Tito.
Tobias Tobia.
Toby *dim. di* Tobias.

Tom(my) *dim. di* Thomas.
Tonkin, Tonking Tonchino.
Tony *dim. di* Ant(h)ony.
Trajan Traiano.
Tristan, Tristram Tristano.
Troy Troia.
Tully Tullio.
Tunis Tunisi.
Turin Torino.
Turkey Turchia.
Tuscany Toscana.
Tyrol Tirolo.
Tyrrhenian Sea Mar Tirreno.

Ukraine Ucraina.
Ulysses Ulisse.
United States of America Stati
Uniti d'America.
Urban Urbano.
Ursula Orsola.
USA Stati Uniti d'America.
USSR URSS (Unione Repubbliche
Socialiste Sovietiche).

Valentine Valentino.
Valerius Valerio.
Vatican Vaticano.
Venetia Veneto.
Venice Venezia.
Venus Venere.
Vesuvius Vesuvio.
Victor Vittorio.
Victoria Vittoria.
Vincent Vincenzo.
Virgil Virgilio.
Vivian Viviana, Viviano.
Vulcan Vulcano.

Wales Galles.
Walter Gualtiero.
Warsaw Varsavia.
Will *dim. di* William.
William Guglielmo.
Willy *dim. di* William.

Xerxes Serse.

Yugoslavia Iugoslavia.

Zachary Zaccaria.
Zurich Zurigo.

SIGLE E ABBREVIAZIONI USATE NEI PAESI DI LINGUA INGLESE

a., 1. *about*: c., circa **2.** *acre*: acro **3.** *approved*: approvato, riconosciuto dallo Stato.

A.A., *Automobile Association*: A.C., Automobile Club.

A.A.R., *against all risks*: contro ogni rischio.

Abp., *Archbishop*: arcivescovo.

abr., 1. *abridged*: ridotto (*di edizione*) **2.** *abridgment*: compendio.

A.C., *alternating current*: c.a., corrente alternata.

a/c, ac., *account*: c., conto.

A.D., *Anno Domini* (= *dopo Cristo*): d.C., dopo Cristo.

adj., *adjourned*: aggiornato.

Adm., *Admiral*: ammiraglio.

adv., *advertisement*: inserzione.

A.E.C., *Atomic Energy Commission*: C.E.A., Commissione per l'energia atomica.

A.F., *Air Force*: A.M., Aeronautica Militare.

Ala., *Alabama*.

Alas., *Alaska*.

alt., 1. *alternate*: alternata **2.** *alternating*: alternata.

a.m., *ante meridiem, before noon*: antimeridiano.

Am(er)., 1. *America*: Am., Amer., America **2.** *American*: am., amer., americano.

anon., *anonymous*: anonimo.

A.P., *Associated Press*: Stampa Associata.

app., *appendix*: app., appendice.

approx., *approximately*: appross., approssimativamente.

Apr., *April*: apr., aprile.

apt., *apartment*: appartamento.

Ariz., *Arizona*.

Ark., *Arkansas*.

arr., 1. *arrival*: arr., arrivo **2.** *arrived*: arr., arrivato.

ass., *association*: ass., associazione.

at. no., *atomic number*: n.a., numero atomico.

att(y)., *attorney*: proc., procuratore.

at. wt., *atomic weight*: p. at., peso atomico.

Aug., *August*: ago., agosto.

avdp., *avoirdupois*: avoirdupois.

ave., *avenue*: v.le, viale.

b., 1. *book*: l., libro **2.** *born*: n., nato.

B.A., *Bachelor of Arts*: diplomato in lettere.

Bap(t)., *Baptist*: Battista.

B.B.C., *British Broadcasting Corporation*: Ente Radiofonico Britannico.

B.C., *Before Christ*: a.C., avanti Cristo.

B/E, b.e., *bill of exchange*: cambiale.

B.E.A., *British European Airways*: Linee Aeree Europee Britanniche.

Beds., *Bedfordshire*.

Berks., *Berkshire*.

bet., *between*: fra.

B/L, *bill of lading*: polizza di carico.

blvd., *boulevard*: boulevard.

B.M., *British Museum*: Museo Britannico.

B.M.A., *British Medical Association*: Associazione Medica Britannica.

B.O.A.C., *British Overseas Airways Corporation*: Società aerea d'oltremare britannica.

B. of A., *Bank of America*: Banca d'America.

B. of E., *Bank of England*: Banca d'Inghilterra.

Bp., *Bishop*: vesc., vescovo.

bros., *brothers*: F.lli, Fratelli.

b.s., 1. *balance sheet*: bilancio di esercizio **2.** *bill of sale*: atto di vendita.

bsh., *bushel*: staio.

Bucks., *Buckinghamshire*.

bul(l)., *bulletin*: boll., bollettino.

c., 1. *centigrade*: c., centigrado **2.** *cent*: cent., centesimo **3.** *chapter*: cap., capitolo.

C/A, *current account*: c/c, conte corrente.

ca., 1. *cathode:* catodo 2. *about:* ca., circa.

Cal(if), *California.*

Cam(b), *Cambridge.*

Cambs., *Cambridgeshire.*

Can., 1. *Canada:* Canada 2. *Canadian:* canadese.

Cantab., *of Cambridge:* cantabrigense.

cap., 1. *chapter:* cap., capitolo 2. *capital:* capitale.

Capt., *Captain:* cap., capitano.

Card., *Cardinal:* card., cardinale.

cc., 1. *chapters:* capp., capitoli 2. *cubic centimetres:* cmc., centimetri cubi.

C.D., *Corps Diplomatique:* C.D., Corpo Diplomatico.

C.E.D., *Community for European Defence:* C.E.D., Comitato per la Difesa Europea.

Celt., *Celtic:* celtico.

cent., 1. *centigrade:* c., centigrado 2. *centimetre:* cm., centimetro 3. *central:* centrale 4. *century:* sec., secolo.

c.f., *cost and freight:* c.f., costo e nolo.

C.F.I., c.f.i., *cost, freight and insurance:* costo, nolo e assicurazione.

Ch., 1. *Church:* Chiesa 2. *China:* Cina 3. *Chinese:* cinese.

ch(ap), *chapter:* cap., capitolo.

Ches(h), *Cheshire.*

Chr., 1. *Christ:* Cristo 2. *Christian:* cristiano.

C.I.A., *Central Intelligence Agency:* Organizzazione centrale d'informazioni (Servizio segreto americano).

c.i.f., *cost, insurance, freight:* c.i.f., costo, assicurazione e nolo.

cm., *centimetre:* cm., centimetro.

Co., 1. *Company:* s., società 2. *County:* contea.

c/o, *care of:* c/o, presso.

C.O.D., c.o.d., *cash on delivery:* pagamento alla consegna.

Col., 1. *Colonel:* col., colonnello 2. *Colorado.*

coll., 1. *colleague:* collega 2. *college:* coll., collegio 3. *colloquial:* fam., familiare.

Colo., *Colorado.*

Conn., *Connecticut.*

Consol., *consolidated:* consolidato.

cont(d)., *continued:* continuo, ininterrotto.

coop., *co-operative:* coop., coopera-

iva.

corp., *corporation:* 1. corporazione 2. *(amer.)* s.r.l., società a responsabilità limitata.

Corn(w), *Cornwall.*

c.o.s., *cash on shipment:* pagamento alla spedizione.

C.P., *Communist Party:* P.C., Partito Comunista.

cp., *compare:* cfr., confrontare.

Ct., *Connecticut.*

cu., *cubic:* c., cubico.

Cumb., *Cumberland.*

C.U.P., *Cambridge University Press:* Edizioni dell'Università di Cambridge.

d., 1. *date:* data 2. *dead:* m., morto 3. *penny, pence:* penny, pence.

d.c., *direct current:* c.c., corrente continua.

D.A.B., *Dictionary of American Biography:* Dizionario della Biografia Americana.

Dak., *Dakota.*

D.C., *District of Columbia:* Distretto della Columbia.

D.D., *Doctor of Divinity:* dottore in teologia.

dd., d/d, *delivered:* consegnato.

Dec., *December:* dic., dicembre.

Del., *Delaware.*

dep., 1. *department:* reparto, ufficio; *(am.)* ministero 2. *deputy:* deputato.

Devon., *Devonshire.*

Dir., *director:* dirett., direttore.

disc., *discount:* sconto.

D. Lit., *Doctor of Literature:* dottore in letteratura.

D.N.B., *Dictionary of National Biography:* Dizionario della Biografia Nazionale.

dol., *dollar:* dollaro.

Dorset., *Dorsetshire.*

doz., *dozen:* dozz., dozzina.

D.P., *Displaced Person:* profugo.

Dr., 1. *Doctor:* dott., dottore 2. *Debtor:* debitore.

dz., *dozen:* dozz., dozzina.

E., 1. *East:* E, Est 2. *English:* inglese.

ea., *each:* cad., cadauno.

E.B., *Encyclopaedia Britannica:* Enciclopedia Britannica.

E.C.A., *Economic Co-operation Administration:* Amministrazione della cooperazione economica.

E.C.M., *European Common Market:* M.E.C., Mercato Comune Europeo.

ed., 1. *edited:* ed., edito **2.** *edition:* ed., edizione.

E.D.C., *European Defence Community:* C.E.D., Comunità per la difesa europea.

edit., V. *ed.*

Edin., *Edinburgh.*

e.g., *for example:* p. es., per esempio.

Emp., *Emperor:* imperatore.

enc(l)., *enclosure:* all., allegato.

Eng., 1. *England:* Inghilterra **2.** *English:* inglese.

esp(ec)., *especially:* spec., specialmente.

Esq., *Esquire (titolo di cortesia usato negli indirizzi):* Egr., egregio.

etc., *and so on:* ecc., eccetera.

Eur., 1. *Europe:* Europa **2.** *European:* europeo.

ex., 1. *examined:* esaminato **2.** *example:* es., esempio **3.** *excepted:* eccetto **4.** *executive:* esecutivo.

exc., *except(ed):* eccettuato.

F., *Fahrenheit:* F., Fahrenheit.

f., *frequency:* f., frequenza.

F.A.O., *Food and Agricultural Organization:* Organizzazione per l'agricoltura e l'alimentazione.

F.B.I., *Federal Bureau of Investigation:* Ufficio federale d'investigazione.

Feb., *February:* feb., febbraio.

Fed., 1. *Federal:* fed., federale **2.** *Federation:* federazione.

Fla., Flor., *Florida.*

F.O., *Foreign Office:* M.A.A.EE., Ministero degli affari esteri.

F.O.B., f.o.b., *free on board:* f.o.b., franco bordo.

fol., *folio:* folio.

fol(l)., *following:* seg., seguente.

Fr., 1. *Father:* P., padre **2.** *France:* Francia **3.** *French:* francese **4.** *Friday:* ven., venerdì.

Fri., *Friday:* ven., venerdì.

ft., *foot, feet:* piede, piedi.

g., 1. *conductance:* conduttanza **2.** *gender:* genere **3.** *gram:* g., grammo **4.** *guinea:* ghinea.

Ga., *Georgia.*

gal(l)., *gallon:* gallone.

G.B., *Great Britain:* Gran Bretagna.

Gen., *General:* gen., generale.

gen., 1. *gender:* genere **2.** *generally:* gen., generalmente.

gent., *gentleman:* gentiluomo, signore.

G.H.Q., *General Headquarters:* Q.G., quartier generale.

G.I., *Government Issue:* promulgazione ministeriale.

Gloster., *Gloucestershire.*

G-Man., *Government Man:* soldato governativo.

G.O.P., *Grand Old Party (U.S. Republican Party):* Partito Repubblicano Americano.

G.P.O., *General Post Office:* Posta centrale.

H, *hydrogen:* H., idrogeno.

h., 1. *hour:* h., ora **2.** *high:* A., alto.

H.B.M., *His (Her) Britannic Majesty:* S.M.B., Sua Maestà Britannica.

H.C., *House of Commons:* Camera dei Comuni.

H.E., *His Excellency:* S.E., Sua Eccellenza.

Hereford., *Herefordshire.*

Herts., *Hertfordshire.*

hf., *half:* metà.

H.H., 1. *His Holiness:* S.S., Sua Santità **2.** *His (Her) Highness:* S.A., Sua Altezza.

hhd., *hogshead:* hogshead (*misura di capacità l. 238,5*).

H.L., *House of Lords:* Camera Alta.

H.M., *His (Her) Majesty:* V.M., Vostra Maestà.

H.M.S., *His (Her) Majesty's Service:* servizio di Sua Maestà.

Hon., *Honourable:* on., onorevole.

H.P., 1. *high pressure:* alta pressione **2.** *horse power:* H.P., cavalli vapore.

hr., *hour:* h., ora.

H.S., *High School:* scuola media superiore.

Hunts., *Huntingdonshire.*

I(a)., *Iowa.*

ib(id)., *in the same place:* ibid., nello stesso luogo.

I.D., *Intelligence Department:* reparto informazioni.

id., *the same:* id., come sopra.

Id(a)., *Idaho.*

i.e., *that is:* cioè.

Ill., *Illinois.*

in., *inch:* pollice (*misura*).

inc., 1. *incorporated*: incorporato 2. *including*: incluso

inst., *instant* (*the present month*): c.m., corrente mese.

I.O.U., *I owe you*: pagherò.

I.Q., *Intelligence Quotient*: Q.I., quoziente d'intelligenza.

Ire., *Ireland*.

Ja(n)., *January*: genn., gennaio.

J.P., *Justice of the Peace*: giudice di pace.

Jr., jun., *junior*: iun., iunior

Kan(s)., *Kansas*.

kg., *kilogram*: kg., chilogrammo.

k||o., 1. *kilogram*: chilogrammo 2. *kilometre*: km., chilometro.

K.K.K., *Ku Klux Klan*: K.K.K., Ku Klux Klan.

km., *kilometre*: km., chilometro.

K.O., *knock out*: fuori combattimento.

kw., *kilowatt*: kw., chilowatt.

Ky., *Kentucky*.

L., *pound*: L.st., lira sterlina.

l., 1. *litre*: l., litro 2. *long*: lungo.

La., *Louisiana*.

Lancs., *Lancashire*.

Lat., *Latin*: latino.

lat., *latitude*: latitudine.

lb., *pound*: libbra.

L.C.D., *lowest common denominator*: m.c.d., minimo comun denominatore.

L.C.M., *least common multiple*: m.c.m., minimo comune multiplo.

Leics., *Leicestershire*.

L.F., *low frequency*: b.f., bassa frequenza.

Lieut., *Lieutenant*: luogotenente.

Lincs., *Lincolnshire*.

LL.D., *Doctor of Laws*: dottore in legge.

Lon., *London*: Londra.

lon(g)., *longitude*: longitudine.

L.P., 1. *Labour Party*: Partito Laburista 2. *Long Play*: microsolco.

L.R., *Lloyd's Register*: Registro dei Lloyd.

Ltd., *limited*: s.r.l., società a responsabilità limitata.

m., 1. *male*: m., maschio 2. *metre*: m., metro 3. *mile*: miglio 4. *minute*: m., minuto 5. *month*: m., mese.

M.A., *Master of Arts*: laureato in lettere.

Mad., Madm., *Madam*: sig.ra, signora.

Maj., *Major*: magg., maggiore.

Mar., *March*: mar., marzo.

Mass., *Massachusetts*.

max., *maximum*: mass., massimo.

M.C., *Member of Congress*: membro del Congresso.

Md., *Maryland*.

M.D., *Doctor of Medicine*: dottore in medicina.

Mdx., *Middlesex*.

Me., *Maine*.

M.F., *medium frequency*: m.f., media frequenza.

mg(m)., *milligram*: mg., milligrammo.

Mich., *Michigan*.

Minn., *Minnesota*.

Miss., *Mississippi*.

mm., *millimetre*: mm., millimetro.

Mo., 1. *Missouri* 2. *Monday*: lun., lunedì.

M.O., *money order*: ordine di pagamento.

Mon., *Monday*: lun., lunedì.

Mont., *Montana*.

M.P., 1. *Military Police*: Polizia militare 2. *Member of Parliament*: membro del Parlamento.

mph., *miles per hour*: miglia orarie.

Mr., *Mister*: sig., signor.

Mrs., *Mistress*: sig.ra, signora.

M/S, *motorship*: M/n, motonave.

MS., *manuscript*: ms., manoscritto.

MSS., *manuscripts*: mss., manoscritti.

Mt., *mount*: M., monte.

mus., 1. *museum*: mus., museo 2. *music*: musica.

N., *North*: N, Nord.

n., 1. *born*: n., nato 2. *number*: n., numero.

N.A.T.O., *North Atlantic Treaty Organization*: P.A., Patto atlantico.

N.B.C., *National Broadcasting Company*: Compagnia radiofonica nazionale.

N.C., *North Carolina*.

N.C.O., *non-commissioned officer*: s. uff., sottufficiale.

N. D(ak)., *North Dakota*.

Neb(r)., *Nebraska*.

Nev., *Nevada*.

New M., *New Mexico*.

N.H., *New Hampshire.*
N.J., *New Jersey.*
N. M(ex)., *New Mexico.*
no., *number:* n., numero.
Norf., *Norfolk.*
Northum(b)., *Northumberland*
nos., *numbers:* numeri.
Notts., *Nottinghamshire.*
Nov., *November:* nov., novembre.
N.Y., *New York:* Nuova York.

O., *Ohio.*
Oct., *October:* ott., ottobre.
O.E.D., *Oxford English Dictionary:* Dizionar.o Inglese Oxford.
Okla., *Oklahoma.*
op. cit., *in the work cited:* op. cit., opera citata.
Ore(g)., *Oregon.*
O.U.P., *Oxford University Press:* Edizioni dell'Università di Oxford.
Ox(f)., *Oxford.*
Oxon., 1. *Oxford* 2. *of Oxford:* osoniese 3. *Oxfordshire ounce:* oncia.

P., *(car-)park:* P., parcheggio.
p., 1. *page:* p., pagina 2. *past:* pass., passato.
Pa., *Pennsylvania.*
P.A.A., *Pan American Airways:* Linee aeree panamericane.
par., *paragraph:* parag., paragrafo.
pat., 1. *patent:* brev., brevetto 2. *patented:* brevettato.
P.A.Y.E., *pay as you earn* (trattenuta di ricchezza mobile): R.M., ricchezza mobile.
pd., *paid:* pagato.
Penn(a). v. *Pa.*
Ph. D., *Doctor of Philosophy:* dottore in filosofia.
P.M., *Prime Minister:* Primo Ministro.
p.m., *post meridiem (after noon):* pomeridiano.
P.O., p.o., 1. *Post Office:* U.P., : ficio postale 2. *postal order:* V., vaglia.
P.O.B., *post office box:* C.P., casella postale.
p.o.d., *pay on delivery:* pagamento alla consegna.
pp., *pages:* pagg., pagine.
prep., *preparation:* preparazione.
Pres., *President:* pres., presidente.
Prof., *Professor:* prof., professore.
prox., *next:* prossimo.
P.S., *postscript:* P.S., poscritto.

p.t.o., *please turn over:* voltare pagina.

Q.M.G., *Quartermaster General:* capo dipartimento amministrazione e alloggi.
qu., 1. *quart:* misura di capacità (l. 1.136) 2. *quarter:* quarto.
quot., *quotation:* citazione.

R., r., 1. *river:* f., fiume 2. *road:* strada.
R.A.C., *Royal Automobile Club:* Regio Automobile Club.
R.A.D.I.A.C., *Radioactivity Detection Identification and Computation:* Rivelazione, identificazione e calcolo della radioattività.
R.A.F., *Royal Air Force:* Regia Aviazione militare.
R.C., 1. *Red Cross:* C.R., Croce Rossa 2. *Roman Catholic:* Cattolico Romano.
R.C.A., *Radio Corporation of America:* Associazione Radiofonica Americana.
re., *reference* 1. ref., referenza 2. riferimento.
rec., 1. *receipt:* ricevuta 2. *record:* record.
reg., 1. *region:* regione 2. *register:* reg., registro 3. *regular:* regolare.
Rev., *Reverend:* rev., reverendo.
R.H., *Royal Highness:* A.R., Altezza Reale.
R.N., *Royal Navy:* Regia Marina.
Rt. Hon., *Right Honourable:* molto onorevole.
Rt. Rev., *Right Reverend:* molto reverendo.
Ry., *Railway:* ferrovia.

S., *South:* S, Sud.
s., 1. *second:* secondo 2. *shilling:* scellino.
Sat., *Saturday:* sab., sabato.
S.C., *South Carolina.*
sch., *school:* sc., scuola.
Scot., 1. *Scotland:* Scozia 2. *Scottish:* scozzese.
S. D(ak)., *South Dakota.*
sec., 1. *second:* secondo 2. *section:* sezione 3. *secretary:* segr., segretario
Sen., 1. *Senate:* senato 2. *senator:* senatore 3. *senior:* senior.
Sept., *September:* sett., settembre.
Sergt., *sergeant:* serg., sergente.
sh., *shilling:* scellino.

S.H.A.P.E., *Supreme Headquarters Allied Powers Europe:* quartier generale delle Forze alleate in Europa.

Shrops., *Shropshire.*

So., 1. *South:* S, Sud **2.** *Southern:* sudista.

Soc., *society:* s., società.

Somerset., *Somersetshire.*

spec., 1. *special:* spec., speciale **2.** *specification:* specificazione.

sp. gr., *specific gravity:* gravità specifica.

sq., *square:* p.za, piazza.

Sr., 1. *senior:* senior **2.** *Sir:* Sir **3.** *sister:* sorella.

SS, S/S, *steamship:* piroscafo.

St., 1. *Saint:* s., santo **2.** *street:* via.

st., *stone:* misura di peso (Kg. 6,350).

Staffs., *Staffordshire.*

ster., stg., *sterling:* L.st., lira sterlina.

St. Ex., *Stock Exchange:* Borsa valori.

Sun(d)., *Sunday:* dom., domenica.

Sup. Ct., *Supreme Court:* C.S., Corte suprema.

supp(l)., *supplement:* supplemento.

Sur., *Surrey.*

Sus., *Sussex.*

S.W., 1. *South Wales:* Galles del sud **2.** *South West:* S.O., sud ovest.

Swit., Swtz., *Switzerland:* Svizzera.

syn., *synonym:* sinonimo

Sy., *Surrey.*

t., 1. *ton:* t., tonnellata **2.** *volume:* v., volume.

T.B., *tuberculosis:* tbc, tubercolosi.

tel., 1. *telegram:* telegramma **2.** *telegraph:* telegrafo **3.** *telephone:* tel., telefono.

Tenn., *Tennessee.*

Tex., *Texas.*

Thur(s)., *Thursday:* giov., giovedì.

T.O., *turn over:* voltare.

T.U., *Trade-Union:* Sindacato.

Tu(es)., *Tuesday:* mar., martedì.

TV., *television:* TV, televisione.

T.W.A., *Trans World Airlines:* linee aeree intercontinentali.

U., 1. *Union:* U., unione **2.** *University:* Università.

U.K., *United Kingdom:* R.U., Regno Unito.

U.N., *United Nations:* N.U., Nazioni Unite.

U.N.E.S.C.O., *United Nations Educational Scientific and Cultural Organization:* Organizzazione culturale, scientifica e per l'educazione delle Nazioni Unite.

U.N.I.C.E.F., *United Nations International Children's Emergency Fund:* Fondo d'emergenza internazionale per l'infanzia delle Nazioni Unite.

U.N.O., *United Nations Organization:* O.N.U., Organizzazione delle Nazioni Unite.

U.P., *United Press:* Stampa associata.

U.S., *United States:* S.U., Stati Uniti.

U.S.A., 1. *United States of America:* S.U.A., Stati Uniti d'America **2.** *United States Army:* Esercito degli Stati Uniti.

U.S.A.E.C., *United States Atomic Energy Commission:* commissione per l'energia atomica degli Stati Uniti.

U.S.A.F., *United States Air Force:* Aviazione militare degli Stati Uniti.

U.S.I.S., *United States Information Service:* Servizio informazioni degli Stati Uniti.

U.S.N., *United States Navy:* Marina degli Stati Uniti.

U.S.S.R., *Union of Soviet Socialist Republics:* U.R.S.S., Unione delle repubbliche socialiste sovietiche.

U.S.S., *United States Ship:* nave degli Stati Uniti.

Ut., *Utah.*

v., *verse:* v., verso.

Va., *Virginia.*

Vat., *Vatican:* Vaticano.

Ven., *Venerable:* Ven., venerabile.

V.H.F., *very high frequency:* altissima frequenza.

Vic(t)., *Victoria.*

V.I.P., *Very Important Person:* Persona molto importante.

viz., *namely:* cioè.

vol., *volume:* vol., volume.

V.P., *Vice-President:* vicepresidente.

vs., *against:* contro.

Vt., *Vermont.*

Vul(g)., *Vulgate:* Vulgata.

vv., *verses:* vv., versi.

w., *watt:* W., watt.

W., 1. *West*: O, Ovest **2.** *Washington.*

w., 1. *week*: settimana **2.** *wife*: moglie **3.** *with*: con.

Warwick., *Warwickshire.*

Wash., *Washington.*

W.D., *War Department*: Ministero della Guerra.

Wed., *Wednesday*: mer., mercoledì.

Westm., *Westminster.*

Westmore., *Westmoreland.*

whf., *wharf*: pontile.

Wis(c)., *Wisconsin.*

wk., 1. *week*: settimana **2.** *work*: lavoro.

w.l., *wave length*: lunghezza d'onda.

Worcs., *Worcestershire.*

W.R.A.C., *Women's Royal Army Corps*: Regio corpo d'armata femminile.

wt., *weight*: peso.

W.Va., *West Virginia*: Virginia dell'ovest.

Wy(o)., *Wyoming.*

Xmas., *Christmas*: Natale.

y., 1. *yard*: iarda **2.** *year*: anno.

yd., *yard*: iarda.

Y.H.A., *Youth Hostels Association*: Associazione Ostelli per la gioventù.

Y.M.C.A., *Young men's Christian Association*: Associazione Cristiana per i giovani.

yr., 1. *year*: anno **2.** *your*: vostro.

Yorks., *Yorkshire.*

yrs., 1. *years*: anni **2.** *yours*: vostri.

Y.W.C.A., *Young Women's Christian Association*: Associazione Cristiana per le giovani.

Z., *atomic number*: n.a., numero atomico.

&, *and*: e.

&c., *and so forth*: etc., ecc., eccetera.

PREFACE TO THE ITALIAN-ENGLISH SECTION OF THE
PICCOLO DIZIONARIO ITALIANO-INGLESE

1. The first part of the English-Italian section of the **Compact Diction-ary** contains information in Italian designed to help in its use. It gives rules of pronunciation, a list of irregular verbs, tables of comparison of the English and American units and metric system, information on the English and American currency, a list of cardinal and ordinal numbers, and an explanatory list of the abbreviations used.

A similar introduction is included here to help in the use of the Italian-English section.

2. Since Italian presents particular problems with its verbs we have pro-vided a list of irregular verbs in general use. We have not included their compounds, as they are conjugated in the same way.

Those verbs which take *essere* as an auxiliary are indicated by means of a single star. Those which take *essere* when used intransitively and *avere* when used transitively have a double star.

With the past definite tense we have shown the 1st person singular only, since the 3rd person singular and the 3rd person plural follow the same pattern, while the 2nd person singular and plural are regular in form e.g.: *prendere* – presi, *prendesti,* prese, *prendemmo, prendeste,* presero.

3. There are two points concerning the current use of verbs which the student of Italian may well find helpful:

a) there is a tendency in modern Italian towards a more frequent use of the perfect tense to represent completed past action (though such irrefut-able statements of the past as, for example, *Dante died in 1321* would still always be translated as *Dante morì . . .*);

b) though the polite form in the singular, with *Lei* and the 3rd person of the verb, is regularly used e.g.: *Lei scrive in inglese?* (Are you writing in English?), the plural form addressed to more than one person is now more frequently the 2nd person plural with *Voi,* instead of the 3rd person plural with *Loro* e.g.: *Voi scrivete in inglese?* rather than *Loro scrivono in inglese?*

4. As some Italian nouns have irregular plurals or do not change their form in the plural we have included a list of the more commonly used ones.

5. In illustrating the possible alternative translations for the Italian words listed, the following symbols have been adopted:

a) a double line (ll) after the initial translation or translations indicates a grammatical change from, for example, an adjective to a noun or a pro-noun to an adverb;

b) a lozenge (♦) indicates something more than just an alternative translation, showing, for example, a figurative or idiomatic use;

c) the numbers printed in large type (1., 2., 3., etc.) indicate the various alternative meanings;

d) the small numbers ([1], [2], [3], etc.) indicate words of identical form but different meaning.

The Alphabet

The Italian alphabet consists of 21 letters only. j *(i lunga)*, k *(cappa)*, w *(doppio vu)*, x *(ics)*, y *(ipsilon)* do not occur in the alphabet, though they are used for the spelling of foreign words e.g.: *judo, kimono, watt, xenofobia, yacht* . In some cases y is replaced by i, e.g. *raion* for rayon. ch replaces k, e.g. *chilogramma* for kilogram. ph is represented by f, e.g. *fobia* for phobia. x occurs in certain expressions such as *ex-presidente, extraterritoriale*, etc.

Letter	Name	Letter	Name
a	*a*	m	*emme*
b	*bi*	n	*enne*
c	*ci*	o	*o*
d	*di*	p	*pi*
e	*e*	q	*cu*
f	*effe*	r	*erre*
g	*gi*	s	*esse*
h	*acca*	t	*ti*
i	*i*	u	*u*
l	*elle*	v	*vu*
		z	*zeta*

Pronunciation

Since Italian is a phonetic language, once the rules of pronunciation are learnt, it is possible to pronounce most words correctly, though it is not always easy to tell on which syllable the tonic stress falls.

The Vowels

Italian vowels are pure sounds and should be pronounced well forward in the mouth:

	A	like a in far	*gala*
close	E	like a in fate	*seta*
open	E	like e in ten	*pelle*
	I	like i in machine	*vino*
close	O	like o in store	*corte*
open	O	like o in spot	*motto*
	U	like oo in spoon	*uso*

The Consonants

In the case of double consonants each consonant is sounded, with the voice rising on them and falling on the following vowel.

The consonants B, D, F, L, M, N, P, Q, T and V are pronounced very much as in English. The rest are as follows:

C   1. before a, o, u, and consonants, including h: like c in cat, as in *casa, crema, chilo*;
       2. before e or i: like ch in chip, as in *cena, cibo*.

G   1. before a, o, u and consonants, including h but not including l and n: like g in gap, as in *gala, grido, ghiro*;
       2. before e or i: like g in gem, as in *gente, gita*.

gli   like lli in billion, as in *figlia*; (a few exceptions have the gli pronounced as in English, e.g. *anglicano, negligente*).

gn   like ni in onion, as in *signore*.

H   is always silent and occurs in very few words, except as shown above to harden the c and g sounds before e and i.

Q   is always followed by u, like qu in quick, as in *quinto*.

R   is rolled, rather as in rr Scottish pronunciation, as in *pera, serra*.

S   1. is voiced, like s in rose, as in *rosa, esatto*, or when followed by b, d, g, l, m, n, r, v, the voiceless consonants, as in *sdegno, svelto*;
       2. is unvoiced like s in sap, at the beginning of a word, or when it is doubled, as in *sega, rosso*.

sc   1. before e or i is like sh in shot, as in *scena*;
       2. before a, o and u is like sk in skate, as in *scarpa, scopo, scudo*;
       3. an h after it and before e or i makes it like sk, as in *schema, schiena*;
       4. an i after it and before a, o or u makes it like sh, as in *scialle, sciocco, sciupare*.

Z   1. voiced like ds in treads, as in *zio*;
       2. unvoiced like ts in wits, as in *forza*.

Accentuation

In printed and written Italian an accent is used to indicate when the toni stress falls on a final vowel such as in *città* or *caffè*. It is also used to distinguish between two words which are spelt and pronounced alike but have different meanings:

     è = is   *e* = and
     dà = he gives   *da* = from, by, of, etc.

It also occurs on some monosyllabic words as in *già* and *più*.

In print the acute accent is used to indicate a stress on a final e as in *perché* or *né*, though in handwriting the grave accent is more usual. In modern Italian the grave accent is normally used elsewhere and we have followed this practice.

As a general rule the tonic stress is on the penultimate syllable, but this is not by any means always so. The grave and acute accents have been used to show where the stress falls when it does not fall on the penultimate syllable. The open and close e are distinguished in the accepted way by means of è and é, e.g. *créscere, crédere, festival, férvido,* and the grave accent is used everywhere else, e.g. *càndido, moltitùdine.*

IRREGULAR ITALIAN VERBS†

Accendere – *p. def.* accesi, *p.p.* acceso
Accludere – see alludere
Addurre – *pres.* adduco, *p. def.* addussi, *fut.* addurrò, *p.p.* addotto
Affliggere – *p. def.* afflissi, *p.p.* afflitto
Alludere – *p. def.* allusi, *p.p.* alluso
Andare* – *pres.* vado, vai, va, andiamo, andate, vanno *fut.* andrò
Annettere – *p. def.* annettei (annessi), *p.p.* annesso
Apparire* – *pres.* apparisco, *p. def.* apparii (apparvi, apparsi), *p.p.* apparso
Appendere – *p. def.* appesi, *p.p.* appeso
Ardere – *p. def.* arsi, *p.p.* arso
Aspergere – *p. def.* aspersi, *p.p.* asperso
Assalire – *pres.* assalgo (assalisco), assalgono
Assolvere – *p. def.* assolsi (assolvei, assolvetti), *p.p.* assolto
Assumere – *p. def.* assunsi, *p.p.* assunto

Bere – *pres.* bevo, *p. def.* bevvi, *fut.* berrò

Cadere* – *p. def.* caddi, *fut.* cadrò
Cedere – *p. def.* cedei (cedetti)
Chiedere – *p. def.* chiesi, *p.p.* chiesto
Chiudere – *p. def.* chiusi, *p.p.* chiuso
Cingere – *p. def.* cinsi, *p.p.* cinto
Cogliere – *pres.* colgo, colgono, *p. def.* colsi, *p.p.* colto
Comprimere – *p. def.* compressi, *p.p.* compresso
Conoscere – *p. def.* conobbi, *p.p.* conosciuto
Consumare – *p. def.* consumai (consunsi), *p.p.* consumato (consunto)
Correre** – *p. def.* corsi, *p.p.* corso
Costruire – *p.p.* costruito (costrutto)
Crescere* – *p. def.* crebbi, *p.p.* cresciuto
Cucire – *pres.* cucio
Cuocere – *pres.* cuocio, cuoci, cuoce, cociamo, cocete, cuociono, *p. def.* cossi, *p.p.* cotto

Dare – *pres.* do, dai, dà, diamo, date, danno, *p. def.* diedi (detti), desti, *fut.* darò, *p.p.* dato

† Verbs which take *essere* are indicated by one star.
  Those taking *avere* and *essere* have two stars.

Decidere – *p. def.* decisi, *p.p.* deciso

Difendere – *p. def.* difesi, *p.p.* difeso

Dipendere** – *p. def.* dipesi, *p.p.* dipeso

Dipingere – *p. def.* dipinsi, *p.p.* dipinto

Dire – *pres.* dico, dite, *p. def.* dissi, *fut.* dirò, *p.p.* detto

Dirigere – *p. def.* diressi, *p.p.* diretto

Discutere – *p. def.* discussi, *p.p.* discusso

Dissolvere – *p. def.* dissolsi (dissolvei), *p.p.* dissolto

Distinguere – *p. def.* distinsi, *p.p.* distinto

Dividere – *p. def.* divisi, *p.p.* diviso

Dolersi* – *pres.* mi dolgo, ti duoli, si duole, ci doliamo, vi dolete, si dolgono, *p. def.* mi dolsi, *fut.* mi dorrò

Dovere – *pres.* devo (debbo), devi, deve, dobbiamo, dovete, devono (debbono), *fut.* dovrò

Eccellere – *p. def.* eccelsi, *p.p.* eccelso

Emergere* – *p. def.* emersi, *p.p.* emerso

Ergere – *p. def.* ersi, *p.p.* erto

Erigere – *p. def.* eressi, *p.p.* eretto

Esigere – *p.p.* esatto

Espellere – *p. def.* espulsi, *p.p.* espulso

Esplodere** – *p. def.* esplosi, *p.p.* esploso

Evadere* – *p. def.* evasi, *p.p.* evaso

Fare – *pres.* faccio (fo), fai, fa, facciamo, fate, fanno, *imper.* facevo, *p. def.* feci, *fut.* farò, *p.p.* fatto

Fendere – *p. def.* fendei (fendetti), *p.p.* fesso (fenduto)

Figgere – *p. def.* fissi, *p.p.* fisso (fitto)

Fingere – *p. def.* finsi, *p.p.* finto

Fondere – *p. def.* fusi, *p.p.* fuso

Frangere – *p. def.* fransi, *p.p.* franto

Friggere – *p. def.* frissi, *p.p.* fritto

Giacere* – *pres.* giaccio, giacciono, *p. def.* giacqui, *p.p.* giaciuto

Giungere* – *p. def.* giunsi, *p.p.* giunto

Godere – *fut.* godrò

Incutere – *p. def.* incussi (incutei), *p.p.* incusso

Indulgere – *p. def.* indulsi, *p.p.* indulto

Intridere – *p. def.* intrisi, *p.p.* intriso

Invadere – *p. def.* invasi, *p.p.* invaso

Ledere – *p. def.* lesi, *p.p.* leso

Leggere – *p. def.* lessi, *p.p.* letto

Mettere – *p. def.* misi, *p.p.* messo

Mordere – *p. def.* morsi, *p.p.* morso
Morire* – *pres.* muoio, muori, muore, moriamo, morite, muoiono, *fut.* morrò, *p.p.* morto
Mungere – *p. def.* munsi, *p.p.* munto
Muovere – *pres.* moviamo, movete, *p. def.* mossi, *p.p.* mosso

Nascere* – *p. def.* nacqui, *p.p.* nato
Nascondere – *p. def.* nascosi, *p.p.* nascosto
Nuocere – *pres.* noccio, nociamo, nocete, nocciono, *p. def.* nocqui, *p.p.* nociuto

Offrire – *p. def.* offrii (offersi), *p.p.* offerto

Parere* – *pres.* paio, paiamo, paiono, *p. def.* parvi, *fut.* parrò, *p.p.* parso
Percuotere – *p.p.* percosso
Perdere – *p. def.* persi (perdei, perdetti), *p.p.* perduto (perso)
Persuadere – *p. def.* persuasi, *p.p.* persuaso
Piacere* – *pres.* piaccio, piaci, piace, piacciamo, piacete, piacciono, *p. def.* piacqui, *p.p.* piaciuto
Piangere – *p. def.* piansi, *p.p.* pianto
Piovere** – *p. def.* piovve, piovvero
Porgere – *p. def.* porsi, *p.p.* porto
Porre – *pres.* pongo, poni, pone, poniamo, ponete, pongono, *p. def.* posi, *fut.* porrò, *p.p.* posto
Potere – *pres.* posso, puoi, può, possiamo, potete, possono, *fut.* potrò
Prediligere – *p. def.* predilessi, *p.p.* prediletto
Prendere – *p. def.* presi, *p.p.* preso
Proteggere – *p. def.* protessi, *p.p.* protetto
Pungere – *p. def.* punsi, *p.p.* punto

Radere – *p. def.* rasi, *p.p.* raso
Redimere – *p. def.* redensi, *p.p.* redento
Reggere – *p. def.* ressi, *p.p.* retto
Rendere – *p. def.* resi, *p.p.* reso
Ridere – *p. def.* risi, *p.p.* riso
Rifulgere** – *p. def.* rifulsi, *p.p.* rifulso
Rispondere – *p. def.* risposi, *p.p.* risposto
Rodere – *p. def.* rosi, *p.p.* roso
Rompere – *p. def.* ruppi, *p.p.* rotto

Radere – *p. def.* rasi, *p.p.* raso
Sapere – *pres.* so, sai, sa, sappiamo, sapete, sanno, *p. def.* seppi, *fut.* saprò
Scegliere – *pres.* scelgo, scelgono, *p. def.* scelsi, *p.p.* scelto
Scendere** – *p. def.* scesi, *p.p.* sceso
Scindere – *p. def.* scissi, *p.p.* scisso

Sciogliere – *pres.* sciolgo, sciolgono, *p. def.* sciolsi, *p.p.* sciolto

Scrivere – *p. def.* scrissi, *p.p.* scritto

Scuotere – *p. def.* scossi, *p.p.* scosso

Sedere* – *pres.* siedo (seggo), siedi, siede, sediamo, sedete, siedono (seggono)

Soddisfare – *pres.* soddisfo (soddisfaccio, soddisfò), soddisfi (soddisfai), soddisfa, soddisfiamo (soddisfacciamo), soddisfate, soddisfano (soddisfanno), *p. def.* soddisfeci, *p.p.* soddisfatto

Sorgere* – *p. def.* sorsi, *p.p.* sorto

Spargere – *p. def.* sparsi, *p.p.* sparso

Spegnere – *p. def.* spensi, *p.p.* spento

Spendere – *p. def.* spesi, *p.p.* speso

Spingere – *p. def.* spinsi, *p.p.* spinto

Stare* – *pres.* sto, stai, sta, stiamo, state, stanno, *imperf.* stavo, *p. def.* stetti, *p.p.* stato

Stringere – *p. def.* strinsi, *p.p.* stretto

Struggere – *p. def.* strussi, *p.p.* strutto

Svellere – *pres.* svello (svelgo), svellono (svelgono), *p. def.* svelsi, *p.p.* svelto

Svenire* – *p. def.* svenni

Tacere – *pres.* taccio, taci, tace, taciamo, tacete, tacciono, *p. def.* tacqui, *p.p.* taciuto

Tendere – *p. def.* tesi, *p.p.* teso

Tenere – *pres.* tengo, tieni, tiene, teniamo, tenete, tengono, *p. def.* tenni, *fut.* terrò

Tingere – *p. def.* tinsi, *p.p.* tinto

Togliere – *pres.* tolgo, tolgono, *p. def.* tolsi, *p.p.* tolto

Torcere – *p. def.* torsi, *p.p.* torto

Trarre – *pres.* traggo, trai, trae, traiamo, traete, traggono, *imperf.* traevo, *p. def.* trassi, *fut.* trarrò, *p.p.* tratto

Uccidere – *p. def.* uccisi, *p.p.* ucciso

Udire – *pres.* odo, odi, ode, udiamo, udite, odono, *fut.* udrò (udirò)

Ungere – *p. def.* unsi, *p.p.* unto

Uscire* – *pres.* esco, esci, esce, usciamo, uscite, escono

Valere** – *pres.* valgo, valgono, *p. def.* valsi, *fut.* varrò, *p.p.* valso

Vedere – *pres.* vedo (veggo), vedono (veggono), *p. def.* vidi, *fut.* vedrò, *p.p.* visto

Venire* – *pres.* vengo, vieni, viene, veniamo, venite, vengono, *p. def.* venni, *fut.* verrò

Vilipendere – *p. def.* vilipesi, *p.p.* vilipeso

Vincere – *p. def.* vinsi, *p.p.* vinto

Vivere** – *p. def.* vissi, *p.p.* vissuto

Volere – *pres.* voglio, vuoi, vuole, vogliamo, volete, vogliono, *p. def.*
  volli, *fut.* vorrò
Volgere – *p. def.* volsi, *p.p.* volto

IRREGULAR PLURALS OF NOUNS

l'autobus	gli autobus
il bar	i bar
il caffè	i caffè
la città	le città
la frutta	le frutta
il re	i re
il braccio	le braccia
il bue	i buoi
il centinaio	le centinaia
il dito	le dita
il ginocchio	le ginocchia
la guancia	le guance
il labbro	le labbra
il lenzuolo	le lenzuola
la mano	le mani
il migliaio	le migliaia
l'orecchio	le orecchie
il paio	le paia
l'uomo	gli uomini

ITALIAN MONEY

Italian bank notes are issued in the following denominations:

500 lire	10,000 lire
1000 lire	50,000 lire
2000 lire	100,000 lire.
5000 lire	

The one hundred thousand lire notes are not negotiable outside Italy.

  Coins are issued in five, ten, twenty, fifty, one hundred and five hundred pieces.

NUMERALS

Cardinal		*Cardinal cont.*	
1	uno	3	tre
2	due	4	quattro

Cardinal

		Cardinal cont.	
5	cinque	29	ventinove
6	sei	30	trenta
7	sette	31	trentuno
8	otto	32	trentadue
9	nove	38	trentotto
10	dieci	40	quaranta
11	undici	50	cinquanta
12	dodici	60	sessanta
13	tredici	70	settanta
14	quattordici	80	ottanta
15	quindici	90	novanta
16	sedici	100	cento
17	diciassette	101	centouno
18	diciotto	105	centocinque
19	diciannove	150	centocinquanta
20	venti	200	duecento
21	ventuno	300	trecento
22	ventidue	1000	mille
23	ventitré	1100	millecento
24	ventiquattro	1200	milleduecento
25	venticinque	2000	duemila
26	ventisei	100,000	centomila
27	ventisette	1,000,000	un milione
28	ventotto		

Ordinal

1st	primo
2nd	secondo
3rd	terzo
4th	quarto
5th	quinto
6th	sesto
7th	settimo
8th	ottavo
9th	nono
10th	decimo
11th	undicesimo *or* decimo primo
12th	dodicesimo *or* decimo secondo
20th	ventesimo
21st	ventunesimo *or* ventesimo primo
22nd	ventiduesimo *or* ventesimo secondo

30th	trentesimo
40th	quarantesimo
50th	cinquantesimo
101st	centunesimo
200th	duecentesimo
1000th	millesimo
1205th	milleduecentocinquesimo
1,000,000th	milionesimo

ABBREVIATIONS USED IN THE DICTIONARY

abbr.	abbreviation	(dial.)	dialect
(aer.)	aviation	dif.	defective
agg.	adjective	dim.	diminutive
(agr.)	agriculture	dimostr.	demonstrative
(amer.)	American		
amm.	administrative	ecc., etc.	etcetera
(anat.)	anatomy	(eccl.)	ecclesiastical
(ant.)	archaic	(econ.)	economics
(arch.)	architecture	(edil.)	building industry
art.	article	(elettr.)	electricity
(arte)	art	escl.	exclamation
assol.	absolute		
(astr.)	astronomy	f.	feminine
attr.	attribute	(fam.)	familiar
aus.	auxiliary	(farm.)	pharmaceutical
(auto)	motoring	(ferr.)	railway
avv.	adverb	(fig.)	figurative
		(fil.)	philosophy
(bot.)	botany	(fis.)	physics
(biol.)	biology	(foto)	photography
		fut.	future
(chim.)	chemistry		
(chir.)	surgery	gen.	genitive
(cine)	cinematography	general.	generally
coll.	collective	(geogr.)	geography
(comm.)	commerce	(geol.)	geology
comp.	comparative	(geom.)	geometry
compl.	complement	ger.	gerund
condiz.	conditional	(gergo)	jargon, slang
cong.	conjunction	(giorn.)	journalism
(costr.)	building	(giur.)	legal
(cuc.)	cooking	(gramm.)	grammar

i.	intransitive	*pl.*	plural
id.	idem	*(poet.)*	poetical
imp.	impersonal	*(pol.)*	political
imperat.	imperative	*(pop.)*	popular
imperf.	imperfect	*poss.*	possessive
ind.	indicative	*p.p.*	past participle
indef.	indefinite	*prep.*	preposition
inf.	infinitive	*pred.*	predicate
int.	interrogative	*pres.*	present
inter.	interjection	*pron.*	pronoun
(iron.)	ironic	*prov.*	proverbial
irr.	irregular	*(psicol.)*	psychology
(itt.)	ichthyology		
		qc.	something
(lat.)	Latin, Latinism	*qu.*	someone
loc. avv.	adverbial phrase		
loc. cong.	conjunctive phrase	*r.*	reflexive
		(radio)	radio
loc. prep.	prepositional phrase	*rec.*	reciprocal
		reg.	regular
(lett.)	literature	*rel.*	relative
		(relig.)	religion
m.	masculine		
(mar.)	naval, maritime	*s.*	masculine and feminine noun
(mat.)	mathematics		
(mecc.)	mechanics	*semidif.*	partly defective
(med.)	medicine	*sf.*	feminine noun
(metal.)	metallurgy	*sm.*	masculine noun
(mil.)	military	*(scherz.)*	humourous
(min.)	mineralogy	*(scol.)*	scolastic
(mit.)	mythology	*(scult.)*	sculpture
(mus.)	music	*sing.*	singular
		so	someone
neg.	negative	*sogg.*	subject
(neol.)	neologism	*sost.*	noun
		spec.	especially
		(spreg.)	pejorative
ogg.	object	*sthg.*	something
(ott.)	optics	*(stor.)*	history
		superl.	superlative
p.	participle		
pass.	past	*t.*	transitive
p. def.	past definite	*(teat.)*	theatre
pers.	personal	*(tec.)*	technical
(pitt.)	painting		

(tel.)	telephony	*v. dif.*	defective verb
(teol.)	theology	*vi.*	instransitive verb
(tip.)	typography	*(v. irr.)*	irregular verb
(tv.)	television	*(volg.)*	vulgar
		vr.	reflexive verb
(us.)	usage	*v. semidif.*	partially defective verb
v.	verb	*vt.*	transitive verb
V.	cf.		
(vezz.)	diminutive	*(zool.)*	zoology

A

a, ad *prep.* **1.** (*termine*) to: *l'ho dato a te*, I gave it to you **2.** (*moto a luogo*) *vado alla stazione*, I am going to the station **3.** (*stato in luogo*) in, at: *vivo a Milano*, I live in Milan; *sono a casa*, I am at home **4.** (*tempo determinato*) at, on, in: *al mio arrivo*, on my arrival **5.** (*iterativo*): *due, tre volte al giorno*, twice, three times a day.

àbaco (*arch.*) *sm.* abacus.

abate *sm.* abbot.

abbacchiare *vt.* (*di frutta*) to beat (*v. irr.*) down. ◆ **abbacchiarsi** *vr.* to feel (*v. irr.*) down-hearted.

abbacchiato *agg.* down-hearted.

abbacinare *vt.* to dazzle.

àbbaco *sm.* elementary arithmetic book.

abbagliante *agg.* dazzling: *fari abbaglianti*, dazzling beams.

abbagliare *vt.* to dazzle, to blind (with).

abbaglio *sm.* **1.** dazzling **2.** (*errore*) blunder.

abbaiare *vi.* to bark.

abbaino *sm.* garret.

abbandonare *vt.* **1.** to leave (*v. irr.*), to forsake (*v. irr.*), to abandon **2.** (*rinunciare*) to give (*v. irr.*) up.

abbandonato *agg.* **1.** (*trascurato*) neglected **2.** (*di casa*) deserted **3.** (*di persona*) forsaken.

abbandono *sm.* **1.** (*di persona che viene abbandonata*) forsaking **2.** (*rinuncia*) giving up.

abbarbicare *vi.* to take (*v. irr.*) root. ◆ **abbarbicarsi** *vr.* to cling (*v. irr.*) (*anche fig.*).

abbaruffarsi *vr.* to quarrel.

abbassamento *sm.* lowering || — *di temperatura*, fall (in temperature).

abbassare *vt.* **1.** to lower, to pull down || — *la testa*, to bend (*v. irr.*) one's head **2.** (*ridurre*) to reduce. ◆ **abbassarsi** *vr.* to stoop (down).

abbasso *avv.* **1.** (*al di sotto*) below **2.** (*giù*) down **3.** (*al piano terreno, dopo aver sceso le scale*) downstairs. ◆ **abbasso!** *inter.* down with!

abbastanza *avv.* **1.** enough **2.** (*discretamente*) quite.

abbàttere *vt.* to pull down. ◆ **abbàttersi** *vr.* to be discouraged.

abbattimento *sm.* **1.** throwing down **2.** (*morale*) dejection.

abbattuto *agg.* disheartened.

abbazia *sf.* abbey.

abbecedario *sm.* primer.

abbellimento *sm.* embellishment.

abbellire *vt.* to embellish.

abbeverare *vt.* to water. ◆ **abbeverarsi** *vr.* to water.

abbeveratoio *sm.* trough.

abbicì *sm.* **1.** alphabet **2.** (*principi elementari*) primer.

abbiente *agg.* well-to-do, wealthy.

abbigliamento *sm.* clothes || *industria dell'—*, clothing industry.

abbigliare *vt.* to dress.

abbinare *vt.* to couple.

abbindolare *vt.* to cheat.

abbisognare *vi.* to need, to be necessary.

abboccamento *sm.* interview.

abboccare *vt. e vi.* **1.** to bite (*v. irr.*) **2.** (*fig.*) to be taken in. ◆ **abboccarsi** *vr.* to confer (with).

abbonacciarsi *vi.* **1.** (*di vento*) to drop **2.** (*di mare*) to smooth down.

abbonamento *sm.* **1.** subscription **2.** (*ferr.*) season-ticket.

abbonare *vt.* **1.** to make (*v. irr.*) (*so.*) a subscriber **2.** (*defalcare*) to make a discount. ◆ **abbonarsi** *vr.* to subscribe (to).

abbonato *sm.* **1.** subscriber **2.** (*ferr.*) season-ticket holder.

abbondante *agg.* plentiful.

abbondanza *sf.* plenty.

abbondare *vi.* to have plenty (of), to be plentiful.

abbonire *vt.* to calm.

abbordàbile *agg.* accessible.

abbordàggio *sm.* boarding.

abbordare *vt.* **1.** (*mar.*) to board **2.** (*una persona*) to open conversation (with).

abborracciare *vi.* to bungle.

abbottonare *vt.* to button (up). ◆ **abbottonarsi** *vr.* to button one's clothes (up).

abbottonatura *sf.* **1.** button-holes **2.** (*l'abbottonarsi*) buttoning.

abbozzare *vt.* to sketch || — *un sorriso*, to smile faintly.

abbozzo *sm.* sketch.

abbozzolarsi *vr.* to cocoon.

abbracciare *vt.* **1.** to embrace **2.** (*comprendere*) to include **3.** (*afferrare*) to grasp **4.** (*con lo sguardo*) to take (v. irr.) in. ♦ **abbracciarsi** vr. to embrace.

abbraccio sm. embrace.

abbrancare vt. to grasp. ♦ **abbrancarsi** vr. to cling (v. irr.) (to).

abbreviare vt. to shorten, to abridge.

abbreviazione sf. abbreviation.

abbrivare vt. to get (v. irr.) under way.

abbrivo sm. freshway.

abbronzare vt. 1. to bronze 2. (al sole) to tan. ♦ **abbronzarsi** vr. to get (v. irr.) tanned.

abbronzatura sf. tanning.

abbruciacchiare vt. to scorch.

abbrustolire vt. to toast, to roast.

abbrutimento sm. brutalization.

abbrutire vt. to brutalize.

abbuffarsi vr. to stuff oneself.

abbuiarsi vr. to get (v. irr.) dark.

abbuono sm. allowance.

abburattare vt. to sift.

abdicare vi. to abdicate.

abdicazione sf. abdication.

aberrare vi. to stray.

aberrazione sf. aberration.

abetaia sf. fir-wood.

abete sm. fir-tree.

abietto agg. abject, base.

abiezione sf. abjection.

abigeato sm. cattle-stealing.

àbile agg. 1. able, skilful 2. (a fare qc.) clever at.

abilità sf. ability, skill.

abilitare vt. to qualify.

abilitazione sf. qualification || esame di —, qualifying examination.

abisso sm. abyss.

abitàbile agg. inhabitable.

abitàcolo sm. (aer.) cockpit.

abitante sm. inhabitant.

abitare vi. to inhabit, to live in.

abitato sm. inhabited place.

abitazione sf. habitation, house.

àbito sm. 1. (da uomo) suit 2. (da donna) dress.

abituale agg. usual, customary.

abituare vt. to accustom. ♦ **abituarsi** vr. to get (v. irr.) used (to).

abitudinario agg. methodical. ♦ **abitudinario** sm. routinist.

abitùdine sf. habit, custom.

abituro sm. slum dwelling.

abiura sf. abjuration.

abiurare vt. to abjure.

ablazione sf. ablation.

abluzione sf. ablution.

abnegazione sf. self-denial.

abnorme agg. abnormal.

abolire vt. to abolish.

abolizione sf. abolition, repeal.

abominare vt. to loathe.

abominévole agg. abominable.

aborìgeni sm. pl. the natives.

aborrimento sm. abhorrence.

aborrire vt. to hate, to loathe.

abortire vi. to miscarry.

aborto sm. miscarriage.

abrasione sf. abrasion.

abrogare vt. 1. to abrogate 2. (giur.) to repeal.

abrogazione sf. 1. abrogation 2. (giur.) repeal.

àbside sf. apse.

abulìa sf. (fig.) lack of will-power.

abùlico agg. (fig.) lacking in will-power.

abusare vi. to abuse.

abusivo agg. abusive.

abuso sm. abuse.

acacia sf. acacia.

acanto sm. acanthus.

acca sf. letter H.

accademia sf. academy.

accadèmico agg. academical. ♦ **accadèmico** sm. academician.

accademismo sm. academism.

accadere vi. to happen.

accaduto sm. event.

accagliarsi vr. 1. to curdle 2. (del sangue) to coagulate.

accalappiacani sm. dog-catcher.

accalappiare vt. 1. to catch (v. irr.) 2. (fig.) to ensnare.

accalcarsi vr. to crowd.

accaldarsi vr. 1. to get (v. irr.) heated 2. (fig.) to get excited.

accaldato agg. hot.

accalorarsi vr. to get (v. irr.) excited.

accampamento sm. camp.

accampare vt. to camp: — diritti, to lay (v. irr.) claims to.

accanimento sm. 1. fury 2. (tenacia) tenacity.

accanirsi vr. 1. (inferire) to rage 2. (ostinarsi) to persist.

accanito agg. 1. (senza pietà) relentless 2. obstinate.

accanto avv. beside, near, by || accanto a, by, near, at the side of.

accantonare vt. to set (v. irr.) aside.

accaparrare vt. to buy (v. irr.) up.

accapigliarsi vr. to come (v. irr.) to blows, to quarrel.

accappatoio sm. bath-gown.

accapponarsi vr. to get (v. irr.) goose-flesh.

accarezzare vt. 1. to caress, to stroke 2. (fig.) to entertain.

accartocciare vt. 1. to wrap up 2. (spiegazzare) to crumple.

accasare vt. to marry, to give (v. irr.) in marriage. ♦ **accasarsi** vr. to get (v. irr.) married.

accasciarsi vi. 1. to fall (v. irr.) to the ground 2. (fig.) to lose (v. irr.) heart.

accatastare vt. to heap up.

accattivarsi vi. to win (v. irr.).

accattonaggio sm. begging.

accattone sm. beggar.

accavallare vt. to overlap: — le gambe, to cross one's legs.

accecamento sm. blinding 2. (fig.) lack of perception.

accecare vt. to blind. ♦ **accecarsi** vr. to blind oneself.

accèdere vi. 1. to approach 2. (entrare) to enter 3. (comm.) to comply (with).

accelerare vt. 1. to quicken 2. (di velocità) to accelerate.

accelerato sm. (ferr.) slow train.

acceleratore sm. accelerator.

accelerazione sf. acceleration.

accèndere vt. 1. to light 2. (di fiammiferi) to strike (v. irr.) 3. (di radio, luce ecc.) to switch on 4. (fig.) to inflame. ♦ **accèndersi** vr. 1. to light up 2. (prender fuoco) to catch (v. irr.) fire || — in volto, to blush.

accendino sm. **accendisìgaro** sm. (cigarette)-lighter.

accennare vi. 1. to make (v. irr.) a sign 2. (menzionare) to mention 3. (alludere) to allude.

accenno sm. 1. sign 2. (fig.) hint.

accensione sf. 1. lighting 2. (mecc.) ignition || chiavetta d'—, ignition-key.

accentare vt. to accent, to stress.

accentazione sf. accentuation, stressing.

accento sm. 1. accent 2. (tonico) stress.

accentramento sm. centralization.

accentrare vt. to centralize.

accentuare vt. to accentuate, to stress. ♦ **accentuarsi** vr. to get (v. irr.) worse, to increase.

accerchiamento sm. surrounding.

accerchiare vt. to surround.

accertamento sm. 1. assurance 2. (controllo) verification.

accertare vt. 1. to assure 2. (verificare) to verify.

acceso agg. 1. lit up 2. (in volto) blushing 3. (d'ira) in a temper.

accessìbile agg. 1. open to 2. (di persona) approachable.

accesso sm. 1. admission 2. (di malattia, passione) fit.

accessorio agg. accessory. ♦ **accessori** sm. pl. fittings.

accetta sf. hatchet.

accettare vt. 1. to accept 2. (consentire) to consent.

accetto agg. welcome.

accezione sf. meaning.

acchiappare vt. to catch (v. irr.).

acchito sm. di primo —, at first sight, at once.

acciacco sm. infirmity.

acciaierìa sf. steel-mill.

acciaio sm. steel.

acciarino sm. 1. flint-lock 2. (di fucile) gun-lock.

accidentale agg. accidental.

accidentato agg. uneven.

accidente sm. chance, accident.

accidenti inter. damn.

accidia sf. sloth.

accigliarsi vr. to frown.

accìngersi vr. to set (v. irr.) about (doing).

acciottolare vt. to cobble.

acciottolato sm. cobbled paving.

acciottolìo sm. clatter.

acciuffare vt. to catch (v. irr.), to seize.

acciuga sf. anchovy.

acclamare vt. 1. to acclaim 2. (applaudire) to applaud.

acclamazione sf. acclamation, applause.

acclimatazione sf. acclimatization.

acclùdere vt. to enclose.

accluso agg. enclosed.

accoccolarsi vr. to squat down.

accodarsi vr. to follow.

accogliente agg. comfortable, hospitable.

accoglienza sf. reception, welcome.

accògliere vt. 1. to receive 2. (fare buona accoglienza) to welcome 3. (una richiesta) to grant.

accòlito sm. acolyte.

accollatura sf. neckline.

accoltellare vt. to stab.

accomiatare vt. 1. to give (v. irr.) leave 2. (licenziare) to dismiss. ◆ **accomiatarsi** vr. to take (v. irr.) leave (of).

accomodamento sm. 1. adjustment 2. (conciliazione) conciliation.

accomodante agg. yielding.

accomodare vt. 1. (riparare) to repair 2. (sistemare) to settle 3. (far comodo) to suit.

accompagnamento sm. 1. (l'accompagnare) accompanying 2. (seguito) retinue 3. (mus.) accompaniment.

accompagnare vt. 1. to accompany 2. (— qu. alla stazione) to see (v. irr.) so. off 3. (mus.) to accompany.

accompagnatore sm. 1. companion 2. (mus.) accompanist.

accomunare vt. 1. to join, to associate. ◆ **accomunarsi** vr. to join.

acconciare vt. 1. to adjust, to adorn 2. (capelli) to dress.

acconciatura sf. hair-style.

acconsentire vi. 1. to consent 2. (annuire) to assent.

accontentare vt. to satisfy. ◆ **accontentarsi** vr. to be content (with).

acconto sm. account.

accoppare vt. to kill.

accoppiamento sm. 1. coupling 2. (di buoi al giogo) yoking 3. (mecc.) connection.

accoppiare vt. 1. to couple 2. (fig.) to match. ◆ **accoppiarsi** vr. to couple, to mate.

accoppiata sf. (ippica) fourecast.

accorato agg. sorrowful.

accorciare vt. to shorten.

accordare vt. 1. to grant 2. (mus.) to tune 3. (armonizzare) to match. ◆ **accordarsi** vr. to agree (upon).

accordatore sm. tuner.

accordo sm. 1. agreement ‖ come d'—, as agreed 2. (mus.) chord 3. (fig.) harmony.

accorgersi vr. 1. (percepire) to perceive 2. (rendersi conto) to realize.

accorgimento sm. 1. sagacity 2. (stratagemma) clever device.

accòrrere vi. to run (v. irr.), to hasten: — in aiuto, to rush to the help.

accortezza sf. sagacity.

accorto agg. shrewd.

accostare vt. 1. to draw (v. irr.) near 2. (porte, finestre ecc.) to set (v. irr.) ajar. ◆ **accostarsi** vr. to come (v. irr.) near.

accotonare vt. to raise.

accotonatura sf. raising.

accozzaglia sf. huddle: un'— di gente, a motley crowd.

accozzare vt. to huddle. ◆ **accozzarsi** vr. to huddle.

accreditamento sm. (comm.) crediting.

accreditare vt. to credit. ◆ **accreditarsi** vr. to gain credit.

accréscere vt. to increase.

accrescimento sm. increase.

accrescitivo agg. e sm. augmentative.

accucciarsi vr. to crouch.

accudire vi. to look after: — alla casa, to do (v. irr.) the housework.

accu nulare vt. to heap up.

accumulatore sm. accumulator.

accuratezza sf. accuracy, care.

accurato agg. careful, precise.

accusa sf. charge.

accusare vt. 1. to accuse, to charge (with) 2. (sentire) to feel (v. irr.) 3. (comm.) to acknowledge.

accusativo agg. e sm. accusative.

accusato agg. accused.

accusatore sm. prosecutor: pubblico —, public prosecutor.

acerbo agg. 1. unripe 2. (acido) sour.

àcero sm. maple.

acetilene sm. acetylene.

aceto sm. vinegar.

acetone sm. acetone.

acidità sf. 1. acidity 2. (di stomaco) hyperchlorhydria.

àcido agg. sour. ◆ **àcido** sm. acid.

acidulo agg. acidulous.

àcino sm. (di uva) grape.

acme sf. 1. acme 2. (di malattia) crisis (pl. -ses).

acne sf. acne.

aconfessionale agg. nondenominational.

acqua sf. 1. water: — marina, sea water; — piovana, rain water; — potabile, drinking water 2. (pioggia) rain: — a catinelle, heavy rain.

acquaforte sf. etching.

acquaio sm. sink.

acquamarina sf. aquamarine.

acquaragia sf. turpentine.

acquario sm. aquarium.

acquasanta sf. holy water.

acquasantiera *sf.* stoup.

acquàtico *agg.* aquatic.

acquattarsi *vr.* 1. to crouch 2. (*nascondersi*) to hide (*v. irr.*).

acquavite *sf.* brandy.

acquazzone *sm.* downpour.

acquedotto *sm.* aqueduct.

acquerellista *sm.* water-colourist.

acquerello *sm.* water-colour.

acquerùgiola *sf.* drizzle.

acquiescente *agg.* acquiescent.

acquiescenza *sf.* acquiescence.

acquirente *sm.* buyer.

acquisire *vt.* to acquire.

acquistare *vt.* 1. (*comperare*) to buy (*v. irr.*) 2. (*ottenere*) to get (*v. irr.*) 3. (*fig.*) to gain || — *terreno*, to make (*v. irr.*) progress.

acquisto *sm.* purchase || *fare acquisti*, to go (*v. irr.*) shopping.

acquitrino *sm.* marsh.

acquolina *sf.* drizzle: *far venire l'— in bocca*, to make (*v. irr.*) so.'s mouth water.

acre *agg.* 1. sour 2. (*fig.*) sarcastic 3. (*pungente*) pungent.

acrèdine *sf.* 1. acridity 2. (*fig.*) acrimony.

acrimònia *sf.* acrimony.

acròbata *s.* acrobat.

acrobàtico *agg.* acrobatic.

acrobazìa *sf.* acrobatics (*pl.*) || *fare delle acrobazie*, to perform stunts.

acròpoli *sf.* acropolis.

acuire *vt.* to sharpen: — *l'interesse*, to stimulate interest.

acùleo *sm.* 1. (*bot.*) prickle 2. (*zool.*) sting.

acume *sm.* insight.

acuminare *vt.* to sharpen.

acùstica *sf.* acoustics.

acutezza *sf.* 1. sharpness 2. (*di mente*) perspicacity.

acutizzare *vt.* to make (*v. irr.*) acute. ◆ **acutizzarsi** *vr.* to grow (*v. irr.*) acute.

acuto *agg.* 1. sharp 2. (*di angoli, accenti*) acute 3. (*intenso*) intense 4. (*di suono*) shrill. ◆ **acuto** *sm.* (*mus.*) high note.

adagiare *vt.* to lay (*v. irr.*) down with care. ◆ **adagiarsi** *vr.* to lie (*v. irr.*) down.

adagio[1] *avv.* 1. slowly 2. (*con cautela*) cautiously 3. (*con delicatezza*) gently.

adagio[2] *sm.* proverb, saying.

adamantino *agg.* adamantine.

adamìtico *agg.* adamic.

adattàbile *agg.* adaptable.

adattamento *sm.* 1. adaptation 2. (*assestamento*) adjustment.

adattare *vt.* to adapt, to fit. ◆ **adattarsi** *vr.* 1. to adapt oneself 2. (*attagliarsi*) to fit.

adatto *agg.* 1. fit, proper 2. (*che va bene*) suitable (for).

addebitare *vt.* to debit.

addèbito *sm.* charge: *fare un — a qu. per qc.*, to charge so. with sthg.

addendo *sm.* addendum (*pl.* -da).

addensamento *sm.* 1. thickening 2. (*di persone*) crowding.

addensare *vt.* 1. to thicken. ◆ **addensarsi** *vr.* 1. to thicken 2. (*di folla*) to crowd.

addentare *vt.* to bite (*v. irr.*).

addentellato *sm.* 1. (*arch.*) toothing 2. (*fig.*) stepping-stone.

addentrarsi *vr.* to penetrate: — *in una questione*, to probe a question.

addentro *avv.* inside.

addestramento *sm.* 1. training 2. (*mil.*) drilling.

addestrare *vt.* 1. to train 2. (*mil.*) to drill.

addetto *agg.* employed (in). ◆ **addetto** *sm.* attaché.

addietro *avv.* 1. (*di spazio*) behind 2. (*di tempo*) before, ago || *era venuto due giorni* —, he had come two days before.

addìo *inter.* good-bye.

addirittura *avv.* 1. quite 2. (*in esclamazioni*) really!

addirsi *vr.* to become (*v. irr.*).

additare *vt.* to point at.

addizionale *agg.* additional.

addizionare *vt.* to sum up.

addizionatrice *sf.* adding-machine, adder.

addizione *sf.* addition.

addobbare *vt.* to adorn.

addobbo *sm.* 1. decoration 2. (*eccl.*) sacred ornaments (*pl.*).

addolcire *vt.* 1. to sweeten 2. (*fig.*) to soften. ◆ **addolcirsi** *vr.* to become (*v. irr.*) soft(er).

addolorare *vt.* to grieve. ◆ **addolorarsi** *vr.* to be grieved.

addolorato *agg.* grieved, sorry.

addome *sm.* abdomen.

addomesticare *vt.* to tame.

addominale *agg.* abdominal.

addormentare *vt.* 1. to send (*v. irr.*) to sleep 2. (*med.*) to anaesthetize. ♦ **addormentarsi** vr. **1.** to fall (v. irr.) asleep **2.** (fig.) to go (v. irr.) to sleep.

addossare vt. **1.** to lean **2.** (attribuire) to lay (v. irr.). ♦ **addossarsi** vr. **1.** (affollarsi) to crowd **2.** (prendere su di sé) to take (v. irr.) upon oneself.

addosso avv. prep. **1.** on, upon: mettere qc. —, to put (v. irr.) sthg. on; togliere qc. d'—, to take (v. irr.) sthg. off **2.** (vicino a) close to: la casa è — alla montagna, the house is close to the mountain || dare —, to assault, to contradict.

addottrinare vt. to instruct. ♦ **addottrinarsi** vr. to instruct oneself.

addurre vt. **1.** to put (v. irr.) forward: — una scusa, to plead **2.** (citare) to quote.

adeguamento sm. **1.** proportionment **2.** (adattamento) adaptation.

adeguare vt. **1.** to proportionate **2.** (adattare) to conform. ♦ **adeguarsi** vr. to conform oneself, to adapt oneself.

adeguato agg. **1.** proportionate **2.** (adatto) convenient, fit **3.** (giusto) fair.

adémpiere vt. **1.** (compiere) to fulfil **2.** (eseguire) to carry out. ♦ **adémpiersi** vr. (avverarsi) to come (v. irr.) true.

adempimento sm. **1.** fulfilment **2.** (esecuzione) carrying out.

adenòidi sf. pl. adenoids.

adepto sm. **1.** adept **2.** (seguace) follower.

aderente agg. **1.** adherent **2.** (di abito) close-fitting.

aderenza sf. **1.** adherence **2.** (med.) adhesion **3.** (pl.) connections.

aderire vi. **1.** (stare vicino e fig.) to adhere, to stick **2.** (consentire) to comply with **3.** (parteggiare per) to take sides (with).

adescamento sm. **1.** enticement **2.** (seduzione) seduction.

adescare vt. **1.** to entice **2.** (sedurre) to seduce.

adesione sf. adhesion: dare la propria — ad un partito, to join a party.

adesivo agg. adhesive.

adesso avv. now, at present, at the moment.

adiacente agg. adjacent.

adibire vt. to use as.

àdipe sm. fat.

adiposo agg. adipose.

adirarsi vr. to get (v. irr.) angry.

adirato agg. angry.

adire vt. (giur.) to apply to: — le vie legali, to take (v. irr.) legal steps.

àdito sm. entry: dare —, to give (v. irr.) rise.

adocchiare vt. **1.** to glance **2.** (scorgere) to catch (v. irr.) sight of.

adolescente agg. teen-aged, adolescent. ♦ **adolescente** sm. teen-ager.

adolescenza sf. adolescence.

adombrare vt. **1.** to shade **2.** (nascondere) to conceal **3.** (simboleggiare) to symbolize. ♦ **adombrarsi** vr. **1.** to resent **2.** (di cavallo) to shy.

adoperare vt. to use. ♦ **adoperarsi** vr. to endeavour.

adoràbile agg. charming.

adorare vt. to adore, to worship.

adorazione sf. adoration, worship.

adornare vt. to adorn.

adorno agg. adorned.

adottare vt. to adopt.

adottivo agg. adoptive.

adozione sf. adoption: patria d'—, adopted country.

adrenalina sf. adrenalin.

adulare vt. to flatter.

adulatore agg. flattering. ♦ **adulatore** sm. flatterer.

adulazione sf. flattery.

adùltera sf. adulteress.

adulterare vt. **1.** to adulterate **2.** (fig.) to falsify.

adulterino agg. adulterine.

adulterio sm. adultery.

adùltero agg. adulterous. ♦ **adùltero** sm. adulterer.

adulto agg. e sm. grown-up, adult.

adunanza sf. meeting.

adunco agg. hooked.

aerare vt. **1.** to air **2.** (chim.) to aerate.

aerazione sf. **1.** airing **2.** (chim.) aeration.

àereo agg. aerial || per via aerea, by air. ♦ **àereo** sm. **1.** plane **2.** (radio) aerial.

aerodinàmica sf. aerodynamics.

aeròdromo sm. aerodrome.

aerolito sm. aerolite.

aeromodello sm. model aircraft.

aeronàuta sm. aeronaut.

aeronàutica sf. aeronautics.

aeronave sf. airship.

aeronavigazione sf. air navigation

aeroplano sm. (aero)plane, aircraft || — a razzo, rocket plane; — passeggeri, passenger plane; — da bombardamento, bomber.

aeroporto sm. airport.

aerosòl sm. aerosol.

aerostàtica sf. aerostatics.

aeròstato sm. aerostat.

aerostazione sf. air-terminal.

aerotassì sm. airtaxi.

aerotrasportare vt. to air-bear.

afa sf. sultriness.

afasia sf. aphasia.

affàbile agg. affable.

affabilità sf. affability, kindness.

affaccendarsi vr. to busy oneself.

affaccendato agg. busy.

affacciare vt. 1. to show (v. irr.) 2. (un dubbio) to raise. ♦ **affacciarsi** vr. 1. to show oneself 2. (su un luogo) to face.

affamare vt. to starve (out).

affamato agg. 1. hungry 2. (fig.) eager. ♦ **affamato** sm. starveling.

affamatore sm. starver.

affannare vt. to trouble, to worry. ♦ **affannarsi** vr. 1. to worry oneself 2. (affaccendarsi) to busy oneself.

affanno sm. 1. breathlessness 2. (pena) worry.

affannoso agg. 1. breathless || respiro —, difficult breathing 2. (ansioso) anxious.

affare sm. 1. affair, business: — di cuore, love affair; questo è — nostro, this is our business 2. (comm.) business: fare affari, to do (v. irr.) business || (pol.) affari esteri, foreign affairs; (in Gran Bretagna) Ministero degli Affari Esteri, Foreign Office.

affarista sm. speculator.

affascinante agg. charming.

affascinare vt. to charm.

affaticamento sm. weariness.

affaticare vt. to tire. ♦ **affaticarsi** vr. 1. to get (v. irr.) tired 2. (lavorare molto) to work hard.

affatto avv. 1. completely, quite 2. (in frasi negative) at all: niente —, not at all.

affatturare vt. to bewitch.

affermare vt. 1. to affirm 2. (fig.) to assert. ♦ **affermarsi** vr. to make (v. irr.) a name for oneself.

affermativo agg. affirmative.

affermazione sf. 1. statement 2. (successo) achievement.

afferrare vt. to grasp 2. (fig.) to seize. ♦ **afferrarsi** vr. to grasp at, to clutch at.

affettare¹ vt. (tagliare a fette) to slice.

affettare² vt. (ostentare) to affect.

affettato¹ agg. sliced.

affettato² agg. (ostentato) affected.

affettatrice sf. slicing machine.

affettazione sf. affectation, show.

affettivo agg. emotional.

affetto¹ sm. affection: portare — a qu., to set (v. irr.) one's affection on so.

affetto² agg. affected (with).

affettuosità sf. tenderness.

affettuoso agg. tender, affectionate.

affezionarsi vr. to grow (v. irr.) fond of.

affezione sf. 1. affection 2. (med.) affection, disease.

affiancare vt. to flank. ♦ **affiancarsi** vr. to line up (with).

affiatamento sm. concord.

affiatare vt. 1. to bring (v. irr.) together 2. (mus.) to tune. ♦ **affiatarsi** vr. to become (v. irr.) familiar (with).

affibbiare vt. 1. to buckle 2. (fig.) to shift (upon).

affidamento sm. trust, confidence: dare —, to inspire confidence.

affidare vt. 1. to entrust 2. (consegnare) to commit. ♦ **affidarsi** vr. to rely upon.

affievolire vt. to weaken. ♦ **affievolirsi** vr. to grow (v. irr.) weak.

affiggere vt. to post up: — lo sguardo, to fix one's eyes (on).

affilare vt. to sharpen. ♦ **affilarsi** vr. (dimagrire) to thin.

affilato agg. 1. sharp 2. (di naso, viso) thin.

affiliare vt. to affiliate.

affiliato sm. member, associate.

affiliazione sf. affiliation.

affinamento sm. 1. refining 2. (fig.) sharpening.

affinare vt. 1. to refine 2. (assottigliare) to make (v. irr.) thin. ♦ **affinarsi** vr. 1. to refine, to improve 2. (assottigliarsi) to become (v. irr.) thin.

affinché cong. so that, in order that.

affine agg. like, similar.

affinità sf. affinity.

affiorare vi. to appear on the surface.

affissare vt. to affix.

affissione sf. bill-posting.

affisso sm. 1. (avviso) bill 2. (cartello) placard 3. (manifesto) poster.

affittacamere sm. e sf. landlord, landlady.

affittare vt. 1. (dare in affitto) to let (v. irr.) 2. (prendere in affitto) to rent 3. (noleggiare) to hire.

affitto sm. rent.

afflato sm. afflatus.

affliggere vt. 1. to drown 2. (di malattie) to afflict. ♦ **affliggersi** vr. to worry.

afflitto agg. sad, sorrowful.

afflizione sf. 1. affliction 2. (flagello) calamity.

afflosciarsi vr. 1. to become (v. irr.) flabby 2. (fig.) to weaken.

affluente sm. affluent.

affluenza sf. 1. (di acque) flow 2. (di persone) crowd 3. (abbondanza) plenty.

affluire vi. 1. (di acque) to flow 2. (di persone) to crowd 3. (di cose) to pour in.

afflusso sm. afflux.

affogamento sm. drowning.

affogare vt. 1. to drown 2. (fig.) to smother. ♦ **affogarsi** vr. to drown oneself.

affogato agg. 1. drowned 2. (fig.) oppressed || uova affogate, poached eggs.

affollamento sm. overcrowding, throng.

affollare vt. 1. to crowd 2. (fig.) to overwhelm. ♦ **affollarsi** vr. to press up.

affollato agg. crowded.

affondare vt. 1. (sommergere) to sink (v. irr.) 2. (immergere) to plunge.

affossamento sm. ditching.

affossare vt. to ditch. ♦ **affossarsi** vr. to become (v. irr.) hollow.

affrancamento sm. release.

affrancare vt. 1. to release 2. (con francobollo) to stamp. ♦ **affrancarsi** vr. to free oneself.

affrancato agg. 1. free 2. (con francobollo) stamped.

affrancatura sf. postage.

affranto agg. broken-hearted || (dalla fatica) worn out.

affratellarsi vr. to fraternize.

affresco sm. fresco.

affrettare vt. 1. to hasten 2. (anticipare) to anticipate. ♦ **affrettarsi** vr. to make (v. irr.) haste.

affrettatamente avv. hastily.

affrettato agg. 1. hasty 2. (trascurato) careless.

affrontare vt. 1. to face 2. (fig.) to deal (v. irr.) with. ♦ **affrontarsi** vr. (venire alle mani) to come (v. irr.) to blows.

affronto sm. insult.

affumicare vt. 1. to fill with smoke 2. (cuc.) to smoke.

affumicato agg. 1. blackened by smoke 2. (cuc.) smoked || lenti affumicate, sun-glasses.

affusolare vt. to taper.

afonia sf. aphonia.

àfono agg. voiceless.

aforisma sm. aphorism.

afoso agg. sultry.

africano agg. e sm. African.

afroasiàtico agg. Afro-Asiatic.

afta sf. aphtha.

àgata sf. agate.

àgave sf. agave.

agenda sf. note-book.

agente sm. agent.

agenzia sf. agency.

agevolare vt. to make (v. irr.) easy.

agevolazione sf. facilitation.

agévole agg. 1. easy 2. (di strada) smooth.

agevolmente avv. easily.

agganciare vt. 1. to hook 2. (ferr.) to couple up.

aggeggio sm. device.

aggettare vi. to jut out.

aggettivo sm. adjective.

agghiacciare vt. to freeze (v. irr.). ♦ **agghiacciarsi** vr. to freeze.

agghindare vt. to array. ♦ **agghindarsi** vr. to dress (oneself) up.

aggiogare vt. to yoke.

aggiornamento sm. 1. (rinvio) adjournment 2. (di un libro) revision.

aggiornare vt. 1. (rinviare) to adjourn 2. (mettere al corrente) to bring (v. irr.) up to date. ♦ **aggiornarsi** vr. to brush up one's knowledge.

aggiornato agg. up-to-date.

aggirare vt. to go (v. irr.) round || ― l'ostacolo, to avoid an obstacle. ♦ **aggirarsi** vr. to wander about, to go about.

aggiudicare vt. to award. ♦ **ag-**

giudicarsi *vr.* to win (*v. irr.*).
aggiudicazione *sf.* award.
aggiùngere *vt.* to add. ♦ aggiùngersi *vr.* to join.
aggiunta *sf.* 1. addition 2. (*aumento*) increase.
aggiunto *agg.* added, joined. ♦ aggiunto *sm.* assistant.
aggiustare *vt.* 1. (*riparare*) to mend 2. (*sistemare*) to arrange. ♦ aggiustarsi *vr.* (*accomodarsi*) to make (*v. irr.*) oneself comfortable.
agglomerato *sm.* agglomerate.
agglutinare *vt.* to agglutinate.
aggraffare *vt.* to seize.
aggranchire *vt.* to benumb.
aggrapparsi *vr.* to cling (*v. irr.*) (to), to get (*v. irr.*) hold (of).
aggravante *agg.* aggravating. ♦ aggravante *sf.* (*giur.*) aggravating circumstance.
aggravare *vt.* to aggravate, to overburden. ♦ aggravarsi *vr.* to grow (*v. irr.*) worse.
aggravato *agg.* 1. overburdened 2. (*med.*) worse.
aggraziare *vt.* to make (*v. irr.*) graceful.
aggredire *vt.* to assault.
aggregare *vt.* to associate. ♦ aggregarsi *vr.* to join.
aggressione *sf.* aggression, assault.
aggressività *sf.* aggressiveness.
aggressivo *agg.* aggressive.
aggressore *sm.* aggressor.
aggrottare *vt.* to frown.
aggrovigliare *vt.* to entangle.
aggrovigliarsi *vr.* to get (*v. irr.*) entangled.
aggruppare *vt.* to group.
agguantare *vt.* to catch (*v. irr.*).
agguato *sm.* ambush.
agguerrire *vt.* to inure (for war).
♦ agguerrirsi *vr.* to get (*v. irr.*) inured.
agiatamente *avv.* in ease and comfort.
agiato *agg.* well-to-do.
àgile *agg.* nimble.
agilità *sf.* nimbleness.
agio *sm.* comfort, ease, leisure.
agiografia *sf.* hagiography.
agire *vi.* to act.
agitare *vt.* 1. to agitate 2. (*scuotere*) to shake (*v. irr.*) 3. to stir (*anche fig.*). ♦ agitarsi *vr.* to be agitated.
agitatore *sm.* 1. agitator 2. (*mecc.*) stirrer.

agitazione *sf.* 1. agitation 2. (*eccitazione*) excitement 3. (*di folla*) tumult.
aglio *sm.* garlic.
agnello *sm.* lamb.
agnosticismo *sm.* agnosticism.
ago *sm.* 1. needle 2. (*mecc.*) tongue.
agognare *vt.* to long (for sthg.).
agonia *sf.* agony, pangs (*pl.*) of death.
agonismo *sm.* athletic spirit.
agonizzante *agg.* dying.
agonizzare *vi.* to be in one's death agony.
agorafobìa *sf.* agoraphobia.
agosto *sm.* August.
agraria *sf.* agriculture.
agrario *agg.* agrarian. ♦ agrario *sm.* 1. land-owner 2. (*esperto*) agriculturist.
agreste *agg.* agrestic, rustic.
agretto *agg.* sourish.
agrìcolo *agg.* agricultural.
agricoltore *sm.* farmer.
agricoltura *sf.* agriculture.
agrifoglio *sm.* holly.
agrimensore *sm.* land-surveyor.
agro *agg.* sour. ♦ agro *sm.* sourness.
agrodolce *agg.* bitter-sweet, sourish.
agronomìa *sf.* agronomy.
agronòmico *agg.* agronomical.
agrònomo *sm.* agronomist.
agrumi *sm. pl.* citrus fruit (*sing.*).
aguzzare *vt.* to sharpen.
aguzzino *sm.* 1. gaoler, jailer 2. (*fig.*) torturer.
aguzzo *agg.* sharp, pointed.
ahimè *inter.* alas.
aia *sf.* threshing-floor.
aio *sm.* tutor.
airone *sm.* heron.
aitante *agg.* vigorous, stout.
aiuola *sf.* flower-bed.
aiutante *sm.* 1. assistant 2. (*mil.*) adjutant: — *di campo*, aide-decamp.
aiutare *vt.* to help. ♦ aiutarsi *vr.* (*ingegnarsi*) to make (*v. irr.*) shift. ♦ aiutarsi *vr. rec.* to help (one another).
aiuto *sm.* 1. help: *chiedere* —, to call for help 2. (*chi aiuta*) help, helper 3. (*pl.*) (*mil.*) reinforcements.
aizzare *vt.* to incite, to rouse.
ala *sf.* wing.
alabarda *sf.* halberd.

alabastro sm. alabaster.

àlacre agg. brisk, industrious.

alacrità sf. alacrity.

alamaro sm. frog.

alambicco sm. still.

alano sm. Great Dane.

alba sf. dawn.

albanese agg. e sm. Albanian.

àlbatro sm. albatross.

albeggiare vi. to dawn.

alberare vt. **1.** to plant with trees **2.** (mar.) to mast.

alberato agg. planted with trees.

alberatura sf. (mar.) masting.

albergatore sm. hotel-keeper.

alberghiero agg. hotel (attributivo): industria alberghiera. hotel trade.

albergo sm. hotel.

àlbero sm. **1.** tree **2.** (mar.) mast **3.** (mecc.) shaft.

albicocca sf. apricot.

albino agg. e sm. albino.

albo sm. **1.** list, roll: — degli avvocati, Law List; — d'onore, roll of honour **2.** (per fotografie ecc.) album **3.** (tavola per affissione) notice-board.

album sm. album.

albume sm. albumen.

albumina sf. albumin.

alca sf. auk.

alcalino agg. e sm. alkaline.

alce sm. elk.

alchimia sf. alchemy.

alcòlico agg. alcoholic.

alcolismo sm. alcoholism.

alcolizzato agg. e sm. alcoholic.

alcool sm. alcohol.

alcova sf. alcove.

alcunché pron. anything, something.

alcuno agg. **1.** (frasi affermative) some, a few **2.** (frasi negative) any. ♦ **alcuno** pron. **1.** (frasi affermative) somebody, someone **2.** (frasi negative) anybody, anyone.

aldilà sm. hereafter.

aleatorio agg. aleatory.

aleggiare vi. **1.** to flutter **2.** (fig.) to hover (about).

alettone sm. aileron.

alfa sf. alpha.

alfabeto sm. alphabet.

aliiere sm. **1.** ensign **2.** (scacchi) bishop.

alga sf. seaweed.

àlgebra sf. algebra.

algèbrico agg. algebraic, algebraical.

aliante sm. glider.

àlibi sm. alibi.

alienare vt. to alienate, to estrange. ♦ **alienarsi** vr. to alienate oneself, to become (v. irr.) estranged.

alienato agg. lunatic, mad; estranged, alienated. ♦ **alienato** sm. **1.** lunatic, madman (pl. -men) **2.** alienated person, estranged person.

alienazione sf. alienation, estrangement.

alienista sm. alienist, psychiatrist.

alieno agg. averse, opposed.

alimentare[1] vt. to feed (v. irr.), to nourish.

alimentare[2] agg. alimentary || generi alimentari, foodstuffs; negozio di generi alimentari, grocery store.

alimentazione sf. nourishment, feeding.

alimento sm. food.

alinea sf. paragraph.

aliquota sf. aliquot, rate.

aliscafo sm. hydrofoil boat.

aliseo sm. trade-wind.

àlito sm. breath.

allacciare vt. **1.** to lace, to connect **2.** (fig.) to establish. ♦ **allacciarsi** vr. **1.** (abbracciarsi) to embrace **2.** (aggrovigliarsi) to get (v. irr.) entangled, to be entangled.

allagare vt. to flood, to inundate.

allampanato agg. lean, lanky.

allargamento sm. widening, enlargement.

allargare vt. to widen, to enlarge, to extend. ♦ **allargarsi** vr. to widen, to extend, to spread (v. irr.).

allarmante agg. alarming.

allarmare vt. to alarm. ♦ **allarmarsi** vr. to get (v. irr.) frightened.

allarme sm. alarm, warning, alert.

allattamento sm. breast-feeding, nursing.

allattare vt. to suckle, to nurse.

alleanza sf. alliance.

allearsi vr. to ally, to become (v. irr.) allies. ♦ **alleato** agg. allied. ♦ **alleato** sm. ally.

allegare vt. **1.** to allege **2.** (accludere) to enclose.

allegato sm. enclosure.

alleggerimento sm. lightening, relief.

alleggerire vt. to lighten, to re-

lieve, to unburden. ♦ **allegge-**
rirsi *vr.* to relieve oneself.

allegoria *sf.* allegory.

allegòrico *agg.* allegoric(al).

allegramente *agg.* cheerfully, merrily.

allegrìa *sf.* cheerfulness, mirth.

allegro *agg.* merry, cheerful, jolly.

allegrone *sm.* jolly fellow.

allenamento *sm.* · training.

allenare *vt.* to train. ♦ **allenarsi**
vr. to train (oneself).

allenatore *sm.* trainer; (*di squadre*)
coach.

allentamento *sm.* **1.** loosening **2.**
(*di velocità*) slackening.

allentare *vt.* to slacken, to loosen,
to relax: — *il freno,* to release
the brake. ♦ **allentarsi** *vr.* to
slacken.

allergìa *sf.* allergy.

allèrgico *agg.* allergic.

allestimento *sm.* preparation, fitting out ‖ — *scenico,* staging.

allestire *vt.* to prepare, to fit out.

allettamento *sm.* enticement, allurement.

allettante *agg.* alluring, enticing.

allettare *vt.* to allure, to entice.

allevamento *sm.* **1.** breeding, raising ‖ (*di bambino*) bringing up
2. (*luogo*) stock-farm ‖ — *di cavalli,* stud-farm.

allevare *vt.* **1.** (*bambini*) to bring
(*v. irr.*) up **2.** (*animali*) to breed
(*v. irr.*), to rear.

allevatore *sm.* breeder.

alleviare *vt.* to relieve, to alleviate.

allibire *vi.* to be left speechless,
to be struck dumb.

allibito *agg.* struck dumb, speechless.

allibratore *sm.* bookmaker.

allietare *vt.* to cheer. ♦ **allietarsi**
vr. to cheer up.

allievo *sm.* **1.** pupil **2.** (*mil.*) cadet.

alligatore *sm.* alligator.

allineamento *sm.* **1.** alignment ‖
(*tip.*) — *di caratteri,* ranging of
characters **2.** (*mil.*) dressing.

allineare *vt.* **1.** to line up, to
align: — *delle cifre,* to tabulate
figures **2.** (*mil.*) to dress; (*in ordine di marcia*) to form up. ♦ **allinearsi** *vr.* **1.** to get (*v. irr.*) into
line **2.** (*mil.*) to dress ‖ *allineatevi,* dress up! **3.** (*pol.*) to be
aligned with.

allocco *sm.* **1.** owl **2.** (*fig.*) fool.

allocuzione *sf.* allocution: *fare
un'—,* to deliver a speech.

allòdola *sf.* skylark, lark.

allogare *vt.* to lodge.

allogazione *sf.* lease.

alloggiare *vt.* **1.** to lodge, to
house, to put (*v. irr.*) up **2.** (*mil.*)
to quarter; (*in casa privata*) to
billet. ♦ **alloggiare** *vi.* **1.** to
lodge, to live **2.** (*mil.*) to quarter;
(*in casa privata*) to be billeted.

alloggio *sm.* · **1.** lodging ‖ *indennità
di —,* living-out allowance **2.**
(*mil.*) quarters (*pl.*).

allontanamento *sm.* **1.** removal **2.**
(*licenziamento*) dismissal.

allontanare *vt.* **1.** to remove, to
drive (*v. irr.*) away: — *un pericolo,* to evert a danger **2.** (*licenziare*) to dismiss, to turn out. ♦
allontanarsi *vr.* to go (*v. irr.*)
away, to depart.

allora *avv.* **1.** then **2.** (*quindi*) so.

allorché *cong.* when.

alloro *sm.* laurel.

alluce *sm.* big toe.

allucinare *vt.* **1.** to dazzle **2.** (*dare
allucinazioni*) to hallucinate.

allucinato *agg.* hallucinated.

allucinazione *sf.* hallucination.

alludere *vi.* to allude (to), to hint
(at).

alluminio *sm.* aluminium.

allunaggio *sm.* mooning.

allunare *vi.* to moon.

allungàbile *agg.* extensible.

allungamento *sm.* lengthening,
stretching.

allungare *vt.* **1.** to lengthen, to
extend, to stretch ‖ — *il passo,* to
quicken one's steps ‖ — *il collo,*
to stretch one's neck ‖ — *gli
orecchi,* to strain one's ears ‖
(*fig.*) — *le mani su qc.,* to lay
(*v. irr.*) hands on sthg. ♦ **allungarsi** *vr.* to lengthen, to grow
(*v. irr.*) longer, to draw (*v. irr.*)
out.

allusione *sf.* allusion, hint.

allusivo *agg.* allusive.

alluvionato *agg.* flooded ‖ *zone
alluvionate,* flood-areas. ♦ **alluvionato** *sm.* flood-victim.

alluvione *sf.* flood.

almanaccare *vi.* to fantasticate.

almanacco *sm.* almanac.

almeno *avv.* at least.

alno *sm.* alder-tree.

aloè *sm.* aloe.

alone *sm.* halo.
alpaca *sm.* alpaca.
alpe *sf.* alp.
alpestre *agg.* alpine.
alpinismo *sm.* (mountain-)climbing, mountaineering.
alpinista *s.* (mountain-)climber.
alpino *agg.* Alpine.
alquanto *avv.* somewhat, rather.
altalena *sf.* swing.
altana *sf.* roof-terrace.
altare *sm.* altar.
alterare *vt.* to alter; (*salute*) to impair; (*cibo*) to adulterate. ◆ **alterarsi** *vr.* 1. to alter, to change 2. (*andare a male*) to go (*v. irr.*) bad 3. (*turbarsi*) to be upset || *la sua voce si alterò*, his voice faltered.
alterazione *sf.* 1. alteration 2. (*deteriorazione*) deterioration 3. (*turbamento*) emotion; (*della voce*) faltering.
altercare *vi.* altercation.
alterigia *sf.* haughtiness.
alternanza *sf.* alternation.
alternare *vt.* to alternate. ◆ **alternarsi** *vr.* to alternate.
alternativa *sf.* alternative.
alterno *agg.* alternate.
altero *agg.* lofty, proud.
altezza *sf.* 1. height 2. (*di tessuto*) width 3. (*di suono*) pitch 4. (*fig.*) *essere all'— di qc.*, to be equal to sthg.; to be up to sthg. 5. (*titolo*) highness.
altezzoso *agg.* haughty.
alticcio *agg.* tight, tipsy.
altimetro *sm.* altimeter.
altitùdine *sf.* altitude.
alto *agg.* 1. high, tall: *un uomo —*, a tall man || *alta direzione*, top management 2. (*di suono*) loud || *ad alta voce*, aloud, loudly 3. (*profondo*) deep: *acqua alta*, deep water 4. (*geogr.*) northern, upper 5. (*stor.*) early. ◆ **alto** *sm.* height || *alti e bassi*, ups and downs. ◆ **alto** *avv.* high, up || *mani in —*, hands up.
altoforno *sm.* blast-furnace.
altolocato *agg.* high-ranking, high-class.
altoparlante *sm.* loud-speaker.
altopiano *sm.* plateau.
altresì *avv.* likewise, also.
altrettanto *agg. correlativo* as much (...as); (*pl.*) as many (...as) || (*neg.*) as (o so) much (...as); (*pl.*)

as (o so) many... (as): *egli ha altrettante possibilità quanto me*, he has as many chances as I. ◆ **altrettanto** *pron.* 1. as much; (*pl.*) as many 2. (*lo stesso*) the same: *— a voi!*, the same to you!. ◆ **altrettanto** *avv.* 1. (*con agg. e avv.*) as (...as); (*neg.*) as (o so) ...as) 2. (*coi verbi*) as much (as).
altrimenti *avv.* otherwise. ◆ **altrimenti** *cong.* otherwise, else.
altro *agg. indef.* 1. other || *un —*, another 2. (*differente*) different 3. (*con pronomi int.*) else: *chi altro?*, who else? 4. (*in più*) more: *leggerò altri due libri*, I shall read two more books 5. (*susseguente*) next: *verrò l'altra domenica*, I shall come next Sunday 6. (*antecedente*) last: *andai l'altro mese*, I went last month.
altronde 1. (*nella loc. avv.*) *d'—*, on the other hand 2. (*tuttavia*) however.
altrove *avv.* elsewhere, somewhere else.
altrùi *agg.* other people's, someone else's. ◆ **l'altrùi** *sm.* the property of others.
altruismo *sm.* unselfishness.
altruìstico *agg.* unselfish.
altura *sf.* height.
alunno *sm.* pupil.
alveare *sm.* beehive.
alveo *sm.* river-bed.
alzaia *sf.* towing-line || *strada d'—*, towing-path.
alzare *vt.* 1. to lift, to raise 2. (*erigere*) to build (*v. irr.*) 3. (*mar.*) to hoist. ◆ **alzarsi** *vr.* (*dal letto*) to get (*v. irr.*) up 2. (*in piedi*) to stand (*v. irr.*) up 3. (*in altezza*) to grow (*v. irr.*) tall.
alzata *sf.* 1. raising 2. (*l'alzarsi*) rising.
amàbile *agg.* amiable.
amabilità *sf.* amiability.
amaca *sf.* hammock.
amàlgama *sm.* amalgam.
amalgamare *vt.* to amalgamate.
amante *s.* 1. lover 2. (*fig.*) fond of 2. (*richiedere*) to require.
amanuense *sm.* copyist.
amaranto *sm.* amaranth.
amare *vt.* 1. to love, to be fond of 2. (*richiedere*) to require.
amareggiare *vt.* 1. to make (*v. irr.*) bitter 2. (*fig.*) to sadden. ◆ **amareggiarsi** *vr.* to worry.
amarena *sf.* sour black cherry.

amaretto *sm.* macaroon.

amarezza *sf.* **1.** bitterness **2.** (*fig.*) sorrow.

amaro *agg.* bitter. ♦ **amaro** *sm.* (*liquore*) bitters (*pl.*).

amatore *sm.* **1.** lover **2.** (*chi si occupa d'arte per diletto*) amateur.

amàzzone *sf.* **1.** Amazon **2.** (*fig.*) masculine woman.

ambage *sf.* ambages (*pl.*) || *senza ambagi*, plainly.

ambasciata *sf.* **1.** embassy **2.** (*messaggio*) message.

ambasciatore *sm.* ambassador.

ambedue *agg.* e *pron.* both.

ambientare *vt.* **1.** to acclimatize **2.** (*fatti, personaggi ecc.*) to place. ♦ **ambientarsi** *vr.* to get (*v. irr.*) accustomed.

ambiente *sm.* **1.** ambient **2.** (*fig.*) milieu **3.** (*stanza*) room.

ambiguità *sf.* ambiguity.

ambiguo *agg.* ambiguous.

ambio *sm.* amble.

ambire *vt.* to desire.

àmbito *sm.* ambit.

ambivalente *agg.* ambivalent.

ambivalenza *sf.* ambivalence.

ambizione *sf.* ambition.

ambizioso *agg.* ambitious.

ambo *sm.* ambo.

ambra *sf.* amber.

ambrosia *sf.* ambrosia.

ambulante *agg.* itinerant || *venditore —*, pedlar.

ambulanza *sf.* ambulance.

ambulatorio *sm.* surgery.

ameba *sf.* amoeba.

amebìasi *sf.* amoebiasis (*pl.* -ses).

amenità *sf.* **1.** amenity **2.** (*facezia*) joke.

ameno *agg.* **1.** pleasant **2.** (*divertente*) funny: *un tipo —*, a funny chap.

americanismo *sm.* Americanism.

americano *agg.* e *sm.* American.

ametista *sf.* amethyst.

amianto *sm.* amianthus.

amichévole *agg.* friendly.

amicizia *sf.* friendship || *fare —*, to make (*v. irr.*) friends with.

amico *sm.* friend.

amidatura *sf.* starching.

àmido *sm.* starch.

ammaccare *vt.* to bruise.

ammaccatura *sf.* bruise.

ammaestramento *sm.* **1.** (*addestramento*) training **2.** (*insegnamento*) teaching **3.** (*di animali*) taming.

ammaestrare *vt.* **1.** (*addestrare*) to train **2.** (*insegnare*) to teach (*v. irr.*) **3.** (*di animali*) to tame.

ammainare *vt.* to furl.

ammalarsi *vr.* to fall (*v. irr.*) ill.

ammalato *agg.* **1.** (*pred.*) ill **2.** (*attr.*) sick. ♦ **ammalato** *sm.* sick person, patient.

ammaliare *vt.* to bewitch.

ammaliatrice *sf.* bewitcher.

ammanco *sm.* shortage || *— di cassa*, deficit.

ammanettare *vt.* to handcuff.

ammannire *vt.* to prepare.

ammansire *vt.* **1.** to tame **2.** (*fig.*) to calm. ♦ **ammansirsi** *vr.* **1.** to become (*v. irr.*) tamed **2.** to calm down.

ammarare *vi.* **1.** to alight (on water) **2.** (*di capsule spaziali*) to splash down.

ammassare *vt.* to heap. ♦ **ammassarsi** *vr.* to gather.

ammasso *sm.* heap.

ammattire *vi.* to get (*v. irr.*) mad.

ammazzare *vt.* to kill.

ammazzatoio *sm.* slaughter-house.

ammenda *sf.* amends (*pl.*).

amméttere *vt.* **1.** (*lasciar entrare*) to admit, to receive **2.** (*concedere, supporre*) to acknowledge, to suppose.

ammezzato *sm.* mezzanine.

ammezzire *vi.* to become (*v. irr.*) over-ripe.

ammiccare *vi.* to wink (at).

ammina *sf.* amine.

amministrare *vt.* **1.** to manage **2.** (*giur.; eccl.*) to administer.

amministrativo *agg.* administrative.

amministratore *sm.* manager.

amministrazione *sf.* management.

ammiràbile *agg.* admirable.

ammiraglio *sm.* admiral.

ammirare *vt.* to admire.

ammiratore *sm.* **1.** admirer **2.** (*di attori ecc.*) fan.

ammirazione *sf.* admiration.

ammirévole *agg.* admirable.

ammissibile *agg.* admissible.

ammobiliamento *sm.* furnishing.

ammobiliare *vt.* to furnish.

ammodernare *vt.* to modernize.

ammodo *agg.* nice, proper.

ammogliare *vt.* to marry. ♦ **ammogliarsi** *vr.* to get (*v. irr.*) married.

ammollare vt. 1. to soak 2. (am-morbidire) to soften.

ammollire vt. to soften.

ammoniaca sf. ammonia.

ammonire vt. 1. to admonish 2. (avvisare) to warn.

ammonizione sf. 1. admonition 2. (rimprovero) reproof 3. (avverti-mento) warning.

ammontare vi. to amount.

ammonticchiare vt. to heap (up).

ammorbare vt. to taint.

ammorbidire vt. to soften.

ammortamento sm. redemption || quota d'—, depreciation allowance.

ammortire vt. to numb.

ammortizzare vt. to redeem.

ammosciare vt. to become (v. irr.) flabby.

ammucchiare vt. to heap (up).

ammuffire vi. 1. to grow (v. irr.) musty 2. (fig.) to languish: — in casa, to languish at home.

ammutinamento sm. mutiny.

ammutinarsi vr. to mutiny.

ammutinato agg. mutinous. ♦ **ammutinato** sm. mutineer.

ammutolire vi. 1. to become (v. irr.) dumb 2. (essere ammutolito da altri) to be struck dumb.

amnesia sf. loss of memory.

amnistia sf. amnesty.

amnistiare vt. to amnesty.

amo sm. fish-hook.

amorale agg. amoral.

amoralità sf. amorality.

amore sm. 1. love || — di sé, self-ishness 2. (persona o cosa amata) beloved || per amore di, for the sake of.

amoreggiare vi. to flirt.

amoretto sm. flirtation.

amorévole agg. loving.

amorevolezza sf. lovingness.

amorfo agg. amorphous.

amorino sm. Cupid.

amoroso agg. 1. loving 2. (fig.) amorous: poesia —, amorous verse.

amovibile agg. movable.

amperòmetro sm. amperometer.

ampiezza sf. width, (anche fig.) breadth.

ampio agg. 1. wide 2. (di abito) comfortable.

amplesso sm. embrace.

ampliamento sm. amplification.

ampliare vt. 1. to amplify 2. (au-mentare) to increase. ♦ **ampliar-**

si vr. to widen.

amplificare vt. 1. to enlarge 2. (fig.; fis.) to amplify.

amplificatore sm. amplifier.

amplificazione sf. amplification.

ampolla sf. 1. phial 2. (per olio, aceto ecc.) cruet.

ampollosità sf. pomposity.

ampolloso agg. pompous: stile —, bombastic style.

amputare vt. to amputate.

amputazione sf. amputation.

amuleto sm. amulet.

anabbaglianti sm. pl. lower beams

anabolismo sm. anabolism.

anacoreta sm. anchorite.

anacronismo sm. anachronism.

anacronistico agg. anachronistic.

anàgrafe sf. registry office.

anagramma sm. anagram.

analcòlico agg. soft.

anale agg. anal.

analfabeta sm. illiterate.

analfabetismo sm. illiteracy.

analgèsico agg. e sm. analgesic.

anàlisi sf. analysis (pl. -ses).

analitico agg. analytical.

analizzare vt. to analyse.

analogamente avv. likewise.

analogia sf. analogy.

anàlogo agg. similar.

ànanas sm. pine-apple.

anarchia sf. anarchy.

anàrchico agg. anarchic. ♦ **anàr-chico** sm. anarchist.

anatema sm. anathema.

anatomia sf. anatomy.

anatòmico agg. anatomic.

anatomista sm. anatomist.

ànatra sf. duck.

anatròccolo sm. duckling.

anca sf. hip.

ancestrale agg. ancestral.

anche avv. 1. (pure) also, too 2. (in frasi neg.) either: anch'io non verrò, I will not come either 3. (con comp.) even, still: ciò è an-che peggio, it is still worse 4. (persino) even. ♦ **anche** cong. (anche se) even if, even though

ancheggiare vi. to waddle.

anchilosare vt. to ankylose.

anchilosi sf. ankylosis.

àncora sf. 1. anchor: levar l'—, to weigh anchor 2. (fig.) hope: — di salvezza, last hope.

ancora avv. 1. (tuttora) still 2. (in frasi neg.) yet 3. (di nuovo) again 4. (davanti a comp.) still, even

5. (*con pron. e agg. quantitativi*) more: — *molte persone*, many more people **6.** («*di più*» *in frasi affermative*) some more: *voglio ancora caffè*, I want some more coffee **7.** («*di più*» *in frasi neg. e dubitative*) any more: *hai ancora caffè?*, have you any more coffee? **8.** (*più a lungo*) longer: *leggi ancora un po'*, read a little longer.

ancoraggio *sm.* anchorage.

ancorare *vt.* to anchor.

ancorché *cong.* even if, even though.

andamento *sm.* **1.** (*tendenza*) trend **2.** (*procedimento*) proceeding.

andante *agg.* **1.** (*scadente*) plain **2.** (*comm.*) current **3.** (*mus.*) andante.

andare *vi.* **1.** (*anche fig.*) to go (*v. irr.*): — *a cavallo*, to go on horseback; — *a far compere*, to go shopping; — *a piedi*, to go on foot; — *a zonzo*, to lounge about; — *e venire*, to come (*v. irr.*) and go; — *in bicicletta*, to ride (*v. irr.*) a bicycle; — *in treno*, to go by train; — *a male*, to go bad **2.** (*essere molto venduto*) to be in demand **3.** (— *bene, di indumento*) to fit || — *avanti* (*di orologi*), to be fast; — *indietro* (*di orologi*), to be slow. ♦ **andàrsene** *vr.* to go away.

andata *sf.* going: — *e ritorno*, going there and back || *biglietto di sola* —, single ticket || *biglietto di* — *e ritorno*, return ticket.

andatura *sf.* **1.** gait **2.** (*velocità*) pace.

andazzo *sm.* habit, custom.

andicappare *vt.* to handicap.

andirivieni *sm.* coming and going.

àndito *sm.* passage.

andrògino *agg.* androgynous. ♦ **andrògino** *sm.* androgyne.

androne *sm.* lobby.

aneddòtico *agg.* anecdotic.

anèddoto *sm.* anecdote.

anelare *vi.* **1.** to gasp **2.** (*fig.*) to long for.

anèlito *sm.* **1.** gasp **2.** (*fig.*) longing for.

anello *sm.* ring: — *di fidanzamento*, engagement ring; — *di matrimonio*, wedding ring || — *di catena*, link of a chain.

anemia *sf.* anaemia.

anèmico *agg.* anaemic.

anèmone *sm.* anemone.

anestesìa *sf.* anaesthesia.

anestesista *s.* anaesthetist.

anestètico *agg.* e *sm.* anaesthetic.

anestetizzare *vt.* to anaesthetize.

anfibio *agg.* amphibious. ♦ **anfibio** *sm.* (*zool.; mil.*) amphibian.

anfiteatro *sm.* amphitheatre.

anfitrione *sm.* amphitryon.

ànfora *sf.* amphora (*pl.* -ae).

anfrattuoso *agg.* anfractuous.

angèlico *agg.* angelic(al).

àngelo *sm.* angel.

angherìa *sf.* vexation.

angina *sf.* angina.

angioma *sm.* angioma.

anglicano *agg.* e *sm.* Anglican.

angolare *agg.* angular.

àngolo *sm.* **1.** corner **2.** (*fis.; geom.*) angle.

angoloso *agg.* angular.

angoscia *sf.* anguish.

angosciare *vt.* to anguish.

angoscioso *agg.* **1.** (*che dà angoscia*) distressing **2.** (*pieno di angoscia*) full of anguish.

anguilla *sf.* **1.** eel **2.** (*fig.*) elusive person.

anguria *sf.* water-melon.

angustia *sf.* **1.** narrowness **2.** (*tribolazione*) distress.

angustiare *vt.* to afflict. ♦ **angustiarsi** *vr.* to worry.

angusto *agg.* **1.** narrow **2.** (*fig.*) mean.

ànice *sm.* anise.

anidride *sf.* anhydride.

anilina *sf.* aniline.

ànima *sf.* **1.** soul || *esalare l'—*, to die || *vender l'—a caro prezzo*, to sell (*v. irr.*) one's life dearly. **2.** (*parte centrale, nerbo*) soul, heart **3.** (*cuore, sentimento*) feeling, heart **4.** (*persona*) person: *Torino ha oltre un milione di anime*, Turin has over one million persons.

animale *sm.* e *agg.* animal.

animalesco *agg.* beastly.

animare *vt.* to enliven, to give (*v. irr.*) life. ♦ **animarsi** *vr.* to become (*v. irr.*) lively.

animatamente *avv.* animatedly.

animato *agg.* **1.** living **2.** (*vivace*) lively.

animatore *sm.* animator.

animazione *sf.* briskness.

animismo *sm.* animism.

ànimo *sm.* **1.** mind: *ho in animo di fare ciò*, I have a mind to do that **2.** (*coraggio*) courage **3.** (*inclinazione*) disposition.

animosità *sf.* animosity.

animoso *agg.* 1. brave 2. (*ostile*) malevolent.

anisetta *sf.* anisette.

ànitra *sf.* duck.

annacquare *vt.* 1. to water 2. (*fig.*) to moderate.

annaffiare *vt.* to water.

annaffiatolo *sm.* watering-can.

annali *sm. pl.* annals.

annaspare *vi.* to grope.

annaspìo *sm.* groping.

annata *sf.* 1. year 2. (*raccolto*) crop.

annebbiare *vt.* 1. to dim 2. (*fig.*) to dull. ◆ **annebbiarsi** *vr.* (*della vista*) to blur.

annegamento *sm.* drowning.

annegare *vt.* to drown. ◆ **annegarsi** *vr.* to drown oneself.

annegato *agg.* drowned.

annerimento *sm.* blackening.

annerire *vt.* to blacken.

annessione *sf.* annexation.

annesso *agg.* 1. connected 2. (*accluso*) enclosed.

annèttere *vt.* to annex.

annichilazione *sf.* annihilation.

annichilimento *sm.* annihilation.

annichilire *vt.* to annihilate.

annidarsi *vr.* 1. to nestle 2. (*nascondersi*) to hide (*v. irr.*).

annientamento *sm.* 1. destruction 2. (*di desideri*) frustration.

annientare *vt.* to destroy.

anniversario *agg. e sm.* anniversary.

anno *sm.* 1. year: — *bisestile*, leap-year || *Capo d'*—, New Year's Day || *durante tutto l'*—, all the year round 2. (*periodo lungo e indeterminato*) a long time 3. (*nell'indicare l'età*) to be ... years old: *ho 10 anni*, I am 10 years old.

annodare *vt.* to knot: — *amicizie*, to make friends.

annoiare *vt.* to bore, to tire. ◆ **annoiarsi** *vr.* to be bored.

annoiato *agg.* bored.

annoiatore *sm.* tiresome person.

annoso *agg.* old.

annotare *vt.* 1. (*corredare di note*) to annotate 2. (*prendere nota*) to take (*v. irr.*) a note (of).

annotazione *sf.* note.

annottare *vi.* to grow (*v. irr.*) dark.

annuale *agg.* yearly.

annuario *sm.* year-book.

annuire *vi.* to nod.

annullamento *sm.* cancellation.

annullare *vt.* 1. to annul 2. (*comm.*) to cancel.

annunciare *vt.* 1. to announce 2. (*predire*) to foretell (*v. irr.*).

annunciatore *sm.* announcer.

annuncio *sm.* 1. notice 2. (*presagio*) presage.

ànnuo *agg.* yearly.

annusare *vt.* 1. to smell 2. (*tabacco*) to take (*v. irr.*) snuff.

annuvolarsi *vr.* 1. to get (*v. irr.*) cloudy 2. (*fig.*) to become (*v. irr.*) gloomy.

ano *sm.* anus.

anòdino *agg.* anodyne.

ànodo *sm.* anode.

anomalìa *sf.* anomaly.

anòmalo *agg.* anomalous.

anònima *sf.* joint-stock company.

anònimo *agg.* anonymous. ◆ **anònimo** *sm.* anonym.

anormale *agg.* abnormal.

anormalità *sf.* abnormality.

ansa *sf.* 1. (*insenatura*) creek 2. (*di fiume*) bend 3. (*manico*) handle.

ansante *agg.* panting.

ansare *vi.* to pant.

ansia *sf.* anxiety.

ansietà *sf.* anxiety.

ansimare *vi.* to pant.

ansioso *agg.* 1. anxious 2. (*desideroso*) eager.

ànsito *sm.* panting.

anta *sf.* 1. shutter 2. (*di armadio*) door.

antagonismo *sm.* antagonism.

antagonista *s.* antagonist.

antàrtico *agg.* Antarctic.

antecedente *agg.* previous. ◆ **antecedente** *sm.* antecedent.

antecessore *sm.* predecessor.

antefatto *sm.* antecedent fact.

anteguerra *sm.* pre-war time.

antenato *sm.* ancestor.

antenna *sf.* 1. (*zool.*) antenna (*pl.* -nae) 2. (*radio*) aerial.

anteporre *vt.* to place before, to put (*v. irr.*) before.

anteprima *sf.* preview.

anteriore *agg.* 1. (*nello spazio*) fore 2. (*nel tempo*) previous, former.

antiabbaglianti *sm. pl.* anti-dazzle.

antiaèreo *agg.* anti-aircraft.

antibattèrico *agg. e sm.* antibacterial.

antibiòtico *agg. e sm.* antibiotic.

anticaglia *sf.* worthless antique.

anticamente *avv.* in ancient times.

anticàmera *sf.* ante-room || *fare* —,

to be kept waiting.

anticarro *agg.* anti-tank.

antichità *sf.* 1. antiquity 2. (*oggetti antichi*) antiques (*pl.*).

anticipare *vt.* 1. to anticipate 2. (*di danaro*) to pay in advance.

anticipatamente *avv.* in advance.

anticipato *agg.* 1. advanced 2. (*comm.*) in advance.

anticipazione *sf.* anticipation.

anticipo *sm.* advance: *essere in* —, to be before time 2. (*caparra*) earnest money.

anticlericale *agg. e s.* anticlerical.

anticlericalismo *sm.* anticlericalism.

antico *agg.* 1. ancient 2. (*all'antica*) old-fashioned.

anticonformista *s.* nonconformist.

anticongelante *sm.* anti-freeze.

anticorpo *sm.* antibody.

anticostituzionale *agg.* anticonstitutional.

antidatare *vt.* to antedate.

antidiluviano *agg. e sm.* antediluvian.

antidoto *sm.* antidote.

antiestètico *agg.* antiaesthetic.

antifascismo *sm.* antifascism.

antifascista *s. e agg.* antifascist.

antifebbrile *sm.* febrifuge.

antifecondativo *sm.* anti-conceptive.

antifona *sf.* antiphon: *capire l'*— to take (*v. irr.*) a hint.

antifurto *sm.* antitheft device.

antigàs *agg.* anti-gas: *maschera* —, gas-mask.

antigiènico *agg.* unhealthy.

antìlope *sf.* antelope.

antimilitarismo *sm.* antimilitarism.

antincendio *agg.* antifire: *pompa* —, fire-pump.

antinebbia *agg.* *faro* —, fog-light.

antinevralgico *agg.* antineuralgic.

antinomìa *sf.* antinomy.

antiparticella *sf.* antiparticle.

antipasto *sm.* hors-d'oeuvre.

antipatìa *sf.* dislike.

antipàtico *agg.* disagreeable.

antìpodi *sm. pl.* antipodes.

antiquariato *sm.* antique-dealing.

antiquario *sm.* antique-dealer.

antiquato *agg.* old-fashioned.

antireumàtico *agg.* antirheumatic.

antirùggine *agg.* anti-rust.

antisemitismo *sm.* anti-Semitism.

ntisèttico *agg. e sm.* antiseptic.

antispàstico *agg.* antispasmodic.

antistante *agg.* before, in front of.

antìtesi *sf.* antithesis (*pl.* -ses).

antitetànico *agg.* antitetanic.

antitètico *agg.* antithetic(al).

antitòssico *agg.* antitoxic.

antivigilia *sf.* the day before the eve.

antologìa *sf.* anthology.

antològico *agg.* anthological.

antonomàsia *sf.* antonomasia || *per* —, antonomastically.

antracite *sf.* anthracite.

antro *sm.* 1. cave 2. (*tana*) den.

antropocentrismo *sm.* anthropocentrism.

antropofagìa *sf.* anthropophagy.

antropòfago *agg.* anthropophagous.

   ♦ **antropòfago** *sm.* cannibal.

antropologìa *sf.* anthropology.

antropòlogo *sm.* anthropologist.

antropomorfo *agg.* anthropomorphous.

anulare *agg.* annular. ♦ **anulare** *sm.* ring-finger.

anzi *cong.* 1. (*al contrario*) on the contrary 2. (*in più*) moreover || — *che*, rather than; — *che no*, rather.

   ♦ **anzi** *avv.* before: — *tempo*, before time.

anzianità *sf.* seniority.

anziano *agg.* 1. elderly 2. (*in cariche, uffici ecc.*) senior.

anziché *cong.* 1. rather than 2. (*invece di*) instead of.

anzidetto *agg.* above-mentioned.

anzitempo *avv.* before time.

aorta *sf.* aorta.

apartìtico *agg.* non-sectarian.

apatìa *sf.* apathy, indifference.

apàtico *agg.* listless.

ape *sf.* bee.

aperitivo *sm.* aperitif.

apertamente *avv.* openly.

aperto *agg.* open.

apertura *sf.* 1. opening 2. (*di mente*) broad-mindedness 3. (*ampiezza di un arco*) span: — *alare*, wing-span.

àpice *sm.* apex.

apicoltura *sf.* bee-keeping.

apnea *sf.* apnoea.

apocalisse *sf.* apocalypse.

apocalìttico *agg.* apocalyptic(al).

apòcrifo *agg.* apocryphal || *libri apocrifi*, Apocrypha.

apòfisi *sf.* apophysis.

apogeo *sm.* apogee.

apòlide *agg.* stateless. ♦ **apòlide** *sm.* stateless person.

apolìtico *agg.* non-political.

apologìa *sf.* apologia.

apologista *s.* apologist.

apòlogo *sm.* apologue.

apoplessìa *sf.* apoplexy.

apoplèttico *agg.* apoplectic: *colpo —*, apoplectic fit.

apostasìa *sf.* apostasy.

apòstata *sm.* apostate.

apòstolo *sm.* apostle.

apostrofare *vt.* to apostrophize.

apòstrofe *sf.* apostrophe.

apòstrofo *sm.* apostrophe.

apoteòsi *sf.* apotheosis.

appagare *vt.* 1. to satisfy, to gratify 2. (*la sete*) to quench one's thirst.

appaiare *vt.* 1. to couple 2. (*armonizzare colori, vestiario ecc.*) to match.

appallottolare *vt.* to roll into a ball.

appaltare *vt.* to give (*v. irr.*) out by contract.

appaltatore *sm.* contractor.

appalto *sm.* contract, bid.

appannaggio *sm.* apanage.

appannamento *sm.* 1. (*di metalli*) tarnishing 2. (*di vetri ecc.*) clouding 3. (*di vista*) dimming.

appannare *vt.* 1. (*di metalli*) to tarnish 2. (*di vetri ecc.*) to cloud 3. (*di vista*) to dim.

apparato *sm.* 1. apparatus 2. (*mostra*) display.

apparecchiare *vt.* to prepare: *— la tavola*, to lay (*v. irr.*) the table.

apparecchio *sm.* 1. set 2. (*aereoplano*) aeroplane || *— fotografico*, camera; *— telefonico*, telephone; *— radio*, radio set.

apparentare *vt.* to relate.

apparente *agg.* 1. (*illusorio*) seeming 2. (*chiaro*) apparent, obvious.

apparentemente *avv.* seemingly.

apparenza *sf.* 1. appearance 2. (*aspetto*) look 3. (*pompa*) show.

apparire *vi.* 1. to appear 2. (*aver l'aspetto*) to look 3. (*risultare*) to result.

appariscente *agg.* 1. striking 2. (*vistoso*) showy.

apparizione *sf.* apparition.

appartamento *sm.* flat.

appartarsi *vr.* to retire.

appartenenza *sf.* belonging.

appartenere *vi.* 1. to belong (to) 2. (*essere membro*) to be a member (of).

appassionare *vt.* to impassion. ♦ appassionarsi *vr.* to become (*v. irr.*) fond of.

appassionato *agg.* 1. passionate 2. (*di musica, arte ecc.*) keen (on).

appassire *vi.* to wither.

appellare *vt.* to name, to call. ♦ appellarsi *vr.* to appeal.

appellativo *sm.* appellative.

appello *sm.* 1. (*giur.*) appeal 2. (*chiamata*) call 3. (*esortazione*) appeal.

appena *avv.* 1. (*a fatica*) hardly 2. (*molto poco*) very little 3. (*da poco*) just: *ero — arrivato*, I had just arrived || *non —*, as soon as.

appèndere *vt.* to hang (*v. irr.*).

appendice *sf.* appendix || *romanzo d'—*, serial.

appendicite *sf.* appendicitis.

appesantire *vt.* to make (*v. irr.*) heavy. ♦ appesantirsi *vr.* to grow (*v. irr.*) heavy.

appestare *vt.* 1. to infect 2. (*spargere odore*) to stink (*v. irr.*).

appestato *agg.* 1. plague-stricken 2. (*fig.*) tainted. ♦ appestato *sm.* plague-stricken person.

appetenza *sf.* 1. appetite 2. (*desiderio*) longing (for sthg.).

appetìbile *agg.* pleasing.

appetire *vt.* to desire.

appetito *sm.* appetite.

appezzamento *sm.* plot of land.

appianare *vt.* 1. to level 2. (*fig.*) to smooth.

appiattarsi *vr.* 1. to crouch 2. (*stare in agguato*) to lie (*v. irr.*) in wait 3. (*nascondersi*) to hide (*v. irr.*).

appiattire *vt.* to flatten.

appiccare *vt.* (*il fuoco*) to set (*v. irr.*) fire.

appiccicare *vt.* 1. to stick (*v. irr.*) 2. (*appioppare*) to palm off.

appiccicoso *agg.* sticky.

appiè *prep.* 1. (*al di sotto*) below 2. (*ai piedi*) at the foot: *— del letto*, at the foot of the bed.

appiedare *vt.* to dismount.

appiedato *agg.* dismounted.

appieno *avv.* fully.

appigliarsi *vr.* to get (*v. irr.*) hold of: *— ad un pretesto*, to take (*v. irr.*) a pretext.

appiglio *sm.* 1. support 2. (*fig.*) pretext.

appiombo *sm.* perpendicularity.

appioppare *vt.* 1. to give (*v. irr.*)

|| — *uno schiaffo*, to slap **2.** (*affibbiare*) to palm off.

appisolarsi *vr.* to doze off.

applaudire *vt. e vi.* to applaud.

applauditore *sm.* applauder.

applàuso *sm.* **1.** applause (*solo sing.*) **2.** (*fig.*) praise.

applicare *vt.* **1.** to apply **2.** (*giur.*) to carry out **3.** (*accostare*) to set (*v. irr.*). ♦ **applicarsi** *vr.* to apply oneself.

applicazione *sf.* **1.** application **2.** (*fig.*) care **3.** (*guarnizione*) trimming.

appoggiare *vt.* **1.** to lean (*v. irr.*) **2.** (*posare*) to lay (*v. irr.*) **3.** (*fig.*) to back. ♦ **appoggiarsi** *vr.* **1.** to lean (*v. irr.*) **2.** (*fig.*) to rely (on).

appoggio *sm.* **1.** support **2.** (*fig.*) assistance **3.** (*colui che dà —*) supporter.

appollaiarsi *vr.* to perch.

apporre *vt.* to affix.

apportare *vt.* **1.** to bring (*v. irr.*) **2.** (*produrre*) to produce.

apporto *sm.* contribution.

appositamente *avv.* on purpose.

appòsito *agg.* **1.** special **2.** (*adatto*) fit.

apposizione *sf.* **1.** (*gramm.*) apposition **2.** (*l'apporre*) affixing.

apposta *avv.* expressly.

appostare *vt.* (*mil.*) to place. ♦ **appostarsi** *vr.* to lie (*v. irr.*) in ambush.

apprèndere *vt.* to learn (*v. irr.*).

apprendista *sm.* apprentice.

apprendistato *sm.* apprenticeship.

apprensione *sf.* **1.** concern **2.** (*l'apprendere*) learning.

appresso *avv.* near, close by. ♦ **appresso** *prep.* near, close to.

apprestamento *sm.* preparation.

apprestare *vt.* to prepare.

apprettare *vt.* to dress.

apprezzàbile *agg.* appreciable.

apprezzamento *sm.* **1.** appreciation **2.** (*giudizio*) opinion.

apprezzare *vt.* **1.** to appreciate **2.** (*valutare*) to value.

approdare *vi.* **1.** to land **2.** (*fig.*) to be of use.

approfittare *vi.* to profit (by). ♦ **approfittarsi** *vr.* **1.** to avail oneself **2.** (*abusare*) to take (*v. irr.*) undue advantage.

approfondire *vt.* **1.** to make (*v. irr.*) deeper **2.** (*fig.*) to examine closely.

approntare *vt.* to make (*v. irr.*) ready.

appropriarsi *vr.* to take (*v. irr.*) possession of.

appropriato *agg.* fit, suitable.

appropriazione *sf.* appropriation: — *indebita*, embezzlement.

approssimarsi *vr.* **1.** to come (*v. irr.*) near **2.** (*di tempo*) to draw (*v. irr.*) near.

approssimativamente *avv.* approximately.

approssimativo *agg.* approximative.

approssimazione *sf.* approximation.

approvare *vt.* **1.** to approve (of) **2.** (*promuovere*) to pass.

approvazione *sf.* approval.

approvvigionamento *sm.* **1.** (*l'approvvigionare*) supplying **2.** (*provviste*) supplies.

approvvigionare *vt.* to supply provisions (to).

appuntamento *sm.* appointment.

appuntare *vt.* **1.** to sharpen **2.** (*prender nota*) to note **3.** (*biasimare*) to blame.

appuntellare *vt.* **1.** to prop **2.** (*fig.*) to support.

appuntino *avv.* nicely.

appuntito *agg.* pointed.

appunto[1] *sm.* **1.** note **2.** (*critica*) blame.

appunto[2] *avv.* exactly, just.

appurare *vt.* to verify.

apribottiglie *sm.* bottle-opener.

aprile *sm.* April: *pesce d'—*, April fool.

aprire *vt.* to open: — *le braccia a qc.*, to welcome so.

apriscàtole *sm.* tin-opener.

àquila *sf.* eagle.

aquilino *agg.* aquiline.

aquilone *sm.* **1.** (*vento del nord*) north wind **2.** (*giocattolo*) kite.

aquilotto *sm.* eaglet.

arabescare *vt.* to decorate with arabesques.

arabesco *sm.* arabesque.

aràbico *agg.* Arabic.

aràbile *agg.* arable.

àrabo *agg. e sm.* Arab.

aràchide *sf.* peanut.

aragosta *sf.* lobster.

aràldico *agg.* heraldic.

araldo *sm.* herald.

arancia *sf.* orange.

aranciata sf. orange squash.

aranciera sf. orangery.

arancio agg. (colore) orange. ♦ **arancio** sm. orange-tree.

arancione agg. orange-coloured.

arare vt. to plough.

aratore sm. ploughman (pl. -men).

aratro sm. plough.

aratura sf. ploughing.

arazzo sm. arras.

arbitraggio sm. **1.** (sport) umpirage **2.** (comm.) arbitrage.

arbitrare vt. **1.** to arbitrate **2.** (calcio, boxe) to referee.

arbitrario agg. arbitrary.

arbitrio sm. **1.** will: libero —, free will **1.** (atto arbitrario) arbitrary act.

àrbitro sm. **1.** (sport) umpire **2.** (calcio, boxe) referee **3.** (giur.) arbitrator.

arboricoltore sm. arboriculturist.

arboricoltura sf. arboriculture.

arboscello sm. shrub.

arbusto sm. shrub.

arca sf. ark || — di scienza, eminent scholar.

arcàdico agg. e sm. Arcadian.

arcàico agg. **1.** archaic **2.** (di parole, stile) obsolete.

arcaismo sm. **1.** archaism **2.** (parola arcaica) obsolete word.

arcàngelo sm. archangel.

arcano agg. mysterious.

archeologia sf. archaeology.

archeològico agg. archaeologic(al).

archeòlogo sm. archaeologist.

archètipo sm. archetype.

archetto sm. **1.** small arch **2.** (mus.) bow.

architettare vt. **1.** to draw (v. irr.) the plans **2.** (fig.) to devise.

architetto sm. architect.

architettònico agg. architectonic.

architettura sf. architecture.

architrave sm. architrave.

archiviare vt. **1.** to place in the archives **2.** (comm.) to file.

archivio sm. **1.** archives (pl.) **2.** (comm.) file.

archivista sm. archivist.

arciduca sm. archduke.

arciere sm. archer.

arcigno agg. gruff.

arcimiliardario sm. multimillion-aire.

arcipèlago sm. archipelago (pl. -goes).

arcivescovado sm. archbishopric.

arcivéscovo sm. archbishop.

arco sm. **1.** (arma) bow **2.** (geom.) arc **3.** (arch.) arch **4.** (mus.) bow.

arcobaleno sm. rainbow.

arcolaio sm. wool-winder.

arcuare vt. **1.** to arch **2.** (piegare) to bend (v. irr.).

ardente agg. **1.** burning **2.** (fig.) passionate.

ardentemente avv. ardently.

àrdere vt. to burn (v. irr.).

ardesia sf. slate.

ardire vi. **1.** to dare **2.** (avere l'impudenza) to have the impudence. ♦ **ardire** sm. **1.** bold **2.** (rischioso) risky.

ardito agg. **1.** bold **2.** (rischioso) risky.

ardore sm. **1.** fierce heat **2.** (fig.) passion.

àrduo agg. **1.** hard **2.** (erto) steep.

àrea sf. **1.** area **2.** (sfera d'azione) sphere.

arena sf. **1.** (sabbia) sand **2.** (arch.) arena.

arenarsi vr. to get (v. irr.) stranded (anche fig.).

arengario sm. tribune.

areòpago sm. Areopagus.

àrgano sm. **1.** (mar.) capstan **2.** (mecc.) windlass.

argentare vt. to silver.

argènteo agg. silvery.

argenterìa sf. silver ware.

argentino agg. silvery.

argento sm. silver.

argilla sf. clay.

argilloso agg. clayey.

arginare vt. **1.** to dam **2.** (fig.) to check.

àrgine sm. bank.

argomentare vt. to infer. ♦ **argomentare** vi. to argue.

argomentazione sf. reasoning.

argomento sm. **1.** subject **2.** (prova a sostegno) argument.

arguire vt. to deduce.

argutezza sf. shrewdness.

arguto agg. **1.** sharp **2.** (faceto) witty.

arguzia sf. wit.

aria sf. **1.** air: — condizionata, air conditioning || corrente d'—, draught || camera d'—, inner tube || andare all'—, to fall (v. irr.) through **2.** (aspetto) look **3.** (mus.) tune.

ariano agg. e sm. Aryan.

aridità sf. **1.** aridity **2.** (di cuore) lack of feeling.

àrido agg. **1.** arid **2.** (di cuore)

lacking feeling.

arieggiare vt. 1. to air 2. (rassomigliare) to look like 3. (imitare) to imitate.

arieggiato agg. aired.

ariete sm. ram.

aringa sf. herring.

arioso agg. airy.

aristocràtico agg. aristocratic. ♦ **aristocràtico** sm. aristocrat.

aristocrazìa sf. aristocracy.

aristotèlico agg. e sm. Aristotelian.

aritmètica sf. arithmetic.

aritmètico agg. arithmetic(al).

arlecchinata sf. harlequinade.

arlecchino sm. harlequin.

arma sf. weapon, arm: armi bianche, side-arms; armi da fuoco, fire-arms || galleria d'armi, armoury.

armadietto sm. (per medicinali, strumenti ecc.) cabinet 2. (per abiti) locker.

armadio sm. 1. (per stoviglie) cupboard 2. (per abiti) wardrobe.

armaiolo sm. armourer.

armamentario sm. 1. instruments (pl.) 2. (armeria) armoury.

armamento sm. arming.

armare vt. to arm.

armata sf. army.

armatore sm. 1. shipbuilder 2. (chi possiede una nave) shipowner.

armatura sf. 1. armour 2. (impalcatura) scaffolding.

armeggiare vi. 1. to handle arms 2. (darsi da fare) to busy oneself 3. (tramare) to manoeuvre.

armeggio sm. 1. handling of arms 2. (l'affaccendarsi) bustling 3. (intrigo) manoeuvre.

armento sm. herd.

armerìa sf. armoury.

armiere sm. gunsmith.

armistizio sm. armistice.

armonìa sf. harmony.

armònica sf. (a bocca) mouth-organ.

armònico agg. harmonic.

armonio sm. harmonium.

armonioso agg. harmonious.

armonista s. harmonist.

armonizzare vt. to harmonize. ♦ **armonizzare** vi. 1. to harmonize 2. (di colori) to match.

arnese sm. 1. (strumento) tool 2. (aggeggio) gadget.

arnia sf. beehive.

aroma sm. flavour.

aromàtico agg. aromatic.

aromatizzare vt. to flavour.

arpa sf. harp.

arpeggiare vi. to play the harp.

arpeggio sm. arpeggio.

arpista s. harpist.

arra sf. earnest.

arrabattarsi vr. to bestir oneself.

arrabbiare vi. 1. to become (v. irr.) angry 2. (di cane) to be affected with rabies. ♦ **arrabbiarsi** vr. to get (v. irr.) angry.

arrabbiato agg. 1. angry 2. (di cane) rabid.

arrabbiatura sf. rage.

arraffare vt. to grasp.

arrampicarsi vr. to climb.

arrampicata sf. climb.

arrampicatore sm. 1. mountain climber 2. (fig.) social climber.

arrancare vi. 1. to plod along 2. (zoppicare) to limp 3. (affaticarsi) to get (v. irr.) tired.

arrangiamento sm. arrangement.

arrangiare vt. to arrange. ♦ **arrangiarsi** vr. to manage.

arrecare vt. 1. to bring (v. irr.) 2. (causare) to cause.

arredamento sm. furnishing.

arredare vt. to furnish.

arredatore sm. internal decorator.

arredo sm. piece of furniture.

arrèndersi vr. 1. to surrender 2. (fig.) to give (v. irr.) it up.

arrendévole agg. 1. pliant 2. (fig.) docile.

arrestare vt. 1. to stop 2. (trarre in arresto) to arrest. ♦ **arrestarsi** vr. to stop.

arresto sm. arrest.

arretrare vt. 1. to pull back 2. (ritirare) to withdraw (v. irr.).

arretrato agg. backward.

arricchimento sm. enrichment.

arricchire vt. to enrich. ♦ **arricchirsi** vr. to grow (v. irr.) rich.

arricciare vt. to curl: — il naso, to turn up one's nose.

arrìdere vi. to be favourable.

arringare vt. to harangue.

arringatore sm. haranguer.

arrischiare vt. to risk. ♦ **arrischiarsi** vr. to venture.

arrivare vi. 1. to arrive (at), (in) 2. (fig.) to attain.

arrivato agg. (fig.) successful.

arrivederci inter. goodbye.

arrivismo sm. social climbing.

arrivista sm. social climber.

arrivo sm. arrival.

arrogante *agg.* arrogant.

arroganza *sf.* arrogance.

arrogarsi *vr.* to arrogate to oneself.

arrossire *vi.* to blush.

arrostire *vt.* 1. to roast 2. (*di pane*) to toast.

arrosto *sm.* roast.

arrotare *vt.* to grind (*v. irr.*): — i denti, to grind one's teeth.

arrotino *sm.* knife-grinder.

arrotolare *vt.* to roll up.

arrotondare *vt.* 1. to round 2. (*di cifre*) to make (*v. irr.*) a round figure.

arrovellarsi *vr.* to worry.

arroventare *vt.* to make (*v. irr.*) red-hot.

arruffare *vt.* to ruffle.

arruffone *sm.* muddler

arrugginire *vi.* to rust.

arruolare *vt.* to enrol.

arsenale *sm.* 1. (*cantiere*) ship-yard 2. (*deposito di armi*) arsenal.

arsènico *sm.* arsenic.

arsura *sf.* 1. (*siccità*) drought 2. (*sete*) parching thirst.

arte *sf.* art || belle arti, fine arts.

artefatto *agg.* adulterated.

artéfice *sm.* maker.

arteria *sf.* 1. artery 2. (*di traffico*) thoroughfare.

arteriosclerosi *sf.* arteriosclerosis.

artesiano *agg.* artesian.

àrtico *agg.* arctic.

articolare *vt.* to articulate.

articolazione *sf.* articulation.

artìcolo *sm.* 1. (*gramm.; di giornale*) article || — di fondo, editorial 2. (*comm.*) item.

artificiale *agg.* artificial.

artificio *sm.* 1. device 2. (*astuzia*) cunning.

artigianato *sm.* handicraft.

artigiano *sm.* craftsman (*pl.* -men).

artigliere *sm.* gunner.

artiglieria *sf.* artillery.

artiglio *sm.* claw.

artista *sm.* artist.

artistico *agg.* artistic(al).

arto *sm.* limb: — artificiale, artificial limb.

artrite *sf.* arthritis (*pl.* -ides).

artrosi *sf.* arthrosis.

arzigògolo *sm.* subtlety.

arzillo *agg.* lively, brisk.

ascella *sf.* armpit.

ascendente *sm.* 1. ascendancy 2. (*antenato*) ancestor.

ascendenza *sf.* ancestry.

ascéndere *vi.* (*anche fig.*) to rise (*v. irr.*).

ascensione *sf.* 1. ascension 2. (*scalata*) climb.

ascensore *sm.* lift.

ascesa *sf.* ascent.

ascesi *sf.* mystical practice.

ascesso *sm.* abscess.

asceta *sm.* ascetic.

ascètico *agg.* ascetical.

ascetismo *sm.* asceticism.

ascia *sf.* axe.

ascissa *sf.* abscissa (*pl.* -sae).

asciugacapelli *sm.* hair-drier.

asciugamano *sm.* towel.

asciugare *vt.* 1. to dry 2. (*con un panno*) to wipe. ♦ **asciugarsi** *vr.* to dry up.

asciugatoio *sm.* towel.

asciutto *agg.* (*anche fig.*) dry 2. (*magro*) thin.

ascoltare *vt.* 1. to listen (to) 2. (*assistere*) to attend: — le lezioni, to attend classes.

ascolto *sm.* listening.

ascrivere *vt.* 1. to count 2. (*attribuire*) to ascribe. ♦ **ascriversi** *vr.* to claim.

asepsi *sf.* asepsis.

asessuale *agg.* asexual.

asèttico *agg.* aseptic.

asfaltare *vt.* to asphalt.

asfalto *sm.* asphalt.

asfissìa *sf.* 1. asphyxia 2. (*da gas*) gassing.

asfissiare *vt.* 1. to asphyxiate 2. (*con gas*) to gas.

asiàtico *agg.* e *sm.* Asiatic.

asilo *sm.* 1. shelter 2. (*scuola materna*) infant-school.

asimmetrìa *sf.* asymmetry.

asimmètrico *agg.* asymmetrical.

asinerìa *sf.* stupidity.

asinità *sf.* asininity.

àsino *sm.* 1. ass 2. (*fig.*) jackass.

asma *sf.* asthma.

asmàtico *agg.* asthmatical.

asociale *agg.* asocial.

àsola *sf.* buttonhole.

asparago *sm.* asparagus.

aspèrgere *vt.* to sprinkle.

asperità *sf.* 1. asperity 2. (*di superfici*) unevenness 3. (*di carattere*) harshness.

aspersorio *sm.* aspergillum.

aspettare *vt.* to wait (for). ♦ **aspettarsi** *vr.* to expect.

aspettativa *sf.* 1. expectation 2.

(esonero temporaneo) temporary retirement.

aspetto *sm.* look || *di bell'aspetto*, good-looking || *sala d'—*, waiting-room.

àspide *sm.* asp.

aspirante *agg.* aspirant. ♦ **aspirante** *sm.* candidate, applicant.

aspirapòlvere *sm.* vacuum cleaner, hoover.

aspirare *vt.* to inspire. ♦ **aspirare** *vi.* to aspire (to).

aspiratore *sm.* aspirator.

aspirazione *sf.* **1.** aspiration **2.** *(mecc.)* suction.

aspirina *sf.* aspirin.

asportare *vt.* **1.** to remove **2.** *(med.)* to extirpate.

asportazione *sf.* **1.** removal **2.** *(med.)* extirpation.

asprezza *sf.* **1.** sourness **2.** *(fig.)* harshness.

asprigno *agg.* sourish.

aspro *agg.* **1.** sour **2.** *(fig.)* harsh.

assaggiare *vt.* to taste.

assaggio *sm.* **1.** tasting **2.** *(campione)* sample.

assai *avv.* **1.** *(con agg. e avv.)* very **2.** *(con comp.)* much: *— meglio*, much better.

assalire *vt.* **1.** to assail **2.** *(di malattia)* to attack.

assalitore *sm.* assailer.

assaltare *vt.* to assault.

assalto *sm.* assault, attack.

assaporare *vt.* **1.** to savour **2.** *(fig.)* to enjoy.

assassinare *vt.* to murder.

assassinio *sm.* murder.

assassino *sm.* murderer.

asse *sf.* **1.** *(tavola di legno)* board **2.** *(geom.)* axis *(pl. axes)* **3.** *(stor.)* Axis.

assecondare *vt.* to favour.

assediare *vt.* to besiege.

assedio *sm.* siege.

assegnamento *sm.* assignment || *fare — su qualcuno*, to rely on so.

assegnare *vt.* **1.** to assign **2.** *(un premio)* to award.

assegno *sm.* cheque: *— al portatore*, cheque to bearer; *— circolare*, banker's draft; *— sbarrato*, crossed cheque.

assemblea *sf.* **1.** meeting **2.** *(corpo deliberante)* assembly.

assembramento *sm.* concourse of people.

assembrarsi *vr.* to assemble.

assennatezza *sf.* common sense.

assennato *agg.* sensible.

assenso *sm.* assent.

assentarsi *vr.* to go *(v. irr.)* away.

assente *agg.* absent.

assenteismo *sm.* absenteeism.

assentire *vi.* **1.** to assent (to) **2.** *(col capo)* to nod (in assent).

assenza *sf.* absence.

assenzio *sm.* absinth.

asserire *vt.* to affirm.

asserragliarsi *vr.* to barricade oneself.

asserto *sm.* assertion.

assertore *sm.* **1.** assertor **2.** *(difensore)* defender, champion.

asservimento *sm.* enslavement.

asservire *vt.* to enslave, to subdue.

asserzione *sf.* statement.

assessorato *sm.* assessorship.

assessore *sm.* **1.** *(alle imposte)* assessor **2.** *(comunale)* councillor responsible for a municipal region.

assestamento *sm.* **1.** adjustment **2.** *(definitivo)* settlement **3.** *(del terreno)* settling.

assestare *vt.* to arrange: *— un colpo*, to deal *(v. irr.)* a blow. ♦ **assestarsi** *vr.* to settle (down).

assetato *agg.* **1.** thirsty **2.** *(fig.)* eager (for).

assetto *sm.* order.

assicurare *vt.* **1.** *(legare)* to fasten **2.** *(promettere)* to assure **3.** *(affermare)* to affirm **4.** *(comm.)* to insure.

assicurata *sf.* registered letter.

assicurato *agg.* insured, assured. ♦ **assicurato** *sm.* insurant.

assicuratore *sm.* insurer.

assicurazione *sf.* **1.** assurance **2.** *(comm.)* insurance.

assideramento *sm.* frost-bite.

assiduità *sf.* assiduity.

assiduo *agg.* assiduous.

assieme *avv.* V. **insieme**.

assieparsi *vr.* to crowd (round).

assillante *agg.* urging.

assillare *vt.* to urge.

assillo *sm.* **1.** urge **2.** *(fig.)* worry.

assimilàbile *agg.* assimilable.

assimilare *vt.* to assimilate, to absorb.

assimilazione *sf.* assimilation.

assioma *sm.* axiom.

assiomàtico *agg.* axiomatic.

assise *sf. pl.* assizes.

assistente *sm.* assistant.

assistenza *sf.* assistance.

assistenziale agg. charitable.
assistere vt. 1. to assist 2. (curare) to nurse. ♦ **assistere** vi. to attend (sthg.).
assito sm. 1. wooden partition 2. (pavimento) plank floor.
asso sm. 1. (carte) ace 2. (sport) champion || piantare in —, to leave (v. irr.) in the lurch.
associare vt. to join. ♦ **associarsi** vr. to associate.
associato sm. member.
associazione sf. association.
assodare vt. 1. to consolidate 2. (accertare) to ascertain.
assoggettare vt. to subject. ♦ **assoggettarsi** vr. to submit oneself.
assolato agg. sunny.
assoldare vt. to recruit.
assolo sm. (mus.) solo.
assolutamente avv. absolutely.
assolutismo sm. absolutism.
assolutista agg. e sm. absolutist.
assoluto agg. e sm. absolute.
assoluzione sf. 1. (eccl.) absolution 2. (giur.) discharge.
assòlvere vt. 1. (teol.) to absolve 2. (giur.) to discharge 3. (eseguire) to accomplish.
assomigliante agg. like.
assomigliare vi. to look like.
assommare vt. e vi. to add, to amount (to).
assonanza sf. assonance.
assonnarsi vr. to fall (v. irr.) asleep.
assonnato agg. sleepy.
assopimento sm. dozing.
assopire vt. to make (v. irr.) dozy. ♦ **assopirsi** vr. to doze off.
assorbente agg. absorbing || carta —, blotting-paper.
assorbimento sm. absorption.
assorbire vt. to absorb.
assordante agg. deafening.
assordare vt. to deafen.
assortimento sm. assortment.
assortire vt. 1. to stock 2. (fig.) to match.
assorto agg. absorbed.
assottigliamento sm. 1. thinning 2. (riduzione) reduction.
assottigliare vt. 1. to thin 2. (diminuire) to reduce. ♦ **assottigliarsi** vr. to grow (v. irr.) thin.
assuefare vt. to accustom. ♦ **assuefarsi** vr. to accustom oneself.
assuefazione sf. custom.
assùmere vt. 1. to assume 2. (in

servizio) to employ 3. (informazioni) to make (v. irr.) inquiries.
assunzione sf. 1. (ascesa) accession 2. (impiego) engagement 3. (teol.) Assumption.
assurdamente avv. absurdly.
assurdità sf. absurdity.
assurdo agg. absurd. ♦ **assurdo** sm. absurdity.
assùrgere vi. to rise (v. irr.).
asta sf. 1. pole 2. (di bandiera) flagstaff 3. (di occhiali) bar 4. (di bilancia) arm (of balance) 5. (vendita all'asta) auction(-sale).
astante agg. present. ♦ **astante** sm. on-looker.
astemio agg. abstemious. ♦ **astemio** sm. teetotaller.
astenersi vr. to abstain.
astenìa sf. asthenia.
astensione sf. abstention.
astensionista sm. abstentionist.
asterisco sm. asterisk.
astèroide sm. asteroid.
asticciola sf. pothook.
astigmàtico agg. astigmatic.
astigmatismo sm. astigmatism.
astinenza sf. abstinence.
astio sm. resentment.
astiosamente avv. resentfully.
astioso agg. resentful.
astracàn sm. astrakhan.
astràgalo sm. 1. (bot.) astragalus (pl. -li) 2. (arch.) astragal.
astrale agg. astral.
astrarre vt. to abstract. ♦ **astrarsi** vr. to think (v. irr.) about sthg. else.
astrattismo sm. (arte) abstractionism.
astratto agg. abstract.
astrazione sf. abstraction.
astringente agg. e sm. astringent.
astro sm. star.
astrolabio sm. astrolabe.
astrologìa sf. astrology.
astròlogo sm. astrologer.
astronàuta sm. astronaut.
astronave sf. space-ship.
astronomìa sf. astronomy.
astronòmico agg. astronomic(al).
astrònomo sm. astronomer.
astrusità sf. abstruseness.
astruso agg. abstruse.
astuccio sm. case, box: — per occhiali, spectacle-case.
astuto agg. cunning.
astuzia sf. 1. (qualità) cunning 2. (atto) trick.

atassìa *sf.* ataxy.

atàvico *agg.* atavic.

atavismo *sm.* atavism.

ateìsmo *sm.* atheism.

àteo *agg.* atheistic. ♦ àteo *sm.* atheist.

atleta *sm.* athlete.

atlètica *sf.* athletics.

atlètico *agg.* athletic.

atmosfèra *sf.* atmosphere.

atollo *sm.* atoll.

atòmico *agg.* atomic.

atomismo *sm.* atomism.

atomìstica *sf.* atomic theory.

atomizzatore *sm.* atomizer.

àtomo *sm.* (*anche fig.*) atom.

atonìa *sf.* atony.

àtono *agg.* atonic.

atrio *sm.* (entrance-)hall.

atroce *agg.* dreadful.

atrocità *sf.* atrocity.

atrofìa *sf.* atrophy.

atrofizzare *vt.* to atrophy.

atrofizzato *agg.* atrophic.

atropìna *sf.* atropine.

attaccabottoni *sm.* buttonholer.

attaccabrighe *sm.* quarrelsome fellow.

attaccamento *sm.* attachment: *avere dell'—*, to entertain an attachment (for).

attaccante *sm.* attacker.

attaccapanni *sm.* cloak-stand.

attaccare *vt.* 1. (*unire*) to attack 2. (*appiccicare*) to stick (*v. irr.*) 3. (*cucire*) to sew (*v. irr.*) 4. (*assalire*) to attack 5. (*mus.*) to open. ♦ attaccarsi *vr.* 1. (*appigliarsi*) to cling (*v. irr.*) 2. (*affezionarsi*) to become (*v. irr.*) fond of.

attaccatura *sf.* junction: *— della manica*, arm-hole.

attacchino *sm.* bill-poster.

attacco *sm.* 1. (*mil.*) attack 2. (*med.*) fit 3. (*mecc.*) connection ‖ *— elettrico*, connecting plug.

attagliarsi *vr.* to suit.

attanagliare *vt.* to pinch.

attardarsi *vr.* to delay.

attecchire *vi.* 1. to take (*v. irr.*) root 2. (*aver fortuna*) to find (*v. irr.*) favour.

atteggiamento *sm.* attitude.

atteggiarsi *vr.* to assume an attitude: *— a vittima*, to pose as a victim.

attempato *agg.* elderly.

attendente *sm.* orderly.

attèndere *vt.* 1. (*aspettare*) to wait for 2. (*aspettarsi*) to expect 3. (*accudire, frequentare*) to attend.

attendìbile *agg.* reliable.

attenere *vi.* to concern. ♦ attenersi *vr.* 1. to cling (*v. irr.*) (on), (to) 2. (*seguire*) to conform.

attentamente *avv.* 1. attentively 2. (*con cura*) carefully.

attentare *vi.* to attempt. ♦ attentarsi *vr.* to dare.

attentato *sm.* attempt (upon).

attenti *sm.* attention: *stare sull'—*, to stand (*v. irr.*) at attention.

attento *agg.* attentive, careful.

attenuante *agg.* extenuating.

attenuare *vt.* 1. to attenuate 2. (*giur.*) to extenuate.

attenuazione *sf.* 1. attenuation 2. (*di colpa*) extenuation.

attenzione *sf.* 1. attention 2. care: *fate —*, take care 3. (*riguardo*) regard.

atterràggio *sm.* landing.

atterrare *vt.* to knock down. ♦ atterrare *vi.* (*aer.*) to land.

atterrire *vt.* to terrify. ♦ atterrirsi *vr.* to take (*v. irr.*) fright.

attesa *sf.* wait.

attestare *vt.* to attest.

attestato *sm.* 1. certificate 2. (*prova*) proof.

atticciato *agg.* sturdy.

àttico *sm.* attic.

attìguo *agg.* adjoining.

attillarsi *vr.* to spruce oneself up.

attillato *agg.* close-fitting.

àttimo *sm.* moment.

attinente *agg.* pertaining.

attinenza *sf.* relationship.

attìngere *vt.* to draw (*v. irr.*): *— acqua da un pozzo*, to draw water from a well; *— denaro da qu.*, to draw on so. for money.

attirare *vt.* to attract, to draw (*v. irr.*) (*anche fig.*).

attitùdine *sf.* turn, disposition.

attivare *vt.* to make (*v. irr.*) active.

attivista *s.* activist.

attività *sf.* 1. activity 2. (*comm.*) profit: *— e passività*, assets and liabilities.

attivizzare *vt.* to make (*v. irr.*) active.

attivo *agg.* active.

attizzare *vt.* to stir up.

attizzatòlo *sm.* poker.

atto[1] *sm.* 1. act 2. (*azione*) action 3. (*fatto*) deed: *un — buono*, a good deed.

atto² *agg.* fit.

attònito *agg.* astonished.

attore *sm.* actor: — *cinematografico*, screen actor.

attorniare *vt.* to surround.

attorno *avv. e prep.* about, round, around: *non c'è nessuno* —, there is nobody about; — *alla tavola*, round the table; *le colline — al villaggio*, the hills around the village || *darsi d'*—, to busy oneself.

attraccaggio *sm.* mooring.

attraccare *vi.* to moor.

attraente *agg.* charming, attractive.

attrarre *vt.* to attract, to draw (*v. irr.*) (*anche fig.*).

attrattiva *sf.* attraction, appeal.

attraversamento *sm.* crossing.

attraversare *vt.* **1.** to cross **2.** (*ostacolare*) to thwart.

attraverso *avv.* **1.** (*di luogo*) across, through: — *il fiume*, across the river **2.** (*di tempo*) through.

attrazione *sf.* attraction, appeal.

attrezzare *vt.* to equip.

attrezzatura *sf.* equipment.

attrezzista *sm.* (*teat.*) property-man.

attrezzo *sm.* tool.

attribuire *vt.* **1.** to attribute **2.** (*assegnare*) to assign **3.** (*addossare*) to put (on).

attributo *sm.* attribute.

attribuzione *sf.* attribution.

attrice *sf.* actress: — *cinematografica*, screen actress.

attrito *sm.* **1.** friction **2.** (*fig.*) dissension.

attruppamento *sm.* trooping.

attrupparsi *vr.* to troop.

attuàbile *agg.* feasible.

attuale *agg.* present.

attualità *sf.* the moment: *cosa d'*—, topical question.

attualmente *avv.* at present.

attuare *vt.* to carry out.

attutire *vt.* to mitigate: — *un rumore*, to deaden a noise.

audace *agg.* bold.

audacia *sf.* boldness.

audiovisivo *agg.* audiovisual.

auditore *sm.* listener.

auditorio *sm.* **1.** auditorium **2.** (*pubblico*) audience.

audizione *sf.* **1.** (*fisiol.*) hearing **2.** (*teat.*) performance.

àuge *sm.* summit: *essere in* —, to enjoy great favour.

augurale *agg.* augural.

augurare *vt.* to wish.

augurio *sm.* wish || *auguri di Natale e Capodanno*, season's greetings.

augusto *agg.* august.

àula *sf.* hall, room: — *di scuola*, school-room.

aumentare *vt.* to increase.

aumento *sm.* increase.

àureo *agg.* **1.** gold **2.** (*dorato*) golden.

aurèola *sf.* halo.

aurìcola *sf.* auricle.

auricolare *agg.* auricular.

aurìfero *agg.* auriferous.

aurora *sf.* dawn (*anche fig.*).

auscultare *vt.* to auscultate.

auscultazione *sf.* auscultation.

ausiliare *agg.* auxiliary.

ausilio *sm.* **1.** help **2.** (*difesa*) defence.

auspicare *vt.* to augur.

auspicio *sm.* **1.** (*stor.*) auspice, omen: *di buon, cattivo* —, of good, ill omen **2.** (*augurio*) wish.

austerità *sf.* austerity.

austero *agg.* austere.

australe *agg.* austral.

australiano *agg. e sm.* Australian.

austrìaco *agg. e sm.* Austrian.

autarchìa *sf.* autarky.

autàrchico *agg.* autarkic.

autenticare *vt.* to certify.

autenticazione *sf.* authentication.

autenticità *sf.* authenticity.

autèntico *agg.* **1.** authentic **2.** (*genuino*) genuine.

autista *sm.* driver: — *di piazza*, taxi-driver.

àuto *sf.* car: — *da corsa*, racing car; — *aperta*, open car; — *di serie*, production-model car; — *fuori serie*, special-body car.

autoambulanza *sf.* ambulance.

auto-attrezzi *sf.* breakdown-lorry.

autobiografia *sf.* autobiography.

autobiògrafo *sm.* autobiographer.

autoblinda *sf.* armoured car.

autobotte *sf.* tank truck.

àutobus *sm.* (motor-) bus.

autoclave *sf.* autoclave.

autocontrollo *sm.* self-control.

autòcrate *sm.* autocrat.

autocrazìa *sf.* autocracy.

autocritica *sf.* self-criticism.

autòctono *agg.* autochthonous. ♦ **autòctono** *sm.* native.

autodafé *sm.* auto-da-fé (*pl. autos-da-fé*).

autodeterminazione *sf.* self-determination.

autodidatta *s.* self-taught person.

autòdromo *sm.* motor-racing track.

autoeducazione *sf.* self-education.

autofinanziamento *sm.* self-financing.

autògeno *agg.* autogenous.

autogoverno *sm.* self-government.

autografare *vt.* to autograph.

autògrafo *agg.* autographic(al). ◆ **autògrafo** *sm.* autograph.

autolesione *sf.* self-injury.

autolesionismo *sm.* self-injuring.

autolettiga *sf.* ambulance.

autolinea *sf.* bus line.

automa *sm.* automaton, robot.

automàtico *agg.* automatic: *pistola, fucile —*, automatic pistol, gun || *distributore —*, slot machine.

automatismo *sm.* automatism.

automazione *sf.* automation.

automòbile *sf.* V. *auto*.

automobilismo *sm.* motoring.

automobilista *sm.* motorist.

automotrice *sf.* rail-car.

autonoleggio *sm.* car rental.

autonomìa *sf.* autonomy: *— di volo*, flight range.

autonomismo *sm.* self-government.

autònomo *agg.* self-governing.

autoparco *sm.* car-park.

autopilota *sm.* automatic pilot.

autopompa *sf.* fire-engine.

autoposteggio *sm.* parking.

autopsìa *sf.* autopsy.

autoradio *sf.* car radio-set.

autore *sm.* author.

autorespiratore *sm.* aqualung.

autorévole *agg.* authoritative.

autorevolezza *sf.* authoritativeness.

autorimessa *sf.* garage.

autorità *sf.* authority.

autoritario *agg.* authoritative.

autoritratto *sm.* self-portrait.

autorizzare *vt.* 1. (*dare autorità*) to empower 2. (*permettere*) to permit.

autorizzazione *sf.* permission, consent.

autoscuola *sf.* driving school.

autostazione *sf.* filling station.

autostòp *sm.* hitch-hiking.

autostoppista *sm.* hitch-hiker.

autostrada *sf.* motor-way.

autosuggestione *sf.* auto-suggestion.

autotreno *sm.* motor-lorry.

autrice *sf.* authoress.

autunnale *agg.* autumnal.

autunno *sm.* autumn.

ava *sf.* 1. grandmother 2. (*antenata*) ancestress.

avallare *vt.* to guarantee.

avallo *sm.* guarantee.

avambraccio *sm.* forearm.

avamposto *sm.* outpost.

avanguardia *sf.* vanguard: *essere all'—*, to be in the van.

avannotto *sm.* fry.

avanscoperta *sf.* scouting party: *andare all'—*, to scout.

avanspettàcolo *sm.* introductory variety turn.

avanti *avv.* 1. (*di luogo*) forward: *andare —*, to move forward 2. (*a chi bussa*) «come in» 3. (*di tempo*) before || (*di orologio*) fast: *il mio orologio è avanti di 20 minuti*, my watch is twenty minutes fast. ◆ **avanti** *prep.* before. ◆ **avanti che** *cong.* before (con ger.).

avantieri *avv.* the day before yesterday.

avanzamento *sm.* 1. advancing 2. (*progresso*) advancement 3. (*promozione*) promotion.

avanzare *vt.* 1. to advance 2. (*fig.*) to put (*v. irr.*) forward 3. (*promuovere*) to promote. ◆ **avanzare** *vi.* to advance. ◆ **avanzarsi** *vr.* to advance.

avanzata *sf.* advance.

avanzato *agg.* 1. advanced 2. (*promosso*) promoted.

avanzo *sm.* remnant || *— di galera*, jail-bird || *— di stoffa*, scrap of cloth.

avarìa *sf.* damage.

avariato *agg.* damaged.

avarizia *sf.* avarice.

avaro *agg.* avaricious.

avena *sf.* oats (*p.*).

avere *vt.* 1. (*general. e come v. ausiliare*) to have: *ho molti libri*, I have many books; *ho letto questo giornale*, I have read this newspaper 2. (*possedere*) to own, to have got: *ha una grande casa*, he owns, has got a big house 3. (*ottenere*) to get (*v. irr.*): *ebbi quell'impiego*, I got that job 4. (*indossare*) to wear (*v. irr.*): *aveva (indosso) un abito rosso*, she was wearing a red dress 5. (*dovere*) to have to: *ho molte cose da fare*,

I have many things to do **6.** (*di anni*) to be ... years old: *bo 10 anni*, I am ten years old.

aviatore *sm.* airman (*pl.* -men), pilot.

aviazione *sf.* **1.** aviation **2.** (*arma*) Air Force.

avicoltura *sf.* bird-rearing.

avidità *sf.* **1.** avidity **2.** (*ingordigia*) greed **3.** (*brama*) eagerness.

avido *agg.* **1.** avid **2.** (*ingordo*) greedy **3.** (*desideroso*) eager.

aviere *sm.* airman (*pl.* -men).

aviogetto *sm.* jet-(plane).

aviolinea *sf.* airline.

aviotrasportare *vt.* to air-bear (*v. irr.*).

aviotrasporto *sm.* air-transport.

avitaminosi *sf.* avitaminosis.

avito *agg.* ancestral.

avo *sm.* **1.** grandfather **2.** (*antenato*) ancestor **3.** (*pl.*) forefathers.

avorio *sm.* ivory.

avulso *agg.* uprooted.

avvalersi *vr.* to avail oneself.

avvaloramento *sm.* strengthening.

avvalorare *vt.* **1.** to give (*v. irr.*) value to **2.** (*rafforzare*) to strengthen.

avvampare *vi.* to flare up (*anche fig.*).

avvantaggiare *vt.* to advantage, to better. ♦ **avvantaggiarsi** *vr.* to profit (by).

avvedersi *vr.* to perceive.

avvedutamente *avv.* shrewdly.

avvedutezza *sf.* shrewdness.

avveduto *agg.* shrewd.

avvelenamento *sm.* poisoning.

avvelenare *vt.* to poison.

avvelenatore *sm.* poisoner.

avvenente *agg.* charming, pretty.

avvenenza *sf.* charm, loveliness.

avvenimento *sm.* event.

avvenire[1] *vi. imp.* to happen.

avvenire[2] *sm.* future.

avventarsi *vr.* to throw (*v. irr.*) oneself.

avventatamente *avv.* rashly.

avventatezza *sf.* rashness.

avventato *agg.* rash.

avventizio *agg.* **1.** temporary **2.** (*giur.*) adventitious.

avvento *sm.* **1.** (*eccl.*) Advent **2.** arrival **3.** (*assunzione al trono*) accession.

avventore *sm.* customer.

avventura *sf.* adventure.

avventurarsi *vr.* to venture.

avventuriero *sm.* adventurer.

avventuroso *agg.* adventurous.

avverarsi *vr.* to come (*v. irr.*) true.

avverbiale *agg.* adverbial.

avverbio *sm.* adverb.

avversare *vt.* to oppose.

avversario *agg.* contrary. ♦ **avversario** *sm.* opponent.

avversione *sf.* aversion, dislike.

avversità *sf.* adversity, misfortune.

avverso *agg.* unfavourable.

avvertenza *sf.* **1.** (*avviso*) warning **2.** (*attenzione, cura*) attention, care.

avvertibile *agg.* perceptible.

avvertimento *sm.* warning.

avvertire *vt.* **1.** (*avvisare*) to inform **2.** (*mettere in guardia*) to warn **3.** (*osservare*) to notice.

avvezzare *vt.* to accustom.

avvezzo *agg.* accustomed, used.

avviamento *sm.* starting.

avviare *vt.* to start.

avvicinamento *sm.* approach.

avvicinare *vt.* to approach. ♦ **avvicinarsi** *vr.* **1.** to approach **2.** (*essere simile*) to be similar.

avvicendare *vt.* to alternate. ♦ **avvicendarsi** *vr.* to alternate.

avvicendamento *sm.* alternation.

avvilente *agg.* **1.** discouraging **2.** (*umiliante*) humiliating.

avvilimento *sm.* **1.** dejection **2.** (*umiliazione*) humiliation.

avvilire *vt.* **1.** (*scoraggiare*) to dishearten **2.** (*umiliare*) to humiliate. ♦ **avvilirsi** *vr.* **1.** to lose heart **2.** (*umiliarsi*) to abase oneself.

avvilito *agg.* **1.** downcast **2.** (*umiliato*) humbled.

avviluppare *vt.* **1.** to wrap up **2.** (*aggrovigliare*) to entangle. ♦ **avvilupparsi** *vr.* **1.** to wrap oneself up **2.** (*aggrovigliarsi*) to get (*v. irr.*) entangled.

avvinazzare *vt.* to get (*v. irr.*) drunk.

avvinazzato *agg.* tipsy.

avvincente *agg.* engaging.

avvincere *vt.* to enthral.

avvinghiarsi *vr.* to cling (*v. irr.*).

avvio *sm.* start: *prendere l'—*, to start off.

avvisaglia *sf.* (*primo segno*) foreshadowing.

avvisare *vt.* **1.** to inform, to let (*v. irr.*) know **2.** (*mettere in guardia*) to warn.

avviso *sm.* **1.** notice **2.** (*consiglio*) warning **3.** (*manifesto*) poster **4.**

(*opinione*) opinion.

avvistare *vt.* to sight.

avvitamento *sm.* spin.

avvitare *vt.* 1. (*mecc.*) to screw 2. (*aer.*) to spin.

avviticchiarsi *vr.* to twist round.

avvocato *sm.* 1. lawyer 2. (*civilista*) solicitor.

avvocatura *sf.* legal profession.

avvòlgere *vt.* 1. to wrap (*anche fig.*) 2. (*arrotolare*) to roll up.

avvolgimento *sm.* 1. winding 2. (*di pacchi*) wrapping up 3. (*elettr.*) winding.

avvoltoio *sm.* vulture (*anche fig.*).

azalea *sf.* azalea.

azienda *sf.* firm, concern: — *industriale*, manufacturing concern; — *agricola*, farm.

aziendale *agg.* firm, concern.

àzimut *sm.* azimuth.

azimutale *agg.* azimuthal.

azionamento *sm.* working.

azionare *vt.* to set (*v. irr.*) in action, to work.

azionario *agg.* share: *capitale* —, share capital.

azione *sf.* 1. action 2. (*comm.*) share.

azionista *s.* shareholder.

azotare *vt.* to azotize.

azoto *sm.* azote.

azteco *agg. e sm.* Aztec.

azzannare *vt.* to seize in the jaws.

azzardare *vt.* to risk, to venture.

azzardo *sm.* hazard || *gioco d'*—, game of chance.

azzeccare *vt.* to guess, to hit (*v. irr.*) the mark.

àzzimo *agg.* unleavened: *pane* —, unleavened bread.

azzoppare *vt.* to lame. ♦ **azzopparsi** *vr.* to become (*v. irr.*) lame.

azzuffarsi *vr.* to come (*v. irr.*) to blows.

azzurro *agg.* blue.

azzurrògnolo *agg.* bluish.

B

babbeo *sm.* blockhead.

babbo *sm.* father, daddy.

babbuccia *sf.* slipper.

babbuino *sm.* baboon.

babele *sf.* babel.

bacare *vi.* **bacarsi** *vr.* to rot.

bacato *agg.* rotten.

bacca *sf.* berry.

baccalà *sm.* stockfish.

baccanale *sm.* bacchanal.

baccano *sm.* uproar.

baccante *sf.* Bacchante.

baccarà *sm.* baccarat.

baccellierato *sm.* bachelorship.

baccelliere *sm.* bachelor.

baccello *sm.* pod.

bacchetta *sf.* 1. rod 2. (*di direttore d'orchestra*) baton 3. (*di tamburo*) drumstick.

bacchettata *sf.* rod stroke.

bacchettone *sm.* bigot.

bacchiare *vt.* to beat (*v. irr.*) down.

bàcchico *agg.* Bacchic.

bacheca *sf.* show-case.

bachelite *sf.* bakelite.

bacherozzo *sm.* 1. (*scarafaggio*) cockroach 2. (*bruco*) maggot.

bachicoltura *sf.* silkworm breeding.

baciamano *sm.* hand-kissing.

baciapile *sm.* bigot.

baciare *vt.* to kiss. ♦ **baciarsi** *vr.* *rec.* to kiss each other.

bacile *sm.* basin.

bacillo *sm.* bacillus (*pl.* -li).

bacinella *sf.* basin.

bacino *sm.* 1. basin 2. (*anat.*) pelvis 3. (*mar.*) dock: — *di carenaggio*, dry dock.

bacio *sm.* kiss.

baciucchiare *vt.* to kiss repeatedly.

baco *sm.* worm: — *da seta*, silkworm.

bada *sf.* (*nella loc.*) *tenere a* — *qu.*, to hold (*v. irr.*) so. at bay.

badare *vi.* to mind (*so.*, *sthg.*): *senza* — *a spese*, regardless of expense.

badessa *sf.* abbess.

badìa *sf.* abbey.

badilante *sm.* navvy.

badile *sm.* shovel.

baffo *sm.* 1. moustache: *portare i baffi*, to wear (*v. irr.*) a moustache || *ridere sotto i baffi*, to laugh in one's sleeve 2. (*sgorbio*) smear.

bagagliaio *sm.* luggage van.

bagaglio *sm.* luggage (*solo sing.*) || *fare i bagagli*, to pack || *disfare i bagagli*, to unpack.

bagarinaggio *sm.* cornering.

bagattella *sf.* trifle.

baggianata *sf.* 1. (*azione*) foolish action 2. (*discorso*) nonsense.

bagliore *sm.* flash.

bagnante *sm.* bather.

bagnare *vt.* **1.** to wet **2.** (*immergere*) to dip **3.** (*di mare, fiume*) to wash. ◆ **bagnarsi** *vr.* **1.** to get (*v. irr.*) wet **2.** (*fare bagni in mare ecc.*) to bathe.

bagnato *agg.* wet.

bagnino *sm.* bathing attendant.

bagno *sm.* **1.** bath: *far un —,* to take (*v. irr.*) a bath; — *di sole,* sun-bath **2.** (*in mare ecc.*) bathe || *fare il —,* to bathe || *costume da —,* bathing-costume.

bagnomaria *sm.* bain-marie.

bagordo *sm.* revelry.

baia¹ *sf.* (*scherzo*) joke || *dare la — a qu.,* to make (*v. irr.*) fun of so.

baia² *sf.* (*geogr.*) bay.

baionetta *sf.* bayonet.

baita *sf.* Alpine hut.

balaustrata *sf.* balustrade.

balbettare *vt. e vi.* to stammer.

balbettio *sm.* stammer.

balbuzie *sf.* stammer.

balbuziente *agg.* stammering. ◆ **balbuziente** *s.* stammerer.

balconata *sf.* balcony.

balcone *sm.* balcony.

baldacchino *sm.* canopy.

baldanza *sf.* boldness.

baldanzoso *agg.* bold.

baldo *agg.* bold.

baldoria *sf.* revel: *far —,* to make (*v. irr.*) merry.

balena *sf.* whale: *stecca di —,* whalebone.

balenare *vi.* **1.** to lighten **2.** (*di idea*) to flash.

baleno *sm.* lightning || *in un —,* in the twinkling of an eye.

balestra *sf.* **1.** crossbow **2.** (*mecc.*) leaf spring.

balia *sf.* wet nurse: — *asciutta,* dry-nurse.

balìa *sf.* mercy: *in — di,* at the mercy of.

balistica *sf.* ballistics.

balla *sf.* **1.** (*di cotone, di lana*) bale **2.** (*volg.; fandonia*) tall story **3.** (*fig.; mucchio*) heap.

ballare *vt. e vi.* to dance.

ballata *sf.* ballad.

ballatoio *sm.* gallery.

ballerina *sf.* **1.** dancer **2.** (*classica*) ballerina.

ballerino *sm.* **1.** dancer **2.** (*classico*) ballet-dancer.

balletto *sm.* ballet.

ballo *sm.* **1.** dance **2.** (*festa*) ball || *essere in —,* to be on the go; *tirare in —,* to call in question.

ballottaggio *sm.* second ballot.

balneare *agg.* bathing || *stazione —,* seaside resort.

balocco *sm.* toy.

balordaggine *sf.* **1.** dullness **2.** (*azione*) foolish action **3.** (*discorso*) nonsense.

balordo *agg. e sm.* stupid.

balsamico *agg.* balmy.

balsamo *sm.* balm.

baluardo *sm.* bulwark.

balza *sf.* **1.** cliff **2.** (*di vestito*) flounce.

balzano *agg.* **1.** queer **2.** (*di cavallo*) white-footed.

balzare *vi.* to jump.

balzo *sm.* jump: *cogliere la palla al —,* to seize an opportunity.

bambagia *sf.* cotton-wool.

bambina *sf.* **1.** little girl, child (*pl.* children) **2.** (*in fasce*) baby.

bambinaia *sf.* nurse.

bambino *sm.* **1.** little boy, child (*pl.* children) **2.** (*in fasce*) baby || *dare alla luce un —,* to bring (*v. irr.*) forth a child.

bamboccio *sm.* **1.** (*bambola*) ragdoll **2.** (*fig.*) simpleton.

bambola *sf.* doll.

bambù *sm.* bamboo.

banale *agg.* banal.

banalità *sf.* banality.

banana *sf.* banana.

banano *sm.* banana-tree.

banca *sf.* bank.

bancarella *sf.* stall.

bancario *agg.* bank: *libretto —,* passbook. ◆ **bancario** *sm.* bank clerk.

bancarotta *sf.* bankruptcy: *fare —,* to go (*v. irr.*) bankrupt.

banchetto *sm.* banquet.

banchiere *sm.* banker.

banchina *sf.* **1.** (*molo*) wharf **2.** (*terrapieno*) bank.

banchisa *sf.* ice-pack.

banco *sm.* **1.** bench **2.** (*di chiesa*) pew **3.** (*di negozio*) counter **4.** (*di nebbia, di sabbia, di gioco*) bank.

banconota *sf.* banknote.

banda *sf.* **1.** (*lato*) side **2.** (*mus.; striscia di stoffa*) band **3.** (*di delinquenti*) gang.

banderuola *sf.* weathercock.

bandiera *sf.* flag, colours (*pl.*).

bandire *vt.* **1.** to proclaim **2.** (*esi-*

liare, eliminare) to banish.
bandito *sm.* outlaw.
bando *sm.* 1. ban 2. (*esilio*) banishment || *essere al —*, to be banished 3. (*annunzio*) announcement.
bar *sm.* bar.
bara *sf.* coffin.
baracca *sf.* hut.
baraccone *sm.* booth.
baraonda *sf.* chaos.
barare *vi.* to cheat.
bàratro *sm.* abyss.
barattare *vt.* to exchange.
baratto *sm.* barter.
baràttolo *sm.* 1. jar 2. (*di metallo*) tin.
barba *sf.* beard: *fare, farsi la —*, to shave || (*fig.*) *in — a*, in spite of.
barbabiètola *sf.* beet-root.
barbarie *sf.* 1. barbarousness 2. (*crudeltà*) barbarity.
bàrbaro *agg.* e *sm.* barbarian.
barbiere *sm.* barber.
barbone *sm.* 1. (*straccione*) tramp 2. (*cane*) poodle.
barbuto *agg.* bearded.
barca *sf.* boat: *andare in —*, to go (*v. irr.*) boating.
barcaiolo *sm.* boatman (*pl.* -men).
barcamenarsi *vr.* to wangle.
barcollare *vi.* to stagger.
barcone *sm.* long boat.
bardare *vt.* to harness. ♦ **bardarsi** *vr.* to dress up.
barella *sf.* stretcher.
barile *sm.* barrel.
barista *sm.* barman (*pl.* -men). ♦ **barista** *sf.* barmaid.
baritonale *agg.* baritone.
barìtono *sm.* baritone.
barlume *sm.* glimmer.
baro *sm.* cheat.
barocco *agg.* e *sm.* baroque.
baromètrico *agg.* barometric(al).
baròmetro *sm.* barometer.
barone *sm.* baron.
baronessa *sf.* baroness.
barra *sf.* 1. bar 2. (*mar.*) helm.
barricare *vt.* to barricade.
barricata *sf.* barricade.
barriera *sf.* 1. barrier 2. (*fig.*) obstacle.
barrire *vi.* to trumpet.
barrito *sm.* trumpet.
barroccio *sm.* cart.
baruffa *sf.* quarrel.
barzelletta *sf.* joke.
basalto *sm.* basalt.

basamento *sm.* base.
basare *vt.* to base.
basco *agg.* e *sm.* Basque. ♦ **basco** *sm.* (*berretto*) beret.
base *sf.* base.
basette *sf. pl.* whiskers.
bàsico *agg.* basic.
basilare *agg.* basic.
basìlica *sf.* basilica.
basìlico *sm.* basil.
basilisco *sm.* basilisk.
bassezza *sf.* baseness.
basso *agg.* 1. low 2. (*di statura*) short 3. (*abietto*) base. ♦ **basso** *avv.* low. ♦ **basso** *sm.* 1. bottom 2. (*mus.*) bass.
bassofondo *sm.* shallow || *i bassifondi della società*, the underworld.
bassopiano *sm.* lowland.
bassorilievo *sm.* bas-relief.
bassotto *agg.* thick-set. ♦ **bassotto** *sm.* (*cane*) dachshund.
bassoventre *sm.* belly.
basta *inter.* stop it!: *— con*, enough of.
bastardo *agg.* e *sm.* 1. bastard 2. (*di animali*) mongrel.
bastare *vi.* to be enough.
bastimento *sm.* ship.
bastione *sm.* 1. rampart 2. (*mil.*) bastion.
basto *sm.* pack-saddle.
bastonare *vt.* to cane.
bastonata *sf.* blow with a cane.
bastonatura *sf.* caning.
bastone *sm.* stick, staff.
batacchio *sm.* clapper.
batisfera *sf.* bathysphere.
batista *sf.* batiste.
batosta *sf.* blow.
batrace *sm.* batrachian.
battaglia *sf.* battle, fight || (*fig.*) *cavallo di —*, favourite subject, favourite piece.
battagliare *vi.* to battle, to fight (*v. irr.*), to struggle.
battagliero *agg.* 1. warlike 2. (*fig.*) fierce.
battaglione *sm.* battalion.
battelliere *sm.* boatman (*pl.* -men).
battello *sm.* boat.
battente *sm.* 1. (*picchiotto*) knocker 2. (*di porta*) wing.
bàttere *vt.* 1. to beat (*v. irr.*), to strike (*v. irr.*) (*anche delle ore*) 2. (*scrivere a macchina*) to type || *— le mani*, to clap hands; *— i piedi*, to stamp; *in un batter d'oc-*

chio, in the twinkling of an eye.
♦ **bàttere** *vi.* **1.** to knock **2.** (*pulsare*) to throb. ♦ **bàttersi** *vr.* to fight (*v. irr.*).

batterìa *sf.* **1.** battery **2.** (*da cucina*) kitchen utensils.

batter:o *sm.* bacterium (*pl.* -ia).

batteriologìa *sf.* bacteriology.

battésimo *sm.* baptism: *nome di* —, Christian name.

battezzare *vt.* to baptize.

battibaleno *sm.* (*nella loc. avv.*) *in un* —, in a twinkling.

battibecco *sm.* squabble.

batticuore *sm.* **1.** throb **2.** (*fig.*) fear.

battimano *sm.* clap.

battipanni *sm.* carpet-beater.

battistero *sm.* baptistery.

battistrada *sm.* **1.** outrider **2.** (*di pneumatico*) tread ‖ *fare da* —, to lead (*v. irr.*) the way.

bàttito *sm.* **1.** beat **2.** (*mecc.*) knock.

battitore *sm.* **1.** beater **2.** (*cricket, baseball*) batsman (*pl.* -men).

battitura *sf.* thrashing.

battuta *sf.* **1.** beating: — *di caccia*, beating **2.** (*di spirito*) witty remark **3.** (*mus.*) bar **4.** (*teat.*) cue **5.** (*tennis*) service.

batùffolo *sm.* flock.

baule *sm.* trunk.

bauxite *sf.* bauxite.

bava *sf.* **1.** slaver **2.** (*di lumaca*) slime.

bavaglino *sm.* bib.

bavaglio *sm.* gag: *mettere il* — *a qu.* (*fig.*), to gag so.

bàvero *sm.* collar.

bazàr *sm.* bazaar.

bazza *sf.* slipper-chin.

bazzècola *sf.* trifle.

bazzicare *vt. e vi.* to frequent.

bazzotto *agg.* soft-boiled.

be' *inter.* well.

beare *vt.* to make (*v. irr.*) so. happy. ♦ **bearsi** *vr.* to rejoice (at).

beatificazione *sf.* beatification.

beatitùdine *sf.* beatitude.

beato *agg.* **1.** happy **2.** (*relig.*) blessed.

beccaccia *sf.* woodcock.

beccaccino *sm.* snipe.

beccare *vt.* **1.** to peck **2.** (*fam. per acchiappare*) to catch (*v. irr.*). ♦ **beccarsi** *vr.* **1.** (*procurarsi*) to get (*v. irr.*) **2.** (*litigare*) to quarrel.

beccata *sf.* peck.

beccheggiare *vi.* to pitch.

beccheggio *sm.* pitching.

becchìme *sm.* birdseed.

becchino *sm.* grave-digger.

becco *sm.* **1.** beak **2.** (*caprone*) billy-goat **3.** (*fig.*) cuckold.

beccuccio *sm.* (*di teiera ecc.*) spout.

beduino *agg. e sm.* Bedouin.

befana *sf.* **1.** "befana" **2.** (*fig. fam.*) hag.

beffa *sf.* mockery: *farsi — di*, to laugh at; (*ingannare*) to make (*v. irr.*) a fool of.

beffardo *agg.* mocking. ♦ **beffardo** *sm.* mocker.

beffare *vt.* to mock. ♦ **beffarsi** *vr.* to laugh at.

beffeggiare *vt.* V. *beffare*.

bega *sf.* **1.** quarrel **2.** (*problema intricato*) entangled affair.

beghina *sf.* bigot.

begonia *sf.* (*bot.*) begonia.

belare *vi.* to bleat.

belato *sm.* bleat.

belga *agg. e sm.* Belgian.

bella *sf.* **1.** beauty **2.** (*innamorata*) sweetheart ‖ *copiare in* —, to make (*v. irr.*) a fair copy.

belladonna *sf.* (*bot.; farm.*) belladonna.

belletto *sm.* rouge.

bellezza *sf.* beauty: *istituto di* —, beauty parlour.

bellicismo *sm.* warlikeness.

bèllico *agg.* **1.** war (*attributivo*) **2.** (*del tempo di guerra*) wartime.

bellicoso *agg.* warlike.

belligerante *agg. e sm.* belligerent.

belligeranza *sf.* belligerence.

bellimbusto *sm.* dandy.

bello *agg.* **1.** fine, beautiful **2.** (*di uomo*) handsome ‖ *nel bel mezzo*, right in the middle. ♦ **bello** *sm.* **1.** (*la bellezza*) beauty **2.** (*innamorato*) sweetheart ‖ *sul più* —, at the right moment; *ora viene il* —, now you'll hear the best of it.

belva *sf.* wild beast.

belvedere *sm.* **1.** observation post **2.** (*arch.*) belvedere.

bemolle *sm.* (*mus.*) flat.

benché *cong.* though.

benda *sf.* bandage.

bendaggio *sm.* bandage.

bendare *vt.* to bandage.

bene *sm.* good: *per il tuo* —, for your sake; *voler* —, to love. ♦

beni sm. pl. property || — immo-
bili, real estate: — di consumo,
consumer goods. ♦ **bene** avv. **1.**
well **2.** (molto) very **3.** (niente-
no) no less than || star —, to be
well; andar —, to suit.

benedetto agg. blessed.

benedire vt. to bless.

benedizione sf. blessing.

benefattore sm. benefactor.

beneficare vt. to help.

beneficenza sf. charity.

beneficiario agg. e sm. beneficiary.

beneficiata sf. benefit.

beneficio sm. **1.** benefit **2.** (eccl.;
giur.) benefice.

benèfico agg. **1.** beneficent **2.** (vantaggioso) beneficial.

benemerenza sf. merit.

benemèrito agg. well-deserving.

beneplàcito sm. consent: a tuo
—, as you like.

benèssere sm. welfare.

benestante agg. well-off. ♦ **benestante** s. well-to-do person.

benestare sm. assent.

benevolenza sf. benevolence.

benèvolo agg. benevolent.

bengala sm. Bengal light.

beniamino sm. darling.

benignità sf. **1.** benignity **2.** (di
clima) mildness.

benigno agg. **1.** benign **2.** (di clima) mild.

beninteso avv. of course.

benpensante agg. sensible || i ben-
pensanti, the right thinking.

benservito sm. testimonial.

bensì cong. but.

benvenuto agg. sm. inter. welcome
|| dare il — a qu., to welcome so.

benvolere vt. to like: farsi —, to
make (v. irr.) oneself liked.

benzina sf. petrol.

benzinaio sm. filling station attendant.

benzolo sm. benzol.

beone sm. drunkard.

beota agg. e sm. Bœotian.

bèrbero agg. e sm. Berber.

berciare vi. to bawl.

bere vt. to drink (v. irr.) || darla
a — (fig.), to tell (v. irr.) tall
stories.

bergamotto sm. (bot.; farm.) bergamot.

berillo sm. beryllium.

berlina sf. **1.** (carrozza) berline **2.**
(automobile) limousine **3.** (gogna)

pillory: mettere alla —, to pillory.

bernòccolo sm. bump.

berretta sf. cap.

berretto sm. cap.: — con visiera,
peaked cap.

bersagliare vt. **1.** to shoot (v. irr.)
(at) **2.** (fig.) to torment.

bersaglio sm. target: tiro al —,
target-shooting || colpire il —, to
hit (v. irr.) the mark.

besciamella sf. cream-sauce.

bestemmia sf. swear.

bestemmiare vi. to swear (v. irr.)

bestia sf. beast || montare in —,
to lose (v. irr.) one's temper.

bestiale agg. beastly.

bestialità sf. **1.** beastliness **2.** (fig.)
foolishness || dire —, to talk non-
sense; fare —, to make (v. irr.)
blunders.

bestiame sm. cattle.

béttola sf. tavern.

betulla sf. birch.

bevanda sf. drink.

beveraggio sm. beverage.

bevitore sm. drinker.

bevuta sf. **1.** draught **2.** (il bere)
drinking.

biada sf. fodder.

biancastro agg. whitish.

bianchegglare vi. e vt. **1.** (essere
bianco) to be white **2.** (diventare,
far diventare bianco) to whiten.

biancherìa sf. linen.

bianco agg. white || in —, blank;
di punto in —, suddenly.

biancore sm. whiteness.

biancospino sm. hawthorn.

biascicare vt. to mumble.

biasimare vt. to blame.

biasimévole agg. blamable.

biàsimo sm. blame.

Bibbia sf. Bible.

bibita sf. drink.

biblico agg. biblical.

bibliografìa sf. bibliography.

bibliogràfico agg. bibliographic(al).

biblioteca sf. **1.** library **2.** (scaffale) bookcase.

bibliotecario sm. librarian.

bica sf. stack.

bicamerale agg. (pol.) bicameral.

bicarbonato sm. bicarbonate.

bicchiere sm. glass.

bicefalo agg. V. bicipite.

bicicletta sf. bicycle: andare in
—, to cycle.

bicìpite agg. two-headed. ♦ **bicìpite** sm. biceps.

bicocca sf. hut.

bicolore agg. two-coloured.

bidè sm. bidet.

bidello sm. porter.

bidente sm. pitchfork.

bidone sm. 1. can 2. (fam.) swindle.

bieco agg. sinister.

biella sf. (mecc.) connecting rod.

biennale agg. biennial.

biètola sf. beet.

biennio sm. biennium (pl. -nia).

bifase agg. (elettr.) two-phase.

bifolco sm. boor.

biforcarsi vr. to fork.

biforcazione sf. fork.

biforcuto agg. forked.

bigamìa sf. bigamy.

bìgamo agg. bigamous. ♦ **bìgamo** sm. bigamist.

bighellonare vi. to lounge.

bighellone sm. lounger.

bigio agg. grey.

bigiotterìa sf. trinkets (pl.).

biglia sf. (biliard-)ball.

bigliettaio sm. 1. conductor 2. (di stazione) booking-clerk.

biglietterìa sf. 1. booking-office 2. (di teatro) box-office.

biglietto sm. 1. card: — di visita, visiting card 2. (di tram ecc.) ticket: — di andata e ritorno, return ticket; mezzo —, half-fare ticket 3. (banconota) bank-note.

bigodino sm. (hair-)curler.

bigotto agg. bigoted. ♦ **bigotto** sm. bigot.

bikini sm. bikini.

bilancia sf. balance, scales (pl.).

bilanciare vt. to balance.

bilanciere sm. 1. balance-wheel 2. (mar.) outrigger.

bilancio sm. budget: fare il —, to strike (v. irr.) the balance.

bilaterale agg. bilateral.

bile sf. 1. bile 2. (ira) anger.

biliardo sm. billiards (pl.).

bìlico sm. 1. balance 2. (fig.) uncertainty || mettere in —, to balance; stare in —, to be balanced.

bilingue agg. bilingual.

bilione sm. billion.

bilioso agg. bilious.

bimba sf. V. bambina.

bimbo sm. V. bambino.

bimensile agg. fortnightly.

bimestrale agg. bimestrial.

bimestre sm. (period of) two months.

bimotore agg. two-engined: aereo —, two-engined plane.

binario sm. track: — morto, dead-end track.

binòcolo sm. binoculars (pl.).

binomio sm. binomial.

biòccolo sm. flock: — di neve, snow-flake.

biochìmica sf. biochemistry.

biofìsica sf. biophysics.

biografìa sf. biography.

biogràfico agg. biographic(al).

biògrafo sm. biographer.

biologìa sf. biology.

biològico agg. biologic(al).

biòlogo sm. biologist.

biondo agg. fair.

biosfera sf. biosphere.

biòssido sm. dioxide.

bipartizione sf. bipartition.

bìpede agg. e sm. biped.

biplano sm. biplane.

bipolare agg. bipolar.

birba sf. scapegrace.

birbante s. rogue.

birbonata sf. knavery.

birbone sm. rogue.

bireattore sm. two-engined jet.

birichino sm. urchin. ♦ **birichino** agg. naughty.

birillo sm. skittle.

biro sf. ball-point pen.

biroccio sm. cart.

birra sf. beer.

birrerìa sf. 1. beer-house 2. (fabbrica) brewery.

bisaccia sf. packsack.

bisbètico agg. cantankerous.

bisbigliare vt. to whisper.

bisbiglio sm. whisper.

bisboccia sf. spree: far —, to revel.

bisca sf. gambling-house.

biscia sf. snake.

biscotto sm. biscuit.

bisessuale agg. bisexual.

bisestile agg. anno —, leap year.

bisettimanale agg. bi-weekly.

bisettrice sf. bisector.

bisìllabo agg. disyllabic. ♦ **bisìllabo** sm. disyllable.

bislacco agg. odd.

bislungo agg. oblong.

bismuto sm. bismuth.

bisnipote s. great-grandchild (pl. -children).

bisnonna sf. great-grandmother.

bisnonno sm. great-grandfather.

bisognare vi. imp. to be necessary, must.

bisogno *sm.* **1.** need **2.** (*povertà*) necessity || aver —, to need.

bisognoso *agg.* needy.

bisonte *sm.* bison.

bissare *vt.* to give (*v. irr.*) an encore (of sthg.).

bistecca *sf.* beefsteak.

bisticciare *vi.* to squabble.

bisticcio *sm.* **1.** squabble **2.** (*gioco di parole*) pun.

bistrattare *vt.* to ill-treat.

bistro *sm.* bistre.

bisturi *sm.* lancet.

bitòrzolo *sm.* bump.

bitume *sm.* bitumen.

bivacco *sm.* bivouac.

bivalente *agg.* bivalent.

bivio *sm.* **1.** fork **2.** (*fig.*) alternative.

bizantino *agg. e sm.* Byzantine.

bizza *sf.* freak || fare le bizze, to be peevish.

bizzarrìa *sf.* **1.** peculiarity **2.** (*cosa*) curiosity **3.** (*atto, detto*) extravagance.

bizzarro *agg.* strange.

bizzoso *agg.* **1.** freakish **2.** (*irascibile*) irascible.

blandire *vt.* to soothe.

blandizia *sf.* blandishment.

blando *agg.* bland.

blasone *sm.* **1.** blazon **2.** (*nobiltà*) nobility.

blaterare *vi. e vt.* to prate.

bleso *agg.* lisping || pronuncia blesa, lisp. ♦ **bleso** *sm.* lisper.

blindare *vt.* (*mil.*) to armour.

bloccare *vt.* to block, to stop. ♦ **bloccarsi** *vr.* to jam.

blocco *sm.* **1.** block **2.** (*mil.*) blockade.

blu *agg. e sm.* blue.

bluff *sm.* bluff.

blusa *sf.* blouse.

boa¹ *sf.* (*mar.*) buoy.

boa² *sm.* (*zool.*) boa.

bobina *sf.* bobbin.

bocca *sf.* mouth: — da incendio, fire-plug; — dello stomaco, pit of the stomach; chiudere la — a qu., to silence so.

boccaccia *sf.* grimace.

boccale *sm.* jug.

boccaporto *sm.* hatchway.

boccata *sf.* mouthful.

boccheggiare *vi.* to gasp.

bocchino *sm.* mouthpiece.

boccia *sf.* **1.** water-bottle **2.** (*sport*) bowl.

bocciare *vt.* **1.** (*respingere*) to reject **2.** (*agli esami*) to fail.

bocciatura *sf.* failure.

boccio *sm.* bud.

boccone *sm.* **1.** bit **2.** (*boccata*) mouthful **3.** (*esca*) bait.

bocconi *avv.* lying face downwards.

boia *sm.* executioner.

boicottare *vt.* to boycott.

bolgia *sf.* **1.** (*fig.*) bedlam **2.** (*di inferno*) pit.

bòlide *sm.* (*astr.*) bolide.

bolla *sf.* **1.** bubble **2.** (*vescica*) blister **3.** (*eccl.*) bull.

bollare *vt.* **1.** (*timbrare*) to stamp **2.** (*a fuoco e fig.*) to brand.

bollato *agg.* **1.** stamped: carta bollata, stamped paper: (*a fuoco e fig.*) branded.

bollente *agg.* boiling.

bolletta *sf.* **1.** bill **2.** (*ricevuta*) receipt || essere in — (*fig.*), to be (*v. irr.*) penniless.

bollettario *sm.* counterfoil-book.

bollettino *sm.* **1.** bulletin **2.** (*comm.*) list, note.

bollire *vi. e vt.* to boil.

bollito *sm.* boiled meat.

bollitore *sm.* **1.** boiler **2.** (*bricco*) kettle.

bollitura *sf.* boiling.

bollo *sm.* stamp.

bollore *sm.* **1.** boil **2.** (*fig.*) excitement.

bolscevico *agg. e sm.* Bolshevist.

bolscevismo *sm.* Bolshevism.

boma *sf.* (*mar.*) boom.

bomba *sf.* bomb.

bombardamento *sm.* bombardment.

bombardare *vt.* to bombard; (*generalmente da aerei*) to bomb.

bombardiere *sm.* **1.** (*soldato*) bombardier **2.** (*aereo*) bomber.

bombetta *sf.* bowler.

bòmbola *sf.* bottle.

bomboniera *sf.* candy-box.

bonaccia *sf.* dead calm.

bonaccione *agg.* good-natured. ♦ **bonaccione** *sm.* good-natured man (*pl.* men).

bonarietà *sf.* good nature.

bonario *agg.* good-natured, friendly.

bonìfica *sf.* reclamation.

bonificare *vt.* **1.** to reclaim **2.** (*comm.*) to grant an allowance.

bonomia *sf.* good nature.

bontà *sf.* goodness.

bonzo *sm.* bonze.

borbottare *vi. e vt.* **1.** to mumble

2. (*lamentarsi*) to grumble.
borbottio *sm.* **1.** mumbling **2.** (*protesta*) grumbling.
bordare *vt.* to border.
bordeggiare *vi.* to tack.
bordello *sm.* bawdyhouse.
bordo *sm.* **1.** edge **2.** (*mar.*) board: *a* —, on board.
bordura *sf.* border.
bòrea *sf.* Boreas.
boreale *agg.* boreal: *aurora* —, aurora borealis.
borgata *sf.* village.
borghese *agg.* **1.** middle-class **2.** (*comune*) plain **3.** (*civile*) civilian: *in* —, in civilian dress. ◆ **borghese** *s.* middle-class person.
borghesia *sf.* middle class(es): *l'alta* —, the upper middle class(es); *la piccola* —, the lower middle class(es).
borgo *sm.* village.
borgomastro *sm.* burgomaster.
bòria *sf.* arrogance.
bòrico *agg.* boric.
borioso *agg.* arrogant.
borotalco *sm.* talcum powder.
borraccia *sf.* flask.
borsa[1] *sf.* bag || — *per documenti*, brief case; — *di studio*, scholarship.
borsa[2] *sf.* (*comm.*) Stock Exchange.
borsaiolo *sm.* pickpocket.
borseggiare *vt.* to pick pockets.
borsellino *sm.* purse.
borsetta *sf.* (hand-)bag.
boscaglia *sf.* brushwood.
boscaiolo *sm.* woodman (*pl.* -men).
boschetto *sm.* grove.
bosco *sm.* wood.
boscoso *agg.* woody.
bòssolo *sm.* cartridge-case.
botànica *sf.* botany.
bòtola *sf.* trap-door.
botta *sf.* **1.** blow **2.** (*battuta*) sarcastic remark || *dare un sacco di botte a qu.*, to whack so.
botte *sf.* barrel.
bottega *sf.* shop.
bottegaio *sm.* shop-keeper.
bottiglia *sf.* bottle.
bottiglieria *sf.* wine shop.
bottino *sm.* booty: *far* —, to plunder.
botto *sm.* blow || *di* —, suddenly.
bottone *sm.* button || *attaccare un* — (*fig.*), to buttonhole.
bovaro *sm.* cowherd.
bovini *sm. pl.* cattle (*sing.*).

bozza *sf.* **1.** (*gonfiore*) swelling **2.** (*tip.*) proof **3.** (*abbozzo*) draft || *correggere le bozze*, to proofread.
bozzetto *sm.* sketch.
bòzzolo *sm.* cocoon.
braccare *vt.* to hunt.
braccetto (*nella loc. avv.*) *a* —, arm-in-arm.
bracciale *sm.* **1.** (*fascia che si porta al braccio*) arm-band **2.** (*braccialetto*) bracelet.
braccialetto *sm.* bracelet.
bracciante *sm.* labourer.
bracciata *sf.* **1.** armful **2.** (*di nuoto*) stroke.
braccio *sm. arm*: *essere in* — *a qu.*, to be in so.'s arms || — *di mare*, sound.
bracco *sm.* hound.
bracconaggio *sm.* poaching.
bracconiere *sm.* poacher.
brace *sf.* embers (*pl.*).
brache *sf. pl.* **1.** trousers **2.** (*mutande*) drawers.
brachicèfalo *agg.* brachycephalous.
braciere *sm.* brazier.
braciola *sf.* chop.
bradicardia *sf.* (*med.*) bradycardia.
brado *agg.* wild.
brama *sf.* longing.
bramare *vt.* to long for (sthg.).
bramosìa *sf.* covetousness.
bramoso *agg.* eager for (sthg.).
branca *sf.* **1.** claw **2.** (*settore*) branch.
branchia *sf.* gill.
branco *sm.* **1.** herd **2.** (*di pecore*) flock **3.** (*di pesci*) shoal **4.** (*di lupi e fig.*) pack.
brancolare *vi.* to grope.
branda *sf.* **1.** camp-bed **2.** (*mar.*) bunk.
brandello *sm.* **1.** rag **2.** (*pezzetto*) bit || *coi vestiti a brandelli*, in rags; *fare a brandelli*, to tear (*v. irr.*) up.
brandire *vt.* to brandish.
brano *sm.* piece.
brasato *sm.* braised beef.
brasiliano *agg. e sm.* Brazilian.
bravata *sf.* bravado.
bravo *agg.* clever, good || —!, well done!; *su, da* —!, be a good boy!
bravura *sf.* **1.** cleverness **2.** (*coraggio*) bravery || (*mus.*) *pezzo di* —, bravura.
breccia *sf.* breach: *essere sulla* —, to stand (*v. irr.*) in the breach.
brefotrofio *sm.* foundling hospital.

bretella sf. brace.
breve agg. short.
brevettare vt. to patent.
brevetto sm. patent.
breviario sm. breviary.
brevità sf. brevity.
brezza sf. breeze.
bricco sm. kettle, pot.
bricconata sf. roguish trick.
briccone sm. rogue.
briciola sf. crumb.
briciolo sm. bit.
briga sf. 1. trouble 2. (lite) quarrel: attaccar —, to pick a quarrel.
brigadiere sm. 1. « brigadiere » 2. (ufficiale nell'Esercito Britannico assegnato al comando di brigata) brigadier.
brigante sm. robber.
brigantino sm. (mar.) brig.
brigare vi. to intrigue.
brigata sf. 1. party 2. (mil.) brigade.
briglia sf. bridle || a — sciolta, at full gallop.
brillante agg. e sm. brilliant.
brillantina sf. brilliantine.
brillare vi. to shine (v. irr.). ◆ **brillare** vt. 1. (riso ecc.) to hull 2. (una mina) to blast.
brillo agg. tipsy.
brina sf. hoarfrost.
brinare vi. imp.: ha brinato, there has been a frost.
brinata sf. hoarfrost.
brindare vi. to toast: — a qu., to toast so.
brindello sm. rag.
brindisi sm. toast.
brio sm. liveliness.
brioso agg. lively.
britannico agg. British.
brivido sm. 1. shiver 2. (di paura, orrore) shudder.
brizzolato agg. grizzled.
brocca sf. jug.
broccato sm. brocade.
bròccolo sm. broccoli.
brodaglia sf. slops (pl.).
brodo sm. broth.
broglio sm. intrigue: — elettorale, gerry-mander.
bromo sm. bromine.
bromuro sm. bromide.
bronchiale agg. bronchial.
bronchite sf. bronchitis.
broncio sm. pout || fare il —, to pout.
bronco sm. bronchus (pl. -chi).

broncopolmonite sf. bronchopneumonia.
brontolare vi. e vt. to grumble.
brontolìo sm. grumbling.
brontolone sm. grumbler.
brontosàuro sm. brontosaurus.
brònzeo agg. 1. bronze (attributivo) 2. (simile a bronzo) bronzy.
bronzo sm. bronze || faccia di —, brazen-faced person.
brossura sf. paper-back binding || in —, paper-bound.
brucare vt. to browse (on).
bruciacchiare vt. to scorch.
bruciacchiatura sf. scorching.
bruciapelo (nella loc. avv.) a —, point-blank.
bruciare vt. e vi. to burn (v. irr.).
bruciatore sm. burner.
bruciatura sf. burn.
bruciore sm. burning, smart (anche fig.).
bruco sm. caterpillar.
brùffolo sm. pimple.
brughiera sf. heath.
brulicare vi. to swarm (with).
brulichìo sm. swarm.
brullo agg. bare.
bruma sf. mist.
brumoso agg. misty.
brunire vt. to burnish.
brunitura sf. burnishing.
bruno agg. brown.
bruscamente avv. roughly.
brusco agg. 1. rough 2. (di sapore) sour.
brusìo sm. buzz.
brutale agg. brutal.
brutalità sf. brutality.
bruto agg. e sm. brute.
bruttezza sf. ugliness.
brutto agg. 1. ugly 2. (cattivo) bad.
bruttura sf. 1. ugly thing 2. (azione) base action.
bùbbola sf. lie.
bubbone sm. bubo.
bubbònico agg. bubonic.
buca sf. hole: — delle lettere, letter-box.
bucaneve sm. snowdrop.
bucaniere sm. buccaneer.
bucare vt. 1. to pierce 2. (una gomma) to puncture 3. (biglietti) to punch.
bucato sm. 1. washing 2. (i panni) laundry.
buccia sf. peel.
bucherellare vt. to riddle.

buco sm. hole.

bucòlico agg. bucolic.

buddismo sm. Buddhism.

buddista s. Buddhist.

budello sm. **1.** bowel **2.** (strada stretta) alley **3.** (tubo) narrow tube.

budino sm. pudding.

bue sm. ox (pl. oxen): carne di —, beef.

bùfalo sm. buffalo.

bufera sf. **1.** storm **2.** (di vento) gale.

buffetto sm. fillip: dare un —, to fillip.

buffo agg. funny || opera buffa, comic opera.

buffonata sf. buffoonery.

buffone sm. **1.** clown, fool **2.** (di corte) court jester **3.** (fig.) unreliable person.

bugìa sf. **1.** lie **2.** (portacandela) flat candlestick.

bugiardo agg. false. ♦ **bugiardo** sm. liar.

bugigàttolo sm. lumber-room.

buio agg. e sm. dark: — pesto, pitch dark.

bulbo sm. **1.** bulb **2.** (di occhio) eyeball.

bùlgaro agg. e sm. Bulgarian.

bulinare vt. to engrave.

bulino sm. burin.

bullonare vt. (mecc.) to bolt.

bullone sm. bolt.

buonanotte sf. good night.

buonasera sf. good evening.

buoncostume sm.: squadra del —, vice squad.

buongiorno sm. **1.** (di mattina) good morning **2.** (di pomeriggio) good afternoon **3.** (a ogni ora incontrandosi, fam.) hullo **4.** (a ogni ora lasciandosi) goodbye.

buongustaio sm. gourmet.

buongusto sm. good taste.

buono agg. **1.** good **2.** (di tempo) fine || alla buona, informal; a buon diritto, by right; di buon grado, willingly. ♦ **buono** sm. **1.** good **2.** (persona) good person **3.** (comm.) bond **4.** (tagliando) coupon.

buonsenso sm. (common) sense.

buontempone sm. merry fellow.

buonumore sm. V. umore.

buonuomo sm. **1.** good-natured man (pl. men) **2.** simple man (pl. men).

burattinaio sm. puppet showman (pl. -men).

burattino sm. puppet.

burbanzoso agg. haughty.

bùrbero agg. gruff.

burla sf. trick || per —, in fun.

burlare vt. to play a trick on (so.). ♦ **burlarsi** vr. to make (v. irr.) fun of.

burlesco agg. farcical.

burlone sm. joker.

buròcrate sm. bureaucrat.

burocràtico agg. bureaucratic.

burocrazìa sf. bureaucracy; (in Inghilterra) Civil Service.

burrasca sf. storm.

burrascoso agg. stormy.

burrificio sm. dairy.

burro sm. butter.

burrone sm. ravine.

burroso agg. buttery.

buscarsi vr. to get (v. irr.) || buscarle, to get a thrashing.

bussare vi. to knock: — alla porta, to knock at the door.

busse sf. pl. blows: prendere le —, to get (v. irr.) a thrashing.

bùssola sf. compass: perdere la — (fig.), to lose (v. irr.) one's head.

bussolotto sm. dice-box || fare il giuoco dei bussolotti (anche fig.), to juggle.

busta sf. **1.** envelope **2.** (astuccio) case.

bustarella sf. bribe.

bustina sf. (mil.) service cap.

busto sm. **1.** bust **2.** (indumento per donna) corset.

butano sm. (chim.) butane.

buttare vt. **1.** to throw (v. irr.) **2.** (sprecare) to waste || — all'aria, to upset (v. irr.); — a terra, to knock down.

butterato agg. pitted.

buzzo sm. belly || di — buono, very eagerly.

C

càbala sf. cab(b)ala.

cabalìstico agg. cab(b)alistic(al).

cabina sf. **1.** box, hut: — balneare, bathing hut; — telefonica, telephone box **2.** (aer.; mar.) cabin.

cablogramma sm. cable.

cabotaggio sm. cabotage: *nave di piccolo —*, coasting vessel.

cacao sm. 1. (*bot.*) cacao 2. (*polvere, bevanda*) cocoa.

cacare vi. to evacuate one's bowels.

cacarella sf. diarrhoea.

cacatoa, cacatùa sm. cockatoo.

cacca sf. excrement.

caccia sf. hunt, hunting || *— grossa*, big game || *cane da —*, sporting dog; *stagione di —*, shooting season; *andare a —*, to go (v. irr.) hunting; *andare a — di uccelli*, to go shooting. ♦ **caccia** sm. (aer.) fighter.

cacciagione sf. game.

cacciare vt. 1. to hunt 2. (*mil.; mar.*) to chase 3. (*scacciare*) to expel 4. (*mettere*) to put (v. irr.).

cacciatore sm. hunter (anche fig.).

cacciatorpediniere sf. (*torpedo-boat*) destroyer.

cacciavite sm. screwdriver.

cachi sm. persimmon.

cacio sm. cheese || *essere alto come un soldo di —*, to be very short.

cacofonìa sf. cacophony.

cactus sm. cactus (pl. cacti).

cadauno agg. e pron. indef. each.

cadàvere sm. corpse.

cadavèrico agg. 1. corpse-like 2. (*pallido*) deadly pale.

cadente agg. 1. falling 2. (*di astri*) setting || *stella —*, shooting star || *età —*, decrepit old age.

cadenza sf. 1. cadence 2. (*ritmo*) rhythm 3. (*accento*) accent.

cadere vi. to fall (v. irr.) (anche fig.): *— bocconi*, to fall flat on one's face; *— in mare*, to fall overboard; *— addormentato*, to fall asleep; *— a proposito*, to fall in the nick of time; *— dal sonno*, to be overcome by sleep; *nell'errore*, to fall into error || *far —*, to knock down; (fig.) to bring (v. irr.) about the fall of 2. (*tramontare, di astri*) to set (v. irr.) 3. (*calare*) to drop 4. (*far fiasco*) to fail.

cadetto agg. e sm. cadet.

caducità sf. caducity.

caduco agg. perishable, decaying.

caduta sf. 1. fall, falling 2. (fig.) downfall, ruin 3. (fis.) drop.

caffè sm. 1. coffee: *— macinato*, ground coffee; *— nero*, black coffee 2. (*locale*) coffee-house.

caffeina sf. caffeine.

caffettiera sf. coffee-pot.

cafone sm. boor.

caglionévole agg. sickly, weak.

cagliarsi vr. to curdle.

cagna sf. bitch.

cagnara sf. 1. furious barking 2. (fig.) uproar.

cagnesco agg. *in —*, surlily || *guardare in —*, to scowl at.

cagnolino s. 1. (*cucciolo*) puppy 2. (*cane piccolo*) small dog.

caimano sm. cayman.

cala sf. 1. creek 2. (mar.) hold.

calabrone sm. hornet.

calamaio sm. ink-stand.

calamaro sm. calamary.

calamita sf. magnet (anche fig.).

calamità sf. calamity, misfortune.

calamitare vt. to magnetize (anche fig.).

calamitoso agg. calamitous.

calandra sf. 1. (zool.) wood-lark 2. (mecc.) calender.

calare vt. to lower, to drop || *cala la tela*, the curtain drops. ♦ **calare** vi. 1. to descend 2. (*di astri*) to set (v. irr.) 3. (*di febbre*) to abate 4. (comm.) to fall (v. irr.). ♦ **calarsi** vr. to let (v. irr.) oneself down.

calata sf. descent.

calca sf. crowd.

calcagno sm. heel || *stare alle calcagna di qu.*, to follow so. closely.

calcare[1] vt. 1. to tread (v. irr.) 2. (*premere*) to press down || *— la mano*, to exaggerate.

calcare[2] sm. limestone.

calcàreo agg. calcareous.

calce sf. lime || *in —* (loc. avv.), at the foot.

calcestruzzo sm. concrete.

calciare vi. to kick.

calciatore sm. footballer.

calcificare vt. to calcify.

calcificazione sf. calcification.

calcina sf. lime.

calcinaccio sm. debris (solo sing.).

calcinare vt. to calcine.

calcio[1] sm. 1. kick 2. (giuoco) football || *— d'inizio*, kick-off; *— di rigore*, penalty 3. (di arma) butt.

calcio[2] sm. (chim.) calcium.

calco sm. 1. (scult.) cast 2. (di disegno) drawing.

calcolàbile agg. computable.

calcolare vt. 1. to calculate, to compute 2. (*prevedere*) to estimate.

calcolatore sm. (electronic) computer || *regolo —*, slide-rule.

calcolatrice *sf.* calculating machine.

càlcolo *sm.* 1. calculation 2. (*med.*) stone.

calcomanìa *sf.* transfer.

caldaia *sf.* 1. kier 2. (*per produzione di vapore*) boiler.

caldamente *avv.* warmly.

caldeggiare *vt.* to favour.

caldeggiatore *sm.* supporter.

calderaio *sm.* tinker.

calderone *sm.* 1. cauldron 2. (*fig.*) medley.

caldo *agg.* 1. warm; (*molto caldo*) hot 2. (*fig.*) ardent. ◆ **caldo** *sm.* heat || *far* —, to be warm, to be hot.

caleidoscopio *sm.* kaleidoscope.

calendario *sm.* calendar.

calende *sf. pl.* kalends || *rimandare alle* — *greche*, to put off till doomsday.

calesse *sm.* gig, calash.

calessino *sm.* gig.

calibrare *vt.* to calibrate.

calibratura *sf.* calibration.

càlibro *sm.* 1. calibre 2. (*di persona*) caliber, importance.

càlice *sm.* 1. (*eccl.*) chalice 2. (*bicchiere*) goblet, drinking-cup.

calìgine *sf.* thick fog, smog.

callifugo *sm.* corn-plaster.

calligrafìa *sf.* handwriting.

calligràfico *agg.* calligraphic.

callìgrafo *sm.* calligrapher: *perito* —, handwriting expert.

callista *sm.* chiropodist.

callo *sm.* corn.

callosità *sf.* callosity.

calloso *agg.* callous.

calma *sf.* calm.

calmante *agg.* calming, soothing. ◆ **calmante** *sm.* (*farm.*) sedative.

calmare *vt.* 1. to calm 2. (*metter pace*) to appease.

calmo *agg.* calm, quiet.

calo *sm.* 1. shrinkage 2. (*comm.*) drop.

calore *sm.* 1. (*forte*) heat; (*moderato*) warmth 2. (*fig.*) warmth, eagerness.

caloria *sf.* calory.

calorìfero *sm.* heating apparatus, radiator.

caloroso *agg.* 1. warm, hearty 2. (*che non sente freddo*) not feeling the cold.

calotta *sf.* 1. cap: — *cranica*, skull-cap 2. (*geom.*) bowl.

calpestare *vt.* to tread (*v. irr.*):

vietato — *l'erba*, keep off the grass.

calpestìo *sm.* trampling (of feet).

calunnia *sf.* slander.

calunniare *vt.* to slander.

calunniatore *sm.* slanderer.

calvìzie *sf.* baldness.

calvo *agg.* bald.

calza *sf.* 1. (*corta*) sock; (*da donna*) stocking 2. (*lavoro a maglia*) knitting || *fare la* —, to knit.

calzamaglia *sf.* tights (*pl.*).

calzare *vt.* to put (*v. irr.*) on. ◆ **calzare** *vi.* to fit.

calzatura *sf.* shoe || *negozio di calzature*, shoe-shop.

calzaturificio *sm.* boot factory.

calzettone *sm.* heavy sock.

calzino *sm.* sock.

calzolaio *sm.* shoemaker.

calzolerìa *sf.* shoemaker's shop.

calzoni *sm. pl.* trousers.

camaleonte *sm.* chameleon (*anche fig.*).

cambiale *sf.* bill (of exchange): — *a vista*, bill at sight; *emettere una* —, to issue a bill; *girare una* —, to endorse a bill; *protestare una* —, to note a bill || — *pagherò*, promissory note.

cambiamento *sm.* change.

cambiare *vt.* to change (*anche fig.*). ◆ **cambiarsi** *vr.* to change.

cambio *sm.* 1. change 2. (*econ.*) exchange 3. (*mecc.*) change-gear 4. (*auto*) gear || *in* —, in exchange for, instead of.

camelia *sf.* (*bot.*) camellia.

càmera *sf.* 1. room: — *da letto*, bedroom; — *dei bambini*, nursery; — *degli ospiti*, guest-room || *musica da* —, chamber music 2. (*pol.*) Chamber House: *camera dei deputati*, Chamber of Deputies 3. (*tec.*) chamber || — *oscura*, dark room; — *d'aria*, inner tube.

camerata¹ *sm.* comrade, mate.

camerata² *sf.* dormitory.

cameratismo *sm.* comradeship.

cameriera *sf.* 1. maid 2. (*di albergo*) chambermaid 3. (*di ristorante*) waitress.

cameriere *sm.* 1. man-servant (*pl. men*-) 2. (*di ristorante*) waiter.

càmice *sm.* 1. overall 2. (*eccl.*) surplice.

camicetta *sf.* blouse.

camicia *sf.* 1. (*da uomo*) shirt || — *da notte* (*da uomo*), night-shirt

2. (*da donna*) chemise || — *da notte* (*da donna*), night-dress **3.** (*tec.*) jacket || *è nato con la —*, he was born with a silver spoon in his mouth.

caminetto *sm.* fireplace.

camino *sm.* **1.** (*focolare*) fireplace **2.** (*comignolo*) chimney.

camion *sm.* lorry.

camioncino *sm.* van.

camionista *sm.* lorry-driver.

cammello *sm.* camel.

cammeo *sm.* cameo.

camminare *vi.* **1.** to walk || — *a grandi passi*, to stride (*v. irr.*) along; — *in punta di piedi*, to walk on tiptoe **2.** (*di meccanismi*) to go (*v. irr.*), to work **3.** (*discorsi, affari ecc.*) to proceed.

camminata *sf.* **1.** walk **2.** (*andatura*) gait.

camminatore *sm.* walker.

cammino *sm.* way.

camomilla *sf.* (*bot.*) camomile: *una tazza di —*, a cup of camomile-tea.

camoscio *sm.* chamois: *pelle di —*, chamois leather.

campagna *sf.* **1.** country: *casa di —*, country-house; *andare in —*, to go (*v. irr.*) into the country; *essere in —*, to be in the country **2.** (*tenuta*) estate **3.** (*mil.*) campaign **4.** (*villeggiatura*) holidays.

campana *sf.* bell.

campanaro *sm.* bell-ringer.

campanello *sm.* door-bell: — *d'allarme*, alarm-bell.

campanile *sm.* bell-tower.

campanilismo *sm.* parochialism.

campare *vi.* to live.

campeggiatore *sm.* camper.

campeggio *sm.* camping.

campestre *agg.* rural, rustic || *corsa —*, cross-country race.

campionario *sm.* set of samples, sample case || *fiera campionaria*, trade fair.

campionato *sm.* championship.

campione *sm.* **1.** champion **2.** (*comm.*) sample.

campo *sm.* **1.** (*mil.*) field **2.** (*sport*) sport ground || — *da tennis*, tennis court **3.** (*terreno*) field || — *di battaglia*, battle-field.

camuffare *vt.* to disguise.

canadese *agg.* e *sm.* Canadian.

canaglia *sf.* **1.** rabble **2.** (*di persona malvagia*) rascal.

canale *sm.* **1.** canal **2.** (*braccio di mare*) channel **3.** (*condotto*) pipe **4.** (*tv.*) channel.

cànapa *sf.* hemp.

canarino *sm.* canary.

cancellare *vt.* **1.** (*a penna*) to cross out; (*con una gomma*) to rub out; (*con un panno*) to wipe out **2.** (*fig.*) efface.

cancellatura *sf.* **1.** erasure **2.** (*fig.*) effacement.

cancellerìa *sf.* **1.** (*pol.*) chancellery **2.** (*materiale di —*) stationery articles **3.** (*giur.*) record-office.

cancelliere *sm.* **1.** (*pol.*) chancellor **2.** (*giur.*) recorder.

cancello *sm.* gate.

cancrena *sf.* gangrene.

cancro *sm.* cancer.

candeggina *sf.* chloride.

candela *sf.* **1.** candle: — *di sego*, tallow candle; *al lume di —*, by candle-light **2.** (*auto*) sparking plug.

candelabro *sm.* branched candlestick.

candeliere *sm.* candlestick.

candelotto *sm.* short thick candle: — *fumogeno*, smoke candle.

candidato *sm.* candidate.

candidatura *sf.* candidature.

càndido *agg.* **1.** snow-white **2.** (*innocente*) innocent.

candito *agg.* candied. ♦ **candito** *sm.* sugar candy.

candore *sm.* **1.** whiteness **2.** (*innocenza*) innocence.

cane *sm.* **1.** dog: — *da caccia*, sporting dog; — *pastore*, sheep dog; — *da guardia*, watch-dog **2.** (*persona spietata*) brute **3.** (*di fucile*) cock.

cànfora *sf.* camphor.

canguro *sm.* kangaroo.

canìcola *sf.* the height of summer.

canile *sm.* kennel.

canino *agg.* canine: *dente —*, canine tooth.

canna *sf.* **1.** reed **2.** (*coltivata*) cane || — *da zucchero*, sugar cane **3.** (*tubo*) pipe **4.** (*di arma*) barrel **5.** (*da pesca*) (fishing-)rod.

cannella *sf.* **1.** (*bot.*) cinnamon **2.** (*di botte*) spout.

cannello *sm.* **1.** torch **2.** (*chim.*) pipe.

canneto *sm.* canebrake.

cannibale *sm.* cannibal.

cannocchiale *sm.* binoculars (*pl.*) || — *da campagna*, field glasses; — *da teatro*, opera glasses.

cannone *sm.* **1.** gun: — *antiaereo*, anti-aircraft gun; — *anticarro*, anti-tank gun **2.** *(fig.)* ace.

cannuccia *sf.* **1.** thin cane: — *per sorbire bibite*, straw.

cànone *sm.* canon: — *d'affitto*, rent; — *della radio*, radio-licence fee.

canònica *sf.* rectory.

canònico *agg.* canonical || *diritti canonici*, canon law. ♦ **canònico** *sm.* canon.

canonizzare *vt.* to canonize.

canoro *agg.* singing.

canottaggio *sm.* **1.** rowing, boating **2.** *(come attività)* boating.

canottiera *sf.* vest.

canotto *sm.* small boat.

canovaccio *sm.* **1.** *(per asciugare stoviglie)* dish-cloth; **2.** *(per ricamo)* canvas **3.** *(trama di un'opera)* plot.

cantante *sm.* singer.

cantare *vt.* **1.** to sing *(v. irr.)* **2.** *(del gallo)* to crow **3.** *(fare la spia)* to squeal.

cantata *sf.* song.

canterellare *vt. e vi.* to sing *(v. irr.)* softly, to hum.

càntico *sm.* hymn.

cantiere *sm.* yard.

cantilena *sf.* sing-song.

cantina *sf.* cellar.

cantiniere *sm.* cellarman *(pl.* -men*).*

cantino *sm.* chanterelle.

canto¹ *sm.* singing.

canto² *sm.* *(angolo)* corner || *dal — mio*, for my part; *da un —*, on one hand.

cantonata *sf.* corner: *prendere una —*, to make *(v. irr.)* a blunder.

canfone *sm.* **1.** corner **2.** *(geogr.)* canton.

cantoniera *sf.* **1.** *(mobile)* corner cupboard **2.** *(casa)* roadman's house **3.** *(ferr.)* signalman's house.

cantoniere *sm.* signalman *(pl.* -men*).*

canuto *agg.* hoary.

canzonare *vt.* to make *(v. irr.)* fun of.

canzone *sf.* song.

canzonetta *sf.* **1.** short song **2.** *(poet.)* canzonet.

canzonettista *s.* **1.** music-hall singer **2.** *(autore di canzoni)* songwriter.

caolino *sm.* kaolin.

caos *sm.* chaos.

capace *agg.* **1.** able **2.** *(idoneo)* fit **3.** *(abile)* clever.

capacità *sf.* **1.** ability, cleverness **2.** *(capienza)* capacity.

capanna *sf.* hut.

capanno *sm.* **1.** *(da caccia)* shooting--box **2.** *(per bagnanti)* bathing-box.

caparbieria *sf.* stubbornness.

caparbio *agg.* stubborn.

caparra *sf.* caution-money.

capeggiare *vt.* to lead *(v. irr.).*

capello *sm.* hair *(solo sing.)* || *acconciatura dei capelli*, hairdress; *farsi tagliare i capelli*, to have one's hair cut; *avere un diavolo per —*, to be furious.

capezzale *sm.* bolster.

capézzolo *sm.* nipple.

capienza *sf.* capacity.

capigliatura *sf.* hair.

capillare *agg.* capillary.

capillarità *sf.* capillarity.

capinera *sf.* blackcap.

capire *vt.* to understand *(v. irr.).*

capitale *sm.* capital. ♦ **capitale** *agg.* **1.** *(che riguarda la vita)* capital **2.** *(principale)* main.

capitalismo *sm.* capitalism.

capitalista *s.* capitalist.

capitalizzare *vt.* to capitalize. ♦ **capitalizzare** *vi.* *(accumulare denaro)* to save.

capitano *sm.* captain, leader.

capitare *vi.* **1.** *(giungere)* to arrive **2.** *(accadere)* to happen, to befall *(v. irr.).*

capitello *sm.* *(arch.)* capital.

capitolare *vi.* to capitulate.

capitolare *sm.* capitulary. ♦ **capitolare** *agg.* capitular.

capitolo *sm.* chapter.

capitòmbolo *sm.* tumble.

capo *sm.* **1.** head || *avere mal di —*, to have a headache; *senza — né coda*, without rhyme or reason **2.** *(estremità)* end || *da un — all'altro*, from end to end; *andare a —*, new line; *in — a un anno*, within a year; *Capo d'Anno*, New Year's day **3.** *(geogr.)* cape **4.** *(chi comanda)* leader.

capobanda *sm.* **1.** *(mus.)* bandmaster **2.** *(di una banda di criminali)* ringleader.

capocuoco *sm.* head cook.

capocordata *sm.* first man on the rope.

capodanno *sm.* New Year's day.

capofamiglia *s.* head of a family.

capofila *sm.* file-leader.
capofitto (*nella loc. avv.*) *a —*, headlong || *cadere, tuffarsi a —*, to fall (*v. irr.*), to dive head first.
capogiro *sm.* dizziness.
capolavoro *sm.* masterpiece.
capolìnea *sm.* terminus (*pl.* -ni).
capolino *sm.* small head || *far —*, to peep in.
capoluogo *sm.* main town.
caporale *sm.* corporal.
caporedattore *sm.* editor in chief.
caposaldo *sm.* **1.** datum point **2.** (*mil.*) stronghold **3.** (*fondamento*) main point.
caposcuola *sm.* leader of a movement.
capostazione *sm.* station-master.
capotare *vi.* **1.** (*di aerei*) to somersault **2.** (*di auto*) to turn over.
capoufficio *sm.* head-clerk.
capoverso *sm.* **1.** (*in poesia*) beginning of a line **2.** (*in prosa*) beginning of a paragraph.
capovòlgere *vt.* to turn upside down. ♦ **capovòlgersi** *vr.* to capsize.
cappa *sf.* **1.** (*mantello*) cloak **2.** (*di prete*) cape **3.** (*fig.*) vault || *del·camino*, chimney.
cappella *sf.* chapel.
cappellano *sm.* chaplain.
cappello *sm.* **1.** hat: *— a cilindro*, top-hat; *— di paglia*, straw hat; **2.** (*introduzione*) preamble.
càppero *sm.* caper.
cappone *sm.* capon.
cappotto *sm.* **1.** coat **2.** (*di gioco*) capot.
cappuccino *sm.* **1.** (*eccl.*) capuchin **2.** (*bevanda*) white coffee.
cappuccio *sm.* hood.
capra *sf.* goat.
capretto *sm.* kid.
capriccio *sm.* whim: *fare i capricci*, to be naughty.
caprino *agg.* goatish.
capriola[1] *sf.* caper: *far capriole*, to cut (*v. irr.*) capers.
capriola[2] *sf.* (*femmina del capriolo*) doe.
capriolo *sm.* roe-deer.
càpsula *sf.* **1.** capsule **2.** (*di dente*) crown.
captare *vt.* (*radio*) to pick up.
capzioso *agg.* captious.
carabina *sf.* carabine.
carabiniere *sm.* carabineer.
caracollare *vi.* to caracole.

caraffa *sf.* **1.** (*per acqua*) carafe **2.** (*per vino*) decanter.
caràmbola *sf.* cannon: *far —*, to cannon.
carambolare *vi.* to cannon.
caramella *sf.* sugar-drop, toffee.
caramellare *vt.* to coat with burnt sugar.
caramello *sm.* caramel.
carato *sm.* carat.
caràttere *sm.* **1.** character, temper **2.** (*caratteristica*) character **3.** (*tip.*) type.
caratterista *s.* character actor (actress).
caratterìstico *agg.* characteristic.
♦ **caratterìstica** *sf.* characteristic.
caravella *sf.* caravel.
carbonaio *sm.* coal merchant.
carbone *sm.* coal || *— di legna*, charcoal; *— fossile*, pit coal; *miniera di —*, coal-mine.
carbonerìa *sf.* Carbonarist movement.
carbonìfero *agg.* carboniferous.
carbonio *sm.* carbon.
carbonizzare *vt.* **1.** to carbonize **2.** (*di legno*) to char.
carburante *sm.* fuel.
carburatore *sm.* carburettor.
carburazione *sf.* carburation.
carcassa *sf.* carcass.
carcerazione *sf.* imprisonment.
càrcere *sm.* prison, jail.
carceriere *sm.* jailer.
carciofo *sm.* artichoke.
cardano *sm.* (*mecc.*) cardan joint.
cardare *vt.* to card.
cardìaco *agg.* cardiac || *disturbi cardiaci*, heart-disease.
cardinale *agg.* e *sm.* cardinal.
càrdine *sm.* **1.** hinge, pivot **2.** (*fig.*) foundation.
cardiòlogo *sm.* cardiologist.
cardiopatìa *sf.* cardiopathy.
cardo *sm.* **1.** (*bot.*) thistle **2.** (*cuc.*) cardoon **3.** (*mecc.*) carding machine.
carena *sf.* (*mar.*) keel **2.** (*aer.*) hull **3.** (*zool.*) càrina (*pl.* -nae).
carenza *sf.* want, lack.
carestìa *sf.* famine.
carezza *sf.* caress.
carezzévole *agg.* caressing.
cariàtide *sf.* caryatid.
cariato *agg.* decayed.
càrica *sf.* **1.** (*pubblico ufficio*) office: *entrare in —*, to take (*v.*

irr.) office **2.** (*mil.*) charge **3.** (*di arma da fuoco*; *elettr.*) charge **4.** (*di orologio*) winding up.

caricare *vt.* **1.** to load **2.** (*mil.*; *elettr.*) to charge **3.** (*di orologio*) to wind (*v. irr.*) up.

caricatore *sm.* **1.** loader **2.** (*di arma*) magazine.

caricatura *sf.* caricature.

càrico¹ *agg.* **1.** loaded, laden (*anche fig.*) **2.** (*di caffè*) strong **3.** (*elettr.*) charged.

càrico² *sm.* **1.** (*di nave*) freight; (*di veicolo*) load; (*di animale da soma*) burden **2.** (*fig.*) load, weight **3.** (*accusa*) charge || (*comm.*) essere a — di qu., to be charged to so.

carie *sf.* decay.

carino *agg.* pretty, nice.

carità *sf.* **1.** (*amore*; *teol.*) charity **2.** (*elemosina*) alms.

carlinga *sf.* cockpit.

carlona (*nella loc. avv.*) alla —, carelessly.

carminio *agg.* carmine.

carnagione *sf.* complexion.

carnale *agg.* carnal.

carne *sf.* **1.** flesh **2.** (*come alimento*) meat || — di manzo, beef; — di vitello, veal; — in scatola, tinned meat; — congelata, frozen meat.

carnéfice *sm.* executioner.

carneficina *sf.* slaughter.

carnevale *sm.* carnival.

carnìvoro *agg.* carnivorous.

caro *agg.* **1.** dear **2.** (*costoso*) dear, expensive.

carogna *sf.* carrion.

carosello *sm.* carousel.

carota *sf.* carrot.

caròtide *sf.* carotid.

carovana *sf.* caravan.

carovita *sm.* high cost of living.

carpa *sf.* carp.

carpentiere *sm.* carpenter.

carpire *vt.* **1.** to snatch **2.** (*con astuzia*) to swindle.

carponi *avv.* on all fours.

carràbile *agg.* cart: passo —, driveway.

carreggiata **1.** (*solco*) track **2.** (*strada*) cartway.

carrellata *sf.* dolly shot.

carrello *sm.* **1.** (*ferr.*) wag(g)on **2.** (*aer.*) landing gear **3.** (*cine*; *tv.*) dolly **4.** (*di macchina per scrivere*)

carriage.

carriera *sf.* career || di gran —, at full speed.

carriola *sf.* wheelbarrow.

carrista *sm.* (*mil.*) tankman (*pl. -men*).

carro *sm.* **1.** (*a due ruote*) cart **2.** (*a quattro ruote*) wag(g)on || — armato, tank.

carrozza *sf.* carriage: — diretta, through coach; — viaggiatori, passenger car.

carrozzàbile *agg.* practicable.

carrozzella *sf.* **1.** cab **2.** (*per bambini*) perambulator; (*fam.*) pram.

carrozzerìa *sf.* body.

carrozziere *sm.* body-maker.

carrozzone *sm.* **1.** lumbering coach **2.** (*di zingari*) caravan.

carruba *sf.*, **carrubo** *sm.* carob.

carrùcola *sf.* pulley.

carta *sf.* paper: — da lettere, writing-paper; — carbone, carbon paper; — d'identità, identity card; — stradale, road-map.

cartaio *sm.* paper-maker.

cartamodello *sm.* dressmaker's pattern.

cartamoneta *sf.* paper-money.

cartapesta *sf.* paper-pulp.

cartavetrata *sf.* sand-paper.

carteggio *sm.* **1.** correspondence **2.** (*collezione di lettere*) collection of letters.

cartella *sf.* **1.** (*da scuola*) satchel **2.** (*di cuoio*) brief-case.

cartello *sm.* **1.** bill **2.** (*pubblicitario*) poster **3.** (*stradale*) traffic sign **4.** (*econ.*) cartel.

cartellone *sm.* **1.** (*pubblicitario*) poster **2.** (*teat.*) bill.

cartellonista *sm.* commercial artist.

cartiera *sf.* paper-mill.

cartilàgine *sf.* cartilage.

cartoccio *sm.* paper-bag.

cartografìa *sf.* cartography.

cartolerìa *sf.* stationer's shop.

cartolina *sf.* postcard: — illustrata, picture postcard.

cartoncino *sm.* thin card.

cartone *sm.* cardboard || cartoni animati, cartoons.

cartuccia *sf.* cartridge || mezza — (*fig.*), shrimp.

casa *sf.* **1.** (*abitazione*) house **2.** (*ambiente familiare*) home || amico di —, family friend; donna di —, housewife; nostalgia di —, home-sickness; *andare a —*, to go (*v. irr.*) home; *restare a —*, to stay at home; *essere in —*, to be in **3.** (*stirpe*) house, dynasty, family.

casacca *sf.* coat.

casaccio (*nella loc. avv.*) *a —*, at random.

casalinga *sf.* housewife.

casalingo *agg.* homely: *cucina casalinga*, plain cooking.

casato *sm.* **1.** (*cognome*) surname **2.** (*origine, nascita*) birth.

cascame *sm.* waste.

cascamorto *sm.* spoel: *fare il —*, to run (*v. irr.*) after.

cascante *agg.* **1.** (*debole*) weak **2.** (*floscio*) flabby (*anche fig.*).

cascare *vi.* **1.** to fall (*v. irr.*) **2.** (*con rumore*) to crash || *— dalle nuvole*, to be struck with amazement; *— dal sonno*, to be overcome with sleep.

cascata *sf.* **1.** (*caduta*) fall **2.** (*d'acqua*) waterfall **3.** (*fig.*) cascade.

cascina *sf.* **1.** dairy farm **2.** (*cascinale*) farmstead.

casco *sm.* **1.** helmet **2.** (*per asciugare i capelli*) dryer.

casella *sf.*: *— postale*, post-box.

casellante *sm.* **1.** (*ferr.*) signalman (*pl.* -men) **2.** (*di passaggio a livello*) crossing keeper.

casellario *sm.* **1.** set of pigeon-holes **2.** (*giur.*) *— penale*, records-office.

casereccio *agg.* homely: *pane —*, home-made bread.

caserma *sf.* barracks (*pl.*).

caso *sm.* **1.** chance **2.** (*fatto*) case **3.** (*possibilità*) way, possibility || *a —*, at random; *per —*, by chance.

càspita *inter.* good gracious!

cassa *sf.* **1.** case, box **2.** (*comm.*) cash || *libro di —*, cash-book; *pagamento per —*, cash-payment; *sportello di —*, cashier's window **3.** (*mus.*) case || *gran —*, bass-drum.

cassaforte *sf.* safe.

cassapanca *sf.* chest.

cassazione *sf.* (*giur.*) cassation.

casseruola *sf.* saucepan.

cassetto *sm.* drawer.

cassettone *sm.* chest of drawers.

cassiere *sm.* cashier.

casta *sf.* caste.

castagna *sf.* chestnut.

castagnaccio *sm.* chestnut-tart.

castagno *sm.* chestnut-tree.

castano *agg.* nut-brown.

castellano *sm.* lord of a castle.

castello *sm.* castle.

castigare *vt.* to punish.

castigatezza *sf.* moderation.

castigato *agg.* **1.** (*casto*) chaste **2.** (*emendato*) castigated.

castigo *sm.* punishment.

castità *sf.* chastity.

casto *agg.* chaste.

castoro *sm.* beaver.

castrare *vt.* to castrate.

castrato *sm.* (*cuc.*) mutton.

castroneria *sf.* stupidity.

casuale *agg.* casual.

casualità *sf.* casualness.

cataclisma *sm.* cataclysm (*anche fig.*).

catacomba *sf.* catacomb.

catafalco *sm.* catafalque.

catafascio (*nella loc. avv.*) *andare a —*, to go (*v. irr.*) to rack and ruin; *a —*, topsyturvy.

catalessi *sf.* catalepsy.

catalizzatore *sm.* catalyst.

catalogare *vt.* to catalogue.

catàlogo *sm.* catalogue.

catapecchia *sf.* hovel.

catapulta *sf.* catapult.

catarifrangente *sm.* reflector.

catarro *sm.* catarrh.

catarsi *sf.* catharsis.

catasta *sf.* pile, heap.

catasto *sm.* cadastre.

catàstrofe *sf.* catastrophe.

catastròfico *agg.* catastrophic(al).

catechismo *sm.* catechism.

catechizzare *vt.* **1.** to catechize **2.** (*fig.*) to persuade.

catecùmeno *sm.* catechumen.

categorìa *sf.* category, class.

categòrico *agg.* categorical, absolute.

catena *sf.* **1.** chain **2.** (*fig.*) bond.

catenaccio *sm.* bolt.

cateratta *sf.* cataract.

caterva *sf.* **1.** (*di persone*) crowd **2.** (*di cose*) great quantity.

catino *sm.* basin.

catione *sm.* (*fis.*) cation.

càtodo *sm.* cathode.

catramare *vt.* to tar.

catrame *sm.* tar.

càttedra *sf.* **1.** desk **2.** (*l'ufficio dell'insegnare*) teaching post **3.** (*di università*) chair.

cattedrale *sf.* cathedral.

cattiverìa *sf.* wickedness.

cattività *sf.* captivity.

cattivo agg. e sm. bad || — scrittore, poor writer.

cattolicésimo sm. catholicism.

cattòlico agg. catholic.

cattura sf. 1. capture 2. (arresto) arrest: mandato di —, warrant of arrest.

catturare vt. 1. to capture 2. (arrestare) to arrest.

caucclù sm. india-rubber.

càusa sf 1. cause 2. (giur.) law suit || far — a qu., to sue so. (for).

causare vt. to cause.

càustico agg. caustic (anche fig.)

cautela sf. caution.

cautelare vt. to protect. ♦ **cautelarsi** vr. to take (v. irr.) precautions.

cauterizzare vt. to cauterize.

càuto agg. cautious, prudent.

cauzione sf. 1. guarantee 2. (per essere rilasciato dalla polizia) bail.

cava sf. quarry.

cavalcare vt. to ride (v. irr.). ♦ **cavalcare** vi. to ride on horseback.

cavalcavìa sm. fly-over bridge.

cavalcioni (a) loc. avv. astride.

cavaliere sm. 1. rider 2. (di ordine cavalleresco) knight.

cavalla sf. mare.

cavallerésco agg. knightly.

cavallerìa sf. 1. (mil.) cavalry 2. (stor.) chivalry.

cavalletta sf. grasshopper.

cavalletto sm. 1. trestle 2. (foto) tripod 3. (per pittori) easel.

cavallo sm. 1. horse: — da corsa, racehorse; — a dondolo, rocking-horse; — da soma, pack-horse; ferro di —, horse-shoe 2. (ginnastica) vaulting-horse 3. (cavallo vapore) horse-power (abbr. H.P.).

cavallone sm. (maroso) billow.

cavare vt. to take (v. irr.) off || — un dente, to pull out a tooth || cavarsela, to get (v. irr.) off.

cavatappi, cavaturàccioli sm. cork-screw.

caverna sf. cave.

cavernoso agg. cavernous || voce cavernosa, very deep voice.

cavezza sf. halter.

cavia sf. cavy.

caviale sm. caviar.

caviglia sf. ankle.

cavillare vi. to cavil (at).

cavillo sm. cavil.

cavità sf. cavity.

cavo agg. hollow, empty. ♦ **cavo** sm. cable, rope.

cavolfiore sm. cauliflower.

càvolo sm. cabbage.

cazzotto sm. punch || fare a cazzotti, to come (v. irr.) to blows.

cazzuola sf. trowel.

cece sm. chick-pea.

cecità sf. blindness (anche fig.).

cecoslovacco agg. e sm. Czechoslovak.

cèdere vt. e vi. 1. (dare) to give (v. irr.) 2. (trasferire) to hand over 3. (vendere) to dispose of. ♦ **cèdere** vi. 1. to surrender 2. (venir meno) to subside 3. (essere inferiore) to be second to.

cedimento sm. 1. yielding 2. (fig.) giving up.

cèdola sf. coupon.

cedrata sf. citron syrup.

cedrina sf. lemon-scented verbena.

cedro sm. 1. citron-tree 2. (frutto) citron.

cedrone agg. e sm. (gallo) capercaillie.

cefalea sf. cephalea.

cefalgìa sf. cephalalgy.

ceffone sm. slap in the face.

celare vt. to conceal, to hide (v. irr.).

celebrare vt. to celebrate || — un anniversario, to keep (v. irr.) an anniversary.

celebrazione sf. celebration.

cèlebre agg. celebrated.

celebrità sf. celebrity.

cèlere agg. quick, swift.

celerità sf. quickness.

celeste agg. 1. light-blue 2. (del cielo) heavenly.

celia sf. jest.

celiare vi. to jest.

celibato sm. bachelorhood.

cèlibe agg. e sm. single. ♦ **cèlibe** sm. bachelor.

cella sf. cell.

cèllula sf. cell.

cellulare agg. cellular || segregazione —, close confinement.

cellulite sf. cellulitis.

celluloide sf. celluloid.

cellulosa sf. cellulose.

celta sm. Celt.

cèltico agg. Celtic.

cémbalo sm. 1. (tamburello) tambourine 2. (spinetta) spinet.

cementare vt. to cement (anche fig.).

cementazione *sf.* cementation.

cementificio *sm.* cement-factory.

cemento *sm.* cement: — *armato*, reinforced concrete.

cena *sf.* **1.** (*pasto serale leggero*) supper **2.** (*pranzo*) dinner || *far* —, to have supper.

cenàcolo *sm.* supper-room **2.** (*di artisti*) artistic coterie || *il* — *di Leonardo da Vinci*, Leonardo's Last Supper.

cenare *vi.* to have (*v. irr.*) supper.

cenciaio *sm.* ragman (*pl.* -men).

cencio *sm.* **1.** rag **2.** (*vestito logoro*) tatters (*pl.*).

cencioso *agg.* ragged, tattered.

cénere *sf.* ash (*general. al pl.*).

cenno *sm.* **1.** (*segno*) sign **2.** (*allusione*) hint **3.** (*breve notizia*) notice || *fare un* — *col capo*, to nod || *a un vostro* — (*comm.*), on hearing from you.

cenobio *sm.* coenobium (*pl.* -ia).

cenone *sm.* **1.** (*di Natale*) Christmas eve dinner **2.** (*di Capodanno*) New Year's eve dinner.

censimento *sm.* census.

censire *vt.* **1.** to take (*v. irr.*) a census of **2.** (*di proprietà*) to assess.

censo *sm.* **1.** (*stor.*) census **2.** (*ricchezza*) wealth.

censore *sm.* **1.** censor **2.** (*fig.*) critic.

censorio *agg.* censorial.

censura *sf.* **1.** (*ufficio di censore*) censorship **2.** (*azione di censura*) censure.

censurare *vt.* **1.** to censor **2.** (*fig.*) to censure.

centauro *sm.* **1.** centaur **2.** (*fig., motociclista*) motorcyclist.

centellinare *vt.* to sip.

centenario *agg. e sm.* **1.** centennial **2.** (*di persona*) centenarian. ♦ **centenario** *sm.* (*commemorazione*) centenary.

centesimale *agg.* centesimal.

centèsimo *agg.* (the) hundredth. ♦ **centèsimo** *sm.* (one) hundredth (of sthg.) **2.** (*di dollaro*) cent **3.** (*di franco*) centime || *non avere un* —, to be penniless.

centigrado *agg.* centigrade.

centigrammo *sm.* centigramme.

centilitro *sm.* centilitre.

centimetro *sm.* centimetre.

centinaio *sm.* hundred.

cento *agg. e num. card.* hundred || — *di questi giorni*, many happy returns of the day.

centrale *agg.* central. ♦ **centrale** *sf.* **1.** — *elettrica*, power station **2.** — *telefonica*, exchange.

centralinista *s.* operator.

centralino *sm.* telephone exchange.

centralismo *sm.* centralism.

centrare *vt.* to hit (*v. irr.*) the centre.

centrifuga *sf.* centrifuge.

centrifugo *agg.* centrifugal.

centrino *sm.* doily.

centripeto *agg.* centripetal.

centrismo *sm.* centrism.

centro *sm.* **1.** centre **2.** (*istituto*) institute.

centuplicare *vt.* **1.** to centuplicate **2.** (*fig.*) to increase.

centuplo *agg. e sm.* centuple.

centuria *sf.* (*stor.*) century.

centurione *sm.* (*stor.*) centurion.

ceppo *sm.* **1.** stump **2.** (*fig.*) stock.

cera *sf.* **1.** wax **2.** (*aspetto*) look || *avere bella* —, to look well.

ceralacca *sf.* sealing-wax.

ceràmica *sf.* **1.** (*arte*) ceramics **2.** (*pezzo*) piece of pottery.

ceramista *sm.* ceramist.

cerato *agg.* waxed || *tela cerata*, wax-cloth.

cerbiatto *sm.* fawn.

cerbottana *sf.* **1.** blowgun **2.** (*giocattolo*) pea-shooter.

cercare *vt.* **1.** to look for **2.** (*per consultazione*) to look up **3.** (*a tentoni*) to fumble for **4.** (*chiedere*) to ask (for). ♦ **cercare** *vi.* to try.

cercatore *sm.* seeker: — *d'oro*, gold-digger; (*amer.*) prospector.

cerchia *sf.* circle.

cerchiare *vt.* to hoop.

cerchiatura *sf.* hooping.

cerchietto *sm.* **1.** small ring **2.** (*gioco*) quoit.

cerchio *sm.* **1.** circle **2.** (*gioco*) hoop.

cerchione *sm.* rim.

cereale *sm.* cereals (*pl.*).

cerebrale *agg.* cerebral.

cèreo *agg.* waxen.

ceretta *sf.* **1.** boot polish **2.** (*per depilare*) wax.

cerimonia *sf.* **1.** ceremony **2.** (*pompa*) pomp.

cerimoniale *sm.* ceremonial.

cerimoniere *sm.* Master of Ceremonies.

cerimonioso *agg.* ceremonious.

cerino *sm.* match.

cerniera *sf.* **1.** (*di occhiali, porte, finestre*) hinge **2.** (*di borsetta*) clasp **3.** (*lampo*) zipper.

cèrnita *sf.* choice, selection.

cero *sm.* large candle.

cerone *sm.* make-up.

cerotto *sm.* plaster.

certamente *avv.* certainly, undoubtedly.

certezza *sf.* certainty.

certificare *vt.* to certify, to attest.

certificato *sm.* certificate.

certo¹ *agg. indef.* **1.** certain: — *Mr. Smith,* a (certain) Mr. Smith **2.** (*qualche*) some: *certe persone lo riconobbero,* some people recognized him; *dopo un — tempo,* after some time **3.** (*tale, di tal genere*) such. ♦ **certi** *pron. indef. pl.* some people.

certo² *agg.* certain. ♦ **certo** *avv.* certainly.

certuni *pron. indef.* some.

cerùleo *agg.* sky-blue.

cerva *sf.* (zool.) hind.

cervella *sf.* brain.

cervelletto *sm.* cerebellum.

cervello *sm.* **1.** brain **2.** (*intelligenza, mente*) understanding, mind.

cervellòtico *agg.* far-fetched.

cervicale *agg.* cervical.

cervice *sf.* nape.

cèrvidi *sm. pl.* cervidae.

cervo *sm.* deer (*inv. al pl.*).

cesàreo *agg.* Caesarean ‖ *taglio* —, Caesarean operation.

cesarismo *sm.* Caesarism.

cesellare *vt.* to chisel (*anche fig.*).

cesellatura *sf.* chisel work.

cesello *sm.* chisel.

cesoia *sf.* shears (*pl.*).

cespuglio *sm.* bush, thicket.

cespuglioso *agg.* bushy.

cessare *vt. e vi.* to cease, to stop.

cessazione *sf.* cessation.

cessione *sf.* transfer.

cesso *sm.* lavatory.

cesta *sf.* basket.

cestaio *sm.* **1.** basket-maker **2.** (*chi vende*) basket-vendor.

cestinare *vt.* (fig.) to refuse.

cestino *sm.* small basket: — *da lavoro,* work-basket; — *da viaggio,* luncheon-basket; — *per la carta straccia,* waste-paper basket.

cesto *sm.* (sport) basket.

cesura *sf.* caesura.

cetàceo *agg. e sm.* cetacean.

ceto *sm.* class, rank.

cetra *sf.* cithern, lyre.

cetriolino *sm.* gherkin.

cetriolo *sm.* cucumber.

che¹ *pron. rel.* **1.** (*sogg., riferito a persone*) who, that: *l'uomo — mi parlò,* the man who (that) spoke to me **2.** (*sogg., riferito a cose e animali*) which, that: *ecco il cane — mi fu regalato,* here is the dog which (that) was given to me **3.** (*ogg., riferito a persone*) whom: *è la ragazza più graziosa — abbia mai incontrato,* she is the prettiest girl whom I ever met **4.** (*ogg., riferito a cose e animali*) which: *questo è il libro — le darò,* this is the book which I shall give her **5.** *il* —, which **6.** (*riferito a tempo*) when.

che² *agg. int.* **1.** what: — *musica preferisci?,* what music do you prefer? **2.** which: — *libro scegli?,* which book do you choose? ♦ **che** *pron. int.* what: — *è questo?,* what is this? ♦ **che** *agg. escl.* what, what a. ♦ **che** *pron. ind.* something.

che³ *cong.* **1.** that **2.** (*comparativo*) than: *è più bella che intelligente,* she is more beautiful than intelligent **3.** (*correlativo*) whether: — *tu venga o no,* whether you come or not. ♦ **che** *inter.* what!

checché *pron. indef.* whatever.

checchessia *pron. indef.* anything.

chepì *sm.* (mil.) kepi.

cherosene *sm.* kerosene.

cherubino *sm.* cherub.

chetamente *avv.* quietly, secretly.

chetare *vt.* to quiet. ♦ **chetarsi** *vr.* to quiet down.

chetichella (*nella loc. avv.*) *alla —,* on the sly, secretly.

cheto *agg.* quiet.

chi *pron. rel.* **1.** (*colui che*) he (*ogg.* him) who (*ogg.* whom) **2.** (*colei che*) she (*ogg.* her) who (*ogg.* whom) **3.** (*coloro che*) they (*ogg.* them) who (*ogg.* whom) **4.** (*gen.*) those, the person who(m). ♦ **chi** *pron. indef.* **1.** whoever, anyone **2.** (*qualcuno che*) someone who. ♦ **chi** *pron. int.* **1.** (*sogg.*) who **2.** (*ogg.*) whom **3.** which: — *di voi?,* which of you? **4.** (*specificazione poss.*) whose: *di — è questa casa?,* whose house is this?

chiàcchiera *sf.* chatter.

chiacchierare *vi.* to chat.

chiacchierata *sf.* chat.

chiacchierone *sm.* chatterbox.

chiamare *vt.* to call ‖ *mandare a* —, to send (*v. irr.*) for; — *al telefono*, to call up. ◆ **chiamarsi** *vr.* to be called ‖ *come ti chiami?*, what's your name?

chiamata *sf.* call, appeal.

chiara *sf.* — *d'uovo*, white (of an egg).

chiaretto *sm.* (*vino*) claret.

chiarezza *sf.* **1.** clearness **2.** (*fig.*) evidence.

chiarificare *vt.* to clarify.

chiarificazione *sf.* **1.** clarification **2.** (*fig.*) frank explanation.

chiarimento *sm.* explanation.

chiarire *vt.* **1.** to clarify, to clear up **2.** (*spiegare*) to explain.

chiaro *agg.* **1.** clear, evident **2.** (*di luce*) light.

chiarore *sm.* **1.** light **2.** (*luce tenue*) faint light.

chiaroscuro *sm.* light and shade.

chiaroveggente *agg.* **1.** clear-sighted **2.** (*che ha facoltà divinatorie*) clairvoyant.

chiassata *sf.* row.

chiasso *sf.* noise, uproar.

chiassone *sm.* noisy person.

chiassoso *agg.* **1.** noisy **2.** (*fig.*) showy.

chiatta *sf.* barge.

chiavarda *sf.* bolt.

chiave *sf.* **1.** key **2.** (*mus.*) clef.

chiavistello *sm.* latch, bolt.

chiazza *sf.* spot, stain.

chicchessia *pron. indef.* anyone.

chicco *sm.* **1.** grain **2.** (*di grandine*) hailstone **3.** (*di caffè*) coffee-bean **4.** (*di uva*) grape.

chiedere *vt.* to ask: — *qc. a qu.*, (*per sapere*) to ask so. sthg., (*per avere*) to ask so. for sthg. **2.** (*riferito a un prezzo*) to charge.

chierichetto *sm.* altar boy.

chiesa *sf.* church.

chiglia *sf.* (*mar.*) keel.

chilo¹ *sm.* (*med.*) chyle ‖ *fare il* —, to take (*v. irr.*) a nap.

chilo² *sm.* kilo.

chilogrammo *sm.* kilogram.

chilometraggio *sm.* distance in kilometres.

chilòmetro *sm.* kilometre.

chilowatt *sm.* kilowatt.

chimera *sf.* chimera.

chimica *sf.* chemistry.

chimico *agg.* chemical. ◆ **chìmico**

sm. chemist.

china *sf.* slope.

chinare *vt.* to bend (*v. irr.*), to bow. ◆ **chinarsi** *vr.* to bend (*v. irr.*) down.

chincaglierìa *sf.* **1.** small fancy articles (*pl.*) **2.** (*negozio*) fancy goods shop.

chinino *sm.* quinine.

chioccia *sf.* brooding-hen.

chiòcciola *sf.* snail ‖ *scala a* —, spiral staircase.

chiodato *agg.* nailed.

chiodo *sm.* **1.** nail **2.** (*fig.*) fixed idea.

chioma *sf.* hair.

chiosco *sm.* **1.** kiosk **2.** (*per giornali, frutta e verdura*) stand.

chiostro *sm.* cloister.

chiromante *s.* chiromancer.

chiromanzìa *sf.* chiromancy.

chirurgìa *sf.* surgery.

chirurgo *sm.* surgeon.

chissà *inter.* goodness knows.

chitarra *sf.* guitar.

chiùdere *vt.* **1.** to shut (*v. irr.*) ‖ — *a chiave*, to lock **2.** (*terminare*) to close **3.** (*rinchiudere*) to shut (*v. irr.*) up.

chiunque *pron.* **1.** (*sogg.*) anyone who, whoever **2.** (*ogg.*) whomever, anyone **3.** (*specificazione possessiva*) *di* —, whosoever.

chiuso *agg.* closed, shut ‖ — *a chiave*, locked.

chiusura *sf.* closing.

ci *pron.* **1.** (*ogg.*) us: *essi* — *amano*, they love us **2.** (*riflessivo*) ourselves: *noi* — *laviamo*, we wash ourselves **3.** (*rec. fra due persone*) each other: *mia madre ed io* — *guardammo*, my mother and I looked at each other **4.** (*rec. fra più persone*) one another **5.** (*dimostrativo*) this, that, it: *non badarci*, pay no attention to it. ◆ **ci** *avv. di luogo* there (*là*), here (*qui*).

ciabatta *sf.* slipper.

ciambella *sf.* ring-shaped cake.

ciambellano *sm.* chamberlain.

ciancia *sf.* idle talk ‖ *ciance!*, nonsense!

cianciare *vi.* to chatter.

cianografìa *sf.* blueprint.

cianuro *sm.* cyanide.

ciao *inter.* **1.** (*incontrandosi*) hullo **2.** (*congedandosi*) bye-bye.

ciarla *sf.* **1.** loquacity **2.** (*notizia*

falsa) false report.
ciarlare *vi.* to talk idly.
ciarlatano *sm.* charlatan.
ciascuno *agg.* every. ◆ **clascuno** *pron.* 1. *(con valore distributivo)* each 2. *(tutti)* everybody, everyone.
cibernètica *sf.* cybernetics.
cibo *sm.* food.
ciborio *sm.* ciborium (*pl.* -ia).
cicala *sf.* cicada.
cicatrice *sf.* scar.
cicatrizzare *vt.* to cicatrize, to heal. ◆ **cicatrizzarsi** *vr.* to cicatrize, to heal.
cicerone *sm.* guide.
ciclamino *sm.* cyclamen.
ciclico *agg.* cyclic.
ciclismo *sm.* cycling.
ciclista *s,* cyclist.
ciclo *sm.* 1. cycle 2. *(di malattia)* course.
ciclone *sm.* hurricane.
ciclòpico *agg.* Cyclopean.
ciclostilare *vt.* to mimeograph.
ciclostile *sm.* cyclostyle.
ciclotrone *sm.* cyclotron.
cicogna *sf.* stork.
cicuta *sf.* hemlock.
cieco *agg.* blind (*anche fig.*). ◆ **cieco** *sm.* blind man.
cielo *sm.* 1. sky 2. *(aria)* air 3. *(paradiso)* Heaven.
cifra *sf.* 1. figure, number 2. *(segno di cifrario)* cipher.
cifrare *vt.* 1. to cipher 2. *(ricamare in cifra)* to mark.
ciglio *sm.* 1. eyelash 2. *(bordo)* edge.
cigno *sm.* swan.
cilecca *sf.* failure || *far —,* to miss fire, *(fig.)* to fail.
cileno *agg.* Chilean.
cilicio *sm.* 1. hairshirt 2. *(relig.)* cilice.
ciliegia *sf.* cherry.
ciliegio *sm.* cherry-tree.
cilindrata *sf.* *(auto)* displacement.
cilindro *sm.* 1. *(geom.; auto)* cylinder 2. *(cappello)* top-hat.
cima *sf.* 1. top, summit: *in —,* at the top 2. *(fig.)* genius.
cìmbali *sm. pl.* essere in *—,* to be tipsy.
cimentare *vt.* to put (*v. irr.*) to the test. ◆ **cimentarsi** *vr.* to venture upon.
cimitero *sm.* cemetery, graveyard.
cinabro *sm.* cinnabar.
cincillà *sf.* chinchilla.

cineasta *sm.* cinematographer.
cinecàmera *sf.* cine-camera.
cinedilettante *sm.* film-amateur.
cinegiornale *sm.* news-reel.
cinema *sm.* 1. cinema, pictures (*pl.*) 2. *(locale)* cinema 3. *(amer.)* movies (*pl.*).
cinemàtica *sf.* kinematics.
cinematografia *sf.* cinematography.
cinematògrafo *sm.* cinema.
cinèreo *agg.* cinereous, ashen-grey.
cinese *agg.* e *sm.* Chinese.
cineteca *sf.* film library.
cinètica *sf.* kinetics.
cingere *vt.* 1. to engird 2. *(circondare)* to surround.
cinghia *sf.* 1. strap 2. *(mecc.)* belt.
cinghiale *sm.* *(zool.)* wild boar.
cinico *agg.* cynical. ◆ **cinico** *sm.* cynic.
cinismo *sm.* cynicism.
cinocèfalo *sm.* cynocephalus (*pl.* -ali).
cinòdromo *sm.* greyhound racing-track.
cinofilìa *sf.* dog-love.
cinquanta *agg.* fifty.
cinquantenario *sm.* fiftieth anniversary.
cinque *agg.* five.
cinquecento *agg.* five hundred.
cinta *sf.* town-walls (*pl.*): *muro di —,* boundary walls.
cinto *sm.* belt. ◆ **cinto** *agg.* surrounded.
cintola *sf.* waist: *dalla — in giù,* below the waist; *dalla — in su,* above the waist.
cintura *sf.* belt.
cinturone *sm.* belt.
ciò *pron.* that, this, it.
ciocca *sf.* *(di capelli)* lock.
cioccolata *sf.* chocolate.
cioccolatino *sm.* chocolate.
cioccolato *sm.* chocolate.
cioè *cong.* that is.
ciondolare *vi.* 1. to dangle 2. *(fig.)* to lounge.
ciòndolo *sm.* pendant.
ciondoloni *avv.* dangling.
ciòtola *sf.* cup, bowl.
ciòttolo *sm.* pebble.
cipolla *sf.* onion.
cipresso *sm.* cypress.
cipria *sf.* powder: *piumino per —,* powder puff.
circa *prep.* e *avv.* about, nearly || *— a,* as to.
circo *sm.* circus.

circolante *agg.* circulating: *moneta* —, currency.

circolare[1] *agg.* circular. ♦ **circolare** *sf.* circular letter.

circolare[2] *vi.* to circulate.

circolatorio *agg.* circulatory.

circolazione *sf.* 1. circulation 2. (*traffico*) traffic 3. (*comm.*) currency.

circolo *sm.* 1. circle 2. (*associazione*) club.

circoncidere *vt.* to circumcise.

circoncisione *sf.* circumcision.

circondare *vt.* to surround (*anche fig.*).

circonferenza *sf.* circumference.

circonflesso *agg.* circumflex.

circonlocuzione *sf.* circumlocution.

circonvallazione *sf.* ring-road.

circonvenire *vt.* to circumvent.

circonvoluzione *sf.* circumvolution.

circoscrivere *vt.* to circumscribe.

circoscrizione *sf.* 1. circumscription 2. (*territorio*) area.

circospetto *agg.* circumspect.

circospezione *sf.* circumspection.

circostante *agg.* 1. surrounding 2. (*attr.*) neighbouring.

circostanza *sf.* circumstance, occasion: *in queste circostanze*, under these circumstances; *in quella* —, on that occasion.

circostanziale *agg.* circumstantial.

circostanziare *vt.* to detail.

circuire *vt.* 1. to surround 2. (*fig.*) to circumvent.

circùito *sm.* circuit.

cirìllico *agg.* cyrillic.

cirrosi *sf.* cirrhosis.

cisalpino *agg.* cisalpine.

cisposo *agg.* blear.

ciste *sf.* cyst.

cisterna *sf.* 1. cistern 2. (*serbatoio*) tank.

cistifèllea *sf.* gall-bladder.

cistite *sf.* cystitis.

citare *vt.* 1. (*menzionare*) to mention 2. (*da un libro o da un discorso ecc.*) to quote 3. (*giur.*) to summon.

citazione *sf.* 1. (*da un discorso, un libro ecc.*) quotation 2. (*giur.*) summons (*pl.*).

citòfono *sm.* interphone.

citologia *sf.* (*biol.*) cytology.

citrato *sm.* citrate.

cìtrico *agg.* citric.

città *sf.* 1. town: — *di provincia*, country town; — *natale*, home

town; *gente di* —, townspeople; *vita di* —, town life 2. (*metropoli*) city.

cittadella *sf.* 1. citadel 2. (*baluardo*) stronghold.

cittadina *sf.* 1. small town 2. (*donna che abita in città*) woman citizen.

cittadinanza *sf.* 1. (*abitanti*) people of the city 2. (*nazionalità*) citizenship: *diritto di* —, right of citizenship.

cittadino *sm.* 1. (*che abita in città*) town-dweller 2. (*che appartiene a uno stato*) citizen. ♦ **cittadino** *agg.* town.

ciuffo *sm.* 1. forelock 2. (*di penne, peli, erba*) tuft.

ciurma *sf.* crew.

civetta *sf.* 1. owl 2. (*fig.*) coquette.

civetteria *sf.* coquetry.

cìvico *agg.* civic.

civile *agg.* 1. civil 2. (*che riguarda la civiltà*) civilized 3. (*gentile*) polite 4. (*non ecclesiastico o non militare*) civilian.

civilizzare *vt.* to civilize.

civilizzazione *sf.* civilization.

civiltà *sf.* 1. civilization 2. (*cortesia*) politeness.

civismo *sm.* civic virtues (*pl.*).

clamore *sm.* uproar.

clamoroso *agg.* noisy.

clandestino *agg.* clandestine, secret.

clarinetto, clarino *sm.* clarinet.

classe *sf.* class || *di* — (*qualità*), first-rate.

classicismo *sm.* classicism.

clàssico *agg.* classical. ♦ **clàssico** *sm.* classic.

classifica *sf.* 1. classification 2. (*sport*) position.

classificare *vt.* to classify.

classificazione *sf.* classification.

claudicare *vi.* to limp.

clàusola *sf.* 1. clause 2. (*riserva*) reserve.

claustrofobìa *sf.* claustrophobia.

clava *sf.* club.

clavicémbalo *sm.* harpsichord.

clavìcola *sf.* collar-bone.

clemente *agg.* clement, mild.

clemenza *sf.* clemency, mildness.

cleptòmane *agg. e sm.* kleptomaniac.

cleptomanìa *sf.* kleptomania.

clericale *agg.* clerical.

clero *sm.* clergy.

cliente *sm.* **1.** customer **2.** (*di medico, avvocato*) client.

clientela *sf.* **1.** customers (*pl.*) **2.** (*di medico, avvocato*) practice **3.** (*comm.*) connection.

clima *sm.* climate.

clinica *sf.* nursing-home.

clinico *agg.* clinical. ♦ **clinico** *sm* clinician.

clistere *sm.* enema.

cloaca *sf.* cloaca.

cloro *sm.* chlorine.

clorofilla *sf.* chlorophyll.

cloroformio *sm.* chloroform.

cloruro *sm.* chloride.

coabitare *vi.* to cohabit.

coabitazione *sf.* cohabitation.

coadiuvante *agg.* coadjuvant.

coadiuvare *vt.* to help.

coagulare *vt.* **1.** to coagulate **2.** (*del latte*) to curdle.

coagulazione *sf.* coagulation.

coagulo *sm.* **1.** curd **2.** (*di sangue*) blood-clot.

coalizione *sf.* alliance, coalition.

coalizzare *vt.* to unite. ♦ **coalizzarsi** *vr.* to form a coalition.

coartare *vt.* to force.

coatto *agg.* forced: *domicilio —,* forced residence.

cobalto *sm.* cobalt.

cobelligerante *agg.* e *sm.* co-belligerent.

cobra *sm.* cobra.

cocaina *sf.* cocaine.

cocainòmane *s.* cocainist.

coccarda *sf.* cockade.

cocchiere *sm.* coachman (*pl.* -men).

cocchio *sm.* coach.

coccige *sm.* cocyx (*pl.* -yges).

coccinella *sf.* ladybird.

cocciniglia *sf.* cochineal.

coccio *sm.* **1.** (*terracotta*) crock, pot **2.** (*pezzo rotto*) fragment of pottery.

cocciutaggine *sf.* stubbornness.

cocciuto *agg.* stubborn.

cocco *sm.* **1.** (*frutto*) coconut **2.** (*albero*) coconut-tree **3.** (*fam. vezz.*) darling.

coccodrillo *sm.* crocodile.

coccolare *vt.* to pet, to fondle.

cocente *agg.* **1.** hot, scalding **2.** (*fig.*) deep, bitter.

cocòmero *sm.* water-melon.

cocuzzolo *sm.* **1.** crown **2.** (*vetta*) top.

coda *sf.* **1.** tail **2.** (*fila*) queue: *fare la —,* to queue up.

codardo *agg.* cowardly. ♦ **codardo** *sm.* coward.

codesto *agg.* **1.** that (*pl.* those) **2.** (*come « tale »*) such. ♦ **codesto** *pron.* that one (*pl.* those ones).

còdice *sm.* **1.** code: *— civile,* Civil Law **2.** (*manoscritto antico*) codex.

codificare *vt.* to codify.

coefficiente *sm.* coefficient.

coercitivo *agg.* coercive.

coercizione *sf.* compulsion.

coerente *agg.* coherent.

coerenza *sf.* coherence.

coesione *sf.* cohesion.

coesistenza *sf.* coexistence.

coesistere *vi.* to coexist.

coetàneo *agg.* e *sm.* contemporary || *Carlo ed io siamo coetanei,* Charles and I are the same age.

cofanetto *sm.* casket: *— di gioielli,* jewel box.

còfano *sm.* **1.** coffer **2.** (*auto*) bonnet.

cògliere *vt.* **1.** to pick up, to pluck **2.** (*sorprendere*) to catch (*v. irr.*) **3.** (*colpire*) to hit (*v. irr.*) **4.** (*afferrare*) to seize: *— la palla al balzo,* to seize the opportunity.

cognata *sf.* sister-in-law.

cognato *sm.* brother-in-law.

cognizione *sf.* **1.** knowledge **2.** (*giur.*) cognizance.

cognome *sm.* surname.

coincidenza *sf.* **1.** coincidence **2.** (*ferr.*) connection.

coincidere *vi.* to coincide, to clash.

coinvòlgere *vt.* to involve.

còito *sm.* coition.

colabrodo *sm.* strainer.

colaggio *sm.* **1.** (*di liquidi*) leakage **2.** (*metal.*) casting.

colare *vt.* **1.** to strain **2.** (*fondere*) to cast (*v. irr.*) ♦ **colare** *vi.* to drip.

colata *sf.* **1.** (*metal.*) casting **2.** (*quantità di metallo fuso*) cast **3.** (*di lava*) flow.

colato *agg.* strained, filtered.

colazione *sf.* **1.** (*del mattino*) breakfast **2.** (*di mezzogiorno*) lunch.

colbacco *sm.* busby.

colei *pron. dimostr.* **1.** (*sogg.*) she; (*ogg.*) her **2.** *— che,* she who, she whom (*sogg.*); her who, her whom (*ogg.*): *— che viene qui è mia sorella,* she who is coming here is my sister; *— che vedi è Maria,* she whom you see is Mary; *vedi — che viene?,* can you see her who is coming?; *sono stata aiutata da —*

che odiavo, I have been helped by her whom I hated.

coleòttero *sm.* coleopter.

colera *sm.* cholera.

colesterolo *sm.* cholesterol.

còlica *sf.* colic.

colino *sm.* strainer.

colite *sf.* colitis.

colla *sf.* glue || — *di farina*, paste.

collaborare *vi.* to collaborate.

collaboratore *sm.* collaborator.

collaborazione *sf.* collaboration.

collaborazionismo *sm.* collaborationism.

collaborazionista *sm.* collaborationist.

collana *sf.* **1.** necklace **2.** (*raccolta*) collection **3.** (*di libri*) series.

collare *sm.* collar.

collasso *sm.* breakdown: — *cardiaco*, heart failure.

collaterale *agg.* collateral.

collaudare *vt.* to test.

collaudatore *sm.* **1.** tester **2.** (*aer.*) test pilot **3.** (*auto*) test-driver.

collàudo *sm.* test: *fare un — di qc.*, to put (*v. irr.*) sthg. to the test.

collazionare *vt.* to collate.

colle *sm.* hill.

collega *sm.* colleague.

collegamento *sm.* **1.** connection **2.** (*mecc.*) linkwork || *essere in —*, to be in touch.

collegare *vt.* to connect, to link.

collegiale *agg.* collegial. ♦ **collegiale** *sm.* boarder.

collegio *sm.* **1.** college **2.** (*scuola con convitto*) boarding-school.

còllera *sf.* anger || *essere in —*, to be angry.

collèrico *agg.* hot-tempered.

colletta *sf.* collection.

collettivismo *sm.* collectivism.

collettività *sf.* collectivity.

collettivizzare *vt.* to collectivize.

collettivizzazione *sf.* collectivization.

collettivo *agg.* collective.

colletto *sm.* collar.

collettore *agg.* collecting. ♦ **collettore** *sm.* **1.** (*esattore; raccoglitore*) collector **2.** (*mecc.*) manifold **3.** (*elettr.*) commutator.

collezionare *vt.* to collect.

collezione *sf.* collection.

collezionista *sm.* collector.

collimare *vi.* **1.** (*essere d'accordo*) to agree (with) **2.** (*coincidere*) to

coincide.

collina *sf.* hill.

collinoso *agg.* hilly.

collirio *sm.* eye-wash.

collisione *sf.* collision (*anche fig.*), impact.

collo *sm.* **1.** neck: *allungare il —*, to crane one's neck || *a rotta di —*, at breakneck speed; *tra capo e —*, unexpectedly **2.** (*pacco*) parcel, package.

collocamento *sm.* **1.** placing **2.** (*impiego*) employment || *agenzia di —*, employment bureau **3.** (*comm.*) disposal.

collocare *vt.* **1.** to place **2.** (*impiegare*) to employ **3.** (*comm.*) to sell (*v. irr.*), to dispose of (sthg.). ♦ **collocarsi** *vr.* **1.** to place oneself **2.** (*impiegarsi*) to get a situation.

collocazione *sf.* **1.** placing **2.** (*comm.*) sale **3.** (*di libri in biblioteche*) press-mark.

colloidale *agg.* colloidal.

colloquio *sm.* **1.** conversation, talk **2.** (*intervista*) interview.

collusione *sf.* collusion.

colluttazione *sf.* scuffle: *venire a —*, to come (*v. irr.*) to grips.

colmare *vt.* **1.** to fill up **2.** (*fig.*) to fill, to overwhelm.

colmo *agg.* full, brimful. ♦ **colmo** *sm.* top, summit, climax || *per — di sfortuna*, as a crowning misfortune; *è il —!*, that beats everything.

colomba *sf.* dove.

colombaia *sf.* dove-cot.

colombo *sm.* pigeon: — *viaggiatore*, carrier-pigeon.

colonia *sf.* colony.

coloniale *agg.* colonial.

colonialismo *sm.* colonialism.

colonialista *sm.* colonialist.

colonizzare *vt.* to colonize.

colonizzatore *sm.* colonizer.

colonizzazione *sf.* colonization.

colonna *sf.* column (*anche fig.*), pillar || — *d'acqua*, fall of water.

colonnato *sm.* colonnade.

colonnello *sm.* colonel.

colono *sm.* **1.** farmer **2.** (*abitante di una colonia*) settler.

colorante *agg.* colouring. ♦ **colorante** *sm.* dye.

colorare *vt.* to colour **2.** ♦ **colorarsi** *vr.* **1.** to colour **2.** (*di persona*) to blush, to flush.

colorazione *sf.* colouring.

colore *sm.* **1.** colour || *biancheria di* —, coloured linen; *gente di* —, coloured people; *colori a olio*, oilpaints **2.** (*aspetto*) look.

colorire *vt.* to colour.

colorito *sm.* complexion.

coloritura *sf.* colouring.

coloro *pron. dimostr.* **1.** they (*sogg.*); them (*compl.*) **2.** — *che*, they who, they whom (*sogg.*); them who, them whom (*compl.*): — *studiano saranno premiati*, they who study will be given a prize; — *tu vedi sono i miei amici*, they whom you see are my friends; *amerò sempre* — *mi amano*, I shall always love them who love me; *ti presenterò a* — *hai visto ieri*, I shall introduce you to them whom you saw yesterday.

colossale *agg.* colossal.

colosso *sm.* colossus (*pl.* -si).

colpa *sf.* **1.** fault **2.** (*colpevolezza*) guilt.

colpévole *agg.* guilty.

colpevolezza *sf.* guilt, guiltiness.

colpire *vt.*: **1.** to hit (*v. irr.*), to strike (*v. irr.*; *anche fig.*) **2.** (*di arma da fuoco*) to shoot (*v. irr.*).

colpo *sm.* **1.** blow, stroke (*anche fig.*): — *di fortuna*, stroke of luck; — *apoplettico*, stroke of apoplexy || — *d'aria*, draught; *a* — *d'occhio*, at a glance; *a* — *sicuro*, without any risk; *senza* — *ferire*, without resistance **2.** (*di arma da fuoco*) shot.

colposo *agg.* unpremeditated: *omicidio* —, manslaughter.

coltellata *sf.* stab.

coltello *sm.* knife: — *a serramanico*, jack-knife; *affilare un* —, to sharpen a knife.

coltivàbile *agg.* cultivable.

coltivare *vt.* to cultivate (*anche fig.*), to till, to farm.

coltivatore *sm.* **1.** tiller, farmer **2.** (*di patate, tabacco ecc.*) grower.

coltivazione *sf.* **1.** tilling, farming **2.** (*di patate, tabacco ecc.*) growing.

colto *agg.* (*istruito*) learned.

coltre *sf.* blanket, coverlet.

colui *pron. dimostr.* **1.** he (*sogg.*) him (*compl.*) **2.** — *che*, he who, he whom (*sogg.*); him who, him whom (*compl.*): — *che ti ha salutato è mio fratello*, he who has greeted you is my brother; — *che vedesti ieri è un mio vecchio ami-*

co, he whom you saw yesterday is an old friend of mine; *daranno il premio a* — *che studierà*, they will give the prize to him who studies; *fui aiutata da* — *che avevo aiutato*, I was helped by him whom I had helped.

coma *sm.* coma.

comandamento *sm.* **1.** command, precept **2.** (*relig.*) commandment.

comandante *sm.* commander.

comandare *vt.* **1.** to order, to command **2.** (*essere al comando*) to command, to be in command of.

comando *sm.* **1.** (*ordine*) order **2.** (*autorità*) command **3.** (*sede del comandante*) headquarters (*pl.*).

comatoso *agg.* comatose.

combaciare *vi.* to fit together.

combattente *sm.* **1.** fighting man **2.** (*soldato*) soldier, service man.

combattentistico *agg.* soldier (like) (*attr.*).

combàttere *vt.* e *vi.* to fight (*v. irr.*) (*anche fig.*).

combattimento *sm.* **1.** combat, fight, battle **2.** (*boxe*) match.

combattività *sf.* pugnacity.

combattivo *agg.* pugnacious.

combinare *vt.* **1.** to combine **2.** (*di colori*) to match **3.** (*concludere*) to conclude **4.** (*progettare*) to plan.

combinazione *sf.* **1.** combination **2.** (*sistemazione*) arrangement **3.** (*caso, coincidenza*) chance, coincidence.

combriccola *sf.* **1.** band **2.** (*comitiva*) party.

combustìbile *agg.* combustible. ♦ **combustìbile** *sm.* fuel.

combustione *sf.* combustion.

combutta *sf.* **1.** gang: *essere in* —, to be hand in glove **2.** (*congiura*) plot.

come *avv.* **1.** (*simile a*) like: *è proprio* — *suo padre*, he is just like his father **2.** (*in qualità di, modale*) as: *ti parlo* — *amico*, I am speaking to you as a friend **3.** (*in comp.*) as ... as; so ... as: *Carlo è studioso* — *me*, Charles is as studious as I; *Carlo non è studioso* — *me*, Charles is not so studious as I **4.** (*int.*) how: — *va?*, How are you? **5.** (*escl.*) how: — *è interessante questo libro!*, How interesting this book is! ♦ **come** *prep.* **1.** (*tempo-*

rale) as, as soon as: — *sentii la sua voce lo riconobbi*, as soon as I heard his voice I recognized him 2. (*come se*) as if: *mi guarda* — *se mi conoscesse*, he is looking at me as if he knew me || — *Dio volle*, in God's good time; — *segue*, as follows; — *d'accordo*, as agreed.

cometa *sf.* comet.

comicità *sf.* comicality.

còmico *agg.* comical, funny. ♦ **còmico** *sm.* comedian.

comìgnolo *sm.* chimney-pot.

cominciare *vt.* to begin (*v. irr.*), to start.

comitato *sm.* committee.

comitiva *sf.* party, company.

comizio *sm.* meeting.

comma *sm.* paragraph.

commedia *sf.* 1. comedy, play 2. (*fig.*) pretence || *recitare la* —, to play a part.

commediante *sm.* 1. player 2. (*fig.*) shammer.

commediògrafo *sm.* playwright.

commemorare *vt.* to commemorate.

commemorativo *agg.* memorial.

commemorazione *sf.* commemoration.

commendàbile *agg.* commendable.

commendatizia *sf.* letter of recommendation.

commensale *sm.* table-companion.

commentare *vt.* to comment (on).

commentario *sm.* (*lett.*) commentary.

commentatore *sm.* commentator.

commento *sm.* commentary.

commerciàbile *agg.* negotiable.

commerciale *agg.* commercial.

commercializzare *vt.* to commercialize.

commerciante *sm.* 1. trader 2. (*uomo d'affari*) business-man (*pl.* -men) || — *all'ingrosso*, wholesale dealer; — *al minuto*, retailer.

commerciare *vi.* to trade, to deal (*v. irr.*) (in).

commercio *sm.* 1. commerce, trade 2. (*affari*) business || — *all'ingrosso*, wholesale trade; — *al minuto*, retail trade; — *d'importazione, esportazione*, import, export trade; *essere in* —, to be on sale; *essere fuori* —, to be out of sale; *essere in* — (*di un commerciante*), to be in business.

commessa *sf.* shop assistant, shop-girl.

commesso *sm.* clerk, shopman (*pl.* -men), shop assistant || — *viaggiatore*, commercial traveller.

commestibile *agg.* eatable. ♦ **commestibili** *sm. pl.* foodstuffs.

comméttere *vt.* 1. to commit, to do (*v. irr.*), to make (*v. irr.*) 2. (*ordinare*) to order.

commiato *sm.* 1. (*preso*) leave 2. (*dato*) dismissal.

commilitone *sm.* fellow-soldier.

comminatoria *sf.* commination.

comminatorio *agg.* comminatory.

commiserare *vt.* to pity.

commiserazione *sf.* pity.

commissariato *sm.* 1. (*carica di commissario*) commissaryship 2. (*ufficio*) commissary's office.

commissario *sm.* commissary.

commissionare *vt.* (*comm.*) to order.

commissionario *sm.* (*comm.*) commission agent.

commissione *sf.* 1. errand: *fare una* —, to go (*v. irr.*) on an errand 2. (*comm.*) commission, order 3. (*comitato*) commission, committee.

commisurare *vt.* to compare.

committente *sm.* purchaser, buyer.

commosso *agg.* moved, affected.

commovente *agg.* moving, touching, affecting.

commozione *sf.* 1. emotion 2. (*med.*) concussion: — *cerebrale*, concussion of the brain.

commuòvere *vt.* to move, to touch. ♦ **commuòversi** *vr.* to be moved.

commutàbile *agg.* commutable.

commutare *vt.* to commute.

commutativo *agg.* commutative.

commutatore *sm.* commutator.

comò *sm.* chest of drawers.

comodino *sm.* night-table.

comodità *sf.* convenience, comfort.

còmodo *agg.* 1. useful 2. (*conveniente*) convenient 3. (*confortevole*) comfortable 4. (*maneggevole*) handy.

compagnìa *sf.* 1. company: *tener* —, to keep (*v. irr.*) company 2. (*gruppo di persone*) party 3. (*società*) company.

compagno *sm.* companion, mate, comrade || — *di giuochi*, playmate; — *di stanza*, room-mate; — *di studi*, fellow-student.

compagnone *sm.* jolly good fellow.

comparàbile *agg.* comparable.

comparare *vt.* to compare.

comparativo *agg.* (*gramm.*) comparative.

comparato *agg.* comparative.

compare *sm.* 1. (*compagno*) comrade, partner 2. (*padrino*) godfather 3. (*testimone di matrimonio*) witness 4. (*complice*) accomplice.

comparire *vi.* 1. to appear 2. (*sembrare*) to show (*v. irr.*) oneself 3. (*far bella mostra*) to show (*v. irr.*) off.

comparizione *sf.* appearance: (*giur.*) mandato di —, summons.

comparsa *sf.* 1. appearance 2. (*teat.; cine*) supernumerary 3. (*giur.*) appearance.

compartecipare *vi.* to share in.

compartimento *sm.* 1. compartment 2. (*circoscrizione*) department.

compartizione *sf.* distribution.

compassato *agg.* 1. stiff, formal 2. (*di discorso*) restrained.

compassione *sf.* pity, commiseration.

compasso *sm.* compasses (*pl.*).

compatìbile *agg.* consistent.

compatibilità *sf.* consistency.

compatimento *sm.* pity, compassion.

compatire *vt.* to pity.

compatriota *sm.* fellow-countryman (*pl.* -men). ♦ **compatriota** *sf.* fellow-countrywoman (*pl.* -women).

compattezza *sf.* 1. compactness 2. (*di associazione, partito*) unity.

compatto *agg.* compact, solid.

compendiare *vt.* to abridge, to sum up.

compendio *sm.* 1. abridgement, summary.

compenetrare *vt.* to penetrate.

compensàbile *agg.* remunerable.

compensare *vt.* 1. to compensate 2. (*ricompensare*) to reward.

compensato *sm.* ply-wood.

compensazione *sf.* 1. compensation, indemnity 2. (*comm.*) clearing.

compenso *sm.* 1. compensation 2. (*rimunerazione*) reward, retribution.

còmpera *sf.* purchase.

competente *agg.* competent.

competenza *sf.* 1. competence 2. (*onorario*) fee.

compètere *vi.* 1. (*gareggiare*) to vie 2. (*spettare*) to be due, to belong.

competitivo *agg.* competitive.

competitore *sm.* competitor, rival.

competizione *sf.* competition.

compiacente *agg.* obliging.

compiacenza *sf.* 1. kindness 2. (*soddisfazione*) satisfaction.

compiacere *vt.* to please, to gratify. ♦ **compiacersi** *vr.* 1. to be pleased (with), to congratulate 2. (*degnarsi*) to condescend.

compiacimento *sm.* 1. satisfaction 2. (*congratulazione*) congratulation.

compiàngere *vt.* 1. to pity, to sympathize (with) 2. (*disprezzare*) to despise.

compianto *agg.* regretted. ♦ **compianto** *sm.* regret.

compiere *vt.* 1. (*finire*) to finish 2. (*eseguire*) to accomplish 3. (*adempiere*) to do (*v. irr.*): — il proprio dovere, to do one's duty 4. (*di età*) ho compiuto 30 anni, I am now 30 years old.

compilare *vt.* to compile: — un documento, to draw (*v. irr.*) up a document; — una lista, to make (*v. irr.*) a list.

compilazione *sf.* 1. compilation 2. (*comm.*) drawing up.

compimento *sm.* 1. (*il compiere*) completion 2. (*conclusione*) achievement.

compitare *vt.* to spell (*v. irr.*).

compitezza *sf.* politeness, refinement.

compito *agg.* polite.

còmpito *sm.* 1. task, duty 2. (*scolastico, a casa*) homework; (*a scuola*) class-work.

compiutamente *avv.* completely.

compiutezza *sf.* completeness.

compiuto *agg.* complete.

compleanno *sm.* birthday: buon —!, happy birthday!.

complementare *agg.* complementary.

complemento *sm.* 1. complement 2. (*gramm.*) — indiretto, indirect object 3. (*mil.*) truppe di —, reserve.

complessato *agg.* neurotic.

complessione *sf.* constitution.

complessità *sf.* complexity.

complessivamente *avv.* on the whole.

complessivo *agg.* total, inclusive.

complesso *agg.* complex, complicated. ♦ **complesso** *sm.* **1.** whole **2.** (*industriale*) plant, set **3.** (*mus.*) band.

completamente *avv.* completely.

completare *vt.* to complete, to finish.

completezza *sf.* completeness.

completo *agg.* **1.** complete, whole **2.** (*pieno*) full. ♦ **completo** *sm.* (*vestito*) suit.

complicare *vt.* to complicate.

complicato *agg.* complicated.

complicazione *sf.* complication: *salvo complicazioni*, if no complications set in.

còmplice *s.* accomplice.

complicità *sf.* accomplicity.

complimentare *vt.* to compliment. ♦ **complimentarsi** *vr.* to congratulate (so.).

complimento *sm.* **1.** compliment **2.** (*congratulazione*) congratulation.

complottare *vi.* to plot.

complotto *sm.* plot, conspiracy.

compluvio *sm.* (*arch.*) compluvium (*pl.* -ia).

componente *agg.* component. ♦ **componente** *sm.* **1.** member **2.** (*chim.*) component.

componimento *sm.* **1.** (*lett.; mus.; scol.*) composition **2.** (*giur.*) settlement.

comporre *vt.* **1.** to compose: — *una poesia*, to write (*v. irr.*) a poem; — *un numero telefonico*, to dial a number **2.** (*chim.*) to compound **3.** (*assestare*) to arrange.

comportamento *sm.* behaviour.

comportare *vt.* to involve, to require. ♦ **comportarsi** *vr.* to behave (oneself).

compòsito *agg.* composite.

compositore *sm.* **1.** (*mus.*) composer **2.** (*tip.*) compositor.

composizione *sf.* **1.** composition **2.** (*conciliazione*) composition, agreement **3.** (*tip.*) composing.

composta *sf.* compote.

compostezza *sf.* **1.** composure **2.** (*dignità*) self-respect.

composto *agg.* **1.** compound **2.** (*ordinato*) tidy **3.** (*calmo*) calm ‖ *stare* —, to sit (*v. irr.*) still. ♦ **composto** *sm.* compound.

comprare *vt.* **1.** to buy (*v. irr.*): — *a credito*, to buy on credit; — *per contanti*, to buy for cash; — *all'ingrosso*, to buy wholesale **2.** (*corrompere*) to bribe.

compratore *sm.* buyer, purchaser.

compravéndita *sf.* marketing.

comprèndere *vt.* **1.** (*includere*) to include, to take (*v. irr.*) in **2.** (*capire*) to understand (*v. irr.*) **3.** (*rendersi conto*) to realize.

comprensibile *agg.* intelligible.

comprensibilità *sf.* intelligibility.

comprensione *sf.* **1.** comprehension, understanding **2.** (*compassione*) sympathy.

comprensivo *agg.* **1.** comprehensive **2.** (*che capisce*) comprehending **3.** (*che prova simpatia*) sympathetic.

compressa *sf.* **1.** tablet **2.** (*di garza*) compress.

compressibilità *sf.* compressibility.

compressione *sf.* compression.

comprìmere *vt.* **1.** to compress **2.** (*fig.*) to restrain, to repress.

compromesso *sm.* compromise.

compromettente *agg.* compromising.

comprométtere *vt.* to compromise, to involve.

comproprietà *sf.* joint ownership.

comproprietario *sm.* joint owner.

comprovare *vt.* to prove.

compunto *agg.* filled with compunction, contrite.

computare *vt.* to compute.

computisterìa *sf.* book-keeping.

còmputo *sm.* reckoning.

comunale *agg.* communal, municipal.

comunardo *sm.* (*stor.*) Communard.

comune[1] *agg.* **1.** common **2.** (*abituale*) frequent, usual.

comune[2] *sm.* **1.** commune **2.** (*edificio*) Town Hall.

comunella *sf.* cabal: *far* — *con qu.*, to consort.

comunemente *avv.* commonly, usually.

comunicàbile *agg.* communicable.

comunicabilità *sf.* communicability.

comunicante *agg.* communicating.

comunicare *vt.* **1.** to communicate, to transmit **2.** (*relig.*) to communicate. ♦ **comunicarsi** *vr.* to receive Holy Communion.

comunicativa *sf.* communicativeness.

comunicativo *agg.* communicative.

comunicato *sm.* bulletin.

comunicazione *sf.* communication.

comunione *sf.* **1.** communion: —

di idee, similarity of ideas **2.** *(relig.)* Holy Communion.
comunismo *sm.* communism.
comunista *s.* communist.
comunità *sf.* community.
comunque *avv.* however, anyhow.
con *prep.* **1.** *(compagnia, unione, strumento)* with: *venne — me,* he came with me; *scrivo — questa penna,* I write with this pen **2.** *(stato, condizione)* in: *— il freddo sto meglio,* in cold weather I feel better **3.** *(mezzo di trasporto)* by: *arriverò col treno delle 3,* I shall arrive by the three o'clock train **4.** *(per mezzo di)* by means of.
conato *sm.* effort || *avere conati di vomito,* to feel *(v. irr.)* sick.
conca *sf.* **1.** basin, pot **2.** *(valle)* valley.
concatenamento *sm.* concatenation.
concatenare *vt.* to concatenate.
concatenazione *sf.* concatenation.
concavo *agg.* concave, hollow.
concèdere *vt.* **1.** to grant, to bestow **2.** *(permettere)* to allow.
concentramento *sm.* concentration: *campo di —,* concentration camp.
concentrare *vt.* to concentrate. ♦ **concentrarsi** *vr.* to concentrate.
concentrato *agg.* concentrated. ♦ **concentrato** *sm.* concentrated food.
concentrazione *sf.* concentration.
concèntrico *agg.* concentric.
concepìbile *agg.* conceivable.
concepimento *sm.* conception.
concepire *vt.* **1.** to conceive **2.** *(nutrire speranze, timori)* to entertain **3.** *(formulare)* to express.
concerìa *sf.* tannery.
concèrnere *vt.* to concern, to relate to.
concertare *vt.* **1.** *(mus.)* to harmonize **2.** *(stabilire)* to plan, to arrange.
concertato *agg.* concerted *(anche mus.),* arranged.
concertista *s.* concert artist.
concertìstico *agg.* concert.
concerto *sm.* concert.
concessionario *sm.* concessionary agent.
concessione *sf.* **1.** concession **2.** *(permesso)* permission.
concetto *sm.* concept.
concettuale *agg.* conceptual.

concezionale *agg.* conceptional.
concezione *sf.* conception.
conchiglia *sf.* shell.
concia *sf.* **1.** *(di pelli)* tanning **2.** *(di tabacco)* curing.
conciare *vt.* **1.** *(pelli)* to tan **2.** *(tabacco)* to cure **3.** *(fig.)* to ill-treat **4.** *(insudiciare)* to soil. ♦ **conciarsi** *vr.* to get *(v. irr.)* dirty.
conciatore *sm.* tanner.
conciatura *sf.* tanning.
conciliàbile *agg.* compatible, consistent.
conciliabilità *sf.* compatibility.
conciliàbolo *sm.* conventicle, secret talk.
conciliante *agg.* conciliatory.
conciliare *vt.* **1.** to reconcile **2.** *(procacciare)* to win *(v. irr.),* to gain. ♦ **conciliarsi** *vr.* to win *(v. irr.).*
conciliare *agg.* conciliar.
conciliativo *agg.* conciliatory. ♦ **conciliatore** *sm.* peacemaker || *giudice —,* Justice of the Peace.
conciliazione *sf.* conciliation.
concilio *sm.* Council.
concimala *sf.* dung-hill, dung-pit.
concimare *vt.* to dung.
concimazione *sf.* dunging.
concime *sm.* **1.** *(organico)* dung **2.** *(chimico)* fertilizer.
concio *sm.* dung.
concionare *vi.* to harangue.
concione *sf.* harangue.
concisione *sf.* concision.
conciso *agg.* concise, brief.
concistoro *sm.* *(eccl.)* consistory.
concitare *vt.* to excite, to stir (up).
concitazione *sf.* excitement, agitation.
concittadino *sm.* fellow-citizen.
conclamare *vt.* to acclaim.
conclave *sm.* *(eccl.)* conclave.
concludente *agg.* **1.** conclusive **2.** *(di persona)* energetic.
conclùdere *vt.* **1.** to conclude, to finish **2.** *(dedurre)* to infer **3.** *(fare)* to do *(v. irr.).*
conclusionale *sf.* *(giur.)* pleadings *(pl.)..*
conclusione *sf.* **1.** conclusion **2.** *(risultato)* issue, result.
conclusivo *agg.* conclusive.
concomitante *agg.* concomitant.
concomitanza *sf.* concomitance.
concordanza *sf.* agreement.
concordare *vi.* to agree. ♦ **concordare** *vt.* **1.** to agree upon **2.**

(*mettere d'accordo*) to reconcile **3.** (*gramm.*) to put (*v. irr.*) in concord.

concordatario *agg.* **1.** (*eccl.*) of concordat **2.** (*giur.; comm.*) composition.

concordato *sm.* **1.** convention **2.** (*eccl.*) concordat **3.** (*giur.; comm.*) agreement, composition.

concorde *agg.* concordant, agreeing: *volontà* —, unanimous will.

concordemente *avv.* concordantly.

concordia *sf.* concord, agreement.

concorrente *agg.* **1.** concurrent **2.** (*rivale*) competing. ♦ **concorrente** *sm.* **1.** candidate **2.** (*rivale*) competitor.

concorrenza *sf.* **1.** (*affluenza*) concourse **2.** (*comm.*) competition ‖ *fare —*, to compete with; — *sleale*, unfair competition.

concorrenziale *agg.* competitive.

concórrere *vi.* **1.** to come (*v. irr.*) together **2.** (*contribuire*) to concur, to contribute **3.** (*partecipare*) to share in **4.** (*mettersi in gara*) to compete.

concorso *sm.* **1.** (*affluenza*) rush, crowd, concourse **2.** (*gara*) competition **3.** (*sport*) contest.

concretare *vt.* **1.** to make (*v. irr.*) concrete **2.** (*concludere*) to realize.

concretezza *sf.* concreteness.

concreto *agg.* **1.** concrete, real **2.** (*solido*) solid.

concrezione *sf.* concretion.

concubina *sf.* concubine.

concubinaggio, concubinato *sm.* concubinage.

conculcare *vt.* to trample on.

concupire *vt.* to covet, to lust after.

concupiscenza *sf.* concupiscence, lust.

concussione *sf.* (*giur.*) concussion.

condanna *sf.* **1.** condemnation **2.** (*sentenza*) sentence: — *a morte*, death sentence **3.** (*pena*) penalty.

condannàbile *agg.* condemnable.

condannare *vt.* **1.** to sentence **2.** (*fig.*) to condemn **3.** (*riprovare*) to blame.

condannato *agg.* sentenced. ♦ **condannato** *sm.* condemned man.

condensàbile *agg.* condensable.

condensabilità *sf.* condensability.

condensazione *sf.* condensation.

condensare *vt.* to condense.

condensatore *sm.* condenser.

condimento *sm.* seasoning, dress-

ing.

condire *vt.* to season; (*anche fig.*) to flavour.

condirettore *sm.* joint manager.

condiscendente *agg.* complying.

condiscendenza *sf.* **1.** compliance **2.** (*degnazione*) condescension.

condiscéndere *vi.* **1.** to comply with **2.** (*degnarsi*) to condescend.

condiscépolo *sm.* schoolfellow.

condivìdere *vt.* to share (*anche fig.*).

condizionale *agg. e sm.* conditional. ♦ **condizionale** *sf.* (*giur.*) conditional sentence.

condizionamento *sm.* conditioning.

condizionare *vt.* to condition.

condizione *sf.* **1.** condition: *a — che*: on condition that **2.** (*ceto*) rank, station.

condoglianza *sf.* condolence.

condominio *sm.* joint ownership.

condòmino *sm.* joint-owner.

condonare *vt.* to remit.

condono *sm.* remission.

condotta *sf.* **1.** conduct, behaviour.

condotto *agg. medico* —, doctor employed by the local authority. ♦ **condotto** *sm.* **1.** conduit, pipeline **2.** (*anat.*) duct.

conducente *sm.* driver.

conducibilità *sf.* (*fis.*) conductibility.

condurre *vt.* **1.** (*guidare*) to lead (*v. irr.*) **2.** (*accompagnare*) to take (*v. irr.*) **3.** (*governare, trattare*) to manage: — *i propri affari*, to manage one's business **4.** (*vivere*) to lead (*v. irr.*): — *una vita triste*, to lead a sad life. ♦ **condurre** *vi.* to lead (*v. irr.*): *questa strada conduce a Milano*, this route leads to Milan. ♦ **condursi** *vr.* to behave.

conduttività *sf.* conductivity.

conduttivo *agg.* conducting.

conduttore *agg.* conducting. ♦ **conduttore** *sm.* **1.** leader, guide **2.** (*di veicoli*) driver **3.** (*fis.*) conductor.

conduttura *sf.* **1.** duct, conduit **2.** (*di tubazioni*) piping.

conduzione *sf.* **1.** management **2.** (*fis.*) conduction.

confabulare *vi.* to confabulate.

confacente *agg.* suitable, proper.

confarsi *vr.* to suit, to become (*v. irr.*).

confederale *agg.* confedearl.

confederare *vt.* to confederate.

confederazione *sf.* 1. Confederation 2. (*alleanza*) confederacy.

conferenza *sf.* 1. lecture 2. (*assemblea*) conference.

conferenziere *sm.* lecturer.

conferimento *sm.* bestowal.

conferire *vt.* to confer, to bestow. ♦ **conferire** *vi.* 1. to `have an interview 2. (*giovare*) to be useful.

conferma *sf.* confirmation.

confermare *vt.* to confirm. ♦ **confermarsi** *vr.* to prove oneself.

confermazione *sf.* confirmation.

confessare *vt.* 1. to confess 2. (*riconoscere, ammettere*) to admit. ♦ **confessarsi** *vr.* (*eccl.*) to go (*v. irr.*) to confession.

confessionale *agg.* confessional. ♦ **confessionale** *sm.* confessional.

confessione *sf.* 1. confession 2. (*ammissione*) admission 3. (*memorie*) memoirs (*pl.*).

confessore *sm.* confessor.

confetteria *sf.* confectionery.

confettiere *sm.* confectioner.

confetto *sm.* comfit.

confettura *sf.* 1. (*confetti*) sweetmeats (*pl.*) 2. (*marmellata*) jam || — *d'arance*, marmalade.

confezionare *vt.* 1. to make (*v. irr.*) up 2. (*di piatti*) to prepare 3. (*di pacchi*) to pack up.

confezione *sf.* 1. manufacture 2. (*preparazione*) preparation 3. (*pl.*) (*abiti*) ready-to-wear clothes 4. (*imballaggio*) packing.

conficcare *vt.* to hammer, to drive (*v. irr.*). ♦ **conficcarsi** *vr.* to run (*v. irr.*) into.

confidare *vt.* to confide. ♦ **confidare** *vi.* 1. to confide, to trust 2. (*fare assegnamento*) to rely (on).

confidente *agg.* trustful. ♦ **confidente** *sm.* 1. confidant 2. (*di polizia*) police spy.

confidenza *sf.* 1. (*fiducia*) confidence 2. (*cosa confidata*) secret 3. (*familiarità*) familiarity || *essere in — con qu.*, to be on familiar terms with so.

confidenziale *agg.* confidential: *strettamente —*, strictly confidential.

confidenzialmente *avv.* confidentially.

configgere *vt.* to drive (*v. irr.*) in.

configurare *vt.* to configure, to shape.

configurazione *sf.* configuration, shape.

confinante *agg.* 1. neighbouring 2. (*fig.*) bordering.

confinare *vi.* to border on. ♦ **confinare** *vt.* 1. to banish 2. (*fig.*) to confine.

confinario *agg.* border.

confinato *agg.* interned.

confine *sm.* 1. border, frontier 2. (*fig.*) limit, boundary.

confino *sm.* internment, political confinement.

confisca *sf.* confiscation.

confiscabile *agg.* confiscable.

confiscare *vt.* to confiscate.

confitto *agg.* 1. nailed, driven in 2. (*fig.*) fixed.

conflagrare *vi.* to break (*v. irr.*) out.

conflagrazione *sf.* 1. conflagration 2. (*fig.*) sudden out-break (of war).

conflitto *sm.* 1. conflict 2. (*fig.*) clash.

confluente *sm.* confluent.

confluenza *sf.* confluence.

confluire *vi.* to flow together.

confóndere *vt.* 1. to confuse 2. (*scambiare una persona per un'altra*) to mistake (*v. irr.*) 3. (*turbare*) to confound. ♦ **confóndersi** *vr.* 1. to get (*v. irr.*) mixed up 2. (*mescolarsi*) to mingle 3. (*turbarsi*) to be disconcerted.

confondìbile *agg.* liable to be confused.

conformare *vt.* to conform. ♦ **conformarsi** *vr.* to conform.

conformato *agg.* shaped.

conformazione *sf.* conformation.

conforme *agg.* 1. conforming 2. (*simile*) similar 3. (*fedele*) true || — *a*, in conformity with. ♦ **conforme a** *loc. avv.* in conformity with.

conformismo *sm.* time-serving.

conformista *s.* 1. time-server 2. (*relig.*) conformist.

conformìstico *agg.* conformist.

conformità *sf.* conformity.

confortàbile *agg.* consolable.

confortante *agg.* consoling.

confortare *vt.* 1. to comfort 2. (*incoraggiare*) to encourage.

confortatore *agg.* comforting. ♦ **confortatore** *sm.* comforter.

confortatòrio *agg.* comforting.

confortévole *agg.* 1. comforting 2. (*comodo*) comfortable.

confortevolmente *avv.* comfortably.

conforto *sm.* **1.** comfort, solace **2.** (*incoraggiamento*) encouragement.

confratello *sm.* brother (*pl.* brethren).

confratèrnita *sf.* brotherhood.

confrontàbile *agg.* comparable.

confrontare *vt.* **1.** to compare **2.** (*giur.*) to confront.

confronto *sm.* **1.** comparison **2.** (*giur.*) confrontation ‖ *nei confronti di,* to, towards; *in — a,* in comparison with.

confucianésimo *sm.* confucianism.

confusamente *avv.* confusedly.

confusionario *agg.* blundering, unmethodical. ♦ **confusionario** *sm.* bungler, muddler.

confusione *sf.* confusion, medley.

confusionismo *sm.* general confusion.

confuso *agg.* **1.** confused, mixed, vague **2.** (*indistinto*) indistinct **3.** (*imbarazzato*) embarrassed.

confutàbile *agg.* confutable.

confutare *vt.* to confute.

confutazione *sf.* confutation.

congedare *vt.* **1.** to dismiss **2.** (*mil.*) to discharge. ♦ **congedarsi** *vr.* to take (*v. irr.*) one's leave.

congedato *sm.* dischargee.

congedo *sm.* **1.** (*commiato*) leave **2.** (*mil.*) leave, discharge ‖ *essere in —,* to be on leave.

congegnare *vt.* **1.** (*mecc.*) to assemble **2.** (*fig.*) to devise.

congegno *sm.* **1.** device, gear **2.** (*fig.*) device, scheme.

congelamento *sm.* **1.** freezing **2.** (*med.*) congelation.

congelare *vt.* to freeze (*v. irr.*), to congeal.

congelato *agg.* congealed, frozen (*anche comm.*).

congelatore *sm.* freezer.

congènere *agg.* **1.** akin (*attr.*) **2.** similar (*pred.*).

congeniale *agg.* congenial.

congènito *agg.* congenital, innate.

congestionare *vt.* to congest.

congestionato *agg.* congested: *viso —,* flushed face.

congestione *sf.* congestion.

congettura *sf.* conjecture, supposition.

congetturare *vt.* to conjecture.

congiùngere *vt.* **1.** to join **2.** (*collegare*) to connect.

congiuntiva *sf.* conjunctiva.

congiuntivite *sf.* conjunctivitis.

congiuntivo *agg.* conjunctive. ♦ **congiuntivo** *sm.* (*gramm.*) subjunctive.

congiunto *agg.* **1.** joined, united **2.** (*collegato*) connected. ♦ **congiunto** *sm.* relative.

congiuntura *sf.* **1.** point of junction **2.** (*circostanza, situazione*) circumstance, situation **3.** (*econ.*) trend, trade cycle.

congiunzione *sf.* **1.** connection **2.** (*gramm.; astr.*) conjunction.

congiura *sf.* conspiracy, plot.

congiurare *vi.* to conspire, to plot.

congiurato *sm.* conspirator, plotter.

conglobamento *sm.* conglobation.

conglobare *vt.* **1.** to conglobate **2.** (*di tasse, debiti ecc.*) to combine.

conglobazione *sf.* conglobation.

conglomerato *sm.* **1.** (*geol.*) conglomerate **2.** (*etnico; pol.*) grouping.

congratularsi *vr.* to congratulate.

congratulazione *sf.* congratulation.

congregazione *sf.* assembly, congregation (*anche eccl.*).

congressista *s.* member of a congress.

congresso *sm.* congress.

congruo *agg.* **1.** (*coerente*) congruous **2.** (*adeguato*) adequate.

conguagliare *vt.* **1.** to equalize **2.** (*comm.*) to balance.

coniare *vt.* to coin (*anche fig.*).

cònico *agg.* conic(al).

conifera *sf.* conifer.

coniglio *sm.* **1.** rabbit **2.** (*fig.*) faint-hearted.

conio *sm.* **1.** (*attrezzo per coniare*) minting die **2.** (*impronta*) coin, brand **3.** (*invenzione di nuove parole*) coinage.

coniugale *agg.* conjugal: *vita —,* married life.

coniugare *vt.* **1.** to conjugate **2.** (*unire in matrimonio*) to marry.

coniugato *agg.* married.

coniugazione *sf.* conjugation.

cònjuge *sm.* husband. ♦ **cònjuge** *sf.* wife.

connaturale *agg.* connatural, innate.

connaturato *agg.* deeply rooted.

connazionale *sm.* fellow-countryman (*pl.* -men). ♦ **connazionale** *sf.* fellow-countrywoman (*pl.* -women).

connessione *sf.* connection.

connesso *agg.* connected.

connèttere *vt.* 1. (*unire*) to connect, to join 2. (*fig.*) to associate, to link ‖ *non connettere*, to talk at random.

connettivo *agg.* connective.

connivente *agg.* conniving (at).

connotato *sm.* description, feature ‖ *i connotati*, description.

connubio *sm.* 1. marriage 2. (*fig.*) union.

cono *sm.* cone: — *gelato*, ice-cream cone.

conoscente *sm.* acquaintance.

conoscenza *sf.* 1. knowledge ‖ *venire a — di qc.*, to become (*v. irr.*) acquainted with sthg. 2. (*persona*) acquaintance 3. (*sensi*) consciousness.

conóscere *vt.* 1. to know (*v. irr.*): — *di vista*, to know by sight; — *di fama*, to know by reputation; — *dalla voce*, to recognize by one's voice 2. (*fare la conoscenza*) to meet (*v. irr.*).

conoscìbile *agg.* 1. knowable 2. (*riconoscibile*) recognizable.

conoscitivo *agg.* cognitive.

conoscitore *sm.* expert, good judge.

conosciuto *agg.* well-known, renowned.

conquista *sf.* conquest.

conquistare *vt.* 1. to conquer 2. (*fig.*) to win (*v. irr.*).

conquistatore *sm.* 1. conqueror 2. (*rubacuori*) lady-killer.

consacrare *vt.* 1. (*eccl.*) to consecrate 2. (*dedicare*) to devote.

consacrazione *sf.* consecration.

consanguineità *sf.* consanguinity.

consanguìneo *agg.* consanguine, akin. ♦ **consanguìneo** *sm.* kinsman (*pl.* -men).

consapévole *agg.* aware, conscious.

consapevolezza *sf.* 1. consciousness 2. (*conoscenza*) knowledge.

conscio *agg.* conscious.

consecutivo *agg.* 1. following 2. (*di seguito*) running: *per due giorni consecutivi*, for two days running 3. (*gramm.*) consecutive.

consegna *sf.* 1. (*comm.*) delivery: — *contro assegno*, cash on delivery; — *mancata*, nondelivery; *ordine di* —, delivery-note; *effettuare la* —, to effect delivery 2. (*deposito*) consignment 3. (*mil.*) orders (*pl.*) ‖ — *in caserma*, confinement to barracks.

consegnare *vt.* 1. to deliver 2. (*mil.*) to confine to barracks.

conseguente *agg.* consequent.

conseguenza *sf.* consequence.

conseguìbile *agg.* attainable.

conseguimento *sm.* attainment.

conseguire *vt.* to attain, to achieve, to get (*v. irr.*).

consenso *sm.* 1. consent 2. (*matrimoniale*) licence.

consensuale *agg.* by mutual consent.

consentire *vi.* to consent, to agree. ♦ **consentire** *vt.* to allow.

consenziente *agg.* consenting.

conserto *agg.* interwoven, folded: *a braccia conserte*, with folded arms.

conserva *sf.* preserve ‖ — *di frutta*, jam; — *di pomodoro*, tomato sauce.

conservare *vt.* to preserve ♦ **conservarsi** *vr.* to keep (*v. irr.*).

conservativo *agg.* conservative.

conservatore *agg.* 1. preserving 2. (*pol.*) conservative. ♦ **conservatore** *sm.* 1. preserver 2. (*pol.*) conservative.

conservatorio *sm.* academy of music.

conservazione *sf.* preservation ‖ *istinto di* —, instinct of self-preservation.

considerare *vt.* 1. to consider, to think (*v. irr.*) of 2. (*reputare*) to deem, to judge. ♦ **considerarsi** *vr.* to consider oneself.

considerato *agg.* considerate ‖ — *che*, considering that.

considerazione *sf.* 1. consideration 2. (*stima*) esteem, regard ‖ *avere — per qu.*, to have regard for so.

considerévole *agg.* considerable.

consigliare *vt.* to advise. ♦ **consigliarsi** *vr.* to ask so.'s advice, to consult (with).

consigliere *sm.* 1. counsellor 2. (*membro di un consiglio*) councillor.

consiglio *sm.* 1. advice (*solo sing.*) 2. (*corpo di persone*) council.

consiliare *agg.* of a council.

consìmile *agg.* similar.

consistente *agg.* firm, substantial.

consistenza *sf.* 1. consistence 2. (*comm.*) on hand: — *di cassa*, cash on hand.

consistere *vi.* to consist.

consociare vt. to associate.

consociato agg. associated.

consociazione sf. association.

consocio sm. co-partner.

consolante agg. cheering.

consolare[1] vt. to console, to comfort. ♦ **consolarsi** vr. to be comforted.

consolare[2] agg. consular.

consolato sm. consulate.

consolatore agg. consoling. ♦ **consolatore** sm. consoler.

consolazione sf. consolation, solace.

console sm. consul.

consolidamento sm. consolidation.

consolidare vt. to consolidate, to strengthen.

consolidato agg. consolidated.

consonante sf. consonant.

consonanza sf. consonance (anche fig.).

consono agg. in accordance (with).

consorella sf. (eccl.) sister.

consorte sm. consort, husband. ♦ **consorte** sf. consort, wife.

consorteria sf. faction.

consorzio sm. society: — agrario, agricultural union.

constare vi. 1. (essere composto) to consist 2. (risultare) to be within one's knowledge || da quanto mi consta, as far as I know.

constatare vt. V. costatare.

constatazione sf. V. costatazione.

consueto agg. usual, customary.

consuetudinario agg. customary, consuetudinary.

consuetudine sf. 1. custom, habit 2. (comm.) rule.

consulente sm. adviser.

consulenza sf. advice.

consulta sf. 1. consultation 2. (corpo consultivo) council.

consultare vt. 1. to consult 2. (esaminare) to examine.

consultazione sf. consultation: libro di —, reference book.

consultivo agg. consultative.

consulto sm. consultation.

consumare vt. 1. to consume 2. (di abiti) to wear (v. irr.) 3. (dissipare) to waste 4. (compiere) to commit.

consumato agg. 1. (perfetto) accomplished 2. (logoro) worn out 3. (divorato) consumed.

consumatore sm. consumer.

consumazione sf. 1. consumption 2. (giur.) consummation 3. (bibi-

ta) drink.

consumo sm. consumption || per proprio uso e —, for one's private use.

consuntivo agg. final: bilancio —, final balance.

consunzione sf. consumption.

contàbile agg. bookkeeping. ♦ **contàbile** sm. bookkeeper.

contabilità sf. bookkeeping.

contachilòmetri sm. speedometer.

contadino sm. countryman (pl. -men), peasant. ♦ **contadino** agg. rustic.

contado sm. countryside.

contagiare vt. to infect.

contagio sm. contagion (anche fig.), infection.

contagioso agg. contagious, infectious (anche fig.).

contagiri sm. revolution counter.

contagocce sm. dropper.

contaminare vt. 1. to pollute, to infect 2. (un testo letterario) to corrupt.

contaminazione sf. contamination (anche fig.), pollution.

contante agg. ready. ♦ **contante** sm. ready money || pagare in contanti, to pay cash.

contare vt. 1. to count, to number 2. (considerare) to consider 3. (proporsi) to think (v. irr.) of || conto di andare a Milano domani, I think of going to Milan tomorrow 4. (aspettarsi) to expect. ♦ **contare** vi. 1. (avere importanza) to count, to be important 2. (fare assegnamento) to rely on.

contatore sm. meter: — del gas, gas-meter; — dell'acqua, water-meter; — della luce, electric power-meter.

contatto sm. contact, touch: essere in —, to be in touch 2. (elettr.) contact.

conte sm. 1. Count 2. (in Gran Bretagna) Earl.

contea sf. 1. earldom 2. (divisione territoriale) county.

conteggiare vt. to count.

conteggio sm. computation.

contegno sm. 1. behaviour 2. (atteggiamento) attitude.

contegnoso agg. 1. dignified 2. (altero) stiff.

contemperare vt. to adapt.

contemplare vt. 1. to behold (v.

irr.), to admire 2. (*giur.*) to consider.

contemplativo *agg.* contemplative.

contemplatore *sm.* contemplator.

contemplazione *sf.* contemplation.

contempo (*nella loc. avv.*) nel —, in the meantime.

contemporaneamente *avv.* at the same time.

contemporaneità *sf.* contemporaneousness.

contemporàneo *agg.* e *sm.* contemporary.

contendente *agg.* contending, opposing. ◆ **contendente** *sm.* opponent, rival.

contèndere *vt.* to contend, to refuse. ◆ **contèndersi** *vr. rec.* to contend.

contenere *vt.* 1. to contain, to hold (*v. irr.*) 2. (*trattenere*) to repress. ◆ **contenersi** *vr.* 1. (*comportarsi*) to behave 2. (*dominarsi*) to contain oneself.

contenitore *sm.* container.

contentare *vt.* 1. to content. ◆ **contentarsi** *vr.* to be content (with).

contentezza *sf.* pleasure, joy.

contento *agg.* content, pleased.

contenuto *sm.* contents (*pl.*).

contenzioso *agg.* contentious.

conterìe *sf. pl.* glass beads.

conterràneo *sm.* fellow-countryman (*pl.* -men) || (*femm.*) fellow-countrywoman (*pl.* -women).

contesa *sf.* 1. contest 2. (*litigio*) quarrel.

contessa *sf.* countess.

contestàbile *agg.* questionable.

contestare *vt.* 1. to contest, to challenge, to deny 2. (*notificare*) to declare.

contestazione *sf.* dispute, objection: *sollevare contestazioni*, to raise objections.

contesto *sm.* context.

contiguità *sf.* contiguity.

contiguo *agg.* neighbouring.

continentale *agg.* continental.

continente *agg.* moderate. ◆ **continente** *sm.* continent.

continenza *sf.* continence.

contingentamento *sm.* allotment.

contingentare *vt.* to allot.

contingenza *sf.* 1. emergency 2. (*circostanza*) circumstance 3. (*fil.*) contingency.

continuamente *avv.* continuously.

continuare *vt.* e *vi.* 1. to go (*v.*

irr.) on (with) 2. (*riprendere*) to resume.

continuativo *agg.* continuative.

continuato *agg.* 1. (*ininterrotto*) continuous 2. (*che si ripete*) continual.

continuatore *sm.* continuator.

continuazione *sf.* continuation.

continuità *sf.* continuity.

continuo *agg.* 1. (*ininterrotto*) continuous 2. (*che si ripete*) continual.

conto *sm.* 1. (*anche comm.*) account: *fare i conti*, to make (*v. irr.*) up accounts 2. (*di albergo ecc.*) bill 3. (*assegnamento*) reliance: *far su*, to rely on 4. (*stima*) regard || *persona di poco —*, person of little account; *rendere — di*, to answer for; *rendersi —*, to realize; *mettersi per proprio —*, to set (*v. irr.*) for oneself.

contòrcere *vt.* to twist. ◆ **contòrcersi** *vr.* to twist.

contorcimento *sm.* twisting.

contornare *vt.* 1. to surround 2. (*con guarnizioni*) to trim.

contorno *sm.* 1. outline 2. (*orlo*) border 3. (*cuc.*) vegetables (*pl.*).

contorsione *sf.* contortion.

contorsionismo *sm.* writhing.

contorsionista *s.* contorsionist.

contorto *agg.* twisted.

contrabbandare *vt.* to smuggle.

contrabbandiere *sm.* smuggler.

contrabbando *sm.* smuggling.

contrabbassista *sm.* double-bass player.

contrabbasso *sm.* double-bass.

contraccambiare *vt.* to return.

contraccambio *sm.* return || *rendere il —*, to retaliate (upon).

contraccolpo *sm.* 1. counterblow 2. (*fig.*) reaction.

contraccusa *sf.* countercharge.

contrada *sf.* 1. quarter 2. (*paese*) country.

contraddanza *sf.* country-dance.

contraddire *vt.* to contradict. ◆ **contraddirsi** *vr.* to contradict oneself. ◆ **contraddirsi** *v. rec.* to contradict one another, each other.

contraddistinguere *vt.* to mark.

contraddittore *sm.* opposer.

contraddittorio *agg.* contradictory. ◆ **contraddittorio** *sm.* debate.

contraddizione *sf.* contradiction, discrepancy.

contraente *agg.* contracting. ◆

contraente *sm.* contractor.
contraèrea *sf.* anti-aircraft artillery.
contraèreo *agg.* anti-aircraft.
contraffare *vt.* to counterfeit.
contraffatto *agg.* counterfeit.
contraffattore *sm.* **1.** (*falsificatore*) counterfeiter **2.** (*imitatore*) imitator.
contrafforte *sm.* buttress.
contraggenio *sm.* dislike || *a* (*di*) —, unwillingly.
contràlbero *sm.* (*mecc.*) countershaft.
contralto *sm.* contralto.
contrammiraglio *sm.* rear-admiral.
contrappasso *sm.* retaliation.
contrappello *sm.* second roll-call.
contrappesare *vt.* to counterbalance.
contrappeso *sm.* counterbalance.
contrapporre *vt.* to oppose, to contrast || — *qc. a qu.*, to set (*v. irr.*) sthg. against so.
contrapposizione *sf.* contraposition.
contrapposto *agg.* opposite || *per* —, on the contrary. ♦ **contrapposto** *sm.* opposite.
contrappunto *sm.* counterpoint.
contrariamente *avv.* on the contrary || — *ad ogni aspettativa*, contrary to all expectation.
contrariare *vt.* **1.** to oppose **2.** (*irritare*) to annoy.
contrarietà *sf.* **1.** opposition **2.** (*avversità*) misfortune.
contrario *agg.* **1.** contrary, opposed **2.** (*nocivo*) harmful **3.** (*riluttante*) unwilling || *al* —, on the contrary. ♦ **contrario** *sm.* contrary.
contrarre *vt.* to contract.
contrassegnare *vt.* to mark.
contrassegno *sm.* **1.** countersign **2.** (*segno*) mark **3.** (*distintivo*) badge.
contrastare *vi.* to be in contrast. ♦ **contrastare** *vt.* to oppose.
contrastato *agg.* opposed.
contrasto *sm.* **1.** contrast **2.** (*dissidio*) conflict.
contrattaccare *vt.* to counterattack.
contrattacco *sm.* counterattack.
contrattare *vt.* to negotiate: — *il prezzo*, to haggle about the price.
contrattazione *sf.* dealing, negotiation.
contrattempo *sm.* **1.** (*incidente*) mishap **2.** (*inconveniente*) inconvenience.

contràttile *agg.* contractile.
contratto *sm.* contract.
contratto *agg.* contracted.
contrattuale *agg.* contractual.
contravveleno *sm.* antidote.
contravvenire *vi.* to infringe.
contravventore *sm.* transgressor.
contravvenzione *sf.* **1.** violation **2.** (*multa*) fine.
contrazione *sf.* contraction.
contribuente *sm.* taxpayer.
contribuire *vi.* to contribute.
contributo *sm.* contribution.
contribuzione *sf.* contribution.
contristarsi *vr.* to grieve.
contrito *agg.* contrite.
contrizione *sf.* contrition.
contro *prep.* **1.** against **2.** (*in opposizione a*) contrary to || — *assegno*, cash on delivery.
controbàttere *vt.* (*confutare*) to disprove, to confute.
controbilanciare *vt.* to counterbalance.
controcampo *sm.* (*cine*) reverse shot.
controcorrente *sf.* counter-current. ♦ **controcorrente** *loc. avv.* against the stream.
controffensiva *sf.* counter-offensive.
controfigura *sf.* double.
controfirmare *vt.* to countersign.
controindicare *vt.* (*med.*) to contra-indicate.
controindicazione *sf.* (*med.*) contra-indication.
controllare *vt.* **1.** to control **2.** (*verificare*) to verify, to check **3.** (*ispezionare*) to inspect **4.** (*comm.*) to audit.
controllo *sm.* **1.** control **2.** (*verifica*) check, verification **3.** (*ispezione*) inspection **4.** (*comm.*) audit.
controllore *sm.* **1.** controller **2.** (*ferr.*) ticket-inspector.
controluce *avv.* against the light. ♦ **controluce** *sf.* counterlight.
contromarca *sf.* pass-out check (ticket).
controparte *sf.* counter-party.
contropartita *sf.* **1.** (*comm.*) counter-item **2.** (*compenso*) compensation.
contropelo *sm.* wrong way of the hair || *fare il* —, to shave against the lie of the hair.
controproducente *agg.* opposite effect.

controproposta sf. counter-proposal.

controprova sf. 1. countercheck 2. (giur.) counter-evidence.

contròrdine sm. counter-order: dare un —, to countermand an order.

controriforma sf. counter-reformation.

controrivoluzione sf. counter-revolution.

controsenso sm. self-contradiction, absurdity.

controspionaggio sm. counterespionage.

controstòmaco avv. reluctantly.

controvelaccio sm. (mar.) main royal.

controvento avv. against the wind.

controversia sf. controversy.

controverso agg. controversial.

controvertibile agg. controvertible.

controvoglia avv. unwillingly.

contumace agg. guilty of default.

contumacia sf. default.

contumaciale agg. (giur.) judgment by default.

contumelia sf. insult, abuse.

contundente agg. blunt: corpo —, blunt instrument.

conturbare vt. 1. to perturb 2. (eccitare) to thrill.

contusione sf. bruise.

contuso agg. bruised.

convalescente agg. e sm. convalescent.

convalescenza sf. convalescence.

convalidare vt. to ratify, to confirm.

convegno sm. meeting.

convenévole agg. convenient, proper. ♦ **convenévoli** sm. pl. compliments.

conveniente agg. 1. convenient (for) 2. (economicamente vantaggioso) profitable.

convenienza sf. 1. convenience 2. (vantaggio economico) profit 3. (buona creanza) propriety.

convenire vi. 1. to convene 2. (essere d'accordo) to agree 3. (essere utile) to be convenient.

convento sm. 1. convent 2. (di suore) nunnery.

conventuale agg. conventual.

convenuto agg. agreed upon. ♦ **convenuto** sm. 1. agreement 2. i convenuti, the persons present.

_venzionale agg. conventional.

convenzionare vt. to make (v. irr.) an agreement.

convenzione sf. convention.

convergente agg. convergent.

convergenza sf. convergence.

convèrgere vi. to converge.

conversare vi. to talk.

conversatore sm. talker.

conversazione sf. conversation, talk.

conversione sf. 1. (anche fig.) conversion 2. (mil.) wheel.

convertibile agg. convertible.

convertire vt. 1. (pol.; relig.) to convert 2. (mutare) to turn, to change. ♦ **convertirsi** vr. to be converted.

convessità sf. convexity.

convesso agg. convex.

convincere vt. to convince, to persuade.

convinto agg. convinced, persuaded.

convinzione sf. persuasion, firm belief.

convitato sm. guest.

convito sm. banquet.

convitto sm. boarding-school.

convivente agg. cohabiting.

convivenza sf. cohabitation, life in common.

convìvere vi. to live together.

convocare vt. to convene, to summon.

convocazione sf. convocation, summoning.

convogliare vt. 1. (scortare) to escort 2. (trasportare) to carry away 3. (indirizzare) to address.

convoglio sm. 1. (treno) train 2. (mil.; mar.) convoy.

convolare vi. to fly (v. irr.) together: — a giuste nozze, to get (v. irr.) married.

convulsione sf. convulsion.

convulso agg. convulsive.

cooperare vi. to co-operate, to collaborate.

cooperativa sf. 1. co-operative society 2. (di consumo) co-operative store.

cooperativo agg. co-operative.

cooperatore sm. co-operator.

cooperazione sf. co-operation, collaboration.

coordinamento sm. co-ordination.

coordinare vt. to co-ordinate.

coordinata sf. co-ordinate.

coordinativo agg. co-ordinative.

coordinato agg. co-ordinate.

coordinatore *agg.* co-ordinative. ♦ **coordinatore** *sm.* co-ordinator.

coordinazione *sf.* co-ordination.

coorte *sf.* 1. (*mil.*) cohort 2. (*folla*) crowd.

copale *sf.* 1. copal 2. (*pelle*) patent leather.

copeco *sm.* copeck.

coperchio *sm.* lid, cover (*anche mecc.*).

coperta *sf.* 1. blanket: — *da viaggio,* rug; — *scozzese,* plaid 2. (*mar.*) deck.

copertina *sf.* cover: — *di libro,* book-cover.

coperto *agg.* 1. (*riparato*) covered, sheltered ‖ — *di ferro,* iron-clad; *mettere al* —, to shelter from 2. (*di cielo*) overcast 3. (*nascosto*) hidden. ♦ **coperto** *sm.* cover.

copertone *sm.* tyre.

copertura *sf.* 1. covering 2. (*di mobili*) cover.

copia *sf.* 1. copy 2. (*foto*) print.

copiare *vt.* to copy.

copiativo *agg. matita copiativa,* copying pencil.

copiatura *sf.* copying.

copione *sm.* script.

copiosamente *avv.* plentifully.

copioso *agg.* plentiful.

copista *sm.* copyist.

coppa *sf.* 1. cup 2. (*auto*) pan.

coppella *sf.* (*metal.*) cupel.

coppellare *vt.* (*metal.*) to cupel.

coppia *sf.* 1. (*di persone e cose*) couple 2. (*di animali*) pair ‖ *una* — *di buoi,* a yoke.

copricapo *sm.* hat.

coprifuoco *sm.* curfew.

copriletto *sm.* coverlet.

coprire *vt.* 1. to cover 2. (*nascondere*) to conceal 3. (*coprire un suono*) to drown.

copto *agg.* coptic. ♦ **copto** *sm.* copt.

copulativo *agg.* (*gramm.*) copulative.

copulazione *sf.* copulation.

coraggio *sm.* 1. courage, bravery, heart 2. (*sfrontatezza*) impudence.

coraggiosamente *avv.* bravely.

coraggioso *agg.* brave, bold.

corale *agg.* choral.

corallifero *agg.* coralliferous.

corallo *sm.* coral.

corazza *sf.* 1. cuirass 2. (*bot.; zool.*) armour, carapace.

corazzare *vt.* 1. to armour 2. (*fig.*) to strengthen. ♦ **corazzarsi** *vr.* to harden oneself.

corazzata *sf.* (*mar.*) battleship.

corazziere *sm.* cuirassier.

corbelleria *sf.* 1. foolish action 2. (*sciocchezza*) nonsense.

corda *sf.* 1. rope 2. (*mus.*) string.

cordaio *sm.* 1. (*chi fabbrica corde*) rope-maker 2. (*chi vende corde*) rope-seller.

cordame *sm.* cordage.

cordata *sf.* rope: *in* —, on the rope.

cordiale *agg.* cordial, hearty. ♦ **cordiale** *sm.* (*liquore*) cordial.

cordialità *sf.* cordiality.

cordialmente *avv.* cordially.

cordicella *sf.* string.

cordigliera *sf.* cordillera.

cordite *sf.* cordite.

cordoglio *sm.* deep sorrow.

cordone *sm.* 1. cord 2. (*mil.*) cordon.

coreano *agg. e sm.* Korean.

coreografia *sf.* choreography.

coreografico *agg.* 1. choreographic 2. (*fig.*) spectacular.

coreografo *sm.* choreographer.

coriaceo *agg.* coriaceous, tough.

coriandolo *sm.* confetti (*pl.*).

coricare *vt.* to lay (*v. irr.*) down. ♦ **coricarsi** *vr.* to lie (*v. irr.*) down.

corifeo *sm.* coryphaeus (*pl. -aei*).

corinzio *agg. e sm.* Corinthian.

corista *sm.* chorus-singer.

cormorano *sm.* (*zool.*) cormorant.

cornacchia *sf.* rook, crow.

cornamusa *sf.* bagpipe.

cornata *sf.* butt.

cornea *sf.* cornea.

cornetta *sf.* cornet.

cornice *sf.* frame.

cornicione *sm.* 1. (*arch.*) cornice 2. (*di finestre, porte*) label 3. (*di gronda*) eaves (*pl.*).

cornificare *vt.* 1. (*di moglie*) to cuckold 2. (*di marito*) to be unfaithful to.

corno *sm.* horn ‖ (*inter.*) *un* —, not at all.

cornuto *agg.* horned. ♦ **cornuto** *sm.* (*fig.*) cuckold.

coro *sm.* 1. chorus 2. (*eccl.*) choir.

corolla *sf.* corolla.

corollario *sm.* corollary.

corona *sf.* 1. crown: — *del rosario,* rosary crown; — *del dente,* crown 2. (*mecc.*) rim 3. (*relig.*) (*tonsura*) tonsure.

coronamento *sm.* 1. crowning 2. (*completamento*) fulfilment.

coronare *vt.* to crown (*anche fig.*).

coronario *agg.* coronary.

corpo *sm.* 1. body || *a — morto*, desperately; *combattere a — a —*, to fight (*v. irr.*) hand to hand; *passare sul — di qu.*, to pass over so. 2. (*cadavere*) corpse 3. (*collettività*) corps || *— insegnante*, teaching staff.

corporale *agg.* corporal.

corporativismo *sm.* (*econ.*) corporative system.

corporativo *agg.* (*econ.*) corporative.

corporatura *sf.* build, size.

corporazione *sf.* corporation.

corpòreo *agg.* corporeal.

corpulento *agg.* corpulent, stout.

corpulenza *sf.* stoutness.

corpuscolare *agg.* corpuscular.

corpùscolo *sm.* corpuscle.

corredare *vt.* 1. to equip 2. (*accompagnare*) to accompany.

corredino *sm.* baby's outfit.

corredo *sm.* 1. outfit 2. (*di sposa*) trousseau 3. (*bagaglio*) wealth, store: *— di cultura*, store of knowledge.

corrèggere *vt.* 1. to correct 2. (*di bevande*) to lace. ♦ corrèggersi *vr.* to amend, to correct oneself.

correggia *sf.* leather strap.

correlativo *agg.* correlative.

correlazione *sf.* correlation.

corrente[1] *agg.* 1. (*che scorre*) running 2. (*circolante*) current 3. (*comm.*) inst. (*abbrev. di instant*) || *conto —*, current account 4. (*andante*) common.

corrente[2] *sf.* 1. current (*anche fig.*), stream 2. (*di aria*) draught.

correntemente *avv.* fluently.

còrrere *vi.* 1. to run (*v. irr.*): *— dietro a qu.*, to run after; *— a gambe levate*, to run as hard as one can || *lasciar —*, to take (*v. irr.*) no notice of sthg. 2. (*di tempo*) to pass 3. (*di voci*) to be abroad.

corresponsàbile *agg.* jointly responsible.

corresponsione *sf.* payment.

correttezza *sf.* 1. correctness 2. (*onestà*) honesty 3. (*decoro, educazione*) propriety, politeness.

correttivo *agg.* e *sm.* corrective.

corretto *agg.* 1. correct, exact 2. (*irreprensibile*) faultless 3. (*di bevanda*) laced.

correttore *sm.* corrector || *— di bozze*, proof-reader.

correzionale *agg.* correctional.

correzione *sf.* 1. correction || *— di bozze*, proof-reading; *casa di —*, house of correction.

corridoio *sm.* 1. passage 2. (*di treno*) corridor.

corridore *sm.* 1. runner 2. (*sport*) racer.

corriera *sf.* coach.

corriere *sm.* 1. messenger 2. (*chi trasporta merci*) carrier 3. (*posta*) mail.

corrimano *sm.* handrail.

corrispettivo *agg.* correlative. ♦ corrispettivo *sm.* 1. equivalent 2. (*compenso*) compensation.

corrispondente *agg.* e *sm.* correspondent.

corrispondenza *sf.* correspondence.

corrispòndere *vi.* 1. to correspond (with) 2. (*ricambiare sentimenti ecc.*) to return. ♦ corrispòndere *vt.* to pay.

corrisposto *agg.* 1. (*contraccambiato*) returned 2. (*pagato*) paid.

corroborante *agg.* e *sm.* corroborant.

corroborare *vt.* to strengthen.

corròdere *vt.* to corrode.

corròmpere *vt.* 1. to corrupt (*anche fig.*), to pollute 2. (*con denaro*) to bribe.

corrosione *sf.* corrosion.

corrosivo *agg.* e *sm.* corrosive.

corrucciarsi *vr.* to get (*v. irr.*) angry.

corrucciato *agg.* angry, worried.

corruccio *sm.* anger, worry.

corrugamento *sm.* corrugation: *— della fronte*, wrinkling of the forehead.

corrugare *vt.* to wrinkle.

corruttibile *agg.* corruptible.

corruttore *agg.* corrupting. ♦ corruttore *sm.* 1. corrupter 2. (*con denaro*) briber.

corruzione *sf.* 1. corruption 2. (*con denaro*) bribery.

corsa *sf.* 1. (*sport*) race 3. (*su veicolo pubblico*) trip || *prezzo della —*, fare; (*ferr.*) *perdere la —*, to miss the train.

corsaro *sm.* corsair.

corsetto *sm.* corset.

corsia *sf.* 1. passage 2. (*di ospedale*) ward 3. (*di strada*) lane.

corsiero sm. steed.
corsivo agg. cursive. ♦ **corsivo** sm. (tip.) italics (pl.).
corso sm. 1. course (anche fig.) 2. (di acque) water-course.
corte sf. 1. court 2. (cortile) courtyard 3. (corteggiamento) courtship.
corteccia sf. 1. bark 2. (anat.) cortex.
corteggiare vt. 1. to woo 2. (adulare) to flatter.
corteggiatore sm. suitor, lover.
corteo sm. train, procession: — funebre, funeral train.
cortese agg. kind.
cortesia sf. 1. kindness, politeness 2. (favore) favour || per —, please.
cortigiano sm. 1. courtier 2. (adulatore) flatterer.
cortile sm. courtyard || animali da —, poultry.
cortina sf. curtain: — di ferro (pol.), iron curtain.
cortisone sm. cortisone.
corto agg. short: a — di, short of.
cortocircùito sm. short circuit.
cortometraggio sm. short (film).
corvetta sf. (mar.) corvette.
corvino agg. 1. corvine 2. (nero) raven(-black).
corvo sm. raven.
cosa sf. 1. thing 2. (faccenda) matter || nessuna —, nothing; ogni —, everything; che —?, what?.
cosacco agg. e sm. Cossack.
coscia sf. 1. thigh 2. (cuc.) leg.
cosciente agg. 1. conscious 2. (conscio) aware.
coscienza sf. 1. conscience 2. (consapevolezza) consciousness.
coscienziosamente avv. conscientiously.
coscienzioso agg. conscientious.
cosciotto sm. leg: — di manzo, leg of beef.
coscritto sm. recruit.
coscrizione sf. conscription.
cosecante sf. cosecant.
coseno sm. (mat.) cosine.
così avv. so: e — via, and so on; — come, — pure, as well as; — ... come, — ... quanto, as ... as; — da, so ... as: non è — sciocco da farlo, he is not so foolish as to do that.
cosicché cong. so that.
cosiddetto agg. so-called.
cosiffatto agg. such, similar.

cosmesi sf. beauty culture.
cosmètico agg. e sm. cosmetic.
còsmico agg. cosmic.
cosmo sm. cosmos.
cosmogonìa sf. cosmogony.
cosmografia sf. cosmography.
cosmògrafo sm. cosmographer.
cosmologìa sf. cosmology.
cosmonàuta s. astronaut.
cosmonàutica sf. astronautics.
cosmopolita agg. e sm. cosmopolitan.
cosmopolitismo sm. cosmopolitanism.
coso sm. (fam.) 1. (cosa) thing 2. (individuo) fellow.
cospàrgere vt. 1. to strew (v. irr.) 2. (sale, zucchero ecc.) to sprinkle.
cospetto sm. presence: al — di, in the presence of.
cospicuità sf. conspicuousness.
cospìcuo agg. 1. (visibile) conspicuous 2. (notevole) remarkable.
cospirare vi. to plot.
cospiratore sm. plotter.
cospirazione sf. plot.
costa sf. 1. coast, shore 2. (venatura) rib 3. (di monte) side 4. (di libro) back.
costà avv. there.
costaggiù avv. down there.
costale agg. costal.
costante agg. steady. ♦ **costante** sf. constant.
costanza sf. 1. firmness 2. (perseveranza) perseverance || con —, steadily.
costare vi. to cost (v. irr.).
costassù avv. up there.
costata sf. chop.
costatare vt. 1. (accertare) to ascertain 2. (notare) to notice.
costatazione sf. 1. ascertainment 2. (osservazione) remark.
costato sm. chest.
costeggiare vt. 1. to follow the coast of 2. (per terra) to skirt. ♦ **costeggiare** vi. to coast along.
costei pron. 1. (sogg.) she 2. (compl.) her 3. this woman, that woman.
costellare vt. to scatter.
costellazione sf. constellation.
costernare vt. to dismay. ♦ **costernarsi** vr. to be dismayed (at).
costernazione sf. dismay.
costì avv. there.
costiera sf. stretch of coast.
costiero agg. coastal || nave costiera, coaster.

costipare *vt.* 1. (*un terreno*) to tamp 2. (*ammassare*) to amass. ♦ **costiparsi** *vr.* 1. (*raffreddarsi*) to catch (*v. irr.*) a cold 2. (*di intestino*) to become (*v. irr.*) constipated.

costipato *agg.* essere —, to have a cold.

costipazione *sf.* 1. (*raffreddore*) cold 2. (*intestinale*) constipation 3. (*di terreno*) tamping.

costituente *agg.* constituent.

costituire *vt.* 1. to constitute, to form 2. (*nominare*) to appoint. ♦ **costituirsi** *vr.* (*consegnarsi*) to give (*v. irr.*) oneself up.

costituito *agg.* constituted.

costitutivo *agg.* constitutive.

costituto *sm.* (*giur.*) interrogation of the accused.

costituzionale *agg.* constitutional.

costituzionalismo *sm.* constitutionalism.

costituzionalità *sf.* constitutionality.

costituzione *sf.* 1. establishment 2. (*pol.; med.*) constitution.

costo *sm.* cost: ad ogni —, at all cost; a nessun —, in no case.

còstola *sf.* rib ‖ stare alle costole, to watch over.

costoletta *sf.* cutlet.

costone *sm.* side.

costoro *pron.* 1. (*sogg.*) they 2. (*compl.*) them 3. these people, those people.

costoso *agg.* expensive, dear.

costringere *vt.* 1. (*stringere*) to press 2. (*obbligare*) to compel.

costrizione *sf.* 1. (*restringimento*) constriction 2. (*obbligo*) compulsion.

costruire *vt.* to build (*v. irr.*).

costruttivo *agg.* constructive.

costruttore *agg.* building. ♦ **costruttore** *sm.* builder.

costruzione *sf.* construction, building.

costui *pron.* 1. (*sogg.*) he 2. (*compl.*) him 3. this man, that man.

costumato *agg.* 1. (*virtuoso*) virtuous 2. (*educato*) polite.

costume *sm.* 1. (*usanza*) custom 2. (*personale*) habit 3. (*condotta*) morals (*pl.*) 4. (*vestito*) costume.

costumista *sm.* costume-designer.

cotangente *sf.* (*mat.*) cotangent.

cotenna *sf.* 1. pigskin 2. (*del cranio*) scalp 3. (*del lardo*) rind.

còtica *sf.* V. cotenna.

cotogna *sf.* quince.

cotognata *sf.* quince jam.

cotoletta *sf.* cutlet.

cotone *sm.* cotton.

cotoniere *sm.* cotton-spinner.

cotoniero *agg.* cotton.

cotonificio *sm.* cotton-mill.

cotonina *sf.* calico.

cotta¹ *sf.* (*eccl.*) surplice.

cotta² *sf.* 1. (*cottura*) cooking 2. (*infornata*) batch 3. (*fam.*) prendere una — per, to have a crush on.

cottimista *sm.* pieceworker.

còttimo *sm.* piecework: lavorare a —, to work by the job; lavoro a —, job-work; contratto a —, job contract.

cotto *sm.* brickwork.

cottura *sf.* 1. cooking 2. (*in forno*) baking.

coturno *sm.* cothurnus (*pl.* -ni).

cova *sf.* 1. (*il covare*) brooding 2. (*nido*) nest.

covare *vt.* 1. to brood 2. (*fig.*) to brood over 3. (*di fuoco; passioni*) to smoulder 4. (*di malattia*) to be latent.

covata *sf.* brood.

covo *sm.* den.

covone *sm.* sheaf (*pl.* sheaves).

cozza *sf.* mussel.

cozzare *vi.* 1. to strike (*v. irr.*) 2. (*venire in collisione*) to collide.

cozzo *sm.* 1. clash, collision 2. (*conflitto*) conflict.

crampo *sm.* cramp.

cranio *sm.* skull.

crasso *agg.* crass, gross: ignoranza crassa, gross ignorance.

cratere *sm.* crater.

cràuti *sm. pl.* sauerkraut (*sing.*).

cravatta *sf.* neck-tie.

creanza *sf.* politeness.

creare *vt.* 1. to create 2. (*causare*) to cause 3. (*nominare*) to appoint 4. (*costituire*) to form.

creativo *agg.* creative.

creato *sm.* creation.

creatore *agg.* creating. ♦ **creatore** *sm.* creator.

creatura *sf.* creature.

creazione *sf.* creation.

credente *sm.* believer.

credenza¹ *sf.* belief.

credenza² *sf.* (*buffet*) sideboard.

credenziale *agg.* credential: lettera —, credential.

crédere vt. e vi. **1.** (pensare) to think (v irr.) **2.** (prestar fede) to believe. ♦ **crédersi** vr. to think (v. irr.) oneself.

credìbile agg. **1.** credible **2.** (di persona) trustworthy.

credibilità sf. credibility.

creditizio agg. credit.

crédito sm. **1.** (comm.) credit: a —, on credit **2.** (stima) esteem.

creditore sm. creditor.

credo sm. creed.

credulità sf. credulity.

credulone agg. credulous.

crema sf. cream.

cremaglièra sf. rack: ferrovia a —, rack-railway.

cremare vt. to cremate.

crematorio agg. crematory: forno —, crematory.

cremazione sf. cremation.

cremerìa sf. creamery.

crèmisi agg. e sm. crimson.

crèolo agg. e sm. creole.

crepa sf. crack.

crepaccio sm. crevasse.

crepacuore sm. heart-break: morire di —, to die of a broken heart.

crepapelle (nella loc. avv.) ridere a —, to roar with laughter; mangiare a —, to eat to excess.

crepare vi. to crack.

crepella sf. crepoline.

crepitare vi. to crackle.

crepitìo sm. crackle.

crepuscolare agg. crepuscular.

crepùscolo sm. twilight.

crescente agg. growing.

crescenza sf. growth.

créscere vi. **1.** to grow (v. irr.) **2.** (aumentare) to increase.

crescione sm. (bot.) water-cress.

créscita sf. **1.** growth **2.** (aumento) increase.

crèsima sf. confirmation.

cresimare vt. to confirm.

creso sm. Croesus.

crespo agg. crisp.

cresta sf. **1.** crest **2.** (di gallo) comb.

crestina sf. maid-servant's cap.

creta sf. clay.

cretinerìa sf. **1.** idiocy **2.** (azione) foolish action **3.** (detto) nonsense.

cretinismo sm. idiocy.

cretino agg. e sm. idiot.

cricca sf. gang.

cricco sm. jack.

criminale agg. e sm. criminal.

criminalista s. **1.** (avvocato) criminal lawyer **2.** (studioso) criminologist.

criminalità sf. criminality.

crimine sm. crime.

criminologìa sf. criminology.

criminosità sf. criminality.

criminoso agg. criminal.

crine sm. horse-hair.

crinièra sf. mane.

crinolina sf. crinoline.

criolite sf. cryolite.

cripta sf. crypt.

crisantemo sm. chrysanthemum.

crisàlide sf. chrysalid.

crisi sf. **1.** crisis (pl. -ses) **2.** (med.) fit.

crisma sm. **1.** (eccl.) chrism **2.** (fig.) approval || con tutti i crismi, approved, praised.

cristallerìa sf. **1.** crystal-ware **2.** (fabbrica) crystal manufactory.

cristallièra sf. glass case.

cristallino agg. e sm. crystalline.

cristallizzare vt. e vi., **cristallizzarsi** vr. to crystallize.

cristallizzazione sf. crystallization.

cristallo sm. **1.** crystal **2.** (lastra di vetro) plate glass.

cristallografìa sf. crystallography.

cristianésimo sm. Christianity.

cristiania sm. (sport) Christiania.

cristianità sf. **1.** (i cristiani) Christendom **2.** (cristianesimo) Christianity.

cristiano agg. e sm. Christian.

criterio sm. **1.** principle **2.** opinion **3.** (buon senso) sense.

crìtica sf. **1.** criticism **2.** (saggio) critical essay **3.** (i critici) the critics (pl.).

criticamente avv. critically.

criticare vt. **1.** to criticize **2.** (biasimare) to blame.

criticismo sm. **1.** criticism **2.** (stor.) critical philosophy.

crìtico agg. critical. ♦ **critico** sm. critic.

criticone sm. fault-finder.

crittògama sf. (bot.) cryptogam.

crittografìa sf. cryptography.

crittogramma sm. cryptogram.

crivellare vt. to riddle.

crivellatura sf. riddling.

crivello sm. riddle.

croato agg. e sm. Croatian.

croccante agg. crisp. ♦ **croccante** sm. almond sweetmeat.

crocchetta *sf.* croquette.

crocchia *sf.* bun.

crocchio *sm.* group.

croce *sf.* cross.

crocerossina *sf.* Red Cross nurse.

crociata *sf.* crusade.

crociata *sf.* cross-road.

crocicchio *sm.* cross-road.

crociera *sf.* 1. cruise 2. *(arch.)* cross-vault.

crocifiggere *vt.* to crucify.

crocifissione *sf.* crucifixion.

crocifisso *sm.* crucifix.

croco *sm.* *(bot.)* crocus.

crogiuolo *sm.* crucible.

crollare *vi.* to fall *(v. irr.)* down.

crollo *sm.* 1. breakdown 2. *(caduta)* falling down.

croma *sf.* *(mus.)* quaver.

cromare *vt.* to chromium-plate.

cromàtico *agg.* chromatic.

cromatismo *sm.* chromatism.

cromatografia *sf.* chromatography.

cromatura *sf.* chromium plating.

cromo *sm.* chromium.

cromolitografia *sf.* chromolithography.

cromosomo *sm.* chromosome.

crònaca *sf.* 1. chronicle 2. *(di giornale)* news.

crònico *agg.* chronic. ♦ **crònico** *sm.* chronic invalid.

cronista *sm.* reporter.

cronistoria *sf.* chronicle.

cronologia *sf.* chronology.

cronològico *agg.* chronological.

cronometraggio *sm.* time-study.

cronometrare *vt.* to time.

cronometria *sf.* timing.

cronòmetro *sm.* stop watch.

crosta *sf.* 1. crust 2. *(tec.)* coating.

crostàcei *sm. pl.* Crustacea.

crostata *sf.* *(cuc.)* tart.

cròtalo *sm.* rattlesnake.

crucciare *vt.*, **crucciarsi** *vr.* to worry.

cruciale *agg.* crucial.

cruciverba *sm.* cross-word puzzle.

crudele *agg.* cruel.

crudeltà *sf.* cruelty.

crudezza *sf.* 1. *(di stagione)* harshness 2. *(di parole)* coarseness 3. *(di cibo)* rawness.

crudo *agg.* 1. raw 2. *(poco cotto)* underdone 3. *(aspro, rigido)* harsh 4. *(rozzo)* coarse.

cruento *agg.* bloody.

crumiro *sm.* blackleg.

cruna *sf.* needle's eye.

crusca *sf.* bran.

cruscotto *sm.* dashboard.

cubaggio *sm.* cubage.

cubano *agg.* e *sm.* Cuban.

cubatura *sf.* cubature.

cubetto *sm.* — *di ghiaccio*, ice cube.

cùbico *agg.* cubic.

cubismo *sm.* cubism.

cubitale *agg.* a caratteri cubitali, in very large letters.

cùbito *sm.* 1. *(misura)* cubit 2. *(avambraccio)* forearm.

cubo *sm.* cube.

cuccagna *sf.* abundance ‖ *albero della* —, greasy pole.

cuccetta *sf.* berth.

cucchiaiata *sf.* spoonful.

cucchiaino *sm.* 1. tea-spoon, coffee-spoon 2. *(il contenuto)* tea-spoonful.

cucchiaio *sm.* spoon.

cuccia *sf.* dog-house.

cùcciolo *sm.* puppy.

cùccuma *sf.* kettle.

cucina *sf.* 1. kitchen 2. *(modo di cucinare)* cooking 3. *(culinaria)* cookery 4. *(stufa)* stove.

cucinare *vt.* to cook.

cuciniere *sm.* man-cook.

cucire *vt.* 1. to sew *(v. irr.)* 2. *(med.)* to stitch.

cucito *sm.* needlework.

cucitrice *sf.* 1. seamstress 2. *(macchinetta)* stapler.

cucitura *sf.* 1. seam 2. *(di fogli)* stapling.

cucù *sm.* *(zool.)* cuckoo.

cucùrbita *sf.* gourd.

cuffia *sf.* 1. cap. 2. *(radio)* headphone.

cugina *sf.* cousin.

cugino *sm.* cousin.

cui *pron. rel.* 1. *(di possesso)* whose; *(di possesso, solo per animali e cose)* of which: *l'uomo la — casa*, the man whose house; *il libro le — pagine*, the book the pages of which 2. *(altri casi, per persone)* whom; *(altri casi, per animali e cose)* which: *l'uomo con — parlai*, the man to whom I spoke; *il libro di — parlai*, the book about which I spoke ‖ *in — (dove)*, where; *in — (quando)* when.

culaccio *sm.* rump.

culatta *sf.* breech.

culinaria *sf.* cookery.

culinario *agg.* culinary.

culla *sf.* cradle.

cullare *vt.* to rock, to lull (*anche fig.*).

culminante *agg.* culminant: *momento* —, climax.

culminare *vi.* to culminate.

culmine *sm.* 1. summit 2. (*fig.*) apex.

culo *sm.* bottom; (*volg.*) ass.

culto *sm.* 1. cult 2. (*religione*) religion 3. (*adorazione*) worship.

cultore *sm.* lover.

cultura *sf.* culture.

culturale *agg.* cultural.

cumulare *vt.* to heap up.

cumulativo *agg.* cumulative.

cumulatore *sm.* hoarder.

cumulazione *sf.* hoarding.

cùmulo *sm.* 1. heap 2. (*nube*) cumulus (*pl.* -li).

cuna *sf.* cradle.

cuneiforme *agg.* cuneiform, wedge--shaped.

cùneo *sm.* wedge.

cunetta *sf.* 1. (*stradale*) road bump 2. (*scolo*) gutter.

cunìcolo *sm.* underground passage, shaft.

cuòcere *vt.* 1. to cook 2. (*in forno, fornace*) to bake.

cuoco *sm.* cook.

cuoiame *sm.* leather and hides.

cuoio *sm.* leather || — *capelluto*, scalp.

cuore *sm.* heart.

cupezza *sf.* 1. darkness 2. (*tristezza*) gloom.

cupidigia *sf.* cupidity, greed.

cùpido *agg.* greedy.

cupo *agg.* 1. dark 2. (*triste*) gloomy 3. (*profondo*) deep.

cùpola *sf.* dome.

cùpreo *agg.* cupreous.

cùprico *agg.* cupric.

cura *sf.* 1. care 2. (*med.*) treatment || *casa di* —, nursing-home.

curàbile *agg.* curable.

curante *agg. medico* —, attending physician.

curare *vt.* 1. (*aver cura di*) to take (*v. irr.*) care of 2. (*med.*) to treat 3. (*una pubblicazione*) to edit. ◆ **curarsi** *vr.* (*seguire una cura*) to follow a treatment.

curaro *sm.* curare.

curato *sm.* vicar.

curatore *sm.* trustee.

curdo *agg.* Kurdish. ◆ **curdo** *sm.* Kurd.

curia *sf.* 1. (*eccl.*) see 2. (*giur.*) court of justice.

curie *sm.* curie.

curiosare *vi.* to pry.

curiosità *sf.* 1. curiosity 2. (*stranezza*) oddity.

curioso *agg.* curious.

currìculum *sm.* curriculum (*pl.* -la).

cursore *sm.* 1. messenger 2. (*mecc.*) slider.

curva *sf.* bend.

curvare *vt.* to bend (*v. irr.*). ◆ **curvarsi** *vr.* 1. to bend (*v. irr.*) 2. (*inclinarsi*) to bow.

curvatura *sf.* 1. bending 2. (*arch.*) sweep.

curvilìneo *agg.* curvilinear.

curvo *agg.* bent.

cuscinetto *sm.* small cushion || — *a sfera*, ball bearing.

cuscino *sm.* 1. cushion 2. (*guanciale*) pillow 3. (*mecc.*) pillow.

custode *sm.* keeper.

custodia *sf.* 1. care 2. (*tutela*) guardianship 3. (*astuccio*) case.

custodire *vt.* 1. to keep (*v. irr.*) 2. (*aver cura di*) to look after.

cutàneo *agg.* skin: *malattia cutanea*, skin disease.

cute *sf.* skin.

D

da *prep.* 1. (*provenienza*) from: *vengo* — *Milano*, I come from Milan 2. (*moto a luogo*) to: *andremo* — *loro*, we shall go to their house 3. (*stato in luogo*) at: *vivo* — *mia zia*, I live at my aunt's 4. (*moto per luogo*) through: *passai* — *Roma*, I passed through Rome 5. (*tempo, durata*) for: *siamo qui* — *due mesi*, we have been here for two months; (*a partire da*) since: *lo conosco dal 1955*, I have known him since 1955 6. (*agente*) by: *fu aiutato* — *sua sorella*, he was helped by his sister 7. (*come*) like: *si comportano* — *bambini*, they are behaving like children || *fare* —, to act as.

dabbasso *avv.* 1. below, down below 2. (*al piano inferiore*) downstairs.

dabbenàggine sf. ingenuousness.
dabbene agg. honest.
daccapo avv. over again, from the beginning.
dacché cong. since.
dadaismo sm. dadaism.
dado sm. 1. die (pl. dice) 2. (cuc.) cube 3. (mecc.) nut.
daffare sm. work || darsi —, to be on the go.
dagherrotipìa sf. daguerreotypy.
dagherròtipo sm. daguerreotype.
dàgli, dài inter. go on.
dàino sm. fallow-deer (invariato al pl.).
dàlia sf. dahlia.
daltònico agg. colour-blind.
daltonismo sm. colour-blindness.
d'altronde avv. on the other hand.
dama sf. 1. lady of rank 2. (al ballo) partner 3. (giuoco) draughts (pl.).
damasco sm. damask.
damerino sm. dandy.
damiere sm. draughtboard.
damigella sf. maid of honour.
damigiana sf. demijohn.
danaroso agg. wealthy.
danese agg. Danish. ♦ **danese** sm. Dane.
dannare vt. to damn || far —, to drive (v. irr.) so. mad. ♦ **dannarsi** 1. to be damned 2. (fig.) to strive (v. irr.) hard.
dannato agg. damned. ♦ **dannato** sm. damned soul.
dannazione sf. damnation: —!, damn!
danneggiamento sm. damage.
danneggiare vt. 1. to damage 2. (di persone) to injure.
danno sm. 1. damage 2. (a persona) injury || recare — a qu., to do (v. irr.) so. harm.
dannoso agg. harmful.
dantesco agg. Dantesque.
danza sf. dance.
danzante agg. dancing: trattenimento —, dance.
danzare vi. e vi. to dance.
danzatore sm. dancer.
dappertutto avv. everywhere.
dappocàggine sf. ineptitude.
dappoco agg. inept.
dappresso avv. near-by.
dapprima avv. at first.
dardeggiare vt. e vi. to dart.
dardo sm. dart.
dare sm. debit. ♦ **dare** vt. to give

(v. irr.): — origine, luogo a qc., to give rise; — a bere a qu. che, to give so. to believe that; — ad intendere, to give to understand; — a pensare, to give food for thought || — atto di qc., to acknowledge; può darsi, maybe; — àla testa, to go (v. irr.) to one's head; — nell'occhio, to stand (v. irr.) out. ♦ **darsi** vr. to devote oneself || — al bere, to take (v. irr.) to drink; — ammalato, to pretend to be ill; — da fare, to busy oneself; darsela a gambe, to take (v. irr.) to one's heels.
dàrsena sf. wet dock.
darvinismo sm. Darwinism.
data sf. date: in — d'oggi, under to-day's date.
datare vt. to date.
dativo agg. dative.
dato agg. 1. given 2. (stabilito) stated 3. (dedito) addicted || — e non concesso, supposing that. ♦ **dato** sm. datum (pl. -ta).
dato che cong. since, as.
datore sm. giver || — di lavoro, employer.
dàttero sm. 1. date 2. (albero) date-palm.
dattilografare vt. to typewrite.
dattilografia sf. typewriting.
dattilògrafo sm. typist.
dattiloscritto agg. typewritten.
dattiloscritto sm. typescript.
dattorno avv. round, about.
davanti avv. before, in front. ♦ **davanti** sm. front. ♦ **davanti** agg. front. ♦ **davanti a** (loc. prep.) before.
davantino sm. ruffle.
davanzale sm. window-sill.
davvero avv. really, indeed.
daziario agg. toll.
daziere sm. exciseman (pl. -men).
dazio sm. 1. toll, duty 2. (ufficio daziario) toll-house 3. (di consumo) excise.
dea sf. goddess.
deambulare vi. to walk about.
deambulatorio agg. e sm. deambulatory.
deambulazione sf. deambulation.
debellare vt. 1. to defeat 2. (fig.) to overcome (v. irr.).
debilitante agg. weakening.
debilitare vt. to weaken.
debilitazione debilitation.

debitamente *avv.* duly.

débito *agg.* due, proper. ♦ **débito** *sm.* debt: *fare un —*, to run (*v. irr.*) into debt.

debitore *sm.* debtor.

débole *agg.* weak.

debolezza *sf.* weakness.

debosciato *agg.* debauched.

debuttante *sm.* **1.** novice **2.** (*di ragazza in società*) debutante.

debuttare *vi.* **1.** to make (*v. irr.*) one's debut **2.** (*di ragazza in società*) to come (*v. irr.*) out.

debutto *sm.* **1.** debut **2.** (*di ragazza in società*) coming out.

dècade *sf.* **1.** (*di giorni*) ten days **2.** (*di anni*) ten years.

decadente *agg.* **1.** decaying **2.** (*lett.*) decadent.

decadenza *sf.* decay, decline.

decadere *vi.* to decline || *— da un diritto*, to lose (*v. irr.*) a right.

decaduto *agg.* impoverished.

decaedro *sm.* decahedron.

decagrammo *sm.* decagram.

decalcare *vt.* to transfer.

decalcificare *vt.* to decalcify.

decàlitro *sm.* decalitre.

decàlogo *sm.* decalogue.

decàmetro *sm.* decametre.

decampare *vi.* **1.** to decamp **2.** (*fig.*) to recede.

decano *sm.* **1.** senior **2.** (*eccl.*) dean.

decantare *vt.* **1.** to extol **2.** (*chim.*) to decant.

decantazione *sf.* (*chim.*) decantation.

decapitare *vt.* to behead.

decappottàbile *agg.* (*auto*) convertible.

decasillabo *agg.* decasyllabic. ♦ **decasillabo** *sm.* decasyllable.

decatissaggio *sm.* decatizing.

decèdere *vi.* to die.

decelerare *vt.* to decelerate.

decennale *agg.* decennial.

decenne *agg.* **1.** ten years old (*predicativo*) **2.** ten-year-old (*attributivo*).

decennio *sm.* ten-year period.

decente *agg.* decent, proper.

decesso *sm.* death.

decìdere *vt.* to decide. ♦ **decìdersi** *vr.* to make (*v. irr.*) up one's

mind.

decifrare *vt.* **1.** to decipher **2.** (*fam.*) to make (*v. irr.*) out.

decifrazione *sf.* deciphering.

decigrammo *sm.* decigram.

decilitro *sm.* decilitre.

decimale *agg.* e *sm.* decimal.

decimare *vt.* to decimate.

decimazione *sf.* decimation.

decimetro *sm.* decimetre.

dècimo *agg.* tenth.

decina *sf.* ten, half-a-score.

decisione *sf.* decision.

decisivo *agg.* decisive.

deciso *agg.* **1.** resolute, firm **2.** (*definito*) decided.

declamare *vt.* e *vi.* to declaim.

declamatorio *agg.* declamatory.

declamazione *sf.* declamation.

declassare *vt.* to degrade.

declinàbile *agg.* declinable.

declinante *agg.* declining.

declinare *vt.* **1.** to decline || *— le proprie generalità*, to say (*v. irr.*) one's name and surname. ♦ **declinare** *vi.* **1.** (*del sole*) to set (*v. irr.*) **2.** (*degradare*) to slope **3.** (*venir meno*) to decline.

declinazione *sf.* (*gramm.*) declension.

declino *sm.* decline.

declivio *sm.* declivity.

decollaggio *sm.* (*aer.*) take-off.

decollare *vi.* to take (*v. irr.*) off.

decollo *sm.* take-off.

decolorante *agg.* decolorating. ♦ **decolorante** *sm.* decolorant.

decolorare *vt.* to decolorate.

decolorazione *sf.* decoloration || *— dei capelli*, hair bleaching.

decomponibile *agg.* decomposable.

decomporre *vt.* to decompose.

decomposizione *sf.* **1.** decomposition **2.** (*putrefazione*) putrefaction.

decongelare *vt.* to defrost.

decongestionare *vt.* to decongest.

decorare *vt.* to decorate: *— al valore*, to decorate for bravery.

decorativo *agg.* decorative.

decoratore *sm.* decorator.

decorazione *sf.* decoration.

decoro *sm.* dignity.

decoroso *agg.* decorous, proper.

decorrenza *sf.* expiration: *con — da*, beginning from.

decòrrere *vi.* **1.** to pass || *a — da*, to begin (*v. irr.*) from **2.** (*comm.*) to run (*v. irr.*), to have effect.

decorso *sm.* **1.** period **2.** (*il passa-*

re) passing.

decrepitezza *sf.* decrepitude.

decrèpito *agg.* decrepit.

decréscere *vi.* to decrease.

decretare *vt.* 1. to decree 2. (*concedere*) to confer.

decreto *sm.* decree: — *legge*, Order in Council.

decuplicare *vt.* to decuple.

dècuplo *sm.* decuple, ten times as much.

decurtare *vt.* to reduce.

dèdalo *sm.* maze.

dèdica *sf.* dedication.

dedicare *vt.* to dedicate. ♦ **dedicarsi** *vr.* to devote oneself.

dedicatorio *agg.* dedicatory.

dèdito *agg.* 1. given up 2. (*a vizio*) addicted.

dedizione *sf.* devotion.

dedurre *vt.* 1. to infer, to deduce 2. (*defalcare*) to deduct.

deduttivo *agg.* deductive.

deduzione *sf.* deduction.

defalcare *vt.* to deduct.

defalco *sm.* deduction.

defecare *vi.* to defecate.

defenestrare *vt.* 1. to throw (*v. irr.*) out of the window 2. (*fig.*) to dismiss.

defenestrazione *sf.* defenestration.

deferente *agg.* deferential.

deferenza *sf.* compliance, deference.

deferire *vt.* 1. to submit 2. (*giur.*) to remit.

defezionare *vi.* to desert.

defezione *sf.* 1. defection 2. (*mil.*) desertion.

deficiente *agg.* 1. insufficient 2. (*idiota*) mentally deficient. ♦ **deficiente** *sm.* idiot.

deficienza *sf.* 1. deficiency, lack 2. (*idiozia*) mental deficiency.

déficit *sm.* deficit.

definìbile *agg.* definable.

definire *vt.* 1. to define 2. (*determinare, risolvere*) to determine.

definitivo *agg.* final.

definito *agg.* definite.

definizione *sf.* 1. definition 2. (*risoluzione*) settlement.

deflagrante *agg.* deflagrating.

deflagrare *vi.* to deflagrate.

deflagrazione *sf.* deflagration.

deflazione *sf.* deflation.

deflèttere *vi.* to deflect.

deflettore *sm.* baffle.

deflorare *vt.* to deflower.

deflorazione *sf.* defloration.

defluire *vi.* to flow down.

deflusso *sm.* 1. downflow 2. (*di marea*) ebb-tide.

deformante *agg.* deforming.

deformare *vt.* 1. to deform, to disfigure 2. (*alterare*) to alter. ♦ **deformarsi** *vr.* 1. (*mecc.*) to warp 2. to get (*v. irr.*) deformed.

deformazione *sf.* 1. deformation 2. (*mecc.*) buckling.

deforme *agg.* deformed.

deformità *sf.* deformity.

defraudare *vt.* to defraud.

defunto *agg.* e *sm.* dead.

degenerare *vi.* to degenerate.

degenerazione *sf.* degeneration.

degènere *agg.* degenerate.

degente *sm.* patient.

degenza *sf.* stay in hospital.

deglutizione *sf.* swallowing.

degnarsi *vr.* to condescend.

degnazione *sf.* condescension.

degno *agg.* worthy, deserving.

degradante *agg.* degrading.

degradare *vt.* to degrade.

degradazione *sf.* degradation.

degustare *vt.* to taste.

deiezione *sf.* dejection.

deificare *vt.* to deify.

deismo *sm.* deism.

deità *sf.* deity.

delatore *sm.* delator.

delazione *sf.* delation, informing.

delèbile *agg.* erasable.

dèlega *sf.* 1. delegation 2. (*procura*) proxy.

delegare *vt.* to delegate.

delegato *sm.* delegate.

delegazione *sf.* 1. delegation 2. (*commissione*) committee.

deleterio *agg.* harmful.

delfino *sm.* 1. (*zool.*) dolphin 2. (*fig.*) probable successor 3. (*stor.*) dauphin.

deliberare *vt.* to decide.

deliberazione *sf.* deliberation.

delicatezza *sf.* delicacy.

delicato *agg.* 1. delicate 2. (*scrupoloso*) scrupulous 3. (*discreto*) discreet, tactful.

delimitare *vt.* to delimit.

delimitazione *sf.* delimitation.

delineare *vt.* to outline.

delineazione *sf.* delineation.

delinquente *sm.* delinquent.

delinquenza *sf.* criminality.

delinquere *vi.* to commit an offence.

deliquio *sm.* swoon.

delirare *vi.* to rave.

delirio *sm.* delirium, frenzy (*anche fig.*).

delitto *sm.* crime.

delittuoso *agg.* criminal.

delizia *sf.* delight.

deliziare *vt.* to delight.

delizioso *agg.* **1.** delightful **2.** (*di sapore, profumo*) delicious.

delta *sm.* delta.

deltòide *agg.* e *sm.* deltoid.

delucidare *vt.* to explain.

delucidazione *sf.* explanation.

delùdere *vt.* to disappoint.

delusione *sf.* disappointment.

demagogìa *sf.* demagogy.

demagògico *agg.* demagogic.

demagogo *sm.* demagogue.

demandare *vt.* to commit.

demaniale *agg.* (owned by the) State.

demanio *sm.* State property.

demarcare *vt.* to mark the boundaries of.

demarcazione *sf.* demarcation.

demente *agg.* insane. ♦ **demente** *sm.* madman (*pl.* -men).

demenza *sf.* insanity.

demeritare *vt.* to forfeit. ♦ **demeritare** *vi.* to deserve censure.

demèrito *sm.* demerit.

demiurgo *sm.* demiurge.

democràtico *agg.* democratic. ♦ **democràtico** *sm.* democrat.

democratizzare *vt.* to democratize.

democrazìa *sf.* democracy.

democristiano *sm.* christian-democrat.

demografìa *sf.* demography.

demogràfico *agg.* demographic(al).

demolire *vt.* to demolish.

demolitore *sm.* **1.** demolisher **2.** (*fig.*) iconoclast.

demolizione *sf.* **1.** demolition **2.** (*fig.*) destruction.

dèmone *sm.* **1.** demon **2.** (*diavolo*) devil.

demonìaco *agg.* demoniac(al).

demonio *sm.* **1.** devil **2.** (*fig.*) demon.

demonologìa *sf.* demonology.

demoralizzare *vt.* to demoralize. ♦ **demoralizzarsi** *vr.* to lose (*v. irr.*) heart.

demoralizzazione *sf.* demoralization.

denaro *sm.* **1.** money **2.** (*moneta antica*) denarius (*pl.* -rii).

denaturare *vt.* to denature.

dendrologìa *sf.* dendrology.

denegare *vt.* to deny.

denicotinizzare *vt.* to denicotinize.

denigrare *vt.* to denigrate.

denigratore *sm.* denigrator.

denigrazione *sf.* denigration.

denominare *vt.* to name.

denominativo *agg.* denominative.

denominatore *sm.* denominator.

denominazione *sf.* denomination.

denotare *vt.* to signify.

densità *sf.* density.

denso *agg.* thick.

dentale *agg.* dental.

dentario *agg.* dental, tooth (*attr.*).

dentato *agg.* toothed.

dentatura *sf.* **1.** set of teeth **2.** (*di ingranaggio*) toothing.

dente *sm.* tooth (*pl.* teeth).

dentellare *vt.* to indent.

dentellatura *sf.* indentation.

dentello *sm.* **1.** (*mecc.*) tooth **2.** (*arch.*) dentil **3.** (*tacca*) notch.

dentiera *sf.* dental plate.

dentifricio *agg.* tooth (*attr.*) ♦ **dentifricio** *sm.* tooth-paste.

dentina *sf.* dentine.

dentista *sm.* dentist.

dentìstico *agg.* dental: *gabinetto* —, dentist's surgery.

dentizione *sf.* teething.

dentro *avv.* in, inside. ♦ **dentro** *prep.* **1.** in, inside **2.** (*di tempo*) (with)in.

denudare *vt.* **1.** to strip **2.** (*scoprire*) to lay (*v. irr.*) bare. ♦ **denudarsi** *vr.* to strip.

denudazione *sf.* denudation.

denuncia *sf.* **1.** denunciation **2.** (*dichiarazione*) statement: — *dei redditi*, statement of one's income.

denunciare *vt.* **1.** to denounce **2.** (*dichiarare*) to report **3.** (*giur.*) — *qu.*, to inform against so.

denutrito *agg.* underfed.

denutrizione *sf.* underfeeding.

deodorante *agg.* deodorizing. ♦ **deodorante** *sm.* deodorant.

deodorare *vt.* to deodorize.

deontologìa *sf.* deontology.

depauperamento *sm.* impoverishment.

depauperare *vt.* to impoverish.

depennare *vt.* to cross out.

deperìbile *agg.* perishable.

deperimento *sm.* **1.** (*di salute*) wasting away **2.** (*per un dolore*) pining away **3.** (*di cose*) deterioration.

deperire *vi.* 1. (*di salute*) to waste away 2. (*per un dolore*) to pine away 3. (*di cose*) to deteriorate.

depilare *vt.* to remove hair (from).

depilatore *sm.* hair-remover.

depilatorio *agg.* hair-removing.

depilazione *sf.* hair-removal.

deplorabile *agg.* deplorable.

deplorare *vt.* 1. (*essere spiacenti*) to deplore 2. (*lagnarsi di*) to complain of.

deplorazione *sf.* 1. (*biasimo*) blame 2. (*rimpianto*) regret.

deplorévole *agg.* 1. deplorable 2. (*biasimevole*) blamable.

deporre *vt.* 1. to lay (*v. irr.*) 2. (*da una carica*) to remove from (an) office 3. (*depositare*) to deposit 4. (*giur.*) to witness. ♦ **deporre** *vi.* (*giur.*) to give (*v. irr.*) evidence.

deportare *vt.* to deport.

deportato *agg.* deported. ♦ **deportato** *sm.* convict.

deportazione *sf.* deportation.

depositante *sm.* depositor.

depositare *vt.* to deposit: — merci, to store goods.

depositario *sm.* trustee.

depòsito *sm.* 1. deposit 2. (*luogo in cui depositare*) warehouse 3. (*per bagagli*) left-luggage room.

deposizione *sf.* deposition.

depravare *vt.* to corrupt.

depravazione *sf.* corruption.

deprecàbile *agg.* deprecable.

deprecare *vt.* to deprecate.

deprecativo *agg.* deprecatory.

deprecazione *sf.* deprecation.

depredamento *sm.* plunder.

depredare *vt.* to plunder, to ravage.

depressione *sf.* depression.

depressivo *agg.* depressing.

depresso *agg.* depressed.

depressore *sm.* depressor.

deprezzamento *sm.* depreciation.

deprezzare *vt.* to depreciate.

deprimente *agg.* depressing.

deprimere *vt.* to depress.

depurare *vt.* to depurate.

depurativo *agg.* depurative.

depuratore *sm.* 1. depurator 2. (*mecc.*) cleaner.

depurazione *sf.* purification, depuration.

deputare *vt.* to depute.

deputato *sm.* deputy.

deputazione *sf.* deputation.

deragliamento *sm.* derailment.

deragliare *vi.* to go (*v. irr.*) off the rails.

derattizzare *vt.* to clear by deratization.

derattizzazione *sf.* deratization.

derelitto *agg.* forlorn.

deretano *sm.* posterior.

deridere *vt.* to laugh at, to make (*v. irr.*) fun of.

derisìbile *agg.* laughable.

derisione *sf.* mockery.

derisorio *agg.* derisory.

deriva *sf.* drift.

derivare *vi.* 1. to derive 2. (*originarsi*) to rise (*v. irr.*). ♦ **derivare** *vt.* to derive.

derivativo *agg.* derivative.

derivato *agg.* derived. ♦ **derivato** *sm.* 1. derivative 2. (*sottoprodotto*) by-product.

derivazione *sf.* 1. derivation 2. (*elettr.*) shunt.

derma *sm.* derm.

dermatologia *sf.* dermatology.

dermatològico *agg.* dermatological.

dermatòlogo *sm.* dermatologist.

dèroga *sf.* derogation.

derogare *vi.* to derogate.

derrata *sf.* 1. victual 2. (*alimentare*) food-stuff.

derubare *vt.* to rob (so. of).

desco *sm.* dinner table.

descrittivo *agg.* descriptive.

descrivere *vt.* to describe.

descrivìbile *agg.* describable.

descrizione *sf.* description.

desèrtico *agg.* desert.

deserto *agg.* e *sm.* desert.

desideràbile *agg.* desirable.

desiderare *vt.* 1. to wish 2. (*desiderare di avere*) to wish for.

desiderio *sm.* wish.

desideroso *agg.* desirous, eager (for).

designare *vt.* to appoint.

designazione *sf.* designation.

desinare *vi.* to dine, to have dinner. ♦ **desinare** *sm.* dinner.

desinenza *sf.* ending.

desistere *vi.* to cease, to leave (*v. irr.*) off.

desolare *vt.* 1. to desolate 2. (*addolorare*) to distress.

desolato *agg.* (*spiacente*) sorry.

desolazione *sf.* 1. desolation 2. (*dolore*) grief, sorrow.

dèspota *sm.* despot.

destare *vt.* 1. to wake (*v. irr.*) 2.

(*suscitare*) to rouse. ♦ **destarsi** *vr.*
to wake (*v. irr.*) up.

destinare *vt.* **1.** to destine **2.** (*devolvere*) to assign.

destinatario *sm.* addressee.

destinazione *sf.* destination.

destino *sm.* **1.** destiny **2.** (*sorte*)
lot.

destituire *vt.* to dismiss.

destituzione *sf.* dismissal.

desto *agg.* awake.

destra *sf.* **1.** right hand **2.** (*parte
destra*) right, right side: *alla tua
—*, on your right; *tenere la —*, to
keep (*v. irr.*) right.

destramente *avv.* skilfully.

destreggiarsi *vr.* to manage.

destrezza *sf.* dexterity.

destriero *sm.* steed.

destrina *sf.* dextrine.

destro *agg.* **1.** right **2.** (*abile*) clever.
♦ **destro** *sm.* opportunity.

desueto *agg.* unusual, obsolete.

desuetùdine *sf.* disuse.

desùmere *vt.* **1.** to infer **2.** (*trarre*)
to draw (*v. irr.*).

detenere *vt.* **1.** to hold (*v. irr.*) **2.**
(*tener prigioniero*) to keep (*v. irr.*)
in prison.

detentore *sm.* holder.

detenuto *agg.* imprisoned. ♦ **detenuto** *sm.* prisoner.

detenzione *sf.* **1.** possession **2.** (*il
detenere*) holding **3.** (*galera*) detention.

detergente *agg.* e *sm.* detergent.

detèrgere *vt.* to cleanse.

deterioramento *sm.* deterioration.

deteriorare *vt.* **1.** to deteriorate **2.**
(*danneggiare*) to damage.

deteriore *agg.* worse.

determinàbile *agg.* determinable.

determinante *agg.* determinant.

determinare *vt.* **1.** to determine
2. (*causare*) to cause.

determinativo *agg.* determinative
|| *articolo —*, definite article.

determinato *agg.* **1.** determinate
2. (*particolare*) special **3.** (*deciso*)
resolute.

determinazione *sf.* determination.

determinismo *sm.* determinism.

deterrente *agg.* e *sm.* deterrent.

detersivo *agg.* e *sm.* detersive.

detestàbile *agg.* detestable.

detestare *vt.* to loathe.

detettore *sm.* detector.

detonante *agg.* explosive.

detonare *vi.* to detonate.

detonatore *sm.* detonator.

detonazione *sf.* explosion.

detrarre *vt.* to deduct.

detrattore *sm.* detractor.

detrazione *sf.* **1.** deduction **2.** (*fig.*)
detraction.

detrimento *sm.* detriment.

detrìtico *agg.* detrital.

detrito *sm.* rubble, debris.

detronizzare *vt.* to depose.

detronizzazione *sf.* dethronement.

detta (*nella loc. avv.*) *a — di qu.*,
according to what so. says.

dettagliante *sm.* retailer.

dettagliare *vt.* to detail.

dettagliatamente *avv.* in detail.

dettaglio *sm.* **1.** detail **2.** (*comm.*)
retail.

dettame *sm.* dictate.

dettare *vt.* **1.** to dictate **2.** (*suggerire*) to suggest || *— la legge*, to
lay (*v. irr.*) down the law.

dettato *sm.* dictation.

detto *agg.* **1.** called **2.** (*sopraddetto*)
said, above-mentioned. ♦ **detto**
sm. saying.

deturpare *vt.* to disfigure.

deturpazione *sf.* disfigurement.

devalutazione *sf.* depreciation.

devastare *vt.* to ravage, to ruin.

devastatore *agg.* ravaging. ♦ **devastatore** *sm.* ravager.

devastazione *sf.* devastation.

deviare *vi.* to deviate || *non —!
(non cambiare discorso*), stick to
the point! ♦ **deviare** *vt.* to divert.

deviazione *sf.* **1.** deviation **2.** (*stradale*) detour || *— ferroviaria*,
shunting.

deviazionismo *sm.* deviationism.

devoluzione *sf.* devolution.

devòlvere *vt.* **1.** (*giur.*) to devolve,
to assign **2.** (*adoperare*) to employ.

devoto *agg.* **1.** devout, affectionate
2. (*relig.*) pious, religious.

devozione *sf.* devotion, piety.

di *prep.* **1.** of **2.** (*partitivo*) some,
any: *dammi del pane*, give me
some bread; *hai dello zucchero?*,
have you any sugar? **3.** (*tempo*) in,
during: *— mattina*, in the morning **4.** (*argomento*) of, about **5.**
(*paragone coi comparativi*) than: *è
più graziosa — sua sorella*, she
is prettier than her sister **6.** (*nei
superl.*) of, in **7.** (*modo*) with, in.

dì *sm.* day.

diabete *sm.* diabetes.

diabètico *agg.* e *sm.* diabetic.

diabòlico *agg.* diabolic(al).

diàcono *sm.* deacon.

diadema *sm.* diadem.

diàfano *agg.* diaphanous.

diaframma *sm.* diaphragm.

diàgnosi *sf.* diagnosis (*pl.* -ses).

diagnosticare *vt.* to diagnose.

diagnòstico *agg.* diagnostic.

diagonale *agg.* diagonal. ♦ **diagonale** *sf.* diagonal.

diagonalmente *avv.* diagonally.

diagramma *sm.* diagram.

dialettale *agg.* dialectal.

dialèttica *sf.* dialectics. ♦ **dialèttico** *sm.* dialectic.

dialèttico *agg.* dialectic. ♦ **dialèttico** *sm.* dialectic.

dialetto *sm.* dialect.

diàlisi *sf.* dialysis (*pl.* -ses).

dialogare *vi.* to hold (*v. irr.*) a dialogue.

diàlogo *sm.* dialogue.

diamante *sm.* diamond.

diametralmente *avv.* diametrically.

diàmetro *sm.* diameter.

dianzi *avv.* just, just now.

diapositiva *sf.* slide.

diarchìa *sf.* diarchy.

diario *sm.* diary.

diarrea *sf.* diarrhoea.

diaspro *sm.* jasper.

diatonìa *sf.* diatony.

diatriba *sf.* diatribe.

diavolerìa *sf.* 1. devilry 2. (*fam.*) trick.

diavoletto *sm.* imp.

diàvolo *sm.* devil.

dibàttere *vt.* to debate. ♦ **dibàttersi** *vr.* to struggle.

dibàttito *sm.* debate, discussion.

dibattuto *agg.* controversial.

diboscamento *sm.* deforestation.

diboscare *vt.* to deforest.

dicastero *sm.* office.

dicembre *sm.* December.

dicerìa *sf.* gossip, rumour.

dichiarare *vt.* to declare.

dichiarato *agg.* declared.

dichiarazione *sf.* declaration.

diciannove *agg.* nineteen.

diciannovenne *agg.* 1. nineteen years old (*pred.*) 2. nineteen-year-old (*attr.*).

diciannovèsimo *agg.* nineteenth.

diciassette *agg.* seventeen.

diciassettenne *agg.* 1. seventeen years old (*pred.*) 2. seventeen-year-old (*attr.*).

diciassettèsimo *agg.* seventeenth.

diciottenne *agg.* 1. eighteen years old (*pred.*) 2. eighteen-year-old (*attr.*).

diciottèsimo *agg.* eighteenth.

diciotto *agg.* eighteen.

dicitore *sm.* speaker.

dicitura *sf.* wording.

didascalìa *sf.* 1. explanation 2. (*cine*) subtitles (*pl.*).

didascàlico *agg.* didactic.

didàttica *sf.* didactics.

didàttico *agg.* didactic(al).

didentro *sm.* inside.

didietro *sm.* back.

dieci *agg.* ten.

diecina *sf.* ten, half a score.

diedro *sm.* dihedral.

dielèttrico *agg.* dielectric.

diesis *sm.* sharp.

dieta *sf.* diet.

dietètico *agg.* dietetic.

dietòlogo *sm.* dietician.

dietro *avv.* behind. ♦ **dietro** *prep.* behind, after. ♦ **dietro** *sm.* back, rear.

dietrofrònt *inter.* about turn!

difatti *avv.* as a matter of fact.

difèndere *vt.* to defend.

difendìbile *agg.* defensible.

difensiva *sf.* defensive.

difensivo *agg.* defensive.

difensore *agg.* defending. ♦ **difensore** *sm.* 1. defender 2. (*giur.*) defending counsel 3. (*di un'idea ecc.*) supporter.

difesa *sf.* defence.

difettare *vi.* to be wanting.

difettivo *agg.* defective.

difetto *sm.* defect.

difettoso *agg.* defective.

diffamare *vt.* to defame.

diffamatore *sm.* defamer.

diffamatorio *agg.* defamatory.

diffamazione *sf.* defamation.

differente *agg.* unlike, different.

differentemente *avv.* differently.

differenza *sf.* difference.

differenziale *agg.* e *sm.* differential.

differenziare *vt.* to differentiate.

differenziato *agg.* differentiated.

differenziazione *sf.* differentiation.

differìbile *agg.* that can be deferred.

differimento *sm.* deferment.

differire *vi.* (*essere diverso*) to differ (from). ♦ **differire** *vt.* to delay.

difficile *agg.* difficult.

difficilmente *avv.* with difficulty.

difficoltà *sf.* difficulty.

difficoltoso *agg.* difficult.

diffida *sf.* warning, intimation.

diffidare *vi.* to distrust. ♦ **diffidare** *vt.* to give (*v. irr.*) warning.

diffidente *agg.* suspicious.

diffidenza *sf.* **1.** distrust **2.** (*sospetto*) suspicion.

diffóndere *vt.* to diffuse, to spread (*v. irr.*). ♦ **diffóndersi** *vr.* to spread (*v. irr.*).

difforme *agg.* **1.** different **2.** shapeless.

difformità *sf.* difference, deformity.

diffrazione *sf.* diffraction.

diffusamente *avv.* diffusely.

diffusione *sf.* **1.** diffusion, spreading **2.** (*di giornale*) circulation.

diffuso *agg.* diffuse.

diffusore *sm.* diffusor.

difilato *avv.* straight.

diftèrico *agg.* diphtheric.

difterite *sf.* diphtheria.

diga *sf.* dam.

digerente *agg.* digestive.

digerìbile *agg.* digestible.

digeribilità *sf.* digestibility.

digerire *vt.* to digest.

digestione *sf.* digestion.

digestivo *agg.* e *sm.* digestive.

digesto *sm.* digest.

digitale *agg.* digital ‖ *impronte digitali*, finger-prints. ♦ **digitale** *sf.* digitalis, (*fam.*) foxglove.

digiunare *vi.* to fast.

digiunatore *sm.* faster.

digiuno¹ *agg.* **1.** fasting **2.** (*fig.*) lacking (in).

digiuno² *sm.* fast.

dignità *sf.* dignity.

dignitario *sm.* dignitary.

dignitosamente *avv.* with dignity.

dignitoso *agg.* dignified.

digradante *agg.* **1.** sloping **2.** (*pitt.*) shading.

digradare *vi.* **1.** to slope down **2.** (*pitt.*) to shade off.

digressione *sf.* digression.

digressivo *agg.* digressive.

digrignare *vt.* to gnash.

digrossamento *sm.* **1.** reducing **2.** (*sbozzo*) rough-hewing.

digrossare *vt.* **1.** to reduce **2.** (*sbozzare*) to rough-hew.

dilacerare *vt.* to tear (*v. irr.*).

dilagare *vi.* to spread (*v. irr.*).

dilaniare *vt.* to tear (*v. irr.*) to

pieces.

dilapidare *vt.* to squander.

dilapidatore *sm.* squanderer.

dilapidazione *sf.* squandering.

dilatàbile *agg.* dilatable.

dilatabilità *sf.* dilatability.

dilatare *vt.*, **dilatarsi** *vr.* **1.** to dilate **2.** (*fis.*) to expand.

dilatazione *sf.* dilatation.

dilatorio *agg.* dilatory.

dilavamento *sm.* washing away.

dilavare *vt.* to wash away.

dilazionare *vt.* to defer.

dilazione *sf.* delay, respite.

dileggiare *vt.* to mock.

dileggio *sm.* mockery.

dileguare *vt.* to disperse. ♦ **dileguarsi** *vr.* to disappear.

dilemma *sm.* dilemma.

dilettante *sm.* amateur.

dilettantismo *sm.* amateurism.

dilettare *vt.* to delight. ♦ **dilettarsi** *vr.* to take (*v. irr.*) delight (in).

dilettévole *agg.* delightful.

diletto *agg.* beloved. ♦ **diletto** *sm.* delight.

diligente *agg.* diligent.

diligenza *sf.* **1.** diligence **2.** (*carrozza*) stage-coach.

dilucidare *vt.* V. *delucidare.*

dilucidazione *sf.* V. *delucidazione.*

diluente *sm.* diluent.

diluire *vt.* **1.** to dilute **2.** (*fig.*) to water down.

diluizione *sf.* dilution.

dilungarsi *vr.* to speak (*v. irr.*) diffusely.

diluviale *agg.* **1.** torrential **2.** (*geol.*) diluvial.

diluviano *agg.* diluvial.

diluviare *vi.* **1.** to pour **2.** (*fig.*) to shower.

diluvio *sm.* deluge, flood.

dimagramento *sm.* thinning.

dimagrante *agg.* slimming.

dimagrare *vi.* to thin.

dimagrire *vi.* V. *dimagrare.*

dimenare *vt.* **1.** (*la coda*) to wag **2.** to wave. ♦ **dimenarsi** *vr.* to move about restlessly.

dimensione *sf.* dimension, size.

dimenticanza *sf.* **1.** (*svista*) oversight **2.** (*oblio*) oblivion.

dimenticare *vt.*, **dimenticarsi** *vr.* to forget (*v. irr.*).

diméntico *agg.* forgetful.

dimesso *agg.* **1.** modest **2.** (*trasandato*) shabby.

dimestichezza *sf.* familiarity.
dimetro *sm.* dimeter.
diméttere *vt.* to dismiss || — *dall'ospedale*, to discharge. ◆ **diméttersi** *vr.* to resign.
dimezzamento *sm.* halving.
dimezzare *vt.* to halve.
diminuendo *sm.* 1. (*mat.*) minuend 2. (*mus.*) diminuendo.
diminuìbile *agg.* diminishable.
diminuire *vt.* e *vi.* to lessen, to diminish.
diminutivo *agg.* e *sm.* diminutive.
diminuzione *sf.* lessening, reduction.
dimissionare *vt.* to oblige (so.) to resign.
dimissionario *agg.* resigning.
dimissione *sf.* resignation || *dare le dimissioni*, to resign.
dimissoria *sf.* dimissory letter.
dimodoché *cong.* so that.
dimora *sf.* residence, lodgings (*pl.*).
dimorare *vi.* to stay, to live.
dimorfismo *sm.* dimorphism.
dimorfo *agg.* dimorphic.
dimostràbile *agg.* demonstrable.
dimostrabilità *sf.* demonstrability.
dimostrante *sm.* demonstrant.
dimostrare *vt.* 1. to show (*v. irr.*) 2. (*provare*) to demonstrate. ◆ **dimostrarsi** *vr.* to show oneself.
dimostrativo *agg.* e *sm.* demonstrative.
dimostratore *sm.* demonstrator.
dimostrazione *sf.* demonstration.
dina *sf.* dyne.
dinàmica *sf.* dynamics.
dinamicamente *avv.* dynamically.
dinamicità *sf.* dynamism, energy.
dinàmico *agg.* 1. dynamic 2. (*fig.*) energetic.
dinamismo *sm.* 1. dynamism 2. (*fig.*) energy.
dinamitardo *sm.* dynamiter.
dinamite *sf.* dynamite.
dìnamo *sf.* dynamo.
dinamòmetro *sm.* dynamometer.
dinanzi *prep.* before, in front of. ◆ **dinanzi** *avv.* before, in front, forward.
dìnaro *sm.* dinar.
dinasta *sm.* dynast.
dinastìa *sf.* dynasty.
dinàstico *agg.* dynastic(al).
dindo *sm.* turkey.
diniego *sm.* denial.
dinoccolato *agg.* slouching.
dinosàuro *sm.* dinosaur.

dintorni *sm. pl.* surroundings.
dintorno *avv.* e *prep.* 1. round, round about 2. (*circa*) about.
dio *sm.* god: *Marte, il — della guerra*, Mars, the god of war. ◆ **Dio** *sm.* God: — *ci assista!*, — *non voglia!*, God help us, God forbid.
diocesano *agg.* diocesan.
diòcesi *sf.* diocese.
dìodo *sm.* diode.
dionea *sf.* dionaea.
dionisìaco *agg.* Dionysiac.
diorama *sm.* diorama.
diorite *sf.* diorite.
diottrìa *sf.* diopter.
diòttrica *sf.* dioptrics.
diòttrico *agg.* dioptric.
dipanamento *sm.* winding into a ball.
dipanare *vt.* 1. to wind (*v. irr.*) into a ball 2. (*fig.*) to disentangle.
dipanatoio *sm.* skein-winder.
dipartimentale *agg.* departmental.
dipartimento *sm.* department.
dipartire *vi.* to depart. ◆ **dipartirsi** *vr.* 1. to go (*v. irr.*) away 2. (*morire*) to pass away.
dipartita *sf.* 1. departure 2. (*morte*) death.
dipendente *agg.* dependent (on). ◆ **dipendente** *sm.* employee.
dipendenza *sf.* dependence (on).
dipèndere *vi.* 1. (*derivare*) to be due 2. (*essere subordinato, vivere a carico*) to depend (on).
dipingere *vt.* to paint.
dipinto *agg.* painted. ◆ **dipinto** *sm.* painting.
diplegìa *sf.* diplegia.
diplococco *sm.* diplococcus (*pl.* -ci).
diploma *sm.* diploma.
diplomare *vt.* to confer a diploma (upon so.). ◆ **diplomarsi** *vr.* to get (*v. irr.*) a diploma.
diplomàtica *sf.* diplomatics.
diplomaticamente *avv.* diplomatically.
diplomàtico *agg.* diplomatic. ◆ **diplomàtico** *sm.* diplomat.
diplomato *agg.* holding a diploma. ◆ **diplomato** *sm.* graduate.
diplomazìa *sf.* diplomacy.
diplopìa *sf.* diplopia.
dìpnoi *sm. pl.* Dipnoi.
dipodìa *sf.* dipody.
dipoi *avv.* then.
diporto *sm.* recreation, diversion ||

viaggiare per —, to travel on pleasure.

dipresso (*nella loc. avv.*) *a un* —, approximately.

diptero *agg.* dipteral.

diradamento *sm.* **1.** thinning **2.** (*di nebbia, gas*) rarefaction.

diradare *vt.* **1.** to thin out **2.** (*rendere meno frequente*) to do (*v. irr.*) less frequent. ♦ **diradarsi** *vr.* **1.** to clear away **2.** (*divenire meno frequente*) to become (*v. irr.*) less frequent.

diramare *vt.* to issue, to spread (*v. irr.*).

diramazione *sf.* **1.** branching **2.** (*diffusione*) diffusion **3.** (*per radio*) broadcasting.

dire *vt.* **1.** (*nel senso di enunciare e quando introduce il discorso diretto e quando introduce il discorso diretto*) to say (*v. irr.*): *dice che ha sonno*, he says he is sleepy; « *venite* », *ci disse*, « come », he said to us **2.** (*nel senso di raccontare e quando è enunciata la persona cui si parla*) to tell (*v. irr.*): *gli dissi di venire*, I told him to come || *si dice*, they say; *mi si dice*, I am told; *inutile — che*, it goes without saying that; *vale a* —, that is to say; *sentir* —, to hear (*v. irr.*); *voler* —, to mean (*v. irr.*).

dire *sm.* words (*pl.*), speech.

direttamente *avv.* directly.

direttissima *sf. per* —, summarily.

direttissimo *sm.* (*ferr.*) fast train.

direttiva *sf.* directions (*pl.*).

direttivo *agg.* **1.** leading **2.** (*comm.*) managing.

diretto *agg.* direct, straight.

direttore *sm.* **1.** (*comm.; amm.*) manager **2.** (*di scuola*) headmaster.

direttoriale *agg.* directorial.

direttorio *sm.* executive board.

direttrice *sf.* **1.** (*comm.; amm.*) manageress **2.** (*di scuola*) headmistress.

direzionale *agg.* directional || *centro* —, office district.

direzione *sf.* **1.** direction, course **2.** (*di società*) management **3.** (*di giornale*) editorship **4.** (*di scuola*) headmastership **5.** (*sede*) administrative office.

dirigente *agg.* directing, leading. ♦ **dirigente** *sm.* director, manager, leader.

dirigere *vt.* **1.** (*indirizzare*) to direct

2. (*guidare*) to lead (*v. irr.*) **3.** (*sovraintendere*) to supervise. ♦ **dirigersi** *vr.* to turn one's steps towards.

dirigibile *sm.* airship.

dirigismo *sm.* state planning.

dirigista *sm.* supporter of state planning.

dirimente *agg.* diriment.

dirimere *vt.* to settle.

dirimpettaio *sm.* person living just opposite.

dirimpetto *avv.* face to face, opposite.

diritta *sf.* right, right-hand: *a* —, on the right.

dirittamente *avv.* straight.

diritto *agg.* straight, upright || *rigare* —, to behave properly.

diritto *sm.* **1.** right **2.** (*tassa, tributo*) due **3.** (*legge*) law.

dirittura *sf.* **1.** straight line **2.** (*rettitudine*) uprightness **3.** (*sport*) — *d'arrivo*, home stretch.

dirizzare *vt.* **1.** to direct **2.** (*erigere*) to raise **3.** (*raddrizzare; fig.*) to put (*v. irr.*) right, to straighten.

dirizzone *sm.* inconsiderate action.

diroccamento *sm.* demolition.

diroccare *vt.* to demolish.

diroccato *agg.* **1.** (*demolito*) dismantled **2.** (*in rovina*) crumbled.

dirompente *agg.* disruptive.

diròmpere *vt.* **1.** (*di lino, canapa ecc.*) to scutch **2.** (*rompere*) to break (*v. irr.*).

dirottare *vt.* to divert. ♦ **dirottare** *vi.* to change course.

dirotto *agg.* excessive: *pianto* —, desperate crying; *piove a* —, it is pouring.

dirozzamento *sm.* **1.** (*lo sbozzare*) rough-hewing **2.** (*fig.*) refinement.

dirozzare *vt.* **1.** (*sbozzare*) to rough-hew **2.** (*fig.*) to refine.

dirugginire *vt.* to remove the rust from.

dirupamento *sm.* **1.** falling down **2.** (*di luogo*) abruptness.

dirupato *agg.* **1.** abrupt **2.** (*roccioso*) rocky.

dirupo *sm.* precipice.

disabbellire *vt.* to spoil the beauty of. ♦ **disabbellirsi** *vr.* to lose (*v. irr.*) one's beauty.

disabitato *agg.* **1.** uninhabited **2.** (*abbandonato*) deserted.

disabituare *vt.* to disaccustom. ♦ **disabituarsi** *vr.* to give (*v. irr.*)

up the habit of.

disaccordo sm. disagreement.

disacerbare vt. to appease.

disadatto agg. 1. unfit 2. (che non si addice) unbecoming.

disadornare vt. to disadorn.

disadorno agg. 1. unadorned 2. (spoglio) bare.

disaffezionarsi vr. to lose (v. irr.) one's affection (for).

disaffezionato agg. estranged.

disaffezione sf. estrangement.

disagévole agg. uncomfortable.

disagiatamente avv. uncomfortably.

disagiato agg. 1. uncomfortable 2. (povero) needy.

disagio sm. 1. uneasiness || essere a —, to be uneasy 2. (disturbo) inconvenience 3. (pl.; privazioni) privations.

disamare vt. to cease to love.

disàmina sf. examination.

disaminare vt. to examine carefully.

disancorarsi vr. 1. to weigh anchor 2. (fig.) to break (v. irr.) all connections (with).

disanimarsi vr. to lose (v. irr.) heart.

disappetenza sf. lack of appetite.

disapprèndere vt. to forget (v. irr.).

disapprovare vt. to disapprove (of).

disapprovazione sf. disapproval.

disappunto sm. disappointment.

disarcionare vt. to unsaddle.

disarmare vt. to disarm.

disarmato agg. disarmed.

disarmo sm. disarmament.

disarmonìa sf. discord.

disarmonicamente avv. discordantly.

disarmònico agg. discordant.

disarmonizzare vt. to disharmonize.

disarticolare vt. to disjoint.

disarticolazione sf. disjointing.

disastro sm. disaster.

disastroso agg. disastrous.

disattento agg. inattentive.

disattenzione sf. inattention: errore di —, a slip of the pen.

disavanzo sm. deficit.

disavveduto agg. heedless.

disavventura sf. 1. mishap 2. (sfortuna) misfortune.

disavvertenza sf. inadvertence.

disavvezzo agg. unaccustomed.

disazotare vt. to remove nitrogen from.

disborso sm. disbursement.

disbrigo sm. dispatch.

disbrogliare vt. to disentangle.

discacciare vt. to turn out.

discapitare vi. to suffer damage.

discàpito sm. disadvantage.

discàrico sm. 1. discharge 2. (scusa) defence.

discendente agg. descending. ◆

discendente sm. descendant.

discendenza sf. 1. descent 2. (discendenti) offspring.

discéndere vt. 1. to descend, to go (v. irr.) down 2. (di astri) to sink (v. irr.) 3. (di prezzi) to fall (v. irr.).

discépolo sm. disciple.

discèrnere vt. 1. to discern 2. (distinguere) to distinguish.

discernìbile agg. discernible.

discernimento sm. discernment.

discesa sf. 1. descent 2. (declivio) slope 3. (caduta) fall 4. (invasione) invasion.

dischiùdere vt. to disclose.

dischiuso agg. disclosed.

discinto agg. ungirt.

disciplina sf. 1. (materia di studio) doctrine 2. (regola) discipline.

disciplinàbile agg. disciplinable.

disciplinare[1] vt. to discipline.

disciplinare[2] agg. disciplinary.

disciplinarmente avv. with discipline.

disciplinatamente avv. with discipline.

disciplinato agg. disciplined.

disco sm. 1. disk 2. (mus.) record 3. (sport) discus 4. (ferr.) disk signal.

discòbolo sm. discus-thrower.

discòide agg. discoid.

discolo sm. wild boy, little scamp.

discolpa sf. excuse.

discolpare vt. to clear.

disconoscente aff. ungrateful.

disconoscenza sf. ungratitude.

disconòscere vt. to refuse to recognize.

disconoscimento sm. 1. refusal to recognize 2. (ingratitudine) ingratitude.

discontinuità sf. discontinuity.

discontinuo agg. discontinuous.

discordante agg. 1. discordant 2. (diverso) different 3. (di colori) clashing.

discordanza sf. discordance.

discordare vi. 1. to disagree 2. (di colori) to clash 3. (di suoni) to jar.

discorde agg. discordant (with).

discordemente avv. discordantly.

discordia sf. discord.

discòrrere vi. to talk.

discorsivo agg. talkative.

discorso sm. speech.

discostare vt. to shift.

discosto agg. far, distant. ♦ **discosto** avv. at some distance.

discoteca sf. record library.

discreditare vt. to discredit.

discrédito sm. discredit.

discrepante agg. differing.

discrepanza sf. discrepancy.

discretamente avv. 1. (con discrezione) discreetly 2. (sufficientemente) fairly 3. (piuttosto) rather.

discreto agg. 1. (che ha discrezione) discreet 2. (moderato) moderate 3. (abbastanza buono) fairly good.

discrezionale agg. discretionary.

discrezione sf. discretion.

discriminante agg. discriminating.

discriminare vt. to discriminate.

discriminazione sf. discrimination.

discussione sf. discussion.

discusso agg. discussed.

discùtere vt. to discuss.

discutibile agg. questionable.

disdegnare vt. to disdain.

disdegno sm. disdain.

disdegnosamente avv. disdainfully.

disdegnoso agg. disdainful.

disdetta sf. 1. (giur.) notice of leave 2. (sfortuna) bad luck.

disdettare vt. to give (v. irr.) notice.

disdicévole agg. unbecoming.

disdire vt. 1. (ritrattare) to take (v. irr.) back, to retract 2. (annullare) to cancel.

disegnare vt. 1. to draw (v. irr.) 2. (progettare) to plan.

disegnatore sm. designer.

disegno sm. 1. drawing 2. (di tessuto) pattern 3. (di edificio) plan 4. (schizzo) sketch 5. (fig.) design, plan.

diseredare vt. to disinherit.

diseredato agg. 1. poor, destitute 2. (privato di eredità) disinherited.

disertare vt. 1. to desert 2. (abbandonare) to leave (v. irr.).

disertore sm. deserter.

diserzione sf. desertion.

disfacimento sm. 1. (il disfare) undoing 2. (decadimento) decay.

disfare vt. 1. to undo (v. irr.) 2. (slegare) to untie.

disfasia sf. dysphasia.

disfatta sf. defeat.

disfattismo sm. defeatism.

disfattista agg. e s. defeatist.

disfatto agg. 1. (distrutto) ruined 2. (slegato) undone 3. (molto stanco) worn out.

disfavore sm. disfavour.

disfida sf. challenge.

disfunzione sf. disorder.

disgelare vt. e vi. to thaw.

disgelo sm. thaw.

disgiùngere vt. to disjoin.

disgiungimento sm. disjoining.

disgiuntamente avv. separately.

disgiuntivamente avv. disjunctively.

disgiuntivo agg. disjunctive.

disgiunto agg. disjoined.

disgiunzione sf. disjunction.

disgrazia sf. 1. misfortune 2. (sfavore) disfavour || cadere in —, to lose (v. irr.) so.'s favour 3. (fatto involontario) accident.

disgraziatamente avv. unfortunately.

disgraziato agg. 1. unlucky, wretched 2. (deforme) misshapen.

disgregamento sm. disintegration.

disgregare vt. to disgregate, to break (v. irr.) up.

disgregazione sf. disgregation.

disguido sm. miscarriage.

disgustare vt. to disgust, to sicken. ♦ **disgustarsi** vr. to become (v. irr.) disgusted (with).

disgusto sm. 1. disgust 2. (avversione) dislike.

disgustoso agg. disgusting.

disidratare vt. to dehydrate.

disidratazione sf. dehydration.

disillùdere vt. to undeceive.

disillusione sf. disillusion.

disilluso agg. undeceived, disappointed.

disimballaggio sm. unpacking.

disimballare vt. to unpack.

disimpacciare vt. to disembarrass.

disimparare vt. to forget (v. irr.).

disimpegnare vt. 1. to redeem 2. (liberare da un impegno) to release. ♦ **disimpegnarsi** *vr.* **1.** to disengage oneself **2.** (*cavarsela*) to manage.

disimpegno *sm.* **1.** redemption **2.** (*il liberarsi da un impegno*) disengagement.

disincagliare *vt.* to get (*v. irr.*) afloat.

disincantare *vt.* to disenchant.

disincanto *agg.* disenchanted.

disincanto *sm.* disenchantment.

disinfestare *vt.* to disinfest.

disinfettante *sm.* disinfectant.

disinfettare *vt.* to disinfect.

disinfezione *sf.* disinfection.

disingannare *vt.* to undeceive.

disinganno *sm.* **1.** undeceiving **2.** (*delusione*) disappointment.

disinnescare *vt.* to defuse.

disinnestare *vt.* to disengage.

disinnesto *sm.* disengagement, release.

disinserire *vt.* to disconnect.

disintegrare *vt.* to disintegrate.

disintegratore *sm.* disintegrator.

disintegrazione *sf.* disintegration.

disinteressare *vt.* **1.** to disinterest **2.** (*comm.*) to buy (*v. irr.*) out. ♦ **disinteressarsi** *vr.* to take (*v. irr.*) no interest (in).

disinteressato *agg.* **1.** disinterested **2.** (*altruistico*) unselfish.

disinteresse *sm.* **1.** indifference **2.** (*altruismo*) unselfishness.

disintossicare *vt.* to unpoison.

disintossicazione *sf.* unpoisoning.

disinvolto *agg.* unconstrained, free-and-easy.

disinvoltura *sf.* unconstraint, free-and-easy way.

disistima *sf.* disesteem.

disistimare *vt.* to disesteem.

dislivello *sm.* **1.** difference of level **2.** (*di acque*) rise **3.** (*di strade*) gradient **4.** (*ineguaglianza*) inequality.

dislocamento *sm.* **1.** displacement **2.** (*mil.*) dislocation.

dislocare *vt.* **1.** to displace **2.** (*mil.*) to dislocate.

dislocazione *sf.* removal, dislocation.

dismisura *sf.* excess || *a —*, excessively.

disobbedire *vi.* V. **disubbidire**.

disobbligare *vt.* to release from duty. ♦ **disobbligarsi** *vr.* to free oneself from duty.

disoccupato *agg.* unemployed. ♦

disoccupato *sm.* unemployed person.

disoccupazione *sf.* unemployment.

disonestà *sf.* **1.** dishonesty **2.** (*atto disonesto*) fraud.

disonesto *agg.* dishonest, fraudulent.

disonorante *agg.* shameful.

disonorare *vt.* to dishonour.

disonore *sm.* dishonour, shame.

disonorévole *agg.* dishonourable.

disopra *avv.* **1.** above, over **2.** (*in cima*) on top **3.** (*ai piani superiori*) upstairs. ♦ **disopra** *sm.* top, upper part. ♦ **al disopra di**, **disopra a** *prep.* above.

disordinare *vt.* to disorder.

disordinatamente *avv.* untidily.

disordinato *agg.* untidy, disorderly.

disórdine *sm.* **1.** disorder, untidiness **2.** (*sregolatezza*) disorderliness **3.** (*tumulto*) disorder, tumult.

disorgànico *agg.* inorganic.

disorganizzare *vt.* to disorganize.

disorganizzato *agg.* disorganized.

disorganizzazione *sf.* disorganization.

disorientamento *sm.* disorientation, confusion.

disorientare *vt.* **1.** to disorientate **2.** (*sconcertare*) to bewilder.

disorientato *agg.* bewildered, puzzled.

disormeggiare *vt.* to unmoor.

disossare *vt.* to bone.

disossidante *sm.* deoxidizer.

disossidare *vt.* to deoxidize.

disossidazione *sf.* deoxidation.

disotto *avv.* **1.** below, underneath **2.** (*al piano inferiore*) downstairs. ♦ **disotto** *sm.* underside, lower part. ♦ **al disotto di**, **disotto a** *prep.* under, beneath, below.

dispaccio *sm.* dispatch.

disparato *agg.* disparate.

disparere *sm.* difference of opinion.

dispari *agg.* odd.

disparità *sf.* disparity.

disparte *avv.* aside, apart: *starsene in —*, to stand (*v. irr.*) aside; (*fig.*) to stand aloof; *mettere in —*, to put (*v. irr.*) aside; (*per uno scopo*) to put by.

dispendio *sm.* **1.** heavy expense **2.** (*di forza, tempo*) waste.

dispendioso *agg.* expensive.

dispensa *sf.* **1.** pantry **2.** (*mobile*) sideboard **3.** (*pubblicazione perio-*

dica) number **4.** (*esenzione; eccl.*) dispensation.

dispensare *vt.* **1.** (*distribuire*) to deal (*v. irr.*) out **2.** (*esentare*) to exempt, to dispense.

dispensario *sm.* dispensary.

dispensato *agg.* exempted.

dispensatore *sm.* distributor, dispenser.

dispepsìa *sf.* dyspepsia.

dispèptico *agg.* dyspeptic.

disperare *vi.* to despair, to lose (*v. irr.*) all hope. ♦ **disperarsi** *vr.* to give (*v. irr.*) oneself up to despair.

disperatamente *avv.* desperately.

disperato *agg.* **1.** despairing **2.** (*senza speranza*) hopeless ‖ *essere — (di malato)*, to be far gone. ♦ **disperato** *sm.* **1.** (*miserabile*) destitute **2.** (*forsennato*) madman (*pl. -men*).

disperazione *sf.* despair.

dispèrdere *vt.* to disperse **2.** (*consumare*) to waste.

dispersione *sf.* **1.** dispersion **2.** (*elettr.*) leak.

dispersivo *agg.* dispersive.

disperso *agg.* missing, lost.

dispetto *sm.* **1.** spite: *a — di*, in spite of **2.** (*stizza*) vexation.

dispettoso *agg.* spiteful.

displacere [1] *vi.* **1.** to dislike ‖ *mi dispiace*, I am sorry; (*in espressioni di cortesia*) *se non vi dispiace*, if you please **2.** (*essere sgradevole*) to be disagreeable.

displacere [2] *sm.* **1.** regret **2.** (*disapprovazione*) displeasure **3.** (*fastidio*) trouble.

dispiegare *vt.* **1.** (*allargare*) to spread (*v. irr.*) out **2.** (*le vele*) to unfurl.

displuvio *sm.* **1.** watershed ‖ *linea di —*, ridge **2.** (*arch.*) hip.

disponìbile *agg.* available.

disponibilità *sf.* availability.

disporre *vt.* **1.** to arrange **2.** (*preparare*) to dispose **3.** (*deliberare*) to order.

dispositivo *sm.* (*mecc.*) device.

disposizione *sf.* **1.** disposition, arrangement **2.** (*ordine*) order, direction ‖ *a —*, at one's disposal **3.** (*inclinazione*) bent.

disposto *agg.* **1.** ready, willing **2.** (*ben disposto fisicamente*) strong.

dispòtico *agg.* despotic.

dispotismo *sm.* despotism.

dispregiativamente *avv.* disparagingly.

dispregiativo *agg.* depreciative. ♦ **dispregiativo** *sm.* (*gramm.*) pejorative.

dispregiatore *sm.* contemner.

dispregio *sm.* contempt.

disprezzàbile *agg.* despicable.

disprezzare *vt.* **1.** to despise **2.** (*considerare di poco conto*) to look down on.

disprezzo *sm.* contempt.

disputa *sf.* discussion.

disputàbile *agg.* disputable.

disputare *vi* e *vt.* to discuss.

disquisizione *sf.* disquisition.

dissaldare *vt.* to unsolder.

dissanguamento *sm.* **1.** bleeding **2.** (*fig.*) impoverishment.

dissanguare *vt.* **1.** to bleed **2.** (*fig.*) to impoverish. ♦ **dissanguarsi** *vr.* (*fig.*) to become (*v. irr.*) impoverished.

dissanguato *agg.* **1.** bloodless **2.** (*fig.*) impoverished.

dissanguatore *sm.* (*fig.*) bloodsucker.

dissapore *sm.* disagreement.

disseccare *vt.* to dissect.

disseccamento *sm.* drying up.

disseccante *agg.* drying up. ♦ **disseccante** *sm.* desiccative.

disseccare *vt.* **1.** to dry up **2.** (*cibo*) to desicate.

disselciare *vt.* to unpave.

disseminare *vt.* to disseminate.

disseminato *agg.* strewn.

disseminatore *agg.* disseminating. ♦ **disseminatore** *sm.* disseminator.

disseminazione *sf.* dissemination.

dissennatamente *avv.* madly.

dissennatezza *sf.* **1.** madness **2.** (*avventatezza*) rashness.

dissennato *agg.* **1.** mad **2.** (*avventato*) rash.

dissensione *sf.* dissension.

dissenso *sm.* dissent.

dissenterìa *sf.* dysentery.

dissentèrico *agg.* dysenteric.

dissentire *vi.* to dissent.

dissenziente *agg.* dissenting. ♦ **dissenziente** *sm.* dissenter.

disseppellimento *sm.* disinterment.

disseppellire *vt.* **1.** to disinter **2.** (*fig.*) to revive.

disserrare *vt.* to unfasten.

dissertare *vi.* to dissertate (on).

dissertatore *sm.* dissertator.

dissertazione *sf.* dissertation.

dissestare *vt.* 1. *(finanziariamente)* to ruin 2. *(mettere fuori posto)* to derange.

dissestato *agg.* *(di persona)* ruined.

dissesto *sm.* 1. trouble 2. *(fallimento)* bankruptcy.

dissetante *agg.* refreshing: *bibita* —, refreshing drink.

dissetare *vt.* to quench the thirst of. ◆ **dissetarsi** *vr.* 1. to quench one's thirst 2. *(bere)* to drink *(v. irr.)*; *(di animali)* to water.

dissezione *sf.* dissection.

dissidente *agg. e sm.* dissident.

dissidenza *sf.* dissidence.

dissidio *sm.* 1. dissension, disagreement 2. *(litigio)* quarrel.

dissigillare *vt.* to unseal.

dissimile *agg.* unlike.

dissimmetria *sf.* dissymmetry.

dissimulare *vt.* to dissemble.

dissimulatamente *avv.* dissemblingly.

dissimulatore *sm.* dissimulator.

dissimulazione *sf.* dissimulation.

dissipare *vt.* to dissipate. ◆ **dissiparsi** *vr.* to dissipate, to vanish.

dissipatezza *sf.* dissipation.

dissipatore *sm.* waster.

dissipazione *sf.* dissipation.

dissociàbile *agg.* dissociable.

dissociare *vt.* to dissociate.

dissociazione *sf.* dissociation.

dissodamento *sm.* tillage.

dissodare *vt.* to till.

dissolùbile *agg.* dissoluble.

dissolubilità *sf.* dissolubility.

dissolutezza *sf.* dissoluteness.

dissoluto *agg.* dissolute.

dissoluzione *sf.* dissolution.

dissolvente *agg. e sm.* dissolvent.

dissòlvere *vt.* 1. to dissolve 2. *(disperdere)* to dispel. ◆ **dissòlversi** *vr.* to dissolve.

dissolvimento *sm.* dissolution.

dissomigliante *agg.* dissimilar (to).

dissomiglianza *sf.* dissimilarity.

dissomigliare *vi.* to be unlike. ◆ **dissomigliarsi** *vr.* to differ from.

dissonante *agg.* dissonant.

dissonanza *sf.* 1. dissonance 2. *(fig.)* discordance.

dissonare *vi.* 1. to be out of tune 2. *(fig.)* to discord (with).

dissotterramento *sm.* disinterment.

dissotterrare *vt.* to disinter.

dissuadere *vt.* to dissuade.

dissuasione *sf.* dissuasion.

distaccamento *sm.* 1. detaching 2. *(mil.)* detachment.

distaccare *vt.* to detach. ◆ **distaccarsi** *vr.* to come *(v. irr.)* off.

distacco *sm.* 1. detaching 2. *(partenza)* leaving 3. *(indifferenza)* unconcern.

distante *agg.* distant. ◆ **distante** *avv.* far, far off, far away.

distanza *sf.* distance.

distanziare *vt.* 1. to space 2. *(lasciare indietro)* to distance.

distanziato *agg.* 1. spaced 2. *(sport)* outdistanced.

distare *vi.* to be far: *quanto dista?,* how far is it?

distèndere *vt.* 1. *(allungare)* to stretch 2. *(spalmare)* to spread *(v. irr.)* 3. *(porre, stendere)* to lay *(v. irr.)*. ◆ **distèndersi** *vr.* 1. to spread *(v. irr.)* 2. *(sdraiarsi)* to lie *(v. irr.)* down 3. *(rilassarsi)* to relax.

distensione *sf.* 1. *(di nervi, tensione)* relaxation 2. *(pol.)* distension.

distensivo *agg.* relaxing.

distesa *sf.* expanse || *a —*, continuously.

distesamente *avv.* diffusely.

disteso *agg.* 1. *(teso)* extended 2. *(giacente)* lying 3. *(esteso)* extensive || *per —*, diffusely.

distico *sm.* couplet.

distillare *vt.* to distil.

distillato *agg.* distilled. ◆ **distillato** *sm.* distillate.

distillatoio *sm.* still.

distillatore *sm.* distiller.

distillazione *sf.* distillation.

distilleria *sf.* distillery.

distinguere *vt.* 1. to distinguish 2. *(contrassegnare)* to mark.

distinta *sf.* list.

distintivo *agg.* distinctive. ◆ **distintivo** *sm.* badge.

distinto *agg.* 1. distinct 2. *(garbato)* distinguished.

distinzione *sf.* 1. distinction 2. *(riguardo)* regard 3. *(raffinatezza)* refinement.

distògliere *vt.* 1. *(dissuadere)* to dissuade 2. *(distrarre)* to divert. ◆ **distògliersi** *vr.* to be distracted.

distorsione *sf.* distortion.

distrarre *vt.* 1. *(distogliere)* to divert 2. *(divertire)* to entertain.

distrattamente *avv.* **1.** absent-mindedly **2.** (*inavvertitamente*) inadvertently.

distratto *agg.* **1.** absent-minded **2.** (*disattento*) inattentive.

distrazione *sf.* **1.** absent-mindedness **2.** (*disattenzione*) inattention **3.** (*divertimento*) recreation.

distretta *sf.* urgent need.

distretto *sm.* district || — *militare*, recruiting centre.

distrettuale *agg.* district.

distribuibile *agg.* distributable.

distribuire *vt.* to distribute.

distributivo *agg.* e *sm.* distributive.

distributore *agg.* distributing. ♦ **distributore** *sm.* distributor || — *di benzina*, petrol pump.

distribuzione *sf.* distribution.

districare *vt.* to disentangle.

distruggere *vt.* **1.** to destroy **2.** (*struggere*) to consume. ♦ **distruggersi** *vr.* (*consumarsi*) to pine (away).

distruggibile *agg.* destroyable.

distruttivo *agg.* destroying.

distrutto *agg.* destroyed.

distruttore *agg.* destroying. ♦ **distruttore** *sm.* destroyer.

distruzione *sf.* destruction.

disturbare *vt.* to disturb.

disturbato *agg.* **1.** disturbed **2.** (*indisposto*) unwell.

disturbatore *sm.* disturber.

disturbo *sm.* **1.** trouble, inconvenience **2.** (*malattia*) trouble, illness **3.** (*radio*) disturbance.

disubbidiente *agg.* disobedient.

disubbidienza *sf.* disobedience.

disubbidire *vi.* to disobey.

disuguaglianza *sf.* **1.** inequality **2.** (*di terreno*) unevenness.

disuguale *agg.* **1.** unequal **2.** (*irregolare*) irregular **3.** (*differente*) different.

disumanamente *avv.* inhumanly.

disumanare *vt.* to divest of humanity.

disumanità *sf.* inhumanity.

disumano *agg.* inhuman.

disumidire *vt.* to dry.

disunione *sf.* disunion.

disunire *vt.* to disunite. ♦ **disunirsi** *vr.* to become (*v. irr.*) disunited.

disunito *agg.* disunited.

disusare *vt.* to disuse.

disusato *agg.* disused.

disuso *sm.* disuse.

ditale *sm.* thimble.

ditata *sf.* finger-mark.

ditirambico *agg.* dithyrambic.

ditirambo *sm.* dithyramb.

dito *sm.* **1.** finger **2.** (*del piede*) toe.

ditta *sf.* firm.

dittafono *sm.* dictaphone.

dittatore *sm.* dictator.

dittatoriale *agg.* dictatorial.

dittatorio *agg.* dictatorial.

dittatura *sf.* dictatorship.

dittico *sm.* diptych.

dittongo *sm.* diphthong.

diuresi *sf.* diuresis.

diuretico *agg.* diuretic.

diurno *agg.* diurnal, daytime.

diuturnamente *avv.* for a long time.

diuturno *agg.* diuturnal.

diva *sf.* **1.** goddess **2.** (*cine*) star.

divagare *vi.* to wander **2.** (*divertire*) to amuse. ♦ **divagarsi** *vr.* **1.** to be distracted **2.** (*divertirsi*) to amuse oneself.

divagazione *sf.* digression.

divampare *vi.* to blaze.

divano *sm.* divan, sofa.

divaricamento *sm.* straddle.

divaricare *vt.* to open wide || — *le gambe*, to part one's legs wide.

divario *sm.* difference.

divedere *vt.* **1.** (*nella loc. avv.*) *dare a* —, to show (*v. irr.*) clearly **2.** (*dar a credere*) to make (*v. irr.*) believe.

divèllere *vt.* to uproot.

divenire[1] *vi.* **1.** to become (*v. irr.*) **2.** (*mutarsi lentamente*) to grow (*v. irr.*).

divenire[2] *sm.* becoming: *l'essere e il* —, being and becoming.

diverbio *sm.* quarrel.

divergente *agg.* divergent.

divergenza *sf.* divergence.

divergere *vi.* **1.** to diverge **2.** (*scostarsi*) to wander.

diversamente *avv.* **1.** differently **2.** (*altrimenti*) otherwise.

diversificare *vt.* to diversify. ♦ **diversificarsi** *vr.* to differ.

diversione *sf.* diversion.

diversità *sf.* diversity.

diversivo *agg.* **1.** deviating **2.** (*che distrae*) diverting. ♦ **diversivo** *sm.* diversion, distraction.

diverso *agg.* different.

divertente *agg.* amusing.

divertimento *sm.* amusement.

divertire *vt.* to amuse, to entertain ♦ **divertirsi** *vr.* to enjoy oneself, to have a good time.

divezzamento *sm.* weaning.

divezzare *vt.* to wean.

dividendo *sm.* dividend.

divìdere *vt.* 1. to divide 2. (*condividere*) to share.

divieto *sm.* prohibition.

divinamente *avv.* divinely.

divinare *vt.* to divine.

divinatore *sm.* diviner.

divinatorio *agg.* divinatory.

divinazione *sf.* divination.

divincolarsi *vr.* to wriggle.

divinità *sf.* divinity.

divinizzare *vt.* to deify.

divino *agg.* divine.

divisa *sf.* 1. uniform 2. (*valuta*) currency.

divisare *vt.* to plan.

divisìbile *agg.* divisible.

divisibilità *sf.* divisibility.

divisionale *agg.* divisional.

divisione *sf.* 1. division 2. (*amm.*) department.

divisionismo *sm.* pointillism.

divisionista *s.* pointillist.

divismo *sm.* stardom, star worship.

diviso *agg.* 1. divided 2. (*separato*) separated 3. (*condiviso*) shared.

divisore *sm.* divisor.

divisorio *agg.* dividing.

divo *sm.* 1. deity 2. (*cine*) star.

divorare *vt.* to devour.

divoratore *agg.* devouring.

divorziare *vi.* to divorce, to be divorced.

divorziato *agg.* divorced. ♦ **divorziato** *sm.* divorcee.

divorzio *sm.* divorce (*anche fig.*).

divulgàbile *agg.* that may be divulged.

divulgare *vt.* to spread (*v. irr.*).

divulgativo *agg.* divulging.

divulgatore *sm.* divulger.

divulgazione *sf.* divulgation, spreading.

dizionario *sm.* dictionary.

dizionarista *s.* lexicographer.

dizione *sf.* 1. diction 2. (*pronuncia*) pronunciation.

do *sm.* (*mus.*) C.

doccia *sf.* shower.

docente *agg.* teaching. ♦ **docente** *sm.* teacher || *libero —*, fully established university lecturer.

docenza *sf.* teaching.

dòcile *agg.* docile.

docilità *sf.* docility.

documentare *vt.* to document.

documentario *sm.* documentary.

documentarista *s.* documentary film-maker.

documentato *agg.* documented.

documentazione *sf.* 1. documentation 2. *pl.* (*documenti*) papers.

documento *sm.* document.

dodecaedro *sm.* dodecahedron.

dodecafonìa *sf.* dodecaphony.

dodecafònico *agg.* dodecaphonic.

dodecàgono *sm.* dodecagon.

dodecasìllabo *agg.* dodecasyllable.

dodicèsimo *agg.* twelfth.

dòdici *agg.* twelve.

doga *sf.* stave.

dogana *sf.* customs (*pl.*).

doganale *agg.* customs (*attr.*): *dichiarazione —*, customs entry.

doganiere *sm.* customs officer.

doge *sm.* doge.

doglia *sf.* 1. sharp pains 2. (*pl., med.*) throes.

dogma *sm.* dogma.

dogmàtico *agg.* dogmatic(al).

dogmatismo *sm.* dogmatism.

dolce *agg.* 1. sweet 2. (*mite*) mild 3. (*tec.*) soft. ♦ **dolce** *sm.* 1. sweet 2. (*torta*) cake.

dolcezza *sf.* 1. sweetness 2. (*di clima*) mildness.

dolciario *agg.* confectionary.

dolciastro *agg.* sweetish.

dolcificare *vt.* 1. to sweeten 2. (*fig.*) to mitigate.

dolcificazione *sf.* sweetening.

dolciumi *sm. pl.* sweets.

dolente *agg.* 1. afflicted, grieved 2. (*spiacente*) sorry.

dolere *vi.* 1. to ache 2. (*rincrescere*) to regret. ♦ **dolersi** *vr.* to regret.

dolicocèfalo *agg.* dolichocephalic.

dòllaro *sm.* dollar.

dolmen *sm.* dolmen.

dolo *sm.* fraud.

dolomite *sf.* dolomite.

dolomìtico *agg.* dolomitic.

dolorante *agg.* aching.

dolore *sm.* 1. pain, ache 2. (*fig.*) sorrow, grief.

dolorosamente *avv.* 1. painfully 2. (*morale*) sadly.

doloroso *agg.* 1. painful 2. (*che causa dolore*) grievous.

doloso *agg.* fraudulent.

domàbile *agg.* tamable.

domanda *sf.* 1. question, request

2. (*richiesta scritta*) application.
domandare *vt.* to ask (so. for sthg.). ◆ **domandarsi** *vr.* to wonder.
domani *avv.* tomorrow.
domare *vt.* **1.** to tame **2.** (*sottomettere*) to subdue.
domatore *sm.* tamer.
domattina *avv.* tomorrow morning.
doménica *sf.* Sunday.
domenicale *agg.* Sunday (*attr.*).
domenicano *agg.* dominican.
domèstica *sf.* maid.
domèstico *agg. e sm.* domestic || *lavori domestici,* household duties.
domiciliare *agg.* domiciliary.
domiciliarsi *vr.* to settle (in).
domiciliato *agg.* resident, living.
domicilio *sm.* **1.** house, dwelling **2.** (*giur.*) domicile.
dominante *agg.* dominant.
dominare *vt.* to dominate.
dominatore *sm.* ruler.
dominazione *sf.* domination.
dominio *sm.* **1.** domination **2.** (*territorio*) dominion **3.** (*giur.*) domain || *di — pubblico,* known to everybody.
dòmino *sm.* domino.
donare *vt.* to give (*v. irr.*) ◆ **donare** *vi.* (*addirsi*) to suit.
donatore *sm.* donor.
donazione *sf.* **1.** donation **2.** (*somma elargita per uno scopo*) grant.
donchisciottesco *agg.* quixotic.
donde *avv.* whence, from where || *ne ha ben —,* he has good reason for it.
dondolamento *sm.* swinging.
dondolare *vt. e vi.* to swing (*v. irr.*). ◆ **dondolarsi** *vr.* to swing, to rock.
dondolio *sm.* swinging.
dòndolo *sm.* (*altalena*) swing || *a —,* rocking.
donna *sf.* woman (*pl.* women).
donnaiolo *sm.* ladies' man (*pl.* men).
donnesco *agg.* womanlike.
dònnola *sf.* weasel.
dono *sm.* gift.
donzella *sf.* damsel.
dopo *avv.* **1.** (*di luogo*) after, next **2.** (*dietro*) behind **3.** (*di tempo*) after, then **4.** (*più tardi*) later. ◆ **dopo** *prep.* (*di luogo e tempo*) after.
dopodomani *avv.* the day after to-

morrow.
dopoguerra *sm.* post-war period.
dopopranzo *sm.* afternoon.
dopotutto *avv.* after all.
doppiaggio *sm.* (*cine*) dubbing.
doppiamente *avv.* **1.** doubly **2.** (*con inganno*) deceitfully.
doppiare *vt.* **1.** to double **2.** (*cine*) to dub.
doppiato *agg.* **1.** doubled **2.** (*cine*) dubbed.
doppiatura *sf.* doubling.
doppietta *sf.* double-barrelled gun.
doppiezza *sf.* **1.** doubleness **2.** (*ambiguità*) double-dealing.
doppio *agg.* **1.** double **2.** (*ambiguo*) double-faced. ◆ **doppio** *sm.* twice as much, twice as many.
doppiofondo *sm.* double bottom.
doppione *sm.* **1.** double **2.** (*di parola*) doublet.
doppiopetto *sm.* double-breasted.
dorare *vt.* to gild.
dorato *agg.* **1.** gilded **2.** (*color oro*) golden.
doratore *sm.* gilder.
doratura *sf.* gilding.
dòrico *agg.* doric.
dorìfora *sf.* potato-beetle.
dormicchiare *vi.* to doze.
dormiente *agg.* sleeping. ◆ **dormiente** *sm.* sleeper.
dormiglione *sm.* sleepy-head.
dormire *vi.* **1.** to sleep (*v. irr.*) || *— tra due guanciali,* to set (*v. irr.*) one's mind at rest **2.** (*fig.*) to remain inactive.
dormita *sf.* sleep.
dormitorio *sm.* dormitory.
dormiveglia *sm.* drowsiness.
dorsale *agg.* dorsal: *spina —,* backbone.
dorso *sm.* **1.** back **2.** (*di monte*) ridge.
dosàbile *agg.* measurable.
dosaggio *sm.* dosage.
dosare *vt.* to proportion: *— le parole,* to weigh one's words.
dosatura *sf.* dosage.
dose *sf.* dose: *una buona — di,* a good deal of.
dossale *sm.* dossal.
dosso *sm.* back: *togliersi di —,* to take (*v. irr.*) off.
dotare *vt.* **1.** to give (*v. irr.*) a dowry **2.** (*fornire di una rendita*) to endow **3.** (*fornire*) to provide (with).
dotato *agg.* **1.** gifted (with) **2.** (*e-*

quipaggiato) provided (with).

dotazione *sf.* endowment.

dote *sf.* **1.** dowry **2.** (*qualità*) endowment.

dotto[1] *agg.* learned. ♦ **dotto** *sm.* scholar.

dotto[2] *sm.* (*anat.*) duct.

dottorale *agg.* doctoral.

dottorato *sm.* doctorate.

dottore *sm.* **1.** doctor **2.** (*laureato*) graduate.

dottoressa *sf.* **1.** (*laureata*) graduate **2.** (*in medicina*) lady doctor.

dottrina *sf.* doctrine.

dottrinale *agg.* doctrinal.

dottrinario *sm.* doctrinaire.

dottrinarismo *sm.* doctrinairism.

dove *avv.* where.

dovere[1] *vi.* **1.** (*obbligo*) must (*v. dif.*): *devi lavorare*, you must work **2.** to have to **3.** (*possibilità, predestinazione*) to be to: *doveva diventare un grande scrittore*, he was to become a great writer **4.** (*devo?, dobbiamo?, nel senso di: vuoi che?*) shall (*v. dif.*): *devo aprire la finestra?*, shall I open the window? **5.** (*al condizionale*) ought to, should (*v. dif.*): *dovresti essere gentile*, you ought to be kind; *dovremmo partire*, we should leave **6.** (*al congiuntivo*) should, were to: *se dovesse venire*, if he should come, if he were to come **7.** (*essere obbligati*) to be obliged, to be forced **8.** (*essere da attribuire, dover arrivare*) to be due: *lo si deve al mio ritardo*, this is due to my being late; *il treno deve arrivare alle 4*, the train is due at 4 a.m. ♦ **dovere** *vt.* (*essere debitore in tutti i sensi*) to owe: *ti devo 1000 lire*, I owe you one thousand lire; *ti devo la vita*, I owe you my life.

dovere[2] *sm.* duty: *fare il proprio —*, to do (*v. irr.*) one's duty.

doverosamente *avv.* dutifully.

doveroso *agg.* dutiful.

dovizia *sf.* plenty.

dovizioso *agg.* abundant.

dovunque *avv.* **1.** everywhere **2.** (*seguito da verbo*) wherever.

dovuto *agg.* **1.** due **2.** (*equo*) fair. ♦ **dovuto** *sm.* due.

dozzina *sf.* dozen.

dozzinale *agg.* cheap, common.

draconiano *agg.* draconian.

draga *sf.* dredger.

dragaggio *sm.* dredging.

dragamine *sm.* mine-sweeper.

dragare *vt.* to dredge.

draglia *sf.* stay.

drago *sm.* dragon.

dragona *sf.* sword-knot.

dragone *sm.* dragon.

dramma *sm.* drama.

drammàtica *sf.* dramatics.

drammaticamente *avv.* dramatically.

drammaticità *sf.* tragicalness.

drammàtico *agg.* dramatic.

drammatizzare *vt.* to dramatise.

drammaturgia *sf.* dramaturgy.

drammaturgo *sm.* dramatist.

drappeggiare *vt.* to drape.

drappeggio *sm.* draping.

drappello *sm.* squad.

drapperia *sf.* drapery.

drappo *sm.* cloth.

dràstico *agg.* drastic.

drenaggio *sm.* drainage.

drenare *vt.* to drain.

drìade *sf.* **1.** (*mit.*) dryad **2.** (*bot.*) dryas (*pl.* -ades).

dribblare *vt.* to dribble.

dritta *sf.* **1.** right hand, right **2.** (*mar.*) starboard.

dritto *agg.* **1.** (*non storto*) straight **2.** (*eretto, onesto*) upright. ♦ **dritto** *sm.* right side.

drizza *sf.* halyard.

drizzare *vt.* to straighten.

droga *sf.* **1.** drug **2.** (*spezia*) spices (*pl.*).

drogare *vt.* **1.** to drug **2.** (*condire*) to spice.

drogheria *sf.* grocery.

droghiere *sm.* grocer.

dromedario *sm.* dromedary.

drùido *sm.* druid.

drupa *sf.* drupe.

dualismo *sm.* dualism.

dualità *sf.* duality.

dubbezza *sf.* dubiousness.

dubbio *sm.* doubt: *mettere in —*, to question. ♦ **dubbio** *agg.* dubious.

dubbioso *agg.* doubtful.

dubitare *vi.* to doubt.

dubitativo *agg.* dubitative.

duca *sm.* duke.

ducale *agg.* ducal.

ducato *sm.* **1.** dukedom **2.** (*moneta*) ducat.

duchessa *sf.* duchess.

due *agg.* two.

duecentèsimo *agg.* two hundredth.

duecentesco *agg.* thirteenth century (*attr.*).

duecento *sm.* two hundred || *il* —, the thirteenth century.

duellare *vi.* to duel.

duello *sm.* duel: — *all'ultimo sangue*, duel to the death.

duetto *sm.* duet.

duna *sf.* dune.

dunque *cong.* 1. (*perciò*) therefore 2. (*rafforzativo*) well, then. ♦ **dunque** *sm. venire al* —, to come (*v. irr.*) to the point.

duodenale *agg.* duodenal.

duodeno *sm.* duodenum.

duomo *sm.* cathedral.

duplicare *vt.* to duplicate.

duplicato *sm.* duplicate.

dùplice *agg.* twofold.

duplicità *sf.* double-dealing.

durabilità *sf.* durability.

duralluminio *sm.* duralumin.

durante *prep.* during.

durare *vi.* 1. to last 2. (*perseverare*) to persist 3. (*resistere*) to hold (*v. irr.*) out. ♦ **durare** *vt.* to endure || *chi la dura la vince*, slow and steady wins the race.

durata *sf.* 1. duration, length 2. (*periodo*) term 3. (*di un oggetto*) endurance.

duraturo *agg.* lasting.

durévole *agg.* durable.

durezza *sf.* 1. hardness 2. (*rigidità*) stiffness.

duro *agg.* 1. hard 2. (*di voce*) harsh || *avere il sonno* —, to sleep (*v. irr.*) like a log; *avere la testa dura*, to be a block-head, to be stubborn.

durone *sm.* hard skin.

dùttile *agg.* ductile.

duttilità *sf.* ductility.

E

e *cong.* and: *e... e*, both... and.

ebanista *sm.* cabinet-maker.

ebanisterìa *sf.* 1. (*bottega*) cabinet-maker's shop 2. (*arte*) cabinet-making.

ebanite *sf.* ebonite.

èbano *sm.* ebony.

ebbene *cong.* well: —?, what about it?

ebbrezza *sf.* 1. drunkenness 2. (*fig.*) elation.

èbbro *agg.* 1. drunken 2. (*fig.*) mad.

ebdomadario *agg.* weekly. ♦ **ebdomadario** *sm.* weekly paper.

èbete *agg.* idiotic. ♦ **èbete** *sm.* idiot.

ebollizione *sf.* boiling.

ebràico *agg.* Hebrew.

ebreo *agg.* Hebrew, Jewish. ♦ **ebreo** *sm.* Hebrew, Jew.

ecatombe *sf.* massacre.

eccedente *agg.* excessive, in excess (*pred.*). ♦ **eccedente** *sm.* (*comm.*) exceeding.

eccedenza *sf.* excess, surplus: — *di peso*, overweight.

eccèdere *vi.* to exceed. ♦ **eccèdere** *vi.* to go (*v. irr.*) too far.

eccellente *agg.* excellent.

eccellenza *sf.* 1. excellence 2. (*titolo*) excellency.

eccèllere *vi.* to excel.

eccelso *agg.* sublime.

eccentricità *sf.* eccentricity.

eccèntrico *agg.* eccentric.

eccepire *vi.* to object.

eccessivo *agg.* excessive.

eccesso *sm.* excess.

eccètera *sm.* et cetera (*abbr.* etc.), and so on.

eccetto *prep.* except, but, save. ♦ **eccetto che** *cong.* 1. except that 2. (*purché*) provided that.

eccettuare *vt.* to except.

eccettuato *agg.* excluded.

eccezionale *agg.* exceptional.

eccezione *sf.* exception.

ecchìmosi *sf.* bruise.

eccidio *sm.* bloodshed.

eccitàbile *agg.* excitable.

eccitabilità *sf.* excitability.

eccitamento *sm.* excitement.

eccitante *agg.* e *sm.* excitant.

eccitare *vt.* to excite. ♦ **eccitarsi** *vr.* to get (*v. irr.*) excited.

eccitatore *agg.* excitative. ♦ **eccitatore** *sm.* exciter.

eccitazione *sf.* excitement.

ecclesiàstico *agg.* ecclesiastical.

ecco *avv.* here, there (*in unione con le voci del verbo* to be *al pres. ind.*): — *il mio cappello!*, here is my hat! || — *tutto*, that's all; *quand'* —, when suddenly.

eccome *inter.* and how!

echeggiare *vi.* to echo (with sthg.).

echinoderma *sm.* echinoderm.

eclèttico *agg.* e *sm.* eclectic.

eclettismo *sm.* eclecticism.

eclissare *vt.* 1. to eclipse 2. (*fig.*) to overshadow.

eclisse, eclissi *sf.* eclipse.

eclittica *sf.* ecliptic.

eclittico *agg.* ecliptic.

eco *sf.* echo.

economato *sm.* 1. steward's office 2. (*in università*) bursar's office.

economia *sf.* 1. economy 2. (*scienza*) economics.

economico *agg.* 1. economic 2. (*a buon prezzo*) cheap.

economista *s.* economist.

economizzare *vt.* to economize.

economo *agg.* economical. ♦ **econònomo** *sm.* 1. steward 2. (*di università*) bursar.

ecumenico *agg.* ecumenical.

eczema *sm.* eczema.

edema *sm.* oedema.

eden *sm.* Eden.

edera *sf.* ivy.

edicola *sf.* newspaper kiosk.

edicolista *sm.* news-agent.

edificante *agg.* edifying.

edificare *vt.* 1. to build (*v. irr.*) (up) 2. (*fig.*) to edify.

edificatore *sm.* 1. builder 2. (*fig.*) edifier.

edificazione *sf.* 1. building 2. (*fig.*) edification.

edificio *sm.* building.

edile *agg.* building: *perito —,* master-builder. ♦ **edile** *sm.* (*stor. romana*) aedile.

edilizia *sf.* building industry.

edilizio *agg.* building (*attr.*).

edito *agg.* published.

editore *sm.* publisher.

editoria *sf.* book industry.

editoriale *agg. e sm.* editorial.

editrice *agg.: casa —,* publishing house.

editto *sm.* edict.

edizione *sf.* edition, issue.

edonismo *sm.* hedonism.

edonista *s.* hedonist.

edotto *agg.* aware: *rendere —,* to inform.

educanda *sf.* boarding-school girl.

educandato *sm.* girls' boarding-school.

educare *vt.* 1. to educate 2. (*allevare*) to bring (*v. irr.*) up.

educativo *agg.* educational.

educato *agg.* well-bred, polite.

educatore *sm.* educator.

educazione *sf.* 1. education 2.

(*buone maniere*) good manners (*pl.*).

edulcorare *vt.* to edulcorate.

efebo *sm.* ephebe.

efelide *sf.* freckle.

effemeride *sf.* ephemeris (*pl.* -ides).

effeminare *vt.* to effeminate. ♦ **effeminarsi** *vr.* to become (*v. irr.*) effeminate.

effeminatezza *sf.* effeminacy.

efferatezza *sf.* brutality.

efferato *agg.* brutal.

effervescente *agg.* sparkling.

effervescenza *sf.* effervescence.

effettivamente *avv.* actually, indeed.

effettivo *agg.* actual.

effetto *sm.* 1. effect, result ‖ *in effetti,* as a matter of fact 2. (*comm.*) bill.

effettuabile *agg.* feasible.

effettuare *vt.* to carry out: — *un piano,* to carry out a plan. ♦ **effettuarsi** *vr.* (*aver luogo*) to take (*v. irr.*) place.

effettuazione *sf.* accomplishment.

efficace *agg.* effective, efficacious.

efficacia *sf.* efficacy.

efficiente *agg.* efficient.

efficienza *sf.* efficiency.

effigiare *vt.* to portray.

effigie *sf.* image.

effimera *sf.* (*fam.*) mayfly.

effimero *agg.* ephemeral.

effluvio *sm.* exhalation.

effondere *vt.* to pour forth. ♦ **effondersi** *vr.* to spread (*v. irr.*) (about).

effrazione *sf.* (*giur.*) house-breaking, burglary.

effusione *sf.* 1. shedding 2. (*cordialità*) cordiality 3. (*pl., manifestazioni*) effusions.

effusivo *agg.* effusive.

egemonia *sf.* hegemony.

egemonico *agg.* hegemonic.

egida *sf.* 1. aegis 2. (*fig.*) protection.

egiziano *agg. e sm.* Egyptian.

egli *pron.* he: — *stesso,* he himself.

egloga *sf.* eclogue.

egocentrico *agg.* egocentric. ♦ **egocentrico** *sm.* egocentric man.

egocentrismo *sm.* egocentrism.

egoismo *sm.* selfishness.

egoista *agg. e sm.* egoist.

egotismo *sm.* self-conceit.

egregiamente *avv.* eminently.

egregio *agg.* eminent ‖ (*nelle lettere*) — *Signore,* Dear Sir.

eguaglianza, eguagliare, eguale ecc. V. *uguaglianza, uguagliare, uguale ecc.*

egualità *sf.* equality.

eiaculare *vi.* to ejaculate.

eiaculazione *sf.* ejaculation.

eiezione *sf.* ejection.

elaborare *vt.* to elaborate.

elaborato *agg.* elaborate.

elaborazione *sf.* **1.** elaboration **2.** (*di piano*) formulation.

elargire *vt.* to lavish.

elargizione *sf.* donation.

elasticità *sf.* **1.** elasticity **2.** (*agilità*) nimbleness.

elasticizzare *vt.* to make (*v. irr.*) elastic.

elàstico *agg.* **1.** elastic **2.** (*agile*) nimble. ◆ **elàstico** *sm.* rubber band.

elce *sm.* ílex.

elefante *sm.* elephant.

elefantesco *agg.* elephantine.

elefantìasi *sf.* elephantiasis.

elegante *agg.* elegant, smart.

eleganza *sf.* smartness.

elèggere *vt.* **1.** to elect **2.** (*nominare*) to appoint.

eleggìbile *agg.* eligible.

eleggibilità *sf.* eligibility.

elegìa *sf.* elegy.

elegìaco *agg.* elegiac.

elementare *agg.* elementary: *scuola —*, primary school.

elemento *sm.* **1.** element **2.** (*componente*) component **3.** (*pl., rudimenti*) rudiments **4.** (*persona*) person.

elemòsina *sf.* alms: *chiedere l'—*, to beg.

elemosinare *vt.* e *vi.* to beg (for).

elencare *vt.* to list.

elenco *sm.* list: *— telefonico*, telephone directory.

elettivo *agg.* elective.

eletto *agg.* elect, chosen.

elettorale *agg.* electoral.

elettorato *sm.* electorate.

elettore *sm.* voter.

elettràuto *sm.* **1.** (*officina*) car electrical repairs (*pl.*) **2.** (*meccanico*) car electrician.

elettricista *sm.* electrician.

elettricità *sf.* electricity.

elèttrico *agg.* electric.

elettrificare *vt.* to electrify.

elettrificazione *sf.* electrification.

elettrizzare *vt.* to electrify.

elettrocalamita *sf.* electro-magnet.

elettrocardiogramma *sm.* electrocardiogram.

elettrodinàmica *sf.* electrodynamics.

elèttrodo *sm.* electrode.

elettrodomèstici *sm. pl.* electrical household appliances.

elettrògeno *agg.* generating electricity.

elettròlisi *sf.* electrolysis.

elettromagnètico *agg.* electro-magnetic.

elettromotore *sm.* dynamo.

elettromotrice *sf.* electric rail car.

elettrone *sm.* electron.

elettrònica *sf.* electronics.

elettrònico *agg.* electronic.

elettrotècnica *sf.* electrical technology.

elettrotreno *sm.* electric train.

elevamento *sm.* elevation.

elevare *vt.* **1.** to elevate **2.** (*erigere*) to erect **3.** (*mat.*) to raise. ◆ **elevarsi** *vr.* to rise (*v. irr.*).

elevatezza *sf.* loftiness.

elevato *agg.* elevated, high.

elevatore *sm.* elevator.

elevazione *sf.* **1.** elevation **2.** (*l'elevare*) rising **3.** (*mat.*) raising.

elezione *sf.* election.

èlica *sf.* **1.** (*aer.*) propeller **2.** (*mar.*) screw.

elicoidale *agg.* helicoidal.

elicòttero *sm.* helicopter.

elìdere *vt.* to annul. ◆ **elìdersi** *vr. rec.* to annul each other.

eliminare *vt.* to eliminate. ◆ **eliminarsi** *vr.* to be eliminated.

eliminatoria *sf.* preliminary heat.

eliminazione *sf.* elimination, expulsion.

elio *sm.* helium.

eliocèntrico *agg.* heliocentric.

eliografìa *sf.* heliography.

elioterapìa *sf.* heliotherapy.

eliotipìa *sf.* heliotypy.

eliporto *sm.* heliport.

elisione *sf.* elision.

elisir *sm.* elixir.

èlitra *sf.* elytrum (*pl.* -ra).

ella *pron.* she: *— stessa*, she herself.

ellènico *agg.* Hellenic.

ellenismo *sm.* Hellenism.

ellenista *s.* Hellenist.

ellisse *sf.* ellipse.

ellissi *sf.* ellipsis (*pl.* -ses).

ellìttico *sm.* elliptic(al).

elmetto *sm.* helmet.

elmo *sm.* helmet.
elocuzione *sf.* elocution.
elogiàbile *agg.* praiseworthy.
elogiare *vt.* to eulogize, to praise.
elogiatore *sm.* eulogist.
elogio *sm.* eulogy, praise.
eloquente *agg.* eloquent.
eloquenza *sf.* eloquence.
elucubrare *vt.* to lucubrate: — *su, intorno a qc.,* to lucubrate on, about sthg.
elucubrazione *sf.* lucubration.
elùdere *vt.* to elude.
elusivo *agg.* elusive.
elvètico *agg.* Helvetic.
elzeviro *sm.* 1. elzevir 2. (*giorn.*) leading literary article.
emaciare *vt.* to emaciate. ♦ **emaciarsi** *vr.* to become (*v. irr.*) emaciated.
emaciato *agg.* emaciated.
emanare *vt.* 1. to issue 2. (*vapori, profumi*) to exhale.
emanazione *sf.* emanation.
emancipare *vt.* to emancipate.
emancipato *agg.* emancipated.
emancipazione *sf.* emancipation.
emàtico *agg.* haematic.
ematoma *sm.* haematoma (*pl.* -ata).
ematosi *sf.* haematosis.
embargo *sm.* embargo.
emblema *sm.* 1. emblem 2. (*simbolo*) symbol.
emblemàtico *agg.* emblematic.
embolìa *sf.* embolism.
èmbolo *sm.* embolus (*pl.* -li).
embrionale *agg.* embryonic.
embrione *sm.* embryo.
emendamento *sm.* 1. amendment 2. (*correzione*) emendation.
emendare *vt.* 1. to amend 2. (*correggere*) to emend.
emergenza *sf.* emergency.
emèrgere *vi.* 1. to emerge 2. (*fig.*) to emerge, to appear.
emèrito *agg.* emeritus.
emeroteca *sf.* newspaper library.
emersione *sf.* emersion.
eméttere *vt.* 1. to emit 2. (*di suono*) to utter 3. (*emanare*) to deliver 4. (*banconote*) to issue.
emiciclo *sm.* hemicycle.
emicrania *sf.* headache.
emigrante *agg. e sm.* emigrant.
emigrare *vi.* to emigrate.
emigrato *sm.* emigrant.
emigrazione *sf.* emigration.
eminente *agg.* outstanding, eminent.
eminenza *sf.* eminence.

emiro *sm.* emir.
emisfèrico *agg.* hemispheric(al).
emisfero *sm.* hemisphere.
emissario *sm.* emissary.
emissione *sf.* 1. emission 2. (*econ.*) issue.
emistichio *sm.* hemistich.
emittente *agg.* issuing || *stazione* — (*radio*), broadcasting station.
emofilìa *sf.* haemophilia.
emoglobina *sf.* haemoglobin.
emolliente *agg.* emollient.
emolumento *sm.* emolument.
emorragìa *sf.* haemorrhage.
emorròidi *sf. pl.* haemorrhoids.
emòstasi *sf.* haemostasis.
emostàtico *agg.* haemostatic.
emoteca *sf.* blood bank.
emotività *sf.* emotionality.
emotivo *agg.* emotional.
emottisi *sf.* haemoptysis.
emozionante *agg.* touching, exciting, thrilling.
emozionare *vt.* to move. ♦ **emozionarsi** *vr.* to get (*v. irr.*) excited.
emozione *sf.* emotion, thrill.
empiastro *sm.* plaster.
empietà *sf.* impiety.
empio *agg.* impious.
empire *vt.* to fill.
empìrico *agg. e sm.* empiric.
empirismo *sm.* empiricism.
emporio *sm.* department store.
emulare *vt.* to emulate.
emulazione *sf.* emulation.
èmulo *sm.* rival.
emulsionare *vt.* to emulsify.
emulsione *sf.* emulsion.
encefalite *sf.* encephalitis.
encèfalo *sm.* encephalon (*pl.* -ala).
enciclica *sf.* encyclic.
enciclopedìa *sf.* encyclopaedia.
enciclopèdico *agg.* encyclopaedic.
enclìtico *agg.* enclitic.
encomiàbile *agg.* praiseworthy.
encomiare *vt.* to commend.
encomio *sm.* panegyric.
endecasìllabo *agg.* hendecasyllabic. ♦ **endecasìllabo** *sm.* hendecasyllable.
endèmico *agg.* endemic.
endocardio *sm.* endocardium.
endocardite *sf.* endocarditis.
endòcrino *agg.* endocrine.
endocrinologìa *sf.* endocrinology.
endovenoso *agg.* intravenous. ♦ **endovenosa** *sf.* intravenous injection.

energètico *agg.* e *sm.* tonic.

energia *sf.* energy.

energicamente *avv.* energetically.

enèrgico *agg.* energetic(al).

energùmeno *sm.* energumen.

ènfasi *sf.* emphasis.

enfàtico *agg.* emphatic.

enfiagione *sf.* swelling.

enfisema *sm.* emphysema.

enfitèusi *sf.* emphyteusis.

enigma *sm.* enigma, puzzle.

enigmàtico *agg.* puzzling.

enigmista *sm.* enigmatographer.

enigmìstica *sf.* enigmatography.

enigmìstico *agg.* puzzle (*attr.*).

ennèsimo *agg.* nth: *ennesima potenza*, nth power.

enologìa *sf.* oenology.

enòlogo *sm.* oenologist.

enorme *agg.* huge.

enormità *sf.* 1. hugeness 2. (*fig.*) absurdity.

ente *sm.* 1. being 2. (*comm.*) body, corporation.

enterite *sf.* enteritis.

enteroclisma *sm.* enema.

enterocolite *sf.* enterocolitis.

entità *sf.* entity.

entomologìa *sf.* entomology.

entomòlogo *sm.* entomologist.

entrambi *pron.* e *agg.* both.

entrante *agg.* (*con espressioni di tempo*) next, coming.

entrare *vi.* to enter, to come (*v. irr.*) in, to go (*v. irr.*) in || *non c'entra*, this has got nothing to do with it; — *correndo*, to run (*v. irr.*) in; — *in carica*, to come (*v. irr.*) into office; — *in società*, to go into partnership (with); — *precipitosamente*, to rush in; — *in giuoco*, to come into play; — *in vigore*, to come into force.

entrata *sf.* 1. entrance, entry 2. (*rendita*) income.

entratura *sf.* entrance.

entro *prep.* 1. (*luogo*) inside 2. (*tempo*) in, within, by: — *due giorni*, within two days; — *lunedì*, by Monday.

entrobordo *sm.* inboard.

entroterra *sm.* inland.

entusiasmante *agg.* exciting.

entusiasmare *vt.* to raise enthusiasm in. ♦ **entusiasmarsi** *vr.* to become (*v. irr.*) enthusiastic.

entusiasmo *sm.* enthusiasm.

entusiasta *agg.* enthusiast: *essere — di qc.*, to be crazy about sthg.

entuslàstico *agg.* enthusiastic(al).

enucleare *vt.* to enucleate.

enucleazione *sf.* enucleation.

enumerare *vt.* to enumerate.

enumerazione *sf.* enumeration.

enunciare *vt.* to state: — *un teorema*, to enunciate a theorem.

enunciato *sm.* proposition, terms (*pl.*).

enunciazione *sf.* enunciation.

enuresi *sf.* enuresis.

enzima *sm.* enzyme.

eòlico *agg.* Aeolian.

epàtico *agg.* hepatic.

epatite *sf.* hepatitis.

èpica *sf.* epic.

epicentro *sm.* epicentre.

èpico *agg.* epic.

epicureismo *sm.* 1. epicurism 2. (*fil.*) epicureanism.

epicureo *agg.* e *sm.* Epicurean.

epidemìa *sf.* epidemic.

epidèmico *agg.* epidemical.

epidèrmico *agg.* epidermic.

epidèrmide *sf.* epidermis, skin.

Epifanìa *sf.* Epiphany, Twelfth Night.

epìgono *sm.* imitator, follower.

epìgrafe *sf.* epigraph.

epigrafìa *sf.* epigraphy.

epigramma *sm.* epigram.

epigrammista *s.* epigrammatist.

epilessìa *sf.* epilepsy.

epilèttico *agg.* e *sm.* epileptic.

epìlogo *sm.* epilogue.

episcopale *agg.* episcopal.

episconato *sm.* episcopacy.

episòdico *agg.* episodic(al).

episodio *sm.* episode.

epistola *sf.* epistle.

epistolare *agg.* epistolary.

epistolario *sm.* letters (*pl.*).

epitaffio *sm.* epitaph.

epitalamio *sm.* epithalamium (*pl.* -ia).

epitelio *sm.* epithelium.

epìteto *sm.* epithet.

epìtome *sf.* epitome.

època *sf.* 1. epoch 2. (*età*) age 3. (*data*) date || *far —*, to mark an epoch.

epopea *sf.* 1. epopee 2. (*serie di fatti eroici*) epos.

eppure *cong.* yet.

epulone *sm.* glutton.

epurare *vt.* to purge.

epurazione *sf.* purge.

equamente *avv.* fairly.

equànime *agg.* equanimous.

equanimità *sf.* equanimity, impartiality.
equatore *sm.* equator.
equatoriale *agg.* equatorial.
equazione *sf.* equation.
equestre *agg.* equestrian.
equidistante *agg.* equidistant.
equidistanza *sf.* equidistance.
equilàtero *agg.* equilateral.
equilibrare *vt.* to balance.
equilibrato *agg.* 1. balanced 2. (*fig.*) well-balanced.
equilibrio *sm.* balance, equilibrium.
equilibrismo *sm.* acrobatics (*pl.*).
equilibrista *s.* acrobat.
equino *agg.* equine.
equinozio *sm.* equinox.
equipaggiamento *sm.* equipment, outfit.
equipaggiare *vt.* to equip, to fit out.
equipaggio *sm.* (*mar.; aer.*) crew.
equiparàbile *agg.* comparable.
equiparare *vt.* to equalize.
equiparazione *sf.* equalization.
equipollente *agg.* equipollent.
equipollenza *sf.* equipollence.
equità *sf.* equity, fairness.
equitazione *sf.* riding.
equivalente *agg.* equivalent.
equivalenza *sf.* equivalence.
equivalere *vi.* to be equivalent. ♦ **equivalersi** *vr.* to be equivalent.
equivocàbile *agg.* mistakable.
equivocare *vi.* to misunderstand (*v. irr.*).
equìvoco *agg.* equivocal, ambiguous. ♦ **equìvoco** *sm.* equivocation.
equo *agg.* fair.
era *sf.* era, epoch.
erariale *agg.* fiscal.
erario *sm.* Treasury.
erba *sf.* grass || in —, green; (*fig.*) budding: un poeta in —, a budding poet.
erbaccia *sf.* weed.
erbàceo *agg.* herbaceous.
erbaggio *sm.* vegetable.
erbario *sm.* herbarium.
erbetta *sf.* new grass.
erbivéndolo *sm.* greengrocer.
erbìvoro *agg.* herbivorous.
erborista *s.* herborist.
erboso *agg.* grassy.
èrcole *sm.* Hercules.
ercùleo *agg.* Herculean.
erede *sm.* heir. ♦ **erede** *sf.* heiress.
eredità *sf.* inheritance.

ereditare *vt.* to inherit.
ereditarietà *sf.* hereditariness.
ereditario *agg.* hereditary.
ereditiera *sf.* heiress.
eremita *sm.* hermit.
eremitaggio *sm.* hermitage.
èremo *sm.* hermitage.
eresia *sf.* heresy.
erètico *agg.* heretical.
erèttile *agg.* erectile.
eretto *agg.* 1. upright 2. (*costruito*) built.
erezione *sf.* 1. erection 2. (*costruzione*) building.
ergastolano *sm.* convict (serving a life sentence).
ergàstolo *sm.* life imprisonment.
èrgere *vt.* to raise. ♦ **èrgersi** *vr.* to rise (*v. irr.*).
èrica *sf.* heather.
erìgere *vt.* to erect, to build (*v. irr.*). ♦ **erìgersi** *vr.* to set up (for).
erma *sf.* herma (*pl.* -ae).
ermafrodito *agg.* hermaphrodite.
ermellino *sm.* ermine.
ermenèuta *sm.* hermeneut.
ermenèutica *sf.* hermeneutics.
ermètico *agg.* 1. (*tec.*) airtight 2. (*oscuro*) obscure.
ermetismo *sm.* obscurity.
ernia *sf.* hernia.
erniario *agg.* hernial.
erodere *vt.* to wear (*v. irr.*) away.
eroe *sm.* hero.
erogare *vt.* 1. to distribute 2. (*elett.; idraulica*) to deliver.
erogazione *sf.* 1. distribution 2. (*elettr.; idraulica*) delivery.
eròico *agg.* heroic.
eroina *sf.* 1. heroine 2. (*farm.*) heroin.
eroismo *sm.* heroism.
eròmpere *vi.* to burst (*v. irr.*) forth.
erosione *sf.* erosion.
erosivo *agg.* erosive.
eròtico *agg.* erotic.
erotismo *sm.* eroticism.
erotòmane *s.* erotomaniac.
èrpete *sm.* herpes.
èrpice *sm.* harrow.
errabondo *agg.* wandering.
errante *agg.* errant.
errare *vi.* 1. (*vagare*) to wander 2. (*sbagliare*) to err.
erràtico *agg.* erratic.
errato *agg.* wrong.
erròneo *agg.* erroneous.

errore *sm.* error, mistake.
erta *sf.* steep || *stare all'—*, to be on the look-out.
erto *agg.* steep.
erudire *vt.* to teach (*v. irr.*). ♦ **erudirsi** *vr.* to get (*v. irr.*) educated.
erudito *agg.* learned. ♦ **erudito** *sm.* scholar.
erudizione *sf.* erudition, learning.
eruttare *vt.* to erupt.
eruttivo *agg.* eruptive.
eruzione *sf.* eruption.
esacerbare *vt.* to embitter.
esacerbazione *sf.* embitterment.
esaedro *sm.* hexahedron.
esagerare *vt.* to exaggerate. ♦ **esagerare** *vi.* to go (*v. irr.*) too far, to exceed.
esagerato *agg.* **1.** exaggerated **2.** (*di prezzo*) exorbitant.
esagerazione *sf.* exaggeration.
esagitare *vt.* to stir violently.
esagonale *agg.* hexagonal.
esàgono *sm.* hexagon.
esalare *vt.* to exhale. ♦ **esalare** *vi.* to exhale, to rise (*v. irr.*).
esalazione *sf.* exhalation.
esaltare *vt.* to exalt. ♦ **esaltarsi** *vr.* **1.** (*vantarsi*) to boast **2.** (*infervorarsi*) to become (*v. irr.*) excited.
esaltato *agg.* excited. ♦ **esaltato** *sm.* hot-head.
esaltazione *sf.* **1.** exaltation **2.** (*eccitazione*) excitement.
esame *sm.* examination: *dare un —*, to take (*v. irr.*) an examination; *essere respinto ad un —*, to fail in an examination.
esàmetro *sm.* hexameter.
esaminando *sm.* candidate.
esaminare *vt.* to examine.
esaminatore *sm.* examiner.
esangue *agg.* bloodless.
esànime *agg.* lifeless.
esasperare *vt.* to exasperate. ♦ **esasperarsi** *vr.* to become (*v. irr.*) irritated.
esasperato *agg.* exasperated.
esasperazione *sf.* exasperation.
esattamente *avv.* exactly, just.
esattezza *sf.* exactitude.
esatto *agg.* exact, right.
esattore *sm.* collector.
esattoria *sf.* collector's office.
esaudimento *sm.* satisfaction.
esaudire *vt.* to grant.
esauriente *agg.* exhaustive.

esaurimento *sm.* exhaustion.
esaurire *vt.* to exhaust. ♦ **esaurirsi** *vr.* to get (*v. irr.*) exhausted.
esaurito *agg.* **1.** exhausted **2.** (*di persona*) worn out **3.** (*che ha l'esaurimento nervoso*) suffering from a nervous breakdown **4.** (*di libro*) out of print.
esàusto *agg.* exhausted.
esautorare *vt.* to deprive of authority.
esazione *sf.* collection.
esborso *sm.* outlay.
esca *sf.* **1.** bait **2.** (*materiale infiammabile*) tinder **3.** (*di esplosivo*) fuse.
escandescenza *sf.* outburst of rage || *dare in escandescenze*, to lose (*v. irr.*) one's temper.
escatologia *sf.* eschatology.
escavatore *sm.* digger.
escavatrice *sf.* digger.
escavazione *sf.* digging out.
eschimese *agg.* e *sm.* Eskimo.
esclamare *vi.* to exclaim.
esclamativo *agg.* exclamatory: *punto —*, exclamation mark.
esclamazione *sf.* exclamation.
esclùdere *vt.* to exclude, to leave (*v. irr.*) out.
esclusione *sf.* exclusion || *ad — di*, except.
esclusiva *sf.* **1.** patent **2.** (*diritto esclusivo*) sole right.
esclusività *sf.* exclusiveness.
esclusivo *agg.* exclusive, sole.
escluso *agg.* **1.** excluded **2.** (*eccettuato*) excepted.
escogitare *vt.* to contrive.
escoriare *vt.* to graze.
escoriazione *sf.* abrasion.
escremento *sm.* excrement.
escrescenza *sf.* excrescence.
escursione *sf.* excursion, trip.
escursionista *s.* excursionist.
escussione *sf.* examination.
esecràbile *agg.* execrable.
esecrare *vt.* to execrate.
esecrazione *sf.* execration.
esecutivo *agg.* executive.
esecutore *sm.* **1.** executor **2.** (*di musica*) performer **3.** (*carnefice*) executioner.
esecuzione *sf.* **1.** execution **2.** (*mus.*) performance.
esedra *sf.* exedra (*pl.* -ae).
esegesi *sf.* exegesis (*pl.* -ses).
esegeta *s.* exegete.
eseguìbile *agg.* feasible.

eseguire vt. 1. to execute, to carry out 2. (mus.) to perform.

esempio sm. 1. example, instance 2. (modello perfetto) pattern.

esemplare agg. exemplary. ◆ **esemplare** sm. 1. pattern, specimen 2. (di libro) copy.

esemplificare vt. to exemplify.

esemplificazione sf. exemplification.

esentare vt. to exempt.

esente agg. exempt, free.

esenzione sf. exemption.

eseque sf. pl. exequies.

esercente sm. shop-keeper.

esercire vt. to manage (a business) || — un negozio, to keep (v. irr.) a shop.

esercitare vt. 1. to exercise 2. (una professione) to practice 3. (addestrare) to train. ◆ **esercitarsi** vr. to practice.

esercitazione sf. 1. exercise 2. (allenamento) training 3. (mil.) drill.

esèrcito sm. army.

esercizio sm. 1. exercise 2. (negozio) shop 3. (comm.) — finanziario, financial year.

esibire vt. to exhibit, to show (v. irr.).

esibizione sf. exhibition, show.

esibizionismo sm. exhibitionism, showing-off.

esibizionista s. exhibitionist.

esigente agg. exacting.

esigenza sf. 1. demand, exigence 2. (pretesa) pretension.

esìgere vt. 1. (comm.) to collect 2. (richiedere con autorità) to insist on 3. (pretendere) to exact.

esigibile agg. 1. exigible 2. (riscuotibile) collectable.

esiguità sf. exiguity.

esiguo agg. exiguous, scanty.

esilarante agg. exhilarating.

esilarare vt. to exhilarate.

èsile agg. slender.

esiliare vt. to exile. ◆ **esiliarsi** vr. to go (v. irr.) into exile.

esiliato agg. banished. ◆ **esiliato** sm. exile.

esìlio sm. exile.

esìmere vt. to free, to excuse. ◆ **esìmersi** vr. to evade (sthg.).

esimio agg. excellent.

esistente agg. 1. existing 2. (di cose) extant.

esistenza sf. existence.

esistenziale agg. existential.

esistenzialismo sm. existentialism.

esistenzialista agg. e s. existentialist.

esìstere vi. to exist.

esitante agg. hesitating: voce —, faltering voice.

esitare vi. 1. to hesitate 2. (di voce) to falter.

esitazione sf. hesitation: senza —, unhesitatingly.

èsito sm. result, outcome.

esiziale agg. ruinous.

èsodo sm. exodus.

esòfago sm. oesophagus.

esògeno agg. exogenous.

esonerare vt. to exonerate.

esònero sm. exoneration.

esorbitante agg. exorbitant.

esorbitanza sf. exorbitance.

esorbitare vi. to exceed.

esorcismo sm. exorcism.

esorcista sm. exorcist.

esorcizzare vt. to exorcize.

esorcizzatore sm. exorcizer.

esordiente agg. beginning. ◆ **esordiente** sm. beginner.

esordio sm. preamble, beginning.

esordire vi. 1. to begin (v. irr.) 2. (in arte) to make (v. irr.) one's debut.

esortare vt. to exhort.

esortativo agg. exhortative.

esortazione sf. exhortation.

esosità sf. greediness.

esoso agg. greedy.

esoterico agg. esoteric.

esotèrmico agg. exothermic.

esòtico agg. exotic.

esotismo sm. exoticism.

espàndere vt. to spread (v. irr.) (out). ◆ **espàndersi** vr. to spread.

espansione sf. expansion.

espansionismo sm. expansionism.

espansività sf. effusiveness.

espansivo agg. effusive.

espatriare vi. to emigrate.

espatrio sm. expatriation.

espediente sm. expedient.

espèllere vt. to expel.

esperanto sm. Esperanto.

esperienza sf. experience.

esperimento sm. 1. experiment 2. (esame) test 3. (tentativo) trial.

esperire vt. to try.

esperto agg. e sm. expert.

espettorante agg. e sm. expectorant.

espettorare vt. to expectorate.

espettorazione *sf.* expectoration.

espiare *vt.* to expiate.

espiatorio *agg.* expiatory: *capro* —, scapegoat.

espiazione *sf.* expiation.

espirare *vt.* e *vi.* to expire.

espirazione *sf.* expiration.

espletare *vt.* to dispatch.

espletazione *sf.* dispatching.

esplicare *vt.* to explicate: — *un'attività*, to have an activity.

esplicativo *agg.* explanatory.

esplicazione *sf.* explication.

esplicito *agg.* explicit.

esplòdere *vi.* to explode, to burst (*v. irr.*).

esplorare *vt.* 1. to explore 2. (*mil.*) to scout.

esploratore *sm.* 1. explorer 2. (*mil.*) scout.

esplorazione *sf.* 1. exploration 2. (*mil.*) scouting expedition.

esplosione *sf.* 1. explosion, blast 2. (*fig.*) outbreak.

esplosivo *agg.* e *sm.* explosive.

esponente *sm.* exponent.

esporre *vt.* 1. to show (*v. irr.*) 2. (*a rischio*) to venture 3. (*spiegare*) to expound 4. (*mettere in vista*) to display. ♦ **esporsi** *vr.* to expose oneself.

esportare *vt.* to export.

esportatore *agg.* exporting. ♦ **esportatore** *sm.* exporter.

esportazione *sf.* export, exportation.

esposimetro *sm.* exposure-meter.

espositore *sm.* exhibitor.

esposizione *sf.* 1. exposure 2. (*mostra*) exhibition 3. (*eloquio*) exposition.

esposto *sm.* petition.

espressamente *avv.* 1. expressly 2. (*appositamente*) on purpose.

espressione *sf.* expression.

espressionismo *sm.* expressionism.

espressionista *s.* expressionist.

espressivo *agg.* expressive.

espresso *agg.* express.

esprimere *vt.* to express.

esprimibile *agg.* expressible.

espropriare *vt.* to dispossess.

espropriazione *sf.* expropriation.

espugnare *vt.* to conquer.

espugnatore *sm.* conqueror.

espugnazione *sf.* conquest.

espulsione *sf.* expulsion.

espulsivo *agg.* e *sm.* expulsive.

espulsore *sm.* ejector.

espùngere *vt.* to expunge.

espurgare *vt.* 1. to expurgate 2. (*un libro*) to bowdlerize.

espurgazione *sf.* 1. expurgation 2. (*un libro*) to bowdlerize.

essa *pron.* 1. (*sogg.*) she, (*compl.*) her 2. (*riferito a cose o animali*) it.

esse *sf.* letter S.: *a* —, S-shaped.

essenza *sf.* essence.

essenziale *agg.* essential.

essenzialità *sf.* essentiality.

èssere *vi.* to be || *c'è*, *ci sono*, there is, there are.

èssere *sm.* 1. being 2. (*esistenza*) existence.

essi *pron.* (*sogg.*) they, (*compl.*) them.

essiccare *vt.* to dry.

essiccatoio *sm.* drier.

essiccazione *sf.* drying process.

esso *pron.* 1. (*sogg.*) he, (*compl.*) him 2. (*per cose o animali*) it.

essudato *sm.* exudate.

essudazione *sf.* exudation.

est *sm.* east.

èstasi *sf.* ecstasy: *andare in* —, to go (*v. irr.*) into ecstasies; *mandare in* —, to throw (*v. irr.*) into ecstasies.

estasiare *vt.* to enrapture. ♦ **estasiarsi** *vr.* to be enraptured.

estate *sf.* summer.

estàtico *agg.* ecstatic.

estemporàneo *agg.* extempore.

estèndere *vt.* to extend.

estendibile *agg.* extensible.

estensione *sf.* 1. extension 2. (*distesa*) expanse, extent 3. (*mus.*) range.

estensivo *agg.* extensive.

estensore *sm.* 1. compiler 2. (*giur.*) drafts-man (*pl.* -men) 3. (*sport*) chest-expander.

estenuante *agg.* exhausting.

estenuare *vt.* to tire out.

estenuazione *sf.* exhaustion.

esteriore *agg.* outward. ♦ **esteriore** *sm.* exterior, outside.

esteriorità *sf.* outward appearance.

esternamente *avv.* externally, outside.

esternare *vt.* to express, to utter.

esterno *agg.* outer, external.

èstero *agg.* foreign. ♦ **èstero** *sm.* foreign countries (*pl.*) || *all'*—, abroad.

esterofilia *sf.* xenomania.

esterrefatto agg. aghast, amazed.

esteso agg. large, wide ‖ per —, in detail.

esteta s. aesthete.

estetica sf. aesthetics.

estetico agg. aesthetic.

estetismo sm. aestheticism.

èstimo sm. estimate.

estinguere vt. 1. to put (v. irr.) out 2. (saldare) to extinguish ‖ — la propria sete, to slake one's thirst. ♦ **estinguersi** vr. (finire) to die.

estinguibile agg. extinguishable.

estinto agg. 1. extinct 2. (morto) dead. ♦ **estinto** sm. deceased man.

estintore sm. extinguisher.

estinzione sf. 1. extinction 2. (di sete) quenching 3. (di debito) paying off.

estirpare vt. 1. to extirpate 2. (di denti) to pull out.

estirpazione sf. 1. extirpation 2. (di denti) extraction.

estivo agg. summer (attr.).

estòrcere vt. to extort.

estorsione sf. extortion.

estradare vt. to extradite.

estradizione sf. extradition.

estràneo agg. extraneous, alien. ♦ **estràneo** sm. stranger.

estraniare vt. to estrange. ♦ **estraniarsi** vr. to get (v. irr.) estranged.

estrarre vt. to draw (v. irr.) out: — a sorte, to draw by lot.

estrattivo agg. extractive.

estratto sm. 1. extract 2. (riassunto) excerpt 3. (comm.) — conto, statement of account.

estrattore sm. extractor.

estrazione sf. 1. extraction 2. (di lotteria) drawing.

estremamente avv. extremely.

estremismo sm. extremism.

estremista s. extremist: — di destra, extreme rightist; — di sinistra, extreme leftist.

estremità sf. extremity, end.

estremo agg. 1. utmost 2. (eccessivo) intense 3. (drastico) drastic. ♦ **estremo** sm. extreme.

estrinsecare vt. to express. ♦ **estrinsecarsi** vr. to be expressed.

estrinsecazione sf. expression.

estrìnseco agg. extrinsic(al).

estro sm. 1. inspiration 2. (capriccio) whim.

estrométtere vt. to turn out.

estromissione sf. expulsion.

estroso agg. 1. (ispirato) inspired 2. freakish.

estroverso agg. extroverted.

estuario sm. estuary.

esuberante agg. exuberant.

esuberanza sf. exuberance.

esulare vi. 1. to go (v. irr.) into exile 2. (fig.) to be beyond.

esulcerare vt. to exulcerate.

esulcerazione sf. exulceration.

èsule sm. 1. exile 2. (profugo) refugee.

esultante agg. rejoicing.

esultanza sf. exultation.

esultare vi. to rejoice.

esumare vt. to exhume.

esumazione sf. exhumation.

età sf. age ‖ che — hai?, how old are you?; avere la stessa —, to be the same age; una persona di mezza —, a middle-aged person.

ètere sm. ether.

etèreo agg. ethereal.

eternare vt. to make (v. irr.) eternal.

eternità sf. eternity.

eterno agg. eternal, everlasting.

eteròclito agg. 1. heteroclite 2. (fig.) irregular.

eterodossìa sf. heterodoxy.

eterodosso agg. heterodox.

eterogeneità sf. heterogeneity.

eterogèneo agg. heterogeneous.

ètica sf. ethics.

etichetta sf. 1. label 2. (galateo) etiquette.

etichettare vt. to stick (v. irr.) a label (on).

ètico agg. ethical.

etilene sm. ethylene.

etìlico agg. ethylic.

etilismo sm. alcoholism.

etimologìa sf. etymology.

etimològico agg. etymologic(al).

ètnico agg. ethnic(al).

etnografìa sf. ethnography.

etnologìa sf. ethnology.

etnòlogo sm. ethnologist.

etrusco agg. e sm. Etruscan.

ettàgono sm. heptagon.

èttaro sm. hectare.

etto sm. hectogram.

ettolitro sm. hectolitre.

ettòmetro sm. hectometre.

eucalipto sm. eucalyptus.

eucaristìa sf. Eucharist, Holy Communion.

eucarìstico *agg.* Eucharistic.
eufemismo *sm.* euphemism.
eufonìa *sf.* euphony.
eufònico *agg.* euphonic(al).
euforbia *sf.* Euphorbia.
euforìa *sf.* euphoria.
eufòrico *agg.* euphoric.
eunuco *sm.* eunuch.
euritmìa *sf.* eurhythmy.
europeismo *sm.* Europeanism.
europeo *agg. e sm.* European.
eurovisione *sf.* Eurovision.
eutanasìa *sf.* euthanasia.
evacuare *vt.* to evacuate.
evacuazione *sf.* evacuation.
evàdere *vi.* to escape. ♦ **evàdere**
vt. (*burocratico*) **1.** to dispatch **2.**
(*eludere*) to evade.
evanescente *agg.* vanishing.
evangèlico *agg.* evangelic(al).
evangelista *sm.* evangelist.
evangelizzare *vt.* to evangelize.
evaporare *vi.* to evaporate.
evaporazione *sf.* evaporation.
evasione *sf.* **1.** escape **2.** (*comm.*)
dare — a una pratica, to dispatch
a business.
evasivo *agg.* evasive.
evaso *sm.* runaway.
evasore *sm.* evader: *— fiscale,* tax
evader.
evenienza *sf.* event, occurrence:
per ogni —, for any occasion.
evento *sm.* event.
eventuale *agg.* possible.
eventualità *sf.* eventuality.
eventualmente *avv.* in case.
evidente *agg.* evident, obvious,
clear.
evidenza *sf.* evidence.
evincere *vt.* (*giur.*) to evict.
evirare *vt.* to evirate.
evitàbile *agg.* avoidable.
evitare *vt.* **1.** to avoid **2.** (*sfuggire*)
to escape.
evo *sm.* age: *il Medio Evo,* the
Middle Ages.
evocare *vt.* to evoke, to recall.
evocativo *agg.* evocative.
evocazione *sf.* evocation.
evolutivo *agg.* evolutive.
evoluto *agg.* well-developed, modern.
evoluzione *sf.* evolution.
evoluzionismo *sm.* evolutionism.
evòlvere *vt.* to evolve.
evviva *inter.* hurray.
ex libris *sm.* ex libris.
extra *agg.* extra.

extraterritoriale *agg.* extraterritorial.
eziologìa *sf.* aetiology.

F

fa¹ *sm.* (*mus.*) F.
fa² *avv.* ago: *un anno —,* a year ago.
fabbisogno *sm.* needs (*pl.*).
fàbbrica *sf.* **1.** factory ǁ *— di au-
tomobili,* motor works; *— di
mattoni,* brickyard; *— di carta,*
paper-mill; *capo —,* fore-man (*pl.
-men*); *marchio di —,* trade-mark
2. (*fabbricazione*) manufacture.
fabbricàbile *agg.* manufacturable ǁ
area —, housing area.
fabbricante *sm.* manufacturer.
fabbricare *vt.* **1.** (*produrre*) to
manufacture **2.** (*costruire*) to build
(*v. irr.*) **3.** (*fare*) to make (*v. irr.*).
fabbricato *sm.* building ǁ *imposta
sui fabbricati,* house tax.
fabbricazione *sf.* **1.** manufacture,
make **2.** (*costruzione*) building.
fabbro *sm.* blacksmith.
fabbroferraio *sm.* blacksmith.
faccenda *sf.* matter; business (*solo
sing.*) ǁ *— di stato,* state affair
2. (*lavori domestici*) housework
(*solo sing.*).
faccendiere *sm.* busybody.
faccetta *sf.* little face **2.** (*geom.*)
facet.
facchinaggio *sm.* porterage.
facchino *sm.* porter.
faccia *sf.* **1.** face: *che — tosta!,*
what a face!; *a — a —,* face to face
2. (*aspetto*) look, expression **3.** (*lato, superficie*) face, side.
facciale *agg.* facial.
facciata *sf.* **1.** front, façade **2.** (*pagina*) page.
face *sf.* torch.
faceto *agg.* facetious, witty.
facezia *sf.* witty remark, joke: *dire delle facezie,* to crack jokes.
fachiro *sm.* fakir.
fàcile *agg.* **1.** easy **2.** (*trattabile*)
docile **3.** (*pronto*) ready **4.** (*incline*) inclined **3.** (*probabile*) likely.
facilità *sf.* **1.** facility **2.** (*attitudine*) aptitude.
facilitare *vt.* to make (*v. irr.*)
easier

facilitazione *sf.* 1. facilitation 2. (*agevolazione*) facility.

facione *sm.* slipshod fellow.

facinoroso *agg.* lawless. ♦ **facinoroso** *sm.* lawless man.

facoltà *sf.* faculty.

facoltativo *agg.* facultative: *fermata facoltativa*, request stop.

facoltoso *agg.* wealthy.

facondia *sf.* eloquence.

facondo *agg.* eloquent.

facsimile *sm.* facsimile.

factotum *sm.* factotum.

faggeto *sm.* beech-wood.

faggio *sm.* beech.

fagiano *sm.* pheasant.

fagiolino *sm.* French bean.

fagiolo *sm.* bean.

fagocita, fagocito *sm.* phagocyte.

fagocitare *vt.* 1. to phagocyte 2. (*fig.*) to absorb.

fagocitosi *sf.* phagocytosis.

fagotto[1] *sm.* bundle.

fagotto[2] *sm.* (*mus.*) bassoon.

faina *sf.* beech-marten.

falange *sf.* phalanx (*pl.* -nges).

falcata *sf.* 1. curvet 2. (*di persona*) stride.

falce *sf.* 1. sickle 2. (*da fieno*) scythe 3. (*di luna*) crescent.

falciare *vt.* 1. to mow (*v. irr.*) 2. (*fig.*) to mow down.

falciatore *sm.* mower.

falciatrice *sf.* mowing-machine.

falciatura *sf.* mowing.

falcidiare *vt.* to reduce.

falco *sm.* hawk: *avere occhi di —*, to be hawk-eyed.

falconeria *sf.* falconry.

falconiere *sm.* hawker.

falda *sf.* 1. (*strato*) stratum (*pl.* -ta) 2. (*di neve*) flake 3. (*di cappello*) brim 4. (*di monte*) slope.

falegname *sm.* joiner.

falegnameria *sf.* 1. joinery 2. (*bottega*) joiner's shop.

falena *sf.* moth.

falla *sf.* leak.

fallace *agg.* false, disappointing.

fallacia *sf.* fallacy.

fallibile *agg.* liable to make mistakes.

fallico *agg.* phallic.

fallimentare *agg.* bankruptcy.

fallimento *sm.* 1. bankruptcy 2. (*fig.*) failure.

fallire *vi.* 1. to fail 2. (*comm.*) to go (*v. irr.*) bankrupt 3. (*fam.*) to go under.

fallito *agg.* 1. (*comm.*) bankrupt 2. (*fig.*) unsuccessful. ♦ **fallito** *sm.* 1. (*comm.*) bankrupt 2. (*fig.*) failure.

fallo *sm.* 1. fault: *senza —*, without fail 2. (*anat.*) phallus (*pl.* -li).

falò *sm.* bonfire.

falpalà *sm.* furbelow.

falsare *vt.* 1. to misrepresent 2. (*falsificare*) to falsify.

falsariga *sf.* 1. ruling paper 2. (*fig.*) pattern, model.

falsario *sm.* 1. forger 2. (*di monete*) coiner.

falsetto *sm.* falsetto.

falsificabile *agg.* falsifiable.

falsificare *vt.* to falsify, to counterfeit.

falsificatore *sm.* 1. falsifier 2. (*di monete*) coiner.

falsificazione *sf.* falsification, forgery.

falsità *sf.* 1. falseness 2. (*menzogna*) falsehood 3. (*ipocrisia*) insincerity.

falso *agg.* 1. false 2. (*falsificato*) forged.

fama *sf.* fame, renown, reputation: *acquistarsi —*, to win (*v. irr.*) fame; *avere cattiva —*, to have a bad reputation.

fame *sf.* 1. hunger: *avere —*, to be hungry: *far morire di —*, to starve 2. (*carestia*) famine.

famelico *agg.* ravenous.

famigerato *agg.* ill-famed.

famiglia *sf.* family.

familiare *agg.* 1. domestic, homely 2. (*intimo, anche fig.*) familiar 3. (*senza cerimonie*) informal. ♦ **familiare** *sm.* relative.

familiarità *sf.* familiarity: *avere — con qu.*, to be familiar with so.

famoso *agg.* famous, celebrated.

fanale *sm.* lamp 2. (*auto*) light: *— anteriore*, head-light; *— di coda*, (*aer.*) tail light, (*auto*) rear lamp; *— di posizione*, parking lights (*pl.*).

fanatico *agg.* fanatical. ♦ **fanatico** *sm.* 1. fanatic 2. (*fam.*) fan.

fanatismo *sm.* fanaticism.

fanatizzare *vt.* to fanaticize.

fanciulla *sf.* young girl.

fanciullaggine *sf.* 1. childishness 2. (*azione infantile*) childish action.

fanciullesco *agg.* childish.

fanciullezza *sf.* childhood.

fanciullo *sm.* young boy, child (*pl.* children).

fandonia *sf.* lie.

fanello *sm.* linnet.

fanfara *sf.* **1.** brass band **2.** (*suono di trombe*) fanfare.

fanfaronata *sf.* boasting.

fanfarone *sm.* boaster.

fangaia *sf.* muddy road.

fanghiglia *sf.* slush.

fango *sm.* **1.** mud: *gettare del — addosso a qu.*, to throw (*v. irr.*) mud at so.; *cadere nel —*, to fall (*v. irr.*) very low **2.** (*med.*) mud-baths (*pl.*).

fangoso *agg.* muddy.

fannullone *sm.* idler.

fanone *sm.* whalebone.

fantaccino *sm.* foot-soldier.

fantascienza *sf.* science fiction.

fantasia *sf.* **1.** imagination, fancy **2.** (*inventiva*) inventiveness **3.** (*articoli fantasia*) fancy goods.

fantasioso *agg.* fanciful.

fantasma *sm.* ghost.

fantasmagoria *sf.* phantasmagoria.

fantasmagòrico *agg.* phantasmagoric.

fantasticare *vt.* to daydream.

fantasticheria *sf.* daydream.

fantàstico *agg.* **1.** fanciful **2.** (*bizzarro*) queer **3.** (*fam.*) extraordinary.

fante *sm.* **1.** infantryman (*pl.* -men) **2.** (*delle carte*) knave, jack.

fanteria *sf.* infantry.

fantesca *sf.* maid-servant.

fantino *sm.* jockey.

fantoccio *sm.* puppet (*anche fig.*).

fantomàtico *agg.* mysterious.

farabutto *sm.* blackguard.

faraona *sf.* guinea-hen.

faraone *sm.* Pharaoh.

farcire *vt.* to stuff.

farcito *agg.* stuffed.

fardello *sm.* **1.** bundle **2.** (*fig.*) burden.

fare *vt.* **1.** (*in senso generale*) to do (*v. irr.*): *cosa fai?*, what are you doing?; *ecco fatto!*, that's done!; *— del proprio meglio*, to do one's best; **2.** (*fabbricare, creare*) to make (*v. irr.*): *— amicizia*, to make friends; *— un errore*, to make a mistake; *— in fretta*, to make haste **3.** (*essere, esercitare una professione*) to be: *faccio l'insegnante*, I am a teacher **4.** (*reputare*) to think (*v. irr.*): *la facevo*

più intelligente, I thought she was more intelligent **5.** (*segnare le ore*): *che ora fa il tuo orologio?*, what time is it by your watch? **6.** (*praticare*) to go (*v. irr.*) in for || *— le carte*, to shuffle; *— fagotto*, to pack up; *— una passeggiata*, to go for a walk; *— colazione*, to have breakfast; *— bella, brutta figura*, to cut (*v. irr.*) a fine, a poor figure; *— compassione*, to rouse compassion; *— aspettare qu.*, to keep (*v. irr.*) so. waiting; *— avere, sapere, vedere a qu.*, to let (*v. irr.*) so. have, know, see. ◆ **fare** *vi.* **1.** (*di condizioni atmosferiche*): *che tempo fa?*, what is the weather like? **2.** (*far caldo, freddo*) to be hot, cold **3.** (*essere adatto*) to suit. ◆ **farsi** *vr.* to become (*v. irr.*), to grow (*v. irr.*) || *— animo*, to take (*v. irr.*) courage.

fare *sm.* manners (*pl*).

faretra *sf.* quiver.

farfalla *sf.* butterfly.

farfugliare *vt.* to mumble.

farina *sf.* meal, flour.

farināceo *agg.* farinaceous.

faringe *sf.* pharynx (*pl.* -nges).

faringite *sf.* pharyngitis.

farinoso *agg.* mealy, floury.

fariseo *agg. e sm.* Pharisee.

farmacèutico *agg.* pharmaceutic.

farmacia *sf.* **1.** pharmacy **2.** (*negozio*) chemist's shop.

farmacista *sm.* chemist.

fàrmaco *sm.* medicine, remedy (*anche fig.*).

farmacologia *sf.* pharmacology.

farmacopea *sf.* pharmacopoeia.

farneticare *vi.* to rave.

faro *sm.* **1.** lighthouse **2.** (*auto*) headlight.

farràgine *sf.* medley, mixture.

farraginoso *agg.* confused.

farsa *sf.* farce.

farsesco *agg.* farcical.

fascetta *sf.* **1.** small band **2.** (*med.*) bandage **3.** (*edit.*) wrapper.

fascia *sf.* **1.** band **2.** (*med.*) bandage **3.** (*dei bambini*) swaddling-band.

fasciame *sm.* planking.

fasciare *vt.* **1.** to bind (*v. irr.*) (up) **2.** (*dei neonati*) to swaddle.

fasciatura *sf.* **1.** dressing **2.** (*di neonato*) swaddling.

fascìcolo *sm.* booklet.

fascina *sf.* faggot.

fàscino sm. charm, fascination.

fascio sm. 1. bundle 2. (geom.) sheaf 3. (di luce) beam.

fascismo sm. Fascism.

fascista agg. e s. Fascist.

fase sf. 1. stage 2. (elettr.) phase 3. (auto) stroke.

fastello sm. faggot.

fastidio sm. 1. trouble: dare — a qu., to give (v. irr.) so. trouble 2. (contrarietà) annoyance.

fastidioso agg. tiresome.

fastigio sm. 1. pediment 2. (fig.) height.

fasto sm. pomp.

fastosità sf. pomp, splendour.

fastoso agg. magnificent.

fasullo agg. false.

fata sf. fairy.

fatale agg. fatal, inevitable.

fatalismo sm. fatalism.

fatalista agg. e s. fatalist.

fatalità sf. fatality.

fatica sf. weariness, fatigue.

faticare vi. to toil, to work hard.

faticata sf. drudgery.

faticoso agg. hard, tiring.

fatìdico agg. fatidical.

fato sm. 1. fate, destiny 2. (sorte) lot.

fatta sf. kind, sort.

fattibile agg. practicable.

fattispecie sf. case in point: nella —, in this case.

fattivo agg. 1. effective 2. (attivo) busy.

fatto sm. 1. fact 2. (azione) deed 3. (avvenimento) event || sapere il — proprio, to know (v. irr.) one's business; venire al`—, to go (v. irr.) to the point; in — di, as regards.

fattore sm. 1. factor 2. (agr.) farmer.

fattoria sf. farm.

fattorino sm. errand-boy.

fattucchiere sm. wizard.

fattura sf. 1. making 2. (lavorazione) work 3. (comm.) invoice 4. (stregoneria) sorcery.

fatturare vt. 1. to adulterate 2. (comm.) to invoice.

fatturazione sf. (comm.) invoicing.

fatuità sf. fatuity.

fatuo agg. 1. fatuous 2. (vanitoso) vain || fuoco —, will-o'-the-visp.

fàuci sf. pl. 1. jaws 2. (di persona) throat (sing.).

fàuna sf. fauna.

fàuno sm. faun.

fàusto agg. propitious.

fautore sm. supporter.

fava sf. broad bean || pigliare due piccioni con una —, to kill two birds with one stone.

favella sf. speech.

favellare vi. to speak (v. irr.).

favilla sf. spark (anche fig.).

favo sm. 1. honeycomb 2. (med.) favus.

fàvola sf. 1. fable 2. (frottola) idle story 3. (oggetto di pettegolezzo) byword.

favoloso agg. fabulous.

favore sm. favour.

favoreggiamento sm. favouring.

favoreggiare vt. to favour.

favoreggiatore sm. abettor.

favorévole agg. favourable.

favorire vt. 1. to favour 2. (aiutare) to help 3. (promuovere) to foster.

favoritismo sm. favouritism.

favorito agg. e sm. favourite.

fazione sf. faction.

fazioso agg. factious.

fazzoletto sm. 1. handkerchief 2. (da collo) neckerchief.

febbraio sm. February.

febbre sf. fever.

febbricitante agg. feverish.

febbrìfugo sm. febrifugal. ♦ febbrìfugo sm. febrifuge.

febbrile agg. feverish.

fecale agg. fecal.

feccia sf. dregs (pl.) (anche fig.).

feci sf. pl. excrement (sing.).

fècola sf. starch.

fecondare vt. to fecundate.

fecondazione sf. fecundation.

fecondità sf. fecundity.

fecondo agg. fecund.

fede sf. 1. faith, belief 2. (fiducia) trust.

fedele agg. faithful.

fedeltà sf. fidelity.

fèdera sf. pillow-case.

federale agg. federal.

federalismo sm. federalism.

federativo agg. federative.

federato agg. federate.

federazione sf. federation.

fedìfrago sm. traitor.

fedina sf. criminal record.

fègato sm. 1. liver 2. (fig.) courage.

fegatoso agg. 1. bilious 2. (fig.) irritable.

felce sf. fern.

feldspato sm. felspar.

felice agg. **1.** happy **2.** (fortunato) lucky **3.** (piacevole) pleasant.

felicità sf. happiness.

felicitarsi vr. to congratulate (so. on sthg.).

felicitazioni sf. pl. congratulation (sing.).

felino agg. e sm. feline.

fellone sm. villain, traitor.

fellonìa sf. felony, treason.

felpato agg. **1.** plushy **2.** (fig.) soft || a passi felpati, stealthily.

feltro sm. felt.

feluca sf. **1.** (mar.) felucca **2.** (cappello) cocked hat.

fémmina sf. female || mala —, bad woman.

femminile agg. **1.** female **2.** (da donna) feminine.

femminilità sf. womanliness.

femminismo sm. feminism.

femminuccia sf. **1.** simple woman **2.** (uomo senza coraggio) coward.

fèmore sm. thigh-bone.

fendente sm. cutting blow.

fèndere vt. to rend (v. irr.).

fenditura sf. cleft, fissure.

fenice sf. phoenix.

fènico agg. phenic.

fenolo sm. phenol.

fenomenale agg. phenomenal.

fenomenismo sm. phenomenalism.

fenòmeno sm. phenomenon (pl. -na).

fenomenologìa sf. phenomenology.

ferace agg. fruitful, rich (anche fig.).

ferale agg. feral, deadly.

fèretro sm. coffin.

ferie sf. pl. holidays.

feriale agg. working: giorno —, working-day.

ferimento sm. wounding.

ferino agg. ferine, wild.

ferire vt. to wound, to hurt (v. irr.).

ferita sf. wound (anche fig.).

ferito agg. wounded, injured.

feritoia sf. loophole.

ferma sf. **1.** (mil.) service **2.** (caccia) pointing.

fermacarte sm. paper-weight.

fermaglio sm. **1.** clasp **2.** (per gioielli) brooch **3.** (per carte) clip.

fermare vt. **1.** to stop, to arrest **2.** (fissare) to fix (anche fig.) **3.** (giur.) to hold (v. irr.). ♦ **fermarsi** vr. **1.** to stop **2.** (soggiornare) to stay **3.** (fare una pausa) to pause.

fermata sf. **1.** stop **2.** (pausa) pause.

fermentare vi. to ferment (anche fig.).

fermentazione sf. fermentation.

fermento sm. **1.** ferment **2.** (fig.) turmoil, ferment.

fermezza sf. firmness, strength.

fermo agg. **1.** still **2.** (irremovibile) steady, firm || mano ferma, firm hand; volontà ferma, unfaltering will. ♦ **fermo** sm. **1.** (mecc.) lock, catch, stop **2.** (giur.) provisional arrest.

fermoposta sm. poste-restante.

feroce agg. fierce, cruel.

ferocia sf. fierceness.

ferraglia sf. scrap-iron.

ferragosto sm. **1.** August holiday **2.** (in Inghilterra) August Bank holiday.

ferraio sm. blacksmith.

ferramenta sf. pl. hardware (sing.).

ferramento sm. iron tool.

ferrare vt. **1.** to fit with iron **2.** (di cavalli) to shoe.

ferrato agg. **1.** ironshod **2.** (di scarpe) hobnailed **3.** (strada ferrata) railway **4.** (fig.) well read.

ferratura sf. shoeing.

fèrreo agg. iron (attr.).

ferriera sf. iron-foundry.

ferro sm. iron: — battuto, wrought iron; — da stiro, flat-iron; — da calza, knitting needle || i ferri del mestiere, the tools of the trade; tocca —!, touch wood!

ferroso agg. ferrous.

ferrovia sf. railway.

ferroviario agg. railway (attr.).

ferroviere sm. railwayman (pl. -men).

ferruginoso agg. ferruginous.

fèrtile agg. fertile (anche fig.).

fertilità sf. fertility.

fertilizzante agg. fertilizing. ♦ **fertilizzante** sm. fertilizer.

fertilizzare vt. to fertilize.

fèrula sf. rod.

fervente agg. burning, ardent (anche fig.).

fèrvido agg. fervid, ardent || fervidi auguri, best wishes.

fervore sm. fervour, heat.

fessura sf. **1.** crack **2.** (per liquidi) leak.

festa sf. **1.** (giorno di riposo) holiday **2.** (religiosa) feast **3.** (anniversario) birthday **4.** (onomasti-

co) Saint's day 5. *(banchetto, ballo)* feast, ball || *giorno di —*, festal day.

festaiolo *sm.* reveller.

festante *agg.* rejoicing.

festeggiamento *sm.* celebration.

festeggiare *vt.* 1. to celebrate 2. *(accogliere festosamente)* to give *(v. irr.)* a hearty welcome.

festévole *agg.* festive.

festino *sm.* feast.

fèstival *sm.* festival.

festività *sf.* festivity.

festivo *agg.* 1. festive 2. *(domenicale)* Sunday *(attr.)*.

festone *sm.* festoon.

festoso *agg.* joyous.

festuca *sf.* straw.

feticcio *sm.* fetish.

feticismo *sm.* fetishism.

feticista *s.* fetishist.

fètido *agg.* foetid, foul.

feto *sm.* foetus.

fetore *sm.* stink.

fetta *sf.* 1. slice 2. *(piccolo pezzo)* piece.

fettuccia *sf.* tape.

feudale *agg.* feudal.

feudalésimo *sm.* feudalism.

feudatario *sm.* feudatory.

fèudo *sm.* feud.

fiaba *sf.* 1. fable 2. *(falsità)* falsehood.

fiabesco *agg.* fairy-like.

fiacca *sf.* weariness || *battere la —* *(fam.)*, to be sluggish.

fiaccare *vt.* to exhaust. ♦ **fiaccarsi** *vr.* to break *(v. irr.)* down.

fiacchezza *sf.* weakness, weariness.

fiacco *agg.* weak, exhausted.

fiàccola *sf.* torch.

fiaccolata *sf.* torchlight procession.

fiala *sf.* phial.

fiamma *sf.* 1. flame 2. *(molto viva)* blaze.

fiammante *agg.* 1. flaming 2. *(fig.)* bright || *nuovo —*, brand-new.

fiammata *sf.* blaze.

fiammeggiante *agg.* blazing, burning.

fiammeggiare *vi.* to blaze, to flame, to burn.

fiammifero *sm.* match: *accendere un —*, to strike *(v. irr.)* a match.

fiammingo *agg.* Flemish. ♦ **fiammingo** *sm.* Fleming.

fiancata *sf.* 1. side 2. *(mar.)* broadside.

fiancheggiare *vt.* 1. to flank 2. *(fig.)* to support.

fiancheggiatore *sm.* flanker, supporter.

fianco *sm.* 1. hip, side *(anche fig.)* 2. *(di animali; mil.)* flank.

fiasca *sf.* flask.

fiasco *sm.* flask || *fare —*, to fail utterly.

fiatare *vi.* to breathe: *senza —*, without speaking.

fiato *sm.* breath.

fibbia *sf.* buckle.

fibra *sf.* 1. fibre 2. *(costituzione)* constitution.

fibroma *sm.* fibroma *(pl. -ata)*.

fibroso *agg.* fibrous.

fibula *sf.* 1. fibula 2. *(med.)* splint-bone.

ficcanaso *sm.* meddler.

ficcare *vt.* to thrust *(v. irr.)*; to drive *(v. irr.)* (in). ♦ **ficcarsi** *vr.* to interfere || *— in testa qc.*, to get *(v. irr.)* sthg. into one's head.

fico *sm.* fig.

fidanzamento *sm.* engagement.

fidanzare *vt.* to engage. ♦ **fidanzarsi** *vr.* to become *(v. irr.)* engaged (to so.).

fidanzata *sf.* fiancée.

fidanzato *sm.* fiancé.

fidare *vi.* to trust. ♦ **fidarsi** *vr.* to trust (upon so., sthg.).

fidato *agg.* reliable.

fideiussione *sf.* suretyship.

fidente *agg.* confiding.

fido *agg.* faithful. ♦ **fido** *sm.* 1. devoted follower 2. *(comm.)* credit.

fiducia *sf.* trust, confidence: *— in se stessi*, self-confidence. ♦ **fiduciario** *agg.* fiduciary. ♦ **fiduciario** *sm.* fiduciary, trustee.

fiducioso *agg.* trusting, hopeful.

fiele *sm.* 1. gall 2. *(fig.)* hatred.

fienagione *sf.* haymaking.

fienile *sm.* hay-loft.

fieno *sm.* hay: *asma da —*, hay-asthma.

fiera *sf.* 1. fair 2. *(esposizione)* exhibition || *— campionaria*, samples fair.

fierezza *sf.* fierceness.

fiero *agg.* proud.

fiévole *agg.* 1. feeble 2. *(di luce, suono)* dim.

,figgere *vt.* to fix.

figlia *sf.* daughter.

figliare *vt.* to bring *(v. irr.)* forth.

figliastra *sf.* step-daughter.
figliastro *sm.* step-son.
figlio *sm.* son.
figlioccia *sf.* goddaughter.
figlioccio *sm.* godson.
figliolanza *sf.* children (*pl.*), family.
figliolo *sm.* son.
figura *sf.* **1.** figure **2.** (*illustrazione*) illustration, picture **3.** (*personaggio di romanzi, opere teatrali ecc.*) character || *fare una bella, brutta* —, to cut (*v. irr.*) a fine, poor figure.
figurare *vt.* **1.** to represent **2.** (*far figura*) to look smart **3.** (*apparire*) to appear.
figurativo *agg.* figurative.
figurato *agg.* **1.** (*illustrato*) illustrated **2.** (*di linguaggio, senso*) figurative.
figurazione *sf.* figuration.
figurinista *s.* dress-designer.
figurino *sm.* fashion-plate.
figuro *sm.* scoundrel.
fila *sf.* **1.** row, file **2.** (*coda*) queue: *fare la* —, to queue (up).
filaccia *sf.* lint.
filamento *sm.* filament.
filamentoso *agg.* filamentous.
filanda *sf.* spinning-mill.
filandaia *sf.* spinner.
filante *agg.*: *stella* — **1.** (*astr.*) falling-star **2.** (*di carta*) (paper) streamer.
filantropia *sf.* philanthropy.
filàntropo *sm.* philanthrope.
filare[1] *vt.* **1.** to spin (*v. irr.*) **2.** (*correre*) to run (*v. irr.*) **3.** (*amoreggiare*) to flirt.
filare[2] *sm.* row, line.
filarmònico *agg. e sm.* philharmonic.
filastrocca *sf.* nursery rhyme.
filatelìa *sf.* stamp-collecting.
filatèlico *agg.* philatelic. ♦ **filatèlico** *sm.* philatelist.
filato *agg.* **1.** spun **2.** (*di seguito*) running.
filatura *sf.* spinning.
filettare *vt.* (*mecc.*) to thread.
filettatura *sf.* (*mecc.*) threading.
filetto *sm.* **1.** (*filo sottile*) thin thread **2.** (*mecc.*) thread || — *della lingua*, fraenum.
filiale *agg.* filial. ♦ **filiale** *sf.* branch house.
filiazione *sf.* filiation.
filibustiere *sm.* **1.** filibuster **2.** (*fig.*) adventurer, rascal.

filiera *sf.* **1.** (*mecc.*) screw cutting die **2.** (*ind. tess.*) spinneret.
filiforme *agg.* threadlike.
filigrana *sf.* **1.** filigree **2.** (*di carta*) watermark.
filìppica *sf.* philippic.
fillòssera *sf.* phylloxera.
film *sm.* picture || *girare un* —, to shoot (*v. irr.*) a picture.
filmare *vt.* to film.
filo *sm.* **1.** thread **2.** (*ind. tessile*) yarn **3.** (*tec.*) wire || *un* — *d'acqua*, a fine stream of water; *un* — *d'aria*, a breath of air.
filobus *sm.* trolley-bus.
filologia *sf.* philology.
filòlogo *sm.* philologist.
filone *sm.* **1.** (*di pane*) long loaf **2.** (*min.*) vein.
filosofare *vi.* to philosophize.
filosofia *sf.* philosophy.
filòsofo *sm.* philosopher.
filovìa *sf.* trolley-bus line.
filtrare *vt.* to filter, to strain.
filtro *sm.* **1.** filter **2.** (*colino*) strainer.
filza *sf.* **1.** string **2.** (*fig.*) series (*pl.*) **3.** (*cucito*) running stitch.
finale *agg.* last, final.
finalità *sf.* aim, end.
finalmente *avv.* **1.** at last **2.** (*in conclusione*) finally.
finanche *avv.* even.
finanza *sf.* finance.
finanziamento *sm.* financing.
finanziare *vt.* to finance.
finanziario *agg.* financial.
finanziatore *sm.* financing capitalist.
finanziere *sm.* financier.
finché *cong.* **1.** till, until **2.** (*per tutto il tempo che*) as long as.
fine[1] *sf.* end || *alla fin* —, after all. ♦ **fine** *sm.* (*scopo*) purpose.
fine[2] *agg.* fine, thin.
finestra *sf.* window.
finestrino *sm.* window.
finezza *sf.* **1.** thinness **2.** (*acume*) subtlety **3.** (*raffinatezza*) refinement **4.** (*gentilezza*) kindness.
fingere *vi.* to pretend. ♦ **fingersi** *vr.* to feign oneself.
finimenti *sm. pl.* harness (*sing.*).
finimondo *sm.* **1.** end of the world **2.** (*fig.*) catastrophe.
finire *vi.* **1.** to finish, to end **2.** (*interrompersi*) to stop || — *con*, to end by: *finii con l'andare*, I ended by going.
finitezza *sf.* perfection.

finìtimo agg. bordering.
finito agg. 1. finished, ended 2. (rovinato) done for.
finitura sf. finishing.
fino prep. 1. (di tempo) till, until, up to: — a dicembre, till December 2. (di spazio) as far as: andammo fino a Roma, we went as far as Rome 3. (fino da) from 4. (a partire da) since.
finocchio sm. fennel.
finora avv. till now, so far.
finta sf. 1. sham 2. (scherma) feint.
fintantoché avv. V. finché.
finto agg. false.
finzione sf. pretence, duplicity.
fio sm. penalty: pagare il —, to pay (v. irr.) the penalty (of).
fioccare vi. 1. to snow 2. (fig.) to shower.
fiocco sm. 1. ribbon 2. (di lana) staple 3. (falda) flake 4. (di neve) snowflake.
fiòcina sf. harpoon.
fioco agg. 1. (ranco) hoarse 2. (debole) weak 3. (di luce) dim 4. (di voce) faint.
fionda sf. sling.
fioraio sm. florist.
fiorame sm. floral design.
fiordaliso sm. bluebottle.
fiordo sm. fjord.
fiore sm. 1. flower 2. (fioritura) bloom: essere in — (anche fig.), to be in bloom 3. (parte scelta) the best part 4. (nelle carte) clubs (pl.).
fiorente agg. 1. blooming 2. (fig.) flourishing.
fioretto sm. 1. little flower 2. (relig.) act of mortification 3. (scherma) foil.
floricultore sm. floriculturist.
fiorino sm. florin.
fiorire vi. 1. to flower, to bloom, to blossom 2. (fig.) to flourish.
fiorista s. florist.
fiorito agg. 1. flowery 2. (in fiore) in bloom.
fioritura sf. 1. flowering 2. (fig.) flourishing.
fiotto sm. wave, stream: a fiotti, in streams.
firma sf. signature.
firmamento sm. firmament.
firmare vt. to sign.
firmatario sm. 1. signatory 2. (comm.) signer.
fisarmònica sf. accordion.

fisarmonicista s. accordionist.
fiscale agg. 1. fiscal 2. (inquisitorio) strict.
fiscalismo sm. rigorism.
fischiare vi. 1. to whistle 2. (di segnale acustico) to hoot 3. (di serpente; per disapprovare) to hiss 4. (nelle orecchie) to buzz 5. (di proiettili) to whiz.
fischiata sf. 1. whistling 2. (di disapprovazione) hissing.
fischiettare vt. to whistle softly.
fischietto sm. whistle.
fischio sm. 1. whistle 2. (di serpente; di disapprovazione) hiss 3. (segnali acustici) hoot 4. (nelle orecchie) buzzing.
fisco sm. public treasury.
fisica sf. physics.
fisico agg. physical, bodily. ♦ **fisico** sm. 1. (scienziato) physicist 2. (costituzione) physique.
fisima sf. caprice, whim.
fisiologia sf. physiology.
fisiològico agg. physiologic(al).
fisiòlogo sm. physiologist.
fisionomìa sf. 1. features (pl.) 2. (carattere) character.
fisionomista sm. physiognomist.
fisioterapìa sf. physiotherapy.
fissaggio sm. fixing.
fissare vt. 1. to fix 2. (guardare fisso) to gaze 3. (prenotare) to book. ♦ **fissarsi** vr. 1. to be fixed 2. (stabilirsi) to settle down.
fissato agg. 1. fixed 2. (fam.) obsessed.
fissatore sm. 1. fixer 2. (foto) fixing bath.
fissazione sf. fixed idea.
fissione sf. fission.
fissità sf. fixity.
fisso agg. fixed.
fistola sf. 1. Pan-pipe 2. (patol.) fistula.
fitologìa sf. phytology.
fitta sf. stitch.
fittavolo sm. tenant farmer.
fittizio agg. fictitious.
fitto[1] agg. 1. (conficcato) driven in 2. (denso) thick.
fitto[2] sm. rent.
fiumana sf. 1. broad stream 2. (fig.) crowd, stream.
fiume sm. 1. river 2. (fig.) flood.
fiutare vt. 1. to smell (v. irr.) 2. (fig.) to guess.
fiuto sm. 1. scent, smell 2. (fig.) intuition.

flàccido agg. flabby.

flacone sm. vial.

flagellare vt. **1.** to flagellate **2.** (fig.) to scourge.

flagellazione sf. flagellation.

flagello sm. **1.** scourge, whip **2.** (fig.) scourge, plague.

flagrante agg. flagrant || cogliere qu. in —, to catch (v. irr.) so. in the open act.

flagranza sf. flagrancy.

flanella sf. flannel.

flato sm. flatus.

flatulenza sf. flatulence.

flautato agg. fluted.

flautista sm. flute-player.

flàuto sm. flute.

flèbile agg. plaintive, feeble.

flebite sf. phlebitis.

fleboclisi sf. phleboclysis.

flebòtomo sm. phlebotomist.

flemma sf. coolness, phlegm.

flemmàtico agg. phlegmatic.

flemmone sm. phlegmon.

flessìbile agg. flexible, pliant (anche fig.).

flessibilità sf. flexibility.

flessione sf. flexion, bending.

flessuosità sf. **1.** flexuosity **2.** (di corpo) suppleness.

flessuoso agg. **1.** flexuous **2.** (di corpo) supple.

flèttere vt. to bend (v. irr.).

flirtare vi. to flirt.

flogìstico agg. (med.) phlogistic.

flora sf. flora.

floreale agg. floral.

floricoltore sm. floriculturist.

floricoltura sf. floriculture.

floridezza sf. prosperity.

flòrido agg. **1.** prosperous **2.** (fig.) buxom **3.** (di colorito) ruddy.

florilegio sm. florilegium (pl. -ia).

floscio agg. flabby.

flotta sf. fleet: — metropolitana (in Gran Bretagna), the Home Fleet.

flottante agg. floating.

flottiglia sf. flotilla.

fluente agg. fluent (anche fig.).

fluidità sf. fluency.

flùido agg. e sm. fluid.

fluire vi. to flow.

fluorescente agg. fluorescent.

fluorescenza sf. **1.** (fig.) fluorescence **2.** (elettr.) glow.

fluorìdrico agg. hydrofluoric.

fluorite sf. fluorite.

fluoro sm. fluorine.

fluoruro sm. fluoride.

flussione sf. fluxion.

flusso sm. **1.** (di marea) flood(-tide) **2.** (fig.) flux.

flutto sm. wave.

fluttuante agg. **1.** fluctuating, floating **2.** (incerto) irresolute.

fluttuare vi. to fluctuate, to waver.

fluttuazione sf. fluctuation.

fluviale agg. river (attr.).

fobìa sf. phobia, aversion.

foca sf. seal.

focaccia sf. cake || rendere pan per —, to give (v. irr.) tit for tat.

focaia sf. pietra —, flint.

focale agg. focal.

foce sf. mouth.

focolaio sm. centre of infection.

focolare sm. **1.** hearth **2.** (caminetto) fireplace **3.** (fig.) home.

focoso agg. hot, fiery.

fòdera sf. lining.

foderare vt. to line.

fòdero sm. scabbard, sheath.

fòga sf. impetuosity.

foggia sf. **1.** (moda) fashion **2.** (maniera) way **3.** (forma) shape.

foggiare vt. to shape.

foglia sf. leaf (pl. leaves) || mangiare la —, to take (v. irr.) the hint.

fogliame sm. foliage, leafage.

foglio sm. sheet.

fogna sf. sewer.

fognatura sf. sewage.

foia sf. lust.

fola sf. **1.** fable **2.** (fandonia) fib.

folata sf. (di vento) gust.

folclore sm. folklore.

folcloristico agg. folkloristic.

folgorante agg. flashing, dazzling.

folgorare vt. to strike (v. irr.) with lightning.

folgorazione sf. **1.** (elettr.) electrocution **2.** (fig.) fulmination.

fòlgore sf. thunderbolt.

folla sf. crowd.

folle agg. **1.** mad **2.** (mecc.) idle **3.** (auto) neutral.

folleggiare vi. **1.** to behave foolishly **2.** (divertirsi) to make (v. irr.) merry.

folletto sm. **1.** imp **2.** (ragazzo) restless child.

follìa sf. madness || amare qu. alla —, to be madly in love with so.

folto agg. thick. ♦ **folto** sm. thick.

fomentare vt. to foster.

fomentatore sm. fomenter.

fomento sm. fomentation.

fonda sf. anchorage || **nave alla —**, ship at anchor.

fondaco sm. draper's shop.

fondale sm. 1. (teat.) background 2. (mar.) depth.

fondamentale agg. fundamental.

fondamento sm. 1. foundation: **gettare le fondamenta**, to lay (v. irr.) the foundation 2. (fig.) basis, ground.

fondare vt. to found. ♦ **fondarsi** vr. to base oneself on.

fondatezza sf. foundation, ground.

fondato agg. well-grounded.

fondatore sm. founder.

fondazione sf. 1. foundation 2. (istituzione) institution.

fondere vt. 1. to melt 2. (fondere in forma) to cast (v. irr.) 3. (unire) to blend.

fonderia sf. foundry.

fondiario agg. land (attr.).

fondista sm. long-distance runner.

fonditore sm. melter, caster.

fonditura sf. 1. melting 2. (colata) casting.

fondo agg. deep. ♦ **fondo** sm. 1. (parte inferiore) bottom 2. (estremità) end 3. (indole) nature 4. (possedimento) estate 5. (capitale) fund || **articolo di —**, leading article.

fonema sm. phoneme.

fonètica sf. phonetics.

fonogramma sm. phonogram.

fonologìa sf. phonology.

fontana sf. fountain.

fontanella sf. (anat.) fontanel.

fonte sf. spring, source (anche fig.).

foraggio sm. forage.

foràneo agg. 1. rural 2. (mar.) outer.

forare vt. 1. to pierce 2. (di pneumatico) to puncture 3. (di biglietti) to punch.

foratura sf. 1. piercing 2. (di pneumatico) puncture.

fòrbici sf. pl. scissors.

forbire vt. 1. to clean 2. (di stile) to polish.

forbito agg. 1. elegant 2. (di stile) polished.

forca sf. 1. fork 2. (patibolo) gallows.

forcella sf. 1. forked stick 2. (mecc.) fork 3. (per capelli) hairpin.

forchetta sf. fork.

forcina sf. hairpin.

fòrcipe sm. forceps (pl.).

forcuto agg. forked.

forense agg. forensic.

foresta sf. forest (anche fig.), wood.

forestale agg. forestal: **guardia —**, forester.

foresterìa sf. guest-rooms (pl.).

forestiero agg. foreign. ♦ **forestiero** sm. foreigner.

fòrfora sf. dandruff, scurf.

forgiare vt. 1. to forge 2. (modellare) to shape.

forma sf. 1. form, shape 2. (tec.) mould.

formaggio sm. cheese.

formale agg. 1. formal 2. (solenne) solemn.

formalismo sm. formalism.

formalista agg. e s. formalist.

formalità sf. formality.

formalizzarsi vr. to be shocked (at, by).

formare vt. 1. to form 2. (fare) to make (v. irr.), to create 3. (modellare) to shape 4. (addestrare) to train. ♦ **formarsi** vr. 1. to form 2. (crescere, affinarsi) to grow (v. irr.), to develop.

formativo agg. formative.

formato sm. 1. form 2. (misura) size 3. (di libro) format.

formazione sf. formation.

formica sf. ant.

formichiere sm. ant-eater.

formicolare vi. 1. to swarm 2. (sentire un formicolio) to tingle.

formicolìo sm. 1. swarming 2. (intorpidimento) tingling.

formidàbile agg. formidable.

fòrmula sf. formula (pl. -ae).

formulare vt. to formulate.

fornace sf. furnace.

fornaio sm. 1. baker 2. (negozio) baker's shop.

fornello sm. stove.

fornire vt. 1. to supply (with), to provide (with) 2. (equipaggiare) to equip (with).

fornito agg. 1. furnished (with), supplied (with) 2. (equipaggiato) equipped (with).

fornitore sm. furnisher, supplier.

fornitura sf. 1. (il fornire) supplying 2. (attrezzatura) furniture, fitting.

forno sm. 1. (da cucina) oven 2. (metal.) furnace.

foro¹ sm. hole.

foro² sm. 1. court of justice 2. (gli avvocati) the Bar 3. (stor.) forum.

forse *avv.* **1.** perhaps, maybe **2.** (*circa*) about.

forsennato *agg.* mad, frantic.

forte *agg.* **1.** strong (*anche fig.*) **2.** (*di mali*) severe **3.** (*violento*) heavy **4.** (*di suono*) loud. ♦ **forte** *sm.* **1.** strong man **2.** (*punto di forza*) strong point **3.** (*fortezza*) fortress. ♦ **forte** *avv.* strongly.

fortezza *sf.* stronghold, fortress.

fortificare *vt.* to strengthen, to fortify (*anche fig.*).

fortificazione *sf.* fortification.

fortino *sm.* block-house.

fortùito *agg.* fortuitous, accidental.

fortuna *sf.* **1.** luck **2.** (*ricchezza*) fortune, wealth **3.** (*riuscita*) success **4.** (*emergenza*) emergency.

fortunale *sm.* storm.

fortunato *agg.* lucky.

fortunoso *agg.* **1.** stormy **2.** (*fig.*) eventful.

forùncolo *sm.* boil.

foruncolosi *sf.* furunculosis.

forviare *vt.* to lead (*v. irr.*) astray.

forza *sf.* **1.** strength **2.** (*fig.*) power || — *di volontà*, will-power; *a* — *di*, by dint of **3.** (*mil.*) force.

forzare *vt.* **1.** to force, to compel **2.** (*scassinare*) to pick the lock of.

forzato *agg.* forced. ♦ **forzato** *sm.* convict.

forziere *sm.* coffer.

forzoso *agg.* forced.

foschia *sf.* haze, mist.

fosco *agg.* **1.** dark, hazy **2.** (*di aspetto*) gloomy.

fosfato *sm.* phosphate.

fosforescente *agg.* phosphorescent.

fosforescenza *sf.* phosphorescence.

fòsforo *sm.* **1.** phosphorus **2.** (*fig.*) intelligence.

fossa *sf.* **1.** ditch **2.** (*cavità*) hollow **3.** (*tomba*) grave.

fossato *sm.* ditch.

fòssile *agg.* e *sm.* fossil || *carbon* —, pit-coal.

fosso *sm.* ditch.

foto *sf.* photo.

fotocèllula *sf.* photoelectric cell.

fotocopia *sf.* photocopy.

fotogènico *agg.* photogenic.

fotografare *vt.* to photograph.

fotografia *sf.* **1.** (*arte fotografica*) photography **2.** (*immagine fotografica*) photograph || — *istantanea*, snapshot; *fare una* —, to take (*v. irr.*) a photograph.

fotògrafo *sm.* photographer.

fotomontaggio *sm.* photomontage.

fra *prep.* V. *tra.*

fra' *sm.* (*relig.*) Brother.

frac *sm.* tail-coat.

fracassare *vt.* to smash, to shatter.

fracasso *sm.* **1.** noise, hubbub **2.** (*di cose rotte*) crash.

fracco *sm.* **1.** a great deal **2.** (*di botte*) a good thrashing.

fràdicio *agg.* **1.** rotten **2.** (*bagnato*) wet through.

fràgile *agg.* **1.** fragile **2.** (*fig.*) frail.

fragilità *sf.* fragility (*anche fig.*).

fràgola *sf.* strawberry.

fragore *sm.* loud noise.

fragoroso *agg.* noisy.

fragrante *agg.* fragrant.

fragranza *sf.* fragrance.

fraintèndere *vt.* · to misunderstand (*v. irr.*).

frammassone *sm.* freemason.

frammassoneria *sf.* freemasonry.

frammentario *agg.* fragmentary.

frammento *sm.* fragment.

framméttere *vt.* to interpose. ♦ **framméttersi** *vr.* to interpose, to intrude.

frammezzare *vt.* to intersperse.

frammezzo *prep.* V. *tra.*

frammischiare *vt.* to intermingle. ♦ **frammischiarsi** *vr.* to intermingle.

frana *sf.* landslide.

franare *vi.* **1.** (*di terreno*) to slide (*v. irr.*) down **2.** (*di casa*) to fall (*v. irr.*) in.

francescano *agg.* e *sm.* Franciscan.

francese *agg.* French. ♦ **francese** *sm.* Frenchman (*pl.* -men).

francesismo *sm.* Gallicism.

franchezza *sf.* frankness, outspokenness.

franchigia *sf.* **1.** immunity **2.** (*postale*) post-free **3.** (*mar.*) furlough.

franco¹ *agg.* **1.** frank, outspoken **2.** (*libero; comm.*) free: *un porto* —, a free port; — *a bordo*, free on board; — *di spese*, free of charge.

franco² *sm.* franc.

francobollo *sm.* stamp.

francotiratore *sm.* sharp-shooter.

frangente *sm.* **1.** (*mar.*) breaker **2.** (*situazione difficile*) emergency.

fràngere *vt.* **1.** to break (*v. irr.*) **2.** (*schiacciare*) to crush.

frangetta *sf.* fringe.

frangia *sf.* **1.** fringe **2.** (*fig.*) embellishment.

frangiare *vt.* to fringe.

frangibile *agg.* frangible.

frangibilità *sf.* frangibility.

frangiflutti *agg. e sm.* breakwater.

frangizolle *sm.* (*agr.*) clod-smasher.

franoso *agg.* crumbling.

frantoio *sm.* oil-mill.

frantumare *vt.* to shatter.

frantume *sm.* fragment || *andare in frantumi,* to break (*v. irr.*) into fragments.

frappé *sm.* shake.

frapporre *vt.* to interpose. ♦ **frapporsi** *vr.* to interpose.

frasario *sm.* jargon.

frasca *sf.* 1. leafy branch 2. (*donna leggera*) coquette.

frascheggiare *vi.* 1. to rustle 2. (*civettare*) to flirt.

fraschetta *sf.* 1. twig 2. (*fig.*) frivolous girl.

frase *sf.* sentence.

fraseggiare *vi.* to phrase.

fraseologia *sf.* phraseology.

fràssino *sm.* ash-tree.

frastagliare *vt.* to indent.

frastagliato *agg.* indented.

frastaglio *sm.* indentation.

frastornare *vt.* to disturb.

frastuono *sm.* noise, uproar, hubbub.

frate *sm.* 1. friar 2. (*come appellativo*) Brother.

fratellanza *sf.* brotherhood, fraternity.

fratellastro *sm.* half-brother.

fratello *sm.* brother || *fratelli siamesi,* Siamese twins.

fraternità *sf.* brotherhood, fraternity.

fraternizzare *vi.* to fraternize.

fraternizzazione *sf.* fraternization.

fraterno *agg.* brotherly.

fratricida *agg.* fratricidal. ♦ **fratricida** *s.* fratricide.

fratricidio *sm.* fratricide.

fratta *sf.* thicket.

frattaglie *sf. pl.* chitterlings.

frattanto *avv.* meantime, meanwhile.

frattempo (*nella loc. avv.*) *nel —,* in the meanwhile.

fratto *agg.* broken, crushed.

frattura *sf.* fracture.

fratturare *vt.* to fracture, to break (*v. irr.*). ♦ **fratturarsi** *vr.* to fracture, to break.

fraudolento *agg.* fraudulent.

fraudolenza *sf.* fraudulence.

frazionamento *sm.* division.

frazionare *vt.* to divide.

frazionario *agg.* fractional.

frazione *sf.* fraction.

freccia *sf.* arrow.

frecciata *sf.* (*fig.*) gibe.

freddare *vt.* 1. to cool 2. (*ammazzare*) to kill.

freddezza *sf.* coldness, coldheartedness.

freddo *agg.* cold. ♦ **freddo** *sm.* cold: *avere —,* to be cold; *tremare di —,* to shiver with cold.

freddoloso *agg.* sensitive to cold.

freddura *sf.* pun.

fregagione *sf.* massage.

fregare *vt.* 1. to rub 2. (*imbrogliare; volg.*) to swindle.

fregata[1] *sf.* rubbing.

fregata[2] *sf.* (*nave*) frigate.

fregatura *sf.* swindle.

fregiare *vt.* to decorate, to adorn.

fregio *sm.* 1. ornament 2. (*arch.*) frieze.

frego *sm.* stroke: *tirare un — su qc.,* to cross sthg. out.

frègola *sf.* heat.

fremente *agg.* quivering: *— d'ira,* fuming.

frèmere *vi.* to quiver, to tremble.

frèmito *sm.* quiver, thrill.

frenare *vt.* 1. to brake 2. (*trattenere*) to restrain.

frenata *sf.* braking.

frenesìa *sf.* 1. frenzy 2. (*desiderio sfrenato*) immoderate desire.

frenètico *agg.* 1. frantic 2. (*entusiastico*) enthusiastic.

freno *sm.* 1. brake || *bloccare i freni,* to jam the brakes; *togliere il —,* to release the brake 2. (*ritegno*) check restraint || *mordere il —,* to fret under restraint; *stringere i freni,* to shorten the reins 3. (*di cavallo*) bit.

frenologia *sf.* phrenology.

frequentare *vt.* 1. to frequent 2. (*di scuola*) to attend 3. (*di luogo pubblico*) to patronize.

frequentato *agg.* 1. frequented 2. (*di scuola*) attended 3. (*di luogo pubblico*) patronized.

frequentatore *sm.* 1. frequenter 2. (*cliente assiduo*) regular customer.

frequente *agg.* frequent.

frequenza *sf.* 1. frequency 2. (*affluenza*) concourse 3. (*assiduità*) attendance.

fresa sf. milling machine.

fresatrice sf. milling machine.

freschezza sf. freshness (anche fig.), coolness.

fresco agg. 1. fresh 2. (di temperatura) cool.

frescura sf. coolness.

fretta sf. haste, hurry: avere —, to be in a hurry.

frettoloso agg. hurried.

freudiano agg. Freudian.

fríabile agg. crumbly.

friabilità sf. friability.

fricassea sf. fricassee.

friggere vt. to fry || andare a farsi —, to go (v. irr.) to the devil.

friggitoria sf. fried food shop.

frigidezza, frigidità sf. frigidity.

frigido agg. frigid (anche fig.).

frignare vi. to whimper.

frigorifero agg. refrigerant. ♦ **frigorifero** sm. 1. refrigerator 2. (fam.) fridge.

fringuello sm. finch.

frittata sf. omelette.

frittella sf. pancake.

fritto agg. fried.

frittura sf. fry.

frivolezza sf. 1. frivolity 2. (cosa frivola) trifle.

frìvolo agg. frivolous.

frizionare vt. to rub, to massage.

frizione sf. 1. rub, rubbing, massage 2. (auto) clutch.

frizzante agg. 1. biting 2. (di bevanda) sparkling.

frizzare vi. 1. to tingle 2. (di bevanda) to sparkle.

frizzo sm. 1. witticism 2. (scherno) gibe.

frodare vt. to defraud.

frodatore sm. defrauder.

frode sf. fraud, swindle.

frodo sm. smuggling || cacciare di —, to poach; cacciatore di —, poacher.

frollare vt. to hang. ♦ **frollare** vi. to become (v. irr.) tender.

frollatura sf. hanging.

frollo agg. tender, high || pasta frolla, pastry.

fronda[1] sf. leafy branch.

fronda[2] sf. (rivolta) rebellion: vento di —, trouble brewing.

frondoso agg. leafy.

frontale agg. frontal.

fronte sf. 1. forehead: ampia, sfuggente, broad, receding forehead 2. (arch.) front || di — a, in front

of; far — a, to face. ♦ **fronte** sm. 1. (mil.) front 2. (pol.) union.

fronteggiare vt. to face.

frontespizio sm. 1. (arch.) frontispiece 2. (di libro) title page.

frontiera sf. frontier, border.

frontone sm. 1. pediment 2. (di porta, finestra) gable.

frònzolo sm. frill || senza fronzoli, plain.

frotta sf. 1. crowd 2. (di animali) flock.

frottola sf. fib.

frugacchiare vi. to rummage.

frugale agg. frugal.

frugalità sf. frugality.

frugare vi. to search, to rummage.

frùgolo sm. lively child.

fruire vi. to enjoy, to avail oneself of.

fruizione sf. fruition.

frullare vi. 1. to whip, to beat (v. irr.) up 2. (di ali) to whir.

frullato sm. — di frutta, fruit-shake.

frullatore sm. mill.

frullino sm. whisk.

frullio sm. whirring.

frullo sm. whir.

frumento sm. wheat.

frusciare vi. to rustle.

fruscio sm. rustle.

frusta sf. 1. whip 2. (cuc.) whisk.

frustare vt. to whip, to lash.

frustata sf. lash.

frustino sm. riding-whip.

frusto agg. worn-out, thread-bare.

frustrare vt. to frustrate.

frutta sf. fruit: — candita, candied fruit; — sciroppata, fruit in syrup; — cotta, compote.

fruttare vi. 1. to bear (v. irr.) fruit, to pay (v. irr.) 2. (comm.) to yield.

frutteto sm. orchard.

frutticultura sf. fruit-growing.

fruttiera sf. fruit-dish.

fruttífero agg. 1. fruitful 2. (econ. interest-bearing: buono —, inter est-bearing security.

fruttificare vi. to bear (v. irr. fruit.

fruttivéndolo sm. greengrocer.

frutto sm. fruit || frutti di mare, edible mussels.

fruttuoso agg. fruitful, profitable.

fu agg. late.

fucilare vt. to shoot (v. irr.).

fucilata sf. shot.

fucilazione sf. shooting.

fucile sm. rifle, gun: — ad aria compressa, air-gun; — da caccia, shotgun; calcio del —, butt; canna del —, gun-barrel; caricare un —, to load a gun.

fucileria sf. 1. rifle fire 2. (insieme di fucili) musketry.

fuciliere sm. rifleman (pl. -men).

fucina sf. forge.

fucinare vt. to forge.

fuco sm. 1. drone 2. (bot.) fucus.

fucsia sf. fuchsia.

fuga sf. 1. flight, escape 2. (di innamorati) elopement 3. (falla, apertura) escape, leak 4. (mus.) fugue.

fugace agg. short-lived, transient.

fugacità sf. fugacity.

fugare vt. 1. to put (v. irr.) to flight, to disperse 2. (scacciare) to dispel.

fuggévole agg. flying, ephemeral.

fuggiasco agg. e sm. runaway.

fuggire vi. 1. to run (v. irr.) away, to flee (v. irr.) 2. (di innamorati) to elope. ♦ **fuggire** vt. to shun.

fuggitivo agg. e sm. fugitive.

fulcro sm. fulcrum (pl. -ra).

fùlgido agg. shining.

fulgore sm. brightness.

fulìggine sf. soot.

fuligginoso agg. sooty.

fulminante agg. fulminant. ♦ **fulminante** sm. 1. (chim.) fulminate 2. (di arma) primer.

fulminare vt. 1. to strike (v. irr.) by lightning 2. (colpire) to strike.

fulminato agg. 1. struck by lightning 2. (fig.) thunder-struck.

fùlmine sm. lightning.

fulmineo agg. flashing.

fulvo agg. tawny.

fumaiolo sm. smoke-stack.

fumante agg. smoking, steaming.

fumare vt. e vi. to smoke.

fumarola sf. fumarole.

fumata sf. 1. smoke 2. (segnale) smoke signal.

fumatore sm. smoker.

fumetto sm. strip cartoon || giornali a fumetti, comics.

fumista s. stove-repairer.

fumo sm. 1. smoke || venditore di —, windbag; andare in —, to end in smoke 2. (vapore) fume (anche fig.) 3. (di pentole) steam.

fumògeno agg. smoke-producing.

fumoso agg. smoky.

funàmbolo sm. rope-dancer.

fune sf. 1. rope 2. (cavo) cable.

fùnebre agg. 1. funeral: canto —, dirge; carro —, hearse 2. (cupo) gloomy.

funerale sm. funeral || i funerali, the obsequies.

funerario agg. funerary.

funèreo agg. funeral.

funestare vt. to afflict.

funesto agg. baneful, woeful.

fungaia sf. mushroom-bed.

fùngere vi. to act (as).

fungo sm. mushroom.

funicolare sf. funicular.

funivìa sf. telpherage.

funzionale agg. functional.

funzionamento sm. working.

funzionare vi. 1. to act (as) 2. (andar bene) to work.

funzionario sm. official.

funzione sf. 1. function 2. (carica) office 3. (relig.) service.

fuochista sm. stoker.

fuoco sm. 1. fire 2. (cine; foto; mat.) focus: mettere a —, to focus.

fuorché cong. except, but.

fuori avv. 1. out, outdoors 2. (all'estero) abroad. ♦ **fuori (di)** prep. out of, outside.

fuoribordo sm. outboard motor.

fuoriclasse sm. first-rater.

fuorigioco sm., agg. e avv. off-side.

fuorilegge sm. outlaw.

fuoriserie agg. e sm. special body car.

fuoruscito sm. exile, refugee.

fuorviare vt. to lead (v. irr.) astray.

furberìa sf. cunning.

furbo agg. cunning, shrewd.

furente agg. furious, mad.

furerìa sf. orderly room.

furetto sm. ferret.

furfante sm. rascal, scamp.

furgoncino sm. small van.

furgone sm. van.

furia sf. fury: montare su tutte le furie, to fly (v. irr.) into a fury.

furibondo agg. furious.

furioso agg. 1. furious 2. (violento) violent.

furore sm. fury: far —, to be a hit.

furoreggiare vi. to be all the rage.

furtivo agg. stealthy.

furto sm. theft.

fuscello sm. 1. twig, straw 2. (fig.) thin person.

fusìbile sm. fuse.

fusione sf. 1. fusion 2. (di società comm.) merging.

fuso *sm.* spindle || — *orario*, time zone.

fusoliera *sf.* fuselage.

fustigare *vt.* to flog.

fusto *sm.* **1.** (*bot.*) stalk **2.** (*tronco umano*) trunk **3.** (*per benzina*) drum **4.** (*di legno per liquori*) barrel **5.** (*giovane prestante*) muscle-man (*pl.* -men) **6.** (*di colonna*) shaft.

fùtile *agg.* trifling.

futilità *sf.* trifle.

futurismo *sm.* futurism.

futurista *agg. e sm.* futurist.

futuro *agg. e sm.* future.

G

gabbamondo *sm.* swindler.

gabbare *vt.* to swindle.

gabbia *sf.* **1.** cage **2.** (*per imballaggio*) crate.

gabbiano *sm.* sea-gull.

gabellare *vt.* (*far credere*) to pass off as.

gabinetto *sm.* **1.** (*studio*) study **2.** (*pol.*) cabinet **3.** (*latrina*) water-closet, toilet.

gagà *sm.* dandy.

gagliardamente *avv.* vigorously.

gagliardetto *sm.* pennon.

gagliardo *agg.* vigorous.

gaglioffo *sm.* rascal.

gaiezza *sf.* **1.** cheerfulness **2.** (*di colore*) brightness.

gaio *agg.* **1.** cheerful **2.** (*di colore*) bright.

gala *sf.* **1.** (*trina*) frill **2.** (*festa*) gala: *abito di* —, gala dress.

galante *agg. e sm.* gallant || *lettera* —, love letter; *fare il* —, to flirt.

galanterìa *sf.* **1.** gallantry **2.** (*complimento*) compliment.

galantina *sf.* galantine.

galantuomo *sm.* honest man.

galassia *sf.* galaxy.

galateo *sm.* **1.** good manners (*pl.*) **2.** (*libro*) book of manners.

galena *sf.* galena.

galeone *sm.* galleon.

galeotto *sm.* **1.** convict **2.** (*mezzano*) pander **3.** (*mar.*) galley-slave.

galera *sf.* **1.** jail **2.** (*mar.*) galley.

galileo *agg. e sm.* Galilean.

galla[1] (*nella loc. avv.*) *a* —, afloat || *stare a* —, to float; *venire a* —, to come (*v. irr.*) to the surface; (*fig.*) to come to light.

galla[2] *sf.* (*bot.*) gall.

galleggiamento *sm.* floating: *linea di* —, water-line.

galleggiante *agg.* floating, afloat (*pred.*). ♦ **galleggiante** *sm.* **1.** float **2.** (*boa*) buoy.

galleggiare *vi.* to float.

galleria *sf.* **1.** tunnel **2.** (*d'arte, in teatro*) gallery.

gallese *agg.* Welsh. ♦ **gallese** *sm.* Welshman (*pl.* -men).

galletta *sf.* biscuit.

gallina *sf.* **1.** hen **2.** (*cibo*) chicken.

gallinàceo *agg. e sm.* gallinacean.

gallio *sm.* gallium.

gallismo *sm.* cocksure behaviour (towards women).

gallo *sm.* **1.** cock **2.** (*stor.*) Gaul.

gallonato *agg.* gallooned.

gallone *sm.* **1.** braid, galloon **2.** (*mil.*) chevron stripes (*pl.*) **3.** (*misura*) gallon.

galoppante *agg.* galloping.

galoppare *vi.* to gallop.

galoppata *sf.* gallop.

galoppatoio *sm.* riding-track.

galoppino *sm.* **1.** errand-boy **2.** (*tirapiedi*) drudge.

galoppo *sm.* gallop: *al* —, at a gallop, (*fig.*) at full speed; *andare al gran* —, to ride (*v. irr.*) full gallop.

galoscia *sf.* galosh.

galvànico *agg.* galvanic.

galvanizzare *vt.* **1.** to galvanize **2.** (*rivestire di metallo*) to electroplate.

galvanizzazione *sf.* **1.** galvanization **2.** (*rivestitura di metallo*) electroplating.

galvanoplàstica *sf.* galvanoplastics.

gamba *sf.* leg || *avere le gambe lunghe*, to be long-legged; *male in* —, down at heel; *in* — (*fig.*), smart.

gambale *sm.* **1.** legging **2.** (*di armatura*) jamb.

gamberetto *sm.* shrimp.

gàmbero *sm.* **1.** (*di mare*) lobster **2.** (*d'acqua dolce*) crayfish || *andare come un* —, to go (*v. irr.*) backwards.

gambo *sm.* stem.

gamma *sf.* range: — *di lunghezza d'onda*, waveband.

ganascia *sf.* jaw || *mangiare a quattro ganasce*, to eat (*v. irr.*) voraciously.

gancio *sm.* hook.

ganga *sf.* gang.

gànghero *sm.* hinge || *andare fuori dai gangheri*, to lose (*v. irr.*) one's temper.

ganglio *sm.* ganglion (*pl.* -ia).

gangsterismo *sm.* gangsterism.

ganimede *sm.* dandy.

gara *sf.* competition.

garagista *sm.* garage keeper.

garante *sm.* 1. warranter 2. (*per un imputato*) bail || *essere* —, to answer for.

garantire *vt.* 1. to warrant 2. (*farsi garante per*) to answer for 3. (*un imputato*) to go (*v. irr.*) bail for.

garanzia *sf.* 1. warranty, guarantee 2. (*somma di* —) security 3. (*cauzione*) bail || *dare, non dare* —, to be reliable, unreliable; *a* — *di*, as a guarantee for.

garbare *vi.* to like.

garbatamente *avv.* politely.

garbatezza *sf.* politeness.

garbato *agg.* polite.

garbo *sm.* politeness || *con bel* —, with a good grace.

garbuglio *sm.* entanglement.

gardenia *sf.* gardenia.

gareggiare *vi.* to compete.

garganella (*nella loc. avv.*) *bere a* —, to gulp down.

gargarismo *sm.* gargle.

gargarizzare *vi.* to gargle.

garibaldino *agg. e sm.* Garibaldian.

garitta *sf.* 1. sentry-box 2. (*torretta*) look-out turret 3. (*di guardiano*) cabin.

garòfano *sm.* carnation || *chiodo di* —, clove.

garrese *sm.* withers (*pl.*).

garretto *sm.* 1. back of heel 2. (*di animale*) hock.

garrire *vi.* 1. (*di bandiere*) to flutter, to flap 2. (*di uccelli*) to chirp.

gàrrulo *agg.* talkative.

garza *sf.* gauze.

garzone *sm.* shop-boy, apprentice.

gas *sm.* gas.

gasolio *sm.* gas oil.

gasometro *sm.* gasholder.

gassare *vt.* to gas.

gassato *agg.* aerated || *acqua gassata*, soda-water.

gassista *sm.* gas-fitter.

gassògeno *sm.* gas producer.

gassoso *agg.* 1. gaseous 2. (*gassato*) aerated.

gàstrico *agg.* gastric.

gastrite *sf.* gastritis.

gastroenterite *sf.* gastroenteritis.

gastronomia *sf.* gastronomy.

gastronòmico *agg.* gastronomic(al).

gatta *sf.* she-cat.

gattabuia *sf.* jail.

gatto *sm.* cat.

gattopardo *sm.* leopard.

gaudente *agg.* 1. jolly 2. (*dissipato*) fast. ♦ **gaudente** *sm.* fast person.

gàudio *sm.* joy.

gavetta *sf.* mess-tin.

gavitello *sm.* buoy.

gazza *sf.* magpie.

gazzarra *sf.* din.

gazzella *sf.* gazelle.

gazzetta *sf.* gazette.

gelare *vt. e vi.* to freeze (*v. irr.*).

gelata *sf.* frost.

gelataio *sm.* ice-cream vendor.

gelateria *sf.* ice-cream shop.

gelatina *sf.* 1. (*cuc.*) jelly 2. (*chim.*) gelatine.

gelatinoso *agg.* gelatinous.

gelato *agg.* frozen, icy. ♦ **gelato** *sm.* ice-cream.

gèlido *agg.* icy (*anche fig.*).

gelo *sm.* 1. intense cold 2. (*fig.*) chill 3. (*ghiaccio*) ice 4. (*brina*) frost.

gelone *sm.* chilblain.

gelosia *sf.* 1. jealousy 2. (*cura*) care 3. (*persiana*) shutter.

geloso *agg.* jealous.

gelso *sm.* mulberry(-tree).

gelsomino *sm.* jasmine.

gemebondo *agg.* groaning.

gemelli *sm. pl.* (*di polsino*) cuff-links.

gemello *agg. e sm.* twin.

gèmere *vi.* to groan.

gèmito *sm.* groan.

gemma *sf.* 1. gem 2. (*bot.*) bud.

gemmare *vi.* (*bot.*) to bud.

gendarme *sm.* policeman (*pl.* -men).

gendarmeria *sf.* 1. police-force 2. (*caserma*) police-station.

genealogia *sf.* genealogy.

genealògico *agg.* genealogical.

generàbile *agg.* generable.

generale[1] *agg.* general || *quartier* —, headquarters (*pl.*).

generale² sm. general.

generalità sf. generality || *dare le proprie —*, to give (v. irr.) one's particulars.

generalizzare vt. to generalize.

generalizzazione sf. generalization.

generare vt. 1. to beget (v. irr.) 2. (*produrre, anche tec.*) to produce. ♦ **generarsi** vr. to be born.

generatore agg. generative. ♦ **generatore** sm. generator.

generazione sf. generation.

gènere sm. 1. kind 2. (*gramm.*) gender 3. (*letterario*) genre 4. (*prodotto*) product || *generi alimentari*, foodstuffs; *generi di prima necessità*, commodities.

genèrico agg. generic, vague.

gènero sm. son-in-law.

generosità sf. generosity.

generoso agg. generous.

gènesi sf. genesis (pl. -ses).

genètica sf. genetics.

genètico agg. genetic.

genetlíaco sm. birthday.

gengiva sf. gum.

genia sf. 1. race 2. (*spreg.*) tribe.

geniale agg. clever.

genialità sf. 1. cleverness 2. (*genio*) genius.

genio sm. genius || *andare a —*, to please.

genitale agg. e sm. genital.

genitivo sm. genitive.

genitore sm. 1. parent 2. (*padre*) father.

genitrice sf. mother.

gennaio sm. January.

genocidio sm. genocide.

gentaglia sf. rabble.

gente sf. people: *c'è molta —*, there are a lot of people; *le genti dell'Asia*, the peoples of Asia.

gentildonna sf. lady.

gentile agg. 1. kind 2. (*cortese*) polite || *è — da parte sua*, it is kind of him.

gentilezza sf. 1. kindness 2. (*cortesia*) politeness 3. (*favore*) favour.

gentilizio agg. noble: *stemma —*, coat of arms.

gentiluomo sm. gentleman (pl. -men).

genuflessione sf. genuflection.

genuflèttersi vr. to kneel down.

genuinità sf. genuineness.

genuino agg. genuine.

genziana sf. gentian.

geodesìa sf. geodesy.

geofisica sf. geophysics.

geografia sf. geography.

geogràfico agg. geographic(al) || *carta geografica*, map.

geògrafo sm. geographer.

geologìa sf. geology.

geològico agg. geologic(al).

geòlogo sm. geologist.

geòmetra sm. 1. geometer 2. (*agrimensore*) land-surveyor.

geometrìa sf. geometry.

geomètrico agg. geometric(al).

geopolìtica sf. geopolitics.

geòrgico agg. georgic.

geranio sm. geranium.

gerarca sm. leader.

gerarchìa sf. hierarchy.

gerente sm. manager.

gerenza sf. management.

gergo sm. 1. slang 2. (*di una classe professionale*) jargon.

germànico agg. Germanic.

germanio sm. germanium.

germanismo sm. Germanism.

germanista s. Germanist.

germanistica sf. Germanic studies.

germano¹ agg. e sm. German.

germano² agg. german: *fratello —*, brother-german.

germe sm. germ.

germicida agg. germicidal. ♦ **germicida** sm. germicide.

germinare vi. V. *germogliare*.

germinazione sf. germination.

germogliare vi. 1. to sprout 2. (*fig.*) to spring (v. irr.) (up).

germoglio sm. germ.

geroglifico sm. hieroglyphic.

gerontologìa sf. gerontology.

gerundio sm. gerund.

gessetto sm. chalk.

gesso sm. 1. chalk 2. (*med.; scult.; edil.*) plaster.

gesta sf. pl. deeds.

gestante sf. pregnant woman.

gestazione sf. gestation.

gesticolare vi. to gesticulate.

gestione sf. management.

gestire vt. to manage.

gestire¹ vi. to gesture.

gesto sm. gesture || *un bel —*, a noble deed.

gestore sm. manager.

gesuita sm. Jesuit.

gesuìtico agg. Jesuitic(al).

gettare vt. 1. to throw (v. irr.), (*anche metal.; edil.*) to cast (v. irr.) 2. (*bot.*) to sprout 3. (*fruttare*) to yield || *— le fondamenta*, to lay (v. irr.) the foundations; — un grido, to utter a cry. ◆ gettarsi vr. (di fiume) to flow.

gettata sf. 1. throw 2. (edil.; metal.) cast 3. (di arma) range 4. (molo) jetty.

gettito sm. (delle imposte) yield.

getto sm. 1. throw 2. (mecc.; di liquidi) jet 3. (bot.) sprout 4. (metal.; edil.) casting || di —, effortlessly; a — continuo, continuously.

gettone sm. 1. counter: — telefonico, telephone counter 2. (contromarca) check || macchina a —, slot-machine.

geyser sm. geyser.

gheriglio sm. kernel.

germinella sf. trick: fare una —, to play a trick (on).

ghermire vt. to clutch.

ghette sf. pl. spats.

ghetto sm. 1. ghetto 2. (insieme degli ebrei) Jewry.

ghiacciaia sf. 1. ice-box 2. (stanza) ice-house.

ghiacciaio sm. glacier.

ghiacciare vi e vt. to freeze (v. irr.).

ghiacciato agg. 1. frozen 2. (molto freddo) icy.

ghiaccio sm. ice.

ghiacciolo sm. icicle.

ghiaia sf. gravel.

ghiaioso agg. gravelly.

ghianda sf. acorn.

ghiandola sf. gland.

ghibellino agg. e sm. Ghibelline.

ghigliottina sf. guillotine.

ghigliottinare vt. to guillotine.

ghignare vi. to grin.

ghigno sm. grin.

ghingheri (nella loc. avv.) mettersi in —, to dress up.

ghiotto agg. 1. greedy 2. (appetitoso) dainty.

ghiottone sm. glutton.

ghiottoneria sf. 1. gluttony 2. (cibo prelibato) dainty.

ghiribizzo sm. whim.

ghirigoro sm. doodle.

ghirlanda sf. wreath.

ghiro sm. dormouse (pl. dormice) || dormire come un —, to sleep (v. irr.) like a log.

ghisa sf. cast iron.

già avv. 1. already 2. (un tempo) once 3. (certamente) of course.

giacca sf. coat, jacket.

giacché cong. as, since.

giacente agg. 1. lying 2. (di capitale) uninvested 3. (di posta) unclaimed.

giacenza sf. lying || capitale in —, uninvested capital; lettera in —, unclaimed letter; merci in —, goods in stock.

giacere vi. to lie (v. irr.).

giaciglio sm. couch.

giacimento sm. (min.) deposit: — di petrolio, oil-field.

giacinto sm. hyacinth.

giacobino sm. e agg. Jacobin.

giada sf. jade.

giaggiolo sm. iris.

giaguaro sm. jaguar.

giallastro agg. yellowish.

giallo agg. yellow || romanzo, film, dramma —, thriller.

giammai avv. never.

giansenismo sm. Jansenism.

giansenista s. Jansenist.

giapponese agg. e sm. Japanese (invariato al pl.).

giara sf. jar.

giardinaggio sm. gardening.

giardinetta sf. station wagon.

giardiniere sm. gardener.

giardino sm. garden || — d'infanzia, nursery-school.

giarrettiera sf. garter.

giavellotto sm. javelin: lancio del —, javelin throwing.

gibbosità sf. hump.

giberna sf. cartridge-pouch.

gigante sm. giant || fare passi da —, to make (v. irr.) rapid progress.

giganteggiare vi. to tower.

gigantesco agg. gigantic.

gigantismo sm. giantism.

gigione sm. ham.

giglio sm. lily.

gilè sm. waistcoat.

gincana sf. gymkhana.

gineceo sm. gynaeceum (pl. -ea).

ginecologia sf. gynaecology.

ginecologico agg. gynaecological.

ginecologo sm. gynaecologist.

ginepraio sm. 1. juniper thicket 2. (fig.) fix: ficcarsi in un —, to get (v. irr.) into a scrape.

ginepro sm. juniper.

ginestra sf. broom.

gingillarsi vr. to dawdle.

gingillo sm. 1. knick-knack 2. (balocco) plaything.

ginnasio sm. 1. grammar school 2.

(*in Italia e stor.*) gymnasium (*pl.* -ia).

ginnasta *sm.* athlete.

ginnàstica *sf.* gymnastics.

ginnico *agg.* gymnastic, athletic.

ginocchiata *sf.* blow with the knee.

ginocchiera *sf.* 1. knee-guard 2. (*mecc.*) toggle.

ginocchio *sm.* 1. knee: *in* —, on one's knees 2. (*mecc.*) bend.

ginocchioni *avv.* on one's knees.

giocare *vi.* 1. to play 2. (*d'azzardo*) to gamble 3. (*scommettere*) to bet (*v. irr.*) 4. (*in borsa*) to speculate. ♦ **giocare** *vt.* 1. to play 2. (*ingannare*) to deceive. ♦ **giocarsi** *vr.* (*beffarsi*) to trifle (with).

giocata *sf.* 1. game 2. (*puntata*) stake.

giocatore *sm.* 1. player 2. (*d'azzardo*) gambler 3. (*in borsa*) stockjobber.

giocàttolo *sm.* toy.

giocherellare *vi.* to toy.

gioco *sm.* 1. play 2. (*regolato da norme*) game 3. (*d'azzardo*) gambling 4. (*scherzo*) joke || *per* —, for fun; — *di pazienza*, puzzle; — *di parole*, pun; *essere in* —, to be involved.

giocoforza *sm.* necessary: *è* —, it is absolutely necessary.

giocoliere *sm.* juggler.

giocondità *sf.* gaiety.

giocondo *agg.* gay.

giocosità *sf.* playfulness.

giocoso *agg.* playful.

giogaia *sf.* mountain range.

giogo *sm.* 1. yoke 2. (*di monte*) summit.

gioia *sf.* 1. joy 2. (*gioiello*) jewel.

gioiellerìa *sf.* 1. jewelry 2. (*negozio*) jeweller's shop.

gioielliere *sm.* jeweller

gioiello *sm.* jewel

gioioso *agg.* joyful.

gioire *vi.* to rejoice (at).

giornalaio *sm.* newsman (*pl.* -men).

giornale *sm.* 1. newspaper 2. (*comm.*) journal || — *radio*, news bulletin; *cine* —, news-reel.

giornaliero *agg.* daily.

giornalismo *sm.* 1. journalism 2. (*la stampa*) press.

giornalista *s.* journalist, reporter.

giornalìstico *agg.* journalistic || *ambiente* —, press.

giornalmente *avv.* daily.

giornata *sf.* day: *lavorare a* —, to work by the day || *donna a* —, charwoman (*pl.* -women).

giorno *sm.* day: *di* —, by day; *a giorni*, in a few days' time; *due volte al* —, twice a day; *un* — (*avv.*), one day || — *festivo*, holiday.

giovamento *sm.* benefit || *trarre* — *da*, to benefit by.

gióvane *agg.* young. ♦ **gióvane** *sm.* young man (*pl.* -men). ♦ **gióvane** *sf.* young woman (*pl.* women).

giovanetta *sf.* girl.

giovanetto *sm.* boy.

giovanile *agg.* 1. juvenile 2. (*da giovane*) youthful.

giovanotto *sm.* young man (*pl.* men).

giovare *vi.* to be of use. ♦ **giovare** *vt.* to be good (for). ♦ **giovarsi** *vr.* to benefit (by).

giovedì *sm.* Thursday.

giovenca *sf.* heifer.

gioventù *sf.* youth.

gioviale *agg.* jolly.

giovialità *sf.* jollity.

giovinastro *sm.* hooligan.

giovincello *sm.* lad.

giovinezza *sf.* youth.

giràbile *agg.* endorsable.

giradischi *sm.* record player.

giradito *sm.* whitlow.

giraffa *sf.* giraffe.

giramento *sm.* turning: — *di capo*, giddiness; *avere un* —, to feel (*v. irr.*) giddy.

giramondo *sm.* 1. wanderer 2. (*turista*) globe-trotter.

giràndola *sf.* 1. (*fuoco d'artificio*) Catherine-wheel 2. (*fig.*) fickle person.

girandolare *vi.* to saunter.

girandolone *sm.* saunterer.

girante *sm.* 1. (*comm.*) endorser 2. (*mecc.*) impeller (*di pompa*), wheel (*di turbina*).

girare *vi. e vt.* 1. to turn 2. (*evitare*) to avoid 3. (*viaggiare*) to tour 4. (*vagare*) to stroll 5. (*comm.*) to endorse 6. (*riprendere un film*) to shoot (*v. irr.*). ♦ **girarsi** *vr.* to turn.

girarrosto *sm.* spit.

girasole *sm.* sunflower.

girata *sf.* 1. turn 2. (*comm.*) endorsement.

giratario *sm.* (*comm.*) endorsee.

giravolta *sf.* 1. turning 2. (*fig.*) shift ‖ *fare una* —, to turn round.

girello *sm.* 1. (*per bambini*) go-cart 2. (*parte di bue*) rump.

giretto *sm.* stroll: *fare un* —, to take (*v. irr.*) a short walk.

girévole *agg.* revolving.

girino *sm.* tadpole.

giro *sm.* 1. turn 2. (*viaggio*) tour 3. (*passeggiata*) stroll 4. (*percorso*) round ‖ *a* — *di posta*, by return of post; — *d'affari*, turnover; *nel* — *di pochi giorni*, in a few days' time; *fare un* — *in auto*, to go (*v. irr.*) for a drive in a car; *fare un* — *in bicicletta*, to take (*v. irr.*) a ride on a bicycle.

girondino *agg. e sm.* Girondist

gironzolare *vi.* to stroll.

giroscopio *sm.* gyroscope.

girotondo *sm.* round dance.

girovagare *vi.* to wander.

giròvago *agg.* wandering. ♦ **giròvago** *sm.* tramp ‖ *venditore* —, pedlar.

gita *sf.* trip: *fare una* —, to take (*v. irr.*) a trip.

gitano *sm.* Spanish gipsy.

gitante *s.* tripper.

giù *avv.* 1. down 2. (*dabbasso*) downstairs ‖ — *per*, down; *su per* —, approximately.

giubba *sf.* coat.

giubbetto *sm.* 1. jacket 2. (*da donna*) bodice.

giubbotto *sm.* (heavy) coat.

giubilare *vi.* to exult.

giubileo *sm.* jubilee.

giùbilo *sm.* rejoicing.

giudàico *agg.* Judaic.

giudaismo *sm.* Judaism.

giudeo *agg.* Jewish. ♦ **giudeo** *sm.* Jew. ♦ **giudea** *sf.* Jewess.

giudicare *vt.* 1. to judge 2. (*pensare*) to think (*v. irr.*).

giùdice *sm.* judge ‖ *i giudici*, the Bench.

giudiziario *agg.* judicial.

giudizio *sm.* 1. judgement 2. (*causa*) trial 3. (*sentenza*) sentence 4. (*buon senso*) common sense ‖ *far* —, to behave oneself; *rinviare a* —, to commit for trial.

giudizioso *agg.* sensible.

giùggiola *sf.* jujube ‖ *andare in brodo di giuggiole*, to be extremely pleased.

giuggiolone *sm.* simpleton.

giugno *sm.* June.

giugulare *agg.* jugular.

giuliano *agg.* Julian.

giulivo *agg.* cheerful.

giullare *sm.* jester.

giumenta *sf.* (*cavalla*) mare.

giunca *sf.* junk.

giunco *sm.* reed.

giùngere *vi.* 1. to arrive (at), to reach (sthg.) 2. (*riuscire*) to succeed (in). ♦ **giùngere** *vt.* (*congiungere*) to join.

giungla *sf.* jungle.

giunta[1] *sf.* 1. addition: *per* —, in addition 2. (*di peso*) make-weight.

giunta[2] *sf.* — *comunale*, town council.

giunto *sm.* (*mecc.*) joint.

giuntura *sf.* juncture.

giunzione *sf.* 1. connection 2. (*giunto*) joint ‖ *fare una* —, to joint.

giuramento *sm.* oath: *sotto* —, on oath.

giurare *vt.* to swear (*v. irr.*).

giurato *sm.* juryman (*pl.* -men) ‖ *i giurati*, the jury (*sing.*).

giuria *sf.* jury.

giurìdico *agg.* juridical: *stato* —, legal status.

giurisdizione *sf.* jurisdiction.

giurisprudenza *sf.* law.

giurista *sm.* jurist.

giustezza *sf.* 1. exactness 2. (*tip.*) measure.

giustificàbile *agg.* justifiable.

giustificare *vt.* to justify.

giustificazione *sf.* justification.

giustizia *sf.* justice.

giustiziare *vt.* to execute.

giustiziato *sm.* executed man.

giustiziere *sm.* 1. executioner 2. (*vendicatore*) avenger.

giusto *agg.* 1. just 2. (*esatto*) right 3. (*legittimo*) legitimate.

glabro *agg.* hairless.

glaciale *agg.* icy: *regione* —, ice region.

glaciazione *sf.* glaciation.

gladiatore *sm.* gladiator.

gladiolo *sm.* gladiolus.

glande *sm.* glans (*pl.* -ndes).

glàndola *sf.* V. *ghiandola*.

glandolare *agg.* glandular.

glassare *vt.* 1. (*con zucchero*) to ice 2. (*con gelatina*) to glaze.

glàuco *agg.* glaucous.

glaucoma *sm.* glaucoma.

gleba *sf.* clod ‖ *servo della* —, serf.

gli[1] *art.* **1.** the **2.** (*in senso generico non si traduce*): — *stranieri amano l'Italia*, foreigners love Italy **3.** (*si traduce col possessivo coi capi di vestiario ecc.*): *si tolse — occhiali*, he took off his glasses.

gli[2] *pron.* **1.** (*per persona*) him, to him **2.** (*per cosa*) it, to it || — *mandai un libro*, I sent him a book, I sent to him.

glicerina *sf.* glycerine.

glìcine *sm.* wistaria.

glicògeno *sm.* glycogen.

glielo *pron.* it (to) him; it (to) her; him to him; him to her; it to it.

globale *agg.* total.

globo *sm.* globe.

globulare *agg.* globular.

glòbulo *sm.* (*biol.*) corpuscle.

gloria *sf.* glory.

gloriarsi *vr.* to glory (in).

glorificare *vt.* to glorify.

glorificazione *sf.* glorification.

glorioso *agg.* glorious.

glossa *sf.* gloss.

glossario *sm.* glossary.

glòttide *sf.* glottis.

glottologìa *sf.* glottology.

glottològico *agg.* glottological.

glottòlogo *sm.* glottologist.

glucosio *sm.* glucose.

glùteo *sm.* gluteus (*pl.* -ei).

glutinato *agg.* gluten (*attr.*).

glùtine *sm.* gluten.

gnomo *sm.* gnome.

gnosticismo *sm.* gnosticism.

gnòstico *agg.* e *sm.* gnostic.

gobba *sf.* **1.** hump (*anche fig.*) **2.** (*donna —*) humpbacked woman.

gobbo *agg.* **1.** humpbacked **2.** (*curvo*) bent. ♦ **gobbo** *sm.* humpback.

goccia *sf.* **goccio** *sm.* drop.

gocciolare *vi.* e *vt.* to drip.

gocciolìo *sm.* dripping.

godere *vi.* e *vt.* to enjoy || *godersela*, to have a good time.

godereccio *agg.* **1.** (*amante dei godimenti*) pleasure-loving **2.** (*che dà godimento*) pleasant.

godimento *sm.* enjoyment.

goffàggine *sf.* **1.** clumsiness **2.** (*atto goffo*) clumsy action.

goffo *agg.* clumsy.

gogna *sf.* pillory: *mettere alla —*, to pillory.

gola *sf.* **1.** throat: *aver mal di —*, to have a sorethroat. **2.** (*golosità*) gluttony: *far —*, to tempt **3.** (*geogr.*) gorge.

goletta *sf.* (*mar.*) schooner.

golf *sm.* **1.** 'jersey **2.** (*gioco*) golf.

golfo *sm.* gulf.

goliàrdico *agg.* of students.

goliardo *sm.* university student.

golosità *sf.* **1.** greediness **2.** (*cibo prelibato*) dainty.

goloso *agg.* greedy. ♦ **goloso** *sm.* glutton.

gòmena *sf.* rope.

gomitata *sf.* nudge || *farsi avanti a gomitate*, to elbow one's way.

gòmito *sm.* **1.** elbow **2.** (*di strada*) sharp bend || — *a —*, side by side.

gomìtolo *sm.* clew.

gomma *sf.* **1.** rubber **2.** (*sostanza resinosa*) gum **3.** (*pneumatico*) tyre.

gommapiuma *sf.* foam rubber.

gòndola *sf.* gondola.

gonfalone *sm.* standard.

gonfiare *vt.* **1.** to swell (*v. irr.*) **2.** (*esagerare*) to exaggerate. ♦ **gonfiarsi** *vr.* to swell (*anche fig.*).

gonfiatura *sf.* **1.** swelling **2.** (*esagerazione*) exaggeration.

gonfio *agg.* **1.** swollen **2.** (*di stile*) bombastic.

gonfiore *sm.* swelling.

gong *sm.* gong.

gongolante *agg.* rejoicing (at).

gongolare *vi.* to rejoice (at).

goniòmetro *sm.* goniometer.

gonna *sf.* **1.** skirt **2.** (*di costume storico anche maschile*) gown.

gonnellino *sm.* — *scozzese*, kilt.

gonzo *sm.* blockhead.

gorgheggiare *vi.* to trill.

gorgheggio *sm.* trill.

gorgo *sm.* whirlpool.

gorgogliare *vi.* to gurgle.

gorgoglìo *sm.* gurgling.

gorilla *sm.* gorilla.

gota *sf.* cheek.

gòtico *agg.* Gothic.

gotta *sf.* gout.

governàbile *agg.* governable.

governante *sm.* **1.** ruler **2.** (*statista*) statesman (*pl.* -men). ♦ **governante** *sf.* **1.** housekeeper **2.** (*bambinaia*) nurse.

governare *vt.* **1.** to govern, to rule **2.** (*badare a*) to look after **3.** (*mar.*) to steer.

governativo *agg.* government (*attributivo*).

governatore *sm.* governor.

governo *sm.* **1.** government **2.** (*dominio*) rule **3.** (*comm.*) management **4.** (*mar.*) steerage || — *della* *casa*, housekeeping.

gozzo *sm.* 1. goitre 2. (*di uccello*) crop.

gozzoviglia *sf.* revelry.

gozzovigliare *vi.* to revel.

gozzuto *agg.* goitrous.

gracchiare *vi.* to croak.

gracidare *vi.* to croak.

gracidìo *sm.* croaking.

gràcile *agg.* frail.

gracilità *sf.* frailty.

gradassata *sf.* boastfulness, brag.

gradasso *sm.* boaster, braggart.

gradatamente *avv.* gradually.

gradazione *sf.* 1. gradation 2. (*sfumatura*) shade.

gradévole *agg.* agreeable.

gradimento *sm.* 1. pleasure 2. satisfaction 3. (*approvazione*) approval.

gradinata *sf.* 1. flight of steps 2. (*negli stadi*) tiers of seats.

gradino *sm.* 1. step 2. (*di stadio*) stage.

gradire *vt.* 1. to like 2. (*accettare*) to accept.

gradito *agg.* 1. (*piacevole*) pleasant 2. (*ben accetto*) welcome.

grado *sm.* 1. degree 2. (*mil.*) rank || *essere in* —, to be able; *di buon* —, willingly.

graduale *agg.* gradual.

gradualità *sf.* graduality.

graduare *vt.* to graduate.

graduato *agg.* 1. graded 2. (*di strumento*) graduated. ♦ **graduato** *sm.* non-commissioned officer.

graduatorìa *sf.* 1. classification 2. (*sport*) position.

graduazione *sf.* graduation.

graffa *sf.* clip.

graffiare *vt.* to scratch.

graffiatura *sf.* scratch.

graffio *sm.* scratch.

graffito *sm.* graffito (*pl.* -ti).

grafia *sf.* 1. writing 2. (*ortografia*) spelling.

gràfico *agg.* graphic. ♦ **gràfico** *sm.* graph.

grafite *sf.* graphite.

grafologìa *sf.* graphology.

grafòlogo *sm.* graphologist.

grafòmane *s.* graphomaniac.

grafomanìa *sf.* graphomania.

gragnuola *sf.* 1. hail 2. (*fig.*) shower.

gramaglie *sf. pl.* mourning (*sing.*): *mettersi in* —, to go (*v. irr.*) into mourning.

gramigna *sf.* couch-grass.

graminàcee *sf. pl.* Gramineae.

grammàtica *sf.* grammar.

grammaticale *agg.* grammatical.

grammàtico *sm.* grammarian.

grammo *sm.* gram.

grammòfono *sm.* gramophone.

gramo *agg.* 1. miserable 2. (*scarso*) scanty.

grana *sf.* 1. grain 2. (*noia*) trouble 3. (*denaro*) dough.

granaglie *sf. pl.* corn (*sing.*).

granaio *sm.* barn.

granata[1] *sf.* (*scopa*) broom.

granata[2] *sf.* (*mil.*) grenade.

granatiere *sm.* grenadier.

granatina *sf.* grenadine.

granato *agg.* 1. garnet red 2. (*fatto a grani*) grainy.

grancassa *sf.* big drum.

granchio *sm.* crab || *prendere un* —, to make (*v. irr.*) a blunder.

grande *agg.* 1. great 2. (*esteso*) large 3. (*grosso*) big 4. (*alto*) high; (*di statura*) tall 5. (*adulto*) grownup.

grandeggiare *vi.* 1. to tower 2. (*ostentare*) to show (*v. irr.*) off.

grandezza *sf.* 1. greatness 2. (*dimensione*) size 3. (*estensione*) largeness 4. (*grandiosità*) grandeur 5. (*liberalità*) liberality 6. (*mat.*) quantity.

grandiloquenza *sf.* magniloquence.

grandinare *vi.* to hail (*anche fig.*).

grandinata *sf.* hail-storm.

gràndine *sf.* hail.

grandiosità *sf.* grandeur.

grandioso *agg.* grand.

granduca *sm.* Grand Duke.

granducato *sm.* Grand Duchy.

granduchessa *sf.* Grand Duchess.

granello *sm.* grain.

granita *sf.* grated-ice drink.

granìtico *agg.* granitic.

granito *sm.* granite.

granìvoro *agg.* granivorous.

grano *sm.* 1. grain 2. (*frumento*) wheat 3. (*ogni cereale*) corn.

granturco *sm.* maize.

granulare *agg.* granular.

granuloma *sm.* granuloma.

granuloso *agg.* granulose.

grappa[1] *sf.* (*per unire blocchi di legno ecc.*) cramp.

grappa[2] *sf.* (*liquore*) "grappa".

gràppolo *sm.* cluster.

grassaggio *sm.* greasing.

grassatore *sm.* robber.

grassazione *sf.* robbery.

grassetto *sm.* (*tip.*) heavytype.

grassezza *sf.* fatness.

grasso *agg.* fat. ♦ **grasso** *sm.* **1.** fat **2.** (*lubrificante*) grease.

grassoccio *agg.* plump.

grata *sf.* grating.

graticciata *sf.* trellis-work.

graticola *sf.* **1.** grill **2.** (*di forno*) grate.

graticolato *sm.* **1.** trellis **2.** (*inferriata*) grating.

gratifica *sf.* bonus.

gratificare *vt.* to gratify.

gratificazione *sf.* gratuity.

gratis *avv.* free.

gratitùdine *sf.* gratitude.

grato *agg.* **1.** grateful **2.** (*gradito*) welcome **3.** (*piacevole*) pleasant.

grattacapo *sm.* trouble.

grattacielo *sm.* skyscraper.

grattare *vt.* **1.** to scratch **2.** (*grattugiare*) to grate.

grattugia *sf.* grater.

grattugiare *vt.* to grate.

gratùito *agg.* **1.** free **2.** (*ingiustificato*) gratuitous.

gravame *sm.* **1.** burden **2.** (*ipoteca*) mortgage.

gravare *vi.* to weigh. ♦ **gravare** *vt.* to burden.

grave *agg.* **1.** grave **2.** (*pesante*) heavy **3.** (*importante, pericoloso*) serious.

gravezza *sf.* **1.** (*pesantezza*) heaviness **2.** (*serietà*) gravity **3.** (*stanchezza*) weariness.

gravidanza *sf.* pregnancy.

gràvido *agg.* **1.** (*di femmina*) pregnant **2.** (*fig.*) fraught (with).

gravità *sf.* **1.** gravity **2.** (*severità*) severity.

gravitare *vi.* to gravitate.

gravitazionale *agg.* gravitational.

gravitazione *sf.* gravitation.

gravosità *sf.* heaviness.

gravoso *agg.* heavy.

grazia *sf.* **1.** grace **2.** (*favore*) favour **3.** (*clemenza*) mercy **4.** (*teol.*) grace **5.** *Sua, Vostra Grazia,* His, Her, Your Grace || *in — di,* owing to.

graziare *vt.* to pardon.

grazie *inter.* thank you!, thanks! — *tante,* many thanks!

grazioso *agg.* pretty, graceful.

greca *sf.* **1.** (*disegno*) Greek fret **2.** (*mil.*) zig-zag braid.

grecale *sm.* north-east wind.

grecismo *sm.* Hellenism.

grecista *s.* Hellenist.

greco *agg.* e *sm.* Greek.

greco-romano *agg.* Graeco-Roman.

gregario *sm.* **1.** follower **2.** (*aiutante*) helper.

gregge *sm.* flock.

greggio *agg.* **1.** raw **2.** (*di tessuto*) unbleached **3.** (*di metallo e fig.*) unrefined.

gregoriano *agg.* Gregorian.

grembiale, grembiule *sm.* apron.

grembo *sm.* **1.** lap **2.** (*ventre materno*) womb **3.** (*fig.*) bosom.

gremire *vt.* to fill.

gremito *agg.* filled (with).

greppia *sf.* crib.

gres *sm.* stoneware.

greto *sm.* **1.** (*di fiume*) gravel bank **2.** (*di mare*) shingly shore.

grettezza *sf.* meanness.

gretto *agg.* mean, narrow-minded.

greve *agg.* heavy.

grezzo *agg.* V. *greggio*.

gridare *vt.* e *vi.* **1.** to cry **2.** (*gridare forte, protestare*) to cry out: *gridò per il dolore,* he cried out with pain.

grido *sm.* cry || *di —,* famous.

grifagno *agg.* **1.** rapacious **2.** (*fig.*) fierce.

grifo *sm.* snout.

grifone *sm.* griffin.

grigiastro *agg.* greyish.

grigio *agg.* grey: — *perla,* pearl grey.

grigiore *sm.* greyness.

griglia *sf.* **1.** (*di finestra*) shutter **2.** (*di forno*) grate **3.** (*grata, graticola*) grill || *cuocere alla —,* to grill.

grilletto *sm.* trigger.

grillo *sm.* **1.** cricket **2.** (*fig.*) fancy.

grillotalpa *sm.* mole-cricket.

grimaldello *sm.* picklock.

grinfia *sf.* clutch.

grinta *sf.* grim face.

grinza *sf.* **1.** (*di pelle*) wrinkle **2.** (*di stoffa*) crease || (*fig.*) *non fa una —,* it is quite correct.

grinzoso *agg.* **1.** (*di pelle*) wrinkly **2.** (*di stoffa*) creasy.

grisù *sm.* fire-damp.

gronda *sf.* eaves (*pl.*).

grondaia *sf.* **1.** gutter **2.** (*tubo di discesa*) gutter pipe.

grondante *agg.* dripping.

grondare *vi.* to drip || — *sangue,* to bleed (*v. irr.*).

groppa *sf.* back.

groppo sm. knot: avere un — in gola, to have a lump in one's throat.

groppone sm. back: piegare il —, to submit.

grossa sf. dormire della —, to sleep (v. irr.) soundly.

grossezza sf. 1. bigness 2. (dimensione) size 3. (spessore) thickness.

grossista s. wholesaler.

grosso agg. 1. (anche fig.) big 2. (denso) thick.

grossolanità sf. coarseness.

grossolano agg. coarse: errore —, blunder.

grotta sf. cave.

grottesco agg. grotesque.

groviera sf. gruyère.

groviglio sm. tangle.

gru sf. (zool.; mecc.) crane.

gruccia sf. 1. crutch 2. (per abiti) dress-hanger 3. (per uccelli) perch.

grufolare vi. to root.

grugnire vi. to grunt.

grugnito sm. grunt.

grugno sm. snout.

grumo sm. clot.

grumoso agg. clotted.

gruppo sm. group.

gruzzolo sm. hoard; (risparmi) savings (pl.).

guadàbile agg. fordable.

guadagnare vt. 1. to gain 2. (col lavoro) to earn.

guadagno sm. 1. earnings (pl.) 2. (comm.) profits (pl.) 3. (fig.) gain.

guadare vt. to ford.

guado sm. ford.

guai inter. woe!

guaina sf. 1. (bot.; fodero per armi) sheath 2. (custodia, astuccio) case 3. (anat.) theca (pl. -ae).

guaio sm. trouble.

guaire vi. to yelp.

guaito sm. yelp.

gualcire vt. to rumple.

gualdrappa sf. saddle-cloth.

guancia sf. cheek.

guanciale sm. pillow || dormire fra due guanciali, to have no worries.

guantaio sm. glover.

guantiera sf. 1. (scatola per guanti) glove-box 2. (vassoio) tray.

guantificio sm. glove-factory.

guanto sm. glove.

guantone sm. boxing-glove.

guardabarriere sm. gate-keeper.

guardaboschi sm. forester.

guardacaccia sm. gamekeeper.

guardacoste sm. coastguard.

guardalinee sm. (sport) linesman (pl. -men).

guardamano sm. (di scala) hand-rail.

guardapesca sm. fishing warden.

guardaportone sm. doorkeeper.

guardare vt. to look (at) 2. (proteggere) to protect. ♦ guardare vi. 1. (tentare) to try 2. (essere orientato) to face. ♦ guardarsi vr. (da), to beware (of).

guardaroba sm. 1. wardrobe 2. (in teatro ecc.) cloak-room.

guardarobiera sf. 1. (nei locali pubblici) cloak-room attendant 2. (in alberghi e case private) linen maid.

guardarobiere sm. (nei locali pubblici) cloak-room attendant.

guardasala sm. ticket-collector.

guardasigilli sm. keeper of the seals.

guardavìa sm. guard-rail.

guardia sf. guard || — medica, first-aid station; fare la — a, to guard; mettere in —, to warn.

guardiamarina sm. midshipman (pl. -men).

guardiano sm. 1. keeper 2. (di armenti) herdsman (pl. -men) || — notturno, night watchman (pl. -men).

guardina sf. guard-room.

guardingo agg. wary.

guardiola sf. guard-room.

guaribile agg. 1. curable 2. (di ferita) healable.

guarigione sf. recovery.

guarire vt. 1. to cure 2. (una ferita) to heal. ♦ guarire vi. 1. to recover 2. (di ferita) to heal.

guaritore sm. healer.

guarnigione sf. garrison.

guarnire vt. 1. to trim 2. (cuc.) to garnish 3. (fornire) to furnish 4. (mecc.) to pack.

guarnitura, guarnizione sf. 1. trimming 2. (cuc.) garniture 3. (mecc.) packing.

guasconata sf. gasconade.

guascone agg. e sm. (anche fig.) Gascon.

guastafeste s. kill-joy.

guastamestieri sm. bungler.

guastare vt. 1. to spoil (v. irr.) 2. (danneggiare) to damage.

guastatore sm. 1. destroyer 2. (mil.) sapper.

guasto agg. 1. damaged 2. (marcio) rotten 3. (corrotto) tainted 4. (mecc.) out of order.

guasto sm. 1. damage 2. (mecc.) breakdown || ci deve essere un —, there must be something wrong.

guatare vt. to gaze (at).

guazzabuglio sm. mess.

guazzare vi. 1. to paddle 2. (rotolarsi) to wallow 3. (di liquidi in recipienti) to splash about.

guazzo sm. (pitt.) gouache.

guelfo agg. e sm. Guelph.

guercio agg. squinting. ♦ **guercio** sm. squinter.

guerra sf. war.

guerrafondaio sm. warmonger.

guerreggiante agg. e sm. belligerent.

guerreggiare vi. to fight (v. irr.), to war.

guerresco agg. 1. war (attr.) 2. (bellicoso) warlike.

guerriero agg. warlike. ♦ **guerriero** sm. warrior.

guerriglia sf. guerrilla.

guerrigliero sm. 1. guerrilla 2. partisan.

gufo sm. owl.

guglia sf. spire.

gugliata sf. needleful.

guida sf. 1. guide 2. (auto) drive || patente di —, driving licence; — telefonica, telephone book.

guidare vt. 1. to guide 2. (auto) to drive (v. irr.).

guidatore sm. driver.

guidoslitta sf. bobsleigh.

guinzaglio sm. leash: mettere al —, to leash.

guisa sf. manner || a — di, like.

guitto sm. strolling player.

guizzante agg. 1. darting 2. (di luce) flashing 3. (di pesci) wriggling.

guizzare vi. 1. to dart 2. (di luce) to flash 3. (di pesci) to wriggle.

guizzo sm. 1. dart 2. (di luce) flash 3. (di pesci) wriggle.

guscio sm. shell.

gustare vt. 1. to enjoy 2. (assaggiare) to taste.

gustativo agg. gustative.

gustatore sm. taster.

gusto sm. 1. taste 2. (gradimento) liking || di, con —, with relish.

gustoso agg. 1. (saporito) tasty 2. (piacevole) pleasant.

guttaperca sf. gutta-percha.

gutturale agg. guttural.

H

harem sm. harem.

hascisc sm. hashish.

hawaiano agg. e sm. Hawaiian.

hurrà inter. hurrah.

i art. the.

iarda sf. yard.

iato sm. hiatus.

iattanza sf. boastfulness.

iattura sf. misfortune.

ibèrico agg. e sm. Iberian.

ibernazione sf. hibernation.

ibisco sm. hibiscus.

ibridazione sf. hybridization.

ibridismo sm. hybridism.

ibrido agg. e sm. hybrid.

icona sf. icon.

iconoclasta sm. iconoclast.

idea sf. idea.

ideàbile agg. imaginable.

ideale agg. e sm. ideal.

idealismo sm. idealism.

idealista s. idealist.

idealìstico agg. idealistic.

idealizzare vt. to idealize.

idealizzazione sf. idealization.

ideare vt. to conceive, to devise.

ideatore sm. inventor, deviser.

ideazione sf. ideation.

idèntico agg. identic.

identificàbile agg. identifiable.

identificare vt. to identify.

identificazione sf. identification.

identità sf. identity.

ideografia sf. ideography.

ideogramma sm. ideogram.

ideologìa sf. ideology.

ideològico agg. ideologic(al).

ideologismo sm. ideology.

ideòlogo sm. ideologist.

idilliaco agg. idyllic.

idillio sm. idyl.

idioma sm. language.

idiomàtico agg. idiomatic.

idiosincrasia sf. idiosyncrasy.

idiota sm. idiot. ♦ **idiota** agg. idiotic.

idiotismo sm. idiom.

idiozìa sf. idiocy.

idolatra sm. idolater.

idolatrare vt. to worship.
idolatria sf. idolatry.
idolo sm. idol.
idoneità sf. fitness.
idòneo agg. fit.
idrante sm. hydrant.
idratare vt. to hydrate.
idrato sm. hydrate.
idràulica sf. hydraulics.
idràulico agg. hydraulic. ◆ **idràulico** sm. plumber.
ìdrico agg. water.
idrocarburo sm. hydrocarbon.
idrocefalìa sf. hydrocephalus.
idrocèfalo sm. hydrocephalus.
idroelèttrico agg. hydroelectric.
idròfilo agg. absorbent: cotone —, cotton wool.
idrofobìa sf. rabies.
idròfobo agg. 1. rabid 2. (fig.) furious.
idrògeno sm. hydrogen.
idrografìa sf. hydrography.
idròlisi sf. hydrolysis (pl. -ses).
idrologìa sf. hydrology.
idròpico agg. dropsical.
idropisìa sf. dropsy.
idroscalo sm. seaplane station.
idrostàtica sf. hydrostatics.
idrovolante sm. seaplane.
idròvora sf. water-scooping machine.
iella sf. bad luck.
iena sf. 1. hyaena 2. (fig.) vixen.
ieràtico agg. hieratic(al).
ieri avv. yesterday.
iettatore sm. evil-eyed man.
iettatura sf. evil-eye.
igiene sf. 1. hygiene 2. (sistema sanitario) sanitation.
igiènico agg. sanitary.
igienista s. hygienist.
ignaro agg. ignorant.
ignavia sf. laziness.
ignavo agg. lazy.
ìgneo agg. igneous.
ignòbile agg. mean.
ignominia sf. ignominy.
ignominioso agg. ignominious.
ignorante agg. e sm. ignorant.
ignoranza sf. ignorance.
ignorare vt. to ignore.
ignoto agg. unknown.
ignudo agg. naked.
igrometria sf. hygrometry.
iguana sf. iguana.
il art. the.
ìlare agg. cheerful.
ilarità sf. hilarity.

ìliaco agg. iliac.
illanguidire vt. to weaken.
illazione sf. illation.
illécito agg. illicit.
illegale agg. illegal.
illegalità sf. illegality.
illeggìbile agg. illegible.
illegittimità sf. illegitimacy.
illegìttimo agg. illegitimate.
illeso agg. unhurt.
illibatezza sf. purity.
illibato agg. pure.
illiberale agg. illiberal.
illimitato agg. unlimited.
illividire vt. to make (v. irr.) livid. ◆ **illividire** vi. to turn livid.
illogicità sf. illogicality.
illògico agg. illogical.
illùdere vt. to delude. ◆ **illùdersi** vr. to delude oneself.
illuminante agg. illuminating.
illuminare vt. to light up.
illuminazione sf. lighting.
illuminismo sm. Illuminism.
illusione sf. illusion.
illusionismo sm. illusionism.
illusionista s. conjurer.
illuso agg. deluded. ◆ **illuso** sm. day-dreamer.
illusorio agg. illusory.
illustrare vt. to illustrate.
illustrativo agg. illustrative.
illustrato agg. illustrated ‖ cartolina illustrata, picture post-card.
illustrazione sf. illustration.
illustre agg. renowned.
imbacuccare vt. to muffle up.
imbaldanzire vt. to embolden. ◆ **imbaldanzirsi** vr. to grow (v. irr.) bold.
'mballàggio sm. packing.
imballare vt. to pack (up). ◆ **imballarsi** vr. (di motori) to race.
imbalsamare vt. 1. to embalm 2. (di animali) to stuff.
imbalsamatore sm. 1. embalmer 2. (di animali) stuffer.
imbalsamazione sf. 1. embalming 2. (di animali) stuffing.
imbambolato agg. dull.
imbandierare vt. to deck with flags.
imbandire vt. 1. (la tavola) to lay (v. irr.) 2. to prepare.
imbarazzante agg. embarrassing.
imbarazzare vt. to embarrass. ◆ **imbarazzarsi** vr. to meddle.
imbarazzato agg. embarrassed.
imbarazzo sm. embarrassment.

imbarcadero *sm.* landing-stage.

imbarcare *vt.* to take (*v. irr.*) on board. ♦ **imbarcarsi** *vr.* to embark.

imbarcazione *sf.* boat.

imbarco *sm.* embarkation.

imbastardire *vt.* to debase.

imbastardito *agg.* debased.

imbastire *vt.* **1.** to tack **2.** (*fig.*) to put (*v. irr.*) together.

imbastitura *sf.* tacking.

imbàttersi *vr.* to meet (*v. irr.*) (with).

imbattibile *agg.* invincible.

imbattibilità *sf.* invincibility.

imbavagliare *vt.* to gag.

imbeccare *vt.* **1.** to feed (*v. irr.*) **2.** (*fig.*) to prompt.

imbeccata *sf.* **1.** beakful **2.** (*fig.*) prompting.

imbecille *agg. e sm.* imbecile.

imbecillità *sf.* imbecility.

imbelle *agg.* weak.

imbellettare *vt.* to make (*v. irr.*) up.

imbellire *vt.* to embellish.

imberbe *agg.* beardless.

imbestialire *vi.* to get (*v. irr.*) furious. ♦ **imbestialirsi** *vr.* to get furious.

imbévere *vt.* to imbue with.

imbiancamento *sm.* whitening.

imbiancare *vt.* **1.** to whiten **2.** (*i muri*) to whitewash.

imbiancatura *sf.* **1.** (*di muri*) whitewashing **2.** (*di tessuti*) bleaching.

imbianchino *sm.* house painter.

imbiondire *vt.* to make (*v. irr.*) fair. ♦ **imbiondire** *vi.* to become (*v. irr.*) fair.

imbizzarrirsi *vr.* **1.** to become (*v. irr.*) restive **2.** (*adirarsi*) to fire up.

imboccare *vt.* **1.** to feed (*v. irr.*) **2.** (*di strada*) to enter.

imboccatura *sf.* **1.** mouth **2.** (*di strumento*) mouthpiece.

imbonimento *sm.* sales talk.

imbonire *vt.* to allure.

imbonitore *sm.* charlatan.

imborghesimento *sm.* getting into middle-class habits.

imborghesire *vt.* to give (*v. irr.*) middle-class habits. ♦ **imborghesirsi** *vr.* to acquire middle-class habits.

imboscare *vt.* **1.** to put (*v. irr.*) into safe keeping **2.** (*mil.*) to help to evade military service. ♦ **im-**boscarsi** *vr.* **1.** to lie (*v. irr.*) in ambush **2.** (*mil.*) to evade military service.

imboscata *sf.* ambush.

imboscato *sm.* shirker.

imboschimento *sm.* afforestation.

imboschire *vt.* to afforest.

imbottigliamento *sm.* bottling || — **stradale**, traffic jam.

imbottigliare *vt.* **1.** to bottle **2.** (*fig.*) to block.

imbottire *vt.* **1.** to stuff **2.** (*di vestiti*) to wad **3.** (*fig.*) — **la testa**, to cram. ♦ **imbottirsi** *vr.* **1.** to fill oneself (with), to stuff oneself (with) **2.** (*coprirsi*) to wrap oneself (into).

imbottita *sf.* quilt.

imbottito *agg.* stuffed, filled || *panino* —, sandwich.

imbottitura *sf.* **1.** stuffing **2.** (*di vestiti*) wadding.

imbracciare *vt.* **1.** to put (*v. irr.*) sthg. on one's hands **2.** (*di fucile*) to bring (*v. irr.*) to firing position.

imbrancare *vt.* to herd.

imbrattacarte *sm.* scribbler.

imbrattamento *sm.* soiling.

imbrattare *vt.* to soil.

imbrattatele *sm.* dauber.

imbrigliamento *sm.* bridling.

imbrigliare *vt.* to bridle.

imbrigliatura *sf.* bridling.

imbroccare *vt.* **1.** to hit (*v. irr.*) **2.** (*fig.*) to guess.

imbrogliare *vt.* **1.** to cheat **2.** (*confondere*) to confuse.

imbroglio *sm.* cheat, swindle.

imbroglione *sm.* cheat, swindler.

imbronciarsi *vr.* to pout.

imbronciato *agg.* sulky.

imbrunire *vi.* **1.** to brown **2.** (*farsi sera*) to get (*v. irr.*) dark.

imbrunire *sm.* nightfall.

imbruttire *vt.* to make (*v. irr.*) ugly. ♦ **imbruttirsi** *vr.* to become (*v. irr.*) ugly.

imbucare *vt.* to post.

imburrare *vt.* to butter.

imbuto *sm.* funnel.

imene *sm.* hymen.

imeneo *sm.* wedding.

imenòttero *sm.* hymenopteron (*pl.* -ra).

imitare *vt.* to imitate.

imitativo *agg.* imitative.

imitatore *sm.* imitator.

imitazione *sf.* imitation.

immacolato agg. spotless.
immagazzinare vt. to store (up).
immaginàbile agg. imaginable.
immaginare vt. to imagine.
immaginario agg. imaginary.
immaginativa sf. imagination.
immaginativo agg. imaginative.
immaginazione sf. imagination.
immàgine sf. image.
immalinconire vt. to make (v. irr.) melancholy. ♦ **immalinconire** vi. to grow (v. irr.) sad.
immancàbile agg. unfailing.
immane agg. 1. huge 2. (fig.) frightful.
immanente agg. immanent.
immanenza sf. immanence.
immangiàbile agg. uneatable.
immarcescìbile agg. incorruptible.
immateriale agg. immaterial.
immaterialità sf. immateriality.
immatricolare vt. to matriculate. ♦ **immatricolarsi** vr. to matriculate.
immatricolazione sf. matriculation.
immaturità sf. immaturity.
immaturo agg. 1. (di frutto) unripe 2. (di persona) immature.
immedesimare vt. 1. to unify. ♦ **immedesimarsi** vr. to identify oneself (with).
immedesimazione sf. unifying.
immediatamente avv. at once.
immediatezza sf. immediateness.
immediato agg. immediate.
immemoràbile agg. immemorial.
immèmore agg. forgetful.
immensità sf. immensity.
immenso agg. immense.
immèrgere vt. to immerse. ♦ **immèrgersi** vr. to immerse oneself.
immeritato agg. undeserved.
immeritévole agg. undeserving.
immersione sf. immersion.
immèttere vt. to let (v. irr.) in. ♦ **immèttersi** vr. to penetrate.
immigrante agg. e sm. immigrant.
immigrare vi. to immigrate.
immigrato agg. immigrated. ♦ **immigrato** sm. immigrant.
immigrazione sf. immigration.
imminente agg. impending.
imminenza sf. imminence.
immischiare vt. to involve. ♦ **immischiarsi** vr. to meddle (with).
immiserimento sm. impoverishing.
immiserire vt. to impoverish. ♦

immiserirsi vr. 1. to become (v. irr.) poor 2. (fig.) to weaken.
immissario sm. affluent.
immissione sf. letting in.
immòbile agg. immobile || beni immòbili, immovables.
immobiliare agg. immovable.
immobilismo sm. ultra-conservatism.
immobilità sf. immobility.
immobilizzare vt. 1. to immobilize 2. (comm.) to lock up.
immobilizzazione sf. 1. immobilization 2. (comm.) locking up.
immoderato agg. immoderate.
immodestia sf. immodesty.
immodesto agg. immodest.
immolare vt. to immolate.
immondezza sf. dirtiness.
immondezzaio sm. garbage heap.
immondìzia sf. 1. filth 2. (spazzatura) garbage.
immondo agg. dirty.
immorale agg. immoral.
immoralità sf. immorality.
immortalare vt. to immortalize.
immortale agg. immortal.
immortalità sf. immortality.
immoto agg. motionless.
immune agg. immune.
immunità sf. immunity.
immunizzare vt. to immunize.
immunizzazione sf. immunization.
immusonirsi vr. to sulk.
immusonito agg. sulky.
immutàbile agg. immutable.
immutabilità sf. immutability.
impacchettare vt. to package.
impacciare vt. to hamper.
impacciato agg. 1. embarrassed 2. (goffo) awkward.
impaccio sm. hindrance.
impacco sm. compress.
impadronirsi vr. to take (v. irr.) possession (of).
impagàbile agg. priceless.
impaginare vt. to make-up.
impaginatore sm. maker-up.
impaginazione sf. making-up.
impagliare vt. 1. to cover with straw 2. (di animali) to stuff with straw.
impagliatore sm. 1. chair-mender 2. (di animali) stuffer.
impagliatura sf. 1. chair-mending 2. (di animali) stuffing.
impalare vt. to impale.
impalato agg. stiff.
impalcatura sf. 1. scaffolding 2.

(di corna di cervo) antlers *(pl.)*.

impallidire *vi.* to turn pale.

impallinare *vt.* to shot.

impalmare *vt.* to marry.

impalpàbile *agg.* impalpable.

impalpabilità *sf.* impalpability.

impanare *vt.* **1.** *(cuc.)* to bread **2.** *(mecc.)* to thread.

impantanare *vt.* to swamp. ♦ **impantanarsi** *vr.* to swamp *(anche fig.)*.

impaperarsi *vr.* to slip up.

impappinarsi *vr.* to stammer.

imparagonàbile *agg.* incomparable.

imparare *vt.* to learn *(v. irr.)*.

impareggiàbile *agg.* unparalleled.

imparentare *vt.* to relate. ♦ **imparentarsi** *vr.* to become *(v. irr.)* related (to).

impari *agg.* unequal.

imparisìllabo *agg. e sm.* imparisyllabic.

imparruccato *agg.* bewigged.

impartire *vt.* to impart.

imparziale *agg.* impartial.

imparzialità *sf.* impartiality.

impassìbile *agg.* impassive, unmoved.

impassibilità *sf.* impassibility.

impastare *vt.* to knead ‖ *– i colori*, to impaste.

impastato *agg.* **1.** kneaded **2.** *(fig.)* full.

impastatore *sm.* kneader.

impastatrice *sf.* kneading-machine.

impasto *sm.* **1.** dough **2.** *(miscuglio)* mixture.

impastoiare *vt.* *(fig.)* to impede.

impatto *sm.* impact.

impaurire *vt.* to frighten. ♦ **impaurirsi** *vr.* to get *(v. irr.)* scared.

impaurito *agg.* afraid: *sguardo —*, fearful look.

impàvido *agg.* fearless.

impaziente *agg.* impatient.

impazientirsi *vr.* to lose *(v. irr.)* one's patience.

impazienza *sf.* impatience.

impazzare *vi.* to be at one's height.

impazzata *(nella loc. avv.)* all'*—*, madly.

impazzire *vi.* to go *(v. irr.)* mad.

impeccàbile *agg.* faultless.

impeciare *vt.* to pitch.

impedimento *sm.* obstacle.

impedire *vt.* to prevent (from).

impegnare *vt.* **1.** *(dare in pegno)* to pawn **2.** *(prenotare)* to reserve,

to book. ♦ **impegnarsi** *vr.* to engage (oneself).

impegnativo *agg.* binding ‖ *lavoro —*, exacting job.

impegno *sm.* engagement.

impegolarsi *vr.* *(fig.)* to get *(v. irr.)* involved.

impelagarsi *vr.* to get *(v. irr.)* in trouble.

impellente *agg.* urgent.

impellicciare *vt.* to fur.

impellicciatura *sf.* veneering.

impenetràbile *agg.* impenetrable.

impenetrabilità *sf.* impenetrableness.

impenitente *agg.* impenitent.

impennacchiare *vt.* to plume.

impennarsi *vr.* **1.** *(di cavallo)* to rear **2.** *(fig.)* to rear up.

impennata *sf.* *(di cavallo)* rearing **2.** *(fig.)* bristling.

impensàbile *agg.* unthinkable.

impensato *agg.* unexpected.

impensierire *vt.* to worry.

imperante *agg.* ruling.

imperare *vi.* to rule (over).

imperativo *agg.* imperative.

imperatore *sm.* emperor.

imperatrice *sf.* empress.

impercettìbile *agg.* imperceptible.

impercettibilità *sf.* imperceptibility.

imperdonàbile *agg.* unpardonable.

imperfetto *agg.* **1.** *(gramm.)* imperfect **2.** *(fig.)* faulty.

imperfezione *sf.* imperfection.

imperiale[1] *agg.* imperial.

imperiale[2] *sm.* imperial.

imperialismo *sm.* imperialism.

imperialista *s.* imperialist.

imperialìstico *agg.* imperialistic

imperio *sm.* command, authority.

imperioso *agg.* imperious.

imperito *agg.* unskilful.

imperituro *agg.* everlasting.

imperizia *sf.* unskilfulness.

imperlare *vt.* to bead. ♦ **imperlarsi** *vr.* to bead.

impermalirsi *vr.* to resent (sthg.).

impermeàbile *agg.* impermeable. ♦ **impermeàbile** *sm.* raincoat.

impermeabilità *sf.* impermeability.

impermeabilizzare *vt.* to waterproof.

impermeabilizzazione *sf.* waterproofing.

imperniare *vt.* to pivot (upon).

impero *sm.* empire.

imperscrutàbile *agg.* inscrutable.

imperscrutabilità *sf.* inscrutableness.

impersonale *agg.* impersonal.

impersonalità *sf.* impersonality.

impersonare *vt.* to impersonate. ♦ **impersonarsi** *vr.* to materialize.

impertèrrito *agg.* undaunted.

impertinente *agg.* impertinent.

impertinenza *sf.* impertinence.

imperturbàbile *agg.* impassive.

imperturbabilità *sf.* imperturbability.

imperturbato *agg.* imperturbed.

imperversare *vi.* to rage.

impervio *agg.* inaccessible.

impeto *sm.* **1.** rush, impetus **2.** (*impulso*) impulse.

impetrare *vt.* to impetrate.

impettito *agg.* stiff.

impetuosità *sf.* impetuosity.

impetuoso *agg.* impetuous.

impiantare *vt.* to found.

impiantito *sm.* **1.** (*di legno*) parquet floor **2.** (*di piastrelle*) tiled floor.

impianto *sm.* plant, installation.

impiastricciare *vt.* to daub.

impiastro *sm.* **1.** plaster **2.** (*fig.*) bore.

impiccagione *sf.* hanging.

impiccare *vt.* to hang.

impiccato *agg.* hanged. ♦ **impiccato** *sm.* hanged man.

impicciare *vt.* to hinder. ♦ **impicciarsi** *vr.* to meddle (in).

impiccio *sm.* hindrance.

impiccolire *vt.* to make (*v. irr.*) smaller.

impiegare *vt.* **1.** to employ **2.** (*spendere*) to spend (*v. irr.*) **3.** (*comm.*) to invest.

impiegatizio *agg.* white-collar (*attributivo*).

impiegato *agg.* employed. ♦ **impiegato** *sm.* employee, clerk.

impiego *sm.* **1.** employment **2.** (*uso*) use.

impietosire *vt.* to move to pity. ♦ **impietosirsi** *vr.* to feel (*v. irr.*) sorry (for).

impietrire *vt.* to petrify.

impigliare *vt.* to entangle.

impigrire *vt.* to make (*v. irr.*) lazy.

impinguare *vt.* **1.** to fatten **2.** (*fig.*) to enrich.

impiombare *vt.* **1.** to plumb **2.** (*otturare*) to fill **3.** (*coprire di piombo*) to lead.

impiombatura *sf.* **1.** plumbing **2.**

(*otturazione*) filling **3.** (*copertura di piombo*) leading.

implacàbile *agg.* implacable.

implacabilità *sf.* implacability.

implicare *vt.* to involve.

implicito *agg.* implicit.

implorare *vt.* to implore.

implorazione *sf.* entreaty.

implume *agg.* featherless.

impolìtico *agg.* impolitic.

impollinare *vt.* to pollinate.

impollinazione *sf.* pollination.

impoltronire *vt.* to make (*v. irr.*) lazy. ♦ **impoltronirsi** *vr.* to grow (*v. irr.*) lazy.

impolverare *vt.* to cover with dust.

impolverato *agg.* dusty.

impomatare *vt.* to pomade. ♦ **impomatarsi** *vr.* to pomade oneself.

imponderàbile *agg.* imponderable.

imponderabilità *sf.* imponderability.

imponente *agg.* imposing.

imponenza *sf.* grandeur, majesty.

imponìbile *agg.* taxable.

imponibilità *sf.* taxability.

impopolare *agg.* unpopular.

impopolarità *sf.* unpopularity.

imporporarsi *vr.* to purple.

imporre *vt.* to impose: — *un nome*, to give (*v. irr.*) a name. ♦ **imporsi** *vr.* **1.** to impose oneself **2.** (*avere successo*) to become (*v. irr.*) popular.

importante *agg.* important.

importanza *sf.* importance.

importare *vi. imp.* to matter, to care. ♦ **importare** *vt.* (*comm.*) to import.

importatore *sm.* importer.

importazione *sf.* import.

importo *sm.* amount.

importunare *vt.* to importune, to bother.

importunità *sf.* importunity.

importuno *agg.* boring. ♦ **importuno** *sm.* bore.

imposizione *sf.* imposition.

impossessarsi *vr.* to take (*v. irr.*) possession (of).

impossìbile *agg.* impossible.

impossibilità *sf.* impossibility.

impossibilitato *agg.* unable.

imposta *sf.* **1.** tax **2.** (*edil.*) shutter.

impostare *vt.* **1.** to start **2.** (*di lettera*) to post.

impostazione *sf.* general lines (*pl.*).

impostore *sm.* impostor.

impostura sf. 1. imposture 2. (frode) fraud.

impotente agg. powerless. ♦ **impotente** agg. e sm. (med.) impotent.

impotenza sf. impotence.

impoverimento sm. impoverishment.

impoverire vt. to impoverish. ♦ **impoverirsi** vr. to become (v. irr.) poor.

impraticàbile agg. impracticable: strada —, impassable road.

impraticabilità sf. impracticability.

impratichire vt. to train. ♦ **impratichirsi** vr. to get (v. irr.) trained.

imprecare vi. to curse.

imprecazione sf. curse.

imprecisàbile agg. indeterminable.

imprecisato agg. undetermined.

imprecisione sf. 1. vagueness 2. (inesattezza) inaccuracy.

impreciso agg. inaccurate.

impregnare vt. to impregnate (with). ♦ **impregnarsi** vr. to become (v. irr.) imbued (with).

imprèndere vt. to undertake (v. irr.).

imprendìbile agg. elusive, invincible.

imprenditore sm. 1. entrepreneur 2. (edil.) contractor.

impreparato agg. unprepared.

impreparazione sf. unpreparedness.

impresa sf. 1. (iniziativa) undertaking 2. (gesta) deed 3. (azienda) firm, company.

impresario sm. 1. contractor 2. (teat.) manager.

imprescindìbile agg. unavoidable.

imprescrittìbile agg. indefeasible.

impressionàbile agg. impressionable.

impressionabilità sf. impressionability.

impressionante agg. frightening.

impressionare vt. 1. to impress 2. (foto) to expose.

impressione sf. impression.

impressionismo sm. impressionism.

impressionista s. impressionist.

impresso agg. printed.

imprestare vt. to lend (v. irr.).

imprevedìbile agg. unforeseeable.

impreveduto agg. unforeseen.

imprevidente agg. improvident.

imprevidenza sf. improvidence.

imprevisto agg. unexpected. ♦ **imprevisto** sm. unforeseen event.

impreziosire vt. to make (v. irr.) precious. ♦ **impreziosirsi** vr. to become (v. irr.) precious.

imprigionamento sm. imprisonment.

imprigionare vt. to imprison.

imprimere vt. to impress.

improbàbile agg. improbable.

improbabilità sf. improbability.

improbo agg. 1. dishonest 2. (faticoso) hard.

improduttività sf. unproductiveness.

improduttivo agg. unproductive.

impronta sf. 1. impression: — del piede, digitale, footprint, fingerprint 2. (fig.) mark.

improntare vt. 1. to prepare 2. (fig.) to mark.

improntitùdine sf. impudence.

impronunciàbile agg. unpronounceable.

improperio sm. insult.

improprietà sf. impropriety.

improprio agg. improper.

improrogàbile agg. undelayable.

improvvisamente avv. suddenly.

improvvisare vt. e vi. to improvise. ♦ **improvvisarsi** vr. to act.

improvvisata sf. surprise.

improvvisatore sm. improviser.

improvvisazione sf. improvisation.

improvviso agg. sudden.

imprudente agg. imprudent.

imprudenza sf. imprudence.

impudente agg. impudent.

impudenza sf. impudence.

impudicizia sf. immodesty.

impudico agg. shameless, immodest.

impugnàbile agg. (giur.) impugnable.

impugnabilità sf. (giur.) impugnment.

impugnare vt. 1. to grasp, to hold 2. (giur.) to impugn.

impugnatura sf. hilt.

impulsività sf. impulsiveness.

impulsivo agg. impulsive.

impulso sm. impulse.

impunemente avv. safely.

impunità sf. impunity.

impunito agg. unpunished.

impuntare vi. to stumbl : (over).

◆ **impuntarsi** vr. 1. to jib 2. (ostinarsi) to stick (v. irr.) (to).
impuntura sf. stitching.
impurità sf. impurity.
impuro agg. impure.
imputàbile agg. 1. imputable 2. (giur.) chargeable (with).
imputare vt. 1. to impute 2. (giur.) to charge (with).
imputato sm. defendant.
imputazione sf. imputation.
imputridimento sm. putrefaction.
imputridire vi. to rot.
in prep. (stato in luogo) in, at: essere — campagna, — città, to be in the country, in town; essere — casa, — chiesa, to be at home, at church 2. (moto a luogo) to: andò — America, he went to America 3. (moto dentro luogo) into: va' nello studio, go into the study 4. (coi mezzi di trasporto) by: sono venuto — treno, I came by train.
inàbile agg. 1. unable 2. (non idoneo) unfit.
inabilità sf. 1. inability 2. (inidoneità) unfitness.
inabilitare vt. to disable.
inabilitazione sf. disability.
inabissamento sm. sinking.
inabissarsi vr. to sink (v. irr.).
inabitàbile agg. uninhabitable.
inabitabilità sf. uninhabitableness.
inabitato agg. 1. uninhabited 2. (deserto) deserted.
inaccessìbile agg. inaccessible.
inaccessibilità sf. inaccessibility.
inaccettàbile agg. unacceptable.
inaccettabilità sf. unacceptableness.
inacerbire vt. to exacerbate. ◆ **inacerbirsi** vr. to grow (v. irr.) bitter.
inacidire vt. to sour. ◆ **inacidirsi** vr. to turn sour.
inacidito agg. sour.
inadattàbile agg. unadaptable.
inadattabilità sf. inadaptability.
inadatto agg. 1. unfit (for) 2. (sconveniente) unbecoming.
inadeguato agg. inadequate.
inadempìbile agg. unfulfillable.
inadempiente agg. defaulting.
inadempienza sf. non-execution.
inafferràbile agg. unseizable.
inalare vt. to inhale.
inalatore sm. inhaler.
inalazione sf. inhalation.

inalberare vt. to hoist. ◆ **inalberarsi** vr. 1. to rear up 2. (fig.) to lose (v. irr.) one's temper.
inalienàbile agg. inalienable.
inalienabilità sf. inalienability.
inalteràbile agg. inalterable.
inalterabilità sf. inalterability.
inalterato agg. unaltered.
inalveare vt. to canalize.
inamidare vt. to starch.
inammissìbile agg. inadmissible.
inammissibilità sf. inadmissibility.
inamovìbile agg. irremovable.
inamovibilità sf. irremovability.
inane agg. inane.
inanellare vt. to curl.
inanimato agg. lifeless.
inanità sf. inanity.
inappagàbile agg. unsatisfiable.
inappagato agg. unsatisfied.
inappellàbile agg. inappellable.
inappetenza sf. inappetence.
inapplicàbile agg. inapplicable.
inapprezzàbile agg. priceless.
inappuntàbile agg. 1. irreproachable 2. (nel vestire) faultlessly dressed.
inarcamento sm. bending, arching.
inarcare vt. to bend (v. irr.) || — le sopracciglia, to raise one's brows. ◆ **inarcarsi** vr. to arch.
inargentare vt. to silver.
inaridire vt. to dry. ◆ **inaridirsi** vr. to dry up.
inarticolato agg. inarticulate.
inascoltato agg. unheard.
inaspettato agg. unexpected.
inasprimento sm. embitterment.
inasprire vt. to embitter. ◆ **inasprirsi** vr. to become (v. irr.) embittered.
inattaccàbile agg. unassailable.
inattendìbile agg. unreliable.
inatteso agg. unexpected.
inattività sf. inactivity.
inattivo agg. inactive.
inattuàbile agg. impracticable.
inattuale agg. outdated.
inaudito agg. unheard of.
inaugurale agg. inaugural.
inaugurare vt. to inaugurate.
inaugurazione sf. inauguration.
inavvedutezza sf. carelessness.
inavveduto agg. careless.
inavvertenza sf. inadvertence.
inavvertito agg. unperceived.
inazione sf. inaction.
incagliare vt. to hinder. ◆ **incagliarsi** vr. to strand.

incaglio *sm* 1. stranding 2. (*fig.*) obstacle.

incalcolàbile *agg.* incalculable.

incallire *vi.* to harden. ♦ **incallirsi** *vr.* to harden.

incallito *agg.* hardened.

incalzante *agg.* 1. pursuing 2. (*fig.*) pressing.

incalzare *vt.* 1. to pursue 2. (*fig.*) to urge.

incameramento *sm.* confiscation.

incamerare *vt.* to confiscate.

incamminare *vt.* to set (*v. irr.*) going. ♦ **incamminarsi** *vr.* to set out (for).

incanalamento *sm.* canalization.

incanalare *vt.* to canalize.

incancellàbile *agg.* indelible.

incancrenire *vi.* to become (*v. irr.*) gangrenous.

incandescente *agg.* white-hot.

incandescenza *sf.* incandescence.

incantamento *sm.* charm.

incantare *vt.* to charm. ♦ **incantarsi** *vr.* to be charmed.

incantato *agg.* enchanted.

incantatore *agg.* enchanting. ♦ **incantatore** *sm.* enchanter.

incantésimo *sm.* spell.

incantévole *agg.* charming.

incanto[1] *sm.* enchantment.

incanto[2] *sm.* (*comm.*) auction: *vendere all'—*, to sell (*v. irr.*) by auction.

incanutire *vi.* to grow (*v. irr.*) hoary.

incapace *agg.* unable.

incapacità *sf.* incapacity.

incaparbirsi *vr.* to become (*v. irr.*) obstinate.

incappare *vi.* to get (*v. irr.*) into, to stumble.

incappucciare *vt.* to hood. ♦ **incappucciarsi** *vr.* to put (*v. irr.*) on one's hood.

incapricciarsi *vr.* to take (*v. irr.*) a fancy (to).

incapsulare *vt.* to capsule.

incarcerare *vt.* to imprison.

incarcerazione *sf.* imprisonment.

incaricare *vt.* to charge (so. with). ♦ **incaricarsi** *vr.* to charge oneself (with).

incaricato *agg.* charged (with). ♦ **incaricato** *sm.* appointee.

incàrico *sm.* task, duty.

incarnare *vt.* to embody. ♦ **incarnarsi** *vr.* to take (*v. irr.*) body.

incarnato *sm.* complexion.

incarnazione *sf.* incarnation.

incarnire *vi.* to grow (*v. irr.*) into flesh.

incartamento *sm.* dossier.

incartapecorire *vi.* to wrinkle.

incartapecorito *agg.* 'wrinkled with age.

incartare *vt.* to wrap in paper.

incarto *sm.* set of papers.

incartocciare *vt.* to wrap up in a cornet.

incasellare *vt.* to put (*v. irr.*) in squares.

incassamento *sm.* 1. boxing 2. (*mecc.; arch.*) embedding.

incassare *vt.* 1. to box 2. (*riscuotere*) to cash.

incassatura *sf.* hollow.

incasso *sm.* 1. collection 2. (*di spettacoli*) receipts (*pl.*).

incastellamento *sm.* 1. fortifications (*pl.*) 2. (*arch.*) scaffolding.

incastellare *vt.* to fortify with battlements.

incastellatura *sf.* 1. frame 2. (*arch.*) scaffolding.

incastonare *vt.* to set (*v. irr.*).

incastonatura *sf.* setting.

incastrare *vt.* 1. to embed 2. (*adattare*) to fit in. ♦ **incastrarsi** *vr.* 1. to fit 2. (*impigliarsi*) to get (*v. irr.*) stuck.

incastro *sm.* joint.

incatenamento *sm.* chaining.

incatenare *vt.* to chain. ♦ **incatenarsi** *vr.* to be linked (with).

incatramare *vt.* to tar.

incattivire *vt.* to exasperate. ♦ **incattivirsi** *vr.* to get (*v. irr.*) crossed.

incàuto *agg.* rash.

incavare *vt.* to hollow out.

incavatura *sf.* hollowness.

incavo *sm.* hollow.

incèdere *vi.* to advance.

incendiare *vt.* to set (*v. irr.*) on fire.

incendiario *agg. e sm.* incendiary.

incendio *sm.* fire.

incenerire *vt.* to reduce to ashes.

incensamento *sm.* 1. incensation 2. (*fig.*) flattery.

incensare *vt.* 1. to incense 2. (*fig.*) to flatter.

incenso *sm.* incense.

incensuràbile *agg.* irreproachable.

incensurato *agg.* blameless: *essere —*, to be a first-offender.

incentivo *sm.* incentive.

inceppamento *sm.* 1. obstacle 2. (*mecc.*) jam.

inceppare *vt.* 1. to clog 2. (*ostacolare*) to encumber. ♦ **inceparsi** *vr.* to jam.

incerare *vt.* to wax.

incertezza *sf.* uncertainty, doubt.

incerto *agg.* uncertain. ♦ **incerto** *sm.* uncertainty.

incespicare *vi.* to stumble.

incessante *agg.* unceasing.

incesto *sm.* incest.

incestuoso *agg.* incestuous.

incetta *sf.* cornering: fare — di, to make (*v. irr.*) a corner in.

incettare *vt.* to corner.

incettatore *sm.* cornerer.

inchiesta *sf.* inquiry, investigation.

inchinare *vt.* to bow (*v. irr.*). ♦ **inchinarsi** *vr.* to bow (down).

inchino *sm.* bow.

inchiodare *vt.* to nail.

inchiodatura *sf.* nailing.

inchiostro *sm.* ink.

inciampare *vi.* to stumble.

inciampo *sm.* obstacle.

incidentale *agg.* 1. incidental 2. (*gramm.*) parenthetic.

incidente *agg.* incident. ♦ **incidente** *sm.* accident.

incidenza *sf.* incidence.

incidere[1] *vt.* 1. to cut (*v. irr.*) 2. (*intagliare*) to engrave 3. (*su disco, nastro ecc.*) to record.

incidere[2] *vi.* to weigh heavily: — sul bilancio, to weigh heavily on one's budget.

incinta *agg. f.* pregnant.

incipiente *agg.* incipient.

incipriare *vt.* to powder. ♦ **incipriarsi** *vr.* to powder (oneself).

incirca (*nella loc. avv.*) all'—, about.

incisione *sf.* 1. cut 2. (*arte*) engraving 3. (*su disco, nastro ecc.*) recording.

incisività *sf.* sharpness.

incisivo *agg.* incisive. ♦ **incisivo** *sm.* (*anat.*) incisor.

inciso *sm.* parenthetic clause: per —, incidentally.

incisore *sm.* engraver.

incitamento *sm.* urge.

incitare *vt.* to urge, to stimulate.

incitrullire *vi.* to become (*v. irr.*) silly.

incivile *agg.* 1. uncivilized 2. (*scortese*) rude.

incivilimento *sm.* civilization.

incivilire *vt.* to civilize. ♦ **incivilirsi** *vr.* to become (*v. irr.*) civilized.

inciviltà *sf.* 1. barbarism 2. (*fig.*) rudeness.

inclassificabile *agg.* unclassifiable.

inclemente *agg.* 1. inclement: tempo —, inclement weather 2. (*spietato*) merciless.

inclemenza *sf.* 1. (*di tempo*) inclemency 2. (*crudeltà*) mercilessness.

inclinare *vt.* to incline, to bend (*v. irr.*).

inclinato *agg.* inclined (*anche fig.*).

inclinazione *sf.* 1. inclination 2. (*attitudine*) bent.

incline *agg.* disposed.

inclito *agg.* famous.

includere *vt.* to include.

inclusione *sf.* inclusion.

inclusivo *agg.* inclusive.

incluso *agg.* 1. included 2. (*accluso*) enclosed.

incoccare *vt.* to nock.

incoercibile *agg.* irrepressible.

incoercibilità *sf.* irrepressibleness.

incoerente *agg.* incoherent.

incoerenza *sf.* incoherence.

incognita *sf.* 1. (*mat.*) unknown quantity 2. (*fig.*) uncertainty.

incognito *agg.* unknown. ♦ **incognito** *sm.* incognito (*pl.* -tos).

incollamento *sm.* pasting.

incollare *vt.* to stick (*v. irr.*). ♦ **incollarsi** *vr.* to stick.

incollatrice *sf.* sizing-machine.

incollatura[1] *sf.* sticking.

incollatura[2] *sf.* (*ippica*) neck.

incollerire *vi.* to get (*v. irr.*) angry. ♦ **incollerirsi** *vr.* to get angry.

incollerito *agg.* angry.

incolonnamento *sm.* column formation.

incolonnare *vt.* to form into columns. ♦ **incolonnarsi** *vr.* to rank.

incolore *agg.* colourless.

incolpabile *agg.* accusable.

incolpare *vt.* to charge (with), to accuse (of). ♦ **incolparsi** *vr.* to accuse oneself.

incolpévole *agg.* blameless.

incolto *agg.* uncultivated.

incòlume *agg.* unhurt.

incolumità *sf.* safety.

incombente *agg.* impending.

incombenza *sf.* errand, task.

incòmbere *vi.* 1. (*spettare*) to be

one's job **2.** (*sovrastare*) to impend (over).

incombustibile *agg.* incombustible.

incominciare *vt.* e *vi.* V. *cominciare.*

incommensurabile *agg.* incommensurable.

incommensurabilità *sf.* incommensurability.

incommerciabile *agg.* not negotiable.

incommutabile *agg.* incommutable.

incomodare *vt.* to annoy. ♦ **incomodarsi** *vr.* to trouble.

incomodità *sf.* uncomfortableness.

incomodo *agg.* uncomfortable || *essere d' —,* to be in the way.

incomparabile *agg.* incomparable.

incompatibile *agg.* incompatible.

incompatibilità *sf.* incompatibility.

incompetente *agg.* incompetent.

incompetenza *sf.* incompetence.

incompiuto *agg.* unfinished.

incompletezza *sf.* incompleteness.

incompleto *agg.* incomplete.

incompostezza *sf.* disorder.

incomposto *agg.* disorderly.

incomprensibile *agg.* incomprehensible.

incomprensibilità *sf.* incomprehensibility.

incomprensione *sf.* incomprehension.

incompreso *agg.* **1.** not understood **2.** (*non apprezzato*) unappreciated.

incomputabile *agg.* incalculable.

incomunicàbile *agg.* incommunicable.

incomunicabilità *sf.* incommunicability.

inconcepibile *agg.* inconceivable.

inconciliabile *agg.* irreconcilable.

inconciliabilità *sf.* irreconcilability.

inconcludente *agg.* **1.** inconclusive **2.** (*di persona*) good-for-nothing.

inconcusso *agg.* unshaken.

incondizionato *agg.* unconditional.

inconfessabile *agg.* unavowable.

inconfessato *agg.* unconfessed.

inconfondibile *agg.* unmistakable.

inconfutabile *agg.* irrefutable.

incongruente *agg.* incongruous.

incongruenza *sf.* incongruity.

incongruo *agg.* incongruous.

inconsapévole *agg.* unconscious, unaware.

inconsapevolezza *sf.* unconsciousness, unawareness.

inconscio *agg.* e *sm.* unconscious.

inconseguente *agg.* inconsequent.

inconseguenza *sf.* inconsequence.

inconsideratezza *sf.* rashness.

inconsiderato *agg.* rash.

inconsistente *agg.* insubstantial.

inconsistenza *sf.* insubstantiality.

inconsolabile *agg.* inconsolable.

inconsueto *agg.* unusual.

inconsulto *agg.* unadvised, rash.

incontaminato *agg.* unpolluted.

incontentabile *agg.* insatiable.

incontentabilità *sf.* insatiability.

incontestabile *agg.* incontestable.

incontinente *agg.* incontinent.

incontinenza *sf.* incontinence.

incontrare *vt.* to meet (*v. irr.*). ♦ **incontrarsi** *vr.* to meet || *i nostri gusti non si incontrano,* our tastes do not agree.

incontrastabile *agg.* incontestable.

incontrastato *agg.* uncontested.

incontro[1] *sm.* **1.** meeting **2.** (*sport*) match.

incontro[2] *prep.* — *a,* towards, to.

incontrollabile *agg.* uncontrollable.

incontrollato *agg.* uncontrolled.

incontrovertibile *agg.* indisputable.

inconveniente *sm.* inconvenience, drawback.

inconvertibile *agg.* inconvertible.

inconvertibilità *sf.* inconvertibility.

incoraggiamento *sm.* encouragement.

incoraggiante *agg.* encouraging.

incoraggiare *vt.* to encourage.

incorniciare *vt.* to frame.

incorniciatura *sf.* framing.

incoronamento *sm.* V. *coronamento.*

incoronare *vt.* V. *coronare.*

incoronazione *sf.* coronation.

incorporare *vt.* to incorporate.

incorporazione *sf.* incorporation.

incorpòreo *agg.* incorporeal.

incorreggibile *agg.* incorrigible.

incòrrere *vi.* to incur, to suffer (*sthg.*).

incorretto *agg.* incorrect.

incorrotto *agg.* incorrupt.

incorruttibile *agg.* incorruptible.

incorruttibilità *sf.* incorruptibility.

incosciente *agg.* **1.** unconscious **2.** (*irresponsabile*) reckless. ♦ **incosciente** *sm.* irresponsible.

incoscienza *sf.* **1.** unconsciousness **2.** (*spericolatezza*) rashness.

incostante *agg.* inconstant: *tempo* —, changeable weather.

incostituzionale *agg.* unconstitutional.

incostituzionalità *sf.* unconstitutionality.

incredibile *agg.* incredible.

incredibilità *sf.* incredibility.

incredulità *sf.* incredulity.

incrèdulo *agg.* incredulous.

incrementare *vt.* to increase.

incremento *sm.* increase.

increscioso *agg.* unpleasant.

increspamento *sm.* 1. (*di acque*) rippling 2. (*di capelli*) ruffling.

increspare *vt.*, **incresparsi** *vr.* 1. (*di acque*) to ripple 2. (*di capelli*) to ruffle.

incretinire *vt.* to make (*v. irr.*) stupid. ♦ **incretinirsi** *vr.* to dull.

incriminàbile *agg.* impeachable.

incriminare *vt.* to impeach.

incriminazione *sf.* 1. (*l'accusare*) crimination 2. (*atto d'accusa*) indictment.

incrinare *vt.* to crack. ♦ **incrinarsi** *vr.* to crack.

incrinatura *sf.* crack.

incriticàbile *agg.* uncensurable.

incrociare *vt.* to cross. ♦ **incrociarsi** *vr.* to cross.

incrociatore *sm.* cruiser.

incrocio *sm.* 1. crossing ‖ — *stradale*, cross-road 2. (*di razze*) crossbreed.

incrollàbile *agg.* unshakable.

incrostare *vt.* to incrust. ♦ **incrostarsi** *vr.* to become (*v. irr.*) incrusted.

incrostazione *sf.* incrustation.

incrudelimento *sm.* toughening.

incrudelire *vi.* to become (*v. irr.*) cruel ‖ — *contro qu.*, to be pitiless towards so.

incrudire *vi.* to grow (*v. irr.*) worse.

incruento *agg.* bloodless.

incubatrice *sf.* incubator.

incubazione *sf.* incubation.

incubo *sm.* nightmare.

incùdine *sf.* anvil.

inculcare *vt.* to inculcate.

incunàbolo *sm.* incunabulum.

incuneare *vt.* to wedge. ♦ **incunearsi** *vr.* to wedge oneself.

incupire *vt.* e *vi.* to darken. ♦ **incupirsi** *vr.* to become (*v. irr.*) gloomy.

incuràbile *agg.* e *sm.* incurable.

incurabilità *sf.* incurability.

incurante *agg.* careless, heedless.

incuria *sf.* heedlessness.

incuriosire *vt.* to make (*v. irr.*) curious. ♦ **incuriosirsi** *vr.* to become (*v. irr.*) curious.

incuriosito *agg.* made curious.

incursione *sf.* raid.

incurvare *vt.* e **incurvarsi** *vr.* to bend (*v. irr.*), to curve.

incurvatura *sf.* bend.

incustodito *agg.* unguarded.

incùtere *vt.* to rouse.

indaco *sm.* indigo.

indaffarato *agg.* busy.

indagare *vt.* to investigate.

indagatore *agg.* investigating.

indàgine *sf.* 1. research, investigation 2. (*giur.*) inquiry.

indebitare *vt.* to involve in debt. ♦ **indebitarsi** *vr.* to run (*v. irr.*) into debt.

indébito *agg.* undue.

indebolimento *sm.* weakening.

indebolire *vt.* to weaken. ♦ **indebolirsi** *vr.* to weaken.

indecente *agg.* indecent.

indecenza *sf.* indecency.

indecifràbile *agg.* 1. indecipherable 2. (*di calligrafia*) illegible.

indecisione *sf.* indecision.

indeciso *agg.* 1. irresolute 2. (*di cose*) undecided.

indeclinàbile *agg.* 1. indeclinable 2. (*che non si può eludere*) unavoidable.

indecoroso *agg.* unseemly.

indefesso *agg.* indefatigable.

indefinìbile *agg.* indefinable.

indefinito *agg.* indefinite.

indeformàbile *agg.* indeformable.

indegno *agg.* 1. unworthy 2. (*spregevole*) disgraceful.

indelèbile *agg.* indelible.

indelicatezza *sf.* indelicacy.

indelicato *agg.* tactless.

indemoniato *agg.* 1. possessed 2. (*fig.*) frantic. ♦ **indemoniato** *sm.* demoniac.

indenne *agg.* undamaged.

indennità *sf.* allowance.

indennizzare *vt.* to indemnify.

indennizzo *sm.* indemnity.

inderogàbile *agg.* intransgressible.

indescrivìbile *agg.* indescribable.

indesideràbile *agg.* undesirable.

indeterminàbile *agg.* indeterminable.

indeterminatezza *sf.* vagueness.

indeterminativo *agg.* (*gramm.*) indefinite.

indeterminato *agg.* indeterminate.

indeterminazione *sf.* indetermination.

indi *avv.* **1.** (*di tempo*) then **2.** (*di luogo*) (from) thence.

indiano *agg.* Indian: — *d'America*, Red Indian; *in fila indiana*, in Indian file.

indiavolato *agg.* frenzied, furious.

indicare *vt.* **1.** to show (*v. irr.*) **2.** (*col dito*) to point at.

indicativo *agg.* indicative.

indicato *agg.* **1.** (*adatto*) suitable **2.** (*consigliabile*) advisable.

indicatore *agg.* indicatory. ♦ **indicatore** *sm.* indicator.

indicazione *sf.* indication.

indice *sm.* **1.** (*dito della mano*) forefinger **2.** (*di libro, statistica ecc.*) index.

indicibile *agg.* inexpressible.

indietreggiare *vi.* to withdraw (*v. irr.*).

indietro *avv.* (*di spazio, tempo*) back, behind.

indifendibile *agg.* indefensible.

indifeso *agg.* undefended.

indifferente *agg.* indifferent.

indifferenza *sf.* indifference.

indifferibile *agg.* undelayable.

indigeno *agg.* e *sm.* native.

indigente *agg.* indigent, poor.

indigenza *sf.* indigence.

indigestione *sf.* indigestion.

indigesto *agg.* **1.** indigestible **2.** (*fig.*) heavy.

indignare *vt.* to make (*v. irr.*) indignant. ♦ **indignarsi** *vr.* to get (*v. irr.*) angry.

indignazione *sf.* indignation.

indimenticabile *agg.* unforgettable.

indimostrabile *agg.* indemonstrable.

indipendente *agg.* independent (*of.*). ♦ **indipendente** *sm.* (*pol.*) independent.

indipendenza *sf.* independence.

indire *vt.* to call, to announce.

indiretto *agg.* indirect.

indirizzare *vt.* to address. ♦ **indirizzarsi** *vr.* **1.** (*dirigersi*) to set (*v. irr.*) out (for) **2.** (*rivolgersi*) to address oneself (to).

indirizzo *sm.* **1.** address **2.** (*linea di condotta*) trend.

indisciplina *sf.* indiscipline.

indisciplinato *agg.* undisciplined.

indiscretezza *sf.* indiscretion.

indiscreto *agg.* indiscreet.

indiscrezione *sf.* indiscretion.

indiscriminato *agg.* indiscriminate.

indiscusso *agg.* undiscussed.

indiscutibile *agg.* unquestionable.

indispensabile *agg.* indispensable.

indispettire *vt.* to vex. ♦ **indispettirsi** *vr.* to become (*v. irr.*) vexed.

indispettito *agg.* vexed.

indisponente *agg.* irritating.

indisporre *vt.* to irritate.

indisposizione *sf.* indisposition.

indisposto *agg.* unwell (*pred.*).

indissolubile *agg.* indissoluble.

indissolubilità *sf.* indissolubility.

indistinto *agg.* indistinct.

indistruttibile *agg.* indestructible.

indisturbato *agg.* undisturbed.

individuale *agg.* individual.

individualismo *sm.* individualism

individualista *s.* individualist.

individualìstico *agg.* individualistic.

individuare *vt.* to single out.

individuo *sm.* individual.

indivisibile *agg.* indivisible.

indivisibilità *sf.* indivisibility.

indiviso *agg.* undivided.

indiziare *vt.* to make (*v. irr.*) suspect.

indiziario *agg.* presumptive.

indiziato *agg.* e *sm.* suspect.

indizio *sm.* **1.** indication **2.** (*giur.*) circumstantial proof.

indòcile *agg.* indocile.

indocilità *sf.* indocility.

indoeuropeo *agg.* e *sm.* Indo-European.

ìndole *sf.* nature, disposition ‖ *un ragazzo di buona —*, a good-natured boy.

indolente *agg.* indolent.

indolenza *sf.* indolence.

idolenzimento *sm.* numbness.

indolenzire *vt.* to numb. ♦ **indolenzirsi** *vr.* to become (*v. irr.*) numb.

indolenzito *agg.* numb.

indolore *agg.* painless.

indomàbile *agg.* untamable.

indomani *sm.* next day ‖ *all' —*, on the day after.

indòmito *agg.* indomitable.

indorare *vt.* V. dorare.

indossare *vt.* **1.** (*avere indosso*) to wear (*v. irr.*) **2.** (*mettere indosso*) to put (*v. irr.*) on.

indossatrice . *sf.* mannequin.
indosso *avv.* on.
indotto *agg.* (*spinto*) driven.
indovinare *vt.* to guess.
indovinello *sm.* riddle.
indovino *sm.* soothsayer.
indubbio *agg.* undoubted.
indubitàbile *agg.* indubitable.
indugiare *vi.* to delay, to hesitate.
indugio *sm.* delay.
indulgente *agg.* indulgent.
indulgenza *sf.* indulgence.
indùlgere *vi.* to indulge (in).
indulto *sm.* **1.** (*eccl.*) indult **2.**
(*giur.*) free pardon.
indumento *sm.* garment.
induriménto *sm.* hardening.
indurire *vt.* e *vi.* to harden. ♦ **in-**
durirsi *vr.* to harden.
indurre *vt.* to induce, to get (*v.*
irr.) || — *in errore*, to mislead (*v.*
irr.) ♦ **indursi** *vr.* to bring (*v.*
irr.) oneself (to).
indùstria *sf.* industry.
industriale *agg.* industrial. ♦ **in-**
dustriale *sm.* industrialist, manufacturer.
industrialismo *sm.* industrialism.
industrializzare *vt.* to industrialize.
industrializzazione *sf.* industri-
alization.
industriarsi *vr.* to do (*v. irr.*) one's
best.
industrioso *agg.* industrious.
induttivo *agg.* inductive.
induttore *sm.* inductor.
induzione *sf.* induction.
inebetire *vt.* e *vi.* to dull.
inebetito *agg.* dull.
inebriante *agg.* inebriating.
inebriare *vt.* **1.** to make (*v. irr.*)
drunk **2.** (*fig.*) to inebriate. ♦
inebriarsi *vr.* **1.** to get (*v. irr.*)
drunk **2.** (*fig.*) to go (*v. irr.*) into
raptures.
ineccepìbile *agg.* unexceptionable.
inedia *sf.* starvation.
inèdito *agg.* unpublished.
ineducato *agg.* ill-bred.
ineffàbile *agg.* ineffable.
inefficace *agg.* ineffective.
inefficacia *sf.* inefficacy.
inefficiente *agg.* inefficient.
inefficienza *sf.* ineffectiveness.
ineguaglianza *sf.* inequality.
ineguale *agg.* **1.** unlike **2.** (*irrego-*
lare) irregular **3.** (*di superficie*)
uneven.

ineleggìbile *agg.* ineligible.
ineleggibilità *sf.* ineligibility.
ineluttàbile *agg.* ineluctable.
ineluttabilità *sf.* inevitableness.
inenarràbile *agg.* unutterable.
inequivocàbile *agg.* unmistakable
inerente *agg.* concerning.
inerme *agg.* unarmed.
inerpicarsi *vr.* to climb (up).
inerte *agg.* inert.
inerzia *sf.* inertness.
inesattezza *sf.* inaccuracy.
inesatto *agg.* incorrect.
inesaudito *agg.* ungranted.
inesaurìbile *agg.* inexhaustible.
inesàusto *agg.* unexhausted.
ineseguìbile *agg.* inexecutable.
inesigìbile *agg.* **1.** uncollectable
2. (*di assegno*) worthless.
inesistente *agg.* inexistent.
inesistenza *sf.* inexistence.
inesoràbile *agg.* inexorable.
inesorabilità *sf.* inexorability.
inesperienza *sf.* inexperience.
inesperto *agg.* unskilled.
inespiàbile *agg.* inexpiable.
inesplicàbile *agg.* inexplicable.
inesploràbile *agg.* inexplorable.
inesplorato *agg.* unexplored.
inespressivo *agg.* inexpressive.
inespresso *agg.* implied.
inesprimìbile *agg.* inexpressible.
inespugnàbile *agg.* inexpugnable.
inespugnabilità *sf.* inexpugnability.
inestimàbile *agg.* inestimable.
inestinguìbile *agg.* unquenchable.
inestirpàbile *agg.* ineradicable.
inestricàbile *agg.* inextricable.
inettitùdine *sf.* unfitness.
inetto *agg.* **1.** unapt **2.** (*dappoco*)
good-for-nothing.
inevaso *agg.* outstanding, unanswered.
inevitàbile *agg.* inevitable.
inezia *sf.* trifle.
infagottare *vt.* to muffle up. ♦ **in-**
fagottarsi *vr.* to muffle oneself
up.
infallìbile *agg.* infallible.
infallibilità *sf.* infallibility.
infamante *agg.* shameful.
infamare *vt.* to defame, to disgrace.
infame *agg.* wicked.
infamia *sf.* infamy.
infangare *vt.* to muddy. ♦ **infan-**
garsi *vr.* to become (*v. irr.*)
muddy.
infanticida *s.* child-murderer.

infanticidio sm. child-murder.

infantile agg. childlike, childish.

infantilismo sm. infantilism.

infanzia sf. 1. infancy 2. (coll.) children (pl.).

infarcire vt. V. farcire.

infarinare vt. to flour. ♦ **infarinarsi** vr. to get (v. irr.) covered with flour.

infarinatura sf. 1. flouring 2. (fig.) smattering.

infarto sm. infarct.

infastidire vt. to annoy. ♦ **infastidirsi** vr. to get (v. irr.) bored.

infaticàbile agg. tireless.

infatti cong. in fact.

infatuare vt. to infatuate. ♦ **infatuarsi** vr. to get (v. irr.) crazy (about).

infatuato agg. crazy (about).

infatuazione sf. infatuation.

infàusto agg. unlucky.

infecondità sf. sterility.

infecondo agg. steril.

infedele agg. unfaithful. ♦ **infedele** sm. infidel.

infedeltà sf. unfaithfulness.

infelice agg. 1. unhappy 2. (non appropriato) ill-timed. ♦ **infelice** s. wretch.

infelicità sf. unhappiness.

inferiore agg. 1. inferior 2. (più basso) lower 3. (al di sotto) below. ♦ **inferiore** sm. inferior.

inferiorità sf. inferiority.

inferire vt. 1. (dedurre) to infer 2. (dare) to inflict.

infermerìa sf. infirmary.

infermiera sf. nurse.

infermiere sm. hospital attendant.

infermità sf. infirmity.

infermo agg. e sm. invalid.

infernale agg. 1. infernal 2. (fig.) awful.

inferno sm. hell.

inferocire vt. to enrage. ♦ **inferocire** vr. to get (v. irr.) fierce.

inferriata sf. grating.

infervorare vt. to excite. ♦ **infervorarsi** vr. to get (v. irr.) excited.

infervorato agg. fervent.

infestare vt. to infest.

infestazione sf. infestation.

infettare vt. to infect. ♦ **infettarsi** vr. to become (v. irr.) infected.

infettivo agg. contagious.

infetto agg. infected.

infezione sf. infection.

infiacchimento sm. weakening.

infiacchire vt. e vi. to weaken. ♦ **infiacchirsi** vr. to become (v. irr.) weak.

infiammàbile agg. inflammable.

infiammabilità sf. inflammability.

infiammare vt. 1. to set (v. irr.) on fire 2. (fig.) to inflame. ♦ **infiammarsi** vr. 1. to take (v. irr.) fire 2. (fig.) to get (v. irr.) excited.

infiammato agg. inflamed (with).

infiammatorio agg. inflammatory.

infiammazione sf. inflammation.

infiascare vt. to put (v. irr.) into flasks.

inficiare vt. 1. to invalidate 2. (giur.) to impugn.

infido agg. false.

infierire vi. to be pitiless.

infìggere vt. 1. to infix 2. (conficcare) to drive (v. irr.) (into).

infilare vt. 1. to thread 2. (introdurre) to insert 3. (passare per) to enter. ♦ **infilarsi** vr. to slip into.

infilata sf. row.

infiltrarsi vr. to penetrate.

infiltrazione sf. infiltration.

infilzare vt. 1. to transfix 2. (conficcare) to stick (v. irr.). ♦ **infilzarsi** vr. 1. to run (v. irr.) oneself through 2. (conficcarsi) to get (v. irr.) stuck.

infilzata sf. string.

ìnfimo agg. lowest.

infine avv. at last.

infingardàggine sf. laziness.

infingardo agg. lazy.

infinità sf. infinity.

infinitamente avv. infinitely.

infinitesimale agg. infinitesimal.

infinito agg. boundless. ♦ **infinito** sm. 1. infinite 2. (gramm.) infinitive.

infioccare vt. to tassel.

infiorare vt. to flower.

infirmare vt. to invalidate.

infischiarsi vr. not to care (about).

infittire vi. to thicken. ♦ **infittirsi** vr. to thicken.

inflazione sf. inflation.

inflazionìstico agg. inflationary.

inflessìbile agg. inflexible.

inflessibilità sf. inflexibility.

inflessione sf. inflexion.

inflìggere vt. to inflict.

influente agg. influential.

influenza sf. 1. influence 2. (med.) (fam.) 'flu.

influenzare vt. to influence.

influire vi. to exert influence (on, upon, over).

influsso sm. influence.

infocare vt. 1. to heat up 2. to inflame.

infocato agg. 1. red hot 2. (fig.) inflamed.

infoltire vi. to thicken.

infondatezza sf. groundlessness.

infondato agg. groundless.

infòndere vt. to infuse.

inforcare vt. 1. to pitchfork 2. (montare a cavalcioni) to get (v. irr.) on || — gli occhiali, to put (v. irr.) on one's glasses.

informale agg. informal.

informare vt. 1. to inform 2. (dare forma) to shape. ♦ **informarsi** vr. to inquire (about).

informativo agg. informative.

informato agg. informed.

informatore sm. informer.

informazione sf. information (solo sing.), news (pl.).

informe agg. shapeless.

infornare vt. to put (v. irr.) into an oven.

infornata sf. batch.

infortunarsi vr. to get (v. irr.) injured.

infortunato agg. injured.

infortunio sm. accident.

infortunìstica sf. industrial accident research.

infossamento sm. hollow.

infossare vt. to hollow. ♦ **infossarsi** vr. to become (v. irr.) hollow.

infradiciare vt. 1. to drench 2. (marcire) to rot (v. irr.).

inframmettenza sf. interference.

inframmèttere vt. to interpose. ♦ **inframméttersi** vr. to meddle (with).

infràngere vt. 1. to shatter 2. (trasgredire) to infringe. ♦ **infràngersi** vr. to break (v. irr.) (up).

infrangìbile agg. unbreakable: vetro —, shatter-proof glass.

infranto agg. 1. shattered, broken 2. (di legge) infringed.

infrarosso sm. infrared.

infrasettimanale agg. midweek.

infrastruttura sf. infrastructure.

infrazione sf. infraction.

infreddolìrsi vr. to feel (v. irr.) cold.

infreddolito agg. chilly.

infrequente agg. infrequent.

infrollìrsi vr. 1. to become (v. irr.) tender 2. (di selvaggina) to become (v. irr.) high.

infruttìfero agg. unfruitful.

infruttuoso agg. 1. unfruitful 2. (fig.) useless.

infuori (loc. prep.) all'—, except.

infuriare vi. to enrage. ♦ **infuriarsi** vr. to flare up.

infusione sf. infusion.

infuso agg. infused. ♦ **infuso** sm. infusion.

infusòrio sm. infusorial.

ingabbiare vt. 1. to cage 2. (fig.) to lock up.

ingaggiare vt. to engage.

ingaggio sm. engagement.

ingagliardire vt. to strengthen. ♦ **ingagliardìrsi** vr. to strengthen.

ingannare vt. to deceive || — il tempo, to while away the time. ♦ **ingannarsi** vr. to be mistaken.

ingannatore agg. deceiving. ♦ **ingannatore** sm. deceiver.

ingannévole agg. deceitful.

inganno sm. deception, fraud.

ingarbugliare vt. to entangle. ♦ **ingarbugliàrsi** vr. to get (v. irr.) mixed up.

ingegnarsi vr. to contrive (to).

ingegnere sm. engineer.

ingegnerìa sf. engineering.

ingegno sm. talent.

ingegnosità sf. ingeniousness.

ingegnoso agg. ingenious.

ingelosire vt. to make (v. irr.) jealous. ♦ **ingelosìrsi** vr. to become (v. irr.) jealous.

ingenerare vt. to engender.

ingeneroso agg. selfish.

ingente agg. huge.

ingentilire vt. to refine.

ingenuità sf. naïveness.

ingenuo agg. naïve.

ingerenza sf. interference.

ingerimento sm. swallowing.

ingerire vt. to swallow.

ingessare vt. to plaster.

ingessatura sf. 1. plastering 2. (med.) plaster cast.

inghiaiare vt. to gravel.

inghiottire vt. 1. to swallow 2. (di acque ecc.) to engulf 3. (sopportare) to lump.

inghirlandare vt. to wreathe.

ingiallire vt. e vi. to yellow.

ingigantire vt. to magnify. ♦ **ingigantire** vi. to become (v. irr.) gigantic.

inginocchiarsi vr. to kneel (v. irr.) (down).

inginocchiatoio sm. kneeler.

ingioiellare vt. to bejewel.

ingiù avv. down, downwards.

ingiùngere vt. to order.

ingiuntivo agg. injunctive.

ingiunzione sf. injunction.

ingiùria sf. insult.

ingiuriare vt. to insult.

ingiurioso agg. insulting.

ingiustamente avv. unjustly.

ingiustificàbile agg. unjustifiable.

ingiustificato agg. unjustified.

ingiustizia sf. unjustice.

ingiusto agg. unjust.

inglese agg. English. ♦ **inglese** sm. Englishman (pl. -men) || gli Inglesi, the English (people).

inglobare vt. to inglobe.

inglorioso agg. inglorious.

ingobbire vi. to become (v. irr.) humpbacked. ♦ **ingobbirsi** vr. to become humpbacked.

ingoiare vt. to swallow.

ingolfarsi vr. (fig.) to throw (v. irr.) oneself (into).

ingollare vt. to gulp down.

ingolosire vt. to make (v. irr.) greedy.

ingombrante agg. cumbersome.

ingombrare vt. to encumber.

ingombro agg. encumbered (with). ♦ **ingombro** sm. encumbrance.

ingommare vt. 1. to gum 2. (in collare) to stick (v. irr.).

ingordigia sf. greed.

ingordo agg. greedy.

ingorgare vt. to choke. ♦ **ingorgarsi** vr. to become (v. irr.) choked.

ingorgo sm. 1. obstruction 2. (del traffico) traffic jam.

ingozzare vt. to gulp.

ingranaggio sm. 1. gear 2. (fig.) mechanism.

ingranare vt. 1. to put (v. irr.) into gear 2. (auto) — una marcia, to engage a gear. ♦ **ingranare** vi. (fam.) to get (v. irr.) along (with).

ingrandimento sm. 1. enlargement 2. (ott.) magnification.

ingrandire vt. 1. to enlarge 2. (ott.) to magnify. ♦ **ingrandirsi** vr. to become (v. irr.) larger.

ingrassare vt. 1. to fatten 2. (lubrificare) to grease. ♦ **ingrassare** vi. to grow (v. irr.) fat.

ingrasso sm. fattening.

ingratitùdine sf. ingratitude.

ingrato agg. ungrateful. ♦ **ingrato** sm. ingrate.

ingravidare vt. to make (v. irr.) pregnant. ♦ **ingravidare** vi. to become (v. irr.) pregnant.

ingraziarsi vr. to get (v. irr.) into so.'s good graces.

ingrediente sm. ingredient.

ingresso sm. 1. entry 2. (entrata) entrance 3. (accesso) admittance.

ingrossamento sm. enlargement.

ingrossare vt. e vi. to enlarge. ♦ **ingrossarsi** vr. to become (v. irr.) bigger.

ingrosso (nella loc. avv.) all'—, wholesale.

inguàlcibile agg. crease-resistant.

inguaribile agg. incurable.

inguinale agg. inguinal.

inguine sm. inguen.

ingurgitare vt. to swallow.

inibire vt. to inhibit.

inibito agg. inhibited.

inibizione sf. inhibition.

iniettare vt. to inject.

iniezione sf. injection.

inimicare vt. to alienate. ♦ **inimicarsi** vr. to estrange from oneself.

inimicizia sf. enmity.

inimitàbile agg. incomparable, inimitable.

inimmaginàbile agg. unimaginable.

inintelligìbile agg. unintelligible.

ininterrotto agg. continuous, unceasing.

iniquità sf. iniquity.

iniquo agg. 1. unfair 2. (malvagio) wicked.

iniziale agg. initial, starting. ♦ **iniziale** sf. initial.

iniziare vt. 1. to begin (v. irr.), to start 2. (introdurre) to initiate.

iniziativa sf. initiative.

iniziato agg. e sm. initiate.

iniziazione sf. initiation.

inizio sm. beginning.

innaffiare vt. to water.

innaffiatoio sm. watering-pot.

innalzamento sm. elevation.

innalzare vt. 1. to raise 2. (rendere più alto) to heighten. ♦ **innalzarsi** vr. to rise (v. irr.).

innamoramento sm. falling in love.

innamorare vt. to charm. ♦ **innamorarsi** vr. to fall (v. irr.) in love (with).

innamorato *agg.* in love (with). ◆ **innamorato** *sm.* lover.

innanzi *avv.* 1. forward, on 2. (*di fronte*) in front of 3. (*più avanti*) further ‖ *d'ora* —, from now on. ◆ **innanzi** *prep.* before.

innato *agg.* inborn.

innaturale *agg.* unnatural.

innegàbile *agg.* undeniable.

inneggiare *vi.* 1. to exalt 2. (*acclamare*) to cheer.

innervare *vt.* to innervate.

innervosire *vt.* to get (*v. irr.*) on so.'s nerves. ◆ **innervosirsi** *vr.* to get nervous.

innescamento *sm.* priming.

innescare *vt.* to prime.

innesco *sm.* primer.

innestare *vt.* 1. (*agr.; med.*) to graft 2. (*mecc.*) to engage.

innesto *sm.* 1. (*agr.; med.*) graft 2. (*mecc.*) clutch.

inno *sm.* hymn ‖ — *nazionale*, national anthem.

innocente *agg.* e *sm.* innocent.

innocenza *sf.* innocence.

innocuità *sf.* innocuousness.

innocuo *agg.* harmless.

innominàbile *agg.* unmentionable.

innovare *vt.* to innovate.

innovatore *agg.* innovating. ◆ **innovatore** *sm.* innovator.

innovazione *sf.* innovation.

innumerévole *agg.* numberless.

inoculare *vt.* to inoculate.

inoculazione *sf.* inoculation.

inodoro *agg.* odourless.

inoffensivo *agg.* harmless.

inoltrare *vt.* to forward. ◆ **inoltrarsi** *vr.* to advance.

inoltrato *agg.* advanced, late.

inoltre *avv.* moreover, besides.

inoltro *sm.* 1. (*di merci*) forwarding 2. (*di documenti*) sending on.

inondare *vt.* to flood.

inondazione *sf.* flood.

inoperosità *sf.* inactivity.

inoperoso *agg.* inactive.

inopinàbile *agg.* inconceivable.

inopinato *agg.* unexpected.

inopportunità *sf.* inopportunity.

inopportuno *agg.* inopportune.

inoppugnàbile *agg.* incontestable.

inoppugnabilità *sf.* incontestability.

inorgànico *agg.* inorganic.

inorgoglire *vt.* to make (*v. irr.*) proud. ◆ **inorgoglirsi** *vr.* to become (*v. irr.*) proud.

inorridire *vt.* to horrify. ◆ **inorridire** *vi.* to be horrified.

inospitale *agg.* inhospitable.

inosservanza *sf.* inobservance.

inosservato *agg.* unobserved.

inossidàbile *agg.* rust-proof ‖ *acciaio* —, stainless steel.

inquadramento *sm.* framing.

inquadrare *vt.* 1. to frame 2. (*fig.*) to set (*v. irr.*) 3. (*mil.*) to rank 4. (*foto, cine*) to frame.

inquadratura *sf.* (*cine*) shot.

inqualificàbile *agg.* despicable.

inquietante *agg.* worrying.

inquietare *vt.* to worry. ◆ **inquietarsi** *vr.* to get (*v. irr.*) angry.

inquieto *agg.* 1. restless 2. (*preoccupato*) worried 3. (*arrabbiato*) angry.

inquietùdine *sf.* 1. restlessness 2. (*preoccupazione*) anxiety.

inquilino *sm.* tenant.

inquinamento *sm.* defilement.

inquinare *vt.* to defile.

inquirente *agg.* investigating.

inquisire *vt.* to investigate. ◆ **inquisire** *vi.* to inquire.

inquisitore *agg.* inquiring. ◆ **inquisitore** *sm.* inquisitor.

inquisizione *sf.* inquisition.

insabbiamento *sm.* (*fig.*) hindering.

insabbiare *vt.* 1. to sand 2. (*fig.*) to hinder.

insaccare *vt.* to sack.

insalata *sf.* salad.

insalatiera *sf.* salad-bowl.

insalubre *agg.* unhealthy.

insalubrità *sf.* insalubrity.

insanàbile *agg.* incurable.

insanguinare *vt.* to cover (with blood). ◆ **insanguinarsi** *vr.* to become (*v. irr.*) bloodstained.

insano *agg.* insane.

insaponare *vt.* to soap.

insaponatura *sf.* soaping.

insaporire *vt.* to flavour.

insaporo *agg.* flavourless.

insaputa *sf.* (*nella loc. avv.*) *all'— di*, unknown to.

insaziàbile *agg.* insatiable.

insaziabilità *sf.* insatiability.

insaziato *agg.* unappeased.

inscatolare *vt.* to tin.

inscenare *vt.* to stage.

inscindìbile *agg.* inseparable.

inscrivere *vt.* 1. (*a una scuola, esame ecc.*) to enrol 2. (*scrivere, scolpire; geom.*) to inscribe.

insediamento *sm.* installation.

insediare *vt.* to install. ◆ **insediarsi** *vr.* to install oneself.

insegna *sf.* 1. insignia (*pl.*) 2. (*bandiera*) flag 3. (*di negozio*) sign-board.

insegnamento *sm.* 1. teaching 2. (*precetto, lezione*) precept, lesson.

insegnante *agg.* teaching. ◆ **insegnante** *s.* teacher.

insegnare *vt.* to teach (*v. irr.*).

inseguimento *sm.* pursuit.

inseguire *vt.* to pursue.

inseguitore *sm.* pursuer.

insellare *vt.* to saddle.

inselvatichire *vi.* to grow (*v. irr.*) wild.

insenatura *sf.* inlet, creek.

insensatezza *sf.* 1. craziness 2. (*atto insensato*) foolish action.

insensato *agg.* foolish, crazy.

insensibile *agg.* 1. insensible 2. (*indifferente*) indifferent 3. (*frigido*) unfeeling.

insensibilità *sf.* 1. insensibility 2. (*indifferenza*) indifference.

insensibilmente *avv.* 1. (*impercettibilmente*) imperceptibly, slightly 2. (*senza sentimento*) insensibly.

inseparàbile *agg.* inseparable.

insepolto *agg.* unburied.

inserimento *sm.* insertion.

inserire *vt.* 1. to insert 2. (*elettr.*) to connect.

inserto *sm.* 1. file, dossier 2. (*cine, stampa*) insert.

inservìbile *agg.* useless.

inserviente *sm.* attendant.

inserzione *sf.* 1. insertion 2. (*pubblicitaria*) advertisement.

inserzionista *sm.* advertiser.

insetticida *agg. e sm.* insecticide.

insettìvoro *agg.* insectivorous. ◆ **insettìvoro** *sm.* insectivore.

insetto *sm.* insect.

insicurezza *sf.* insecurity.

insidia *sf.* 1. snare 2. (*pericolo*) danger.

insidiare *vt.* to endanger || — *la vita di una persona*, to attempt a person's life.

insidioso *agg.* insidious.

insieme *avv.* 1. together 2. (*allo stesso tempo*) at the same time. ◆ **insieme** *prep.* together (with). ◆ **insieme** *sm.* whole: *nell'—*, as a whole || *sguardo d'—*, comprehensive view.

insigne *agg.* famous.

insignificante *agg.* insignificant.

insignire *vt.* to confer (sthg. upon).

insincerità *sf.* insincerity.

insincero *agg.* insincere.

insindacàbile *agg.* undisputable.

insinuante *agg.* insinuating.

insinuare *vt.* to hint. ◆ **insinuarsi** *vr.* to insinuate oneself.

insinuazione *sf.* hint, insinuation.

insipidezza *sf.* insipidness.

insìpido *agg.* 1. tasteless 2. (*fig.*) insipid.

insistente *agg.* 1. insistent, steady 2. (*molesto*) irritating.

insistenza *sf.* insistence.

insìstere *vi.* to insist (on).

ìnsito *agg.* inborn, inherent.

insoddisfatto *agg.* dissatisfied (with).

insoddisfazione *sf.* dissatisfaction (with).

insofferente *agg.* intolerant.

insofferenza *sf.* intolerance.

insoffrìbile *agg.* unbearable.

insolazione *sf.* sunstroke.

insolente *agg. e sm.* insolent.

insolentire *vt.* to insult.

insolenza *sf.* insolence.

insòlito *agg.* unusual.

insolùbile *agg.* insoluble.

insolubilità *sf.* insolubility.

insoluto *agg.* 1. unsolved 2. (*non pagato*) unpaid.

insolvente *agg.* insolvent.

insolvenza *sf.* insolvency.

insolvìbile *agg.* 1. (*di debito*) unpayable 2. (*di persona*) insolvent.

insolvibilità *sf.* insolvency.

insomma *avv.* finally, in short.

insondàbile *agg.* unfathomable.

insonne *agg.* sleepless.

insonnia *sf.* insomnia.

insonnolito *agg.* drowsy, sleepy.

insopportàbile *agg.* unbearable.

insopprimìbile *agg.* insuppressible.

insòrgere *vi.* 1. to rise (*v. irr.*) 2. (*protestare*) to protest, to rebel 3. (*manifestarsi*) to arise (*v. irr.*).

insormontàbile *agg.* insurmountable.

insorto *sm.* rebel.

insospettàbile *agg.* beyond suspicion.

insospettato *agg.* unsuspected.

insospettire *vt.* to make (*v. irr.*) suspicious. ◆ **insospettirsi** *vr.* to grow (*v. irr.*) suspicious.

insostenìbile *agg.* unsustainable.

insostituìbile *agg.* irreplaceable.

insozzare *vt.* **1.** to soil **2.** (*fig.*) to disgrace.

insperàbile *agg.* beyond hope.

insperato *agg.* unhoped for.

inspiegàbile *agg.* inexplicable.

inspirare *vt.* to breathe in.

inspirazione *sf.* breathing in, inhalation.

instàbile *agg.* unstable || *tempo* —, unsettled weather.

instabilità *sf.* **1.** instability **2.** (*fig.*) fickleness.

installare *vt.* to install. ♦ **installarsi** *vr.* to settle.

installazione *sf.* installation.

instancàbile *agg.* untiring.

instaurare *vt.* to set (*v. irr.*) up.

instaurazione *sf.* establishment.

instradare *vt.* to direct, to coach.

insú *avv.* up, upwards.

insubordinatezza *sf.* insubordination.

insubordinato *agg.* insubordinate.

insubordinazione *sf.* insubordination.

insuccesso *sm.* failure.

insudiciare *vt.* to soil.

insufficiente *agg.* insufficient.

insufficienza *sf.* **1.** insufficiency **2.** (*scol.*) low mark.

insulare *agg.* insular.

insulina *sf.* insulin.

insulsàggine *sf.* **1.** silliness **2.** (*cosa insulsa*) nonsense.

insulso *agg.* silly.

insultare *vt.* to insult.

insulto *sm.* insult.

insuperàbile *agg.* insuperable.

insuperato *agg.* unsurpassed.

insuperbire *vt.* to elate. ♦ **insuperbirsi** *vr.* to pride oneself (on).

insurrezionale *agg.* insurrectional.

insurrezione *sf.* insurrection.

insussistente *agg.* unfounded.

intaccare *vt.* **1.** to notch **2.** (*chim.*) to etch **3.** (*fig.*) to injure.

intacco *sm.* notch.

intagliare *vt.* **1.** to carve **2.** (*incidere*) to engrave.

intaglio *sm.* **1.** carving **2.** (*incisione*) engraving.

intangìbile *agg.* intangible.

intanto *avv.* meanwhile.

intarsiare *vt.* to inlay.

intarsio *sm.* inlay.

intasamento *sm.* obstruction.

intasare *vt.* to obstruct.

intascare *vt.* to pocket.

intatto *agg.* intact.

intavolare *vt.* **1.** to plank **2.** (*iniziare*) to begin (*v. irr.*), to start.

integèrrimo *agg.* strictly honest.

integràbile *agg.* integrable.

integrale *agg.* integral; (*mat.*) *calcolo* —, integral calculus.

integrante *agg.* integrant.

integrare *vt.* to integrate.

integrazione *sf.* integration.

integrità *sf.* integrity

ìntegro *agg.* **1.** integral **2.** (*onesto*) honest.

intelaiatura *sf.* **1.** framework **2.** (*di finestre*) sash.

intellettivo *agg.* intellective.

intelletto *sm.* intellect.

intellettuale *agg. e sm.* intellectual.

intellettualismo *sm.* intellectualism.

intelligente *agg.* intelligent.

intelligenza *sf.* intelligence.

intelligìbile *agg.* intelligible.

intelligibilità *sf.* intelligibility.

intemerata *sf.* reprimand.

intemerato *agg.* faultless.

intemperante *agg.* intemperate.

intemperanza *sf.* intemperance.

intemperie *sf. pl.* inclemency of the weather (*sing.*).

intempestività *sf.* untimeliness.

intempestivo *agg.* untimely.

intendente *agg.* expert. ♦ **intendente** *sm.* superintendent.

intendenza *sf.* superintendence.

intèndere *vt.* **1.** (*capire*) to understand (*v. irr.*) **2.** (*significare*) to mean (*v. irr.*) **3.** (*avere intenzione di*) to intend to. ♦ **intèndersi** *vr.* **1.** (*avere cognizione*) to be a good judge **2.** (*mettersi d'accordo*) to come (*v. irr.*) to an agreement.

intendimento *sm.* **1.** understanding **2.** (*intenzione*) intention.

intenditore *sm.* **1.** good judge **2.** (*d'arte*) connoisseur.

intenerimento *sm.* **1.** softening **2.** (*fig.*) tenderness.

intenerire *vt.* **1.** to soften **2.** (*fig.*) to move to pity. ♦ **intenerirsi** *vr.* to be moved to pity.

intensificare *vt.* to intensify.

intensificazione *sf.* intensification.

intensità *sf.* intensity.

intensivo *agg.* intensive.

intenso *agg.* intense.

intentàbile *agg.* **1.** unattemptable **2.** (*giur.*) suable.

intentare vt. to bring (v. irr.).
intento agg. intent. ♦ **intento** sm. aim, purpose.
intenzionale agg. deliberate.
intenzionato agg. disposed.
intenzione sf. intention.
intepidire vt. to warm, to make (v. irr.) tepid. ♦ **intepidirsi** vr. to get (v. irr.) tepid.
interamente avv. wholly, entirely.
intercalare agg. intercalary. ♦ **intercalare** sm. pet phrase.
intercalare vt. to intercalate.
intercambiàbile agg. interchangeable.
intercèdere vi. to intercede, to plead.
intercessione sf. intercession.
intercessore sm. intercessor.
intercettare vt. to intercept.
intercettatore sm. interceptor.
intercettazione sf. interception.
intercomunale sf. (tel.) long-distance call.
intercontinentale agg. intercontinental.
intercòrrere vi. 1. to pass 2. (accadere) to happen.
intercostale agg. intercostal.
interdetto agg. 1. prohibited 2. (giur.) interdicted. ♦ **interdetto** sm. interdict.
interdipendente agg. interdependent.
interdipendenza sf. interdependence.
interdire vt. to interdict.
interdizione sf. interdiction.
interessamento sm. concern.
interessante agg. interesting.
interessare vt. 1. to interest 2. (riguardare) to concern. ♦ **interessarsi** vr. 1. to be interested (in) 2. (provvedere) to take (v. irr.) care (of).
interessato agg. interested.
interesse sm. interest.
interessenza sf. share, profit.
interezza sf. wholeness.
interferenza sf. interference.
interferire vi. to interfere.
interiezione sf. interjection.
interinale agg. temporary.
interiora sf. pl. entrails.
interiore agg. inner. ♦ **interiore** sm. interior, inside.
interiorità sf. inwardness.
interiormente avv. 1. (intimamente) innerly 2. (nell'interno) inside.

interlinea sf. 1. interline 2. (tip.) lead.
interlineare vt. 1. to interline 2. (tip.) to lead (v. irr.).
interlineare vt. to interline.
interlocutore sm. interlocutor.
interlocutorio agg. interlocutory.
interloquire vi. to join in the conversation.
interludio sm. interlude.
intermediario agg. intermediary. ♦ **intermediario** sm. 1. go-between 2. (comm.) middleman (pl. -men).
intermedio agg. intermediate, middle.
intermezzo sm. 1. intermission 2. (mus.) intermezzo.
interminàbile agg. endless.
intermittente agg. intermittent.
intermittenza sf. intermittence.
internamento sm. internment.
internare vt. to intern.
internato agg. interned. ♦ **internato** sm. (scol.) boarding-school.
internazionale agg. international.
internazionalismo sm. internationalism.
internazionalizzare vt. to internationalize.
interno agg. 1. internal, interior 2. (interiore) inner. ♦ **interno** sm. interior.
intero agg. 1. whole 2. (intatto) intact.
interpellanza sf. interrogation.
interpellare vt. 1. (pol.) to interpellate 2. (giur.) to summon 3. (chiedere) to ask.
interplanetario agg. interplanetary.
interpolare vt. to interpolate.
interpolazione sf. interpolation.
interporre vt. to interpose.
interpretare vt. 1. to interpret, to render 2. (teat.) to play.
interpretativo agg. interpretative.
interpretazione sf. 1. interpretation 2. (cine) starring 3. (mus.) performance 4. (teat.) acting.
intèrprete s. 1. interpreter 2. (teat.; cine) actor, player.
interpunzione sf. punctuation.
interramento sm. burial.
interrare vt. 1. to bury 2. (riempire di terra) to fill up with earth.
interrogare vt. to question.
interrogativo agg. interrogative || punto —, question mark. ♦ **interrogativo** sm. interrogative.

interrogatore *agg.* interrogating. ♦ **interrogatore** *sm.* examiner.

interrogatorio *sm.* examination.

interrogazione *sf.* 1. interrogation 2. (*scol.*) oral test.

interròmpere *vt.* to interrupt. ♦ **interròmpersi** *vr.* to stop.

interrotto *agg.* interrupted || *strada interrotta*, blocked road.

interruttore *sm.* (*elettr.*) switch.

interruzione *sf.* interruption.

intersecare *vt.* to intersect.

intersezione *sf.* intersection.

interstizio *sm.* interstice.

intervallare *vt.* to space.

intervallo *sm.* 1. interval 2. (*spazio*) space.

intervenire *vi.* 1. to intervene 2. (*essere presenti*) to be present.

interventismo *sm.* interventionism.

interventista *s.* interventionist.

intervento *sm.* 1. intervention 2. (*presenza*) presence 3. (*chir.*) operation.

intervenuto *agg.* present. ♦ **intervenuto** *sm.* person present.

intervista *sf.* interview.

intervistare *vt.* to interview.

intesa *sf.* agreement.

inteso *agg.* 1. agreed (upon) 2. (*mirante*) aiming (at).

intèssere *vt.* to interweave (*v. irr.*).

intestare *vt.* to head, to register. ♦ **intestarsi** *vr.* to be determinated.

intestatario *sm.* holder.

intestato *agg.* 1. headed 2. (*giur.*) registered 3. (*senza testamento*) intestate 4. (*ostinato*) stubborn.

intestazione *sf.* 1. title 2. (*di lettera ecc.*) heading.

intestinale *agg.* intestinal.

intestino *sm.* intestine.

intimare *vt.* 1. (*ordinare*) to order 2. (*ingiungere*) to summon.

intimazione *sf.* 1. order 2. (*ingiunzione*) summons.

intimidatorio *agg.* intimidatory.

intimidazione *sf.* intimidation.

intimidire *vt.* 1. to make (*v. irr.*) shy 2. (*impaurire*) to intimidate.

intimità *sf.* 1. privacy 2. (*familiarità*) familiarity.

intimo *agg.* 1. intimate 2. (*profondo*) deep. ♦ **intimo** *sm.* 1. (*amico*) intimate 2. (*animo*) soul || *nell'—*, at heart.

intimorire *vt.* to frighten. ♦ **intimorirsi** *vr.* to get (*v. irr.*)

frightened.

intìngere *vt.* to dip.

intìngolo *sm.* 1. gravy 2. (*salsa*) sauce.

intirizzire *vt.* to benumb.

intitolare *vt.* 1. to entitle 2. (*dedicare*) to dedicate.

intoccàbile *agg. e sm.* untouchable.

intolleràbile *agg.* intolerable.

intollerante *agg.* intolerant.

intolleranza *sf.* intolerance.

intonacare *vt.* to plaster.

intonacatura *sf.* plastering.

intonaco *sm.* plaster.

intonare *vt.* 1. to tune 2. (*cantilenare*) to intone. ♦ **intonarsi** *vr.* 1. to harmonize (with) 2. (*di colori*) to match.

intonato *agg.* 1. in tune 2. (*di colori*) matching.

intonazione *sf.* 1. intonation 2. (*di strumenti*) tuning 3. (*di colori, voce*) tone.

intonso *agg.* (*di libri*) uncut.

intontimento *sm.* stunning.

intontire *vt.* to stun.

intoppare *vt.* to stumble (on).

intoppo *sm.* 1. obstacle 2. (*fig.*) hitch.

intorbidare *vt.* to make (*v. irr.*) muddy. ♦ **intorbidarsi** *vr.* to become (*v. irr.*) muddy.

intorno *avv.* round, around. ♦ **intorno a** *prep.* 1. round, around 2. (*circa, su di*) about.

intorpidimento *sm.* numbness.

intorpidire *vt.* to benumb. ♦ **intorpidirsi** *vr.* to grow (*v. irr.*) numb.

intossicare *vt.* to poison.

intossicazione *sf.* poisoning.

intraducìbile *agg.* untranslatable.

intralciare *vt.* to hinder, to interfere.

intralcio *sm.* hindrance.

intrallazzo *sm.* 1. plotting 2. (*imbroglio*) swindle.

intramezzare *vt.* to interpose, to alternate.

intramontàbile *agg.* everlasting.

intramuscolare *agg.* intermuscular.

intransigente *agg.* strict, intransigent.

intransigenza *sf.* intransigence.

intransitivo *agg. e sm.* intransitive.

intrappolare *vt.* to entrap.

intraprendente *agg.* enterprising.

intraprendenza *sf.* enterprise.

intraprèndere vt. 1. to undertake (v. irr.), to start 2. (una professione) to go (v. irr.) in for.

intrattàbile agg. intractable.

intrattenere vt. to entertain. ♦ **intrattenersi** vr. 1. to linger 2. (dilungarsi) to dwell (v. irr.).

intravedere vt. 1. (vedere di sfuggita) to catch (v. irr.) a glimpse of 2. (vedere indistintamente) to see (v. irr.) indistinctly.

intrecciare vt. 1. to interlace || — danze, to dance 2. (capelli, nastri) to plait.

intréccio sm. 1. interlacement 2. (di romanzi) plot.

intrèpido agg. brave, fearless.

intricare vt. to tangle. ♦ **intricarsi** vr. to get (v. irr.) entangled.

intrico sm. tangle.

intrìdere vt. to soak.

intrigante agg. crafty. ♦ **intrigante** sm. intriguer.

intrigare vi. to intrigue. ♦ **intrigarsi** vr. to meddle (with).

intrigo sm. intrigue, plot.

intrìnseco agg. intrinsic.

intristire vi. 1. to pine away 2. (incattivire) to grow (v. irr.) wicked.

introdotto agg. 1. (importato) imported 2. (conosciuto) well-known.

introdurre vt. 1. to introduce 2. (far entrare) to show (v. irr.) in. ♦ **introdursi** vr. to get (v. irr.) into, to slip into.

introduttivo agg. introductory.

introduzione sf. introduction.

introitare vt. to cash.

intròito sm. profit.

introméttere vt. to introduce. ♦ **introméttersi** vr. to interfere.

intromissione sf. intrusion.

intronare vt. to stun.

introspettivo agg. introspective.

introspezione sf. introspection.

introvàbile agg. not to be found.

introversione sf. introversion.

introverso agg. introverted. ♦ **introverso** sm. introvert.

intrufolarsi vr. to intrude (in).

intruglio sm. bad mixture.

intruppamento sm. trooping.

intrupparsi vr. to troope.

intrusione sf. intrusion.

intruso sm. intruder.

intuìbile agg. guessable.

intuire vt. to guess, to perceive.

intuitivo agg. intuitive.

intùito sm. intuition, insight.

intuizione sf. intuition.

inturgidimento sm. swelling.

inturgidire vi. to swell (up). **inturgidirsi** vr. to swell (up).

inuguale agg. unlike.

inumanità sf. inhumanity.

inumano agg. inhuman.

inumare vt. to inter.

inumazione sf. interment.

inumidire vt. to moisten. ♦ **inumidirsi** vr. to moisten.

inurbanità sf. incivility.

inurbano agg. uncivil.

inurbarsi vr. to inurbate.

inusitato agg. unusual.

inùtile agg. useless.

inutilità sf. uselessness.

inutilizzàbile agg. unusable.

invadente agg. intrusive.

invadenza sf. intrusiveness.

invàdere vt. to invade.

invaghimento sm. fancy (for).

invaghirsi vr. to take (v. irr.) a fancy (for), to fall (v. irr.) in love (with).

invaghito agg. fond (of), infatuated.

invalere vi. to prevail.

invalicàbile agg. impassable.

invalidare vt. to invalidate.

invalidazione sf. invalidation.

invalidità sf. invalidity.

invàlido agg. e sm. invalid.

invalso agg. prevailed.

invano avv. in vain.

invariàbile agg. 1. invariable 2. (di tempo) unchangeable.

invariabilità sf. invariability.

invariato agg. unchanged.

invasamento sm. obsession.

invasare vt. to possess.

invasato agg. possessed. ♦ **invasato** sm. possessed person.

invasione sf. invasion.

invasore sm. invader.

invecchiamento sm. ageing.

invecchiare vt. to make (v. irr.) old. ♦ **invecchiare** vi. to grow (v. irr.) old.

invece avv. on the contrary || — di, instead of.

inveire vi. to rail (at).

invelenire vt. to embitter.

invendìbile agg. unsaleable.

invendicato agg. unavenged.

invenduto agg. unsold.

inventare *vt.* to invent.
inventariare *vt.* to inventory.
inventario *sm.* inventory ‖ *con beneficio d'—*, with reservation.
inventiva *sf.* inventiveness.
inventivo *agg.* inventive.
inventore *sm.* inventor.
invenzione *sf.* invention.
inverdire *vi.* to turn green.
inverecondia *sf.* immodesty.
inverecondo *agg.* immodest.
inverificàbile *agg.* unverifiable.
invernale *agg.* 1. winter (*attr.*) 2. (*da inverno*) wintry.
invernata *sf.* wintertime.
inverno *sm.* winter.
invero *avv.* indeed.
inverosimiglianza *sf.* unlikelihood.
inverosimile *agg.* unlikely.
inversione *sf.* inversion.
inverso *agg.* 1. (*mat.*) inverse 2. opposite, contrary. ♦ **inverso** *sm.* opposite, contrary.
invertebrato *agg.* e *sm.* invertebrate.
invertibile *agg.* invertible.
invertire *vt.* to invert ‖ *— la marcia*, to reverse.
invertito *sm.* invert.
invertitore *sm.* reverse gear.
investigare *vt.* to inquire.
investigativo *agg.* investigative.
investigatore *sm.* detective.
investigazione *sf.* investigation.
investimento *sm.* 1. investment 2. collision 3. (*stradale*) running down.
investire *vt.* 1. to invest (with) 2. (*comm.*) to invest 3. (*assalire*) to assail 4. (*auto*) to run (*v. irr.*) down.
investitore *sm.* (*comm.*) investor.
investitura *sf.* investiture.
inveterato *agg.* inveterate.
invetriata *sf.* glass window.
invettiva *sf.* invective.
inviare *vt.* to send (*v. irr.*).
inviato *sm.* 1. messenger 2. (*in diplomazia*) envoy 3. (*in giornalismo*) correspondent.
invidia *sf.* envy: *per —*, out of envy.
invidiàbile *agg.* enviable.
invidiare *vt.* to envy.
invidioso *agg.* envious.
invigorire *vt.* to strengthen. ♦ **invigorirsi** *vr.* to strengthen.
inviluppare *vt.* to envelop, to wrap up.
invincìbile *agg.* invincible.

invincibilità *sf.* invincibility.
invio *sm.* 1. (*per posta*) mailing 2. (*di merci*) forwarding 3. (*per nave*) shipment 4. (*di danaro*) remittance.
inviolàbile *agg.* inviolable.
inviolabilità *sf.* inviolability.
inviperirsi *vr.* to become (*v. irr.*) furious.
inviperito *agg.* furious.
invischiare *vt.* 1. to lime 2. (*fig.*) to entangle. ♦ **invischiarsi** *vr.* to get (*v. irr.*) entangled.
invisìbile *agg.* invisible.
invisibilità *sf.* invisibility.
inviso *agg.* disliked.
invitante *agg.* inviting.
invitare *vt.* 1. to invite 2. (*domandare*) to request.
invitato *agg.* invited. ♦ **invitato** *sm.* guest.
invito *sm.* invitation.
invitto *agg.* unconquered.
invocare *vt.* to invoke.
invocazione *sf.* invocation.
invogliare *vt.* to tempt.
involare *vt.* to abduct. ♦ **involarsi** *vr.* to flee, to run (*v. irr.*) away.
involontario *agg.* unintentional.
involto *agg.* bundle, parcel.
invòlucro *sm.* 1. envelope 2. (*bot.*) involucre.
involutivo *agg.* involutionary.
involuto *agg.* involved.
involuzione *sf.* 1. involution 2. (*decadenza*) decline.
invulneràbile *agg.* invulnerable.
invulnerabilità *sf.* invulnerability.
inzaccherare *vt.* to muddy. ♦ **inzaccherarsi** *vr.* to get (*v. irr.*) muddy.
inzuppare *vt.* 1. to soak 2. (*intingere*) to dip.
io *pron.* I: *— stesso*, I myself.
iodato *agg.* iodized. ♦ **iodato** *sm.* iodate.
iodio *sm.* iodine.
iole *sf.* gig.
ione *sm.* ion.
iònico *agg.* Ionic.
ionizzazione *sf.* ionization.
ionosfera *sf.* ionosphere.
iosa (*nella loc. avv.*) *a —*, in plenty.
iperalimentazione *sf.* hypernutrition.
ipèrbole *sf.* hyperbole.
iperbòlico *agg.* hyperbolic(al).
iperbòreo *agg.* hyperborean.

ipercrìtico agg. hypercritical.
ipermetropìa sf. hypermetropia.
ipermètrope agg. hypermetropic.
ipernutrizione sf. hypernutrition.
ipersensìbile agg. hypersensitive.
ipersensibilità sf. hypersensitivity.
ipertensione sf. hypertension.
iperteso agg. e sm. hypertensive.
ipertrofìa sf. hypertrophy.
ipnosi sf. hypnosis.
ipnòtico agg. hypnotic.
ipnotismo sm. hypnotism.
ipnotizzare vt. to hypnotize.
ipnotizzatore sm. hypnotizer.
ipocondrìa sf. hypochondria.
ipocondrìaco agg. e sm. hypochondriac.
ipocrisìa sf. hypocrisy.
ipòcrita agg. hypocritical. ♦ **ipòcrita** sm. hypocrite.
ipodèrmico agg. hypodermic.
ipodermoclisi sf. hypodermoclysis.
ipòfisi sf. hypophysis.
ipoteca sf. mortgage.
ipotecare vt. to mortgage.
ipotenusa sf. hypotenuse.
ipòtesi sf. 1. hypothesis (pl. -ses) 2. (supposizione) supposition.
ipotètico agg. hypothetical.
ìppica sf. horse-racing.
ìppico agg. horse (attr.).
ippocampo sm. hippocampus (pl. -pi).
ippocastano sm. horse-chestnut.
ippòdromo sm. race-course.
ippopòtamo sm. hippopotamus.
ira sf. anger, rage.
iracondo agg. irascible.
irascìbile agg. irritable.
irascibilità sf. irritability.
irato agg. angry.
iridato agg. iridescent.
ìride sf. iris.
iridescente agg. iridescent.
iridescenza sf. iridescence.
irlandese agg. Irish.
ironìa sf. irony.
irònico agg. ironic(al).
ironizzare vi. to make (v. irr.) ironical remarks.
ìroso agg. wrathful.
irradiamento sm. irradiation.
irradiare vt. to irradiate.
irradiazione sf. V. irradiamento.
irraggiare vt. V. irradiare.
irraggiungìbile agg. unreachable.
irragionévole agg. unreasonable.
irrancidire vi. to grow (v. irr.) rank.

irrazionale agg. irrational.
irrazionalità sf. irrationality.
irreale agg. unreal.
irrealizzàbile agg. unrealizable.
irrealtà sf. unreality.
irreconciliàbile agg. irreconcilable.
irrecuperàbile agg. irrecoverable.
irrefrenàbile agg. unrestrainable.
irrefutàbile agg. irrefutable.
irregolare agg. irregular.
irregolarità sf. irregularity.
irremovìbile agg. 1. immovable 2. (inflessibile) inflexible.
irreparàbile agg. irreparable.
irreperìbile agg. elusive: rendersi —, to hide (v. irr.) oneself.
irreprensìbile agg. irreproachable.
irrequietezza sf. restlessness.
irrequieto agg. restless.
irresistìbile agg. irresistible.
irresolutezza sf. irresolution.
irresoluto agg. hesitating.
irrespiràbile agg. unbreathable.
irresponsàbile agg. irresponsible.
irresponsabilità sf. irresponsibility.
irrestringìbile agg. unshrinkable.
irretire vt. to snare.
irreversìbile agg. irreversible.
irreversibilità sf. irreversibility.
irrevocàbile agg. irrevocable.
irriconoscìbile agg. unrecognizable.
irrìdere vt. to laugh at.
irriducìbile agg. irreducible.
irriflessione sf. thoughtlessness.
irriflessivo agg. thoughtless.
irrigàbile agg. irrigable.
irrigare vt. to irrigate.
irrigazione sf. irrigation.
irrigidimento sm. stiffening.
irrigìdire vt. to stiffen. ♦ **irrigidirsi** vr. to stiffen.
irriguo agg. well-watered.
irrilevante agg. insignificant.
irrimediàbile agg. irremediable.
irrisione sf. mockery.
irrisorio agg. derisory, paltry.
irrispettoso agg. disrespectful.
irritàbile agg. 1. (di persona) irritable 2. (di pelle) sensitive.
irritabilità sf. 1. (di persona) irritability 2. (di pelle) sensitiveness.
irritante agg. irritating.
irritare vt. to irritate. ♦ **irritarsi** vr. 1. to grow (v. irr.) angry 2. (di pelle) to become (v. irr.) irritated.
irritazione sf. 1. irritation 2. (di pelle) inflammation.

irriverente agg. disrespectful.

irriverenza sf. irreverence.

irrobustire vt. to strengthen. ◆
irrobustirsi vr. to strengthen.

irròmpere vi. 1. to break (v. irr.)
into 2. (di acque) to overflow.

irrorare vt. to sprinkle.

irroratrice sf. sprayer.

irruente agg. impetuous.

irruenza sf. impetuosity.

irruvidire vt. to roughen.

irruzione sf. irruption: fare —,
to rush into.

irsuto agg. shaggy.

irto agg. bristling (with).

iscritto sm. member.

iscrivere vt. 1. (a scuola, esami
ecc.) to enrol 2. (registrare) to record 3. (scolpire) to engrave. ◆
iscriversi vr. to enter, to join.

iscrizione sf. 1. inscription 2. (a
scuola, esami ecc.) entry || do-
manda d'—, application.

islàmico agg. Islamic.

islamismo sm. Islamism.

isocronismo sm. isochronism.

isola sf. island.

isolamento sm. 1. isolation 2.
(elettr.) insulation || — acustico,
sound-proofing.

isolano agg. insular. ◆ **isolano** sm.
islander.

isolante agg. insulating. ◆ **isolante** sm. insulator.

isolare vt. 1. to isolate 2. (elettr.)
to insulate || — acusticamente, to
soundproof. ◆ **isolarsi** vr. to
seclude oneself.

isolato agg. 1. isolated 2. (elettr.)
insulated. ◆ **isolato** sm. (edil.)
block.

isolatore sm. insulator.

isolazionismo sm. isolationism.

isolazionista s. isolationist.

isolotto sm. islet.

isomorfismo sm. isomorphism.

isomorfo agg. isomorphous.

isòscele agg. isosceles.

isotèrmico agg. isothermal.

isòtopo sm. isotope.

isòtropo sm. isotrope.

ispànico agg. Hispanic.

ispanismo sm. Hispanicism.

ispanista s. Hispanist.

ispettorato sm. inspectorate.

ispettore sm. inspector.

ispezionare vt. to inspect.

ispezione sf. inspection.

ispido agg. hispid.

ispirare vt. to inspire (with). ◆
ispirarsi vr. to draw (v. irr.) one's
inspiration (from).

ispirato agg. 1. inspired 2. (basato)
imbued (with).

ispiratore agg. inspiring. ◆ **ispiratore** sm. inspirer.

ispirazione sf. inspiration.

israeliano agg. e sm. Israeli.

israelita agg. e s. Israelite.

issare vt. to hoist.

istantànea sf. snapshot: fare un'—,
to snapshot.

istantaneità sf. instantaneousness.

istantàneo agg. instantaneous.

istante sm. instant || all'—, sull'—,
instantly.

istanza sf. 1. request, instance 2.
(supplica) entreaty 3. (domanda
scritta) application.

istèrico agg. hysteric(al). ◆ **istèrico** sm. hysterical man (pl. -men).

isterilire vt. to sterilize. ◆ **isteri-
lirsi** vr. to become (v. irr.) barren.

isterismo sm. hysteria.

istigare vt. to instigate.

istigatore sm. instigator.

istigazione sf. instigation.

istintivo agg. instinctive.

istinto sm. instinct.

istituire vt. 1. to institute 2. (fondare) to found 3. (giur.) to appoint.

istituto sm. 1. institute 2. (istituzione) institution 3. (scuola)
school.

istitutore sm. tutor.

istitutrice sf. governess.

istituzionale agg. institutional.

istituzione sf. institution.

istmo sm. isthmus (pl. -mi).

istologia sf. histology.

istrice sm. hedgehog.

istrione sm. 1. (teat.) histrion 2.
(ciarlatano) quack.

istriònico agg. histrionic.

istruire vt. 1. to teach (v. irr.) 2.
(dare istruzioni) to instruct, to direct 3. (giur.) to institute. ◆
istruirsi vr. to educate oneself.

istruito agg. learned.

istruttivo agg. instructive.

istruttore sm. instructor: giudice
—, examining magistrate.

istruttoria sf. examination || apri-
re l'—, to open proceedings.

istruzione sf. 1. education 2. (cultura) learning 3. (insegnamento)
teaching 4. (ordine) instruction.

istupidire vt. to make (v. irr.) stupid. ♦ **istupidirsi** v.r. to become (v. irr.) stupid.

italiano agg. e sm. Italian.

itinerario sm. itinerary.

itterizia sf. jaundice.

ittiologia sf. ichthyology.

ittiòlogo sm. ichthyologist.

iugoslavo agg. e sm. Yugoslav.

iugulare agg. jugular.

iuta sf. jute.

ivi avv. there.

L

la[1] art. the. ♦ **la** pron. **1.** (per donna) her **2.** (per animale e cosa) it **3.** (forma di cortesia) you.

la[2] sm. (mus.) A.

là avv. there || l'al di —, the hereafter; — per —, on the spot; al di — di, beyond; più in —, (spazio) further on, (tempo) later on.

labbro sm. lip.

labiale agg. labial.

làbile agg. fleeting: memoria —, weak memory.

labirinto sm. labyrinth.

laboratorio sm. **1.** laboratory **2.** (artigianale) workshop.

laboriosità sf. laboriousness.

laborioso agg. laborious.

laburismo sm. labourism.

laburista agg. labour || partito —, Labour Party. ♦ **laburista** s. Labourite.

lacca sf. lacquer.

laccare vt. to lacquer.

laccatura sf. lacquering.

laccio sm. **1.** string || lacci da scarpe, shoe-laces **2.** (trappola) snare || prendere al — (fig.), to ensnare.

laceramento sm. tearing.

lacerante agg. rending.

lacerare vt. to tear (v. irr.) (up), to rend (v. irr.) (anche fig.). ♦ **lacerarsi** vr. to tear.

lacerazione sf. laceration.

làcero agg. **1.** torn **2.** (med.) lacerated.

laconicità sf. laconicism.

lacònico agg. laconic(al).

làcrima sf. tear.

lacrimale agg. lachrymal.

lacrimare vi. to weep (v. irr.).

lacrimazione sf. lachrymation.

lacrimévole agg. tearful.

lacrimògeno agg. lachrymatory: gas —, tear-gas.

lacrimoso agg. tearful.

lacuna sf. gap.

lacunoso agg. lacunous.

lacustre agg. lacustrine.

laddove cong. whereas. ♦ **laddove** avv. (there) where.

ladra sf. woman thief.

ladro agg. thieving. ♦ **ladro** sm. thief: al —!, stop thief!

ladrocinio sm. theft.

ladrone sm. robber.

ladroneria sf. robbery.

laggiù avv. down there.

lagna sf. lament.

lagnanza sf. complaint.

lagnarsi vr. to complain (of).

lago sm. lake.

laguna sf. lagoon.

lagunare agg. lagoon (attr.).

laicato sm. laity.

laicismo sm. laicism.

laicizzare vt. to laicize.

làico agg. laic. ♦ **làico** sm. layman (pl. -men).

laidezza sf. ugliness, foulness.

làido agg. **1.** dirty **2.** (brutto) ugly.

lama[1] sf. blade.

lama[2] sm. (zool.) llama.

lama[3] sm. (monaco buddista) lama.

lambiccare vt. to distil || lambiccarsi il cervello, to rack one's brains.

lambiccato agg. **1.** distilled **2.** (ricercato) over-elaborate.

lambicco sm. alembic.

lambire vt. to lick.

lamella sf. lamella (pl. -lae).

lamentare vt. to lament. ♦ **lamentarsi** vr. to moan.

lamentazione sf. lamentation.

lamentela sf. complaint.

lamentévole agg. mournful.

lamento sm. moan.

lamentoso agg. mournful.

lametta sf. razor-blade.

lamiera sf. sheet.

làmina sf. lamina (pl. -nae).

laminare vt. to laminate.

laminato agg. **1.** (tessuto) lamé **2.** (metallo) rolled section.

laminatoio sm. rolling-mill.

làmpada sf. lamp.

lampadario sm. chandelier, lamp holder.

lampadina *sf.* bulb.

lampante *agg.* glaring, evident.

lampeggiamento *sm.* 1. flashing, lightning 2. *(di fari, semafori ecc.)* winking 3. *(di auto)* to blink.

lampeggiare *vi.* 1. to flash, to lighten 2. *(di fari, semafori ecc.)* to wink.

lampeggiatore *sm.* 1. winking light 2. *(di auto)* blinker.

lampione *sm.* street-lamp.

lampo *sm.* 1. lightning 2. *(luce istantanea, anche fig.)* flash || *chiusura* —, zip-fastener.

lampone *sm.* raspberry.

lampreda *sf.* lamprey.

lana *sf.* wool.

lancetta *sf.* 1. *(di quadrante)* hand 2. *(di chirurgo)* lancet.

lancia[1] *sf.* lance.

lancia[2] *sf.* *(mar.)* launch || — *di salvataggio,* lifeboat.

lanciafiamme *sm.* flame-thrower.

lanciare *vt.* 1. to throw *(v. irr.)* 2. *(fig.)* to launch || — *un'occhiata,* to cast *(v. irr.)* a glance. ♦ **lanciarsi** *vr.* to dash.

lanciatore *sm.* thrower.

lanciere *sm.* lancer.

lancinante *agg.* piercing.

lancio *sm.* 1. throwing 2. *(pubblicitario)* launching.

landa *sf.* moor.

languido *agg.* languid.

languire *vi.* to languish.

languore *sm.* languor.

laniero' *agg.* woollen.

lanificio *sm.* wool factory.

lanolina *sf.* lanolin.

lanoso *agg.* woolly.

lanterna *sf.* lantern.

lanugine *sf.* down.

laparatomia *sf.* laparotomy.

lapidare *vt.* to stone.

lapidario *agg.* lapidary.

lapidazione *sf.* lapidation.

lapide *sf.* 1. tablet 2. *(sepolcrale)* tombstone.

lapis *sm.* pencil.

lardellare *vt.* to lard.

lardo *sm.* lard, bacon.

larga *(nella loc. avv.)* **alla** —, away (from).

largheggiare *vi.* to abound (with).

larghezza *sf.* 1. breadth 2. *(liberalità)* liberality 3. *(abbondanza)* plenty.

largire *vt.* to bestow (upon).

largitore *sm.* bestower.

largizione *sf.* bestowal.

largo *agg.* broad, wide. ♦ **largo** *sm.* 1. *(mar.)* open sea 2. *(piazza)* square || *prendere il* —, to set *(v. irr.)* sail; *(fig.)* to run *(v. irr.)* away; *andare al* —, to take *(v. irr.)* to the open sea; *fare* —, to make *(v. irr.)* room.

larice *sm.* larch.

laringe *sf.* larynx.

laringite *sf.* laryngitis.

larva *sf.* larva *(pl. -ae)*.

lasciapassare *sm.* pass.

lasciare *vt.* 1. to leave *(v. irr.)* 2. *(permettere)* to let *(v. irr.)*, to allow. ♦ **lasciarsi** *vr. rec. (separarsi)* to part.

làscito *sm.* legacy.

lascivia *sf.* lust.

lascivo *agg.* lustful.

lassativo *agg. e sm.* laxative.

lasso *sm.* lapse: *dopo un certo — di tempo,* after a lapse of time.

lassù *avv.* up there.

lastra *sf.* 1. *(vetro)* glass' sheet 2. *(di pietra)* slab 3. *(di metallo, foto)* plate.

lastricare *vt.* to pave.

lastricatura *sf.* paving.

làstrico *sm.* pavement || *essere sul* — *(fig.)*, to be destitute.

latente *agg.* latent.

laterale *agg.* side: *via* —, by-street.

lateralmente *avv.* sideways.

laterizi *sm. pl.* bricks.

làtice *sm.* latex.

latifondista *sm.* landowner.

latifondo *sm.* large landed estate.

latinismo *sm.* Latinism.

latinista *s.* Latinist.

latinità *sf.* Latinity.

latino *agg. e sm.* Latin.

latitante *agg.* absconding: *essere* —, to be in hiding. ♦ **latitante** *s.* absconder.

latitanza *sf.* hiding: *darsi alla* —, to evade arrest.

latitùdine *sf.* latitude.

lato[1] *sm.* 1. side 2. *(fig.)* point of view || *d'altro* —, on the other hand; *da un* —, on the one hand.

lato[2] *agg.* wide || *in senso* —, in a broad sense.

latore *sm.* bearer.

latrare *vi.* to bark.

latrato *sm.* barking.

latrina *sf.* lavatory.

latta *sf.* tin.

lattaio *sm.* milkman (*pl.* -men).
lattante *agg.* unweaned. ♦ **lattante** *s.* suckling (baby).
latte *sm.* milk.
làtteo *agg.* milky.
latterìa *sf.* dairy.
latticini *sm. pl.* dairy products.
lattiera *sf.* milk-jug.
lattiginoso *agg.* 1. milky 2. (*bot.*) lactescent.
lattoniere *sm.* tinker.
lattòsio *sm.* lactose.
lattuga *sf.* lettuce.
laudativo *agg.* laudatory.
làurea *sf.* degree.
laureare *vt.* to confer a degree (on). ♦ **laurearsi** *vr.* to graduate.
laureato *agg.* graduated. ♦ **laureato** *sm.* graduate || — *in lettere*, Doctor of Literature Degree.
làuro *sm.* laurel.
làuto *agg.* sumptuous || *lauti guadagni*, large profits.
lava *sf.* lava.
lavàbile *agg.* washable.
lavabo *sm.* washbowl.
lavaggio *sm.* washing: — *a secco*, dry cleaning.
lavagna *sf.* 1. blackboard 2. (*ardesia*) slate.
lavanda[1] *sf.* 1. washing 2. (*med.*) lavage.
lavanda[2] *sf.* (*bot.*) lavender.
lavandaia *sf.* laundress.
lavanderìa *sf.* laundry.
lavandino *sm.* sink.
lavapiatti *s.* dish-washer.
lavare *vt.* to wash: — *a secco*, to dry-clean. ♦ **lavarsi** *vr.* to wash (oneself).
lavata *sf.* wash || *dare una — di capo* (*fig.*), to scold.
lavativo *sm.* 1. (*med.*) enema 2. (*fig.*) lazy-bones.
lavatoio *sm.* 1. wash-house 2. (*asse per lavare*) wash-board.
lavatrice *sf.* 1. washer 2. (*lavabiancheria*) washing machine.
lavatura *sf.* washing.
lavina *sf.* landslip.
lavorante *sm.* worker.
lavorare *vi. e vt.* to work.
lavorativo *agg.* working || *ora lavorativa*, man-hour.
lavoratore *sm.* worker. ♦ **lavoratore** *sm.* worker — *a giornata*, day-labourer.
lavorazione *sf.* 1. processing 2. (*fattura*) work 3. (*agr.*) tilling ||

— *a mano*, handwork.
lavorìo *sm.* intense activity.
lavoro *sm.* 1. work 2. (*occupazione*) job || — *a ore*, work by the hour; *lavori di casa*, housework; — *su ordinazione*, work to order; *eccesso di* —, overwork; — *in proprio*, self-employment.
lazzaretto *sm.* lazaretto.
lazzarone *sm.* slacker.
lazzo *sm.* joke.
le *art.* the. ♦ **le** *pron.* 1. (*sing.*) her, to her 2. (*pl.*) them 3. (*forma di cortesia*) you, to you.
leale *agg.* 1. loyal 2. (*corretto*) fair.
lealtà *sf.* 1. loyalty 2. (*correttezza*) fairness.
lebbra *sf.* leprosy.
lebbrosario *sm.* leper hospital.
lebbroso *agg.* leprous. ♦ **lebbroso** *sm.* leper.
leccapiedi *sm.* bootlicker.
leccare *vt.* to lick. ♦ **leccarsi** *vr.* to lick (oneself).
leccata *sf.* licking.
leccornìa *sf.* dainty.
lécito *agg.* 1. lawful 2. (*giusto*) right 3. (*permesso*) allowed. ♦ **lécito** *sm.* right.
lèdere *vt.* 1. to injure 2. (*danneggiare*) to damage.
lega *sf.* 1. league 2. (*di metalli*) alloy || *di buona* —, genuine; *di cattiva* —, low.
legàccio *sm.* string.
legale *agg.* legal, lawful || *procedere per vie legali*, to have recourse to the law. ♦ **legale** *sm.* lawyer.
legalità *sf.* legality.
legalizzare *vt.* 1. to legalize 2. (*autenticare*) to authenticate.
legalizzazione *sf.* 1. legalization 2. (*autenticazione*) authentication.
legame *sm.* 1. string 2. (*vincolo*) tie 3. (*connessione*) link.
legamento *sm.* 1. string 2. (*anat.*) ligament.
legare[1] *vt.* 1. to tie 2. (*di metalli*) to alloy (with) 3. (*aver connessione*) to be connected. ♦ **legarsi** *vr.* to bind (*v. irr.*) oneself.
legare[2] *vt.* (*giur.*) to bequeath.
legatario *sm.* legatee.
legato[1] *sm.* 1. ambassador 2. (*eccl.*) legate.
legato[2] *sm.* (*giur.*) legacy.
legatore *sm.* binder.
legatorìa *sf.* bookbinder's establishment.

legatura *sf.* **1.** binding **2.** (*mus.; med.*) ligature.
legazione *sf.* legation.
legge *sf.* **1.** law **2.** (*singola*) act **3.** (*regola*) rule || *progetto di —*, bill; *a norma di —*, according to the law; *a termini di —*, as bv law enacted.
leggenda *sf.* legend.
leggendario *agg.* legendary.
lèggere *vt.* to read (*v. irr.*).
leggerezza *sf.* lightness.
leggero *agg.* light.
leggiadrìa *sf.* loveliness.
leggiadro *agg.* lovely.
leggìbile *agg.* readable.
leggìo *sm.* **1.** reading-desk **2.** (*mus.*) music-stand.
legiferare *vi.* to legislate.
legionario *agg. e sm.* legionary.
legione *sf.* legion.
legislativo *agg.* legislative.
legislatore *sm.* legislator.
legislatura *sf.* legislature.
legislazione *sf.* legislation.
legittimare *vt.* to legitimate.
legittimazione *sf.* legitimation.
legittimìtà *sf.* legitimacy.
legìttimo *agg.* legitimate.
legna *sf.* wood || *— da ardere*, fire-wood.
legnaia *sf.* wood-store.
legname *sm.* **1.** wood **2.** (*da costruzione*) timber.
legnata *sf.* blow with a cudgel.
legno *sm.* wood || *di —*, wooden.
legnosità *sf.* woodiness.
legnoso *agg.* **1.** woody **2.** (*duro*) tough.
legume *sm.* legume.
leguminoso *agg.* leguminous.
lei *pron.* **1.** (*sogg.*) she, (*compl.*) her **2.** (*forma di cortesia*) you.
lembo *sm.* **1.** edge **2.** (*pezzo*) strip.
lemma *sm.* lemma.
lèmure *sm.* lemur. ♦ **lèmuri** *sm. pl.* (*mit.*) lemures.
lena *sf.* **1.** energy **2.** (*respiro*) breath.
lenire *vt.* to soothe.
lenone *sm.* pander.
lente *sf.* lens: *— d'ingrandimento*, magnifying lens || *lenti*, glasses.
lentezza *sf.* slowness.
lenticchia *sf.* lentil.
lentìggine *sf.* freckle.
lentigginoso *agg.* freckly.
lento *agg.* **1.** slow **2.** (*non teso*) loose.

lenza *sf.* fishing-line.
lenzuolo *sm.* sheet.
leone *sm.* lion.
leonessa *sf.* lioness.
leonino *agg.* leonine.
leopardo *sm.* leopard.
lèpido *agg.* witty.
lepidòttero *sm.* lepidopteron (*pl. -era*).
leporino *agg.* leporine || *labbro —*, hare-lip.
lepre *sf.* hare.
lercio *agg.* filthy.
lèsbica *agg. e sf.* Lesbian.
lésina *sf.* awl.
lesinare *vi.* to be stingy. ♦ **lesinare** *vt.* to be stingy.
lesionare *vt.* to damage, to injure.
lesione *sf.* **1.** lesion, injury **2.** (*danno*) damage.
lesivo *agg.* harmful.
leso *agg.* **1.** injured **2.** (*danneggiato*) damaged.
lessare *vt.* to boil.
lessicale *agg.* lexical.
lèssico *sm.* lexicon.
lessicografìa *sf.* lexicography.
lessicologìa *sf.* lexicology.
lesso *agg.* boiled. ♦ **lesso** *sm.* boiled meat.
lestezza *sf.* quickness.
lesto *agg.* quick.
lestofante *sm.* swindler.
letale *agg.* lethal.
letamaio *sm.* dunghill.
letame *sm.* dung.
letàrgico *agg.* **1.** lethargic **2.** (*di animali, in inverno*) hibernating; (*id., in estate*) estivating.
letargo *sm.* **1.** lethargy **2.** (*di animali, in inverno*) hibernation; (*id., in estate*) estivation.
letizia *sf.* joy.
lèttera *sf.* letter || *alla —*, literally.
letterale *agg.* literal.
letterario *agg.* literary.
letterato *agg.* lettered. ♦ **letterato** *sm.* literary man.
letteratura *sf.* literature.
lettiga *sf.* stretcher.
letto *sm.* bed || *camera da —*, bed-room; *vagone —*, sleeping-car.
lettore *sm.* reader.
lettura *sf.* reading.
leucemìa *sf.* leukaemia.
leucociti *sm. pl.* leucocytes.
leucoma *sm.* leucoma.
leva[1] *sf.* **1.** lever **2.** (*fig.*) stimulus || *far — sui sentimenti di qu.*, to

play on so.'s feelings.

leva² sf. (mil.) draft: essere di —, to be due for draft.

levante sm. 1. east 2. (vento) levanter.

levare vt. 1. (sollevare) to raise 2. (togliere) to take (v. irr.) off. ♦ **levarsi** vr. 1. to rise (v. irr.) 2. (togliersi) to take off.

levata sf. 1. (di sole) rising 2. (di posta) collection || — di scudi rebellion.

levataccia sf. early rising.

levatoio agg. ponte —, drawbridge.

levatrice sf. midwife (pl. -wives).

levatura sf. intelligence.

levigare vt. to smooth.

levigatezza sf. smoothness.

levigato agg. smooth.

levitazione sf. levitation.

levriere sm. greyhound.

lezione sf. 1. lesson 2. (universitaria) lecture 3. (lett.) reading.

leziosàggine sf. affectation.

lezioso agg. affected.

lezzo sm. stench.

li pron. them.

lì avv. there: — vicino, near there; — dentro, in there || — per —, at first; di — a poco, soon after; giù di — (press'a poco), thereabouts; essere — per, to be on the point of.

liana sf. liana.

libagione sf. libation.

libbra sf. pound.

libeccio sm. Southwest wind.

libello sm. libel.

libèllula sf. dragonfly.

liberale agg. e sm. liberal.

liberalismo sm. liberalism.

liberalità sf. generosity.

liberalizzare vt. to liberalize.

liberare vt. 1. to free 2. (da pericoli) to rescue 3. (sbarazzare) to rid (v. irr.) (of). ♦ **liberarsi** vr. (sbarazzarsi) to get (v. irr.) rid (of).

liberatore agg. liberating. ♦ **liberatore** sm. deliverer.

liberazione sf. liberation.

libero agg. free.

liberoscambista agg. e sm. free-trader.

libertà sf. liberty, freedom.

libertario agg. e sm. libertarian.

liberticida agg. e s. liberticide.

libertinaggio sm. libertinage.

libertino agg. e sm. libertine.

libìdine sf. lust.

libidinoso agg. lustful.

libido sf. lustfulness.

libraio sm. bookseller.

librarsi vr. to hover.

librerìa sf. 1. bookshop 2. (mobile) bookcase.

libresco agg. bookish.

libretto sm. 1. booklet 2. (d'opera) libretto || — di assegni, cheque-book; — di risparmio, savings-book; — personale, record-book.

libro sm. book.

licenza sf. 1. (abuso) licence 2. (permesso) permission, leave 3. (documento) licence.

licenziamento sm. dismissal.

licenziare vt. to dismiss. ♦ **licenziarsi** vr. to give (v. irr.) up one's job.

licenziosità sf. licentiousness.

licenzioso agg. licentious.

lichene sm. lichen.

licitazione sf. sale by auction.

lido sm. shore.

lieto agg. glad.

lieve agg. slight.

lievitare vi. to rise (v. irr.). ♦ **lievitare** vt. to leaven.

lievitazione sf. leavening.

lièvito sm. 1. yeast 2. (fermento) ferment.

ligio agg. faithful, observant (of).

lignaggio sm. lineage.

ligneo agg. wooden.

lignite sf. lignite.

lilla sm. lilac.

lillipuziano agg. e sm. Lilliputian.

lima sf. file.

limaccioso agg. slimy.

limare vt. 1. to file 2. (fig.) to polish.

limatrice sf. (mecc.) shaping-machine.

limatura sf. filing.

limbo sm. limbo.

limitare vt. to limit. ♦ **limitarsi** vr. (controllarsi) to check oneself.

limitatezza sf. limitation.

limitativo agg. limitative.

limitato agg. limited.

limitazione sf. limitation: — delle nascite, birth-control.

lìmite sm. limit: — di velocità, speed-limit || — di rottura, breaking-point.

limìtrofo agg. neighbouring.

limo sm. slime.

limonata sf. lemonade.

limone *sm.* lemon.

limpidezza *sf.* clearness.

limpido *agg.* limpid, clear.

lince *sf.* lynx.

linciaggio *sm.* lynching.

linciare *vt.* to lynch.

lindo *agg.* neat.

linea *sf.* line || **aereo di** —, air-liner; **mantenere la** —, to keep (*v. irr.*) one's figure.

lineamenti *sm. pl.* 1. features 2. (*linee essenziali*) outlines.

lineare *agg.* 1. linear 2. (*fig.*) unswerving.

lineetta *sf.* 1. dash 2. (*trattino d'unione*) hyphen.

linfa *sf.* (*biol.*) lymph.

linfatico *agg.* lymphatic.

linfatismo *sm.* lymphatism.

lingotto *sm.* ingot.

lingua *sf.* 1. tongue 2. (*linguaggio*) language.

linguacciuto *agg.* talkative.

linguaggio *sm.* language.

linguetta *sf.* 1. flap 2. (*mecc.*; *di scarpe*) tongue.

linguista *s.* linguist.

linguistica *sf.* linguistics.

linguistico *agg.* linguistic.

linimento *sm.* liniment.

lino *sm.* flax.

linoleum *sm.* linoleum.

linone *sm.* lawn.

linotipia *sf.* linotyping.

linotipista *s.* linotypist.

liquefare *vt.* to liquefy. ♦ **liquefarsi** *vr.* to liquefy.

liquefazione *sf.* liquefaction.

liquidare *vt.* 1. to liquidate 2. (*comm.*) to sell (*v. irr.*) off, to settle || — **una questione**, to settle a question.

liquidatore *sm.* liquidator.

liquidazione *sf.* liquidation, sale.

liquido *agg. e sm.* liquid || **denaro** —, cash.

liquirizia *sf.* liquorice.

liquore *sm.* liqueur || **i liquori**, spirits.

liquoroso *agg.* liqueur-like.

lira *sf.* 1. (*moneta*) lira 2. (*mus.*) lyre.

lirica *sf.* 1. lyric poetry 2. (*teatro lirico*) opera.

lirico *agg.* lyric(al). ♦ **lirico** *sm.* lyrist.

lirismo *sm.* lyrism.

lisciare *vt.* 1. to smooth 2. (*adulare*) to flatter. ♦ **lisciarsi** *vr.* to

sleek oneself.

liscio *agg.* 1. smooth 2. (*di bevanda*) undiluted 3. (*semplice*) plain 4. (*di capelli*) sleek.

lisciva *sf.* lye.

liso *agg.* threadbare.

lista *sf.* 1. (*elenco*) list, note 2. (*striscia*) stripe.

listare *vt.* 1. to stripe 2. (*bordare*) to border.

listino *sm.* list.

litania *sf.* litany.

lite *sf.* 1. quarrel, wrangle 2. (*giur.*) lawsuit.

litigante *sm.* 1. wrangler 2. (*giur.*) litigant.

litigare *vi.* 1. to quarrel 2. (*giur.*) to litigate.

litigio *sm.* quarrel.

litigioso *agg.* quarrelsome.

litografia *sf.* 1. lithography 2. (*pezzo singolo*) lithograph.

litografico *agg.* lithographic.

litorale *agg.* littoral. ♦ **litorale** *sm.* coast.

litro *sm.* litre.

liturgia *sf.* liturgy.

liturgico *agg.* liturgic(al).

liuto *sm.* lute.

livellamento *sm.* levelling.

livellare *vt.* to level.

livellatrice *sf.* bulldozer.

livello *sm.* level: **a** — **del mare**, at sea-level; **passaggio a** —, level-crossing; **essere allo stesso** — **di**, to be on a level with.

livido *agg.* livid. ♦ **livido** *sm.* bruise.

livore *sm.* 1. (*invidia*) envy 2. (*odio*) hatred.

livrea *sf.* livery.

lizza *sf.* competition, lists (*pl.*) || **essere in** — (*fig.*), to be competing.

lo *art.* the. ♦ **lo** *pron.* 1. (*per uomo*) him 2. (*per animale, cosa*) it || — **credo**, I think so.

lobo *sm.* lobe.

locale *agg.* local. ♦ **locale** *sm.* 1. room 2. (*ritrovo*) place.

località *sf.* locality, spot.

localizzare *vt.* to localize.

localizzazione *sf.* localization.

locanda *sf.* inn.

locandiere *sm.* innkeeper.

locandina *sf.* play-bill.

locare *vt.* to rent.

locatario *sm.* tenant.

locativo *agg.* locative || **valore** —, rental value.

locatore *sm.* lessor.
locazione *sf.* lease.
locomotiva *sf.* locomotive.
locomotore *agg. e sm.* locomotive.
locomozione *sf.* locomotion.
locusta *sf.* locust.
locuzione *sf.* locution.
lodàbile *agg.* laudable.
lodare *vt.* to praise.
lodatore *sm.* praiser.
lode *sf.* praise.
lodévole *agg.* praiseworthy.
logaritmo *sm.* logarithm.
loggia *sf.* 1. (*arch.*) loggia 2. (*massonica*) lodge.
loggione *sm.* gallery.
lògica *sf.* logic.
logicità *sf.* logicality.
lògico *agg.* logical. ♦ **lògico** *sm.* logician.
logística *sf.* logistics.
logístico *agg.* logistic(al).
loglio *sm.* darnel.
logomachìa *sf.* logomachy.
logoramento *sm.* 1. wear 2. (*fig.*) wasting away.
logorante *agg.* wearing.
logorare *vt.* to wear (*v. irr.*) (out, down). ♦ **logorarsi** *vr.* to wear (out, down).
logorìo *sm.* wear and tear.
lògoro *agg.* worn (out, down).
lombàggine *sf.* lumbago.
lombardo *agg. e sm.* Lombard.
lombare *agg.* lumbar.
lombi *sm. pl.* loins.
lombrico *sm.* earth-worm.
longànime *agg.* forbearing.
longanimità *sf.* forbearance.
longevità *sf.* longevity.
longevo *agg.* longevous.
longitudinale *agg.* longitudinal.
longitùdine *sf.* longitude.
lontananza *sf.* distance: *in —*, in the distance.
lontano *agg.* 1. far 2. (*nel tempo*) far off, distant 3. (*vago*) vague. ♦ **lontano** *avv.* far || *da —*, from afar.
lontra *sf.* otter.
loquace *agg.* talkative.
loquacità *sf.* talkativeness.
loquela *sf.* glibness.
lordare *vt.* to soil. ♦ **lordarsi** *vr.* to get (*v. irr.*) dirty.
lordo *agg.* 1. (*sporco*) filthy 2. (*di peso*) gross.
loro *agg. poss.* their. ♦ **loro** *pron. poss.* theirs. ♦ **loro** *pron. pers.*

1. (*sogg.*) they, (*compl.*) them 2. (*forma di cortesia*) you.
losanga *sf.* lozenge.
losco *agg.* 1. (*bieco*) sinister 2. (*sospetto*) suspicious.
loto *sm.* 1. (*fango*) mud 2. (*bot.*) lotus.
lotta *sf.* 1. struggle 2. (*sport*) wrestling.
lottare *vi.* 1. to struggle 2. (*sport*) to wrestle.
lottatore *sm.* 1. struggler 2. (*sport*) wrestler.
lotterìa *sf.* lottery.
lottizzare *vt.* to lot.
lottizzazione *sf.* division into lots.
lotto *sm.* 1. lot 2. (*gioco*) state lottery.
lozione *sf.* lotion.
lubricità *sf.* lubricity.
lùbrico *agg.* 1. lubricous 2. (*fig.*) lascivious.
lubrificante *agg.* lubricating. ♦ **lubrificante** *sm.* lubricant.
lubrificare *vt.* to lubricate.
lubrificazione *sf.* lubrication.
lucchetto *sm.* padlock.
luccicante *agg.* glittering.
luccicare *vi.* to glitter.
luccichìo *sm.* glitter.
lùcciola *sf.* 1. firefly 2. (*senz'ali*) glow-worm.
luce *sf.* light || *alla — del sole* (*fig.*), openly; *dare alla — un bambino;* to give (*v. irr.*) birth to a child; *mettere in —*, to show (*v. irr.*); *venire alla — (nascere)*, to be born.
lucente *agg.* bright.
lucentezza *sf.* brightness.
lucerna *sf.* oil-lamp.
lucernario *sm.* skylight.
lucèrtola *sf.* lizard.
lucidare *vt.* to polish.
lucidatrice *sf.* 1. floor-polisher 2. (*mecc.*) polishing machine.
lucidatura *sf.* polishing.
lucidezza *sf.* 1. brightness 2. (*di mente*) lucidness.
lucidità *sf.* lucidity.
lùcido *agg.* 1. lucid 2. (*lucidato*) glossy. ♦ **lùcido** *sm.* 1. (*per scarpe*) shoe-polish 2. (*lucidezza*) shine.
lucignolo *sm.* wick.
lucrare *vt.* to profit.
lucrativo *agg.* profitable.
lucro *sm.* profit: *a scopo di —*, for the sake of gain.
ludibrio *sm.* mockery

luglio sm. July.

lùgubre agg. lugubrious.

lui pron. **1.** (sogg.) he **2.** (compl.) him.

lumaca sf. snail.

lume sm. light ‖ al — di candela, by candle-light; perdere il — della ragione, to be blinded by anger.

lumeggiare vt. (fig.) to put (v. irr.) in evidence.

luminare sm. luminary.

luminescenza sf. luminescence.

luminosità sf. brightness.

luminoso agg. bright.

luna sf. moon: — calante, waning moon; — crescente, waxing moon ‖ chiaro di —, moonlight; — di miele, honeymoon; avere la — (fig.), to be in the sulks.

lunare agg. lunar.

lunario sm. almanac ‖ sbarcare il —, to make (v. irr.) both ends meet.

lunàtico agg. moody.

lunazione sf. lunation.

lunedì sm. Monday.

lunetta sf. lunette.

lungàggine sf. slowness, delay.

lunghezza sf. length.

lungimirante agg. far-sighted.

lungo agg. **1.** long: a —, long; e — andare, in the long run **2.** (lento) slow ‖ in — e in largo, far and wide; di gran lunga, by far. ♦ **lungo** prep. **1.** along **2.** (durante) during.

lungofiume sm. embankment.

lungolago sm. lake-front.

lungomare sm. sea-front.

lungometraggio sm. feature film.

luogo sm. place: — di nascita, birthplace; sul —, on the spot; aver —, to take (v. irr.) place; dar —, to cause.

luogotenente sm. lieutenant.

lupa sf. she-wolf.

lupanare sm. brothel.

lupara sf. shotgun.

lupino sm. (bot.) lupine.

lupo sm. wolf ‖ — di mare, sea-dog; in bocca al —!, good luck!

lùppolo sm. hop.

lùrido agg. dirty.

luridume sm. dirt.

lusinga sf. allurement, flattery.

lusingare vt. to allure, to flatter.

lusinghiero agg. alluring, flattering.

lussare vt. to dislocate.

lussazione sf. dislocation.

lusso sm. luxury.

lussuoso agg. luxurious, rich.

lussureggiante agg. luxuriant.

lussureggiare vi. to thrive (v. irr.).

lussuria sf. lust.

lussurioso agg. lustful.

lustrale agg. lustral.

lustrare vt. to polish.

lustrascarpe sm. shoeblack.

lustratura sf. polish.

lustrino sm. spangle.

lustro agg. shining, shiny. ♦ **lustro** sm. lustre.

luteranésimo sm. Lutheranism.

luterano agg. e sm. Lutheran.

lutto sm. mourning: mettere il —, to go (v. irr.) into mourning.

luttuoso agg. mournful.

M

ma cong. **1.** but **2.** (tuttavia) however, still.

màcabro agg. macabre.

macaco sm. **1.** macaque **2.** (fig.) runt.

macché inter. you don't say it!

maccheroni sm. pl. macaroni (sing.).

macchia¹ sf. spot, stain.

macchia² sf. (boscaglia) bush: darsi alla —, to take (v. irr.) to the bush.

macchiare vt. to stain. ♦ **macchiarsi** vr. **1.** to get (v. irr.) stained **2.** (fig.) to soil oneself.

macchiato agg. spotted.

macchietta sf. **1.** caricature **2.** (di persona) character.

màcchina sf. **1.** engine, machine: — calcolatrice, calculating machine; — per cucire, sewing-machine; — da presa, cine-camera; — per scrivere, typewriter; — fotografica, camera; fatto a —, machine-made; andare in — (di giornali), to go (v. irr.) to press **2.** (automobile) car.

macchinale agg. mechanical.

macchinare vt. to plot.

macchinario sm. machinery.

macchinazione sf. machination.

macchinista sm. **1.** (ferr.) engine-driver **2.** (teat.) scene-shifter.

macchinoso agg. complicated.

macedonia *sf.* (*cuc.*) fruit-salad.

macellaio *sm.* butcher.

macellare *vt.* to slaughter.

macelleria *sf.* butcher's shop.

macello *sm.* **1.** (*luogo dove si macella*) slaughter-house **2.** (*massacro*) slaughter.

macerare *vt.* **1.** to soak **2.** (*di lino, canapa*) to ret. ♦ **macerarsi** *vr.* (*fig.*) to waste (away).

maceratoio *sm.* rettery.

macerazione *sf.* **1.** soaking **2.** (*industria tessile*) retting.

macerie *sf. pl.* rubble (*sing.*), ruins.

màcero *sm.* (*per canapa e lino*) retting-ground: *carta da* —, wastepaper.

machiavèllico *agg.* Machiavellian.

machiavellismo *sm.* Machiavellism.

macigno *sm.* boulder.

macilènto *agg.* emaciated.

macilènza *sf.* emaciation.

màcina *sf.* grindstone.

macinacaffè *sm.* coffee-mill.

macinapepe *sm.* pepper-mill.

macinare *vt.* **1.** to grind (*v. irr.*), to mince.

macinino *sm.* grinder.

maciullare *vt.* to crush.

macrocèfalo *agg.* macrocephalous.

macrocosmo *sm.* macrocosm.

macromolècola *sf.* macromolecule.

macroscòpico *agg.* macroscopic.

maculato *agg.* spotted.

madia *sf.* **1.** kitchen cupboard **2.** (*per pane*) kneading trough.

màdido *agg.* wet: — *di sudore*, bathed in sweat.

madonna *sf.* **1.** (*titolo*) Lady, My Lady **2.** (*relig.*) The Virgin Mary, Our Lady **3.** (*pitt.*) Madonna.

madornale *agg.* huge.

madre *sf.* mother.

madrepatria *sf.* mother-country.

madreperla *sf.* mother-of-pearl.

madreperlàceo *agg.* pearly.

madrèpora *sf.* madrepore.

madrepòrico *agg.* madreporic.

madrevite *sf.* **1.** nut screw **2.** (*utensile*) die.

madrigale *sm.* madrigal.

madrina *sf.* godmother.

maestà *sf.* majesty.

maestosità *sf.* majesty.

maestoso *agg.* majestic.

maestra *sf.* (*scol.*) teacher.

maestrale *sm.* mistral.

maestranza *sf.* skilled workers (*pl.*).

maestria *sf.* skill, ability.

maestro *sm.* **1.** (*scol.*) teacher **2.** (*uomo dotto*) master **3.** (*mus.*) conductor, "maestro" || *albero* —, mainmast.

mafia *sf.* "Mafia".

maga *sf.* sorceress.

magagna *sf.* flaw, imperfection.

magari *inter.* if only! ♦ **magari** *avv.* (*forse*) perhaps, maybe. ♦ **magari** *cong.* even if.

magazzinaggio *sm.* storage.

magazziniere *sm.* store-keeper.

magazzino *sm.* warehouse || *fondi di* —, unsold stock.

maggese *sm.* fallow land.

maggio *sm.* May.

maggiolino *sm.* May-bug.

maggiorana *sf.* marjoram.

maggioranza *sf.* majority, most (of).

maggiorare *vt.* to increase.

maggiorazione *sf.* increase, charge.

maggiordomo *sm.* butler.

maggiore *agg.* **1.** (*più grande, ampio*) greater, larger **2.** (*più vecchio*) older: *il* —, the oldest **3.** (*di fratelli*) elder (*fra due*), eldest (*fra molti*). ♦ **maggiore** *sm.* **1.** (*mil.*) major **2.** (*superiore*) superior.

maggiorenne *agg.* of age: *diventare* —, to come (*v. irr.*) of age. ♦ **maggiorenne** *sm.* major.

maggiorente *sm.* notable.

maggioritario *agg.* majority (*attr.*).

maggiormente *avv.* more, much more.

magia *sf.* magic.

màgiaro *agg.* e *sm.* Magyar.

magicamente *avv.* magically.

màgico *agg.* magical.

magistrale *agg.* **1.** magisterial || *scuola* —, teachers' institute **2.** (*eccellente*) masterly.

magistralmente *avv.* skilfully.

magistrato *sm.* Magistrate.

magistratura *sf.* magistracy.

maglia *sf.* **1.** (*di lavoro a maglia*) stitch || *lavorare a* —, to knit (*v. irr.*) **2.** (*indumento*) vest **3.** (*di catena*) link.

magliaia *sf.* knitter.

maglieria *sf.* hosiery.

maglificio *sm.* hosiery.

maglio *sm.* **1.** mallet **2.** (*mecc.*) hammer.

maglione *sm.* sweater.

magma *sm.* magma.

magnanimità *sf.* magnanimity.

magnànimo *agg.* magnanimous.

magnate *sm.* magnate.

magnesia *sf.* magnesia.

magnesio *sm.* magnesium. *lampo al —*, flash.

magnete *sm.* magnet.

magnètico *agg.* magnetic.

magnetismo *sm.* magnetism.

magnetite *sf.* magnetite.

magnetizzare *vt.* to magnetize.

magnetizzatore *sm.* magnetizer.

magnetizzazione *sf.* magnetization.

magnetòfono *sm.* tape-recorder.

magnetòmetro *sm.* magnetometer.

magnificamente *avv.* magnificently.

magnificare *vt.* to extol, to glorify.

magnificenza *sf.* magnificence.

magnìfico *agg.* magnificent.

magniloquente *agg.* magniloquent.

magniloquenza *sf.* magniloquence.

magnolia *sf.* magnolia.

mago *sm.* wizard.

magra *sf.* (*di fiumi*) low water.

magrezza *sf.* thinness.

magro *agg.* 1. thin 2. (*di carni*) lean.

mah *inter.* who knows!

mai *avv.* 1. ever 2. (*non mai*) never: — *e poi* —, never never; — *più*, never more; *caso* —, if; *non si sa* —, you never can tell; *meglio tardi che* —, better late than never.

maiale *sm.* 1. pig 2. (*carne*) pork.

maièutica *sf.* maieutics.

maiòlica *sf.* majolica.

maionese *sf.* mayonnaise

mais *sm.* maize.

maiùscola *sf.* capital letter.

maiuscoletto *sm.* small capitals.

maiùscolo *agg.* capital.

malaccorto *agg.* ill-advised

malachite *sf.* malachite.

malacreanza *sf.* rudeness.

malafede *sf.* bad faith.

malaffare *sm.* 1. *donna di* —, whore 2. *gente di* —, crooks (*pl.*).

malagévole *agg.* difficult, hard.

malagrazia *sf.* bad grace.

malalingua *sf.* backbiter.

malamente *avv.* badly.

malandato *agg.* in bad condition.

malandrino *sm.* 1. brigand 2. (*fam.*) rogue.

malànimo *sm.* malevolence.

malanno *sm.* 1. calamity 2. (*malattia*) illness.

malapena (*nella loc. avv.*) *a —*, hardly.

malaria *sf.* malaria.

malaticcio *agg.* sickly.

malato *agg.* sick, ill. ♦ **malato** *sm.* patient.

malattia *sf.* sickness, disease.

malauguratamente *avv.* unluckily.

malaugurato *agg.* ill-fated.

malaugurio *sm.* ill-omen.

malavita *sf.* underworld.

malavoglia *sf.* unwillingness || *di —*, reluctantly.

malcapitato *agg.* unlucky. ♦ **malcapitato** *sm.* victim.

malconcio *agg.* 1. battered 2. (*contuso*) bruised.

malcontento *agg.* dissatisfied (with). ♦ **malcontento** *sm.* discontent.

malcostume *sm.* immorality, corruption.

maldestro *agg.* awkward.

maldicente *agg.* disparaging. ♦ **maldicente** *sm.* slanderer.

maldicenza *sf.* backbiting.

maldisposto *agg.* ill-disposed, hostile.

male *sm.* 1. evil 2. (*malattia*) illness, disease 3. (*dolore fisico*) pain || *— di testa*, headache. ♦ **male** *avv.* badly, ill.

maledettamente *avv.* awfully.

maledetto *agg.* cursed.

malèdico *agg.* slanderous.

maledire *vt.* to curse.

maledizione *sf.* curse, malediction || *—!* (*inter.*), damn!

maleducato *agg.* rude, impolite.

maleducazione *sf.* rudeness.

malefatta *sf.* mischief.

maleficio *sm.* sorcery.

malèfico *agg.* harmful.

malerba *sf.* weed.

malese *agg.* e *sm.* Malay.

malèssere *sm.* 1. malaise 2. (*disagio*) uneasiness.

malestro *sm.* mischief.

malevolenza *sf.* malevolence.

malèvolo *agg.* malevolent.

malfamato *agg.* ill-famed.

malfatto *agg.* 1. ill-shaped 2. (*di abito*) ill-fitting.

malfattore *sm.* evil-doer.

malfermo *agg.* shaky || *salute malferma*, poor health.

malfido *agg.* unreliable.

malfondato *agg.* ill-grounded.

malformato *agg.* malformed.

malformazione *sf.* malformation.

malgarbo *sm.* bad grace.

malgoverno *sm.* misgovernment, misrule.

malgrado *prep. e avv.* in spite of. ♦ **malgrado (che)** *cong.* though, although.

malìa *sf. (fascino)* fascination.

maliarda *sf.* 1. *(donna affascinante)* fascinating woman 2. *(maga)* witch.

malignamente *avv.* maliciously.

malignare *vi.* to speak *(v. irr.)* ill (of).

malignità *sf.* malice.

maligno *agg.* malicious: *tumore* —, malignant tumor.

malinconìa *sf.* melancholy.

malinconicamente *avv.* sadly.

malincònico *agg.* melancholy.

malincuore *(nella loc. avv.) a* —, unwillingly.

malintenzionato *agg.* ill-disposed.

malinteso *agg.* misplaced. ♦ **malinteso** *sm.* misunderstanding.

malizia *sf.* 1. malice 2. *(astuzia)* cunning.

maliziosamente *avv.* artfully.

malizioso *agg.* malicious, mischievous.

malleàbile *agg.* malleable.

malleabilità *sf.* malleability.

mallevería *sf.* bail.

malloppo *sm.* swag.

malmenare *vt.* to manhandle.

malmesso *agg.* poorly dressed.

malnato *agg.* ill-bred.

malocchio *sm.* evil eye.

malora *sf.* ruin || *va alla* —!, go to the devil!

malore *sm.* illness.

malpensante *agg.* wrong-thinking.

malsano *agg.* unhealthy.

malsicuro *agg.* unsafe.

malta *sf.* mortar.

maltempo *sm.* bad weather.

maltenuto *agg.* untidy.

maltese *agg. e sm.* Maltese.

malto *sm.* malt.

maltolto *agg.* ill-gotten. ♦ **maltolto** *sm.* ill-gotten property.

maltosio *sm.* maltose.

maltrattamento *sm.* maltreatment.

maltrattare *vt.* to maltreat.

maltusianismo *sm.* Malthusianism.

maltusiano *agg. e sm.* Malthusian.

malumore *sm.* ill-humour.

malva *sf.* mallow.

malvagio *agg.* wicked.

malvagità *sf.* wickedness.

malversatore *sm.* embezzler.

malversazione *sf.* embezzlement.

malvisto *agg.* unpopular (with).

malvivente *sm.* gangster.

malvivenza *sf.* delinquency.

malvolere *sm.* ill-will.

malvolere *vi.* to dislike.

mamma *sf.* mama, mummy.

mammalucco *sm. (fam.)* simpleton.

mammella *sf.* 1. mamma *(pl. -ae)* 2. *(di animali da latte)* udder.

mammìfero *agg.* mammiferous. ♦ **mammìfero** *sm.* mammal.

màmmola *sf.* sweet-smelling violet.

mammùt *sm.* mammoth.

manata *sf.* slap.

manca *sf.* 1. left hand 2. *(parte sinistra)* left || *a dritta e a* —, on all sides.

mancante *agg.* incomplete.

mancanza *sf.* 1. lack, shortage 2. *(fallo)* fault || *sentire la — di qu.*, to miss so.

mancare *vi.* 1. to be lacking (in) 2. *(non esserci)* to be missing 3. *(venir meno)* to fail 4. *(agire scorrettamente)* to wrong (so.).

mancato *agg.* unsuccessful.

manchévole *agg.* defective.

manchevolezza *sf.* defect, fault.

mancia *sf.* tip || *dare la — a qu.*, to tip so.

manciata *sf.* handful.

mancina *sf.* left-hand.

mancino *agg.* left-handed. ♦ **mancino** *sm.* left-hander.

manco *avv.* not even.

mandamento *sm.* district.

mandante *sm.* 1. instigator 2. *(giur.)* principal.

mandare *vt.* 1. to send *(v. irr.)* 2. *(spedire)* to forward 3. *(emettere)* to give *(v. irr.)* out.

mandarino *sm.* mandarin.

mandata *sf.* batch || *— di chiave*, turn.

mandatario *sm.* mandatary.

mandato *sm.* 1. mandate 2. *(comm.)* agency 3. *(giur.)* warrant.

mandìbola *sf.* mandible.

mandola *sf.* mandola.

mandolinista *s.* mandolinist.

mandolino *sm.* mandolin.

màndorla *sf.* almond.

màndorlo *sm.* almond-tree.

mandràgora sf. mandrake.
mandria sf. herd.
mandriano sm. herdsman (pl. -men).
maneggévole agg. handy.
maneggiare vt. to handle.
maneggio sm. 1. (equitazione) riding-ground 2. (uso) use 3. (intrigo) plot.
manesco agg. rough, aggressive.
manette sf. pl. handcuff (sing.).
manforte sf. help.
manganellare vt. to cudgel.
manganello sm. cudgel.
manganese sm. manganese.
mangereccio agg. eatable.
mangiàbile agg. eatable.
mangiare vt. to eat (v. irr.).
mangiata sf. square meal.
mangiatoia sf. manger.
mangime sm. fodder.
mangiucchiare vt. to nibble (at).
mania sf. mania.
maniaco agg. 1. maniac 2. (fig.) crazy. ◆ **maniaco** sm. maniac.
mànica sf. sleeve || essere di — larga, stretta, to be indulgent, strict.
manicheismo sm. Manicheism.
manicheo agg. e sm. Manichean.
manichino sm. manikin.
mànico sm. handle.
manicomio sm. mental hospital.
manicotto sm. 1. muff 2. (mecc.) sleeve.
maniera sf. manner, way.
manierato agg. affected.
manierismo sm. mannerism.
maniero sm. castle.
manifattura sf. manufacture.
manifatturiero agg. manufacturing.
manifestante s. demonstrator.
manifestare vt. 1. to manifest, to show (v. irr.) 2. (pol.) to demonstrate.
manifestazione sf. 1. manifestation 2. (pol.) demonstration.
manifesto agg. manifest, clear, obvious. ◆ **manifesto** sm. 1. (affisso) poster 2. (volantino) leaflet 3. (dichiarazione) manifesto.
maniglia sf. handle.
manigoldo sm. scoundrel.
manioca sf. manioc.
manipolare vt. to manipulate.
manipolatore sm. manipulator.
manipolazione sf. manipulation.
manipolo sm. (eccl.; stor.) maniple.
maniscalco sm. blacksmith.

manna sf. 1. manna 2. (fig.) blessing.
mannaia sf. 1. axe 2. (della ghigliottina) knife.
mannaro agg. lupo —, werewolf.
mano sf. hand: fatto a —, handmade; stringere la —, to shake (v. irr.) hands with || a — armata, by force of arms; sotto —, underhand.
manodòpera sf. labour.
manòmetro sm. manometer.
manométtere vt. to tamper with.
manomissione sf. tampering.
manòpola sf. 1. knob 2. (impugnatura) handle.
manoscritto agg. handwritten. ◆ **manoscritto** sm. manuscript.
manovale sm. hodman (pl. -men).
manovella sf. crank.
manovra sf. manoeuvre, operation.
manovràbile agg. manoeuvrable.
manovrare vt. 1. to manoeuvre 2. (mecc.) to operate.
manovratore sm. operator, driver.
manrovescio sm. back-handed slap.
mansarda sf. mansard.
mansione sf. function.
mansuefare vt. to tame.
mansueto agg. meek, mild.
mansuetùdine sf. meekness.
mantella sf. cape.
mantello sm. cloak.
mantenere vt. to keep (v. irr.), to maintain: — la parola, to keep one's word.
mantenimento sm. maintenance.
màntice sm. bellows (pl.).
manto sm. cloak.
manuale agg. manual. ◆ **manuale** sm. handbook.
manubrio sm. 1. handle 2. (di bicicletta ecc.) handle-bar.
manufatto agg. hand-made. ◆ **manufatto** sm. hand-manufactured article.
manutèngolo sm. abettor.
manutenzione sf. maintenance, servicing.
manzo sm. 1. (zool.) steer 2. (carne) beef.
maomettano agg. e sm. Mohammedan.
mappa sf. map.
mappamondo sm. globe.
marachella sf. trick.
marasma sm. 1. (med.) marasmus 2. (fig.) decadence.
maratona sf. marathon race.

marca *sf.* brand: — *di fabbrica*, trade mark.

marcare *vt.* 1. to mark 2. (*sport*) to score.

marcato *agg.* marked, branded.

marcatore *sm.* 1. marker 2. (*sport*) scorer.

marcatura *sf.* 1. marking 2. (*sport*) scoring.

marchesa *sf.* 1. marchioness 2. (*se non è inglese*) marquise.

marchesato *sm.* marquisate.

marchese *sm.* marquis.

marchiano *agg.* enormous, glaring.

marchiare *vt.* to brand.

marchiatura *sf.* branding.

marchio *sm.* 1. stamp 2. (*a fuoco*) brand 3. (*fig.; comm.*) mark.

marcia *sf.* 1. (*auto*) gear 2. (*mil.; mus.*) march.

marciapiede *sm.* 1. pavement 2. (*ferr.*) platform.

marciare *vi.* to march.

marciatore *sm.* (*sport*) road-walker.

marcio *agg.* 1. rotten 2. (*fig.*) corrupted. ♦ marcio *sm.* (*fig.*) corruption.

marcire *vi.* 1. (*guastarsi*) to go (*v. irr.*) bad 2. (*decomporsi*) to rot (*v. irr.*).

marciume *sm.* rottenness.

marco *sm.* mark.

marconigrafia *sf.* marconigraphy.

mare *sm.* sea.

marea *sf.* tide.

mareggiata *sf.* sea-storm.

maremma *sf.* maremma (*pl. -me*).

maremoto *sm.* seaquake.

mareògrafo *sm.* tide-gauge.

maresciallo *sm.* marshal.

margarina *sf.* margarine.

margherita *sf.* daisy.

marginale *agg.* marginal.

marginare *vt.* 1. to border 2. (*tip.*) to margin.

marginatura *sf.* 1. edging 2. (*tip.*) furniture.

màrgine *sm.* 1. border, edge 2. (*fig.*) margin.

marina *sf.* 1. navy 2. (*costa*) seashore 3. (*pitt.*) sea-scape.

marinaio *sm.* sailor.

marinara *sf.* 1. (*cappotto*) duffle coat 2. (*cappello*) sailor hat.

marinare *vt.* (*cuc.*) to pickle || *la scuola*, to play truant.

marinaresco *agg.* sailor-like.

marinaro *agg.* 1. maritime 2. sailor-like. ♦ marinaro *sm.* sailor.

marineria *sf.* 1. seamanship 2. (*marina*) navy.

marino *agg.* sea (*attr.*).

mariolo *sm.* rogue.

marionetta *sf.* puppet.

maritale *agg.* marital.

maritare *vt.* to marry. ♦ maritarsi *vr.* to get (*v. irr.*) married.

marito *sm.* husband.

marittimo *agg.* maritime || *città marittima*, sea-town; *commercio* —, shipping business. ♦ marittimo *sm.* seafarer || *i marittimi*, seafolk (*sing.*).

marmaglia *sf.* rabble.

marmellata *sf.* 1. jam 2. (*d'arance*) marmalade.

marmista *sm.* marble-cutter.

marmitta *sf.* 1. (*cuc.*) stock-pot 2. (*auto*) silencer's muffler.

marmo *sm.* marble.

marmocchio *sm.* kid.

marmòreo *agg.* marble.

marmotta *sf.* 1. marmot 2. (*di persona*) lazy-bones

marna *sf.* marl.

marocchino *agg.* Moroccan. ♦ marocchino *sm.* 1. (*persona*) Moroccan 2. (*cuoio*) Morocco leather.

maroso *sm.* billow.

marra *sf.* 1. (*agr.*) hoe 2. (*mar.*) fluke.

marrone *agg.* brown. ♦ marrone *sm.* chestnut.

martedì *sm.* Tuesday.

martellamento *sm.* hammering.

martellare *vt.* 1. to hammer 2. (*mil.*) to pound 3. (*pulsare*) to throb.

martellata *sf.* hammer-blow.

martello *sm.* hammer.

martinetto *sm.* jack.

martingala *sf.* half-belt.

màrtire *sm. e f.* martyr.

martirio *sm.* martyrdom.

martirizzare *vt.* to martyrize.

martirologio *sm.* martyrology.

màrtora *sf.* marten.

martoriare *vt.* to torture.

marxismo *sm.* Marxism.

marxista *agg. e s.* Marxist.

marzapane *sm.* marzipan.

marziale *agg.* martial.

marziano *sm.* Martian.

marzo *sm.* March.

mascalzonata *sf.* knavery.

mascalzone *sm.* rascal.

mascella *sf.* jaw.

mascellare agg. jaw (attr.).

màschera sf. 1. mask 2. (figura mascherata) masker 3. (cosmesi) face-pack 4. (inserviente di cinema, teatro) usher.

mascheramento sm. masking.

mascherare vt. to mask.

mascherata sf. masquerade.

maschietto sm. male.

maschile agg. male.

maschio¹ agg. 1. male 2. (virile) manly. ◆ **maschio** sm. 1. (di animale) (uccelli) cock, (mammiferi) bull (attributivi) 2. (di uomo) male 3. (bambino) boy.

maschio² sm. (torre) donjon.

mascolinità sf. masculinity.

masnada sf. gang.

masnadiere sm. highwayman (pl. -men).

masochismo sm. masochism.

masonite sf. masonite.

massa sf. mass, heap.

massacrante agg. exhausting.

massacrare vt. to massacre.

massacratore sm. slaughterer.

massacro sm. massacre.

massaggiare vt. to massage.

massaggiatore sm. masseur.

massaggiatrice sf. masseuse.

massaggio sm. massage.

massaia sf. housewife (pl. -wives).

massello sm. ingot.

masseria sf. farm.

masserizie sf. pl. household goods.

massicciata sf. road-bed.

massiccio agg. solid. ◆ **massiccio** sm. massif.

màssima sf. maxim, rule || in linea di —, on the whole; accordo di —, general agreement.

massimalismo sm. Maximalism.

massimalista s. Maximalist.

màssimo agg. 1. greatest, highest 2. (l'estremo) utmost 3. (il più lungo) longest. ◆ **màssimo** sm. 1. most 2. (il meglio) best 3. (mat.; fis.) maximum.

masso sm. boulder.

massone sm. freemason.

massoneria sf. freemasonry.

mastello sm. tub.

masticare vt. to chew.

masticazione sf. mastication.

màstice sm. rubber.

mastino sm. mastiff.

mastite sf. mastitis.

mastodonte sm. 1. (zool.) mastodon 2. (fig.) giant.

mastodòntico agg. colossal.

mastòide sf. mastoid.

mastoidite sf. mastoiditis.

mastro sm. 1. (libro) ledger 2. (appellativo) Master.

masturbazione sf. masturbation.

matassa sf. 1. hank 2. (fig.) tangle.

matemàtica sf. mathematics.

matemàtico agg. mathematical. ◆ **matemàtico** sm. mathematician.

materasso sm. mattress.

materia sf. matter, subject.

materiale agg. 1. material 2. (rozzo) rough. ◆ **materiale** sm. material.

materialismo sm. materialism.

materialista s. materialist.

materialìstico agg. materialistic.

materializzare vt. to materialize.

maternità sf. maternity.

materno agg. motherly, maternal || scuola materna, nursery-school.

matita sf. pencil.

matriarcato sm. matriarchy.

matrice sf. 1. matrix (pl. matrices) 2. (comm.) counterfoil.

matricida s. matricide.

matricidio sm. matricide.

matricola sf. 1. matricula, register || numero di —, matriculation number 2. (scol.) freshman (pl. -men).

matricolato agg. matriculated || briccone —, arrant knave.

matrigna sf. stepmother.

matrimoniale agg. matrimonial.

matrimonio sm. 1. marriage 2. (cerimonia nuziale) wedding.

matrona sf. matron.

matta sf. 1. mad woman (pl. women) 2. (al gioco) jolly joker.

mattacchione sm. joker.

mattatoio sm. slaughter-house.

matterello sm. rolling-pin.

mattina sf. morning.

mattinata sf. 1. morning 2. (teat.) matinée.

mattiniero agg. early-rising.

mattino sm. morning.

matto¹ agg. mad, crazy. ◆ **matto** sm. madman (pl. -men).

matto² agg. 1. (non lucido) mat 2. (di gioielli) false.

mattone sm. 1. brick 2. (fig.) bore.

mattonella sf. tile.

mattutino agg. morning (attr.). ◆ **mattutino** sm. (eccl.) matins (pl.).

maturare vi. e vt. to ripen, to mature (anche fig.).

maturazione *sf.* maturation, ripening (*anche fig.*).

maturità *sf.* ripening, maturity (*anche fig.*).

maturo *agg.* ripe, mature (*anche fig.*).

mausoleo *sm.* mausoleum.

mazurca *sf.* mazurka.

mazza *sf.* **1.** (*clava*) club **2.** (*martello di legno*) mallet.

mazzata *sf.* heavy blow (*anche fig.*).

mazziere *sm.* **1.** mace-bearer **2.** (*di carte*) dealer.

mazzo *sm.* **1.** bunch **2.** (*di carte*) pack || *fare il —*, to shuffle **3.** (*di fiori*) bouquet.

mazzolino *sm.* (*di fiori*) posy.

mazzuolo *sm.* mallet.

me *pron.* **1.** me **2.** (*me stesso*) myself.

meandro *sm.* **1.** meander **2.** (*labirinto*) maze.

meato *sm.* meatus.

meccànica *sf.* mechanics.

meccànico *agg.* mechanical. ♦ **meccànico** *sm.* mechanic.

meccanismo *sm.* **1.** gear **2.** (*movimento*) motion.

meccanizzare *vt.* to mechanize.

meccanizzazione *sf.* mechanization.

meccanografìa *sf.* mechanography.

meccanogràfico *agg.* mechanographic.

mecenate *sm.* Maecenas.

mecenatismo *sm.* patronage.

medaglia *sf.* medal.

medaglione *sm.* **1.** locket **2.** (*arch.*) medallion.

medaglista *sm.* **1.** (*incisore*) medallist **2.** (*collezionista*) collector of medals.

medésimo *agg. e pron.* V. *stesso.*

media *sf.* **1.** average: *alla — di*, at an average of **2.** (*mat.*) mean.

mediana *sf.* median line.

mediànico *agg.* mediumistic.

mediano *agg.* **1.** medial, middle (*attr.*) **2.** (*geom.; anat; bot.*) median. ♦ **mediano** *sm.* (*sport*) half-back.

mediante *prep.* by, by means of, through.

mediato *agg.* indirect.

mediatore *sm.* **1.** mediator **2.** (*comm.*) broker.

mediazione *sf.* **1.** mediation **2.** (*comm.*) brokerage.

medicamento *sm.* medicament.

medicare *vt.* to dress.

medicastro *sm.* quack (doctor).

medicazione *sf.* **1.** medication **2.** (*di ferita*) dressing.

medicina *sf.* medicine.

medicinale *sm.* medicinal.

mèdico *agg.* medical. ♦ **mèdico** *sm.* physician, doctor.

medievale *agg.* medieval.

medio *sm.* **1.** (*dito*) middle finger **2.** (*mat.*) mean. ♦ **medio** *agg.* **1.** middle **2.** (*normale, che risulta da una media*) average.

mediocre *agg.* second-rate.

mediocrità *sf.* mediocrity.

medioevo *sm.* Middle Ages (*pl.*).

meditabondo *agg.* thoughtful.

meditare *vt.* **1.** to ponder **2.** (*avere un'intenzione*) to meditate.

meditativo *agg.* meditative.

meditazione *sf.* meditation.

mediterràneo *agg.* **1.** inland **2.** Mediterranean.

medium *sm.* medium.

medusa *sf.* medusa (*pl.* -ae).

mefistofèlico *agg.* satanic.

mefitico *agg.* poisonous.

megaciclo *sm.* megacycle.

megàfono *sm.* megaphone.

megalòmane *sm.* megalomaniac.

megalomanìa *sf.* megalomania.

megatone *sm.* megaton.

meglio *avv.* **1.** (*comp.*) better **2.** (*superl. rel.*) best. ♦ **meglio** *agg.* **1.** (*comp.*) better: *questo vestito è — di quello*, this dress is better than that **2.** (*superl. rel.*) best. ♦ **meglio** *sm.* best, best thing || *in mancanza di —*, for lack of anything better. ♦ **meglio** *sf.* *avere la —*, to have the better || *alla —*, as well as possible.

mela *sf.* apple.

melacotogna *sf.* quince.

melagrana *sf.* pomegranate.

melanismo *sm.* melanism.

melanzana *sf.* aubergine.

melassa *sf.* molasses (*pl.*).

melato *agg.* **1.** sweetened with honey **2.** (*fig.*) honeyed.

melenso *agg.* dull, silly.

mellifluo *agg.* honeyed.

melma *sf.* slime.

melmoso *agg.* slimy.

melo *sm.* apple-tree.

melodia *sf.* melody.

melòdico *agg.* melodic.

melodioso *agg.* melodious.

melodramma *sm.* **1.** opera **2.** (*fig.*) melodrama.

melodrammàtico agg. **1.** operatic **2.** (fig.) melodramatic.

melograno sm. pomegrancte-tree.

melòmane s. melomaniac.

melomanìa sf. melomania.

melone sm. melon.

membra sf. pl. limbs.

membrana sf. membrane.

membratura sf structure.

membro sm. **1.** member **2.** (anat.) limb.

memoràbile agg. memorable.

memorandum sm. memorandum (pl. -da).

mèmore agg. mindful.

memoria sf. **1.** memory: — di ferro, cast-iron memory || a —, by heart **2.** (ricordo) memory, recollection.

memoriale sm. **1.** (petizione) memorial **2.** (libro di memorie) memoirs (pl.).

memorialista s. memorialist.

menabò sm. dummy.

menadito (nella loc. avv.) a —, perfectly || sapere qc. a —, to have sthg. at one's finger-tips.

menagramo sm. bearer of ill-luck.

menare vt. (condurre) to lead (v. irr.) || — vanto, to boast; — il can per l'aia, to beat (v. irr.) about the bush; — buono, gramo, to bring (v. irr.) good, bad luck.

mendace agg. mendacious, false.

mendacia sf. mendacity.

mendicante sm. beggar.

mendicare vi. to beg.

mendicità sf. mendicity.

mendico agg. e sm. mendicant.

menestrello sm. minstrel.

meninge sf. meninx (pl. meninges).

menisco sm. meniscus.

meno avv. **1.** (comp.) less **2.** (superl. rel.) least || fare a —, to do (v. irr.) without; non poter fare a —, cannot help: non posso fare a — di andare, I cannot help going **3.** (mat.) minus. ◆ **meno** prep. but for || a — che (non), unless. ◆ **meno** agg. **1.** (comp. sing.) less: è — bella di sua sorella, she is less beautiful than her sister **2.** (comp. con s. pl.) fewer: ho — libri di te, I have fewer books than you **3.** (superl. rel. sing.) the least: è il — intelligente dei miei amici, he is the least intelligent of my friends **4.** (superl. rel. con s. pl.) the fewest (raro).

◆ **meno** sm. **1.** (comp.) less **2.** (superl. rel.) the least.

menomare vt. to lessen.

menomato agg. **1.** lessened **2.** (di vista, udito) impaired.

menomazione sf. **1.** lessening **2.** (di arti, sensi) impairment **3.** (di persona) disablement.

menopàusa sf. menopause.

mensa sf. table.

mensile agg. monthly. ◆ **mensile** sm. **1.** (salario) month's salary **2.** (pubblicazione mensile) monthly.

mensilità sf. monthly instalment || tredicesima —, Christmas bonus.

mensilmente avv. monthly, once a month.

mènsola sf. **1.** bracket **2.** (scaffale) shelf (pl. -lves).

menta sf. mint.

mentale agg. mental.

mentalità sf. mentality.

mente sf. mind: persona dalla — ristretta, narrow-minded person; aguzzare la —, to sharpen one's wits.

mentecatto agg. insane. ◆ **mentecatto** sm. madman (pl. -men).

mentina sf. peppermint-drop.

mentire vi. to lie.

mentito agg. false: sotto mentite spoglie, under false pretences.

mentitore sm. liar.

mento sm. chin.

mentolo sm. menthol.

mèntore sm. mentor.

mentre cong. **1.** (temporale) while, as, when **2.** (avversativo) whereas, while **3.** (finché) as long as, while. ◆ **mentre** sm. moment: in quel —, at that moment.

menzionare vt. to mention.

menzione sf. mention.

menzogna sf. falsehood.

menzognero agg. **1.** (di persona) mendacious **2.** (di cosa) false.

meraviglia sf. wonder: sopraffatto dalla —, wonder-struck; non fa — che, nessuna — che, no wonder.

meravigliare vt. to astonish.

meravigliarsi vr. to be astonished (at).

meravigliato agg. astonished.

meraviglioso agg. wonderful.

mercante sm. merchant.

mercanteggiare vi. (tirare sul prezzo) to bargain, to haggle.

mercantile agg. mercantile. ◆ **mercantile** sm. cargo boat.

mercantilismo sm. mercantilism.
mercanzia sf. merchandise.
mercato sm. market || a buon —, cheap.
merce sf. goods (pl.).
mercé sf. mercy.
mercede sf. pay, reward.
mercenario agg. e sm. mercenary.
merceologia sf. technology of marketable goods.
merceria sf. 1. haberdashery 2. (negozio) haberdasher's shop.
mercerizzato agg. mercerized.
merciaio sm. haberdasher.
mercoledì sm. Wednesday: — delle Ceneri, Ash Wednesday.
mercurio sm. mercury, quicksilver.
merenda sf. afternoon snack.
meretrice sf. prostitute.
meretricio sm. prostitution.
meridiana sf. sun-dial.
meridiano agg. e sm. meridian.
meridionale agg. Southern. ♦ **meridionale** sm. Southerner.
meridione sm. south.
meringa sf. meringue.
merino sm. merino.
meritare vt. to deserve.
meritévole agg. deserving.
mèrito sm. merit || in — a, as to.
meritorio agg. meritorious, deserving.
merletto sm. lace.
merlo sm. 1. blackbird 2. (sciocco) simpleton.
merluzzo sm. codfish.
mero agg. 1. pure 2. (fig.) mere.
mesata sf. 1. month 2. (paga di un mese) month's pay.
méscere vt. to pour (out).
meschinità sf. meanness.
meschino agg. mean. ♦ **meschino** sm. wretch.
méscita sf. pouring (out).
mescolanza sf. 1. mixing 2. (miscuglio) mixture.
mescolare vt. 1. to mix 2. (tè, caffè, liquori, tabacco) to blend. ♦ **mescolarsi** vr. to mingle.
mescolatrice sf. mixer.
mese sm. month.
messa sf. 1. (eccl.) Mass 2. (azione del mettere) putting, setting: — a punto, setting up || — a fuoco, focusing.
messaggero sm. messenger.
messaggio sm. 1. message 2. (allocuzione) address.
messale sm. missal.

messe sf. crop, harvest.
messia sm. Messiah.
messiànico agg. Messianic.
messianismo sm. Messianism.
messicano agg. e sm. Mexican.
messinscena sf. staging.
mestare vt. to stir.
mestiere sm. 1. trade 2. (perizia) skill 3. (lavoro) work.
mestizia sf. sadness.
méstola sf. ladle.
méstolo sm. ladle.
mestruazione sf. menstruation.
meta sf. 1. destination 2. (scopo) aim, purpose: senza —, aimless.
metà sf. 1. half (pl. halves) 2. (parte mediana) middle 3. (coniuge) la mia —, my better half.
metabolismo sm. metabolism.
metafisica sf. metaphysics.
metàfora sf. metaphor.
metafòrico agg. metaphoric(al).
metàllico agg. metallic.
metallo sm. metal.
metallurgia sf. metallurgy.
metallùrgico agg. metallurgic(al). ♦ **metallùrgico** sm. metallurgist.
metalmeccànico sm. metallurgist and mechanic.
metamòrfico agg. metamorphic.
metamorfismo sm. metamorphism.
metamòrfosi sf. metamorphosis (pl. -ses).
metano sm. methane.
metapsìchica sf. metapsychics.
metapsìchico agg. metapsychic(al).
metàstasi sf. metastasis (pl. -ses).
metempsicosi sf. metempsychosis (pl. -ses).
metèora sf. meteor.
meteòrico agg. meteoric.
meteorite sm. meteorite.
meteorologia sf. meteorology.
meteorològico agg. meteorological || previsioni meteorologiche, weather-forecast (sing.).
meteoròlogo sm. meteorologist.
meticcio agg. e sm. mestizo (pl. -za).
meticoloso agg. meticulous.
metodicità sf. methodicalness.
metòdico agg. methodical.
metodista agg. e s. Methodist.
mètodo sm. method.
metodologia sf. methodology.
metodològico agg. methodological.
mètopa sf. metope.
metraggio sm. 1. length (in metres) 2. (cine) corto, lungo —, short, full-length film.

mètrica sf. prosody.

mètrico agg. metric.

metrite sf. metritis.

metro sm. 1. metre 2. (strumento per misurare) rule.

metrònomo sm. metronome.

metronotte sm. night-watch.

metròpoli sf. metropolis (pl. -ses).

metropolitana sf. underground.

metropolitano agg. metropolitan.

méttere vt. 1. to put (v. irr.) || — in chiaro qc., to make (v. irr.) sthg. clear; — in dubbio qc., to doubt sthg.; — in serbo, to lay (v. irr.) aside; — in moto, to start; — in luce, to emphasize; — in guardia qu., to put so. on his guard; — le mani su qc., to take (v. irr.) possession of; — le mani sul fuoco per qu., to speak (v. irr.) for so. 2. (impiegare, di tempo) to take 3. (indossare) to put on 4. (paragonare) to compare. ◆ **mettersi** vr. 1. to put oneself || — in contatto con qu., to get (v. irr.) in touch with so.; — in testa di fare qc., to take into one's head to do sthg.; — sotto, to get down to it 2. (incominciare) to begin (v. irr.) 3. (indossare) to put (v. irr.) on.

mettifoglio sm. (tip.) feeder.

mezzadrìa sf. métayage.

mezzadro sm. métayer.

mezzaluna sf. 1. half-moon 2. (emblema islamico) crescent 3. (cuc.) mincing-knife.

mezzana¹ sf. (mar.) mizzen sail.

mezzana² sf. procuress.

mezzano agg. middle. ◆ **mezzano** sm. go-between.

mezzanotte sf. midnight.

mezzatinta sf. half-tone.

mezzo¹ agg. 1. half 2. (medio) middle. ◆ **mezzo** avv. half. ◆ **in mezzo a** prep. 1. in the middle of 2. (fra molti) among 3. (fra due) between.

mezzo² sm. 1. means 2. (fis.) medium.

mezzo³ agg. (marcio) rotten.

mezzobusto sm. bust.

mezzocerchio sm. semicircle.

mezzodì sm. midday, noon.

mezzofondo sm. middle-distance race.

mezzogiorno sm. 1. midday 2. (Sud) South.

mezzosoprano sm. mezzo-soprano.

mi¹ pron. 1. me 2. (me stesso) myself 3. (a me) to me.

mi² sm. (mus.) E, mi.

miagolare vi. to mew.

miagolìo sm. mewing.

miasma sm. miasms.

mica sf. mica.

mìccia sf. fuse.

michetta sf. roll.

micidiale agg. lethal, deadly.

micino sm. kitten, pussy.

micosi sf. mycosis (pl. -ses).

micròbio sm. microbe.

microbiologìa sf. microbiology.

microcosmo sm. microcosm.

microfilm sm. microfilm.

microfono sm. microphone.

microfotografìa sf. microphotography.

micrometrìa sf. micrometry.

micròmetro sm. micrometer.

micron sm. micron.

microrganismo sm. microorganism.

microscopìa sf. microscopy.

microscòpico agg. microscopic(al).

microscopio sm. microscope.

microsolco sm. long-playing record.

microtelèfono sm. microtelephone.

midolla sf. crumb.

midollare agg. medullar.

midollo sm. marrow: — spinale, spinal cord.

miele sm. honey.

mìetere vt. to reap.

mietitrice sf. reaper.

mietitura sf. reaping.

migliaio sm. thousand.

miglio¹ sm. (bot.) millet.

miglio² sm. (misura di lunghezza) mile.

miglioramento sm. improvement.

migliorare vt. to better, to improve.

migliore agg. 1. (comp.) better: questo libro è — di quello, this book is better than that 2. (superl.) the best: è il — alunno della classe, he is the best pupil in his class.

migliorìa sf. improvement.

mignatta sf. leech.

mìgnolo sm. little finger.

migrare vi. to migrate.

migratore agg. migratory. ◆ **migratore** sm. migrant.

migratorio agg. migratory.

migrazione sf. migration.

miliardario sm. multi-millionaire.

miliardo *sm.* a thousand millions.
miliare *agg.* **pietra** —, milestone.
milionario *sm.* millionaire.
milione *sm.* million.
milionèsimo *agg.* millionth.
militante *agg.* militant.
militare[1] *agg.* military. ♦ **militare** *sm.* soldier.
militare[2] *vi.* **1.** to be a soldier **2.** (*lavorare a favore di*) to support.
militaresco *agg.* soldierlike.
militarismo *sm.* militarism.
militarista *sm.* militarist.
militarizzare *vt.* to militarize.
militarizzazione *sf.* militarization.
militarmente *avv.* militarily.
milite *sm.* militiaman (*pl.* -men).
milizia *sf.* Army.
miliziano *sm.* militiaman (*pl.* -men).
millantare *vt.* to boast of. ♦ **millantarsi** *vr.* to boast.
millantatore *sm.* boaster.
millanterìa *sf.* boasting.
mille *agg.* one thousand.
millenario *agg.* e *sm.* millenary.
millennio *sm.* millennium.
millepiedi *sm.* millepede.
millèsimo *agg.* thousandth.
milligrammo *sm.* milligram.
millimetro *sm.* millimetre.
milza *sf.* spleen.
mimare *vt.* e *vi.* to mime.
mimètico *agg.* mimetic.
mimetismo *sm.* **1.** (*di animali*) mimicry **2.** (*mil.*) camouflage.
mimetizzare *vt.* to camouflage.
mimetizzazione *sf.* camouflage.
mìmica *sf.* **1.** (*teat.*) mimic art **2.** (*di gesti*) gesticulation.
mìmico *agg.* miming, mimic.
mimo *sm.* mime.
mimosa *sf.* mimosa.
mina *sf.* mine.
minaccia *sf.* threat.
minacciare *vt.* to threaten.
minaccioso *agg.* threatening.
minare *vt.* **1.** to mine **2.** (*fig.*) undermine.
minareto *sm.* minaret.
minatore *sm.* miner.
minatorio *agg.* threatening.
minchione *sm.* simpleton.
minerale *agg.* mineral. ♦ **minerale** *sm.* mineral.
mineralizzare *vt.* to mineralize.
mineralogìa *sf.* mineralogy.
minerario *agg.* mining (*attr.*).
mìnestra *sf.* soup.
mingherlino *agg.* slim.

miniare *vt.* **1.** to paint in miniature **2.** (*di manoscritti*) to illuminate.
miniato *agg.* illuminated.
miniatura *sf.* miniature.
miniaturista *sm.* miniaturist.
miniera *sf.* mine.
minigonna *sf.* miniskirt.
minimamente *avv.* not in the least.
minimizzare *vt.* to minimize.
mìnimo *agg.* least, slightest, smallest. ♦ **mìnimo** *sm.* minimum..
minio *sm.* red lead.
ministeriale *agg.* ministerial.
ministero *sm.* ministry: — *dell'Istruzione*, ministry of Education || — *degli Esteri, dell'Interno*, Foreign, Home Office; — *del Tesoro*, Treasury.
ministro *sm.* minister.
minoranza *sf.* minority.
minorare *vt.* to diminish.
minorato *agg.* disabled.
minorazione *sf.* **1.** (*diminuzione*) reduction **2.** (*invalidità*) disablement.
minore *agg.* **1.** (*comp.*) (*più piccolo*) smaller, less; (*più basso*) lower; (*più corto*) shorter; (*più giovane*) younger **2.** (*superl.*) the smallest, least, lowest, shortest, youngest.
minorile *agg.* juvenile.
minorenne *agg.* under age. ♦ **minorenne** *s.* minor.
minorile *agg.* juvenile.
minorità *sf.* minority.
minoritario *agg.* minority (*attr.*).
minuetto *sm.* minuet.
minugia *sf.* gut.
minùscolo *agg.* small letter.
minuta *sf.* rough copy.
minutaglia *sf.* bits and pieces (*pl.*).
minuto[1] *agg.* **1.** minute **2.** (*dettagliato*) detailed.
minuto[2] *sm.* minute.
minuto[3] *sm.* (*comm.*) retail.
minuzia *sf.* trifle.
minuziosamente *avv.* minutely.
minuziosità *sf.* minuteness.
minuzioso *agg.* minute, detailed.
minùzzolo *sm.* crumb.
mìo *agg.* my. ♦ **mìo** *pron.* mine
miocardìa *sf.* myocardia.
miocardio *sm.* myocardium.
miocardite *sf.* myocarditis.
miocene *sm.* miocene.
mìope *agg.* short-sighted.
miopìa *sf.* myopia.

mira *sf.* **1.** aim: *prendere la —*, to take (*v. irr.*) aim **2.** (*fig.*) aim, design.

miràbile *agg.* admirable.

mirabìlia *sf. pl.* wonders.

mirabolante *agg.* astonishing.

miràcolo *sm.* miracle: *fare miràcoli*, to do (*v. irr.*) miracles, (*fig.*) to work wonders.

miracoloso *agg.* miraculous.

miràggio *sm.* mirage.

mirare *vt.* to look at. ♦ **mirare** *vi.* to aim (at).

mirìade *sf.* myriad.

miriagrammo *sm.* myriagram.

miriàmetro *sm.* myriametre.

miriàpodi *sm. pl.* Myriapoda.

mirìfico *agg.* wondrous.

mirino *sm.* **1.** sight **2.** (*foto*) view-finder.

mirra *sf.* myrrh.

mirtillo *sm.* bilberry.

mirto *sm.* myrtle.

misantropìa *sf.* misanthropy.

misàntropo *sm.* misanthrope.

miscela *sf.* **1.** mixture **2.** (*di caffè, tè, liquori, tabacco*) blend.

miscelare *vt.* **1.** to mix **2.** (*di caffè, tabacco, liquori ecc.*) to blend.

miscellànea *sf.* miscellany.

mischia *sf.* fray.

mischiare *vt.* to mix, to mingle.

mischiatura *sf.* **1.** (*il mischiare*) mixing **2.** (*miscuglio*) mixture.

misconóscere *vt.* not to acknowledge.

miscredente *agg.* misbelieving. ♦ **miscredente** *sm.* misbeliever.

miscredenza *sf.* misbelief.

miscuglio *sm.* **1.** mixture **2.** (*amalgama*) blend.

miseràbile *agg.* **1.** miserable **2.** (*scarso*) poor **3.** (*vile*) despicable, mean. ♦ **miseràbile** *sm.* wretch.

miserando *agg.* miserable.

miserévole *agg.* miserable, pitiable.

misèria *sf.* **1.** misery, poverty **2.** (*scarsità*) lack **3.** (*inezia*) trifle.

misericòrdia *sf.* mercy.

misericordioso *agg.* merciful.

misero *agg.* **1.** poor, scanty **2.** (*meschino*) wretched.

misfatto *sm.* misdeed.

misoginìa *sf.* misogyny.

misògino *agg.* misogynous. ♦ **misògino** *sm.* misogynist.

misoneìsmo *sm.* misoneism.

missàggio *sm.* mixing.

missile *sm.* missile.

missionàrio *sm.* missionary.

missione *sf.* mission.

missiva *sf.* letter.

misteriosamente *avv.* mysteriously.

misterioso *agg.* mysterious.

mistero *sm.* mystery.

mìstica *sf.* mysticism.

misticismo *sm.* mysticism.

mìstico *agg.* mystic.

mistificare *vt.* to mystify.

mistificatore *sm.* mystifier.

mistificazione *sf.* mystification.

misto *agg.* mixed.

mistura *sf.* mixture.

misura *sf.* **1.** (*misurazione, precauzione*) measure **2.** (*taglia*) size **3.** (*limite*) limit.

misuràbile *agg.* measurable.

misurare *vt.* **1.** to measure **2.** (*tec.*) to gauge **3.** (*limitare*) to limit. ♦ **misurarsi** *vr.* to compete.

misurato *agg.* measured.

misuratore *sm.* **1.** (*persona che misura*) measurer **2.** (*strumento*) gauge.

misurazione *sf.* measurement.

misurino *sm.* small measure.

mite *agg.* gentle, meek.

mitezza *sf.* gentleness, meekness.

mìtico *agg.* mythical.

mitigare *vt.* **1.** to mitigate **2.** (*passioni*) to appease **3.** (*dolori*) to relieve. ♦ **mitigarsi** *vr.* to be appeased.

mitigazione *sf.* **1.** mitigation **2.** (*di passioni*) appeasement **3.** (*di dolore*) relief.

mìtilo *sm.* mussel.

mito *sm.* myth.

mitologìa *sf.* mythology.

mitològico *agg.* mythological.

mitòmane *s.* mythomaniac.

mitomanìa *sf.* mythomania.

mitra[1] *sf.* (*eccl.*) mitre.

mitra[2] *sm.* (*mil.*) tommy-gun.

mitraglia *sf.* grape-shot.

mitragliare *vt.* to machine-gun.

mitragliatore *sm.* machine-gunner.

mitragliatrice *sf.* machine-gun.

mitragliere *sm.* machine-gunner.

mitrale *agg.* mitral.

mitrato *agg.* mitred.

mitridàtico *agg.* mithridatic.

mitridatismo *sm.* mithridatism.

mittente *sm.* sender.

mnemònica *sf.* mnemonics.

mnemònico *agg.* mnemonic.

mo' (*nella loc. prep.*) *a — di*, like.

mòbile agg. 1. movable || scala —, escalator; beni mobili, personal property 2. (mutevole) inconstant. ♦ mòbile sm. piece of furniture.

mobilia sf. furniture.

mobiliare[1] agg. movable, personal.

mobiliare[2] vt. to furnish.

mobilità sf. 1. mobility 2. (fig.) inconstancy.

mobilitare vt. to mobilize.

mobilitazione sf. mobilization.

mocassino sm. moccasin.

moccioso agg. snivelling. ♦ moccioso sm. young scoundrel, brat.

mòccolo sm. 1. candle-end 2. (bestemmia) curse.

moda sf. 1. fashion: di —, in fashion; fuori —, out of fashion || alla —, fashionable 2. (abitudine, modo) manner, way: alla — di, after the manner of.

modale agg. modal.

modalità sf. modality.

modanatura sf. moulding.

mòdano sm. model.

modella sf. model.

modellare vt. to model, to shape.

modellatore sm. modeller.

modellazione sf. modelling.

modello sm. 1. model, pattern 2. (stampo) mould.

moderare vt. to moderate, to check.

moderato agg. moderate.

moderatore agg. moderating. ♦ moderatore sm. moderator.

moderazione sf. moderation.

modernismo sm. modernism.

modernità sf. modernity.

modernizzare vt. to modernize.

moderno agg. modern, up-to-date (attr.).

modestia sf. modesty: — a parte, modesty apart.

modesto agg. modest.

modicità sf. 1. moderateness 2. (di prezzi) cheapness.

mòdico agg. moderate: a prezzo —, cheap.

modifica sf. alteration, change.

modificare vt. to modify.

modificazione sf. V. modifica.

modista sf. milliner.

modisteria sf. milliner's shop.

modo sm. 1. way, manner 2. (gramm.) mood 3. (mezzo) means: in nessun —, by no means || di — che, so (that); in — da, so as to; in che —, how; in qualche —, anyhow; oltre —, beyond measure.

modulare vt. to modulate.

modulato agg. modulated.

modulazione sf. modulation.

mòdulo sm. form.

moffetta sf. skunk.

mògano sm. mahogany.

moggio sm. bushel.

mogio agg. depressed.

moglie sf. wife (pl. wives).

moina sf. simpering.

mola[1] sf. 1. (di mulino) millstone 2. (per arrotare) grindstone.

mola[2] sf. (itt.) sun-fish.

molare[1] vt. to grind (v. irr.).

molare[2] agg. molar. ♦ molare sm. (dente) molar (tooth).

molatura sf. grinding.

molazza sf. muller.

mole sf. 1. mass, bulk 2. (dimensione) size.

molècola sf. molecule.

molecolare agg. molecular.

molestare vt. to molest, to tease.

molestatore sm. molesting. ♦ molestatore sm. molester.

molestia sf. nuisance, trouble.

molesto agg. troublesome.

molibdeno sm. molybdenum.

molitorio agg. molinary.

molla sf. 1. spring 2. (incentivo) spur.

mollare vt. 1. (allentare) to slacken 2. (mar.) to let (v. irr.) go. ♦ mollare vi. to give (v. irr.) in.

molle agg. 1. soft 2. (floscio) flabby 3. (debole) weak 4. (inzuppato) soaking wet. ♦ molle sf. pl. tongs.

molleggiamento sm. 1. (elasticità) springiness 2. (di veicoli) springing system.

molleggiare vi. to be springy.

molleggiato agg. sprung.

molleggio sm. (di veicoli) suspension.

molletta sf. 1. (per il bucato) clothes-peg 2. (per i capelli) hair-pin.

mollettiere sf. pl. puttees.

mollettone sm. thick flannel.

mollezza sf. 1. (morbidezza) softness 2. (debolezza) weakness.

mollica sf. crumb.

mollo agg. damp: mettere a —, to steep.

mollusco sm. mollusc.

molo sm. pier, wharf.

moltéplice agg. manifold.

molteplicità sf. multiplicity.

moltìplica *sf.* (*mecc.*) chain gearing.
moltiplicando *sm.* multiplicand.
moltiplicare *vt.* to multiply.
moltiplicatore *sm.* multiplier.
moltiplicazione *sf.* multiplication.
moltìssimo *agg. indef.* 1. very much (*pl.* very many) 2. (*di tempo*) very long. ♦ **moltìssimo** *avv.* a great deal, very much.
moltitùdine *sf.* multitude.
molto *agg. indef.* 1. (*sing.*) much, a great deal of, a lot of, plenty of 2. (*pl.*) many, a good many, a lot of, plenty of 3. (*di tempo*) long. ♦ **molto** *avv.* 1. very 2. (*con comp.*) much, far 3. (*di tempo*) long, a long time.
momentaneamente *avv.* at the moment.
momentàneo *agg.* momentary.
momento *sm.* 1. moment ‖ *dal* — *che*, since 2. (*tempo, circostanza*) time 3. (*opportunità*) chance.
mònaca *sf.* nun.
monacale *agg.* monastic.
mònaco *sm.* monk.
mònade *sf.* monad.
monarca *sm.* monarch.
monarchìa *sf.* monarchy.
monàrchico *agg.* monarchic.
monastero *sm.* monastery.
monàstico *agg.* monastic.
moncherino *sm.* stump.
monco *agg.* 1. maimed 2. (*fig.*) incomplete.
moncone *sm.* stump.
mondanità *sf.* 1. society life 2. worldliness.
mondano *agg.* worldly.
mondare *vt.* 1. to clean ‖ — *il grano*, to winnow the corn 2. (*fig.*) to cleanse.
mondiale *agg.* world-wide, world (*attr.*).
mondina *sf.* rice-weeder.
mondo[1] *sm.* world: *fare il giro del* —, to go (*v. irr.*) round the world; *da che* — *è* —, since the world began.
mondo[2] *agg.* clean.
monelleria *sf.* prank.
monello *sm.* little rascal, urchin.
moneta *sf.* 1. money (*solo sing.*) 2. (*ogni singolo pezzo*) coin 3. (*spiccioli*) change.
monetario *agg.* monetary.
monetizzare *vt.* to monetize.
mongolfiera *sf.* montgolfier.
mongolismo *sm.* mongolism.

mòngolo *agg.* Mongolian. ♦ **mòngolo** *sm.* Mongol.
mongolòide *agg. e sm.* mongoloid.
monile *sm.* jewel.
monismo *sm.* monism.
mònito *sm.* warning.
monoblocco *sm.* monobloc.
monòcolo *sm.* monocle.
monocromàtico *agg.* monochromatic.
monòcromo *agg.* monochrome.
monodìa *sf.* monody.
monogamìa *sf.* monogamy.
monògamo *agg.* monogamous. ♦ **monògamo** *sm.* monogamist.
monografìa *sf.* monograph.
monogràfico *agg.* monographic.
monogramma *sm.* monogram.
monolìtico *agg.* monolithic.
monòlogo *sm.* monologue, soliloquy.
monometallismo *sm.* monometallism.
monomio *sm.* monomial.
monopàttino *sm.* scooter.
monoplano *sm.* monoplane.
monopolio *sm.* monopoly.
monopolista *sm.* monopolist.
monopolizzare *vt.* to monopolize.
monoposto *agg. e sm.* single-seater.
monorotaia *sf.* monorail.
monosillàbico *agg.* monosyllabic.
monosìllabo *sm.* monosyllable.
monoteìsmo *sm.* monotheism.
monoteìsta *s.* monotheist.
monoteìstico *agg.* monotheistic.
monotipo *sm.* monotype.
monotonìa *sf.* monotony.
monòtono *agg.* monotonous.
monovalente *agg.* monovalent.
monsignore *sm.* monsignor (*pl.* -ri).
monsone *sm.* monsoon.
montacàrichi *sm.* goods-lift.
montaggio *sm.* 1. assembly: *linea di* —, assembly line 2. (*cine*) editing 3. (*foto*) montage.
montagna *sf.* mountain.
montagnoso *agg.* mountainous.
montanaro *agg.* mountain (*attr.*). ♦ **montanaro** *sm.* mountaineer.
montante *sm.* 1. (*boxe*) uppercut 2. (*mecc.; edil.*) vertical rod.
montare *vt.* 1. (*mettere insieme*) to assemble 2. (*cavalcare*) to ride (*v. irr.*) 3. (*di panna*) to whip. ♦ **montare** *vi.* 1. to climb 2. (*alzarsi, aumentare*) to rise (*v. irr.*). ♦ **montarsi** *vr.* to get (*v. irr.*) excited.

montatore sm. assembler.
montatura sf. **1.** fitting **2.** (fig.) hot hair.
montavivande sm. dumb-waiter.
monte sm. **1.** mount (seguito dal nome) **2.** mountain ‖ andare a —, to come (v. irr.) to nothing; mandare a —, to cause to fail.
montone sm. **1.** ram **2.** (carne) mutton.
montuosità sf. hilliness.
montuoso agg. hilly.
monumentale agg. monumental.
monumento sm. monument.
mora¹ sf. (bot.) mulberry.
mora² sf. (giur.) delay.
morale agg. moral. ♦ **morale** sm. morale. ♦ **morale** sf. **1.** morals (pl.) **2.** (fil.) ethics **3.** (conclusione) moral.
moralismo sm. moralism.
moralista s. moralist.
moralistico agg. moralistic.
moralità sf. morality.
moralizzare vt. to moralize.
moralizzazione sf. moralization.
moratorio agg. moratory.
morbidezza sf. softness.
mòrbido agg. soft.
morbillo sm. measles (pl.).
morbo sm. disease, plague.
morbosità sf. morbidity.
morboso agg. morbid.
mordace agg. biting, pungent.
mordacità sf. mordacity.
mordente sm. **1.** (mus.) mordent **2.** (spirito aggressivo) bite.
mòrdere vt. **1.** to bite (v. irr.) **2.** (tormentare) to torment ‖ — il freno, to strain at the leash; — la polvere, to bite the dust.
morena sf. moraine.
morènico agg. morainic.
morente agg. dying. ♦ **morente** sm. dying man.
moresco agg. Moorish.
morfina sf. morphine.
morfinòmane s. morphinomaniac.
morfologìa sf. morphology.
morfològico agg. morphologic(al).
morganàtico agg. morganatic.
moribondo agg. dying. ♦ **moribondo** sm. dying man.
morigeratezza sf. moderation.
morigerato agg. moderate, sober.
morire vi. **1.** to die **2.** (di luci e colori) to fade **3.** (di suoni) to die out **4.** (tramontare) to set (v. irr.) ♦ **morire** sm. death.

mormone agg. e sm. Mormon.
mormorare vt. to murmur. ♦ **mormorare** vi. (parlar male) to gossip.
mormorio sm. **1.** murmur **2.** (lamento) complaining **3.** (malignità) evil gossip.
moro agg. dark. ♦ **moro** sm. **1.** moor **2.** (bot.) mulberry-tree.
morra sf. "morra".
morsa sf. vice.
morsetto sm. (mecc.) clamp.
morsicare vt. to bite (v. irr.).
morsicatura sf. bite.
morsicchiare vt. to nibble.
morso sm. **1.** bite **2.** (puntura, stimolo) sting, pang **3.** (del cavallo) bit **4.** (boccone) morsel, bit.
mortaio sm. mortar.
mortale agg. mortal, deadly.
mortalità sf. mortality.
mortalmente avv. mortally.
mortaretto sm. cracker.
morte sf. death ‖ pena di —, capital punishment; dar la — a qu., to kill so.; odiare a — qu., to hate so. like poison.
mortella sf. myrtle.
mortìfero agg. lethal.
mortificare vt. **1.** to humiliate **2.** (reprimere) to mortify.
mortificato agg. humiliated.
mortificazione sf. mortification.
morto agg. **1.** dead ‖ natura morta (pitt.), still life; stanco —, dead tired **2.** (senza vivacità) dull. ♦ **morto** sm. dead man.
mortorio sm. funeral.
mortuario agg. mortuary.
mosaicista s. mosaicist.
mosàico sm. mosaic.
mosca sf. fly.
moscatello sm. muscatel.
moscato sm. (vino) muscatel. ♦ **moscato** agg. noce moscata, nutmeg.
moscerino sm. gnat.
moschea sf. mosque.
moschettiere sm. musketeer.
moschetto sm. musket.
moscio agg. flabby.
moscone sm. blue-bottle.
mossa sf. **1.** movement **2.** (spostamento al gioco; fig.) move **3.** (sport) starting post.
mossiere sm. (sport) starter.
mosso agg. **1.** (di mare) rough **2.** (di capelli) wavy.
mosto sm. must.

mostra *sf.* **1.** (*esposizione*) show, exhibition **2.** (*vetrina*) shop-window **3.** (*ostentazione*) display.

mostrare *vt.* **1.** to show (*v. irr.*) **2.** (*ostentare*) to show (*v. irr.*) off **3.** (*dimostrare*) to prove **4.** (*fingere*) to pretend.

mostrina *sf.* collar badge.

mostro *sm.* monster.

mostruosamente *avv.* monstrously.

mostruosità *sf.* monstrosity. for **2.** (*giur.*) to allege.

mostruoso *agg.* monstrous.

mota *sf.* mud, mire.

motivare *vt.* **1.** to state the reason

motivazione *sf.* **1.** motivation **2.** (*giur.*) opinion.

motivo *sm.* **1.** reason ‖ *a — di*, owing to; *senza —*, groundless **2.** (*mus.*) theme.

moto *sm.* **1.** motion, movement **2.** (*esercizio fisico*) exercise **3.** (*impulso*) impulse. ♦ **moto** *sf.* motor-cycle.

motobarca *sf.* motor-boat.

motocarrozzetta *sf.* side-car.

motocicletta *sf.* motor-cycle.

motociclismo *sm.* motor-cycling.

motociclista *s.* motor-cyclist.

motofurgone *sm.* van.

motore *agg.* motor, driving. ♦ **motore** *sm.* engine, motor.

motorista *sm.* engineer.

motorizzare *vt.* to motorize. **motorizzarsi** *vr.* to buy (*v. irr.*) a car, a motor-cycle.

motorizzazione *sf.* motorization.

motoscafo *sm.* motor-boat.

motoveicolo *sm.* motor vehicle.

motrice *sf.* **1.** tractor **2.** (*ferr.*) engine.

motteggiare *vt.* to make (*v. irr.*) fun of. ♦ **motteggiare** *vi.* to joke.

motteggiatore *agg.* joking. ♦ **motteggiatore** *sm.* joker.

motteggio *sm.* **1.** (*il motteggiare*) raillery **2.** (*detto arguto*) joke.

mottetto *sm.* motet.

motto *sm.* **1.** word **2.** (*proverbio*) saying **3.** (*facezia*) witticism.

movente *sm.* motive, cause.

movenza *sf.* movements (*pl.*).

movibile *agg.* movable.

movimentare *vt.* to enliven.

movimentato *agg.* **1.** lively **2.** (*pieno di movimento*) eventful.

movimento *sm.* **1.** movement **2.**

(*traffico, trambusto*) traffic, bustle.

moviola *sf.* film-editing machine.

mozione *sf.* motion.

mozzare *vt.* to cut (*v. irr.*) off.

mozzicone *sm.* **1.** stump **2.** (*di sigaretta*) butt.

mozzo¹ *agg.* cut (off).

mozzo² *sm.* **1.** (*di ruota*) hub **2.** (*mar.*) ship-boy.

mucca *sf.* cow.

mucchio *sm.* heap, mass.

mùcido *agg.* mouldy. ♦ **mùcido** *sm.* mould.

muco *sm.* mucus.

mucosa *sf.* mucous membrane.

mucoso *agg.* mucous.

muffa *sf.* mould.

muffire *vi.* to mildew.

muflone *sm.* moufflon.

mugghiare *vi.* **1.** to bellow **2.** (*fig.*) to roar **3.** (*del vento*) to howl.

mugghio *sm.* **1.** bellow **2.** (*fig.*) roar **3.** (*del vento*) howl.

muggire *vi.* V. *mugghiare*.

muggito *sm.* V. *mugghio*.

mughetto *sm.* lily of the valley.

mugnaio *sm.* miller.

mugolare *vi.* **1.** to howl **2.** (*piagnucolare*) to whimper.

mugolìo *sm.* **1.** howling **2.** (*piagnucolìo*) whimpering.

mugugnare *vi.* to mumble.

mulattiera *sf.* mule-track.

mulattiere *sm.* mule-driver.

mulatto *sm.* mulatto.

muliebre *agg.* feminine, womanly.

mulinare *vt.* **1.** to whirl **2.** (*fig.*) to brood (over).

mulinello *sm.* **1.** (*d'acqua*) whirl- pool **2.** (*d'aria*) whirlwind **3.** (*rapido movimento*) twirl.

mulino *sm.* mill.

mulo *sm.* mule.

multa *sf.* fine.

multare *vt.* to fine.

multicolore *agg.* many-coloured.

multiforme *agg.* multiform.

mùltiplo *agg.* e *sm.* multiple.

mummia *sf.* mummy.

mummificare *vt.* to mummify.

mummificazione *sf.* mummification.

mùngere *vt.* to milk.

mungitore *sm.* milker.

mungitura *sf.* milking.

municipale *agg.* municipal.

municipalità *sf.* municipality.

municipalizzare *vt.* to municipalize.

municipalizzazione sf. municipalization.

municipio sm. **1.** municipality **2.** (palazzo) townhall **3.** (stor.) municipium (pl. -ia).

munificenza sf. munificence.

munifico agg. munificent.

munire vt. **1.** (fortificare) to fortify **2.** (provvedere) to supply (with).

munizione sf. munition.

muòvere vt. to move. ♦ **muòversi** vr. to move, to stir ‖ muoviti! hurry up!

mura[1] sf. (mar.) tack.

mura[2] sf. pl. walls.

muraglia sf. wall.

muraglione sm. massive wall.

murale agg. mural.

murare vt. **1.** to wall up **2.** (cingere di mura) to wall.

murario agg. building (attr.).

murata sf. ship's side.

muratore sm. bricklayer.

muratura sf. masonry ‖ lavoro in —, brickwork.

murena sf. moray.

muriàtico agg. muriatic.

muricciolo sm. low wall.

murice sm. murex.

muro sm. wall ‖ armadio a —, built-in cupboard; — del suono, sound barrier.

musa sf. muse.

muschiato agg. musky.

muschio[1] sm. (sostanza odorosa) musk.

muschio[2] sm. (bot.) moss.

muscolare agg. muscular.

muscolatura sf. musculature.

mùscolo sm. muscle.

muscoloso agg. muscular.

muscoso agg. mossy.

museo sm. museum.

museruola sf. muzzle.

mùsica sf. music.

musicale agg. musical.

musicalità sf. musicality.

musicante sm. musician.

musicare vt. to set (v. irr.) to music.

musicista sm. musician.

mùsico sm. musician.

musicologìa sf. musicology.

musicòlogo sm. musicologist.

musivo agg. mosaic (attr.).

muso sm. **1.** muzzle **2.** (broncio) long face; fare il —, to pull a long face.

musone sm. **1.** large muzzle **2.** (persona che tiene il broncio) sulky person.

musonerìa sf. sulkiness.

mussare vi. to froth.

mussolina sf. muslin.

mustèlidi sm. pl. mustelidae.

musulmano agg. e sm. Muslim.

muta sf. **1.** (di cani) pack of hounds **2.** (della guardia) change **3.** (biol.) moult.

mutàbile agg. changeable.

mutabilità sf. **1.** (di cosa) changeability **2.** (di persona) fickleness.

mutamento sm. change.

mutande sf. pl. drawers.

mutandine sf. pl. trunks.

mutare vt. **1.** to change **2.** (di animali) to shed (v. irr.), to moult. ♦ **mutarsi** vr. to change.

mutazione sf. change.

mutévole agg. changeable.

mutilare vt. **1.** to maim **2.** (fig.) to mutilate.

mutilato agg. **1.** maimed **2.** (fig.) mutilated. ♦ **mutilato** sm. cripple.

mutilazione sf. **1.** maiming **2.** (fig.) mutilation.

mùtilo agg. mutilated.

mutismo sm. dumbness.

muto agg. **1.** dumb ‖ carta geografica muta, blank map **2.** (fonetica) mute.

mutria sf. stand-offishness.

mutua sf. national insurance ‖ medico della —, panel doctor.

mutualistico agg. insurance (attr.).

mutualità sf. mutual help.

mutuare vt. **1.** (dare in mutuo) to lend (v. irr.) **2.** (prendere a mutuo) to borrow.

mutuatario sm. borrower.

mutuato agg. insured.

mutuo agg. mutual. ♦ **mutuo** sm. loan.

N

nababbo sm. nabob.

nàcchera sf. castanet.

nafta sf. **1.** oil **2.** (chim.) naphtha.

naftalina sf. moth-balls (pl.).

naia[1] sf. (zool.) cobra.

naia[2] sf. (mil.) fare la —, to do (v. irr.) one's bit.

nàiade sf. naiad.

nàilon sm. nylon.

nandù sm. nandu.

nanismo sm. nanism.

nano sm. dwarf.

nappa sf. tassel.

narcisismo sm. narcissism.

narcisista sm. narcissist.

narciso sm. narcissus.

narcosi sf. narcosis (pl. -ses).

narcòtico agg. e sm. narcotic.

narcotizzare vt. to narcotize.

narice sf. nostril.

narrare vt. to tell (v. irr.).

narrativa sf. fiction.

narrativo agg. narrative.

narratore sm. 1. story-teller 2. (scrittore) writer.

narrazione sf. narration.

narvalo sm. narwhal.

nasale agg. nasal.

nascente agg. rising.

nàscere vi. 1. to be born 2. (di piante) to spring (v. irr.) up 3. (di fiume; sorgere) to rise (v. irr.) 4. (avere origine) to originate || far —, to give (v. irr.) rise to.

nàscita sf. 1. birth 2. (origine) origin.

nascituro sm. unborn child.

nascòndere vt. to hide (v. irr.). ◆ **nascòndersi** vr. to hide (oneself).

nascondiglio sm. hiding-place.

nascosto agg. hidden || di —, secretly.

nasello sm. (itt.) whiting.

naso sm. nose || a lume di —, by guesswork; ficcare il — in qc., to poke one's nose into sthg.; avere buon —, to be shrewd.

nassa sf. bow-net.

nastro sm. 1. ribbon 2. (tec.) tape.

natale agg. native. ◆ **Natale** sm. Christmas.

natalità sf. birth-rate.

natalizio agg. Christmas (attr.).

natante agg. floating. ◆ **natante** sm. watercraft.

natatoia sf. fin.

natatorio agg. swimming (attr.).

nàtica sf. buttock.

natività sf. nativity.

nativo agg. 1. native 2. (innato) inborn.

nato agg. born.

natura sf. nature.

naturale agg. natural.

naturalezza sf. naturalness, simplicity.

naturalismo sm. naturalism.

naturalista s. naturalist.

naturalizzare vt. to naturalize.

naturalizzazione sf. naturalization.

naturalmente avv. naturally, of course.

naturismo sm. naturism.

naturista s. naturist.

naufragare vi. 1. to be shipwrecked 2. (fig.) to be wrecked.

naufragio sm. 1. shipwreck 2. (fig.) wreck.

nàufrago sm. shipwrecked person.

nàusea sf. disgust, nausea || avere la —, to feel (v. irr.) sick.

nauseabondo agg. nauseating.

nauseare vt. to make (v. irr.) sick.

nàutica sf. navigation.

nàutico agg. nautical.

navale agg. naval.

navata sf. 1. (centrale) nave 2. (laterale) aisle.

nave sf. ship.

navetta sf. shuttle.

navicella sf. (aer.) nacelle.

navigàbile agg. navigable.

navigabilità sf. navigability.

navigare vi. to sail.

navigato agg. (fig.) cunning.

navigatore sm. navigator.

navigazione sf. navigation.

naviglio sm. 1. fleet 2. (nave) craft.

nazionale agg. national.

nazionalismo sm. nationalism.

nazionalista s. nationalist.

nazionalità sf. nationality.

nazionalizzare vt. to nationalize.

nazionalizzazione sf. nationalization.

nazionalsocialismo sm. National Socialism.

nazione sf. nation.

nazismo sm. Nazism.

nazista agg. e sm. Nazi.

nazzareno agg. e sm. Nazarene.

ne pron. 1. of him, about him; of her, about her; of it, about it; of them, about them; of this, about this; of that, about that 2. (partitivo) some: — ho, I have some; any: non — ho, I haven't any. ◆ **ne** (particella avv. di moto da luogo) from there.

né cong. 1. neither, not 2. (né... né...) neither... nor; (in presenza di altra negazione) either... or.

neanche avv. not even. ◆ **neanche** cong. neither; nor: essi non anda-

rono e — io, they did not go and neither did I.

nebbia *sf.* fog.

nebbioso *agg.* foggy.

nebulizzare *vt.* to nebulize.

nebulizzatore *sm.* nebulizer.

nebulosa *sf.* nebula (*pl.* -ae).

nebulosità *sf.* 1. nebulosity 2. (*fig.*) haziness.

nebuloso *agg.* 1. nebulous 2. (*fig.*) vague.

necessario *agg.* necessary. ♦ **necessario** *sm.* 1. necessary 2. (*l'indispensabile*) necessities (*pl.*).

necessità *sf.* 1. necessity 2. (*bisogno*) need.

necessitare *vi.* to need.

necrologia *sf.* obituary-notice.

necrologio *sm.* 1. necrology 2. (*annuncio*) obituary.

necròpoli *sf.* necropolis.

necrosi *sf.* necrosis (*pl.* -ses).

necrotizzare *vt.* to necrotize.

nefandezza *sf.* wickedness.

nefando *agg.* wicked.

nefasto *agg.* ill-omened.

nefrite *sf.* nephritis.

nefrìtico *agg.* nephritic. ♦ **nefrìtico** *sm.* nephritic subject.

negare *vt.* 1. to deny 2. (*rifiutare*) to refuse.

negativa *sf.* (*anche foto*) negative.

negativo *agg.* negative.

negato *agg.* 1. refused, denied 2. (*inadatto*) unfit (for).

negatore *agg.* negatory. ♦ **negatore** *sm.* denier.

negazione *sf.* 1. denial 2. (*gramm.*) negative 3. (*cosa diametralmente opposta all'altra*) negation.

neghittoso *agg.* slothful.

negletto *agg.* 1. neglected 2. (*di aspetto*) slovenly.

negligente *agg.* negligent, careless.

negligenza *sf.* negligence, carelessness.

negoziàbile *agg.* negotiable.

negoziante *sm.* 1. merchant, trader 2. (*chi ha negozio*) shopkeeper.

negoziare *vt.* to negotiate.

negoziato *agg.* negotiated. ♦ **negoziato** *sm.* negotiation.

negozio *sm.* 1. shop 2. (*commercio*) trade 3. (*faccenda*) affair.

negriero *agg.* slave (*attr.*). ♦ **negriero** *sm.* slave-trader.

negro *agg. e sm.* 1. negro 2. (*spreg.*) nigger.

negròide *agg. e s.* negroid.

negromante *sm.* necromancer.

negromanzìa *sf.* necromancy.

nembo *sm.* 1. raincloud 2. (*fig.*) multitude.

nèmesi *sf.* nemesis (*pl.* -ses).

nemico *agg.* 1. adverse 2. (*del nemico*) enemy (*attr.*). ♦ **nemico** *sm.* enemy.

neo¹ *sm.* 1. mole 2. (*fig.*) flaw.

neo² *agg.* neo.

neocapitalismo *sm.* neo-capitalism.

neocapitalista *agg. e sm.* neo-capitalist.

neocapitalìstico *agg.* neo-capitalistic.

neoclassicismo *sm.* neo-classicism.

neoclàssico *agg.* neo-classic.

neofascismo *sm.* neofascism.

neofascista *agg. e s.* neofascist.

neòfita *sm.* 1. neophyte 2. (*fig.*) beginner.

neolitico *agg.* .Neolithic.

neologismo *sm.* neologism.

neon *sm.* neon: *insegna al —,* neon sign.

neonato *agg.* new-born. ♦ **neonato** *sm.* (new-born) baby.

neorealismo *sm.* Neorealism.

neorealista *agg. e sm.* neorealist.

neozelandese *agg.* New Zealand (*attr.*). ♦ **neozelandese** *s.* New Zealander.

nepotismo *sm.* 'nepotism.

nerastro *agg.* blackish.

nerbo *sm.* 1. sinew 2. (*fig.*) strength, vigour.

nerboruto *agg.* brawny.

neretto *agg.* (*tip.*) boldface.

nerezza *sf.* blackness.

nero *agg.* black.

nerofumo *sm.* lamp-black.

nerògnolo *agg.* blackish.

nerume *sm.* mass of black.

nervatura *sf.* ribbing.

nervo *sm.* nerve.

nervosamente *agg.* nervously.

nervosismo *sm.* nervousness.

nervoso *agg.* nervous, irritable.

nèspola *sf.* medlar.

nèspolo *sm.* medlar(-tree).

nesso *sm.* connection.

nessuno *agg.* 1. no 2. (*in presenza di altra neg.*) any. ♦ **nessuno** *pron.* 1. (*per persone*) nobody, no one; (*per cose*) none 2. (*in presenza di altra neg.*) anybody (*solo per persone*), anyone, any || — *di,* none of, (*in presenza di altra neg.*) any of.

nèttare sm. nectar.

nettare vt. to clean.

nettezza sf. cleanness: — urbana, municipal street cleansing.

netto agg. 1. clean, spotless (anche fig.) 2. (comm.) net.

nettunio sm. neptunium.

neurite sf. neuritis.

neurochirurgìa sf. neurosurgery.

neurologìa sf. neurology.

neuròlogo sm. neurologist.

neuropàtico agg. neuropathic. ◆ **neuropàtico** sm. neuropath.

neuropatologìa sf. neuropathology.

neurosi sf. neurosis (pl. -es).

neurovegetativo agg. vegetative nervous.

neutrale agg. neutral.

neutralismo sm. neutralism.

neutralista s. neutralist.

neutralità sf. neutrality.

neutralizzare vt. to neutralize.

neutralizzazione sf. neutralization.

nèutro agg. 1. neutral 2. (gramm.; bot.; zool.) neuter.

neutrone sm. neutron.

neve sf. snow.

nevicare vi. to snow: nevica, it is snowing.

nevicata sf. snowfall.

nevischio sm. sleet.

nevoso agg. snowy.

nevralgìa sf. neuralgia.

nevràlgico agg. neuralgic.

nevrastenìa sf. neurasthenia.

nevrastènico agg. neurasthenic.

nevròtico agg. e sm. neurotic.

nibbio sm. kite.

nicchia sf. niche.

nicchiare vi. to shilly-shally.

nichel sm. nickel.

nichelare vt. to nickel.

nichelatura sf. nickel-plating.

nichelino sm. nickel coin.

nichilismo sm. nihilism.

nichilista s. nihilist.

nicotina sf. nicotine.

nidiata sf. 1. nest 2. (covata) brood || una — di bambini, a swarm of children.

nidificare vi. to nest.

nido sm. nest.

niente pron. 1. nothing 2. (in presenza di altre negazioni) anything.

nimbo sm. halo.

ninfa sf. nymph.

ninfea sf. water-lily.

ninfòmane sf. nymphomaniac.

ninnananna sf. lullaby.

ninnolo sm. 1. knick-knack 2. (balocco) plaything.

nipote sm. 1. (di nonno) grand-son 2. (di zio) nephew. ◆ **nipote** sf. 1. (di nonno) grand-daughter 2. (di zio) niece.

nipponico agg. e sm. Japanese.

nirvana sm. nirvana.

nitidezza sf. neatness.

nitido agg. neat, clear.

nitrato sm. nitrate.

nitrico agg. nitric.

nitrire vi. to whinny.

nitrito[1] sm. (di cavallo) whinny.

nitrito[2] sm. (chim.) nitrite.

nitroglicerina sf. nitroglycerin.

niveo agg. snowy.

no avv. no.

nòbile agg. e sm. noble.

nobiliare agg. nobiliary.

nobilitare vt. to ennoble.

nobilitazione sf. ennobling.

nobilmente avv. nobly.

nobiltà sf. nobility.

nocca sf. knuckle.

nocchiere sm. helmsman (pl. -men).

nocciola sf. hazel-nut.

nòcciolo sm. 1. stone 2. (ciò che è essenziale) heart.

nocciolo sm. (bot.) hazel-tree.

noce sm. walnut-tree. ◆ **noce** sf. walnut || guscio di — (barchetta), cockle-shell; — moscata, nutmeg.

nocivo agg. noxious, harmful.

nodo sm. knot.

nodoso agg. knotty.

noi pron. 1. (sogg.) we 2. (compl.) us.

noia sf. 1. boredom 2. (fastidio) worry, nuisance.

noioso agg. 1. boring 2. (molesto) annoying.

noleggiante sm. (mar.) charterer.

noleggiare vt. 1. to hire 2. (di navi) to charter.

noleggiatore sm. hirer.

noleggio sm. 1. hire 2. (mar.) freight.

nolente agg. unwilling || volente o —, willy-nilly.

nolo sm. 1. hire 2. (mar.) freight.

nòmade agg. e s. nomad.

nomadismo sm. nomadism.

nome sm. 1. name 2. (di battesimo) Christian name || senza —, nameless; a — di, on behalf of; per —, by name 3. (gramm.) noun.

nomea sf. notoriety.

nomenclatura sf. nomenclature.
nomìgnolo sm. nickname.
nòmina sf. appointment.
nominale agg. nominal.
nominalismo sm. nominalism.
nominalista s. nominalist.
nominalmente avv. nominally.
nominare vt. 1. to name 2. (eleggere) to appoint.
nominativo agg. 1. nominative 2. (comm.) registered. ♦ **nominativo** sm. name.
non avv. not.
nona sf. 1. (eccl.) Nones (pl.) 2. (mus.) ninth.
nonagenario agg. ninety years old (pred.); ninety-year-old (attr.). ♦ **nonagenario** sm. nonagenarian.
nonconformista s. non-conformist.
noncurante agg. careless.
noncuranza sf. carelessness.
nondimeno avv. nevertheless.
nonna sf. grandmother.
nonno sm. grandfather: i miei nonni, my grandparents.
nonnulla sm. trifle.
nono agg. ninth.
nonostante prep. notwithstanding || — che, though, although.
nonsenso sm. nonsense.
non-ti-scordar-di-me sm. forget-me-not.
nord sm. north.
nordamericano agg. e sm. North American.
nòrdico agg. 1. northern 2. (dell'Europa settentrionale) Nordic. ♦ **nòrdico** sm. 1. Northerner 2. (dell'Europa settentrionale) Nordic.
nordista sm. (stor. amer.) Federal.
norma sf. 1. rule, norm 2. (istruzioni) instruction, direction || a — di legge, according to law.
normale agg. e sm. 1. normal 2. (che dà una norma) standard.
normalità sf. normality.
normalizzare vt. to normalize.
normalizzazione sf. normalization.
normalmente avv. usually.
normanno agg. e sm. Norman: anglo—, (stor.) Anglo-Norman.
normativo agg. normative.
normògrafo sm. stencil.
norvegese agg. e sm. Norwegian.
nosocòmio sm. hospital.
nostalgia sf. home-sickness.
nostàlgico agg. homesick.
nostrano agg. home (attr.), national.

nostro agg. our: i nostri amici, our friends. ♦ **nostro** pron. ours: questa casa è nostra, this house is ours. ♦ **nostro** sm. 1. viviamo del —, we live on our own income 2. il Nostro (di autore), the Author 3. i nostri, our family.
nostromo sm. boatswain.
nota sf. 1. note 2. (lista) list.
notàbile agg. notable.
notaio sm. notary.
notare vt. to note.
notariato sm. profession of notary.
notarile agg. notarial.
notazione sf. notation.
notévole agg. remarkable, notable.
notevolmente avv. remarkably.
notìfica sf. 1. notification 2. (giur.) service.
notificare vt. 1. to notify 2. (informare) to inform 3. (giur.) to serve.
notizia sf. news (pl. con construzione sing.), piece of news (solo sing.) 2. (informazione) information (solo sing.) 3. (dato) note: notizie biografiche, biographical notes.
notiziario sm. news (pl., con costruzione sing.).
noto agg. well-known. ♦ **noto** sm. the known.
notoriamente avv. notoriously.
notorietà sf. notoriety.
notorio agg. 1. (in senso sfavorevole) notorious 2. well-known.
nottàmbulo agg. noctambulous. ♦ **nottàmbulo** sm. night-bird.
nottata sf. night.
notte sf. night.
nottetempo avv. by night.
notturno agg. night (attr.). ♦ **notturno** sm. (mus.) nocturne.
novanta agg. ninety.
novantenne agg. 1. ninety years old (pred.) 2. ninety-year-old (attr.).
novantèsimo agg. ninetieth.
novatore sm. innovator.
nove agg. nine.
novecento agg. nine hundred.
novella sf. short story, tale.
novellino agg. inexperienced. ♦ **novellino** sm. beginner.
novellista s. short-story writer.
novellìstica sf. story-telling.
novello agg. 1. new, spring (attr.) 2. (nuovo) second: un — Raffaello, a second Raffaello.

novembre *sm.* November.

novena *sf.* novena (*pl.* -ae).

nòvero *sm.* number 2. (*categoria*) class.

novilunio *sm.* new moon.

novità *sf.* 1. novelty 2. (*notizia*) news (*pl.* con costruzione sing.), piece of news (*solo sing.*).

noviziato *sm.* novitiate.

novizio *sm.* novice.

nozione *sf.* notion.

nozze *sf. pl.* wedding (*sing.*).

nube *sf.* cloud.

nubifragio *sm.* downpour.

nùbile *agg.* unmarried, single. ◆ nùbile *sf.* single woman.

nuca *sf.* nape.

nucleare *agg.* nuclear.

nucleina *sf.* nuclein.

nùcleo *sm.* nucleus (*pl.* -ei).

nudismo *sm.* nudism.

nudista *s.* nudist.

nudità *sf.* nakedness.

nudo *agg.* naked, bare.

nùgolo *sm.* cloud.

nulla *pron.* V. *niente.*

nullaosta *sm.* permit.

nullatenente *agg.* without property. ◆ nullatenente *s.* person without property.

nullità *sf.* 1. (*di cose*) nullity 2. (*di persone*) nonentity.

nullo *agg.* (*giur.*) null, void.

nume *sm.* numen, deity.

numeràbile *agg.* numerable.

numerabilità *sf.* numerability.

numerale *agg.* numeral.

numerare *vt.* 1. to count 2. (*segnare con numero*) to number.

numerato *agg.* 1. counted 2. (*segnato con un numero*) numbered.

numerario *agg.* numerary. ◆ numerario *sm.* (*comm.*) ready cash.

numeratore *sm.* (*mat.*) numerator.

numerazione *sf.* 1. numbering 2. (*mat.*) numeration.

numericamente *avv.* numerically.

numèrico *agg.* numerical.

nùmero *sm.* number.

numeroso *agg.* numerous.

numismàtica *sf.* numismatics.

numismàtico *agg.* numismatic. ◆ numismàtico *sm.* numismatist.

nunziatura *sf.* (*eccl.*) nunciature.

nunzio *sm.* nuncio.

nuòcere *vi.* to damage, to harm.

nuora *sf.* daughter-in-law.

nuotare *vi.* to swim (*v. irr.*).

nuotata *sf.* swim.

nuotatore *sm.* swimmer.

nuoto *sm.* swimming: *gara di —,* swimming-race.

nuova *sf.* news (*pl.* con costruzione *sing.*), piece of news (*solo sing.*).

nuovamente *avv.* again.

nuovo *agg.* new: *— di zecca, fiammante,* brand-new.

nutazione *sf.* nutation.

nutrice *sf.* wet-nurse.

nutriente *agg.* nourishing.

nutrimento *sm.* 1. feeding 2. (*fig.*) nourishment.

nutrire *vt.* 1. to feed (*v. irr.*) 2. (*mantenere*) to maintain 3. (*di sentimenti, passioni*) to foster. ◆ nutrirsi *vr.* to feed (on).

nutritivo *agg.* nourishing.

nutrito *agg.* fed, nourished.

nutrizione *sf.* 1. feeding 2. (*fig.*) nourishment.

nùvola *sf.* cloud.

nuvoloso *agg.* overcast, cloudy.

nuziale *agg.* wedding (*attr.*).

O

o *cong.* or ‖ *o ... o,* either ... or: *— tu — tua madre dovete venire,* either you or your mother must come; *— l'uno — l'altro,* either: *prendi — l'uno — l'altro,* take either.

òasi *sf.* oasis (*pl.* -ses).

obbligare *vt.* to compel. ◆ obbligarsi *vr.* to bind (*v. irr.*) oneself.

obbligatorietà *sf.* compulsoriness.

obbligatorio *agg.* compulsory.

obbligazione *sf.* 1. obligation 2. (*comm.*) bond.

obbligazionista *sm.* bond-holder.

òbbligo *sm.* obligation: *assumersi l'—,* to undertake (*v. irr.*).

obbrobrio *sm.* disgrace.

obbrobrioso *agg.* disgraceful.

obelisco *sm.* obelisk.

oberare *vt.* to burden.

obesità *sf.* obesity.

obeso *agg.* obese.

òbice *sm.* howitzer.

obiettare *vt.* to object.

obiettivamente *avv.* objectively.

obiettivismo *sm.* objectivism.

obiettività *sf.* objectivity.

obiettivo agg. objective. ♦ **obiettivo** sm. **1.** (mil.) objective **2.** (scopo) aim **3.** (foto) lens.

obiettore sm. objector: — di coscienza, conscientous objector.

obiezione sf. objection.

obitorio sm. morgue.

oblatore sm. donor.

oblazione sf. donation.

obliare vt. to forget (v. irr.).

oblio sm. oblivion.

obliquamente avv. obliquely.

obliquità sf. obliquity.

obliquo agg. oblique.

obliterare vt. to obliterate.

obliterazione sf. obliteration.

oblò sm. porthole.

oblungo agg. oblong.

òboe sm. oboe.

òbolo sm. offering.

obsoleto agg. obsolete.

oca sf. goose (pl. geese): pelle d'—, goose flesh; penna d'—, goose-quill.

occasionale agg. occasional.

occasionalismo sm. occasionalism.

occasionalmente avv. occasionally.

occasione sf. occasion.

occhiaia sf. eye-socket || avere le occhiaie, to have rings under one's eyes.

occhiali sm. pl. spectacles, glasses.

occhialuto agg. spectacled, wearing spectacles (pred.).

occhiata sf. look, glance.

occhiataccia sf. glare.

occhieggiare vt. to cast (v. irr.) glances (at). ♦ **occhieggiare** vi. to peep (at).

occhiello sm. **1.** button-hole **2.** (mecc.) eye.

occhietto sm. fare l'— a qu., to wink at so.

occhio sm. eye || costare un —, to be terribly expensive; chiudere un — su, to turn a blind eye to; dare nell'—, to strike (v. irr.) the eye; tenere d'—, to keep (v. irr.) an eye on; in un batter d'—, in the twinkling of an eye.

occidentale agg. west, western. ♦ **occidentale** s. westerner.

occidentalizzare vt. to occidentalize.

occidente sm. west.

occipitale agg. occipital.

occipite sm. occiput (pl. occipita).

occlusione sf. occlusion.

occlusivo agg. occlusive.

occorrente agg. necessary. ♦ **occorrente** sm. the necessary.

occorrenza sf. all'—, in case of need.

occòrrere vi. **1.** (imp.) to be necessary **2.** (abbisognare) to need.

occultamento sm. concealment.

occultare vt. to hide (v. irr.), to conceal. ♦ **occultarsi** vr. to hide.

occultatore sm. hider.

occultismo sm. occultism.

occulto agg. **1.** occult **2.** (nascosto) hidden.

occupante agg. occupying. ♦ **occupante** s. occupant.

occupare vt. **1.** to occupy **2.** (ingaggiare) to employ. ♦ **occuparsi** vr. **1.** (impiegarsi) to find (v. irr.) a job **2.** (badare) to attend (to).

occupato agg. engaged || essere — (fare un lavoro), to work.

occupazione sf. **1.** occupation **2.** (lavoro) job.

oceànico agg. oceanic.

ocèano sm. ocean.

oceanografia sf. oceanography.

ocello sm. ocellus (pl. -li).

ocra sf. ochre.

oculare agg. ocular, eye (attr.). ♦ **oculare** sm. (fis.) eyepiece.

oculatezza sf. shrewdness.

oculato agg. prudent.

oculista sm. oculist.

oculìstica sf. ophthalmology.

odalisca sf. odalisque.

ode sf. ode.

odiare vt. to hate.

odierno agg. of today, today's.

odio sm. hatred.

odioso agg. hateful.

odontàlgico agg. odontalgic.

odontoiatra s. odontologist, dentist.

odontoiatrìa sf. odontology.

odontoiàtrico agg. odontological.

odorare vt. e vi. to smell (v. irr.).

odorato sm. smell.

odore sm. smell.

odorifero agg. odoriferous.

odoroso agg. fragrant.

offèndere vt. to offend. ♦ **offendersi** vr. to be offended (at, by); to feel (v. irr.) hurt (by).

offensiva sf. offensive.

offensivo agg. offensive.

offensore sm. offender.

offerente s. **1.** offerer **2.** (a un'asta) bidder.

offerta *sf.* offer, donation.

offesa *sf.* offence.

offeso *agg.* offended, injured.

officiare *vi.* to officiate.

officina *sf.* workshop.

officinale *agg.* officinal.

offrire *vt.* to offer. ♦ **offrirsi** *vr.* to offer (oneself).

offuscamento *sm.* 1. dimming 2. *(oscurità)* dimness.

offuscare *vt.* to dim. ♦ **offuscarsi** *vr.* to grow *(v. irr.)* dim.

oftalmia *sf.* ophthalmia.

oftalmico *agg.* ophthalmic.

oftalmologia *sf.* ophthalmology.

oftalmoscopia *sf.* ophthalmoscopy.

oftalmoscopio *sm.* ophthalmoscope.

oggettivamente *avv.* objectively.

oggettivare *vt.* to objectify.

oggettivazione *sf.* objectification.

oggettivismo *sm.* objectivism.

oggettività *sf.* objectivity.

oggettivo *agg.* objective.

oggetto *sm.* object.

oggi *avv.* today.

ogiva *sf.* ogive.

ogivale *agg.* ogival.

ogni *agg.* every, each || *in — modo,* anyhow; *in — luogo,* everywhere.

ogniqualvolta *cong.* whenever.

ognuno *pron.* everybody, everyone || *— di,* each of.

oleandro *sm.* oleander.

oleario *agg.* oil *(attr.).*

oleato *agg.* oiled || *carta oleata,* grease-proof paper.

oleificio *sm.* oil mill.

oleodotto *sm.* oil pipeline.

oleografia *sf.* 1. oleography 2. *(pezzo singolo)* oleograph.

oleoso *agg.* oily.

olezzare *vi.* to smell *(v. irr.)* sweetly.

olezzo *sm.* fragrance.

olfattivo *agg.* olfactory.

olfatto *sm.* smell.

oliare *vt.* to oil.

oliatore *sm.* oil-can.

oliera *sf.* cruet.

oligarca *sm.* oligarch.

oligarchia *sf.* oligarchy.

oligarchico *agg.* oligarchic(al).

oligocene *sm.* Oligocene.

olimpiaco *agg.* V. *olimpico.*

olimpiade *sf.* Olympiad || *le Olimpiadi,* Olympic games.

olimpico *agg.* Olympic.

olimpionico *agg.* Olympic games *(attr.).* ♦ **olimpionico** *sm.*

Olympic champion.

olio *sm.* oil.

oliva *sf.* olive.

olivastro *agg.* olive.

oliveto *sm.* olive-grove.

olivo *sm.* olive.

olmo *sm.* elm.

olocausto *sm.* holocaust.

olografo *agg.* holograph.

oltraggiare *vt.* to outrage.

oltraggio *sm.* outrage.

oltraggioso *agg.* outrageous.

oltramontano *agg. e sm.* ultramontane.

oltranza *sf. (nella loc. avv.) a —,* to the bitter end.

oltranzista *sm.* extremist.

oltre *avv.* 1. *(di luogo)* further, farther 2. *(di tempo)* longer. ♦ **oltre** *prep.* 1. *(di luogo)* beyond 2. *(più di)* over 3. *(in aggiunta)* in addition to. ♦ **oltre a, che** *cong.* besides.

oltrecortina *avv.* beyond the Iron Curtain.

oltremare *avv.* overseas: *d'—,* overseas *(attr.).*

oltremodo *avv.* extremely.

oltrepassare *vt.* to go *(v. irr.)* beyond || *— i limiti* (*fig.*), to go *(v. irr.)* too far.

oltretomba *sm.* hereafter.

omaccione *sm.* burly man *(pl. men).*

omaggio *sm.* 1. homage 2. *(offerta)* gift.

ombelicale *agg.* umbilical.

ombelico *sm.* navel.

ombra *sf.* 1. shade *(anche spettro)* 2. *(immagine proiettata, parvenza)* shadow || *dar — a qu.,* to overshadow so.

ombreggiare *vt.* to shade.

ombreggiatura *sf.* shading.

ombrella *sf. (bot.)* umbel.

ombrellifero *agg.* umbelliferous.

ombrellino *sm.* parasol.

ombrello *sm.* umbrella.

ombrellone *sm.* sunshade.

ombretto *sm.* eye shadow.

ombrina *sf.* umbrina.

ombrosità *sf.* 1. shadiness 2. *(di persona)* touchiness 3. *(di cavallo)* skittishness.

ombroso *agg.* 1. shady 2. *(di persona)* touchy 3. *(di cavallo)* skittish.

omega *sm.* omega.

omelia *sf.* homily.

omeopatia *sf.* homeopathy.

omeopàtico *agg.* homeopathic. ♦
omeopàtico *sm.* homeopath.

omèrico *agg.* Homeric.

òmero *sm.* humerus (*pl.* -ri).

omertà *sf.* silence.

omesso *agg.* omitted.

ométtere *vt.* to omit, to leave out.

omicida *agg.* homicidal. ♦ **omicida** *s.* homicide.

omicidio *sm.* homicide.

omissione *sf.* omission.

òmnibus *sm.* bus.

omogeneità *sf.* homogeneity.

omogeneizzare *vt.* to homogenize.

omogèneo *agg.* homogeneous.

omologare *vt.* 1. to homologate 2.
(*sport*) to ratify.

omologazione *sf.* 1. homologation
2. (*sport*) ratification.

omòlogo *agg.* homologous.

omonimìa *sf.* homonymy.

omònimo *agg.* homonymous. ♦
omònimo *sm.* homonym.

omosessuale *agg. e s.* homosexual.

omosessualità *sf.* homosexuality.

oncia *sf.* ounce.

onda *sf.* wave || *mettere in —* (*radio*), to broadcast (*v. irr.*).

ondata *sf.* wave: *a ondate*, in
waves.

onde *avv.* 1. whence 2. (*affinché*) so
that 3. (*cosicché*) therefore 4. (*da,
con cui*) from, by, with which.

ondeggiamento *sm.* 1. waving 2.
(*di barca*) rolling 3. (*esitazione*)
wavering.

ondeggiante *agg.* 1. waving 2. (*di
barca*) rolling 3. (*esitante*) wavering.

ondeggiare *vi.* 1. to wave 2. (*di
barca*) to roll 3. (*esitare*) to waver.

ondina *sf.* undine.

ondoso *agg.* undulatory.

ondulare *vt.* to wave.

ondulato *agg.* 1. wavy 2. (*tec.*) corrugated.

ondulatorio *agg.* undulatory.

ondulazione *sf.* 1. undulation 2.
(*di capelli*) wave.

onerare *vt.* to burden.

ònere *sm.* burden || — *fiscale*, tax.

oneroso *agg.* burdensome.

onestà *sf.* 1. honesty 2. (*castità*)
chastity.

onesto *agg.* 1. honest 2. (*casto*)
chaste.

ònice *sf.* onyx.

onìrico *agg.* oneiric.

onnipotente *agg.* omnipotent. ♦
Onnipotente (l') *sm.* the Almighty.

onnipotenza *sf.* omnipotence.

onnipresente *agg.* omnipresent.

onnisciente *agg.* omniscient.

onniscienza *sf.* omniscience.

onniveggente *agg.* omnipercipient.

onnìvoro *agg.* omnivorous. ♦ **onnìvoro** *sm.* omnivore.

onomàstico *agg.* onomastic. ♦
onomàstico *sm.* name-day.

onomatopea *sf.* onomatopoeia.

onomatopèico *agg.* onomatopoeic.

onoràbile *agg.* honourable.

onorabilità *sf.* honourableness.

onoranza *sf.* honour.

onorare *vt.* to honour. ♦ **onorarsi** *vr.* to be proud (of).

onorario *agg.* honorary. ♦ **onorario** *sm.* fee.

onorato *agg.* 1. honoured 2. (*onesto*) honourable.

onore *sm.* honour || *farsi —*, to excel; *a onor del vero*, to tell (*v. irr.*) the truth; *serata d'—*, gala night.

onorévole *agg.* honourable.

onorificenza *sf.* 1. honour 2. (*decorazione*) decoration.

onorìfico *agg.* honorific(al).

onta *sf.* 1. shame 2. (*offesa*) insult || *ad — di*, in spite of.

ontano *sm.* alder.

ontologìa *sf.* ontology.

ontològico *agg.* ontological.

opacità *sf.* opacity.

opaco *agg.* 1. opaque 2. (*di suoni,
colori*) dull.

opale *sm.* opal.

opalescente *agg.* opalescent.

opalino *agg.* opaline.

òpera *sf.* 1. work 2. (*melodramma*)
opera 3. (*istituto*) institution.

operàbile *agg.* 1. workable. 2. (*chir.*) operable.

operaio *agg.* working. ♦ **operaio** *sm.* worker: — *specializzato*, skilled worker.

operante *agg.* operating.

operare *vi.* to work, to operate (*anche med.*).

operativo *agg.* operative.

operato *agg.* (*di tessuto*) diapered.
♦ **operato** *sm.* 1. (*condotta*)
behaviour 2. (*chi ha subito un'operazione*) operated patient.

operatore *sm.* 1. operator 2. (*cine*)
cameraman (*pl.* -men).

operatorio agg. operating.

operazione sf. operation: *fare un'— a qu.*, to perform an operation on so.; *subire un'—*, to undergo (v. irr.) an operation.

operetta sf. operetta.

operistico agg. opera (attr.).

operosità sf. industry.

operoso agg. industrious.

opificio sm. factory.

opimo agg. fertile.

opinàbile agg. thinkable.

opinare vi. to think (v. irr.).

opinione sf. opinion: *secondo l'— di qu.*, in so.'s opinion.

opossum sm. opossum.

oppiare vt. to opiate.

oppiato agg. e sm. opiate.

oppio sm. opium.

oppiòmane s. opium-addict.

opponente agg. e sm. opponent.

opponìbile agg. opposable.

opporre vt. 1. to oppose 2. (*obiettare*) to object. ♦ **opporsi** vr. to object (to), to be opposed.

opportunismo sm. opportunism.

opportunista s. opportunist.

opportunistico agg. opportunistic.

opportunità sf. 1. (*occasione*) opportunity 2. (*l'essere opportuno*) timeliness.

opportuno agg. 1. opportune 2. (*giusto*) right.

oppositore sm. opponent.

opposizione sf. opposition || *fare — (a qu., qc.)*, to oppose (so., sthg.).

opposto agg. e sm. opposite.

oppressione sf. oppression.

oppressivo agg. oppressive.

oppresso agg. oppressed.

oppressore sm. oppressor.

opprimente agg. oppressive.

opprìmere vt. to oppress.

oppugnare vt. to assail.

oppure cong. 1. or 2. (*altrimenti*) or else.

optare vi. to opt.

opulento agg. opulent.

opulenza sf. opulence.

opùscolo sm. pamphlet.

opzione sf. option.

ora¹ sf. 1. hour 2. (*tempo*) time: *che — è?*, what time is it?; *— di punta*, rush hour; *all'—*, by the hour; *di — in —*, hourly; *di buon'—*, early; *legale*, summer time; *non veder l'— di*, to look forward to.

ora² avv. now || *— come —*, at the moment; *d'— in poi*, from now on; *fino ad —*, so far; *sin d'—*, now; *prima d'—*, before; *or —*, just. ♦ **ora che** cong. now (that).

oràcolo sm. oracle.

òrafo sm. goldsmith.

orale agg. e sm. oral.

oralmente avv. orally.

oramai avv. V. ormai.

orango sm. orang-outang.

orario agg. 1. time (attr.) 2. (*all'ora*) per hour. ♦ **orario** sm. 1. hours (pl.) 2. (*tabella*) time-table || *in —*, on time.

orata sf. dory.

oratore sm. orator.

oratoria sf. oratory.

oratorio sm. oratory.

orazione sf. 1. oration 2. (*preghiera*) prayer.

orbare vt. to bereave (v. irr.).

orbene avv. well.

òrbita sf. orbit.

orbitale agg. orbital.

orbo agg. (di un occhio) one-eyed.

orchestra sf. orchestra.

orchestrale agg. orchestral. ♦ **orchestrale** s. member of an orchestra.

orchestrare vt. to orchestrate.

orchestrazione sf. orchestration.

orchestrina sf. band.

orchidea sf. orchid.

orcio sm. pitcher.

orco sm. ogre.

orda sf. horde.

ordigno sm. device.

ordinale agg. e sm. ordinal.

ordinamento sm. 1. arrangement 2. (*regolamento*) code, system.

ordinanza sf. 1. order 2. (*attendente mil.*) batman (pl. -men).

ordinare vt. 1. to order 2. (*mettere in ordine*) to put (v. irr.) in order 3. (*eccl.*) to ordain 4. (*med.*) to prescribe. ♦ **ordinarsi** vr. 1. to straighten up 2. (*mil.*) to draw (v. irr.) up.

ordinario agg. e sm. ordinary.

ordinata sf. 1. (*mat.*) ordinate 2. (*aer.; mar.*) frame.

ordinatamente avv. tidily.

ordinato agg. tidy, orderly.

ordinazione sf. 1. order 2. (*med.*) prescription 3. (*eccl.*) ordination.

òrdine sm. order || *— d'idee*, scheme of things; *all'— del giorno*, on the agenda; *per — di*, by order of; *parola d'—*, password; *di prim'—*, firstclass (*attr.*).

ordire *vt.* **1.** to warp **2.** (*fig.*) to plot.

ordito *sm.* warp.

orecchiàbile *agg.* catchy.

erecchino *sm.* earring.

orecchio *sm.* ear.

orecchioni *sm. pl.* mumps.

oréfice *sm.* jeweller.

oreficerìa *sf.* **1.** jeweller's art **2.** (*negozio*) jeweller's shop.

òrfano *agg. e sm.* orphan.

orfanotrofio *sm.* orphanage.

organetto *sm.* barrel-organ || *suonatore di —*, organ-grinder.

organicità *sf.* organic unity.

organico[1] *agg.* organic.

organico[2] *sm.* staff.

organismo *sm.* **1.** organism **2.** (*ente*) body.

organista *s.* organist.

organizzàbile *agg.* organizable.

organizzare *vt.* to organize.

organizzatore *sm.* organizer.

organizzazione *sf.* organization.

òrgano *sm.* organ.

organza *sf.* organza.

organzino *sm.* organzine.

orgasmo *sm.* orgasm.

orgia *sf.* orgy.

orgiàstico *agg.* orgiastic.

orgoglio *sm.* pride.

orgoglioso *agg.* proud.

orientale *agg.* eastern.

orientalista *s.* orientalist.

orientamento *sm.* orientation || *perdere l'—*, to lose (*v. irr.*) one's bearings.

orientare *vt.* to orient. ♦ **orientarsi** *vr.* **1.** to find (*v. irr.*) one's bearings **2.** (*tendere*) to tend.

oriente *sm.* east.

orifiamma *sf.* oriflamme.

orifizio *sm.* orifice.

orìgano *sm.* origan.

originale *agg.* **1.** original **2.** (*strano*) odd. ♦ **originale** *sm.* **1.** original **2.** (*persona eccentrica*) eccentric.

originalità *sf.* **1.** originality **2.** (*stranezza*) oddity.

originare *vt. e vi.* to originate.

originariamente *avv.* originally.

originario *agg.* original.

origine *sf.* origin || *avere —*, to originate; *dare —*, to cause.

origliare *vi.* to eavesdrop.

orina *sf.* urine.

orinale *sm.* chamber pot.

orinare *vi.* to urinate.

orinatoio *sm.* public lavatory.

orizzontale *agg.* horizontal.

orizzontalmente *avv.* horizontally.

orizzontare *vt.*, **orizzontarsi** *vr.* V. orientare, orientarsi.

orizzonte *sm.* horizon.

orlare *vt.* **1.** (*bordare*) to edge **2.** (*fare l'orlo*) to hem.

orlatura *sf.* hemming.

orlo *sm.* **1.** (*di abito ecc.*) hem **2.** (*bordatura*) border **3.** (*estremità*) edge **4.** (*di oggetto rotondo*) rim || *— a giorno*, hem-stitch; *sull'— della rovina*, on the verge of ruin.

orma *sf.* **1.** mark **2.** (*traccia*) trace **3.** (*di piede*) footprint || *seguire le orme di qu.*, to follow in so.'s footsteps; *tornare sulle proprie orme*, to go (*v. irr.*) back on one's tracks.

ormai *avv.* **1.** (by) now **2.** (*al passato*) (by) then.

ormeggiare *vt.* to moor. ♦ **ormeggiarsi** *vr.* to moor.

ormeggio *sm.* mooring.

ormone *sm.* hormone.

ormònico *agg.* hormonic.

ornamentale *agg.* ornamental.

ornamentazione *sf.* ornamentation.

ornamento *sm.* ornament.

ornare *vt.* to adorn.

ornato *agg.* **1.** adorned (with) **2.** (*di stile*) ornate.

ornitologìa *sf.* ornithology.

ornitològico *agg.* ornithological.

ornitòlogo *sm.* ornithologist.

oro *sm.* gold || *d'—*, golden.

orografìa *sf.* orography.

orogràfico *agg.* orographic(al).

orologerìa *sf.* **1.** (*arte*) horology **2.** (*negozio*) watchmaker's shop || *movimento d'—*, clock movement.

orologiaio *sm.* watchmaker.

orologio *sm.* **1.** watch **2.** (*a muro, da tavolo*) clock.

oròscopo *sm.* horoscope.

orpello *sm.* tinsel.

orrendamente *avv.* dreadfully.

orrendo *agg.* dreadful.

orrìbile *agg.* horrible.

orribilmente *avv.* horribly.

òrrido *agg.* frightful.

orripilante *agg.* terrifying.

orrore *sm.* horror.

orsa *sf.* she-bear: *— Maggiore*,

Great Bear; — **Minore**, Little Bear.

orsacchiotto *sm.* 1. young bear 2. (*giocattolo*) Teddy bear.

orso *sm.* bear.

ortaggio *sm.* vegetable.

ortensia *sf.* hydrangea.

ortica *sf.* nettle.

orticaria *sf.* nettle-rash.

orticultore *sm.* horticulturist.

orticultura *sf.* horticulture.

orto *sm.* 1. kitchen garden 2. (*ds orticoltore*) market garden.

ortodossìa *sf.* orthodoxy.

ortodosso *agg.* orthodox.

ortofrutticolo *agg.* horticultural.

ortogonale *agg.* orthogonal.

ortografìa *sf.* orthography, spelling.

ortogràfico *agg.* orthographic(al).

ortolano *sm.* 1. market-gardener 2. (*negoziante*) greengrocer.

ortopedìa *sf.* orthopedics.

ortopèdico *agg.* orthopedic. ♦ **ortopèdico** *sm.* orthopedist.

orzaiolo *sm.* sty.

orzata *sf.* (*bibita*) orgeat.

orzo *sm.* barley.

osanna *sf.* hosanna.

osare *vi.* to dare (*v. semidif.*). ♦ **osare** *vt.* (*tentare*) to attempt.

oscenità *sf.* obscenity.

osceno *agg.* obscene.

oscillare *vi.* 1. to swing (*v. irr.*) 2. (*di fiamma; opinioni*) to waver 3. (*elettr.*) to oscillate 4. (*di prezzi*) to fluctuate.

oscillatore *sm.* oscillator.

oscillatorio *agg.* oscillatory.

oscillazione *sf.* 1. swing 2. (*di fiamma; opinioni*) wavering 3. (*elettr.*) oscillation 4. (*di prezzi*) fluctuation.

oscillògrafo *sm.* oscillograph.

oscurantismo *sm.* obscurantism.

oscurantista *agg. e s.* obscurantist.

oscurare *vt.* 1. to darken 2. (*fig.*) to overshadow. ♦ **oscurarsi** *vr.* to darken.

oscurità *sf.* 1. darkness 2. (*fig.*) obscurity.

oscuro *agg.* 1. dark 2. (*sconosciuto, umile*) obscure 3. (*difficile*) hard, difficult 4. (*sconosciuto*) unknown.

osmosi *sf.* osmosis (*pl.* **-ses**).

ospedale *sm.* hospital.

ospedaliero *agg.* hospital (*attr.*).

ospitale *agg.* hospitable.

ospitalità *sf.* hospitality.

ospitare *vt.* to entertain.

òspite *s.* 1. (*chi ospita, uomo*) host; (*id.*, *donna*) hostess 2. (*chi è ospitato*) guest.

ospizio *sm.* 1. (*per poveri*) alms-house 2. (*per trovatelli*) foundling hospital 3. (*per vecchi ecc.*) home (for the old etc.).

ossario *sm.* charnel-house, ossuary.

ossatura *sf.* 1. skeleton 2. (*di edificio, discorso*) framework.

òsseo *agg.* bony.

ossequente *agg.* respectful.

ossequio *sm.* 1. homage 2. (*obbedienza*) obedience 3. (*saluti*) regards (*pl.*).

ossequiosità *sf.* deference.

ossequioso *agg.* deferential.

osservàbile *agg.* observable.

osservante *agg.* observant.

osservanza *sf.* 1. observance 2. (*ossequio*) regards (*pl.*).

osservare *vt.* 1. to observe 2. (*esaminare*) to examine.

osservatore *agg.* observing. ♦ **osservatore** *sm.* observer.

osservatorio *sm.* observatory.

osservazione *sf.* 1. observation: **in** —, under observation 2. (*rimprovero*) reproach.

ossessionante *agg.* haunting.

ossessionare *vt.* to haunt.

ossessione *sf.* obsession.

ossessivo *agg.* haunting.

ossesso *sm.* person possessed.

ossìa *cong.* (*cioè*) that is.

ossidàbile *agg.* oxidizable.

ossidare *vt.* to oxidize. ♦ **ossidarsi** *vr.* to oxidize.

ossidazione *sf.* oxidation.

òssido *sm.* oxide.

ossìdrico *agg.* oxyhydrogen.

ossificare *vt.* to ossify. ♦ **ossificarsi** *vr.* to ossify.

ossificazione *sf.* ossification.

ossigenare *vt.* 1. to oxygenate 2. (*di capelli*) to peroxide.

ossigenato *agg.* 1. oxygenated 2. (*di capelli*) peroxided ‖ **acqua ossigenata**, hydrogen peroxide.

ossìgeno *sm.* oxygen.

osso *sm.* bone ‖ **in carne e ossa**, in flesh and blood; **avere le ossa rotte**, to be aching all over.

ossuto *agg.* bony.

ostacolare *vt.* to hamper.

ostàcolo *sm.* 1. obstacle 2. (*sport*) hurdle ‖ **corsa ippica ad ostacoli**, steeple-chase.

ostaggio *sm.* hostage.

oste *sm.* innkeeper.

osteggiare *vt.* to oppose.

ostello *sm.* — *della gioventù,* (youth) hostel.

ostensorio *sm.* monstrance.

ostentare *vt.* 1. to show (*v. irr.*) off 2. (*fingere*) to feign.

ostentatamente *avv.* ostentatiously.

ostentazione *sf.* ostentation.

osteologia *sf.* osteology.

osteria *sf.* pub.

ostètrica *sf.* midwife (*pl.* -wives).

ostetricia *sf.* obstetrics.

ostètrico *sm.* obstetrician.

ostia *sf.* 1. wafer 2. (*eccl.*) host.

òstico *agg.* 1. irksome 2. (*di sapore*) unpalatable 3. (*fig.*) difficult.

ostile *agg.* hostile.

ostilità *sf.* hostility.

ostinarsi *vr.* to persist (in).

ostinato *agg.* stubborn.

ostinazione *sf.* obstinacy.

ostracismo *sm.* ostracism.

òstrica *sf.* oyster.

ostricaio *sm.* oyster-seller.

ostricultura *sf.* oyster-breeding.

ostruire *vt.* to obstruct.

ostruzione *sf.* obstruction.

ostruzionismo *sm.* obstructionism.

ostruzionista *s.* obstructionist.

otaria *sf.* otary.

otite *sf.* otitis.

otorinolaringoiatra *s.* otorhinolaryngologist.

otorinolaringoiatria *sf.* otorhinolaryngology.

ottaedro *sm.* octahedron.

ottagonale *agg.* octagonal.

ottàgono *sm.* octagon.

ottanta *agg.* eighty.

ottantenne *agg.* eighty years old, eighty-year-old (*attr.*).

ottantèsimo *agg.* eightieth.

ottava *sf.* octave.

ottavo *agg. e sm.* eighth.

ottemperanza *sf.* compliance.

ottemperare *vi.* to comply (with).

ottenebrare *vt.* to cloud.

ottenere *vt.* to obtain, to get (*v. irr.*).

ottetto *sm.* octet.

òttica *sf.* optics.

òttico *agg.* optic(al). ♦ **òttico** *sm.* optician.

ottimismo *sm.* optimism.

ottimista *s.* optimist.

ottimìstico *agg.* optimistic.

òttimo *agg.* best, very good. ♦ **òttimo** *sm.* optimum (*pl.* -ma).

otto *agg.* eight.

ottobre *sm.* October.

ottocento *agg.* eight hundred. ♦ **ottocento** *sm. l'*—, the nineteenth century.

ottomana *sf.* ottoman.

ottomano *agg. e sm.* Ottoman.

ottone *sm.* brass.

ottuagenario *agg. e sm.* octogenarian.

otturare *vt.* to stop. ♦ **otturarsi** *vr.* to stop.

otturatore *sm.* (*foto*) shutter.

otturazione *sf.* stopping.

ottusità *sf.* obtuseness.

ottuso *agg.* obtuse.

ovaia *sf.* ovary.

ovale *agg. e sm.* oval.

ovatta *sf.* 1. wadding 2. (*cotone idròfilo*) cotton-wool.

ovattare *vt.* to stuff with wadding.

ovazione *sf.* ovation.

ove *avv.* where.

ovest *sm.* west.

ovile *sm.* fold.

ovino *agg.* ovine. ♦ **ovino** *sm.* sheep (*invariato al pl.*).

ovìparo *agg.* oviparous.

ovòide *agg.* egg-shaped.

òvolo *sm.* (*fungo*) agaric.

ovulazione *sf.* ovulation.

òvulo *sm.* ovule.

ovunque *avv.* 1. everywhere 2. (*in qualsiasi posto*) anywhere. ♦ **ovunque** *cong.* wherever.

ovvero *cong.* or.

ovviare *vi.* to obviate (sthg.).

ovvio *agg.* obvious.

oziare *vi.* to loaf, to idle.

ozio *sm.* idleness.

oziosamente *avv.* idly.

ozono *sm.* ozone.

P

pacare *vt.* to calm.

pacatezza *sf.* calmness.

pacato *agg.* calm.

pacca *sf.* slap.

pacchetto *sm.* packet.

pacchia *sf.* godsend.

pacchianata *sf.* coarse action.

pacchiano *agg.* coarse.

pacco *sm.* 1. (*postale*) parcel 2. (*collo*) package.

paccottiglia *sf.* cheap stuff.

pace *sf.* peace || *darsi —*, to set (*v. irr.*) one's mind at rest.

pachiderma *sm.* pachyderm.

pachistano *agg.* e *sm.* Pakistani.

pacificare *vt.* 1. to pacify 2. (*riconciliare*) to reconcile. ♦ **pacificarsi** *vr.* to become (*v. irr.*) reconciled.

pacificazione *sf.* 1. pacification 2. (*riconciliazione*) reconciliation.

pacifico *agg.* 1. pacific 2. (*evidente*) self-evident.

pacifismo *sm.* pacifism.

pacifista *s.* pacifist.

pacioccone *sm.* easy-going person.

padella *sf.* frying-pan.

padiglione *sm.* pavilion.

padre *sm.* father.

padrino *sm.* godfather.

padronale *agg.* (*privato*) private || *casa —*, manor-house.

padronanza *sf.* mastery: — *di sé*, self-control.

padrone *sm.* 1. master 2. (*proprietario*) owner 3. (*di casa, albergo*) landlord || *essere — di sé*, to have self-control; *padronissimo!*, do as you like!

paesaggio *sm.* landscape.

paesano *agg.* rural. ♦ **paesano** *sm.* peasant.

paese *sm.* 1. (*nazione, territorio*) country 2. (*villaggio*) village.

paesista *s.* landscape painter.

paffuto *agg.* chubby.

paga *sf.* pay, wages (*pl.*): *libro —*, wages book; *giorno di —*, pay day.

pagàbile *agg.* payable.

pagaia *sf.* paddle.

pagamento *sm.* payment.

paganésimo *sm.* paganism.

pagano *agg.* e *sm.* pagan.

pagare *vt.* to pay (*v. irr.*).

pagella *sf.* schoolreport.

paggio *sm.* page.

pagherò *sm.* promissory note.

pàgina *sf.* page.

paglia *sf.* straw.

pagliacciata *sf.* buffoonery.

pagliaccio *sm.* clown.

pagliaio *sm.* strawstack.

pagliericcio *sm.* paillasse.

paglierino *agg.* straw-coloured.

paglietta *sf.* 1. (*cappello*) straw-hat 2. (*paglia di ferro*) steel-wool 3. (*trucioli per imballaggio*) wood-shavings (*pl.*) 4. (*trucioli, di carta*) paper-wool.

pagnotta *sf.* round loaf (*pl.* -aves).

pagoda *sf.* pagoda.

paio *sm.* 1. (*di cose necessariamente unite*) pair 2. (*due*) couple.

pala *sf.* 1. shovel 2. (*di remo, elica*) blade 3. (*di ruota*) paddle || — *d'altare*, altar-piece.

paladino *sm.* 1. paladin 2. (*fig.*) champion.

palafitta *sf.* 1. pile 2. (*abitazione*) pile-dwelling.

palafreniere *sm.* groom.

palafreno *sm.* palfrey.

palanchino *sm.* palanquin.

palata *sf.* 1. shovelful 2. (*colpo*) blow with a shovel || *a palate* (*fig.*), in plenty.

palatale *agg.* palatal.

palatino *agg.* palatine.

palato *sm.* palate.

palazzo *sm.* palace.

palco *sm.* 1. (*di teatro*) box 2. (*pedana*) stand.

palcoscènico *sm.* stage.

paleocristiano *agg.* paleo-christian.

paleografia *sf.* paleography.

paleògrafo *sm.* paleographer.

paleontologìa *sf.* paleontology.

paleontològico *agg.* paleontologic(al).

paleontòlogo *sm.* paleontologist.

palesare *vt.* to reveal.

palese *agg.* evident.

palestra *sf.* gymnasium.

paletta *sf.* (*di capostazione*) signal stick.

palinodìa *sf.* palinode.

palissandro *sm.* rosewood.

palizzata *sf.* palisade.

palla *sf.* 1. ball 2. (*pallottola*) bullet.

pallacanestro *sf.* basket-ball.

pallanuoto *sf.* water-polo.

pallavolo *sf.* volley-ball.

palleggiare *vi.* (*calcio*) to dribble. ♦ **palleggiare** *vt.* to toss. ♦ **palleggiarsi** *vr. rec.* to shift on one another.

palleggio *sm.* 1. (*calcio*) dribbling 2. (*tennis*) tossing.

palliativo *agg.* e *sm.* palliative.

pallidezza *sf.* paleness.

pàllido *agg.* pale.

pallino *sm.* 1. (*di fucile*) shot 2. (*mania*) craze.

palloncino *sm.* 1. balloon 2. (*lampioncino*) Chinese lantern.

pallone *sm.* ball || *gioco del —*, football.

pallore *sm.* pallor.

pallòttola *sf.* 1. pellet 2. (*mil.*) bullet.

pallottoliere *sm.* abacus (*pl.* -ci).

palma¹ *sf.* (*della mano*) palm.

palma² *sf.* (*albero*) palm(-tree).

palmare *agg.* 1. (*anat.*) palmar 2. (*evidente*) clear.

palmato *agg.* 1. (*bot.*) palmate 2. (*zool.*) webbed.

palmeto *sm.* palm-grove.

palmìpede *agg.* e *sm.* palmiped.

palmo *sm.* palm.

palo *sm.* 1. pole 2. (*per fondamenta, ormeggio*) pile || — indicatore, signpost; *fare il —*, to be on the lookout.

palombaro *sm.* diver.

palpàbile *agg.* tangible.

palpare *vt.* 1. to finger 2. (*med.*) to palpate.

palpebra *sf.* eyelid || *battere le palpebre*, to blink.

palpitante *agg.* 1. throbbing 2. (*fig.*) fascinating.

palpitare *vi.* to throb (with sthg.).

palpitazione *sf.* 1. throbbing 2. (*med.*) palpitation.

pàlpito *sm.* throb.

paltò *sm.* overcoat.

palude *sf.* marsh.

paludoso *agg.* marshy.

pàmpino *sm.* vine-leaf (*pl.* -leaves).

panacea *sf.* panacea.

panare *vt.* to bread.

panca *sf.* bench.

pancetta *sf.* 1. (*cu persona*) pot-belly.

panchina *sf.* bench.

pancia *sf.* belly.

panciera *sf.* body-belt.

panciotto *sm.* waistcoat.

panciuto *agg.* pot-bellied.

pancotto *sm.* panada.

pàncreas *sm.* pancreas.

pancreàtico *agg.* pancreatic.

pandemonio *sm.* pandemonium.

pane *sm.* bread.

panegìrico *sm.* panegyric.

panetteria *sf.* bakery.

panettiere *sm.* baker.

pànfilo *sm.* yacht.

pangermanismo *sm.* Pan-Germanism.

pànico *agg.* e *sm.* panic.

panico *sm.* (*bot.*) millet.

paniere *sm.* basket.

panificare *vi.* to make (*v. irr.*) bread.

panificazione *sf.* bread-making.

panificio *sm.* bakery.

panino *sm.* roll: — *imbottito*, sandwich.

panna¹ *sf.* cream: — *montata*, whipped cream.

panna² *sf. restare in* —, to have a breakdown.

pannello *sm.* 1. (*edil.*) panel 2. (*di stoffa*) light cloth.

panno *sm.* 1. cloth (*pl.* cloths) 2. *pl.* (*vestiti*) clothes.

pannocchia *sf.* cob.

pannolino *sm.* 1. (*per bambini*) napkin 2. (*assorbente igienico*) sanitary towel.

panorama *sm.* view.

panslavismo *sm.* Pan-slavism.

pantagruèlico *agg.* Pantagruelian.

pantaloni *sm. pl.* trousers || — *corti*, shorts.

pantano *sm.* 1. mire 2. (*luogo pantanoso; fig.*) quagmire.

panteismo *sm.* pantheism.

panteista *s.* pantheist.

panteìstico *agg.* pantheistic(al).

pantera *sf.* panther.

pantòfola *sf.* slipper.

pantògrafo *sm.* pantograph.

pantomima *sf.* pantomime.

panzana *sf.* fib.

paonazzo *agg.* purple.

papa *sm.* pope.

papà *sm.* daddy.

papale *agg.* papal.

papalina *sf.* skull-cap.

papato *sm.* papacy.

papàvero *sm.* poppy || *alto* —, (*fig.*) bigwig.

pàpera *sf.* 1. (*zool.*) duckling 2. (*errore*) slip 3. (*teat.*) fluff.

papilla *sf.* papilla (*pl.* -ae).

papillare *agg.* papillary.

papiro *sm.* papyrus (*pl.* -ri).

papirologìa *sf.* papyrology.

papismo *sm.* popery.

papista *s.* papist.

pappa *sf.* pap.

pappagallo *sm.* parrot || *ripetere a* —, to parrot.

pappagorgia *sf.* double chin.

pappare *vt.* to gorge. ♦ **papparsi** *vr.* to eat up.

pàprica *sf.* paprika.

paràbola *sf.* 1. parable 2. (*geom.; mil.*) parabola.

parabòlico *agg.* parabolic.

parabrezza *sm.* windscreen.

paracadutare *vt.* to parachute. ♦

paracadutarsi vr. to bail out.
paracadute sm. parachute.
paracadutismo sm. parachutism.
paracadutista sm. 1. parachutist 2. (mil.) paratrooper.
paracarro sm. wayside post.
paradigma sm. paradigm.
paradisiaco agg. paradisiac(al).
paradiso sm. paradise.
paradossale agg. paradoxical.
paradosso sm. paradox.
parafango sm. mudguard.
paraffina sf. paraffin.
parafrasare vt. to paraphrase.
paràfrasi sf. paraphrase.
parafùlmine sm. lightning-rod.
paragonàbile agg. comparable.
paragonare vt. to compare.
paragone sm. comparison: a — di, in comparison with.
paràgrafo sm. paragraph.
paràlisi sf. palsy.
paralitico agg. e sm. paralytic.
paralizzare vt. to paralyze.
parallela sf. parallel: le parallele (sport), parallel bars.
parallelepìpedo sm. parallelepiped (pl. -da).
parallelismo sm. parallelism.
parallelo agg. e sm. parallel.
parallelogrammo sm. parallelogram.
paralume sm. lamp-shade.
paramento sm. 1. hanging 2. (eccl.) vestment.
paràmetro sm. parameter.
paraninfo sm. paranymph.
paranoia sf. paranoia.
paranòico agg. e sm. paranoiac.
paraocchi sm. pl. blinkers.
parapetto sm. 1. parapet 2. (davanzale) sill.
parapiglia sm. turmoil.
paraploggia sm. umbrella.
parare vt. 1. (riparare) to shield 2. (evitare) to parry 3. (ornare) to decorate || andare a —, to drive (v. irr.) at. ♦ **pararsi** vr. 1. (comparire) to appear 2. (adornarsi) to deck oneself.
parasole sm. parasol.
parassita agg. parasitic. ♦ **parassita** s. parasite.
parassitismo sm. parasitism.
parastatale agg. State controlled || ente —, semi-governmental body.
parata sf. 1. parade 2. (sport) parry || fare una — (sport), to parry.
paratìa sf. bulkhead.

paratifo sm. paratyphoid.
parato sm. hanging || carta da parati, wallpaper.
paratola sf. cataract.
paraurti sm. bumper.
paravento sm. screen.
parcella sf. fee.
parcheggiare vt. to park.
parcheggio sm. 1. parking 2. (luogo) car park.
parco¹ sm. park: — di divertimenti, fun-fair.
parco² agg. sparing.
parecchio agg. quite a lot of. ♦ **parecchio** avv. quite a lot, quite (+ agg.). ♦ **parecchio** pron. a good deal of it, several (pl.).
pareggiare vt. 1. (livellare) to level 2. (comm.) to balance 3. (parificare una scuola) to recognize officially. ♦ **pareggiare** vi. (sport) to draw (v. irr.).
pareggio sm. 1. (comm.) balance 2. (sport) draw, tie.
parentado sm. V. parentela.
parente sm. relative.
parentela sf. 1. relationship 2. (i parenti) relatives.
parèntesi sf. 1. parenthesis (pl. -ses) 2. (segno grafico) bracket.
parere¹ vi. 1. to seem 2. (essere simile a) to look like 3. (pensare) to think (v. irr.) (of).
parere² sm. opinion.
paresi sf. paresis.
parete sf. wall: — divisoria, partition.
pàrgolo sm. little child (pl. children).
pari agg. 1. equal, same 2. (simile) like 3. (divisibile per due) even. ♦ **pari** sm. equal, peer.
paria sm. pariah.
parietale agg. parietal.
parificazione sf. 1. (comm.) balance 2. (scuola) official recognition 3. (livellamento) levelling.
parigino agg. e sm. Parisian.
pariglia sf. pair.
parimenti avv. likewise.
parità sf. equality.
paritario agg. equalitarian.
parlamentare¹ agg. parliamentary. ♦ **parlamentare** sm. Member of Parliament.
parlamentare² vi. to parley.
parlamentarismo sm. parliamentarianism.

parlamento *sm.* parliament.

parlantina *sf.* talkativeness || *aver buona* —, to be a glib talker.

parlare *vi.* to speak (*v. irr.*), to talk.

parlare *sm.* **1.** (*discorso*) speech **2.** (*chiacchiere*) talk **3.** (*idioma*) language.

parlato *agg. cinema* —, talkies (*pl.*).

parlatore *sm.* speaker.

parlatorio *sm.* parlour.

parlottare *vi.* to mutter.

parodìa *sf.* parody.

parodiare *vt.* to parody.

parodista *s.* parodist.

parola *sf.* **1.** word **2.** (*facoltà di parlare, discorso*) speech || *parole incrociate*, crosswords; *gioco di parole*, pun; *far* —, to mention; *restare senza* —, to be left speechless; *venire a parole con*, to have words with; *rivolgere la* — *a qu.*, to address so.; *avere la* — *facile*, to be a glib talker.

parolaccia *sf.* nasty word: *dire parolacce*, to swear (*v. irr.*).

parolaio *sm.* **1.** chatterbox **2.** (*di scrittore*) word-monger.

paroliere *sm.* « lyrics » writer.

parossismo *sm.* paroxysm.

paròtide *sf.* parotid.

parricida *s.* parricide.

parricidio *sm.* parricide.

parrocchia *sf.* parish.

parrocchiale *agg.* parish (*attr.*).

parrocchiano *sm.* parishioner.

pàrroco *sm.* **1.** (*cattolico*) parish priest **2.** (*protestante*) parson.

parrucca *sf.* wig.

parrucchiere *sm.* hairdresser.

parsimonia *sf.* thriftiness.

parsimonioso *agg.* thrifty.

parte *sf.* **1.** part **2.** (*lato*) side **3.** (*porzione*) share **4.** (*pol.; comm.; giur.*) party || *da* —, aside: *da* — *di*, from; *da* — *a* —, right through; *da una* — ... *dall'altra*, on one hand ... on the other; *la maggior* — *di*, most (of); *a* — *ciò*, apart from that; *farsi da* —, to get (*v. irr.*) out of the way; *fare la* —, to play.

partecipante *s.* **1.** sharer **2.** (*chi annuncia*) spokesman (*pl.* -men) **3.** (*chi presenzia*) the bystander.

partecipare *vi.* **1.** to share (in) **2.** (*esser presente*) to be present. ♦

partecipare *vt.* to announce.

partecipazione *sf.* **1.** sharing **2.**

(*esser presente*) presence **3.** (*annuncio*) announcement **4.** (*biglietto*) card.

partécipe *agg.* **1.** sharing **2.** (*informato*) acquainted || *rendere* — *qu. di qc.*, to acquaint so. with sthg.

parteggiare *vi.* to take (*v. irr.*) sides (with).

partenogènesi *sf.* parthenogenesis.

partenza *sf.* **1.** departure, leaving **2.** (*sport*) start || *punto di* —, starting-point; *essere in* —, to be leaving.

particella *sf.* particle.

participiale *agg.* participial.

participio *sm.* participle.

particolare *agg.* particular. ♦ **particolare** *sm.* detail.

particolareggiato *agg.* detailed.

particolarismo *sm.* particularism.

particolarità *sf.* **1.** particularity **2.** (*dettaglio*) detail.

partigiano *agg. e sm.* partisan.

partire¹ *vi.* **1.** to leave (*v. irr.*) **2.** (*muoversi, iniziare, anche fig.*) to start || *a* — *da*, (*beginning*) from.

partire² *vt.* to separate.

partita *sf.* **1.** (*giocata*) game, match **2.** (*di merce*) lot **3.** (*in contabilità*) entry || *dar* — *vinta* (*fig.*), to give (*v. irr.*) in.

partitivo *agg. e sm.* partitive.

partito *sm.* party.

partitura *sf.* (*mus.*) score.

partizione *sf.* division.

parto *sm.* **1.** delivery **2.** (*fig.*) product.

partoriente *agg.* parturient. ♦ **partoriente** *sf.* lying-in woman.

partorire *vt.* to bring (*v. irr.*) forth, to beget (*v. irr.*) (*anche fig.*).

parvenza *sf.* **1.** appearance **2.** (*ombra*) shadow.

parziale *agg.* partial.

parzialità *sf.* partiality.

parzialmente *avv.* partially.

pàscere *vt. e vi.* **1.** to feed (*v. irr.*) **2.** (*al pascolo*) to graze. ♦ **pàscersi** *vr.* to feed (on).

pascià *sm.* pasha.

pasciuto *agg.* fed.

pascolare *vt. e vi.* to pasture.

pàscolo *sm.* pasture || *essere al* —, to be grazing.

Pasqua *sf.* Easter.

pasquale *agg.* Easter (*attr.*).

passàbile *agg.* passabl∎

passabilmente *avv.* passably.

passaggio *sm.* 1. passage 2. (*traversata*) crossing ‖ *dare un —in macchina*, to give (*v. irr.*) a lift; *vietato il —*, no thoroughfare; *di —*, of transition; (*incidentalmente*) incidentally.

passamanerìa *sf.* passementerie.

passamano *sm.* (*fettuccia*) braid.

passamontagna *sm.* snow-cap.

passante *sm.* 1. (*di cinghia ecc.*) loop 2. (*persona*) passer-by.

passaporto *sm.* passport.

passare *vi.* 1. to pass 2. (*andare*) to call (on so., at sthg.). ♦ **passare** *vt.* 1. to pass 2. (*di tempo*) to spend (*v. irr.*) 3. (*sopportare, trafiggere*) to pass through.

passatempo *sm.* pastime.

passatista *s.* traditionalist.

passato *agg.* 1. past 2. (*scorso*) last. ♦ **passato** *sm.* 1. past 2. (*cuc.*) mash.

passaverdura *sm.* vegetable masher.

passeggero *agg.* passing. ♦ **passeggero** *sm.* passenger.

passeggiare *vi.* to walk, to take (*v. irr.*) a walk.

passeggiata *sf.* 1. walk 2. (*in auto*) drive 3. (*in bicicletta, a cavallo*) ride 4. (*lungomare*) promenade.

passeggino *sm.* perambulator.

passeggio *sm.* 1. walk 2. (*gente che passeggia*) promenaders (*pl.*) ‖ *andare a —*, to go (*v. irr.*) for a walk.

passeràceo *sm.* e *agg.* passerine.

passerella *sf.* 1. (*ponte pedonale*) footbridge 2. (*provvisoria*) trestle-bridge 3. (*mar.; edil.*) gangway 4. (*teat.*) parade.

pàssero *sm.* sparrow.

passibile *agg.* liable (to).

passiflora *sf.* passion-flower.

passino *sm.* strainer.

passionale *agg.* 1. passional 2. (*appassionato*) passionate.

passione *sf.* passion.

passivamente *avv.* passively.

passività *sf.* 1. passivity 2. (*comm.*) liabilities (*pl.*).

passivo *agg.* passive. ♦ **passivo** *sm.* 1. passive 2. (*comm.*) liabilities (*pl.*).

passo *sm.* 1. step 2. (*andatura*) pace 3. (*di montagna*) pass 4. (*brano, passaggio*) passage 5. (*cine*)

gauge 6. (*tec.*) pitch ‖ *passo passo*, very slowly; *segnare il —*, to mark time; *camminare a grandi passi*, to stride (*v. irr.*).

pasta *sf.* 1. paste 2. (*pasticcino*) cake 3. (*per minestre*) "pasta".

pasteggiare *vi.* to feed (*v. irr.*) (on).

pastella *sf.* (*cuc.*) batter.

pastello *sm.* pastel: *matita, disegno a —*, pastel.

pasticca *sf.* tablet.

pasticcerìa *sf.* confectionery.

pasticciare *vt.* e *vi.* to make (*v. irr.*) a mess (of).

pasticciere *sm.* confectioner.

pasticcino *sm.* cake.

pasticcio *sm.* 1. (*cuc.*) pie 2. (*fig.*) mess ‖ *essere nei pasticci*, to be in trouble.

pasticcione *sm.* bungler.

pastificio *sm.* «pasta» factory.

pastiglia *sf.* tablet.

pasto *sm.* meal.

pastoia *sf.* hobble.

pastone *sm.* mash.

pastorale *agg.* pastoral.

pastore *sm.* 1. shepherd 2. (*relig.*) parson.

pastorizìa *sf.* stock-raising.

pastorizzare *vt.* to pasteurize.

pastorizzazione *sf.* pasteurization.

pastosità *sf.* 1. mellowness 2. (*morbidezza*) doughiness.

pastoso *agg.* 1. mellow 2. (*morbido*) doughy.

pastrano *sm.* overcoat.

pastura *sf.* pasture.

patacca *sf.* 1. (*macchia*) spot 2. (*cosa senza valore*) worthless object.

patata *sf.* potato: — *americana*, sweet potato ‖ — *fritta*, chip; (*id., croccante*) crisp.

patema *sm.* worry.

patentato *agg.* licenced.

patente *agg.* patent. ♦ **patente** *sf.* licence.

patereccio *sm.* whitlow.

paterna *sf.* scolding ‖ *fare una — a qu.*, to lecture so.

paternalismo *sm.* paternalism.

paternalìstico *agg.* paternalistic.

paternità *sf.* paternity.

paterno *agg.* paternal.

pateticamente *avv.* pathetically.

patètico *agg.* e *sm.* pathetic.

patìbolare *agg.* sinister.

patìbolo *sm.* scaffold.

patimento *sm.* pain.

pàtina *sf.* 1. patina 2. (*di vernice*)

coat of varnish 3. (sulla lingua) coat 4. (su carta, terracotta) glaze.

patinare vt. 1. to varnish 2. (carta, terracotta) to glaze.

patire vt. e vi. to suffer: — il freddo, to suffer from the cold || — la fame, to starve.

patio agg. sickly. ♦ **patito** sm. (fig.) fan.

patògeno agg. pathogenic.

patologìa sf. pathology.

patològico agg. pathologic(al).

patòlogo sm. pathologist.

patria sf. 1. country, fatherland 2. (luogo natale) birthplace.

patriarca sm. patriarch.

patriarcale agg. patriarchal.

patriarcato sm. patriarchate.

patricida s. V. parricida.

patrigno sm. stepfather.

patrimoniale agg. patrimonial.

patrimonio sm. patrimony.

patrio agg. 1. native 2. (paterno) paternal.

patriota s. patriot.

patriottardo sm. e agg. jingoist.

patriòttico agg. patriotic.

patriottismo sm. patriotism.

patriziato sm. patriciate.

patrizio sm. e agg. patrician.

patrocinante sm. pleader.

patrocinare vt. 1. (sostenere) to support 2. (giur.) to plead.

patrocinio sm. 1. support 2. (giur.) pleading.

patronato sm. 1. patronage 2. (istituto benefico) charitable institution.

patronessa sf. patroness.

patrono sm. 1. patron 2. (giur.) counsel for the defence.

patteggiare vi. to come (v. irr.) to terms.

pattinaggio sm. skating.

pattinare vi. to skate.

pattinatore sm. skater.

pàttino sm. 1. (a rotelle) roller-skate 2. (da ghiaccio) ice-skate 3. (di slitta) shoe 4. (aer.) skid 5. (mecc.) sliding-block.

patto sm. 1. agreement, pact 2. (condizione) term || a — che, provided that; a nessun —, by no means.

pattuglia sf. patrol.

pattugliare vi. to patrol.

pattuire vi. to reach an agreement (upon). ♦ **pattuire** vt. to agree (on).

pattume sm. rubbish.

pattumiera sf. dust-bin.

pauperismo sm. pauperism.

paura sf. 1. fear, dread 2. (spavento) fright, scare.

pauroso agg. fearful.

pàusa sf. pause.

pavesare vt. to dress (with flags).

pavese sm. (mar.) hoist.

pavimentare vt. 1. to pave 2. (una stanza) to floor.

pavimento sm. floor.

pavone sm. peacock.

pavoneggiarsi vr. to show (v. irr.) off.

pazientare vi. to have patience.

paziente agg. e sm. patient.

pazienza sf. patience || —!, never mind!

pazzesco agg. foolish.

pazzìa sf. 1. madness 2. (azione, idea pazza) folly || fare pazzie, to act like a fool.

pazzo agg. mad. ♦ **pazzo** sm. madman (pl. -men).

pecca sf. fault || senza —, faultless.

pe ccaminoso agg. sinful.

peccare vi. 1. to sin 2. (errare) to err 3. (esser manchevole) to lack (sthg.).

peccato sm. sin || che —!, what a pity!; è un — che, it is a pity that.

peccatore sm. sinner.

pece sf. pitch.

pècora sf. 1. sheep (pl. invariato) 2. (femmina) ewe.

pecoraio sm. shepherd.

peculato sm. peculation.

peculiare agg. peculiar.

peculiarità sf. peculiarity.

pecùlio sm. money.

pecuniario agg. pecuniary.

pedaggio sm. toll.

pedagogìa sf. pedagogy.

pedagògico agg. pedagogic(al).

pedagogista s. pedagogist.

pedagogo sm. pedagogue.

pedalare vi. to pedal.

pedale sm. pedal.

pedaliera sf. 1. (aer.) rudder-bar 2. (mus.) pedal keyboard.

pedana sf. 1. (sport) spring-board 2. (piedistallo) stand.

pedante agg. pedantic. ♦ **pedante** s. pedant.

pedanterìa sf. pedantry.

pedantesco agg. pedantic.

pedata sf. 1. kick 2. (impronta) footprint.

pedemontano *agg.* piedmont.

pederasta *sm.* homosexual.

pederastia *sf.* homosexuality.

pedestre *agg.* pedestrian.

pediatra *s.* pediatrist.

pediatria *sf.* pediatrics.

pedicure *s.* chiropodist.

pediluvio *sm.* foot-bath.

pedina *sf.* 1. (*alla dama*) piece 2. (*agli scacchi*) pawn || *muovere una — (anche fig.)*, to make (*v. irr.*) a move.

pedinare *vt.* to shadow.

pedonale *agg.* pedestrian (*attr.*): *passaggio —*, pedestrian crossing.

pedone *sm.* pedestrian || *strada riservata ai pedoni*, footpath.

peduncolo *sm.* stalk.

peggio *agg.* (*comp.*) worse. ♦ **peggio** *sm.* the worst. ♦ **peggio** *avv.* 1. (*comp.*) worse 2. (*superl. rel.*) the worst || *— per lui*, so much the worse for him; *alla —*, at worst; *avere la —*, to get (*v. irr.*) the worst of it.

peggioramento *sm.* aggravation.

peggiorare *vt.* to make (*v. irr.*) worse. ♦ **peggiorare** *vi.* to get (*v. irr.*) worse.

peggiorativo *agg. e sm.* pejorative.

peggiore *agg.* 1. (*comp.*) worse: *questo libro è — di quello*, this book is worse than that 2. (*superl. rel.*) the worst: *era il suo — nemico*, he was his worst enemy.

pegno *sm.* pledge || *dare qc. in —*, to pledge sthg.; *polizza di —*, pawn-ticket; *agenzia di pegni*, pawnshop.

pelàgico *agg.* pelagic.

pelame *sm.* hair.

pelapatate *sm.* potato peeler.

pelare *vt.* 1. to unhair 2. (*sbucciare*) to peel 3. (*spellare*) to skin 4. (*far pagare caro*) to fleece. ♦ **pelarsi** *vr.* to lose (*v. irr.*) one's hair.

pelato *agg.* bald.

pelatura *sf.* 1. unhairing 2. (*sbucciatura*) peeling.

pellaio *sm.* furrier.

pellame *sm.* hides (*pl.*).

pelle *sf.* skin; (*di animale grosso*) hide || *articoli in —*, leather articles; *amici per la —*, bosom friends.

pellegrina *sf.* (*mantella*) tippet.

pellegrinaggio *sm.* pilgrimage: *in —*, on a pilgrimage.

pellegrinare *vi.* to wander, to roam.

pellegrino *sm.* pilgrim.

pellerossa *agg. e sm.* redskin.

pelletteria *sf.* 1. leather goods 2. (*negozio*) leather goods shop.

pellicano *sm.* pelican.

pelliccerìa *sf.* 1. furriery 2. (*negozio*) furrier's shop

pelliccia *sf.* fur.

pellicciaio *sm.* furrier.

pellicola *sf.* film: *— a passo ridotto*, substandard film.

pelo *sm.* hair: *per un —*, by a hair's breadth; *cercare il — nell'uovo*, to split (*v. irr.*) hairs || *non avere peli sulla lingua*, to be outspoken.

peloso *agg.* hairy.

pelota *sf.* pelota.

peltro *sm.* pewter.

peluria *sf.* down || *coperto di —*, downy.

pelvi *sf.* pelvis.

pèlvico *agg.* pelvic.

pena *sf.* 1. (*punizione*) punishment 2. (*dolore*) pain 3. (*disturbo*) trouble || *essere in —*, to worry; *aver — di*, to pity; *a mala —*, hardly; *non ne vale la —*, it is not worth while.

penale *agg.* 1. criminal 2. (*relativo alla pena*) penal.

penalista *sm.* criminal lawyer.

penalità *sf.* penalty.

penalizzare *vt.* to penalize.

penare *vi.* 1. to suffer 2. (*far fatica*) to be hardly able.

pendaglio *sm.* pendant.

pendente *agg.* 1. pendent 2. (*inclinato*) leaning. ♦ **pendente** *sm.* pendant.

pendenza *sf.* 1. slope 2. (*grado d'inclinazione*) gradient 3. (*giur.*) pending suit 4. (*comm.*) outstanding account.

pèndere *vi.* 1. to hang (*v. irr.*) 2. (*inclinare*) to lean (*v. irr.*) 3. (*essere in declino*) to slope 4. (*incombere*) to overhang (*v. irr.*) 5. (*essere incerto*) to waver.

pendìo *sm.* slope.

pèndola *sf.* pendulum-clock.

pendolare *agg.* pendular.

pèndolo *sm.* pendulum.

pendulo *agg.* pendulous.

pene *sm.* penis.

penetràbile *agg.* penetrable.

penetrabilità *sf.* penetrability.

penetrante *agg.* piercing.

penetrare *vi.* e *vt.* **1.** to penetrate **2.** (*con fatica; di freddo, suono*) to pierce **3.** (*furtivamente*) to steal (*v. irr.*) (into).

penetrazione *sf.* penetration.

penicillina *sf.* penicillin.

peninsulare *agg.* peninsular.

penisola *sf.* peninsula.

penitente *agg.* e *s.* penitent.

penitenza *sf.* **1.** (*teol.*) penance **2.** (*pentimento*) repentance **3.** (*nei giochi*) forfeit.

penitenziale *agg.* penitential.

penitenziario¹ *agg.* penitentiary. ◆ **penitenziario²** *sm.* jail.

penna *sf.* **1.** pen **2.** (*di uccello*) feather.

pennacchio *sm.* **1.** plume **2.** (*mil.*) panache.

pennecchio *sm.* wool on the distaff.

pennellare *vi.* **1.** to brush **2.** (*med.*) to paint.

pennellata *sf.* touch (of the brush).

pennellessa *sf.* flat brush.

pennello *sm.* brush.

pennino *sm.* nib.

pennone *sm.* (*mar.*) yard.

pennuto *agg.* ~feathered. ◆ **pennuto** *sm.* bird.

penombra *sf.* half-light.

penoso *agg.* painful.

pensare *vi.* e *vt.* **1.** to think (*v. irr.*) (of) **2.** (*badare*) to look after || *pensa ai fatti tuoi*, mind your own business.

pensata *sf.* thought, idea.

pensatore *sm.* thinker.

pensiero *sm.* **1.** thought **2.** (*opinione*) mind, opinion **3.** (*ansia*) worry.

pensieroso *agg.* thoughtful.

pènsile *agg.* hanging || *giardino —*, roof garden.

pensilina *sf.* **1.** penthouse **2.** (*di attesa*) shelter.

pensionàbile *agg.* pensionable.

pensionante *s.* boarder.

pensionato¹ *agg.* retired. ◆ **pensionato** *sm.* pensioner, retired person.

pensionato² *sm.* (*istituto*) hostel.

pensione *sf.* (*assegno vitalizio*) pension || *essere in —*, to be retired; *mettere in —*, to pension off **2.** (*albergo*) boarding-house || *essere a —*, to be boarding (at); *— completa*, full board.

pensoso *agg.* pensive.

pentaedro *sm.* pentahedron.

pentàgono *sm.* pentagon.

pentagramma *sm.* (*mus.*) pentagram.

pentàmetro *sm.* pentameter.

pentano *sm.* pentane.

Pentecoste *sf.* Pentecost, Whitsunday.

pentimento *sm.* repentance.

pentirsi *vr.* **1.** to repent **2.** (*rimpiangere*) to regret.

pèntodo *sm.* pentode.

péntola *sf.* pot.

penùltimo *agg.* e *sm.* last but one.

penuria *sf.* shortage, penury.

penzolare *vi.* to dangle.

penzoloni *agg.* **1.** (*dondolante*) dangling **2.** (*pèndente*) hanging.

peòcio *sm.* mussel.

peonia *sf.* peony.

pepaiola *sf.* pepper-box.

pepare *vt.* to pepper.

pepato *agg.* peppery (*anche fig.*).

pepe *sm.* pepper.

peperone *sm.* pepper: *peperoni sott'aceto*, pickled peppers.

pepita *sf.* nugget.

peplo *sm.* peplum.

pepsina *sf.* pepsin.

peptone *sm.* peptone.

per *prep.* **1.** for: *fallo — me*, do it for me **2.** (*moto per luogo*) through: *passai per Roma*, I passed through Rome **3.** (*entro, per mezzo di*) by: *devo farlo — la fine dell'anno*, I have to do it by the end of the year; *— telegramma*, by telegram **4.** (*causa*) owing to, because of: *non potemmo andare — la nebbia*, we couldn't go owing to (because of) fog || *— l'addietro*, in the past; *— caso*, by chance; *— nulla*, not at all; *— sempre*, for ever; *— tempo*, early. ◆ **per** *cong.* **1.** (*finale*) to, in order to **2.** (*causale*) for.

pera *sf.* pear.

peràcido *sm.* peracid.

perbacco *inter.* by Jove.

perbene *agg.* respectable.

percalle *sm.* percale.

percentuale *agg.* per cent. ◆ **percentuale** *sf.* percentage.

percepìbile *agg.* **1.** perceptible **2.** (*di somme*) receivable.

percepire *vt.* **1.** to perceive **2.** (*di stipendio*) to receive.

percettibile *agg.* perceptible.
percettivo *agg.* perceptive.
percezione *sf.* perception.
perché *cong.* 1. (*int.*) why 2. (*nelle risposte*) because 3. (*affinché*) so that. ◆ **perché** *sm.* reason, why: *chiedersi il* —, to wonder why.
perciò *cong.* therefore, so.
perclorato *sm.* perchlorate.
percòrrere *vt.* 1. to cover 2. (*attraversare*) to run (*v. irr.*) through.
percorso *sm.* 1. (*distanza*) distance 2. (*tragitto*) way 3. (*tracciato*) course.
percossa *sf.* blow.
percuòtere *vt.* to strike (*v. irr.*).
percussione *sf.* percussion.
percussore *sm.* percussion-pin.
perdente *agg.* losing. ◆ **perdente** *s.* loser.
pèrdere *vt.* 1. to lose (*v. irr.*) 2. (*di treno, occasione*) to miss 3. (*far acqua*) to leak. ◆ **pèrdersi** *vr.* 1. to get (*v. irr.*) lost 2. (*svanire*) to fade 3. (*rovinarsi*) to be ruined || — *d'animo*, to lose heart.
perdifiato (*nella loc. avv.*) *a* —, with all one's strength.
perdigiorno *sm.* idler.
pèrdita *sf.* 1. loss 2. (*falla, fuga*) leak.
perditempo *sm.* waste of time.
perdizione *sf.* perdition.
perdonàbile *agg.* pardonable.
perdonare *vt.* 1. to forgive (*v. irr.*) 2. (*risparmiare*) to spare. ◆ **perdonarsi** *vr.* to forgive oneself. ◆ **perdonarsi** *v. rec.* to forgive each other (one another).
perdono *sm.* forgiveness || *chiedere* —, to beg one's pardon.
perdurare *vi.* to continue.
perdutamente *avv.* desperately.
perduto *agg.* lost.
peregrinare *vi.* to wander, to roam.
peregrinazione *sf.* wandering, roaming.
peregrino *agg.* rare.
perenne *agg.* 1. perennial 2. (*eterno*) everlasting.
perennemente *avv.* 1. perennially 2. (*per sempre*) for ever.
perentorio *agg.* peremptory.
perequazione *sf.* equalization.
perfettamente *avv.* perfectly.
perfettìbile *agg.* perfectible.
perfettibilità *sf.* perfectibility.
perfetto *agg.* perfect. ◀ **perfetto**

sm. (*gramm.*) perfect.
perfezionamento *sm.* perfecting.
perfezionare *vt.* 1. to perfect 2. (*migliorare*) to improve. ◆ **perfezionarsi** *vr.* to improve.
perfezione *sf.* perfection: *alla* —, to perfection.
perfidamente *avv.* wickedly.
perfidia *sf.* wickedness.
pèrfido *agg.* wicked.
perfino *avv.* even.
perforare *vt.* 1. to pierce 2. (*d biglietti, schede*) to punch 3. (*mecc.*) to drill, to bore.
perforatore *agg.* perforating. ◆ **perforatore** *sm.* perforator.
perforatrice *sf.* (*macchina*) drill, punch.
perforazione *sf.* 1. perforation 2. (*mecc.*) drilling 3. (*di biglietti, schede*) punching.
pergamena *sf.* parchment.
pèrgola *sf.* bower.
pergolato *sm.* arbour.
pericardio *sm.* pericardium (*pl.* -ia).
pericolante *agg.* tottering.
pericolo *sm.* danger || *mettere in* —, to endanger; *correre un* —, to be in danger.
pericolosamente *avv.* dangerously.
pericoloso *agg.* dangerous.
periferia *sf.* 1. periphery 2. (*di città*) suburbs (*pl.*).
perifèrico *agg.* 1. peripheral 2. (*suburbano*) suburban.
perifrasi *sf.* periphrasis (*pl.* -ses).
perifràstico *agg.* periphrastic.
perigeo *sm.* perigee.
perimetro *sm.* perimeter.
periodicità *sf.* periodicity.
periòdico *agg.* e *sm.* periodical.
periodo *sm.* period.
peripezia *sf.* vicissitude.
perìplo *sm.* circumnavigation.
perire *vi.* to perish.
periscopio *sm.* periscope.
peristilio *sm.* peristyle.
perito *sm.* 1. expert 2. (*comm.*) estimator.
peritonite *sf.* peritonitis.
perituro *agg.* perishable.
perizia *sf.* 1. (*abilità*) skill 2. (*valutazione*) survey.
perla *sf.* pearl.
perlàceo *agg.* pearly.
perlìfero *agg.* pearl (*attr.*).
perlomeno *avv.* at least.
perlustrare *vt.* 1. to reconnoitre 2. (*di polizia*) to patrol.

perlustratore *sm.* scout.

perlustrazione *sf.* **1.** reconnaissance **2.** (*di polizia*) patrol || *essere in* —, to be on a reconnaissance.

permalosità *sf.* touchiness.

permaloso *agg.* touchy.

permanente *agg.* permanent. ◆ **permanente** *sf.* permanent wave.

permanentemente *avv.* permanently.

permanenza *sf.* **1.** permanence **2.** (*soggiorno*) stay.

permanere *vi.* **1.** to remain **2.** (*durare*) to last.

permanganato *sm.* permanganate.

permeàbile *agg.* permeable.

permeabilità *sf.* permeability.

permeare *vt.* to permeate.

permesso *agg.* allowed. ◆ **permesso** *sm.* **1.** leave: *in* —, on leave **2.** (*autorizzazione*) licence || *documento di* —, permit.

perméttere *vt.* to allow || *permettete?*, may I? ◆ **perméttersi** *vr.* (*prendersi la libertà*) to take (*v. irr.*) the liberty (of) || *il lusso*, to afford.

pèrmuta *sf.* exchange.

permutàbile *agg.* exchangeable.

permutare *vt.* to exchange.

permutazione *sf.* permutation.

pernice *sf.* partridge.

pernicioso *agg.* pernicious.

perno *sm.* pivot.

pernottamento *sm.* overnight stay.

pernottare *vi.* to stay overnight.

pero *sm.* pear-tree.

però *cong.* but.

peronòspora *sf.* mildew.

perorare *vt.* to plead.

perorazione *sf.* pleading.

peròssido *sm.* peroxide.

perpendicolare *agg. e sf.* perpendicular.

perpetrare *vt.* to perpetrate.

perpetuamente *avv.* perpetually.

perpetuare *vt.* to perpetuate. ◆ **perpetuarsi** *vr.* to last.

perpetuità *sf.* perpetuity.

perpetuo *agg.* perpetual: *in* —, perpetually.

perplessità *sf.* perplexity.

perplesso *agg.* perplexed: *rendere* —, to perplex.

perquisire *vt.* to search.

perquisizione *sf.* search.

persecutore *sm.* persecutor.

persecuzione *sf.* persecution.

perseguìbile *agg.* (*giur.*) prosecutable.

perseguire *vt.* **1.** to pursue **2.** (*giur.*) to prosecute.

perseguitare *vt.* to persecute.

perseguitato *sm.* persecuted person.

perseverante *agg.* persevering.

perseveranza *sf.* perseverance.

perseverare *vi.* to persevere.

persiana *sf.* shutter.

persiano *agg. e sm.* Persian.

persistente *agg.* persistent.

persistenza *sf.* persistence.

persistere *vi.* to persist.

persona *sf.* person: *di* —, personally; — *giuridica*, artificial person.

personaggio *sm.* **1.** personage **2.** (*di romanzo ecc.*) character.

personale *agg.* personal. ◆ **personale** *sm.* **1.** staff **2.** (*corporatura*) figure.

personalità *sf.* personality: — *giuridica*, legal status.

personalmente *avv.* personally.

personificare *vt.* **1.** to personify **2.** (*teat.*) to play.

personificazione *sf.* personification.

perspicace *agg.* shrewd.

perspicacia *sf.* shrewdness.

perspicuo *agg.* perspicuous.

persuadere *vt.* to persuade. ◆ **persuadersi** *vr.* to convince oneself.

persuasione *sf.* persuasion.

persuasivo *agg.* persuasive.

pertanto *cong.* therefore.

pèrtica *sf.* perch.

pertinace *agg.* pertinacious.

pertinacia *sf.* pertinacity.

pertinente *agg.* pertinent.

pertinenza *sf.* pertinence.

pertosse *sf.* whooping cough.

pertugio *sm.* hole.

perturbare *vt.* to disturb.

perturbatore *agg.* disturbing. ◆ **perturbatore** *sm.* disturber.

perturbazione *sf.* disturbance.

pervàdere *vt.* to pervade.

pervenire *vi.* to arrive (at).

perversione *sf.* perversion.

perversità *sf.* perversity.

perverso *agg.* perverse.

pervertire *vt.* to pervert. ◆ **pervertirsi** *vr.* to go (*v. irr.*) astray.

pervicace *agg.* obstinate.

pervicacia *sf.* obstinacy.

pervinca *sf.* periwinkle.

pesa *sf.* **1.** (*luogo*) weigh-house **2.** (*apparecchio*) weighing-machine.

pesante *agg.* heavy.

pesantezza *sf.* heaviness.

pesare *vt.* to weigh. ◆ **pesare** *vi.* 1. to weigh 2. (*fig.*) to lie (*v. irr.*) heavy.

pesata *sf.* weighing.

pesca[1] *sf.* (*bot.*) peach.

pesca[2] *sf.* 1. (*il pescare*) fishing 2. (*industria*) fishery 3. (*il pescato*) catch.

pescaggio *sm.* (*mar.*) draught.

pescare *vt.* 1. to fish 2. (*fig.*) to fish out 3. (*cogliere sul fatto*) to catch (*v. irr.*) red-handed 4. (*carte*) to draw (*v. irr.*). ◆ **pescare** *vi.* to draw.

pescatore *sm.* 1. fisher 2. (*con lenza*) angler.

pesce *sm.* fish: — *rosso*, goldfish; — *persico*, perch.

pescecane *sm.* shark.

peschereccio *agg.* fishing. ◆ **peschereccio** *sm.* fishing-boat.

pescheria *sf.* 1. fish-shop 2. (*mercato*) fish-market.

peschiera *sf.* fish-pond.

pescialola *sf.* (*cuc.*) fish-kettle.

pesco *sm.* peach-tree.

pescoso *agg.* fishy.

pesista *sm.* weight thrower.

peso *sm.* weight: *a* —, by weight.

pessimismo *sm.* pessimism.

pessimista *agg.* pessimistic. ◆ **pessimista** *s.* pessimist.

pessimistico *agg.* pessimistic.

pèssimo *agg.* worst, very bad.

pesta *sf.* 1. track 2. (*difficoltà*) difficulty.

pestaggio *sm.* scuffle.

pestare *vt.* 1. to pound 2. (*picchiare*) to beat (*v. irr.*) 3. (*calpestare*) to tread (*v. irr.*) on.

pestata *sf.* 1. (*lo schiacciare*) pounding 2. (*il calpestare*) treading.

peste *sf.* plague.

pestello *sm.* pestle.

pestìfero *agg.* pestiferous.

pestilenza *sf.* plague.

pestilenziale *agg.* pestilential.

pesto *agg.* pounded: *buio* —, pitch dark; *avere gli occhi pesti*, to have rings under one's eyes.

pètalo *sm.* petal.

petardo *sm.* petard.

petizione *sf.* petition.

petraia *sf.* 1. (*cava*) quarry 2. (*mucchio di pietre*) heap of stones.

petrografìa *sf.* petrography.

petroliera *sf.* tanker.

petrolìfero *agg.* oil (*attr.*).

petrolio *sm.* oil.

pettégola *sf.* gossiper.

pettegolare *vi.* to gossip.

pettegolezzo *sm.* gossip.

pettégolo *agg.* gossipy. ◆ **pettégolo** *sm.* gossiper.

pettinare *vt.* to comb. ◆ **pettinarsi** *vr.* to comb one's hair.

pettinato *sm.* worsted.

pettinatrice *sf.* 1. hairdresser 2. (*industria tessile*) comber.

pettinatura *sf.* 1. hairdo 2. (*industria tessile*) combing.

pèttine *sm.* comb.

pettirosso *sm.* robin.

petto *sm.* 1. breast 2. (*torace*) chest || — *a* —, face to face; *prendere di* —, to face.

pettorale *agg.* e *sm.* pectoral.

pettorina *sf.* stomacher.

pettoruto *agg.* 1. full-breasted 2. (*fig.*) haughty.

petulante *agg.* pert.

petulanza *sf.* pertness.

petunia *sf.* petunia.

pezza *sf.* 1. patch 2. (*macchia*) spot || — *di stoffa*, roll.

pezzato *agg.* spotted.

pezzente *agg.* beggarly. ◆ **pezzente** *s.* ragamuffin.

pezzo *sm.* piece: *fare a pezzi*, to tear (*v. irr.*) to pieces; *a pezzi e bocconi*, piecemeal; — *grosso* (*fig.*), bigwig; — *di ricambio*, spare part.

pezzuola *sf.* handkerchief.

piacente *agg.* pleasant.

piacere[1] *sm.* 1. pleasure 2. (*favore*) favour || *per* —, please; —! (*nelle presentazioni*), how do you do!

piacere[2] *vi.* to like: *gli piace leggere*, he likes reading, he likes to read; *come pare e piace*, as one pleases.

piacévole *agg.* pleasant.

piacimento *sm.* pleasure, liking: *a* —, as much as one likes.

piaga *sf.* 1. sore 2. (*calamità*) plague 3. (*fig.*) nuisance.

piagnisteo *sm.* moaning.

piagnucolare *vi.* to whimper.

piagnucolìo *sm.* whimper.

piagnucoloso *agg.* whimpering.

pialla *sf.* plane.

piallare *vt.* to plane.

piallatrice *sf.* planer.

piallatura *sf.* 1. planing 2. (*trucioli*) shavings (*pl.*).

piana *sf.* plane.

pianeggiante *agg.* level.

pianella sf. 1. (pantofola) slipper 2. (mattonella) flat tile.

pianeròttolo sm. landing.

pianeta sm. planet.

piangente agg. weeping, crying.

piàngere vi. to cry, to weep (v. irr.). ◆ **piàngere** vt. to weep 2. (un lutto) to mourn || — a calde lacrime, to weep one's heart out.

pianificare vt. to plan.

pianificazione sf. planning.

pianista s. pianist.

piano¹ agg. 1. flat 2. (chiaro) clear 3. (semplice) simple.

piano² sm. 1. plain 2. (di casa) floor, storey 3. (strato) layer 4. (superficie piana) level, livello) plane 5. (progetto) plan 6. (cine) primo —, close up || — stradale, roadway; in primo —, in the foreground.

piano³ avv. 1. (lentamente) slowly 2. (sommessamente) softly 3. (con cautela) gently.

pianoforte sm. piano.

pianola sf. barrel-organ.

pianta sf. 1. plant 2. (carta topografica) map 3. (del piede) sole || di sana — (completamente), completely; (di nuovo) anew.

piantagione sf. plantation.

piantare vt. 1. to plant 2. (conficcare) to drive (v. irr.) 3. (lasciare) to leave (v. irr.) || piantarla, to stop.

piantatore sm. planter.

pianterreno sm. ground-floor.

pianto sm. 1. tears (pl.): scoppiare in —, to burst (v. irr.) into tears 2. (dolore) grief.

piantonamento sm. guarding.

piantonare vt. to guard.

piantone¹ sm. soldier on guard.

piantone² sm. (agr.) shoot.

pianura sf. plain.

piastra sf. 1. plate 2. (di marmo) slab 3. (moneta) piastre.

piastrella sf. tile.

piastrellare vt. to tile.

piastrellatura sf. tiling.

piastrina sf. plaque.

piattaforma sf. platform.

piattello sm. pan || tiro al —, trap-shooting.

piattino sm. saucer.

piatto¹ agg. flat.

piatto² sm. 1. dish 2. (portata) course 3. (di lama) flat 4. (di grammofono) turn-table.

piazza sf. 1. square 2. (comm.) market || mettere qc. in —, to make (v. irr.) sthg. public.

piazzaforte sf. stronghold.

piazzale sm. large square.

piazzamento sm. place.

piazzare vt. to place. ◆ **piazzarsi** vr. (sport) to be placed.

piazzista sm. salesman (pl. -men).

picaresco agg. picaresque.

picca sf. pike || picche (alle carte), spades (pl.).

piccante agg. 1. piquant 2. (salace) spicy.

piccarsi vr. to plume oneself (on).

piccato agg. resentful.

picchettare vt. 1. to peg out 2. (mil.) to picket.

picchetto sm. 1. peg 2. (mil.) pickets: essere di —, to be on picket.

picchiare vt. e vi. 1. (percuotere) to beat (v. irr.) 2. (battere) to strike (v. irr.) 3. (bussare) to knock 4. (aer.) to pitch || — in testa (di motore), to ping. ◆ **picchiarsi** vr. rec. to fight (v. irr.).

picchiata sf. 1. beating 2. (aer.) dive || scendere in —, to dive.

picchiatello agg. slightly crazy.

picchiettare vt. 1. (battere) to tap 2. (chiazzare) to spot.

picchiettato agg. spotted.

picchiettìo sm. tapping.

picchio¹ sm. 1. (colpo) blow 2. (alla porta) knock.

picchio² sm. (zool.) woodpecker.

picchiotto sm. door-knocker.

piccinerìa sf. meanness.

piccino agg. 1. little 2. (fig.) mean.

piccionaia sf. 1. pigeon-house 2. (teat.) gallery.

piccione sm. pigeon.

picco sm. peak || a —, vertically; colare a —, mandare a —, to sink (v. irr.).

piccolezza sf. 1. smallness 2. (meschinità) meanness 3. (inezia) trifle.

piccolo agg. 1. small, little 2. (di statura, breve) short 3. (giovane) young 4. (meschino) mean 5. (leggero) light.

piccone sm. pick(axe).

piccozza sf. axe.

pidocchierìa sf. meanness.

pidocchio sm. 1. louse (pl. lice) 2. (fig.) miser.

pidocchioso agg. 1. lousy 2. (fig.) stingy.

piede sm. foot (pl. feet): a piedi, on foot ‖ a — libero, on bail; prender —, to get (v. irr.) a footing.

piedistallo sm. pedestal.

piega sf. 1. fold 2. (fatta ad arte) pleat 3. (segno) crease ‖ messa in — (di capelli), set.

piegàbile agg. folding.

piegamento sm. 1. folding 2. (flessione) flexing.

piegare vt. 1. to fold 2. (flettere, anche fig.) to bend (v. irr.). ♦ **piegare** vi. 1. (voltare) to turn 2. (curvarsi) to bend. ♦ **piegarsi** vr. to bend.

piegatrice sf. (mecc.) bending-machine.

pieghettare vt. to pleat.

pieghévole agg. 1. pliable 2. (atto a essere piegato) folding. ♦ **pieghévole** sm. folder.

pieghevolezza sf. pliability.

piena sf. 1. flood, spate 2. (folla) crowd.

pienamente avv. fully.

pienezza sf. 1. fullness 2. (massimo grado) height.

pieno agg. full: — zeppo, full up; in — (completamente), fully, (esattamente), exactly, (nel mezzo) in the middle; in — giorno, in broad daylight. ♦ **pieno** sm. (il colmo) middle ‖ fare il — (auto), to fill up.

pietà sf. 1. pity 2. (relig.) piety ‖ aver — di, to have mercy on; far —, to arouse pity; per —!, for pity's sake!

pietanza sf. 1. main course 2. (piatto) dish.

pietismo sm. pietism.

pietosamente avv. pitifully.

pietoso agg. pitiful.

pietra sf. stone: posare la prima —, to lay the foundation stone.

pietraia sf. V. petraia.

pietrificare vt. to petrify. ♦ **pietrificarsi** vr. to petrify.

pietrina sf. flint.

pietrisco sm. rubble.

pietroso agg. stony.

piffero sm. pipe.

pigiama sm. pyjamas (pl.).

pigia pigia sm. awful crush.

pigiare vt. to press. ♦ **pigiarsi** vr. to crowd.

pigione sf. rent: stare a — presso, to lodge with.

pigmentato agg. pigmented.

pigmentazione sf. pigmentation.

pigmento sm. pigment.

pigmeo sm. pigmy.

pigna sf. pinecone.

pignatta sf. pot.

pignolería sf. faultfinding.

pignolo sm. 1. (bot.) pine-seed 2. (fig.) faultfinder.

pignoramento sm. attachment.

pignorare vt. to distrain.

pigolare vi. to peep.

pigolìo sm. peep.

pigramente avv. 1. lazily 2. (lentamente) sluggishly.

pigrizia sf. 1. laziness 2. (lentezza) sluggishness.

pigro agg. 1. lazy 2. (lento) sluggish.

pila sf. pile: — a secco, dry battery.

pilastro sm. pillar.

pillola sf. pill: — anticoncezionale, contraceptive (pill), the "pill".

pilone sm. 1. pylon 2. (di ponte) pier ‖ — d'ormeggio, mooring-mast.

piloro sm. pylorus (pl. -ri).

pilota sm. 1. pilot 2. (di auto) driver.

pilotaggio sm. pilotage: scuola di —, flying-school.

pilotare vt. 1. to pilot 2. (un'auto) to drive (v. irr.).

piluccare vt. to nibble.

piluccone sm. nibbler.

pinacoteca sf. picture-gallery.

pinastro sm. pinaster.

pindàrico agg. Pindaric.

pineta sf. pinewood.

pingue agg. 1. fat 2. (ricco) rich.

pinguèdine sf. fatness.

pinguino sm. penguin.

pinna sf. 1. fin 2. (sport) flipper.

pinnàcolo[1] sm. pinnacle.

pinnàcolo[2] sm. (gioco) pinochle.

pino sm. pine (-tree).

pinolo sm. pine-seed.

pinta sf. pint.

pinza sf. pliers (pl.), pincers (pl.).

pinzetta sf. tweezers (pl.).

pio agg. pious ‖ opera pia, charitable organization.

pioggia sf. rain: sotto la —, in the rain.

piolo sm. V. piuolo.

piombare vt. 1. to plumb 2. (tip.) to lead ‖ — un dente, to stop a tooth. ♦ **piombare** vi. 1. (cade-

re) to fall (*v. irr.*) heavily 2. (*assalire*) to assail 3. (*precipitarsi*) to rush.

piombatura *sf.* sealing, leading.

piombino *sm.* 1. plummet 2. (*sigillo*) leaden seal.

piombo *sm.* 1 lead 2. (*sigillo*) leaden seal 3. (*pallottola*) bullet ‖ *filo a —*, plumb line; *a —*, perpendicularly; *di —*, leaden; *andare coi piedi di —*, to proceed very cautiously.

pioniere *sm.* pioneer.

pioppeto *sm.* poplargrove.

pioppo *sm.* poplar.

piorrea *sf.* pyorrhoea.

piovano *agg.* rain (*attr.*).

piovasco *sm.* shower.

piòvere *vi.* to rain, to pour (*anche fig.*).

piovigginare *vi.* to drizzle.

piovigginoso *agg.* drizzly, rainy.

piovoso *agg.* rainy.

piovra *sf.* octopus.

pipa *sf.* pipe.

pipetta *sf.* (*chim.*) pipette.

pipistrello *sm.* bat.

pipita *sf.* agnail.

pira *sf.* pyre.

piramidale *ag.* pyramidal.

piràmide *sf.* pyramid.

pirata *sm.* pirate ‖ *— della strada*, hit-and-run driver.

pirateria *sf.* piracy.

pirico *agg. polvere pirica*, gunpowder.

pirite *sf.* pyrite(s).

piroetta *sf.* pirouette.

piroettare *vi.* to pirouette.

piroga *sf.* pirogue.

pirografia *sf.* pyrography.

piròscafo *sm.* steamer.

pirotècnica *sf.* pyrotechnics.

pirotècnico *agg.* pyrotechnic(al): *spettacolo —*, fireworks. ♦ **pirotècnico** *sm.* pyrotechnist.

piscia *sf.* piss.

pisciare *vi.* to piss.

pisciata *sf.* piss.

pisciatoio *sm.* urinal.

piscicoltura *sf.* pisciculture.

piscina *sf.* swimming-pool.

pisello *sm.* pea.

pisolino *sm.* nap.

pista *sf.* 1. (*traccia*) track 2. (*di animale*) trail 3. (*aer.*) strip.

pistacchio *sm.* pistachio.

pistillo *sm.* pistil.

pistola *sf.* pistol

pistone *sm.* piston.

pitagòrico *agg.* e *sm.* Pythagorean: *tavola pitagorica*, multiplication table.

pitale *sm.* chamber pot.

pitocco *agg.* 1. mean 2. (*fig.*) stingy. ♦ **pitocco** *sm.* 1. beggar 2. (*fig.*) mean person.

pitone *sm.* python.

pitonessa *sf.* pythoness.

pittore *sm.* painter.

pittoresco *agg.* picturesque.

pittòrico *agg.* pictorial.

pittrice *sf.* paintress.

pittura *sf.* 1. painting 2. (*dipinto, descrizione*) picture 3. (*vernice*) paint.

pitturare *vt.* to paint.

più *avv.* 1. (*comp. di maggioranza con agg. polisillabi, con s., v. e avv.*) more: *questo libro è — costoso di quello*, this book is more expensive than that; *ho — libri di te*, I have more books than you; *lavoro — di te*, I work more than you 2. (*comp. di maggioranza con agg. e avv. monosillabi e bisillabi terminanti in y, er, ow*) ...er: *è — gentile di lui*, he is kinder than he is 3. (*superl. rel., corrispondente a "more"*) the most, the more (*fra due*): *è il libro — costoso di tutti*, it is the most expensive book of all; *la — bella delle due sorelle*, the more beautiful of the two sisters 4. (*superl. rel., corrispondente a "...er"*) the ...est, the ...er (*fra due*): *è la persona — felice che conosca*, she is the happiest person I know; *è la — graziosa delle due sorelle*, she is the prettier of the sisters 4. (*di tempo*) no longer, no more, not again ‖ *mai —*, never again. ♦ **più** *agg.* 1. more 2. (*diversi*) several. ♦ **più** *sm.* most: *il — è fatto*, most of it is done ‖ *i —*, most people (*al sing.*).

piuma *sf.* 1. feather, down 2. (*ornamento*) plume.

piumaggio *sm.* plumage.

piumino *sm.* 1. down 2. (*copriletto*) eiderdown 3. (*per la cipria*) powder-puff 4. (*per spolverare*) duster.

piuttosto *avv.* rather. ♦ **piuttosto che, di** *cong.* rather than.

piuolo *sm.* 1. peg: *scala a piuoli*, ladder 2. (*paletto*) post.

piva *sf.* bagpipe.

pivello *sm.* greenhorn.

piviere *sm.* plover.

pizzicàgnolo *sm.* delicatessen seller.

pizzicare *vt.* 1. to pinch, to nip 2. (*di insetti*) to bite (*v. irr.*) 3. (*di sostanza acre*) to burn (*v. irr.*) 4. (*con parole*) to tease 5. (*sorprendere*) to catch (*v. irr.*). ♦ **pizzicare** *vi.* (*prudere*) to itch, to tingle.

pizzicheria *sf.* 1. delicatessen shop 2. (*merci*) delicatessen.

pizzico *sm.* 1. pinch 2. (*pizzicore*) itch 3. (*fig.*) bit.

pizzicore *sm.* itch.

pizzicotto *sm.* pinch.

pizzo *sm.* 1. lace (*solo sing.*) 2. (*di montagna*) peak 3. (*barba*) pointed beard.

placare *vt.* to appease: — *la fame di qu.*, to satisfy so.'s hunger; — *la sete di qu.*, to quench so.'s thirst. ♦ **placarsi** *vr.* to calm down.

placca *sf.* plaque.

placcare *vt.* to plate (sthg. with).

placcatura *sf.* plating.

placenta *sf.* placenta.

placidità *sf.* placidity.

plàcido *agg.* placid.

plaga *sf.* region.

plagiare *vt. e vi.* to plagiarize. ♦ **plagiario** *agg.* plagiaristic. ♦ **plagiario** *sm.* plagiarist.

plagio *sm.* plagiarism.

planare *vi.* to glide down.

planata *sf.* glide.

plancia *sf.* (*mar.*) deck.

plancton *sm.* plankton.

planetario *agg.* planetary. ♢ **planetario** *sm.* planetarium (*pl.* -ia).

planimetria *sf.* planimetry, plan.

planimètrico *agg.* planimetric(al).

planisfero *sm.* planisphere.

plantìgrado *agg. e sm.* plantigrade.

plasma *sm.* plasma.

plasmare *vt.* to mould.

plàstica *sf.* 1. (*operazione*) plastic operation 2. (*materiale*) plastic.

plasticare *vt.* to plasticize.

plasticità *sf.* plasticity.

plàstico *agg.* plastic. ♦ **plàstico** *sm.* 1. plastic model 2. (*carta topografica*) relief map.

plastilina *sf.* plasticine.

plàtano *sm.* plane (-tree).

platea *sf.* pit: *poltrona di* —, stall.

plateale *agg.* coarse.

platinare *vt.* 1. to platinize 2. (*di capelli*) to bleach.

plàtino *sm.* platinum.

platònico *agg.* Platonic.

plaudente *agg.* applauding.

plausìbile *agg.* plausible.

plàuso *sm.* 1. applause 2. (*lode*) praise.

plebaglia *sf.* mob.

plebe *sf.* populace.

plebeo *agg. e sm.* plebeian.

plebiscitario *agg.* plebiscitary.

plebiscito *sm.* plebiscite.

plenario *agg.* plenary.

plenilunio *sm.* plenilune.

plenipotenziario *agg. e sm.* plenipotentiary.

pleonasmo *sm.* pleonasm.

pleonàstico *agg.* pleonastic.

plesso *sm.* plexus.

plètora *sf.* plethora.

plètorico *agg.* plethoric.

plettro *sm.* plectrum (*pl.* -ra).

plèura *sf.* pleura (*pl.* -rae).

pleurite *sf.* pleurisy.

plico *sm.* 1. packet 2. (*busta*) cover: *in* — *separato*, under separate cover.

plotone *sm.* platoon.

plùmbeo *agg.* leaden.

plurale *agg. e sm.* plural.

pluralismo *sm.* pluralism.

pluralità *sf.* plurality.

pluricellulare *agg.* multicellular.

plusvalore *sm.* plus value.

plutòcrate *sm.* plutocrat.

plutocrazìa *sf.* plutocracy.

pneumàtico *agg.* pneumatic, inflatable. ♦ **pneumàtico** *sm.* (*di auto*) tyre.

pneumatorace *sm.* pneumothorax.

pochezza *sf.* (*scarsità, ristrettezza*) scantiness, insufficiency.

pochìssimo *agg. e avv.* 1. very little 2. (*rarissimamente*) very seldom. ♦ **pochìssimi** *sm. pl.* very few.

poco *avv.* 1. not very (*con agg. e avv.*), little (*con comp., p. passati, verbi*): *a* — *a* —, little by little; *per volta*, a little at a time 2. (*di tempo*) a short time || *fra* —, soon. ♦ **poco** *agg.* 1. little (*pl.* few) 2. (*di tempo*) short. ♦ **poco** *pron.* very little (*pl.* few): *un* — *di*, a little.

podere *sm.* farm.

poderoso *agg.* powerful.

podio *sm.* platform.

podismo sm. **1.** walking **2.** (sport) foot-racing.

podista sm. (sport) foot-racer.

podistico agg. foot (attr.).

poema sm. poem.

poesia sf. **1.** poetry **2.** (composizione poetica) poem.

poeta sm. poet.

poetare vi. to write (v. irr.) poetry.

poetico agg. poetic(al).

poggiapiedi sm. footstool.

poggiare vi. e vt. to rest. ♦ **poggiarsi** vr. to lean (v. irr.) against.

poggio sm. hillock.

poi avv. **1.** then **2.** (più tardi) later || d'ora in —, from now on.

poiché cong. since, as.

polacca sf. (mus.) polonaise.

polacco agg. Polish. ♦ **polacco** sm. Pole.

polare agg. polar || stella —, pole-star.

polarità sf. polarity.

polarizzare vt. to polarize.

polarizzatore agg. polarizing. ♦ **polarizzatore** sm. polarizer.

polarizzazione sf. polarization.

polca sf. polka.

polemica sf. polemic.

polemico agg. e sm. polemic.

polemista s. polemist.

polemizzare vi. to polemize.

poliandria sf. polyandry.

policlinico sm. polyclinic.

policromia sf. polychromy.

policromo agg. polychrome.

poliedrico agg. **1.** polyhedral **2.** (fig.) versatile.

poliedro sm. polyhedron.

polifonia sf. polyphony.

polifonico agg. polyphonic.

poligamia sf. polygamy.

poligamo agg. polygamous. ♦ **poligamo** sm. polygamist.

poliglotta s. polyglot.

poligono sm. polygon || — di tiro, shooting-range.

polimerizzazione sf. polymerization.

polimero agg. polymeric. ♦ **polimero** sm. polymer.

polimorfismo sm. polymorphism.

poliomielite sf. poliomyelitis.

poliomielitico agg. polio (attr.). ♦ **poliomielitico** sm. person who has had polio.

polipo sm. polyp.

polisillabo agg. polysyllabic(al). ♦ **polisillabo** sm. polysyllable.

politecnico agg. e sm. polytechnic.

politeismo sm. polytheism.

politeista agg. polytheistic. ♦ **politeista** s. polytheist.

politica sf. **1.** politics **2.** (linea di condotta) policy.

politicante sm. petty politician.

politico agg. **1.** political **2.** (sagace) politic || uomo —, politician.

polivalente agg. polyvalent.

polizia sf. police (us. al pl.).

poliziesco agg. **1.** police (attr.) **2.** (di film ecc.) detective (attr.).

poliziotto sm. policeman (pl. -men).

polizza sf. **1.** policy **2.** (ricevuta) bill.

polla sf. spring.

pollaio sm. hen-house.

pollame sm. poultry.

pollastra sf. pullet.

pollastro sm. cockerel.

pollice sm. **1.** thumb **2.** (del piede) big toe **3.** (misura) inch.

pollicoltore sm. poultryman (pl. -men).

pollicoltura sf. poultry-farming.

polline sm. pollen.

pollivendolo sm. poulterer.

pollo sm. **1.** chicken **2.** (fig.) dupe.

polmonare agg. pulmonary.

polmone sm. lung: — d'acciaio, iron lung.

polmonite sf. pneumonia.

polo¹ sm. pole.

polo² sm. (sport) polo.

polpa sf. **1.** (di frutta) pulp **2.** (carne) lean meat.

polpaccio sm. calf (pl. calves).

polpastrello sm. finger-tip.

polpetta sf. meat-ball, croquette.

polposo agg. pulpy.

polsino sm. cuff.

polso sm. **1.** wrist **2.** (fig.) energy **3.** (pulsazione) pulse **4.** (polsino) cuff || tastare il — a qu., to feel (v. irr.) so.'s pulse; uomo di —, energetic man.

poltiglia sf. **1.** pulp **2.** (fanghiglia) mud.

poltrire vi. to idle.

poltrona sf. **1.** armchair **2.** (teat.) stall.

poltrone agg. idle. ♦ **poltrone** sm. idler.

poltroneria sf. idleness.

polvere sf. **1.** dust **2.** (sostanza polverizzata) powder || togliere la —, to dust.

polveriera sf. powder-magazine.

polverizzare vt. to pulverize. ◆
polverizzarsi vr. to pulverize.

polverone sm. cloud of dust.

polveroso agg. dusty.

pomata sf. salve.

pomello sm. 1. (di porta ecc.) knob
2. (di guancia) cheek-bone.

pomeridiano agg. 1. afternoon
(attr.) 2. (con le ore) p. m. (post
meridiem): alle 5 pomeridiane,
at five o'clock.

pomeriggio sm. afternoon.

pòmice sf. pumice.

pomo sm. 1. (mela) apple 2. (di
porta ecc.) knob.

pomodoro sm. tomato.

pompa sf. 1. pump 2. (fasto) pomp
3. (ostentazione) display || impresa
di pompe funebri, undertaker's
business; far — di sé, to show (v.
irr.) off.

pompare vt. 1. to pump 2. (fig.)
to puff up.

pompelmo sm. grapefruit.

pompiere sm. fireman (pl. -men).

pompòsità sf. pomposity.

pomposo agg. pompous.

ponderàbile agg. ponderable.

ponderabilità sf. ponderability.

ponderare vt. to ponder.

ponderatamente avv. after reflection.

ponderatezza sf. circumspection.

ponderato agg. pondered.

ponderazione sf. consideration.

ponderoso agg. ponderous.

ponente sm. west.

ponte sm. 1. bridge: — girevole,
swing bridge 2. (mar.) deck 3.
(impalcatura) scaffold || rompere i
ponti con (fig.), to break (v. irr.)
with.

pontéfice sm. pope.

pontificale agg. pontifical.

pontificare vi. to pontificate.

pontificato sm. pontificate.

pontificio agg. papal.

pontile sm. landing-stage.

pontone sm. pontoon.

ponzare vi. to rack one's brains.

popolamento sm. peopling.

popolano agg. common. ◆ **popola-
no** sm. man of the people || i
popolani, the common people.

popolare[1] vt. to people. ◆ **popo-
larsi** vr. to become (v. irr.) popu-
lated.

popolare[2] agg. 1. popular 2. (tradizionale) folk (attr.).

popolaresco agg. popular-like.

popolarità sf. popularity.

popolarizzare vt. to popularize.

popolazione sf. population.

pòpolo sm. 1. (gente) people (pl.)
2. (nazione) people.

popoloso agg. populous.

popone sm. melon.

poppa[1] sf. 1. (mar.) stern || avere il
vento in —, to sail before the
wind; a —, astern.

poppa[2] sf. breast.

poppante s. suckling.

poppare vt. to suck.

poppata sf. suck: ora della —,
feeding-time.

poppatoio sm. feeding-bottle.

populismo sm. populism.

populista agg. populistic. ◆ **populista** s. populist.

porcaro sm. swineherd.

porcellana sf. china (solo sing.).

porcherìa sf. 1. dirt 2. (azione di-
sonesta) dirty trick 3. (detto indecente) obscene word 4. (atto indecente) obscene act 5. (cibo cattivo) revolting stuff 6. (cose senza
valore) rubbish.

porcile sm. pigsty.

porcino agg. pig (attr.). ◆ **porcino** sm. (fungo) boletus.

porco sm. 1. pig 2. (cuc.) pork.

porcospino sm. porcupine.

pòrfido sm. porphyry.

pòrgere vt. 1. to hand 2. (offrire)
to offer.

pornografìa sf. pornography.

pornogràfico agg. pornographic.

poro sm. pore.

porosità sf. porosity.

poroso agg. porous.

pòrpora sf. purple.

porporato sm. Cardinal.

porre vt. 1. to put (v. irr.) 2. (sup-
porre) to suppose || — le fonda-
menta, to lay (v. irr.) the founda-
tions; — mano, to begin (v. irr.).

porro sm. 1. leek 2. (med.) wart.

porta sf. 1. door 2. (di mura ecc.)
gate 3. (sport) goal.

portabagagli sm. 1. luggage-rack
2. (facchino) porter.

portabandiera sm. ensign.

portacarte sm. portfolio.

portacénere sm. ash-tray.

portachiavi sm. key-holder.

portacipria sm. compact.

portaèrei sf. aircraft carrier.

portaferiti sm. stretcher-bearer.

portafiori *sm.* flower-holder.

portafoglio *sm.* 1. wallet 2. (*pol.*) portfolio.

portafortuna *sm.* mascot.

portagioielli *sm.* jewel-case.

portalèttere *sm.* ·postman (*pl.* -men).

portamento *sm.* 1. gait 2. (*condotta*) behaviour.

portamonete *sm.* purse.

portantina *sf.* sedan-chair.

portaombrelli *sm.* umbrella-stand.

portaòrdini *sm.* messenger.

portapacchi *sm.* carrier.

portapenne *sm.* penholder.

portare *vt.* 1. (*verso chi parla o ascolta*) to bring (*v. irr.*) 2. (*lontano da chi parla, accompagnare*) to take (*v. irr.*) 3. (*trasportare*) to carry 4. (*condurre*) to lead (*v. irr.*) 5. (*indossare*) to wear (*v. irr.*) 6. (*avere*) to have.

portasapone *sm.* soap-dish.

portasigarette *sm.* cigarette-case.

portaspilli *sm.* pincushion.

portata *sf.* 1. (*di pranzo*) course 2. (*di arma, strumento ottico*) range 3. (*di fiume*) flow 4. (*di ponte, auto ecc.*) capacity 5. (*stazza*) tonnage 6. (*fig.*) importance.

portàtile *agg.* portable.

portatore *sm.* bearer.

portauovo *sm.* egg-cup.

portavoce *sm.* spokesman (*pl.* -men).

portello *sm.* hatch.

portento *sm.* prodigy.

portentosamente *avv.* prodigiously.

portentoso *agg.* prodigious.

porticato *sm.* arcade.

pòrtico *sm.* 1. (*loggia*) porch 2. (*porticato*) arcade.

portiera¹ *sf.* (*porta*) door.

portiera² *sf.* doorkeeper.

portiere *sm.* 1. (*sport*) goal-keeper 2. porter.

portinaio *sm.* door keeper.

portineria *sf.* porter's lodge.

porto¹ *sm.* 1. port (*anche fig.*) 2. (*bacino*) harbour (*anche fig.*).

porto² *sm.* (*trasporto*) carriage: *franco di* —, carriage paid || — *d'armi*, shooting licence; *condurre in* — (*fig.*), to carry out.

portoghese *agg. e sm.* Portuguese.

portone *sm.* main door.

portuale *agg.* harbour (*attr.*): *città* —, port. ◆ **portuale** *sm.* docker.

porzione *sf.* portion.

posa *sf.* 1. (*il porre*) laying 2. (*posizione*) posture 3. (*affettazione*) pose 4. (*pausa*) pause 5. (*foto*) exposure || *mettersi in* —, to pose; *senza* —, incessantly.

posare *vt.* to lay (*v. irr.*). ◆ **posare** *vi.* 1. (*aver fondamento*) to rest 2. (*assumere un atteggiamento non spontaneo*) to pose 3. (*di liquido*) to stand (*v. irr.*). ◆ **posarsi** *vr.* 1. to settle 2. (*aer.: di uccello*) to alight.

posata *sf.* 1. (*coltello*) knife (*pl.* knives) 2. (*forchetta*) fork 3. (*cucchiaio*) spoon.

posato *agg.* staid.

poscritto *sm.* postscript.

positiva *sf.* (*foto*) positive.

positivamente *avv.* positively.

positivismo *sm.* positivism.

positivista *s.* positivist.

positivo *agg.* positive.

posizione *sf.* position.

posologia *sf.* posology.

posporre *vt.* 1. to place after 2. (*posticipare*) to postpone.

possedere *vt.* to possess.

possedimento *sm.* V. *possesso*.

possente *agg.* powerful.

possessivo *agg.* possessive.

possesso *sm.* 1. possession 2. (*proprietà*) property.

possessore *sm.* possessor, owner.

possibile *agg.* possible: *il più presto* —, as soon as possible; *fare il* —, to do (*v. irr.*) one's best.

possibilità *sf.* 1. possibility 2. (*potere*) power || — *finanziarie*, means.

possidente *sm.* 1. man (*pl.* -men) of property 2. (*terriero*) landowner.

posta *sf.* 1. post, mail 2. (*ufficio postale*) post-office || *fermo* —, poste restante; *a giro di* —, by return of post; *per* —, by mail 3. (*al gioco*) stake.

postale *agg.* postal, post (*attr.*), mail (*attr.*): *per pacco* —, by parcel post; *spese postali*, postage.

postazione *sf.* stationing.

postbèllico *agg.* post-war (*attr.*).

postdatare *vt.* to postdate.

posteggiare *vt.* to park.

posteggiatore *sm.* 1. car-park attendant 2. (*venditore*) stall-keeper.

posteggio *sm.* car-park || — *di taxi*, taxi rank.

postelegrafònico *agg.* postal telegraph and telephone (*attr.*). ◆

postelegrafònico *sm.* post-office clerk.

postema *sf.* aposteme.

pòsteri *sm. pl.* descendants.

posteriore *agg.* 1. (*nel tempo*) following 2. (*nello spazio*) back, rear.

posterità *sf.* posterity.

posticcio *agg.* false. ◆ **posticcio** *sm.* toupee.

posticipare *vt.* to postpone.

posticipazione *sf.* deferment.

postiglione *sm.* postilion.

postilla *sf.* (marginal) note.

postillare *vt.* to annotate.

postino *sm.* postman (*pl.* -men).

posto *sm.* 1. place 2. (*spazio*) room 3. (*lavoro*) job 4. (*posto a sedere*) seat 5. (*stazione*) station || *al — di*, instead of.

postoperatòrio *agg.* postoperative.

postribolo *sm.* brothel.

postulante *sm.* 1. petitioner 2. (*eccl.*) postulant.

postulare *vt.* to petition (for sthg.).

postulato *sm.* postulate.

pòstumo *agg.* posthumous.

potàbile *agg.* drinkable.

potare *vt.* to prune.

potassa *sf.* potash.

potàssico *agg.* potassic.

potàssio *sm.* potassium.

potatore *sm.* pruner.

potatura *sf.* pruning.

potente *agg.* powerful.

potenza *sf.* power || *in — (avv.)*, potentially, (*agg.*) potential.

potenziale *agg.* e *sm.* potential.

potenzialità *sf.* potentiality.

potenziamento *sm.* 1. (*rafforzamento*) strengthening 2. (*sviluppo*) development.

potenziare *vt.* 1. (*rafforzare*) to strengthen 2. (*sviluppare*) to develop.

potere¹ *vi.* 1. can (*pres.*), could (*pass., condiz.*), to be able: *non può venire*, he cannot come 2. (*eventualità, augurio, permesso*) may (*pres.*), might (*pass., condiz.*), to be allowed to: *può darsi*, maybe; *può darsi che venga*, he may come.

potere² *sm.* power.

potestà *sf.* power, authority.

poveràccio *sm.* poor devil.

pòvero *agg.* poor.

povertà *sf.* poverty.

pozione *sf.* potion.

pozza *sf.* pool.

pozzànghera *sf.* puddle.

pozzetto *sm.* 1. (*di motore*) sump 2. (*di fognatura*) drain well.

pozzo *sm.* well: *— nero*, cesspool; *— carbonifero*, coal-pit.

pragmatismo *sm.* pragmatism.

pragmatista *s.* pragmatist.

pragmatìstico *agg.* pragmatist.

prammàtica *sf.* custom: *di —*, customary.

prammàtico *agg.* pragmatic.

pranzare *vi.* to dine.

pranzo *sm.* 1. dinner 2. (*di mezzogiorno*) lunch.

prassi *sf.* praxis.

prataiolo *agg.* field (*attr.*).

praterìa *sf.* prairie.

pràtica *sf.* 1. practice 2. (*affare*) matter 3. (*esperienza*) experience 4. (*incartamento*) file 5. (*trattativa*) dealing 6. (*passo presso un'autorità*) step || *far —*, to practise; *aver — di*, to be familiar with.

praticàbile *agg.* practicable.

praticabilità *sf.* practicability.

praticàccia *sf.* practical knowledge.

praticante *agg.* practising.

praticare *vt.* 1. to practise 2. (*frequentare*) to frequent 3. (*fare*) to make (*v. irr.*).

praticità *sf.* practicality.

pràtico *agg.* 1. practical 2. (*esperto*) skilled || *esser — di*, to be familiar with.

prativo *agg.* grass (*attr.*).

prato *sm.* 1. meadow 2. (*artificiale*) lawn.

pratolina *sf.* daisy.

pravo *agg.* perverse.

preallarme *sm.* prewarning.

preàmbolo *sm.* preface.

preannunziare *vt.* to portend.

preavvertire *vt.* to forewarn.

preavvisare *vt.* to forewarn.

preavviso *sm.* 1. forewarning 2. (*disdetta*) notice.

prebèllico *agg.* pre-war (*attr.*).

prebenda *sf.* 1. (*eccl.*) prebend 2. (*salario*) salary.

precarietà *sf.* precariousness.

precario *agg.* precarious.

precauzionale *agg.* precautionary.

precauzione *sf.* 1. precaution 2. (*cautela*) caution.

precedente *agg.* previous. ◆ **precedente** *sm.* precedent || *i precedenti* (*condotta*), record.

precedenza *sf.* precedence || *in —*, previously.

precèdere *vt.* to precede. ♦ **precèdere** *vi.* to come (*v. irr.*) first.

precessione *sf.* precession.

precettare *vt.* **1.** (*giur.*) to summon **2.** (*mil.*) to call to arms.

precetto *sm.* **1.** precept **2.** (*mil.*) call-up notice.

precettore *sm.* tutor.

precipitare *vt.* to precipitate. ♦ **precipitare** *vi.* **1.** to fall (*v. irr.*) **2.** (*chim.*) to precipitate. ♦ **precipitarsi** *vr.* to dash.

precipitato *agg. e sm.* precipitate.

precipitazione *sf.* **1.** (*atmosferica*) precipitation **2.** (*furia*) haste.

precipitoso *agg.* **1.** (*impetuoso*) headlong **2.** (*frettoloso*) hasty **3.** (*scosceso*) precipitous.

precipizio *sm.* precipice: *a — (precipitosamente)*, headlong; (*a picco*) perpendicularly.

precipuo *agg.* principal.

precisare *vt.* to specify.

precisazione *sf.* specification.

precisione *sf.* **1.** precision **2.** (*chiarezza*) clarity.

preciso *agg.* **1.** precise **2.** (*accurato*) careful **3.** (*definito*) definite **4.** (*identico*) identical **5.** (*di ore*) sharp.

preclaro *agg.* prominent.

preclùdere *vt.* to preclude.

precoce *agg.* **1.** precocious **2.** (*di frutto, stagione*) early **3.** (*prematuro*) premature.

precocità *sf.* precociousness.

preconcetto *agg.* preconceived. ♦ **preconcetto** *sm.* prejudice.

preconizzare *vt.* to foretell (*v. irr.*).

precordi *sm. pl.* praecordia.

precòrrere *vt.* to anticipate.

precursore *agg.* precursory. ♦ **precursore** *sm.* forerunner.

preda *sf.* **1.** prey **2.** (*bottino*) booty ‖ *cadere in — a*, to fall (*v. irr.*) a prey to; *far — di*, to plunder.

predace *agg.* predacious.

predare *vt.* to plunder.

predatore *agg.* predatory. ♦ **predatore** *sm.* plunderer.

predatorio *agg.* predatory.

predecessore *sm.* forerunner.

predella *sf.* **1.** platform **2.** (*sgabello*) stool.

predellino *sm.* **1.** (*di vettura*) footboard **2.** (*poggiapiedi*) footstool.

predestinare *vt.* to predestine.

predestinazione *sf.* **1.** predestina-

tion **2.** (*destino*) destiny.

predeterminare *vt.* to predetermine.

predeterminazione *sf.* predetermination.

predetto *agg.* **1.** (*suddetto*) above mentioned **2.** (*presagito*) foretold (*pred.*).

prediale *agg.* praedial.

prèdica *sf.* sermon: *fare la — a qu.*, to lecture so.

predicabile *agg.* predicable.

predicare *vt. e vi.* to preach.

predicativo *agg.* predicate.

predicato *sm.* predicate: *essere in — per*, to be considered for.

predicatore *sm.* preacher.

predicatorio *agg.* preachifying.

predicazione *sf.* preaching.

predicozzo *sm.* lecture.

predigestione *sf.* preliminary digestion.

prediletto *agg.* favourite. ♦ **prediletto** *sm.* pet.

predilezione *sf.* predilection.

predilìgere *vt.* to prefer.

predire *vt.* to foretell (*v. irr.*).

predisporre *vt.* **1.** to predispose **2.** (*provvedere*) to arrange. ♦ **predisporsi** *vr.* to prepare oneself.

predisposizione *sf.* **1.** (*med.*) predisposition **2.** (*inclinazione*) bent.

predizione *sf.* prediction.

predominante *agg.* prevailing.

predominanza *sf.* prevalence.

predominare *vi.* to prevail.

predominio *sm.* predomination.

predone *sm.* plunderer.

preesistente *agg.* pre-existing.

preesistenza *sf.* pre-existence.

preesistere *vi.* to pre-exist.

prefabbricare *vt.* to prefabricate.

prefazio *sm.* preface.

prefazione *sf.* preface.

preferenza *sf.* preference: *di —*, generally.

preferenziale *agg.* preferential.

preferibile *agg.* preferable.

preferire *vt.* to prefer.

preferito *agg. e sm. V. prediletto.*

prefettizio *agg.* prefectorial.

prefetto *sm.* prefect.

prefettura *sf.* prefecture.

prefiggere *vt.* to (pre-)establish. ♦ **prefiggersi** *vr.* to be resolved: *— uno scopo*, to propose an aim to oneself.

prefigurare *vt.* to prefigure.

prefigurazione *sf.* prefiguration.

prefisso *sm.* prefix.
preformare *vt.* to preform.
pregare *vt.* 1. to pray 2. (*chiedere*) to beg.
pregévole *agg.* valuable.
preghiera *sf.* 1. prayer 2. (*domanda*) request.
pregiare *vt.* to esteem. ♦ **pregiarsi** *vr.* to beg (to).
pregiato *agg.* valuable: *vino* —, vintage wine.
pregio *sm.* 1. (*valore*) value 2. (*merito*) merit || *di* —, valuable.
pregiudicare *vt.* to prejudice.
pregiudicato *sm.* previous offender.
pregiudiziale *agg.* prejudicial.
pregiudizio *sm.* prejudice.
pregnante *agg.* pregnant.
pregno *agg.* 1. pregnant (with) 2. (*pieno*) full (of).
pregustare *vt.* to foretaste.
preistoria *sf.* prehistory.
preistòrico *agg.* prehistoric.
prelatizio *agg.* prelatic.
prelato *sm.* prelate.
prelazione *sf.* pre-emption.
prelevamento *sm.* drawing: *fare un* — (*comm.*), to draw (*v. irr.*).
prelevare *vt.* to draw (*v. irr.*).
prelibare *vt.* to foretaste.
prelibato *agg.* excellent.
prelievo *sm.* V. prelevamento.
preliminare *agg.* preliminary.
prelùdere *vi.* to prelude (sthg.), to foreshadow (sthg.).
preludiare *vi.* to prelude.
preludio *sm.* prelude.
prematuro *agg.* premature.
premeditare *vt.* to premeditate.
premeditato *agg.* premeditated.
premeditazione *sf.* premeditation.
prèmere *vi.* 1. to press 2. (*importare*) to interest 3. (*essere urgente*) to be urgent. ♦ **prèmere** *vt.* to press.
premessa *sf.* introduction.
premesso *agg.* previous.
preméttere *vt.* 1. to premise 2. (*mettere prima*) to put (*v. irr.*) before.
premiare *vt.* 1. to give (*v. irr.*) a prize 2. (*ricompensare*) to reward.
premiazione *sf.* awarding of prizes.
preminente *agg.* pre-eminent.
preminenza *sf.* pre-eminence.
premio *sm.* 1. prize 2. (*ricompensa*) reward 3. (*comm.*) premium.
prèmito *sm.* tenesmus.

premolare *agg.* e *sm.* premolar.
premonitore *agg.* premonitory.
premorire *vi.* to predecease.
premunire *vt.* to forearm. ♦ **premunirsi** *vr.* to secure.
premura *sf.* 1. (*cura*) care 2. (*fretta*) hurry 3. (*gentilezza*) kindness || *aver* —, to be in a hurry.
premuroso *agg.* 1. (*servizievole*) helpful 2. (*gentile*) obliging.
prèndere *vt.* 1. to take (*v. irr.*) 2. (*sorprendere, afferrare*) to catch (*v. irr.*) 3. (*comprare, ottenere*) to get (*v. irr.*). ♦ **prèndersi** *vr.* to take || *che ti prende?*, what's the matter with you?
prendisole *sm.* sun-suit.
prenome *sm.* praenomen (*pl.* -mina).
prenotare *vt.* to book. ♦ **prenotarsi** *vr.* to engage oneself.
prenotazione *sf.* booking.
prènsile *agg.* prehensile.
prensione *sf.* prehension.
preoccupante *agg.* worrying.
preoccupare *vt.* to worry. ♦ **preoccuparsi** *vr.* to be worried (about).
preoccupazione *sf.* worry.
preordinare *vt.* to prearrange.
preparare *vt.* to prepare. ♦ **prepararsi** *vr.* to get (*v. irr.*) ready.
preparativo *sm.* preparation.
preparato *agg.* ready. ♦ **preparato** *sm.* (*med.*) preparation.
preparatore *sm.* preparer.
preparatorio *agg.* preparatory.
preparazione *sf.* preparation.
preponderante *agg.* preponderant.
preponderanza *sf.* preponderance.
preporre *vt.* 1. to put (*v. irr.*) before 2. (*preferire*) to prefer 3. (*mettere a capo*) to put at the head.
prepositivo *agg.* prepositional.
preposizione *sf.* preposition.
preposto *sm.* 1. provost 2. (*relig., prevosto*) parish priest.
prepotente *agg.* overbearing.
prepotentemente *avv.* overbearingly.
prepotenza *sf.* 1. arrogance 2. (*azione*) overbearing action.
preraffaellismo *sm.* Pre-Raphaelitism.
preraffaellita *agg.* e *s.* Pre-Raphaelite.
prerogativa *sf.* 1. prerogative 2. (*di persona*) faculty 3. (*di cosa*) property.
presa *sf.* 1. taking 2. (*stretta*) grip

3. (*cattura*) capture 4. (*elettr.*) plug 5. (*pizzico*) pinch || *macchina da —*, camera; *far — (di cemento)*, to set (*v. irr.*).

presagio *sm.* presage, omen.

presagire *vt.* 1. to foresee (*v. irr.*) 2. (*essere presagio di*) to forebode.

presago *agg.* essere — *di* (*prevedere*), to have a presentiment of.

presbiopia *sf.* long-sightedness.

prèsbite *agg.* long-sighted.

presbiterianismo *sm.* Presbyterianism.

presbiteriano *agg. e sm.* Presbyterian.

presbiterio *sm.* presbytery.

prescégliere *vt.* to choose (*v. irr.*).

prescelto *agg.* chosen.

prescienza *sf.* prescience.

prescindere *vi.* to leave (*v. irr.*) out of consideration: *a — da*, apart from.

prescritto *sm.* prescript.

prescrìvere *vt.* to prescribe.

prescrizione *sf.* 1. regulation 2. (*med.; giur.*) prescription: *caduto in —*, invalidated by prescription.

presentàbile *agg.* presentable.

presentare *vt.* 1. to present 2. (*mostrare*) to show (*v. irr.*) 3. (*far conoscere*) to introduce. ♦ **presentarsi** *vr.* 1. to present oneself 2. (*capitare*) to occur.

presentatore *sm.* 1. announcer 2. (*teat.*) showman (*pl. -men*).

presentazione *sf.* 1. presentation 2. (*di una persona*) introduction.

presente *agg. e s.* present || *i presenti*, the people present; *la —* (*lettera*), this letter.

presentemente *avv.* now.

presentimento *sm.* presentiment.

presentire *vt.* to foresee (*v. irr.*).

presenza *sf.* 1. presence 2. (*frequenza*) attendance.

presenziare *vt. e vi.* to be present (at).

presepio *sm.* crib.

preservare *vt.* to preserve.

preservativo *agg. e sm.* preservative.

preservazione *sf.* preservation.

prèside *sm.* headmaster. ♦ **prèside** *sf.* headmistress.

presidente *sm.* 1. president 2. (*di assemblea*) chairman (*pl. -men*).

presidenza *sf.* 1. presidency 2. (*di assemblea*) chairmanship 3. (*di società*) management 4. (*insieme di direttori*) board of directors 5. (*di scuola*) headmastership.

presidenziale *agg.* presidential.

presidiare *vt.* to garrison.

presidio *sm.* garrison.

presièdere *vt. e vi.* to preside (over, at).

pressa *sf.* press.

pressacarte *sm.* paper-weight.

pressante *agg.* pressing.

pressantemente *avv.* pressingly.

pressappoco *avv.* approximately.

pressare *vt.* to press.

pressi *sm. pl.* 1. neighbourhood (*sing.*) 2. (*sobborghi*) outskirts.

pressione *sf.* pressure: *fare — su qu.* (*fig.*), to put (*v. irr.*) pressure on so.

presso *avv.* nearly: *a un di —*, *press'a poco*, approximately; *da —*, closely. ♦ **presso** *prep.* 1. near 2. (*a casa di*) at 3. (*nell'ufficio di*) with 4. (*fra*) among 5. (*negli indirizzi*) c/o (care of).

pressoché *avv.* almost.

pressurizzare *vt.* to pressurize.

pressurizzazione *sf.* pressurization.

prestabilire *vt.* to pre-arrange.

prestamente *avv.* quickly.

prestanome *sm.* man of straw.

prestante *agg.* good-looking.

prestanza *sf.* fine appearance.

prestare *vt.* V. **imprestare**. ♦ **prestarsi** *vr.* to volunteer.

prestatore *sm.* lender: *— d'opera*, workman (*pl. -men*).

prestazione *sf.* 1. (*prestito*) loan 2. (*servizio*) service 3. (*sport*) performance.

prestezza *sf.* quickness.

prestidigitatore *sm.* conjurer.

prestigio *sm.* prestige || *gioco di —*, conjuring trick.

prestigioso *agg.* 1. (*affascinante*) glamorous 2. (*favoloso*) fabulous.

prèstito *sm.* loan: *prendere in —*, to borrow; *dare in —*, to lend (*v. irr.*).

presto[1] *agg. — di mano*, dexterous.

presto[2] *avv.* 1. soon 2. (*di buon'ora*) early 3. (*in fretta*) quickly || *— o tardi*, sooner or later; *al più —*, as soon as possible. ♦ **presto!** *inter.* quick!

presùmere *vt.* to presume.

presumìbile *agg.* presumable.

presumibilmente *avv.* presumably.

presuntivo *agg.* presumptive.

presunto *agg.* supposed.

presuntuosamente *avv.* presumptuously.

presuntuosità *sf.* conceit.

presuntuoso *agg.* presumptuous.

presunzione *sf.* presumption.

presupporre *vt.* 1. to presuppose 2. (*supporre*) to suppose.

presupposizione *sf.* 1. presupposition 2. (*supposizione*) supposition.

presupposto *sm.* V. *presupposizione*.

prete *sm.* priest.

pretendente *sm.* 1. pretender 2. (*corteggiatore*) suitor.

pretèndere *vt.* 1. to pretend 2. (*esigere*) to want. ♦ **pretèndere** *vi.* to claim.

pretensione *sf.* pretension.

pretenzioso *agg.* 1. pretentious 2. (*presuntuoso*) conceited.

preterintenzionale *agg.* unintentional.

preterito *agg. e sm.* past.

pretesa *sf.* 1. pretence 2. (*richiesta*) claim || *avere molte pretese*, to be hard to please; *avanzare pretese su*, to claim rights over.

pretesto *sm.* 1. pretext 2. (*occasione*) occasion.

pretore *sm.* magistrate.

prettamente *avv.* purely.

pretto *agg.* pure.

pretura *sf.* magistrate's court.

prevalente *agg.* prevailing.

prevalenza *sf.* prevalence.

prevalere *vi.* to prevail.

prevaricare *vi.* 1. to prevaricate 2. (*abusare del potere*) to abuse one's office.

prevaricatore *sm.* prevaricator.

prevaricazione *sf.* 1. prevarication 2. (*abuso di potere*) abuse of office.

prevedere *vt.* 1. to foresee (*v. irr.*) 2. (*di legge, contratto*) to provide (for).

prevedibile *agg.* foreseeable.

preveggente *agg.* foreseeing.

preveggenza *sf.* foresight.

prevenire *vt.* 1. (*precedere*) to forestall 2. (*evitare*) to prevent 3. (*avvertire*) to warn.

preventivamente *avv.* 1. beforehand 2. (*in modo preventivo*) preventively.

preventivare *vt.* to estimate.

preventivo *agg.* 1. preventive 2. (*comm.*) estimated || *bilancio —*, budget. ♦ **preventivo** *sm.* estimate

preventorio *sm.* preventive sanatorium.

prevenuto *agg.* essere — *contro*, to have a prejudice against.

prevenzione *sf.* 1. prejudice 2. (*il prevenire*) prevention.

previdente *agg.* provident.

previdenza *sf.* providence: — *sociale*, social security.

previdenziale *agg.* social security (*attr.*).

previo *agg.* 1. previous 2. (*soggetto a*) subject to.

previsione *sf.* 1. forecast 2. (*comm.*) estimate.

previsto *agg.* 1. foreseen 2. (*comm.*) estimated 3. (*giur.*) provided.

prevosto *sm.* V. *preposto*.

preziosismo *sm.* preciosity.

preziosità *sf.* preciousness.

prezioso *agg.* precious. ♦ **prezioso** *sm.* jewel.

prezzèmolo *sm.* parsley.

prezzo *sm.* 1. price, cost 2. (*valore*) value || *a — di*, at the cost of.

prezzolare *vt.* to hire.

prezzolato *agg.* (*mercenario*) mercenary.

prigione *sf.* 1. prison 2. (*pena*) imprisonment.

prigionia *sf.* imprisonment.

prigioniero *agg.* imprisoned. ♦ **prigioniero** *sm.* prisoner.

prillare *vi.* to twirl.

prima[1] *avv.* 1. before 2. (*in anticipo*) in advance 3. (*un tempo*) once 4. (*più presto*) earlier, sooner 5. (*per prima cosa*) first || *— o poi*, sooner or later; *quanto —*, soon. ♦ **prima** *prep.* before. ♦ **prima che**, *di cong.* before.

prima[2] *sf.* 1. (*ferr.; scuola*) first class 2. (*teat.*) première.

primario *agg.* primary. ♦ **primario** *sm.* head physician.

primate *sm.* (*eccl.*) primate.

primati *sm. pl.* (*zool.*) Primates.

primaticcio *agg.* early.

primatista *s.* record-holder.

primato *sm.* 1. supremacy 2. (*sport*) record.

primavera *sf.* spring.

primaverile *agg.* spring (*attributivo*), springlike.

primeggiare *vi.* to excel.

primigenio *agg.* primigenial.

primipara *sf.* primipara (*pl.* -ae).

primitivo *agg. e sm.* primitive.

primizia *sf.* 1. (*frutta*) early fruit

2. (*verdura*) early vegetable 3. (*novità*) novelty.

primo *agg.* 1. first 2. (*principale*) chief 3. (*iniziale*) early 4. (*prossimo*) next ‖ *in un — tempo*, at first.

primogènito *agg.* e *sm.* first-born.

primogenitura *sf.* primogeniture.

primordiale *agg.* primeval.

primordi *sm. pl.* beginnings.

primula *sf.* primrose.

principale *agg.* principal. ♦ **principale** *sm.* master, boss.

principato *sm.* principality.

prìncipe *sm.* prince.

principesco *agg.* princely.

principessa *sf.* princess.

principiante *sm.* beginner.

principiare *vt.* e *vi.* to begin (*v. irr.*).

principio *sm.* 1. (*inizio*) beginning 2. (*norma*) principle: *per —*, on principle.

priora *sf.* prioress.

priorato *sm.* priorate.

priore *sm.* prior.

priorità *sf.* priority.

prisma *sm.* prism.

prismàtico *agg.* prismatic(al).

prìstino *agg.* former.

privare *vt.* to deprive.

privatista *s.* external student.

privativa *sf.* 1. (*esclusiva*) sole right 2. (*monopolio*) monopoly 3. (*tabaccheria*) tobacconist's shop.

privativo *agg.* privative.

privato *agg.* 1. private 2. (*privo*) deprived. ♦ **privato** *sm.* private citizen.

privazione *sf.* 1. (*disagio*) privation 2. (*perdita*) loss.

privilegiare *vt.* to privilege.

privilegiato *agg.* 1. privileged 2. (*comm.*) preferred.

privilegio *sm.* privilege.

privo *agg.* devoid: — *di padre*, fatherless; — *di madre*, motherless.

pro[1] *prep.* for.

pro[2] *sm.* *a che —?*, what is the use of?

proavo *sm.* great grandfather.

probàbile *agg.* probable.

probabilismo *sm.* probabilism.

probabilità *sf.* probability.

probante *agg.* probatory.

probativo *agg.* probative.

probità *sf.* uprightness.

probiviri *sm. pl.* arbiters.

problema *sm.* problem.

problematicità *sf.* problematic nature.

problemàtico *agg.* problematic(al).

probo *agg.* upright.

proboscidati *sm. pl.* Proboscidea.

probòscide *sf.* trunk.

procaccia *sm.* postman (*pl.* -men).

procacciare *vt.* to get (*v. irr.*). ♦ **procacciarsi** *vr.* to get.

procacciatore *sm.* procurer.

procace *agg.* 1. (*provocante*) provoking 2. (*inverecondo*) immodest.

procacità *sf.* 1. provocativeness 2. (*inverecondia*) immodesty.

pro capite *loc. avv.* each.

procèdere *vi.* 1. to proceed, to go (*v. irr.*) on 2. (*agire*) to act.

procedimento *sm.* 1. (*progressione*) course 2. (*condotta*) behaviour 3. (*giur.*) proceedings (*pl.*) 4. (*tec.*) process.

procedura *sf.* 1. procedure 2. (*giur.*) practice.

procedurale *agg.* procedural.

procella *sf.* storm.

procellaria *sf.* stormy-petrel.

procelloso *agg.* stormy.

processare *vt.* to try: *far —*, to prosecute.

processionaria *sf.* processioner.

processione *sf.* procession.

processo *sm.* 1. (*giur.*) trial 2. (*med.*; *chim.*; *tec.*) process ‖ *andare sotto —*, to be tried; *intentare un —*, to bring (*v. irr.*) an action.

processuale *agg.* trial (*attr.*).

procinto (*nella loc. avv.*) *in — di*, on the point of.

proclama *sm.* proclamation.

proclamare *vt.* to proclaim.

proclamatore *sm.* proclaimer.

proclamazione *sf.* proclamation.

proclive *agg.* inclined.

proclività *sf.* inclination.

procònsole *sm.* proconsul.

procrastinare *vt.* to postpone. ♦ **procrastinare** *vi.* to procrastinate.

procrastinazione *sf.* procrastination.

procreare *vt.* to procreate.

procreatore *sm.* procreator.

procreazione *sf.* procreation.

procura *sf.* 1. proxy: *per —*, by proxy 2. (*documento*) letter of attorney.

procurare *vt.* 1. to get (*v. irr.*) 2. (*causare*) to cause 3. (*cercare*) to try. ♦ **procurarsi** *vr.* to get (*v. irr.*).

procuratore *sm.* attorney.

prode *agg.* brave.

prodezza *sf.* 1. bravery 2. (*azione*) brave deed.

prodiere *sm.* bowman (*pl.* -men).

prodiero *agg.* forward.

prodigalità *sf.* lavishness.

prodigare *vt.* to lavish. ♦ **prodigarsi** *vr.* to do (*v. irr.*) all one can.

prodigio *sm.* prodigy.

prodigiosità *sf.* prodigiousness.

prodigioso *agg.* prodigious.

pròdigo *agg.* lavish.

proditoriamente *avv.* treacherously.

proditorio *agg.* treacherous.

prodotto *sm.* 1. product 2. (*risultato*) result 3. (*agr.*) produce.

pròdromo *sm.* 1. warning sign 2. (*med.*) symptom.

produrre *vt.* to produce. ♦ **prodursi** *vr.* 1. (*causarsi*) to cause oneself 2. (*accadere*) to happen 3. (*esibirsi*) to perform (before).

produttività *sf.* productivity.

produttivo *agg.* productive.

produttore *agg.* productive. **produttore** *sm.* producer.

produzione *sf.* production.

proemio *sm.* proem.

profanamente *avv.* profanely.

profanare *vt.* to profane.

profanatore *agg.* profaning. **profanatore** *sm.* profaner.

profanazione *sf.* profanation.

profanità *sf.* profanity.

profano *agg.* profane. ♦ **profano** *sm.* (*persona inesperta*) layman (*pl.* -men) || *i profani*, the laity.

proferire *vt.* 1. to pronounce 2. (*dire*) to utter.

professare *vt.* to profess.

professionale *agg.* professional: *scuola* —, vocational school.

professione *sf.* profession.

professionismo *sm.* professionalism.

professionista *sm.* 1. professional man 2. (*sport*) professional.

professorale *agg.* professorial.

professore *sm.* 1. teacher 2. (*ordinario di università*) professor.

profeta *sm.* prophet.

profetare *vt.* to prophesy.

profètico *agg.* prophetic(al).

profetizzare *vt.* V. *profetare*.

profezìa *sf.* prophecy.

profferire *vt.* 1. (*offrire*) to offer 2. (*pronunciare*) to utter.

profferta *sf.* offer.

proficuo *agg.* profitable.

profilare *vt.* 1. to profile 2. (*orlare*) to edge. ♦ **profilarsi** *vr.* 1. to be outlined 2. (*apparire*) to loom.

profilassi *sf.* prophylaxis.

profilato *agg.* 1. (*delineato*) outlined 2. (*afilato*) sharp 3. (*orlato*) edged. ♦ **profilato** *sm.* section.

profilàttico *agg.* e *sm.* prophylactic.

profilo *sm.* 1. (*contorno*) outline 2. (*di viso*) profile 3. (*studio letterario*) monograph.

profittare *vi.* 1. (*trar profitto*) to avail oneself (of) 2. (*progredire*) to make (*v. irr.*) progress 3. (*guadagnare*) to make profits.

profittatore *sm.* profiteer.

profittévole *agg.* profitable.

profitto *sm.* profit: *trar* —, to profit (by); *mettere qc. a* —, to make (*v. irr.*) good use of sthg.

profluvio *sm.* flood.

profondamente *avv.* deeply: *dormire* —, to sleep (*v. irr.*) soundly.

profòndere *vt.* to lavish. ♦ **profòndersi** *vr.* to be profuse (in, of).

profondità *sf.* depth.

profondo *agg.* deep. ♦ **profondo** *sm.* depth.

pròfugo *sm.* refugee.

profumare *vt.* to scent. ♦ **profumarsi** *vr.* to spray oneself with scent.

profumatamente *avv.* (*fig.*) dearly.

profumeria *sf.* perfumery.

profumiere *sm.* perfumer.

profumo *sm.* perfume, scent.

profusamente *avv.* 1. profusely 2. (*lungamente*) at length.

profusione *sf.* profusion.

progenerare *vt.* to procreate.

progenie *sf.* progeny.

progenitore *sm.* ancestor.

progettare *vt.* to plan.

progettazione *sf.* planning.

progettista *s.* planner.

progetto *sm.* plan.

prognatismo *sm.* prognathism.

prognato *agg.* prognathous.

prògnosi *sf.* prognosis (*pl.* -ses).

programma *sm.* program(me).

programmare *vt.* to program(me).

programmatore *sm.* programmist.

programmazione *sf.* programming.

programmista *sm.* programmer.
progredire *vi.* **1.** to advance **2.** (*fig.*) to get (*v. irr.*) on **3.** (*far progressi*) to make (*v. irr.*) progress.
progressione *sf.* progression.
progressista *agg. e s.* progressive.
progressivamente *avv.* progressively.
progressivo *agg.* progressive.
progresso *sm.* progress.
proibire *vt.* **1.** to forbid (*v. irr.*) **2.** (*impedire*) to prevent.
proibitivo *agg.* prohibitive.
proibizione *sf.* prohibition.
proibizionismo *sm.* prohibitionism.
proibizionista *agg. e s.* prohibitionist.
proiettare *vt.* **1.** to project **2.** (*cine*) to show (*v. irr.*) ♦ **proiettare** *vi.* to project. ♦ **proiettarsi** *vr.* to be projected.
proièttile *sm.* shell.
proiettore *sm.* **1.** (*riflettore*) searchlight **2.** (*cine*) projector.
proiezione *sf.* **1.** projection **2.** (*cine*) movie show ‖ *macchina da* —, projector; *sala di* —, projection room.
prole *sf.* issue.
proletariato *sm.* proletariat.
proletario *agg. e sm.* proletarian.
proliferare *vi.* to proliferate.
proliferazione *sf.* proliferation.
prolìfico *agg.* prolific.
prolissità *sf.* prolixity.
prolisso *agg.* prolix.
pròlogo *sm.* prologue.
prolungàbile *agg.* extendable.
prolungamento *sm.* extension.
prolungare *vt.* **1.** to extend **2.** (*differire*) to postpone. ♦ **prolungarsi** *vr.* **1.** to extend **2.** (*dilungarsi*) to dwell (*v. irr.*) (on).
prolusione *sf.* opening lecture.
promemoria *sm.* memorandum (*pl.* -da).
promessa *sf.* promise.
promettente *agg.* promising.
prométtere *vt.* to promise: — *bene*, to be full of promise.
prominente *agg.* prominent.
prominenza *sf.* prominence.
promiscuità *sf.* promiscuity.
promiscuo *agg.* mixed, promiscuous.
promontorio *sm.* promontory.
promosso *agg.* **1.** (*a scuola*) successful **2.** (*sostenuto*) promoted.

promotore *sm.* promoter.
promozione *sf.* promotion.
promulgare *vt.* to promulgate.
promulgatore *sm.* promulgator.
promulgazione *sf.* promulgation.
promuòvere *vt.* **1.** to promote **2.** (*a scuola*) to pass.
pronao *sm.* pronaos (*pl.* -aoi).
pronipote *sm.* **1.** (*di bisnonno*) great-grandson, great-grandchild (*pl.* -children) **2.** (*di prozio*) grand-nephew ‖ *i pronipoti* (*discendenti*), descendants. ♦ **pronipote** *sf.* **1.** (*di bisnonno*) great-granddaughter, great-grandchild **2.** (*di prozio*) grandniece.
prono *agg.* prone.
pronome *sm.* pronoun.
pronominale *agg.* pronominal.
pronosticare *vt.* **1.** to forecast (*v. irr.*) **2.** (*predire*) to foretell (*v. irr.*) **3.** (*far prevedere*) to portend.
pronòstico *sm.* forecast.
prontezza *sf.* readiness.
pronto *agg.* **1.** (*preparato*) ready **2.** (*veloce*) prompt **3.** (*al telefono*) hallo ‖ — *soccorso*, first aid.
prontuario *sm.* handbook.
pronuncia *sf.* pronunciation.
pronunciamento *sm.* pronouncement.
pronunciare *vt.* **1.** to pronounce **2.** (*proferire*) to utter ‖ — *un discorso*, to deliver a speech. ♦ **pronunciarsi** *vr.* to give (*v. irr.*) one's opinion.
pronunciato *agg.* pronounced.
propaganda *sf.* **1.** propaganda **2.** (*comm.*) advertising: *far* — (*comm.*), to advertise **3.** (*pol.*) canvass.
propagandare *vt.* **1.** to propagandize **2.** (*comm.*) to advertise.
propagandista *s.* **1.** propagandist **2.** (*comm.*) advertiser.
propagandìstico *agg.* **1.** propagandist **2.** (*comm.*) advertising.
propagare *vt.* to propagate. ♦ **propagarsi** *vr.* to propagate.
propagatore *sm.* propagator.
propagazione *sf.* propagation.
propagginare *vt.* (*agr.*) to layer.
propàggine *sf.* **1.** (*agr.*) layer **2.** (*geogr.*) ramification **3.** (*discendenza*) offspring.
propalare *vt.* to spread (*v. irr.*).
propano *sm.* propane.
propedèutica *sf.* propaedeutics.
propedèutico *agg.* propaedeutic(al).

propellente *agg.* propellent. ♦ **propellente** *sm.* propellant.

propèndere *vi.* to be inclined.

propensione *sf.* propensity.

propenso *agg.* inclined.

propilene *sm.* propylene.

propileo *sm.* propylaeum (*pl.* -laea).

propina *sf.* examiner's fee.

propinare *vt.* to give (*v. irr.*).

propiziare *vt.* to propitiate. ♦ **propiziarsi** *vr.* to gain so.'s favour.

propiziatore *sm.* propitiator.

propiziatorio *agg.* propitiatory.

propiziazione *sf.* propitiation.

propizio *agg.* favourable.

proponimento *sm.* resolution: *far —*, to resolve.

proporre *vt.* **1.** to propose **2.** (*suggerire*) to suggest. ♦ **proporsi** *vr.* to intend, to mean (*v. irr.*).

proporzionale *agg.* proportional.

proporzionalità *sf.* proportionality.

proporzionare *vt.* to proportion.

proporzionato *agg.* (*adeguato*) proportionate: *ben —*, well-proportioned.

proporzione *sf.* **1.** proportion **2.** (*rapporto*) ratio.

propòsito *sm.* **1.** purpose **2.** (*intenzione*) intention || *di —*, on purpose; *a — di*, with regard to; *a —* (*inter.*), by the way; *a —* (*al momento giusto*), at the right moment.

proposizione *sf.* sentence.

proposta *sf.* proposal.

proprietà *sf.* **1.** property **2.** (*l'essere proprietario*) ownership **3.** (*correttezza*) propriety || *— letteraria*, copyright.

proprietario *agg.* proprietary. ♦ **proprietario** *sm.* **1.** owner **2.** (*di locanda*) landlord **3.** (*possidente*) man of property || *— terriero*, landowner.

proprio *agg.* **1.** (*rafforzativo del poss.*) own **2.** (*adatto*) suitable **3.** (*mat.; gramm.*) proper || *vero e —*, real. ♦ **proprio** *avv.* **1.** (*esattamente*) exactly **2.** (*veramente*) really || *— ora*, just now; *— così*, just like that.

propugnare *vt.* to support.

propugnatore *sm.* supporter.

propulsione *sf.* propulsion.

propulsivo *agg.* propulsive.

propulsore *sm.* propeller.

prora *sf.* bow.

proravìa (*nella loc. avv.*) *a —*, at the bow.

pròroga *sf.* **1.** (*giur.*) adjournment **2.** (*dilazione*) extension.

prorogàbile *agg.* **1.** (*giur.*) adjournable **2.** extensible.

prorogare *vt.* **1.** to delay, to extend **2.** (*giur.*) to postpone.

proromퟢ펴re *vi.* **1.** to burst (out).

proròmpere *vi.* **1.** to burst-(*v. irr.*) (out) **2.** (*di liquidi*) to gush out.

prosa *sf.* prose || *teatro di —*, drama; *compagnia di —*, dramatic company.

prosaicità *sf.* prosaism.

prosàico *agg.* prosaic.

prosapia *sf.* race.

prosàstico *agg.* prose (*attr.*).

prosatore *sm.* prose-writer.

proscenio *sm.* proscenium.

proscimmie *sf. pl.* lemurs.

prosciògliere *vt.* **1.** (*da un obbligo*) to release **2.** (*giur.*) to acquit.

proscioglimento *sm.* **1.** release **2.** (*giur.*) acquittal.

prosciugamento *sm.* **1.** drying up **2.** (*artificiale*) draining.

prosciugare *vt.* **1.** to dry up **2.** (*artificialmente*) to drain. ♦ **prosciugarsi** *vr.* to dry up.

prosciutto *sm.* ham.

proscritto *sm.* exile.

proscrivere *vt.* to banish.

proscrizione *sf.* banishment.

prosecuzione *sf.* prosecution.

proseguimento *sm.* continuation.

proseguire *vt.* to continue. ♦ **proseguire** *vi.* to go (*v. irr.*) on.

proselitismo *sm.* proselytism.

proselito *sm.* proselyte.

prosieguo *sm.* course.

prosodìa *sf.* prosody.

prosopopèa *sf.* (*fig.*) haughtiness.

prosperare *vi.* to prosper.

prosperità *sf.* prosperity.

pròspero *agg.* prosperous.

prosperoso *agg.* **1.** prosperous **2.** (*in salute*) healthy.

prospettare *vt.* **1.** (*indicare*) to point out **2.** (*guardare*) to look on to.

prospèttico *agg.* perspective (*attr.*).

prospettiva *sf.* **1.** perspective **2.** (*possibilità*) prospect.

prospetto *sm.* **1.** view **2.** (*fronte*) front **3.** (*specchietto, programma*) prospectus.

prospezione *sf.* prospecting.

prospiciente *agg.* facing.

prossimità *sf.* closeness: *in — di*, near.

pròssimo *agg.* 1. (*vicino*) near 2. (*seguente*) next. ♦ **pròssimo** *sm.* fellow creatures (*pl.*), neighbour.

pròstata *sf.* prostate.

prosternare *vt.* to prostrate.

prostituire *vt.* to prostitute.

prostituta *sf.* prostitute.

prostituzione *sf.* prostitution.

prostrare *vt.* to prostrate. ♦ **prostrarsi** *vr.* to bow down.

prostrazione *sf.* prostration.

protagonista *s.* protagonist.

protèggere *vt.* to protect.

proteico *agg.* protein (*attr.*).

proteìna *sf.* protein.

protèndere *vt.* to stretch (out): *— lo sguardo*, to gaze. ♦ **protèndersi** *vr.* to stretch oneself.

protervia *sf.* insolence.

protervo *agg.* insolent.

pròtesi *sf.* prosthesis.

protesta *sf.* protest.

protestante *agg. e s.* protestant.

protestantésimo *sm.* Protestantism.

protestare *vt. e vi.* to protest.

protesto *sm.* protest: *in —*, under protest; *lasciar andare una cambiale in —*, to dishonour a bill.

protettivo *agg.* protective.

protetto *agg.* protected. ♦ **protetto** *sm.* favourite.

protettorato *sm.* protectorate.

protettore *sm.* 1. protector 2. (*patrono*) patron.

protezione *sf.* 1. protection 2. (*patronato*) patronage.

protezionismo *sm.* protectionism.

protezionista *s.* protectionist.

proto *sm.* overseer.

protocollare *agg.* protocol (*attr.*).

protocollo *sm.* 1. protocol 2. (*registro*) record || *mettere a —*, to record; *carta —*, foolscap.

protone *sm.* proton.

protoplasma *sm.* protoplasm.

protòtipo *sm.* prototype.

protozoi *sm. pl.* Protozoa.

protrarre *vt.* 1. to protract 2. (*differire*) to defer. ♦ **protrarsi** *vr.* to go (*v. irr.*) on.

protrazione *sf.* 1. protraction 2. (*differimento*) deferment.

protuberanza *sf.* bulge.

prova *sf.* 1. proof 2. (*giur.*) evidence (*solo sing.*) 3. (*esperimento, esame*) test 4. (*tentativo*) try 5.

(*sventura*) trial 6. (*teat.*) rehearsal 7. (*di abito*) fitting || *in —*, on trial; *dar — di essere*, to prove to be; *superare una —*, to pass a test.

provare *vt.* 1. to prove 2. (*tentare, mettere alla prova*) to try 3. (*sentire*) to feel (*v. irr.*) 4. (*di abiti*) to try on 5. (*teat.*) to rehearse 6. (*collaudare*) to test. ♦ **provarsi** *vr.* 1. (*tentare*) to try 2. (*cimentarsi*) to engage (in).

provenienza *sf.* origin.

provenire *vi.* to come (*v. irr.*).

provento *sm.* 1. proceeds (*pl.*) 2. (*reddito*) income.

proverbiale *agg.* proverbial

proverbio *sm.* proverb.

provetta *sf.* test-tube.

provetto *agg.* skilled.

provincia *sf.* province.

provinciale *agg. e s.* provincial: *strada —*, main road.

provincialismo *sm.* provincialism.

provino *sm.* 1. (*teat.*) tryout 2. (*cine*) test film.

provocante *agg.* 1. provocative 2. (*procace*) immodest.

provocare *vt.* 1. to provoke 2. (*causare*) to cause.

provocatore *sm.* provoker.

provocazione *sf.* provocation.

provvedere *vi.* 1. to provide (for) 2. (*badare a*) to see (*v. irr.*) (to) 3. (*aver cura di*) to take (*v. irr.*) care of. ♦ **provvedere** *vt.* 1. to provide 2. (*preparare*) to prepare.

provvedimento *sm.* measure.

provveduto *agg.* 1. provided (with) 2. (*accorto*) wary.

provvidenza *sf.* providence: *essere una —*, to be providential.

provvidenziale *agg.* providential.

pròvvido *agg.* provident.

provvigione *sf.* 1. (*comm.*) commission 2. (*provvista*) supply.

provvisorietà *sf.* temporariness.

provvisorio *agg.* temporary: *in via provvisoria*, temporarily.

provvista *sf.* supply, provision (*specialmente di cibo*).

provvisto *agg.* 1. supplied (with) 2. (*fig.*) well-off.

prua *sf.* bow.

prudente *agg.* 1. prudent 2. (*cauto*) careful.

prudenza *sf.* 1. prudence 2. (*cautela*) care 3. (*precauzione*) precaution.

prùdere *vi.* to itch.

prugna *sf.* plum.

prugno *sm.* plum-tree.

pruno *sm.* 1. thorn-bush 2. (*spina*) thorn.

pruriginoso *agg.* itching

prurito *sm.* itch.

prùssico *agg.* prussic.

pseudònimo *sm.* pseudonym.

psicanàlisi *sf.* psychoanalysis.

psicanalista *s.* psychoanalyst.

psicanalìtico *agg.* psychoanalytic(al).

psicanalizzare *vt.* to psychoanalyze.

psiche *sf.* psyche.

psichiatra *s.* psychiatrist.

psichiatrìa *sf.* psychiatry.

psichiàtrico *agg.* psychiatric(al).

psìchico *agg.* psychic(al).

psicologìa *sf.* psychology.

psicològico *agg.* psychologic(al).

psicòlogo *sm.* psychologist.

psicometrìa *sf.* psychometry.

psicopatìa *sf.* psychopathy.

psicopàtico *agg. e sm.* psychopathic.

psicopatologìa *sf.* psychopathology.

psicòsi *sf.* psychosis (*pl.* -ses).

psicoterapìa *sf.* psychotherapy.

psittacòsi *sf.* psittacosis.

pubblicàbile *agg.* publishable.

pubblicano *sm.* publican.

pubblicare *vt.* 1. to publish 2. (*di leggi ecc.*) to issue.

pubblicazione *sf.* publication: *fare le pubblicazioni di matrimonio*, to put up the banns.

pubblicista *s.* journalist.

pubblicità *sf.* 1. publicity 2. (*propaganda*) advertising || *fare* —, to advertise.

pubblicitàrio *agg.* advertising.

pùbblico *agg.* public. ♦ **pùbblico** *sm.* 1. public 2. (*in teatro ecc.*) audience 3. (*cine*) moviegoers (*pl.*).

pube *sm.* pubis (*pl.* -bes).

pubertà *sf.* puberty.

pudibondo *agg.* demure.

pudicìzia *sf.* demureness.

pudìco *agg.* demure.

pudore *sm.* decency.

puericoltura *sf.* puericulture.

puerile *agg.* childish.

puerilità *sf.* childishness.

puèrpera *sf.* childwife (*pl.* -wives)

pugilato *sm.* boxing: *fare del* —, to box

pùgile *sm.* boxer.

pugnalare *vt.* to stab.

pugnalata *sf.* 1. stab 2. (*fig.*) blow.

pugnale *sm.* dagger.

pugno *sm.* 1. fist 2. (*colpo*) punch 3. (*manciata*) handful || *colpire col* —, to punch; *in* —, in one's hand; *di proprio* —, in one's own handwriting; *fare a pugni*, to fight (*v. irr.*), (*fig.*) to clash.

pula *sf.* chaff.

pulce *sf.* flea: — *in un orecchio*, suspicion.

pulcino *sm.* chick.

puledro *sm.* colt.

puleggia *sf.* pulley.

pulire *vt.* to clean: *pulirsi la bocca*, to wipe one's mouth.

pulito *agg.* clean.

pulitore *sm.* cleaner.

pulizìa *sf.* 1. (*il pulire*) cleaning 2. (*l'essere pulito*) cleanliness.

pullulare *vi.* to swarm (with).

pùlpito *sm.* pulpit.

pulsante *sm.* push button.

pulsare *vi.* to beat (*v. irr.*)

pulsazione *sf.* beat.

pulverulento *agg.* dusty.

pulvìscolo *sm.* dust: — *atmosferico*, motes (*pl.*).

puma *sm.* puma.

pungente *agg.* 1. prickly 2. (*fig.*) biting.

pùngere *vt.* 1. to sting (*v. irr.*) 2. (*di ago*) to prick 3. (*fig.*) to tease. ♦ **pùngersi** *vr.* to prick oneself.

pungiglione *sm.* sting.

pungitopo *sm.* (*bot.*) butcher's broom.

pungolare *vt.* to goad.

pùngolo *sm.* goad.

punìbile *agg.* punishable.

punire *vt.* to punish: — *una offesa*, to revenge an insult.

punitivo *agg.* punitive.

punitore *agg.* punitory. ♦ **punitore** *sm.* punisher.

punizione *sf.* punishment.

punta *sf.* 1. point 2. (*estremità*) tip 3. (*cima*) top 4. (*un po'*) bit 5. (*dolore, fitta*) twinge || *sulla — dei piedi*, on tiptoe; *avere qc. sulla — delle dita*, to have sthg. at one's finger-tips.

puntale *sm.* (*di bastone ecc.*) ferrule.

puntamento *sm.* aim.

puntare *vt.* 1. to point (at) 2. (*mirare*) to aim (at) 3. (*spingere*) to push **4.** (*scommettere*) to bet (*v. irr.*) || — *i piedi* (*fig.*), to put (*v. irr.*) one's foot down. ♦ **puntare** *vi.* to head.

puntata *sf.* **1.** (*al gioco*) stake **2.** (*di romanzo*) instalment.

puntatore *sm.* **1.** (*mil.*) marksman (*pl.* -men) **2.** (*al gioco*) better.

punteggiare *vt.* **1.** to punctuate **2.** (*nel disegno*) to dot.

punteggiatura *sf.* **1.** punctuation **2.** (*nel disegno*) dotting.

punteggio *sm.* (*sport*) score.

puntellare *vt.* to prop.

puntellatura *sf.* propping.

puntello *sm.* prop.

punteruolo *sm.* punch.

puntiglio *sm.* **1.** punctilio **2.** (*ostinazione*) obstinacy || *per* —, out of pique.

puntigliosamente *avv.* **1.** punctiliously **2.** (*ostinatamente*) obstinately.

puntiglioso *agg.* **1.** punctilious **2.** (*ostinato*) obstinate.

puntina *sf.* **1.** (*da fonografo*) needle **2.** (*da disegno*) drawing-pin.

puntino *sm.* dot: *puntini di sospensione*, dots || *a* —, properly.

punto[1] *sm.* **1.** point **2.** (*di cucito*) stitch **3.** (*voto*) mark **4.** (*gramm.*) full stop **5.** (*macchiolina*) dot || *due punti*, colon; — *e virgola*, semicolon; *mettere a* —, to set (*v. irr.*) up.

punto[2] *avv.* not at all.

punto[3] *agg. e pron.* not ... any.

puntone *sm.* (*edil.*) strut.

puntuale *agg.* punctual.

puntualità *sf.* punctuality.

puntualizzare *vt.* to stress.

puntualmente *avv.* punctually.

puntura *sf.* **1.** (*di insetto*) sting **2.** (*di ago*) prick **3.** (*iniezione*) injection **4.** (*dolore, fitta*) pain.

puntuto *agg.* pointed.

punzecchiamento *sm.* **1.** (*d'insetto*) stinging **2.** (*d'ago*) pricking **3.** (*fig.*) teasing.

punzecchiare *vt.* **1.** (*di insetti*) to sting (*v. irr.*) **2.** (*fig.*) to tease.

punzonare *vt.* to punch.

punzonatrice *sf.* (*mecc.*) punch.

punzonatura *sf.* punching.

punzone *sm.* punch.

pupàttola *sf.* doll.

pupazzetto *sm.* (*disegno*) sketch.

pupazzo *sm.* puppet.

pupilla *sf.* pupil.

pupillo *sm.* pupil.

pupo *sm.* baby.

purché *cong.* provided (that).

pure *avv.* **1.** (*anche*) also, too **2.** (*eppure*) yet **3.** (*di concessione*) as you like, of course. ♦ **pure** *cong.* **1.** (*con frasi concessive*) even though **2.** (*tuttavia*) but, yet. ♦ **pure di** *cong.* if only.

purè *sm.* purée: — *di patate*, mashed potatoes; *fare un* — *di verdura*, to mash vegetables.

purezza *sf.* purity.

purga *sf.* purgative, purge.

purgante *sm.* purgative, purge.

purgare *vt.* **1.** to purge **2.** (*di scritti*) to expurgate.

purgativo *agg.* purgative.

purgatorio *sm.* purgatory.

purificare *vt.* to purify.

purificatore *agg.* purificatory.

purificazione *sf.* purification.

purismo *sm.* purism.

purista *s.* purist.

puritanésimo *sm.* Puritanism.

puritano *agg. e sm.* Puritan.

puro *agg.* **1.** pure **2.** (*mero*) mere.

purosangue *sm.* thoroughbred.

purpùreo *agg.* purple.

purpurina *sf.* purpurin.

purtroppo *avv.* unfortunately.

purulento *agg.* purulent.

pus *sm.* pus.

pusillànime *agg.* pusillanimous. ♦ **pusillànime** *s.* coward.

pusillanimità *sf.* pusillanimity.

pùstola *sf.* pustule.

putacaso *loc. avv.* supposing.

putativo *agg.* putative.

putiferio *sm.* uproar: *sollevare un* —, to make (*v. irr.*) an uproar.

putrèdine *sf.* **1.** putridness **2.** (*cosa putrefatta*) rot.

putrefare *vi.* to rot. ♦ **putrefarsi** *vr.* to rot.

putrefatto *agg.* rotten.

putrefazione *sf.* putrefaction.

putrella *sf.* iron beam.

putrescenza *sf.* putrescence.

putrescìbile *agg.* putrescible.

putridità *sf.* rottenness.

pùtrido *agg.* rotten.

putridume *sm.* rot.

putto *sm.* putto (*pl.* -ti).

puzza *sf.* V. *puzzo*.

puzzare *vi.* to stink (*v. irr.*).

puzzo *sm.* stench.

pùzzola *sf.* polecat.

puzzolente *agg.* stinking.

Q

qua *avv.* here: *di — di*, on this side of; *per di —*, this way; *da quando in —?*, since when?

quàcchero *agg. e sm.* Quaker.

quaderno *sm.* exercise-book.

quadrangolare *agg.* quadrangular.

quadràngolo *sm.* quadrangle.

quadrante *sm.* 1. quadrant 2. *(di orologio)* dial.

quadrare *vt.* 1. *(geom.)* to square 2. *(formare)* to shape. ♦ **quadrare** *vi.* *(corrispondere)* to suit.

quadrato *agg.* 1. square 2. *(fig.)* strong. ♦ **quadrato** *sm.* 1. square 2. *(sport)* ring.

quadratura *sf.* 1. squaring 2. *(mat.)* quadrature.

quadrettato *agg.* 1. squared 2. *(di tessuto)* chequered.

quadriennale *agg.* quadrennial.

quadriennio *sm.* quadrennium *(pl. -ia)*.

quadrifoglio *sm.* four-leaved clover.

quadriglia *sf.* quadrille.

quadrilatero *sm.* quadrilateral.

quadrimotore *sm.* four-engined aircraft.

quadrivio *sm.* cross-roads.

quadro *agg.* V. *quadrato*. ♦ **quadro** *sm.* 1. picture 2. *(tabella)* table 3. *(teat.)* scene 4. *(elettr.)* board 5. *(mil.)* cadre || *galleria di quadri*, picture-gallery; — *riassuntivo*, summary; — *degli interruttori*, switch board.

quadrùmane *agg.* quadrumanous. ♦ **quadrùmane** *sm.* quadrumane.

quadrùpede *agg. e sm.* quadruped.

quadruplicare *vt.* to quadruple. ♦ **quadruplicarsi** *vr.* to quadruple.

quadruplo *agg. e sm.* 1. quadruple 2. *(quattro volte tanto)* four times as much.

quaggiù *avv.* down here.

quaglia *sf.* quail.

qualche *agg.* *(in frasi affermative e interrogative che aspettano risposta affermativa)* some; *(in frasi interrogative, dubitative, condizionali)* any || — *volta*, sometimes; *in — luogo*, somewhere; *in — modo*, somehow.

qualcosa *pron.* something, anything *(per l'uso V. qualche)*.

qualcuno *pron.* 1. somebody, someone 2. *(alcuni)* some, any: — *di*, some, any of *(per l'uso V. qualche)*.

quale *pron. rel.* 1. *(per persone)* who *(sogg.)*, whom *(altri casi)* 2. *(per animali, cose)* which 3. *(per tutti, solo sogg. e ogg.)* that || *del* — *(poss.)*, whose: *l'uomo la casa del* —, the man whose house. ♦ **quale** *agg. e pron. int.* 1. *(di che tipo)* what 2. *(scelta tra numero limitato)* which. ♦ **quale** *agg. escl.* what. ♦ **quale** *pron. (correlativo di "tale")* is || *è tale e — suo fratello*, he is just like his brother.

qualifica *sf.* 1. qualification 2. *(titolo)* title.

qualificare *vt.* to qualify.

qualificativo *agg.* qualifying.

qualificato *agg.* qualified: *operaio* —, skilled worker.

qualificazione *sf.* qualification.

qualità *sf.* 1. quality 2. *(specie)* kind 3. *(ufficio)* capacity.

qualitativo *agg.* qualitative.

qualora *cong.* in case.

qualsiasi *agg.* V. *qualunque*.

qualunque *agg.* 1. any 2. *(quale che sia)* whatever; *(riferito a numero limitato)* whichever 3. *(comune)* ordinary || *uno* —, anybody; — *cosa*, anything; *in — posto*, anywhere; *in — modo*, anyhow.

quando *avv. e cong.* when || *da* —, since; *da —?*, since when?; *quand'anche*, even though; *di — in* —, now and then.

quantità *sf.* quantity: *una gran* — *di*, a great deal of.

quantitativo *agg.* quantitative. ♦ **quantitativo** *sm.* V. *quantità*.

quanto *agg.* how much *(pl. how many)* || *tanto ...* —, as much... as; *tanti... quanti*, as many... as; — *tempo?* how long? ♦ **quanto** *avv.* how, how much || *tanto* —, as much as; *tanto ...* —, as... as; *tanto ...* — *(sia... sia)* both... and; — *più... tanto più*, the more... the more; — *più... tanto meno*, the more... the less; — *a*, as for; — *prima*, soon; *per* —, however; *fa?*, how much is it?

quantunque *cong.* though, although.

quaranta *agg.* forty.

quarantena *sf.* quarantine.

quarantenne *agg.* forty years old, forty-year-old *(attr.)*.

quarantèsimo *agg.* fortieth.

quarantina *sf.* about forty: *aver*

passato la —, to be over forty.

quarésima sf. Lent.

quartetto sm. quartet.

quartiere sm. 1. (di una città) quarter 2. (rione amministrativo) district || — generale, headquarters (pl.).

quartina sf. quatrain.

quarto agg. fourth. ♦ **quarto** sm. quarter.

quarzo sm. quartz.

quasi avv. almost: — mai, hardly ever.

quassù avv. up here.

quaterna sf. set of four numbers.

quaternario agg. quaternary. ♦ **quaternario** sm. (verso di una poesia) line of four syllables.

quatto agg. 1. squatting 2. (silenzioso) silent || — —, very quietly.

quattordicèsimo agg. fourteenth.

quattòrdici agg. fourteen.

quattrini sm. pl. money (us. al sing.): star male a —, to be hard up.

quattro agg. four || in — e — otto, in no time; fare il diavolo a —, to make (v. irr.) a hullabaloo; farsi in —, to do (v. irr.) one's utmost.

quattrocchi (nella loc. avv.) a —, privately.

quattrocento agg. four hundred. ♦ **quattrocento** sm. il —, the fifteenth century.

quattromila agg. four thousand.

quegli agg. V. quelli. ♦ **quegli** pron. V. egli.

quel agg. e pron. V. quelli.

quella agg. e pron. V. quello.

quelle agg. e pron. V. quelle.

quelli agg. those. ♦ **quelli** pron. those, the ones.

quello agg. that. ♦ **quello** pron. that, the one || — che (ciò che), what; tutto — che, all that.

quercia sf. oak.

querela sf. 1. complaint 2. (giur.) action; sporger —, to bring (v. irr.) an action.

querelante s. plaintiff.

querelare vt. to proceed (against).

querelato sm. defendant.

quèrulo agg. querulous.

quesito sm. question.

questa agg. e pron. V. questo.

queste agg. e pron. V. questi.

questi agg. these. ♦ **questi** pron. 1. these 2. (sing.) this (man).

questionare vi. to quarrel.

questionario sm. questionnaire.

questione sf. 1. question 2. (lite) quarrel.

questo agg. this. ♦ **questo** pron. this, that || —...quello (il primo... il secondo) the former... the latter.

questore sm. questor.

questua sf. 1. begging 2. (in chiesa) collection.

questuante agg. begging. ♦ **questuante** s. beggar.

questuare vi. to beg.

questura sf. police-headquarters (pl.).

questurino sm. cop.

qui avv. here: per di —, this way; — vicino, close by; da — innanzi, from now on; di — a un anno, a year from now; di — a otto giorni, a week today; fin — (di tempo), so far.

quiescenza sf. quiescence.

quietanza sf. receipt.

quietare vt. to quiet. ♦ **quietarsi** vr. to quiet down.

quiete sf. quiet.

quietismo sm. quietism.

quieto agg. quiet || star — (zitto), to keep (v. irr.) quiet; star — (fermo), to keep (v. irr.) still; — —, very quietly.

quindi avv. 1. therefore 2. (poi) then.

quindicenne agg. fifteen years old, fifteen-year-old (attr.).

quindicèsimo agg. fifteenth.

quìndici agg. fifteen.

quindicina sf. 1. about fifteen 2. (salario) a fortnight's wages || una — di giorni, about a fortnight.

quindicinale agg. fortnightly.

quinquennale agg. quinquennial.

quinta sf. (teat.) wing || dietro le quinte, behind the scenes.

quintale sm. quintal.

quinterno sm. five sheets (pl.).

quintessenza sf. quintessence.

quintetto sm. quintet(te).

quinto agg. fifth.

quintuplicare vt. to quintuple.

quìntuplo agg. e sm. quintuple.

quisquìlia sf. trifle.

quivi avv. here.

quota sf. 1. share 2. (aer.) altitude 3. (mar.) depth || perdere —, to lose (v. irr.) height; prender —, to climb.

quotare vt. to quote. ♦ **quotarsi** vr. to subscribe.

quotato agg. 1. quoted 2. (fig.) esteemed.

quotazione sf. quotation.

quotidianamente avv. daily.

quotidiano agg. e sm. daily: vita quotidiana, everyday life.

quoziente sm. quotient.

R

rabàrbaro sm. rhubarb.

rabberciamento sm. patching (up).

rabberciare vt. to patch (up).

rabbia sf. 1. rage 2. (idrofobia) rabies || far — a qu., to make (v. irr.) so. angry.

rabbino sm. rabbi.

rabbioso agg. 1. (med.) rabid 2. (fig.) angry.

rabbonire vt. to calm down.

rabbrividire vi. 1. (di freddo) to shiver 2. (di paura ecc.) to shudder.

rabbuffare vt. 1. to ruffle 2. (risaproverare) to reprimand.

rabbuffo sm. rebuke.

rabbuiarsi vr. to darken.

rabdomante s. dowser.

rabdomanzìa sf. dowsing.

rabesco sm. V. arabesco.

raccapezzare vt. 1. (raccogliere) to gather 2. (capire) to understand (v. irr.). ♦ **raccapezzarsi** vr. to see (v. irr.) one's way.

raccapricciante agg. horrifying.

raccapricciare vt. to horrify. ♦ **raccapricciarsi** vr. to be horrified.

raccapriccio sm. horror.

raccattare vt. to pick up.

racchétta sf. racket.

racchio agg. ugly.

racchiùdere vt. to contain.

raccògliere vt. 1. to pick (up) 2. (radunare) to gather 3. (far collezione) to collect 4. (accogliere) to shelter 5. (agr.) to reap. ♦ **raccògliersi** vr. 1. to gather 2. (concentrarsi) to collect one's thoughts.

raccoglimento sm. 1. concentration 2. (meditazione) meditation.

raccogliticcio agg. picked up at random.

raccoglitore sm. 1. picker 2. (collezionista) collector 3. (cartella) folder.

raccolta sf. 1. (agr.) harvest; (di frutta, cotone) picking 2. (collezione) collection 3. (adunanza) gathering || fare la —, to harvest; chiamare a —, to collect.

raccoltamente avv. intently

raccolto sm. harvest.

raccomandàbile agg. recommendable.

raccomandare vt. 1. to recommend 2. (esortare) to urge 3. (di lettere, pacchi) to register. ♦ **raccomandarsi** vr. to beg (so.).

raccomandata sf. registered letter: fare una —, to register a letter.

raccomandazione sf. 1. recommendation 2. (consiglio) advice 3. (di lettere, pacchi) registration.

raccomodare vt. to mend.

raccontare vt. to tell (v. irr.) || si racconta, it is said.

racconto sm. 1. tale 2. (resoconto) relation.

raccorciare vt. to shorten. ♦ **raccorciarsi** vr. to grow (v. irr.) shorter.

raccordare vt. to connect.

raccordo sm. 1. connection 2. (mecc.) union 3. (ferr.) siding.

ràchide sf. rachis (pl. -ides).

rachìtico agg. rickety.

rachitismo sm. rickets.

racimolare vt. to glean.

rada sf. roadstead.

radar sm. radar.

raddobbare vt. 1. (mar.) to repair 2. (riparare) to refit.

raddobbo sm. (mar.) repair.

raddolcimento sm. 1. sweetening 2. (fig.) softening.

raddolcire vt. 1. to sweeten 2. (fig.) to soften 3. (alleviare) to soothe. ♦ **raddolcirsi** vr. 1. to soften 2. (alleviarsi) to be soothed 3. (mitigarsi) to grow (v. irr.) milder.

raddoppiamento sm. doubling.

raddoppiare vt. to double. ♦ **raddoppiarsi** vr. to double.

raddoppio sm. doubling.

raddrizzamento sm. 1. straightening 2. (correzione) redressing.

raddrizzare vt. 1. to straighten 2. (correggere) to redress.

radente agg. 1. shaving 2. (rasente) grazing.

ràdere vt. 1. to shave 2. (sfiorare) to graze 3. (distruggere) to raze.

radezza sf. 1. thinness 2. (rarità) infrequency.

radiale agg. radial.

radiante agg. radiant.

radiare vt. 1. to radiate 2. (espellere) to expel 3. (un nome) to strike (v. irr.) off.

radiatore sm. radiator.

radiazione sf. 1. radiation 2. (espulsione) expulsion.

radicale agg. radical.

radicalismo sm. radicalism.

radicare vi. to root. ♦ **radicarsi** vr. to root.

radicato agg. deep-rooted.

radice sf. root.

radio[1] sm. (anat.) radius (pl. -dii).

radio[2] sm. (chim.) radium.

radio[3] sf. radio, wireless: ponte —, radiolink; alla —, on the radio; — portatile ricevente e trasmittente, walkie-talkie.

radioattività sf. radioactivity.

radioattivo agg. radioactive.

radioaudizione sf. 1. broadcasting 2. (ascolto) listening.

radiocomunicazione sf. wireless communication.

radiocrònaca sf. running commentary, radio account.

radiocronista s. radio commentator, wireless commentator.

radiodiffusione sf. broadcast.

radioestesia sf. sensitivity to radiation.

radiofaro sm. radio beacon.

radiogoniòmetro sm. radio compass.

radiografare vt. to radiograph.

radiografia sf. 1. radiograph 2. (scienza) radiography.

radiogramma sm. radiogram.

radiogrammòfono sm. radio-gramophone.

radiologìa sf. radiology.

radiòlogo sm. radiologist.

radioscopìa sf. radioscopy.

radioscòpico agg. radioscopic.

radiosità sf. radiance.

radioso agg. bright.

radiotècnica sf. radioengineering.

radiotècnico sm. radioengineer.

radiotelefonìa sf. radiotelephony.

radiotelèfono sm. radiotelephone.

radiotelegrafìa sf. radiotelegraphy.

radiotelegràfico agg. radiotelegraphic, wireless (attr.).

radiotelegrafista s. telegraphist.

radiotelevisione sf. radio and television.

radioterapìa sf. radiotherapy.

radiotrasméttere vt. to broadcast (v. irr.).

rado agg. 1. thin 2. (non frequente) infrequent || di —, seldom.

radunare vt. to gather. ♦ **radunarsi** vr. to gather.

raduno sm. gathering.

radura sf. glade.

raffazzonare vt. to patch up.

raffermo agg. stale.

ràffica sf. 1. gust 2. (di arma) burst 3. (fig.) hail.

raffigurare vt. to represent. ♦ **raffigurarsi** vr. (immaginare) to imagine.

raffinamento sm. 1. refining 2. (fig.) refinement.

raffinare vt. to refine. ♦ **raffinarsi** vr. to become (v. irr.) refined, to refine.

raffinatamente avv. refinedly.

raffinatezza sf. refinement.

raffinato agg. refined (anche fig.).

raffinazione sf. refining.

raffinerìa sf. refinery.

raffio sm. grapnel.

rafforzamento sm. strengthening.

rafforzare vt. to strengthen. ♦ **rafforzarsi** vr. to grow (v. irr.) stronger.

raffreddamento sm. 1. cooling 2. (fig.) coolness.

raffreddare vt. 1. to cool 2. (fig.) to lessen. ♦ **raffreddarsi** vr. 1. to cool 2. (fig.) to wane 3. (prendere un raffreddore) to catch (v. irr.) a cold.

raffreddato agg. essere —, to have a cold.

raffreddatore sm. cooler.

raffreddore sm. cold.

raffrenare vt. to restrain.

raffrontare vt. to compare.

raffronto sm. comparison.

rafia sf. raffia.

ràgadi sf. pl. rhagades.

raganella sf. 1. tree-frog 2. (strumento) rattle.

ragazza sf. girl.

ragazzaglia sf. crowd of youngsters.

ragazzata sf. escapade.

ragazzo sm. boy: da —, as a boy.

raggelare vt. to freeze (v. irr.). ♦ **raggelarsi** vr. to freeze.

raggiante agg. radiant (with).

raggiare vi. 1. to shine (v. irr.) (with sthg.) 2. (fig.) to beam (with sthg.). ♦ **raggiare** vt. to radiate.

raggiera sf. halo of rays: a —, radially.

raggio sm. 1. ray 2. (geom.) radius 3. (d'azione) range 4. (di ruota) spoke || — di sole, sunbeam

raggirare vt. to cheat.

raggiro sm. cheat.

raggiùngere vt. to reach.

raggiungimento sm. reaching.

raggiustare vt. 1. to repair 2. (riordinare) to rearrange.

raggomitolare vt. to roll up. ♦ **raggomitolarsi** vr. to roll oneself up.

raggranellare vt. to scrape together.

raggrinzire vt. to wrinkle. ♦ **raggrinzirsi** vr. to wrinkle, to become (v. irr.) wrinkled.

raggrumare vt. to clot. ♦ **raggrumarsi** vr. to clot.

raggruppamento sm. 1. grouping 2. (gruppo) group.

raggruppare vt. to group. ♦ **raggrupparsi** vr. to gather.

ragguagliare vt. 1. (livellare) to level 2. (informare) to inform 3. (paragonare) to compare 4. (comm.) to balance.

ragguaglio sm. 1. (informazione) information (solo sing.) 2. (paragone) comparison 3. (comm.) balance.

ragguardévole agg. considerable.

ragia sf. resin: acqua —, turpentine.

ragionamento sm. reasoning.

ragionare vi. 1. to reason (about) 2. (discutere) to discuss (sthg.).

ragionatore sm. reasoner.

ragione sf. 1. reason 2. (diritto) right 2. (rapporto) rate || la — per cui, the reason why; a — veduta, after due consideration; aver —, to be right; a maggior —, all the more reason; aver — di qu., to get (v. irr.) the better of so.; — sociale (comm.), style.

ragioneria sf. bookkeeping.

ragionévole agg. 1. reasonable 2. (di buon senso) sensible.

ragionevolezza sf. reasonableness.

ragioniere sm. bookkeeper.

ragliare vi. to bray.

raglio sm. bray.

ragnatela sf. cobweb.

ragno sm. spider.

ragù sm. ragout.

raion sm. rayon.

rallegramenti sm. pl. congratulations.

rallegrare vt. to cheer (up). ♦ **rallegrarsi** vr. 1. to rejoice (at) 2. (congratularsi) to congratulate (so. on sthg.).

rallentamento sm. slowing down.

rallentare vt. to slacken. ♦ **rallentare** vi. 1. to slacken 2. (di velocità) to slow down. ♦ **rallentarsi** vr. to get (v. irr.) slack.

rallentatore sm. (cine) slow motion.

ramaiolo sm. ladle.

ramanzina sf. scolding.

ramare vt. to copper.

ramarro sm. green lizard.

ramazza sf. broom.

rame sm. copper.

ramìfero agg. copper-bearing (attr.).

ramificare vt. to ramify. ♦ **ramificarsi** vr. to ramify.

ramificazione sf. ramification.

ramingo agg. roving.

rammagliare vt. to mend a run.

rammaricare vt. to afflict. ♦ **rammaricarsi** vr. 1. to be sorry 2. (lamentarsi) to complain (of).

rammàrico sm. sorrow.

rammendare vt. to darn.

rammendatrice sf. darner.

rammendo sm. 1. darning 2. (parte rammendata) darn.

rammentare vt. to remember: — qc. a qu., to remind so. of sthg. ♦ **rammentarsi** vr. to remember.

rammollimento sm. softening.

rammollire vt. to soften. ♦ **rammollirsi** vr. to soften, to go (v. irr.) soft.

rammollito agg. soft: un vecchio —, a dotard. ♦ **rammollito** sm. imbecile.

ramo sm. branch.

ramoscello sm. twig.

ramoso agg. branched.

rampa sf. 1. ramp 2. (di scale) flight.

rampante agg. rampant.

rampicante agg. climbing: pianta —, creeper.

rampino sm. hook.

rampogna sf. reproach.

rampollare vi. to spring (v. irr.).

rampollo sm. 1. (d'acqua) spring 2. (di albero) shoot 3. (discendente) offspring.

rampone sm. 1. (mar.) harpoon 2. (da montagna) crampon.

rana sf. frog: uomo —, frogman (pl. -men); nuotare a —, to swim (v. irr.) the breast stroke.

ràncido agg. 1. rancid 2. (fig.) trite || sapere di —, to have a rancid taste.

rancio sm. (mil.) mess.

rancore sm. grudge.

randagio agg. stray.

randellare vt. to cudgel.

randellata sf. blow with a cudgel.

randello sm. cudgel.

ranetta sf. rennet.

rango sm. rank.

rannicchiarsi vr. to crouch.

rannuvolamento sm. clouding over.

rannuvolare vi. to become (v. irr.) cloudy, to cloud over. ♦ **rannuvolarsi** vr. to get (v. irr.) cloudy.

ranocchio sm. frog.

rantolare vi. 1. to wheeze 2. (in punto di morte) to have the death-rattle.

ràntolo sm. 1. wheeze 2. (di morte) death-rattle.

ranùncolo sm. buttercup.

rapa sf. turnip.

rapace agg. greedy. ♦ **rapace** sm. bird of prey.

rapacità sf. greed.

rapare vt. to crop (so.'s hair).

rapato agg. shorn.

ràpida sf. rapid.

rapidità sf. swiftness.

ràpido agg. swift. ♦ **ràpido** sm. express (train).

rapimento sm. 1. kidnapping 2. (di donna) abduction 3. (fig.) rapture.

rapina sf. robbery.

rapinare vt. to rob.

rapinatore sm. robber.

rapire vt. 1. to kidnap 2. (una donna) to abduct 3. (fig.) to ravish.

rapitore sm. 1. kidnapper 2. (di donna) abductor.

rappacificare vt. to reconcile. ♦ **rappacificarsi** vr. to become (v. irr.) reconciled.

rappacificazione sf. reconciliation.

rappezzare vt. to patch.

rappezzatura sf. 1. patching 2. (parte rappezzata) patch.

rapporto sm. 1. relation 2. (relazione) report 3. (mat.) ratio || chiamare a —, to summon; andare a

— da, to report to; essere in buoni rapporti, to be on good terms; sotto tutti i rapporti, in every respect.

rapprèndere vi. to coagulate. ♦ **rapprèndersi** vr. to coagulate.

rappresaglia sf. retaliation: far —, to retaliate.

rappresentàbile agg. performable.

rappresentante s. 1. representative 2. (comm.) agent.

rappresentanza sf. 1. representation 2. (comm.) agency || in — di, on behalf of.

rappresentare vt. 1. to represent 2. (comm.) to be agent (for) 3. (una parte) to play 4. (un'opera teatrale) to stage. ♦ **rappresentarsi** vr. to imagine.

rappresentativo agg. representative.

rappresentazione sf. 1. representation 2. (teat.) performance 3. (cine) exhibition.

rapsodia sf. rhapsody.

rarefare vt. to rarefy. ♦ **rarefarsi** vr. to rarefy.

rarefatto agg. rarefied.

rarefazione sf. rarefaction.

rarità sf. rarity.

raro agg. rare: rare volte, seldom; una bestia rara (fig.), a queer fish.

rasare vt. 1. to shave 2. (un prato) to mow (v. irr.) 3. (lisciare) to smooth. ♦ **rasarsi** vr. to shave.

rasato agg. 1. shaven 2. (liscio) smooth 3. (simile a raso) satin (attributivo).

rasatura sf. 1. shave 2. (di prato) mowing.

raschiamento sm. 1. scraping 2. (med.) curettage.

raschiare vt. 1. to scrape 2. (med.) to curette || raschiarsi la gola, to clear one's throat.

raschiata sf. scraping.

raschiatoio sm. 1. scraper 2. (med.) curette.

raschiatura sf. scraping.

raschietto sm. 1. scraper 2. (per cancellare) eraser.

rasciugare vt. to dry.

rasentare vt. 1. to graze 2. (confinare) to border (on).

rasente prep. close to: passare —, to skim.

raso agg. V. rasato. ♦ **raso** sm. satin.

rasoio sm. razor.

raspa sf. rasp.

raspamento sm. rasping.

raspare vt. 1. to rasp 2. (con le unghie) to scratch 3. (frugare) to rummage.

rassegna sf. 1. (rivista, recensione) review 2. (esame) survey || passare in —, to inspect.

rassegnare vt. to hand in: — le dimissioni, to resign. ♦ **rassegnarsi** vr. to resign oneself.

rassegnato agg. resigned.

rassegnazione sf. resignation.

rasserenare vt. 1. to clear 2. (fig.) to cheer up. ♦ **rasserenarsi** vr. to clear up.

rassettare vt. 1. to tidy 2. (riparare) to mend.

rassicurante agg. reassuring.

rassicurare vt. to reassure. ♦ **rassicurarsi** vr. to be reassured.

rassicurazione sf. reassurance.

rassodamento sm. consolidation.

rassodare vt. 1. to consolidate 2. (indurire) to harden. ♦ **rassodarsi** vr. to harden.

rassomigliante agg. like, alike (pred.).

rassomiglianza sf. likeness.

rassomigliare vi. to be like. ♦ **rassomigliarsi** vr. rec. to be alike.

rassottigliare vt. V. assottigliare.

rastrellamento sm. 1. raking 2. (mil.) mopping up 3. (di polizia) combing 4. (dragaggio) dragging.

rastrellare vt. 1. to rake 2. (mil.) to mop up 3. (di polizia) to comb 4. (dragare) to drag.

rastrelliera sf. rack.

rastrello sm. rake.

rastremare vt. to taper. ♦ **rastremarsi** vr. to taper.

rata sf. instalment: a rate, by instalments.

rateale agg. by instalments.

rateare vt. to divide into instalments.

ratifica sf. ratification.

ratificare vt. to ratify.

ratificatore sm. ratifier.

ratificazione sf. V. ratifica.

ratto[1] sm. 1. kidnapping 2. (di donna) rape.

ratto[2] sm. (topo) rat.

rattoppare vt. to patch (up).

rattoppo sm. 1. patching up 2. (toppa) patch.

rattrappimento sm. 1. (intorpidi-mento) benumbing 2. (contrazione) contraction.

rattrappire vt. 1. (contrarre) to contract 2. (intorpidire) to benumb.

rattristare vt. to grieve. ♦ **rattristarsi** vr. 1. (divenir triste) to become (v. irr.) sad 2. (essere triste) to be sad.

raucedine sf. hoarseness: avere la —, to have a hoarse voice.

rauco agg. hoarse.

ravanello sm. radish.

ravvedersi vr. to mend one's way.

ravvedimento sm. reformation.

ravviamento sm. tidying (up).

ravviare vt. to tidy (up).

ravvicinamento sm. 1. approach 2. (conciliazione) reconciliation.

ravvicinare vt. 1. to bring (v. irr.) closer 2. (riconciliare) to reconcile 3. (confrontare) to compare. ♦ **ravvicinarsi** vr. 1. to draw (v. irr.) closer 2. (riconciliarsi) to become (v. irr.) reconciled.

ravvisabile agg. recognizable.

ravvisare vt. to recognize.

ravvivamento sm. revival.

ravvivare vt. 1. to revive 2. (rallegrare) to brighten up || — il fuoco, to poke the fire. ♦ **ravvivarsi** vr. 1. to revive 2. (rallegrarsi) to brighten up.

raziocinante agg. reasoning.

raziocinio sm. 1. reason 2. (buon senso) common sense.

razionale agg. rational.

razionalismo sm. rationalism.

razionalista s. rationalist.

razionalità sf. rationality.

razionamento sm. rationing.

razionare vt. to ration.

razione sf. ration.

razza[1] sf. 1. race 2. (di animali) breed 3. (genere) kind.

razza[2] sf. (itt.) ray.

razzia sf. 1. raid 2. (insetticida) insecticide || far —, to plunder.

razziale agg. racial.

razziare vt. to plunder.

razziatore sm. plunderer.

razzismo sm. racialism.

razzista s. racialist.

razzo sm. rocket.

razzolare vi. to scratch about.

re[1] sm. king.

re[2] sm. (mus.) D, re.

reagente sm. reagent.

reagire vi. to react.

reale[1] *agg.* real.
reale[2] *agg. (del re)* royal.
realismo *sm.* realism.
realista[1] *agg. e s.* realist.
realista[2] *agg. e s. (del re)* royalist.
realistico *agg.* realistic.
realizzàbile *agg.* realizable.
realizzare *vt.* to realize. ◆ **realizzarsi** *vr.* 1. to be realized 2. *(avverarsi)* to come *(v. irr.)* true.
realizzatore *sm.* realizer.
realizzazione *sf.* 1. realization 2. *(teat.)* staging 3. *(cine)* production.
realtà *sf.* reality.
reame *sm.* kingdom.
reato *sm.* 1. offence 2. *(crimine)* crime.
reattivo *agg.* reactive. ◆ **reattivo** *sm.* reagent.
reattore *sm.* 1. reactor 2. *(aereo)* jet.
reazionario *agg. e sm.* reactionary.
reazione *sf.* reaction: *motore a —*, jet engine; *aereo a —*, jet.
rebante *agg.* 1. thundering 2. *(fig.)* bombastic.
rebus *sm.* rebus.
recalcitrare *vi.* V. *ricalcitrare.*
recapitare *vt.* to deliver.
recàpito *sm.* 1. *(consegna)* delivery 2. *(indirizzo)* address.
recare *vt.* 1. to bring *(v. irr.)* 2. *(fig.)* to bear *(v. irr.)* 3. *(causare)* to cause. ◆ **recarsi** *vr.* to go *(v. irr.)*.
recèdere *vi.* to withdraw *(v. irr.)*.
recensione *sf.* review.
recensire *vt.* to review.
recensore *sm.* reviewer.
recente *agg.* recent.
recentemente *avv.* recently.
recentissime *sf. pl.* latest news.
recessione *sf.* recession.
recessivo *agg.* receding.
recesso *sm.* 1. recess 2. *(recessione)* recession 3. *(giur.)* withdrawal.
recettivo *agg.* V. *ricettivo.*
recezione *sf.* reception.
recìdere *vt.* to cut *(v. irr.)* off.
recidiva *sf.* relapse.
recidività *sf.* 1. *(giur.)* recidivism 2. *(med.)* relapse.
recidivo *agg.* 1. *(giur.)* recidivous 2. *(med.)* relapsing. ◆ **recidivo** *sm.* 1. *(giur.)* recidivist 2. *(med.)* relapser.
recintare *vt.* to fence.
recinto *sm.* enclosure.
recipiente *sm.* vessel.

reciprocamente *avv.* reciprocally.
reciprocità *sf.* reciprocity.
recìproco *agg.* reciprocal.
recisamente *avv.* resolutely.
recisione *sf.* excision.
reciso *agg.* 1. cut 2. *(fig.)* resolute.
rècita *sf.* performance.
recitare *vt.* 1. to recite 2. *(teat.)* to act || *— una parte*, to play a part.
recitativo *sm.* recitative.
recitazione *sf.* 1. recitation 2. *(teat.)* acting.
reclamante *sm.* claimant.
reclamare *vt.* to claim. ◆ **reclamare** *vi.* to complain.
reclamìstico *agg.* advertising.
reclamizzare *vt.* to advertise.
reclamo *sm.* complaint.
reclinare *vt.* to bow.
reclusione *sf.* 1. seclusion 2. *(prigionia)* imprisonment.
recluso *agg.* 1. secluded 2. *(imprigionato)* imprisoned. ◆ **recluso** *sm.* prisoner.
rècluta *sf.* 1. recruit 2. *(fig.)* novice.
reclutamento *sm.* enlistment.
reclutare *vt.* to enlist, to recruit.
recòndito *agg.* hidden.
recriminare *vi.* 1. to recriminate 2. *(lamentarsi)* to complain.
recriminazione *sf.* 1. recrimination 2. *(lamentela)* complaint.
recrudescente *agg.* recrudescent.
recrudescenza *sf.* recrudescence.
redarguire *vt.* to reproach.
redattore *sm.* 1. drawer 2. *(di giornale)* member of the editorial staff || *— capo*, editor.
redazionale *agg.* editorial.
redazione *sf.* 1. drawing up 2. *(di giornale)* editing 2. *(i redattori)* editorial staff 3. *(ufficio)* editorial office.
redditività *sf.* profitableness.
redditizio *agg.* profitable.
rèddito *sm.* 1. income 2. *(dello Stato)* revenue.
redento *agg.* redeemed.
redentore *sm.* redeemer.
redenzione *sf.* redemption.
redìgere *vt.* to draw *(v. irr.)* up.
redìmere *vt.* to redeem.
redimìbile *agg.* redeemable.
rèdini *sf. pl.* reins.
redivivo *agg.* 1. restored to life 2. *(nuovo)* new.
rèduce *agg.* back from. ◆ **rèduce** *sm.* veteran.

referendum *sm.* referendum.

referenza *sf.* reference.

referenziare *vt.* to give (*v. irr.*) references.

referto *sm.* report.

refettorio *sm.* refectory.

refezione *sf.* meal.

refrattario *agg.* refractory: *terra refrattaria*, fireclay.

refrigerante *agg.* e *sm.* refrigerant.

refrigerare *vt.* to refrigerate.

refrigeratore *sm.* refrigerator.

refrigerazione *sf.* refrigeration.

refrigerio *sm.* 1. cool 2. (*sollievo*) relief.

refurtiva *sf.* stolen goods (*pl.*).

refuso *sm.* misprint, wrong fount.

regalare *vt.* 1. to present (so. with sthg.) 2. (*vendere a poco prezzo*) to sell (*v. irr.*) cheap.

regalato *agg.* (*venduto a buon prezzo*) cheap.

regale *agg.* regal.

regalia *sf.* (*mancia*) gratuity.

regalo *sm.* present: *in —*, **as a** present.

regata *sf.* regatta.

reggente *agg.* e *sm.* regent.

reggenza *sf.* regency.

règgere *vt.* 1. (*sorreggere*) to hold (*v. irr.*) 2. (*dirigere*) to run (*v. irr.*) 3. (*gramm.*) to govern || *— una prova*, to stand (*v. irr.*) a test. ♦ **règgere** *vi.* 1. (*resistere*) to hold (out) 2. (*stare in piedi, anche fig.*) to stand. ♦ **règgersi** *vr.* 1. (*sostenersi*) to stand 2. (*appoggiarsi a*) to hold (on, to).

reggia *sf.* royal palace.

reggicalze *sm.* girdle.

reggimento *sm.* (*mil.*) regiment.

reggipetto *sm.* bra.

reggiseno *sm.* V. *reggipetto*.

reggitore *sm.* ruler.

regìa *sf.* 1. (*teat.*) production 2. (*cine*) direction || *— di*, produced, directed by.

regicida *sm.* regicide.

regicidio *sm.* regicide.

regime *sm.* 1. regime 2. (*mecc.*) speed 3. (*dieta*) diet || *essere a —*, to be on a diet.

regina *sf.* queen.

regio *agg.* royal.

regionale *agg.* regional.

regionalismo *sm.* regionalism.

regionalista *s.* regionalist.

regione *sf.* 1. region 2. (*divisione amministrativa; fig.*) province.

regista *sm.* 1. (*teat.*) producer 2. (*cine*) director.

registràbile *agg.* registrable, recordable.

registrare *vt.* 1. to register 2. (*comm.*) to book 3. (*segnare; cine*) to record 4. (*su nastro*) to tape-record 5. (*mecc.*) to adjust.

registratore *sm.* 1. (*persona*) registrar 2. (*strumento*) register: *— di cassa*, cash-register || (*magnetofono*) taperecorder.

registrazione *sf.* 1. registration 2. (*comm.*) entry 3. (*di suoni*) recording.

registro *sm.* 1. register 2. (*comm.*) book 3. (*ufficio governativo*) registry.

regnante *agg.* reigning. ♦ **regnante** *s.* sovereign.

regnare *vi.* to reign.

regno *sm.* 1. reign 2. (*territorio; fig.*) kingdom.

règola *sf.* 1. rule 2. (*esempio*) example 3. (*misura*) moderation || *in —*, in order; *è di —*, it is the custom.

regolamentare *agg.* prescribed: *non essere —*, to be against the rules.

regolamentarmente *avv.* according to the rules.

regolamentazione *sf.* ● regulations (*pl.*).

regolamento *sm.* regulation: *— dei conti*, settlement.

regolare[1] *vt.* 1. to regulate 2. (*sistemare*) to settle 3. (*sintonizzare*) to tune (in). ♦ **regolarsi** *vr.* 1. to act 2. (*controllarsi*) to control oneself.

regolare[2] *agg.* regular.

regolarità *sf.* regularity.

regolarizzare *vt.* to regularize.

regolarizzazione *sf.* regularization.

regolatamente *avv.* 1. regularly 2. (*con moderazione*) moderately.

regolatezza *sf.* sobriety.

regolato *agg.* regular.

regolatore *agg.* regulating: *piano —*, townplan. ♦ **regolatore** *sm.* regulator.

regolazione *sf.* regulation.

règolo *sm.* rule: *— calcolatore*, slide rule.

regredire *vi.* to regress.

regressione *sf.* regression.

regressivo *agg.* regressive.

regresso *sm.* regress.

reietto *agg.* rejected. ♦ **reietto** *sm.* outcast.

reiezione *sf.* rejection.

reincarnare *vt.* to reincarnate. ♦ **reincarnarsi** *vr.* to be reincarnated.

reincarnazione *sf.* reincarnation.

reintegrare *vt.* 1. to restore 2. (*risarcire*) to indemnify.

reintegrazione *sf.* 1. restoration 2. (*risarcimento*) indemnification.

reità *sf.* 1. (*colpevolezza*) guiltiness 2. (*malvagità*) wickedness.

reiterare *vt.* to reiterate.

reiterazione *sf.* reiteration.

relativamente *avv.* comparatively: — *a*, as regards.

relativismo *sm.* relativism.

relativistico *agg.* relativistic.

relatività *sf.* relativity.

relativo *agg.* 1. relative 2. (*rispettivo*) respective 3. (*attinente*) pertinent.

relatore *sm.* 1. relator 2. (*di leggi*) proposer.

relazionare *vt.* to relate.

relazione *sf.* 1. report 2. (*legame*) relation 3. (*contatto*) touch 4. (*conoscenza*) acquaintance || *aver* — *con*, to be connected with; *essere in buone relazioni*, to be on good terms; *mettersi in* — *con*, to get (*v. irr.*) into touch with; — *amorosa*, love affair.

relegare *vt.* to relegate.

relegazione *sf.* relegation.

religione *sf.* 1. religion 2. (*culto*) worship.

religiosità *sf.* piety.

religioso *agg. e sm.* religious.

reliquia *sf.* relic.

reliquiario *sm.* reliquary.

relitto *sm.* 1. wreckage 2. (*di persona*) outcast.

remare *vi.* 1. to row 2. (*con pagaia*) to paddle.

remata *sf.* 1. row 2. (*colpo di remo*) stroke.

rematore *sm.* oarsman (*pl.* -men).

remiganti *sf. pl.* remiges.

remigare *vi.* 1. to row 2. (*di ali*) to flap.

reminiscenza *sf.* reminiscence.

remissione *sf.* (*giur.*) remission.

remissività *sf.* submissiveness.

remissivo *agg.* submissive.

remo *sm.* oar.

rèmora *sf.* 1. (*ostacolo*) obstacle 2. (*indugio*) delay 3. (*zool.*) remora.

remoto *agg.* remote: *passato* — (*gramm.*) past simple tense.

remunerare *vt.* to remunerate.

remunerativo *agg.* remunerative.

remunerazione *sf.* remuneration.

rena *sf.* sand.

renale *agg.* renal.

rèndere *vt.* 1. to render 2. (*fruttare*) to yield || — *conto di*, to account for; — *giustizia a qu.*, to do (*v. irr.*) so. justice. ♦ **rèndersi** *vr.* to become (*v. irr.*) || — *conto di*, to realize.

rendiconto *sm.* 1. statement 2. (*resoconto*) report.

rendimento *sm.* 1. rendering 2. (*resa*) output 3. (*efficienza*) efficiency.

rèndita *sf.* 1. revenue 2. (*privata*) income.

rene *sm.* kidney.

renella *sf.* gravel.

reni *sf. pl.* back (*sing.*).

renitente *agg.* reluctant || *essere* — *alla leva*, to fail to appear at the draft.

renitenza *sf.* reluctance || — *alla leva*, failure to register for national service.

renna *sf.* reindeer (*pl. invariato*).

renoso *agg.* sandy.

reo *agg.* guilty. ♦ **reo** *sm.* culprit.

reòmetro *sm.* rheometer.

reòstato *sm.* rheostat.

reparto *sm.* 1. department 2. (*mil.*) detachment.

repellente *agg.* repulsive.

repentaglio *sm.* danger: *a* —, in danger.

repentino *agg.* sudden.

reperìbile *agg.* to be found (*pred.*).

reperire *vt.* to find (*v. irr.*).

reperto *sm.* 1. (*giur.*) evidence 2. (*med.*) report.

repertorio *sm.* (*teat.*) repertoire.

rèplica *sf.* 1. reply 2. (*obiezione*) objection 3. (*copia*) copy 4. (*teat.*) performance || *avere molte repliche* (*teat.*), to have a long run.

replicare *vt.* 1. to reply 2. (*obiettare*) to object 3. (*ripetere*) to repeat.

reprensìbile *agg.* reprehensible.

reprensione *sf.* reprehension.

repressione *sf.* repression.

repressivo *agg.* repressive.

represso *agg.* repressed.

reprimenda *sf.* reprimand.

reprìmere *vt.* to repress.

rèprobo agg. e sm. reprobate.

repùbblica sf. republic.

repubblicano agg. e sm. republican.

reputare vt. 1. to consider 2. (pensare) to think (v. irr.).

reputazione sf. reputation.

requie sf. rest.

requisire vt. to requisition.

requisito sm. qualification.

requisitoria sf. 1. indictment 2. (giur.) summing up.

requisizione sf. requisition.

resa sf. (rendimento) yield 2. (capitolazione) surrender || — dei conti, rendering of accounts.

rescindere vt. to rescind.

rescindibile agg. rescindable.

rescissione sf. rescission.

reseda sf. reseda.

resezione sf. resection.

residente agg. e sm. resident.

residenza sf. residence.

residenziale agg. residential.

residuare vi. to be left.

residuato agg. residual. ♦ **residuato** sm. — di guerra, war surplus.

residuo agg. remaining. ♦ **residuo** sm. residue: residui radioattivi, radioactive waste.

rèsina sf. resin.

resinoso agg. resinous.

resipiscenza sf. resipiscence.

resistente agg. 1. resistant 2. (forte) strong.

resistenza sf. resistance.

resistere vi. 1. to resist 2. (sopportare) to endure.

resoconto sm. report.

respingente sm. buffer.

respingere vt. 1. to repel 2. (rimandare) to return 3. (rifiutare) to reject 4. (scol.) to pluck.

respinta sf. V. parata.

respiràbile agg. breathable.

respirare vt. e vi. to breathe.

respiratore sm. respirator.

respiratorio agg. respiratory.

respirazione sf. respiration, breathing.

respiro sm. 1. breath 2. (riposo) respite.

responsàbile agg. responsible (for).

responsabilità sf. responsibility.

responso sm. 1. response 2. (opinione) opinion.

responsorio sm. responsory.

ressa sf. crowd: far — intorno a

qu., to crowd round so.

resta sf. 1. (di cipolla, aglio ecc.) string 2. (di lancia) rest.

restante agg. e sm. V. rimanente.

restare vi. V. rimanere.

restaurare vt. to restore.

restauratore sm. restorer.

restaurazione sf. restoration.

restàuro sm. restoration: in —, under repair.

restìo agg. loath, reluctant.

restituire vt. 1. to return 2. (reintegrare) to restore.

restituzione sf. 1. return 2. (reintegrazione) restoration.

resto sm. 1. rest 2. (mat.) remainder 3. (di denaro) change || resti, remains; del —, on the other hand.

restringente sm. astringent.

restringere vt. 1. (contrarre) to contract 2. (limitare) to limit 3. (un vestito) to tighten. ♦ **restringersi** vr. 1. to get (v. irr.) narrower 2. (contrarsi) to contract 3. (affollarsi) to close up 4. (di tessuti) to shrink (v. irr.).

restringimento sm. 1. narrowing 2. (contrazione) contraction 3. (limitazione) limitation 4. (di tessuto) shrinking 5. (di vestito) tightening.

restrittivo agg. restrictive.

restrizione sf. restriction.

retaggio sm. heritage.

retata sf. 1. haul 2. (di polizia) roundup.

rete sf. 1. net 2. (di letto) wire netting 3. (intreccio) network.

reticella sf. 1. (per capelli) hair-net 2. (per bagagli) luggage-rack.

reticente agg. reticent.

reticenza sf. reticence.

reticolato sm. 1. (mil.) barbed-wire entanglement 2. (tracciato di linee) network.

reticolo sm. 1. (anat.) reticulum (pl. -la) 2. (ott.) reticle.

rètina sf. retina.

retina sf. V. reticella.

rètore sm. rhetorician.

retòrica sf. rhetoric.

retòrico agg. rhetorical.

retrarre vt. to retract.

retràttile agg. retractile.

retrattilità sf. retractility.

retribuire vt. to pay (v. irr.).

retribuzione sf. payment.

retrìvo agg. reactionary.

retro sm. back.

retroattività sf. retroactivity.

retroattivo agg. retroactive.

retrobottega sm. back of the shop.

retrocèdere vi. to withdraw (v. irr.). ♦ **retrocèdere** vt. 1. (mil.) to degrade 2. to retrocede.

retrocessione sf. 1. retrocession 2. (mil.) degradation.

retrodatare vt. to date back.

retrògrado agg. 1. out-of-date 2. (reazionario) reactionary.

retroguardia sf. rear-guard.

retromarcia sf. reverse-gear.

retroscena sf. 1. back of the stage 2. (fig.) intrigue.

retrospettivo agg. retrospective.

retrostante agg. at the back.

retroterra sm. hinterland.

retroversione sf. 1. retroversion 2. (di traduzione) back version.

retrovie sf. pl. zone behind the front (sing).

retrovisore sm. specchietto —, driving mirror.

retta[1] sf. (geom.) straight line.

retta[2] sf. (di pensione) terms (pl.).

retta[3] sf. dar — a qu., to listen to so.

rettale agg. rectal.

rettamente avv. 1. (giustamente) rightly 2. (onestamente) honestly.

rettangolare agg. rectangular.

rettàngolo sm. rectangle.

rettìfica sf. 1. rectification 2. (mecc.) grinding.

rettificare vt. 1. to rectify 2. (mecc.) to grind (v. irr.).

rettificatrice sf. grinder.

rettificazione sf. V. rettìfica.

rettifilo sm. straight, stretch.

rèttile sm. reptile.

rettilìneo agg. rectilinear. ♦ **rettilìneo** sm. straight, stretch.

rettitùdine sf. righteousness, honesty.

retto agg. 1. straight 2. (geom.; giusto) right. ♦ **retto** sm. (anat.) rectum (pl. -ta).

rettorato sm. rectorship.

rettore sm. 1. rector 2. (di università) chancellor.

rèuma sm. rheumatism.

reumàtico agg. e sm. rheumatic.

reumatismo sm. V. reuma.

reverendo agg. reverend. ♦ **reverendo** sm. clergyman (pl. -men).

reversìbile agg. reversible.

reversibilità sf. reversibility.

reversione sf. reversion.

revisionare vt. 1. (mecc.) to overhaul 2. (comm.) to audit.

revisione sf. 1. revision 2. (mecc.) overhaul 3. (comm.) audit.

revisionismo sm. revisionism.

revisore sm. 1. reviser 2. (comm.) auditor.

reviviscenza sf. reviviscence.

rèvoca sf. revocation.

revocàbile agg. revocable.

revocare vt. 1. (richiamare) to recall 2. (giur.) to revoke.

revocazione sf. revocation.

revolverata sf. revolver shot.

revulsione sf. revulsion.

revulsivo agg. revulsive.

riabbottonare vt. to button again.

riabilitare vt. to rehabilitate.

riabilitazione sf. rehabilitation.

riaccèndere vt. 1. to relight 2. (radio, luce ecc.) to turn on again. ♦ **riaccèndersi** vr. 1. to brighten again 2. (riprender fuoco) to catch (v. irr.) fire again.

riaccompagnare vt. to take (v. irr.) home.

riacquistare vt. 1. to buy (v. irr.) again 2. (riprendere) to recover.

riadattare vt. to adapt again. ♦ **riadattarsi** vr. (rassegnarsi) to resign oneself again.

riaddormentare vt. to send (v. irr.) to sleep again. ♦ **riaddormentarsi** vr. to fall (v. irr.) asleep again.

riaffacciare vt. to present again. ♦ **riaffacciarsi** vr. to reappear, to appear again.

riaffermare vt. to affirm again. ♦ **riaffermarsi** vr. to reaffirm oneself.

riafferrare vt. to grasp again. ♦ **riafferrarsi** vr. to catch (v. irr.) hold of (so., sthg.) again.

riallacciare vt. 1. to fasten again 2. (riprendere) to resume.

riallargare vt. to widen again. ♦ **riallargarsi** vr. to widen again.

rialto sm. rise, height.

rialzamento sm. 1. raising 2. (rialzo) rise, height.

rialzare vt. 1. to raise 2. (rendere più alto) to make (v. irr.) higher. ♦ **rialzarsi** vr. to rise (v. irr.) again.

rialzato agg. piano —, ground floor.

rialzo sm. 1. rise 2. (di sostegno) support.

riamare vt. to love again.

riammèttere vt. to readmit.

rianimare vt. to revive. ♦ **rianimarsi** vr. 1. (riprendere allegria) to cheer up 2. (riprendere coraggio) to take (v. irr.) courage again.

riapertura sf. reopening.

riapparire vi. to reappear.

riaprire vt. to open again. ♦ **riaprirsi** vr. to open again.

riarmare vt. to rearm. ♦ **riarmarsi** vr. to rearm.

riarmo sm. rearmament.

riarso agg. parched.

riassestare vt. to readjust. ♦ **riassestarsi** vr. to readjust.

riassettare vt. to put (v. irr.) in order again.

riassetto sm. rearrangement.

riassorbire vt. to reabsorb.

riassùmere vt. 1. (assumere di nuovo) to take (v. irr.) on again 2. (riepilogare) to sum up 3. (riprendere) to resume.

riassuntivo agg. summarizing.

riassunto sm. summary.

riattaccare vt. 1. (con colla) to stick (v. irr.) again 2. (ricucire) to sew (v. irr.) 3. (riprendere) to begin (v. irr.) again 4. (mil.) to attack again 5. (tel.) to hang (v. irr.) up. ♦ **riattaccarsi** vr. to stick again.

riattamento sm. repair.

riattare vt. to repair.

riattivare vt. to restore.

riavere vt. 1. to have again 2. (ricuperare) to get (v. irr.) back. ♦ **riaversi** vr. to recover.

riavvicinare vt. 1. to approach again 2. (riconciliare) to reconcile. ♦ **riavvicinarsi** vr. to approach again 2. (riconciliarsi) to be reconciled.

ribadire vt. to rivet.

ribalderìa sf. rascality.

ribaldo sm. rascal.

ribalta sf. 1. (teat.) footlights (pl.) 2. (fig.) limelight.

ribaltàbile agg. overturnable.

ribaltare vt. to overturn. ♦ **ribaltarsi** vr. to capsize.

ribassare vt. to reduce. ♦ **ribassare** vi. to fall (v. irr.).

ribasso sm. 1. fall 2. (sconto) discount.

ribàttere vt. 1. to beat (v. irr.) again 2. (ribadire) to rivet 3. (confutare) to confute. ♦ **ribàttere** vi. to insist.

ribattezzare vt. to rename.

ribellarsi vr. to rebel.

ribelle agg. rebellious. ♦ **ribelle** s. rebel.

ribellione sf. rebellion.

ribes sm. gooseberry.

riboccante agg. overflowing (with).

riboccare vi. to overflow (with).

ribollimento sm. ebullition.

ribollire vi. to boil.

ribollitura sf. reboiling.

ribrezzo sm. disgust: fare —, to disgust.

ributtante agg. disgusting.

ributtare vt. 1. to throw (v. irr.) again 2. (respingere) to repel 3. (disgustare) to disgust.

ricacciare vt. 1. (respingere) to push (out, back) 2. (ficcare di nuovo) to thrust (v. irr.) again. ♦ **ricacciarsi** vr. to plunge again.

ricadere vi. 1. to fall (v. irr.) again 2. (avere una ricaduta) to relapse 3. (pendere) to hang (v. irr.).

ricaduta sf. relapse.

ricalcare vt. 1. to pull down 2. (un disegno) to transfer || — le orme di qu., to tread (v. irr.) in so.'s steps.

ricalcitrante agg. recalcitrant.

ricalcitrare vi. to recalcitrate.

ricamare vt. e vi. to embroider.

ricamatore sm. embroiderer.

ricamatrice sf. embroideress.

ricambiare vt. 1. to change again 2. (contraccambiare) to return.

ricambio sm. 1. replacement 2. (med.) metabolism || di —, spare (agg. attr.).

ricamo sm. embroidery: un —, a piece of embroidery.

ricapitolare vt. to summarize || ricapitolando, in short.

ricapitolazione sf. summary.

ricaricare vt. 1. to reload 2. (di batteria) to recharge 3. (di orologio) to wind (v. irr.) up again.

ricascare vi. V. ricadere.

ricattare vt. to blackmail.

ricattatore sm. blackmailer.

ricattatorio agg. blackmailing.

ricatto sm. blackmail.

ricavare vt. 1. to draw (v. irr.) 2. (ottenere) to get (v. irr.).

ricavato sm. proceeds (pl.).

ricavo sm. V. ricavato.

riccamente avv. richly.

ricchezza sf. wealth (solo sing.).

riccio[1] agg. curly.

riccio² *sm.* **1.** curl **2.** (*bot.*) chestnut husk **3.** (*zool.*) hedgehog **4.** (*di mare*) sea-urchin.

ricciuto *agg.* curly.

ricco *agg.* rich: — *di*, rich in.

ricerca *sf.* **1.** search **2.** (*scientifica*) research **3.** (*indagine*) investigation.

ricercare *vt.* **1.** (*cercare*) to seek (*v. irr.*) for **2.** (*investigare*) to investigate **3.** (*cercare di nuovo*) to look for (so., sthg.) again.

ricercatezza *sf.* refinement.

ricercato *agg.* **1.** (*richiesto*) sought-after **2.** (*raffinato*) refined **3.** (*insolito*) far-fetched **4.** (*dalla polizia*) wanted.

ricercatore *sm.* **1.** searcher **2.** (*scientifico*) researcher.

ricetta *sf.* **1.** (*med.*) prescription **2.** (*cuc.*) recipe.

ricettàcolo *sm.* receptacle.

ricettare *vt.* (*custodire cose rubate*) to receive.

ricettario *sm.* **1.** (*med.*) book of prescriptions **2.** (*cuc.*) book of recipes.

ricettatore *sm.* receiver.

ricettazione *sf.* receiving of stolen goods.

ricettività *sf.* receptivity.

ricettivo *agg.* receptive.

ricevente *agg.* receiving. ♦ **ricevente** *s.* receiver.

ricévere *vt.* to receive.

ricevimento *sm.* **1.** receipt **2.** (*festa*) party.

ricevitore *sm.* receiver.

ricevitorìa *sf.* receiving-office.

ricevuta *sf.* receipt: *accusare* —, to acknowledge receipt.

ricezione *vt.* reception.

richiamare *vt.* **1.** to call again **2.** (*far tornare*) to recall **3.** (*attirare*) to attract **4.** (*rimproverare*) to rebuke ‖ — *all'ordine*, to call to order. ♦ **richiamarsi** *vr.* (*riferirsi*) to refer.

richiamata *sf.* recall.

richiamato *sm.* (*mil.*) re-drafted soldier.

richiamo *sm.* **1.** recall **2.** (*allettamento*) call.

richiedente *s.* applicant.

richièdere *vt.* **1.** to ask (for sthg., so.) again **2.** (*chiedere*) to ask for **3.** (*in restituzione*) to ask (for sthg.) back **4.** (*necessitare di*) to require.

richiesta *sf.* **1.** request: *dietro* —, at request **2.** (*comm.*) demand.

richiùdere *vt.* to close again. ♦ **richiùdersi** *vr.* to close again.

rìcino *sm.* castor-oil plant: *olio di* —, castor-oil.

ricognitore *sm.* (*mil.*) scout.

ricognizione *sf.* reconnaissance.

ricollegare *vt.* to connect. ♦ **ricollegarsi** *vr.* to be connected.

ricollocamento *sm.* replacement.

ricolmare *vt.* **1.** to fill up **2.** (*fig.*) to load.

ricolmo *agg.* **1.** full **2.** (*fig.*) loaded (with).

ricominciare *vt.* to begin (*v. irr.*) again.

ricomparire *vi.* to reappear.

ricompensa *sf.* reward: *in* —, as a reward.

ricompensare *vt.* to reward.

ricomperare *vt.* to buy (*v. irr.*) again.

ricomporre *vt.* to recompose.

ricomposizione *sf.* recomposition.

riconciliare *vt.* to reconcile. ♦ **riconciliarsi** *vr.* to be reconciled.

riconciliatore *sm.* reconciler.

riconciliazione *sf.* reconciliation.

ricondurre *vt.* to take (*v. irr.*) back, to bring (*v. irr.*) back.

riconferma *sf.* reconfirmation.

riconfermare *vt.* to reconfirm.

riconfortare *vt.* to cheer up. ♦ **riconfortarsi** *vr.* to cheer up.

ricongiùngere *vt.* to join again. ♦ **ricongiùngersi** *vr.* to join again.

ricongiungimento *sm.* reunion.

riconnèttere *vt.* to connect again.

riconoscente *agg.* grateful.

riconoscenza *sf.* gratitude.

riconòscere *vt.* to recognize.

riconoscìbile *agg.* recognizable.

riconoscimento *sm.* **1.** recognition **2.** (*ammissione*) admission.

riconquista *sf.* recapture.

riconquistare *vt.* to conquer again.

riconsegna *sf.* return.

riconsegnare *vt.* to redeliver.

riconsiderare *vt.* to reconsider.

riconversione *sf.* reconversion.

riconvocare *vt.* to resummon.

riconvocazione *sf.* resummons.

ricopiare *vt.* to copy.

ricopiatura *sf.* (re)copying.

ricoprire *vt.* **1.** to cover **2.** (*coprire di nuovo*) to cover again **3.** (*fig.*) to load.

ricordare *vt.* **1.** to remember **2.** *(chiamare alla memoria altrui)* to remind (so. of sthg.) **3.** *(nominare)* to mention. ♦ **ricordarsi** *vr.* to remember.

ricordo *sm.* **1.** memory **2.** *(oggetto ricordo)* souvenir **3.** *(memorie)* *(lett.)* memoirs *(pl.)*.

ricorrente *agg.* recurrent.

ricorrenza *sf.* **1.** recurrence **2.** *(anniversario)* anniversary **3.** *(occasione)* occasion.

ricórrere *vi.* **1.** *(ripetersi)* to recur **2.** *(rivólgersi)* to appeal **3.** *(fare appello)* to appeal **4.** *(valersi)* to resort.

ricorso *sm.* **1.** *(ritorno)* return **2.** *(appello)* appeal ‖ *su — di*, on a petition by.

ricostituente *agg.* e *sm.* tonic.

ricostituire *vt.* to form again. ♦ **ricostituirsi** *vr.* to form again.

ricostituzione *sf.* reconstitution.

ricostruire *vt.* to reconstruct.

ricostruttore *agg.* reconstructive. **ricostruttore** *sm.* reconstructor.

ricostruzione *sf.* reconstruction.

ricoverare *vt.* to shelter: *— in ospedale*, to hospitalize. ♦ **ricoverarsi** *vr.* to take *(v. irr.)* shelter.

ricòvero *sm.* **1.** sheltering **2.** *(in ospedale)* hospitalization **3.** *(ospizio)* home.

ricreare[1] *vt.* to re-create.

ricreare[2] *vt.* *(divertire)* to recreate. ♦ **ricrearsi** *vr.* to recreate.

ricreativo *agg.* recreative.

ricreazione *sf.* recreation: *ora della —*, playtime.

ricrédersi *vr.* to change one's mind.

ricréscere *vi.* to grow *(v. irr.)* again.

ricréscita *sf.* fresh growth.

ricucire *vt.* **1.** to sew *(v. irr.)* up **2.** *(cucire di nuovo)* to sew *(v. irr.)* again.

ricucitura *sf.* sewing up.

ricuòcere *vt.* e *vi.* **1.** to cook again **2.** *(al forno)* to bake again.

ricuperàbile *agg.* recoverable.

ricuperare *vt.* **1.** to recover **2.** *(di tempo)* to make *(v. irr.)* up for.

ricùpero *sm.* recovery.

ricurvare *vt.* **1.** to bend *(v. irr.)* **2.** *(curvare di nuovo)* to bend again.

ricurvo *agg.* bent.

ricusàbile *agg.* refusable.

ricusare *vt.* to refuse.

ridacchiare *vi.* to giggle.

ridanciano *agg.* jolly.

ridare *vt.* **1.** to give *(v. irr.)* again **2.** *(restituire)* to return.

ridda *sf.* turmoil.

ridente *agg.* **1.** smiling **2.** *(di luogo)* charming.

ridere *vi.* to laugh (at): *per —*, for fun. ♦ **ridersi** *vr.* to make *(v. irr.)* fun (of).

ridestare *vt.* **1.** to wake *(v. irr.)* (up) again **2.** *(destare)* to awaken. ♦ **ridestarsi** *vr.* **1.** to wake (up) again **2.** *(destarsi)* to awake.

ridìcolàggine *sf.* nonsense *(solo sing.)*.

ridìcolo *agg.* ridiculous. ♦ **ridìcolo** *sm.* ridicule.

ridimensionare *vt.* to reorganize.

ridire *vt.* **1.** to say *(v. irr.)* again, to tell *(v. irr.)* again **2.** *(riferire)* to repeat **3.** *(obiettare)* to object.

ridiscéndere *vi.* to come *(v. irr.)* down again, to go *(v. irr.)* down again.

ridiscórrere *vi.* to talk again.

ridiventare *vi.* to become *(v. irr.)* again.

ridomandare *vt.* to ask again.

ridonare *vt.* **1.** to give *(v. irr.)* again **2.** *(restituire)* to give back.

ridondante *agg.* redundant.

ridondanza *sf.* redundancy.

ridondare *vi.* **1.** to be redundant **2.** *(risultare)* to redound.

ridosso *(nella loc. avv.)* *a — di*, close to.

ridotta *sf.* redoubt.

ridotto *agg.* **1.** reduced **2.** *(di libro)* abridged ‖ *mal —*, in a sorry plight. ♦ **ridotto** *sm.* *(teat.)* foyer.

riducente *agg.* reducing. ♦ **riducente** *sm.* reducer.

riducìbile *agg.* reducible.

ridurre *vt.* **1.** to reduce **2.** *(adattare)* to adapt **3.** *(un libro)* to abridge. ♦ **ridursi** *vr.* **1.** to be reduced **2.** *(restringersi)* to shrink *(v. irr.)*.

riduttore *agg.* e *sm.* V. **riducente**.

riduzione *sf.* **1.** reduction **2.** *(sconto)* discount **3.** *(cine; tv)* adaptation **4.** *(di libro)* abridgement.

riecheggiare *vt.* e *vi.* to re-echo.

riedificare *vt.* to rebuild *(v. irr.)*.

riedificazione *sf.* rebuilding.

rieducare *vt.* to re-educate.

rieducazione *sf.* re-education.

rielaborare *vt.* to re-elaborate.

rielèggere vt. to re-elect.

rieleggìbile agg. re-elegible.

rielezione sf. re-election.

riemèrgere vi. to re-emerge.

riemersione sf. re-emergence.

riempire vt. to fill. ◆ **riempirsi** vr. to fill.

riempitivo sm. filling.

rientrante agg. receding.

rientranza sf. recess.

rientrare vi. 1. to re-enter 2. (tornare) to return 3. (far parte) to be part (of) 4. (piegare in dentro) to recede.

rientro sm. 1. recess 2. (astronautica) retro-firing 3. (ritorno) return.

riepilogare vt. to recapitulate.

riepilogo sm. recapitulation.

riesame sm. re-examination.

riesaminare vt. to re-examine.

rièssere vi. to be again.

riesumare vt. 1. to exhume 2. (fig.) to bring (v. irr.) to light.

rievocare vt. to recall.

rievocazione sf. recalling.

rifacimento sm. 1. reconstruction 2. (adattamento) adaptation.

rifare vt. 1. to do (v. irr.) again, to make (v. irr.) again 2. (ripercorrere) to retrace 3. (riparare) to repair 4. (imitare) to imitate 5. (indennizzare) to indemnify. ◆ **rifarsi** vr. 1. to make up 2. (vendicarsi) to revenge oneself 3. (risalire) to go (v. irr.) back.

rifasciare vt. 1. to bandage again 2. (un bambino) to swaddle again.

riferìbile agg. 1. referable 2. (raccontabile) fit to be told.

riferimento sm. reference: linea, punto di —, datum-line, datum-point.

riferire vt. 1. to report 2. (attribuire) to ascribe. ◆ **riferirsi** vr. to refer.

rificcare vt. to thrust (v. irr.) again.

rifilare vt. 1. to spin again 2. (tagliare a filo) to trim 3. (appioppare) to palm off.

rifilatura sf. 1. trimming 2. (bordo) border.

rifinimento sm. finishing touch.

rifinire vt. to finish.

rifinitura sf. V. rifinimento.

rifiorire vi. to blossom again 2. (fig.) to flourish again.

rifioritura sf. reflorescence.

rifiutàbile agg. refusable.

rifiutare vt. to refuse.

rifiuto sm. refusal || rifiuti, waste (solo sing.); i rifiuti della società, the dregs of society.

riflessione sf. reflection.

riflessivo agg. 1. reflective 2. (gramm.) reflexive.

riflesso agg. reflected, reflex (anche fig.). ◆ **riflesso** sm. 1. reflection 2. (di colore) tint 3. (med.) reflex || di —, as a consequence; per —, indirectly.

riflèttere vt. e vi. to reflect. ◆ **riflèttersi** vr. to be reflected.

riflettore sm. 1. reflector 2. (lampada) searchlight.

rifluire vi. 1. to flow again 2. (fluire indietro) to flow back.

riflusso sm. ebb.

rifocillare vt. to give (v. irr.) refreshment. ◆ **rifocillarsi** vr. to take (v. irr.) refreshment.

rifóndere vt. 1. to melt again 2. (rimborsare) to refund.

riforma sf. reformation.

riformare vt. 1. to reform 2. (mil.) to declare unfit for military service.

riformatore sm. reformer.

riformatorio sm. reformatory.

riformismo sm. reformism.

riformista s. reformist.

rifornimento sm. 1. supplying 2. (aer.; auto) refuelling 3. (scorta) supply || stazione di —, filling-station; far — di benzina, to fill up the tank.

rifornire vt. to supply (so. with).

rifornitore sm. supplier.

rifràngere vt. to refract. ◆ **rifràngersi** vr. to be refracted.

rifrangibilità sf. refrangibility.

rifrattore sm. refractor.

rifrazione sf. refraction.

rifritto agg. 1. fried again 2. (fig.) stale.

rifuggire vi. 1. to escape again 2. (essere alieno) to shrink (v. irr.).

rifugiarsi vr. to take (v. irr.) shelter.

rifugiato agg. e sm. refugee.

rifugio sm. 1. shelter 2. (di montagna) mountain hut.

rifulgere vi. to shine (v. irr.) brightly (with sthg.).

rifusione sf. 1. re-melting 2. (rimborso) repayment.

riga sf. 1. line 2. (fila) row 3. (regolo) rule 4. (striscia) stripe 5. (scriminatura) parting 6. (mus.

stave || *mettersi in* —, to line up.

rigaglie *sf.* pl. giblets.

rigagnolo *sm.* 1. rivulet 2. (*scolo*) gutter.

rigare *vt.* 1. to rule 2. (*solcare*) to furrow || — *diritto*, to behave well.

rigato *agg.* 1. ruled 2. (*a strisce*) striped 3. (*solcato*) furrowed.

rigattiere *sm.* second-hand dealer.

rigatura *sf.* 1. ruling 2. (*di arma*) rifling.

rigenerare *vt.* 1. to regenerate 2. (*mecc.*) to repair.

rigenerativo *agg.* regenerative. ◆ **rigeneratore** *sm.* regeneratot.

rigenerazione *sf.* regeneration.

rigettare *vt.* 1. to throw (*v. irr.*) again 2. (*gettare indietro*) to throw back 3. (*vomitare*) to vomit 4. (*respingere*) to reject..

rigetto *sm.* rejection.

righello *sm.* ruler.

rigidezza *sf.* 1. stiffness 2. (*di clima*) rigour.

rigidità *sf.* V. rigidezza.

rigido *agg.* 1. stiff 2. (*di clima*) rigorous.

rigirare *vt.* 1. to turn again 2. (*cambiare*) to change. ◆ **rigirare** *vi.* to walk about. ◆ **rigirarsi** *vr.* to turn about.

rigiro *sm.* 1. turning round 2. (*di parole*) involved expression.

rigo *sm.* V. riga.

rigoglio *sm.* bloom.

rigogliosità *sf.* luxuriancy.

rigoglioso *agg.* flourishing.

rigonfiamento *sm.* swelling.

rigonfiare *vt.* to swell (*v. irr.*). ◆ **rigonfiarsi** *vr.* to swell.

rigonfio *agg.* swollen (with). ◆ **rigonfio** *sm.* swelling.

rigore *sm.* 1. rigour 2. (*esattezza*) exactness || *di* —, compulsory; *a* —, according to the rules; *a* — *di termini*, in the strict sense, *area di* — (*sport*), penalty-area.

rigorismo *sm.* rigorism.

rigorista *s.* rigorist.

rigorosità *sf.* 1. rigour 2. (*esattezza*) preciseness.

rigoroso *agg.* 1. rigorous 2. (*esatto*) exact.

rigovernare *vt.* 1. to govern again 2. (*di piatti*) to wash up.

rigovernatura *sf.* washing-up.

riguadagnare *vt.* 1. to earn again 2. (*ricuperare, raggiungere*) to regain.

riguardare *vt.* 1. to look at (*so., sthg.*) again 2. (*esaminare*) to examine 3. (*considerare*) to regard. ◆ **riguardarsi** *vr.* to take (*v. irr.*) care of oneself.

riguardata *sf.* look.

riguardévole *agg.* 1. considerable 2. (*importante*) important.

riguardo *sm.* 1. regard 2. (*cura*) care || *persona di* —, person of consequence; — *a*, as regards; *a questo* —, in this connection.

riguardoso *agg.* respectful.

rigurgitare *vi.* 1. to overflow 2. (*di stomaco*) to regurgitate 3. (*brulicare*) to swarm (with).

rigùrgito *sm.* 1. overflow 2. (*di stomaco*) regurgitation 3. (*travaso*) extravasation 4. (*gorgo*) eddy.

rilanciare *vt.* 1. to throw (*v. irr.*) again 2. (*lanciare indietro*) to throw back 3. (*un'offerta*) to raise.

rilancio *sm.* 1. new throw 2. (*di offerta*) raising.

rilasciare *vt.* 1. to release 2. (*concedere*) to grant 3. (*emettere*) to issue. ◆ **rilasciarsi** *vr.* 1. to slacken 2. (*med.*) to prolapse 3. (*rilassarsi*) to relax.

rilascio *sm.* 1. release 2. (*concessione*) granting 3. (*emissione*) issue.

rilassamento *sm.* 1. slackening 2. (*med.*) prolapse 3. (*riposo*) relaxation.

rilassare *vt.* 1. to slacken 2. (*distendere*) to relax. ◆ **rilassarsi** *vr.* 1. to slacken 2. (*distendersi*) to relax.

rilassatezza *sf.* laxity.

rilegare *vt.* 1. to tie again 2. (*libri*) to bind (*v. irr.*).

rilegatura *sf.* binding.

rilèggere *vt.* to reread (*v. irr.*), to read (*v. irr.*) again.

rilento (*nella loc. avv.*) *a* —, slowly.

rilevamento *sm.* 1. (*topografico*) survey 2. (*mar.*) bearing 3. (*cambio*) relieving.

rilevante *agg.* prominent.

rilevare *vt.* 1. to take (*v. irr.*) off again 2. (*notare*) to notice 3. (*far notare*) to point out 4. (*prendere*) to take 5. (*topografia*) to survey 6. (*sostituire*) to relieve 7. (*comm.*) to take over.

rilevazione *sf.* V. rilievo.

rilievo *sm.* 1. relief 2. (*importanza*) importance 3. (*osservazione*) remark 4. (*topografico*) survey 5. (*comm.*) taking over ‖ *mettere in* —, to stress.

rilucente *agg.* glittering.

rilùcere *vi.* to glitter.

riluttante *agg.* reluctant.

riluttanza *sf.* reluctance.

riluttare *vi.* to reluct (at).

rima *sf.* rhyme ‖ *rispondere per le rime*, to give (*v. irr.*) tit for tat.

rimandare *vt.* 1. to send (*v. irr.*) again 2. (*restituire*) to send back 3. (*posporre*) to postpone 4. (*far riferimento*) to refer 5. (*agli esami*) to make (*v. irr.*) (so.) repeat (an exam).

rimando *sm.* 1. returning 2. (*differimento*) postponement 3. (*segno di richiamo*) reference-mark.

rimaneggiamento *sm.* 1. rearrangement 2. (*di opera letteraria*) adaptation 3. (*pol.*) shuffle.

rimaneggiare *vt.* 1. to rearrange 2. (*modificare*) to change 3. (*pol.*) to shuffle.

rimanente *agg.* remaining. ♦ **rimanente** *sm.* rest.

rimanenza *sf.* remainder.

rimanere *vi.* 1. to remain 2. (*avanzare*) to be left 3. (*essere sorpreso*) to be astonished.

rimangiare *vt.* to eat (*v. irr.*) again. ♦ **rimangiarsi** *vr.* to take (*v. irr.*) back.

rimarchévole *agg.* remarkable.

rimare *vt. e vi.* to rhyme.

rimarginare *vt.* to heal. ♦ **rimarginarsi** *vr.* to heal.

rimaritare *vt.* to marry again. ♦ **rimaritarsi** *vr.* to marry again.

rimasticare *vt.* 1. to chew again 2. (*fig.*) to muse.

rimasuglio *sm.* remains (*pl.*).

rimatore *sm.* rhymer.

rimbalzare *vi.* to rebound.

rimbalzello *sm.* ducks and drakes.

rimbalzo *sm.* rebound: *di* —, on the rebound.

rimbambimento *sm.* dotage.

rimbambire *vi.* to reach one's dotage.

rimbambito *agg.* in one's dotage (*pred.*): *un vecchio* —, a dotard.

rimbeccare *vt.* to retort.

rimbecco *sm.* retort.

rimbecillire *vi.* 1. to grow (*v. irr.*) stupid 2. (*per età*) to reach one's dotage.

rimbecillito *agg.* doting.

rimboccare *vt.* to tuck up. ♦ **rimboccarsi** *vr.* to tuck up.

rimbombante *agg.* thundering.

rimbombare *vi.* 1. to thunder 2. (*risuonare*) to resound.

rimbombo *sm.* roar.

rimborsàbile *agg.* repayable.

rimborsare *vt.* to reimburse.

rimborso *sm.* reimbursement.

rimboscare *vt.* V. rimboschire.

rimboschimento *sm.* reafforestation.

**irr.*) wooded again.

rimboschire *vt.* to reafforest. ♦ **rimboschirsi** *vr.* to become (*v. irr.*).

rimbrottare *vt.* to reproach.

rimbrotto *sm.* reproach.

rimediàbile *agg.* remediable.

rimediare *vi.* to find (*v. irr.*) a remedy (for).

rimedio *sm.* remedy.

rimembranza *sf.* memory.

rimembrare *vt.* to remember.

rimeritare *vt.* to reward.

rimescolamento *sm.* 1. stir 2. (*turbamento*) shock.

rimescolare *vt.* 1. to stir again 2. (*mescolare*) to stir. ♦ **rimescolarsi** *vr.* to be upset ‖ *gli si rimescolò il sangue* (*per rabbia*), his blood boiled, (*per paura*), his blood ran cold.

rimescolìo *sm.* confusion.

rimessa *sf.* 1. replacing 2. (*per auto*) garage 3. (*di denaro*) remittance 4. (*di merci*) consignment ‖ — *in gioco*, throw-in.

rimesso *agg.* 1. (*falso*) false 2. (*ristabilito*) well again 3. (*perdonato*) forgiven.

rimestare *vt.* V. rimescolare.

riméttere *vt.* 1. to put (*v. irr.*) again, to put back 2. (*consegnare*) to hand 3. (*mandare, perdonare*) to remit 4. (*affidare*) to leave (*v. irr.*) 5. (*vomitare*) to vomit ‖ — *in gioco*, to throw (*v. irr.*) in; *rimetterci*, to lose (*v. irr.*). ♦ **riméttersi** *vr.* 1. (*affidarsi*) to rely on 2. (*ristabilirsi*) to recover 3. (*rasserenarsi*) to clear up.

rimirare *vt.* to gaze (at). ♦ **rimirarsi** *vr.* to admire oneself.

rimisurare *vt.* to measure again.

rimodellare *vt.* to remodel.

rimodernamento *sm.* modernizazione.

rimodernare *vt.* to modernize. ♦ **rimodernarsi** *vr.* to become up-to-date.

rimondare *vt.* to clean again.

rimonta *sf.* 1. (*mil.*) remount 2. (*sport*) catching up.

rimontare *vt.* 1. to go (*v. irr.*) up 2. (*ricomporre*) to reassemble. ♦ **rimontare** *vi.* 1. to remount 2. (*fig.*) to go back 3. (*sport*) to catch (*v. irr.*) up || — in auto, to get (*v. irr.*) into a car again.

rimorchiare *vt.* to tow.

rimorchiatore *sm.* tug.

rimorchio *sm.* 1. tow 2. (*veicolo*) trailer.

rimòrdere *vt.* 1. to bite (*v. irr.*) again 2. (*fig.*) to prick.

rimorso *sm.* remorse.

rimosso *agg.* removed.

rimostranza *sf.* remonstrance: *fare le proprie rimostranze*, to remonstrate.

rimostrare *vi.* to remonstrate.

rimovìbile *agg.* removable.

rimozione *sf.* removal.

rimpacchettare *vt.* to package again.

rimpadronirsi *vr.* to seize again.

rimpagliare *vt.* 1. to re-cover with straw 2. (*imbottire*) to re-stuff with straw.

rimpallo *sm.* counterblow.

rimpannucciarsi *vr.* (*fig.*) to improve one's financial position.

rimpastare *vt.* 1. to knead again 2. (*fig.*) to rearrange.

rimpasto *sm.* 1. kneading again 2. (*fig.*) rearrangement 3. (*pol.*) reshuffle.

rimpatriare *vt.* to repatriate. ♦ **rimpatriare** *vi.* to return to one's country.

rimpatrio *sm.* repatriation.

rimpetto *avv.* opposite.

rimpiàngere *vt.* 1. to regret 2. (*una perdita*) to mourn.

rimpianto *sm.* regret.

rimpiattarsi *vr.* to hide (*v. irr.*) oneself.

rimpiattino *sm.* hide-and-seek.

rimpiazzare *vt.* to replace.

rimpiazzo *sm.* replacement.

rimpicciolire *vt.* to lessen. ♦ **rimpicciolirsi** *vr.* to lessen.

rimpiegare *vt.* to re-employ.

rimpiego *sm.* re-employment.

rimpinguare *vt.* 1. to fatten 2. (*arricchire*) to enrich. ♦ **rimpinguarsi** *vr.* 1. to fatten 2. (*arricchirsi*) to grow (*v. irr.*) rich.

rimpinzare *vt.* to stuff (with).

rimpolpare *vt.* V. *rimpinguare*.

rimproverare *vt.* to reproach.

rimpròvero *sm.* reproach: *muovere un —*, to reproach.

rimuginare *vt.* to brood over.

rimunerare *vt.* to remunerate.

rimuòvere *vt.* 1. to remove 2. (*dissuadere*) to dissuade 3. (*da una carica*) to dismiss.

rimutare *vt.* to change again.

rinascenza *sf.* Renaissance.

rinàscere *vi.* to revive.

rinascimentale *agg.* Renaissance (*attr.*).

rinascimento *sm.* Renaissance.

rinàscita *sf.* 1. rebirth 2. (*fig.*) revival.

rincagnarsi *vr.* to frown.

rincagnato *agg.* pug (*attr.*).

rincalzare *vt.* 1. (*rimboccare*) to tuck in 2. (*sostenere*) to prop up.

rincalzo *sm.* support: *a — di*, in support of.

rincantucciare *vt.* to put (*v. irr.*) in a corner. ♦ **rincantucciarsi** *vr.* to hide (*v. irr.*) in a corner.

rincarare *vt.* 1. to raise the price of 2. (*esagerare*) to exaggerate. ♦ **rincarare** *vi.* to become (*v. irr.*) more expensive.

rincaro *sm.* rise in prices.

rincasare *vi.* to return home.

rinchiùdere *vt.* to shut (*v. irr.*) up.

rincitrullire *vt.* to make (*v. irr.*) silly. ♦ **rincitrullirsi** *vr.* to grow (*v. irr.*) silly.

rincivilire *vt.* to civilize. ♦ **rincivilirsi** *vr.* 1. to become (*v. irr.*) civilized 2. (*raffinarsi*) to become refined.

rincollare *vt.* to paste again.

rincominciare *vt.* to begin (*v. irr.*) again.

rincontrare *vt.* to meet (*v. irr.*) again. ♦ **rincontrarsi** *vr.* to meet again.

rincontro *sm.* meeting.

rincoramento *sm.* encouragement.

rincorare *vt.* to encourage. ♦ **rincorarsi** *vr.* to pluck up courage.

rincórrere *vt.* to run (*v. irr.*) after.

rincorsa *sf.* run-up.

rincréscere *vi.* 1. to be sorry: *mi*

rincresce, I am sorry 2. (dar noia) to mind: ti rincresce aprire la finestra?, do you mind opening the window?

rincrescimento sm. regret: con mio —, to my regret.

rincrudimento sm. aggravation.

rincrudire vi. 1. to aggravate 2. (esacerbare) to embitter 3. (del tempo) to get (v. irr.) worse.

rinculare vi. to recoil.

rinculo sm. recoil.

rinfacciare vt. to throw (v. irr.) (sthg.) in so.'s face.

rinfiancare vt. to support.

rinfilare vt. 1. to thread again 2. (rinserire) to insert again. ♦ **rinfilarsi** vr. 1. (introdursi) to slip again 2. (rindossare) to slip on again.

rinfiorare vt. to adorn with flowers again.

rinfittire vt. 1. to thicken 2. (rendere più frequenti) to make (v. irr.) more frequent. ♦ **rinfittirsi** vr. (di lana) to shrink (v. irr.).

rinfocolare vt. 1. to poke 2. (fig.) to stir up (again).

rinfoderare vt. to sheathe (again).

rinforzamento sm. strengthening.

rinforzare vt. 1. to strengthen 2. (mecc.) to stiffen. ♦ **rinforzarsi** vr. to become (v. irr.) stronger.

rinforzo sm. 1. strengthening 2. (mil.) reinforcements (pl.) 3. (fig.) support 4. (mecc.) stiffener.

rinfrancare vt. to encourage. ♦ **rinfrancarsi** vr. 1. (migliorare) to improve 2. (riprendere coraggio) to pluck up courage.

rinfrescamento sm. cooling.

rinfrescante agg. refreshing.

rinfrescare vt. 1. to cool 2. (ristorare) to refresh 3. (rinnovare) to renovate. ♦ **rinfrescare** vi. to cool.

rinfresco sm. 1. refreshments (pl.) 2. (ricevimento) cocktail party.

rinfusa (nella loc. avv.) alla —, in confusion.

ringalluzzire vt. to make (v. irr.) cocky. ♦ **ringalluzzirsi** vr. to become (v. irr.) cocky.

ringentilire vt. to refine.

ringhiare vi. to snarl.

ringhiera sf. 1. railing 2. (di scale) banisters (pl.).

ringhio sm. snarl.

ringhioso agg. snarling

ringiovanimento sm. rejuvenation.

ringiovanire vt. 1. to make (v. irr.) young again 2. (far sembrare più giovane) to make (so.) look younger. ♦ **ringiovanire** vi. 1. to grow (v. irr.) young again 2. (sembrare più giovane) to look younger.

ringiovanito agg. young again.

ringoiare vt. to swallow up again.

ringranare vt. to re-engage.

ringraziamento sm. thanks (pl.).

ringraziare vt. to thank.

ringuainare vt. V. rinfoderare.

rinite sf. rhinitis.

rinnegàbile agg. deniable.

rinnegamento sm. disowning.

rinnegare vt. to disown.

rinnegato agg. e sm. renegade.

rinnegatore sm. disowner.

rinnestare vt. 1. (agr.) to graft again 2. (mecc.) to re-engage.

rinnesto sm. 1. (agr.) new grafting 2. (mecc.) re-engagement.

rinnovàbile agg. renewable.

rinnovamento sm. renewal.

rinnovare vt. to renew. ♦ **rinnovarsi** vr. (riaccadere) to happen again.

rinnovatore sm. renewer.

rinnovazione sf. renewal.

rinnovellare vt. to renew. ♦ **rinnovellarsi** vr. to be renewed.

rinnovo sm. renewal.

rinoceronte sm. rhinoceros.

rinolaringite sf. rhinolaryngitis.

rinologia sf. rhinology.

rinomanza sf. renown.

rinomato agg. renowned.

rinominare vt. 1. to name again 2. (designare di nuovo) to reappoint.

rinoplàstica sf. rhinoplasty.

rinoscopia sf. rhinoscopy.

rinoscopio sm. rhinoscope.

rinsaccare vt. to pack again. ♦ **rinsaccarsi** vr. to shrug one's shoulders.

rinsaldamento sm. consolidation.

rinsaldare vt. to consolidate.

rinsanguare vt. 1. to supply with new blood 2. (fig.) to reinvigorate. ♦ **rinsanguarsi** vr. 1. to recover 2. (finanziariamente) to re--establish one's financial condition.

rinsanire vi. 1. to recover 2. (rinsavire) to return to reason.

rinsavimento sm. return to reason.

rinsavire vi. to recover one's wits.

rinsecchire vi. 1. to dry up 2. (di persone) to get (v. irr.) thin 3.

(avvizzire) to wither.

rinserrare vt. **1.** to shut (v. irr.) up (again).

rintanarsi vr. to shut (v. irr.) one-self up.

rintascare vt. to pocket again.

rintavolare vt. to start again.

rintoccare vi. **1.** (di orologio) to strike (v. irr.) **2.** (di campana) to toll.

rintocco sm. **1.** (di orologio) stroke **2.** (di campana) toll.

rintontire vt. to stun. ♦ **rinton-tirsi** vr. to be stunned.

rintracciare vt. **1.** to trace **2.** (tro-vare) to find (v. irr.) out.

rintronamento sm. booming.

rintronare vt. **1.** to deafen **2.** (stor-dire) to stun. ♦ **rintronare** vi. to boom.

rintuzzare vt. **1.** to blunt **2.** (ri-battere) to retort.

rinuncia sf. renouncement.

rinunciare vi. to renounce (sthg.).

rinunciatario agg. releasee.

rinvenimento sm. recovery.

rinvenire vt. to find (v. irr.). ♦ **rinvenire** vi. **1.** to recover one's senses **2.** (riprendere freschezza) to revive **3.** (riprendere morbidezza) to soften.

rinverdire vt. (ravvivare) to reawaken. ♦ **rinverdire** vi. **1.** to turn green again **2.** (ravvivarsi) to revive.

rinvestimento sm. reinvestment.

rinvestire vt. **1.** to restore to the possession of **2.** (comm.) to reinvest.

rinviare vt. **1.** to put (v. irr.) off **2.** (mandare indietro) to return.

rinvigorimento sm. reinvigoration.

rinvigorire vt. to reinvigorate. ♦ **rinvigorirsi** vr. to regain strength.

rinvilire vt. to lower. ♦ **rinvilire** vi. to become (v. irr.) cheaper.

rinvio sm. **1.** postponement **2.** (il ri-mandare indietro) returning.

rinvoltare vt. to wrap up again.

rinzaffare vt. **1.** to bung again **2.** (arch.) to rough in.

rinzaffatura sf. (arch.) roughing-in coat.

rio¹ sm. rivulet.

rio² agg. evil.

rioccupare vt. to reoccupy.

rioccupazione sf. reoccupation.

rionale agg. local, ward (attr.).

rione sm. ward, district.

riordinare vt. **1.** to tidy up **2.** (or-ganizzare) to reorganize **3.** (coman-dare di nuovo) to order again.

riordinatore sm. **1.** rearranger **2.** (riorganizzatore) reorganizer.

riordinazione sf. **1.** rearrangement **2.** (riorganizzazione) reorganization **3.** (nuova ordinazione) new order.

riordino sm. V. riordinazione.

riorganizzare vt. to reorganize.

riorganizzatore sm. reorganizer.

riorganizzazione sf. reorganiza-tion.

riottosità sf. **1.** turbulence **2.** (in-docilità) indocility.

riottoso agg. **1.** turbulent **2.** (indo-cile) indocile.

ripa sf. **1.** bank **2.** (scarpata) scarp.

ripagare vt. **1.** to repay (v. irr.) **2.** (pagare di nuovo) to pay (v. irr.) again.

riparare vt. **1.** (proteggere) to shel-ter **2.** (aggiustare) to repair **3.** (ri-sarcire) to redress ‖ — un esame, to repeat an exam. ♦ **riparare** vi. **1.** (porre rimedio) to remedy **2.** (rifugiarsi) to take (v. irr.) shel-ter. ♦ **ripararsi** vr. to take shelter.

riparatore agg. repairing. ♦ **ripa-ratore** sm. repairer.

riparazione sf. **1.** repair: in —, under repair **2.** (fig.) reparation.

riparlare vi. to speak (v. irr.) again.

riparo sm. **1.** shelter **2.** (rimedio) remedy **3.** (mecc.) guard.

ripartire¹ vi. to start again.

ripartire² vt. to divide.

ripartizione sf. division.

ripassare vi. to pass again **2.** (far visita) to call again. ♦ **ripas-sare** vt. **1.** (riattraversare) to cross again **2.** (dare di nuovo) to pass again **3.** (rileggere, rivedere) to go (v. irr.) through **4.** (mecc.) to overhaul.

ripassata sf. **1.** (revisione) revision **2.** (mecc.) overhauling **3.** (pulita) cleaning **4.** (mano di vernice) new coat.

ripasso sm. **1.** (ritorno) return **2.** (revisione) revision **3.** (di lezioni) review.

ripensamento sm. reflection: avere un —, to change one's mind.

ripensare vi. **1.** to think (v. irr.) (of sthg., so.) again **2.** (riconside-

rare) to think over 3. (*cambiar parere*) to change one's mind: *ci ho ripensato*, I have changed my mind.

ripercòrrere *vt.* to travel over (*sthg.*) again.

ripercuòtere *vt.* to strike (*v. irr.*) again. ♦ **ripercuòtersi** *vr.* 1. to reverberate 2. (*fig.*) to influence (*so., sthg.*).

ripercussione *sf.* repercussion.

ripescare *vt.* 1. to catch (*v. irr.*) again 2. (*ritrovare*) to find (*v. irr.*) again.

ripetente *s.* repeater.

ripètere *vt.* to repeat.

ripetitore *sm.* 1. repeater 2. (*scol.*) private tutor.

ripetizione *sf.* 1. (*rifacimento*) repetition 2. (*ripasso*) revision 3. (*lezione privata*) private lesson || *arma a —*, repeater.

ripetuto *agg.* repeated.

ripiano *sm.* 1. (*terreno*) terrace 2. (*pianerottolo*) landing 3. (*scaffale*) shelf (*pl.* -lves).

ripicco *sm.* spite: *per —*, out of spite.

ripidezza *sf.* steepness.

ripido *agg.* steep.

ripiegamento *sm.* 1. folding 2. (*il curvare*) bending 3. (*mil.*) withdrawal.

ripiegare *vt.* 1. to bend (*v. irr.*) again 2. (*piegare*) to fold. ♦ **ripiegare** *vi.* 1. to bend 2. (*ritirarsi*) to withdraw (*v. irr.*). ♦ **ripiegarsi** *vr.* to bend.

ripiegatura *sf.* 1. folding 2. (*piega*) fold 2. (*curva*) bend.

ripiego *sm.* 1. expedient 2. (*rimedio*) remedy.

ripienezza *sf.* fullness.

ripieno *agg.* 1. full 2. (*cuc.*) stuffed (with). ♦ **ripieno** *sm.* 1. filling 2. (*cuc.*) stuffing.

ripigliare *vt.* V. *riprendere*.

ripiombare *vt.* to plunge back. ♦ **ripiombare** *vi.* to fall (*v. irr.*) again.

ripopolamento *sm.* 1. repeopling 2. (*di animali*) restocking.

ripopolare *vt.* 1. to repeople 2. (*di animali*) to restock.

riporre *vt.* 1. to replace 2. (*metter via*) to put (*v. irr.*) away 3. (*porre*) to place. ♦ **riporsi** *vr.* (*riprendere*) to resume.

riportare *vt.* 1. to bring (*v. irr.*)

again, to take (*v. irr.*) again 2. (*portare indietro*) to bring back, to take back 3. (*riferire*) to report 4. (*citare*) to quote 5. (*ricevere*) to get (*v. irr.*) 6. (*mat.*) to carry. ♦ **riportarsi** *vr.* (*tornare*) to go (*v. irr.*) back.

riporto *sm.* 1. (*mat.*) carry over 2. (*in borsa*) contango 3. (*ornamento*) appliqué.

riposante *agg.* restful.

riposare *vt.* 1. to rest 2. (*posare di nuovo*) to place back. ♦ **riposare** *vi.* to rest. ♦ **riposarsi** *vr.* to rest.

riposato *agg.* 1. (*fresco*) fresh 2. (*tranquillo*) quiet.

riposo *sm.* rest: *andare a —*, to retire.

ripostiglio *sm.* cupboard.

riprèndere *vt.* 1. to take (*v. irr.*) again 2. (*riavere*) to take back 3. (*riassumere, ricominciare*) to resume 4. (*ricuperare*) to recover 5. (*rimproverare*) to reprove 6. (*teat.*) to revive 7. (*cine*) to shoot (*v. irr.*). ♦ **riprèndersi** *vr.* 1. to recover 2. (*da turbamento*) to collect oneself 3. (*correggersi*) to correct oneself.

riprensione *sf.* reprehension.

riprensivo *agg.* reprehensive.

ripresa *sf.* 1. renewal 2. (*teat.; rinascita*) revival 3. (*riconquista*) recapture 4. (*da malattia*) recovery 5. (*cine*) shot 6. (*auto*) acceleration 7. (*registrazione*) recording 8. (*di pugilato*) round 9. (*sport*) second half.

ripresentare *vt.* to present again.

ripristinare *vt.* 1. to restore 2. (*rimettere in vigore*) to re-establish.

ripristino *sm.* 1. restoration 2. (*il rimettere in vigore*) re-establishment.

riproducìbile *agg.* reproducible.

riprodurre *vt.* to reproduce. ♦ **riprodursi** *vr.* to reproduce.

riproduttivo *agg.* reproductive.

riproduttore *agg.* reproducing. ♦ **riproduttore** *sm.* reproducer.

riproduzione *sf.* reproduction.

ripromèttere *vt.* to promise again. ♦ **ripromèttersi** *vr.* 1. to intend 2. (*aspettarsi*) to expect.

riproporre *vt.* to re-propose. ♦ **riproporsi** *vr.* to re-propose.

riprova *sf.* (new) proof.

riprovare *vt.* 1. to try again 2. (*sentire di nuovo*) to feel (*v. irr.*)

again 3. (*disapprovare*) to criticize 4. (*scol.*) to fail.

riprovazione *sf.* reprobation.

riprovévole *agg.* **1.** blamable 2. (*spregevole*) despicable.

ripubblicare *vt.* to republish.

ripudiare *vt.* to repudiate.

ripudio *sm.* repudiation.

ripugnante *agg.* repugnant.

ripugnanza *sf.* repugnance.

ripugnare *vi.* **1.** (*disgustare*) to disgust 2. (*essere contrario*) to be repugnant.

ripulire *vt.* **1.** to clean again 2. (*pulire*) to clean 3. (*fig.*) to polish 4. (*saccheggiare*) to ransack.

ripulita *sf.* clean: *darsi una* —, to tidy oneself up.

ripulsa *sf.* repulse.

ripulsione *sf.* repulsion.

ripulsivo *agg.* repulsive.

riquadrare *vt.* **1.** to square 2. (*una stanza*) to decorate.

riquadratura *sf.* **1.** square 2. (*decorazione*) decoration.

riquadro *sm.* **1.** square 2. (*su parete*) panel.

risacca *sf.* surf.

risaia *sf.* rice-field.

risalire *vt.* **1.** to go (*v. irr.*) up again 2. (*contro corrente*) to go up: — *la corrente*, to go upstream. ♦ **risalire** *vi.* **1.** to go up again 2. (*nel tempo*) to go back.

risaltare¹ *vi.* **1.** to shine (*v. irr.*) up 2. (*di persona*) to stand (*v. irr.*) out.

risaltare² *vt.* to jump again.

risalto *sm.* **1.** prominence 2. (*rilievo*) relief.

risanàbile *agg.* **1.** curable 2. (*bonificabile*) reclaimable.

risanamento *sm.* **1.** curing 2. (*guarigione*) recovery 3. (*bonifica*) reclamation 4. (*fig.*) reformation || — *di quartiere*, slum-clearance.

risanare *vt.* **1.** to cure 2. (*bonificare*) to reclaim 3. (*un quartiere*) to clear (a slum). ♦ **risanare** *vi.* to recover.

risanatore *agg.* healing. ♦ **risanatore** *sm.* healer.

risapere *vt.* to come (*v. irr.*) to know.

risaputo *agg.* well-known.

risarcìbile *agg.* that can be indemnified.

risarcimento *sm.* indemnity.

risarcire *vt.* to indemnify.

risata *sf.* laugh: *scoppiare in una* —, to burst (*v. irr.*) out laughing.

riscaldamento *sm.* heating.

riscaldare *vt.* **1.** to warm (up) 2. (*di casa*) to heat 3. (*fig.*) to excite. ♦ **riscaldarsi** *vr.* to warm up.

riscaldo *sm.* inflammation.

riscattàbile *agg.* redeemable.

riscattare *vt.* to redeem.

riscatto *sm.* **1.** ransom 2. (*redenzione*) redemption.

rischiaramento *sm.* brightening.

rischiarare *vt.* to light (*v. irr.*) (up). ♦ **rischiararsi** *vr.* **1.** to light up 2. (*diventare più chiaro*) to get (*v. irr.*) clearer 3. (*di cielo*) to clear up.

rischiare *vt.* to risk. ♦ **rischiare** *vi.* to run (*v. irr.*) the risk (of).

rischio *sm.* risk.

rischioso *agg.* risky.

risciacquare *vt.* to rinse. ♦ **risciacquarsi** *vr.* to rinse.

risciacquata *sf.* rinse.

risciacquatura *sf.* **1.** rinsing 2. (*acqua*) dish-water.

riscontare *vt.* to rediscount.

risconto *sm.* rediscount.

riscontrare *vt.* **1.** (*controllare*) to check 2. (*trovare*) to find (*v. irr.*) 3. (*confrontare*) to compare.

riscontro *sm.* **1.** (*controllo*) checking 2. (*confronto*) comparison 3. (*risposta*) reply 4. (*corrispondenza simmetrica*) pendant.

riscoprire *vt.* to discover again.

riscossa *sf.* **1.** (*rivolta*) revolt 2. (*riscatto*) redemption || *andare alla* —, to counterattack.

riscossione *sf.* collection.

riscotìbile *agg.* collectable.

riscotimento *sm.* collection.

riscrivere *vt.* **1.** to rewrite (*v. irr.*) 2. (*in risposta*) to write (*v. irr.*) back.

riscuòtere *vt.* **1.** (*denaro*) to collect 2. (*conseguire*) to win (*v. irr.*) 3. (*scuotere*) to shake (*v. irr.*). ♦ **riscuòtersi** *vr.* (*trasalire*) to start.

riseccare *vt.* to dry up. ♦ **riseccarsi** *vr.* to dry up.

risedersi *vr.* to sit (*v. irr.*) down again.

risega *sf.* **1.** (*arch.*) offset 2. (*della pelle*) fold.

riseminare *vt.* to sow (*v. irr.*) again.

risentimento *sm.* resentment: *con* —, resentfully.

risentire vt. 1. (sentire di nuovo) to feel (v. irr.) again 2. (riudire) to hear (v. irr.) again 3. (sentire) to feel || — di qc., to show (v. irr.) traces of sthg.; (di persona) to feel the effect of sthg. ♦ **risentirsi** vr. to take (v. irr.) offence (at).

risentito agg. (sdegnato) resentful.

riserbare vt. V. riservare.

riserbo sm. 1. reserve 2. (discrezione) discretion.

riserva sf. 1. reserve 2. (di caccia, pesca) preserve.

riservare vt. to reserve ♦ **riservarsi** vr. (ripromettersi) to intend: — la diagnosi, to refuse to formulate a definite diagnosis.

riservatezza sf. reservedness.

riservato agg. 1. reserved 2. (segreto) private.

risibile agg. laughable.

risicoltore sm. rice-grower.

risicoltura sf. rice-growing.

risièdere vi. to reside.

risma sf. 1. ream 2. (fig.) kind.

riso[1] sm. (bot.) rice.

riso[2] sm. laugh.

risolare vt. to resole.

risolatura sf. resoling.

risollevare vt. 1. to raise again 2. (confortare) to cheer up. ♦ **risollevarsi** vr. 1. to rise again 2. (confortarsi) to cheer up.

risolutezza sf. resolution.

risolutivo agg. resolutive.

risoluto agg. resolute.

risoluzione sf. 1. resolution 2. (giur.) cancellation.

risòlvere vt. 1. to resolve 2. (rescindere) to rescind. ♦ **risòlversi** vr. 1. (decidersi) to make (v. irr.) up one's mind 2. (mutarsi) to turn (into) 3. (di malattia) to clear up.

risolvibile agg. resolvable 2. (rescindibile) rescindable.

risonante agg. resonant.

risonanza sf. resonance.

risonare vt. 1. to play again 2. (un campanello) to ring (v. irr.) again. ♦ **risonare** vi. to resound.

risòrgere vi. 1. to rise (v. irr.) again 2. (rifiorire) to revive || far —, to revive.

risorgimento sm. revival.

risorsa sf. resource.

risparmiare vt. 1. to save 2. (evitare, salvare) to spare.

risparmiatore agg. thrifty. ♦ **risparmiatore** sm. saver.

risparmio sm. saving: senza —, lavishly.

rispecchiare vt. to reflect. ♦ **rispecchiarsi** vr. to be reflected.

rispedire vt. 1. to send: (v. irr.) again 2. (spedire indietro) to send back.

rispettàbile agg. respectable.

rispettabilità sf. respectability.

rispettare vt. 1. to respect 2. (onorare) to honour.

rispettivo agg. respective.

rispetto sm. respect: — a, as regards; a — di, in comparison to; mancare di — a, to be disrespectful to.

rispettoso agg. respectful.

risplendente agg. shining.

risplèndere vi. to shine (v. irr.).

rispolverare vt. 1. to dust again 2. (fig.) to brush up.

rispondente agg. answering (to).

rispondenza sf. correspondence.

rispóndere vt. e vi. 1. to answer (so., sthg.) 2. (obbedire) to respond || — di qu., qc., to answer for so., sthg.

risposare vt. V. rimaritare.

risposta sf. answer, reply.

rispuntare vi. 1. to reappear 2. (risorgere) to rise (v. irr.) again 3. (di germogli) to sprout again.

rissa sf. brawl.

rissare vi. to brawl.

rissoso agg. quarrelsome.

ristabilimento sm. 1. restoration 2. (di salute) recovery.

ristabilire vt. to restore. ♦ **ristabilirsi** vr. 1. to settle again 2. (rimettersi) to recover.

ristagnamento sm. 1. stagnation 2. (di sangue) staunching.

ristagnare vi. to stagnate. ♦ **ristagnare** vt. to staunch.

ristagno sm. (econ.) slackness.

ristampa sf. reprint: essere in —, to be reprinting.

ristampare vt. to reprint.

ristare vi. 1. (cessare) to stop 2. (rimanere) to remain.

ristoràbile agg. restorable.

ristorante sm. restaurant.

ristorare vt. to refresh, to restore (anche fig.).

ristoratore agg. refreshing. ♦ **ristoratore** sm. restorer.

ristoro sm. 1. relief 2. (cibo, be-

vanda) refreshment || *luogo di —*, refreshment-room.

ristrettezza *sf.* **1.** narrowness **2.** (*insufficienza*) lack || *— di idee*, narrow-mindedness.

ristretto *agg.* **1.** narrow **2.** (*condensato*) condensed.

ristringere *vt.* **1.** to tighten again **2.** (*premere di nuovo*) to press again || *— la mano a qu.*, to shake (*v. irr.*) hands with so. again.

ristuccare *vt.* **1.** (*edil.*) to replaster **2.** (*nauseare*) to surfeit.

ristuccatura *sf.* (*edil.*) replastering.

ristudiare *vt.* to study again.

risucchiare *vt.* to suck (again).

risucchio *sm.* whirlpool.

risultante *agg. e sf.* resultant.

risultanza *sf.* result.

risultare *vi.* **1.** to result **2.** (*venire a sapere*) to turn out || *mi risulta*, I know.

risultato *sm.* result.

risurrezione *sf.* resurrection.

risuscitamento *sm.* resuscitation.

risuscitare *vt. e vi.* to resuscitate.

risvegliare *vt.* to wake (*v. irr.*) (up). ◆ **risvegliarsi** *vr.* to wake up.

risveglio *sm.* **1.** awakening **2.** (*fig.*) revival.

risvoltare *vt.* to turn up.

risvolto *sm.* **1.** (*di giacca*) lapel **2.** (*di calzoni*) turn-up.

ritagliare *vt.* **1.** to cut (*v. irr.*) out **2.** (*tagliare di nuovo*) to cut again.

ritaglio *sm.* **1.** (*di stoffa*) remnant **2.** (*di giornale*) clipping || *ritagli di tempo*, odd moments.

ritardare *vt.* to delay. ◆ **ritardare** *vi.* **1.** to be late **2.** (*di orologio*) to be slow.

ritardatario *sm.* late-comer.

ritardo *sm.* delay: *in —*, late.

ritegno *sm.* **1.** reserve **2.** (*freno*) restraint **3.** (*riluttanza*) reluctance.

ritemprare *vt.* **1.** to strengthen **2.** (*metalli*) to harden again. ◆ **ritemprarsi** *vr.* to get (*v. irr.*) stronger.

ritenere *vt.* **1.** to hold (*v. irr.*) **2.** (*giudicare*) to consider **3.** (*pensare*) to think (*v. irr.*).

ritentare *vt.* **1.** to tempt again **2.** (*riprovare*) to try again.

ritenuta *sf.* deduction.

ritenzione *sf.* retention.

ritingere *vt.* to dye again.

ritirare *vt.* **1.** to withdraw (*v. irr.*)

2. (*farsi consegnare*) to collect. ◆ **ritirarsi** *vr.* **1.** to retire **2.** (*di stoffa*) to shrink (*v. irr.*).

ritirata *sf.* **1.** retreat **2.** (*latrina*) lavatory.

ritiro *sm.* **1.** withdrawal **2.** (*il ritirarsi*) retirement **3.** (*luogo appartato*) retreat **4.** (*il farsi consegnare*) collection.

ritmare *vt.* to mark.

ritmica *sf.* rhythmic(s).

ritmico *agg.* rhythmic(al).

ritmo *sm.* rhythm.

rito *sm.* rite: *essere di —*, to be customary.

ritoccare *vt.* to retouch.

ritoccatore *sm.* retoucher.

ritocco *sm.* retouch.

ritogliere *vt.* **1.** to take (*v. irr.*) off again **2.** (*riappropriarsi*) to take back. ◆ **ritogliersi** *vr.* to take off again.

ritorcere *vt.* **1.** to twist again **2.** (*torcere*) to twist **3.** (*rivolgere*) to retort. ◆ **ritorcersi** *vr.* **1.** to get (*v. irr.*) twisted **2.** (*fig.*) to recoil (on, upon).

ritorcitura *sf.* twisting.

ritornare *vi.* to return.

ritornello *sm.* refrain.

ritorno *sm.* return: *— di fiamma*, backfire; *essere di —*, to be back.

ritorsione *sf.* retortion.

ritorto *agg.* twisted.

ritrarre *vt.* **1.** to withdraw (*v. irr.*) **2.** (*distogliere*) to turn away **3.** (*rappresentare*) to represent **4.** (*dedurre*) to understand (*v. irr.*). ◆ **ritrarsi** *vr.* to withdraw.

ritrattare *vt.* **1.** to retract **2.** (*trattare di nuovo*) to treat again.

ritrattazione *sf.* **1.** retraction **2.** (*nuova trattazione*) new treatment.

ritrattista *s.* portraitist.

ritrattistica *sf.* portraiture.

ritratto *sm.* portrait.

ritrazione *sf.* retraction.

ritrito *agg.* stale.

ritrosìa *sf.* **1.** (*riluttanza*) reluctance **2.** (*timidezza*) shyness.

ritroso *agg.* **1.** (*riluttante*) reluctant **2.** (*timido*) shy || *a —*, backwards.

ritrovamento *sm.* finding.

ritrovare *vt.* **1.** to find (*v. irr.*) again **2.** (*ricuperare*) to recover **3.** (*scoprire*) to discover. ◆ **ritrovarsi** *vr.* **1.** to find oneself **2.** (*rincontrarsi*) to meet (*v. irr.*) again.

ritrovato *sm.* **1.** invention **2.** (*scoperta*) discovery.

ritrovo *sm.* meeting-place, haunt.

ritto *agg.* upright.

rituale *agg.* e *sm.* ritual.

rituffare *vt.* to plunge again. ♦ **rituffarsi** *vr.* to plunge again.

riudire *vt.* to hear (*v. irr.*) again.

riunione *sf.* meeting.

riunire *vt.* **1.** to re-unite **2.** (*raccogliere*) to gather **3.** (*unire*) to join. ♦ **riunirsi** *vr.* **1.** to come (*v. irr.*) together again **2.** (*unirsi*) to unite **3.** (*incontrarsi*) to meet (*v. irr.*).

riuscire *vi.* **1.** to succeed (in), to be good (at) **2.** (*risultare*) to be **3.** (*uscire di nuovo*) to go (*v. irr.*) out again.

riuscita *sf.* **1.** issue **2.** (*successo*) success.

riutilizzare *vt.* to utilize again.

riva *sf.* **1.** (*di mare, lago*) shore **2.** (*di fiume*) bank.

rivale *agg.* e *sm.* rival.

rivaleggiare *vt.* to rival (so., sthg.).

rivalere *vr.* **1.** to make (*v. irr.*) up for one's losses **2.** (*valersi di nuovo*) to make use again.

rivalicare *vt.* to recross.

rivalità *sf.* rivalry.

rivalsa *sf.* **1.** (*rivincita*) revenge **2.** (*risarcimento*) compensation **3.** (*comm.*) recourse.

rivalutare *vt.* to revalue **2.** (*elevare*) to raise.

rivalutazione *sf.* **1.** revaluation **2.** (*aumento*) rise.

rivangare *vt.* e *vi.* to dig (*v. irr.*) up again.

rivedere *vt.* **1.** to see (*v. irr.*) again **2.** (*revisionare*) to revise.

riveduta *sf.* look, revision.

rivelare *vt.* to reveal. ♦ **rivelarsi** *vr.* **1.** to reveal oneself **2.** (*dimostrarsi*) to prove.

rivelatore *agg.* revealing. ♦ **rivelatore** *sm.* **1.** revealer **2.** (*radio*) detector.

rivelazione *sf.* **1.** revelation **2.** (*fis.; radio*) detection.

rivéndere *vt.* to resell (*v. irr.*) **1.** **2.** (*al dettaglio*) to retail.

rivendicare *vt.* **1.** to claim **2.** (*vendicare*) to revenge.

rivendicatore *agg.* **1.** claiming **2.** (*vendicatore*) revenging. ♦ **rivendicatore** *sm.* **1.** claimant **2.** (*vendicatore*) revenger.

rivendicazione *sf.* claim.

rivéndita *sf.* **1.** resale **2.** (*spaccio*) shop.

rivenditore *sm.* retailer.

rivendùgliolo *sm.* V. *rigattiere*.

riverberare *vt.* to reverberate. ♦ **riverberarsi** *vr.* to reverberate.

rivèrbero *sm.* reverberation: *di —*, indirectly.

riverente *agg.* reverent.

riverenza *sf.* **1.** reverence **2.** (*inchino*) bow.

riverenziale *agg.* reverential.

riverire *vt.* **1.** to revere **2.** (*salutare*) to pay (*v. irr.*) one's respects (to).

riversare *vt.* **1.** to pour again **2.** (*versare*) to pour **3.** (*di fiume*) to flow. ♦ **riversarsi** *vr.* to flow.

riverso *avv.* on one's back.

rivestimento *sm.* **1.** covering **2.** (*interno*) lining.

rivestire *vt.* **1.** to dress again **2.** (*foderare*) to line (with sthg.) **3.** (*coprire*) to cover (with sthg.) **4.** (*fig.*) to hold (*v. irr.*).

riviera *sf.* coast || *la Riviera*, the Riviera.

rivierasco *agg.* coast (*attr.*).

rivincere *vt.* **1.** to win (*v. irr.*) again **2.** (*recuperare*) to win back.

rivincita *sf.* **1.** (*vendetta*) revenge **2.** (*sport*) return match **3.** (*al gioco*) return game.

rivista *sf.* **1.** review **2.** (*teat.*) revue **3.** (*mil.*) parade || *passare in —*, to review.

rivivere *vi.* e *vt.* to live again.

rivo *sm.* stream.

rivolere *vt.* **1.** to want again **2.** (*volere indietro*) to want back.

rivòlgere *vt.* **1.** to turn **2.** (*indirizzare*) to address. ♦ **rivòlgersi** *vr.* **1.** to turn **2.** (*parlando*) to address (so.) **3.** (*ricorrere, riferirsi*) to apply (to).

rivolgimento *sm.* **1.** upheaval **2.** (*cambio*) change.

rivolo *sm.* streamlet.

rivolta *sf.* revolt.

rivoltante *agg.* revolting.

rivoltare *vt.* **1.** to turn (over) again **2.** (*rovesciare*) to turn **3.** (*capovolgere*) to turn upside-down **4.** (*con l'interno all'esterno*) to turn inside out **5.** (*fig.*) to upset (*v. irr.*). ♦ **rivoltarsi** *vr.* **1.** to turn round **2.** (*rigirarsi*) to turn over **3.** (*ribellarsi*) to revolt **4.** (*fig.*) to turn.

rivoltella *sf.* revolver.

rivoltoso *agg.* e *sm.* rebel.

rivoluzionare *vt.* to revolutionize.

rivoluzionario *agg.* e *sm.* revolutionary.

rivoluzione *sf.* revolution.

rizoma *sm.* rhizome.

rizzare *vt.* to raise: — le orecchie, to prick one's ears. ♦ **rizzarsi** *vr.* 1. to stand (*v. irr.*) up 2. (*di capelli*) to stand on end.

roba *sf.* stuff, things (*pl.*).

robaccia *sf.* rubbish.

robinia *sf.* locust-tree.

robustezza *sf.* robustness.

robusto *agg.* robust.

rocambolesco *agg.* daring.

rocca[1] *sf.* 1. stronghold 2. (*roccia*) rock.

rocca[2] *sf.* (*conocchia*) distaff.

roccaforte *sf.* stronghold.

rocchetto *sm.* 1. (*di tronco*) log 2. (*di colonna*) drum.

roccia *sf.* rock.

rocciatore *sm.* rock-climber.

roccioso *agg.* rocky.

roco *agg.* hoarse.

rodaggio *sm.* (*auto*) running in.

rodare *vt.* to run (*v. irr.*) in.

ròdere *vt.* 1. to gnaw 2. (*corrodere*) to corrode. ♦ **ròdersi** *vr.* 1. to worry 2. (*di rabbia ecc.*) to be consumed (with).

rodimento *sm.* 1. gnawing 2. (*fig.*) anxiety.

roditore *agg.* e *sm.* rodent.

rododendro *sm.* rhododendron.

rogare *vt.* to draw (*v. irr.*) up.

rogatoria *sf.* request.

rogazioni *sf. pl.* rogations.

roggia *sf.* irrigation ditch.

rògito *sm.* deed.

rogna *sf.* 1. scabies 2. (*fig.*) trouble.

rognone *sm.* kidney.

rognoso *agg.* scabby.

rogo *sm.* 1. fire 2. (*pira*) pyre 3. (*supplizio*) stake.

rollare *vi.* to roll.

rollio *sm.* roll.

romancio *agg.* Romansh.

romànico *agg.* 1. (*arch.*) Romanesque 2. Romanic.

romano *agg.* e *sm.* Roman.

romanticheria *sf.* 1. (*atteggiamento*) romantic attitude 2. (*azione*) romantic deed.

romanticismo *sm.* Romanticism.

romàntico *agg.* e *sm.* romantic.

romanza *sf.* romance.

romanzare *vt.* to romanticize.

romanzesco *agg.* romantic.

romanziere *sm.* novelist.

romanzo[1] *agg.* Romance.

romanzo[2] *sm.* 1. novel 2. (*storia incredibile*) romance || — a puntate, serial; — a fumetti, comics.

romba *sf.* roar.

rombare *vi.* to rumble.

ròmbico *agg.* rhombic(al).

rombo[1] *sm.* (*rumore*) rumble.

rombo[2] *sm.* (*geom.*) rhomb.

rombo[3] *sm.* (*itt.*) brill.

romboèdrico *agg.* rhombohedral.

romboedro *sm.* rhombohedron (*pl.* -ra).

romboidale *agg.* rhomboid(al).

romboide *agg.* e *sm.* rhomboid.

romeno *agg.* e *sm.* Rumanian.

romeo *sm.* pilgrim.

romitaggio *sm.* hermitage.

romito *agg.* solitary. ♦ **romito** *sm.* hermit.

romitorio *sm.* hermitage.

ròmpere *vt.* to break (*v. irr.*): — i ponti con qu., to break with so. ♦ **rómpersi** *vr.* to break (up).

rompicapo *sm.* puzzle.

rompicollo *sm.* madcap: a —, headlong.

rompighiaccio *sm.* ice-breaker.

rompiscàtole *s.* nuisance.

rompitore *sm.* breaker.

ronca *sf.* pruning-knife (*pl.* -ives).

ronciglio *sm.* hook.

ròncola *sf.* pruning-hook.

ronda *sf.* 1. rounds (*pl.*) 2. (*pattuglia*) patrol.

rondella *sf.* washer.

ròndine *sf.* swallow: a coda di —, swallow-tailed.

rondinotto *sm.* young swallow.

rondò *sm.* 1. (*mus.*) rondo 2. (*poet.*) rondel 3. (*piazza circolare*) circus.

rondone *sm.* swift.

ronfare *vi.* to snore.

ronzare *vi.* 1. to buzz 2. (*fig.*) to hang (*v. irr.*) around.

ronzino *sm.* nag.

ronzìo *sm.* buzz.

ròrido *agg.* 1. (*bagnato*) wet 2. (*rugiadoso*) dewy.

rosa *sf.* rose || all'acqua di rose (*fig.*), moderate. ♦ **rosa** *agg.* e *sm.* pink.

rosàceo *agg.* rosy.

rosaio *sm.* rose-bush.

rosario *sm.* rosary.

rosato agg. rosy.

ròseo agg. rosy.

roseòla sf. roseola.

roseto sm. rose-garden.

rosetta sf. **1.** rosette **2.** (diamante) rose **3.** (mecc.) washer.

rosicchiare vt. to gnaw.

rosmarino sm. rosemary.

rosolare vt. to brown. ♦ **rosolarsi** vr. **1.** to get (v. irr.) brown **2.** (prendere il sole) to bask.

rosolìa sf. German measles (pl.).

rosolio sm. rosolio.

rosone sm. rose-window.

rospo sm. toad.

rossastro agg. reddish.

rosseggiare vi. to be reddish.

rossetto sm. **1.** (per labbra) lipstick **2.** (per guance) rouge.

rossiccio agg. ruddy.

rosso agg. e sm. red: — d'uovo, yolk; diventar —, to flush.

rossore sm. flush.

rosticcerìa sf. rotisserie.

rosticciere sm. owner of a rotisserie.

rostro sm. **1.** rostrum (pl. -ra) **2.** (becco) beak.

rotàbile agg. carriage (attr.).

rotaia sf. **1.** rail **2.** (solco) rut.

rotare vi. e vt. to rotate, to revolve.

rotativa sf. rotary press.

rotativo agg. rotary.

rotatorio agg. rotating.

rotazione sf. rotation.

roteare vt. **1.** to swing (v. irr.) **2.** (gli occhi) to roll. ♦ **roteare** vi. to wheel.

rotella sf. small wheel.

rotocalco sm. **1.** rotogravure **2.** (rivista) illustrated magazine.

rotolamento sm. rolling.

rotolare vt. e vi. to roll. ♦ **rotolarsi** vr. to roll.

ròtolo sm. roll || andare a rotoli, to go (v. irr.) to rack and ruin; mandare a rotoli, to ruin.

rotolone sm. V. ruzzolone.

rotonda sf. rotunda.

rotondità sf. roundness.

rotondo agg. **1.** round **2.** (grassoccio) plump.

rotore sm. rotor.

rotta sf. **1.** course **2.** (rottura) breach **3.** (sconfitta) rout || a — di collo, headlong; essere in — con, to be on bad terms with; mettere in —, to rout.

rottame sm. **1.** wreck **2.** (di scarto)

scraps (pl.).

rotto agg. **1.** broken **2.** (stracciato) torn **3.** (avvezzo) accustomed.

rottura sf. break(ing).

ròtula sf. knee-cap.

rovente agg. red-hot.

ròvere sm. oak.

rovesciamento sm. **1.** overthrowing **2.** (cambiamento) reversal.

rovesciare vt. **1.** to overturn **2.** (capovolgere) to turn upside down **3.** (gettare) to throw (v. irr.) **4.** (rivoltare) to turn inside out **5.** (versare intenzionalmente) to pour **6.** (versare accidentalmente) to spill **7.** (abbattere) to overthrow (v. irr.). ♦ **rovesciarsi** vr. **1.** to overturn **2.** (riversarsi) to pour.

rovescio sm. **1.** reverse **2.** (opposto) opposite **3.** (di pioggia) heavy shower **4.** (di critiche ecc.) hail || a — (capovolto), upside down.

roveto sm. bramble-bush.

rovina sf. ruin.

rovinare vt. **1.** to ruin **2.** (sciupare) to spoil (v. irr.). ♦ **rovinare** vi. to crash.

rovinìo sm. **1.** downfall **2.** (rumore) crash.

rovinoso agg. ruinous.

rovistare vt. e vi. to rummage.

rovo sm. blackberry bush.

rozza sf. jade.

rozzezza sf. roughness.

rozzo agg. rough.

ruba sf. andare a —, to sell (v. irr.) like wildfire.

rubacchiare vt. to pilfer.

rubacuori agg. bewitching. ♦ **rubacuori** sm. lady-killer.

rubare vt. to steal (v. irr.).

ruberìa sf. theft.

rubicondo agg. ruddy.

rubinetterìa sf. plumbing fixtures (pl.).

rubi netto sm. tap.

rubino sm. ruby.

rubizzo agg. hale.

rublo sm. rouble.

rubrica sf. **1.** (di giornale) column **2.** (per indirizzi) addressbook.

rude agg. rough.

rùdere sm. ruin.

rudezza sf. roughness.

rudimentale agg. rudimentary.

rudimento sm. rudiment.

ruffiano sm. pander.

ruga sf. wrinkle.

ruggente agg. roaring.

rùggine sf. 1. rust 2. (fig.) grudge.
rugginoso agg. rusty.
ruggire vi. to roar.
ruggito sm. roar.
rugiada sf. dew: goccia di —, dew-drop.
rugiadoso agg. dewy.
rugosità sf. 1. wrinkledness 2. (scabrosità) ruggedness.
rugoso agg. 1. wrinkled 2. (scabro) rugged.
rullaggio sm. pista di —, taxi-track.
rullare vi. 1. to roll 2. (di aereo) to taxi.
rullino sm. roll.
rullìo sm. roll.
rullo sm. 1. roll 2. (mecc.) roller.
rum sm. rum.
ruminante agg. e sm. ruminant.
ruminare vt. to ruminate.
ruminazione sf. rumination.
rùmine sm. rumen.
rumore sm. 1. noise 2. (diceria) rumour || far — (fig.), to arouse great interest.
rumoreggiare vi. 1. to rumble 2. (fig.) to rumour.
rumorìo sm. noise.
rumorista sm. noise-maker.
rumoroso agg. noisy.
ruolino sm. (di marcia) time schedule.
ruolo sm. 1. roll, list 2. (teat.) role 3. (amm.) roster.
ruota sf. wheel.
rupe sf. cliff.
rupestre agg. rocky.
rurale agg. rural || i rurali, country people.
ruscello sm. brook.
ruspa sf. scraper.
ruspare vi. (razzolare) to scratch about.
russare vi. to snore.
russo agg. e sm. Russian.
rusticità sf. rusticity.
rùstico agg. 1. rustic 2. (ritroso) unsociable.
ruta sf. rue.
rutilante agg. glowing.
ruttare vi. to belch.
rutto sm. belch.
rùvido agg. rough.
ruzzare vi. to romp.
ruzzolare vt. to roll. ♦ **ruzzolare** vi. 1. to roll 2. (cadere) to tumble down.
ruzzolone sm. tumble: fare un —, to tumble down.

S

sàbato sm. Saturday.
sabba sm. witches' Sabbath.
sabbia sf. sand.
sabbiare vt. to sand.
sabbiatura sf. sand-bath.
sabbioso agg. sandy.
sabotaggio sm. sabotage.
sabotare vt. to sabotage.
sabotatore sm. saboteur.
sacca sf. bag.
saccarina sf. saccharine.
saccarosio sm. saccharose.
saccente agg. pedantic. ♦ **saccente** s. ped.nt.
saccheggiare vt. to sack.
saccheggio sm. sack.
sacchetto sm. small bag.
sacco sm. 1. sack, bag || colazione al —, picnic; mettere qu. nel —, to take (v. irr.) so. in 2. (grande quantità) a lot of.
saccoccia sf. pocket.
saccone sm. palliasse.
sacerdotale agg. sacerdotal.
sacerdote sm. priest.
sacerdozio sm. priesthood.
sacrale agg. sacral.
sacramentale agg. sacramental.
sacramentare vi. (fig.) to swear (v. irr.).
sacramento sm. sacrament.
sacrario sm. shrine.
sacrificare vt. to sacrifice.
sacrificio sm. sacrifice.
sacrilegio sm. sacrilege.
sacrìlego agg. sacrilegious.
sacrista sm. sacristan.
sacro agg. sacred, holy.
sacrosanto agg. 1. sacrosanct 2. (indiscutibile) absolute.
sàdico agg. sadistic. ♦ **sàdico** sm. sadist.
sadismo sm. sadism.
saetta sf. 1. arrow 2. (fulmine) thunderbolt.
saettare vt. 1. to shoot (v. irr.) arrows at 2. (fig.) to dart. ♦ **saettare** vi. to dart.
sàffico agg. Sapphic.
sagace agg. sagacious.
sagacia sf. sagacity.
saggezza sf. wisdom.
saggiare vt. to assay, to test.
saggiatore sm. 1. assayer 2. (bilancia) assay balance.
saggina sf. sorghum.

saggio[1] *agg.* wise. ♦ **saggio** *sm.* wise man (*pl.* men).

saggio[2] *sm.* **1.** essay **2.** (*campione*) sample **3.** (*saggio ginnico*) display.

saggista *s.* essayist.

sagittario *sm.* **1.** archer **2.** (*astr.*) Sagittarius.

sagoma *sf.* shape || è una —! (*fam.*), he is a character!

sagomare *vt.* to shape.

sagra *sf.* festival.

sagrato *sm.* church-square.

sagrestano *sm.* sacristan.

sagrestia *sf.* sacristy.

saia *sf.* serge.

saio *sm.* habit.

sala *sf.* hall, room: — da pranzo, dining-room.

salace *agg.* salacious.

salacità *sf.* salacity.

salamandra *sf.* salamander.

salame *sm.* salami (*pl.*).

salamelecco *sm.* salaam.

salamoia *sf.* pickle.

salare *vt.* to salt.

salariale *agg.* salary (*attr.*).

salariato *agg.* wage-earning. ♦ **salariato** *sm.* wage-earner.

salario *sm.* wages (*pl.*).

salassare *vt.* to bleed (*v. irr.*).

salasso *sm.* **1.** bleeding **2.** (*fig.*) extortion.

salato *agg.* **1.** salty **2.** (*costoso*) dear **3.** (*salace*) keen.

salatura *sf.* salting.

salda *sf.* starch-water.

saldamente *avv.* firmly.

saldare *vt.* **1.** to solder, to weld **2.** (*un conto*) to settle.

saldatore *sm.* solderer, welder.

saldatrice *sf.* welding machine.

saldatura *sf.* soldering, welding.

saldezza *sf.* firmness.

saldo[1] *agg.* firm.

saldo[2] *sm.* balance: — attivo, passivo, credit, debit balance.

sale *sm.* salt.

salesiano *agg.* e *sm.* Salesian.

salgemma *sf.* rock-salt.

sàlice *sm.* willow.

salicilato *sm.* salicylate.

saliente *agg.* important.

saliera *sf.* salt-cellar.

salina *sf.* salt-pit.

salino *agg.* saline, salt (*attr.*).

salire *vi.* **1.** to rise (*v. irr.*), to go (*v. irr.*) up **2.** (*di prezzi*) to increase.

saliscendi *sm.* **1.** latch **2.** (*alter-

narsi di salite e discese*) ups and downs (*pl.*).

salita *sf.* **1.** slope, ascent **2.** (*aumento*) rise.

saliva *sf.* saliva, spittle.

salivare *agg.* salivary.

salivare *vi.* to salivate.

salivazione *sf.* salivation.

salma *sf.* corpse.

salmastro *agg.* saltish.

salmo *sm.* psalm.

salmodìa *sf.* psalmody.

salmodiare *vi.* to sing (*v. irr.*) psalms.

salmone *sm.* salmon.

salnitro *sm.* saltpetre.

salone *sm.* large hall, reception--room.

salottiero *agg.* drawing-room (*attr.*).

salotto *sm.* sitting-room.

salpare *vi.* to set (*v. irr.*) sails.

salsa *sf.* sauce.

salsèdine *sf.* saltness.

salsiccia *sf.* sausage.

salsiera *sf.* sauce-boat.

salso *agg.* salt (*attr.*).

saltare *vt.* e *vi.* to jump, to leap (*v. irr.*): — di palo in frasca, to jump from one subject to another; far — una serratura, to break (*v. irr.*) a lock.

saltatore *agg.* jumping. ♦ **saltatore** *sm.* jumper.

saltellare *vi.* to hop.

saltimbanco *sm.* tumbler.

salto *sm.* jump, leap.

saltuario *agg.* desultory.

salubre *agg.* healthy.

salubrità *sf.* healthiness.

salume *sm.* salted meat.

salumiere *sm.* delicatessen seller.

salumeria *sf.* delicatessen.

salutare[1] *agg.* healthy.

salutare[2] *vt.* to greet, to hail.

salute *sf.* health.

saluto *sm.* greeting, salute.

salva *sf.* volley (*anche fig.*): colpo a —, blank shot.

salvacondotto *sm.* safe-conduct.

salvadanaio *sm.* money-box.

salvagente *sm.* **1.** life-belt **2.** (*marciapiede*) traffic island.

salvaguardare *vt.* to safeguard.

salvaguardia *sf.* safeguard.

salvare *vt.* **1.** to save (*anche fig.*) **2.** (*trarre in salvo*) to rescue. ♦ **salvarsi** *vr.* to save oneself.

salvataggio *sm.* rescue.

salvatore *sm.* saviour, saver.

salve *inter.* hail.

salvezza *sf.* salvation.

salvia *sf.* sage.

salvietta *sf.* towel.

salvo *agg.* safe. ♦ **salvo** *prep.* except, save. ♦ **salvo che** *cong.* except that, unless.

sanàbile *agg.* curable, remediable.

sanare *vt.* to heal.

sanatorio *sm.* sanatorium (*pl.* -ia).

sancire *vt.* to sanction.

sanculotto *sm.* sansculotte.

sàndalo¹ *sm.* (*calzatura*) sandal.

sàndalo² *sm.* (*mar.*) punt.

sandolino *sm.* small canoe.

sangue *sm.* blood: *spargimento di* —, bloodshed; *perdita di* —, bleeding; — *freddo*, coolness; *a* — *freddo*, in cold blood; *farsi cattivo* —, to worry over; *buon* — *non mente*, blood will tell.

sanguigno *agg.* sanguineous, blood (*attr.*).

sanguinaccio *sm.* blood-sausage.

sanguinante *agg.* bleeding.

sanguinare *vi.* to bleed (*v. irr.*).

sanguinario *agg.* e *sm.* sanguinary: *uomo* —, bloodthirsty man.

sanguinoso *agg.* bloody.

sanguisuga *sf.* leech.

sanità *sf.* soundness, sanity.

sanitario *agg.* sanitary.

sano *agg.* 1. healthy 2. (*fig.*) sound 3. (*intero, intatto*) intact.

sansa *sf.* husk.

sànscrito *sm.* Sanskrit.

santarellina *sf.* goody-goody.

santificante *agg.* sanctifying.

santificare *vt.* to canonize: — *le feste*, to observe holy days.

santificazione *sf.* sanctification.

santino *sm.* small holy picture.

santìssimo *agg.* most holy: *il* — *Sacramento*, the Blessed Sacrament.

santità *sf.* holiness.

santo *agg.* 1. holy 2. (*seguito da nome proprio*) saint. ♦ **santo** *sm.* saint.

santone *sm.* santon.

santuario *sm.* sanctuary.

sanzionare *vt.* to ratify.

sanzione *sf.* sanction.

sapere¹ *vt.* 1. to know (*v. irr.*): *non* — *che fare*, to be at a loss what to do; *chi sa!*, who knows!; *non si sa mai*, you never know; *venire a* —, to hear (*v. irr.*) 2. (*essere capace*) can, to be able: *sai parlare inglese?*, can you speak English?; *non so farlo*, I am not able to do it. ♦ **sapere** *vi.* (*aver sapore*) to taste.

sapere² *sm.* 1. knowledge 2. (*cultura*) learning.

sàpido *agg.* sapid.

sapiente *agg.* wise. ♦ **sapiente** *sm.* sage.

sapienza *sf.* wisdom.

saponaria *sf.* soapwort.

saponata *sf.* lather (*solo sing.*).

sapone *sm.* soap: — *da barba*, shaving-soap; — *da bagno*, bath soap.

saponetta *sf.* cake of soap.

saponificare *vt.* to saponify.

saponificazione *sf.* saponification.

saponificio *sm.* soap-works (*pl. con costruzione sing.*).

sapore *sm.* taste, flavour (*anche fig.*).

saporire *vt.* to flavour.

saporitamente *avv.* savourily || *dormire* —, to sleep (*v. irr.*) soundly.

saporito *agg.* savoury, tasty.

saputello *sm.* wiseacre.

saputo *agg.* 1. learned 2. (*noto*) well-known.

sarabanda *sf.* saraband.

saraceno *sm.* saracen.

saracinesca *sf.* rolling-shutter.

sarcasmo *sm.* sarcasm.

sarcàstico *agg.* sarcastic.

sarchiare *vt.* to weed.

sarchiatore *agg.* weeding. ♦ **sarchiatore** *sm.* weeder.

sarchiatura *sf.* weeding.

sarchio *sm.* hoe.

sarcòfago *sm.* sarcophagus (*pl.* -gi).

sardina *sf.* sardine.

sardònico *agg.* sardonic.

sarmento *sm.* runner.

sarta *sf.* dressmaker.

sartie *sf. pl.* shrouds.

sartina *sf.* grisette.

sarto *sm.* tailor.

sartorìa *sf.* 1. (*da uomo*) tailor's 2. (*da donna*) dressmaker's.

sassaia *sf.* stony place.

sassaiuola *sf.* 1. shower of stones 2. (*battaglia di sassi*) stone-fight.

sassata *sf.* blow with a stone.

sasso *sm.* stone: *a un tiro di* — *da*, within a stone's throw of.

sassofonista *sm.* saxophonist.

sassòfono *sm.* saxophone.

sassolino *sm.* pebble.

sàssone *agg.* e *sm.* Saxon.

sassoso agg. stony.

satànico agg. Satanic.

satèllite sm. satellite.

sàtira sf. satire.

satìrico agg. satirical.

sàtiro sm. satyr.

satollare vt. to satiate.

satollo agg. satiated.

sàtrapo sm. satrap.

saturare vt. to saturate.

saturazione sf. saturation.

saturnali sm. pl. saturnalia.

sàturo agg. saturated.

sàuro agg. sorrel.

savana sf. savannah.

savio agg. wise. ♦ **savio** sm. sage.

saziàbile agg. satiable.

saziare vt. to satisfy, to glut. ♦ **saziarsi** vr. to get (v. irr.) full.

sazietà sf. satiety: mangiare, bere a —, to eat (v. irr.), to drink (v. irr.) one's fill.

sazio agg. replete, full.

sbaciucchiare vt. to smother with kisses.

sbadatàggine sf. carelessness.

sbadato agg. careless.

sbadigliare vi. to yawn.

sbadiglio sm. yawn.

sbafare vi. to scrounge.

sbafatore sm. scrounger.

sbafo (nella loc. avv.) prendere qc. a —, to scrounge sthg.

sbagliare vi. to mistake (v. irr.). ♦ **sbagliarsi** vr. to make (v. irr.) a mistake.

sbagliato agg. wrong.

sbaglio sm. mistake.

sbalestrare vt. 1. to send (v. irr.) 2. (fig.) to flounder.

sballare vt. to unpack.

sballato agg. (fig.) foolhardy.

sballottamento sm. jolting.

sballottare vt. to jolt (about), to toss (about).

sbalordimento sm. amazement.

sbalordire vt. to amaze.

sbalorditivo agg. amazing.

sbalordito agg. amazed.

sbalzamento sm. 1. overthrow 2. (fig.) dismissal.

sbalzare¹ vt. to throw (v. irr.), to toss.

sbalzare² vt. (arte) to emboss.

sbalzato agg. (arte) embossed.

sbalzo sm. 1. bound, jump 2. (cambio) change.

sbancare vt. to leave (v. irr.) broke.

sbandamento sm. 1. dispersal 2. (auto) skid 3. (mar.) list.

sbandare vt. 1. to disperse 2. (auto) to cause a skid.

sbandata sf. V. sbandamento.

sbandato sm. straggler.

sbandierare vt. (fig.) to display.

sbaragliare vt. to rout.

sbaraglio sm. jeopardy: mettere allo —, to jeopardize.

sbarazzare vt. to clear up. ♦ **sbarazzarsi** vr. to get (v. irr.) rid (of).

sbarazzino agg. free and easy. ♦ **sbarazzino** sm. little scamp.

sbarbare vt. to shave.

sbarbatello sm. young colt.

sbarcare v. e vi. to land, to disembark.

sbarco sm. 1. (di passeggeri) landing 2. (di merci) unloading.

sbarra sf. 1. bar 2. (del timone) tiller.

sbarramento sm. 1. barricade 2. (di acque) dam 3. (mil.) barrage.

sbarrare vt. 1. to bar: — un assegno, to cross a cheque 2. (spalancare) to open wide.

sbarrato agg. blocked || occhi sbarrati, wide open eyes.

sbattacchiamento sm. banging, slamming.

sbattacchiare vt. to bang, to slam.

sbàttere vt. 1. (urtare contro) to knock 2. (scaraventare) to throw (v. irr.) 3. (chiudere violentemente) to slam 4. (di panna, uova) to whip, to beat (v. irr.).

sbattezzare vt. to force to abjure Christianity.

sbattimento sm. banging.

sbattiuova sm. egg-whisk.

sbattuto agg. 1. depressed: viso —, tired face 2. (di uova) beaten.

sbavare vi. 1. to dribble 2. (tip.) to smudge.

sbavatura sf. 1. dribble 2. (tip.) smudge.

sbellicarsi vr. — dalle risa, to split (v. irr.) one's sides with laughter.

sbendare vt. to unbandage.

sberla sf. slap.

sberleffo sm. grimace.

sbertucciare vt. 1. to mock 2. (sgualcire) to crumple.

sbiadire vi. to fade.

sbiancare vt. to bleach. ♦ **sbiancare** vi. to turn white. ♦ **sbiancarsi** vr. to turn white.

sbieco *agg.* slanting: *guardare qu. di* —, to look askance at so.; *tagliare una stoffa di* —, to cut (*v. irr.*) a cloth on the bias.

sbigottimento *sm.* dismay.

sbigottire *vt.* to dismay. ♦ **sbigottirsi** *vr.* to be dismayed.

sbigottito *agg.* dismayed.

sbilanciare *vt.* to unbalance. ♦ **sbilanciarsi** *vr.* 1. to lose (*v. irr.*) one's balance 2. (*fig.*) to commit oneself.

sbilancio *sm.* lack of balance; disproportion.

sbilenco *agg.* crooked.

sbirciare *vt.* to cast (*v. irr.*) a sidelong glance.

sbirraglia *sf.* police (*us. al pl.*).

sbirro *sm.* policeman (*pl. -men*).

sbizzarrirsi *vr.* to satisfy one's whims.

sbloccare *vt.* to raise the blockade: — *gli affitti*, to decontrol rents.

sblocco *sm.* 1. raising the blockade 2. (*mecc.*) releasing the brake 3. (*econ.*) decontrol.

sboccare *vi.* 1. (*di corso d'acqua*) to flow 2. (*di strada*) to lead (*v. irr.*).

sboccato *agg.* (*fig.*) coarse.

sbocciare *vi.* to open, to blossom.

sboccio *sm.* blooming.

sbocco *sm.* outlet, exit.

sboccconcellare *vt.* to nibble.

sbollire *vi.* (*fig.*) to cool down.

sbolognare *vt.* to palm off.

sbornia *sf.* drunkenness: *prendere la* —, to get (*v. irr.*) drunk.

sborsamento *sm.* paying out.

sborsare *vt.* to pay (*v. irr.*) out.

sborso *sm.* 1. payment 2. (*denaro sborsato*) outlay.

sbottare *vi.* to burst (*v. irr.*) out.

sbotto *sm.* outburst.

sbottonare *vt.* to unbutton. ♦ **sbottonarsi** *vr.* 1. to undo (*v. irr.*) one's buttons 2. (*fig.*) to disclose one's feelings.

sbozzare *vt.* to sketch out.

sbracare *vt.* to unbreech.

sbracato *agg.* (*fig.*) unseemly.

sbracciare *vi.* to gesticulate. ♦ **sbracciarsi** *vr.* 1. to roll up one's sleeves 2. (*agitarsi*) to strive (*v. irr.*).

sbracciato *agg.* (*di persona*) with bare arms.

sbraitare *vi.* to shout.

sbranamento *sm.* tearing to pieces.

sbranare *vt.* to tear (*v. irr.*) to pieces.

sbrancare *vt.* to separate. ♦ **sbrancarsi** *vr.* to scatter.

sbrattare *vt.* to clean.

sbriciolamento *sm.* crumbling.

sbriciolare *vt.* to crumble.

sbrigare *vt.* to finish off, to get (*v. irr.*) through. ♦ **sbrigarsi** *vr.* to hurry up.

sbrigativo *agg.* quick, hasty.

sbrigliare *vt.* to unbridle.

sbrinamento *sm.* defrosting.

sbrinare *vt.* to defrost.

sbrindellare *vt.* to tear (*v. irr.*) to ribbons.

sbrodolare *vt.* to spill (*v. irr.*).

sbrodolone *sm.* 1. slovenly eater 2. (*chi parla a lungo*) babbler.

sbrogliare *vt.* to disentangle. ♦ **sbrogliarsi** *vr.* to extricate oneself.

sbronza *sf.* V. *sbornia*.

sbronzarsi *vr.* to get (*v. irr.*) drunk.

sbronzo *agg.* drunk.

sbruffare *vt.* to besprinkle. ♦ **sbruffare** *vi.* (*fig.*) to brag.

sbruffo *sm.* sprinkle.

sbruffone *sm.* braggart.

sbucare *vi.* 1. to come (*v. irr.*) out 2. (*fig.*) to spring (*v. irr.*).

sbucciare *vt.* 1. to peel 2. (*sgranare*) to shell.

sbucciatura *sf.* 1. peeling 2. (*scalfittura*) scratch.

sbudellamento *sm.* stabbing.

sbudellare *vt.* to stab.

sbuffare *vi.* 1. to pant, to puff 2. (*per noia, ira*) to snort.

sbuffo *sm.* 1. puff 2. (*per noia, ira*) snort.

sbugiardare *vt.* to give (*v. irr.*) the lie to.

sbullonare *vt.* to unbolt.

scabbia *sf.* scabies.

scabbioso *agg.* scabby.

scabro *agg.* rough.

scabrosità *sf.* 1. roughness 2. (*fig.*) difficulty.

scabroso *agg.* 1. rough 2. (*fig.*) scabrous.

scacchiera *sf.* chess-board.

scacchiere *sm.* (*stor.*) Exchequer.

scacchista *sm.* chess-player.

scaccacani *sf.* dummy pistol.

scacciare *vt.* 1. to drive (*v. irr.*) away 2. (*da scuola*) to expel.

scacciata *sf.* expulsion.

scaccino *sm.* church cleaner.

scacco *sm.* **1.** (*quadratino*) square **2.** (*disegno su tessuti*) check **3.** (*giuoco*) chess || — *matto*, checkmate.

scadente *agg.* **1.** poor **2.** (*comm.*) falling due.

scadenza *sf.* (*comm.*) maturity: *a breve, lunga scadenza* (*comm.*), at short, long maturity || *a breve* —, in a short time.

scadenzario *sm.* discount bill-book.

scadere *vi.* **1.** to expire **2.** (*di pagamenti ecc.*) to become (*v. irr.*) due **3.** (*peggiorare*) to fall (*v. irr.*) off.

scadimento *sm.* decay.

scafandro *sm.* diving-suit.

scaffalare *vt.* to shelve.

scaffalatura *sf.* shelving.

scaffale *sm.* shelf (*pl.* shelves).

scafo *sm.* hull, body.

scagionare *vt.* to acquit. ♦ **scagionarsi** *vr.* to exculpate oneself.

scaglia *sf.* **1.** scale **2.** (*di legno, pietra*) chip.

scagliare *vt.* to fling (*v. irr.*), to throw (*v. irr.*).

scaglionare *vt.* to divide into groups.

scaglione *sm.* **1.** group **2.** (*mil.*) echelon.

scaglioso *agg.* scaly.

scala *sf.* **1.** stairs (*pl.*) **2.** (*trasportabile*) ladder **3.** (*scala graduata*) scale || *salire, scendere le scale*, to go (*v. irr.*) upstairs, downstairs.

scalare[1] *agg.* gradual.

scalare[2] *vt.* **1.** to climb (up) **2.** (*diminuire*) to scale down.

scalata *sf.* climbing.

scalatore *sm.* climber.

scalcagnato *agg.* down-at-heel, shabby.

scalciare *vi.* to kick.

scalcinato *agg.* **1.** unplastered **2.** (*sciatto*) shabby.

scaldabagno *sm.* water-heater.

scaldaletto *sm.* bed-warmer.

scaldapiedi *sm.* foot-warmer.

scaldare *vt.* to heat, to warm. ♦ **scaldarsi** *vr.* to warm oneself, to get (*v. irr.*) warm.

scaldavivande *sm.* dish-warmer.

scaldino *sm.* hand-warmer.

scalea *sf.* flight of stairs.

scaleno *agg.* scalene.

scalfire *vt.* to scratch.

scalfittura *sf.* scratch.

scalinata *sf.* flight of steps.

scalino *sm.* step.

scalmanarsi *vr.* (*fig.*) to get (*v. irr.*) excited.

scalmanato *agg.* out of breath, excited.

scalmo *sm.* rowlock.

scalo *sm.* **1.** (*mar.; aer.*) port of call: *volo senza* —, non-stop flight **2.** (*ferr.*) goods station || *fare* — *a*, to touch at.

scalogna *sf.* bad luck.

scalognato *agg.* unlucky.

scalone *sm.* great staircase.

scaloppina *sf.* veal cutlet.

scalpellare *vt.* to chisel.

scalpellino *sm.* stone-cutter.

scalpello *sm.* chisel.

scalpicciare *vi.* to shuffle.

scalpiccio *sm.* shuffling.

scalpitare *vi.* **1.** to paw **2.** (*di persona*) to stamp.

scalpitìo *sm.* **1.** pawing **2.** (*di persona*) stamping.

scalpore *sm.* fuss, noise.

scaltrezza *sf.* shrewdness.

scaltrire *vt.* to sharpen so.'s wits. ♦ **scaltrirsi** *vr.* to become (*v. irr.*) sharp.

scaltro *agg.* shrewd.

scalzacane *sm.* **1.** (*incompetente*) botcher **2.** (*malridotto*) down-and-out.

scalzare *vt.* **1.** to take (*v. irr.*) so.'s shoes and socks off **2.** (*fig.*) to undermine.

scalzo *agg.* barefoot.

scambiare *vt.* **1.** to exchange **2.** (*sbagliarsi*) to mistake (*v. irr.*).

scambiévole *agg.* reciprocal.

scambio *sm.* **1.** exchange **2.** (*ferr.*) points (*pl.*).

scambista *sm.* (*ferr.*) pointsman (*pl.* -men).

scamiciato *agg.* shirt-sleeved (*attr.*).

scamosciare *vt.* to chamois.

scamosciato *agg.* shammy.

scampagnata *sf.* trip into the country.

scampanare *vi.* to chime.

scampanellare *vi.* to ring (*v. irr.*) long and loudly.

scampanellata *sf.* loud long ring.

scampare *vi.* to escape || *l'hai scampata bella!*, you have had a narrow escape.

scampato *sm.* survivor.

scampo[1] *sm.* escape: *via di* —, escape.

scampo² *sm.* (*itt.*) shrimp.

scàmpolo *sm.* remnant.

scanalare *vt.* to channel.

scanalatura *sf.* groove.

scandagliare *vt.* to sound.

scandaglio *sm.* sounding-lead.

scandalizzare *vt.* to shock.

scandalizzato *agg.* shocked.

scàndalo *sm.* scandal: *fare uno —,* to stir up a scandal.

scandaloso *agg.* scandalous, shocking.

scandire *vt.* **1.** to scan **2.** (*parole*) to syllabize **3.** (*mus.*) to stress.

scannare *vt.* **1.** to cut (*v. irr.*) **2.** (*uccidere crudelmente*) to slaughter.

scannatoio *sm.* slaughter-house.

scanno *sm.* seat.

scansafatiche *sm.* lazy-bones.

scansare *vt.* to avoid, to shun. ♦ **scansarsi** *vr.* to step aside.

scansìa *sf.* shelves (*pl.*).

scantinato *sm.* basement.

scantonamento *sm.* (*l'evitare*) avoiding.

scantonare *vt.* (*evitare*) to avoid. ♦ **scantonare** *vi.* to turn the corner.

scanzonato *agg.* unconventional.

scapaccione *sm.* slap.

scapataggine *sf.* recklessness.

scapestrato *agg. e sm.* madcap.

scapigliare *vt.* to dishevel.

scapigliato *agg.* **1.** dishevelled **2.** (*fig.*) unruly.

scàpito *sm.* damage, detriment: *a — di,* to the detriment of.

scàpola *sf.* shoulder-blade.

scapolare *agg. e sm.* scapular.

scàpolo *agg.* single. ♦ **scàpolo** *sm.* bachelor.

scappamento *sm.* **1.** escape **2.** (*di motori*) exhaust.

scappare *vi.* to escape, to run (*v. irr.*) away ‖ *lasciarsi —,* to miss.

scappata *sf.* **1.** escape **2.** (*breve visita*) call.

scappatella *sf.* prank.

scappatoia *sf.* loop-hole.

scappellarsi *vr.* to take (*v. irr.*) off one's hat.

scappellata *sf.* raising one's hat.

scappellotto *sm.* slap.

scarabeo *sm.* scarab.

scarabocchiare *vt. e vi.* to scribble.

scarabocchio *sm.* scribble.

scarafaggio *sm.* black-beetle.

scaramanzìa *sf. per —,* for luck.

scaramuccia *sf.* skirmish.

scaraventare *vt.* to hurl.

scarcerare *vt.* to release (from prison).

scarcerazione *sf.* release (from prison).

scardinare *vt.* to unhinge.

scàrica *sf.* **1.** (*di armi da fuoco; elettr.*) discharge **2.** (*di proiettili, frecce; fig.*) shower.

scaricabarilli *sm. fare a —,* to lay (*v. irr.*) the blame on so. else.

scaricamento *sm.* unloading.

scaricare *vt.* to discharge.

scaricatoio *sm.* **1.** wharf **2.** (*tubo*) waste-pipe.

scaricatore *sm.* unloader: *— di porto,* docker.

scàrico *sm.* **1.** (*scolo*) drain **2.** (*di merci*) discharge. ♦ **scàrico** *agg.* **1.** (*di arma*) unloaded **2.** discharged.

scarlattina *sf.* scarlet fever.

scarlatto *agg.* scarlet.

scarmigliare *vt.* to dishevel.

scarnire *vt.* to take (*v. irr.*) flesh off.

scarno *agg.* thin, lean.

scarpa *sf.* shoe: *— col tacco alto,* high-heeled shoe; *lucido per scarpe,* shoe polish.

scarpata *sf.* scarp.

scarpone *sm.* boot.

scarroccio *sm.* (*mar.*) leeway.

scarrozzare *vt. e vi.* to drive (*v. irr.*) about.

scarsamente *avv.* scarcely.

scarseggiare *vi.* to be lacking (in).

scarsità *sf.* shortage, lack.

scarso *agg.* scanty, lacking in.

scartabellare *vt.* to look through.

scartafaccio *sm.* note-book.

scartamento *sm.* (*ferr.*) gauge: *— ridotto,* narrow gauge.

scartare¹ *vt.* (*mettere da parte*) to reject.

scartare² *vi.* to unwrap.

scartare³ *vt.* (*sport*) to swerve.

scarto¹ *sm.* **1.** (*cosa scartata*) discard **2.** (*lo scartare*) discarding.

scarto² *sm.* (*deviazione*) swerve.

scartocciare *vt.* to unwrap.

scartoffie *sf. pl.* heap of papers.

scassare *vt.* (*rompere*) to force open.

scassinare *vt.* to break (*v. irr.*) open.

scassinatore *sm.* **1.** house-breaker **2.** (*di notte*) burglar.

scasso *sm.* lock-picking, house--breaking: *furto con* — (*di giorno*), house-breaking; (*di notte*) burglary.

scatenamento *sm.* (*fig.*) outburst.

scatenare *vt.* 1. (*aizzare*) to stir up 2. (*suscitare*) to rouse. ♦ **scatenarsi** *vr.* 1. to break (*v. irr.*) loose 2. (*fig.*) to break out.

scàtola *sf.* 1. box 2. (*di latta*) tin.

scatolame *sm.* 1. tins (*pl.*) 2. (*cibo in scatola*) tinned food.

scattare *vi.* 1. (*adirarsi*) to lose (*v. irr.*) one's temper 2. to go (*v. irr.*) off; to spring (*v. irr.*). ♦ **scattare** *vt.* (*foto*) to shoot (*v. irr.*).

scatto *sm.* 1. (*d'ira*) outburst || *di* —, suddenly; *a scatti*, in jerks 2. (*rumore*) click 3. (*di stipendio*) increase.

scaturire *vi.* 1. to spring (*v. irr.*) 2. (*derivare*) to originate.

scavalcare *vt.* 1. (*gettare da cavallo*) to unhorse 2. (*fig.*) to supplant 3. (*passare sopra*) to step, to jump over.

scavare *vt.* 1. to dig (*v. irr.*) 2. (*archeologia*) to excavate.

scavatrice *sf.* excavator.

scavezzacollo *sm.* reckless fellow.

scavo *sm.* 1. digging 2. (*archeologia*) excavation.

scégliere *vt.* to choose (*v. irr.*), to pick out.

sceicco *sm.* sheik.

scelleratezza *sf.* 1. wickedness 2. (*atto scellerato*) misdeed.

scellerato *agg.* wicked. ♦ **scellerato** *sm.* wicked person.

scellino *sm.* shilling: *mezzo* —, sixpence.

scelta *sf.* choice.

scelto *agg.* choice, selected.

scemare *vi.* to diminish.

scemenza *sf.* stupidity.

scemo *agg.* e *sm.* stupid.

scempiare *vt.* to halve.

scempio¹ *agg.* stupid, foolish.

scempio² *sm.* havoc.

scena *sf.* 1. scene 2. (*palcoscenico*) stage: *colpo di* —, stage effect.

scenario *sm.* scenery.

scenata *sf.* row.

scéndere *vi.* 1. to go (*v. irr.*) down, to come (*v. irr.*) down 2. (*da un veicolo*) to get (*v. irr.*) off; (*da cavallo*), to dismount (from a horse) 3. (*declinare*) to slope down 4. (*di astri*) to sink (*v. irr.*) 5. (*avere origini*) to descend.

scendiletto *sm.* bedside-carpet.

sceneggiare *vt.* to arrange into scenes.

sceneggiatore *sm.* scenarist.

sceneggiatura *sf.* screenplay.

scenicamente *avv.* scenically.

scenografia *sf.* scenography.

scèrnere *vt.* to choose (*v. irr.*).

scervellarsi *vr.* to rack one's brains.

scervellato *agg.* brainless. ♦ **scervellato** *sm.* brainless person.

scetticismo *sm.* scepticism.

scèttico *agg.* sceptical. ♦ **scèttico** *sm.* sceptic.

scettro *sm.* sceptre.

sceverare *vt.* to discern.

scevro *agg.* exempt.

scheda *sf.* card: — *elettorale*, voting-paper.

schedario *sm.* card-index.

scheggia *sf.* splinter, chip.

scheggiare *vt.* to chip, to splinter.

scheletrico *agg.* skeletal.

schèletro *sm.* skeleton.

schema *sm.* 1. scheme 2. (*tec.*) diagram.

schemàtico *agg.* schematic.

schematismo *sm.* schematism.

scherma *sf.* fencing.

schermaglia *sf.* skirmish.

schermare *vt.* 1. to screen 2. (*elettr.*) to shield.

schermirsi *vr.* to act coy.

schermitore *sm.* fencer.

schermo *sm.* 1. protection 2. (*cine*) screen 3. (*fis.*) shield 4. (*foto*) filter.

schernire *vt.* to laugh at.

scherno *sm.* mockery, derision.

scherzare *vi.* 1. to joke 2. (*considerare con leggerezza*) to trifle with.

scherzo *sm.* 1. joke: *per* —, for fun 2. (*effetto*) effects (*pl.*).

scherzosamente *avv.* playfully.

scherzoso *agg.* playful.

schettinare *vi.* to roller-skate.

schettini *sm. pl.* roller-skates.

schiaccianoci *sm.* nut-cracker.

schiacciante *agg.* (*decisivo*) overwhelming.

schiacciare *vt.* to crush, to squash.

schiacciasassi *sm.* steam-roller.

schiaffare *vt.* to hurl.

schiaffeggiare *vt.* to slap.

schiaffo *sm.* 1. slap 2. (*affronto*) slap in the face.

schiamazzare *vi.* to make (*v. irr.*) a din.

schiamazzo *sm.* din, uproar.

schiantare vt. to break (v. irr.). ♦ **schiantarsi** vr. to break, to crash.

schiarimento sm. (spiegazione) explanation.

schiarire vt. to clear, to make (v. irr.) clear: — i capelli, to bleach one's hair. ♦ **schiarirsi** vr. (fig.) to brighten.

schiarita sf. 1. clearing 2. (miglioramento) improvement.

schiattare vi. to burst: — di rabbia, to burst with rage.

schiavista sm. 1. anti-abolitionist 2. (mercante di schiavi) slave-trader.

schiavitù sf. slavery.

schiavo agg. e sm. slave.

schidionata sf. spitful.

schidione sm. spit.

schiena sf. 1. back 2. (di monte) ridge.

schienale sm. back.

schiera sf. 1. formation 2. (gruppo di persone) group.

schieramento sm. array.

schierare vt. to array. ♦ **schierarsi** vr. 1. to draw (v. irr.) up 2. (parteggiare) to side with.

schiettezza sf. openness, purity.

schietto agg. pure, open.

schifare vt. to loathe. ♦ **schifarsi** vr. to feel (v. irr.) disgusted (at).

schifezza sf. disgusting thing.

schifiltoso agg. squeamish.

schifo[1] sm. disgust.

schifo[2] sm. (mar.) skiff.

schifoso agg. disgusting.

schioccare vi. 1. to crack 2. (le dita) to snap 3. (le labbra) to smack.

schiocco sm. 1. crack 2. (di labbra) smack.

schiodare vt. to unnail.

schiodatura sf. unnailing.

schioppettata sf. shot.

schioppo sm. gun.

schiùdere vt. to open. ♦ **schiùdersi** vr. to open.

schiuma sf. 1. foam 2. (di vino, birra) froth 3. (di sapone) lather.

schiumare vt. to skim. ♦ **schiumare** vi. 1. to foam 2. (di bevande) to froth.

schiumarola sf. skimmer.

schiumoso agg. 1. (di mare) foamy 2. (di bevande) frothy 3. (di sapone) lathery.

schiuso agg. open.

schivare vt. to avoid.

schivata sf. dodge.

schivo agg. shy, bashful.

schizofrenia sf. schizophrenia. ♦

schizofrenico agg. schizophrenic. ♦ **schizofrenico** sm. schizophrene.

schizzare vt. 1. to splash, to spatter 2. (abbozzare) to sketch. ♦ **schizzare** vi. to spurt.

schizzata sf. splashing.

schizzatoio sm. spray.

schizzetto sm. spray.

schizzinoso agg. squeamish, fussy.

schizzo sm. 1. splash, squirt 2. (pitt.) sketch.

sci sm. ski.

scia sf. 1. (mar.) wake 2. (traccia) trail.

scià sm. shah.

sciàbica sf. trawl.

sciàbola sf. sabre.

sciabolata sf. sabre-cut.

sciabolatore sm. sabreur.

sciabordare vi. to wash.

sciabordìo sm. washing, lapping.

sciacallo sm. 1. jackal 2. (fig.) profiteer.

sciacquare vt. to rinse (out).

sciacquatura sf. 1. rinsing 2. (acqua) rinsing-water.

sciacquìo sm. rinsing.

sciacquone sm. flush.

sciagura sf. misfortune.

sciagurato agg. 1. unlucky 2. (malvagio) wicked. ♦ **sciagurato** sm. wretch.

scialacquare vt. to squander.

scialacquatore sm. squanderer.

scialacquìo sm. squandering.

scialare vt. to squander money.

scialbare vt. to plaster.

scialbo agg. pale, wan.

scialle sm. shawl.

scialo sm. waste.

scialuppa sf. boat.

sciamannato agg. slovenly.

sciamano sm. shaman.

sciamare vi. to swarm.

sciame sm. swarm.

sciancarsi vr. to become (v. irr.) lame.

sciancato agg. lame.

sciarada sf. charade.

sciare[1] vi. to ski.

sciare[2] vi. (mar.) to back water.

sciarpa sf. scarf.

sciàtica sf. sciatica.

sciàtico agg. sciatic.

sciatore sm. skier.

sciatterìa *sf.* slovenliness.

sciatto *agg.* 1. slovenly, untidy 2. (*di stile ecc.*) careless.

scibile *sm.* knowledge.

sciccherìa *sf.* smartness.

scientìfico *agg.* scientific.

scienza *sf.* science.

scienziato *sm.* scientist.

scilinguàgnolo *sm.* glib tongue.

scimitarra *sf.* scimitar.

scimmia *sf.* monkey, ape (*anche fig.*).

scimmiesco *agg.* monkeyish.

scimmiottare *vt.* to ape.

scimmiotto *sm.* young monkey.

scimpanzé *sm.* chimpanzee.

scimunito *agg.* silly. ◆ scimunito *sm.* blockhead.

scìndere *vt.* to divide: — *le questioni*, to deal (*v. irr.*) with each matter separately.

scintilla *sf.* spark.

scintillamento *sm.* sparkling.

scintillante *agg.* sparkling.

scintillare *vi.* to sparkle.

scintillìo *sm.* sparkling.

scintoismo *sm.* Shintoism.

scintoista *sm.* Shintoist.

scioccamente *avv.* foolishly.

scioccchezza *sf.* 1. foolishness 2. foolish thing 3. trifle.

sciocco *agg.* silly.

sciògliere *vt.* 1. to melt 2. (*slegare, disfare*) to untie 3. (*liberare*) to release 4. (*risolvere*) to solve. ◆ sciògliersi *vr.* to dissolve, to get (*v. irr.*) loose.

scioglilingua *sm.* tongue-twister.

scioglimento *sm.* 1. dissolution, breaking up 2. (*epilogo*) unravelling.

sciolina *sf.* ski wax.

scioltezza *sf.* 1. agility 2. (*spigliatezza*) ease 3. (*nel parlare*) fluency.

sciolto *agg.* 1. melted 2. (*slegato*) untied 3. (*agile*) agile 4. (*disinvolto*) easy || *capelli sciolti*, loose hair; *avere la lingua sciolta*, to have a ready tongue; — *da obblighi*, free from obligations.

scioperante *sm.* striker.

scioperare *vi.* to strike (*v. irr.*).

scioperataggine *sf.* laziness.

scioperato *agg.* lazy. ◆ scioperato *sm.* lazy fellow.

sciòpero *sm.* strike.

sciorinare *vt.* to air, to display (*anche fig.*).

sciovìa *sf.* ski-lift.

scivinismo *sm.* chauvinism.

sciovinista *sm.* chauvinist.

scipitàggine *sf.* insipidity (*anche fig.*).

scipito *agg.* insipid.

scirocco *sm.* sirocco.

sciroppare *vt.* to syrup.

sciroppato *agg.* in syrup.

sciropposo *agg.* syrupy.

scisma *sm.* schism.

scismàtico *agg. e sm.* schismatic.

scissione *sf.* 1. scission, split (*anche fig.*) 2. (*fis.; biol.*) fission.

scisso *agg.* divided.

scissura *sf.* 1. cleft, split 2. (*fig.*) dissension.

sciupare *vt.* 1. to spoil (*v. irr.*), to damage 2. (*sprecare*) to waste.

sciupato *agg.* 1. spoilt 2. (*sprecato*) wasted.

sciupìo *sm.* waste.

sciupone *agg.* wasteful. ◆ sciupone *sm.* waster.

scivolamento *sm.* sliding.

scivolare *vi.* 1. to slide (*v. irr.*) 2. (*involontariamente*) to slip.

scivolata *sf.* 1. slide 2. (*involontaria*) slip.

scivolo *sm.* 1. (*aer.; mar.*) slipway 2. skid.

scivolone *sm.* slip.

scivoloso *agg.* slippery.

sclerosi *sf.* sclerosis.

scleròtica *sf.* sclerotic.

scleròtico *agg.* sclerotic.

scoccare *vt. e vi.* 1. to shoot (*v. irr.*) 2. (*l'ora*) to strike (*v. irr.*).

scocciare *vt.* to bother.

scocciatore *sm.* bore.

scocciatura *sf.* bother.

scodella *sf.* bowl.

scodellare *vt.* to dish up.

scodinzolare *vi.* to wag the tail.

scodinzolìo *sm.* tail-wagging.

scogliera *sf.* cliff.

scoglio *sm.* 1. rock 2. (*fig.*) difficulty.

scoiare *vt.* V. *scuoiare*.

scoiàttolo *sm.* squirrel.

scolapasta *sm.* colander.

scolara *sf.* pupil, schoolgirl.

scolare *vt.* 1. to drain 2. (*in un colabrodo*) to strain.

scolaresca *sf.* student-body.

scolaro *sm.* pupil, schoolboy.

scolàstica *sf.* scholasticism.

scolàstico *agg.* 1. school (*attr.*) 2. (*dispregiativo*) bookish.

scolatoio *sm.* drain.

scolatura *sf.* draining.

scoliosi *sf.* scoliosis.

scollacciato *agg.* 1. (*di abito*) low--necked 2. (*fig.*) coarse.

scollare[1] *vt.* to cut (*v. irr.*) away the neck of.

scollare[2] *vt.* (*staccare*) to unglue.

scollato[1] *agg.* (*di abito*) low-necked.

scollato[2] *agg.* unglued.

scollatura *sf.* neckline.

scollo *sm.* neck-opening.

scolo *sm.* draining.

scolorare *vt.* to discolour. ♦ **scolorarsi** *vr.* to grow (*v. irr.*) pale.

scolorimento *sm.* discolouration.

scolorire *vt.* to bleach.

scolorito *agg.* faded, pale.

scolpare *vt.* to exculpate.

scolpire *vt.* to sculpture.

scombinare *vt.* to upset (*v. irr.*).

scombinato *agg.* screwy.

scombussolamento *sm.* upsetting.

scombussolare *vt.* to upset (*v. irr.*).

scommessa *sf.* bet.

scomméttere *vt.* to bet (*v. irr.*).

scommettitore *sm.* bettor.

scomodamente *avv.* uncomfortably.

scomodare *vt.* to trouble, to bother.

scomodità *sf.* lack of comfort.

scòmodo *agg.* uncomfortable.

scompaginamento *sm.* upsetting, upset.

scompaginare *vt.* to upset (*v. irr.*).

scompagnare *vt.* to break (*v. irr.*) up (a pair).

scompagnato *agg.* odd.

scomparire *vi.* 1. to disappear 2. (*non spiccare*) not to stand (*v. irr.*) out.

scomparsa *sf.* 1. disappearance 2. (*morte*) death.

scomparso *agg.* 1. disappeared 2. (*morto*) dead.

scompartimento *sm.* 1. partition 2. (*ferr.*) compartment.

scompartire *vt.* to divide, to share out.

scomparto *sm.* V. *scompartimento*.

scompenso *sm.* lack of balance: — *cardiaco*, cardiac decompensation.

scompiacenza *sf.* unkindness.

scompigliare *vt.* 1. to upset (*v. irr.*) 2. (*arruffare*) to ruffle.

scompigliatamente *avv.* confusedly.

scompiglio *sm.* confusion, disorder.

sccomponìbile *agg.* decomposable.

scomponimento *sm.* decomposition.

scomporre *vt.* 1. to decompose 2. (*i lineamenti*) to distort.

scompostamente *avv.* in an unseemly manner.

scompostezza *sf.* unseemliness.

scomposto *agg.* 1. (*sguaiato*) unseemly 2. decomposed.

scomùnica *sf.* excommunication.

scomunicare *vt.* to excommunicate.

scomunicato *agg.* e *sm.* excommunicate.

sconcertante *agg.* disconcerting.

sconcertare *vt.* to disconcert, to baffle.

sconcertato *agg.* disconcerted.

sconcerto *sm.* perturbation.

sconcezza *sf.* indecency.

sconciamente *avv.* indecently.

sconcio *agg.* indecent.

sconclusionatamente *avv.* inconclusively.

sconclusionato *agg.* inconclusive.

scondito *agg.* 1. unseasoned 2. (*di insalata*) undressed.

sconfessare *vt.* to disown.

sconfessione *sf.* disowning.

sconfiggere *vt.* to defeat.

sconfinamento *sm.* 1. (*in paese straniero*) crossing the frontier 2. (*in proprietà privata*) trespass.

sconfinare *vi.* 1. (*in paese straniero*) to cross the frontier 2. (*in proprietà privata*) to trespass.

sconfinato *agg.* boundless.

sconfitta *sf.* defeat.

sconfitto *agg.* defeated.

sconfortante *agg.* discouraging.

sconfortare *vt.* to discourage.

sconfortato *agg.* discouraged.

sconforto *sm.* 1. discouragement 2. (*dolore*) sorrow.

scongiurare *vt.* 1. to beseech (*v. irr.*) 2. (*evitare*) to avoid.

scongiuro *sm.* exorcism.

sconnessione *sf.* disconnectedness.

sconnesso *agg.* 1. disconnected 2. (*fig.*) rambling.

sconnèttere *vt.* to disconnect. ♦ **sconnèttere** *vi.* to wander.

sconoscente *agg.* ungrateful.

sconoscenza *sf.* ingratitude.

sconòscere *vt.* to disown.

sconosciuto *agg.* unknown. ♦ **sconosciuto** *sm.* stranger.

sconquassare vt. to shatter.
sconquassato agg. ramshackle.
sconquasso sm. mess, disorder.
sconsacrare vt. to deconsecrate.
sconsideratezza sf. rashness.
sconsiderato agg. thoughtless.
sconsigliare vt. to advise against.
sconsigliato agg. rash.
sconsolante agg. discouraging.
sconsolare vt. to dishearten.
sconsolato agg. disconsolate.
scontàbile agg. discountable.
scontare vt. **1.** (comm.) to discount **2.** (detrarre) to deduct **3.** (espiare) to expiate.
scontato agg. (previsto) expected.
scontentare vt. to displease.
scontentezza sf. discontent.
scontento agg. displeased.
sconto sm. discount.
scontrarsi vr. to clash.
scontrino sm. ticket, check.
scontro sm. **1.** encounter **2.** (di veicoli) crash **3.** (fig.) clash.
scontrosamente avv. peevishly.
scontrosità sf. bad temper.
scontroso agg. bad-tempered.
sconveniente agg. **1.** unprofitable **2.** (indecente) unseemly.
sconvenientemente avv. unbecomingly.
sconvenienza sf. **1.** unprofitableness **2.** (mancanza di correttezza) unseemliness.
sconvolgente agg. upsetting.
sconvòlgere vt. to upset (v. irr.).
sconvolgimento sm. upsetting, confusion.
sconvolto agg. upset.
scopa sf. broom.
scopare vt. to sweep (v. irr.).
scoperchiare vt. to take (v. irr.) off the lid.
scoperta sf. discovery.
scopertamente avv. openly.
scoperto agg. uncovered || automobile scoperta, open car; a capo —, bare-headed; giocare a carte scoperte, to act openly.
scopino sm. street-sweeper.
scopo sm. aim, purpose: senza —, aimless.
scopolamina sf. scopolamine.
scoppiare vi. **1.** to burst (v. irr.) **2.** (di guerre, epidemie ecc.) to break (v. irr.) out.
scoppiettamento sm. crackling.
scoppiettare vi. to crackle.
scoppiettìo sm. crackling.

scoppio sm. **1.** burst, explosion: motore a —, piston-engine **2.** (di guerre, rivoluzioni ecc.) outbreak.
scoprimento sm. **1.** discovering **2.** (di monumento) unveiling.
scoprire vt. **1.** to discover **2.** (avvistare) to sight **3.** (togliere ciò che copre) to uncover **4.** (palesare) to show (v. irr.). ♦ **scoprirsi** vr. (rivelarsi) to reveal oneself.
scopritore sm. discoverer.
scoraggiamento sm. discouragement.
scoraggiante agg. discouraging.
scoraggiare vt. to discourage. ♦ **scoraggiarsi** vr. to get (v. irr.) discouraged.
scoraggiato agg. discouraged.
scoramento sm. discouragement.
scorato agg. disheartened.
scorbùtico agg. **1.** (med.) scorbutic **2.** (fig.) ill-tempered.
scorbuto sm. scurvy.
scorciare vt. to shorten.
scorciatoia sf. short cut.
scorcio sm. **1.** foreshortening **2.** (spazio di tempo) end, close.
scordare[1] vt. to forget (v. irr.).
scordare[2] vt. (mus.) to untune.
scordato[1] agg. forgotten.
scordato[2] agg. (mus.) untuned.
scòrfano sm. **1.** sea-scorpion **2.** (di persona) fright: che —!, what a fright!
scòrgere vt. to perceive, to discern.
scoria sf. **1.** (metal.) dross **2.** (fig.) scum.
scornare vt. **1.** to horn **2.** (fig.) to humiliate.
scornato agg. humiliated.
scorno sm. shame.
scorpacciata sf. blow out: fare una — di, to stuff oneself with.
scorpione sm. scorpion.
scorporare vt. to disembody.
scòrporo sm. breaking up.
scorrazzare vi. to run (v. irr.) about.
scòrrere vt. **1.** to run (v. irr.) **2.** (scivolare) to glide **3.** (fluire) to flow **4.** (di tempo) to fly (v. irr.).
scorreria sf. raid.
scorrettezza sf. incorrectness.
scorretto agg. **1.** incorrect **2.** (di costumi) dissolute **3.** (maleducato) rude.
scorrèvole agg. **1.** sliding **2.** (fig.) fluent.

scorrevolezza sf. fluency.

scorribanda sf. incursion, raid.

scorrimento sm. sliding.

scorsa sf. glance.

scorso agg. last, past.

scorsoio agg. running.

scorta sf. 1. escort 2. (provvista) supply || ruota di —, spare wheel.

scortare vt. to escort.

scortecciare vt. 1. to peel 2. (un albero) to bark.

scortese agg. rude, impolite.

scortesia sf. rudeness.

scorticare vt. to skin.

scorticatura sf. scratch.

scortichino sm. flaying-knife.

scorza sf. 1. (corteccia) bark 2. (buccia) skin, rind.

scoscéndere vt. to split (v. irr.).

scoscendimento sm. 1. collapse 2. (di terreno) break.

scosceso agg. steep, sloping.

scossa sf. shock, shake.

scosso agg. 1. shaken 2. (fig.) upset.

scossone sm. 1. shake 2. (strattone) jerk.

scostare vt. to shift, to move away.
♦ **scostarsi** vr. 1. to move away 2. (staccarsi) to turn off.

scostumatezza sf. dissoluteness.

scostumato agg. dissolute. ♦ **scostumato** sm. dissolute person.

scotennare vt. to scalp.

scottante agg. burning.

scottare vt. 1. to burn (v. irr.) 2. (cuc.) to half-cook 3. (fig.) to hurt (v. irr.).

scottatura sf. burn.

scotto[1] sm. score: pagare lo —, to pay (v. irr.) one's piper.

scotto[2] agg. overdone.

scovare vt. 1. to put (v. irr.) up 2. (scoprire) to discover.

scozzare vt. to shuffle.

scozzese agg. Scotch, Scottish. ♦ **scozzese** sm. Scotchman (pl. -men).

scozzonare vt. 1. to break (v. irr.) in 2. (fig.) to teach (v. irr.) the first elements.

screanzatamente avv. rudely.

screanzato agg. rude, impolite. ♦ **screanzato** sm. rude person.

screditare vt. to discredit.

screditato agg. discredited.

scrédito sm. discredit.

scremare vt. to skim.

scremato agg. skimmed: latte —, skim-milk.

scrematura sf. skimming.

screpolare vi. 1. to crack 2. (della pelle) to get (v. irr.) chapped.

screpolatura sf. 1. crack 2. (della pelle) chap.

screziare vt. to variegate.

screziato agg. variegated.

screziatura sf. variegation.

screzio sm. disagreement.

scribacchiare vt. e vi. to scribble.

scribacchino sm. scribbler.

scricchiolare vi. 1. to creak 2. (di denti) to grind (v. irr.).

scricchiolio sm. 1. creaking 2. (di denti) grinding.

scrigno sm. casket: — di gioielli, jewel-case.

scriminatura sf. (hair-)parting.

scriteriato agg. senseless.

scritta sf. 1. inscription 2. (cartello) notice 3. (dicitura) caption.

scritto sm. writing.

scrittoio sm. writing-desk.

scrittore sm. writer.

scrittrice sf. woman writer.

scrittura sf. 1. writing: — a macchina, typewriting; — a mano, handwriting 2. (teat.) engagement 3. (giur.) deed.

scritturare vt. to engage.

scrivania sf. writing-desk.

scrivano sm. clerk, copyist.

scrivere vt. to write (v. irr.): — a mano, to write by hand; — a penna, a matita, to write in pen, in pencil; — sotto dettatura, to write from dictation; — a macchina, to typewrite (v. irr.) 2. (registrare) to enter, to record.

scroccare vt. to scrounge.

scrocco sm. vivere a —, to sponge one's living.

scroccone sm. sponger.

scrofa sf. sow.

scrofoloso agg. scrofulous.

scrollamento sm. 1. shaking 2. (di spalle) shrugging.

scrollare vt. 1. to shake (v. irr.) 2. (le spalle) to shrug.

scrollata sf. 1. (di testa) shake 2. (di spalle) shrug.

scrosciante agg. (di risa ecc.) roaring: pioggia —, pelting rain.

scrosciare vi. 1. (di pioggia) to pelt down 2. (fig.) to roar.

scroscio sm. 1. (di cascata, torrente ecc.) roar 2. (fig.) roar, burst || — di pioggia, shower.

scrostamento sm. peeling.

scrostare vt. **1.** to take (v. irr.) the crust off, to peel off **2.** (dei muri) to remove the plaster from a wall. ♦ **scrostarsi** vr. to fall (v. irr.) off, to peel off.

scrùpolo sm. scruple.

scrupolosamente avv. scrupulously.

scrupolosità sf. scrupulosity.

scrupoloso agg. scrupulous.

scrutare vt. to search, to scan.

scrutatore agg. searching, inquisitive. ♦ **scrutatore** sm. **1.** searcher **2.** (di elezioni) scrutineer.

scrutinare vt. to scrutinize.

scrutinio sm. **1.** (di elezioni) poll **2.** (scolastico) assignment of a term's marks **3.** (attento esame) scrutiny.

scucire vt. to unsew (v. irr.), to unstitch. ♦ **scucirsi** vr. to rip.

scucito agg. **1.** unsewn **2.** (fig.) incoherent.

scucitura sf. unsewing.

scuderìa sf. stable.

scudetto sm. **1.** small shield **2.** (sport) (championship) shield.

scudiero sm. squire.

scudisciare vt. to lash.

scudisciata sf. lash.

scudiscio sm. switch, lash.

scudo sm. shield.

scuffia sf. (sbornia) drunkenness.

sculacciare vt. to spank.

sculacciata sf. spank.

sculettare vi. to waddle.

scultore sm. sculptor.

scultòreo agg. sculptural.

scultura sf. sculpture.

scuolare vt. to skin.

scuola sf. school: — diurna, day-classes; — elementare, primary school; — media inferiore, superiore, secondary school; — pubblica, State school; maestro di —, schoolmaster.

scuòtere vt. **1.** to shake (v. irr.) (anche fig.) **2.** (agitare) to stir.

scuotimento sm. shaking.

scure sf. axe.

scurire vt. **1.** to darken **2.** (pitt.) to tone down. ♦ **scurirsi** vr. to grow (v. irr.) dark.

scuro agg. dark || faccia scura, grim face.

scurrile agg. scurrilous.

scurrilità sf. scurrility.

scusa sf. **1.** excuse, apology **2.** (pretesto) pretext.

scusàbile agg. excusable.

scusare vt. to excuse, to forgive (v. irr.) || scusi!, scusate!, sorry!, excuse me! ♦ **scusarsi** vr. to apologize.

sdebitarsi vr. **1.** to pay (v. irr.) off one's debts **2.** (disobbligarsi) to return a kindness.

sdegnare vt. **1.** to disdain **2.** (provocare lo sdegno) to enrage.

sdegnato agg. indignant.

sdegno sm. disdain, indignation.

sdegnosamente avv. disdainfully.

sdegnoso agg. **1.** (di atti e parole) disdainful **2.** (di persona) haughty.

sdentare vt. to break (v. irr.) the teeth.

sdentato agg. toothless.

sdilinquimento sm. mawkishness.

sdilinquirsi vr. to melt away.

sdoganamento sm. clearing (through the customs).

sdolcinato agg. sugary, affected.

sdolcinatura sf. mawkishness.

sdoppiamento sm. splitting.

sdoppiare vt. to split.

sdraia sf. deck-chair.

sdraiarsi vr. to lie (v. irr.) down.

sdrucciolare vi. to slip, to slide.

sdrucciolévole agg. slippery.

sdrucciolone sm. slip.

sdrucire vt. to tear (v. irr.).

sdrucito agg. torn.

se cong. **1.** if **2.** (dubitativo) whether || — mai, in case; — non altro, at least; — non che, except that; anche —, even if.

sé pron. pers. **1.** one, him, her, it, them **2.** (riflessivi) oneself, himself, herself, itself, themselves || una donna piena di —, a conceited woman; essere fuori di —, to be beside oneself; tornare in —, to recover consciousness; amore di —, selfishness; padronanza di —, self-control; un uomo sicuro di —, a self-confident man; un uomo che si è fatto da —, a self-made man; rispetto di —, self-respect.

sebàceo agg. sebaceous.

sebbene cong. though, although.

sebo sm. sebum.

secante sf. secant.

secca sf. **1.** shoal **2.** (siccità) drought.

seccamente avv. coldly.

seccante agg. (fig.) annoying, irritating || una cosa, persona —, a nuisance.

seccare vt. 1. to dry up 2. (annoiare) to annoy, to irritate. ♦ **seccarsi** vr. (infastidirsi) to be annoyed (with).

seccatore sm. bother.

seccatura sf. 1. (essiccamento) drying 2. (noia) bother, nuisance.

secchia sf. pail, bucket.

secchiello sm. bucket.

secchio sm. V. secchia.

secco agg. 1. dry 2. (appassito) withered 3. (magro) thin 4. (brusco) sharp 5. (freddo) cold.

secentesco agg. of the seventeenth century.

secèrnere vt. to secrete.

secessione sf. secession.

secessionista agg. e sm. secessionist.

seco pron. with him, with her, with them.

secolare agg. 1. secular 2. (in opposizione a ecclesiastico) lay.

secolarizzare vt. to secularize.

secolarizzazione sf. secularization.

secolo sm. 1. century 2. (epoca) epoch, age || Padre Carlo, al — John Smith, Father Charles, in the world John Smith.

seconda sf. (auto) second gear || a — di (loc. prep.), according to.

secondare vt. to favour.

secondario agg. secondary.

secondino sm. warder.

secondo[1] agg. 1. second 2. (favorevole) favourable. ♦ **secondo** sm. 1. (minuto) second 2. (ufficiale in seconda) executive officer.

secondo[2] prep. according to. ♦ **secondo** avv. second.

secrezione sf. secretion.

sèdano sm. celery.

sedare vt. to soothe.

sedativo agg. e sm. sedative.

sede sf. 1. seat, centre 2. (residenza) residence 3. (eccl.) see 4. (edificio per pubblici uffici) office.

sedentario agg. sedentary.

sedere[1] vi. 1. (stare seduto) to sit (v. irr.), to be sitting 2. (mettersi a sedere) to sit (down).

sedere[2] sm. bottom.

sedia sf. chair: — a dondolo, rocking-chair.

sedicenne agg. 1. (attr.) sixteen--year-old 2. (pred.) sixteen years old.

sedicente agg. would-be.

sedicèsimo agg. sixteenth.

sèdici agg. sixteen.

sedile sm. seat, chair.

sedimentario agg. sedimentary.

sedimentazione sf. sedimentation.

sedimento sm. sediment.

sedizione sf. sedition.

sedizioso agg. seditious.

seducente agg. 1. alluring 2. (affascinante) charming.

sedurre vt. to seduce, to tempt.

seduta sf. sitting, session.

seduttore agg. seducing. ♦ **seduttore** sm. seducer.

seduzione sf. 1. seduction 2. (attrazione) attraction.

sega sf. saw.

ségala sf. rye.

segaligno agg. 1. rye (attr.) 2. (di persona) wiry.

segare vt. to saw (v. irr.).

segatura sf. sawdust.

seggio sm. chair, seat: — elettorale, poll.

sèggiola sf. chair.

seggiovia sf. chair-lift.

segherìa sf. saw-mill.

seghettare vt. to jag.

segmentazione sf. segmentation.

segmento sm. segment.

segnalare vt. 1. to signal 2. (far notare) to point out. ♦ **segnalarsi** vr. to distinguish oneself.

segnalatore sm. 1. signaller 2. (segnalatore di direzione) direction indicator.

segnalazione sf. signal: — stradale, traffic signal.

segnale sm. signal: — di pericolo, allarme, danger, alarm signal; — di linea libera, occupata (tel.), ringing, engaged tone; — di passaggio a livello, level-crossing signal.

segnalètica sf. signals (pl.).

segnalètico agg. descriptive.

segnalibro sm. book-mark.

segnare vt. 1. to mark 2. (indicare) to show (v. irr.) 3. (sport) to score. ♦ **segnarsi** vr. to cross oneself.

segnatura sf. 1. marking 2. (sport) scoring.

segno sm. 1. sign, mark: passare il —, to overstep the mark 2. (limite) limit 3. (simbolo) symbol.

sego sm. tallow.

segregare vt. to segregate.

segregazione sf. segregation.

segreta sf. dungeon.

segretamente *avv.* in secret.
segretariato *sm.* secretariate.
segretario *sm.* secretary.
segreteria *sf.* **1.** secretariat **2.** (*di ministero*) secretariat of State.
segretezza *sf.* secrecy.
segreto *agg.* secret. ♦ **segreto** *sm.* **1.** secret: *nel — del cuore*, in the depths of one's heart **2.** (*parte interna, intimità*) secrecy.
seguace *sm.* follower, supporter.
seguente *agg.* following, next.
segugio *sm.* bloodhound.
seguire *vt.* e *vi.* **1.** to follow **2.** (*sorvegliare*) to supervise **3.** (*frequentare regolarmente*) to attend.
séguito *sm.* **1.** (*corteo*) retinue **2.** (*successione, sequela*) series **3.** (*continuazione*) continuation || *il — alla prossima puntata*, to be continued **4.** (*comm.*): *a — di*, following up.
sei *agg.* six.
seicento *agg.* six hundred. ♦ **seicento** *sm.* the seventeenth century.
selce *sf.* flint.
selciare *vt.* to pave.
selciato *sm.* pavement.
selenio *sm.* selenium.
selenite *agg.* lunar. ♦ **selenite** *sf.* selenite.
selettività *sf.* selectivity.
selettivo *agg.* selective.
selettore *sm.* selector.
selezionare *vt.* to select.
selezione *sf.* selection.
sella *sf.* saddle.
sellaio *sm.* saddler.
sellare *vt.* to saddle.
sellino *sm.* saddle.
selva *sf.* **1.** wood **2.** (*fig.*) mass.
selvaggina *sf.* game.
selvaggio *agg.* wild, primitive. ♦ **selvaggio** *sm.* savage.
selvàtico *agg.* **1.** wild **2.** (*non socievole*) unsociable.
selvoso *agg.* woody.
semàforo *sm.* traffic-lights (*pl.*).
semàntica *sf.* semantics.
semàntico *agg.* semantic.
sembianza *sf.* features (*pl.*).
sembrare *vi.* **1.** to seem **2.** (*somigliare*) to look like.
seme *sm.* **1.** seed **2.** (*carte da giuoco*) suit.
sementa *sf.* **1.** seeds (*pl.*) **2.** (*epoca della semina*) seed-time.
semente *sf.* seeds (*pl.*).
semenza *sf.* seeds (*pl.*).

semenzaio *sm.* seed-bed.
semestrale *agg.* six-monthly (*attr.*).
semestralmente *avv.* twice a year.
semestre *sm.* half-year.
semiaperto *agg.* half-open.
semicerchio *sm.* semicircle.
semichiuso *agg.* half-closed.
semicircolare *agg.* semicircular.
semiconduttore *sm.* semiconductor.
semidiàmetro *sm.* semi-diameter.
semidìo *sm.* demigod.
semifinale *sf.* semifinal.
semilavorato *agg.* e *sm.* semi-manufactured.
sémina *sf.* sowing.
seminàbile *agg.* fit to be sown.
seminagione *sf.* sowing.
seminare *vt.* to sow (*v. irr.*).
seminario *sm.* seminary.
seminarista *sm.* seminarist.
seminato *agg.* **1.** sown **2.** (*fig.* strewn.
seminatore *sm.* sower.
seminfermità *sf.* partial infirmity: *— mentale*, partial insanity.
seminudo *agg.* half-naked.
semiserio *agg.* half-serious.
semisfera *sf.* hemisphere.
semita *s.* Semite.
semìtico *agg.* Semitic.
semitono *sm.* semitone.
semivivo *agg.* half-alive.
sémola *sf.* bran.
semolino *sm.* semolina.
semovente *agg.* self-moving.
sempiterno *agg.* everlasting.
sémplice *agg.* simple.
semplicione *sm.* simpleton.
semplicismo *sm.* superficiality.
semplicìstico *agg.* superficial.
semplicità *sf.* simplicity.
semplificare *vt.* to simplify.
semplificazione *sf.* simplification
sempre *avv.* **1.** always: *— avanti! always onward!*; *— meglio, peggio*, better and better, worse and worse; *per —*, for ever; *una volta per —*, once for all **2.** (*tuttora*) still: *vivi — qui?*, do you still live here?
sempreverde *sm.* evergreen.
sènape *sf.* mustard.
senato *sm.* senate.
senatore *sm.* senator.
senatoriale *agg.* senatorial.
senescenza *sf.* senescence.
senile *agg.* senile.
senilità *sf.* senility.
senno *sm.* sense, wisdom.

seno sm. 1. breast, bosom 2. (grembo) womb.

sensale sm. broker.

sensatezza sf. good sense.

sensato agg. sensible.

sensazionale agg. sensational.

sensazione sf. sensation, feeling.

sensibile agg. sensitive.

sensibilità sf. sensitiveness.

sensibilizzare vt. to sensitize.

sensibilmente avv. 1. sensitively 2. (notevolmente) sensibly.

sensitività sf. sensitivity.

sensitivo agg. 1. sensory 2. (sensibile) sensitive.

senso sm. 1. sense 2. (sensazione) sensation 3. (direzione) direction, way 4. (modo) way, manner.

sensorio agg. sensorial.

sensuale agg. sensual.

sensualità sf. sensuality.

sensualmente avv. sensually.

sentenza sf. 1. sentence 2. (massima) saying.

sentenziare vi. to judge, to hold (v. irr.).

sentenziosamente avv. sententiously.

sentenzioso agg. sententious.

sentiero sm. path.

sentimentale agg. sentimental.

sentimentalismo sm. sentimentalism.

sentimentalità sf. sentimentality.

sentimento sm. 1. sentiment 2. (disposizione spirituale) feeling.

sentinella sf. sentry.

sentire vt. 1. to feel (v. irr.) 2. (udire) to hear (v. irr.) 3. (gustare) to taste 4. (odorare) to smell (v. irr.) 5. (ascoltare) to listen to. ♦ **sentirsi** vr. to feel.

sentitamente avv. heartily.

sentito agg. 1. heart-felt 2. (udito) heard ‖ per — dire, by hearsay.

sentore sm. inkling: aver — di, to suspect.

senza prep. without: — scarpe, barefoot; — fine, endless; — confronto, unrivalled; — numero, countless; — testa, thoughtless.

senzatetto s. homeless person.

separare vt. to separate. ♦ **separarsi** vr. to separate.

separatamente avv. separately.

separatismo sm. separatism.

separatista s. separatist.

separativo agg. separative.

separato agg. separated.

separazione sf. separation.

sepolcrale agg. sepulchral.

sepolcro sm. sepulchre, tomb.

sepolto agg. buried.

sepoltura sf. burial.

seppellimento sm. burial.

seppellire vt. to bury.

seppia sf. cuttle-fish.

seppure cong. even if.

sequela sf. series (invariato al pl.).

sequenza sf. 1. series 2. (cine) sequence.

sequestràbile agg. seizable.

sequestrare vt. to seize.

sequestro sm. 1. seizure 2. (per debiti) distress.

sequoia sf. sequoia.

sera sf. evening.

seràfico agg. seraphic.

serafino sm. seraph.

serale agg. evening (attr.).

serata sf. 1. evening 2. (ricevimento serale) party.

serbare vt. 1. (mettere in serbo) to put (v. irr.) aside 2. (conservare) to keep (v. irr.) ‖ — odio, rancore, to nourish hatred, rancour. ♦ **serbarsi** vr. to keep, to remain.

serbatoio sm. reservoir, tank.

serbo (nella loc.) tenere in —, to keep (v. irr.) aside.

serenamente avv. serenely.

serenata sf. serenade.

serenìssimo agg. Serene Highness.

serenità sf. serenity.

sereno agg. serene, clear ‖ giudizio —, objective judgement.

sergente sm. sergeant.

sèrico agg. silk (attr.), silky.

sericoltore sm. silkgrower.

sericoltura sf. sericulture.

serie sf. 1. series (invariato al pl.): in —, mass-produced 2. (assieme) set 3. (fila) row.

serietà sf. seriousness.

serio agg. serious, earnest.

sermone sm. 1. sermon 2. (rimprovero) lecture.

seròtino agg. evening (attr.).

serpe sf. snake.

serpeggiante agg. winding.

serpeggiare vi. to wind (v. irr.).

serpente sm. snake, serpent.

serpentina sf. 1. coil 2. (di strada) winding road.

serpentino agg. snakelike. ♦ **serpentino** sm. serpentine.

serra sf. greenhouse.

serraglio *sm.* **1.** menagerie **2.** (*del sultano*) seraglio.

serramànico (*nella loc. avv.*) coltello a —, flick-knife.

serramento *sm.* lock.

serrare *vt.* **1.** to shut (*v. irr.*), to close **2.** (*a chiave*) to lock **3.** (*stringere*) to tighten **4.** (*concludere*) to conclude.

serrata *sf.* (*econ.*) lockout.

serratura *sf.* lock: *buco della —,* keyhole.

serva *sf.* maid-servant.

servìbile *agg.* usable.

servigio *sm.* service, favour.

servile *agg.* servile.

servilismo *sm.* servility.

servire *vt.* **1.** to serve **2.** (*di persona di servizio*) to wait on **3.** (*le carte*) to deal (*v. irr.*). ♦ **servire** *vi.* (*occorrere*) to need: *vi serve qualcosa?,* can I help you? ♦ **servirsi** *vr.* **1.** to use **2.** (*a tavola*) to help oneself (to).

servitore *sm.* servant.

servitù *sf.* **1.** servitude, slavery **2.** (*personale di servizio*) servants (*pl.*).

servizièvole *agg.* obliging.

servizio *sm.* **1.** service **2.** (*lavoro*) work: *fuori —,* off duty **3.** (*favore*) favour.

servo *sm.* **1.** servant **2.** (*schiavo*) slave.

servofreno *sm.* brake booster.

sèsamo *sm.* sesame.

sessanta *agg.* sixty.

sessantenne *agg.* **1.** (*attr.*) sixty- -year-old **2.** (*pred.*) sixty years old. ♦ **sessantenne** *s.* sixty-year-old person.

sessantèsimo *agg.* sixtieth.

sessantina *sf.* about sixty: *un uomo sulla —,* a man in his sixties.

sessione *sf.* session.

sesso *sm.* sex.

sessuale *agg.* sexual.

sessualità *sf.* sexuality.

sestante *sm.* sextant.

sesterzio *sm.* sesterce.

sestetto *sm.* sextet.

sesto[1] *agg.* sixth.

sesto[2] *sm.* **1.** order **2.** (*arch.*) curve.

sèstuplo *agg. e sm.* sextuple.

seta *sf.* silk.

setacciare *vt.* to sieve.

setaccio *sm.* sieve.

sete *sf.* thirst: *avere —,* to be thirsty.

seterìa *sf.* **1.** silk factory **2.** (*negozio di seta*) silk shop.

setificio *sm.* silk factory.

sétola *sf.* **1.** bristle **2.** (*crine*) hair.

setta *sf.* sect.

settanta *agg.* seventy.

settantenne *agg.* **1.** (*attr.*) seventy- -year-old **2.** (*pred.*) seventy years old. ♦ **settantenne** *s.* seventy- -year-old person.

settantèsimo *agg.* seventieth.

settario *agg.* sectarian.

settarismo *sm.* sectarianism.

sette *agg.* seven.

settecentesco *agg.* of eighteenth century.

settecento *agg.* seven hundred. ♦ **settecento** *sm.* the eighteenth century.

settembre *sm.* September.

settentrionale *agg.* northern.

settentrione *sm.* north.

setticemia *sf.* septicaemia.

sèttico *agg.* septic.

settimana *sf.* week.

settimanale *agg.* weekly. ♦ **settimanale** *sm.* weekly magazine.

settimino *sm.* seven months' child.

setto *sm.* septum (*pl.* -ta).

settore *sm.* **1.** (*geom.*) sector **2.** (*campo*) field.

settoriale *agg.* sectorial.

severità *sf.* severity.

severo *agg.* severe, strict.

sevizia *sf.* torture.

seviziare *vt.* to torture.

sezionamento *sm.* dissection.

sezionare *vt.* (*anat.*) to dissect.

sezione *sf.* **1.** section **2.** (*reparto*) department **3.** (*di scuola*) side.

sfaccendato *agg.* idle. ♦ **sfaccendato** *sm.* idler.

sfaccettare *vt.* to facet.

sfacchinare *vi.* to drudge.

sfacciatàggine *sf.* impudence.

sfacciato *agg.* **1.** impudent, cheeky **2.** (*di colori*) gaudy.

sfacelo *sm.* break-up.

sfaldamento *sm.* flaking.

sfaldarsi *vr.* to flake away.

sfamare *vt.* to appease so.'s hunger.

sfarfallare *vi.* to flutter about.

sfarzo *sm.* pomp.

sfarzoso *agg.* sumptuous.

sfasamento *sm.* **1.** (*mecc.; elettr.*) phase-displacement, phase-difference **2.** (*fig.*) inconsequence.

sfasato *agg.* **1.** out of phase **2.** (*fig.*) inconsequent.

sfasciare[1] *vt.* (*togliere le fasce*) to unbandage.

sfasciare[2] *vt.* to smash. ♦ **sfasciarsi** *vr.* to collapse.

sfasciato *agg.* (*rotto*) in pieces.

sfatare *vt.* to discredit.

sfaticato *agg.* lazy. ♦ **sfaticato** *sm.* lazy-bones.

sfatto *agg.* undone.

sfavillante *agg.* shining.

sfavillare *vi.* to shine (*v. irr.*), to sparkle.

sfavore *sm.* disfavour, discredit.

sfavorévole *agg.* unfavourable.

sfebbrato *agg.* without a temperature.

sfegatarsi *vr.* to wear (*v. irr.*) oneself out.

sfegatato *agg.* fanatic.

sfenòide *sm.* sphenoid.

sfera *sf.* **1.** sphere **2.** (*lancetta*) hand **3.** (*mecc.*) ball.

sfericità *sf.* sphericity.

sfèrico *agg.* spherical.

sferragliare *vi.* to clang.

sferrare *vt.* **1.** (*un attacco*) to launch **2.** (*un colpo*) to land a blow. ♦ **sferrarsi** *vr.* to hurl oneself (at).

sferruzzare *vi.* to knit (*v. irr.*).

sferza *sf.* whip, lash (*anche fig.*).

sferzare *vt.* **1.** to whip, to lash **2.** (*fig.*) to reprimand.

sferzata *sf.* **1.** lash **2.** (*fig.*) sharp rebuke.

sfiancare *vt.* to wear (*v. irr.*) out.

sfiatare *vi.* to leak. ♦ **sfiatarsi** *vr.* to talk oneself hoarse.

sfiatato *agg.* out of breath.

sfiatatolo *sm.* vent.

sfibbiare *vt.* to unbuckle.

sfibramento *sm.* enfeeblement.

sfibrante *agg.* exhausting.

sfibrare *vt.* to weaken, to wear (*v. irr.*) out.

sfibratura *sf.* breaking.

sfida *sf.* challenge: *in tono di —,* defiantly.

sfidante *sm.* challenger.

sfidare *vt.* **1.** to challenge **2.** (*affrontare*) to face, to dare: *— la morte,* to face death.

sfiducia *sf.* mistrust: *avere —,* to mistrust.

sfiduciare *vt.* to discourage. ♦ **sfiduciarsi** *vr.* to become (*v. irr.*) discouraged.

sfiduciato *agg.* discouraged.

sfigurare *vt.* to spoil (*v. irr.*). ♦

sfigurare *vi.* to cut (*v. irr.*) a poor figure.

sfigurato *agg.* disfigured.

sfilacciare *vt.* to fray.

sfilacciato *agg.* frayed.

sfilare[1] *vt.* to unthread, to unstring (*v. irr.*).

sfilare[2] *vi.* to parade.

sfilata *sf.* **1.** march, parade **2.** (*fila*) line, string.

sfinge *sf.* sphinx.

sfinimento *sm.* exhaustion.

sfinire *vt.* to exhaust.

sfinitezza *sf.* extreme weakness.

sfinito *agg.* worn out.

sfintere *sm.* sphincter.

sfiorare *vt.* to graze, to touch on.

sfiorire *vi.* to wither, to fade.

sfiorito *agg.* faded, withered (*anche fig.*).

sfittare *vt.* to vacate.

sfitto *agg.* vacant.

sfocato *agg.* out of focus.

sfociare *vi.* to flow.

sfoderare *vt.* **1.** to unline **2.** (*sguainare*) to unsheathe **3.** (*ostentare*) to display.

sfoderato *agg.* **1.** unlined **2.** (*sguainato*) unsheathed.

sfogare *vt.* to give (*v. irr.*) vent to. ♦ **sfogarsi** *vr.* to relieve one's feelings.

sfoggiare *vi.* to show (*v. irr.*) off.

sfoggio *sm.* show, ostentation.

sfoglia *sf.* **1.** (*lamina*) foil **2.** (*cuc.*) pastry.

sfogliare[1] *vt.* to pluck the petals off.

sfogliare[2] *vt.* **1.** (*voltare le pagine*) to turn over the pages **2.** (*dare un'occhiata*) to glance through.

sfogliata *sf.* **1.** (*cuc.*) puff-pastry **2.** (*di libro*) thumbing.

sfogo *sm.* vent, outlet.

sfolgoramento *sm.* blazing.

sfolgorante *agg.* flaming.

sfolgorare *vi.* to blaze.

sfolgorìo *sm.* blaze.

sfollagente *sm.* truncheon.

sfollamento *sm.* **1.** dispersal **2.** (*mil.*) evacuation.

sfollare *vt. e vi.* to disperse **2.** (*mil.*) to evacuate.

sfollato *agg.* **1.** evacuated. ♦ **sfollato** *sm.* evacuee.

sfoltire *vt.* to thin.

sfondamento *sm.* breaking.

sfondare *vt.* **1.** (*rompere il fondo*) to break (*v. irr.*) the bottom **2.**

(*mil.*) to break through. ♦ **sfondare** *vi.* to have success.

sfondato *agg.* 1. without a bottom ‖ *scarpe sfondate*, worn-out shoes 2. (*insaziabile*) voracious.

sfondo *sm.* background.

sforbiciare *vt.* to cut (*v. irr.*) with scissors.

sformare *vt.* 1. to pull out of shape 2. (*togliere dalla forma*) to remove from the mould. ♦ **sformarsi** *vr.* to get (*v. irr.*) out of shape.

sformato *agg.* shapeless.

sfornare *vt.* 1. to take (*v. irr.*) out of the oven 2. (*produrre*) to bring (*v. irr.*) out.

sfornito *agg.* destitute, lacking (in).

sfortuna *sf.* bad luck.

sfortunato *agg.* unlucky.

sforzare *vt.* to strain, to force. ♦ **sforzarsi** *vr.* to try hard.

sforzatamente *avv.* 1. with much effort 2. (*in modo forzato*) forcedly.

sforzato *agg.* 1. forced 2. (*fig.*) false.

sforzatura *sf.* (*cosa sforzata*) far-fetched thing.

sforzo *sm.* 1. effort 2. (*mecc.*) stress.

sfottere *vt.* to pull so.'s legs.

sfracellare *vt.* to smash. ♦ **sfracellarsi** *vr.* to smash.

sfrangiare *vt.* to undo (*v. irr.*), to form a fringe. ♦ **sfrangiarsi** *vr.* to fray.

sfrangiatura *sf.* fraying.

sfrattare *vt.* to evict.

sfratto *sm.* eviction.

sfrecciare *vi.* to dart.

sfregamento *sm.* rubbing.

sfregare *vt.* to rub.

sfregiare *vt.* to disfigure.

sfregiato *agg.* disfigured.

sfregio *sm.* slash, scar.

sfrenare *vt.* to unbridle.

sfrenatezza *sf.* unrestraint.

sfrenato *agg.* wild, unbridled.

sfrigolare *vi.* to sizzle.

sfrigolio *sm.* sizzle.

sfringuellare *vi.* to twitter.

sfrondare *vt.* 1. to strip off leaves 2. (*fig.*) to curtail.

sfrontatezza *sf.* effrontery.

sfrontato *agg.* brazen, impudent. ♦ **sfrontato** *sm.* impudent fellow.

sfrusciare *vi.* to rustle.

sfruscio *sm.* rustling.

sfruttamento *sm.* exploitation.

sfruttare *vt.* to exploit.

sfruttatore *sm.* profiteer.

sfuggente *agg.* receding: *sguardo* —, elusive look.

sfuggévole *agg.* transitory.

sfuggire *vi.* to escape, to slip. ♦ **sfuggire** *vt.* to avoid.

sfuggita *sf. di* —, quickly: *vedere qu. di* —, to have a glimpse of so.

sfumare *vt.* to shade. ♦ **sfumare** *vi.* 1. to evaporate 2. (*fig.*) to come (*v. irr.*) to nothing.

sfumatamente *avv.* softly.

sfumato *agg.* 1. vanished 2. (*di colori*) soft.

sfumatura *sf.* 1. (*lo sfumare*) shading 2. (*gradazione*) shade.

sfuriata *sf.* outburst.

sgabello *sm.* stool.

sgabuzzino *sm.* closet.

sgambettare *vi.* to kick (one's legs) about.

sgambetto *sm.* trip: *fare lo* —, to trip (so.); (*fig.*) to supplant.

sganasciamento *sm.* dislocation (of so.'s jaw).

sganasciarsi *vr.* — *dalle risa*, to laugh oneself silly.

sganascione *sm.* slap.

sganciare *vt.* 1. to unhook 2. (*ferr.*) to uncouple 3. (*di bombe*) to release. ♦ **sganciarsi** *vr.* (*liberarsi di qu.*) to get (*v. irr.*) away (so.).

sgangherare *vt.* to unhinge.

sgangherato *agg.* 1. unhinged 2. (*sguaiato*) wild.

sgarbatamente *avv.* impolitely.

sgarbato *agg.* rude, impolite.

sgarberia *sf.* rudeness.

sgarbo *sm.* offence.

sgargiante *agg.* gaudy.

sgarrare *vi.* 1. to be wrong 2. (*di orologio*) (*se è avanti*) to gain; (*se è indietro*) to lose (*v. irr.*).

sgattaiolare *vi.* to slip away.

sgelare *vi.* to thaw. ♦ **sgelarsi** *vr.* to thaw.

sgelo *sm.* thawing.

sghembo *agg.* oblique: *di* —, obliquely.

sgherro *sm.* hired assassin.

sghignazzare *vi.* to guffaw.

sghignazzata *sf.* guffaw.

sghimbescio (*nella loc. avv.*) *di* —, awry.

sghiribizzo *sm.* whim.

sgobbare *vi.* to work hard.

sgobbone *sm.* 1. hard worker 2. (*studentesco*) swot.

sgocciolare vi. to drip.

sgocciolio sm. dripping.

sgolarsi vr. to shout oneself hoarse.

sgombrare vt. to clear.

sgombro agg. 1. clear (of) 2. (fig.) free (from).

sgomentare vt. to dismay.

sgomento agg. dismayed. ♦ **sgomento** sm. dismay.

sgominare vt. to rout.

sgonfiamento sm. deflation.

sgonfiare vt. to deflate.

sgonfio agg. deflated.

sgorbia sf. gouge.

sgorbiare vt. to scrawl.

sgorbio sm. 1. scrawl 2. (pittura mal fatta) daub 3. (fig.) deformed man (pl. men).

sgorgare vi. to gush, to flow.

sgozzare vt. to cut (v. irr.) so.'s throat.

sgradévole agg. unpleasant.

sgradito agg. 1. disagreeable 2. (mal accetto) unwelcome.

sgrammaticato agg. ungrammatical.

sgranare vt. 1. to shell: — gli occhi, to open one's eyes wide 2. (mangiare) to devour.

sgranatrice sf. husker.

sgranchire vt. to stretch.

sgranocchiare vt. to munch.

sgrassare vt. to take (v. irr.) the grease off: — il brodo, to skim the grease from the broth.

sgravare vt. 1. to lighten 2. (fig.) to relieve.

sgravio sm. 1. lightening 2. (fig.) relief.

sgraziato agg. awkward.

sgretolamento sm. pounding.

sgretolare vt. to pound. ♦ **sgretolarsi** vr. to crumble.

sgridare vt. to scold.

sgroppare[1] vt. (sciogliere) to untie.

sgroppare[2] vi. (di cavallo) to buck.

sgroppata sf. bucking.

sgrossamento sm. rough-shaping.

sgrossare vt. 1. to rough 2. (dirozzare) to refine.

sgrovigliare vt. to unravel.

sgualato agg. 1. unbecoming 2. (volgare) coarse.

sguainare vt. to unsheathe.

sgualcire vt. to crease.

sgualdrina sf. harlot, whore.

sguardo sm. look, glance: dare uno —, to have a look.

sguarnire vt. 1. to untrim 2. (mil.) to dismantle.

sguattero sm. scullery-boy.

sguazzare vi. to wallow.

sguinzagliare vt. to unleash.

sgusciare vt. to shell. ♦ **sgusciare** vi. to slip away.

si[1] pron. 1. (riflessivo) oneself, himself, herself, itself, themselves 2. (rec.) (fra due) each other; (fra molti) one another 3. (pron. indef.) one, people, we, they: — dice, people say.

sì[2] sm. (mus.) si, B.

sì avv. yes: penso di —, I think so; — certo, certainly; e — che, yet; uno —, uno no, every other one; forse che —, forse che no, maybe yes, maybe no.

sia cong. 1. (o l'uno o l'altro) whether... or, either... or 2. (entrambi) both... and.

siamese agg. e s. Siamese.

sibarita s. sybarite.

siberiano agg. Siberian.

sibilante agg. 1. hissing 2. (fonetica) sibilant.

sibilare vi. to whistle, to hiss.

sibilla sf. sibyl.

sibillino agg. sibylline.

sibilo sm. hiss, whistle.

sicario sm. cut-throat.

sicché cong. 1. so... that 2. (dunque) therefore.

siccità sf. drought.

siccome cong. as, since.

siciliano agg. e sm. Sicilian.

sicomoro sm. sycamore.

sicumera sf. presumption.

sicura sf. safety belt.

sicurezza sf. 1. (certezza) certainty 2. (immunità da pericoli) safety || dispositivo di —, safety device; misura di —, precautionary measure; uscita di —, emergency door; rasoio, spilla di —, safety-razor, pin.

sicuro agg. 1. (certo) sure: — di sé, self-confident 2. (immune da pericoli) safe 3. (che non sbaglia) unfailing 4. (calmo, saldo) calm, steady 5. (esperto) skilful.

siderale agg. sidereal.

siderurgìa sf. metallurgy of iron.

siderúrgico agg. iron (attr.): stabilimento —, iron-works (pl.). ♦ **siderúrgico** sm. iron worker.

sidro sm. cider.

siepe sf. hedge.

siero *sm.* serum.

sieroso *agg.* serous.

sieroterapia *sf.* serotherapy.

siesta *sf.* nap.

siffatto *agg.* such.

sifilide *sf.* syphilis.

sifone *sm.* siphon.

sigaraia *sf.* cigar-seller.

sigaretta *sf.* cigarette.

sigaro *sm.* cigar.

sigillare *vt.* to seal.

sigillatura *sf.* sealing.

sigillo *sm.* seal.

sigla *sf.* monogram.

siglare *vt.* to initial.

significare *vt.* 1. to mean (*v. irr.*) 2. (*comunicare*) to signify 3. (*simboleggiare*) to represent.

significativo *agg.* meaningful.

significato *sm.* 1. meaning 2. (*valore*) import.

signora *sf.* 1. lady, woman (*pl.* women) 2. (*seguito da cognome*) Mrs: *la — Smith*, Mrs. Smith 3. (*vocativo*) Madam: *buon giorno —*, good morning Madam 4. (*padrona*) mistress 5. (*donna ricca*) rich lady 6. (*moglie*) wife (*pl.* wives).

signore *sm.* 1. gentleman, man (*pl.* -men) 2. (*seguito da cognome*) Mr.: *il — Smith*, Mr. Smith 3. (*padrone*) master 4. (*vocativo*) Sir: *sì —!* yes, Sir! 5. (*uomo ricco*) lord 6. (*Dio*) God, Lord.

signoreggiare *vt.* to rule.

signoria *sf.* 1. (*di uomo*) Lordship; (*di donna*) Ladyship 2. (*dominio*) dominion.

signorile *agg.* 1. (*riferito a uomo*) gentlemanlike; (*riferito a donna*) ladylike 2. (*elegante*) luxury.

signorilità *sf.* distinction, high class.

signorina *sf.* 1. young lady 2. (*seguito da cognome*) Miss: *la — Smith*, Miss Smith 3. (*vocativo*) Madam: *Buon giorno —*, good morning Madam 4. (*padroncina*) young mistress 5. (*donna non sposata*) unmarried woman.

signorotto *sm.* squire.

silenziatore *sm.* silencer.

silenzio *sm.* silence.

silenzioso *agg.* silent || *una strada silenziosa*, a noiseless street.

silfide *sf.* sylph.

silfo *sm.* sylph.

silice *sf.* silica.

silicio *sm.* silicon.

silicone *sm.* silicone.

silicosi *sf.* silicosis.

sillaba *sf.* syllable.

sillabare *vt.* to syllabize.

sillabo *sm.* summary.

sillogismo *sm.* syllogism.

sillogistico *agg.* syllogistic.

silo *sm.* silo (*pl.* silos).

siluramento *sm.* 1. torpedoing 2. (*fig.*) firing.

silurante *sf.* torpedo-boat.

silurare *vt.* 1. to torpedo 2. (*fig.*) to dismiss.

siluriano *agg.* e *sm.* Silurian.

siluro *sm.* (*mil.; zool.*) torpedo.

silvestre *agg.* sylvan.

silvicoltore *sm.* forester.

silvicoltura *sf.* forestry.

simbiosi *sf.* symbiosis.

simboleggiare *vt.* to symbolize.

simbòlico *agg.* 1. symbolic 2. (*nominale*) nominal.

simbolismo *sm.* symbolism.

simbolista *agg.* e *sm.* symbolist.

simbolo *sm.* symbol.

similare *agg.* similar.

simile *agg.* 1. like, similar 2. (*pred.*) alike 3. (*tale*) such. ♦ **simile** *sm.* fellow-creature.

similitùdine *sf.* 1. likeness 2. (*lett.*) simile.

simmetria *sf.* symmetry.

simmètrico *agg.* symmetric(al).

simonìa *sf.* simony.

simonìaco *agg.* e *sm.* simoniac.

simpatìa *sf.* liking.

simpàtico *agg.* nice, pleasant.

simpatizzante *agg.* sympathizing. ♦ **simpatizzante** *s.* sympathizer.

simpatizzare *vi.* 1. to sympathize 2. (*rec.*) to take (*v. irr.*) a liking to each other.

simposio *sm.* symposium (*pl.* -ia).

simulacro *sm.* 1. simulacre 2. (*finzione*) sham.

simulare *vt.* to feign.

simulato *agg.* simulated.

simulatore *sm.* simulator.

simulazione *sf.* simulation.

simultaneità *sf.* simultaneity.

simultàneo *agg.* simultaneous (with).

sinagoga *sf.* synagogue.

sincerarsi *vr.* to make (*v. irr.*) sure.

sincerità *sf.* sincerity.

sincero *agg.* sincere, true.

sincopare *vt.* to syncopate.

sincopato agg. syncopated.
sincope sf. 1. (med.) syncope 2. (mus.; gramm.) syncopation.
sincronismo sm. synchronism.
sincronizzare vt. to synchronize.
sincronizzazione sf. synchronization.
sindacale agg. trade-union (attr.).
sindacalismo sm. trade-unionism.
sindacalista s. trade-unionist.
sindacare vt. 1. to control 2. (criticare) to criticize.
sindacato sm. trade-union.
sindaco sm. 1. mayor 2. (di società) auditor.
sindrome sf. syndrome.
sinecura sf. sinecure.
sinfonia sf. symphony.
sinfonico agg. symphonic.
singhiozzare vi. to hiccup.
singhiozzo sm. 1. hiccup 2. (di pianto) sob.
singolare agg. 1. singular 2. (singolo) single.
singolarità sf. singularity.
singolarmente avv. 1. (ad uno ad uno) singly 2. (segnatamente) particularly.
singolo agg. single, individual.
singulto sm. 1. hiccup 2. (di pianto) sob.
sinistra sf. 1. left: alla mia —, on my left 2. (mano) left hand 3. (parte) left-hand side || uomo di — (pol.), left-winger.
sinistramente avv. sinisterly.
sinistrato agg. 1. (di edificio) bomb-damaged 2. (di persona) injured. ◆ **sinistrato** sm. (damage) sufferer.
sinistro agg. 1. (truce) sinister, grim. ◆ **sinistro** sm. 1. accident, mishap 2. (boxe) left.
sinologo sm. Sinologist.
sinonimia sf. synonymy.
sinonimo agg. synonymous. ◆ **sinonimo** sm. synonym.
sinora avv. till now, so far.
sinovite sf. synovitis.
sintassi sf. syntax.
sintesi sf. synthesis (pl. -ses).
sintetico agg. synthetic.
sintetizzare vt. to synthetize.
sintomatico agg. symptomatic.
sintomo sm. symptom.
sintonia sf. syntony.
sintonizzare vt. to tune in.
sinuosità sf. winding.

sinuoso agg. winding.
sinusite sf. sinusitis.
sionismo sm. Zionism.
sionista s. Zionist.
sipario sm. curtain.
sirena sf. 1. (mit.) siren, mermaid 2. (acustica) hooter.
siringa sf. syringe.
siringare vt. to syringe.
sismico agg. seismic.
sismografo sm. seismograph.
sismologia sf. seismology.
sismologo sm. seismologist.
sistema sm. system: — di vita, way of life.
sistemare vt. 1. (mettere in ordine) to arrange 2. (definire) to settle.
sistematico agg. systematic(al).
sistemazione sf. 1. (ordine) arrangement 2. (collocazione di macchinari) layout 3. (il sistemarsi) settling 4. (lavoro) job.
sito sm. place.
situare vt. to place.
situazione sf. situation.
slabbrare vt. to chip the rim of.
slabbratura sf. chipping.
slacciare vt. 1. to untie 2. (sbottonare) to unbutton.
slanciarsi vr. to rush.
slanciato agg. slim.
slancio sm. 1. rush 2. (energia) energy.
slargare vt. to widen.
slattamento sm. weaning.
slattare vt. to wean.
slavato agg. pale.
slavina sf. landslide; (di neve) snowslide.
slavo agg. e sm. Slav.
sleale agg. unfair.
slealtà sf. disloyalty.
slegare vt. to untie.
slegato agg. 1. untied 2. (di discorso ecc.) disconnected.
slitta sf. sleigh.
slittamento sm. skidding.
slittare vi. 1. to slide (v. irr.) 2. (di ruote) to skid.
slogamento sm. dislocation.
slogare vt. to dislocate.
slogatura sf. dislocation.
sloggiare vi. to clear out. ◆ **sloggiare** vt. to drive (v. irr.) out.
smaccato agg. sickly-sweet.
smacchiare vt. to clean.
smacchiatore sm. stain-remover.
smacchiatura sf. cleaning.
smacco sm. mortification.

smagliante agg. dazzling.

smagliare vt. to unravel. ♦ **smagliarsi** vr. (di calze) to ladder.

smagliato agg. unravelled.

smagliatura sf. 1. (di calze) ladder.

smagnetizzare vt. to demagnetize.

smagnetizzazione sf. demagnetization.

smagrire vt. e vi. to thin.

smagrito agg. thin, grown thin.

smaliziare vt. to smarten up. ♦ **smaliziarsi** vr. to wisen.

smaliziato agg. cunning.

smaltare vt. to enamel: — le unghie, to paint one's nails.

smaltato agg. 1. enamelled 2. (di unghie) painted.

smaltire vt. to digest: — la sbornia, to get (v. irr.) over one's drunkenness.

smalto sm. enamel: — per unghie, nail-polish.

smanceria sf. mawkishness.

smangiare vt. to corrode.

smania sf. 1. great desire 2. (agitazione) frenzy.

smaniare vi. 1. to yearn (for) 2. (essere agitati) to be restless.

smanioso agg. 1. eager 2. (agitato) restless.

smantellamento sm. dismantling.

smantellare vt. to dismantle.

smarcare vt. to unmark.

smargiassata sf. swagger.

smargiasseria sf. bragging.

smargiasso sm. braggart.

smarginare vt. to trim the edge.

smarrimento sm. 1. loss 2. (turbamento) bewilderment.

smarrire vt. to lose (v. irr.). ♦ **smarrirsi** vr. 1. to lose one's way 2. (di lettera, pacco) to miscarry 3. (turbarsi) to be bewildered.

smascellarsi vr. to dislocate one's jaws.

smascherare vt. to unmask.

smembramento sm. dismemberment.

smembrare vt. to dismember.

smemorataggine sf. 1. lack of memory 2. (dimenticanza) lapse of memory.

smemorato agg. absent-minded.

smentire vt. to deny. ♦ **smentirsi** vr. 1. to contradict oneself 2. (venir meno) to be untrue to oneself.

smentita sf. denial.

smeraldo sm. emerald.

smerciare vt. to sell (v. irr.) off.

smercio sm. sale.

smerigliare vt. 1. to polish with emery 2. (di vetri) to frost glass.

smerigliato agg. emery: carta smerigliata, emery paper; vetro —, frosted glass.

smeriglio sm. emery.

smerlo sm. scallop.

smesso agg. cast off.

smettere vt. to stop, to leave (v. irr.) off: — un vestito, to cast (v. irr.) off a dress.

smezzare vt. to halve.

smidollato agg. (di persona) spineless.

smilitarizzare vt. to demilitarize.

smilitarizzazione sf. demilitarization.

smilzo agg. thin.

sminuire vt. to diminish. ♦ **sminuirsi** vr. to belittle oneself.

sminuzzare vt. 1. (tritare) to mince 2. (tagliuzzare) to chop up 3. (sbriciolare) to crumble.

smistamento sm. 1. clearing 2. (ferr.) shunting 3. (di corrispondenza) sorting.

smistare vt. 1. (di corrispondenza) to sort out 2. (ferr.) to shunt.

smisuratamente avv. beyond measure.

smisurato agg. enormous, huge.

smobilitare vt. to demobilize.

smobilitazione sf. demobilization.

smoccolare vt. to snuff.

smoccolatoio sm. snuffers (pl.).

smoccolatura sf. snuffing.

smodato agg. immoderate.

smoderatezza sf. immoderateness.

smoderato agg. immoderate.

smontàbile agg. demountable.

smontaggio sm. disassembling.

smontare vt. 1. (far scendere) (da cavallo) to unhorse; (da un'automobile) to drop 2. (scomporre in parti) to take (v. irr.) to pieces 3. (mecc.) to disassemble 4. (fig.) to dishearten, to cool. ♦ **smontare** vi. 1. (da un treno, tram ecc.) to get (v. irr.) off 2. (da un'automobile) to get (v. irr.) out 3. (da cavallo) to dismount 4. (dal lavoro) to go (v. irr.) off duty 5. (sbiadire) to fade.

smorfia sf. grimace.

smorfioso agg. affected.

smorto agg. pale.

smorzamento sm. 1. (di luci) shad-

ing 2. (di colori) toning down
3. (di suoni) lowering 4. (di sete;
fig.) quenching.

smorzare vt. 1. (di luci) to shade
2. (di colori) to tone down 3. (di
suoni) to lower 4. (di sete; fig.) to
quench 5. (spegnere) to put (v.
irr.) down.

smottamento sm. landslip.

smottare vi. to slip.

smozzicare vt. 1. to hack to pieces
2. (di parole) to clip.

smunto agg. pale.

smuòvere vt. 1. to shift 2. (fig.)
to move.

smussare vt. 1. to round off 2.
(fig.) to soften.

smussato agg. 1. blunted 2. (fig.)
softened.

snaturare vt. to pervert.

snaturato agg. unnatural.

snazionalizzare vt. to denationalize.

snebbiare vt. 1. to dispel the fog
2. (fig.) to clear.

snellezza sf. slenderness.

snellire vt. 1. to make (v. irr.)
slender 2. (fig.) to simplify. ◆
snellirsi vr. to grow (v. irr.)
slender.

snello agg. slender.

snervante agg. enervating.

snervare vt. to enervate.

snidare vt. 1. to flush 2. (fig.) to
dislodge.

snobbare vt. to snob.

snobismo sm. snobbery.

snocciolare vt. 1. to stone 2. (fig.)
to tell (v. irr.).

snodare vt. 1. to untie 2. (rendere
agile) to make (v. irr.) supple. ◆
snodarsi vr. (di strade) to wind
(v. irr.).

snodato agg. 1. supple 2. (di cosa)
jointed.

snodo sm. joint.

soave agg. sweet.

soavità sf. sweetness.

sobbalzare vi. 1. to jerk 2. (trasalire) to start.

sobbalzo sm. 1. jerk 2. (sussulto)
start.

sobbarcarsi vr. to take (v. irr.)
upon oneself.

sobborgo sm. suburb.

sobillare vt. to stir up.

sobillatore sm. instigator.

sobrietà sf. sobriety.

sobrio agg. sober.

socchiùdere vt. 1. to half-close 2.
(aprire un po') to half-open.

socchiuso agg. half-closed, half-
open.

sòccida sf. agistment.

soccòmbere vi. to succumb.

soccòrrere vt. to help, to assist.

soccorritore agg. helpful. ◆ **soccorritore** sm. helper.

soccorso sm. help || pronto —, first
aid.

socialdemocràtico agg. socialdem-
ocratic.

socialdemocrazìa sf. socialdem-
ocracy.

sociale agg. social.

socialismo sm. Socialism.

socialista agg. e sm. Socialist.

socialità sf. sociality.

socializzare vt. to socialize.

socializzazione sf. socialization.

società sf. 1. society 2. (comm.)
company: — anonima, joint-stock
company; — a responsabilità limi-
tata, limited company || entrare in
—, to enter into partnership.

socièvole agg. sociable.

socievolezza sf. sociability.

socio sm. 1. member 2. (comm.)
partner.

sociologìa sf. sociology.

sociològico agg. sociological.

sociòlogo sm. sociologist.

socràtico agg. Socratic.

soda sf. soda.

sodalizio sm. 1. society 2. (confraternita) brotherhood.

sodare vt. to consolidate.

sodatura sf. (tessile) fulling.

soddisfacente agg. satisfactory.

soddisfare vt. 1. to satisfy 2. (a-
dempiere) to fulfil 3. (far fronte
a) to discharge 4. (riparare) to
make (v. irr.) amends.

soddisfazione sf. satisfaction.

sodio sm. sodium.

sodo agg. solid, firm: uovo —,
hard-boiled egg; darle sode a qu.,
to strike (v. irr.) so. hard.

sofferente agg. 1. suffering 2. (malaticcio) poorly.

sofferenza sf. pain.

soffermare vt. to stop. ◆ **soffer-
marsi** vr. to stop.

soffiare vt. e vi. to blow (v. irr.):
soffiarsi il naso, to blow one's
nose.

soffiata sf. puff.

soffiato agg. puffed.

soffiatore *sm.* blower.
soffiatura *sf.* blowing.
sòffice *agg.* soft.
soffietto *sm.* **1.** bellows (*pl.*) **2.** (*edit.*) blurb.
soffio *sm.* puff, whiff.
soffione *sm.* **1.** blow-pipe **2.** (*geol.*) fumarole.
soffitta *sf.* garret.
soffitto *sm.* ceiling.
soffocamento *sm.* choking.
soffocante *agg.* choking: *caldo —,* sultry heat.
soffocare *vt.* **1.** to choke **2.** (*reprimere*) to repress.
soffocato *agg.* choked.
sòffoco *sm.* sultriness.
soffòndere *vt.* to suffuse.
soffriggere *vt.* to fry slightly.
soffrire *vt.* **1.** to suffer **2.** (*sopportare*) to stand (*v. irr.*).
soffuso *agg.* suffused.
sofisma *sm.* sophism.
sofista *sm.* sophist.
sofistica *sf.* sophistry.
sofisticare *vi.* to quibble. ♦ **sofisticare** *vt.* to adulterate.
sofisticato *agg.* **1.** sophisticated **2.** (*adulterato*) adulterated.
sofisticazione *sf.* adulteration.
sofisticherìa *sf.* quibbling.
sofistico *agg.* sophistical.
soggettista *sm.* scenario writer.
soggettivismo *sm.* subjectivism.
soggettività *sf.* subjectivity.
soggettivo *agg.* subjective.
soggetto *agg.* e *sm.* subject.
soggezione *sf.* **1.** subjection **2.** (*timidezza*) shyness.
sogghignare *vi.* to sneer.
sogghigno *sm.* sneer.
soggiacere *vi.* to be subjected
soggiogare *vt.* to subdue.
soggiornare *vi.* to stay.
soggiorno *sm.* stay: *stanza di —,* living-room.
soggiùngere *vt.* to add.
soglia *sf.* threshold.
sògliola *sf.* sole.
sognante *agg.* dreaming: *occhi sognanti,* dreamy eyes.
sognare *vt.* to dream (*v. irr.*): *— ad occhi aperti,* to have day-dreams.
sognatore *agg.* dreaming. ♦ **sognatore** *sm.* dreamer.
sogno *sm.* dream.
soia *sf.* soya.
solaio *sm.* attic.

solamente *avv.* only.
solare *agg.* **1.** solar **2.** (*radioso*) radiant.
solatìo *agg.* sunny.
solcare *vt.* **1.** to plough **2.** (*fig.*) to furrow.
solcato *agg.* **1.** ploughed **2.** (*fig.*) furrowed.
solcatura *sf.* ploughing, furrowing.
solco *sm.* **1.** (*agr.*) furrow **2.** (*ruga*) wrinkle **3.** (*mar.*) wake **4.** (*di ruota sul terreno*) track.
solcòmetro *sm.* log.
soldataglia *sf.* soldiery.
soldatesco *agg.* soldierly.
soldato *sm.* soldier.
soldo *sm.* **1.** penny **2.** (*denaro*) money **3.** (*salario*) pay: *essere al — di qu.,* to be in so.'s pay.
sole *sm.* sun: *bagno di —,* sun-bathing; *colpo di —,* sunstroke; *un giorno di —, senza —,* a sunny day, a sunless day; *tramonto del —,* sunset.
soleggiare *vt.* to sun-dry.
soleggiato *agg.* sunny.
solenne *agg.* solemn.
solennità *sf.* **1.** solemnity **2.** (*cerimonia*) ceremony.
solennizzare *vt.* to solemnize.
solenòide *sm.* solenoid.
solere *vi.* to use (*usato solo al passato*).
solerte *agg.* diligent.
solerzia *sf.* diligence.
soletta *sf.* sole.
solfa *sf.* **1.** scale **2.** (*fig.*) old story.
solfara *sf.* sulphur mine.
solfare *vt.* to sulphur.
solfatara *sf.* solfatara.
solfato *sm.* sulphate.
solfeggiare *vt.* to sol-fa.
solfeggio *sm.* solfeggio.
solfito *sm.* sulphite.
solfuro *sm.* sulphide.
solidale *agg.* solid (for).
solidamente *avv.* solidly.
solidarietà *sf.* solidarity.
solidarizzare *vi.* to be solid (for).
solidificare *vt.* to solidify.
solidificazione *sf.* solidification.
solidità *sf.* **1.** solidity **2.** (*di colori*) fastness.
sòlido *agg.* **1.** solid **2.** (*di colori*) fast **3.** (*fig.*) sound. ♦ **sòlido** *sm.* solid.
soliloquio *sm.* soliloquy.
solipsismo *sm.* solipsism.
solista *s.* soloist.

solitamente *avv.* usually.
solitario¹ *agg.* solitary. ♦ **solitario** *sm.* 1. hermit 2. *(brillante)* solitaire.
solitario² *sm.* *(a carte)* solitaire.
sòlito *agg.* usual, customary: *essere —,* to be used to (doing); *di —,* usually.
solitùdine *sf.* loneliness.
sollazzare *vt.* to amuse.
sollazzo *sm.* amusement.
sollecitante *agg.* urging.
sollecitare *vt.* 1. *(far premura)* to urge 2. *(brigare)* to solicit 3. *(affrettare)* to hurry up.
sollecitazione *sf.* 1. solicitation 2. *(preghiera)* entreaty.
sollécito *agg.* 1. *(rapido)* prompt 2. *(preoccupato)* solicitous 3. *(premuroso)* obliging.
sollecitùdine *sf.* 1. *(rapidità)* promptness 2. *(interessamento)* concern 3. *(gentilezza)* kindness.
solleone *sm.* dog-days *(pl.).*
solleticante *agg.* alluring.
solleticare *vt.* to tickle.
sollético *sm.* 1. tickle: *soffrire il —,* to be ticklish 2. *(fig.)* itch.
sollevamento *sm.* lifting.
sollevare *vt.* 1. to lift 2. *(issare)* to hoist 3. *(fig.)* to raise 4. *(dar sollievo)* to relieve. ♦ **sollevarsi** *vr.* 1. to rise *(v. irr.)* 2. *(riaversi)* to recover 3. *(insorgere)* to rebel.
sollevato *agg.* *(rasserenato)* cheered up.
sollevazione *sf.* *(rivolta)* rising.
sollievo *sm.* relief.
sollùchero *sm.* *andare in —,* to go *(v. irr.)* into raptures.
solo *agg.* 1. alone *(pred.)*: *da —,* by oneself 2. *(unico)* only. ♦ **solo** *avv.* only.
solstizio *sm.* solstice.
soltanto *avv.* only.
solùbile *agg.* soluble.
solubilità *sf.* solubility.
soluzione *sf.* solution.
solvente *agg. e sm.* solvent.
solvenza *sf.* *(comm.)* solvency.
solvìbile *agg.* solvent.
solvibilità *sf.* solvency.
soma *sf.* load, burden.
somaràggine *sf.* stupidity.
somaro *sm.* ass.
somàtico *agg.* somatic.
somigliante *agg.* alike, similar.
somiglianza *sf.* likeness.
somigliare *vi.* to look like.

somma *sf.* 1. *(mat.)* addition 2. *(di denaro)* sum.
sommamente *avv.* extremely.
sommare *vt.* to add.
sommariamente *avv.* summarily.
sommario *agg. e sm.* summary.
sommèrgere *vt.* to submerge.
sommergìbile *agg.* submersible. ♦ **sommergìbile** *sm.* submarine.
sommergibilista *sm.* submariner.
sommersione *sf.* submersion.
sommerso *agg.* submerged.
sommessamente *avv.* 1. submissively 2. *(a bassa voce)* in a low voice.
sommesso *agg.* 1. submissive 2. *(di voce)* low.
somministrare *vt.* to administer.
somministratore *sm.* giver.
somministrazione *sf.* giving.
sommissione *sf.* V. *sottomissione.*
sommità *sf.* summit, top.
sommo¹ *agg.* 1. highest 2. *(fig.)* supreme.
sommo² *sm.* summit, top.
sommossa *sf.* rising.
sommovimento *sm.* movement, agitation.
sommozzatore *sm.* frogman *(pl. -men).*
sommuòvere *vt.* to stir up.
sonagliera *sf.* collar with bells.
sonaglio *sm.* 1. harness-bell 2. *(giocattolo)* rattle ‖ *serpente a sonagli,* rattlesnake.
sonante *agg.* resounding ‖ *denaro —,* ready money.
sonare *vt.* 1. to sound 2. *(musica)* to play 3. *(di orologio)* to strike *(v. irr.).* ♦ **sonare** *vi.* *(di campanello)* to ring *(v. irr.).*
sonata *sf.* *(mus.)* sonata.
sonatore *sm.* player.
sonda *sf.* 1. *(mar.)* sounding line 2. *(med.)* probe 3. *(min.)* drill.
sondaggio *sm.* 1. sounding 2. *(med.)* probing 3. *(min.)* drilling.
sondare *vt.* 1. to sound 2. *(fig.)* to throw *(v. irr.)* out.
soneria *sf.* 1. *(di orologio)* striking-mechanism 2. alarm.
sonetto *sm.* sonnet.
sonnacchiosamente *avv.* drowsily.
sonnacchioso *agg.* 1. sleepy 2. *(fig.)* torpid.
sonnambulismo *sm.* sleep-walking.
sonnàmbulo *sm.* sleep-walker.
sonnecchiare *vi.* to doze.
sonnellino *sm.* nap.

sonnífero *sm.* sleeping pills (*pl.*).
sonno *sm.* sleep: — *profondo*, sound sleep.
sonnolento *agg.* drowsy.
sonnolenza *sf.* drowsiness.
sonoramente *avv.* sonorously.
sonorità *sf.* sonority.
sonorizzare *vt.* to post-score.
sonorizzazione *sf.* post-scoring.
sonoro *agg.* **1.** sonorous **2.** (*rumoroso*) loud **3.** (*cine*) sound.
sontuosamente *avv.* sumptuously.
sontuosità *sf.* sumptuousness.
sontuoso *agg.* sumptuous.
soperchierìa *sf.* V. *soverchierìa.*
sopire *vt.* **1.** to make (*v. irr.*) drowsy **2.** (*calmare*) to soothe.
sopore *sm.* doze.
soporìfero *agg.* soporific.
sopperire *vi.* **1.** to provide (for) **2.** (*supplire*) to make (*v. irr.*) up (for).
soppesare *vt.* **1.** to weigh in one's hand **2.** (*considerare*) to weigh.
soppiantare *vt.* to supplant.
soppiatto (*nella loc. avv.*) *di —*, stealthily.
sopportàbile *agg.* bearable.
sopportabilità *sf.* bearableness.
sopportabilmente *avv.* bearably.
sopportare *vt.* to bear (*v. irr.*).
sopportazione *sf.* endurance.
soppressare *vt.* to press.
soppressione *sf.* **1.** suppression **2.** (*abolizione*) abolition.
soppresso *agg.* **1.** suppressed **2.** (*abolito*) abolished.
sopprìmere *vt.* **1.** to suppress **2.** (*abolire*) to abolish.
sopra *prep.* **1.** (*con contatto*) on, upon **2.** (*senza contatto*) over **3.** (*al di sopra*) above ◆ **sopra** *avv.* **1.** above **2.** (*al piano superiore*) upstairs.
soprabbondanza *sf.* V. *sovrabbondanza.*
soprabbondare *vi.* V. *sovrabbondare.*
sopràbito *sm.* overcoat.
sopraccaricare *vt.* V. *sovraccaricare.*
sopraccàrico *sm.* V. *sovraccàrico.*
sopraccennato *agg.* above-mentioned.
sopracciglio *sm.* eyebrow.
sopraccitato *agg.* V. *sopraddetto.*
sopraccoperta *sf.* **1.** (*di libro*) jacket **2.** (*di letto*) counterpane.
◆ **sopraccoperta** *avv.* (*mar.*) on deck.

sopraddetto *agg.* above-mentioned.
sopraelevare *vt.* **1.** (*edil.*) to increase the height of **2.** (*di strade, rotaie ecc.*) to bank.
sopraelevazione *sf.* **1.** (*edil.*) heightening **2.** (*di strade, rotaie ecc.*) superelevation.
sopraffare *vt.* to overwhelm.
sopraffazione *sf.* **1.** overwhelming **2.** (*abuso*) abuse.
sopraffino *agg.* first-rate.
sopraggiùngere *vi.* **1.** to arrive **2.** (*accadere*) to happen.
sopraggiunta *sf.* addition.
sopraindicato *agg.* V. *sopraddetto.*
sopralluogo *sm.* investigation on the spot.
soprammercato (*nella loc. avv.*) *per —*, moreover.
soprammèttere *vt.* to place on.
soprammòbile *sm.* knick-knack.
soprannaturale *agg.* supernatural.
soprannome *sm.* nickname.
soprannominare *vt.* to nickname.
soprannùmero *sm.* excess.
soprano *sm.* soprano.
soprappassaggio *sm.* overbridge.
soprappensiero *avv.* lost in thought.
soprappiù *sm.* extra, addition.
soprapprezzo *sm.* extra charge.
soprascarpa *sf.* galosh.
soprascritta *sf.* inscription.
soprascritto *agg.* above-written.
soprasensìbile *agg.* supersensible.
soprassalto *sm.* jerk: *di —*, all of a sudden.
soprassedere *vi.* **1.** to wait **2.** (*rimandare*) to postpone.
soprassoldo *sm.* extra pay.
soprastruttura *sf.* superstructure.
soprattassa *sf.* extra tax.
soprattutto *avv.* above all.
sopravanzare *vt.* **1.** (*superare*) to surpass **2.** (*avanzare*) to be left over.
sopravanzo *sm.* surplus.
sopravvalutare *vt.* to overrate.
sopravvenire *vi.* **1.** (*di persone*) to turn up **2.** (*di cose*) to come (*v. irr.*) about.
sopravvento *sm.* **1.** (*mar.*) windward **2.** (*fig.*) upper hand: *prendere il —*, to get (*v. irr.*) the upper hand.
sopravvissuto *agg.* e *sm.* surviving. ◆ **sopravvissuto** *sm.* survivor.
sopravvivenza *sf.* survival.

sopravvìvere *vi.* to survive.

sopruso *sm.* abuse of power.

soqquadro *sm.* confusion: *a* —, topsy-turvy.

sorbettare *vt.* to freeze (*v. irr.*).

sorbetto *sm.* sherbet.

sorbire *vt.* to sip. ♦ **sorbirsi** *vr.* to put (*v. irr.*) up with.

sorcio *sm.* mouse (*pl.* mice).

sordamente *avv.* dully.

sordidamente *avv.* filthily.

sordidezza *sf.* filthiness.

sòrdido *agg.* filthy.

sordina *sf.* (*mus.*) mute: *in* — (*fig.*), on the sly.

sordità *sf.* deafness.

sordo *agg.* deaf.

sordomuto *sm.* deaf-mute.

sorella *sf.* sister.

sorellastra *sf.* half-sister.

sorgente *sf.* spring, source.

sòrgere *vi.* to rise (*v. irr.*).

sorgiva *sf.* spring-water.

sorgivo *agg.* spring (*attr.*).

soriano *agg.* syrian: *gatto* —, tabby cat.

sormontare *vt.* 1. to surmount 2. (*superare*) to overcome (*v. irr.*).

sornione *agg.* sly. ♦ **sornione** *sm.* sly person.

sorpassare *vt.* 1. to overtake (*v. irr.*) 2. (*sport*) to outrun (*v. irr.*).

sorpassato *agg.* old-fashioned.

sorpasso *sm.* overtaking.

sorprendente *agg.* surprising.

sorprèndere *vt.* 1. (*cogliere inaspettatamente*) to catch (*v. irr.*) 2. (*meravigliare*) to surprise.

sorpresa *sf.* surprise: *di* —, by surprise.

sorrèggere *vt.* to support.

sorridente *agg.* smiling.

sorrìdere *vi.* to smile 2. (*attrarre*) to appeal.

sorriso *sm.* smile.

sorsata *sf.* sip.

sorseggiare *vt.* to sip.

sorso *sm.* gulp, sip.

sorta *sf.* kind, sort.

sorte *sf.* 1. destiny; lot 2. (*avvenire*) future.

sorteggiare *vt.* to draw (*v. irr.*) lots (for).

sorteggio *sm.* draw.

sortilegio *sm.* witchcraft.

sortire[1] *vt.* to get (*v. irr.*).

sortire[2] *vi.* to come (*v. irr.*) out.

sortita *sf.* sally.

sorvegliante *sm.* overseer.

sorveglianza *sf.* overseeing.

sorvegliare *vt.* to oversee (*v. irr.*).

sorvolare *vt.* 1. to fly (*v. irr.*) over 2. (*passar sopra*) to pass over.

sorvolo *sm.* flying over.

sosia *sm.* double.

sospèndere *vt.* 1. (*attaccare*) to suspend 2. (*interrompere*) to defer.

sospensione *sf.* 1. (*incertezza; chim.*) suspension 2. (*interruzione*) interruption.

sospensiva *sf.* suspension.

sospensivo *agg.* suspensive.

sospeso *agg.* 1. hanging 2. (*interrotto*) suspended.

sospettàbile *agg.* liable to suspicion.

sospettare *vt.* to suspect.

sospetto *sm.* suspicion.

sospettosamente *avv.* suspiciously.

sospettoso *agg.* suspicious.

sospingere *vt.* to drive (*v. irr.*) || *ad ogni piè sospinto*, at every moment.

sospirare *vi.* 1. to sigh 2. (*fig.*) to pine. ♦ **sospirare** *vt.* to long (for).

sospirato *agg.* (*desiderato*) longed for.

sospiro *sm.* sigh.

sosta *sf.* 1. (*fermata*) stop 2. (*pausa*) pause.

sostantivamente *avv.* substantively.

sostantivare *vt.* to substantivize.

sostantivo *agg.* substantive, noun.

sostanza *sf.* substance || *in* — (*in breve*), in short.

sostanziale *agg.* substantial.

sostanzialmente *avv.* substantially.

sostanzioso *agg.* substantial.

sostare *vi.* to stop.

sostegno *sm.* support.

sostenere *vt.* 1. to support 2. (*affermare*) to maintain 3. (*tener alto*) to keep (*v. irr.*) up.

sostenìbile *agg.* 1. supportable 2. (*di opinioni*) maintainable.

sostenimento *sm.* 1. support 2. (*sostentamento*) sustenance.

sostenitore *sm.* supporter.

sostentamento *sm.* sustenance.

sostenuto *agg.* 1. stiff, distant 2. (*comm.*) steady.

sostituìbile *agg.* replaceable.

sostituire *vt.* to replace.

sostituto *sm.* substitute.

sostituzione *sf.* replacement.

sostrato *sm.* substratum (*pl.* -ta).

sottacere vt. to keep (v. irr.) (sthg.) from.

sottaceti sm. pl. pickles.

sottana sf. 1. skirt 2. (di prete) cassock.

sottecchi (nella loc. avv.) di —, stealthily.

sotterfugio sm. subterfuge.

sotte.ramento sm. burial.

sotterrànea sf. underground.

sotterràneo agg. underground. ♦ **sotterràneo** sm. 1. (di basilica) vault 2. (di castello) dungeon.

sotterrare vt. to bury.

sottigliezza sf. 1. thinness 2. (acutezza) subtlety.

sottile agg. 1. thin 2. (fig.) subtle.

sottilizzare vi. to split (v. irr.) hairs.

sottilmente avv. 1. finely 2. (con acutezza) subtly.

sottintèndere vt. to imply.

sottinteso agg. implied. ♦ **sottinteso** sm. allusion.

sotto prep. 1. under 2. (al di sotto, più in basso) below, beneath 3. (in espressioni di tempo) — Natale, at Christmas; essere — gli esami, to be close to the exams. ♦ **sotto** avv. 1. underneath, below 2. (al piano di sotto) downstairs.

sottobanco loc. avv. underthe-counter.

sottobosco sm. underbrush.

sottocchio avv. in front of: tenere qc. —, to keep (v. irr.) an eye on sthg.

sottochiave avv. under lock and key.

sottocoperta sf. (mar.) below deck.

sottocoppa sf. saucer.

sottocutàneo agg. subcutaneous.

sottofondo sm. 1. (edil.) foundation 2. (sfondo) background.

sottogamba (nella loc. avv.) prendere qc. —, to make (v. irr.) light of sthg.

sottolineare vt. 1. to underline 2. (fig.) to lay (v. irr.) stress (on).

sottolineatura sf. underlining.

sottomano avv. 1. (di nascosto) underhand 2. (a portata di mano) at hand.

sottomarino agg. e sm. submarine.

sottomesso agg. 1. subdued 2. (obbediente) submissive.

sottométtere vt. to subject. ♦ **sottométtersi** vr. to submit (oneself).

sottomissione sf. 1. subdual 2. (obbedienza) submission.

sottopassaggio sm. subway.

sottoporre vt. 1. (al giudizio di qu.) to submit 2. (subire, far subire) to subject 3. (esporre) to expose.

sottoposto agg. subordinate.

sottoprodotto sm. by-product.

sottoscritto agg. subscribed. ♦ **sottoscritto** sm. undersigned.

sottoscrivere vt. 1. to sign 2. (comm.) to underwrite. ♦ **sottoscrivere** vi. to subscribe.

sottoscrizione sf. subscription.

sottosegretario sm. under-secretary.

sottosopra avv. 1. upside down 2. (in disordine) topsy-turvy.

sottospecie sf. subspecies (invariato al pl.).

sottostante agg. below.

sottostare vi. 1. (essere sotto) to be below 2. (essere soggetto) to be subjected 3. (sottomettersi) to submit.

sottosuolo sm. subsoil.

sottotenente sm. second lieutenant.

sottotitolo sm. subtitle.

sottovalutare vt. to undervalue.

sottovento avv. (mar.) leeward.

sottoveste sf. petticoat.

sottovoce avv. in a low voice.

ottrarre vt. 1. (mat.) to subtract 2. (portar via) to take (v. irr.) away 3. (rubare) to steal (v. irr.) 4. (salvare da) to deliver. ♦ **sottrarsi** vr. to avoid (sthg.).

sottrazione sf. subtraction.

sottufficiale sm. non-commissioned officer.

sovente avv. often, frequently.

soverchiare vi. to overcome (v. irr.).

soverchieria sf. oppression.

soviètico agg. e sm. Soviet.

sovrabbondante agg. superabundant.

sovrabbondanza sf. superabundance.

sovrabbondare vi. to superabound.

sovraccaricare vt. to overload.

sovraccàrico sm. overload.

sovraccoperta sf. e avv. V. sopraccoperta.

sovranità sf. 1. sovereignty 2. (supremazia) supremacy.

sovrannaturale agg. V. soprannaturale.

sovrano agg. sovereign.

sovrappopolare vt. to overpopulate.

sovrappopolato agg. overpopulated.

sovrappopolazione sf. overpopulation.

sovrapporre vt. to superimpose.

sovrapposizione sf. superimposition.

sovrastampa sf. overprint.

sovrastante agg. impending, overhanging.

sovrastare vi. 1. to overhang (v. irr.) over 2. (fig.) to impend 3. (essere superiore) to be superior.

sovreccedente agg. superabundant.

sovreccedenza sf. surplus.

sovreccitàbile agg. overexcitable.

sovreccitabilità sf. overexcitability.

sovreccitare vt. to overexcite.

sovreccitazione sf. overexcitement.

sovrimposta sf. additional tax.

sovrimpressione sf. (foto; cine) superimposure.

sovrintendente sm. superintendent.

sovrintendenza sf. superintendence.

sovrumano agg. superhuman.

sovvenzionare vt. to subsidize.

sovvenzione sf. subsidy.

sovversione sf. overthrow.

sovversivo agg. subversive. ♦ **sovversivo** sm. subverter.

sovvertimento sm. subversion.

sovvertire vt. to overthrow (v. irr.).

sozzo agg. filthy.

sozzume sm. filth.

spaccalegna sm. wood-cutter.

spaccamontagne sm. braggart.

spaccapietre sm. stone-breaker.

spaccare vt. 1. to split (v. irr.) 2. (rompere) to break (v. irr.) || il mio orologio spacca il minuto, my watch is dead right; il sole spacca le pietre, the sun is blazing down.

spaccatura sf. split, cleft.

spacchettare vt. to unpack.

spacciare vt. 1. (vendere) to sell (v. irr.) 2. (mettere in circolazione) to circulate 3. (far credere) to make (v. irr.) (so.) believe 4. (uccidere) to kill. ♦ **spacciarsi** vr. to pretend to be || lo danno per spacciato (di malato), they give him up.

spacciato agg. done for.

spacciatore sm. 1. seller 2. (di monete false) forger.

spaccio sm. 1. shop 2. (vendita) sale.

spacco sm. 1. split 2. (di abiti) vent.

spacconata sf. bluff.

spaccone sm. boaster.

spada sf. sword.

spadaccino sm. fencer.

spadino sm. court-sword.

spadroneggiare vi. to lord it.

spaesato agg. (fig.) lost.

spaghetto sm. 1. (piccolo spago) string 2. (fam.) (paura) fright.

spagliare vt. to take (v. irr.) the straw off.

spagnoletta sf. 1. (di filo) spool 2. (arachide) peanut.

spagnolismo sm. Hispanicism.

spagnolo agg. Spanish. ♦ **spagnolo** sm. Spaniard.

spago sm. string.

spaiare vt. to uncouple.

spaiato agg. odd.

spalancare vt. to open wide.

spalancato agg. wide open.

spalare vt. to shovel away.

spalatore sm. shoveller.

spalatura sf. shovelling.

spalla sf. 1. shoulder 2. (pl.) back (sing.) 3. (teat.) stooge man || alle spalle, behind; vivere alle spalle di qu., to live on so.

spallata sf. 1. push with the shoulders 2. (alzata di spalle) shrug.

spalleggiare vt. to back.

spalletta sf. parapet.

spalliera sf. 1. back 2. (di piante) espalier.

spallina sf. 1. shoulder-strap 2. (mil.) epaulette.

spalluccia sf. far spallucce, to shrug one's shoulders.

spalmare vt. to smear.

spalto sm. glacis.

spampanare vt. to strip a vine of its leaves.

spàndere vt. 1. to spread (v. irr.) 2. (versare) to shed (v. irr.) 3. (scialacquare) to squander.

spanna sf. span.

spannare vt. to skim.

spannocchiare vt. to husk.

spappolare vt. to pulp. ♦ **spappolarsi** vr. to become (v. irr.) mushy.

sparare[1] vt. to shoot (v. irr.), to fire.

sparare[2] *vt. (squartare)* to split (*v. irr.*).

sparata *sf.* **1.** discharge **2.** (*spacconata*) brag.

sparato *sm.* (*di camicia*) shirt-front.

sparatore *sm.* shooter.

sparatoria *sf.* shooting.

sparecchiare *vt.* to clear.

spareggio *sm.* **1.** disparity **2.** (*sport*) deciding game.

spàrgere *vt.* **1.** to scatter **2.** (*divulgare*) to spread (*v. irr.*) **3.** (*versare; di luce*) to shed (*v. irr.*).

spargimento *sm.* **1.** spreading **2.** (*versamento*) shedding || — *di sangue*, bloodshed.

sparigliare *vt.* to unmatch.

sparire *vi.* to disappear.

sparizione *sf.* disappearance.

sparlare *vi.* to speak (*v. irr.*) badly.

sparo *sm.* shot.

sparpagliare *vt.* to scatter. ♦ **sparpagliarsi** *vr.* to scatter.

sparso *agg.* **1.** (*versato*) shed **2.** (*sciolto*) loose.

spartano *agg.* Spartan.

spartiacque *sm.* watershed.

spartineve *sm.* snow-plough.

spartire *vt.* to share out.

spartito *sm.* score.

spartizione *sf.* sharing.

sparuto *agg.* lean, spare.

sparviero *sm.* sparrow-hawk.

spasimante *sm.* wooer.

spasimare *vi.* **1.** to suffer agonies **2.** (*fig.*) to yearn.

spàsimo *sm.* pang.

spasmo *sm.* spasm.

spasmodicamente *avv.* spasmodically.

spasmòdico *agg.* spasmodic.

spassare *vt.* to amuse || *spassarsela*, to have a very good time.

spassionato *agg.* impartial.

spasso *sm.* **1.** amusement: *che —!*, what fun! **2.** (*passeggiata*) *andare a —*, to go (*v. irr.*) for a walk; *essere a —*, to be out of work.

spassoso *agg.* funny, amusing.

spàstico *agg.* spastic.

spato *sm.* spar.

spàtola *sf.* broad knife.

spatriare *vt.* V. *espatriare.*

spauracchio *sm.* **1.** scarecrow **2.** (*fig.*) bugbear.

spaurire *vt.* to frighten. ♦ **spaurirsi** *vr.* to get (*v. irr.*) frightened.

spaurito *agg.* frightened.

spavalderìa *sf.* boldness.

spavaldo *agg.* bold, arrogant.

spaventapàsseri *sm.* scarecrow.

spaventare *vt.* to frighten, to scare. ♦ **spaventarsi** *vr.* to be frightened.

spaventato *agg.* frightened, scared.

spavento *sm.* fright.

spaventoso *agg.* dreadful, frightful.

spaziale *agg.* space (*attr.*).

spaziare *vt.* to space. ♦ **spaziare** *vi.* to range.

spaziatura *sf.* spacing.

spazieggiare *vt.* to space.

spazientirsi *vr.* to lose (*v. irr.*) one's patience.

spazio *sm.* **1.** space **2.** (*posto*) room.

spazioso *agg.* wide.

spazzacamino *sm.* chimney-sweep.

spazzamine *sm.* mine-sweeper.

spazzaneve *sm.* snow-plough.

spazzare *vt.* to sweep (*v. irr.*).

spazzata *sf.* sweep.

spazzatura *sf.* (*rifiuti*) sweepings (*pl.*): *bidone della —*, dust-bin; *carro della —*, dust-cart.

spazzino *sm.* **1.** road-sweeper **2.** (*spazzaturaio*) dustman (*pl. -men*).

spàzzola *sf.* brush || *capelli a —*, crew-cut.

spazzolare *vt.* to brush.

spazzolata *sf.* brush.

spazzolino *sm.* (small) brush: — *da denti*, tooth-brush.

spazzolone *sm.* scrubbing-brush.

specchiarsi *vr.* **1.** to look at oneself in a mirror **2.** (*riflettersi*) to be mirrored.

specchiera *sf.* looking-glass.

specchietto *sm.* **1.** hand-mirror **2.** (*tabella*) table || — *retrovisore*, driving-mirror.

specchio *sm.* **1.** mirror **2.** (*prospetto*) register **3.** (*modello*) model || — *d'acqua*, sheet of water.

speciale *agg.* special.

specialista *s.* specialist.

specialità *sf.* speciality.

specializzare *vt.* to specialize. ♦ **specializzarsi** *vr.* to specialize.

specializzazione *sf.* specialization.

specie *sf.* **1.** kind **2.** (*scientifico; teol.*) species (*pl. invariato*) || *far —*, to surprise.

specificamente *avv.* specifically.

specificare *vt.* to specify.

specificazione *sf.* specification.

specìfico *agg. e sm.* specific.

specioso *agg.* specious.

speculare¹ *vi.* to speculate (on): — *al rialzo, al ribasso,* to speculate for the advance, for the fall.

speculare² *agg.* mirror-like.

speculativo *agg.* speculative.

speculatore *agg.* speculative. ♦ **speculatore** *sm.* speculator.

speculazione *sf.* speculation.

spedire *vt.* 1. to send (*v. irr.*) 2. (*via mare*) to ship 3. (*via terra*) to forward.

speditamente *avv.* 1. quickly 2. (*correntemente*) fluently.

speditezza *sf.* 1. quickness 2. (*nel parlare*) fluency.

spedito *agg.* 1. (*svelto*) quick 2. (*nel parlare*) fluent.

speditore *sm.* sender.

spedizione *sf.* 1. forwarding 2. (*per mare*) shipment 3. (*di lettere, pacchi*) dispatch 4. (*scientifico; mil.*) expedition || — *per via aerea,* air-freight.

spedizioniere *sm.* forwarding agent.

spègnere *vt.* 1. (*un fuoco*) to put (*v. irr.*) out 2. (*gas, luce ecc.*) to turn off 3. (*fig.*) to stifle || — *la sete,* to quench one's thirst. ♦ **spègnersi** *vr.* 1. to go (*v. irr.*) out 2. (*fig.*) to fade 3. (*morire*) to pass away.

spegnimento *sm.* extinction.

spegnitoio *sm.* snuffer.

spelacchiare *vt.* to tear (*v. irr.*) out the hair of. ♦ **spelacchiarsi** *vr.* to lose (*v. irr.*) one's hair.

spelacchiato *agg.* 1. scanty-haired 2. (*di stoffe, pellicce*) worn-out.

spelare *vt.* to balden. ♦ **spelarsi** *vr.* V. *spelacchiarsi.*

spelato *agg.* 1. hairless 2. (*di indumento*) worn.

spelatura *sf.* 1. hairless patch 2. (*di indumento*) worn patch.

speleologìa *sf.* speleology.

speleològico *agg.* speleological.

speleòlogo *sm.* speleologist.

spellare *vt.* to skin. ♦ **spellarsi** *vr.* to peel.

spellatura *sf.* 1. skinning 2. (*parte spellata*) graze.

spelonca *sf.* den.

spendaccione *sm.* spendthrift.

spèndere *vt.* to spend (*v. irr.*) (*anche fig.*).

spennacchiare *vt.* to pluck. ♦ **spennacchiarsi** *vr.* to lose (*v. irr.*) one's feathers.

spennare *vt.* to pluck.

spennellare *vt.* 1. to brush 2. (*med.*) to paint.

spennellata *sf.* touch of the brush.

spennellatura *sf.* (*med.*) painting.

spensieratamente *avv.* thoughtlessly.

spensieratezza *sf.* thoughtlessness.

spensierato *agg.* thoughtless.

spento *agg.* 1. extinguished, out (*pred.*) 2. (*estinto*) extinct 3. (*smorto*) dull.

speràbile *agg.* to be hoped (for).

speranza *sf.* hope.

speranzoso *agg.* hopeful.

sperare *vt.* e *vi.* to hope (for sthg., in so.).

sperdersi *vr.* 1. to get (*v. irr.*) lost 2. (*dileguare*) to vanish.

sperduto *agg.* 1. scattered 2. (*isolato*) secluded 3. (*smarrito*) lost.

sperequazione *sf.* inequality.

spergiurare *vi.* to swear (*v. irr.*) falsely: *giurare e* —, to swear again and again.

spergiuro *sm.* 1. perjury 2. (*di persona*) perjurer.

spericolato *agg.* reckless. ♦ **spericolato** *sm.* daredevil.

sperimentale *agg.* experimental.

sperimentalismo *sm.* experimentalism.

sperimentalmente *avv.* experimentally.

sperimentare *vt.* 1. to experiment (with) 2. (*mettere alla prova*) to test.

sperimentato *agg.* 1. (*provato*) tried 2. (*esperto*) experienced.

sperimentatore *sm.* experimenter.

sperimentazione *sf.* experimentation.

sperma *sm.* sperm.

spermatozoo *sm.* spermatozoon (*pl.* -zoa).

speronare *vt.* 1. (*mar.*) to ram 2. (*un cavallo*) to spur.

speronata *sf.* 1. (*mar.*) ramming 2. (*colpo di sperone*) spur.

sperone *sm.* V. *sprone.*

sperperamento *sm.* squandering.

sperperare *vt.* to squander.

sperperatore *sm.* squanderer.

spèrpero *sm.* dissipation.

sperticato *agg.* excessive.

spesa *sf.* 1. expense: *far fronte a una* —, to meet (*v. irr.*) an expense 2. (*compera*) shopping: *andare a far spese,* to go (*v. irr.*) shopping.

spesare vt. to maintain.

spesato agg. essere —, to have all expenses paid.

spessire vt. to thicken. ♦ **spessirsi** vr. to thicken.

spesso[1] agg. 1. thick 2. (frequente) frequent.

spesso[2] avv. often.

spessore sm. thickness.

spettàbile agg. respectable.

spettàcolo sm. 1. spectacle 2. (teat.) performance.

spettacoloso agg. spectacular.

spettante agg. due.

spettanze sf. pl. dues.

spettare vi. 1. to be (for so.) 2. (essere dovuto) to be due.

spettatore sm. 1. spectator 2. (testimone) witness || gli spettatori, the audience.

spettegolare vi. to gossip.

spettinare vt. to ruffle so.'s hair. ♦ **spettinarsi** vr. to ruffle one's hair.

spettinato agg. uncombed.

spettrale agg. spectral.

spettro sm. 1. ghost 2. (fis.) spectrum (pl. -ra).

spettroscopìa sf. spectroscopy.

spettroscòpico agg. spectroscopic(al).

spettroscopio sm. spectroscope.

speziale sm. (farmacista) chemist.

spezie sf. pl. spices.

spezzàbile agg. breakable.

spezzare vt. to break (v. irr.). ♦ **spezzarsi** vr. to break.

spezzatino sm. stew.

spezzato agg. broken.

spezzettamento sm. chopping.

spezzettare vt. to chop.

spezzone sm. 1. (mil.) incendiary bomb 2. (metal.) cut-down size.

spia sf. 1. spy 2. (indizio) evidence 3. (di porta) peep-hole || — luminosa, warning light; fare la —, to play the spy.

spiaccicare vt. to squash. ♦ **spiaccicarsi** vr. to get (v. irr.) squashed.

spiacente agg. sorry.

spiacere vi. V. dispiacere.

spiacévole agg. unpleasant.

spiacevolmente avv. unpleasantly.

spiaggia sf. 1. beach 2. (riva) (sea)shore.

spianamento sm. 1. levelling 2. (il radere al suolo) razing.

spianare vt. 1. to level 2. (radere al suolo) to raze 3. (appianare, lisciare) to smooth. ♦ **spianarsi** vr. to become (v. irr.) smooth.

spianata sf. 1. levelling 2. (luogo spianato) open space 3. (arch.) esplanade 4. (in un bosco) clearing.

spianato agg. 1. levelled 2. (liscio) smooth.

spiano (nella loc. avv.) a tutto —, profusely; (sodo) hard.

spiantare vt. 1. to pull out 2. (rovinare) to ruin. ♦ **spiantarsi** vr. (rovinarsi) to go (v. irr.) to ruin.

spiantato agg. (fig.) penniless. ♦ **spiantato** sm. (fig.) pauper.

spiare vt. 1. to spy (upon) 2. (aspettare) to watch (for).

spiattellare vt. to blab (out).

spiazzo sm. 1. open space 2. (nel bosco) clearing.

spiccare vt. 1. to pick 2. (tagliare) to cut (v. irr.) off 3. (pronunciare) to enunciate distinctly 4. (emettere) to issue || — un salto, to take (v. irr.) a leap; — il volo, to fly (v. irr.) up; — una tratta, to draw (v. irr.) a bill. ♦ **spiccare** vi. to stand (v. irr.) out.

spiccatamente avv. distinctly.

spiccato agg. 1. (marcato) marked 2. (nitido) clear.

spicchio sm. 1. slice 2. (di agrumi) segment 3. (di aglio) clove 4. (geom.) sector || a spicchi, sliced.

spicciare vt. to dispatch ♦ **spicciarsi** vr. to hurry up.

spicciativo agg. V. spiccio.

spiccicare vt. 1. to detach 2. (pronunciare) to utter.

spiccio agg. 1. quick 2. (franco) straightforward || andar per le spicce, to go (v. irr.) straight to the point; moneta spiccia, small change.

spicciolata (nella loc. avv.) alla —, few at a time.

spiccioli sm. pl. change (solo sing.).

spicco sm. far —, to stand (v. irr.) out.

spidocchiare vt. to delouse.

spiedo sm. spit.

spiegàbile agg. explainable.

spiegamento sm. 1. spreading out 2. (mil.) deployment.

spiegare vt. 1. to explain 2. (stendere) to spread (v. irr.) out 3. (di vele) to unfurl 4. (mil.) to deploy. ♦ **spiegarsi** vr. 1. (farsi *capire*) to make (*v. irr.*) oneself understood 2. (*stendersi*) to spread out.

spiegazione *sf.* explanation.

spiegazzare *vt.* to crumple.

spietatamente *avv.* ruthlessly.

spietatezza *sf.* ruthlessness.

spietato *agg.* ruthless.

spifferare *vt.* to blurt out.

spiffero *sm.* draught.

spiga *sf.* 1. spike 2. (*di cereali*) ear.

spigare *vi.* to ear.

spighetta *sf.* braid.

spigliatamente *avv.* easily.

spigliatezza *sf.* ease.

spigliato *agg.* easy.

spigo *sm.* lavender.

spigolare *vt.* to glean (*anche fig.*).

spigolatore *sm.* gleaner.

spigolatrice *sf.* gleaner.

spigolatura *sf.* gleaning.

spigolo *sm.* edge.

spigoloso *agg.* edgy.

spilla *sf.* 1. pin 2. (*gioiello*) brooch.

spillare *vt.* 1. to draw (*v. irr.*) 2. (*fig.*) to worm.

spillo *sm.* pin: — *da balia*, safety-pin.

spillone *sm.* (*per cappello*) hat-pin.

spilorcería *sf.* stinginess.

spilorcio *agg.* stingy. ♦ **spilorcio** *sm.* miser.

spilungona *sf.* lanky woman.

spilungone *sm.* lanky man.

spina *sf.* 1. thorn 2. (*lisca*) fishbone 3. (*elettr.*) plug 4. (*mecc.*) pin 5. (*di botte*) bung 6. (*fig.*) sorrow, grief || — *dorsale*, backbone; *a* — *di pesce*, herring-bone.

spinacio *sm.* spinach (*solo sing.*).

spinale *agg.* spinal.

spinare *vt.* (*pesce*) to bone.

spinato *agg.* (*a spina di pesce*) herring-bone || *filo* —, barbed wire.

spinetta *sf.* spinet.

spingere *vt.* 1. to push 2. (*condurre*) to drive (*v. irr.*) 3. (*stimolare*) to urge 4. (*portare*) to carry. ♦ **spingersi** *vr.* to push.

spino *sm.* thorn.

spinone *sm.* (*cane*) griffon.

spinosità *sf.* thorniness.

spinoso *agg.* thorny.

spinta *sf.* 1. push 2. (*stimolo*) incentive 3. (*mecc.; edil.*) thrust.

spinterògeno *sm.* (battery) coil ignition.

spinto *agg.* 1. (*eccessivo*) excessive 2. (*audace*) risky.

spintone *sm.* shove || *farsi avanti a spintoni*, to elbow one's way forward.

spiombare *vt.* to unseal.

spionaggio *sm.* espionage.

spioncino *sm.* peep-hole.

spione *sm.* spy.

spiovente *agg.* 1. drooping 2. (*inclinato*) sloping. ♦ **spiovente** *sm.* 1. slope 2. (*sport*) high kick.

spiòvere *vi.* 1. to stop raining 2. (*ricadere*) to come (*v. irr.*) down.

spira *sf.* coil.

spiraglio *sm.* 1. small hole 2. (*barlume*) gleam.

spirale *sf.* 1. spiral 2. (*molla*) spring.

spirante *agg.* 1. (*soffiante*) blowing 2. (*morente*) passing away 3. (*esalante*) exhaling.

spirare *vi.* 1. (*soffiare*) to blow (*v. irr.*) 2. (*morire*) to pass away (*v. scadere*) to expire 4. (*emanare*) to emanate. ♦ **spirare** *vt.* to exhale.

spiritato *agg.* 1. possessed 2. (*spaventato*) frightened.

spiritico *agg.* spiritualistic.

spiritismo *sm.* spiritualism.

spiritista *s.* spiritualist.

spiritìstico *agg.* V. *spiritico*.

spirito *sm.* 1. spirit 2. (*fantasma*) ghost 3. (*arguzia*) wit 4. (*alcool*) alcohol || *far dello* —, to be witty.

spiritosàggine *sf.* witticism.

spiritosamente *avv.* wittily.

spiritoso *agg.* 1. witty 2. (*alcoolico*) alcoholic.

spirituale *agg.* spiritual.

spiritualismo *sm.* spiritualism.

spiritualista *agg.* spiritualistic. ♦ **spiritualista** *s.* spiritualist.

spiritualità *sf.* spirituality.

spiritualizzare *vt.* to spiritualize.

spiritualmente *avv.* spiritually.

spizzicare *vt.* to nibble.

spizzico (*nella loc. avv.*) *a* —, little by little.

splendente *agg.* brign.

splèndere *vi.* to shine (*v. irr.*).

splèndido *agg.* splendid.

splendore *sm.* splendour.

spocchia *sf.* haughtiness. ⸮

spocchioso *agg.* haughty.

spodestamento *sm.* 1. dispossession 2. (*da posizione autorevole*) dethronement.

spodestare *vt.* 1. to dispossess 2. (*detronizzare*) to dethrone.

spoetizzare *vt.* to disenchant.

spoglia sf. 1. (di animale) skin 2. (veste) dress 3. (bottino) spoils (pl.) || spoglie mortali, mortal remains.

spogliare vt. 1. to strip 2. (derubare) to rob 3. (saccheggiare) to plunder. ♦ **spogliarsi** vr. 1. to strip 2. (di alberi) to shed (v. irr.) 3. (privarsi) to strip oneself (of).

spogliarello sm. strip-tease.

spogliatoio sm. 1. dressing-room 2. (teat. ecc.) cloak-room.

spoglio agg. bare. ♦ **spoglio** sm. 1. (computo) counting 2. (esame) examination 3. (vestito smesso) cast-off || fare lo —, to go (v. irr.) through.

spola sf. shuttle.

spoletta sf. 1. spool 2. (di arma) fuse.

spoliazione sf. spoliation.

spolmonarsi vr. to talk oneself hoarse.

spolpare vt. 1. to take (v. irr.) the flesh off 2. (fig.) to skin.

spolpato agg. 1. stripped of the flesh 2. (fig.) skinned.

spolverare vt. to dust.

spolveratura sf. 1. dusting 2. (fig.) smattering.

spolverino sm. dust-coat.

spolverizzare vt. to dust.

spòlvero sm. 1. dusting 2. (disegno) perforated pattern.

sponda sf. 1. edge 2. (di fiume) bank 3. (di mare) shore 4. (parapetto) parapet.

sponsali sm. pl. nuptials.

spontaneamente avv. spontaneously.

spontaneità sf. spontaneity.

spontàneo agg. spontaneous.

spopolamento sm. depopulation.

spopolare vt. to depopulate. ♦ **spopolarsi** vr. to become (v. irr.) depopulated.

spopolato agg. (deserto) deserted.

spora sf. spore.

sporàdico agg. sporadic.

sporcaccione sm. dirty man

sporcare vt. to dirty.

sporcizia sf. dirt.

sporco agg. dirty.

sporgente agg. protruding.

sporgenza sf. protrusion.

spòrgere vi. to put (v. irr.) out. ♦ **spòrgere** vt. to put (v. irr.) out. ♦ **spòrgersi** vr. to lean (v. irr.) out.

sport sm. sport.

sporta sf. basket.

sportello sm. 1. door 2. (di biglietteria) ticket-window 3. (di ufficio postale ecc.) counter.

sportivamente avv. sportingly.

sportivo agg. sporting. ♦ **sportivo** sm. sportsman (pl. -men).

sporto agg. 1. leaning out 2. (proteso) outstretched.

sposa sf. bride.

sposalizio sm. wedding.

sposare vt. to marry. ♦ **sposarsi** vr. to get (v. irr.) married.

sposo sm. bridegroom.

spossamento sm. exhaustion.

spossante agg. exhausting.

spossare vt. to exhaust.

spossatezza sf. V. spossamento.

spossato agg. weary.

possessare vt. to dispossess.

spostàbile agg. shiftable.

spostamento sm. 1. shifting 2. (cambiamento) change.

spostare vt. 1. to shift, to move 2. (cambiare) to change. ♦ **spostarsi** vr. to shift.

spostato agg. out of one's place (pred.). ♦ **spostato** sm. misfit.

spranga sf. bar.

sprangare vt. to bar.

sprazzo sm. flash: — d'ingegno, brain-wave.

sprecare vt. to waste.

spreco sm. waste.

sprecone sm. waster.

spregévole agg. despicable.

spregiare vt. to scorn.

spregiativo agg. 1. scornful 2. (gramm.) pejorative. ♦ **spregiativo** sm. (gramm.) pejorative.

spregio sm. contempt.

spregiudicatamente avv. open-mindedly.

spregiudicatezza sf. open-mindedness.

spregiudicato agg. open-minded.

sprèmere vt. 1. to squeeze 2. (torcere) to wring (v. irr.) out. ♦ **spremersi** vr. to rack oneself

spremilimoni sm. lemon-squeezer.

spremitura sf. 1. squeezing 2. (di panni bagnati) wringing.

spremuta sf. squash.

spremuto agg. 1. squeezed 2. (di panni) wrung.

spretare vt. to unfrock. ♦ **spretarsi** vr. to renounce one's priesthood.

spretato *agg.* unfrocked. ♦ **spretato** *sm.* unfrocked priest.

sprezzante *agg.* scornful.

sprezzare *vt.* V. *disprezzare*.

sprezzo *sm.* scorn.

sprigionamento *sm.* 1. exhalation 2. (*violento*) bursting out.

sprigionare *vt.* to emit. ♦ **sprigionarsi** *vr.* 1. to be emitted 2. (*con violenza*) to burst (*v. irr.*) out.

sprimacciare *vt.* to shake (*v. irr.*) up.

sprizzare *vt. e vi.* to spurt: — *scintille,* to spit (*v. irr.*) sparks; — *gioia,* to burst (*v. irr.*) with joy.

sprizzo *sm.* spurt.

sprofondamento *sm.* 1. sinking 2. (*crollo*) collapse.

sprofondare *vt.* (*far cadere*) to cause to collapse. ♦ **sprofondare** *vi.* 1. to sink (*v. irr.*) 2. (*crollare*) to collapse 3. (*fig.*) to be absorbed. ♦ **sprofondarsi** *vr.* 1. to sink 2. (*crollare*) to collapse 3. (*fig.*) to be absorbed.

sproloquio *sm.* long rigmarole.

spronare *vt.* to spur.

spronata *sf.* spurring.

sprone *sm.* 1. spur 2. (*mar.*) ram || *a spron battuto,* at full speed.

sproporzionato *agg.* disproportionate, out of proportion (*pred.*).

sproporzione *sf.* disproportion.

spropositato *agg.* 1. full of blunders 2. (*fig.*) enormous.

sproposito *sm.* 1. blunder 2. (*eccesso*) excess || *a* —, off the point.

sprovveduto *agg.* 1. (*incauto*) unwary 2. (*sprovvisto*) devoid 3. (*impreparato*) unprepared.

sprovvisto *agg.* devoid || *alla sprovvista,* unawares.

spruzzare *vt.* 1. to spray 2. (*inzaccherare*) to splash.

spruzzata *sf.* spray.

spruzzatore *sm.* sprayer.

spruzzatura *sf.* spraying.

spruzzo *sm.* 1. spray 2. (*di liquido sporco*) splash.

spudoratezza *sf.* shamelessness.

spudorato *agg.* shameless.

spugna *sf.* 1. sponge 2. (*tessuto*) sponge-cloth || *cancellare con la* —, to sponge; *bere come una* —, to drink (*v. irr.*) like a fish.

spugnatura *sf.* sponge down.

spugnosità *sf.* sponginess.

spugnoso *agg.* spongy.

spulciare *vt.* 1. to look for fleas 2. (*esaminare; fig.*) to peruse 3. (*raccogliere; fig.*) to gather here and there.

spuma *sf.* foam.

spumante *agg.* foaming. ♦ **spumante** *sm.* sparkling wine.

spumare *vi.* to foam.

spumeggiante *agg.* foaming.

spumeggiare *vi.* to foam.

spumoso *agg.* foamy.

spuntare[1] *vt.* 1. (*smussare*) to blunt 2. (*tagliare*) to trim 3. (*staccare*) to unpin || *spuntarla,* to succeed. ♦ **spuntarsi** *vr.* 1. (*smussarsi*) to get (*v. irr.*) blunt 2. (*staccarsi*) to become (*v. irr.*) unpinned.

spuntare[2] *vi.* 1. (*sorgere*) to rise (*v. irr.*) 2. (*germogliare*) to sprout 3. (*di capelli*) to begin (*v. irr.*) to grow 4. (*apparire*) to appear.

spuntato *agg.* pointless.

spuntatura *sf.* 1. (*lo smussare*) blunting 2. (*il tagliare*) trimming.

spuntino *sm.* snack.

spunto *sm.* 1. cue 2. (*punto di partenza*) starting point.

spurgare *vt.* 1. to clean 2. (*med.*) to discharge. ♦ **spurgarsi** *vr.* (*espettorare*) to expectorate.

spurgo *sm.* 1. (*lo spurgare*) discharging 2. (*l'espettorare*) expectorating 3. (*ciò che viene espulso*) discharge.

spurio *agg.* spurious.

sputacchiare *vi.* V. *sputare*.

sputacchiera *sf.* spittoon.

sputacchio *sm.* spittle.

sputare *vt.* to spit (*v. irr.*).

sputasentenze *sm.* wiseacre.

sputo *sm.* spit.

squadra *sf.* 1. (*da disegno*) square 2. (*gruppo; sport*) team 3. (*di operai*) gang 4. (*mil.*) squad 5. (*mar.*) squadron || — *mobile,* flying squad.

squadrare *vt.* 1. to square 2. (*guardare*) to look (so.) up and down.

squadratura *sf.* squaring.

squadriglia *sf.* squadron.

squadro *sm.* squaring.

squadrone *sm.* squadron.

squagliamento *sm.* melting.

squagliare *vt.* to melt. ♦ **squagliarsi** *vr.* 1. to melt 2. (*andar via*) to steal (*v. irr.*) away.

squalifica *sf.* disqualification.

squalificare vt. to disqualify.

squàllido agg. dreary.

squallore sm. dreariness.

squalo sm. shark.

squama sf. scale.

squamare vt. to scale. ♦ **squamarsi** vr. to scale.

squamoso agg. scaly.

squarciagola (nella loc. avv.) a —, at the top of one's voice.

squarciamento sm. tearing.

squarciare vt. 1. to tear (v. irr.) 2. (fig.) to dispel. ♦ **squarciarsi** vr. to be torn.

squarcio sm. gash.

squartare vt. to mangle.

squartatore sm. mangler.

squassare vt. to jolt.

squasso sm. jolt.

squattrinato agg. penniless.

squilibrare vt. to unbalance. ♦ **squilibrarsi** vr. to lose (v. irr.) one's balance.

squilibrato agg. unbalanced. ♦ **squilibrato** sm. lunatic.

squilibrio sm. 1. lack of balance 2. (mentale) derangement.

squillante agg. 1. shrill 2. (di trombe) blaring 3. (di campane) pealing.

squillare vi. 1. to ring (v. irr.) 2. (di trombe) to blare.

squillo sm. 1. ring 2. (di tromba) blare.

squinternare vt. 1. to ruin 2. (fig.) to upset (v. irr.).

squisitezza sf. exquisiteness.

squisito agg. exquisite.

squittìo sm. squeak.

squittire vi. to squeak.

sradicare vt. to uproot.

sragionare vi. to talk nonsense.

sregolatezza sf. disorderliness.

sregolato agg. disorderly.

stabbio sm. 1. sty 2. (letame) manure.

stàbile . sm. building. ♦ **stàbile** agg. 1. stable 2. (permanente) permanent: in pianta —, on the permanent staff.

stabilimento sm. 1. (fabbrica) factory 2. (edificio, lo stabilire) establishment.

stabilire vt. 1. to establish 2. (decidere) to decide. ♦ **stabilirsi** vr. to settle.

stabilità sf. stability.

stabilizzare vt. to stabilize.

stabilizzatore sm. stabilizer.

stabilizzazione sf. stabilization.

stabilmente avv. firmly.

stacanovismo sm. Stakhanovism.

staccàbile agg. detachable.

staccare vt. 1. to take (v. irr.) off 2. (tagliare) to cut (v. irr.) off 3. (separare) to separate 4. (slegare) to unfasten || — un assegno, to issue a cheque. ♦ **staccarsi** vr. 1. to come (v. irr.) off 2. (sciogliersi) to break (v. irr.) loose 3. (scostarsi) to move away 4. (separarsi) to part 5. (distaccarsi) to pull ahead (of) 6. (esser diverso) to differ.

stacciare vt. to sieve.

staccio sm. sieve.

staccionata sf. fence.

stacco sm. detachment.

stadera sf. steelyard.

stadio sm. 1. stadium (pl. -ia), sports ground 2. (fase) stage.

staffa sf. stirrup || perder le staffe (fig.), to lose (v. irr.) one's self-control.

staffetta sf. 1. courier 2. (sport) relay race.

staffilare vt. to lash.

staffilata sf. lash.

staffile sm. whip.

stafilococco sm. staphylococcus (pl. -ci).

staggio sm. 1. (di scala) shaft 2. (di sedia) back leg.

stagionale agg. seasonal.

stagionare vt. to season.

stagionato agg. 1. seasoned 2. (fig.) oldish.

stagionatura sf. seasoning.

stagione sf. season.

stagnaio sm. tinsmith.

stagnante agg. stagnant.

stagnare[1] vi. to stagnate.

stagnare[2] vt. 1. to tin 2. (saldare) to solder 3. (impermeabilizzare) to waterproof 4. (fermare) to staunch.

stagnatura sf. tinning.

stagnino sm. tinker.

stagno[1] sm. tin.

stagno[2] sm. (bacino d'acqua) pond.

stagno[3] agg. water-tight.

stagnola sf. tin-foil.

staio sm. bushel.

stalagmite sf. stalagmite.

stalattite sf. stalactite.

stalla sf. stable.

stalliere sm. stable-boy.

stallo sm. stall.

stallone sm. stallion.

stamattina *avv.* this morning.

stambecco *sm.* ibex.

stamberga *sf.* hovel.

stambugio *sm.* hole.

stame *sm.* (*bot.*) stamen.

stamigna *sf.* bunting.

stampa *sf.* 1. print 2. (*atto di stampare*) printing 3. (*periodici, giornali*) press 4. (*genere*) stamp || *agenzia di —*, news-agency; *errore di —*, misprint.

stampare *vt.* 1. to print 2. (*mecc.*) to press 3. (*coniare*) to coin. ♦ **stamparsi** *vr.* — *in mente*, to impress (sthg.) firmly on one's mind.

stampatello *sm.* block letters (*pl.*).

stampato *sm.* 1. printed matter 2. (*modulo*) form.

stampatore *sm.* printer.

stampatrice *sf.* printing-press.

stampella *sf.* crutch.

stamperia *sf.* printing-office.

stampigliare *vt.* to stamp.

stampo *sm.* 1. die, mould 2. (*genere*) stamp.

stanare *vt.* to drive (*v. irr.*) out.

stancare *vt.* 1. to tire 2. (*infastidire*) to annoy. ♦ **stancarsi** *vr.* 1. to get (*v. irr.*) tired 2. (*annoiarsi*) to get bored.

stanchezza *sf.* tiredness.

stanco *agg.* tired.

standardizzare *vt.* to standardize.

stanga *sf.* 1. bar 2. (*di carro*) shaft 3. (*di passaggio a livello*) barrier.

stangare *vt.* 1. to bar 2. (*percuotere*) to thrash.

stanghetta *sf.* 1. (*degli occhiali*) bar 2. (*di serratura*) bolt.

stanotte *avv.* tonight.

stantio *agg.* stale.

stantuffo *sm.* 1. piston 2. (*di pompa ecc.*) plunger.

stanza *sf.* 1. room 2. (*strofa*) stanza || *prendere, avere —*, to settle.

stanziamento *sm.* appropriation.

stanziare *vt.* to appropriate. ♦ **stanziarsi** *vr.* to settle.

stappare *vt.* to uncork.

stare *vi.* 1. to stay 2. (*abitare*) to live 3. (*di salute, essere*) to be 4. (*in piedi*) to stand (*v. irr.*) 5. (*dipendere*) to depend (on) 6. (*spettare*) to be up 7. (*andare*) to go (*v. irr.*) 8. (*di abito*) to suit || *— per*, to be going (to); *lasciar —*, to leave (*v. irr.*) alone; *sta' a sentire!*, listen!; *ben ti sta!*, it

serves you right!

starnazzare *vi.* to flutter.

starnutire *vi.* to sneeze.

starnuto *sm.* sneeze.

stasare *vt.* to unclog.

stasera *avv.* this evening.

stasi *sf.* 1. standstill 2. (*med.*) stasis (*pl. -ses*).

statale *agg.* State (*attr.*), of the State. ♦ **statale** *s.* State employee.

statica *sf.* statics.

statico *agg.* static.

statista *sm.* statesman (*pl. -men*).

statistica *sf.* statistics.

statizzare *vt.* to nationalize.

statizzazione *sf.* nationalization.

stato *sm.* 1. state, condition (*anche posizione sociale*) 2. (*giur.*) status 3. (*pol.*) State || *ufficio di — civile*, registry office; *ufficiale di — civile*, registrar.

statua *sf.* statue.

statuaria *sf.* statuary.

statuario *agg.* statuesque.

statuire *vt.* to decree.

statunitense *agg.* United States (*attr.*). ♦ **statunitense** *sm.* United States citizen.

statura *sf.* stature.

statuto *sm.* statute.

stazionamento *sm.* standing.

stazionare *vi.* 1. to stay 2. (*di vetture*) to be parked.

stazionario *agg.* stationary.

stazione *sf.* station.

stazza *sf.* tonnage.

stazzare *vt.* to have the tonnage of.

stecca *sf.* 1. (*di ombrello, ventaglio*) rib 2. (*da biliardo*) cue 3. (*di persiana*) slat 4. (*di busto*) whalebone 5. (*stonatura*) false note.

steccare *vt.* 1. (*chiudere con steccato*) to fence in 2. (*mus.*) to fluff. ♦ **steccare** *vi.* 1. (*cantando*) to sing (*v. irr.*) a false note 2. (*suonando*) to play a false note.

steccato *sm.* fence.

stecchito *agg.* 1. (*secco*) dried up 2. (*magro*) skinny 3. (*morto*) stone dead.

stecco *sm.* 1. stick 2. (*persona magra*) bag of bones.

stecconata *sf.* paling.

stele *sf.* stele (*pl. -lae*).

stella *sf.* star: *— marina*, starfish; *a forma di —*, starlike.

stellare *agg.* 1. stellar 2. (*a forma di stella*) star-shaped.

stellato *agg.* starry.

stelletta *sf.* 1. (*tip.*) asterisk 2. (*mil.*) star.

stelloncino *sm.* short paragraph.

stelo *sm.* stem.

stemma *sm.* coat-of-arms.

stemperare *vt.* 1. to mix 2. (*diluire*) to spin out. ♦ **stemperarsi** *vr.* to dissolve.

stempiarsi *vr.* to go (*v. irr.*) bald.

stendardo *sm.* standard.

stèndere *vt.* 1. to spread (*v. irr.*) 2. (*allungare*) to stretch 3. (*scrivere*) to draw (*v. irr.*) up 4. (*rilassare*) to relax || — *il bucato*, to hang (*v. irr.*) out the washing. ♦ **stèndersi** *vr.* 1. to stretch 2. (*adagiarsi*) to lie (*v. irr.*) down.

stenodattilografia *sf.* shorthand and typewriting.

stenografare *vt.* to write (*v. irr.*) down in shorthand.

stenografia *sf.* shorthand.

stenògrafo *sm.* shorthand-writer.

stentare *vi.* 1. to have difficulty (in) 2. (*mancare del necessario*) to be in need.

stentato *agg.* 1. hard 2. (*cresciuto a stento*) stunted.

stento *sm.* privation: *a* —, hardly, with difficulty.

stentòreo *agg.* stentorian.

steppa *sf.* steppe.

sterco *sm.* dung.

stereofonìa *sf.* stereophony.

stereofònico *agg.* stereophonic.

stereografìa *sf.* stereography.

stereogràfico *agg.* stereographic(al).

stereoscopìa *sf.* stereoscopy.

stereoscòpio *sm.* stereoscope.

stereotipato *agg.* stereotyped.

stereotipìa *sf.* stereotyping.

stèrile *agg.* barren.

sterilità *sf.* barrenness.

sterilizzare *vt.* to sterilize.

sterilizzatore *agg.* sterilizing. ♦ **sterilizzatore** *sm.* sterilizer.

sterilizzazione *sf.* sterilization.

sterlina *sf.* pound.

sterminare *vt.* to exterminate.

sterminatezza *sf.* immensity.

sterminato *agg.* (*smisurato*) immense.

sterminatore *sm.* exterminator.

sterminio *sm.* extermination.

sterno *sm.* breast-bone.

sterpàglia *sf.* brushwood.

sterpo *sm.* dry twig.

sterrare *vt.* to dig (*v. irr.*) up.

sterratore *sm.* navvy.

sterzare *vt.* to steer.

sterzata *sf.* sudden turn.

sterzo *sm.* (*auto*) steering-gear.

stesso *agg.* 1. (*medesimo*) same 2. (*intensivo*) *se* —, oneself; *io, me* —, myself; *tu, te* —, yourself; *egli, lui* —, himself; *ella, lei stessa*, herself; *esso* —, itself; *noi stessi*, ourselves; *voi stessi*, yourselves; *loro stessi*, themselves 3. (*proprio*) very. ♦ **stesso** *agg.* same. ♦ **stesso** *avv.* all the same

stesura *sf.* 1. (*redazione*) draft 2. (*di contratto*) drawing up.

stetoscòpio *sm.* stethoscope.

stigmate *sf. pl.* 1. stigmata (*pl.*) 2. (*marchio*) brand (*sing.*).

stigmatizzare *vt.* to stigmatize.

stilare *vt.* to draw (*v. irr.*) up.

stile *sm.* style: *aver* —, to be stylish; *con* —, stylishly.

stilettata *sf.* stab.

stilista *s.* stylist.

stilìstica *sf.* stylistics.

stilizzare *vt.* to stylize.

stilizzazione *sf.* stylization.

stilla *sf.* drop.

stillare *vi.* e *vt.* to ooze. ♦ **stillarsi** *vr.* — *il cervello*, to rack one's brain.

stillicìdio *sm.* dripping.

stilo *sm.* stylus.

stilogràfica *sf.* fountainpen.

stilogràfico *agg.* stylographic(al).

stima *sf.* 1. (*valutazione*) estimate 2. (*buona opinione*) esteem.

stimàbile *agg.* estimable.

stimare *vt.* 1. (*valutare*) to estimate 2. (*tenere in considerazione*) to esteem 3. (*ritenere*) to consider.

stimatore *sm.* estimator.

stimolante *agg.* stimulating. ♦ **stimolante** *sm.* stimulant.

stimolare *vt.* to stimulate.

stìmolo *sm.* 1. stimulus (*pl.* -li) 2. (*pungolo*) goad.

stinco *sm.* shin.

stingere *vt.* to fade. ♦ **stingersi** *vr.* to fade.

stinto *agg.* faded.

stipare *vt.* to cram.

stipato *agg.* crammed (with).

stipendiare *vt.* to pay (*v. irr.*) a salary (to so.).

stipèndio *sm.* salary.

stìpite *sm.* jamb.

stipulante *agg.* stipulating. ♦ **stipulante** *s.* stipulator.

stipulare *vt.* to stipulate.

stipulazione *sf.* stipulation.

stiracchiare *vt.* **1.** to stretch **2.** (*distorcere*) to twist.

stiracchiato *agg.* (*fig.*) forced.

stiramento *sm.* **1.** stretching **2.** (*muscolare*) strain.

stirare *vt.* **1.** to stretch **2.** (*col ferro da stiro*) to iron.

stiratura *sf.* ironing.

stireria *sf.* (*e tintoria*) laundry shop.

stirpe *sf.* **1.** stock **2.** (*progenie*) issue.

stitichezza *sf.* constipation.

stitico *agg.* constipated.

stiva *sf.* hold.

stivale *sm.* boot.

stivaletto *sm.* ankle-boot.

stizza *sf.* anger.

stizzire *vt.* to vex. ♦ **stizzirsi** *vr.* to get (*v. irr.*) cross.

stizzito *agg.* cross.

stizzoso *agg.* peevish.

stoccata *sf.* thrust: *lanciare una —* (*fig.*), to gibe (at).

stoffa *sf.* **1.** cloth **2.** (*fig.*) stuff.

stoicismo *sm.* stoicism.

stoico *agg. e sm.* stoic.

stoino *sm.* door-mat.

stola *sf.* stole.

stolidità *sf.* stolidity.

stolido *agg.* stolid.

stoltezza *sf.* foolishness.

stolto *agg.* foolish. ♦ **stolto** *sm.* fool.

stomacare *vt.* to sicken. ♦ **stomacarsi** *vr.* to sicken.

stomachévole *agg.* sickening.

stòmaco *sm.* stomach: *dare di —*, to vomit; *restare sullo —*, to lie (*v. irr.*) on one's stomach.

stomatite *sf.* stomatitis.

stomatologia *sf.* stomatology.

stonare *vi.* **1.** to be out of tune **2.** (*fig.*) to be out of place **3.** (*di colori*) to clash. ♦ **stonare** *vt.* to upset (*v. irr.*).

stonato *agg.* **1.** out of tune **2.** (*fig.*) out of place **3.** (*turbato*) upset **4.** (*di nota*) false.

stonatura *sf.* false note.

stoppa *sf.* tow.

stoppaccio *sm.* wad.

stoppare *vt.* **1.** to plug **2.** (*sport*) to stop.

stoppia *sf.* stubble.

stoppino *sm.* wick.

stopposo *agg.* **1.** towy **2.** (*di carne*) stringy.

stòrcere *vt.* **1.** to twist **2.** (*un'articolazione*) to sprain || *— gli occhi*, to roll one's eyes. ♦ **stòrcersi** *vr.* **1.** to twist **2.** (*lussarsi, slogarsi*) to wrench.

stordimento *sm.* **1.** dizziness **2.** (*meraviglia*) bewilderment.

stordire *vt.* **1.** to stun **2.** (*di alcoolici*) to dull **3.** (*assordare*) to deafen **4.** (*innervosire*) to drive (*v. irr.*) crazy. ♦ **stordirsi** *vr.* to dull one's senses.

stordito *agg.* **1.** (*sbalordito*) bewildered **2.** (*sbadato*) heedless **3.** (*sciocco*) foolish.

storia *sf.* **1.** history **2.** (*racconto*) story.

storicismo *sm.* historical method.

storicità *sf.* historicity.

storico *agg.* historical. ♦ **storico** *sm.* historian.

storiografia *sf.* historiography.

storiografo *sm.* historiographer.

stormire *vi.* to rustle.

stormo *sm.* **1.** flight **2.** (*folla*) crowd || *suonare a —*, to ring (*v. irr.*) the tocsin.

stornare *vt.* to divert.

stornello¹ *sm.* ditty.

stornello² *sm.* (*zool.*) starling.

storno¹ *agg.* dapple-grey.

storno² *sm.* (*zool.*) starling.

storno³ *sm.* (*comm.*) transfer.

storpiare *vt.* **1.** to cripple **2.** (*rovinare*) to mangle.

storpiatura *sf.* **1.** crippling **2.** (*fig.*) mangling **3.** (*cosa malfatta*) botch.

storpio *sm.* cripple.

storta *sf.* **1.** twist **2.** (*in una articolazione*) sprain **3.** (*chim.*) retort.

storto *agg.* **1.** twisted **2.** (*piegato*) crooked **3.** (*di occhi*) squinting **4.** (*sbagliato*) wrong.

stortura *sf.* **1.** deformity **2.** (*errore*) mistake.

stoviglie *sf. pl.* kitchenware (*sing.*).

stràbico *agg.* squinting. ♦ **stràbico** *sm.* squinter.

strabiliante *agg.* amazing.

strabiliare *vt.* to amaze (*anche far strabiliare*). ♦ **strabiliare** *vi.* to be amazed. ♦ **strabiliarsi** *vr.* to be amazed.

strabismo *sm.* squint.

straboccare *vi.* **1.** to overflow **2.** (*fig.*) to abound (in).

strabocchévole *agg.* overflowing.

strabuzzare *vt.* — *gli occhi*, to roll one's eyes.

stracarico *agg.* overloaded (with).

stracciare *vt.* to tear (*v. irr.*). ♦ **stracciarsi** *vr.* to tear.

stracciato *agg.* 1. torn 2. (*di persona*) in rags.

straccio *agg.* torn, in rags || *carta straccia*, waste paper. ♦ **straccio** *sm.* rag: — *per la polvere*, duster.

straccione *sm.* ragamuffin.

stracivéndolo *sm.* rag-and-bone--man (*pl.* -men).

stracotto *agg.* overdone. ♦ **stra-cotto** *sm.* stew.

strada *sf.* 1. road 2. (*di città*) street 3. (*percorso; fig.*) way || — *a senso unico*, one-way street; — *ferrata*, railway; — *maestra*, main road.

stradale *agg.* road (*attr.*), of the road: *fondo* —, road-bed.

stradino *sm.* roadman (*pl.* -men).

strafalcione *sm.* blunder.

strafare *vi.* to overdo (*v. irr.*).

strafottente *agg.* 1. (*noncurante*) unconcerned 2. (*arrogante*) arrogant.

strage *sf.* 1. slaughter 2. (*distruzione*) destruction || *fare una* —, to slaughter.

stragrande *agg.* enormous.

stralciare *vt.* 1. (*comm.*) to remove 2. (*fig.*) to take (*v. irr.*) off.

stralcio *sm.* 1. removal 2. (*estratto*) extract.

strale *sm.* dart.

stralunare *vt.* — *gli occhi*, to roll one's eyes, to open one's eyes wide.

stralunato *agg.* 1. (*di occhi*) rolling, wild-eyed 2. (*di persona*) upset.

stramazzare *vi.* to fall (*v. irr.*) heavily.

stramberia *sf.* oddity.

strambo *agg.* odd.

strame *sm.* litter.

strampalato *agg.* queer.

stranezza *sf.* oddity.

strangolamento *sm.* strangling.

strangolare *vt.* to strangle.

strangolatore *sm.* strangler.

straniero *agg.* foreign. ♦ **straniero** *sm.* foreigner.

strano *agg.* strange.

straordinario *agg.* extraordinary.

strapazzare *vt.* 1. to ill-use 2. (*sgridare*) to scold 3. (*far lavorare troppo*) to overwork 4. (*di uova*) to scramble. ♦ **strapazzarsi** *vr.* to overwork oneself.

strapazzata *sf.* 1. scolding 2. (*fatica*) overwork.

strapazzo *sm.* overwork: *abiti da* —, working-clothes; *scrittore da* —, hack.

strapieno *agg.* full up.

straplombare *vi.* 1. to lean (*v. irr.*) 2. (*scendere a precipizio*) to fall (*v. irr.*) perpendicularly.

straplombo *sm.* precipice: *a* —, sheer.

strapotente *agg.* very powerful.

strappare *vt.* 1. (*lacerare*) to tear (*v. irr.*) 2. (*togliere*) to snatch 3. (*estirpare*) to pull up 4. (*un dente*) to pull out 5. (*estorcere*) to wring (*v. irr.*). ♦ **strapparsi** *vr.* (*lacerarsi*) to tear.

strappo *sm.* 1. tear 2. (*strappata*) pull 3. (*infrazione*) breach || — *muscolare*, sprain.

strapuntino *sm.* folding seat.

straricco *agg.* immensely rich.

straripamento *sm.* overflowing.

straripare *vi.* to overflow.

strascicare *vt.* 1. to drag 2. (*i piedi*) to shuffle 3. (*le parole*) to drawl.

strascico *sm.* 1. train 2. (*residuo*) after-effect 3. (*rete*) trawl.

strascinare *vt.* V. *trascinare*.

stratagemma *sm.* stratagem.

stratega *sm.* strategist.

strategia *sf.* strategy.

stratégico *agg.* strategic(al).

stratificare *vt.* to stratify.

stratificazione *sf.* stratification.

strato *sm.* 1. layer 2. (*di rivestimento*) coat 3. (*della società*) class.

stratosfera *sf.* stratosphere.

stratosférico *agg.* stratospheric(al).

strattone *sm.* 1. pull 2. (*sobbalzo*) jerk || *a strattoni*, jerkily; (*a intervalli*) by fits and starts.

stravagante *agg.* odd, queer.

stravaganza *sf.* oddity.

stravecchio *agg.* very old.

stravedere *vi.* to see (*v. irr.*) badly: — *per qu.*, to be crazy about so.

stravincere *vt.* to crush. ♦ **stra-vincere** *vi.* to win (*v. irr.*) all along the line.

stravizio *sm.* excess.

stravòlgere *vt.* 1. to twist 2. (*gli occhi*) to roll.

stravolto *agg.* 1. (*turbato*) upset 2. (*di occhi*) rolling.

straziante *agg.* tormenting, heart-rending (*solo fig.*).

straziare *vt.* to tear (*v. irr.*).

strazio *sm.* torment: *far — di*, to play havoc with.

strega *sf.* witch.

stregare *vt.* to bewitch.

stregone *sm.* wizard.

stregoneria *sf.* witchcraft.

stremare *vt.* to exhaust.

stremo *sm.* extreme.

strenna *sf.* gift.

strenuo *agg.* brave.

strepitare *vi.* to shout.

strèpito *sm.* din, uproar.

strepitoso *agg.* uproarious: *successo —*, striking success.

streptococco *sm.* streptococcus (*pl.* -ci).

streptomicina *sf.* streptomycin.

stretta *sf.* **1.** grasp **2.** (*calca*) press **3.** (*gola*) gorge || *— di mano*, handshake; *essere alle strette*, to be in dire straits; *mettere alle strette qu.*, to put (*v. irr.*) so. with his back against the wall.

strettezza *sf.* **1.** narrowness **2.** (*povertà*) financial difficulty.

stretto *agg.* **1.** narrow **2.** (*serrato, piccolo*) tight **3.** (*rigoroso*) strict **4.** (*pigiato*) packed. ♦ **stretto** *sm.* strait.

strettoia *sf.* narrow passage.

stria *sf.* streak.

striare *vt.* to streak.

stricnina *sf.* strychnine.

stridente *agg.* **1.** shrill **2.** (*discordante*) jarring.

stridere *vi.* **1.** to creak **2.** (*di insetti*) to chirp **3.** (*contrastare*) to jar.

stridìo *sm.* **1.** creaking **2.** (*di insetti*) chirping.

strido *sm.* **1.** scream **2.** (*di animale*) screech.

stridulo *agg.* shrill.

striglia *sf.* curry-comb.

strigliare *vt.* **1.** to curry **2.** (*fig.*) to rebuke.

strillare *vi.* to scream.

strillo *sm.* scream.

strillone *sm.* newsboy.

striminzito *agg.* **1.** stunted **2.** (*di persona*) thin.

strimpellare *vt.* **1.** (*di violino*) to scrape **2.** (*di pianoforte*) to strum.

strinare *vt.* to singe.

stringa *sf.* lace.

stringare *vt.* **1.** to lace tightly **2.** (*fig.*) to condense.

stringato *agg.* **1.** laced **2.** (*fig.*) concise.

stringente *agg.* **1.** (*urgente*) urgent **2.** (*convincente*) persuasive.

stringere *vt.* **1.** to press **2.** (*restringere, avvitare*) to tighten **3.** (*abbracciare*) to clasp **4.** (*impugnare*) to grasp **5.** (*fare*) to make (*v. irr.*) || *— la mano a*, to shake (*v. irr.*) hands with; *— i pugni*, to clench one's fists; *stringi stringi*, in conclusion. ♦ **stringere** *vi.* to be tight. ♦ **stringersi** *vr.* **1.** to press (against) **2.** (*far spazio*) to squeeze up || *— nelle spalle*, to shrug one's shoulders.

stringimento *sm.* **1.** pressing **2.** (*restringimento, legamento, avvitamento*) tightening **3.** (*l'impugnare*) clasp **4.** (*fitta*) pang.

striscia *sf.* **1.** strip **2.** (*riga*) stripe **3.** (*scia*) trail || *a strisce*, striped.

strisciante *agg.* **1.** creeping **2.** (*servile*) fawning.

strisciare *vi.* **1.** to creep (*v. irr.*) **2.** (*fig.*) to grovel. ♦ **strisciare** *vt.* **1.** to drag **2.** (*i piedi*) to shuffle **3.** (*radere*) to graze **4.** (*fig.*) to fawn (on).

stritolamento *sm.* crushing.

stritolare *vt.* to crush.

strizzare *vt.* **1.** to squeeze **2.** (*torcere*) to wring (*v. irr.*) || *— l'occhio*, to wink (at so.).

strizzata *sf.* **1.** squeeze **2.** (*il torcere*) wring.

strofa *sf.* stanza.

strofinaccio *sm.* **1.** duster **2.** (*per asciugare*) towel.

strofinamento *sm.* rubbing.

strofinare *vt.* to rub.

strombatura *sf.* splay.

strombazzare *vt. e vi.* to trumpet.

strombettare *vi.* **1.** to blow (*v. irr.*) a trumpet **2.** (*auto*) to honk.

stroncare *vt.* **1.** to break (*v. irr.*) off **2.** (*fig.*) to demolish.

stroncatura *sf.* harsh criticism.

stronzio *sm.* strontium.

stropicciare *vt.* **1.** to rub **2.** (*i piedi*) to shuffle **3.** (*sgualcire*) to crease. ♦ **stropicciarsi** *vr.* **1.** (*gli occhi*) to rub oneself **2.** (*sgualcirsi*) to crease.

stropiccìo *sm. — di piedi*, shuffling.

strozzare *vt.* **1.** to strangle **2.** (*ostruire*) to obstruct **3.** (*fig.*) to choke.

strozzato *agg.* **1.** strangled **2.** (*soffocato*) choked **3.** (*con strozzature*) with narrow passages **4.** (*med.*)

strangulated **5.** (*ostruito*) obstructed.

strozzatura *sf.* **1.** strangling **2.** (*il soffocare*) choking **3.** (*ostruzione*) obstruction **4.** (*restringimento*) narrow passage **5.** (*med.*) strangulation.

strozzinaggio *sm.* usury.

strozzino *sm.* usurer.

struggente *agg.* pining.

struggere *vt.* **1.** to melt **2.** (*fig.*) to wear (*v. irr.*) out. ♦ **struggersi** *vr.* **1.** to melt **2.** (*affliggersi*) to be distressed **3.** (*languire*) to be consumed (with), to pine (for).

struggimento *sm.* longing.

strumentale *agg.* instrumental.

strumentalismo *sm.* instrumentalism.

strumentare *vt.* to instrument.

strumentazione *sf.* instrumentation.

strumento *sm.* instrument.

strusciare *vt.* **1.** to rub **2.** (*adulare*) to fawn (on). ♦ **strusciarsi** *vr.* to rub (oneself).

strutto *sm.* lard.

struttura *sf.* structure.

strutturale *agg.* structural.

strutturare *vt.* to structure.

strutturazione *sf.* structure.

struzzo *sm.* ostrich.

stuccare[1] *vt.* **1.** to stucco **2.** (*turare*) to fill.

stuccare[2] *vt.* **1.** (*nauseare*) to sicken **2.** (*annoiare*) to bore. ♦ **stuccarsi** *vr.* **1.** to get (*v. irr.*) sick **2.** (*annoiarsi*) to get bored.

stuccatura *sf.* **1.** plastering **2.** (*di dente*) filling.

stucchévole *agg.* **1.** filling **2.** (*nauseante*) sickening **3.** (*noioso*) boring.

stucco *sm.* **1.** stucco **2.** (*per vetri*) putty ‖ *restare di —,* to be nonplussed.

studente *sm.* student.

studentesco *agg.* student (*attr.*).

studiacchiare *vt.* to study fitfully.

studiare *vt.* to study. ♦ **studiarsi** *vr.* to try.

studiato *agg.* (*affettato*) affected.

studio *sm.* **1.** study **2.** (*progetto*) plan **3.** (*cine*) studio ‖ *programma di studi,* curriculum; *essere allo —,* to be under consideration.

studioso *agg.* studious. ♦ **studioso** *sm.* scholar.

stufa *sf.* stove.

stufare *vt.* **1.** to stew **2.** (*fig.*) to bore. ♦ **stufarsi** *vr.* to get (*v. irr.*) bored.

stufato *sm.* stew.

stufo *agg.* fed up (with).

stuoia *sf.* mat.

stuolo *sm.* crowd.

stupefacente *agg.* stupefying. ♦ **stupefacente** *sm.* drug.

stupefare *vt.* to stupefy. ♦ **stupefarsi** *vr.* to be stupefied.

stupefazione *sf.* stupefaction.

stupendamente *avv.* wonderfully.

stupendo *agg.* wonderful.

stupidàggine *sf.* stupidity.

stupidità *sf.* stupidity.

stùpido *agg.* e *sm.* stupid.

stupire *vt.* to astonish. ♦ **stupirsi** *vr.* to be astonished.

stupito *agg.* astonished.

stupore *sm.* astonishment.

stupro *sm.* rape.

sturare *vt.* **1.** to uncork **2.** (*botti*) to unbung.

stuzzicadenti *sm.* tooth-pick.

stuzzicare *vt.* **1.** to prod **2.** (*frugare*) to pick **3.** (*molestare*) to tease **4.** (*stimolare*) to whet.

su *prep.* **1.** on **2.** (*senza contatto; rivestimento*) over **3.** (*al di sopra di*) above **4.** (*circa*) about ‖ *nove volte — dieci,* nine times out of ten. ♦ *su avv.* **1.** up **2.** (*al piano superiore*) upstairs **3.** (*indosso*) on ‖ *— per giù,* more or less; *in —* (*in avanti*), onwards; *più —,* further up; *—, andiamo!* come on!

sua *agg.* e *pron.* V. *suo.*

suadente *agg.* persuasive.

subàcqueo *agg.* underwater (*attr.*). ♦ **subàcqueo** *sm.* frogman (*pl.* -men*).

subaffittare *vt.* to sublease.

subaffitto *sm.* sublease.

subalpino *agg.* subalpine.

subalterno *agg.* e *sm.* subaltern.

subbuglio *sm.* **1.** turmoil **2.** (*disordine*) mess.

subconscio *sm.* subconscious.

subcosciente *agg.* e *sm.* subconscious.

subdolamente *avv.* underhand.

sùbdolo *agg.* sly.

subentrare *vi.* to take (*v. irr.*) the place (of).

subire *vt.* to undergo (*v. irr.*).

subissare *vt.* **1.** (*sprofondare*) to sink (*v. irr.*) **2.** (*fig.*) to overwhelm.

subisso *sm.* (*gran quantità*) shower.

subitaneità *sf.* suddenness.

subitaneo *agg.* sudden.

subito *avv.* 1. at once 2. (*presto*) soon || — *prima*, just before; — *dopo*, just after.

sublimare *vt.* to sublimate.

sublimato *sm.* sublimate.

sublimazione *sf.* sublimation.

sublime *agg. e sm.* sublime.

sublimità *sf.* sublimity.

sublocazione *sf.* subletting.

sublunare *agg.* sublunar.

subodorare *vt.* to suspect.

subordinare *vt.* to subordinate.

subordinata *sf.* subordinate clause.

subordinato *agg. e sm.* subordinate.

subordinazione *sf.* subordination.

subornare *vt.* to suborn.

subornazione *sf.* subornation.

substrato *sm.* substratum (*pl.* -ta).

suburbano *agg.* suburban.

suburbio *sm.* suburb.

succèdere *vi.* 1. to succeed 2. (*capitare*) to happen. ♦ **succèdersi** *vr.* to follow one another.

successione *sf.* succession.

successivamente *avv.* afterwards.

successivo *agg.* following.

successo *sm.* 1. success 2. (*esito*) outcome || *aver* —, to be successful.

successore *sm.* successor.

succhiare *vt.* to suck.

succhiata *sf.* suck.

succhiello *sm.* gimlet.

succinto *agg.* 1. (*di abiti*) scanty 2. (*conciso*) concise.

succo *sm.* 1. juice 2. (*fig.*) pith.

succosità *sf.* 1. juiciness 2. (*fig.*) pithiness.

succoso *agg.* 1. juicy 2. (*fig.*) pithy.

succubo *agg.* entirely dominated (by).

succulento *agg.* 1. juicy 2. (*gustoso*) rich.

succursale *sf.* branch.

sud *sm.* south: *del* —, southern, south (*attr.*); *verso* —, southwards.

sudare *vi.* to sweat: — *sette camicie*, to toil hard; — *freddo*, to be in a cold sweat.

sudario *sm.* shroud.

sudata *sf.* sweat.

sudaticcio *agg.* clammy.

sudato *agg.* 1. sweaty 2. (*fig.*) hard-earned.

suddetto *agg.* above-mentioned.

suddiàcono *sm.* subdeacon.

sudditanza *sf.* subjection.

sùddito *sm.* subject.

suddividere *vt.* to subdivide.

suddivisione *sf.* subdivision.

sùdicio *agg.* dirty.

sudicione *sm.* dirty fellow.

sudiciume *sm.* dirt.

sudore *sm.* 1. sweat 2. (*fig.*) toil.

sudorifero *agg.* 1. (*che secerne sudore*) sudoriferous 2. (*che produce sudore*) sudorific.

sue *agg. e pron.* V. *suo*.

sufficiente *agg.* 1. sufficient 2. (*altezzoso*) conceited 2. (*voto sufficiente*) pass mark.

sufficienza *sf.* 1. sufficiency 2. (*alterigia*) conceit 3. (*voto sufficiente*) pass mark || *aria di* —, superior air; *a* —, enough.

suffisso *sm.* suffix.

suffragare *vt.* 1. to support 2. (*eccl.*) to pray for.

suffragio *sm.* 1. suffrage 2. (*approvazione*) approval.

suggellare *vt.* to seal.

suggello *sm.* seal.

suggerimento *sm.* 1. suggestion 2. (*teat.*) prompting.

suggerire *vt.* 1. to suggest 2. (*dar l'imbeccata; teat.*) to prompt.

suggeritore *sm.* prompter.

suggestionàbile *agg.* impressionable.

suggestionabilità *sf.* impressionability.

suggestionare *vt.* to influence. ♦ **suggestionarsi** *vr.* to will oneself (to do sthg.), to be influenced.

suggestione *sf.* suggestion.

suggestività *sf.* suggestiveness.

suggestivamente *avv.* evocatively.

suggestivo *agg.* evocative.

sùghero *sm.* 1. cork 2. (*albero*) cork-tree.

sugna *sf.* pork fat.

sugo *sm.* 1. juice 2. (*di carne*) gravy 3. (*di pomodoro*) sauce 4. (*fig.*) gist.

sugosità *sf.* V. *succosità*.

sugoso *agg.* V. *succoso*.

suicida *agg.* suicidal. ♦ **suicida** *s.* suicide.

suicidarsi *vr.* to commit suicide.

suicidio *sm.* suicide.

suino *agg.* swine (*attr.*) || *carne suina*, pork. ♦ **suino** *sm.* swine (*pl. invariato*).

sulfamìdico *sm.* sulphonamide.

sulfùreo *agg.* sulphureous.

sultanato *sm.* sultanate.

sultanina *sf.* sultana.

sultano *sm.* sultan.

summenzionato *agg.* aforesaid.

sunto *sm.* summary.

suo *agg.* 1. (*di lui*) his 2. (*di lei*) her 3. (*di esso*) its 4. (*formula di cortesia*) your. ♦ **suo** *pron.* 1. (*di lui*) his 2. (*di lei*) hers 3. (*di esso*) its 4. (*formula di cortesia*) yours || **i suoi** (*famigliari*), his, her family.

suòcera *sf.* mother-in-law.

suòcero *sm.* father-in-law.

suol *agg. e pron.* V. *suo*.

suola *sf.* sole.

suolo *sm.* soil, ground.

suonare *vt.* V. *sonare*.

suono *sm.* sound.

suora *sf.* nun, sister.

superàbile *agg.* surmountable.

superaffollato *agg.* overcrowded.

superalimentare *vt.* 1. to overish 2. (*mecc.*) to overcharge.

superalimentazione *sf.* 1. overfeeding 2. (*mecc.*) overcharging.

superamento *sm.* 1. overcoming 2. (*auto*) overtaking.

superare *vt.* 1. (*oltrepassare*) to exceed 2. (*auto*) to overtake (*v. irr.*) 3. (*attraversare*) to cross 4. (*vincere*) to overcome (*v. irr.*) 5. (*una persona*) to surpass 6. (*un esame, una prova*) to pass.

superbia *sf.* pride.

superbo *agg.* 1. proud 2. (*magnifico*) superb.

superdotato *agg.* highly gifted.

superficiale *agg.* superficial.

superficialità *sf.* superficiality.

superficie *sf.* 1. surface 2. (*area*) area.

superfluo *agg.* superfluous. ♦ **superfluo** *sm.* surplus.

superiora *sf.* Mother Superior.

superiore *agg.* 1. superior 2. (*sovrastante*) upper 3. (*più avanzato*) advanced. ♦ **superiore** *sm.* superior.

superiorità *sf.* superiority.

superlativo *agg. e sm.* superlative.

supermercato *sm.* supermarket.

supernutrizione *sf.* overfeeding.

supersònico *agg.* supersonic.

supèrstite *agg.* surviving. ♦ **supèrstite** *s.* survivor.

superstizione *sf.* superstition.

superstizioso *agg.* superstitious.

superuomo *sm.* superman (*pl.* -men).

supervisione *sf.* supervision.

supervisore *sm.* supervisor.

supinamente *avv.* supinely.

supino *agg.* supine.

suppellèttile *sf.* furnishings (*pl.*).

supplementare *agg.* supplementary.

supplemento *sm.* 1. supplement 2. (*spesa supplementare*) additional charge 3. (*di biglietto ferroviario*) excess fare.

supplente *agg.* temporary. ♦ **supplente** *s.* temporary teacher.

supplenza *sf.* temporary post.

suppletivo *agg.* supplementary.

sùpplica *sf.* 1. entreaty 2. (*petizione*) petition.

supplicante *agg. e s.* suppliant.

supplicare *vt.* to entreat.

supplichévole *agg.* entreating.

supplire *vi.* 1. (*compensare*) to make (*v. irr.*) up (for) 2. (*sostituire*) to substitute (for). ♦ **supplire** *vt.* to take (*v. irr.*) the place of.

supplizio *sm.* torment: *andare al —*, to go (*v. irr.*) to the scaffold.

supporre *vt.* to suppose.

supporto *sm.* support.

supposizione *sf.* supposition.

supposta *sf.* suppository.

supposto che *cong.* suppose (that).

suppurare *vi.* to suppurate.

suppurazione *sf.* suppuration.

supremazia *sf.* supremacy.

supremo *agg.* supreme: *Comando — (mil.)*, headquarters (*pl.*).

surclassare *vt.* to outclass.

surgelare *vt.* to deep-freeze (*v. irr.*).

surrealismo *sm.* surrealism.

surrealista *agg. e s.* surrealist.

surrealistico *agg.* surrealistic.

surrenale *agg.* suprarenal.

surrettizio *agg.* surreptitious.

surriscaldamento *sm.* overheating.

surriscaldare *vt.* to overheat. ♦ **surriscaldarsi** *vr.* to get (*v. irr.*) overheated.

surrogàbile *agg.* replaceable.

surrogare *vt.* to replace.

surrogato *sm.* substitute.

surrogazione *sf.* (*giur.*) surrogation.

suscettìbile *agg.* 1. susceptible 2. (*permaloso*) touchy.

suscettibilità *sf.* 1. susceptibility 2. (*permalosità*) touchiness || *urtare la — di qu.*, to hurt (*v. irr.*) so.'s feelings.

suscitare vt. **1.** to provoke **2.** (eccitare) to stir up.

suscitatore sm. provoker.

susina sf. plum.

susino sm. plum-tree.

susseguente agg. following.

susseguire vi. to follow. ✦ **susseguirsi** vr. to follow.

sussidiare vt. **1.** to support **2.** (di governo) to subsidize.

sussidiario agg. subsidiary.

sussidio sm. subsidy.

sussiego sm. haughtiness.

sussistenza sf. **1.** existence **2.** (sostentamento) subsistence **3.** (mil.) Catering Corps.

sussistere vi. **1.** to subsist **2.** (reggere) to hold (v. irr.) water.

sussultare vi. **1.** to start **2.** (di cose) to shake (v. irr.).

sussulto sm. start.

sussurrare vt. e vi. **1.** to whisper **2.** (criticare) to murmur.

sussurro sm. whisper.

sutura sf. suture.

suturare vt. to suture.

svagare vt. **1.** to divert **2.** (divertire) to amuse. ✦ **svagarsi** vr. **1.** to divert one's mind **2.** (divertirsi) to amuse oneself.

svagatezza sf. absent-mindedness.

svagato agg. absent-minded.

svago sm. amusement.

svaligiamento sm. **1.** robbery **2.** (di una casa) burglary.

svaligiare vt. **1.** to rob **2.** (una casa) to burgle.

svaligiatore sm. **1.** robber **2.** (di case) burglar.

svalutare vt. **1.** to devaluate **2.** (sottovalutare) to undervalue.

svalutazione sf. devaluation.

svanire vi. **1.** to disappear **2.** (dileguarsi, di luce ecc.) to fade.

svanito agg. **1.** (dileguato) vanished **2.** (di mente) feeble-minded.

svantaggio sm. disadvantage.

svantaggioso agg. disadvantageous.

svaporamento sm. evaporation.

svaporare vi. to evaporate.

svariare vt. to vary.

svariato agg. various.

svarione sm. blunder.

svasare vt. (mecc.) to flare.

svasato agg. (di abito) bell-shaped.

svasatura sf. **1.** (di abito) bell-shaping **2.** (mecc.; lo svasare) flaring **3.** (apertura) countersink.

svàstica sf. swastika.

svecchiamento sm. renewal.

svecchiare vt. to renew.

svedese agg. Swedish. ✦ **svedese** sm. Swede.

sveglia sf. **1.** early call **2.** (orologio) alarm clock **3.** (mil.) reveille.

svegliare vt. to wake (v. irr.) (up). ✦ **svegliarsi** vr. to wake (up).

sveglio agg. **1.** awake (pred.) **2.** (fig.) quick-witted.

svelare vt. **1.** to reveal, to disclose **2.** (togliere il velo) to unveil.

svelenire vt. (fig.) to remove the sting from.

svèllere vt. to extirpate.

sveltezza sf. quickness.

sveltire vt. **1.** to quicken **2.** (scaltrire) to wake (v. irr.) up **3.** — la figura, to slim. ✦ **sveltirsi** vr. **1.** to become (v. irr.) quick(er) **2.** (scaltrirsi) to wake up.

svelto agg. **1.** quick **2.** (slanciato) slender **3.** (intelligente) smart. ✦ **svelto** avv. fast || —!, hurry up!

svenare vt. to open so.'s veins. ✦ **svenarsi** vr. to cut (v. irr.) one's veins.

svéndere vt. to undersell (v. irr.).

svéndita sf. (clearance) sale.

svenévole agg. maudlin.

svenimento sm. faint.

svenire vi. to faint.

sventagliare vt. to fan.

sventare vt. to baffle.

sventatezza sf. **1.** thoughtlessness **2.** (atto sventato) thoughtless action.

sventato agg. (sbadato) thoughtless. ✦ **sventato** sm. scatter-brain.

svèntola sf. (schiaffo) slap.

sventolare vt. e vi. to wave. ✦ **sventolarsi** vr. to fan oneself.

sventolìo sm. waving.

sventramento sm. **1.** disembowelment **2.** (demolizione) demolition.

sventrare vt. **1.** to disembowel **2.** (demolire) to demolish.

sventura sf. misfortune: per —, unluckily; per colmo di —, to crown it all.

sventuratamente avv. unfortunately.

sventurato agg. unfortunate.

svenuto agg. unconscious.

svergognare vt. to shame.

svergognatamente avv. shamelessly.

svergognato agg. shameless.

svernamento sm. wintering.

svernare vi. to winter.

svestire *vt.* to undress. ♦ svestirsi *vr.* to undress.

svettare *vt.* to lop. ♦ svettare *vi.* to stand (*v. irr.*) out.

svezzamento *sm.* weaning.

svezzare *vt.* to wean.

sviamento *sm.* 1. diversion 2. (*il traviare*) leading astray 3. (*il traviarsi*) going astray.

sviare *vt.* 1. to divert 2. (*traviare*) to lead (*v. irr.*) astray. ♦ sviarsi *vr.* 1. to be diverted 2. (*traviarsi*) to go (*v. irr.*) astray.

sviato *agg.* led astray (*pred.*).

svignàrsela *vr.* to slink (*v. irr.*) away.

svigorire *vt.* to weaken. ♦ svigorirsi *vr.* to grow (*v. irr.*) weak.

svilimento *sm.* depreciation.

svilire *vt.* to depreciate.

sviluppare *vt.* 1. to develop 2. (*sciogliere*) to loosen 3. (*sprigionare*) to generate. ♦ svilupparsi *vr.* to develop.

sviluppatore *sm.* (*foto*) developer.

sviluppo *sm.* 1. development 2. (*sprigionamento*) generation.

svincolamento *sm.* 1. release 2. (*doganale*) clearance 3. (*riscatto*) redemption.

svincolare *vt.* 1. to release 2. (*sdoganare*) to clear 3. (*riscattare*) to redeem. ♦ svincolarsi *vr.* to get (*v. irr.*) free.

svisare *vt.* (*travisare*) to twist.

sviscerare *vt.* 1. to disembowel 2. (*fig.*) to dissect.

svisceratо *agg.* passionate.

svista *sf.* oversight.

svitare *vt.* to unscrew.

svìzzero *agg.* e *sm.* Swiss.

svogliatezza *sf.* 1. unwillingness 2. (*pigrizia*) laziness.

svogliato *agg.* 1. unwilling 2. (*pigro*) lazy. ♦ svogliato *sm.* lazy-bones.

svolazzare *vi.* to flutter.

svolazzo *sm.* 1. fluttering 2. (*tratto di penna*) flourish.

svòlgere *vt.* 1. to unwind (*v. irr.*) 2. (*trattare*) to develop 3. (*mettere in opera*) to carry out. ♦ svòlgersi *vr.* 1. to unwind 2. (*svilupparsi*) to develop 3. (*accadere*) to take (*v. irr.*) place.

svolgimento *sm.* 1. unwinding 2. (*trattazione*) treatment 3. (*corso*) course 4. (*sviluppo*) development.

svolta *sf.* 1. turn 2. (*fig.*) turning

point || *fare una* —, to turn.

svoltare *vi.* to turn.

svuotamento *sm.* emptying.

svuotare *vt.* to empty 2. (*fig.*) to deprive.

T

tabaccaio *sm.* tobacconist.

tabaccare *vt.* to snuff.

tabaccherìa *sf.* tobacconist's.

tabacchiera *sf.* snuff-box.

tabacco *sm.* tobacco.

tabella *sf.* 1. (*lista*) list 2. (*quadro*) board.

tabellone *sm.* notice board.

tabernàcolo *sm.* tabernacle.

tabù *sm.* taboo.

tabulatore *sm.* tabulator.

tacca *sf.* 1. notch 2. (*fig.*) condition.

taccagnerìa *sf.* stinginess.

taccagno *agg.* stingy. ♦ taccagno *sm.* miser.

tacchino *sm.* turkey.

taccia *sf.* 1. reputation 2. (*accusa*) charge.

tacciare *vt.* to charge (with).

tacco *sm.* heel.

taccuino *sm.* note-book.

tacere *vi.* to be silent: *far* —, to silence.

tachicardìa *sf.* tachycardia.

tachìmetro *sm.* tachometer.

tacitare *vt.* 1. to hush up 2. (*un creditore*) to pay (*v. irr.*) off.

tàcito *agg.* 1. silent 2. (*non espresso*) tacit.

taciturno *agg.* silent.

tafano *sm.* gad-fly.

tafferuglio *sm.* brawl.

taglia *sf.* 1. (*riscatto*) ransom 2. (*ricompensa*) reward 3. (*misura*) size.

tagliacarte *sm.* paper-knife (*pl.* -knives).

taglialegna *sm.* wood-cutter.

tagliando *sm.* coupon.

tagliapietre *sm.* stone-cutter.

tagliare *vt.* 1. to cut (*v. irr.*) 2. (*attraversare*) to cut across: — *via*, to cut off || — *a pezzi*, to cut into pieces; — *la corda* (*fig.*), to run (*v. irr.*) away; — *la strada a qu.*, to bar so.'s way. ♦ tagliarsi *vr.* to cut.

tagliatelle *sf. pl.* noodles.

tagliato *agg.* 1. cut 2. (*inclinato, disposto*) cut out, fit: *essere — fuori,* to be cut off.

tagliatore *sm.* cutter.

taglieggiare *vt.* to ransom.

tagliente *agg.* sharp.

tagliere *sm.* trencher.

taglio *sm.* 1. cut 2. (*il tagliare*) cutting 3. (*parte tagliente, orlo*) edge 4. (*dimensione*) size 5. (*raccolto*) harvest.

tagliola *sf.* snare.

taglione *sm.* retaliation.

tagliuzzare *vt.* to mince.

talare *agg.* talaric: *veste —,* cassock.

talco *sm.* talc: *— borato,* talcum powder.

tale *agg.* 1. such 2. (*per tralasciare i dati determinati*) such and such: *il — giorno,* on such and such day 3. (*suddetto*) above-mentioned || *— e quale,* exactly like, exactly as. ♦ **tale** *pron. indef.* someone.

talea *sf.* scion.

talento *sm.* talent.

talismano *sm.* talisman.

tallonare *vi.* to follow.

talloncino *sm.* slip.

tallone *sm.* heel.

talora *avv.* sometimes.

talpa *sf.* mole.

taluno *agg.* some. ♦ **taluno** *pron.* someone (*pl. some* people).

talvolta *avv.* V. *talora.*

tamarindo *sm.* tamarind.

tambureggiare *vi.* to drum.

tamburellare *vi.* to drum one's fingers on.

tamburino *sm.* drummer.

tamburo *sm.* 1. drum 2. (*mecc.*) cylinder.

tamponamento *sm.* 1. plugging 2. (*med.*) tamponage 3. (*auto*) bumping.

tamponare *vt.* 1. to plug 2. (*med.*) to tampon 3. (*auto*) to bump (against).

tampone *sm.* 1. plug 2. (*med.*) tampon 3. (*di carta asciugante*) blotter.

tana *sf.* den.

tanfo *sm.* stench.

tangente *agg.* e *sf.* tangent.

tangenza *sf.* tangency: *punto di —,* tangential point.

tangenziale *agg.* tangential.

tànghero *sm.* boor.

tangìbile *agg.* tangible.

tangibilità *sf.* tangibility.

tànnico *agg.* (*chim.*) tannic.

tannino *sm.* tannin.

tanto *avv.* i. so 2. (*coi verbi*) so much 3. (*di tempo*) so long 4. (*ad ogni modo*) anyhow || *— quanto,* as much as; *— quanto, as... as (sia... sia)* both ... and; *— meglio,* so much the better; *— per cambiare,* just for a change. ♦ **tanto** *agg.* so much (*pl.* so many): *— ... quanto,* as much... as (*pl.* as many... as). ♦ **tanto che** *cong.* so (that).

tapiro *sm.* tapir.

tappa *sf.* 1. (*luogo*) halting-place 2. (*parte di viaggio*) stage 3. (*sport*) lap.

tappare *vt.* 1. to stop 2. (*con tappo*) to cork.

tapparella *sf.* rolling shutter.

tappeto *sm.* carpet.

tappezzare *vt.* 1. (*con carta*) to paper 2. (*coprire*) to cover 3. (*foderare*) to upholster.

tappezzerìa *sf.* 1. (*di carta*) paper 2. (*di stoffa*) tapestry.

tappezziere *sm.* 1. (*per pareti*) paper hanger 2. (*per divani ecc.*) upholsterer.

tappo *sm.* 1. plug 2. (*per bottiglia*) cap.

tara *sf.* 1. tare 2. (*med.; difetto*) taint.

taràntola *sf.* tarantula.

tarare *vt.* 1. (*mecc.*) to set (*v. irr.*) 2. (*calibrare*) to calibrate 3. (*comm.*) to tare.

tarato *agg.* 1. (*comm.*) tared 2. (*mecc.*) set 3. (*med.*) with a taint 4. (*fig.*) corrupted.

tarchiato *agg.* sturdy.

tardare *vi.* to be late. ♦ **tardare** *vt.* to delay.

tardi *avv.* late: *far —,* to be late.

tardivo *agg.* 1. (*arretrato*) backward 2. (*che viene tardi*) tardy.

tardo *agg.* 1. tardy 2. (*ottuso*) dull 3. (*di tempo*) late || *a tarda notte,* late in the night; *tarda età,* old age.

targa *sf.* 1. (*di metallo*) plate 2. (*di marmo*) slab 3. (*auto*) number-plate.

targare *vt.* (*auto*) to give (*v. irr.*) a number-plate (to a car).

tariffa *sf.* tariff.

tarlarsi *vr.* to get (*v. irr.*) worm-caten.

tarlatura *sf.* worm-hole.

tarlo *sm.* **1.** woodworm **2.** (*fig.*) gnawings (*pl.*).

tarma *sf.* moth.

tarmarsi *vr.* to get (*v. irr.*) moth-eaten.

tarpare *vt.* to clip.

tartagliare *vi.* to stammer.

tartàrico *agg.* tartaric.

tàrtaro *sm.* tartar.

tartaruga *sf.* tortoise.

tartassare *vt.* to harass.

tartina *sf.* canapé.

tartufo *sm.* truffle.

tasca *sf.* pocket.

tascàbile *agg.* pocket (*attributivo*).

tassa *sf.* **1.** tax **2.** (*d'iscrizione*) fee.

tassàbile *agg.* taxable.

tassàmetro *sm.* taximeter: — *di parcheggio*, parking meter.

tassare *vt.* to tax.

tassativo *agg.* peremptory.

tassazione *sf.* taxation.

tassello *sm.* dowel.

tassì *sm.* taxi.

tassista *sm.* taxi-driver.

tasso[1] *sm.* (*comm.*) rate.

tasso[2] *sm.* (*bot.*) yew.

tasso[3] *sm.* (*zool.*) badger.

tastare *vt.* to feel (*v. irr.*): — *il terreno* (*fig.*), to feel one's way.

tastiera *sf.* keyboard.

tasto *sm.* **1.** key **2.** (*tatto*) feel **3.** (*argomento*) subject.

tastoni *avv.* *a —*, gropingly; *andare a —*, to grope.

tàttica *sf.* tactics.

tàttico *agg.* tactical. ♦ **tàttico** *sm.* tactician.

tàttile *agg.* tactile.

tatto *sm.* **1.** touch **2.** (*fig.*) tact || *con —*, tactfully.

tatuaggio *sm.* tattoo.

tatuare *vt.* to tattoo.

taumatùrgico *agg.* thaumaturgic(al).

taumaturgo *sm.* thaumaturge.

taurino *agg.* bull-like (*attr.*): *dal collo —*, bull-necked.

tauromachia *sf.* bullfight.

tautologia *sf.* tautology.

taverna *sf.* tavern.

taverniere *sm.* tavern-keeper.

tàvola *sf.* **1.** table **2.** (*asse*) board **3.** (*di marmo*) slab **4.** (*illustrazione*) plate.

tavolaccio *sm.* plank-bed.

tavolato *sm.* **1.** (*di pavimento*) plank floor **2.** (*mar.*) planking **3.**

(*geogr.*) plateau.

tavolozza *sf.* palette.

tazza *sf.* cup: — *da tè*, tea-cup.

te *pron.* you.

tè *sm.* tea.

teatrale *agg.* theatrical.

teatro *sm.* theatre: — *di posa*, studio.

tècnica *sf.* technique.

tecnicismo *sm.* technicality.

tècnico *agg.* technical. ♦ **tècnico** *sm.* technician.

tecnologia *sf.* technology.

tecnològico *agg.* technological.

tedesco *agg.* e *sm.* German.

tediare *vt.* to bore.

tedio *sm.* boredom.

tedioso *agg.* boring.

tegame *sm.* saucepan.

teglia *sf.* bakepan.

tégola *sf.* tile: *coprire di tegole*, to tile.

teiera *sf.* tea-pot.

teismo *sm.* theism.

tela *sf.* **1.** cloth **2.** (*teat.*) curtain **3.** (*dipinto*) painting **4.** (*per dipingere*) canvas || — *cerata*, oilcloth; — *di sacco*, sackcloth; — *di lino*, linen; — *di ragno*, cobweb.

telaio *sm.* **1.** loom **2.** (*ossatura, cornice*) frame.

telecàmera *sf.* camera.

telecomandare *vt.* to radiocontrol.

telecomunicazione *sf.* telecommunication.

telefèrica *sf.* cableway.

telefonare *vt.* to (tele)phone.

telefonata *sf.* (telephone) call.

telefonia *sf.* telephony.

telefònico *agg.* telephone (*attr.*): *cabina telefonica*, telephone booth.

telefonista *sm.* (telephone) operator. ♦ **telefonista** *sf.* switchboard girl.

telefono *sm.* (tele)phone: *dare un colpo di —*, to ring (*v. irr.*) up.

telefoto *sf.* telephotograph.

telegiornale *sm.* (television) news (-reel).

telegrafare *vt.* to telegraph.

telegrafia *sf.* telegraphy.

telegràfico *agg.* telegraphic(al).

telegrafista *sm.* telegraphist.

telègrafo *sm.* **1.** telegraph **2.** (*ufficio*) telegraph-office.

telegramma *sm.* telegram, wire: *fare un — a qu.*, to wire so.

telèmetro *sm.* **1.** telemeter **2.** (*in arma da fuoco; foto*) rangefinder.

teleobiettivo *sm.* telephoto lens.

teleologia *sf.* teleology.

telepatia *sf.* telepathy.

telerie *sf. pl.* linen (*sing.*): *commerciante in* —, linen-draper.

teleschermo *sm.* television screen.

telescopio *sm.* telescope.

telescrivente *sf.* teletypewriter.

teleselezione *sf.* long distance dialing.

telespettatore *sm.* televiewer.

teletipia *sf.* teletype.

teletrasméttere *vt.* to telecast (*v. irr.*).

televisione *sf.* television: *guardare la* —, to watch television; *alla* —, on television; *trasmettere per* —, to telecast.

televisivo *agg.* televisional, television (*attr.*): *trasmissione televisiva*, telecast.

televisore *sm.* television set

tellùrico *agg.* telluric.

telo *sm.* sheet.

telone *sm.* 1. (*teat.*) curtain 2. (*cine*) screen.

tema¹ *sf.* (*paura*) fear: *per* — *che*, lest.

tema² *sm.* 1. theme 2. (*scolastico*) composition.

temàtica *sf.* themes (*pl.*).

temàtico *agg.* thematic(al).

temerarietà *sf.* rashness.

temerario *agg.* rash.

temere *vt.* e *vi.* 1. to fear 2. (*patire*) not to stand (*v. irr.*) || *temo di sì*, I fear so; *temo di no*, I fear not.

temibile *agg.* dreadful.

tèmpera *sf.* 1. (*metal.*) hardening 2. (*pitt.*) distemper || *dipingere a* —, to distemper.

temperamatite *sm.* pencil-sharpener.

temperamento *sm.* 1. temperament 2. (*alleviamento*) mitigation.

temperante *agg.* temperate.

temperanza *sf.* temperance.

temperare *vt.* 1. to temper 2. (*matite*) to sharpen.

temperato *agg.* 1. temperate 2. (*di matita*) sharpened.

temperatura *sf.* temperature.

temperino *sm.* penknife (*pl. -knives*).

tempesta *sf.* tempest, storm.

tempestare *vt.* 1. (*assalire*) to assail 2. (*importunare*) to harass 3. (*cospargere*) to strew (*v. irr.*) (*sthg.*

with). ♦ **tempestare** *vi.* 1. to storm 2. (*grandinare*) to hail.

tempestività *sf.* timeliness.

tempestivo *agg.* timely.

tempestoso *agg.* stormy.

tempia *sf.* temple.

tempio *sm.* temple.

tempo *sm.* 1. time 2. (*atmosferico*) weather 3. (*gramm.*) tense 4. (*fase*) stage 5. (*cine*) part || *un* —, once; *col passare del* —, in the long run; *molto* — *prima, dopo*, long before, after; *a* — *perso*, in one's spare time; *per* —, early.

temporale¹ *agg.* temporal.

temporale² *agg.* (*anat.*) temporal.

temporale³ *sm.* storm.

temporalesco *agg.* stormy.

temporaneità *sf.* temporariness.

temporàneo *agg.* temporary.

temporeggiare *vi.* to temporize.

tempra *sf.* 1. temper 2. (*metal.*) hardening 3. (*fig.*) character.

temprare *vt.* 1. to temper 2. (*fig.*) to strengthen 3. (*plasmare*) to form.

temprato *agg.* (*abituato*) inured.

tenace *agg.* tenacious.

tenacia *sf.* tenacity.

tenaglia *sf.* pincers (*pl.*).

tenda *sf.* 1. curtain 2. (*da campo*) tent.

tendaggio *sm.* curtain.

tendente *agg.* tending.

tendenza *sf.* 1. tendency 2. inclination.

tendenziale *agg.* tendential.

tendenziosità *sf.* tendentiousness.

tendenzioso *agg.* tendentious.

tèndere *vt.* 1. (*protendere*) to stretch (out) 2. (*mettere in tensione*) to tighten. ♦ **tèndere** *vi.* 1. to tend 2. (*mirare*) to aim (at).

tendina *sf.* curtain.

tèndine *sm.* tendon.

tenditore *sm.* turnbuckle.

tènebra *sf.* darkness.

tenebroso *agg.* 1. dark 2. (*sinistro*) sinister.

tenente *sm.* lieutenant.

tenere *vt.* 1. to keep (*v. irr.*) 2. (*sostenere, considerare, contenere*) to hold (*v. irr.*) || — *una lezione*, to give (*v. irr.*) a lesson. ♦ **tenersi** *vr.* (*seguire*) to follow: — *al corrente*, to keep tabs on.

tenerezza *sf.* tenderness.

tènero *agg.* tender. ♦ **tènero** *sm.* 1. (*parte tenera*) tender part 2. (*affetto*) sympathy.

tenia sf. tapeworm.

tennis sm. tennis.

tennista s. tennis-player.

tenore sm. tenor.

tenorile agg. tenor (attr.).

tensione sf. tension.

tentacolare agg. tentacular.

tentàcolo sm. tentacle.

tentare vt. 1. to tempt 2. (provare) to try.

tentativo sm. attempt.

tentatore agg. tempting. ♦ **tentatore** sm. tempter.

tentazione sf. temptation.

tentennamento sm. 1. shaking 2. (traballamento) tottering 3. (esitazione) hesitation.

tentennare vt. to shake (v. irr.). ♦ **tentennare** vi. 1. to totter 2. (esitare) to waver.

tentoni agg. gropingly.

tenue agg. 1. small 2. (leggero) soft.

tenuità sf. 1. smallness 2. (levità) slightness.

tenuta sf. 1. (proprietà) estate 2. (capacità) capacity 3. (àbiti) clothes (pl.) 4. (tec.) seal ‖ — di strada, roadability; a — d'acqua, watertight.

teocràtico agg. theocratic(al).

teocrazia sf. theocracy.

teologale agg. theological.

teologia sf. theology.

teològico agg. theologic(al).

teòlogo sm. theologian.

teorema sm. theorem.

teoria sf. 1. theory 2. (fila) string.

teòrico agg. theoretic(al).

teorizzare vi. to theorize.

tepore sm. lukewarmness.

teppa sf. rabble.

teppista sm. teddy-boy.

terapèutico agg. therapeutic(al).

terapìa sf. therapy.

terebinto sm. terebinth.

tèrgere vt. to wipe (off).

tergicristallo sm. windscreen wiper.

tergiversare vi. to hesitate.

tergiversazione sf. hesitation.

tergo sm. back: segue a —, please turn over.

termale agg. thermal: stazione —, spa.

terme sf. pl. thermal springs.

tèrmico agg. thermic.

terminale agg. terminal.

terminare vt. e vi. to end.

tèrmine sm. 1. term 2. (limite) limit 3. (fine) end ‖ contratto a —, time-contract; portare a —, to carry out.

terminologìa sf. terminology.

tèrmite sf. termite.

termocoperta sf. thermal blanket.

termodinàmica sf. thermodynamics.

termoelèttrico agg. thermoelectric(al).

termòforo sm. warming pad.

termògeno agg. thermogenetic.

termoiònico agg. thermionic.

termòmetro sm. thermometer: il — segna..., the thermometer stands at...

termonucleare agg. thermonuclear.

termos sm. vacuum bottle.

termosifone sm. (radiatore) radiator.

termòstato sm. thermostat.

ternario agg. ternary.

terno sm. tern. ♦ **terno** agg. triple.

terra sf. 1. (globo terracqueo) earth 2. (paese; l'opposto del mare) land 3. (terreno) ground ‖ — —, earth bound; raso —, to the ground.

terracotta sf. terracotta: vasellame di —, earthenware.

terraferma sf. dry land.

terraglia sf. pottery.

terranova sm. (cane) Newfoundland dog.

terrapieno sm. 1. bank 2. (di fiume) embankment.

terràqueo agg. terraqueous.

terrazza sf. 1. terrace 2. (balcone) balcony.

terrazziere sm. digger.

terrazzo sm. V. terrazza.

terremoto sm. earthquake.

terreno[1] agg. earthly.

terreno[2] sm. ground.

tèrreo agg. 1. earthy 2. (di colorito) wan, sallow.

terrestre agg. terrestrial, earthly.

terrìbile agg. terrible.

terriccio sm. mould.

terriero agg. land (attr.).

terrificante agg. terrifying.

terrificare vt. to terrify.

terrina sf. tureen.

territoriale agg. territorial.

territorio sm. territory.

terrore sm. terror: incutere — a qu., to strike (v. irr.) so. with terror.

terrorismo sm. terrorism.

terrorista *s.* terrorist.
terroristico *agg.* terroristic.
terrorizzare *vt.* to terrorize.
terroso *agg.* earthy.
terso *agg.* clear.
terza *sf.* 1. (*di scuola, treno*) third class 2. (*di auto*) third gear.
terzetto *sm.* trio.
terziario *agg. e sm.* tertiary.
terzina *sf.* tercet.
terzino *sm.* (*sport*) full back.
terzo *agg.* third. ◆ **terzo** *sm.* 1. third 2. (*terza persona*) third person || *terzi*, third party.
terzùltimo *agg. e sm.* last but two.
tesa *sf.* brim.
tesaurizzare *vt.* to treasure.
teschio *sm.* skull.
tesi *sf.* thesis (*pl.* -ses).
teso *agg.* taut.
tesoreria *sf.* treasury.
tesoriere *sm.* treasurer.
tesoro *sm.* 1. treasure 2. (*pol.*) treasury.
tèssera *sf.* 1. card 2. (*di mosaico*) tessera (*pl.* -rae).
tesseramento *sm.* 1. rationing 2. (*reclutamento*) enrolment.
tesserare *vt.* 1. to ration 2. (*arruolare*) to enrol.
tèssere *vt.* to weave (*v. irr.*).
tèssile *agg.* textile. ◆ **tèssile** *sm.* weaver.
tessitore *sm.* weaver.
tessitura *sf.* 1. weaving 2. (*disposizione dei fili*) texture.
tessuto *sm.* 1. fabric 2. (*med.; fig.*) tissue || *negozio di tessuti*, draper's shop.
testa *sf.* head: *colpo di* —, rash act; *essere in* — *a tutti*, to be ahead of everybody.
testamentario *agg.* testamentary.
testamento *sm.* will.
testardàggine *sf.* stubbornness.
testardo *agg.* stubborn.
testata *sf.* 1. head 2. (*colpo*) butt 3. (*di giornale*) heading.
teste *s.* witness: — *d'accusa, di difesa,* witness for the prosecution, the defence.
testicolo *sm.* testicle.
testimonianza *sf.* 1. witness 2. (*prova*) evidence || *far* —, to bear (*v. irr.*) witness.
testimoniare *vt. e vi.* 1. to witness 2. (*attestare*) to testify.
testimonio *sm.* witness.
testo *sm.* text.

testuale *agg.* 1. textual 2. (*esatto*) exact.
tetànico *agg.* tetanic.
tètano *sm.* tetanus.
tetraedro *sm.* tetrahedron.
tetràggine *sf.* gloom.
tetràgono *agg.* (*fig.*) steadfast.
tetralogìa *sf.* tetralogy.
tetro *agg.* gloomy.
tettarella *sf.* dummy.
tetto *sm.* roof: — *a capanna,* saddle roof.
tettoia *sf.* shed.
tettònica *sf.* tectonics.
teutònico *agg.* Teutonic. ◆ **teutònico** *sm.* Teuton.
ti *pron.* 1. you, to you 2. (*r.*) yourself.
tiara *sf.* tiara.
tibia *sf.* tibia.
tic *sm.* tic.
ticchettare *vi.* to tick.
ticchettìo *sm.* ticking.
ticchio *sm.* fancy.
tièpido *agg.* tepid.
tifo *sm.* 1. typhus 2. (*fig.*) fanaticism.
tifone *sm.* typhoon.
tifoso *sm.* 1. typhus patient 2. (*fig.*) fan.
tiglio *sm.* lime.
tigna *sf.* ringworm.
tignola *sf.* moth.
tigrato *agg.* striped.
tigre *sf.* tiger.
timbrare *vt.* 1. to stamp 2. (*lettere*) to postmark || — *a secco,* to emboss.
timbratura *sf.* 1. stamping 2. (*postale*) postmarking.
timbro *sm.* 1. stamp 2. (*di suono*) timbre 3. (*postale*) postmark || — *a secco,* embossed stamp.
timidezza *sf.* shyness.
timido *agg.* shy.
timo *sm.* thyme.
timone *sm.* helm.
timoniere *sm.* helmsman (*pl.* -men).
timorato *agg.* 1. respectful 2. (*scrupoloso*) scrupulous.
timore *sm.* fear: *aver* —, to fear, to be afraid.
timoroso *agg.* fearful.
tìmpano *sm.* 1. eardrum 2. (*mus.*) kettle-drum 3. (*arch.*) gable.
tinca *sf.* tench.
tinello *sm.* living-room.
tìngere *vt.* to dye (*v. irr.*). ◆ **tìngersi** *vr.* to dye oneself.

tino *sm.* vat.

tinozza *sf.* tub.

tinta *sf.* 1. (*colore*) hue 2. (*materia colorante*) dye 3. (*tingitura*) dyeing.

tinteggiare *vt.* to paint.

tintinnare *vi.* to tinkle.

tintinnìo *sm.* tinkling.

tintore *sm.* 1. dyer 2. (*anche per lavature a secco*) cleaner.

tintorìa *sf.* 1. dyeworks (*pl.*) 2. (*negozio anche per lavature a secco*) dry cleaners' shop.

tintura *sf.* V. **tinta**.

tìpico *agg.* typical.

tipo *sm.* 1. type 2. (*modello*) pattern 3. (*individuo*) fellow.

tipografìa *sf.* 1. typography 2. (*mecc.*) letterpress printing.

tipogràfico *agg.* typographic(al).

tipògrafo *sm.* typographer.

tiràggio *sm.* draught.

tiralìnee *sm.* drawing-pen.

tiranneggiare *vt.* to tyrannize.

tirannìa *sf.* tyranny.

tirànnico *agg.* tyrannical.

tirànnide *sf.* tyranny.

tiranno *sm.* tyrant.

tirante *sm.* 1. (*mecc.*) connecting rod 2. (*arch.*) tie-beam.

tirapiedi *sm.* drudge.

tirare *vt.* 1. to draw (*v. irr.*), to pull 2. (*scagliare*) to throw (*v. irr.*) ♦ **tirare** *vi.* 1. (*sparare*) to shoot (*v. irr.*) 2. (*di tiraggio*) to draw 3. (*di vestito*) to be tight. ♦ **tirarsi** *vr.* to draw.

tirata *sf.* 1. pull 2. (*invettiva*) tirade.

tiratore *sm.* shooter.

tiratura *sf.* 1. (*tip.*) printing 2. (*numero di copie stampate*) circulation.

tirchierìa *sf.* niggardliness.

tìrchio *agg.* niggardly.

tiritera *sf.* rigmarole.

tiro *sm.* 1. (*trazione*) draught 2. (*lancio*) throw 3. (*sparo*) shot 4. (*scherzo*) trick.

tirocìnio *sm.* apprenticeship.

tiròide *sf.* thyroid.

tisana *sf.* ptisan.

tisi *sf.* consumption.

tìsico *agg. e sm.* consumptive.

tisiologìa *sf.* phthisiology.

tisiòlogo *sm.* phthisiologist.

titànico *agg.* titanic.

titillare *vt.* to tickle.

titolare *agg.* 1. regular 2. (*nominale*) titular. ♦ **titolare** *s.* 1. regular holder 2. (*proprietario*) owner 3. (*capo*) principal.

titolato *agg.* titled.

tìtolo *sm.* 1. title 2. (*qualifica*) qualification 3. (*documento*) document 4. (*comm.*) security.

titubante *agg.* hesitating.

titubanza *sf.* hesitation.

titubare *vi.* to hesitate.

tizianesco *agg.* 1. Titianesque 2. (*di capelli*) titian.

tìzio *sm.* fellow.

tizzone *sm.* brand.

toccare *vt.* to touch || — *un porto*, to call at. ♦ **toccare** *vi.* 1. (*capitare*) to happen 2. (*spettare*) to fall (*v. irr.*).

toccasana *sm.* cure-all.

tocco[1] *agg.* (*pazzoide*) touched.

tocco[2] *sm.* 1. touch 2. (*battito*) knock 3. (*rintocco*) toll || *al —*, at one o'clock.

tocco[3] *sm.* (*berretto*) toque.

toga *sf.* gown.

togato *agg.* gowned.

tògliere *vt.* 1. to take (*v. irr.*) 2. (*liberare*) to relieve. ♦ **tògliersi** *vr.* 1. to get (*v. irr.*) off 2. (*un indumento*) to take off || — *la vita*, to commit suicide.

toletta *sf.* toilet.

tolleràbile *agg.* tolerable.

tollerante *agg.* tolerant.

tolleranza *sf.* tolerance.

tollerare *vt.* 1. to tolerate 2. (*sopportare*) to bear (*v. irr.*).

tomaia *sf.* vamp.

tomba *sf.* grave.

tombale *agg.* grave (*attr.*).

tombino *sm.* manhole.

tòmbola *sf.* 1. (*gioco*) "tombola" 2. (*caduta*) tumble.

tombolare *vi.* to tumble down.

tomismo *sm.* Thomism.

tomista *agg. e sm.* Thomist.

tomo *sm.* 1. tome 2. (*persona*) chap.

tònaca *sf.* frock: *gettare la —*, to give (*v. irr.*) up the frock.

tonalità *sf.* tonality.

tonante *agg.* thundering.

tondeggiante *agg.* roundish.

tondeggiare *vi.* to be roundish.

tondello *sm.* round.

tondo *agg. e sm.* round || *chiaro e —*, clearly.

tonfo *sm.* splash.

tònico *agg. e sm.* tonic.

tonificare *vt.* to brace.

tonnellàggio *sm.* tonnage.

tonnellata *sf.* ton.

tonno *sm.* tunny.

tono sm. **1.** tone **2.** (accordo) tune **3.** (mus.) strain.

tonsilla sf. tonsil.

tonsillectomìa sf. tonsillectomy.

tonsillite sf. tonsillitis.

tonsura sf. tonsure.

tonsurare vt. to tonsure.

tonto agg. dull. ♦ **tonto** sm. dunce.

topàia sf. (fig.) hovel.

topàzio sm. topaz.

tòpica sf. **1.** topic **2.** (errore) blunder.

tòpico agg. topical.

topo sm. mouse (pl. mice), rat || — di biblioteca (fig.), bookworm; — di albergo (fig.), hotel thief.

topografìa sf. topography.

topogràfico agg. topographic(al).

topologìa sf. topology.

toponomàstica sf. toponymy.

toppa sf. **1.** (pezza) patch **2.** (di serratura) keyhole || mettere una —, to patch up.

torace sm. thorax, chest.

torba sf. peat.

torbidezza sf. **1.** turbidity **2.** (esser fosco) gloominess.

tòrbido agg. **1.** turbid **2.** (fosco) gloomy **3.** (inquieto) troubled. ♦ **tòrbido** sm. (disordine) disorder: pescare nel —, to fish in troubled water.

torbiera sf. peat-bog.

tòrcere vt. **1.** to wring (v. irr.) **2.** (attorcigliare) to twist || dare del filo da —, to give (v. irr.) a lot of trouble; — il naso (fig.), to turn up one's nose (at). ♦ **tòrcersi** vr. to twist.

torchiare vt. to press.

torchiatura sf. pressing.

tòrchio sm. press.

tòrcia sf. torch.

torcicollo sm. stiff-neck.

torcitore sm. twister.

torcitura sf. twist.

tordo sm. thrush.

torero sm. bullfighter.

torma sf. swarm.

tormalina sf. tourmaline.

tormenta sf. blizzard.

tormentare vt. to torment. ♦ **tormentarsi** vr. to worry.

tormentato agg. (inquieto) restless.

tormento sm. torment.

tormentoso agg. tormenting.

tornaconto sm. profit.

tornado sm. tornado.

tornante sm. bend.

tornare vi. **1.** to return **2.** (di conti) to be correct.

tornasole sm. litmus.

torneo sm. tournament.

tornio sm. lathe.

tornire vt. **1.** (mecc.) to turn **2.** (fig.) to polish.

tornito agg. **1.** (rotondo) round **2.** (ben fatto) well-shaped.

tornitore sm. turner.

toro sm. bull.

torpediniera sf. torpedo-boat.

torpedo sf. torpedo.

torpedone sm. (motor-)coach.

tòrpido agg. torpid.

torpore sm. torpor.

torre sf. tower.

torrefare vt. **1.** to torrefy **2.** (caffè) to roast.

torrefazione sf. **1.** torrefaction **2.** (di caffè) roasting **3.** (negozio) coffee store.

torreggiare vi. to tower.

torrente sm. torrent.

torrentizio agg. torrent-like.

torrenziale agg. torrential.

torretta sf. (mil.; mar.) turret.

tòrrido agg. torrid.

torrione sm. donjon.

torrone sm. nougat.

torsione sf. torsion.

torso sm. **1.** trunk **2.** (di statua) torso.

tòrsolo sm. **1.** (di verdura) stump **2.** (di frutta) core.

torta sf. cake.

tortiera sf. bakepan.

torto agg. **1.** (piegato) bent **2.** (contorto) twisted.

torto sm. **1.** wrong **2.** (colpa) fault || aver —, to be wrong; far — a qu., to wrong so.; a —, wrongly.

tòrtora sf. turtle-dove.

tortuosità sf. tortuosity.

tortuoso agg. tortuous.

tortura sf. torture.

torturare vt. to torture. ♦ **torturarsi** vr. to worry.

torvo agg. grim.

tosare vt. to shear (v. irr.).

tosatrice sf. clippers (pl.).

tosatura sf. shearing.

toscano agg. e sm. Tuscan.

tosse sf. cough.

tossicchiare vi. to keep (v. irr.) on coughing.

tossicità sf. toxicity.

tòssico agg. toxic. ♦ **tòssico** sm. toxicant.

tossicologìa sf. toxicology.
tossicòlogo sm. toxicologist.
tossicomania sf. toxicomania.
tossina sf. toxin.
tossire vi. to cough.
tostapane sm. toaster.
tostare vt. 1. to toast 2. (caffè) to roast.
tosto¹ avv. at once.
tosto² agg. hard || faccia tosta, cheek.
tosto³ sm. toast.
totale agg. e sm. total: in —, in all.
totalità sf. 1. totality 2. (numero complessivo) mass.
totalitario agg. totalitarian.
totalitarismo sm. totalitarianism.
totalizzare vt. 1. to totalize 2. (sport) to score.
totalizzatore sm. totalizer.
tovaglia sf. (table-)cloth.
tovagliolo sm. napkin.
tozzo¹ agg. squat, stocky.
tozzo² sm. piece: un — di pane, a crust of bread.
tra prep. 1. (fra due persone, cose, gruppi) between 2. (fra più di due) among 3. (nel mezzo di) amid 4. (di tempo) (with)in.
traballare vi. 1. to stagger 2. (di vettura) to jolt || entrare, uscire traballando, to stagger in, out.
trabeazione sf. trabeation.
trabiccolo sm. ramshackle vehicle.
traboccare vi. to overflow.
trabocchetto sm. trap.
tracagnotto agg. squat.
tracannare vt. to gulp down.
traccia sf. 1. trace 2. (segno) mark 3. (orme) footsteps (pl.) 4. (schema) outline.
tracciare vt. to trace (out): — a grandi linee, to outline.
tracciato sm. layout.
tracciatore sm. tracer.
trachea sf. windpipe.
tracheale agg. tracheal.
tracheite sf. tracheitis.
tracolla sf. baldric: portare qc. a —, to carry sthg. across one's back.
tracollare vi. 1. to lose (v. irr.) one's balance 2. (cadere) to collapse.
tracollo sm. collapse: portare al —, to bring (v. irr.) to ruin.
tracoma sm. trachoma.
tracotante agg. haughty.
tracotanza sf. haughtiness.

tradimento sm. 1. treason 2. (infedeltà) betrayal || a — (agg.), treacherous, (avv.) treacherously.
tradire vt. 1. to betray 2. (di coniuge) to be unfaithful (to).
traditore agg. treacherous. ♦ **traditore** sm. traitor.
tradizionale agg. traditional.
tradizionalismo sm. traditionalism.
tradizionalista s. traditionalist.
tradizione sf. tradition: per —, traditionally.
tradotta sf. troop-train.
traducìbile agg. translatable.
tradurre vt. to translate: — in atto, to carry out; — in carcere, to take (v. irr.) to prison.
traduttore sm. translator.
traduzione sf. translation.
traente s. (comm.) drawer.
trafelato agg. breathless.
trafficante sm. dealer.
trafficare vi. 1. to deal (v. irr.) 2. (affaccendarsi) to bustle about.
traffico sm. 1. traffic 2. (comm.) trade.
trafiggere vt. to pierce (through).
trafila sf. 1. procedure 2. (mecc.) draw-plate.
trafilare vt. to draw (v. irr.).
trafiletto sm. paragraph.
traforare vt. 1. to perforate 2. (ricamare) to embroider with open-work.
traforato agg. 1. perforated 2. (ricamato a traforo) open-work (attr.).
traforatrice sf. fret-sawing machine.
traforo sm. 1. perforation 2. (galleria) tunnel 3. (falegnameria) fretwork 4. (ricamo) open-work.
trafugamento sm. stealing.
trafugare vt. to steal (v. irr.).
tragedia sf. tragedy.
tragediògrafo sm. tragedian.
traghettare vt. to ferry.
traghetto sm. ferry-boat.
tragicità sf. tragicalness.
tràgico agg. tragical. ♦ **tràgico** sm. tragedian.
tragicòmico agg. tragicomic(al).
tragicommedia sf. tragicomedy.
tragitto sm. 1. way 2. (viaggio) journey.
traguardo sm. goal.
traiettoria sf. trajectory.
trainare vt. to haul.
tràino sm. 1. haulage 2. (carro) truck.

tralasciare *vt.* to leave (*v. irr.*) out, to omit.

tralcio *sm.* shoot.

traliccio *sm.* 1. (*tela*) ticking 2. (*per costruzioni*) trellis || – *di ferro*, iron framework.

tralice (*nella loc. avv.*) *in* –, askance.

tralignamento *sm.* degeneration.

tralignare *vi.* to degenerate.

tralúcere *vi.* to shine (*v. irr.*) (through).

tram *sm.* tramcar.

trama *sf.* 1. weft 2. (*fig.*) plot.

tramaglio *sm.* trammel.

tramandare *vt.* to hand down.

tramare *vt.* 1. to weave (*v. irr.*) 2. (*fig.*) to plot.

trambusto *sm.* bustle.

tramenare *vt.* e *vi.* to move about.

tramenìo *sm.* bustle.

tramestare *vt.* to rummage.

tramestìo *sm.* 1. rummaging 2. (*trepestio*) stamping.

tramezzare *vt.* to partition.

tramezzino *sm.* sandwich.

tramezzo *sm.* partition.

tràmite *sm.* path: – *qu.*, through so.

tramoggia *sf.* hopper.

tramontana *sf.* 1. north 2. (*vento*) north wind || *perder la* –, to lose (*v. irr.*) one's head.

tramontare *vi.* 1. to set (*v. irr.*) 2. (*svanire*) to fade.

tramonto *sm.* 1. setting 2. (*del sole*) sunset 3. (*declino*) decline.

tramortimento *sm.* swoon.

tramortire *vt.* to stun.

trampoliere *sm.* wader.

trampolino *sm.* spring-board.

tràmpolo *sm.* stilt.

tramutare *vt.* to change. ♦ **tramutarsi** *vr.* to change.

trancia *sf.* 1. shears (*pl.*) 2. (*fetta*) slice.

tranciare *vt.* to shear.

tranello *sm.* snare.

trangugiare *vt.* to swallow.

tranne *prep.* but.

tranquillante *agg.* tranquillizing. ♦ **tranquillante** *sm.* tranquillizer.

tranquillità *sf.* calmness.

tranquillizzare *vt.* to calm 2. (*rassicurare*) to reassure.

tranquillo *agg.* calm: *star* –, to keep (*v. irr.*) quiet; *sta'* –!, do not worry!

transalpino *agg.* transalpine.

transatlàntico *agg.* transatlantic. ♦ **transatlàntico** *sm.* liner.

transazione *sf.* 1. transaction 2. (*accomodamento*) arrangement 3. (*compromesso*) compromise.

transcontinentale *agg.* transcontinental.

transetto *sm.* transept.

trànsfuga *s.* runaway.

transigere *vt.* e *vi.* to compromise.

transistore *sm.* transistor.

transitàbile *agg.* practicable.

transitabilità *sf.* practicability.

transitare *vi.* to pass through.

transitivo *agg.* e *sm.* transitive.

trànsito *sm.* transit.

transitorio *agg.* transitory.

transizione *sf.* transition.

transoceànico *agg.* transoceanic.

transustanziazione *sf.* transubstantiation.

tranvìa *sf.* tramway.

tranviario *agg.* tramcar (*attr.*).

tranviere *sm.* 1. tram-driver 2. (*bigliettario*) tram-conductor.

trapanare *vt.* 1. to drill 2. (*med.*) to trepan.

trapanazione *sf.* 1. drilling 2. (*med.*) trepanation.

tràpano *sm.* 1. drill 2. (*med.*) trepan.

trapassare *vt.* to pierce through. ♦ **trapassare** *vi.* (*morire*) to die.

trapasso *sm.* 1. (*morte*) death 2. (*giur.; comm.*) transfer.

trapelare *vi.* to leak out.

trapezio *sm.* 1. trapezium 2. (*da ginnastica*) trapeze.

trapiantare *vt.* to transplant. ♦ **trapiantarsi** *vr.* (*stabilirsi*) to settle.

trapianto *sm.* 1. transplantation 2. (*tessuto trapiantato*) graft.

trappista *sm.* Trappist.

tràppola *sf.* trap: *prendere in* –, to trap.

trapunta *sf.* quilt.

trapuntare *vt.* 1. to quilt 2. (*ricamare*) to embroider.

trapunto *agg.* 1. quilted 2. (*ricamato*) embroidered || – *di stelle*, starry.

trarre *vt.* 1. to draw (*v. irr.*) 2. (*ottenere*) to get (*v. irr.*). ♦ **trarsi** *vr.* to draw.

trasalire *vi.* to startle: *far* –, to startle.

trasandato *agg.* shabby.

trasbordare vt. **1.** to transfer **2.** (traghettare) to ferry.

trasbordo sm. **1.** transfer **2.** (traghetto) ferrying across.

trascendentale agg. transcendental.

trascendentalismo sm. transcendentalism.

trascendente agg. transcendent.

trascendenza sf. transcendence.

trascéndere vt. to transcend. ♦ **trascéndere** vi. to let (v. irr.) oneself go.

trascinare vt. **1.** to drag **2.** (affascinare) to fascinate.

trascòrrere vt. (il tempo) to spend (v. irr.) ♦ **trascòrrere** vi. **1.** (di tempo) to pass **2.** (lasciar correre) to pass over.

trascorso agg. past. ♦ **trascorso** sm. (errore) slip.

trascrittore sm. transcriber.

trascrivere vt. **1.** to transcribe **2.** (giur.) to register.

trascrizione sf. **1.** transcription **2.** (giur.) registration **3.** (trapasso) transfer.

trascuràbile agg. negligible.

trascurare vt. to neglect. ♦ **trascurarsi** vr. not to care of oneself.

trascuratezza sf. **1.** negligence **2.** (sciatteria) slovenliness.

trascurato agg. **1.** (negligente) careless **2.** (sciatto) sloven.

trasecolare vi. to be amazed.

trasecolato agg. amazed.

trasferìbile agg. transferable.

trasferimento sm. transfer.

trasferire vt. to transfer. ♦ **trasferirsi** vr. to (re)move.

trasferta sf. **1.** transfer **2.** (indennità) travelling allowance || in —, on transfer; partita in — (sport), out match.

trasfigurare vt. to transfigure. ♦ **trasfigurarsi** vr. to become (v. irr.) transfigured.

trasfigurazione sf. transfiguration.

trasfòndere vt. **1.** to transfuse **2.** (fig.) to instil.

trasformàbile agg. convertible.

trasformare vt. to change, to turn. ♦ **trasformarsi** vr. to change.

trasformatore sm. transformer.

trasformazione sf. transformation.

trasformismo sm. transformism.

trasfusione sf. transfusion.

trasgredire vt. e vi. to infringe.

trasgressione sf. infringement.

trasgressore sm. infringer.

traslazione sf. **1.** transfer **2.** (fis.; eccl.) translation.

traslocare vt. e vi. to move.

trasloco sm. removal.

traslùcido agg. translucent.

trasméttere vt. to transmit.

trasmettitore sm. transmitter.

trasmigrare vi. to transmigrate.

trasmigrazione sf. transmigration.

trasmissìbile agg. transmissible.

trasmissione sf. **1.** transmission **2.** (giur.) transfer **3.** (mecc.) drive || — radio, broadcast; — televisiva, telecast.

trasmittente agg. transmitting.

trasognato agg. dreamy.

trasparente agg. transparent.

trasparenza sf. transparence.

trasparire vi. **1.** to shine (v. irr.) through **2.** (esser trasparente) to be transparent || lasciar —, to betray.

traspirare vi. to transpire.

traspirazione sf. transpiration.

trasporre vt. to transpose.

trasportàbile agg. transportable.

trasportare vt. **1.** to carry **2.** (fig.) to carry away. ♦ **trasportarsi** vr. to go (v. irr.).

trasportatore sm. conveyer: — a nastro, belt-conveyer.

trasporto sm. transport: nave da —, cargo; spese di —, carriage.

trasposizione sf. transposition.

trastullare vt. to amuse. ♦ **trastullarsi** vr. **1.** (giocare) to play **2.** (scherzare) to trifle.

trastullo sm. **1.** plaything **2.** (divertimento) amusement.

trasudamento sm. sweating.

trasudare vt. e vi. to sweat.

trasversale agg. transversal, cross (attr.). ♦ **trasversale** sf. **1.** transversal **2.** (strada) cross-road.

trasvolare vt. to fly (v. irr.) across.

trasvolata sf. flight (across).

tratta sf. **1.** (traffico) trade **2.** (comm.) draft || — a vista, sight draft; spiccare una — su qu., to draw (v. irr.) upon so.

trattàbile agg. **1.** tractable **2.** (di argomento) that can be dealt with.

trattabilità sf. tractability.

trattamento sm. **1.** treatment **2.** (paga) salary.

trattare vt. **1.** to treat **2.** (maneggiare) to handle **3.** (commerciare) to deal (v. intr.) (in) **4.** (negoziare) to negotiate **5.** (un argomento) to deal (with). ♦ **trattarsi** v. imp. to be a question of, to be involved.

trattativa *sf.* negotiation.

trattato *sm.* **1.** (*patto*) treaty **2.** (*libro*) treatise.

trattazione *sf.* treatment.

tratteggiare *vt.* **1.** to outline **2.** (*ombreggiare*) to hatch.

tratteggio *sm.* **1.** (*abbozzo*) outline **2.** (*ombreggiatura*) hatching.

trattenere *vt.* **1.** to keep (*v. irr.*) **2.** (*dedurre*) to deduct **3.** (*frenare*) to refrain ‖ — *il respiro,* to hold (*v. irr.*) one's breath. ◆ **trattenersi** *vr.* (*fermarsi*) to stay ‖ *non posso trattenermi dal fare,* I cannot help doing.

trattenimento *sm.* (*festa*) party.

trattenuta *sf.* deduction.

trattino *sm.* **1.** dash **2.** (*di unione*) hyphen.

tratto *sm.* **1.** (*tirata*) pull **2.** (*colpo*) stroke **3.** (*linea*) line **4.** (*brano*) passage **5.** (*estensione di spazio*) way **6.** (*lineamento*) feature **7.** (*comportamento*) manners (*pl.*) ‖ *d'un* —, suddenly; *di* — *in* —, now and then.

trattore[1] *sm.* (*mecc.*) tractor.

trattore[2] *sm.* (*oste*) inn-keeper.

trattoria *sf.* inn.

tratturo *sm.* cattle-track.

tràuma *sm.* trauma.

traumàtico *agg.* traumatic.

traumatologìa *sf.* traumatology.

travagliare *vt.* V. *tormentare.*

travaglio *sm.* **1.** (*fatica*) labour **2.** (*cruccio*) trouble.

travasare *vt.* to pour off.

travaso *sm.* **1.** pouring off **2.** (*med.*) effusion.

travatura *sf.* truss.

trave *sf.* beam.

travéggole *sf. pl.* avere le —, to mistake (*v. irr.*) one thing for another.

traversa *sf.* **1.** (*sbarra*) cross-bar **2.** (*via*) side-road.

traversata *sf.* crossing.

traversìa *sf.* misfortune.

traversina *sf.* sleeper.

traverso *agg.* **1.** transverse, cross (*attr.*) **2.** (*obliquo*) slanting ‖ *di* —, askance; *andare per* — (*fig.*), to go (*v. irr.*) wrong with.

travestimento *sm.* disguise.

travestire *vt.* to disguise (as).

traviamento *sm.* corruption.

traviare *vt.* to mislead (*v. irr.*). ◆ **traviarsi** *vr.* to go (*v. irr.*) astray.

travisamento *sm.* alteration.

travisare *vt.* to alter.

travolgente *agg.* sweeping.

travòlgere *vt.* **1.** to sweep (*v. irr.*) away **2.** (*investire*) to run (*v. irr.*) over.

trazione *sf.* traction.

tre *agg.* three.

trebbiare *vt.* to thrash.

trebbiatrice *sf.* thrasher.

trebbiatura *sf.* thrashing.

treccia *sf.* plait: *farsi le trecce,* to plait one's hair.

trecento *agg.* three hundred ‖ *il* — (*secolo*), the fourteenth century.

tredicenne *agg.* thirteen years old, thirteen-year-old (*attr.*).

tredicèsimo *agg.* thirteenth.

trédici *agg.* thirteen.

tregua *sf.* **1.** truce **2.** (*riposo*) rest.

tremante *agg.* **1.** trembling **2.** (*di freddo*) shivering.

tremare *vi.* **1.** to tremble **2.** (*di freddo*) to shiver.

tremendo *agg.* awful.

trementina *sf.* turpentine.

tremila *agg.* three thousand.

trèmito *sm.* **1.** tremble **2.** (*di freddo*) shiver.

tremolante *agg.* **1.** trembling **2.** (*di luce*) flickering **3.** (*di stelle*) twinkling.

tremolare *vi.* **1.** to tremble **2.** (*di luce*) to flicker **3.** (*di stelle*) to twinkle.

tremolìo *sm.* **1.** tremble **2.** (*di luce*) flickering **3.** (*di stelle*) twinkle.

◆**tremore** *sm.* V. **trèmito.**

treno *sm.* train: — *accelerato,* slow train; — *direttissimo,* fast train; — *rapido,* express train **2.** (*tenore*) way of living, routine.

trenta *agg.* thirty.

trentenne *agg.* thirty years old, thirty-year-old (*attr.*).

trentennio *sm.* period of thirty years.

trentèsimo *agg.* thirtieth.

trentina *sf.* about thirty.

trepestìo *sm.* stamping.

trepidante *agg.* anxious.

trepidare *vi.* to be anxious.

trepidazione *sf.* anxiety.

treppiede *sm.* tripod.

tresca *sf.* intrigue.

tréspolo *sm.* trestle.

trìade *sf.* triad.

triangolare *agg.* triangular.

triangolazione *sf.* triangulation.

triàngolo sm. triangle.

tribale agg. tribal.

tribolare vi. 1. to toil 2. (soffrire) to suffer. ♦ **tribolare** vt. to vex.

tribolazione sf. suffering.

tribordo sm. starboard.

tribù sf. tribe.

tribuna sf. 1. (per oratori) platform 2. (sport) stand.

tribunale sm. court.

tribuno sm. tribune.

tributare vt. to bestow.

tributario agg. 1. tributary 2. (fiscale) fiscal. ♦ **tributario** sm. tributary.

tributo sm. tribute.

tricheco sm. walrus.

triciclo sm. tricycle.

triclinio sm. triclinium (pl. -nia).

tricolore agg. e sm. tricolour.

tricorno sm. tricorn.

tricromìa sf. 1. trichromatism 2. (pezzo singolo) trichromatic print.

tridente sm. 1. trident 2. (per fieno) hayfork.

tridimensionale agg. tridimensional.

triedro sm. trihedron.

triennale agg. e sm. triennial.

triennio sm. period of three years.

trifase agg. three-phase (attr.).

trifoglio sm. clover.

trigèmino agg. e sm. trigeminal: parto —, birth of triplets.

trigèsimo agg. thirtieth: nel — della sua morte, on the thirtieth day after his death.

trigonometrìa sf. trigonometry.

trilione sm. 1. (in sistema italiano, francese e americano = 1000⁶) billion; (amer.) trillion 2. (in sistema inglese e tedesco = 1000⁹) trillion; (amer.) quintillion.

trillare vi. 1. to trill 2. (squillare) to ring (v. irr.).

trillo sm. 1. trill 2. (di sveglia, telefono) ring.

trilogìa sf. trilogy.

trimestrale agg. quarterly.

trimestre sm. 1. quarter 2. (scol.) term 3. (paga trimestrale) quarterage.

trimotore agg. three-engined aeroplane.

trina sf. lace.

trincare vt. to gulp. ♦ **trincare** vi. to drink (v. irr.).

trincea sf. trench.

trincerare vt. to entrench.

trincetto sm. shoemaker's knife (pl. knives).

trinchetto sm. albero di —, foremast; vela di —, foresail.

trinciante agg. sharp. ♦ **trinciante** sm. carver.

trinciare vt. 1. to cut (v. irr.) (up) 2. (carne) to carve || — giudizi, to judge rashly.

trinciato sm. cut-tobacco.

trinità sf. trinity.

trinomio sm. trinomial.

trionfante agg. triumphant.

trionfare vi. to triumph.

trionfatore sm. triumpher.

trionfo sm. triumph.

tripartito agg. tripartite.

tripartizione sf. tripartition.

triplicare vt. to treble.

triplo agg. triple. ♦ **triplo** sm. 1. triple 2. (tre volte tanto) three times as much.

trippa sf. (cuc.) tripe.

tripudiare vi. to exult.

tripudio sm. exultation.

trisàvolo sm. great-great-grand-father.

trisìllabo agg. trisyllabic. ♦ **trisìllabo** sm. trisyllable.

triste agg. sad.

tristezza sf. 1. sadness 2. (dolore) grief.

tristo agg. wicked.

tritacarne sm. mincer.

tritare vt. to mince.

tritatutto sm. mincer.

trito agg. (fig.) trite.

tritolo sm. trinitrotoluene.

trìttico sm. triptych.

trittongo sm. triphthong.

tritume sm. crumbs (pl.).

triturare vt. to triturate.

triumvirato sm. triumvirate.

triùmviro sm. triumvir.

trivalente agg. trivalent.

trivella sf. 1. (min.) drill 2. (falegnameria) auger.

trivellare vt. to drill.

trivellazione sf. drilling: torre di —, derrick.

triviale agg. coarse.

trivialità sf. 1. coarseness 2. (detto triviale) coarse expression.

trofeo sm. trophy.

troglodita sm. troglodyte.

troglodìtico agg. troglodytic(al).

trògolo sm. trough.

troia sf. (zool.) sow.

tromba sf. 1. trumpet 2. (di scale)

well || — d'aria, tornado; — d'acqua, water-spout.

trombettiere sm. trumpeter.

trombone sm. **1.** (mus.) trombone **2.** (schioppo) blunderbuss || suonatore di —, trombonist.

trombosi sf. thrombosis.

troncare vt. **1.** to cut (v. irr.) off **2.** (fig.) to break (v. irr.) off.

tronco¹ agg. **1.** cut off **2.** (fig.) broken.

tronco² sm. **1.** trunk **2.** (d'albero abbattuto) log **3.** (geom.) frustum || — ferroviario, railway section; licenziare in —, to sack on the spot.

troncone sm. stump.

troneggiare vi. to dominate (sthg.).

tronfio agg. **1.** conceited **2.** (di stile) bombastic.

trono sm. throne.

tropicale agg. tropical.

tròpico sm. tropic.

tropismo sm. tropism.

troposfera sf. troposphere.

troppo avv. **1.** (con agg. e avv.) too **2.** (con v.) too much **3.** (di tempo) too long. ♦ **troppo** agg. e pron. too much (pl. too many): anche —, only too; essere di —, to be unwelcome.

trota sf. trout (pl. invariato).

trottare vi. to trot: far — qu. (fig.) to make (v. irr.) so. run.

trottata sf. trot.

trottatore sm. trotter.

trotterellare vi. **1.** to trot along **2.** (di bambini) to toddle.

trotto sm. trot: mettere un cavallo al —, to trot a horse.

tròttola sf. top.

trovare vt. **1.** to find (v. irr.) **2.** (far visita) to see (v. irr.) **3.** (pensare) to think (v. irr.). ♦ **trovarsi** vr. **1.** (essere) to be **2.** (sentirsi) to feel (v. irr.).

trovata sf. trick.

trovatello sm. foundling.

trovatore sm. troubadour.

truccare vi. **1.** to make (v. irr.) up **2.** (sport) to fix.

truccatore sm. maker-up.

truccatura sf. make-up.

trucco sm. **1.** trick **2.** (cosmetici) make-up **3.** (inganno) deceit.

truce agg. grim.

trucidare vt. to slay (v. irr.).

trùciolo sm. shaving.

truculento agg. truculent.

truffa sf. cheat.

truffaldino agg. cheating.

truffare vt. to cheat.

truffatore sm. cheat.

truismo sm. truism.

truppa sf. troop.

tu pron. you.

tua agg. e pron. V. tuo.

tuba sf. **1.** tuba **2.** (cappello) top-hat.

tubare vi. to coo.

tubatura sf. piping.

tubercolare agg. tubercular.

tubercolina sf. tuberculin.

tubercolosario sm. sanatorium.

tubercolosi sf. tuberculosis: — polmonare, consumption.

tubercoloso agg. tuberculous. ♦ **tubercoloso** sm. consumptive.

tùbero sm. tuber.

tuberosa sf. tuberose.

tubino sm. bowler-hat.

tubo sm. **1.** tube **2.** (di conduttura) pipe **3.** (anat.) canal.

tubolare agg. tubular.

tue agg. e pron. V. tuo.

tuffare vt. to plunge, to dip. ♦ **tuffarsi** vr. to plunge, to dive.

tuffatore sm. diver.

tuffo sm. plunge, dive.

tufo sm. tuff.

tugurio sm. hovel.

tulipano sm. tulip.

tumefare vt. to swell (v. irr.). ♦ **tumefarsi** vr. to swell.

tumefatto agg. swollen.

tumefazione sf. swelling.

tùmido agg. tumid: labbra tumide, thick lips.

tumore sm. tumour.

tumulare vt. to bury.

tumulazione sf. burial.

tùmulo sm. **1.** tumulus (pl. -li) **2.** (tomba) grave.

tumulto sm. tumult.

tumultuante agg. riotous.

tumultuare vi. to riot.

tumultuoso agg. tumultuous.

tundra sf. tundra.

tungsteno sm. tungsten.

tùnica sf. tunic.

tunnel sm. tunnel.

tuo agg. your. ♦ **tuo** pron. yours.

tuoi agg. e pron. V. tuo || i —, your family.

tuonare vi. to thunder.

tuono sm. thunder.

tuorlo sm. yolk.

turàcciolo sm. **1.** stopper **2.** (di su-

ghero) cork || mettere il *— a una bottiglia*, to cork a bottle.

turare *vt.* to stop, to fill up. ♦ **turarsi** *vr.* **1.** to stop **2.** (*chiudersi*) to shut oneself up.

turba[1] *sf.* crowd.

turba[2] *sf.* (*med.*) trouble.

turbamento *sm.* **1.** perturbation **2.** (*eccitazione*) excitement **3.** (*sconvolgimento*) upsetting.

turbante *sm.* turban.

turbare *vt.* **1.** to upset (*v. irr.*) **2.** (*agitare intorbidando*) to muddy. ♦ **turbarsi** *vr.* to get (*v. irr.*) upset.

turbina *sf.* turbine.

turbinare *vi.* to whirl.

turbine *sm.* **1.** whirl **2.** (*uragano*) hurricane.

turbinio *sm.* whirling.

turbinoso *agg.* **1.** whirling **2.** (*tumultuoso*) tumultuous.

turbolento *agg.* boisterous.

turbolenza *sf.* boisterousness.

turbomotore *sm.* turbojet engine.

turbonave *sf.* turboship.

turboreattore *sm.* (*aer.*) turbojet.

turcasso *sm.* quiver.

turchese *sm.* turquoise.

turchino *agg.* deep blue.

turco *agg.* Turkish. ♦ **turco** *sm.* Turk.

turgidezza *sf.* turgidity.

tùrgido *agg.* turgid.

turibolo *sm.* censer.

turismo *sm.* tourism.

turista *s.* tourist.

turistico *agg.* tourist (*attr.*).

turlupinare *vt.* to swindle.

turlupinatura *sf.* swindle.

turno *sm.* **1.** turn **2.** (*servizio*) duty || *di —*, on duty; *a —*, on turn.

turpe *agg.* filthy.

turpiloquio *sm.* coarse language.

turpitùdine *sf.* baseness.

turrito *agg.* turreted.

tuta *sf.* overalls (*pl.*): *— spaziale*, spacesuit.

tutela *sf.* **1.** guardianship **2.** (*protezione*) protection.

tutelare *vt.* to guard.

tutelare *agg.* tutelary.

tutore *sm.* guardian.

tuttavia *cong.* yet.

tutto *agg.* all, whole (*pl.* all); (*ogni*) every || *tutt'e due*, both; *tutt'al più*, at the most; *tutt'altro che*, anything but; *tutt'altro!*, on the contrary! ♦ **tutto** *pron.* all,

everything (*pl.* all); (*ognuno*) everybody. ♦ **tutto** *s.s.* whole: *del —*, quite.

tuttofare *agg.* cameriera *—*, maid-of-all-work.

tuttora *avv.* still.

U

ubbia *sf.* whim.

ubbidiente *agg.* obedient.

ubbidienza *sf.* obedience.

ubbidire *vi.* to obey (so., sthg.).

ubicare *vt.* to locate.

ubicato *agg.* situated.

ubicazione *sf.* location.

ubiquità *sf.* ubiquity.

ubriacare *vt.* to make (*v. irr.*) drunk. ♦ **ubriacarsi** *vr.* to get (*v. irr.*) drunk.

ubriacatura *sf.* intoxication.

ubriachezza *sf.* drunkenness.

ubriaco *agg.* drunk. ♦ **ubriaco** *sm.* drunken man (*pl.* men).

ubriacone *sm.* drunkard.

uccellagione *sf.* feathered game.

uccellare *vi.* to fowl.

uccelliera *sf.* aviary.

uccello *sm.* bird.

uccìdere *vt.* **1.** to kill **2.** (*assassinare*) to murder **3.** (*con pugnale*) to stab to death **4.** (*con arma da fuoco*) to shoot (*v. irr.*). ♦ **uccìdersi** *vr.* **1.** to get (*v. irr.*) killed **2.** (*suicidarsi*) to commit suicide, to kill oneself.

uccisione *sf.* killing.

uccisore *sm.* killer.

udibile *agg.* audible.

udienza *sf.* hearing.

udire *vt.* to hear (*v. irr.*).

uditivo *agg.* auditory.

udito *sm.* hearing.

uditore *sm.* **1.** listener **2.** (*nella scuola*) auditor.

uditorio *sm.* audience.

ufficiale *agg.* official. ♦ **ufficiale** *sm.* **1.** officer **2.** (*governativo, postale*) official.

ufficialità *sf.* official character.

ufficialmente *avv.* officially.

ufficiare *vi.* to officiate.

ufficio *sm.* office: *capo —*, head clerk; *d'—*, officially; *— informazioni*, information bureau.

ufficiosamente *avv.* unofficially.

ufficioso *agg.* unofficial.

ufo (*nella loc. avv.*) **a —**, without paying.

uggia *sf.* boredom: *questo libro mi è venuto in —*, I have grown tired of this book.

uggiolare *vi.* to whine.

uggioso *agg.* dull.

ùgola *sf.* 1. uvula 2. (*voce*) voice.

uguaglianza *sf.* equality.

uguagliare *vt.* 1. to be equal (to) 2. (*rendere uguale*) to make (*v. irr.*) equal.

uguale *agg.* 1. equal 2. (*simile*) like, alike (*pred.*) 3. (*stesso*) same.

ugualitario *agg.* equalitarian.

ugualmente *avv.* 1. equally 2. (*lo stesso*) all the same.

ùlcera *sf.* ulcer.

ulcerare *vt.* to ulcerate. ♦ **ulcerarsi** *vr.* to ulcerate.

ulcerato *agg.* ulcerated.

ulcerazione *sf.* ulceration.

ulceroso *agg.* ulcerous.

ulteriore *agg.* further.

ulteriormente *avv.* further on.

ultimamente *avv.* 1. recently 2. (*da ultimo*) finally.

ultimare *vt.* to finish.

ultimazione *sf.* corclusion.

ùltimo *agg.* 1. last 2. (*il più recente*) latest 3. (*estremo*) utmost.

ultramicroscòpico *agg.* ultramicroscopic(al).

ultramoderno *agg.* ultramodern.

ultrasensìbile *agg.* ultrasensitive.

ultrasònico *agg.* ultrasonic.

ultrasuono *sm.* ultrasound.

ultraterreno *agg.* supernatural.

ultravioletto *agg.* ultraviolet.

ululare *vi.* 1. to howl 2. (*di sirena*) to hoot.

ululato *sm.* 1. howl 2. (*di sirena*) hoot.

umanésimo *sm.* Humanism.

umanista *sm.* humanist.

umanìstico *agg.* humanistic.

umanità *sf.* humanity.

umanitario *agg.* humanitarian.

umanitarismo *sm.* humanitarianism.

umanizzare *vt.* to humanize.

umaro *agg.* 1. human 2. (*comprensivo*) humane.

umerale *agg.* humeral.

umettare *vt.* to moisten.

umidità *sf.* humidity, dampness.

ùmido *agg.* damp.

ùmile *agg.* humble.

umiliante *agg.* humiliating.

umiliare *vt.* to humble.

umiliazione *sf.* humiliation.

umiltà *sf.* 1. humbleness 2. (*virtù dell'umile*) humility.

umore *sm.* humour: *essere di buon —*, to be in a good humour.

umorismo *sm.* humour.

umorista *s.* humorist.

umorìstico *agg.* humorous.

una *art. e agg.* V. **uno**.

unànime *agg.* unanimous.

unanimità *sf.* unanimity: *all'—*, unanimously.

uncinare *vt.* to hook.

uncinato *agg.* hooked ǁ *croce uncinata*, swastika.

uncinetto *sm.* crochet-hook: *lavorare all'—*, to crochet.

uncino *sm.* hook.

undicèsimo *agg.* eleventh.

ùndici *agg.* eleven.

ùngere *vt.* to grease.

unghia *sf.* 1. nail 2. (*di equino*) hoof 3. (*fig.*) clutch.

unghiata *sf.* scratch: *dare un'—*, to scratch.

unguento *sm.* ointment.

ungulato *agg.* hoofed.

unicamente *avv.* only.

unicellulare *agg.* unicellular.

unicità *sf.* uniqueness.

ùnico *agg.* 1. only 2. (*senza uguale*) unique.

unificare *vt.* 1. to unify 2. (*uniformare*) to standardize.

unificatore *agg.* unifying. ♦ **unificatore** *sm.* unifier.

unificazione *sf.* 1. unification 2. (*uniformazione*) standardization.

uniformare *vt.* 1. to conform 2. (*rendere conforme*) to standardize. ♦ **uniformarsi** *vr.* to conform (to).

uniforme[1] *agg.* uniform.

uniforme[2] *sf.* uniform.

uniformemente *avv.* uniformly.

uniformità *sf.* uniformity.

unigènito *sm.* only child.

unilaterale *agg.* unilateral.

unilateralmente *avv.* unilaterally.

uninominale *agg.* uninominal.

unione *sf.* union.

unionista *sm.* unionist.

unipolare *agg.* unipolar.

unire *vt.* to unite, to join. ♦ **unirsi** *vr.* to unite, to join.

unìsono *sm.* unison.

unità *sf.* **1.** unity **2.** (*fis.; mat.; mil.*) unit.

unitamente *avv.* unitedly: — *a*, together with.

unitario *agg.* unitary.

unito *agg.* **1.** united **2.** (*accluso*) enclosed.

universale *agg.* universal.

universalità *sf.* universality.

universalizzare *vt.* to universalize.

università *sf.* university.

universitario *agg.* university (*attr.*). ♦ **universitario** *sm.* university student.

universo *agg.* whole. ♦ **universo** *sm.* universe.

univoco *agg.* univocal.

uno, un, una *art.* a, an (*davanti a vocale e h muta*). ♦ **uno, un, una** *agg.* one. ♦ **uno, un, una** *pron.* **1.** one **2.** (*un tale*) a man; (*una tale*) a woman || — *a* —, one by one; *l' — e l'altro*, both; *l' — o l'altro*, either; *né l' — né l'altro*, neither; *l' — l'altro*, each other; *un po' per —*, a part each; *costano 5 sterline l'—*, they cost 5 pounds each.

unto *agg.* greasy.

untume *sm.* grease.

untuosamente *avv.* (*fig.*) unctuously.

untuosità *sf.* **1.** greasiness **2.** (*fig.*) unctuousness.

untuoso *agg.* **1.** greasy **2.** (*fig.*) unctuous.

unzione *sf.* unction.

uomo *sm.* man (*pl.* men): *un — da nulla*, a nobody.

uopo *sm.* esser *d'—*, to be necessary; *all'—*, if necessary.

uovo *sm.* egg: *rosso d'—*, yolk; *cercare il pelo nell'—*, to split (*v. irr.*) hairs.

uragano *sm.* hurricane.

uranìfero *agg.* uranic.

urànio *sm.* uranium.

uranite *sf.* uranite.

uranografìa *sf.* uranography.

urbanésimo *sm.* urbanization.

urbanista *s.* town planner.

urbanìstica *sf.* town-planning.

urbanìstico *agg.* town-planning.

urbanità *sf.* urbanity.

urbanizzare *vt.* to urbanize.

urbanizzazione *sf.* urbanization.

urbano *agg.* **1.** urban **2.** (*cortese*) urbane.

ùrea *sf.* urea.

uremìa *sf.* uraemia.

urèmico *agg.* uraemic.

uretra *sf.* urethra.

urgente *agg.* urgent.

urgentemente *avv.* urgently.

urgenza *sf.* urgency.

ùrgere *vt.* to urge. ♦ **ùrgere** *vi.* to be urgent.

uricemìa *sf.* uricaemia.

ùrico *agg.* uric.

urina *sf.* V. *orina*.

urinare *vi.* V. *orinare*.

urlare *vt.* e *vi.* **1.** to shout, to scream **2.** (*di vento, animale; per il dolore*) to howl.

urlatore *agg.* shouting. ♦ **urlatore** *sm.* shouter.

urlo *sm.* **1.** shout **2.** (*di vento, animale; per il dolore*) howl.

urna *sf.* **1.** urn **2.** (*per i voti*) ballot-box || *andare alle urne*, to go (*v. irr.*) to the polls.

urogallo *sm.* grouse.

urologìa *sf.* urology.

uròlogo *sm.* urologist.

urtante *agg.* irritating.

urtare *vt.* **1.** to knock **2.** (*infastidire*) to irritate **3.** (*offendere*) to hurt (*v. irr.*). ♦ **urtarsi** *vr.* to get (*v. irr.*) cross. ♦ **urtarsi** *vr. rec.* to collide.

urticante *agg.* urticating.

urticaria *sf.* nettle rash.

urto *sm.* **1.** push **2.** (*scontro, contrasto*) collision || *essere in —*, to be at variance.

urtone *sm.* shove.

usanza *sf.* **1.** custom **2.** (*abitudine personale*) habit.

usare *vt.* to use: — *una cortesia*, to do (*v. irr.*) a favour. ♦ **usare** *vi.* **1.** to be accustomed; (*solo al passato*) to use **2.** (*essere di moda*) to be fashionable.

usato *agg.* **1.** used **2.** (*in uso*) in use **3.** (*abituale*) usual **4.** (*non nuovo*) second-hand.

uscente *agg.* **1.** retiring **2.** (*con espressioni di tempo*) closing.

usciere *sm.* **1.** usher **2.** (*ufficiale giudiziario*) bailiff.

uscio *sm.* door: *abitare — a — (con)*, to live next door — (to).

uscire *vi.* **1.** to go (*v. irr.*) out, to come (*v. irr.*) out **2.** (*sboccare*) to lead (*v. irr.*) **3.** (*uscire di strada*) to go off || *uscirne bene, male*, to come off well, badly.

uscita *sf.* 1. way out 2. (*atto di uscire*) going out, coming out 3. (*spese*) expense || **strada senza —**, blind-alley.

usignolo *sm.* nightingale.

uso[1] *agg.* accustomed.

uso[2] *sm.* use: **d'—**, usual; **all'— di**, after the fashion of.

ùssaro *sm.* hussar.

ustionare *vt.* to scald.

ustionato *agg.* scalded.

ustione *sf.* scald.

usuale *agg.* usual.

usufruire *vi.* to benefit (by).

usufrutto *sm.* usufruct.

usufruttuario *agg. e sm.* usufructuary.

usura *sf.* 1. usury 2. (*logorio*) wear and tear.

usuraio *sm.* usurer.

usurpare *vt.* to usurp.

usurpatore *agg.* usurping. ♦ **usurpatore** *sm.* usurper.

usurpazione *sf.* usurpation.

utènsile *sm.* utensil.

utente *s.* user.

uterino *agg.* uterine.

ùtero *sm.* uterus (*pl.* -ri).

ùtile *agg.* useful. ♦ **ùtile** *sm.* profit.

utilità *sf.* 1. usefulness 2. (*vantaggio*) profit || **non ne vedo l'—**, I do not see the use of it.

utilitaria *sf.* (*auto*) utility car.

utilitario *agg. e sm.* utilitarian.

utilitarismo *sm.* utilitarianism.

utilistico *agg.* V. **utilitario**.

utilizzàbile *agg.* utilizable.

utilizzare *vt.* to utilize.

utilizzatore *agg.* utilizing. ♦ **utilizzatore** *sm.* utilizer.

utilizzazione *sf.* utilization.

utopìa *sf.* utopia.

utopista *s.* utopian.

utopìstico *agg.* utopian.

uva *sf.* grapes (*pl.*): **— passa**, raisin.

uxoricida *sm.* uxoricide.

uxoricidio *sm.* uxoricide.

V

vacante *agg.* vacant.

vacanza *sf.* 1. holiday 2. (*posto vacante*) vacancy.

vacca *sf.* cow.

vaccaro *sm.* cowherd.

vaccherìa *sf.* cowhouse.

vacchetta *sf.* cowhide.

vaccinàbile *agg.* that can be vaccinated.

vaccinare *vt.* to vaccinate.

vaccinazione *sf.* vaccination.

vaccino *sm.* vaccine.

vaccinògeno *agg.* vaccinogenous.

vaccinoterapìa *sf.* vaccinotherapy.

vacillamento *sm.* 1. unsteadiness 2. (*di luce*) flickering 3. (*fig.*) wavering.

vacillante *agg.* 1. unsteady 2. (*di luce*) flickering 3. (*fig.*) uncertain.

vacillare *vi.* 1. to be unsteady 2. (*di luce*) to flicker 3. (*fig.*) to waver.

vacuità *sf.* vacuity.

vacuo *agg.* vacuous.

vademecum *sm.* vade-mecum.

vagabondaggio *sm.* vagrancy.

vagabondare *vi.* to wander.

vagabondo *agg.* vagabond. ♦ **vagabondo** *sm.* vagrant.

vagamente *avv.* vaguely.

vagante *agg.* wandering.

vagare *vi.* to wander.

vagheggiamento *sm.* longing (for).

vagheggiare *vt.* to long (for).

vagheggino *sm.* gallant.

vaghezza *sf.* 1. charm 2. (*indeterminatezza*) vagueness.

vagina *sf.* vagina (*pl.* -nae).

vagire *vi.* to wail.

vagito *sm.* wail.

vaglia[1] *sf.* (*valore*) worth.

vaglia[2] *sm.* money order: **— postale**, postal order.

vagliare *vt.* to sieve 2. (*fig.*) to weigh.

vagliatura *sf.* screening.

vaglio *sm.* 1. sieve 2. (*fig.*) sifting.

vago *agg.* 1. vague 2. (*leggiadro*) pretty.

vagoncino *sm.* wag(g)on.

vagolare *vi.* to rove.

vagone *sm.* carriage, coach.

vaio[1] *agg.* dark grey.

vaio[2] *sm.* vair.

vaiolo *sm.* smallpox.

valanga *sf.* avalanche.

valchirìa *sf.* Walkyrie.

valente *agg.* 1. skilful 2. (*valoroso*) brave.

valentemente *avv.* 1. skilfully 2. (*valorosamente*) bravely.

valentìa *sf.* 1. skill 2. (*valore*) worth.

valentuomo *sm.* worthy man.

valenza *sf.* valence.

valere *vi.* **1.** to be worth: — *la pena*, to be worth while; *far — i propri diritti*, to assert one's rights; *farsi —*, to make (*v. irr.*) oneself appreciated **2.** (*contare*) to count **3.** (*servire*) to be of use **4.** (*essere valido*) to be valid. ♦ **valersi** *vr.* to avail oneself (of).

valeriana *sf.* valerian.

valévole *agg.* valid.

valicàbile *agg.* that can be crossed.

valicare *vt.* to cross.

vàlico *sm.* pass.

validamente *avv.* validly.

validità *sf.* validity.

vàlido *agg.* **1.** valid **2.** (*fondato*) well-grounded **3.** (*forte*) strong.

valigeria *sf.* leatherware shop.

valigia *sf.* suit-case; *fare le valigie*, to pack up.

vallata *sf.* valley.

valle *sf.* valley.

valletto *sm.* valet.

vallo *sm.* rampart.

vallone *agg.* e *sm.* Walloon.

valore *sm.* **1.** value **2.** (*coraggio*) bravery.

valorizzare *vt.* **1.** to turn to account **2.** (*accentuare*) to emphasize.

valorizzazione *sf.* **1.** turning to account **2.** (*comm.*) valorization.

valorosamente *avv.* bravely.

valoroso *agg.* brave.

valsente *sm.* commercial value.

valuta *sf.* **1.** value **2.** (*moneta*) currency: — *estera*, foreign currency.

valutàbile *agg.* valuable.

valutare *vt.* **1.** to value **2.** (*considerare*) to consider.

valutazione *sf.* **1.** evaluation **2.** (*considerazione*) careful consideration.

valva *sf.* valve.

vàlvola *sf.* **1.** valve **2.** (*elettr.*) fuse **3.** (*radio*) valve, tube.

valvolare *agg.* valvular.

valzer *sm.* waltz: *ballare il —*, to waltz.

vampa *sf.* **1.** blaze **2.** (*al viso*) flush.

vampata *sf.* **1.** blaze **2.** (*folata*) blast **3.** (*al viso*) flush.

vampeggiante *agg.* blazing.

vampeggiare *vi.* to blaze.

vampiro *sm.* vampire.

vanagloria *sf.* vainglory.

vanagloriarsi *vr.* to boast.

vanaglorioso *agg.* boastful.

vanamente *avv.* vainly.

vandàlico *agg.* vandalic.

vandalismo *sm.* vandalism.

vàndalo *agg.* e *sm.* vandal.

vaneggiamento *sm.* raving.

vaneggiare *vi.* to rave.

vanesio *agg.* foppish. ♦ **vanesio** *sm.* fop.

vanga *sf.* spade.

vangare *vt.* to spade.

vangata *sf.* blow with a spade.

vangatore *sm.* spademan.

vangatura *sf.* spading.

vangelo *sm.* Gospel.

vaniglia *sf.* vanilla.

vanigliato *agg.* vanilla-flavoured.

vaniloquio *sm.* empty talk.

vanità *sf.* vanity.

vanitoso *agg.* conceited.

vano[1] *agg.* vain.

vano[2] *sm.* space, room.

vantaggio *sm.* **1.** advantage **2.** (*sport*) lead.

vantaggiosamente *avv.* advantageously.

vantaggioso *agg.* advantageous.

vantare *vt.* **1.** to boast (of) **2.** (*lodare*) to praise **3.** (*millantare*) to brag. ♦ **vantarsi** *vr.* to boast (of).

vanteria *sf.* boast.

vanto *sm.* boast.

vànvera (*nella loc. avv.*) *a —*, at random.

vapore *sm.* **1.** steam **2.** (*mar.*) steamer.

vaporetto *sm.* steamboat.

vaporiera *sf.* steam-engine.

vaporizzare *vt.* to vaporize.

vaporizzatore *sm.* vaporizer.

vaporizzazione *sf.* vaporization.

vaporosità *sf.* **1.** haziness **2.** (*di abito*) gauziness.

vaporoso *agg.* **1.** hazy **2.** (*di abito*) gauzy.

varare *vt.* to launch (*anche fig.*).

varcare *vt.* to cross, to pass.

varco *sm.* passage, opening: *aprirsi un — fra la folla*, to force one's way through the crowd.

variàbile *agg.* variable, unsteady.

variabilità *sf.* variability, unsteadiness.

variante *sf.* variant.

variare *vt.* **1.** to vary **2.** (*di mercato*) to fluctuate.

variato *agg.* V. *vario*.

variazione *sf.* variation, change.

varice *sf.* varix (*pl.* varices).
varicella *sf.* chicken-pox.
varicoso *agg.* varicose.
variegato *agg.* variegated.
varietà *sf.* variety.
vario *agg.* 1. varied 2. (*differente*) various 3. (*parecchi*) several.
variopinto *agg.* many-coloured.
varo *sm.* launch.
vasaio *sm.* potter.
vasca *sf.* basin: — *da bagno*, bath (tub).
vascello *sm.* vessel.
vascolare *agg.* vascular.
vaselina *sf.* vaseline.
vasellame *sm.* 1. (*di terracotta*) earthenware 2. (*di porcellana*) china 3. (*d'argento, d'oro*) silver, gold plate.
vaso *sm.* 1. vase 2. (*rotondo*) pot 3. (*recipiente; anat.*) vessel.
vasocostrittore *agg. e sm.* vasoconstrictor.
vasodilatatore *agg. e sm.* vasodilator.
vasomotore *agg.* vasomotor.
vasomotorio *agg.* vasomotor.
vassallaggio *sm.* 1. (*stor.*) vassalage 2. subjection.
vassallo *agg. e sm.* 1. (*stor.*) vassal 2. subject.
vassoio *sm.* tray.
vastità *sf.* 1. vastness 2. (*estensione*) expanse.
vasto *agg.* wide, large.
vate *sm.* 1. prophet 2. (*poeta*) poet.
Vaticano *agg.* Vatican.
vaticinare *vt.* to prophesy.
vaticinio *sm.* prophecy.
vattelappesca *inter.* who knows!
ve *pron.* you: — *lo scrissi*, I wrote it to you. ♦ **ve** *avv.* there: — *ne sono due*, there are 'two.
ve' *inter.* look, see.
vecchiaia *sf.* old age.
vecchiezza *sf.* great age.
vecchio *agg.* 1. old 2. (*antico*) ancient 3. (*stantio*) stale. ♦ **vecchio** *sm.* old man.
veccia *sf.* vetch.
vece *sf.* stead, place.
vedere *vt.* to see (*v. irr.*): — *la luce* (*nascere*), to be born; *far* —, to show (*v. irr.*); *farsi* —, to show oneself; *non* — *l'ora di*, to look forward to (*con gerundio*). ♦ **vedersi** *vr.* 1. to see oneself 2. (*vedersela*) to deal (*v. irr.*) with.
vedetta *sf.* 1. (*sentinella*) watchman

(*pl.* -men) 2. (*posto di osservazione*) look-out.
vedova *sf.* widow.
vedovanza *sf.* widowhood.
vedovile *agg.* 1. (*di vedova*) of a widow 2. (*di vedovo*) of a widower.
vedovo *sm.* widower.
vedretta *sf.* small steep glacier.
veduta *sf.* 1. sight, view 2. (*opinione*) view, idea.
veemente *agg.* vehement.
veemenza *sf.* vehemence.
vegetale *agg. e sm.* vegetable.
vegetare *vi.* to vegetate.
vegetariano *agg. e sm.* vegetarian.
vegetativo *agg.* vegetative.
vegetazione *sf.* vegetation.
vègeto *agg.* 1. (*di pianta*) thriving 2. (*di persona*) vigorous, strong ‖ *vivo e* —, hale and hearty
veggente *sm.* seer.
veglia *sf.* 1. waking 2. (*il vegliare*) watch.
vegliardo *sm.* old man.
vegliare *vi.* 1. to be awake 2. (*far la veglia*) to watch.
veglione *sm.* masked ball.
veicolo *sm.* vehicle.
vela *sf.* sail.
velame *sm.* 1. veil 2. (*mar.*) sails (*pl.*).
velare *vt.* to veil.
velario *sm.* curtain.
velatura *sf.* sails (*pl.*).
veleggiare *vi.* to sail.
veleno *sm.* poison.
velenoso *agg.* poisonous, venomous.
veletta *sf.* 1. (*mar.*) topsail 2. (*di cappello*) veil.
veliero *sm.* sailing-ship.
velina *sf.* tissue-paper.
velismo *sm.* sailing.
velìvolo *sm.* aeroplane.
velleità *sf.* foolish ambition, fancy.
vellicare *vt.* to tickle.
vello *sm.* fleece.
vellutato *agg.* velvety: *pelle vellutata*, downy skin.
velluto *sm.* velvet.
velo *sm.* veil.
veloce *agg.* fast, quick, swift.
velocipede *sm.* velocipede.
velocità *sf.* speed, velocity: *a tutta* —, at full speed; *limite di* —, speed limit; *cambio di* — (*auto*), gearbox; *indicatore di* —, speedometer.
velòdromo *sm.* cycle-racing track.

veltro *sm.* greyhound.

vena *sf.* vein.

venale *agg.* venal.

venalità *sf.* venality.

venare *vt.* 1. to vein 2. (*di legno*) to grain.

venato *agg.* 1. veined 2. (*di legno*) grained.

venatorio *agg.* venatorial.

venatura *sf.* 1. vein 2. (*di legno*) grain.

vendemmia *sf.* vintage.

vendemmiare *vi.* to gather grapes.

vendemmiatore *sm.* vintager.

véndere *vt.* to sell (*v. irr.*): — *a buon mercato*, to sell cheaply; — *a credito*, to sell on credit; — *all'ingrosso, al minuto*, to sell wholesale, by retail; — *a rate*, to sell by instalments.

vendetta *sf.* revenge.

vendibile *agg.* salable.

vendicare *vt.* to revenge.

vendicativo *agg.* revengeful.

vendicatore *sm.* revenger.

véndita *sf.* sale: — *all'asta*, auction.

venditore *sm.* seller.

venduto *agg.* 1. sold 2. (*fig.*) corrupted.

veneficio *sm.* poisoning.

venéfico *agg.* poisonous.

venerábile *agg.* venerable.

venerando *agg.* venerable.

venerare *vt.* to worship.

venerazione *sf.* worship.

venerdì *sm.* Friday: — *Santo*, Good Friday.

vènere *sf.* 1. Venus 2. (*fig.*) beauty.

venèreo *agg.* venereal.

veneziana *sf.* Venetian-blind.

veniale *agg.* venial.

venire *vi.* 1. to come (*v. irr.*): — *al sodo*, to come to the point; — *in mente*, to come into one's head; — *meno*, to faint; — *alla luce*, to come to light 2. (*riuscire*) to turn out 3. (*derivare*) to derive.

venoso *agg.* venous.

ventaglio *sm.* fan.

ventata *sf.* gust of wind.

ventèsimo *agg.* twentieth.

venti *agg.* twenty.

ventilare *vt.* to ventilate.

ventilato *agg.* airy, windy.

ventilatore *sm.* fan.

ventilazione *sf.* ventilation.

ventina *sf.* score: *essere sulla — (di anni)*, to be about twenty.

vento *sm.* wind.

ventosa *sf.* sucker.

ventosità *sf.* flatulence.

ventoso *agg.* windy.

ventrale *agg.* ventral.

ventre *sm.* 1. abdomen 2. (*fam.*) tummy.

ventricolo *sm.* ventricle.

ventriera *sf.* body-belt.

ventriglio *sm.* gizzard.

ventriloquio *sm.* ventriloquism.

ventriloquo *sm.* ventriloquist.

ventura *sf.* chance, fortune.

venturo *agg.* next, coming.

venustà *sf.* beauty.

venusto *agg.* beautiful.

venuta *sf.* coming, arrival.

vera *sf.* wedding-ring.

verace *agg.* true.

veracità *sf.* veracity, truth.

veramente *avv.* really, truly, indeed.

veranda *sf.* verandah.

verbale *agg.* verbal. ♦ **verbale** *sm.* minutes (*pl.*).

verbalizzare *vt.* to record.

verbo *sm.* 1. verb 2. (*parola*) word.

verbosità *sf.* verbosity.

verboso *agg.* verbose.

verdastro *agg.* greenish.

verde *agg.* green.

verdeggiante *agg.* verdant.

verdeggiare *vi.* to be verdant.

verdemare *sm.* sea-green.

verderame *sm.* verdigris.

verdetto *sm.* verdict.

verdògnolo *agg.* greenish.

verdura *sf.* vegetables (*pl.*).

verecondia *sf.* modesty.

verecondo *agg.* modest.

verga *sf.* 1. twig 2. (*bacchetta*) rod.

vergare *vt.* (*scrivere*) to write (*v. irr.*).

vergata *sf.* blow with a rod.

vergato *agg.* 1. striped 2. (*scritto*) written || *carta vergata*, laid paper.

verginale *agg.* virginal.

vérgine *agg. e sf.* virgin.

vergíneo *agg.* virginal.

verginità *sf.* virginity.

vergogna *sf.* shame: *aver —*, to be ashamed.

vergognarsi *vr.* to be, to feel (*v. irr.*) shamed.

vergognosamente *avv.* shamefully.

vergognoso *agg.* 1. shameful 2. (*timido*) shy.

veridicamente *avv.* veraciously.

veridicità *sf.* veracity.

verídico *agg.* veracious.

verifica *sf.* verification.

verificàbile *agg.* verifiable.

verificare *vt.* to verify, to check.

verificatore *sm.* verifier.

verificazione *sf.* V. *verifica.*

verismo *sm.* realism.

verista *sm.* realist.

verìstico *agg.* realistic.

verità *sf.* truth: *dire la —,* to tell (*v. irr.*) the truth.

veritiero *agg.* truthful.

verme *sm.* worm.

vermìfugo *agg.* e *sm.* vermifuge.

vermiglio *agg.* bright red.

verminoso *agg.* verminous.

vernàcolo *agg.* vernacular.

vernice *sf.* 1. paint 2. (*apparenza*) varnish.

verniciare *vt.* to paint, to varnish.

verniciatura *sf.* painting, varnishing.

vero *agg.* true, real.

verosimigliante *agg.* likely.

verosimiglianza *sf.* iikelihood.

verosìmile *agg.* likely, probable.

verricello *sm.* windlass.

verro *sm.* boar.

verruca *sf.* wart.

versamento *sm.* 1. pouring 2. (*comm.*) payment, deposit.

versante *sm.* side, slope.

versare *vt.* 1. to pour 2. (*rovesciare*) to spill (*v. irr.*) 3. (*comm.*) to pay (*v. irr.*).

versàtile *agg.* versatile.

versatilità *sf.* versatility.

versato *agg.* 1. poured out 2. (*esperto*) versed.

verseggiare *vi.* to versify.

verseggiatore *sm.* versifier.

versetto *sm.* 1. short line 2. (*della Bibbia*) verse.

versificare *vt.* to versify.

versificatore *sm.* versifier.

versificazione *sf.* versification.

versione *sf.* version, translation.

verso[1] *sm.* 1. verse, line 2. (*suono*) sound 3. (*direzione*) way.

verso[2] *prep.* 1. towards, to 2. (*contro*) against 3. (*circa*) about.

vèrtebra *sf.* vertebra (*pl.* -rae).

vertebrale *agg.* vertebral.

vertebrato *agg.* e *sm.* vertebrate.

vertenza *sf.* 1. dispute 2. (*giur.*) litigation.

vèrtere *vi.* to be about, to concern.

verticale *agg.* vertical.

verticalità *sf.* verticality.

vèrtice *sm.* 1. vertex (*pl.* vertices) 2. (*fig.*) height, top.

vertigine *sf.* dizziness (*solo sing.*).

vertiginoso *agg.* dizzy.

verza *sf.* cabbage.

vescica *sf.* bladder.

vescovado *sm.* bishop's residence.

vescovile *agg.* episcopal.

véscovo *sm.* bishop.

vespa *sf.* wasp.

vespaio *sm.* 1. wasps' nest 2. (*fig.*) hornets' nest.

vespro *sm.* 1. evening 2. (*relig.*) evensong.

vessare *vt.* to vex.

vessatorio *agg.* vexatious.

vessazione *sf.* vexation.

vessillo *sm.* flag.

vestaglia *sf.* dressing-gown.

vestale *sf.* vestal.

veste *sf.* 1. dress 2. (*eccl.*) vestment 3. (*qualità*) capacity.

vestiario *sm.* clothes (*pl.*).

vestìbolo *sm.* hall.

vestigio *sm.* vestige.

vestimento *sm.* V. *veste.*

vestire *vt.* 1. to dress 2. (*fig.*) to clothe 3. (*indossare*) to wear (*v. irr.*). ◆ **vestirsi** *vr.* to dress oneself.

vestito *sm.* 1. (*da uomo*) suit 2. (*da donna*) frock, dress.

vestizione *sf.* 1. (*eccl.*) ceremony of taking the habit 2. (*di monaca*) ceremony of taking the veil.

veterano *sm.* veteran.

veterinaria *sf.* veterinary science.

veterinario *agg.* veterinary.

veto *sm.* veto.

vetraio *sm.* glazier.

vetrame *sm.* glassware.

vetrata *sf.* glass partition: *— a colori,* stained glass window.

vetrato *agg.* glazed: *carta vetrata,* glass-paper.

vetreria *sf.* glass-work.

vetrificàbile *agg.* vitrifiable.

vetrificare *vt.* to vitrify.

vetrificazione *sf.* vitrification.

vetrina *sf.* shop-window.

vetrioleggiare *vt.* to vitriolize.

vetriolo *sm.* vitriol.

vetro *sm.* 1. glass 2. (*di finestra*) window-pane.

vetrocromìa *sf.* glass-painting.

vetroso *agg.* glassy.

vetta *sf.* top, summit.

vettore *sm.* vector.

vettoriale *agg.* vectorial.

vettovagliamento *sm.* provisio-ning.

vettovagliare *vt.* to provision.

vettura *sf.* 1. coach 2. (*automobile*) car || — *di piazza*, taxi-cab.

vetturino *sm.* cabman (*pl.* -men).

vetustà *sf.* antiquity.

vetusto *agg.* ancient.

vezzeggiare *vt.* to fondle.

vezzeggiativo *sm.* petname.

vezzo *sm.* 1. habit 2. (*collana*) necklace.

vezzosamente *avv.* charmingly.

vezzoso *agg.* charming.

vi¹ *pron.* you, to you.

vi² *avv.* 1. (*qui*) here 2. (*là*) there.

via¹ *sf.* 1. street 2. (*strada di comunicazione*) road 3. (*cammino*) way (*anche fig.*) 4. (*linea di condotta*) course. ♦ **via** *sm.* dare il —, to give (*v. irr.*) the starting.

via² *avv.* away: *andar* —, to go (*v. irr.*) away.

viabilità *sf.* state of a road.

viadotto *sm.* viaduct.

viaggiante *agg.* travelling.

viaggiare *vi.* to travel: — *in treno, automobile, aereo*, to travel by train, by car, by air.

viaggiatore *sm.* traveller: — *di commercio*, commercial traveller.

viaggio *sm.* 1. journey, trip 2. (*per mare*) voyage 3. (*in aereo*) flight.

viale *sm.* avenue; (*di giardino*) alley.

viandante *sm.* wayfarer.

viatico *sm.* viaticum (*pl.* -ca).

viavai *sm.* coming-and-going.

vibrante *agg.* vibrating (with).

vibrare *vi.* 1. to vibrate 2. (*colpi*) to strike (*v. irr.*).

vibratile *agg.* vibratile.

vibrato *agg.* energetic.

vibratore *sm.* vibrator.

vibrazione *sf.* vibration.

vicariato *sm.* vicariate.

vicario *sm.* vicar.

viceconsole *sm.* vice-consul.

vicedirettore *sm.* assistant-director.

vicegovernatore *sm.* vice-governor.

vicenda *sf.* 1. vicissitude 2. (*evento*) event 3. (*successione*) succession.

vicendévole *agg.* mutual.

vicendevolmente *avv.* mutually.

vicepresidente *sm.* vice-president.

viceré *sm.* viceroy.

vicesegretario *sm.* vice-secretary.

viceversa *avv.* vice versa. ♦ **viceversa** *cong.* whereas.

vicinale *sf.* local road.

vicinanza *sf.* 1. vicinity: *in — di*, close to 2. (*adiacenze*) neighbourhood: *nelle vicinanze*, in the neighbourhood.

vicinato *sm.* 1. neighbourhood 2. (*i vicini*) neighbours (*pl.*).

vicino¹ *agg.* near, close. ♦ **vicino** *sm.* neighbour.

vicino² *avv.* near, near by. ♦ **vicino** *prep.* near, close to.

vicissitùdine *sf.* vicissitude.

vicolo *sm.* lane, alley.

video *sm.* video.

vidimare *vt.* 1. (*firmare*) to sign 2. (*autenticare*) to authenticate.

vidimazione *sf.* 1. (*firma*) signature 2. (*autenticazione*) authentication.

vietare *vt.* to forbid (*v. irr.*).

vietato *agg.* forbidden: — *fumare*, no smoking; — *entrare*, no admittance.

vieto *agg.* antiquated.

vigente *agg.* in force.

vigere *vi.* to be in force.

vigilante *agg.* watchful.

vigilanza *sf.* watch.

vigilare *vt.* to watch over.

vigilato *agg.* watched.

vigile *agg.* watchful. ♦ **vigile** *sm.* policeman (*pl.* -men).

vigilia *sf.* 1. eve 2. (*relig.*) fast.

vigliaccamente *avv.* in a cowardly way.

vigliaccherìa *sf.* 1. cowardice 2. (*azione vigliacca*) cowardly action.

vigliacco *agg.* cowardly.

vigna *sf.* vineyard.

vigneto *sm.* vineyard.

vignetta *sf.* cartoon.

vigore *sm.* vigour: *in* —, in force.

vigoroso *agg.* vigorous.

vile *agg.* 1. cowardly 2. (*meschino*) mean 3. (*basso*) low.

vilipèndere *vt.* to despise.

vilipendio *sm.* contempt.

villa *sf.* villa.

villaggio *sm.* village.

villanìa *sf.* 1. rudeness 2. (*azione villana*) rude action.

villano *agg.* rude. ♦ **villano** *sm.* peasant, countryman (*pl.* -men).

villeggiante *s.* holiday-maker.

villeggiatura *sf.* holiday: *luogo di* —, (holiday) resort.

villino *sm.* cottage.

villoso *agg.* hairy.

viltà *sf.* 1. cowardice 2. (*azione vile*) cowardly action.

vilucchio *sm.* bearbind.

viluppo *sm.* tangle.

vimine *sm.* withe: *paniere di vimini*, wicker basket.

vinaccia *sf.* dregs of pressed grapes (*pl.*).

vinaio *sm.* wine-merchant.

vinario *agg.* wine (*attr.*).

vincente *agg.* winning. ♦ **vincente** *sm.* winner.

vincere *vt.* 1. to win (*v. irr.*) 2. (*battere*) to beat (*v. irr.*) 3. (*sopraffare*) to overcome (*v. irr.*) 4. (*superare*) to outdo (*v. irr.*).

vincibile *agg.* conquerable.

vincita *sf.* 1. win 2. (*denaro vinto*) winnings (*pl.*).

vincitore *agg.* winning. ♦ **vincitore** *sm.* winner.

vinco *sm.* withe.

vincolare *vt.* 1. to bind (*v. irr.*) 2. (*comm.*) to lock up.

vincolato *agg.* 1. bound 2. (*comm.*) locked up.

vincolo *sm.* tie, bond.

vinello *sm.* light wine.

vinicolo *agg.* wine (*attr.*).

vinificazione *sf.* wine-making.

vino *sm.* wine.

vinto *agg.* 1. that has been won 2. (*sconfitto*) beaten 3. (*sopraffatto*) overcome || *darsi* —, to give (*v. irr.*) in. ♦ **vinto** *sm.* 1. (*al giuoco o in qualsiasi contesa*) loser 2. (*in battaglia*) vanquished man.

viola[1] *sf.* 1. violet: — *del pensiero*, pansy. ♦ **viola** *agg. e sm.* violet.

viola[2] *sf.* (*mus.*) viola.

violacee *sf. pl.* violaceae.

violaceo *agg.* violet.

violare *vt.* to violate.

violatore *sm.* violator.

violazione *sf.* violation: — *di domicilio*, house-breaking.

violentare *vt.* 1. to violate, to rape 2. (*fig.*) to do (*v. irr.*) violence to.

violento *agg.* violent.

violenza *sf.* violence, rape.

violetto *agg.* violet.

violinista *s.* violin-player.

violino *sm.* violin.

violoncellista *s.* violoncellist.

violoncello *sm.* violoncello.

viòttola *sf.* path, lane.

viòttolo *sm.* path, lane.

vipera *sf.* 1. adder 2. (*fig.*) viper.

viperino *agg.* viperous.

viraggio *sm.* (*foto*) toning.

virago *sf.* virago.

virare *vt. e vi.* 1. to veer: — *di bordo*, to veer round 2. (*fig.*) to turn about.

virata *sf.* veer.

virginale *agg.* virginal.

virginia *sm.* Virginia.

virgola *sf.* 1. (*gramm.*) comma 2. (*mat.*) point.

virgolette *sf. pl.* inverted commas: *tra* —, in inverted commas.

virgulto *sm.* shoot.

virile *agg.* manly.

virilità *sf.* 1. manliness 2. (*età virile*) manhood.

virilmente *avv.* manfully.

virologia *sf.* virology.

virosi *sf.* virosis (*pl.* -ses).

virtù *sf.* virtue.

virtuale *agg.* virtual.

virtualità *sf.* virtuality.

virtuosismo *sm.* virtuosity.

virtuoso *agg.* virtuous.

virulento *agg.* virulent.

virulenza *sf.* virulence.

virus *sm.* virus.

viscerale *agg.* visceral.

viscere *sm.* 1. vital organ 2. (*f. pl.*) *le viscere*, viscera.

vischio *sm.* 1. mistletoe 2. (*pania*) bird-lime.

vischiosità *sf.* stickiness.

vischioso *agg.* sticky.

viscidità *sf.* viscidity.

viscido *agg.* 1. sticky 2. (*scivoloso*) slippery.

visciola *sf.* wild cherry.

visconte *sm.* viscount.

viscontessa *sf.* viscountess.

viscosità *sf.* viscosity.

viscoso *agg.* viscous.

visibile *agg.* visible, clear.

visibilio *sm.* great number: *andare in* —, to go (*v. irr.*) into raptures.

visibilità *sf.* visibility.

visiera *sf.* 1. (*di elmo*) visor 2. (*di berretto*) peak.

visionario *agg. e sm.* visionary.

visione *sf.* vision: *prendere* — *di*, to look over; *prima* — (*cine*) first screening.

visita *sf.* 1. visit, call: *fare una* —, to pay (*v. irr.*) a visit 2. (*persona che visita*) visitor 3. (*med.*) examination.

visitare *vt.* to visit.

visitatore *sm.* visitor.

visivo *agg.* visual.

viso *sm.* face: — *a* —, face to face.

visone *sm.* mink.

vispo *agg.* lively, brisk.
vista *sf.* 1. sight 2. (*occhi*) eyes (*pl.*).
vistare *vt.* to visa.
visto[1] *sm.* visa.
visto[2] *agg.* seen || — *che*, since as.
vistoso *agg.* 1. showy 2. (*fig.*) considerable.
visuale *agg.* visual. ♦ **visuale** *sf.* sight.
vita[1] *sf.* 1. life (*pl.* lives): *a* —, for life; *in* —, during one's life 2. (*necessario per vivere*) living: *costo della* —, cost of living.
vita[2] *sf.* (*anat.*) waist.
vitaiolo *sm.* bon viveur.
vitalba *sf.* clematis.
vitale *agg.* vital.
vitalità *sf.* vitality.
vitalizio *agg.* for life. ♦ **vitalizio** *sm.* annuity.
vitamina *sf.* vitamin.
vitaminico *agg.* vitaminic.
vite[1] *sf.* vine.
vite[2] *sf.* (*mecc.*) screw.
vitello *sm.* calf (*pl.* calves).
viticcio *sm.* vine-tendril.
viticolo *agg.* viticultural.
viticoltore *sm.* viticulturist.
viticoltura *sf.* grape-growing.
vitreo *agg.* vitreous.
vittima *sf.* victim.
vittimismo *sm.* victimization.
vitto *sm.* 1. food 2. (*pasti in pensione o albergo*) board: — *e alloggio*, board and lodging.
vittoria *sf.* victory.
vittorioso *agg.* victorious.
vituperare *vt.* to vituperate.
vituperio *sm.* insult.
viuzza *sf.* lane.
viva *inter.* hurrah!
vivacchiare *vi.* to live poorly.
vivace *agg.* 1. lively, sprightly 2. (*pronto, sveglio*) quick 3. (*di colori*) bright.
vivacemente *avv.* 1. lively 2. (*prontamente*) quickly 3. (*vivamente*) brightly.
vivacità *sf.* 1. liveliness 2. (*di colori*) brightness.
vivaio *sm.* 1. (*di pesci*) fish-pond 2. (*di piante*) nursery.
vivamente *avv.* deeply, keenly.
vivanda *sf.* food.
vivandiere *sm.* sutler.
vivente *agg.* alive (*pred.*), living. ♦ **vivente** *sm.* living being.
vivere *vt. e vi.* to live: *cessare di*

—, to die; *insegnare a* — *a qu.*, to teach (*v. irr.*) so. good manners; — *alle spalle di qu.*, to sponge on so.
viveri *sm. pl.* victuals.
vivido *agg.* vivid.
vivificare *vt.* to enliven.
vivificatore *agg.* vivifying. ♦ **vivificatore** *sm.* vivifier.
viviparo *agg. e sm.* viviparous.
vivisezione *sf.* vivisection.
vivo *agg.* 1. living, alive (*pred.*) || *a viva forza*, by main force; *argento* —, quicksilver; *calce viva*, quicklime; *farsi* —, to turn up 2. (*vivace*) lively 3. (*profondo, acuto*) deep, sharp 4. (*vivido*) vivid 5. (*di colori*) bright.
viziare *vt.* 1. to spoil (*v. irr.*) 2. (*guastare*) to vitiate.
viziato *agg.* 1. spoilt 2. (*guasto*) vitiated.
vizio *sm.* 1. vice 2. (*cattiva abitudine*) bad habit.
vizioso *agg.* vicious. ♦ **vizioso** *sm.* vicious man.
vocabolario *sm.* 1. vocabulary 2. (*dizionario*) dictionary.
vocabolo *sm.* word.
vocale[1] *agg.* vocal.
vocale[2] *sf.* vowel.
vocalizzare *vt. e vi.* to vocalize.
vocalizzo *sm.* vocalization.
vocativo *agg. e sm.* vocative.
vocazione *sf.* vocation, bent.
voce *sf.* 1. voice: *a* — *alta, bassa*, in a loud, low voice; *parlare sotto* —, to whisper 2. (*diceria*) rumour 3. (*articolo di elenco*) item.
vociare *vi.* to shout.
vociferare *vi.* 1. to shout 2. (*spargere una voce*) to rumour.
vocìo *sm.* shouting.
voga[1] *sf.* (*mar.*) rowing.
voga[2] *sf.* 1. (*moda*) fashion 2. (*energia*) energy.
vogare *vi.* (*mar.*) to row.
vogata *sf.* row.
vogatore *sm.* rower.
voglia *sf.* 1. wish: *aver* —, to feel (*v. irr.*) like 2. (*volontà*) will.
voglioso *agg.* desirous, willing.
voi *pron.* you: — *stessi*, you yourselves.
volano *sm.* battledore and shuttlecock.
volante[1] *agg.* flying: *cervo* —, kite; *foglio* —, loose sheet. ♦ **volante** *sf.* (*di polizia*) flying squad.

volante² sm. steering-wheel.

volantino sm. leaflet.

volare vi. to fly (v. irr.): far —, to blow (v. irr.).

volata sf. 1. flight 2. (corsa) rush 3. (sport) final sprint.

volàtile¹ agg. (chim.) volatile.

volàtile² sm. bird.

volatilizzare vt. to volatilize. ♦ **volatilizzarsi** vr. to volatilize.

volente agg. — o nolente, willy-nilly.

volenterosamente avv. willingly.

volenteroso agg. V. volonteroso.

volentieri avv. willingly.

volere¹ vt. 1. (forte volontà) (pres. indicativo e congiuntivo) will; (passato indicativo e congiuntivo, condizionale) would 2. (desiderio) to want, to wish: voglio che egli venga, I want him to come 3. (gradire) to like (costr. pers.): vorrei, avrei voluto, I should like, I should have liked 4. (desiderio intenso) to wish: vorrei essere ricco!, I wish I were rich! 5. (aver bisogno di) to need, to require 6. (con espressioni di tempo) to take (v. irr.): ci vogliono due ore per andare alla stazione, it takes two hours to go to the station 7. (cercare) to ask for: c'è qualcuno che ti cerca, there is somebody asking for you 8. (essere disposti) to be willing || che tu voglia o no, whether you like it or not; vuoi ... vuoi (sia ... sia), both ... and; Dio lo voglia, Dio non voglia!, God grant it, God forbid!

volere² sm. will, wish.

volgare agg. vulgar, common.

volgarità sf. vulgarity.

volgarizzare vt. to divulge.

volgarizzatore sm. popularizer.

volgarizzazione sf. popularization.

volgarmente avv. vulgarly, commonly.

vòlgere vt. to turn.

vòlgere sm. course.

volgo sm. common people.

voliera sf. aviary.

volitivo agg. 1. strong-willed 2. (gramm.) volitive.

volo sm. flight: prendere il —, to run (v. irr.) away; capire qc. al —, to grasp sthg. immediately.

volontà sf. will: di sua spontanea —, of his own free-will.

volontariamente avv. voluntarily.

volontario agg. voluntary. ♦ **volontario** sm. volunteer.

volontarismo sm. voluntarism.

volonteroso agg. willing.

volenti avv. V. volentieri.

volpe sf. fox.

volpino agg. foxy: cane —, Pomeranian.

volpone sm. old fox.

volta¹ sf. 1. time: una —, once; due, tre volte, twice, three times; ancora una —, once again; una — e mezzo, half as much; una — o l'altra, sooner or later; rare volte, seldom; una — tanto, once in a while; c'era una —, once upon a time there was 2. (turno): a mia —, in my turn.

volta² sf. 1. (curva) bend 2. (arch.) vault.

voltafaccia sm. volte-face.

voltaggio sm. voltage.

voltàmetro sm. voltameter.

voltare vt. to turn.

voltastòmaco sm. sickness.

voltata sf. bend, turning, curve.

volteggiare vi. 1. to whirl 2. (svolazzare) to fly (v. irr.) about.

volteggio sm. vaulting.

volto¹ sm. 1. face 2. (aspetto) aspect.

volto² agg. 1. turned 2. (rivolto) directed.

volùbile agg. changeable.

volubilità sf. inconstancy.

volume sm. volume.

volumètrico agg. volumetric.

voluminoso agg. voluminous, bulky.

voluta sf. volute.

volutamente avv. intentionally.

voluttà sf. 1. delight 2. (dei sensi) voluptuousness.

voluttuario agg. voluptuary.

voluttuosamente avv. voluptuously.

voluttuoso agg. voluptuous.

vòmere sm. 1. ploughshare 2. (anat.) vomer.

vomitare vt. to vomit, to be sick.

vòmito sm. vomiting: conato di —, retch.

vòngola sf. mussel.

vorace agg. voracious, greedy.

voracità sf. voracity, greed.

voràgine sf. chasm.

vorticare vi. to whirl.

vòrtice sm. whirl: — di vento, whirlwind.

vorticosamente *avv.* in whirls.

vorticoso *agg.* whirling.

vostro *agg. poss.* your || *in vece vostra,* instead of you. ♦ **vostro** *pron. poss.* yours || *rispondiamo alla vostra del 3 giugno* (*comm.*), in reply to your letter of June 3rd; *sono dalla vostra,* I am on your side.

votante *agg.* voting. ♦ **votante** *sm.* voter.

votare *vt.* to vote. ♦ **votarsi** *vr.* to devote oneself.

votato *agg.* 1. passed 2. (*dedicato*) devoted.

votazione *sf.* voting.

votivo *agg.* votive.

voto *sm.* 1. (*promessa solenne*) vow 2. (*augurio*) wish 3. (*per elezioni*) vote 4. (*scolastico*) mark: *prendere un bel, brutto —,* to get (*v. irr.*) a good, bad mark.

vulcànico *agg.* volcanic.

vulcanismo *sm.* vulcanism.

vulcanizzare *vt.* to vulcanize.

vulcanizzato *agg.* vulcanized.

vulcanizzazione *sf.* vulcanization.

vulcano *sm.* volcano.

vulneràbile *agg.* vulnerable.

vulnerabilità *sf.* vulnerability.

vuotare *vt.* to empty: *— il sacco,* to speak (*v. irr.*) out one's mind.

vuoto *agg.* 1. empty 2. (*sprovvisto*) devoid. ♦ **vuoto** *sm.* 1. empty space 2. (*recipiente vuoto*) empty 3. (*vacuità*) emptiness.

X

xenofobìa *sf.* xenophobia.

xenòfobo *sm.* xenophobe.

xilòfono *sm.* xylophone.

xilografìa *sf.* 1. (*incisione*) xylograph 2. (*arte*) xylography.

Z

zaffata *sf.* whiff.

zafferano *sm.* saffron.

zaffiro *sm.* sapphire.

zàino *sm.* knapsack.

zampa *sf.* 1. paw 2. (*con zoccolo*) hoof 3. (*di uccello*) claw 4. (*di insetto*) leg || *zampe di gallina* (*scrittura*), scrawl; (*rughe*) crow's feet.

zampata *sf.* blow with a paw.

zampettare *vt.* to toddle.

zampillante *agg.* gushing.

zampillare *vi.* to gush.

zampillo *sm.* gush.

zampino *sm.* little paw || *mettere lo — in una faccenda,* to have a hand in the matter.

zampogna *sf.* 1. reed-pipe 2. (*cornamusa*) bag-pipe.

zampognaro *sm.* piper.

zanna *sf.* 1. fang 2. (*di elefante*) tusk.

zanzara *sf.* mosquito.

zanzariera *sf.* mosquito-net.

zappa *sf.* hoe.

zappare *vt.* to hoe.

zappata *sf.* blow with a hoe.

zappatore *sm.* 1. hoer 2. (*mil.*) pioneer.

zappatura *sf.* hoeing.

zar *sm.* czar.

zarina *sf.* czarina.

zarista *s.* czarist.

zàttera *sf.* raft.

zavorra *sf.* 1. ballast 2. (*fig.*) rubbish.

zavorrare *vt.* to ballast.

zàzzera *sf.* mane.

zazzeruto *agg.* shockheaded.

zebra *sf.* zebra.

zebrato *agg.* striped.

zebratura *sf.* stripes (*pl.*).

zebù *sm.* zebu.

zecca[1] *sf.* mint: *nuovo di —,* brand-new.

zecca[2] *sf.* (*zool.*) tick.

zecchino *sm.* sequin: *oro —,* first-quality-gold.

zèfiro *sm.* zephyr.

zelante *agg.* zealous.

zelantemente *avv.* zealously.

zelo *sm.* zeal.

zènit *sm.* zenith.

zénzero *sm.* ginger.

zeppo *agg.* crammed (with).

zerbino *sm.* door-mat.

zerbinotto *sm.* dandy.

zero *sm.* 1. nought 2. (*in graduazioni*) zero 3. (*tel.*) 0 || *ridursi a —,* to come (*v. irr.*) to nought.

zia *sf.* aunt.

zibaldone *sm.* miscellany.

zibellino *sm.* sable.

zigano *agg. e sm.* tzigane.

zìgomo *sm.* cheek-bone.

zigrinare *vt.* to knurl.

zigrinato *agg.* knurled.

zig-zag (*nella loc. avv.*) *a* —, zigzag.

zigzagare *vi.* to zigzag.

zimbello *sm.* 1. decoy 2. (*fig.*) laughing-stock.

zincare *vt.* to zinc.

zincatura *sf.* zinc-plating.

zinco *sm.* zinc.

zincografia *sf.* zincography.

zingaresco *agg.* gipsy (*attr.*).

zingaro *sm.* gipsy.

zio *sm.* uncle.

zircone *sm.* zircon.

zirconio *sm.* zirconium.

zitella *sf.* spinster.

zittire *vi.* to hiss.

zitto *agg.* silent: *star* —, to be silent.

zizzania *sf.* 1. darnel 2. (*fig.*) discord.

zoccolaio *sm.* clog-maker.

zoccolare *vi.* to clatter about with one's clogs.

zoccolo *sm.* 1. clog 2. (*di animale*) hoof 3. (*piedistallo*) base.

zodiacale *agg.* zodiacal.

zodiaco *sm.* zodiac.

zolfanello *sm.* match.

zolfatara *sf.* V. *solfatara*.

zolfatura *sf.* sulfurization.

zolfo *sm.* sulphur.

zolla *sf.* clod.

zolletta *sf.* lump.

zona *sf.* zone, area.

zonzo (*nella loc. avv.*) *andare a* —, to loaf.

zoo *sm.* zoo.

zoofilia *sf.* zoophilia.

zoofilo *agg.* zoophilous. ♦ **zoofilo** *sm.* animal-lover.

zoofobia *sf.* zoophobia.

zoologia *sf.* zoology.

zoologico *agg.* zoological.

zoologo *sm.* zoologist.

zootecnia *sf.* zootechny.

zootecnico *agg.* zootechnic: *patrimonio* —, live-stock. ♦ **zootecnico** *sm.* animal expert.

zoppicamento *sm.* limping.

zoppicante *agg.* lame.

zoppicare *vi.* 1. to limp 2. (*di mobile*) to be shaky.

zoppo *agg.* 1. lame 2. (*di mobile*) shaky. ♦ **zoppo** *sm.* lame person.

zoticaggine *sf.* boorishness.

zotico *agg.* boorish. ♦ **zotico** *sm.* boor.

zuavo *sm.* zouave || *calzoni alla zuava*, knickerbockers.

zucca *sf.* 1. pumpkin 2. (*testa*) pate.

zuccherare *vt.* to sugar.

zuccherato *agg.* sugared.

zuccheriera *sf.* sugar-basin.

zuccherificio *sm.* sugar-refinery.

zuccherino *sm.* 1. sweet 2. (*fig.*) sugar-plum.

zucchero *sm.* sugar.

zucchina *sf.* vegetable marrow.

zucconaggine *sf.* 1. (*ottusità*) dullness 2. (*ostinatezza*) stubbornness.

zuccone *sm.* 1. (*ottuso*) blockhead 2. (*testardo*) donkey.

zuffa *sf.* brawl.

zufolare *vt. e vi.* to whistle.

zufolio *sm.* whistle.

zufolo *sm.* 1. whistle 2. (*mus.*) pipe.

zuppa *sf.* soup.

zuppiera *sf.* tureen.

zuppo *agg.* soaked.

zuzzurellone *sm.* skittish boy.

NOMI PROPRI, STORICI E GEOGRAFICI

Abele Abel.
Abissinia Abyssinia.
Abramo Abraham.
Achille Achilles.
Ada Ada.
Adamo Adam.
Adolfo Adolph.
Adone Adonis.
Adriano Hadrian.
Adriatico (Mar) Adriatic Sea.
Afganistan Afghanistan.
Africa Africa.
Afrodite Aphrodite.
Agamennone Agamemnon
Agata Agatha.
Agnese Agnes.
Agostino Augustin.
Aia (L') The Hague.
Aiace Ajax.
Albania Albania.
Alberto Albert.
Aldo Aldous.
Alessandra Alexandra.
Alessandro Alexander.
Alessio Alexis.
Alfredo Alfred.
Algeri Algiers.
Algeria Algeria.
Alice Alice.
Alpi Alps pl.
Alsazia Alsace.
Amazzoni (Rio delle) Amazon.
Ambrogio Ambrose.
Amburgo Hamburg.
Amelia Amelia.
America America.
Amleto Hamlet.
Andalusia Andalusia.
Ande Andes pl.
Andrea Andrew.
Angelo Angel.
Anna Ann(e).
Annibale Hannibal.
Antartide Antarctica.
Antonino Antoninus.
Antonio Ant(h)ony.
Apollo Apollo.
Appennini Apennines pl.
Arabia Arabia.
Aragona Aragon.
Arcadia Arcadia.
Archimede Archimedes.

Argentina Argentina.
Arianna Ariadne.
Aristofane Aristophanes.
Aristotele Aristotle.
Armando Armand.
Arnaldo Arnold.
Aroldo Harold.
Arrigo Henry.
Arturo Arthur.
Asia Asia.
Atene Athens.
Atlantico Atlantic.
Augusta Augusta.
Augusto Augustus.
Australia Australia.
Austria Austria.
Azzorre Azores pl.

Babele Babel.
Babilonia Babylon.
Bacco Bacchus.
Balcani Balkans pl.
Baldassarre Balthazar.
Baleari Balearic Islands pl.
Baltico (Mar) Baltic Sea.
Baltimora Baltimore.
Barbara Barbara.
Barcellona Barcelona.
Barnaba Barnaby, Barnabas.
Bartolomeo Bartholomew.
Basilea Basel.
Basilio Basil.
Battista Baptist.
Beatrice Beatrix.
Belgio Belgium.
Belgrado Belgrade.
Benedetto Benedict.
Bengala Bengal.
Beniamino Benjamin.
Berenice Berenice.
Berlino Berlin.
Bermude Bermudas pl.
Bernardo Bernard.
Berta Bertha.
Betlemme Bethlehem.
Bianca Blanche.
Birmania Burma.
Boemia Bohemia.
Bolivia Bolivia.
Bonifacio Boniface.
Bosforo Bosporus.

Brandeburgo Brandenburg.
Brasile Brazil.
Bretagna Brittany.
Bruto Brutus.
Bulgaria Bulgaria.

Cadice Cadiz.
Caino Cain.
Caio Caius.
Cairo Cairo.
California California.
Calvino Calvin.
Cambogia Cambodia.
Campidoglio Capitol.
Canadà Canada.
Caraibi (Mar dei) Caribbean Sea.
Carlo Charles.
Carlomagno Charlemagne.
Carlotta Charlotte.
Carolina Caroline.
Carpazi Carpathian Mountains *pl.*
Cartagine Carthage.
Cascemir Cashmere, Kashmir.
Caspio (Mar) Caspian Sea.
Cassio Cassius.
Cassiopea Cassiopeia.
Castiglia Castile.
Caterina Catherine.
Catone Cato.
Caucaso Caucasus.
Cecilia Cecily.
Cecilio Cecil.
Cecoslovacchia Czechoslovakia.
Cenerentola Cinderella.
Cesare Caesar.
Chiara Clara.
Cicerone Cicero.
Cile Chile.
Cina China.
Cinzia Cynthia.
Cipro Cyprus.
Cirillo Cyril.
Ciro Cyrus.
Clara Clara.
Claudio Claudius, Claude.
Clemente Clement.
Clementina Clementine.
Cleopatra Cleopatra.
Clitennestra Clytemnestra.
Colombia Colombia.
Colonia Cologne.
Congo Congo.
Corea Korea.
Corfù Corfu.
Corinto Corinth.
Cornelio Cornelius.
Cornovaglia Cornwall.
Corrado Conrad.

Corsica Corsica.
Costantino Constantine.
Costantinopoli Constantinople.
Costanza Constance.
Creta Crete.
Crimea Crimea.
Cristina Christine.
Cristo Christ.
Cristoforo Christopher.
Cuba Cuba.

Dafne Daphne.
Damasco Damascus.
Damocle Damocles.
Daniele Daniel.
Danimarca Denmark.
Danubio Danube.
Danzica Danzig.
Dardanelli Dardanelles *pl.*
Dario Darius.
Davide David.
Debora Deborah.
Delfo Delphi.
Democrito Democritus.
Demostene Demosthenes.
Desdemona Desdemona.
Diana Diana.
Didone Dido.
Diocleziano Diocletian.
Diogene Diogenes.
Dionigi, Dionisio Dionysius.
Domenico Dominic.
Domiziano Domitian.
Dorotea Dorothy.
Dublino Dublin.

Ebridi Hebrides *pl.*
Edgardo Edgar.
Edimburgo Edinburgh.
Edipo Oedipus.
Edmondo Edmund.
Edoardo Edward.
Egeo (Mar) Aegean Sea.
Egitto Egypt.
Elena Helen.
Eleonora Eleanor.
Elettra Electra.
Elia Elias, Elijah.
Elisa Eliza.
Elisabetta Elizabeth.
Eliade Hellas.
Emanuele Emanuel.
Emilia Emily.
Enea Aeneas.
Enrichetta Henrietta, Harriet.
Enrico Henry, Harry.
Epaminonda Epaminondas.

Epicuro Epicurus.
Eraclito Heraclitus.
Erasmo Erasmus.
Erberto Herbert.
Ercole Hercules.
Eritrea Eritrea.
Ermete Hermes.
Ernesto Ernest.
Erode Herod.
Erodoto Herodotus.
Esaù Esau.
Eschilo Aeschylus.
Esiodo Hesiod.
Esopo Aesop.
Ester Esther.
Etiopia Ethiopia.
Ettore Hector.
Euclide Euclid.
Eufrate Euphrates.
Eugenio Eugene.
Euripide Euripides.
Europa Europe.
Eva Eve.
Evelina Evelyn.
Ezechiele Ezekiel.

Farsalo Pharsalus.
Fausto Faust(us).
Federico Frederic.
Fedra Phaedra.
Felice Felix.
Ferdinando Ferdinand.
Filadelfia Philadelphia.
Filippi Philippi.
Filippine Philippines *pl.*
Filippo Philip.
Finlandia Finland.
Firenze Florence.
Formosa Formosa.
Francesca Frances.
Francesco Francis.
Francia France.
Franco Frank.
Francoforte Frankfurt.

Gabriele Gabriel.
Galilea Galilee.
Galles Wales.
Gallia Gaule.
Genova Genoa.
Geova Jehovah.
Gerardo Gerard.
Geremia Jeremiah.
Gerico Jericho.
Germania Germany.
Gerolamo Jerome.
Gerusalemme Jerusalem.

Gesù Jesus.
Giacobbe Jacob.
Giacomo James.
Giamaica Jamaica.
Giappone Japan.
Giasone Jason.
Giava Java.
Gibilterra Gibraltar.
Gilberto Gilbert.
Ginevra Geneva.
Giobbe Job.
Giona Jonah, Jonas.
Gionata Jonathan.
Giordano Jordan.
Giorgio George.
Giosuè Joshua.
Giovanna Jane, Jean, Joan.
Giovanni John.
Giove Jove, Jupiter.
Giovenale Juvenal.
Giuda Judas, Jude.
Giudea Judea.
Giuditta Judith.
Giulia Julia, Julie.
Giuliana Juliana.
Giuliano Julian.
Giulietta Juliet.
Giulio Julius.
Giunone Juno.
Giuseppe Joseph.
Giuseppina Josephine.
Goffredo Geoffrey, Jeffrey.
Golgota Golgotha.
Golia Goliath.
Gran Bretagna Great Britain.
Grazia Grace.
Grecia Greece.
Gregorio Gregory.
Groenlandia Greenland.
Guaiana Guiana.
Gualtiero Walter.
Guascogna Gascony.
Guglielmo William.
Guido Guy.
Guinea Guinea.
Gustavo Gustavus.

Iacopo James.
Iberia Iberia.
Icaro Icarus.
Ignazio Ignatius.
Ilario Hilary.
Imalaia Himalaya.
India India.
Indostan Hindustan.
Inghilterra England.
Innocenzo Innocent.
Ionio (Mar) Ionian Sea.

Ippolito Hippolytus.
Irene Irene.
Iride Iris.
Irlanda Ireland.
Irlanda (Stato Libero di) Eire.
Isabella Isabel.
Isacco Isaac.
Isaia Isaiah.
Iside Isis.
Islanda Iceland.
Ismaele Ishmael.
Israele Israel.
Italia Italy.
Iugoslavia Yugoslavia.

Lamberto Lambert.
Lancillotto Launcelot.
Laocoonte Laocoon.
Lapponia Lapland.
Laura Laura.
Lazio Latium.
Lazzaro Lazarus.
Leandro Leander.
Leonardo Leonard.
Leone Leo(n).
Leonida Leonidas.
Leopoldo Leopold.
Lete Lethe.
Letizia Letitia.
Libano Lebanon.
Libia Libya.
Licurgo Lycurgus
Lidia Lydia.
Liegi Liege.
Lione Lyons.
Lisbona Lisbon.
Livio Livy.
Livorno Leghorn.
Lodovico Ludwig.
Lombardia Lombardy.
Londra London.
Lorena Lorraine.
Lorenzo Lawrence.
Losanna Lausanne.
Lotario Lothar.
Lovanio Louvain.
Luca Luke.
Lucerna Lucerne.
Lucia Lucy.
Luciano Lucian.
Lucifero Lucifer.
Lucio Lucius.
Lucrezio Lucretius.
Luigi Louis, Lewis.
Luigia, Luisa Louise.
Lussemburgo Luxemburg.
Lutero Luther.

Maddalena Magdalene.
Maiorca Majorca.
Malesia Malaya.
Malta Malta.
Manciuria Manchuria.
Manfredi Manfred.
Manica (La) The Channel.
Mantova Mantua.
Maometto Mohammed.
Maratona Marathon.
Marcello Marcellus.
Marco Mark.
Margherita Margaret.
Maria Mary.
Marianna Marianne.
Mario Marius.
Marocco Morocco.
Marta Martha.
Marte Mars.
Martino Martin.
Marziale Martial.
Massimiliano Maximilian.
Matilde Matilda.
Matteo Matthew.
Matusalemme Methuselah.
Maurizio Maurice.
Mecca, La Mecca.
Mecenate Maecenas.
Mediterraneo Mediterranean.
Medusa Medusa.
Mefistofele Mephistopheles.
Melanesia Melanesia.
Menelao Menelaus.
Mercurio Mercury.
Merlino Merlin.
Mesopotamia Mesopotamia.
Messalina Messalina.
Messico Mexico.
Micene Mycenae.
Michele Michael.
Mida Midas.
Milano Milan.
Minerva Minerva.
Minosse Minos.
Minotauro Minotaur.
Mitridate Mithridates.
Molucche Moluccas pl.
Monaco (Principato di) Monaco.
Monaco di Baviera Munich.
Mongolia Mongolia.
Mosa Meuse.
Mosca Moscow.
Mosè Moses.
Mozambico Mozambique.

Napoleone Napoleon.
Napoli Naples.
Narciso Narcissus.

Nerone Nero.
Nettuno Neptune.
Nicola, Niccolò Nicholas.
Nilo Nile.
Nizza Nice.
Noè Noah.
Normandia Normandy.
Norvegia Norway.
Nuova Zelanda New Zealand.

Oceania Oceania.
Ofelia Ophelia.
Olanda Holland.
Olimpo Olympus.
Oliviero Oliver.
Omero Homer.
Orazio Horace, Horatio.
Orcadi Orkneys *pl.*
Oreste Orestes.
Orfeo Orpheus.
Orione Orion.
Orlando Roland.
Orsola Ursula.
Osiride Osiris.
Osvaldo Oswald.
Otello Othello.
Ovidio Ovid.

Pacifico Pacific.
Padova Padua.
Paesi Bassi Netherlands *p.*.
Palestina Palestine.
Pancrazio Pancras.
Paola Paula.
Paolina Pauline.
Paolo Paul.
Papuasia Papua.
Paride Paris.
Parigi Paris.
Parnaso Parnassus.
Partenone Parthenon.
Patagonia Patagonia.
Patrizia Patricia.
Patrizio Patrick.
Pechino Peking.
Peloponneso Peloponnesus.
Penelope Penelope.
Pensilvania Pennsylvania.
Pericle Pericles.
Perseo Perseus.
Persia Persia.
Perù Peru.
Piemonte Piedmont.
Pietro, Piero Peter.
Pigmalione Pigmalion.
Pindaro Pindar.
Pio Pius.

Pirenei Pyrenees *pl.*
Pireo Piraeus.
Pitagora Pythagoras.
Platone Plato.
Plinio Pliny.
Plutarco Plutarch.
Polinesia Polynesia.
Polonia Poland.
Pompeo Pompey.
Portogallo Portugal.
Praga Prague.
Prometeo Prometheus.
Prussia Prussia.
Puglia Apulia.

Quintino Quentin.

Rachele Rachel.
Raffaele, Raffaello Raphael.
Raimondo Raymond.
Ramsete Ramses.
Rebecca Rebecca.
Remo Remus.
Reno Rhine.
Riccardo Richard.
Roberto Robert.
Rodano Rhone.
Rodi Rhodes.
Rodolfo Rudolph.
Rodrigo Roderick.
Rolando Roland.
Roma Rome.
Romania Ro(u)mania.
Romeo Romeo.
Romolo Romulus.
Rosa Rose.
Rosalia Rosalie.
Rosalinda Rosalind.
Rossana Roxana.
Rubicone Rubicon.
Ruggero Roger.
Russia Russia.

Saffo Sappho.
Salomone Solomon.
Samuele Samuel.
Sansone Samson.
Sara Sarah.
Sardegna Sardinia.
Sassonia Saxony.
Satana Satan.
Saturno Saturn.
Saul Saul.
Savoia Savoy.
Scandinavia Scandinavia.
Scipione Scipion.

Scozia Scotland.
Sebastiano Sebastian.
Sempione Simplon.
Serse Xerxes.
Siam Siam.
Siberia Siberia.
Sibilla Sibyl.
Sicilia Sicily.
Silla Sulla.
Silvestro Silvester.
Silvia Sylvia.
Simeone Simeon.
Simone Simon.
Siracusa Syracuse.
Siria Syria.
Smirne Smyrna.
Socrate Socrates.
Sodoma Sodom.
Sofia Sophia.
Sofocle Sophocles.
Somalia Somaliland.
Spagna Spain.
Sparta Sparta.
Stati Uniti United States (of America - U.S.A.).
Stefano Stephen.
Stoccolma Stockholm.
Strasburgo Strasbourg.
Sudan S(o)udan.
Susanna Susan(nah).
Svezia Sweden.
Svizzera Switzerland.

Tacito Tacitus.
Tailandia Thailand.
Tamigi Thames.
Tangeri Tangier(s).
Tasmania Tasmania.
Tebe Thebes.
Telemaco Telemachus.
Temistocle Themistocles.
Teodorico Theodoric.
Terenzio Terence.
Teresa Theresa.
Termopili Thermopylae *pl.*
Terranova Newfoundland.
Teseo Theseus.
Tevere Tiber.
Tiberio Tiberius.
Tirolo Tirol, Tyrol.

Tirreno (Mar) Tyrrhenian Sea.
Tito Titus.
Tiziano Titian.
Tobia Tobias.
Tolomeo Ptolemy.
Tommaso Thomas.
Tonchino Tonkin, Tongking.
Torino Turin.
Toscana Tuscany.
Traiano Trajan.
Tristano Tristan, Tristram.
Troia Troy.
Tullio Tully.
Tunisi Tunis.
Tunisia Tunisia.
Turchia Turkey.

Uberto Hubert.
Ucraina Ukraine.
Ugo Hugh.
Ulisse Ulysses.
Umberto Humbert.
Ungheria Hungary.
Urbano Urban.
URSS USSR (Union of Socialist Soviet Republics).

Valentino Valentine.
Valeria Valeria.
Valerio Valerius.
Varsavia Warsaw.
Vaticano Vatican.
Venere Venus.
Veneto Venetia.
Venezia Venice.
Vesuvio Vesuvius.
Vienna Vienna.
Vincenzo Vincent.
Virgilio Virgil.
Virginia Virginia.
Vittoria Victoria.
Vittorio Victor.
Viviana, Viviano Vivian.
Vulcano Vulcan.

Zaccaria Zachary.
Zurigo Zurich.

SIGLE E ABBREVIAZIONI USATE IN ITALIA

A., *alto:* H., high.

A.C., *Automobile Club:* A.A., Automobile Association.

a.C., *avanti Cristo:* B.C. Before Christ.

A.D., *Anno Domini, nell'anno del Signore:* A.D., Anno Domini, (After Christ).

ago., *Agosto:* Aug., August.

A.M., *Aeronautica Militare:* A.F., Air Force.

am., amer., *americano:* Am., American.

anon., *anonimo:* anon., anonymous.

app., *appendice:* app., appendix.

appross., *approssimativo:* approx., approximate.

apr., *aprile:* Apr., April.

A.R., *altezza reale:* R.H., Royal Highness.

ar., *arrivo:* arr., arrival.

ass., *associazione:* ass., association.

b.f., *bassa frequenza:* L.F., low frequency.

boll., *bollettino:* bull., bulletin.

brev., *brevetto:* pat., patent.

C., *centigradi:* cent., centigrade.

c., **1.** *conto:* acc., account **2.** *cubico:* cu., cubic.

ca., **1.** *circa:* a., about **2.** *corrente alternata:* a.c., alternating current.

cad., *cadauno:* ea., each.

Cap., *capitano:* Capt., captain.

cap., *capitolo:* c., chapter.

capit., *capitolo:* c., chapter.

Capp., *capitoli:* cc., chapters.

Card., *Cardinale:* Card., cardinal.

C/c, *conto corrente:* c/a, current account.

cc., *corrente continua:* dc., direct current.

C.D., *Corpo Diplomatico:* C.D., Corps Diplomatique.

C.E.E.A., *Comunità europea per l'energia atomica:* A.E.C., Atomic Energy Commission.

cent., centg., *centigrado:* cent., centigrade.

Cf., *confronta:* cp., compare.

cm., *centimetro:* cent., centimetre.

c.m., *corrente mese:* inst., instant.

cm.c., *centimetro cubo:* c.c., cubic centimetre.

Col., *colonnello:* col., colonel.

coll., *collegio:* coll., college.

coop., *cooperativa:* coop., co-operative.

C.P., *Casella Postale:* P.O.B., Post Office Box.

C.S., *Corte Suprema:* Sup. Ct., Supreme Court.

D., *dottore:* dr., doctor.

d.C., *dopo Cristo:* A.D., Anno Domini.

dic., *dicembre:* Dec., December.

Dirett., *direttore:* dir., director.

dom., *domenica:* Sun., Sunday.

dott., *dottore:* dr., doctor.

dozz., *dozzina:* doz., dozen.

E, *est:* E, East.

ecc., *eccetera:* etc., and so on.

ed., **1.** *edito:* ed., edited **2.** *edizione:* ed., edition.

Egr., *egregio:* Esq, Esquire.

es., *esempio:* ex., example.

feb., *febbraio:* Feb., February.

fed., *federazione:* fed., federation.

F.lli, *fratelli:* br., bros., brothers.

g., *grammo:* g., gram.

Gen., *generale:* Gen., General.

gen., **1.** *generale:* gen., general **2.** *gennaio:* Jan., January.

giov., *giovedì:* Thur., Thursday.

h., *ora:* h., hour.

H.P., *cavallo vapore:* H.P., horse power.

ibid., *ibidem, nello stesso luogo:* ibid., in the same place.

id., *idem, come sopra:* id., the same.

iun., *junior, giovane:* jr., junior.

kg., *chilogrammo*: kg., kilogram.
km., *chilometro*: km., kilometre.
kw., *chilowatt*: kw., kilowatt.

l., 1. *latino*: Lat., Latin 2. *litro*: l., litre.
lat., *latitudine*: lat., latitude.
llb., *libro*: b., book.
long., *longitudine*: long., longitude.
L.st., *Lira sterlina*: L., pound.
lun., *lunedì*: Mon., Monday.

M., *monte*: Mt., mount.
m., 1. *morto*: d., dead 2. *mese*: m., month 3. *metro*: m., metre 4. *minuto*: m., minute.
M.AA.EE., *Ministero degli Affari Esteri*: F.O., Foreign Office.
Magg., *Maggiore*: Maj., Major.
mar., *marzo*: Mar., March.
mart., *martedì*: Tues., Tuesday.
mass., *massimo*: max., maximum.
m.c.d., *minimo comun denominatore*: L.C.D., Lowest Common Denominator.
m.c.m., *minimo comune multiplo*: L.C.M., Least Common Multiple.
M.E.C., *Mercato Comune Europeo*: E.C.M., European Common Market.
mer(c)., *mercoledì*: Wed., Wednesday.
mg., *milligrammo*: mg., milligram.
mm., *millimetro*: mm., millimetre.
M/n., *motonave*: Ms., motorship.
ms., *manoscritto*: ms., manuscript.
mss., *manoscritti*: mss., manuscripts.
Mus., *museo*: mus., museum.

N., 1. *nato*: b., born 2. *Nord*: N., North 3. *numero*: N., Number.
nov., *novembre*: Nov., November.
N.U., *Nazioni Unite*: U.N., United Nations.

O., *ovest*: W., West.
on., *onorevole*: hon., honourable.
O.N.U., *Organizzazione Nazioni Unite*: U.N.O., United Nations Organization.
ott., *ottobre*: Oct., October.

P., *padre*: ft., father.
p., *pagina*: p., page.
P.A., *Patto Atlantico*: N.A.T.O., North Atlantic Treaty Organization.
paragr., *paragrafo*: par., paragraph.
p.at., *peso atomico*: a.w., atomic weight.
P.C., *Partito Comunista*: C.P., Communist Party.
p.e., *per esempio*: e.g., for example (exempli gratia).
pres., *presidente*: pres., president.
proc., *procuratore*: att., attorney.
prof., *professore*: prof., professor.
P.S., *poscritto*: P.S., postscript.
p.za, *piazza*: sq., square.

Q.G., *Quartier Generale*: G.H., General Headquarters.

ref., *referenze*: ref., reference.
reg., *registro*: reg., register.
Rev., *Reverendo*: rev., Reverend.
R.M., *ricchezza mobile*: PAYE, Pay As You Earn.
R.U., *Regno Unito*: U.K., United Kingdom.

S., 1. *Santo*: St., Saint 2. *secolo*: cen., century 3. *società*: co., Company 4. *Sud*: S., South.
sab., *sabato*: Sat., Saturday.
S.A.R., *Sua Altezza Reale*: H.R.H., His (Her) Royal Highness.
Sc., *scuola*: sch., school.
S.E., *Sua Eccellenza*: H.E., His Excellency.
segg., *seguenti*: fol., following.
segr., *segretario*: sec., secretary.
serg., *sergente*: sergt., sergeant.
sett., *settembre*: Sept., September.
sig., *signore*: Mr., Mister.
sig.na, *signorina*: Miss.
sig.ra, *signora*: Mrs., Mistress.
S.M.B., *Sua Maestà Britannica*: H.B.M., His (Her) Britannic Majesty.
S.O., *Sud Ovest*: S.W., South West.
s.p.a., *società per azioni*: inc., incorporated.
spec., 1. *speciale*: spec., special 2. *specialmente*: spec., specially.
s.r.l., *società a responsabilità limitata*: ltd., limited (in inglese); corp., corporation (in americano).
S.S., *Sua Santità*: H.H., His Holiness.
S.U., *Stati Uniti*: U.S., United States.

S.U.A., *Stati Uniti d'America*: U.S.A., United States of America.

T., *tonnellata*: t., ton.

T.B.C., *tubercolosi*: T.B., Tuberculosis.

tel., *telefono*: tel. telephone.

U., *unione*: U., Union.

U.P., *Unione postale*: P.U., Postal Union.

U.R.S.S., *Unione Repubbliche So-* *cialiste Sovietiche*: U.S.S.R., Union of Socialist Soviet Republics.

V., 1. *vaglia*: P.O., Postal Order **2.** *volume*: vol., volume.

v., *verso*: v., verse.

Ven., *Venerabile*: Ven., Venerable.

ven., *venerdì*: Fr., Friday.

vesc., *vescovo*: Bp., Bishop.

v.le, *viale*: Ave., Avenue.

vol., *volume*: vol., volume.

voll., *volumi*: voll., volumes.

vv., *versi*: vv., verses.